D1216471

PsycINFO RETROSPECTIVE:

MENTAL RETARDATION

an Abstracted Bibliography, 1971-1980

MIDDLEBURY COLLEGE LIBRARY

THE AMERICAN PSYCHOLOGICAL ASSOCIATION, INC.
WASHINGTON, D.C.

Other volumes in this Series include:

Learning and Communication Disorders: an Abstracted Bibliography, 1971-1980

370
.M4117
1982

©1982 by the American Psychological Association

Library of Congress Catalog Number 82-071774
ISBN: 0-912704-73-X
Printed in the United States of America

TABLE OF CONTENTS

INTRODUCTION

Why a 10-year Retrospective?

The significance of theoretical and much empirical research often becomes apparent only with time. An historical perspective is required to detect trends and developing areas of study. For this reason, a ten-year retrospective bibliography is an appropriate method for revealing developments in the literature and the current understanding in a specific area.

Why in Mental Retardation?

Public awareness of government funding for research and treatment/educational facilities for the mentally retarded brought about a surge of interest in this area in the early 1970's. With this surge came reports of new research on the causes of retardation, treatment methods for the physical and behavioral problems associated with retardation, and books, monographs, and journals that focused on the training and educational techniques that could be used with the mentally retarded. In spite of this increase in the amount of research being done in this area, no reference tool has been available to at once acquaint the interested reader with the vast amount of work being done in the area and present this information in a single, usable document.

Why Abstracts?

As short summaries of published works, abstracts provide the reader with key information about a journal article, monograph, or book. Abstracts identify subject populations, research methodologies, educational techniques, treatment variables, and theories being tested. With this information, one can select specific articles that are of most interest as well as determine which articles might be of potential interest. Abstracts serve as a valuable guide to the literature. They assist the reader in sorting through all of the available information.

Why PsycINFO?

Psychological Abstracts Information Services (PsycINFO), a service of the American Psychological Association, regularly scans more than 1000 psychological, educational, medical and social science publications published in the United States and other countries each year. Over 34,000 relevant articles are abstracted and indexed by our professional staff each year and appear in PsycINFO print and database products.

Because of the lack of organized, convenient reference material dealing with mental retardation, PsycINFO began work in 1981 to develop a reference tool that would provide a view of the literature published in this area from 1971 through 1980, inclusively. Designed for parents, educators, researchers, and practitioners, the aim of this volume is to provide in a concise, informative manner, abstracts that chronicle the developments in mental retardation during this 10-year period.

An examination of the literature included in the PsycINFO database from 1971 to 1980 revealed that there were more than 3,000 abstracts of articles containing original research, case histories, practical applications, literature reviews, and other material related to mental retardation. The scope of the Retrospective bibliography was determined by a core group of 22 index terms. These terms, drawn from the *Thesaurus of Psychological Index Terms* (3rd Ed.), were considered relevant to the areas of autism and mental retardation. Because of the amount of published research, the Retrospective bibliography was limited to studies concerning children and adolescents (ages up to 19 years).

The 3,000 abstracts selected from the total body of literature published in *Psychological Abstracts* from 1971-1980 are grouped into three major areas:

> Theories, Research, and Assessment
> Treatment and Rehabilitation
> Educational Issues

Each of these areas is further divided into seven sections that deal with specific disorders. Entries are arranged in chronological order, from earliest to latest, in order to help the reader identify trends in mental retardation. An author index is provided to allow the researcher to trace the work of individual researchers, theoreticians, or educators through the decade; the subject index provides additional points of access to particular areas (e.g., head banging).

Finding the original document abstracted or cited in a bibliography may present a substantial challenge. Each abstract in this Retrospective is accompanied by complete bibliographic data to facilitate retrieval of the document from a library or requests for reprints from the author or publisher. For some publications that might not otherwise be available, there are document provision services which provide copies to requestors for a fee. Information on these services may be obtained by writing:

> PsycINFO
> American Psychological Assn.
> 1200 Seventeenth St., N.W.
> Washington, D.C. 20036

The abstracted bibliographic citation

Each abstract published in the Retrospective bibliography contains a number of elements to provide information concerning the original document.

Abstract elements

The following is an example of a PsycINFO abstract as it appears in the Retrospective bibliography. Each element of the abstract is number coded to provide a definition and give information which will be helpful to the reader.

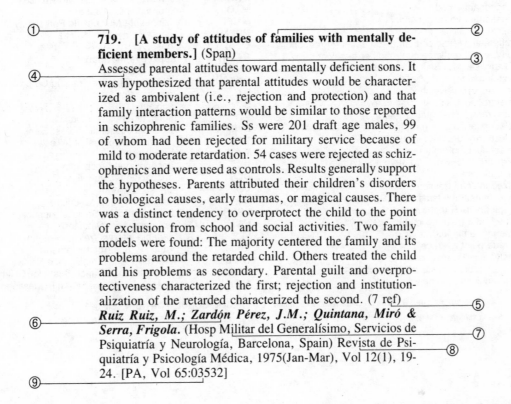

① **719.** **[A study of attitudes of families with mentally deficient members.]** ② (Span) ③

④ Assessed parental attitudes toward mentally deficient sons. It was hypothesized that parental attitudes would be characterized as ambivalent (i.e., rejection and protection) and that family interaction patterns would be similar to those reported in schizophrenic families. Ss were 201 draft age males, 99 of whom had been rejected for military service because of mild to moderate retardation. 54 cases were rejected as schizophrenics and were used as controls. Results generally support the hypotheses. Parents attributed their children's disorders to biological causes, early traumas, or magical causes. There was a distinct tendency to overprotect the child to the point of exclusion from school and social activities. Two family models were found: The majority centered the family and its problems around the retarded child. Others treated the child and his problems as secondary. Parental guilt and overprotectiveness characterized the first; rejection and institutionalization of the retarded characterized the second. (7 ref) ⑤

⑥ ***Ruiz Ruiz, M.; Zardón Pérez, J.M.; Quintana, Miró & Serra, Frigola.*** (Hosp Militar del Generalísimo, Servicios de ⑦ Psiquiatría y Neurología, Barcelona, Spain) Revista de Psiquiatría y Psicología Médica, 1975(Jan-Mar), Vol 12(1), 19- ⑧ 24. [PA, Vol 65:03532]

⑨

1. Record number
Records are numbered consecutively within the Retrospective bibliography.

2. Article title
All titles are in English. Brackets are used to indicate a translated title.

3. Language in which the article was originally published
See list of language abbreviations.

4. Text of abstract or annotation
Note: Occasionally, an abstract may contain a reference to another study, giving the author's name, and the volume and abstract number under which the material was originally published in *Psychological Abstracts*. These references may be traced by looking up the name of the reference

author in the Author Index to the Retrospective bibliography, or by consulting the appropriate volume and issue of *Psychological Abstracts*.

5. References
Number of references [cited in the article] is included.

6. Author(s) or Editor(s)
As many as four authors are listed; if there are more than four, the first author is listed with the notation "et al."

7. Affiliation of first-named author/editor only, at the time of original publication

8. Primary publication title and bibliographic data

9. Volume and abstract number as originally published in *Psychological Abstracts*

ABBREVIATIONS

In addition to commonly understood abbreviations* (including all units of measurement, educational degrees, standard statistical abbreviations, and standard Latin and reference terms), standard abbreviations used are:

ACTH	= adrenocorticotrophic hormone		**ip**	= intraperitoneal(ly) (injections)
ANOVA	= analysis of variance		**IPAT**	= Institute for Personality and Ability Testing
CA	= chronological age		**iv**	= intravenous(ly) (injections)
CNS	= central nervous system		**LSD**	= lysergic acid diethylamide
CR	= conditioned response		**MA**	= mental age
CS	= conditioned stimulus		**MANOVA**	= multivariate analysis of variance
CV	= consonant vowel		**MAO**	= monoamine oxidase
CVC	= consonant vowel consonant		**MMPI**	= Minnesota Multiphasic Personality Inventory
DNA	= deoxyribonucleic acid		**NREM**	= nonrapid eye movement
DRL	= differential reinforcement of low rates (of responding)		**O**	= observer
DRO	= differential reinforcement of other behavior		**REM**	= rapid eye movement
DSM	= Diagnostic and Statistical Manual of Mental Disorders		**RNA**	= ribonucleic acid
E	= experimenter		**ROTC**	= Reserve Officer's Training Corps
ECS	= electroconvulsive shock		**RT**	= reaction time
ECT	= electroconvulsive shock therapy		**S**	= subject
EEG	= electroencephalogram (graph)		**sc**	= subcutaneous(ly) (injection)
EKG	= electrocardiogram (graph)		**SVIB**	= Strong Vocational Interest Blank
EMG	= electromyogram (graph)		**TAT**	= Thematic Apperception Test
EOG	= electrooculogram (graph)		**TV**	= television
EPPS	= Edwards Personal Preference Schedule		**UCR**	= unconditioned response
Exp	= experiment		**UCS**	= unconditioned stimulus
FI	= fixed interval (reinforcement)		**UK**	= United Kingdom
FIRO-B	= Fundamental Interpersonal Relations Orientation		**US**	= United States of America
(or F)	[subtests B (behavior) or F (feelings)]		**USSR**	= Union of Soviet Socialist Republics
FR	= fixed ratio (reinforcement)		**VA**	= Veterans Administration
GABA	= gamma-aminobutyric acid		**VI**	= variable interval (reinforcement)
GPA	= grade point average		**VR**	= variable ratio (reinforcement)
GSR	= galvanic skin response		**WAIS**	= Wechsler Adult Intelligence Scale
icv	= intracerebroventricular(ly) (injections)		**WISC**	= Wechsler Intelligence Scale for Children
im	= intramuscular(ly) (injections)		**16PF**	= Sixteen Personality Factor Questionnaire

Computer languages and computer names will also be used without definition, e.g., **ALGOL, COBOL, FORTRAN, IBM 360.**

*Consult *Webster's New Collegiate Dictionary.*

Language abbreviations used after translated titles are:

Afri	= Afrikaans	**Germ**	= German	**Polh**	= Polish
Alba	= Albanian	**Grek**	= Greek	**Port**	= Portuguese
Arab	= Arabic	**Hind**	= Hindi	**Romn**	= Romanian
Bulg	= Bulgarian	**Hebr**	= Hebrew	**Russ**	= Russian
Chin	= Chinese	**Hung**	= Hungarian	**Sloe**	= Slovene
Czec	= Czech	**Iran**	= Iranian	**Slok**	= Slovak
Danh	= Danish	**Ital**	= Italian	**Span**	= Spanish
Duth	= Dutch	**Japn**	= Japanese	**Srcr**	= Serbo-Croatian
Finn	= Finnish	**Kore**	= Korean	**Swed**	= Swedish
Flem	= Flemish	**Lith**	= Lithuanian	**Turk**	= Turkish
Fren	= French	**Mala**	= Malay	**Ukrn**	= Ukranian
Geor	= Georgian	**Norg**	= Norwegian	**Yugo**	= Yugoslavian

MENTAL RETARDATION

An Abstracted Bibliography, 1971-1980

Theories, Research & Assessment

Autism

1. Intellectuality in parents of psychotic, subnormal, and normal children.
Studied intellectual functioning in parents of 33 autistic children, 30 mentally retarded or brain-damaged children, and 33 matched normals. Ss were diagnosed according to the DeMyer-Churchill diagnostic criteria. Parental intellectuality was measured according to intellectual interests, a preference for people with ideational orientations, academic attitudes, and reading material as assessed in an interview, as well as IQ scores. Results indicate that fewer parents of autistic children emphasized intellectual pursuits and academic success than parents of normal children. There were no differences in attitudes or desired personality characteristics. IQs of the autistic children's fathers were significantly higher than the brain-damaged children's fathers, but mother's IQs were similar to each other. The parents at the time of the birth of the child were older in the autistic and brain-damaged groups than for the parents of the normals.
Allen, John, et al. (Indiana U., Medical School, Indianapolis) Journal of Autism & Childhood Schizophrenia, 1971(Jul), Vol. 1(3), 311-326. [PA, Vol 47:10897]

2. Disturbed children under reduced auditory input: A pilot study.
Examined the effects of reduced auditory stimulation on the behavior of 20 seriously disturbed children (autistic and psychotic; mean age = 8.2). Reduced stimulation was produced by use of an ear protector and a control condition was produced by a placebo device. Classroom attention (by teacher rating) improved under reduced stimulation (p < .01; 2-tailed). The combined scores on a pegboard task, a sorting task, a cancellation task, an echo drum task (repeating numbers of taps), and a story task (S listened then selected the most appropriate picture) improved under reduced stimulation (p < .01). The sorting task did not contribute to this effect. Data indicated that reduced auditory input has a beneficial effect on certain behaviors of a significant number of autistic children. (15 ref.)
Fassler, Joan & Bryant, N. Dale. (Teachers College, Columbia U.) Exceptional Children, 1971(Nov), Vol. 38(3), 197-204. [PA, Vol 49:07137]

3. Formulation of the dynamic economic factors underlying infantile autism.
Presents a theoretical framework and clinical material from the Developmental Center for Autistic Children and attempts to reconstruct step-by-step the dynamic mechanisms which are responsible for infantile autism. 25 autistic children and their mothers were studied for 9 yr. and treated in a day care center. It is hypothesized that the child's mother did not offer adequate protection from overwhelming stimuli and gratifications, nor give the child a sense of security. Autism is described as a defensive mode of behavior which the child adopts in order to cope with stress and frustration.
Fraknoi, Julia & Ruttenberg, Bertram A. (U. Pennsylvania, Medical School) Journal of the American Academy of Child Psychiatry, 1971(Oct), Vol. 10(4), 713-738. [PA, Vol 48:09446]

4. Malabsorption and cerebral dysfunction: A multivariate and comparative study of autistic children.
Investigated biological abnormalities and autism in 15 autistic children randomly selected from cooperating families. All had been the product of difficult pregnancies and now manifested signs of neurological dysfunction. Control groups of normal children, sibling, normal adults, and schizophrenic adults were used. All measures, physiological and behavioral, were made blind to the S's diagnoses. The autistic children exhibited a unique DC burst on the transcephalic DC electrophysiologic recording, as well as elevated blood cortisol levels associated with decreased eosinophil counts. Giladin abolished the normal circadian cortisol rhythm and had differing effects on frontal transcephalic DC base-line activity. Autistic Ss displayed different abnormalities than adult schizophrenics. The conclusion hypothesis concerns a maturational failure of a brain control system and fundamental neurobiological dysfunction in autism. (15 ref.)
Goodwin, Mary S.; Cowen, Murray A. & Goodwin, T. Campbell. (Dept. of Mental Hygiene, Albany, N.Y.) Journal of Autism & Childhood Schizophrenia, 1971(Jan), Vol. 1(1), 48-62. [PA, Vol 47:05288]

5. Psychological studies of childhood autism: Can autistic children make sense of what they see and hear?
Studied cognitive functioning of autistic children by means of several different experimental tasks involving language and nonlanguage stimuli. Autistic children between 7-15 yr. old were compared with normal and subnormal Ss matched for MA. Results indicate the following: (a) memory for sentence messages in comparison to random messages is much greater in nonautistic Ss, but not in autistic Ss. (b) Autistic Ss recall the last words of a message better than the 1st part, even if the 1st words are a meaningful sentence. (c) Autistic Ss do not cluster as do nonautistic Ss. And (d) redundancy patterns in the message do not benefit autistic Ss. No difference in response patterns on an unstructured task was observed. It is concluded that the responding of the autistic Ss was characterized by a lack of sensitivity to the inherent pattern of the input, combined with a tendency to impose simple patterns in different situations. This imposition is seen as detrimental in situations governed by definite rules.
Hermelin, Beate & Frith, Uta. (Medical Research Council, Developmental Psychology Unit, London, England) Journal of Special Education, 1971(Sum), Vol. 5(2), 107-117. [PA, Vol 48:09448]

6. Follow-up study of eleven autistic children originally reported in 1943.
Outlines a further description of the life courses of 11 autistic children 1st reported in 1943. A brief account of each child's development, family, clinical course, and later life is included. The present status is considerably variable with some of the patients employed at an occupation while others have been institutionalized all of their lives. The diagnosis and etiology of autism is reviewed against this background of biographical data. The early onset of the affective disturbance, the predominance of boys, the stereotypic behavior, and the variability in present status among the Ss is discussed.
Kanner, Leo. (Johns Hopkins U., Medical School) Journal of Autism & Childhood Schizophrenia, 1971(Apr), Vol. 1(2), 119-145. [PA, Vol 47:05294]

7. Response latencies to auditory stimuli in autistic children engaged in self-stimulatory behavior.
Studied 3 groups of children (mute autistics, autistics with echolalic speech, and normals) under 2 conditions (while Ss were engaged in self-stimulation vs. free from self-stimulatory behavior). Ss were trained to approach a dispenser, for candy reinforcement, at the sound of a tone. The time interval between the onset of the tone and S's approach was labeled his response latency. Results indicate that (a) the presence of self-stimulatory behavior was associated with increased response latencies for the mute autistics; (b) the response latencies of the latter group decreased as Ss received increased training in responding to the auditory stimulus; (c) the amount of self-stimulatory behavior varied with the magnitude of reinforcement for other behavior; and (d) in a preliminary way, some control over the response latencies was obtained by experimentally manipulating the amount of self-stimulatory behavior. The data were conceptualized in terms of competing reinforcers.
Lovaas, O. Ivar; Litrownik, Alan & Mann, Ronald. (U. California, Los Angeles) Behaviour Research & Therapy, 1971(Feb), Vol. 9(1), 39-49. [PA, Vol 47:01319]

8. Selective responding by autistic children to multiple sensory input.
Reinforced 6 autistic, 5 retarded, and 5 normal children for responding to a complex stimulus involving the simultaneous presentation of auditory, visual, and tactile cues. After discrimination was established, elements of the complex were presented separately to assess which aspects of the complex stimulus had acquired control over the S's behavior. It was found that (a) the autistics responded primarily to only 1 of the cues, normals to all 3 cues, and retardates to 2 cues; and (b) conditions could be arranged such that a cue which had remained nonfunctional when presented in association with other cues could be established as functional when trained separately. Data fail to support theories that any 1 sense modality is impaired in autistic children. When presented with a stimulus complex, autistic Ss' attention was overselective. Findings are related to the literature on selective attention. Since much learning involves contiguous or near-contiguous pairing of 2 or more stimuli, failure to respond to 1 of the stimuli may be an important factor in the development of autism. (27 ref.)
Lovaas, O. Ivar; Schreibman, Laura; Koegel, Robert & Rehm, Richard. (U. California, Los Angeles) Journal of Abnormal Psychology, 1971(Jun), Vol. 77(3), 211-222. [PA, Vol 46:07203]

9. Stimulus overselectivity of autistic children in a two stimulus situation.
Trained autistic and normal children to respond to a complex stimulus involving an auditory component (white noise) and a visual component (red floodlight). After Ss had acquired this discrimination, the individual components were presented singly to assess their control over Ss' behavior. Autistic Ss, unlike the normals, demonstrated stimulus overselectively in that 7 out of 9 responded to only 1 of the components. Results are consistent with those of a previous study where autistics showed stimulus overselectivity in an experiment involving 3 modalities. In both experiments, the previously nonfunctional stimulus was made functional when trained separately.
Lovaas, O. Ivar & Schreibman, Laura. (U. California, Los Angeles) Behaviour Research & Therapy, 1971(Nov), Vol. 9(4), 305-310. [PA, Vol 48:03383]

10. Effects of adult verbal requests on the behavior of autistic children.
The failure of autistic children to respond appropriately to verbal request may be due to developmental receptive aphasia or to the interpersonal conflicts of the autistic child. Using 2 8- and 10-yr-old boys as Ss, the effects of adult verbal request on the performance of autistic children were investigated in verbal discrimination tasks. Results demonstrate that the Ss' performances on a series of discrimination tasks shifted abruptly from random to better-than-chance discrimination when 1 of the objects to be discriminated was replaced by another object. Data is interpreted as indicating that failure to discriminate was not caused by inability to understand the request, but rather may have been due to Ss' conflicts concerning compliance and resistance to adult requests.
Morrison, Delmont; Miller, Dale & Mejia, Berta. (U. California, Medical Center, San Francisco) American Journal of Mental Deficiency, 1971(Jan), Vol. 75(4), 510-518. [PA, Vol 46:03449]

11. [Suggestions for a classification of autistic childhood syndromes.] (Germ)
Complemented the typical psychopathic and preschizophrenic forms of autism on the basis of available theories and observations of psychogenic and somatogenic autistic childhood syndromes and demarcated by a defectogenic "pseudo-autism." it is believed that an inherited genetic autism underlies all autistic childhood syndromes. This autism can emerge under a strong environmental strain from latency and lead to a psychogenic autism, manifesting in a psychopathic syndrome or in a preschizophrenic syndrome, or appearing, due to a brain-organic lesion, as a somatogenic autism. The differential typological classification of various autistic childhood syndromes, including inherited, peristatic, and somatic factors, offers simplified diagnostic possibilities for a prognosis of typically autistic cases of the psychogenetic preschizophrenic, psychopathic, and somatogenic syndromes. The above is valid for the therapy as well. (15 ref.)
Nissen, G. (City Clinic for Child & Juvenile Psychiatry, Berlin, W. Germany) Nervenarzt, 1971(Jan), Vol. 42(1), 35-39. [PA, Vol 47:01322]

12. Social class factors in autism.
Reported studies in which autistic children's parents were found to be highly educated, emotionally detached, and from higher socioeconomic classes than other normal or disturbed children's parents. To investigate these social class factors a large metropolitan institution systematically evaluated all admissions. 74 autistic children were matched for sex and age with other children with neurotic, organic, and behavior disorders. Using education and occupation variables for social class assignment, the parents were evaluated for age, social class, religion, and ethnic origin. Results indicate no differences were found between the parents of autistic and matched parents on any of the social class variables. One statistically significant finding was that fewer mothers of autistic children were employed. The autistic Ss were also more racially heterogeneous. The possibility of different potential patient population and different patient selection procedures accounting for the significant social class factors found in other reported studies is discussed. (25 ref.)
Ritvo, Edward R., et al. (U. California, Center for the Health Sciences, Los Angeles) Journal of Autism & Childhood Schizophrenia, 1971(Jul), Vol. 1(3), 297-310. [PA, Vol 47:11291]

13. Studies on blood platelets, blood enzymes, and leucocyte chromosome breakage in childhood schizophrenia.
Uptake of labeled serotonin by blood platelets did not increase in autistic children with increasing CA. Several studies indicated some minor and some statistically significant differences between autistic children and nonautistic or nonschizophrenic children with respect to lactate dehydrogenase, aldolase, glucose 6-phosphate isomerase, and adenosine triphosphatase (ATPase). Significant differences were found in ATPase activity before and after lysising the blood. This indicates probable red cell membrane differences between autistic and nonautistic children. Autistic schizophrenic children showed a higher incidence of chromosome breakage in leucocytes in culture. These studies provide evidence for biological defects in childhood autistic schizophrenia.
Sankar, D. V. (Creedmoor State Hosp., Queens Village, N.Y.) Behavioral Neuropsychiatry, 1971(Feb), Vol. 2(11-12), 2-10. [PA, Vol 47:03389]

14. Parents of psychotic children as scapegoats.
Describes how G. Allport's dimensions of scapegoating behavior apply to professional attitudes toward parents of autistic children. It is concluded that the professional should examine his motives in classifying parents as primary agents, particularly in

light of recent findings that autism may be linked to genetic, constitutional, and biochemical predispositions.

Schopler, Eric. (Memorial Hosp., Chapel Hill, N.C.) Journal of Contemporary Psychotherapy, 1971(Win), Vol. 4(1), 17-22. [PA, Vol 48:01359]

15. CNV responses of autistic and normal children.

Studied the contingent negative variation (CNV) in autistic children. The objective was to examine differences in central nervous mechanisms between 5 inpatient autistic children and 5 normal controls. The design was a counterbalanced sequence of clicks and flashes followed by projection of an image on a screen including S, another child, S's mother, and a strange women. Slow potential (DC) recording was carried on throughout the procedure. Constant presentation resulted in increased negative responding for both groups. While the controls were able to discriminate slide on-slide off in their responding, as well as exhibit differential responding to content with the strange woman causing the most negative responding, autistic Ss were less discriminating. The autistic Ss only responded selectively to the intermittent-constant variable while the normals were consistent. A discussion of physiological functioning is included.

Small, Joyce G.; DeMyer, Marian K. & Milstein, Victor. (LaRue D. Carter Memorial Hosp., Indianapolis, Ind.) Journal of Autism & Childhood Schizophrenia, 1971(Apr), Vol. 1(2), 215-231. [PA, Vol 47:05318]

16. Intellectual and personality characteristics of parents of autistic children.

Studied 5 sets of parents with autistic children, and 2 with schizophrenic offspring. Demographic, intelligence, and personality data on their families were examined. Rimland's retrospective checklist (Form E-1) was useful in distinguishing between autistic and schizophrenic disorders. Demographic and IQ findings were not supportive of conjectures about parents' remarkable intelligence and achievement levels. Parental MMPI and "A-B therapist" measures (the Kemp version of the Whitehorn-Betz A-B scale) seemed contradictory to related psychogenic hypotheses about severe childhood disturbances. Results are contrary both to positions depicting parents of autistic children as exceedingly brilliant people and as "emotional refrigerators." (26 ref.)

Wolff, Wirt M. & Morris, Larry A. (U. Texas, Southwestern Medical School, Dallas) Journal of Abnormal Psychology, 1971(Apr), Vol. 77(2), 155-161. [PA, Vol 46:03465]

17. [Schizophrenia, autism, and symbiosis: Psychoanalytical approach.] (Span)

Discusses problems in differentiating autism, schizophrenia, and the symbiotic aspects of schizophrenia. It is suggested that the concept of narcissism be abandoned, that the pathological splitting be considered as the essential condition of schizophrenia, and that schizophrenia be considered as having the character of symbiotic illness.

Bleger, José Acta Psiquiátrica y Psicológica de América Latina, 1972(Aug), Vol. 18(4), 227-231. [PA, Vol 49:11550]

18. Uptake and loss of 14C-dopamine by platelets from children with infantile autism.

Studied 4 male and 1 female autistic children 9-19 yrs old. Results are compared with those obtained from normal, age-matched controls. There were no significant differences in the uptake or loss of dopamine in the autistic group, but there was much greater variation in individual values. In 1 S, dopamine uptake and loss were both abnormally high, which may be indicative of a body defect for dopamine in platelets of autistic children. As endogenous 14C-5 hydroxytryptamine and adenosine triphosphate were normal, the defect would not involve an abnormality in dopamine: adenosine triphosphate complex formation. It is suggested that these results highlight the need for more extensive investigation of brain biochemistry in autism.

Boullin, David J. & O'Brien, Robert A. (British Industrial Biological Research Assn., Carshalton, England) Journal of Autism & Childhood Schizophrenia, 1972(Jan), Vol. 2(1), 67-74. [PA, Vol 50:11440]

19. Short-term memory and cross-modal information processing in autistic children.

Tested short-term memory and cross-modal information processing capacities of 7 male autistic or schizophrenic 3-6 yr. olds. Visual-visual and auditory-visual matching and sequencing tasks were presented under 3 conditions: (a) simultaneous, (b) successive, and (c) delayed. Although there were large individual differences in the patterning of intact functions, most Ss showed severe visual-visual short-term memory deficits and several Ss were unable to make cross-modal associations between auditory and visual stimuli. Results suggest that perceptual disabilities rather than emotional disturbance may underly the delayed intellectual and language development of psychotic children and may contribute to the development of bizarre behavior patterns. (18 ref.)

Bryson, Carolyn Q. (Marion County Assn. for Retarded Children, Indianapolis, Ind.) Journal of Learning Disabilities, 1972(Feb), Vol. 5(2), 81-91. [PA, Vol 48:05303]

20. Looking and approach behavior of psychotic and normal children as a function of adult attention or preoccupation.

Studied 14 hospitalized 3-7 yr. olds who had been diagnosed as autistic (5 boys, 3 girls) or early childhood schizophrenic (3 boys, 3 girls). A control group consisted of 14 nonhospitalized Ss matched for age, sex, and socioeconomic status. Each S was observed 3 times/day, 1 day/wk, for 3 consecutive wk. in a room containing a 1-way mirror, a small cubicle seating 1 adult, and 4 zones containing sets of identical toys. An S was left in the room 1st with no adult present, and then with an unfamiliar female who was seated in the cubicle in an attentive and then a preoccupied manner. Measures of approach and attention behavior were recorded. All groups spent the largest amount of time in Zone 2 (where they could see and be seen by the adult), and most Ss looked more at the attentive than the preoccupied adult. Gross differences between psychotic and normal Ss were found in style of play and interpersonal contact. No support was found for the hypothesis that adult attention drives away autistic or schizophrenic children. (20 ref.)

Churchill, Don W. & Bryson, Carolyn Q. (Indiana U., Medical Center) Comprehensive Psychiatry, 1972(Mar), Vol. 13(2), 171-177. [PA, Vol 50:09122]

21. The parents of autistic children.

Reports a celebration speech on the 10th anniversary of the United Kingdom National Society for Autistic Children. The concept of autism is stressed as a condition that can be adapted to, possibly overcome, but as an illness with an unknown cause which cannot be expected to completely disappear in response to an appropriate cure.

Creak, Mildred. Developmental Medicine & Child Neurology, 1972(Oct), Vol. 14(5), 659-661. [PA, Vol 50:03189]

22. Imitation in autistic, early schizophrenic, and non-psychotic subnormal children.

Compared 12 psychotic children (mean age = 66 mo.) with 5 nonpsychotic subnormals (mean age = 72 mo.). Body imitation, motor-object imitation, spontaneous object use, and the influence of task class and difficulty were used as referants. Psychotic Ss did poorly in body, better in motor-object imitation, and best in object use. Controls achieved higher body and motor-object imitation scores. Task difficulty equally affected the performances of Ss and controls. Body imitation failure, traced to neurophysiological deficiencies, combined with severe central language disorders in the psychotic group, precluded nonverbal and verbal interpersonal communication. It is suggested that during early life, psychotic children, unlike the subnormal who have less severe visual-motor or language processing handicaps, cannot use parents' help to interpret environment. (46 ref.)

deMeyer, Marian K., et al. (LaRue D. Carter Memorial Hosp., Clinical Center for Early Childhood Schizophrenia, Indianapolis, Ind.) Journal of Autism & Childhood Schizophrenia, 1972(Jul), Vol. 2(3), 264-287. [PA, Vol 50:07240]

23.   Parental practices and innate activity in normal, autistic, and brain-damaged infants.
Compared infant care practices and innate activity in a study of 96 families representing 33 autistic and early schizophrenic, 33 matched normal, and 30 subnormal children. Data from objectively rated interviews indicate that parents of psychotic and normal children were alike in infant care practices, total stimulation scores, and factor analytically derived scores. Parents of subnormals were the least stimulating and coldest, providing fewer contacts and less physical freedom to the infants than other parents. Normal infants were more active but autistic and subnormal did not differ on any infant rating item. Infant factor scores showed that autistic and subnormal infants were most alike in the Alertness factor, both below normal infants. Social factors did not differ. Brain damage indices were highest in subnormal and lowest in normal, all differing significantly. Results are discussed and interpreted to substantiate criticism of theories that attribute autism to parental or organic-environmental causation during infancy. (34 ref.)
DeMyer, Marian K., et al. (LaRue D. Carter Memorial Hosp., Clinical Research Center for Early Childhood Schizophrenia, Indianapolis, Ind.) Journal of Autism & Childhood Schizophrenia, 1972(Jan), Vol. 2(1), 49-66. [PA, Vol 50:11467]

24.   A comparison of adaptive, verbal, and motor profiles of psychotic and non-psychotic subnormal children.
Constructed a test battery designed to evaluate intellectual, verbal, motor, perceptual-motor, and perceptual task performance levels of preschool psychotic children. The battery was used in an experimental comparison of psychotic (11 early schizophrenic, 19 primary autistic, and 35 secondary autistic) and nonpsychotic subnormal (n = 29) children whose CA group means ranged from 56.1-71.8 mo. The comparison involved selected adaptive (nonverbal intellectual and perceptual-motor), verbal, and motor tasks, all also performed by 3 normal Ss. Subnormal Ss were significantly more advanced than the schizophrenic Ss in 2 motor tasks, and than the primary autistic, in all excepting the Seguin formboard and stair climbing. Primary autistic Ss were better at stair climbing than the schizophrenic Ss whose motor performance profiles proved similar to those of lower functioning autistic. The discussion is focused on etiological implications of results. (30 ref.)
DeMyer, Marian K.; Barton, Sandra & Norton, James A. (LaRue D. Carter Memorial Hosp., Clinical Research Center for Early Childhood Schizophrenia, Indianapolis, Ind.) Journal of Autism & Childhood Schizophrenia, 1972(Oct), Vol. 2(4), 359-377. [PA, Vol 50:06978]

25.   Cognitive mechanisms in autism: Experiments with color and tone sequence production.
Conducted experiments in which 20 5-17 yr old autistic, 20 normal, and 20 severely subnormal children, matched for MA, produced spontaneous sequences of colors and tones. Underlying rules of patterns depended on MA in all groups. However, tendency to use simple rules rigidly, restrict available elements, and avoid rare patterns was specific to severely retarded Ss, a basic abnormality not accounted for by mental retardation. Severely subnormal Ss produced sequences similar to those of normal, using simple rules less strictly, making use of all elements, and frequently producing unique patterns. Complexity and originality rose with increasing choice of elements for building sequences. Modality made little difference, but tone sequences produced by autistic Ss were superior to their color sequences approaching normal pattern characteristics. Lack of flexibility in self-generated rules is linked to a critical period in language development. It is suggested that spontaneous pattern production may facilitate diagnostic differentiation.
Frith, Uta. (Medical Research Council, Developmental Psychology Unit, London, England) Journal of Autism & Childhood Schizophrenia, 1972(Apr), Vol. 2(2), 160-173. [PA, Vol 50:11720]

26.   Locating events in space and time: Experiments with autistic, blind, and deaf children.
Compared autistic, blind, deaf (10 in each handicapped group), and 20 normal children in 2 experiments focused on responses to stimuli in situations allowing for alternative strategies and coding processes. The autistic (6-14 yr. old) and control groups were matched for levels of cognitive development or for task performance relevant to the functions tested. Like the normal and unlike the blind or blindfolded, autistic Ss used visual rather than tactile cues to locate stimuli. On the other hand, like the deaf, but unlike the hearing, they organized visually presented verbal items in a spatial rather than temporal ordered sequence. It is suggested that autistic children do not necessarily process visual stimuli inadequately. Rather, processing capacity seems to depend on the availability of codes for organization, which may be relatively independent of the modality in which stimuli are presented.
Hermelin, Beate. (Medical Research Council Developmental Psychology Unit, London, England) Journal of Autism & Childhood Schizophrenia, 1972(Jul), Vol. 2(3), 288-298. [PA, Vol 50:07005]

27.   Infantile autism: Some notes on recent research studies.
Reports the findings of a study group held under the auspices of the Institute for Mental Retardation. (22 ref)
Ives, L. A. (U Manchester, England) Association of Educational Psychologists Journal & Newsletter, 1972(Fal), Vol 3(2), 47-52. [PA, Vol 53:05505]

28.   How far can autistic children go in matters of social adaptation?
Discusses case histories of 8 male and 1 female autistic children selected from a total of 96 so diagnosed at Johns Hopkins Hospital prior to 1953. Ss, first evaluated and given the diagnosis at an age ranging from 2 yrs, 10 mo to 8 yrs, 1 mo are presently in their 20s and 30s. Their development is traced from acute psychotic infancy until the end of 1971. Having made a sufficient social adjustment, they manage to function as self-dependent individuals, mostly well educated and all gainfully employed. Attention is drawn to differences between this group and other autistic patients, maturational and environmental issues, and past and present patterns of behavior and personality structure.
Kanner, Leo; Rodriguez, Alejandro & Ashenden, Barbara. (Johns Hopkins U., Medical School) Journal of Autism & Childhood Schizophrenia, 1972(Jan), Vol. 2(1), 9-33. [PA, Vol 50:11517]

29.   [Object relation in the autistic child: Essay on the economy of relational movements in the psychotic child: On the observation of an autistic child and his productions.] (Fren)
Considers autism not only as a symptomatological entity, but also as a defensive system which permits a child to live within the boundaries of his psychosis. Theories are developed in which notions of object permanence and identity or constancy of the environment appear to be opposed. The exigency of identity or of environmental constancy, if this constitutes a normal preliminary step of permanent object accession, represents the obstacle point in the evolution of object relation. The role of family and fantasy development (especially with regard to mother-son relations) is elaborated and illustrated by the case history of an autistic boy whose progress in a familial and institutional environment is related from birth to 11 yrs old. The S's institutionalization is shown to be a vehicle for the realization of fantasies. Questions are raised concerning the roles of transitional function with regard to the autistic child's object relations and the connections between family and fetish object.
Lanouzière, Jacqueline & Lainé, Tony. (U. Paris, Lab. of General Psychology, France) Psychiatrie de l'Enfant, 1972, Vol. 15(2), 287-398. [PA, Vol 51:01259]

30.   [Object relation of an autistic child.] (Fren)
Discusses the relationship of the autistic child to his environment. Such a child chooses to select certain objects to which he maintains a privileged and narrow relationship. S was a hospitalized autistic 7-yr-old male. Topics discussed in the context of this

S's illness include (a) narcissism and the assumption of a body image and (b) metabolization of the loss of his mother. It is pointed out that a certain rapport exists between the activity of the autistic child and his graphic production, and that the presence of another attentive person is a source of pleasure to him.
Lanouziere, Jacqueline & Laine, Tony. (U. Paris V, Lab. of General Psychology, France) Perspectives Psychiatriques, 1972(Apr), No. 36, 53-61. [PA, Vol 51:11285]

31. The effect of stimulus interval on the auditory evoked response during sleep in autistic children.
Measured the averaged auditory evoked response to pairs of clicks separated by a 500-msec intrapair interval in 10 29-61 mo old autistic children during Stage 2 and REM sleep. The long interval between paired clicks varied from 2-6.5 secs. Lengthening the interpair interval significantly increased amplitudes of responses to both clicks of each pair during Stage 2 and to the 1st during REM. With no effect during Stage 2, it significantly increased the response latency to the 2nd click during REM. Such lengthening did not affect the amplitude recovery ratio during Stage 2 or REM nor the latency recovery ratio in Stage 2, while increasing the latter during REM. It induced a significantly greater increase in latency ratio in autistic than age-matched normal Ss during REM. However, no difference was noted in recovery ratio between autistic and normal Ss at either interpair stimulus interval.
Ornitz, Edward M., et al. (U. California, Medical School, Los Angeles) Journal of Autism & Childhood Schizophrenia, 1972(Apr), Vol. 2(2), 140-150. [PA, Vol 50:11572]

32. [Language developmental disorder as the primary disturbance of childhood autism.] (Japn)
Reviews recent theories of infantile autism, and endorses the hypothesis by M. Rutter, J. K. Wing, and L. Wing that language-cognitive impairment is a primary symptom and stereotype behaviors are secondary ones. To examine the hemispheric malfunctioning, the dexterity of autistic children was compared with that of retarded children. The incidence of left-handedness was about the same below age 5 but above age 6 was greater in autistic children, suggesting the possibility of minimum brain damage in the left hemisphere of older autistic children. Clinical observation of early behavior problems supported the above hypothesis. Mutism and autistic behaviors after age 3 need special attention and early treatment. (English summary) (36 ref)
Takagi, Ryuro. (Kyoto U, Medical School, Japan) Japanese Journal of Child Psychiatry, 1972(Sep), Vol 13(5), 285-294. [PA, Vol 53:05583]

33. [Perinatal anoxia and "cerebral dysfunction."] (Span)
Briefly describes 8 children, 3 ½-11 yr. old, whose behavior presented symptoms of possible cerebral dysfunction. It is suggested that in each case drug-induced parturition or instrumental delivery of infant S may have produced anoxia which could have been responsible for the present behavioral abnormalities (motor and sensory hyperactivity, autistic tendencies, and dysphasia). (English summary)
Vidal, Fidel & Mendez Vites, Santiago. Archivos de Neurobiología, 1972(Jul), Vol. 35(4), 339-346. [PA, Vol 50:07133]

34. A comparison of personality variables in autistic and mentally retarded children.
Compared personality characteristics of 35 severely mentally retarded children, including 11 with Down's syndrome and 32 autistic children evaluated on the basis of the Behavior Rating Instrument for Autistic Children. Ss, 48 boys and 19 girls, were 4-12 yrs old. Ratings on 5 scales pertaining to nature and degree of relationship to an adult as a person, communication, vocalization and expressive speech, drive for mastery, and psychosexual development indicate that the severely retarded group scored significantly higher in each area. Also higher for that group were the correlations between various scales. It is suggested that severely retarded children, particularly those with Down's syndrome, are less disturbed and better integrated than autistic children, and also that fragmentation, compartmentalization,

and lack of generalization between key areas of function are specific factors in the autistic process. (28 ref.)
Wolf, Enid G.; Wenar, Charles & Ruttenberg, Bertram A. (Developmental Center for Special Education, Washington, D.C.) Journal of Autism & Childhood Schizophrenia, 1972(Jan), Vol. 2(1), 92-108. [PA, Vol 50:11640]

35. Prognosis in autism: A follow-up study.
Presents and discusses a follow-up study to 2 studies by M. Rutter and L. Lockyer (see PA, Vol. 42:5827, and Vol. 42:5828). 85 autistic boys and 35 girls, 5½ yrs of age at initial evaluation and 12 yrs at follow-up, served as Ss. Measures, also applied to 26 nonpsychotic subnormal controls, included speech, social, educational, and family adequacy ratings, IQ's, and neurological data. Most autistic Ss remained educationally retarded and 42% were institutionalized. Results indicate the following prognosis in autism: 1-2% recovery to normal, 5-15% borderline, 16-25% fair, and 60-75% poor. The best predictor of functional capacity in a work/school setting was S's rating at intake. Performance IQ and severity of illness were next to best predictors. Case histories of 20 Ss with the best outcome, including 2 functioning normally, are compared and analyzed. Etiological implications of results are outlined which support theories linking the cause of autism to biological factors. (3 p ref)
DeMyer, Marian K. et al. (LaRue D. Carter Memorial Hosp., Clinical Research Center for Early Childhood Schizophrenia, Indianapolis, Ind.) Journal of Autism & Childhood Schizophrenia, 1973(Jul), Vol. 3(3), 199-246. [PA, Vol 51:07268]

36. On the echolalia of the blind and of the autistic child.
Discusses similarities in echolalia exhibited by autistic children and blind infants in terms of the human desire for communication, arrested language development, difficulties in comprehension and self-differentiation, and parental reactions. It is concluded that the direct effects of sensory restriction in the blind and perceptual restriction in the autistic delay acquisition of the meaning and structure systems of language. (1½ p ref)
Fay, Warren H. (U. Oregon Medical School, Portland) Journal of Speech & Hearing Disorders, 1973(Nov), Vol. 38(4), 478-489. [PA, Vol 51:07242]

37. A study of children with hyperlexia.
A syndrome of precocious and compulsive reading against a background of intellectual slowness and autistic behavior recently has been delineated. 3 boys with this syndrome were observed, 1 S for 4 yrs. Neurologic and psychologic examinations were carried out when the Ss were between the ages of 4 and 6. Ss had marked apraxic disorders, manifested by inability to copy simple figures or to draw. While they read fluently, their comprehension of both spoken and written language was limited. A set of 2- and 3-part commands was given in both spoken and written form. In spoken form, these commands can be carried out by the average child at the age of 4½. The 3 Ss could complete only about half of the commands, doing equally well on written and spoken presentation. Primary speech functions and verbal memory were intact; Ss were able to repeat 10-word sentences, and they often learned long passages verbatim. The basic language defect appeared to be in the association between speech symbols and meaning. The occurrence of this deficit together with apraxia suggests a parietal lobe disorder. The syndrome occurs almost exclusively in boys (14 out of 15 cases so far reported) and most likely is caused by a congenital developmental defect.
Huttenlocher, Peter R. & Huttenlocher, Janellen. (Yale U., Medical School) Neurology, 1973(Oct), Vol. 23(10), 1107-1116. [PA, Vol 51:11462]

38. A cybernetic approach to childhood psychosis.
Presents a theoretical approach to childhood psychoses, focusing on insights gained from the development of computer techniques. Such insights are applicable to the study and treatment of autism and related psychoses in early life, leading to an understanding of psychotic behavior in terms of a defect of the process rather than defect of result. It is assumed that the aim of adaptation in children and adults is to correlate present perception with past experience so as to build up internal models of the world which

aid in formulating and choosing beneficial courses of action. This process is described cybernetically in terms of programing and hardware, with the understanding that as the thinking mechanism matures physiologically, the program is continually modified by experience. Childhood psychoses can be classified in terms of defects in the program and hardware, and it is postulated that the resulting theory has clear and testable consequences for therapy and future research. (23 ref.)
Kahn, Roy M. & Arbib, Michael A. (California State U., San Francisco) Journal of Autism & Childhood Schizophrenia, 1973(Jul), Vol. 3(3), 261-273. [PA, Vol 51:07287]

39. Selective responding to the components of multiple visual cues by autistic children.
Trained 15 normal and 15 profoundly retarded, autistic children (mean ages 9 and 6 yrs, respectively) to respond to a card containing 2 visual cues. After this training discrimination was established, Ss were tested on the single cues in order to assess whether 1 or both stimuli had acquired control over their responding. 12 autistic Ss gave evidence for stimulus overselectivity in that they responded correctly to only 1 of the 2 component cues. On the other hand, 12 normals showed clear evidence of control by both component cues of the training card. Results are consistent with previous studies, where autistics showed overselectivity when presented with multiple sensory input in several modalities. However, autistic Ss appeared to have difficulty responding to multiple cues even when both cues were in the same modality. Results are discussed in relation to the experimental literature on selective attention in normally functioning organisms. (17 ref.)
Koegel, Robert L. & Wilhelm, Hannelore. (U. California, Inst. for Behavioral Science, Santa Barbara) Journal of Experimental Child Psychology, 1973(Jun), Vol. 15(3), 442-453. [PA, Vol 51:03345]

40. Comparative study of conditioning of averaged evoked responses by coupling sound and light in normal and autistic children.
Compared the conditioning of averaged evoked potentials in 11 psychotic and 11 normal 6-14 yr old children. Evoked potentials, like the blocking of alpha rhythm, can be conditioned by coupling a short sound of low intensity with an intense light flash. In normal Ss, the amplitude of the potential evoked by sound at the occipital region was small and quite variable. Its amplitude increased and its variability diminished after coupling of sound and light. Its form resembled the potential evoked by light, especially in its rhythmic aftereffects. In psychotic Ss auditory evoked responses were variable and small and remained so during the coupling of sound and light. These Ss responded to sound with a late slow wave which was strong and generalized. It was particularly prominent during conditioning and resembled the slow waves which follow the visual evoked potentials in autistic Ss. This slow wave resembles in certain ways those provoked by movement or its anticipation in normal Ss, but it appeared here during sensorial conditioning which required no movement. It is suspected that this slow wave may reflect a diffuse motor component in the perceptual and associative processes of these autistic children.
Lelord, G.; Laffont, F.; Jesseaume, P. & Stephant, J. L. (Bretonneau Hosp., Faculty of Medicine, Tours, France) Psychophysiology, 1973(Jul), Vol. 10(4), 415-425. [PA, Vol 51:03350]

41. GC-MS identification of bufotenin in urine samples from patients with schizophrenia or infantile autism.
Found bufotenin in urine samples from 2 drug-free chronic schizophrenic patients and 2 autistic children, but not from 4 normal controls. The identification was based on thin layer chromatography of the tertiary amine fraction using a specific ophthalaldehyde spray, and also on gas chromatography. Unambiguous proof of the identity of bufotenine was provided by gas chromatography-mass spectrum analysis of the bufotenine-positive samples through its trimethylsilyl derivative.
Narasimhachari, Nedathur & Himwich, Harold E. (Galesburg State Research Hosp., Thudichum Psychiatric Research Lab.,

Ill.) Life Sciences, 1973(May), Vol. 12(10, Pt. 2), 475-478. [PA, Vol 51:01271]

42. The spatial or temporal organization of short-term memory.
In 4 experiments children were shown 3 visually displayed digits. The digits were exposed successively in 3 windows in such a way that the left-to-right order never corresponded with the temporal-sequential order. When asked to recall or recognize the digits, 20 8-yr-old normal children responded in terms of temporal order. 10 deaf, 10 autistic and 10 subnormal children, recalled or recognized the spatial (i.e., the left-to-right) order. The relationship between hearing and/or speech and the temporal ordering of visual displays is discussed.
O'Connor, N. & Hermelin, B. M. (Medical Research Council, Psychology Unit, London, England) Quarterly Journal of Experimental Psychology, 1973(Aug), Vol. 25(3), 335-343. [PA, Vol 51:07252]

43. Effect of vestibular and auditory stimulation on the REMs of REM sleep in autistic children.
Studied the influence of vestibular and auditory stimulation on the oculomotor output during REM sleep in 6 normal and 5 autistic children (age range, 39.3-128 mo). One index of the ocular activity from the entire night, which measured the degree of REM clustering without reference to REM sleep time, was significantly smaller for the autistic than for the normal Ss under the influence of vestibular stimulation. The duration and organization of the REM bursts significantly increased during the course of the night in the normals in response to the vestibular stimulation and showed no response during the course of the night in the autistic Ss. The induced changes are manifestations of a specific effect on the phasic activity of REM sleep since no changes in the percent of REM sleep time or the nocturnal sleep cycle occurred. (35 ref)
Ornitz, Edward M.; Forsythe, Alan B. & de la Peña, Augustin. (U. California, Medical School, Center for the Health Sciences, Los Angeles) Archives of General Psychiatry, 1973(Dec), Vol. 29(6), 786-791. [PA, Vol 52:03231]

44. The assessment and treatment of pre-school autistic children.
Considers principles upon which a service for preschool autistic children should be established and outlines the organizational requirements. It is argued that there are serious drawbacks to regional assessment centers for autistic children, and broad-based appraisal, including developmental evaluation, behavioral assessment, medical investigation, and environmental study is required. Since this would necessitate access to a wide range of skills, one person is needed to have the responsibility for coordinating care. Assessment and treatment are seen as inextricably linked, and both must be viewed from a developmental perspective with re-evaluation as the children change with age. Treatment should be mainly focused on aiding social and linguistic development and reducing the tendency to develop rigid stereotyped patterns. A home-based approach founded upon developmental and behavioral principles is considered appropriate. Inpatient care is described as of only limited usefulness and unnecessary for most children.
Rutter, Michael. (U. London, Inst. of Psychiatry, England) Early Child Development & Care, 1973, Vol. 3(1), 13-29. [PA, Vol 52:10331]

45. Sex ratios in families of autistic children.
It is an accepted fact that males are more often affected with autism than females irrespective of the precise definition used for diagnosis. Preliminary reports in the literature indicate that the deviation in sex ratio might be a more general phenomenon in these families. A study of 47 families with autistic children, including 5 families with 2 affected children, indicates that deviations from the expected 1:1 sex ratio do occur. Maternal siblings showed a significant deviation in the direction of the sex of the S. Paternal siblings showed just the opposite deviation for female Ss only. There was also a significant deviation in the paternal 1st cousins of the male Ss. No simple explanation can be provided for these results.

Spence, M. A.; Simmons, J. Q.; Brown, N. A. & Wikler, L. (U. California, Los Angeles) American Journal of Mental Deficiency, 1973(Jan), Vol. 77(4), 405-407. [PA, Vol 50:03329]

46. Problems of differential diagnosis between mental retardation and autismus infantum.
Considers that the intelligence level of autistic children does not exceed that of the mentally retarded, raising the problem of differentiation. On first glance, the child seems intelligent, then, imbecilic. Standardized tests make the level moronic. Autismus infantum, however, must be differentiated from feeble-mindedness since it is a syndrome caused by different factors.
van Krevelen, D. Arn. Acta Paedopsychiatrica, 1973, Vol. 39(8-10), 199-203. [PA, Vol 50:09709]

47. A study of aetiological factors at critical periods of development in autistic children.
Over a 10-yr period, 97 autistic children were seen, treated, and studied along with their families. Data on these cases were analyzed in terms of etiology as known, social class of parents, year of onset, its relationship to the presence of an organic cerebral defect, and outcome in terms of the present educational placement of the child. Findings suggest that infantile autism is a disorder with a multiple etiology and the causes, both organic and environmental, are interrelated. It is postulated that the most consistent effect present in the early backgrounds of these children was a history of sensory deprivation at a critical period of development.
Williams, Sara & Harper, Juliet. (Psychiatric Centre, North Ryde, New South Wales, Australia) Australian & New Zealand Journal of Psychiatry, 1973(Sep), Vol. 7(3), 163-168. [PA, Vol 52:01181]

48. The use of personal pronouns by autistic children.
Eight spontaneously echolalic autistic children (mean age, 9 yrs, 7 mo) who had never used the pronoun I were exposed to short sentences containing several personal pronouns in all positions in a 3-word utterance. It was found that there was no tendency for children to avoid the repetition of I, once sentence position was controlled. A number of children echoed the final word of the sentence while others repeated the whole utterance. Findings provide no support for a psychogenic theory of speech behavior in autistic children.
Bartak, Lawrence & Rutter, Michael. (U London, England) Journal of Autism & Childhood Schizophrenia, 1974(Sep), Vol 4(3), 217-222. [PA, Vol 56:08103]

49. Deictic categories in the language of autistic children.
Tested the hypothesis that autistic children are handicapped in the acquisition of syntactic structures and that the development of some or all of the syntactic and morphological aspects of their language deviates from that of normal and mentally retarded children. A pilot investigation of the production of tense markers in 3 autistic (MA, 3.1-5.4 yrs), 3 mentally retarded (MA, 3.8-4.5 yrs) and 2 normal children (MA, 6.4 and 4.5 yrs) is reported. Testing for the production of tense inflections in a standardized structured test situation using pictures and toys produced results which were scored according to the appearance of a certain tense form. Significant differences were found in the production of the past tense; the percent of correct responses was 80 for normal Ss, 8 for autistic Ss, and mentally retarded Ss fell in between with 60%. It is concluded that the hypothesis of deviance of language acquisition in childhood autism, particularly in areas related to language deixis, is strengthened. (30 ref)
Bartolucci, Giampiero & Albers, Robert J. (St Joseph's Hosp, McMaster Psychiatric Unit, Hamilton, Canada) Journal of Autism & Childhood Schizophrenia, 1974(Mar), Vol 4(2), 131-141. [PA, Vol 56:09985]

50. On some language parameters of autistic echolalia.
Investigated whether the processes involved in autistic echolalia include anything beyond rote mechanical parroting. The S was a 5½-yr-old white male. His was a normal delivery, full-term, and his development proceeded normally to the age of 2 yrs. He then became hyperactive and exhibited bizarre mannerisms. At 5½ yrs he was diagnosed as a childhood psychotic with autism. The test

included 16 sentences which varied in the complexity of the verb phrase. Results confirm the position that S recognized certain grammatical relations in his sentence repetitions. This finding is in accord with D. I. Slobin (1971) and others who suggest that recognition of syntactical structures and meaning play important roles in memory for speech.
Buium, Nissan & Stuecher, Heinrich U. (U Minnesota, Research & Development Ctr) Language & Speech, 1974(Oct-Dec), Vol 17(4), 353-357. [PA, Vol 54:11946]

51. Biogenic amines in autistic and atypical children.
Studied central nervous system biogenic amine metabolism in 35 3-11 yr old children suffering from autism, atypical development, epilepsy, and movement disorders. After oral administration of probenecid, a membrane blocking compound, a cerebrospinal fluid (CSF) sample was obtained for assay of homovanillic acid (HVA), 5-hydroxyindoleacetic acid (5HIAA), and probenecid. The concentrations of HVA and 5HIAA in the CSF were thought to reflect the rate of formation in the brain of their parent amines, dopamine and serotonin, respectively. There were statistically significant differences in CSF HVA and 5HIAA levels between the psychotic and epileptic children. The HVA and 5HIAA were significantly correlated with each other. Each of these acid metabolites covaried with the CSF levels of probenecid. Interpretation of the significance of CSF HVA and 5HIAA requires simultaneous measurement of probenecid concentration. (29 ref)
Cohen, Donald J.; Shaywitz, Bennett A.; Johnson, Warren T. & Bowers, Malcolm. (Yale U, Child Study Ctr) Archives of General Psychiatry, 1974(Dec), Vol 31(6), 845-853. [PA, Vol 53:09746]

52. The measured intelligence of autistic children.
Presents a study with a focus on IQ measurements of subnormal and autistic children analyzed for repeatability and also for relationship to other factors such as severity of illness and outcome of treatment. Initial IQ measurements correlated well with those obtained about 5 yrs later. Of the 115 autistic children (mean age, 64 mo) tested, 94% had general IQs in the retarded range (< 68) at initial evaluation. IQ estimates were significantly related to the severity of symptoms and effectively predicted performance at school. Ss with IQ > 50 at initial evaluation, who were subsequently treated, showed a greater increase in IQ than untreated Ss in the same IQ range. Treatment was without differential effect for children with < 40 IQs. After treatment, verbal IQ gains tended to be maintained or improved in groups with higher initial IQs but stagnated or were even lost in the lower IQ groups.
DeMyer, Marian K. et al. (LaRue D. Carter Memorial Hosp, Clinical Research Ctr for Early Childhood Schizophrenia, Indianapolis, IN) Journal of Autism & Childhood Schizophrenia, 1974(Jan-Mar), Vol 4(1), 42-60. [PA, Vol 56:10002]

53. The near-normal autistic adolescent: Nonreciprocal speech.
A panel of 6 parents and professionals compared, by letter, their impressions of approximately 50 mildly autistic adolescents they had known. When communication problems and social adjustments were examined, it was found that (a) these Ss typically used nonreciprocal speech, with such recurrent problems as failing to listen, interpreting words too literally, and making irrelevant comments; and (b) they were apprehensive, having experienced unpleasant consequences of errors in judgment.
Dewey, Margaret A. & Everard, Margaret P. (National Society for Autistic Children, Adult Programs, Ann Arbor, MI) Journal of Autism & Childhood Schizophrenia, 1974(Dec), Vol 4(4), 348-356. [PA, Vol 56:10003]

54. Specific motor disabilities in Down's syndrome.
Compared 17 children with Down's syndrome with 19 severely subnormal autistic children and with 23 normal children on 2 simple motor tasks (pursuit rotor tracking and finger tapping). It was hypothesized that Down's syndrome is associated with specific difficulties in using long-term motor programs and that mongoloid children may, therefore, be dependent on simple feedback processes to perform motor tasks. Results show that although the groups were matched on initial tracking perfor-

mance, Down's syndrome children failed to show any improvement after a 5-min rest, while both comparison groups showed a very marked improvement. On the finger tapping task, Down's syndrome children were abnormally slow compared to the other groups. Neither the level of mental development nor the degree of general mental retardation can account for these deficits. (26 ref)

Frith, Uta & Frith, Christopher D. (MRC Developmental Psychology Unit, London, England) Journal of Child Psychology & Psychiatry & Allied Disciplines, 1974(Oct), Vol 15(4), 293-301. [PA, Vol 53:09763]

55. Infantile autism: Subclassification on the basis of neurological impairment.
Reviewed case history data on 131 autistic children (mean age = 10.8 yrs) to test the proposition that subclassification based on the presence or absence of positive neurological findings is of prognostic value. Results indicate that this measure was of limited use in defining subclusters of the epidemiological data included in the research. However, it did suggest that reproductive complications were a frequent variable in the etiological histories of the organic group and that environmental stresses were associated with the non-organic group. With respect to follow-up on intellectual functioning and language development, evidence of neurological impairment had no predictive significance. (21 ref)

Harper, Juliet. (New South Wales Coll of Paramedical Studies, Sydney, Australia) Australian Journal of Mental Retardation, 1974(Jun), Vol 3(2), 49-55. [PA, Vol 53:11867]

56. Autistic syndromes in children and adolescents.
Discusses several variants of autism (excluding childhood schizophrenia and Kanner's early infantile autism), stressing the specificity of the organization of cognitive processes, the inconsistency of behavior, and the strange nature of interests and communications characteristic of autistic psychopaths. Peculiarities of autistic manifestations within the framework of organic autism depend on insufficient psychic tension, underdeveloped space-time notions, insufficiency of intelligence as a whole, and the presence of epileptic seizures. Autism may also occur in the form of somatogenic or psychogenic reactions and pathological personality development. It seems to be a nonspecific syndrome of childhood. Peculiar clinical manifestations are associated with peculiarities of the basic disorder. Correlations of clinical, psychological, EEG, and pneumoencephalography data are suggestive of defects and distortions in the system of motivation and behavior planning.

Isaev, D. N. & Kagan, V. E. (Pediatric Medical Inst, Leningrad, USSR) Acta Paedopsychiatrica, 1974, Vol 40(5), 182-189. [PA, Vol 53:03302]

57. [An analysis of the changing behavior patterns in autistic children.] (Japn)
Examined the overt behavior of 15 male and 3 female 3.3–8.0 yr old autistic children during an 18-mo period. The Ss were on nonverbal, subverbal and verbal speech levels with one of the following diagnoses: early infantile autism, autistic child, organic pseudo-autism, minimal brain dysfunction, mental developmental disorder, or emotional deprivation. Three raters used a 16-item behavior checklist to evaluate Ss' behavior 4 times during the 18-mo period. Four behavior patterns characteristic of autistic children were (a) rocking, rotating, repeating a simple motion; (b) patting or touching warm or cold objects or playing with water; (c) throwing a temper tantrum directed toward a definite object or person; and (d) behaving compulsively. Although there were no large differences in the changing behavior patterns based on age, diagnosis, or therapy, children with verbal abilities improved markedly over children lacking such abilities. (English summary) (41 ref)

Ito, Norihiro & Yamazaki, Kosuke. (Hokkaido U School of Education, Sapporo, Japan) Japanese Journal of Child Psychiatry, 1974(Mar–Apr), Vol 15(2), 55–68. [PA, Vol 63:03392]

58. Hair amino acids in childhood autism.
Studied the hair samples of 61 autistic and 15 normal children for changes in amino acid content to determine whether an altered amino acid pattern is present in autistic Ss. No significant differences in hair amino acid composition between autistic and control Ss were seen, nor were age or sex differences apparent. Shampoo used, hair texture, hair color, or hair fragility showed no correlation with amino acid content. Although no amino acid metabolic abnormality appeared in the hair protein of autistic Ss, it is suggested that further attention be given to the examination of urine specimens for ninhydrin-positive substances, and that further study of the peculiar rancid-like hair odor of autistic children be conducted.

Johnson, Robert J.; Wiersema, Vernon & Kraft, I. A. (Texas Research Inst of Mental Sciences, Houston) Journal of Autism & Childhood Schizophrenia, 1974(Mar), Vol 4(2), 187-188. [PA, Vol 56:10023]

59. Response to multiple visual cues of color, size, and form by autistic children.
Describes a study of visual discrimination learning in which 20 autistic males were compared with 20 Down's syndrome and 20 normal controls. Ss, all males, were trained to discriminate between 2 visual stimuli varying in color, form, and size. They were then tested on the 3 parameters presented separately and in combinations of 2. It was found that normal children and those who were classified as verbal autistic did not differ in overall performance or in the effective use of double cues, but were superior to retardates, and retardates were superior to nonverbal autistic children. There was no cue dominance in normal, verbal autistic, and retarded children, but size and color were significantly preferred to form by the nonverbal autistic group. (16 ref)

Kovattana, Patricia M. & Kraemer, Helena C. Journal of Autism & Childhood Schizophrenia, 1974(Sep), Vol 4(3), 251-261. [PA, Vol 56:08119]

60. Factors related to outcome in autistic children.
32 autistic children, identified by V. Lotter (see PA, Vol 41:7561) in an epidemiological survey in England when they were 8-10 yrs old, were followed up 8 yrs later. The best single predictor of outcome was a measure of speech. Speech and IQ together correlated more highly with outcome than did any other combination of variables. The frequency of family mental illness was similar to that found in comparable studies. Onset of fits in adolescence in some autistic children confirms that evidence of neurological abnormalities increases with age. Subclassification among autistic children is urged, and a scheme is offered which identifies main areas of uncertainty in classification. (17 ref)

Lotter, Victor. (U Guelph, Canada) Journal of Autism & Childhood Schizophrenia, 1974(Sep), Vol 4(3), 263-277. [PA, Vol 56:08122]

61. Labeling: A study of an "autistic" child.
Describes the case of a 10-yr-old autistic boy to demonstrate the drastic effects of "psychiatric labeling" on the social status of and behavior toward a child, which inevitably results in negative behavioral changes. It is suggested that the use of such labels (i.e., "autistic") by the parents to significant others in the child's environment influences these persons to view the child in a similar framework of ignorance. How dramatic behavioral changes were induced in the child after introducing his parents and significant others to the principles of cognitive learning theory is outlined. (Spanish & French abstracts)

Morrison, James K. (Capital District Psychiatric Ctr, Cohoes, NY) Journal of Family Counseling, 1974(Fal), Vol 2(2), 71-80. [PA, Vol 53:09788]

62. [Patterns of intelligence in autistic children: I. Analyses by the WISC.] (Japn)
Of 16 autistic children 8-15 yrs old, 6 could not be tested, 2 scored below 60, 3 between 60 and 75, and 5 over 80. Analysis of subtest results showed that scores on "digit span" and "block design" were comparatively high, but on "comprehension" and "picture arrangement" scores were extremely low. Results also indicate that as autistic children grow their overall IQ may

increase, but the standard scores on "comprehension" and "picture arrangement" will remain stable. The evidence thus suggests that an inability to solve these 2 subtests of the WISC is the salient feature of intelligence patterns in autistic children 8-15 yrs old. (English summary)
Murata, Toyohisa; Nawa, Akiko & Okuma, Hiroko. (Fukuoka U, Medical School, Japan) Kyushu Neuro-psychiatry, 1974, Vol 20(3-4), 206-212. [PA, Vol 54:09878]

63.   Concept formation in the speaking autistic child.
Attempted to determine the structure of concept formation on different levels of its development in 4 speaking autistic female Ss 8.9-14.4 yrs old compared with a similar group of 4 normal Ss. The task, a modified form of the test of concept formation by E. Hanfmann and J. Kasanin (1937), consisted of 22 cardboard blocks with 1 of 4 "names" (nonsense syllables) written on the bottom of each block. Ss were required to sort the blocks on the basis of these names. Results show that concept formation by the autistic Ss was definitely impaired. It is suggested that therapy for such children should begin at an early stage of development with the improvement of their perceptual abilities, and proceeding through abstraction and generalization to concept formation.
Noach, Marlene. (U Witwatersrand, Johannesburg, South Africa) International Journal of Mental Health, 1974(Spr), Vol 3(1), 100-109. [PA, Vol 55:00854]

64.   The recovery cycle of the averaged auditory evoked response during sleep in autistic children.
Studied the recovery cycle of the averaged auditory evoked response (AER) during sleep in 28 autistic and 23 normal 22-68 mo old children by measuring the amplitudes and latencies of wave N_2 of the 1st response (R_1) and the 2nd response (R_2) to paired clicks. No significant differences in the recovery ratios (R_2: R_1) were found between autistic and normal children in either Stage 2 or REM sleep at within-pair stimulus separations of 250, 160, 80, and 40 msec. (French summary)
Ornitz, Edward M. et al. (U California, Medical School, Los Angeles) Electroencephalography & Clinical Neurophysiology, 1974(Aug), Vol 37(2), 173-174. [PA, Vol 53:03333]

65.   Effect of visual input on vestibular nystagmus in autistic children.
Reports that a stimulus to oculomotor fixation in the absence of light and a retinal stimulation in the absence of ocular fixation caused greater suppression of postrotatory nystagmus in 21 36-69 mo old autistic children than in 25 38-90 mo old normal children. The former confirmed earlier reports of suppressed vestibular nystagmus in autistic children under conditions permitting optic fixation. The latter suggests a more profound interaction of visual and vestibular systems underlying the suppression of postrotatory nystagmus in autistic children than can be explained by their enhanced ability to use ocular fixation to suppress vestibular nystagmus. Data are consistent with a vestibular dysfunction theory underlying their disordered sensorimotor integration. This is further supported by a less constant time course of the vestibular response of autistic children in darkness. (37 ref)
Ornitz, Edward M.; Brown, Morton B.; Mason, Anne & Putnam, Nicholas H. (U California, Ctr for the Health Sciences, Los Angeles) Archives of General Psychiatry, 1974(Sep), Vol 31(39, 369-375. [PA, Vol 53:05544]

66.   Light and number: Ordering principles in the world of an autistic child.
Describes part of a complex system of ideas in which a 12-yr-old autistic female united concepts of number with elements of sunlight and weather, and seeks to explain some of her reasoning. Certain prime numbers were endowed with positive or negative affect, which persisted even when they were multiplied to form composite numbers. The numbers were associated with 29 kinds of weather, real and fictitious, which also had strong affect attached to them. It is conjectured that the system was an ingenious and laborious attempt by the child to compensate for her failure to endow events and emotions with ordinary social and emotional meaning by the invention of an entirely personal

kind of meaning in whose terms at least some elements of daily experience could be ordered and understood.
Park, David & Youderian, Philip. (Williams Coll) Journal of Autism & Childhood Schizophrenia, 1974(Dec), Vol 4(4), 313-323. [PA, Vol 56:10042]

67.   Infantile autism: Status of research.
Notes that research on autism is hindered by unreliability of diagnosis. When 2 clinicians diagnosed 373 children, agreement on whether the children were autistic was at chance level. Hoping to improve reliability of diagnosis, the present author developed a checklist of autistic symptoms and characteristics. Children getting high scores on this checklist had higher levels of serotonin in their blood platelets and responded better to therapy with massive dosages of vitamins, than those with low checklist scores. (French summary)
Rimland, Bernard. (Inst for Child Behavior, San Diego, CA) Canadian Psychiatric Association Journal, 1974(Apr), Vol 19(2), 130-133. [PA, Vol 54:09886]

68.   Rejoinder to Murray's article.
Suggests that what M. Murray (see PA, Vol 52:10436) considers meaningful speech may have been an instance of delayed echolalia.
Schreibman, Laura & Lovaas, O. Ivar. (Claremont Men's Coll.) Journal of Humanistic Psychology, 1974(Spr), Vol. 14(2), 61-62. [PA, Vol 52:10332]

69.   The effects of stimulus-fading on acquisition of a visual position discrimination in autistic, retarded, and normal children.
Trial-and-error training on a visual position-discrimination task was given to 8 autistic children (mean CA, 6.4 yrs), 8 retarded children (IQ, 36-55), and 8 children of approximately normal intelligence (74-136). Ss sat before an apparatus containing 3 translucent response panels (left, right, and center). A correct response was to press whichever outside panel was closer to a small black square projected to the right or left of center on the center panel (criterion discrimination). Apart from 3 additional normal-IQ Ss who learned the criterion discrimination (and who were excluded from the experiment proper), performance remained at a chance level for all 3 groups. The remaining 24 children received a 60-trial stimulus-fading program designed to teach the discrimination. Normal-IQ Ss performed best on the program, followed by retarded and autistic Ss. The autistic and retarded groups did not differ in performance, and the normal-IQ Ss performed reliably better than the autistic Ss. All 3 groups improved markedly on the criterion-discrimination task as a result of the stimulus-fading program. Implications for teaching autistic children are discussed. (20 ref)
Sherman, T. W. & Webster, C. D. (U Toronto, Canada) Journal of Autism & Childhood Schizophrenia, 1974(Dec), Vol 4(4), 301-312. [PA, Vol 56:10058]

70.   [Families of autistic children.] (Japn)
Describes the family relationships and characteristics of 4 autistic children and their parents. The Ss, and the fathers, were the only males in the family. All 4 fathers had lost their own fathers in early childhood, and had weak masculine identity and obsessive tendencies; they were insecure, dependent, withdrawn, defensive, and rigid. The mothers were defensive and distrustful, and had a tendency to intellectualize. The marital relationship suffered from disagreement, dependency of the husband, defensiveness of the wife, and lack of communication. It is concluded that the psychological development of these autistic children was disturbed by the fathers' obsessiveness and by the lack of maternal acceptance and support.
Takatomi, Takeshi; Suzuki, Koji; Dendo, Hisako & Watanabe, Takayoshi. (National Inst of Mental Health, Ichikawa, Japan) Journal of Mental Health, 1974(Mar), Vol 48(22), 95-112. [PA, Vol 54:05502]

71.   Ethology and stress diseases.
Reviews some of the author's Nobel Prize winning theories concerning the application of behavioral concepts to the field of medicine, contributing specifically to the relief of human suffer-

ing caused by stress. 2 examples of the value of the old method of "watching and wondering" are detailed: (a) the derivation of new facts and views on the nature of early childhood autism, providing evidence from observations, reports in the literature, and current research that neither for genetic abnormalities nor for gross brain damage is there any convincing, direct proof of causality; and (b) the application of F. M. Alexander's (1932) corrective "use" of the manipulation of body musculature to alleviate such symptoms of stress as high blood pressure, poor breathing and sleep habits, and mental slackness. It is emphasized that openminded observation is of the highest importance to medical science and that, by using this basic scientific method, both autism and general misuse of the body can be shown to be due, in a large measure, to modern stressful conditions. (48 ref) *Tinbergen, Nikolaas.* (U. Oxford, England) Science, 1974(Jul), Vol. 185(4145), 20-27. [PA, Vol 52:12834]

72.   [An epidemiological report on the conditions of autistic children at the psychiatric clinic of Nagoya University Hospital.] (Japn)
The prevalence of child autism in Japan; its clinical features, therapeutic methods; history of consultation; epidemiological comparison with other psychological, neurological, and developmental disorders; and other clinical statistical data are discussed. In 1971 15.4% of children who were patients at Nagoya University Hospital were diagnosed as autistic. This high percentage is due to Nagoya's position as a central receiving center for autistic children and its prestige as a university hospital. 79.8% of the autistic children were 2–6 yrs old, and 75.9% exhibited retarded speech development. This factor was the main reason that parents sought professional help. 49.1% of the children were also mentally retarded. The treatment history of a 6.1-yr-old boy is presented in detail. (English summary) (33 ref)
Wakabayashi, Shinichiro; Ohi, Masami; Kaneko, Toshiko & Tanaka, Tohru. (Nagoya U School of Medicine, Japan) Japanese Journal of Child Psychiatry, 1974(Mar–Apr), Vol 15(2), 69–83. [PA, Vol 63:03435]

73.   A study of etiological factors at critical periods of development in autistic children.
Analyzes information about 97 autistic children in New South Wales, observed for 10 yrs, whose parents have been under different forms of treatment. It was noted that these children tended to come from the upper socioeconomic class. Early infantile autism is regarded as a malignant disorder with multiple etiologies. The causes, both organic and environmental, were experienced by the patients as additive in decreasing their sensory experiences. It appeared that the longer the psychosis was active, the more severe were the intellectual deficiencies. Follow-up analysis demonstrated that the outcome of treatment was not encouraging in terms of educational adjustment.
Williams, Sara & Harper, Juliet. (North Ryde Psychiatric Clinic, Australia) International Journal of Mental Health, 1974(Spr), Vol 3(1), 90-99. [PA, Vol 55:02487]

74.   [Characteristics of emotional behavior of autistic children: Clarification of the term "autistic."] (Japn)
Based on clinical observations, the author attempts to more clearly define emotional reactions and behavior patterns symptomatic of affective contact disorders in autistic children. 20 cases are presented to illustrate such symptoms as flattening of affect, extreme negativism, absence of response to physical injury, emotional fluctuation without external stimulus, repetitious behavior, extreme interest in mechanical objects and a disinterest in humans, extremely selective response patterns in human interactions, extremely agitated response when patterned behavior is interrupted, senseless smiling, crying but strong resistance to expressions of sympathy, and sudden change of intentions before achieving goals. The extreme self-centeredness and negativism exhibited by the autistic child and such patterned behavior as rigid maintenance in the order of external objects demonstrates a hypersensitivity and a precarious balance between the child's inner and outer worlds. The ritualization in behavior represents an attempt by the child to enforce order in a

world that overwhelms his limited perceptions and capabilities. (English summary) (17 ref)
Yamagami, Masako. (Shiga Prefectural Child Guidance Clinic, Otsu, Japan) Japanese Journal of Child Psychiatry, 1974(May–Jun), Vol 15(3), 132–144. [PA, Vol 62:13851]

75.   The invulnerable parent.
Uses E. J. Anthony's (1974) description of the invulnerable child of schizophrenic parents as the basis for discussing the invulnerable parent of an autistic child. The following factors are identified and discussed as essential to invulnerability: (a) genetic factors, (b) stress, and (c) recognition, understanding, and acceptance of the nature of the stress. According to Anthony, the most beneficial means of decreasing vulnerability is the establishment of trustful, supportive relationships, based on the deliberate nonuse of reproachful and guilt-provoking techniques, relationships geared to reality and rationality, communications that are single-minded and unequivocal, and feelings that correlate directly with experience and are not incongruous with it.
Akerley, Mary S. (National Society for Autistic Children, Silver Spring, MD) Journal of Autism & Childhood Schizophrenia, 1975(Sep), Vol 5(3), 275-281. [PA, Vol 57:01295]

76.   Intrafamilial incidence of autism, cerebral palsy, and mongolism.
A comparative study of developmentally disturbed children as well as normal children is presented with a focus on their position in the family. Demographic data were compared for 119 autistic, 292 cerebral palsied, and 144 trisomic (trisomy 21 mongoloid) Japanese children (mean age 4 yrs 7 mo). The areas compared were maternal age at birth, ratio of males to females, number of siblings, birth order, and age interval between the S and the closest younger sibling. 128 normal kindergarten children with a mean age of 4 yrs, 6 mo, as well as the Japanese general population, were also compared for these demographic items. The findings on maternal age and sex ratios for these 3 nosological groups are consistent with recent studies. Although the reproduction of mothers of either cerebral palsied or mongoloid children ceased after the birth of the propositi, the reproduction of mothers of autistic children did not show a significant difference from that of normal children's mothers. The age intervals between the Ss and the closest younger sibling did not differ among the 3 groups or in the normal group. (20 ref)
Ando, Haruhiko & Tsuda, Katsuya. (Central Hosp, Aichi Prefectural Colony, Japan) Journal of Autism & Childhood Schizophrenia, 1975(Sep), Vol 5(3), 267-274. [PA, Vol 57:01283]

77.   Comment: The invulnerable parent.
Supports M. S. Akerley's (see PA Vol 57:1295) comparison of the invulnerable child of schizophrenic parents and parents of the autistic or otherwise handicapped child. Several points are made regarding these invulnerable groups, some of which are that (a) "good" environments providing more than adequate care may carry certain hazards, (b) "well" children from "bad" environments not only survive but thrive, and (c) the invulnerable parent or child should not be made to feel guilty.
Anthony, E. James. Journal of Autism & Childhood Schizophrenia, 1975(Sep), Vol 5(3), 281-282. [PA, Vol 57:01297]

78.   Systematic observation of play behavior in autistic children.
Play behavior, defined as interaction with peers and objects, of 5 male autistic 3.3–6.7 yr olds was systematically observed in 4 environments: a stark environment, a theraplay unit, a playroom, and an outside play deck. Preliminary results suggest that (a) with some Ss environment has little or no effect on their play behavior; (b) with multiple objects, Ss frequently related to the objects rather than to their peers; (c) object play was most frequently at the manipulative stage and often included repetitive and negative behavior; (d) within a confined space with no objects present, Ss frequently engaged in solitary repetitive behavior; and (e) within a confined space designed to facilitate a movement flow (theraplay), Ss modeled and imitated and were involved in gross motor play together.

Black, Maureen; Freeman, B. J. & Montgomery, Joanne. (U California Medical School, Los Angeles) Journal of Autism & Developmental Disorders, 1975(Dec), Vol 5(4), 363–371. [PA, Vol 59:01182]

79. Multiple response to sound in dysfunctional children.
Applied methods of linguistic-kinesic microanalysis to sound films of 25 dysfunctional 2 mo–17 yr olds. 17 Ss were markedly dysfunctional (autistic-like) while 8 Ss had milder reading problems. Results show that all Ss appeared to respond to sound more than once: when it actually occurred and again after a delay ranging from a fraction of a second up to a full second, depending on the child. Most of the Ss did not seem to actually hear the sound more than once; however, there is some indication that a few Ss may have done so. Evidence was also found suggesting a continuum from the longer delay of autistic-like children to the briefer delay of children with reading problems.
Condon, William S. (Boston U Medical School) Journal of Autism & Developmental Disorders, 1975(Mar), Vol 5(1), 37–56. [PA, Vol 59:01192]

80. Cognitive processing and linguistic reference in autistic children.
Notes that mutism or echolalia and failure to analyze sentences for their deep structure are characteristics of the language behavior of autistic children. The experimental literature indicates that cognitive processes which underlie the construction of a lexicon or the learning of ordering rules may be disturbed in these children. The inability to coordinate visual and aural stimulation inhibits lexical development, while difficulties in sequencing and use of inappropriate sequencing codes inhibit the growth of a productive grammar. It is suggested that remedial programs which include training in these processes may prove beneficial, and that substitute modes of information processing which the autistic child uses may be exploited to teach language forms. (20 ref)
Dalgleish, Barrie. (U Queensland, Brisbane, Australia) Journal of Autism & Developmental Disorders, 1975(Dec), Vol 5(4), 353–361. [PA, Vol 59:01194]

81. Childhood psychosis: The problem of differential diagnosis.
In 4 interrelated studies of 66 former psychiatric patients (aged 8-10 yrs at time of admission during 1955-1964 or 1945-1954), Form E-1 of B. Rimland's Diagnostic Check List for Behavior-Disturbed Children (DCL) was found to be an effective instrument for differentiating autistic, other psychotic, and nonpsychotic disturbed children. Follow-up study revealed more favorable outcomes in nonpsychotic cases, with significant associations between DCL scores and improvement following discharge. Scores indicative of autism on the DCL were also significantly associated with being Jewish.
Davids, Anthony. (Emma Pendleton Bradley Hosp, Riverside, RI) Journal of Autism & Childhood Schizophrenia, 1975(Jun), Vol 5(2), 129-138. [PA, Vol 57:01315]

82. Differential effects of communication on operant behavior in children.
Performance on a free-operant differentiation device which required Ss to press 1 of 2 panels for candy and money was used to study the effects of nonvisual communication and listening to a story in 5 normal and 2 exceptional 3½–8 yr olds and in 1 24-yr-old adult. Differential responding to the panel that produced reinforcement was acquired by all Ss in the 1st session. Communication by a relevant adult (mother) decreased reinforced and nonreinforced responding and increased talking. Listening to a story decreased reinforced and nonreinforced responding but did not increase talking. Communication had no effect on any of the behaviors of the autistic child and increased the speech of the retarded child the least of the Ss who talked. The effect of crying in 1 child also decreased responding.
Edwards, Joseph S.; Edwards, Diane D. & Lucas, Joanne. (U Missouri, Kansas City) Bulletin of the Psychonomic Society, 1975(Jul), Vol 6(1), 90–92. [PA, Vol 59:07991]

83. Age and type of onset as critical variables in early infantile autism.
A retrospective study of 131 autistic 3–22 yr olds was made in which 2 groups, Natal and Acquired, were defined on the bases of age at onset and type of onset. Prenatal and perinatal variables were found to be significantly related to Natal onset, whereas in the Acquired group the significant variables were those occurring in early childhood, between yrs 1 and 3. Follow-up data on intellectual functioning and language development indicated a better prognosis for the Acquired group. An inability to cope with stress is postulated as an underlying feature in both instances, present from birth in the Natal group and occurring in the face of developmental stresses in the Acquired group. (27 ref)
Harper, Juliet & Williams, Sara. (New South Wales Coll of Paramedical Studies, Sydney, Australia) Journal of Autism & Developmental Disorders, 1975(Mar), Vol 5(1), 25–36. [PA, Vol 59:01208]

84. The recall of digits by normal, deaf and autistic children.
10 normal, 10 autistic, and 10 deaf children (10-12 yrs old) were tested for their immediate memory of visually presented digits. The digits were exposed either with or without a left to right spatial display arrangement and had to be recalled forwards as well as backwards. Normal and deaf Ss tended to be sensitive to both display conditions and recall requirements, whereas autistic Ss were mainly affected by direction of recall. Serial position effects in the normal and deaf groups were more dependent on order of retrieval than on input order.
Hermelin, B. & O'Connor, N. (MRC Developmental Psychology Unit, London, England) British Journal of Psychology, 1975(May), Vol 66(2), 203-209. [PA, Vol 54:05423]

85. Location and distance estimates by blind and sighted children.
3 groups of 24 blindfolded normal, blindfolded autistic, and congenitally blind children (mean age = 13 yrs) made reproduction location and distance estimates of an arm movement. For each task Ss first experienced a standard vertical movement of a predetermined extent. In the test tasks which followed, Ss either reproduced the movement exactly, reproduced the end point although commencing from a different starting position, or reproduced the same distance from a different starting point. Sighted normal Ss and blind Ss performed very similarly on both the reproduction and the location task. However, on distance reproduction the blind Ss underestimated the longer distances more markedly than did the normals. Autistic Ss resembled the blind in their attempts to reproduce the longer distances. Autistic Ss also had a tendency to overshoot over short distances in all tasks. Results are discussed in terms of the role of a visual reference system for different aspects of motor movements.
Hermelin, B. & O'Connor, N. (MRC Developmental Psychology Unit, London, England) Quarterly Journal of Experimental Psychology, 1975(May), Vol 27(2), 295-301. [PA, Vol 54:07740]

86. "Blindisms": Some observations and propositions.
Similarities between "blindisms" and autistic behavior are discussed. Many believe that "blindisms" are attempts by the child at self-stimulation; other theoretical causes are discussed, such as parental inadequacy, transitional adaptation in development, and understimulation. Some treatment procedures are reported, including acceptance, punishment, reinforcement for non-self-stimulatory behavior, diverting activities, and a specific procedure—overcorrection.
Hoshmand, Lisa T. (U Mississippi, Medical Ctr, Jackson) Education of the Visually Handicapped, 1975(May), Vol 7(2), 56-60. [PA, Vol 54:05532]

87. Cardiac arrhythmia and behaviour in autistic children.
Simultaneously videorecorded the behavior and heart rate of 9 4-12 yr old children in a standard situation. 6 normal, age-matched and 6 normal 2-yr-old controls were also studied. It was found that the heart rate of the autistic Ss was characteristically highly variable and more so than that of normal controls of the same age or younger. This variability (arrhythmia) was behavior-dependent in all Ss, involvement in a task resulting in suppression

of the arrhythmia. It was at a maximum in the autistic Ss during the performance of stereotyped behaviors. The functional implications of these behavior-heart rate associations are discussed. (36 ref)
Hutt, C.; Forrest, S. J. & Richer, J. (U Keele, England) Acta Psychiatrica Scandinavica, 1975(Jun), Vol 51(5), 361-372. [PA, Vol 54:11966]

88. On the organic nature of some forms of schizoid or autistic psychopathy.
Presents 4 case histories to illustrate the typical clinical features of autistic psychopathy. These patients—10, 13, 14, and 15 yrs old—showed several clinical features compatible with organic encephalopathy. Physical signs suggesting the presence of an underlying cerebral dysgenesis were particularly frequent. The patients superficially resembled schizophrenics but differed in their delayed and peculiar intellectual development, their response to external stimuli, and their frequent and severe motoric defects. From these observations and a review of the literaure, it is concluded that the patients described have an organic deficiency of brain function that is determined congenitally or in the early postnatal period. (33 ref)
Mnukhin, S. S. & Isaev, D. N. Journal of Autism & Childhood Schizophrenia, 1975(Jun), Vol 5(2), 100-108. [PA, Vol 57:01358]

89. A note on the validity of the Rimland Diagnostic Checklist.
Parents and teachers of 9 psychotic (autistic) children, ages 3-8 yrs, completed the Rimland Diagnostic Check List. Discrepancies between parents' and teachers' assessments of the children indicated that teachers tended to see the children as more abnormal than did the parents in certain areas of behavior and in ability levels. Although differences were not gross enough to invalidate the Checklist, findings indicate that responses to the Checklist should be considered an underestimation of the severity of the child's handicap.
Prior, Margot & Bence, Robyn. (Monash U, Clayton, Australia) Journal of Clinical Psychology, 1975(Jul), Vol 31(3), 510-513. [PA, Vol 56:09009]

90. Learning set acquisition in autistic children.
Compared the performance of 19 autistic 5-13 yr olds (mean MA 4 yrs, 3 mo) on an object discrimination learning set task with that of MA and IQ matched control groups of normal and retarded Ss. All but 2 of the autistic Ss acquired a learning set. About ½ of the Ss in each control group also acquired a learning set. However, the mean number of problems to criterion was similar for both the autistic and control groups of Ss who acquired a learning set. It is suggested that the superior performance of autistic Ss on a task which is believed to be related to MA indicates that the MA of these children may be higher than that which is usually obtained with standard measuring techniques. Results provided somewhat equivocal evidence for a relation between MA, IQ, and learning set formation in the normal and retarded Ss. (24 ref)
Prior, Margot R. & Chen, C. S. (Monash U, Clayton, Australia) Journal of Abnormal Psychology, 1975(Dec), Vol 84(6), 701-708. [PA, Vol 55:07312]

91. Kanner's syndrome or early-onset psychosis: A taxonomic analysis of 142 cases.
Case history data on 142 psychotic 3-13 yr olds were obtained using the Rimland E-2 scale, a diagnostic checklist. A numerical taxonomy was used to classify Ss into subgroups on the basis of responses on the checklist. A comparison was made between a classification of Kanner's syndrome vs no Kanner's syndrome and a classification using random classes as starting points. The best classification of the data was one in which 2 classes were obtained, one containing all the Kanner's syndrome Ss plus other early-onset, nonrelating psychotic Ss and the other containing Ss with later onset and more varied symptoms. Those attributes which significantly differentiated between the classes both in the best classification and in the Kanner's syndrome classification were extracted. A distinction between Kanner Ss and other similar Ss was found only for 3 specific behaviors: (a) obsessive

desire for sameness, (b) islets of special ability, and (c) skillful manipulation of small objects. (27 ref)
Prior, Margot; Perry, Dennis & Gajzago, Christine. (Monash U, Clayton, Australia) Journal of Autism & Developmental Disorders, 1975(Mar), Vol 5(1), 71–80. [PA, Vol 59:01233]

92. Language, communication, and the use of symbols in normal and autistic children.
Describes the characteristics of language and other forms of communication in normal and autistic children. The main basis of comparison is the extent to which each group can comprehend and use spoken and nonspoken language and also develop inner language. It is suggested that the central problem in early childhood autism is an impairment of complex symbolic function affecting all forms of communication. This problem can occur on its own, but, in the majority of cases, it is associated with other impairments of the CNS. The relationship of early childhood autism to mental retardation and to normal intellectual function is discussed. (52 ref)
Ricks, Derek M. & Wing, Lorna. (Harperbury Hosp, St Albans, England) Journal of Autism & Childhood Schizophrenia, 1975(Sep), Vol 5(3), 191-221. [PA, Vol 57:01372]

93. Effects of within-stimulus and extra-stimulus prompting on discrimination learning in autistic children.
Compared 2 different prompting procedures to teach visual and auditory discriminations to 6 autistic 8-14 yr olds. The 1st procedure involved presenting an added cue as an extra-stimulus prompt. This required the S to respond to both prompt and training stimulus. The 2nd procedure involved the use of a within-stimulus prompt. This consisted of an exaggeration of the relevant component of the training stimulus and thus did not require that the S respond to multiple cues. Results indicate that (a) Ss usually failed to learn the discriminations without a prompt, (b) Ss always failed to learn when the extra-stimulus prompt was employed but usually did learn with the within-stimulus prompt, and (c) these findings were independent of which modality (auditory or visual) was required for the discrimination. (15 ref)
Schreibman, Laura. (Claremont Men's Coll) Journal of Applied Behavior Analysis, 1975(Spr), Vol 8(1), 91-112. [PA, Vol 54:03348]

94. Language patterns of adolescent autistics.
Analyzed language samples obtained during interviews with 7 verbal autistic 14–21 yr olds. Linguistic deficits were compared to characteristics reported by W. Goldfarb et al (see PA, Vol 50:6999) for preteen autistics and described structurally. Results show that only 4 Ss demonstrated linguistic impairments. These clustered primarily in the area of prosodic features, semantic co-occurrence constraints, and general disfluency. No such clustering had been reported for the preteen population. No correlation between linguistic deficits, IQ, and age was found. However, performance on the Seashore Test of Musical Talents correlated highly with linguistic performance. Results suggest that (a) autism includes linguistically, and possibly etiologically, distinct subgroups; (b) the basic linguistic deficits in autism may be more specific than thought previously; and (c) perception of prosodic features may be crucial for decoding and encoding linguistic signals. It is noted that autistic children may be lacking in this ability. (32 ref)
Simmons, James Q. & Baltaxe, Christiane. (U California Neuropsychiatric Inst, Los Angeles) Journal of Autism & Developmental Disorders, 1975(Dec), Vol 5(4), 333–351. [PA, Vol 59:01240]

95. Echolalic speech in childhood autism: Consideration of possible underlying loci of brain damage.
Research indicates that the speech of echolalic autistic children is specifically lacking in appropriate use of expressive-intonational features, but the echolalic child's clear articulation of words and phrases indicates that discrimination of phonemic features is intact. The impairment in aphasic disorders is just the reverse. Failure to attend to auditory stimuli and the characteristic language disorder are among the most consistent findings in

autistic children, and they could be related. Discrimination of differential stress emphasis is the way the normal young child extracts major morphemic word stems and syntactic features from environmental speech; this may be a primitive perceptual function of brainstem auditory centers. The brainstem auditory system is especially vulnerable to perinatal injury. Damage to this system is an example of the kind of lesion that might lead to behavioral handicaps without neurological signs. (72 ref)
Simon, Nicole. (Bolt Beranek & Newman, Behavioral Sciences Div, Cambridge, MA) Archives of General Psychiatry, 1975(Nov), Vol 32(1), 1439-1446. [PA, Vol 56:04161]

96. Minor physical anomalies in normal, neurotic, learning disabled, and severely disturbed children.
A high incidence of minor physical anomalies in a childhood schizophrenic population has been previously reported by W. Goldfarb (1956, 1967). In the present study, 108 4–12 yr old boys from 4 different clinical populations were examined, utilizing a standardized anomaly scoring system for which a high interrater reliability was obtained. The patient populations were (a) generally pediatric ward patients, (b) psychoneurotic outpatients at a university child guidance clinic, (c) learning disabled children, and (d) autistic, borderline, and atypical children from 2 residential treatment centers. Results show that both the learning disabled and residential treatment populations had higher mean anomaly scores than did the 1st 2 groups, but did not differ significantly from each other. There was a trend for Ss with multiple anomalies to have had more frequent history of prenatal insults or paternal psychopathology. Results indicate that the development of these minor anatomical anomalies which are formed in the 1st 3 mo of fetal development may parallel early developmental deviation of the CNS. The finding of high anomalies in the residential treatment groups supports the idea that some of these Ss share a common etiology with the other developmental deviations, such as speech delay or mental retardation, for which high anomaly scores have also been reported. (18 ref)
Steg, John P. & Rapoport, Judith L. (Georgetown U Medical School) Journal of Autism & Developmental Disorders, 1975(Dec), Vol 5(4), 299–307. [PA, Vol 59:01176]

97. Hunches on some biological factors in autism.
Speculates that there might exist a basic biochemical (or other) error common to autism, celiac disease, rheumatoid arthritis (RA), and depression. Reports from parents of autistic children and the relevant literature are discussed. The seemingly high incidence of RA in families of autistic children, the low incidence of RA in schizophrenics, the common incidence of celiac disease among autistic children and their families, parent reports of abdominal pain both in themselves and in their autistic children, and findings of depression (instead of schizophrenia) in the families of autistic children are examined. It is recommended that a "listing place" be established for parents' observations for further research. (27 ref)
Sullivan, Ruth C. (National Society for Autistic Children, Huntington, WV) Journal of Autism & Childhood Schizophrenia, 1975(Jun), Vol 5(2), 177-184. [PA, Vol 57:01389]

98. [A study on the prognosis for autistic children.] (Japn)
Reviews reports of follow-up studies and prognosis for autistic children in Japan and other countries and examines data on autistic children at a Japanese university hospital. Findings are as follows: (a) According to the literature, the prognosis for autistic children is pessimistic (i.e., in many studies, only about 10% showed a good prognosis). When fair reports were included, only 30% of Ss showed a favorable prognosis, while 60–70% indicated a poor outcome. (b) Only a few Ss had paying jobs and were socially adjusted, and it appeared that characteristics of autistic disturbance had remained. (c) 56 of 311 children who were diagnosed between 1952 and 1971 were older than 16, and in 34 of them the outcome status was as follows: Three Ss were good (8.8%), 6 were fair (17.6%), and 21 were poor (61.8%). 50% of the 311 Ss never attended school, and 23% were institutionalized. (d) The prognosis for autistic children depends

on speech development, IQ, initial evaluation, therapeutic methods, schooling, and institutional care. (57 ref)
Wakabayashi, Shinichiro & Mizuno, Mayumi. (Aichi Prefectural Colony Inst for Developmental Research, Kasugai, Japan) Japanese Journal of Child Psychiatry, 1975, Vol 16(3), 177–197. [PA, Vol 65:10613]

99. Negativism in verbal and nonverbal responses of autistic children.
Studied negativism in 9 autistic, 9 behavior-disturbed, and 9 normal 5-12 yr olds in 3 different stimulus conditions (verbal requests for verbal responses, verbal requests for nonverbal responses, and nonverbal requests for nonverbal responses). Each condition included 2 tasks, which were requested 15 consecutive times. Ss demonstrated that they could perform the tasks before testing, and their responses were scored according to the similarity between the response and the request. Results demonstrate that the autistic and behavior-disturbed Ss responded similarly, except when requests required verbal responses, in which case the autistic Ss were much more negative. Results suggest applications to diagnostic and therapeutic interventions. (17 ref)
Wallace, Bruce R. (Rehabilitation Ctr, Charlottetown, Prince Edward Island, Canada) Journal of Abnormal Psychology, 1975(Apr), Vol 84(2), 138-143. [PA, Vol 54:09821]

100. [Clinical observations on the developmental structure of autistic children: Change in environment and the mother–child relationship in the ego-formation process.] (Japn)
Compared the behavioral development of 10 autistic children 5–13 yrs old (6 males, 4 females) with that of 11 of their siblings 6–10 yrs old (5 males, 6 females) by evaluating mother–child relationships as measured by the Children's Apperception Test. The anticipated activities at each of the 5 stages of normal development, and the corresponding roles of the mother are presented in detail. The autistic children were divided into 4 groups based on successful completion of developmental phases. Most mothers of children in the well-developed group established wide-ranging and deep rapport with the children under various circumstances. Mothers of the poorly-developed group exhibited significantly less interaction with their children. This difference was true for both the autistic children and their siblings. (English summary) (8 ref)
Yabuki, Kazumi & Saito, Keiko. (National Research Inst for Special Education, Yokosuga City, Japan) Japanese Journal of Child Psychiatry, 1975(Nov), Vol 16(5), 296–306. [PA, Vol 63:03440]

101. An application of neuroendocrinological studies in autistic children and Heller's syndrome.
Investigated the response of plasma 11-hydroxycorticosteroids (11-OHCS) to pyrogen (.005 µg/kg, iv) as well as the circadian rhythm of plasma 11-OHCS levels in 7 autistic 6–10 yr olds and in 2 4–5 yr olds with Heller's syndrome. Results show that in autistic Ss the stress response, which is acquired in an earlier stage of development, was adequately sustained. However, the circadian rhythm, which seems to appear at a later stage with the maturity of the CNS, frequently revealed abnormal patterns. Similar findings were obtained in the Heller's syndrome cases, indicating organic changes in the brain. On the basis of these results, it is postulated that in early infantile autism there exist some functional changes in the CNS that show a close correlation to the regulatory mechanism of ACTH secretion. (22 ref)
Yamazaki, Kosuke et al. (Shiritsu Sapporo Byoin Fuzoku Seiryoin, Children's Ward, Japan) Journal of Autism & Developmental Disorders, 1975(Dec), Vol 5(4), 323–332. [PA, Vol 59:01252]

102. Uptake and efflux of serotonin from platelets of autistic and nonautistic children.
Examined the in vitro uptake and efflux of serotonin by platelets from 12 3-6 yr old autistic children, 15 5.5-11.5 yr old nonautistic hospitalized comparison cases, and normal 5-12 yr olds. Hospitalized comparison Ss were utilized to assess possible environmental and dietary influences. Two efflux procedures were

utilized to explore the possibility that methodological factors accounted for previously reported differences between autistic and comparison groups. Results fail to indicate statistically significant differences in uptake or efflux between the autistic and the hospitalized comparison groups or the normals. Methodologic considerations which could possibly account for the failure to confirm previous findings are discussed in detail. (16 ref)
Yuwiler, Arthur et al. (VA Hosp, Neurobiochemistry Lab, Los Angeles, CA) Journal of Autism & Childhood Schizophrenia, 1975(Jun), Vol 5(2), 83-98. [PA, Vol 57:01400]

103. Phonological investigation of verbal autistic and mentally retarded subjects.
Used the Edinburgh Articulation Test to investigate speech sound systems of 9 verbal autistic and 12 mentally retarded children (mean ages 12.04 and 11.75 yrs, respectively), matched on nonverbal MA (as measured by the Arthur adaptation of the Leiter International Performance Scale). Findings show a delay in phoneme acquisition, as well as a relative uniformity of error types in both groups. Autistic Ss, however, differed significantly from the mentally retarded in the phonemic substitutions which they made. Autistics also exhibited a high correlation between frequency of phonological errors and level of overall language development. Findings are interpreted as supporting the hypothesis that autistics show a more global delay in language development than do retardates. (19 ref)
Bartolucci, Giampiero; Pierce, Sandra; Streiner, David & Eppel, Patricia T. (St Joseph's Hosp, Hamilton, Canada) Journal of Autism & Childhood Schizophrenia, 1976(Dec), Vol 6(4), 303-316. [PA, Vol 58:03429]

104. Articulation in early childhood autism.
Used the Edinburgh Articulation Test to make comparisons between the articulation of 73 autistic children, predominantly subnormal language matched controls, and developmental receptive dysphasic controls (CA range 6.10-16.1 yrs). It was noted that the articulation of autistics was significantly superior to that of both control groups. Findings are discussed in relation to differences in the pattern of language impairment in the 3 groups.
Boucher, Jill. (Charles Burns Clinic, Birmingham, England) Journal of Autism & Childhood Schizophrenia, 1976(Dec), Vol 6(4), 297-302. [PA, Vol 58:03447]

105. Memory deficits in early infantile autism: Some similarities to the amnesic syndrome.
Conducted 5 experiments which compared autistic children (N = 29) with control children (N = 28) on tasks in which retention was tested by different methods. In 3 tests of recall, using named pictures, written words, and spoken words as stimuli, autistic children were impaired in comparison with age-matched normal children and with controls matched for verbal and nonverbal ability. In 1 test of forced-choice recognition of pictures, autistic children were impaired in comparison with ability-matched controls (N = 36). In 3 tests of cued recall, using named pictures, written words, and spoken words as test stimuli, and acoustic, graphemic, and semantic cues, autistic children were not impaired in comparison with normal age-matched controls. In 1 test of paired-associate learning, using nonrelated word pairs as stimuli, autistic children were not impaired in comparison with normal age-matched controls. These experimental paradigms were similar to some that have been used to investigate the amnesic syndrome in man. Thus findings on paired-associate learning differ in autistic and amnesic Ss, but findings on recall, recognition, and cued recall are comparable. A possible parallel between autism and amnesia is discussed. (37 ref)
Boucher, Jill & Warrington, Elizabeth K. (U Birmingham, England) British Journal of Psychology, 1976(Feb), Vol 67(1), 73-87. [PA, Vol 56:09992]

106. Primary childhood aphasia and childhood autism: Clinical, biological, and conceptual observations.
Reviews the literature, delineates aphasia and autism as 2 parallel but related syndromes, and presents case illustrations. Congenital, developmental, and idiopathic acquired aphasia form a spectrum of primary childhood aphasias characterized by profound disturbances in expressive language, relatively much better language comprehension; by the capacity for inner language, imaginative play, gesture, mime, and warm social relations; and by a variety of associated behavioral and cognitive difficulties. The presence of paroxysmal EEG abnormalities suggests cortical dysfunction. In contrast to this spectrum, childhood autism appears earlier in life (during a prelinguistic developmental phase) and is characterized by an impoverishment of inner language; paucity of mime, gesture, and imitation; and much greater disturbance in social attachment and regulation of anxiety. Midbrain and brain-stem dysfunctions involving catecholamine pathways may underlie some aspects of this syndrome. Because of complex, reciprocal effects between various neurological systems in the CNS, there may be mixed aphasic-autistic syndromes and familial clustering of both types of disorders. Intensive language training starting in the preschool years and systematic sign language may be useful for both groups. (4 p ref)
Cohen, Donald J.; Caparulo, Barbara & Shaywitz, Bennett. (Yale U Medical School, Child Study Ctr) Journal of the American Academy of Child Psychiatry, 1976(Aut), Vol 15(4), 604-645. [PA, Vol 59:07988]

107. Creatine phosphokinase levels in children with severe developmental disturbances.
Studied serum creatine phosphokinase (CPK) levels in 110 individuals: 40 psychotic children suffering from childhood autism, atypical personality development, and childhood schizophrenia; 5 children with childhood aphasia; 22 children with severe personality disorders; 29 normal children and normal siblings of psychotic children; and 14 normal parents of psychotic children. Ages of Ss ranged from 4-15 yrs; normal children and normal siblings were 3-21 yrs old. CPK levels from the entire population of adults and children were normally distributed, and the mean CPK levels for the 8 diagnostic groups were within normal limits. Those 22 children with personality disorders had significantly higher CPK levels than the other diagnostic groups. This relatively higher level of CPK may be related to vulnerability to later development of schizophrenic spectrum disorders. There was no apparent relationship between CPK levels and motor activity, nor was there any change in the level of CPK during a trial of psychoactive medication. CPK levels remained relatively stable on test-retest determination. (22 ref)
Cohen, Donald J.; Johnson, Warren; Caparulo, Barbara K. & Young, Gerald. (Yale U Child Study Ctr) Archives of General Psychiatry, 1976(Jun), Vol 33(6), 683-686. [PA, Vol 56:06113]

108. The effects of fluorescent and incandescent illumination upon repetitive behaviors in autistic children.
Observed the repetitive behaviors of 6 autistic children (mean CA, 55.6 mo; mean MA, 26.5 mo) under 2 conditions of background illumination. During 2 sessions, the room was illuminated by fluorescent light and, during 2 other sessions, by equal intensity incandescent light. Ss spent significantly more time engaged in repetitive behavior under fluorescent light. Previous research suggested that such findings were related to the flickering nature of fluorescent illumination. Practical and theoretical implications are discussed. Further experimentation is suggested to assess relationships between flickering illumination and arousal. (17 ref)
Colman, Richard S.; Frankel, Fred; Ritvo, Edward & Freeman, B. J. (U California, Los Angeles) Journal of Autism & Childhood Schizophrenia, 1976(Jun), Vol 6(2), 157-162. [PA, Vol 57:03442]

109. Neuropathologic aspects of psychosis in children.
A search of the literature and extensive inquires of clinicians revealed 33 instances (including 6 sibling pairs) of possible neurological changes in cases of childhood autism or psychosis. Available case material is presented along with some tentative suggestions for further research. (27 ref)
Darby, John K. Journal of Autism & Childhood Schizophrenia, 1976(Dec), Vol 6(4), 339-352. [PA, Vol 58:03451]

110.   A case report of an autistic boy: Selective responding to components of bidimensional visual and auditory stimuli.
Results in a 9-yr-old autistic male did not demonstrate that he showed overselective responding, nor did his responses come under the control of just one stimulus dimension as would have been predicted by an overselectivity theory. He responded during each presentation of the stimulus pair composed of the 2 previously reinforced stimuli and never responded in the presence of the other stimulus pairs. Results conflict with those of previous studies.
Edwards, Jean L.; Shigley, R. H. & Edwards, R. P. (Columbia City School, SC) Journal of Autism & Childhood Schizophrenia, 1976(Jun), Vol 6(2), 139-146. [PA, Vol 57:03447]

111.   Linguistic performance in vulnerable and autistic children and their mothers.
Studied the language patterns of 8 schizophrenic mothers and their 4-yr-old (mean age) children and compared them with the speech of 8 normal mothers and children and 11 normal mothers with autistic children. Children of schizophrenic mothers showed lags in language development and language distortions less severe than, but in some ways similar to those seen in autistic children. Schizophrenic mothers were more likely to produce more deficient and/or distorted language in interactions with their children. Mothers of autistic children produced language that was equal to or above that of mothers of normal children on most parameters and adjusted their language to the chronological rather than the linguistic age of the child. (22 ref)
Frank, Sheldon M.; Allen, Doris A.; Stein, Lorrayne & Myers, Beverly. (New York U Medical Ctr, Millhauser Lab) American Journal of Psychiatry, 1976(Aug), Vol 133(8), 909-915. [PA, Vol 57:01321]

112.   Effects of frequency of photic stimulation upon autistic and retarded children.
Conducted a study to determine if frequency of repetitive photic stimulation could affect the response rate of an operant upon which such stimulation was made contingent. Six autistic and 5 retarded children, equated for mental age (range, 20-51 mo), were trained to pull a lever to obtain photic stimulation of different frequencies. Response rates of autistic Ss were related to the frequency of stimulation, while retarded Ss showed no such consistency. The 2 groups did not differ in the average duration of time they engaged in stereotypies. During a subsequent extinction session, 2 autistic Ss ceased responding, but 1 of 2 retarded Ss did not. Noncontingent photic stimulation suppressed a food-motivated operant in 1 autistic S. Results provide evidence for frequency-dependent properties of repetitive visual feedback in autistic children. In addition, support is given to the position that performance deficits in autistic children correlating with the occurrence of stereotypies result from competition of different sources of reinforcement. (20 ref)
Frankel, Fred et al. (U California, Los Angeles) American Journal of Mental Deficiency, 1976(Jul), Vol 81(1), 32-40. [PA, Vol 56:09967]

113.   The effects of response contingent vestibular stimulation on the behavior of autistic and retarded children.
Examined the reinforcing effects of repetitive vestibular stimulation (i.e., body rocking) on the behavior of 13 autistic and retarded children. While all Ss were observed to push a button for vestibular stimulation, frequency of stimulation was an important parameter for autistics but not for retardates. Results are interpreted as evidence for central rather than peripheral locus of control of motility disturbances in autistic children.
Freeman, B. J.; Frankel, Fred & Ritvo, E. R. (U California Medical School, Los Angeles) Journal of Autism & Childhood Schizophrenia, 1976(Dec), Vol 6(4), 353-358. [PA, Vol 58:03432]

114.   Mental retardation and stress on the parents: A contrast between Down's syndrome and childhood autism.
Mothers of 100 autistic, 100 Down's syndrome, and 100 outpatient psychiatric clinic children completed a questionnaire about their attitudes toward the identified child and the effects of the child on themselves and their families. A canonical correla-

tion between the 15 questionnaire scales and 3 groups revealed a general retardation-social dependency factor separating the mothers of the 2 retarded groups from the clinic sample. The autism group was differentiated from the Down's syndrome group by scales measuring severity of the child's handicap and family integration problems more than by scales measuring stress on the mother. The hypothesis that mothers of autistic children would report more problems than both other groups was supported; the hypothesis that mothers of Down's syndrome children would report more problems than mothers of outpatient clinic children was not. (17 ref)
Holroyd, Jean & McArthur, David. (U California Neuropsychiatric Inst, Los Angeles) American Journal of Mental Deficiency, 1976(Jan), Vol 80(4), 431-436. [PA, Vol 56:00796]

115.   Identification of consistent responding to auditory stimuli by a functionally deaf autistic child.
Measured the responses of a 5-yr-old autistic male to determine if there was a pattern to his responding. There was consistent responding to both stimuli, white noise and the sound of a candy machine delivering candy. The thresholds for responding to the white noise were always consistent on a given day but varied from day to day. Responding to the candy machine always occurred at sound levels well below the thresholds for the white noise. Implications for understanding the lack of speech development in mute autistic children are discussed. (20 ref)
Koegel, Robert L. & Schreibman, Laura. (U California, Inst for Applied Behavioral Science, Santa Barbara) Journal of Autism & Childhood Schizophrenia, 1976(Jun), Vol 6(2), 147-156. [PA, Vol 57:03463]

116.   The autistic child.
Discusses autism—including problems in diagnosis, a case study, guidelines to parents, possible causal factors, treatment, and results of the author's own research. This research—based on the diagnoses of and treatment of 26 male and 6 female children over a period of 14 yrs—revealed that for 12 children treatment was successful; for 10 it was moderately successful; and for 10 it was minimally successful. (Success was measured in terms of improvements in communication capabilities, simple perceptual and motor abilities, and capacities for socializing and self-care). Parents who suspect they have an autistic child are urged to consult their general practitioner, request a special diagnosis from a professional, and apply constructive rearing and educational techniques.
Lowenstein, L. F.   News & Views, 1976(Mar), Vol 2(7), 21-26. [PA, Vol 57:12910]

117.   Short-term and serial memory in autistic, retarded, and normal children.
Experimental data on memory ability of autistic children is scarce and contradictory. It is suggested that this may in part be the result of failure to control for acquisition of the correct response before memory is tested. In Exp I, acquisition was controlled in a delayed-response visual discrimination task. The performance of 9 autistic children (mean MA, 5 yrs 1 mo) was compared with 9 MA-matched normal and 9 MA-matched retarded controls. Recall deteriorated with increasing delay interval in each group. There were no significant group differences. Exp II measured the effects of interference on memory, using a serial memory task. No differences were found among groups in rate of learning, although autistic Ss improved significantly on the 2nd and longer series. There was no relationship between performance on the short-term memory and the serial memory tasks over the same time intervals for any group. Results support the view that when MA and response acquisition level are equated with normal and retarded children in a memory task, autistic children do not show any specific memory deficits.
Prior, Margot R. & Chen, C. S. (Monash U, Clayton, Australia) Journal of Autism & Childhood Schizophrenia, 1976(Jun), Vol 6(2), 121-131. [PA, Vol 57:03416]

118.   An epidemiological study of autistic and psychotic children in the four eastern states of Australia.
Presents findings from a study of the general behavioral and etiological characteristics of 146 autistic and psychotic children from the 4 eastern states of Australia. Both inter- and intra-study comparisons with reference to a number of factors considered significant in childhood psychosis were in accord with those of similar overseas studies, although methodological and diagnostic differences limited the conclusions. A notable finding was that of an excess of "organic" indications in a sub-group of early onset, severely withdrawn "autistic" children, suggesting that further neurological and EEG testing of autistic children is desirable. (36 ref)
Prior, Margot R.; Gajzago, Christine C. & Knox, Dianne T. (Monash U, Clayton, Australia) Australian & New Zealand Journal of Psychiatry, 1976(Jun), Vol 10(2), 173-184. [PA, Vol 57:06019]

119.   The social-avoidance behaviour of autistic children.
Direct observation and previous studies suggested autistic children actively avoid social encounters more than normal children and concommitantly, act as if threatened by the mere proximity or nonthreatening approaches of others. This hypothesis was tested through observations of 3 groups of Ss. Group A included 8 autistic children aged 7 yrs 11 mo to 10 yrs 3 mo, selected from a larger population of hospitalized psychotic children. All of these Ss had Vineland Social Quotients below 70. Group B included 8 nonautistic "disturbed" and retarded children from the same hospital matched for age and sex with Group A. Group C Ss were 9 2-5 yr old normal nursery school children. Groups A and B were videotaped in their outdoor school playgrounds during 25-min morning and afternoon breaks. Each S was observed for a total of 10 2.5-min periods. Group C was observed directly, without videotaping. Results support the hypothesis. The cognitive-language handicap theory of autism is criticized in light of these findings. (27 ref)
Richer, John. (Park Hosp, Headington, England) Animal Behaviour, 1976(Nov), Vol 24(4), 898-906. [PA, Vol 63:03354]

120.   Gaze aversion in autistic and normal children.
Autistic children rarely engage in eye contact, and while observation suggests this is due to a specific avoidance of eye contact, some experimental studies have challenged this. In the present study the effects on 10 autistic (ages, 5-11 yrs) and 9 age- and sex-matched normal children of an adult looking at them with both eyes, with 1 eye covered, or apparently not looking at them (both eyes covered) were investigated. As expected, autistic children looked more at the adult with his eyes covered, and also engaged in less flight behavior. They looked less when 2 eyes were exposed than 1 confirming the potency of the 2-*eye pattern* in provoking gaze aversion. Normal children engaged in much more eye contact than the autistic children, with fewer flight behaviors and stereotypies, supporting the hypothesis that autistic children are predominantly flight motivated. Other, sometimes conflicting, results of previous studies are discussed. Teachers and nurses are cautioned not to make efforts to engage autistic children even in friendly eye contact as this provokes more flight behavior. (29 ref)
Richer, John M. & Coss, R. G. (Smith Hosp, Henley-on-Thames, England) Acta Psychiatrica Scandinavica, 1976(Mar), Vol 53(3), 193-210. [PA, Vol 56:06174]

121.   Platelet monoamine oxidase activity in children and adolescents.
Measured platelet monoamine oxidase activity in a group of 33 preadolescent, adolescent, and postadolescent individuals. The platelet oxidase activity was highest in the females in all 3 populations examined. Ss diagnosed as having primary autism did not display differences in their platelet oxidase activity as compared to Ss of similar age and sex. (22 ref)
Roth, Jerome A.; Young, J. Gerald & Cohen, Donald J. (Yale U Medical School) Life Sciences, 1976(May), Vol 18(9), 919-924. [PA, Vol 56:04204]

122.   Speech patterns of five psychotic children now in adolescence.
Speech samples of 5 autistic children currently between 12 and 19 yrs were analyzed and compared to earlier (8-12 yrs ago) speech descriptions. The adolescents show patterns consisting of varying combinations of constraint in length of utterance, echoing, syntactic disturbance, semantic concreteness, context inappropriateness, and disorders of prosody. This spectrum of disorders is examined against a normal developmental schema to show that childhood psychosis is best viewed as a developmental disorder. Early descriptions of these children were reliably matched to later speech samples by 10 psychiatrists (working blind), showing continuity in style of deviance. (32 ref)
Shapiro, Theodore & Huebner, Hans F. (New York U-Bellevue Medical Ctr) Journal of the American Academy of Child Psychiatry, 1976(Spr), Vol 15(2), 278-293. [PA, Vol 59:05843]

123.   What is an autistic child?
Autism is ill-defined and controversial, but knowledge about the disorder is increasing. Outdated assumptions, commonly held, interfere with the objective assessment of an autistic child. (19 ref)
Stephenson, P. Susan. (U British Columbia, Div of Child Psychiatry, Vancouver, Canada) Canada's Mental Health, 1976(Dec), Vol 24(4), 5-7. [PA, Vol 64:05827]

124.   Autistic children exhibit undetectable hemagglutination-inhibition antibody titers despite previous rubella vaccination.
The etiology of autism is unknown, but autism has been associated with a number of diseases, including prenatal rubella. Rubella vaccine challenge was used in an attempt to retrospectively diagnose prenatal rubella in autistic children. This test was selected because unresponsiveness of antibody titer has been reported as helpful in retrospective diagnosing of prenatal rubella. 15 autistic children and 8 controls matched for age (7-10 yrs) were challenged with rubella vaccine. Rubella vaccine challenge did not differentiate autistic Ss from control Ss; however, 5 of 13 autistic Ss had undetectable titers despite previous vaccine, while all control Ss had detectable titers. Findings suggest that these autistic children may have an altered immune response.
Stubbs, E. Gene. (U Oregon Health Sciences Ctr, Portland) Journal of Autism & Childhood Schizophrenia, 1976(Sep), Vol 6(3), 269-274. [PA, Vol 57:10504]

125.   Rapid eye movement (REM) activity in normal and autistic children during REM sleep.
30 normal Ss aged 3-68 mo and 16 autistic Ss aged 36-62 mo were studied during nonmedical sleep, and data pertaining to REM were measured during the 1st 3 REM periods of the night. When time of night from which data were gathered was held constant, normal Ss showed a significant relationship between age and the organization of eye movements into discrete bursts. When autistic Ss were compared to age-matched normal controls, they showed an immaturity in this phenomena, their results being similar to those found in children less than 18 mo of age. Such an immaturity could result from dysfunction at a number of diverse levels and sites in the CNS. (31 ref)
Tanguay, Peter E.; Ornitz, Edward M.; Forsythe, Alan B. & Ritvo, Edward R. (U California, Los Angeles) Journal of Autism & Childhood Schizophrenia, 1976(Sep), Vol 6(3), 275-288. [PA, Vol 57:10508]

126.   [A study on autism in siblings of autistic children.] (Japn)
Five of the 276 siblings of 242 autistic children were themselves autistic, a much higher rate (1.8%) than that in the general population (0.045%). This is in disagreement with the concept that almost all siblings of autistic children are normal, and it suggests that genetic factors may be involved in autism. (English summary) (39 ref)
Wakabayashi, Shinichiro & Mizuno, Mayumi. (Aichi Prefectural Colony Inst for Developmental Research, Kasugai, Japan) Japanese Journal of Child Psychiatry, 1976, Vol 17(3), 154-164. [PA, Vol 64:12682]

127.   The use of BRIAC for evaluating therapeutic effectiveness.
Evaluated 46 3-9 yr olds in 8 different psychotherapeutic settings at the beginning and at the end of a 12-mo period by means of the Behavior Rating Instrument for Autistic Children. The 3-6 yr olds were initially more severely disturbed and improved significantly more than the 7-9 yr olds. The large, bleak, custodial residential center produced significantly less improvement in the children than did the other settings. However, among good programs (e.g., those that were sensitive to the behaviors and needs of the children and which were skillfully implemented by a dedicated and attentive staff) there was little evidence of differences in therapeutic effectiveness, regardless of whether the therapy was behavior modification, education, psychoanalytically oriented relationship therapy, or activity therapy.
Wenar, Charles & Ruttenberg, Bertram A. (Ohio State U) Journal of Autism & Childhood Schizophrenia, 1976(Jun), Vol 6(2), 175-191. [PA, Vol 57:01544]

128.   The aetiology of childhood autism: A criticism of the Tinbergens' ethological theory.
L. Kanner's (1943) descriptions of children showing the abnormal behavior pattern he observed and named "early infantile autism" are summarized. E. A. Tinbergen and N. Tinbergen's (1972) ethological theory of the etiology of this syndrome is outlined and criticized. It is suggested that the major problem in evaluating the theory, apart from the absence of any evidence in its favor, is the lack of precision with which the Tinbergens use the terms "autism" and "Kanner's syndrome." (66 ref)
Wing, Lorna & Ricks, Derek M. (MRC Social Psychiatry Unit, U London Inst of Psychiatry, England) Psychological Medicine, 1976(Nov), Vol 6(4), 533-543. [PA, Vol 58:05552]

129.   Pragmatic deficits in the language of autistic adolescents.
Investigated patterns of deficits in pragmatic competence in 5 high-level-verbal autistic males, 14–21 yrs of age. Pragmatic competence relates to language use in context and represents an interface between social, cognitive, and linguistic development. Three areas of pragmatic deficits are discussed which could not be accounted for by specific phonological, syntactic, or semantic deficits on the sentence level. These relate to impairment in speaker–hearer role relationship, impairment in rules of conduct governing a dialogue, and impairment in the foregrounding and backgrounding of information. (30 ref)
Baltaxe, Christiane A. (U California, Neuropsychiatric Inst, Los Angeles) Journal of Pediatric Psychology, 1977, Vol 2(4), 176–180. [PA, Vol 62:06122]

130.   Bedtime soliloquies and linguistic competence in autism.
Investigated the linguistic competence of an autistic child by means of her bedtime soliloquies. The usefulness of such monologues as a diagnostic tool is suggested, and the interrelationship between echolalia and language development is discussed. Three bedtime soliloquies of an 8-yr-old echolalic-autistic girl were analyzed along the dimensions of echolalia vs propositional speech, types of ungrammaticality produced, and connected discourse. Results are compared with those of a normal 2.5-yr-old boy studied previously by R. Weir (1962). The present results demonstrate the difficulties in judging the propositional vs echolalic speech. The types of ungrammaticality were found to be useful indicators of apparent differences between the acquisition process in the normal and the autistic child. They revealed that the autistic child may use specific linguistic strategies only minimally utilized by the normal child. The discourse analysis demonstrated additional differences as well as similarities in the way the autistic S organized her utterances in connected discourse. It also showed that the autistic child had specific but limited linguistic competence. It is hypothesized that the autistic S acquires more functional, useful language by a process of gradually breaking down echolalic patterns. In terms of therapy, these findings would support the use of echolalia as a basis for language training. (30 ref)
Baltaxe, Christiane A. & Simmons, James Q. (U California, Los Angeles) Journal of Speech & Hearing Disorders, 1977(Aug), Vol 42(3), 376–393. [PA, Vol 59:09975]

131.   A preliminary comparison of phonological development in autistic, normal, and mentally retarded subjects.
Early childhood autism is a syndrome which appears during the 1st 30 mo of life and is typified by a severe disturbance in language development, among other behavioral abnormalities. Since no systematic linguistic investigation of autistic children is available, an investigation of the phonological characteristics of 10 autistic children was carried out, in the areas of both production and perception of speech sounds. In order to investigate the possibility of atypical phonological characteristics in this group, they were compared with 10 normal and 10 mentally retarded children matched on a nonlinguistic test (Leiter International Performance Scale) of IQ. Results suggest that the autistic group showed a delayed pattern of acquisition of phonological characteristics similar to that found in the mentally retarded group. (31 ref)
Bartolucci, Giampiero & Pierce, Sandra J. (St Joseph's Hosp, Hamilton, Canada) British Journal of Disorders of Communication, 1977(Oct), Vol 12(2), 137–147. [PA, Vol 60:11816]

132.   Hand preference in autistic children and their parents.
Two experiments tested hand preference in groups of between 40 and 50 autistic children and in sex-, age-, and ability-matched controls. Data were also compared with existing findings on normal children. Small differences occurred between the groups in the directions which would be predicted on the assumption that mental subnormality is associated with delayed development of normal patterns of handedness, and on the hypothesis that autistic children as a group will show a persistent slightly increased tendency to use the left hand. Parents of the autistic group were also assessed for handedness. Contrary to the prediction of slightly increased sinistrality in this group of Ss, some indication of increased dextrality occurred. Results are discussed in relation to possible genetic factors in the etiology of autism. (26 ref)
Boucher, Jill. (Charles Burns Clinic, Birmingham, England) Journal of Autism & Developmental Disorders, 1977(Jun), Vol 7(2), 177–187. [PA, Vol 59:09999]

133.   Alternation and sequencing behaviour, and response to novelty in autistic children.
Compared a group of 21 relatively able autistic children (mean CA 9 yrs, 7 mo) with 21 controls (mean CA, 10 yrs) who were matched for sex, age, and nonverbal ability (Raven Coloured Progressive Matrices) in a test of alternation and sequencing behavior, and response to novelty. Autistic Ss showed reduced alternation and response to novelty. Their sequences also showed a tendency to follow strict rules at all ages and ability levels, which was not the case in the control group; rulebound sequencing correlated negatively with response to novelty by the autistic Ss which, again, was not the case in the control group. Results are discussed primarily in relation to the possibility of perseveration as a fundamental disturbance in autism. The potential relevance of the findings to hypotheses concerning the neuropathology of autism is also discussed. (18 ref)
Boucher, Jill. (Charles Burns Clinic, Birmingham, England) Journal of Child Psychology & Psychiatry & Allied Disciplines, 1977(Jan), Vol 18(1), 67–72. [PA, Vol 59:01185]

134.   Families of autistic and dysphasic children: II. Mothers' speech to the children.
Tested various hypotheses about deviance in the communication of mothers to their autistic children. The language of mothers of 13 autistic boys was compared to the language of mothers of 13 boys with developmental receptive dysphasia. The 2 groups of boys were of similar age (mean ages 9 yrs 0 mo and 9 yrs 7 mo, respectively), nonverbal intelligence (IQ at least 70), and language level. The language samples came from hour-long taped interactions between the mothers and their children in their homes. Aspects of maternal communication examined included the following: amount of language used, frequency usage of different types of utterances, syntactic complexity of utterances, grammaticality of utterances, clarity of communication, and tones of voice used. No differences were found between the 2 groups of mothers in level of language usage, pattern of

functional interaction, or in overall clarity of communication. Findings provide *no* support for the suggestion that autism is due wholly or in part to deviant patterns of mother–child communication. (43 ref)

Cantwell, Dennis P.; Baker, Lorian & Rutter, Michael. (U California Medical School, Los Angeles) Journal of Autism & Childhood Schizophrenia, 1977(Dec), Vol 7(4), 313–327. [PA, Vol 60:11841]

135.   The analysis of language level and language function: A methodological study.

Reports a method of analyzing speech and language in young children which encompasses both level of development and abnormalities in usage. It was developed initially to (a) measure changes in the language usage of autistic children as a result of a treatment program, (b) compare the language characteristics of autistic and developmental "dysphasic" children, and (c) compare the language of young normal children with that of both language-disordered groups. There were no significant differences between experimental and control Ss at the initial assessment, but while controls remained very similar on all measures (e.g., total number of utterances, percent of socialized utterances, and percent of nonverbal utterances) over 6 mo, the treatment group showed many changes (e.g., the amount of speech used increased significantly). The 13 autistic and 13 dysphasic Ss were closely comparable in their level of language development, but the autistic group showed a much higher level of inappropriate echolalia and no socialized utterances. The analysis of 30-min audio tape-recorded speech samples obtained during a period of unstructured mother–child interaction at home provided useful measures of both language level and functional language usage. (56 ref)

Cantwell, Dennis P.; Howlin, P. & Rutter, Michael. (U London Inst of Psychiatry, England) British Journal of Disorders of Communication, 1977(Oct), Vol 12(2), 119–135. [PA, Vol 60:10747]

136.   Follow-up report on autism in congenital rubella.

A longitudinal study conducted by the author (see PA, Vol 47:5285) of 243 children with congenital rubella showed a high rate of autism and recovery. Examination of the data suggested that the rubella virus was the primary etiologic agent. The present follow up study assessed 205 of the children at ages 8–9 yrs. Analysis of 22 Ss' cases showed that the course of autism was that of a chronic infection in which recovery, chronicity, improvement, worsening, and delayed appearance of the autistic syndrome all were found. Other rubella consequences such as blindness, deafness, and cardiac and neuromuscular defects remained present except as modified by operations and prostheses. Degree of mental retardation initially was related to the outcome of autism, but shifts in mental retardation over time did not correlate significantly with shift in the autistic symptoms.

Chess, Stella. (New York U Medical Ctr) Journal of Autism & Developmental Disorders, 1977(Mar), Vol 7(1), 69–81. [PA, Vol 59:01346]

137.   Compliance and resistance in autistic children.

Explored, in 3 experiments, factors related to negativism in autistic children, where negativism was defined as the consistent avoidance of a correct response in a multiple choice discrimination task. 27 autistic 7–14 yr olds, assigned to 1 of 4 categories of spoken language ability, served as Ss. In Exp I, a design employed in an earlier study of autistic children by P. A. Cowan et al (see PA, Vol 40:4417) was modified to allow a more detailed examination of patterning of the S's responses. Results show a positive relationship between use of spoken language and successful performance of the task. However, no S was negativistic. Of the Ss tested, 18 had a near perfect performance and 9 scored at chance level. Exp II, an exact replication of the Cowan et al method, still failed to produce any negativism. Exp III, using a more difficult discrimination task, produced a higher rate of errors but still no negativism. Possible reasons for the failure to replicate are discussed. (23 ref)

Clark, Peter & Rutter, Michael. (U London Inst of Psychiatry, England) Journal of Autism & Developmental Disorders, 1977(Mar), Vol 7(1), 33–38. [PA, Vol 59:01189]

138.   Dopamine and serotonin metabolism in neuropsychiatrically disturbed children.

Lumbar cerebrospinal fluid (CSF), homovanillic acid (HVA), 5-hydroxyindoleacetic acid (5-HIAA), and probenecid were measured in 4 subgroups of neuropsychiatrically disturbed children (autism, aphasia, early-onset nonautistic psychosis, and attentionally and cognitively impaired; $N = 34$) and a contrast group of 9 pediatric patients. With the exception of a serotonin metabolite difference between autistic and nonautistic psychotic Ss, there were no significant differences in metabolite concentrations among autistic, nonautistic psychotic, aphasic, and cognitively and attentionally impaired groups, or between the developmentally disabled and contrast groups. Younger Ss had higher concentrations of HVA than older Ss. Girls had significantly lower HVA/probenecid ratios than boys, which did not appear to be related to underlying neuropsychiatric disorder. Significant probenecid-metabolite correlations indicate the importance of measuring probenecid in the CSF in clinical studies. (48 ref)

Cohen, Donald J.; Caparulo, Barbara K.; Shaywitz, Bennett A. & Bowers, Malcolm B. (Yale U Child Study Ctr) Archives of General Psychiatry, 1977(May), Vol 34(5), 545–550. [PA, Vol 59:05771]

139.   Primary childhood aphasia and childhood autism.

Congenital, developmental, and idiopathic acquired aphasia form a spectrum of primary childhood aphasias characterized by profound disturbances in expressive language; better language comprehension; the capacity for inner language, imaginative play, gesture, mime, and warm social relations; and a variety of associated behavioral and cognitive difficulties (e.g., dependency, immaturity). The presence of paroxysmal EEG abnormalities suggests cortical dysfunction. In contrast, childhood autism appears earlier in life and is characterized by an impoverishment of inner language; paucity of mime, gesture, and imitation; and greater disturbance in social attachment and regulation of anxiety. Midbrain and brainstem dysfunctions involving catecholamine pathways may underlie some aspects of this syndrome. Intensive language training starting in the preschool years and possibly introduction of systematic sign language may be useful for both groups and especially valuable for aphasic children with more intact language competence. 10 case studies are described. (5 p ref)

Cohen, Donald J.; Caparulo, Barbara K. & Shaywitz, Bennett A. (Yale U School of Medicine) Annual Progress in Child Psychiatry & Child Development, 1977, 545–587. [PA, Vol 66:05902]

140.   Creatine phosphokinase levels in children with severe developmental disturbances.

Studied serum creatine phosphokinase (CPK) levels in 110 Ss aged 3–21 yrs and 32–49 yrs: 40 psychotic children with childhood autism, atypical personality development, and childhood schizophrenia; 5 children with childhood aphasia; 22 children with severe personality disorders; 29 normal children and normal siblings of psychotic children; and 14 normal parents of psychotic children. CPK levels in all Ss were normally distributed, and the mean CPK levels for the 8 diagnostic groups were within normal limits. Those 22 children with personality disorders had significantly higher CPK levels than the other diagnostic groups. This may be related to vulnerability to later development of schizophrenic spectrum disorders. There was no relationship between CPK levels and motor activity, nor was there any change in the level of CPK during a trial of psychoactive medication. (22 ref)

Cohen, Donald J.; Johnson, Warren; Caparulo, Barbara K. & Young, J. Gerald. (Yale U School of Medicine) Annual Progress in Child Psychiatry & Child Development, 1977, 204–212. [PA, Vol 66:05901]

141. Cardiovascular correlates of attention in normal and psychiatrically disturbed children: Blood pressure, peripheral blood flow, and peripheral vascular resistance.

Measured blood pressure, peripheral blood flow, and peripheral vascular resistance in 28 normal adults and children and in 18 5–20 yr old males with autism and severe disturbances in personality development while the individuals were engaged in a variety of attentional tasks. The tasks were designed to elicit outward direction of attention (and intake of sensory input, e.g., reading a passage and reading letters and numbers) or inward direction of attention (and relative rejection of external sensory input, e.g., mental arithmetic and recall). During tasks involving sensory rejection, normal adults and normal children showed increased blood flow and decreased peripheral vascular resistance; with sensory intake, blood flow was decreased and resistance was increased. The most severely impaired Ss showed little alteration in their physiological response to task requirements. Autistics had higher mean blood flow and lower peripheral vascular resistance than normal children and adults. Some autistic children characteristically may be in a state of sensory rejection associated with generally higher levels of arousal or defense against environmental bombardment. (52 ref)
Cohen, Donald J. & Johnson, Warren T. (Yale U Child Study Ctr) Archives of General Psychiatry, 1977(May), Vol 34(5), 561–567. [PA, Vol 59:05798]

142. Handedness in autistic children.

Tested the handedness of 20 autistic and 25 normal 2.2–6.9 yr olds. Results show that the frequency of non–right-handedness in normal Ss was 12%, whereas it was 65% in autistic Ss. The significance of this difference for the etiology of autism is discussed.
Colby, Kenneth M. & Parkison, Carole. (U California Medical School, Los Angeles) Journal of Autism & Developmental Disorders, 1977(Mar), Vol 7(1), 3–9. [PA, Vol 59:01190]

143. Infantile autism: A genetic study of 21 twin pairs.

Conducted a systematic study of a representative group of 11 monozygotic (MZ) and 10 dizygotic (DZ) 5–23 yr old same-sexed twin pairs in which at least 1 twin showed the syndrome of infantile autism. Data were collected through parental interviews and examinations of the twins. Results show that there was a 36% pair-wise concordance rate for autism in MZ pairs compared with 0% concordance in DZ pairs. The concordance for cognitive abnormalities was 82% in MZ pairs and 10% in DZ pairs. It is concluded that there were important hereditary influences concerning a cognitive deficit which included but was not restricted to autism. In 12 out of 17 pairs discordant for autism, the presence of autism was associated with a biological hazard liable to cause brain damage. It is concluded that brain injury in the infancy period may lead to autism on its own or in combination with a genetic predisposition. Uncertainty remains about the mode of inheritance and exactly what is inherited. Case reports of each twin are presented. (2¾ p ref)
Folstein, Susan & Rutter, Michael. (U London Inst of Psychiatry, England) Journal of Child Psychology & Psychiatry & Allied Disciplines, 1977(Sep), Vol 18(4), 297–321. [PA, Vol 60:05365]

144. Motor development of autistic monozygotic twins: A case study.

Assessed a pair of autistic monozygotic twins on relevant portions of the Geddes Psychomotor Inventory. Overall motor development of the 3½-yr-old twins was similar and is considered to be a partial consequence of the same genotype and comparable environmental experiences from birth. The twins exhibited poor or unsuccessful performance on tasks requiring abilities in language, communication, and appropriate relationships to objects; superior performance on specific fine manual motor skills, walking balance board, and climbing; at-age performance on tasks which were considered measures of patterned gross movement, balance, postural maintenance, and spatial orientation; and few typical autistic motor characteristics.
Geddes, Dolores. (U Southern California) Perceptual & Motor Skills, 1977(Aug), Vol 45(1), 179–186. [PA, Vol 60:05368]

145. Hyperserotonemia and amine metabolites in autistic and retarded children.

Attempted to (a) replicate laboratory findings that blood serotonin (5-hydroxytryptamine, 5-HT) levels are elevated in some severely retarded and autistic children, and (b) determine the mechanisms for the increases in blood 5-HT levels in those individual children who have hyperserotonemia. Mean whole blood 5-HT levels were elevated in groups of autistic and severely retarded children. Eight of 27 autistic children, 13 of 25 severely retarded children, 2 of 23 mildly retarded children, and none of the control children had statistically significant blood 5-HT levels elevations (hyperserotonemia). Hyperserotonemic autistic children excreted more urinary 5-HT, 5-hydroxyindole-acetic acid (5-HIAA), tryptamine, and vanillylmandelic acid than did mildly retarded children with normal blood 5-HT levels. Rates of depletion and repletion of blood of 5-HT levels in these 2 groups following reserpine therapy were identical. Oral tryptophan administration doubled urinary 5-HIAA excretion in both groups and raised urinary 5-HT levels in hyperserotonemic autistic children, but lowered urinary 5-HT in mildly retarded, normal blood 5-HT children. No clear mechanism for hyperserotonemia was found; the rationale for further investigations is discussed. (88 ref)
Hanley, Henry G.; Stahl, Stephen M. & Freedman, Daniel X. (VA Hosp, Lexington, KY) Archives of General Psychiatry, 1977(May), Vol 34(5), 521–531. [PA, Vol 59:05775]

146. A case report of an autistic girl with an extra bisatellited marker chromosome.

Cytogenetic examination of a 14-yr-old severely retarded girl revealed a karyotype of 47 chromosomes with an extra bisatellited chromosome, a translocation between No. 22, and a chromosome in the D group. Data from child psychiatric examinations at 5 and 14 yrs are presented. The importance of giving parents information as early as possible about biological causes of mental retardation and mental illness is stressed.
Hansen, Annelise et al. Journal of Autism & Childhood Schizophrenia, 1977(Sep), Vol 7(3), 263–267. [PA, Vol 60:05337]

147. Diurnal cortisol and temperature variation of normal and autistic children.

Blood samples and temperature measurements were taken over a 24-hr period for 1 female and 5 male children (mean age 7.83 yrs) with autistic features and 1 male and 2 female normal control children of approximately the same age. Normal Ss showed relatively adult diurnal rhythmicity in cortisol and temperature. In contrast, 4 of 6 autistic Ss showed abnormal patterns in both measures. It is suggested that irregularities in the 2 systems are consistent with the idea that a neurointegrative defect of the pituitary–adrenocortical system is a factor in autism.
Hill, Suzanne D.; Wagner, Emily A.; Shedlarski, Joseph G. & Sears, Suzanne P. (U New Orleans) Developmental Psychobiology, 1977(Nov), Vol 10(6), 579–583. [PA, Vol 60:07586]

148. On the etiology of the borderline syndrome in the family groups demonstrated by a case study of an autistic reaction.

Describes in detail the case of a 5-yr-old girl who stopped her emotional and verbal contact at age 3 after a period of normal language development. The patient had previously showed borderline symptoms, however, and both parents were borderline personalities. When the unstable symbiotic balance of the parents could no longer be maintained, the child was expected to save the marriage and mediate as the 3rd object between the parents and create a symbiosis of 3 organisms. At the same time the child was a danger, with the father jealous and fearful of losing his wife. The mother expected the child to be a partner who would not leave her but at the same time would spoil her professional success. When the father left the family and the mother was hospitalized after a suicide attempt, the child reacted with psychotic withdrawal from reality to overcome her own fear of destruction and death. In therapy, drawing became an important connecting medium.
Hirsch, Mathias. Dynamische Psychiatrie, 1977, Vol 10(1), 38–41. [PA, Vol 61:03749]

149.   [Idea and speech content of autistic children.] (Germ)
Describes the speech content peculiarities of autistic children, using numerous examples, such as unintelligible words and neologisms, with special reference to the body, its parts, and its functions to illness, accidents, and death; to destructive desires; and to special circumscribed spheres of interest. The author explains these speech peculiarities by referring to dysfunctions of the perception process, perseveration tendencies, examples supplied by adults, and operant reinforcements at all levels of verbal messages. (French & Spanish summaries)
Kehrer, Hans E. (Westfälische Wilhelms-U Münster, Psychiatrischen und Nervenklinik, West Germany) Acta Paedopsychiatrica, 1977, Vol 43(1), 15–22. [PA, Vol 61:03755]

150.   Increased norepinephrine levels and decreased dopamine-β-hydroxylase activity in primary autism.
Evaluated the sympathetic nervous system in 11 8–35 yr old primary autistic patients and their families. The plasma levels of norepinephrine (NE), the neurotransmitter of the sympathetic nervous system, was higher in the patients than in age-controlled normal volunteers both while supine and after standing. The plasma activity of dopamine-β-hydroxylase, the enzyme that converts dopamine to NE, was significantly lower in the autistic patients and their healthy relatives than in control groups. Dopamine-β-hydroxylase does not appear to provide an index of sympathetic activity in this group of patients who, on the basis of the elevated plasma levels of NE, may demonstrate a chronic state of hyperactivity of the sympathetic nervous system. Low enzyme activity found in both the autistic patients and their immediate families may be associated with this disorder. (46 ref)
Lake, C. Raymond; Ziegler, Michael G. & Murphy, Dennis L. (NIMH Lab of Clinical Science, Bethesda, MD) Archives of General Psychiatry, 1977(May), Vol 34(5), 553–556. [PA, Vol 59:05824]

151.   Advocacy and research: A parent's perspective.
The reduction in public expenditures for research and the rise in consumerism have combined to make parent advocate groups a potentially powerful and active force on behalf of research. This article outlines this present situation from the parents' viewpoint (the 1st author is the parent of an autistic child), including parental hesitation about research and researchers, suggestions on developing a "research constituency," areas of research of particular interest to parents, the rights of human subjects, and the implications of parent involvement in accountability. (21 ref)
Lapin, Constance L. & Donnellan-Walsh, Anne. (National Society for Autistic Children, Los Angeles, CA) Journal of Pediatric Psychology, 1977, Vol 2(4), 191–196. [PA, Vol 62:06176]

152.   Cognitive characteristics of parents of autistic children.
The parents of 15 autistic boys with a nonverbal IQ of at least 80 were compared with a matched group of parents of normal boys on the Goldstein-Scheerer Object Sorting Test and the Bannister-Fransella Grid Test of Thought Disorder. It was necessary to control for social class effects as abnormal scores on the thought disorder tests were more frequent in parents of the manual-labor social class. It was found that (a) there was a lack of agreement between the 2 tests of thought disorder, (b) the parents of autistic children showed thought disorder scores closely comparable to those of the parents of normals, and (c) there was no consistent association between thought disorder and anxiety. The methodological and substantive implications of the findings are discussed in relation to the results of previous investigations. (43 ref)
Lennox, Carolyn; Callias, Maria & Rutter, Michael. (Integra Foundation, Toronto, Canada) Journal of Autism & Developmental Disorders, 1977(Sep), Vol 7(3), 243–261. [PA, Vol 60:05378]

153.   Some observations on the nonextinguishability of children's speech.
Tested the notion that the reinforcing stimuli that maintain high rates of speech may not consist solely of events extrinsic to the person but may involve (sensory) stimulation generated by the behavior itself. Three 10–16 yr old psychotic, autistic children and 3 normal 3–4 yr olds were placed in a variety of environments, and their verbal behavior was recorded while they were alone, with no apparent social reinforcement for their speech. Data show very little change in the Ss' verbal output over rather extensive observations and suggest that the verbal behavior may in part provide its own source of (sensory) reinforcement.
Lovaas, O. Ivar; Varni, James W.; Koegel, Robert L. & Lorsch, Nancy. (U California, Los Angeles) Child Development, 1977(Sep), Vol 48(3), 1121–1127. [PA, Vol 60:01235]

154.   Research related to family factors in autism.
Recent studies do not support the position that parents of autistic children have extreme personality characteristics, such as coldness, obsessiveness, and introversion. In terms of personality characteristics, these parents were found to be similar to parents of other problem children. However, they were likely to be more affluent, and the fathers were more likely to be brighter and better educated. The continual stress of dealing with an autistic child may eventually result in personality changes for these parents. Recent studies support the idea of genetic inheritance which may not involve the complete syndrome of autism but may involve a language-cognitive component. (30 ref)
McAdoo, W. George & DeMyer, Marian K. (Indiana U Medical School, Riley Child Guidance Clinic) Journal of Pediatric Psychology, 1977, Vol 2(4), 162–166. [PA, Vol 62:06187]

155.   [A study on autistic children in twins.] (Japn)
Out of 415 autistic children treated at a Japanese hospital, there were 7 pairs of twins, which is a rate that is more than 3 times that for the general population. All twins were monozygous, and 6 sets were male. Although these findings support the theory of genetic factors of autism, the influence of nongenetic factors should not be neglected. (English summary) (37 ref)
Mizuno, Mayumi & Wakabayashi, Shinichiro. (Aichi Prefectural Colony Inst of Developmental Research, Kasugai, Japan) Japanese Journal of Child Psychiatry, 1977(Jul–Aug), Vol 18(4), 235–246. [PA, Vol 64:12648]

156.   A case report on the artistic talent of an autistic idiot savant.
Suggests that the performance of the idiot savant can best be explained by the hypothesis that a narrowing of the stimuli resulting in funneling of a response occurs in cases where there is at least average cognitive ability. The case of an autistic Japanese artist reported here demonstrates that a consistent high degree of a response can be nurtured through the initiation of elaborate instructional tactics by the teacher.
Morishima, Akira & Brown, Louis F. (U Iowa Coll of Education) Mental Retardation, 1977(Apr), Vol 15(2), 33–36. [PA, Vol 59:01165]

157.   A simultaneous discrimination procedure for the measurement of vision in nonverbal children.
Few nonverbal developmentally disabled children ever receive adequate vision assessment because of their limited language skills. The present study details a simultaneous discrimination procedure for measuring subjective visual acuity in such children. A stimulus fading procedure was used to train a discrimination between Snellen E's differing in orientation, and a psychophysical tracking method was used to determine acuity thresholds. The procedure was tested with 11 nonverbal autistic and schizophrenic 5–16 yr old and validated with 4 nonpsychotic behavior disordered 10–15 yr olds who were normal language users. Eight of the psychotic children were successfully examined in 1 to 3 sessions. Two of these children were identified as having significant acuity losses. The validity assessment showed that the experimental procedure resulted in thresholds equal to or slightly lower than those obtained with the Illiterate E chart. (26 ref)
Newsom, Crighton D. & Simon, Karen M. (Suffolk Child Development Ctr, Smithtown, NY) Journal of Applied Behavior Analysis, 1977(Win), Vol 10(4), 633–644. [PA, Vol 61:01562]

158.   [A follow up study of "Die autistische Psychopathie nach Asperger, H."] (Japn)
A 13-yr follow-up study of 5 typical autistic children shows the following: (a) Ss had poor interpersonal relationships and lack of

sympathy from infancy through adolescence; (b) their interests evolved from Gestalt of objects in infancy to simple causal relations between things; (c) they had difficulty adapting to society after graduation; and (d) they regressed in thinking and personality. It is concluded that autism belongs to the same category as F. Robinson's (see PA, Vol 29:5956) "circumscribed interest patterns." (English summary) (16 ref)

Ohue, Masatoshi. Japanese Journal of Child Psychiatry, 1977, Vol 18(3), 141–155. [PA, Vol 64:12654]

159. The early development of autistic children.
74 young autistic children (mean age 45.2 mo) were selected and defined by direct observation of specific behaviors and clinical assessment of the presence or absence of associated pathological conditions. Retrospective developmental data on these children and 38 age-matched normal children were gathered by means of a written inventory completed by the parents when the children were relatively young (mean age less than 4 yrs). The autistic children were reported to have had significant delays in the development of motor abilities, speech, communication, comprehension, and, to a lesser extent, perception during their 1st and 2nd yrs. (24 ref)

Ornitz, Edward M.; Guthrie, Donald & Farley, Arthur H. (U California, Los Angeles) Journal of Autism & Childhood Schizophrenia, 1977(Sep), Vol 7(3), 207–229. [PA, Vol 60:05384]

160. The syndrome of autism: A critical review.
Reviews the clinical features and behavioral characteristics of autism; differential diagnosis of the syndrome; clinical, neurophysiological, and biochemical research; and its medical management and treatment. It is concluded that autism is a behaviorally defined, specific syndrome that is manifested at birth or shortly thereafter. Its symptoms are expressive of an underlying neuropathophysiological process that affects developmental rate; modulation of perception; language, cognitive, and intellectual development; and the ability to relate. The long-term prognosis is guarded; almost all patients manifest severe symptomatology throughout their lives. Further basic research into the neuropathophysiological process underlying the syndrome is necessary in order to reach the ultimate goal of developing etiologically specific treatment programs. (151 ref)

Ornitz, Edward M. & Ritvo, Edward R. (U California School of Medicine, Los Angeles) Annual Progress in Child Psychiatry & Child Development, 1977, 501–530. [PA, Vol 66:05990]

161. [Electroencephalographic follow-up on autistic children.] (Japn)
Conducted a 5-yr follow-up EEG study of 20 children (aged 3–10 yrs at 1st examination) with autistic symptoms. In the 1st EEG examinations, 8 Ss showed abnormal patterns, and this number increased to 13 in later examinations, indicating that EEG irregularities increased as the Ss grew older. Results indicate that the pathological processes in the brain related to autistic symptoms included difficulties in human relationships, retarded speech, and stereotyped behavior. Findings, however, do not provide clear-cut evidence of a relationship between EEG patterns and clinical symptoms. (28 ref)

Otsuki, Noriko et al. (Osaka U Medical School, Japan) Japanese Journal of Child Psychiatry, 1977(Sep–Nov), Vol 18(5), 321–329. [PA, Vol 64:12655]

162. Late onset echolalia in autism and allied disorders.
Argues that perseverating immediate echolalia (echophrasia) in children suffering from early infantile psychoses, especially autism, is a deviant form of noted normal language development and that the key to its progressive eradication in therapy is the view that the condition itself is a necessary stage of language acquisition. Case notes and observations support the ideas put forward. It is not claimed that deeper seated disorders in autism are in any way solved by this therapy but that it effectively allows them to be reached by other therapies and techniques that rely on language. (37 ref)

Philips, Gloria M. & Dyer, Christopher. (Belchertown State School, MA) British Journal of Disorders of Communication, 1977(Apr), Vol 12(1), 47–59. [PA, Vol 59:05836]

163. A syntactic investigation of verbal autistic, mentally retarded, and normal children.
Compared the syntax used by 10 verbal autistic children matched for nonlinguistic MA with a group of 10 mentally retarded Ss and normal controls. Two different means of assessing syntactic development were utilized: L. Lee's developmental sentence analysis and N. Chomsky's transformational analysis. The autistic group ranked significantly lower than either the mentally retarded or the normal group in terms of developmental sentence scores. When transformational grammar was used to describe the language samples, the autistic children were typified by higher error rates and lower levels of complexity compared to the other 2 groups. However, the results also indicate that the grammatical system of autistic children is rule-governed and probably not unlike that of young normal or retarded children. In conclusion, it appears that the syntactic abnormalities characteristic of autism are attributable to an extreme delay in language development as well as to an impaired ability to make use of linguistic rules. (35 ref)

Pierce, Sandra & Bartolucci, Giampiero. (McMaster U, Hamilton, Canada) Journal of Autism & Developmental Disorders, 1977(Jun), Vol 7(2), 121–134. [PA, Vol 59:10034]

164. Conditional matching learning set performance in autistic children.
Studied 8 autistic and 8 normal children (mean MAs of both groups 5 yrs 2 mo) to test the following hypotheses: (a) If autistic children were able to learn conditional matching learning sets (CMLS) problems this would be an indication that their "real" ability was greater than their apparent ability as shown by standard testing. (b) If normal children of the same MA were able to learn the CMLS whereas autistic children were not, this would indicate a deficit other than that related to low MA in the autistic children. The CMLS involves the use of conditional cues for correct solution to problems. Results show that autistic children performed poorly on the task, where learning depended on higher order processing involving adaptation to positive and negative symbols or signs. The performance of the autistic children was, with one exception, at chance level or below, and the group data showed no evidence of improvement over trials or with retesting. By contrast, 5 of the 8 normal Ss did show improvement between problems and with retesting a month later on the same problems. It is suggested that autistic children suffer from a particular deficit which is exposed in their inability in the CMLS task to make use of symbolic information. (16 ref)

Prior, Margot R. (Monash U, Clayton, Australia) Journal of Child Psychology & Psychiatry & Allied Disciplines, 1977(Apr), Vol 18(2), 183–189. [PA, Vol 59:05837]

165. Psycholinguistic disabilities of autistic and retarded children.
Used the Illinois Test of Psychological Abilities (revised version) to assess and compare language related functioning in 20 autistic Ss (mean CA 11.5 yr) and 20 retarded Ss (mean CA 11.8 yr). Results show that higher functioning groups of both diagnoses differed from lower functioning groups overall and specifically on a number of the subtests. For both high and low functioning autistic Ss, verbal and manual expressive performance was particularly impoverished and indicated a severe deficit in spontaneous communicative ability. Findings are compared with those of V. K. Tubbs (see PA, Vol 41:4792), and in general there is some support for her earlier and widely quoted conclusions. (18 ref)

Prior, Margot R. (Latrobe U, Bundoora, Australia) Journal of Mental Deficiency Research, 1977(Mar), Vol 21(1), 37–45. [PA, Vol 59:05781]

166. Some motivational properties of sensory stimulation in psychotic children.
Assessed the reinforcing properties of sensory stimulation for autistic children. Three different types of sensory stimulation were used: music, visual flickering stimulation (e.g., strobe light), and visual movement (e.g., windshield wiper). In a given session, 1 of the 3 kinds of sensory stimulation was presented for 5 sec contingent upon the children's bar pressing (FR5). In Phase 1,

which was designed to assess the differential reinforcement value of these events, 4 children participated in sessions with each of the sensory events. In Phase 2, designed to assess variables influencing the maintenance of responding for the sensory events, 2 children continued to participate in sessions with their preferred sensory event until satiation occurred. Results show the following: (a) Sensory events could be used as reinforcing stimuli to produce a high rate of responding which was relatively durable over time. (b) The reinforcement function of the sensory events was idiosyncratic across children, with 1 child preferring 1 kind of sensory event, and another child preferring a different kind. (c) There was substantial variability in daily response rates. (d) When a child satiated on a particular sensory event, a relatively small change in the sensory event was sufficient to recover a high rate of responding. Results suggest that sensory reinforcers can profitably be used in behavior therapy with autistic children. (27 ref)
Rincover, Arnold; Newsom, Crighton D.; Lovaas, O. Ivar & Koegel, Robert L. (U North Carolina, Greensboro) Journal of Experimental Child Psychology, 1977(Oct), Vol 24(2), 312–323. [PA, Vol 60:05391]

167.   Biochemical studies of children with the syndromes of autism, childhood schizophrenia and related developmental disabilities: A review.
Reviews research concerning abnormalities in serotonin metabolism, bufotenin excretion, tryptophan metabolism, catecholamines, and enzymes. (1½ p ref)
Ritvo, Edward R. (U California Medical School, Mental Retardation & Child Psychiatry Program, Los Angeles) Journal of Child Psychology & Psychiatry & Allied Disciplines, 1977(Sep), Vol 18(4), 373–379. [PA, Vol 60:05345]

168.   Current status of biochemical research in autism.
Reviews biochemical studies of children diagnosed as having syndromes of autism, childhood schizophrenia, childhood psychosis, and related developmental disabilities. Studies are grouped in chronological order under the following headings: serotonin, tryptophan, catecholamines, and enzyme studies. Three major methodological issues limit cross-comparison of research results: lack of diagnostic specificity, differences in biochemical assay techniques, and a paucity of normal developmental data. In the conclusion, the studies that are felt to warrant replication are indicated, and promising avenues for future investigation are suggested. (28 ref)
Ritvo, Edward R. & Freeman, B. J. (U California, Neuropsychiatric Inst, Los Angeles) Journal of Pediatric Psychology, 1977, Vol 2(4), 149–152. [PA, Vol 62:06210]

169.   National Society for Autistic Children definition of the syndrome of autism.
Autism is a severely incapacitating developmental disability which typically appears during the 1st 3 yrs of life in 5 out of every 10,000 children; it is 4 times more common in boys than in girls. Symptoms are caused by physical disorders of the brain that must be documented in history or present on examination. The symptoms include (a) disturbances in the rate of appearance of physical, social, and language skills; (b) abnormal responses to sensations; (c) absent or delayed speech and language, with possible presence of specific thinking capabilities; and (d) abnormal ways of relating to people, events, and objects. Autism occurs by itself or in association with disorders that affect the function of the brain (e.g., viral infections or epilepsy). 60% of autistic individuals have IQs below 50, 20% between 50 and 70, and only 20% greater than 70. The severe form of the syndrome may include extreme forms of self-injurious, repetitive, unusual, and aggressive behaviors. Such behaviors may be persistent and resistant to change, often requiring unique management, treatment, or teaching strategies. Special educational programs using behavioral methods and designed for specific individuals have proven most helpful. Supportive counseling may be helpful for families with autistic members. Medication to decrease specific symptoms may help certain autistic people live more satisfactory lives.

Ritvo, Edward R. & Freeman, B. J. (U California, Neuropsychiatric Inst, Los Angeles) Journal of Pediatric Psychology, 1977, Vol 2(4), 142–145. [PA, Vol 62:06211]

170.   Depressed lymphocyte responsiveness in autistic children.
Notes that host defense against the etiologic agents postulated to be responsible for the autism-associated syndromes is believed to be primarily of the cell-mediated type. The cellular immune function of 12 autistic 2–12 yr olds and 13 control Ss was assessed in vitro by phytohemagglutinin (PHA) stimulation of lymphocyte cultures. The autistic group exhibited a depressed lymphocyte transformation response to PHA when compared to controls.
Stubbs, E. Gene; Crawford, Mary L.; Burger, Denis R. & Vandenbark, Arthur A. (U Oregon Health Sciences Ctr, Portland) Journal of Autism & Developmental Disorders, 1977(Mar), Vol 7(1), 49–55. [PA, Vol 59:01246]

171.   Intellectual characteristics of adolescent childhood psychotics with high verbal ability.
Investigated the cognitive processes of a group of verbal adolescents with a diagnosis of childhood psychosis made early in life. The 20 autistic children in Group 1 (mean age 189 mo) were matched as closely as possible on age, Full Scale WISC or WAIS IQ (88.4), and sex (16 males and 4 females) with the 20 contrasting children (5 mentally retarded, 11 learning disabled, 1 behavior problem, and 3 normals; IQ 89.2) in Group 2. It was necessary to include several Group 2 Ss in the lower socioeconomic levels to obtain IQ matches for the Group 1 Ss in the mildly mentally retarded range; consequently, the autistic group generally occupied a higher socioeconomic level. Between- and within-group differences were analyzed for each of the WISC or WAIS subtests. Results show that the autistic Ss were significantly superior to Group 2 Ss on the Block Design subtest, but were significantly inferior to Group 2 Ss on the Comprehension subtest. There were no intragroup differences among subtests in Group 2, but there were several in Group 1 due to poor performance on the Comprehension, Coding, and Picture Arrangement subtests. Results indicate that in autistic children, intellectual deficits, characterized by an inability to synthesize information and to interpret social nuances, persist into adolescence.
Tymchuk, A. J.; Simmons, J. Q. & Neafsey, Shonagh. (U California Ctr for the Health Sciences, Los Angeles) Journal of Mental Deficiency Research, 1977(Jun), Vol 21(2), 133–138. [PA, Vol 60:01257]

172.   [A study of imitation in autistic children.] (Japn)
Reports that in cases of autism with good prognoses, the development of imitative behavior and echolalia seemed to play an important role in the child's general development, especially in speech acquisition. In cases with poor prognoses, imitative behavior and imitative vocalizations served no positive function and children remained developmentally retarded due to defects of cognitive function, poor intellectual facilities, or abulia. (67 ref)
Wakabayashi, Shinichiro; Mizuno, Mayumi & Nishimura, Bensaku. (Aichi Prefectural Colony Inst for Developmental Research, Kasugai, Japan) Japanese Journal of Child Psychiatry, 1977(Sep–Nov), Vol 18(5), 271–286. [PA, Vol 64:12683]

173.   Incidence of minor physical anomaly in autism.
74 4–25 yr old Ss diagnosed as autistic were matched by age and sex with 74 controls and examined for presence of minor physical anomalies. Of the 16 anomalies scored, autistic children demonstrated a significant accumulation greater than the number exhibited by normal children. Three of the stigmata—low seating of ears, hypertelorism, and syndactylia—were expressed differentially in the 2 groups, and high palate as well as unusual cranial circumference were significantly high in both groups. Clusters of stigmata that might be associated with known chromosomal disorders could not be identified. The increased number of anomalies suggests that among autistic children such congenital markers indicate a deviant intrauterine experience.

Walker, Harry A. (Children's Brain Research Clinic, Washington, DC) Journal of Autism & Developmental Disorders, 1977(Jun), Vol 7(2), 165–176. [PA, Vol 59:09995]

174. A dermatoglyphic study of autistic patients.
Compared the dermatoglyphic patterns of the fingers and palms of autistic 4–25 yr olds to those of control Ss matched socioeconomically and by age and sex. Analysis of dermal ridge patterns and ridge counts resulted in significant differences between the autistic and normal Ss. Autistic Ss had a reduced number of whorls and increased number of arches, lowered ridge counts, and less distinctness in formation of ridge line. It is concluded that evidence was sufficient to indicate the existence of congenital factors in the etiology of autism. (22 ref)
Walker, Harry A. (Children's Brain Research Clinic, Washington, DC) Journal of Autism & Developmental Disorders, 1977(Mar), Vol 7(1), 11–21. [PA, Vol 59:01250]

175. [Toe walking in children.] (Germ)
66 normal children and children suffering from oligophrenia, mental retardation, and Kanner's syndrome were observed for toe-walking behavior. This gait is observed in many normal children when they are learning to walk and can persist for several months. In autistic and oligophrenic children, walking on the front of the foot can be regarded as a prolonged fixation at a stage of normal motor development or as a motor symptom of retardation. This symptom tends to persist longer in autistic children than in other developmentally disabled children; it can be helpful in differentiating autism from childhood schizophrenia. (28 ref)
Weber, Doris. (Philipps-U Marburg, Inst für Ärztlich-Pädagogische Jugendhilfe, West Germany) Zeitschrift für Kinder- und Jugendpsychiatrie, 1977(Jun), Vol 5(2), 115–127. [PA, Vol 63:03360]

176. Symbolic play in severely mentally retarded and in autistic children.
Used the Camberwell (England) Register to identify 108 children (ages 5–14 yrs) who were being treated for severe mental retardation or had shown signs of early childhood autism. Ss were divided into 3 groups: (a) 42 with no symbolic play; (b) 23 with stereotyped, repetitive, copying play; and (c) 43 who had flexible, varied symbolic play. The last occurred only in children with language comprehension age above the 19-mo level, and was seen in less than half of the school-age severely retarded children. The majority of children with no symbolic play or with stereotyped play had marked autistic features or the full autistic syndrome. Only 2 of those with true symbolic play had any behavior like that found in autism, and none had the full syndrome. A small group of children with "repetitive" speech and stereotyped play was identified, and the relationship with childhood autism is discussed. The educational implications of the findings are discussed. (31 ref)
Wing, Lorna; Gould, Judith; Yeates, Sybil R. & Brierley, Lorna M. (MRC Social Psychiatry Unit, U London Inst of Psychiatry, England) Journal of Child Psychology & Psychiatry & Allied Disciplines, 1977(Apr), Vol 18(2), 167–178. [PA, Vol 59:05786]

177. [Electroencephalographic studies of child psychosis.] (Japn)
Subjected 3 clinical groups of outpatients (147 autistic, 104 speech retarded, and 79 behavior disordered children) to EEG examinations. EEG abnormalities were found in 23.2% of the autistic, 38.5% of the speech retarded, and 41.8% of the behavior disordered Ss. EEG spike or sharp wave activity was more frequently observed than spike and wave, or positive spike, high voltage slow activity. However, no clearly characteristic findings were obtained in any of the clinical groups. Seizures were present in both the EEG abnormal group and the normal group, and there were no significant correlations between EEG abnormalities and seizures. Nearly half of the Ss had some kind of perinatal disturbance, but no association with EEG abnormalities could be drawn. (16 ref)

Yamauchi, Toshio et al. (Hokkaido U School of Medicine, Japan) Japanese Journal of Child Psychiatry, 1977, Vol 18(2), 72–80. [PA, Vol 65:03464]

178. [A comparative study of the speech skill levels and speech disorder patterns in autistic and mentally retarded children.] (Japn)
In a study with 66 autistic and 161 mentally retarded children (mean ages 4 yrs 8 mo and 3 yrs 11 mo, respectively), there were no significant differences between the 2 groups' speech skill levels and prevalence of composition errors of words or sentences, reversal of personal pronouns, and mechanical repetition of questioning. Echolalia, habitual use of mime, monolog, and a history of lost speech were significantly more prevalent among the autistic Ss than among the mentally retarded. (14 ref)
Ando, Haruhiko & Yoshimura, Ikuko. (Aichi Prefectural Colony Central Hosp, Japan) Japanese Journal of Child Psychiatry, 1978, Vol 19(3), 194–200. [PA, Vol 64:12569]

179. [Physical development milestones of autistic and mentally retarded children.] (Japn)
Results of a study with 57 male autistic and 113 male nonorganically mentally retarded children show that there were no significant differences between the 2 groups in terms of birth weight. Neither of the groups showed significant differences in birth weights from the male children in the general population. The age distribution of the 1st unaided walking of the mentally retarded Ss was delayed significantly more than that of the autistic Ss. It is suggested that autistic children have relatively good developmental milestones in early infancy and poor motor skills when they reach school age. (10 ref)
Ando, Haruhiko & Yoshimura, Ikuko. (Aichi Prefectural Colony Central Hosp, Kasugai, Japan) Japanese Journal of Child Psychiatry, 1978(Mar–Apr), Vol 19(2), 101–106. [PA, Vol 64:12568]

180. Autistic children: A study of learning characteristics and programming needs.
Studied learning-acquisition characteristics of 6 autistic 4–8 yr olds. Study 1 showed that the 1st step of a color-cued sequencing task required 4 times more trials to learn than did the remaining 5 steps, producing a significant learning-to-learn curve. Study 2 confirmed earlier findings that extra-stimulus prompts are comparatively ineffective with autistic children when compared to within-stimulus prompts and showed extra-stimulus prompting to be effective following the use of within-stimulus prompting on a similar task.
Arick, Joel R. & Krug, David A. (Good Samaritan Hosp, Portland, OR) American Journal of Mental Deficiency, 1978(Sep), Vol 83(2), 200–202. [PA, Vol 62:06118]

181. Handedness in autistics, retardates, and normals of a wide age range.
Tests of handedness were carried out with 34 autistic children, ages 4 yrs 10 mo to 18 yrs 11 mo, and with sex-, age-, and IQ-matched retardates and sex- and age-matched normals. No significant differences were found between the groups on frequency of handedness, degree of right-hand usage, or degree of dominant-hand usage. There was, however, a significant increase in the variance of dominant-hand usage from normals and retardates to autistics. These results are taken to indicate that earlier reports of handedness differences in young autistic children may reflect a developmental lag rather than a specific etiology of autism. Some support for this hypothesis is obtained from a comparison of age-trends between the groups. The relationship of such a developmental delay to the etiology of autism is discussed. (9 ref)
Barry, Robert J. & James, Angela L. (U New South Wales, School of Education, Sydney, Australia) Journal of Autism & Childhood Schizophrenia, 1978(Sep), Vol 8(3), 315–323. [PA, Vol 62:03697]

182. Cerebral asymmetry and the development of early infantile autism.
Two experiments involving listening preferences of autistic and normal Ss were conducted to test the hypothesis that the right

cerebral hemisphere is more active than the left hemisphere in autistic children. Ss in Exp I were 10 autistic children, mean age 9 yrs 4 mo, and 10 normal Ss, mean age 8 yrs 2 mo. Ss in Exp II were 11 autistic children, mean age 10.3 yrs and 18 normal undergraduates (mean age 19.1 yrs). Results show that when given a choice between verbal and musical material, the autistic children preferred music, while normal children showed no preference. Secondly, autistic children listened to both types of material predominantly with the left ear. Although normal Ss showed greater variation among themselves, they tended to listen to music more often with the left ear and to listen to verbal material more often with the right. Results support the notion that some autistic children are predominantly right-hemisphere processors. (32 ref)
Blackstock, Edward G. (York U, Toronto, Canada) Journal of Autism & Childhood Schizophrenia, 1978(Sep), Vol 8(3), 339–353. [PA, Vol 62:03729]

183.   Echoic memory capacity in autistic children.
Assessed capacity of echoic memory, or recency effect capacity, in 10 relatively able autistic children (mean CA 14.2 yrs) and 10 normal age-matched controls. Test stimuli were lists of words 5 or 6 letters in length. Two sets of 3 10-word lists were used. One set was used for delayed recall, and the other for immediate recall. Capacity was found to be the same for both groups; echoic memory may, therefore, be said to represent a peak ability in more able autistic children. This finding is discussed in relation to another known peak ability, namely the digit span, and in relation to echoic and nonechoic components of autistic children's free recall scores. (14 ref)
Boucher, Jill. (Charles Burns Clinic, Birmingham, England) Journal of Child Psychology & Psychiatry & Allied Disciplines, 1978(Apr), Vol 19(2), 161–166. [PA, Vol 63:01088]

184.   Minor physical anomalies in young psychotic children.
Examined 3 groups of children (aged 1 yr 4 mo–14 yrs 3 mo) for minor physical anomalies: 52 autistic children, 34 nonautistic siblings of these patients, and 29 normal controls. The total number of anomalies and the weighted scores were significantly higher in the autistic children. It is noted that the formation of these anomalies in the 1st 3 mo of fetal life may concur with the developmental deviation of the CNS in some of these individuals. (22 ref)
Campbell, Magda et al. (New York U Medical Ctr) American Journal of Psychiatry, 1978(May), Vol 135(5), 573–575. [PA, Vol 61:13503]

185.   A comparative study of infantile autism and specific developmental receptive language disorder: IV. Analysis of syntax and language function.
Compared 12 autistic boys (mean age 9.2 yrs) with an age and IQ matched sample of 12 developmental "dysphasic" boys on reliable measures of syntax and language functions. The groups did not differ on syntactical usage as determined by morphological, transformational, and phrase structure rules. However, autistic Ss were significantly less likely to make spontaneous remarks and significantly more likely to use delayed echoes, thinking aloud/action accompaniments, and inappropriate echoes of themselves. It is concluded that the autistic child's language deviance is not just a reflection of language impairment. (52 ref)
Cantwell, Dennis P.; Baker, Lorian & Rutter, Michael. (U California Neuropsychiatric Inst, Los Angeles) Journal of Child Psychology & Psychiatry & Allied Disciplines, 1978(Oct), Vol 19(4), 351–362. [PA, Vol 64:05756]

186.   Follow-up report on autism in congenital rubella.
A longitudinal study of 243 children with congenital rubella showed a high rate of autism (A) and a high rate of recovery. Examination of the data suggested that the rubella virus was the primary etiologic agent. It is hypothesized that the course of A was that of a chronic infection in which recovery, chronicity, improvement, worsening, and delayed appearance of the A were found. Other rubella consequences (e.g., blindness, deafness, and cardiac and neuromuscular defects) remained present except as

modified by operations and prostheses. Degree of mental retardation (MR) initially was related to the outcome of A but shifts in MR over time did not correlate significantly for the group with shift in the A symptoms. (10 ref)
Chess, Stella. (New York U Medical Ctr) Annual Progress in Child Psychiatry & Child Development, 1978, 486–498. [PA, Vol 66:12901]

187.   Sensorimotor functioning and communication in mute autistic children.
Examined the sensorimotor functioning of mute autistic children and the relationship between their sensorimotor performance and nonverbal communication. 12 mute children, diagnosed autistic, ranging from 4 yrs 9 mo to 12 yrs of age, were administered 4 scales of sensorimotor development from the I. C. Uzgiris and J. M. Hunt (1975) series: object permanence, gestural imitation, means for obtaining environmental events, and causality. Ss performed most poorly on the imitation scale, with 9 of 12 Ss performing below Piaget's 5th sensorimotor stage. In contrast, performance was highest on the object permanence scale: No child scored below Stage 5. Regarding the Ss' nonverbal communication, Stage 5 performance on the means and causality scales and Stage 3 on the imitation scale appeared to form minimal prerequisites for intentional communication in a variety of situations. None of the Ss, even those with relatively complete sensorimotor development, spontaneously used what E. Bates (1976) has called "protodeclarative" gestures to point out or show objects to adults. The absence of protodeclarative gestures may represent a qualitatively distinct pattern of prelinguistic development in certain autistic children. (18 ref)
Curcio, Frank. (Boston U) Journal of Autism & Childhood Schizophrenia, 1978(Sep), Vol 8(3), 281–292. [PA, Vol 62:03738]

188.   A neurological model for childhood autism.
Analyzes the behavioral and motor disturbances in childhood autism. On the basis of analogy to signs and conditions seen in adult neurology, it is proposed that the syndrome results from dysfunction in a system of bilateral neural structures that includes the ring of mesolimbic cortex located in the mesial frontal and temporal lobes, the neostriatum, and the anterior and medial nuclear groups of the thalamus. The mesolimbic cortex is cytoarchitectonically, angioarchitectonically, and neurochemically distinct and, along with the striatum, forms the entire target area of dopaminergic mesencephalic neurons. This raises the possibility that autism is related to neuromediator imbalance in those structures. Such dysfunction might be the result of macroscopic or microscopic changes in the target area or in structures functionally influencing them, consequent to a variety of causes such as perinatal viral infection, insult to the periventricular watershed area, or genetically determined neurochemical abnormalities. (198 ref)
Damasio, Antonio R. & Maurer, Ralph G. (Iowa City U Hospital & Clinic) Archives of Neurology, 1978(Dec), Vol 35(12), 777–786. [PA, Vol 63:09969]

189.   Childhood autism, its process, as seen in a Victorian fairy tale.
A Victorian fairy tale by L. L. Clifford, "Wooden Tony," is presented and analyzed for its excellent and chilling insight into childhood autism. It traces, with commentary, Tony's progressive breaking with reality, withdrawal, deanimation, and dehumanization, until at the end he becomes a figure in a clock—a wooden figure in a symbolic hospital. (2 ref)
Ekstein, Rudolf. American Imago, 1978(Spr–Sum), Vol 35(1–2), 124–145. [PA, Vol 64:01181]

190.   Genetic influences and infantile autism.
Studied a systematically collected sample of 21 pairs of same-sexed twins, one or both of whom had autism as diagnosed by the criteria of L. Kanner (1943) and M. Rutter (1971). Except for 2 pairs in which dermatoglyphics were used, zygosity was determined by blood grouping in all cases not markedly different in physical appearance. Diagnoses were made from case summaries, numbered randomly to prevent sorting by pair. Results show a significantly higher rate of concordance in monozygotic com-

pared with dizygotic pairs for both autism and cognitive abnormalities, indicating the importance of genetic factors in the etiology of autism. The finding of an association between biological hazards (especially brain injuries) in the perinatal period and autism also demonstrates the important role of environmental influences for the causation of autism (but not cognitive disorder). (6 ref)
Folstein, Susan & Rutter, Michael. (U London, Inst of Psychiatry, England) Annual Progress in Child Psychiatry & Child Development, 1978, 437–441. [PA, Vol 66:12957]

191.   Evidence for language recoding in autistic, retarded and normal children: A re-examination.
In a replication and extension of studies by B. Hermelin and N. O'Connor (see PA, Vols 41:7560 and 42:12161), language recoding abilities in 20 autistic, retarded, and normal children matched for MA and digit span were compared in a verbal recall task. Random word lists, sentences, and anomalous sentences were presented, and the number of words recalled from each type of input was scored. All low span Ss recalled sentences better than they did random lists, with normal Ss superior to retarded and autistic Ss and the latter group poorer than the retarded group. Autistic Ss showed a recency effect with both types of input. There were no group differences among high span Ss, and sentences were again better recalled than random lists. In Exp II, sentences were better recalled than anomalous sentences, with autistic and retarded Ss equivalent in performance and poorer than normal Ss. Although low span autistic Ss were clearly deficient in recall of sentence material when compared with the 2 control groups, the effect of conditions showed that they were able to use structure to improve recall. Since high span autistic Ss did not perform differently from controls, it is suggested that results from this kind of study may not be generalizable and that claims for a specific coding deficit in autistic children need further substantiation. (27 ref)
Fyffe, Christine & Prior, Margot.   British Journal of Psychology, 1978(Aug), Vol 69(3), 393–402. [PA, Vol 63:05530]

192.   Hormonal and cardiac response of autistic children to changes in environmental stimulation.
Studied the physiological responses of 5 6.1–8.9 yr old autistic children to variations in environmental load to examine the under- vs overarousal dichotomy. Measures of urinary mucoprotein excretion and mean heart rate and 3 measures of heart rate variability were compared with matched controls (5 6.3–10.7 yr old severely educationally subnormal children) in conditions of normal, high, and low total environmental load. Results suggest that, although behaviorally unresponsive, the autistic Ss responded physiologically, were generally in a lower state of arousal than the control group, and were labile in response to changes in stimulation. (35 ref)
Graveling, R. A. & Brooke, J. D. (U Salford Human Performance Lab, England) Journal of Autism & Childhood Schizophrenia, 1978(Dec), Vol 8(4), 441–455. [PA, Vol 62:06151]

193.   Plasma zinc, copper, and amino acid levels in the blood of autistic children.
Measured plasma zinc, copper, and amino acid levels in 20 7–16 yr old autistic children. Ss were divided into 2 groups—12 who fully met L. Kanner's criteria and 8 who were atypical on 1 of 3 areas of abnormality (social relationships, language, obsessive/stereotyped play). Ss were compared to 30 normal 7–17 yr old controls. All 3 variables were found to be normal. These findings are in disagreement with previously reported results and suggest that autism cannot simply be attributed to a disorder of zinc metabolism. (18 ref)
Jackson, Malcolm J. & Garrod, Peter J. (U London, University College Hosp & Medical School, England) Journal of Autism & Developmental Disorders, 1978(Jun), Vol 8(2), 203–208. [PA, Vol 62:03769]

194.   Comments on autism and stimulus overselectivity.
Addresses the findings of A. J. Litrownik et al (see PA, Vol 62:6103) that mentally retarded, not autistic children show stimulus overselectivity. Topics examined include the S population, description of the stimuli, effects of testing procedures, IQ and MA, and the meaning of stimulus overselectivity. (10 ref)
Koegel, Robert L. & Lovaas, O. Ivar. (U California Social Process Research Inst, Santa Barbara) Journal of Abnormal Psychology, 1978(Oct), Vol 87(5), 563–565. [PA, Vol 62:06100]

195.   Recognition of faces: An approach to the study of autism.
40 normal, 20 autistic, and 20 subnormal children in 2 age groups were tested for their ability to recognize the faces of peers from isolated facial features and inverted photographs. The normal and subnormal Ss found the upper regions of the face most helpful for identification, whereas the younger autistic children found the lower features more helpful. The older autistic children showed no specific reliance on any one area, but were found to have error scores as low as those of the younger autistic children on the recognition of lower parts and error scores as low as the controls on recognizing upper portions. Results favor a hypothesis in which the autistic child's familiarity with the mouth and/or eye areas is related to a cognitive deficit which affects the processing of both verbal and nonverbal interpersonal communication. (28 ref)
Langdell, Tim. (MRC Developmental Psychology Unit, London, England) Journal of Child Psychology & Psychiatry & Allied Disciplines, 1978(Jul), Vol 19(3), 255–268. [PA, Vol 63:01119]

196.   Restricted stimulus control and inferred attentional deficits in autistic and retarded children.
Seven autistic, 7 Down's syndrome, and 7 normal children (mean CAs 83.1, 65.7, and 45.3 mo; mean MAs 42, 36.7, and 50.6 mo; mean IQs 46.3, 45.3, and 98.6, respectively) were initially trained on a single dimension, simultaneous match-to-sample problem. Following criterion performance, each S's simultaneous matching of 4 new dimensions (2 attributes/dimension) was assessed in order to clarify the relation between autism, retardation, and attentional deficits. The Down's syndrome Ss matched significantly fewer attributes than did the autistic and normal Ss, who were equivalent in their performances. Based on these results, it is suggested that Down's syndrome and not autistic children suffer from attentional deficits. Performance in this simultaneous match-to-sample paradigm, which better assesses attentional mechanisms, was related to performances in previous serial and simultaneous discrimination paradigms, in which autistic children reportedly evidenced overselective attention. (23 ref)
Litrownik, Alan J.; McInnis, Elizabeth T.; Wetzel-Pritchard, Anne M. & Filipelli, Debra L. (San Diego State U) Journal of Abnormal Psychology, 1978(Oct), Vol 87(5), 554–562. [PA, Vol 62:06103]

197.   Childhood autism in Africa.
Mentally handicapped children, mostly in institutions, were screened in 5 countries in Africa in order to explore the usefulness of Western criteria for the recognition of childhood autism in developing countries. Approximately 1,300 children were seen, of whom 30 had some autistic-like behavior. Nine were autistic according to Western criteria. Autistic behavior was found in speaking and nonspeaking children of all grades; in sex ratio, occurrence of epilepsy, and social background the African group was broadly comparable to Western groups. Behavioral comparison with a British sample suggests some prominent features of the syndrome are very uncommon in Africa. Implications for recognition and classification are discussed. (34 ref)
Lotter, Victor. (U Guelph, Canada) Journal of Child Psychology & Psychiatry & Allied Disciplines, 1978(Jul), Vol 19(3), 231–244. [PA, Vol 63:01121]

198.   [Psychoses in the period of development.] (Srcr)
Maintains that even though "dementia precocissima" has been diagnosed in children, childhood psychoses were treated separately only after L. Kanner differentiated one psychosis of early childhood and called it autism, using the Bleuler term "autistic thinking." In early childhood, however, anaclitic depression, as opposed to depression in adulthood, leads to impaired development (as in autism), so that L. Krepelin's basic criterion, dementia, is not as related to autism as it is to schizophrenia in the adult. Later in childhood, new types of psychoses occur, the

most characteristic of which are prepubertal restitutional symptoms. (26 ref)

Matić, Vojin. (U Belgrade, Yugoslavia) Psihijatrija Danas, 1978, Vol 10(2), 133–140. [PA, Vol 65:05584]

199. The utilization of non-vocal communication with handicapped children.

Although it has been in use for a long time, sign language was only recently accepted for use with deaf people; there is only limited acceptance of its use for those with other handicaps. Controversy exists about whether sign language should approximate Standard English or be treated as a separate language. The 2 most commonly used systems are referenced. Sign languages differ from written or spoken English in dimensionality of expression and possible simultaneity, but information can be conveyed at about the same rate. Some signs are learned by deaf children at ages that are younger than those at which hearing children normally begin vocal speech. Limited sign systems have been used with autistic children, language-delayed children, and nonvocal handicapped children. Such use may increase, but the form of languages to be used is as yet undecided. (31 ref)

Moores, Donald F. (Pennsylvania State U) School Psychology Digest, 1978(Nov–Dec), Vol 7(4), 44–54. [PA, Vol 62:06105]

200. Methodological problems in the study of parental cognitive characteristics.

Responds to the study by C. Lennox et al (see PA, Vol 60:5378), which found that parents of autistics do not differ from control parents on the Grid Test of Thought Disorder. The present note attempts to explain the difference between the findings of these authors and those of C. Netley et al (1975). It is suggested that Lennox et al studied unrepresentative cases. A highly significant difference existed in the fact that 18 of the 30 parents of autistic Ss scored above the ceiling of the Progressive Matrices, while only 1 of the 40 control parents obtained such a score. This difference suggests that, although mean parental IQs were not much different, the proportion of exceptionally bright parents was higher in the autistic parent group than in the controls.

Netley, C. & Lockyer, Linda. (Hosp for Sick Children, Toronto, Canada) Journal of Autism & Developmental Disorders, 1978(Mar), Vol 8(1), 115–117. [PA, Vol 61:13562]

201. Self-recognition and stimulus preference in autistic children.

A common notion regarding autistic children is that they do not show self-recognition. In the present study, 7 male autistic Ss, ages 5.5–11.4 yrs, were compared to 10 normal infants at the age of self-recognition. Based on prior research by B. Amsterdam (see PA, Vol 49:8778) and on a pilot study by the present authors, 14 mo was taken as the lower cutoff for the age of controls. Controls ranged in age from 14 mo to 2.7 yrs. Using a videotape "mirror image" and an objective self-recognition criterion, it was observed that 6 of the 7 autistic Ss exhibited self-recognition. In a 2-choice preference situation, autistic Ss tended to prefer the more predictable mirror image to a previously taped film of self. (11 ref)

Neuman, Cynthia J. & Hill, Suzanne D. (U New Orleans) Developmental Psychobiology, 1978(Nov), Vol 11(6), 571–578. [PA, Vol 63:07711]

202. [A longitudinal study of speech acquisition in autistic children.] (Japn)

The verbal behavior of 17 autistic children was recorded for 2–4 yrs during play therapy or in training situations. Verbal behavior was divided into 6 categories: address, response, soliloquy, repetition, vocalization with communicative intention, and vocalization without communicative intention. Linguistic structure of speech was analyzed by measuring the quantity of uttered words and vocabulary, sentence length, and articulatory differentiation. In Group 1 (retarded without speech), Ss' inability to speak was viewed as resulting from a difficulty in organizing vocal sounds. In Group 2 (retarded with speech), Ss' speech was generally soliloquy and echolalia, suggesting that they were unable to generate speech. In Group 3 (relatively well-developed speech), while there was still autistic speech in these Ss, such language

played an important role in the acquisition of useful language. (53 ref)

Nishimura, Bensaku; Mizuno, Mayumi & Wakabayashi, Shinichiro. (Aichi Prefectural Colony Inst for Developmental Research, Japan) Japanese Journal of Child Psychiatry, 1978(Sep–Nov), Vol 19(5), 269–289. [PA, Vol 64:12653]

203. Living with autism.

The mothers of 25 3–14 yr old Irish autistic children were interviewed at home to elucidate the problems that arise in the rearing of autistic children. Topics examined included (a) daily management of the autistic child (e.g., feeding, toilet-training, dressing, sleeping and bedtime behavior, play, and general discipline) and (b) the effects of the handicapped child on the rest of the family (e.g., behavior of siblings, social contacts, shopping and outings, holidays, mothers' health and attitudes to subsequent pregnancies). In contrast to previous findings, the majority of siblings appeared to be well-adjusted to the problems imposed on their families by the presence of an autistic child. However, this finding might have been different had the present siblings been externally assessed. The majority of mothers suffered from depression, for which few sought medical help. (17 ref)

O'Moore, Mona. (U Dublin, Trinity Coll, Ireland) Irish Journal of Psychology, 1978(Win), Vol 4(1), 33–52. [PA, Vol 64:08195]

204. Condon's multiple-response phenomenon in severely dysfunctional children: An attempt at replication.

Attempted to replicate the findings of W. Condon (see PA, Vol 59:1192) on multiple entrainment and dyssynchronous behavioral organization in autistic children. Three autistic and 2 normal 5.3–12.5 yr old children were filmed while being presented with 5 discrete auditory stimuli. Microkinesic analyses of Ss' motor responses were performed in relation to 3 hypotheses designed to support the double-response and dyssynchrony effects. No firm evidence of multiple-responding to single sound was found for the autistic or normal Ss. There was some indication of dyssynchronous, or awkward, response organization for the autistic Ss, in comparison to the smooth-flowing body movements of the normal Ss. (9 ref)

Oxman, Joel; Webster, Christopher D. & Konstantareas, M. Mary. (Clarke Inst of Psychiatry, Toronto, Canada) Journal of Autism & Developmental Disorders, 1978(Dec), Vol 8(4), 395–402. [PA, Vol 62:06198]

205. Amino compounds and organic acids in CSF, plasma, and urine of autistic children.

Amino compounds were measured with an amino acid analyzer in the fasting plasma of 34 patients (mean age 10 yrs) with childhood psychoses (28 having infantile autism) and 40 control children, and in the cerebrospinal fluid (CSF) of 19 of the psychotic children and 23 controls. Organic acids were determined by gas chromatography in urine, plasma, and CSF of the psychotic Ss. The mean concentration of ethanolamine in CSF was significantly higher in psychotic Ss than in control Ss. A subgroup of autistic Ss may possibly have a brain disorder involving ethanolamine metabolism. None of the known inherited diseases of organic acid metabolism was found in any of the psychotic Ss, but future studies utilizing sophisticated gas chromatography/mass spectrometry/computer techniques might disclose abnormal organic acid content in the CSF of such patients. (23 ref)

Perry, Thomas L.; Hansen, Shirley & Christie, R. George. (U British Columbia, Vancouver, Canada) Biological Psychiatry, 1978(Oct), Vol 13(5), 575–586. [PA, Vol 63:07714]

206. Variables affecting stimulus fading and discriminative responding in psychotic children.

Overselective attention in autistic children has proven detrimental to learning when prompt-fading techniques are used, as autistics often respond exclusively to the prompt (the extra guiding stimulus) and fail to learn about the training stimuli. Exp I investigated stimulus variables in prompt fading that might reduce the attentional requirements for discrimination learning. Ss were 8 institutionalized autistic children, each of whom was either mute or echolalic, with minimal intelligible verbal behav-

ior. Two variables were assessed: distinctive vs nondistinctive feature fading, which signified whether a prompt was a feature contained only in the positive stimulus (S+) or contained both in S+ and in the negative stimulus, and within- vs extrastimulus fading, which signified whether the prompt was superimposed on S+ during fading or presented spatially separate from S+. Significant main effects were found for both variables, due to the success of the within-stimulus and the distinctive feature conditions; the combination of within-stimulus and distinctive feature fading was the most effective procedure. Exp II was conducted with the same Ss to assess whether they were still responding only to that pretrained feature after fading. Results show that discriminative responding was maintained when the pretrained feature was made irrelevant, showing that Ss attended to multiple features of S+, but that it was disrupted when the whole letter containing the pretrained feature was made irrelevant, showing that Ss still learned a restricted portion of the S+ word. (48 ref)
Rincover, Arnold. (U North Carolina, Greensboro) Journal of Abnormal Psychology, 1978(Oct), Vol 87(5), 541–553. [PA, Vol 62:06209]

207. Diagnosis and definitions of childhood autism.
Discusses a behavioral definition of childhood autism in terms of 4 criteria: onset before 30 mo of age; impaired social development; delayed and deviant language development; and insistence on sameness, as shown by stereotyped play patterns, abnormal preoccupations, or resistance to change. In addition, the validity of the autistic syndrome, and autism and mental retardation, schizophrenia, neurosis, and developmental language disorders, are discussed. Types of autistic disorders, including Kanner's syndrome, and other infantile psychoses and neurological abnormalities are described. It is concluded that although the 4 criteria appear to offer the best definition of autism, intelligence level and neurological or medical status must also be considered. (4½ p ref)
Rutter, Michael. (U London Inst of Psychiatry, London, England) Journal of Autism & Childhood Schizophrenia, 1978(Jun), Vol 8(2), 139–161. [PA, Vol 62:03805]

208. National Society for Autistic Children definition of the syndrome of autism.
Describes autism as a behaviorally defined syndrome that is manifested prior to 30 mo of age and includes disturbances of (a) developmental rates and/or sequences; (b) responses to sensory stimuli; (c) speech, language, and cognitive capacities; and (d) capacities to relate to people, events, and objects. Associated features (disturbances of thought, mood, and behavior), impairment, etiology, incidence and sex ratio, and complications are discussed. Differential diagnoses, including mental retardation, specific sensory deficits, schizophrenia, and degenerative organic brain syndromes, are also described. This definition of autism is contrasted with that of M. Rutter (see PA, Vol 62:3805). (4 ref)
Schopler, Eric (Ed.)
(Ed). (U North Carolina Medical School, Chapel Hill) Journal of Autism & Childhood Schizophrenia, 1978(Jun), Vol 8(2), 162–167. [PA, Vol 62:03806]

209. Linguistic negation in autistic and normal children.
Six severely maladaptive autistic children, 5.11–12.5 yrs old, with some speech competence were compared to 6 normally developing 3-yr-olds and 7 5-yr-olds of lower- and middle-class families on negation tasks. Ss were shown 12 sets of cards depicting negative contrasts designed to elicit semantic categories of nonexistence, denial, and rejection and were tested for production, imitation, and comprehension. Syntactic and semantic analysis revealed that autistic Ss were superior imitators and poor producers but showed skills in comprehension comparable to a 4-yr-old's level of functioning. While retarded in some functions, the experimental groups produced syntactic structures that were more rigid than normal, suggesting the significantly greater use of imitation as a major strategy in linguistic coding. (23 ref)
Shapiro, Theodore & Kapit, Richard. (Cornell U Medical Ctr, New York, NY) Journal of Psycholinguistic Research, 1978(Sep), Vol 7(5), 337–351. [PA, Vol 63:05621]

210. Echoing in autistic children: A chronometric study of semantic processing.
Notes that the time required to produce a verbal response has been used extensively as an index of the complexity of the mental operations that underlie the comprehension and production of language. An analysis of the discourse of 5 autistic children with an adult demonstrates that echoic speech depends on simpler, more limited decoding of adult utterances than the child's creative original speech. By contrast, 2 normal children show no significant difference in reaction times between imitative and spontaneous productions using the same measure. This finding lends support to the notion that autistic children rely on 2 strategies for their language production made necessary by a cognitive deficit. (15 ref)
Shapiro, Theodore & Lucy, Peter. (Cornell U Medical Coll, New York) Journal of Child Psychology & Psychiatry & Allied Disciplines, 1978(Oct), Vol 19(4), 373–378. [PA, Vol 64:05820]

211. Differential development of autistic symptoms in a pair of fraternal twins.
Reports the differential development of autistic symptoms over a 9-yr period in a pair of fraternal twins. The Ss were tested at various times with the Vineland Social Maturity Scale, the Stanford-Binet Intelligence Scale, the Peabody Picture Vocabulary Test, the Peabody Individual Achievement Test, the Psychoeducational Profile, the WISC-R, the Developmental Test of Visual-Motor Integration, and the Merrill-Palmer Scale of Mental Tests. Neither of the twins developed normally. Evaluations revealed that although the older (male) twin showed some early signs of pathology and suffered from frequent illnesses, he ultimately developed more normally than his sister, who likely sustained brain damage as a result of perinatal anoxia. Significant improvement occurred in both cases. Diagnostic, etiological, and treatment implications are discussed. (28 ref)
Sloan, Jerry L. (Southeastern TEACCH Ctr, Wilmington, NC) Journal of Autism & Developmental Disorders, 1978(Jun), Vol 8(2), 191–202. [PA, Vol 62:03813]

212. Directional dyslexia in autistic children.
Discusses S. Sogame's theory that the occurrence of word dyslexia depends on a specific direction of sequential arrangement of letters. Sogame's research on directional dyslexia is examined. He divides directional dyslexia into 2 kinds: horizontal and vertical. The use of the division in comparative and transcultural research on dyslexia is advocated. (15 ref)
Sogame, Shiro & Kubo, Yoshikazu. (Takachaya Mental Hosp, Children's Dept, Japan) Japanese Journal of Child Psychiatry, 1978(Sep–Nov), Vol 19(5), 290–298. [PA, Vol 64:12596]

213. Auditory nerve and brain-stem evoked responses in normal, autistic, minimal brain dysfunction and psychomotor retarded children.
In several forms of abnormal behavior in infants and children, the cause is either uncertain or an unspecified organic brain lesion is assumed to be present. In the present study, evoked averaged auditory nerve (AN) and brainstem (BS) responses to click stimuli were recorded from 18 4–10 yr old normal, 13 4–12 yr old autistic, 16 3–11 yr old minimal brain dysfunction (MBD), and 10 2–8 yr old psychomotor-retarded (PR) children. Most of the controls were awake and most of the experimental Ss were in sedated sleep, but records were also made from some Ss while awake and asleep; no change was seen in the response traces. In several of the autistic Ss, there were no electrophysiological responses (indicating a profound hearing loss). In several of the PR Ss, responses from the region of the inferior colliculus were absent. In the other experimental Ss, AN and BS responses were recorded with normal response thresholds but longer-than-normal AN latencies. Also, BS transmission time, measured as the time interval from the negative peak of the AN response to the positive trough of the response from the inferior colliculus, was shortest in the controls and longest in the MBD group. Results provide electrophysiological evidence for the existence of an organic brain lesion in these children, at least in the BS regions concerned with auditory function. These and previous data support the conclusion that most of the abnormal behavior seen

in such patients is due to a diffuse brain lesion. (French summary) (29 ref)
Sohmer, H. & Student, M. (Hebrew U–Hadassah Medical School, Jerusalem, Israel) Electroencephalography & Clinical Neurophysiology, 1978(Mar), Vol 44(3), 380–388. [PA, Vol 62:06112]

214.   Evidence from auditory nerve and brainstem evoked responses for an organic brain lesion in children with autistic traits.
To determine whether children with autistic traits have an organic nervous system lesion, auditory nerve and brain-stem evoked responses were recorded in a group of 15 4–12 yr old children with autistic traits. 14 control Ss—12 normal Ss and 2 children in a coma—were also studied. The most obvious results included a longer response latency of the auditory nerve and a longer brainstem transmission time, compared to normal children. Five of the autistic Ss were found to be profoundly deaf. These strengthen the theory that an organic lesion of the nervous system can give rise to autistic traits. (29 ref)
Student, M. & Sohmer, H. (Tel Aviv U, Ramat-Aviv, Israel) Journal of Autism & Developmental Disorders, 1978(Mar), Vol 8(1), 13–20. [PA, Vol 61:13576]

215.   The hostage parent.
Discusses the effects an autistic child has on his or her parents. The importance of a philosophy and a structure in dealing with the child are emphasized. Effects of the child on parenting and the benefits of a global rather than personal focus are described. It is concluded that being the parent of an autistic child provides an opportunity for growth and self-knowledge and encourages the development of insights into the problems of others. (1 ref)
Sullivan, Ruth C.   Journal of Autism & Developmental Disorders, 1978(Jun), Vol 8(2), 234–240. [PA, Vol 62:03816]

216.   Autistic withdrawal of a small child under stress.
Presents the case of a 2-yr-old girl who became autistic following the death of her father. Immediately following the father's death, the S was emotionally neglected by her family. She became depressed and arrested in her development and later regressed, withdrawn, and autistic despite therapy. With her mother's marked improvement the patient progressed, but her ego remained brittle, and she was unable to overcome the loss of her father, who seemed to have been her symbiotic partner. It is doubtful whether she will be able to regain health. (German, French & Spanish summaries) (19 ref)
Susz, E. & Marberg, H. M. (Tel-Aviv U, Israel) Acta Paedopsychiatrica, 1978(May), Vol 43(4), 149–158. [PA, Vol 62:13844]

217.   [Autism and childhood schizophrenia—with special reference to the differences in their autistic states.] (Japn)
Reports the results of clinical examinations of 2 male children (13 and 16 yrs old). The 13-yr-old had been diagnosed as autistic and was being treated for childhood autism, the other had been diagnosed as a childhood schizophrenic. The autistic child showed interpersonal relationships based on tactual stimuli, poor value judgments, and dutiful participation in group activities. The schizophrenic showed interpersonal relationships based on visual stimulation, judgment based on a simple "good and bad" dichotomy, and passive participation in group activities; however, he was fairly aware of (or attuned to) the situation. The major cause for the confusion of the autistic child was damage to his geometric thought processes, while that of the schizophrenic child was caused by his uneasy feeling about interpersonal relationships. (English summary) (13 ref)
Toki, Shinji. (Fukuoka U School of Medicine, Japan) Kyushu Neuro-psychiatry, 1978, Vol 24(1), 132–136. [PA, Vol 63:03430]

218.   "Toe-walking" in children with early childhood autism.
"Toe-walking," which should be properly labelled forefoot-walking, can be observed not only in children with pyramidal symptomatology but also—sometimes for years—in children with early childhood autism or other developmental disturbances. Furthermore, forefoot-walking is not infrequent in normal children while they are learning to walk. 66 children with Kanmer's autism and a number of normal children with forefoot-

walking were observed by their parents and by the authors. Results confirm the assumption that this foot posture of both autistic and nonautistic children with developmental disturbances arises from the fixation of a normal transient stage of development. (French, Spanish & German summaries) (28 ref)
Weber, Doris. (Philipps-U Marburg/Lahn, Inst für Ärztlich-pädagogische Jugendhilfe, West Germany) Acta Paedopsychiatrica, 1978, Vol 43(2–3), 73–83. [PA, Vol 61:11092]

219.   Association between platelet monoamine oxidase activity and hematocrit in childhood autism.
Platelet MAO activity was strongly negatively associated with hematocrit and hemoglobin in 29 4–21 yr old male autistic children, unlike the nonsignificant positive relation in 15 normal male controls. Platelet MAO activity and hematocrit were also negatively related, although with less strength, in other childhood psychiatric patients (34 Ss) and in male relatives (27 Ss) of autistic children. (50 ref)
Young, J. Gerald; Cohen, Donald J. & Roth, Jerome A. (Yale U School of Medicine, Child Study Ctr) Life Sciences, 1978(Aug), Vol 23(8), 797–806. [PA, Vol 63:03441]

220.   The misdiagnosis of Matthew.
Matthew, the youngest of 3 children born to a lower middle income family, was referred for testing because of moodiness and tantrums in school. Because he did not respond to any pure tone presented to the left ear, he was fitted for a hearing aid and considered for placement in a preschool for the deaf. At school, Matthew would let out unrestrained shrill cries and was difficult to manage despite behavior modification efforts. Subsequent diagnosis at the Guidance Center revealed many autistic mannerisms, including rapid hand shaking, smelling testing materials, and emission of unintelligible sounds. A neurologist placed him on medication, and his parents were given counseling. After he was correctly diagnosed, appropriate training was offered. Temper tantrums declined in number, success in reading readiness activity was achieved, and 200 words were learned.
Adkins, P. G. & Ainsa, T. A. (Region XIX Education Service Ctr, El Paso, TX) Academic Therapy, 1979(Jan), Vol 14(3), 335–339. [PA, Vol 66:01357]

221.   Effects of age on communication skill levels and prevalence of maladaptive behaviors in autistic and mentally retarded children.
Investigated the effect of age on communication and maladaptive behavior in 47 autistic and 128 mentally retarded 6–14 yr olds in a special school. The cross-sectional method was used to compare junior and senior groups, and ratings on communication skills and maladaptive behaviors were obtained from teachers. It was found that the skills of comprehension and conversation in the autistic Ss improved significantly with age, and speech improved somewhat. In spite of this improvement in communication skills, maladaptive behaviors in the autistic Ss other than hyperactivity did not change significantly with age. Withdrawal improved significantly with age in the mentally retarded but not in the Ss. (29 ref)
Ando, Haruhiko & Yoshimura, Ikuko. (Aichi Prefectural Colony, Central Hosp, Kasugai, Japan) Journal of Autism & Developmental Disorders, 1979(Mar), Vol 9(1), 83–93. [PA, Vol 62:11080]

222.   Speech skill levels and prevalence of maladaptive behaviors in autistic and mentally retarded children: A statistical study.
Assessed 47 autistic and 128 mentally retarded 6–14 yr olds from a special school in terms of 9 maladaptive behaviors (self-injury, attacks on others, destruction of property, hyperactivity, withdrawal, lack of eye contact, stereotyped behavior, tantrums, and fear) and speech skill levels. Results indicate that the mentally retarded children with withdrawal had significantly lower speech skill levels than those without withdrawal, and the autistic children with self-injury had significantly lower speech skill levels than those without self-injury. (13 ref)

Ando, Haruhiko & Yoshimura, Ikuko. (Central Hosp, Aichi Prefectural Colony, Japan) Child Psychiatry & Human Development, 1979(Win), Vol 10(2), 85–90. [PA, Vol 63:05521]

223. Comprehension skill levels and prevalence of maladaptive behaviors in autistic and mentally retarded children.
Compared the verbal comprehension skills of 2 groups of 6–14 yr old children—47 autistic Ss and 128 nonorganic mentally retarded (MR) Ss. Teacher judgments were used as measures of comprehension skills and maladaptive behaviors. The following maladaptive behaviors were assessed: self injury, attack against other individuals, destruction of property, hyperactivity, withdrawal, lack of eye-to-eye gaze, stereotyped behavior, tantrum, and fear. Comparisons were made between the Ss with maladaptive behavior and those without it in each of the 2 diagnostic groups (i.e., autistic and MR). Results show that the MR Ss with hyperactivity or withdrawal had significantly lower comprehension skill levels than those without these behaviors. No significant differences in comprehension skill levels were found between the groups of MR Ss with and without each of the other 7 maladaptive behaviors. No significant differences in comprehension skills were found between the groups of autistic Ss with and without any of the maladaptive behaviors. (10 ref)
Ando, Haruhiko & Yoshimura, Ikuko. (Central Hosp, Kasugai, Japan) Child Psychiatry & Human Development, 1979(Spr), Vol 9(3), 131–136. [PA, Vol 62:06085]

224. Measuring musical abilities of autistic children.
Three normal 14–18 yr olds with reported musical ability and 3 age-matched autistic Ss were tested for the ability to imitate individual tones and series of tones delivered by voice, piano, and synthesizer. Two independent observers judged that autistic Ss performed as well as or better than normal Ss. Implications for neurological and clinical research are considered. (18 ref)
Applebaum, Edward; Egel, Andrew L.; Koegel, Robert L. & Imhoff, Barbara. (U California, Santa Barbara) Journal of Autism & Developmental Disorders, 1979(Sep), Vol 9(3), 279–285. [PA, Vol 63:01079]

225. [Abnormal movement stereotypies and arousal: An integration.] (Germ)
Discusses stereotyped behavior of animals reared in isolation, autistic children, acute catatonic schizophrenics, and stereotyped behavior elicited by amphetamines in reference to the 2-factor arousal hypothesis of A. Routtenberg (see PA, Vols 42:5112 and 47:2291). A relationship to reticular arousal dominance is hypothesized. (25 ref)
Asendorpf, Jens. (Justus Liebig-U Giessen, West Germany) Archiv für Psychologie, 1979, Vol 131(4), 293–300. [PA, Vol 65:04928]

226. Adult recollections of a formerly autistic child.
Describes the life history, current status, and memories of a 31-yr-old man who, as a child, had been diagnosed as autistic by L. Kanner and others. Prognostic criteria as related to this individual's outcome are discussed. Some speculations about the inner life of autistic children are advanced on the basis of his recollections, and some hypotheses for further research are suggested. (4 ref)
Bemporad, Jules R. (Harvard Medical School, Massachusetts Mental Health Ctr) Journal of Autism & Developmental Disorders, 1979(Jun), Vol 9(2), 179–197. [PA, Vol 62:11102]

227. [Disorders of cognitive development in autistic children.] (Fren)
Reports disorders of cognitive development in psychotic, autistic children, especially disturbances of language: mute children, and verbose children speaking in a void. These observations challenge some conceptions about autism.
Brauner, Françoise & Brauner, Alfred. Etudes Psychothérapiques, 1979(Jun), Vol 10(2), 117–124. [PA, Vol 66:10461]

228. Families of autistic and dysphasic children: I. Family life and interaction patterns.
Patterns of parent–child interaction and family functioning were systematically examined in well-matched groups of 15 autistic and 14 dysphasic children. The measures used included a 24-hr standard day analysis, an interview measure of positive interaction, family interaction scales (based on a 4–6 hr period of home observation, specially developed time-sampled measures of observed mother–child interaction at home), and the Eysenck Personality Inventory. Findings from all measures show that family life and interaction patterns were very similar in the 2 groups. Results are compared with those of previous investigations. It is concluded that autism is most unlikely to be due to abnormal psychogenic influences in the family. (6 ref)
Cantwell, Dennis P.; Baker, Lorian & Rutter, Michael. (U California Neuropsychiatric Inst, Ctr for the Health Sciences, Los Angeles) Archives of General Psychiatry, 1979(Jun), Vol 36(6), 682–687. [PA, Vol 64:08108]

229. Task difficulty and task performance in autistic children.
Examined the effects on the performance of autistic children of varying the cognitive demands made on the children. The Board Form of the Raven Coloured Progressive Matrices was administered to 30 autistic 8–17 yr olds and then, if necessary, either a range of easier, "matrices-type" problems or the more difficult Standard Progressive Matrices. Distribution and type of errors suggested that for most Ss, success or failure on any item was best predicted by the intrinsic difficulty of that item rather than by the S's lack of cooperation. However, it did appear that for some of the lower functioning Ss, early experience of failure did interfere with subsequent performance. (15 ref)
Clark, Peter & Rutter, Michael. (U London Inst of Psychiatry, England) Journal of Child Psychology & Psychiatry & Allied Disciplines, 1979(Oct), Vol 20(4), 271–285. [PA, Vol 65:03386]

230. The incidence of seizures among children with autistic symptoms.
In a study of 183 children with autistic symptoms, it was found that the age-specific incidence rates of seizures in this sample were between 3 and 28 times the rates for children in the general population. Ss classified as totally autistic were at high risk of developing seizures from early childhood well into adolescence, but especially so at puberty. Partially autistic Ss had an increased risk of seizures only up to age 10. It is suggested that the high incidence of seizures at puberty may be specific to children with total autistic symptomatology and may represent a distinct pathological process associated with autism. (14 ref)
Deykin, Eva Y. & MacMahon, Brian. (Harvard U School of Public Health, Boston) American Journal of Psychiatry, 1979(Oct), Vol 136(10), 1310–1312. [PA, Vol 63:03381]

231. Lauretta Bender on autism: A review.
L. Bender, a pioneer in the field of child psychiatry, has written extensively on autism and other forms of childhood disturbance. The development of her theories on autism, especially as it relates to childhood schizophrenia, is reviewed. Bender believes that the condition is one of the manifestations of schizophrenia occurring in earliest childhood. The development and elaboration of this view are traced through her writings and personal contacts, and the influences of P. Schilder, A. Gesell, and others on her work are discussed. (24 ref)
Faretra, Gloria. (Queens Children's Psychiatric Ctr, Bellerose, NY) Child Psychiatry & Human Development, 1979(Win), Vol 10(2), 118–129. [PA, Vol 63:05577]

232. Personal pronouns and the autistic child.
The long-recognized difficulties that speaking autistic children have with the use and nonuse of personal pronouns ("reversals" and "avoidance") have been generally attributed either to the nondifferentiation of the self or to the frequently coexisting symptom of echolalia. These explanations are reconsidered in an analysis of current theory and research on development of self and language. Emphasis is on studies of normal development of personal pronouns and the roles played in that process by listening, echoic memory, mitigated echolalia (recoding), and person deixis. It is concluded that multiple developmental obstacles of a social, cognitive, and grammatical nature underlie the more obvious symptoms and militate against the child's

resolution of labels and their referents. Treatment alternatives that deemphasize the primacy of *I* are offered. (42 ref)
Fay, Warren H. (U Oregon Health Sciences Ctr, Crippled Children's Div) Journal of Autism & Developmental Disorders, 1979(Sep), Vol 9(3), 247–260. [PA, Vol 63:01106]

233.   Stimulus generalization in autistic and normal children.
Eight 10-yr-old psychotic children, 6 of whom fulfilled the criteria for infantile autism, and 8 9-yr-old normal children were tested in a stimulus generalization paradigm, using simple and complex figures. No differences appeared between the normal and psychotic Ss with the simple stimuli, but the psychotic Ss tended to overgeneralize when the test stimuli were certain specific variations of a complex figure. It is suggested that the psychotic Ss did not have a tendency to over- or undergeneralize per se, but that they responded to fewer features of a stimulus than the normal Ss. It remains unclear whether this over-selectivity is pathognomonic of the cognition in childhood psychoses, or whether it reflects these children's delayed cognitive development. (13 ref)
Fein, Deborah; Tinder, Paula & Waterhouse, Lynn. (Boston U School of Medicine) Journal of Child Psychology & Psychiatry & Allied Disciplines, 1979(Oct), Vol 20(4), 325–335. [PA, Vol 65:03395]

234.   Cues and clues to differential diagnosis in childhood autism.
There has been considerable disagreement as to the nature of autism. Since the problem has not yet been clearly defined, etiology remains nebulous, and treatment varies among therapists. An attempt is made to develop a definition of autism by drawing from a variety of reliable sources describing the disorder, and, with reference to these sources, some diagnostic procedures that seem to be effective are discussed. This suggested diagnostic assessment is based on observation, history taking, and a limited use of treatment technique. Diagnostic intervention in the form of intrusion and interaction is most instrumental in reaching diagnostic decisions. When tested in such areas as tactile, kinesthetic, and spatial intrusion, nonautistic children respond in a manner widely disparate from autistic children. No one single manifestation of an autisticlike response is a sufficient diagnostic clue; rather, there is a whole set of reactions upon which a clinical judgment rests. (16 ref)
Fine, Harold J. (U Tennessee, Knoxville) Psychotherapy: Theory, Research & Practice, 1979(Win), Vol 16(4), 452–459. [PA, Vol 64:05772]

235.   Pre-, peri-, and neonatal factors and infantile autism.
Examined unfavorable pre-, peri-, and neonatal events in the birth records of 23 autistic children, and compared the rate of these factors with the expected rate in the general population and in 15 of the Ss' nonautistic siblings. Several potentially neuropathogenic factors occurred at a significantly high rate in the autistic Ss, including breech delivery, the presence of amniotic meconium, low birth weight, low Apgar score, elevated serum bilirubin, hemolytic disease, and respiratory distress syndrome. Autistic Ss had significantly more unfavorable factors than did controls. The study supports the findings of investigations that concluded that autistic children have suffered a high rate of obstetrical events that may have caused brain damage. (36 ref)
Finegan, Jo-Anne & Quarrington, Bruce. (York U, Toronto, Canada) Journal of Child Psychology & Psychiatry & Allied Disciplines, 1979(Apr), Vol 20(2), 119–128. [PA, Vol 64:10493]

236.   Behavior Observation Scale: Preliminary analysis of the similarities and differences between autistic and mentally retarded children.
35 autistic and 30 mentally retarded children matched for mean CA and MA were observed in a playroom. The frequencies of occurrence of 67 objectively defined behaviors (such as staring and whirling) were coded on the Behavior Observation Scale. Data indicate that there is a great deal of overlap in behaviors exhibited by both autistic and retarded children. Only 2 variables—hand flapping and social smile—differentiated the

groups. Implications for determining the objective diagnosis of autism are discussed. (11 ref)
Freeman, B. J. et al. (U California School of Medicine, Neuropsychiatric Inst, Los Angeles) Psychological Reports, 1979(Apr), Vol 44(2), 519–524. [PA, Vol 64:10494]

237.   Generalization by autistic-type children of verbal responses across settings.
Assessed generalization of verbal behavior by autistic-type children across different settings. Four 6–7 yr old boys learned responses to common questions in 2 settings at school and were probed to determine transfer of learning to home. Three Ss demonstrated little generalization to home when trained in a cubicle. Greater generalization was indicated when they received training at varied locations. The 4th S generalized most responses to his home regardless of training setting. Simple manipulations of the school environment to more closely simulate home conditions may facilitate transfer of training to the natural environment. (19 ref)
Handleman, Jan S. (Rutgers U, Douglass Coll, New Brunswick) Journal of Applied Behavior Analysis, 1979(Sum), Vol 12(2), 273–282. [PA, Vol 65:10565]

238.   A comparative dermatoglyphic study of autistic, retarded, and normal children.
Made dermatoglyphic comparisons among 32 autistic children aged 4–18 yrs; 32 sex-, age-, and IQ-matched retarded children; and 32 sex- and age-matched normal children. Significant differences were found between the autistic and normal Ss for distribution of dermal patterns and ridge line disruption, but no significant differences were found for the total mean ridge counts or mean ridge count rankings. Apart from the right hand of the autistic Ss, there were no unusual scores for digital dispersion ratios. Autistic and retarded Ss differed only in their distribution of dermal patterns, with autistic Ss apparently intermediate between retarded and normal groups. Results indicate that conclusions of unique congenital disturbance in the etiology of autism inferred from different dermatoglyphics may be premature and that dermatoglyphics may be ineffective in delineating autistic children from other atypical populations. (29 ref)
Hartin, Phillip J. & Barry, Robert J. (U New South Wales, Sydney, Australia) Journal of Autism & Developmental Disorders, 1979(Sep), Vol 9(3), 233–246. [PA, Vol 63:01054]

239.   Autism and unfavorable left–right asymmetries of the brain.
Used computerized brain tomography to judge left–right morphologic asymmetries of the parietooccipital region in 16 autistic patients (mean age 14.7 yrs), 44 mentally retarded patients, and 100 miscellaneous neurological patients. In 57% of autistic Ss, the right parietooccipital region was wider than the left, while this pattern of cerebral asymmetry was found in only 23% of mentally retarded and 25% of neurological Ss. It is suggested that unfavorable morphologic asymmetries of the brain near the posterior language zone may contribute to the difficulties experienced by autistic children in acquiring language. (18 ref)
Hier, Daniel B.; LeMay, Marjorie & Rosenberger, Peter B. (Massachusetts General Hosp, Boston) Journal of Autism & Developmental Disorders, 1979(Jun), Vol 9(2), 153–159. [PA, Vol 62:11118]

240.   [Mental development in autistic children: A survey of recent studies.] (Japn)
Reviews recent studies on autistic children's mental abilities and language. It is determined that results of intelligence tests vary according to the particular disorder, the same discrimination learning ability level is exhibited in normal children of the same mental age, and retarded vocabulary development characterizes speech, although some autistic children acquire normal facility. Thus, while organic damage to the CNS impairs the autistic child's mental abilities, development does occur, however slowly. (99 ref)
Hirano, Nobuyoshi. (Hinomoto Gakuen Junior Coll, Hyogo, Japan) Japanese Journal of Child & Adolescent Psychiatry, 1979, Vol 20(4), 271–288. [PA, Vol 65:12914]

241.   The effects of schedule of reinforcement on stimulus overselectivity in autistic children.
Research has demonstrated that when autistic children are presented a discrimination task with multiple cues, they typically respond to an abnormally limited number, usually one, of the available cues. This phenomenon, termed "stimulus overselectivity," has been implicated as a possible basis for many of the behavioral deficits characteristic of autism. The present investigation analyzed the effects of changing the schedules of reinforcement during discrimination training on subsequent stimulus overselectivity. 12 autistic children were taught a discrimination involving multiple visual cues on a continuous reinforcement schedule (CRF). The Ss were then overtrained on either the same (CRF) schedule or on a partial (VR3) reinforcement schedule. Subsequent overselectivity on single-cue test trials was then assessed. Results suggested that significantly less overselectivity occurred when the Ss were presented with the VR3 schedule during overtraining. Results are discussed in terms of variables in influencing overselectivity and in terms of implications for designing treatment procedures for autistic children. (41 ref)
Koegel, Robert L.; Schreibman, Laura; Britten, Karen & Laitinen, Richard. (U California, Social Process Research Inst, Santa Barbara) Journal of Autism & Developmental Disorders, 1979(Dec), Vol 9(4), 383–397. [PA, Vol 63:08052]

242.   Stimulus overselectivity in autism: A review of research.
Reviews a series of investigations that suggest that autistic children show "stimulus overselectivity," a response to only a limited number of cues in their environment, and discusses how such overselectivity may relate to several of the behavioral deficits in autism. These include failure to develop normal language or social behavior, failure to generalize newly acquired behavior to new stimulus situations, failure to learn from traditional teaching techniques that use prompts, and a general difficulty in learning new behaviors. Several studies that suggest possible remedial procedures are discussed, and the concept of stimulus overselectivity is related to the literature on attentional or response deficits in adult schizophrenia, mental retardation, learning disabilities, and autism. (2½ p ref)
Lovaas, O. Ivar; Koegel, Robert L. & Schreibman, Laura. (U California, Los Angeles) Psychological Bulletin, 1979(Nov), Vol 86(6), 1236–1254. [PA, Vol 63:05600]

243.   Biophysical bases of autism.
Reviews biophysical variables (e.g., cerebral anoxia, chromosomal disorders, inborn errors of metabolism) that contribute to autism or its symptoms. The roles of parents, teachers, and developmental change agents for the delayed child are discussed, and the nature and manifestations of psychobiological variables are examined in terms of the need for individual yet comprehensive educational interventions and family support services. (34 ref)
Menolascino, Frank J. & Eyde, Donna R. (U Nebraska Medical Ctr, Omaha) Behavioral Disorders, 1979(Nov), Vol 5(1), 41–47. [PA, Vol 65:03427]

244.   [On the I.R.M. dysfunction theory of early childhood autism.] (Japn)
Suggests that mental retardation in autistic children is a function of the degree to which innate learning dispositions are defective, and that imbalanced social behavior and language are caused by dysfunction of the innate releasing mechanism (IRM). (35 ref)
Nakayama, Osamu.   Japanese Journal of Child & Adolescent Psychiatry, 1979, Vol 20(4), 259–270. [PA, Vol 65:12942]

245.   [The nature of early childhood autism: A follow-up study of three groups of autistic children.] (Japn)
Studied 52 autistic children (for periods ranging from 6 to 18 yrs) who had developed poor interpersonal relationships, retarded speech and language development, and ritualistic and compulsive behavior before 3 yrs of age. Based on language development, intelligence, and behavioral changes over time, Ss were divided into 3 groups: (a) severe autistic disturbances in interpersonal relationships, poor symbolic functioning, and intellectual deficiencies; (b) improved interpersonal relationships and intellectual

abilities with the beginning of symbolic functioning; and (c) generalized severe retardation with immature language development and interpersonal relationships. It is concluded that only the 1st group's characteristics should be attributed to early childhood autism. (41 ref)
Nawa, Akiko. (Kyushu U, Faculty of Medicine, Fukuoka, Japan) Japanese Journal of Child & Adolescent Psychiatry, 1979, Vol 20(4), 214–237. [PA, Vol 65:12943]

246.   Chinese autistic children.
Found that the 14 Hong Kong Chinese autistic children studied had similar backgrounds and symptomatology to their Western counterparts. They differed in being more socialized and more aware of themselves. On a 204-item questionnaire, 10 of 14 parents indicated their child had very sensitive hearing. Auditory hyperacuity might explain an autistic child's apparent aversion to communicating. (30 ref)
Ney, P.; Lieh-Mak, F.; Cheng, R. & Collins, W. (U British Columbia Health Sciences Ctr, Vancouver, Canada) Social Psychiatry, 1979, Vol 14(3), 147–150. [PA, Vol 65:05518]

247.   A psychopathogenesis of autism.
Suggests that it is possible that autistic children are not neurophysiologically abnormal but children with hearing hyperacuity, born into an environment that cannot adapt to them. If so, to them human sounds are not soothing but frightening. Environmental noises do not arouse curiosity but hurt so much the child withdraws. Because of self-imposed isolation, the child's brain hungers for stimulation, increasing the level of arousal which results in an anxiety-evoking experience of sound in addition to pain. Parents mistake the withdrawal as a signal for them to try to communicate more vigorously, thereby increasing the child's fear of them. Parents eventually learn to remain cool and aloof, but this deprives the child of alternate forms of stimulation. The net result is an information-deprived brain, an inability to interpret auditory symbols, and eventually, irreversible retardation. (46 ref)
Ney, Philip G. (U British Columbia Health Sciences Ctr, Vancouver, Canada) Child Psychiatry & Human Development, 1979(Sum), Vol 9(4), 195–205. [PA, Vol 62:06194]

248.   A psychopathological study of the recognition of "person" in children.
Studied a 2½-yr-old autistic female and a 12-yr-old schizophrenic male to determine how children learn to recognize a significant adult (the mother) under conditions of emotional stress. Three levels of recognition were determined: neuropsychological prosopognosia, a rigid pattern in which the mother was recognized only in a particular social role, and a pattern in which recognition was linked to the S's affective evaluation of the mother. Results are discussed in terms of K. Lorenz's (1968) theory of imprinting and L. Kanner's (1943) theory of "splitting." (Japanese abstract) (4 ref)
Okada, Sachio & Kaku, Reigetsu. (Kinki U School of Medicine, Osaka, Japan) Japanese Journal of Child & Adolescent Psychiatry, 1979(Sep–Nov), Vol 20(5), 305–310. [PA, Vol 66:01468]

249.   Overview of selected basic research in autism.
A review shows that there is mounting indication, but inconclusive evidence, of unique physiologic disturbances etiologically related to autism. Additionally, there is indication that some of the physiologic disturbances found in autistic children are also present in children with other developmental disorders. Children called autistic probably represent a complex of clinically similar manifestations in a variety of subgroups of children, each subgroup representing a basically different physiologic disturbance. However, the possibility remains that there is only one basic disturbance that in varying degrees affects many body systems and manifests in a variety of overlapping syndromes. Objective markers are needed to allow the demarcation of subgroups of autistic children for further study. Possible markers may be decreased duration of postrotatory nystagmus, auditory evoked response deviations, lymphocytic hyporesponsivity, increased blood platelet serotonin efflux, and/or the presence of urinary N-N-dimethyltryptamine or bufotenin. (72 ref)

Piggott, L. R. (Lafayette Clinic, Detroit, MI) Journal of Autism & Developmental Disorders, 1979(Jun), Vol 9(2), 199–218. [PA, Vol 62:11135]

250. Cognitive abilities and disabilities in infantile autism: A review.
A review of the literature on various aspects of learning and performance in autistic children indicates very little that is specific to autism. Inadequate and inconsistent methodology precludes generalizations concerning the nature of the disorder. Future research should control for developmental influences on performance and investigate higher functioning autistic children who are less governed by retardation factors. The current evidence supports an hypothesis of abnormal hemisphere functioning in this group of children. (6½ p ref)
Prior, Margot R. (La Trobe U, Bundoora, Australia) Journal of Abnormal Child Psychology, 1979(Dec), Vol 7(4), 357–380. [PA, Vol 65:03433]

251. Comprehension of transitive and intransitive phrases by autistic, retarded, and normal children.
12 autistic children were compared with 12 retarded and 12 normal control children (mean CAs 12 yrs 1 mo, 9 yrs 6 mo, and 2 yrs 10 mo, respectively) in a verbal comprehension task. Ss were asked to select from 4 pictures the one that illustrated a 2-word intransitive or 3-word transitive phrase that was described verbally. Distractor pictures differed from the target picture by 1, 2, or all 3 features. Autistic Ss were poorer in performance than the control groups; however, the hierarchy of difficulty of discrimination was common to all 3 groups, with transitive phrases more difficult than intransitive phrases. Word type did not affect comprehension for the autistic Ss although control Ss evidenced most difficulty with the verb or middle word. Results are interpreted as supporting the hypothesis that a severe and global language disorder is characteristic of autism. (20 ref)
Prior, Margot R. & Hall, Lesley C. (LaTrobe U, Bundoora, Australia) Journal of Communication Disorders, 1979(Apr), Vol 12(2), 103–111. [PA, Vol 64:03409]

252. Do autistic children come from upper-middle-class parents?
Most studies have reported autistic children as coming from upper socioeconomic status (SES) families, while a few studies have not found such bias. A study was conducted on a statewide sample of 522 families with autistic children and children with related communications handicaps. It was hypothesized that autistic children from high-SES families would be associated with 7 social class selection factors: (1) early age of onset, (2) early age of treatment admission, (3) normal cognitive potential, (4) complex rituals with maintenance of sameness, (5) long distance traveled for treatment, (6) limited availability of services, and (7) highly detailed child history. Factors 1, 5, 6, and 7 distinguished high- from low-SES families in the predicted direction. Implications for research and treatment are discussed. (36 ref)
Schopler, Eric; Andrews, Carol E. & Strupp, Karen. (U North Carolina, Chapel Hill) Journal of Autism & Developmental Disorders, 1979(Jun), Vol 9(2), 139–152. [PA, Vol 62:11145]

253. [Language faults and the severity of symptoms in autistic children.] (Japn)
Examined the relationship between the language faults of 125 autistic children, the general severity of their symptoms, and their ages. Ss were given an autistic child's developmental scale and were assigned to 1 of 3 groups according to a mean level of profile (MLP, derived from an 11-scale general average profile and standard deviations calculated from the developmental scale). Ss were then divided into 3 age groups: 3–6 yrs, 7–9 yrs, and 10–13 yrs. Factor analysis of 57 language fault items showed that verbal content faults increased rapidly when speech skill level reached 3-or-more word sentences. The severity of symptoms and level of speech skills were highly correlated, and inappropriate replies were significantly higher in the Low MLP group than the other 2 groups at all age levels. (16 ref)
Uchida, Issei. Japanese Journal of Child & Adolescent Psychiatry, 1979(Sep–Nov), Vol 20(5), 311–324. [PA, Vol 66:01492]

254. Utilization of an experimenter-controlled manikin in analysis of social stimuli maintaining behavior of an autistic-like child.
In Phase I, the frequency and duration of 7 behaviors emitted in the presence of a male, female, or manikin (M) were recorded. Phase II measured 8 behaviors emitted during 6 conditions that varied in the M's degree of resemblance to humans. The 10-yr-old male S's behaviors in the presence of the M during Phase I were similar to those observed in the presence of humans. In Phase II, the S's behaviors were systematically varied as a function of the degree to which the M resembled and behaved like a human. (9 ref)
Van Dercar, D. H.; Powell, S.; Sandler, Jack & Van Dercar, C. M. (U South Florida) Psychological Reports, 1979(Aug), Vol 45(1), 47–57. [PA, Vol 65:03456]

255. An analysis of observational learning in autistic and normal children.
15 autistic 5–16 yr olds and 15 normal 1–6 yr olds watched an adult model engage in a set of behaviors under specific instructions. Ss were then tested to determine what they had acquired through observation. Results show that (a) the majority of the autistic and the youngest normal Ss acquired only some limited features of the observational situation, and (b) CA was related to the amount of learning through observation in normal Ss but not in the autistics. The deficit that the autistics showed may be related to a failure to discriminate or attend to the total stimulus input presented. Their failure in observational learning can be seen to contribute in a major way to the severely impoverished behavioral repertoires of these children. (31 ref)
Varni, James W.; Lovaas, O. Ivar; Koegel, Robert L. & Everett, Nancy L. (Children's Hosp, Div of Hematology-Oncology, Los Angeles, CA) Journal of Abnormal Child Psychology, 1979(Mar), Vol 7(1), 31–43. [PA, Vol 64:05836]

256. Minor physical anomalies in exceptional children.
Examined the variation of 14 minor physical anomalies (MPAs) in 1,046 children: (a) 42 normal 9th graders (JHs), (b) 244 kindergartners from middle-income neighborhoods (MKs), (c) 596 kindergartners from low-income areas (LKs), (d) 52 14–16 yr old behaviorally disturbed Ss with normal IQs (BDs), (e) 70 14–16 yr old learning-disabled Ss (LDs), (f) 32 elementary special education day school students (SEs), and (g) 10 5–6 yr old autistic Ss (AUs). The 14 MPAs studied were limited to those of the face, head, palate, hands, and toes. Overall, the intraclass correlation was significantly high at .92 and did not drop below .80 for any MPA. Results show that MPAs varied significantly among the groups. The most normal groups—MKs and JHs—had fewer anomalies ($p = .0001$) than all the other groups. The LKs and BDs each had approximately the same number of MPAs and had significantly fewer MPAs than did the LDs, SEs, and AUs. The LDs and SEs had significantly fewer MPAs than did the AUs. (36 ref)
von Hilsheimer, George & Kurko, Virginia. (Growth Inst, DeLand, FL) Journal of Learning Disabilities, 1979(Aug–Sep), Vol 12(7), 462–469. [PA, Vol 63:03358]

257. A case of infantile autism associated with Down's syndrome.
There is increasing recognition that autism is a syndrome, not a disease entity. But it is not yet clear why some children develop autistic behavior more readily than others. It has been noted that autistic symptoms occur more frequently in children with mental retardation, blindness, congenital rubella, and phenylketonuria and that there are few cases of classical infantile autism in the general population. Autism has rarely been associated with Down's syndrome. A report of a case of Down's syndrome combined with infantile autism is presented, and possible etiological processes are discussed. (26 ref)
Wakabayashi, Shinichiro. (U Nagoya School of Medicine, Japan) Journal of Autism & Developmental Disorders, 1979(Mar), Vol 9(1), 31–36. [PA, Vol 62:11094]

258.   The current status of childhood autism.
Suggests that L. Kanner's (1943) view that impairment of affective contact is a major aspect of childhood autism is still accepted, but that some authorities now consider autism to result from a defect in the cognitive skills underlying the development of social communication, symbolic language, and complex verbal reasoning. (37 ref)
Wing, Lorna. (MRC Social Psychology Unit, U London Inst of Psychiatry, England) Psychological Medicine, 1979(Feb), Vol 9(1), 9–12. [PA, Vol 64:05839]

259.   Differentiation of retardation and autism from specific communication disorders.
Describes characteristic features of childhood autism and compares the behavior of children suffering from this disorder with that of mentally retarded children and children with communication disorders. Clues to diagnosis among these groups and between them and normal children are given for various ages and in terms of speech comprehension, inner language and pretend play, repetitive movements, gesture and mime, social interaction, responses to sensory stimuli, and motor development. Difficulties in diagnosis are discussed. (5 ref)
Wing, Lorna. (MRC Social Psychiatry Unit, U London Inst of Psychiatry, England) Child Care, Health & Development, 1979(Jan–Feb), Vol 5(1), 57–68. [PA, Vol 62:03725]

260.   Schizoid personality in childhood: A comparative study of schizoid, autistic and normal children.
Eight schizoid children (clinically resembling H. Asperger's [1944] autistic psychopaths), 8 high-grade speaking autistic children, and 8 normal children individually matched for age, sex, and intelligence were compared on a battery of tests, including the WISC and the Illinois Test of Psycholinguistic Abilities. Results suggest that Ss with schizoid personality disorders are distinct from autistic children on the one hand and from normal children on the other. In all cognitive, language, and memory tests the schizoid Ss were more distractible than the normal group. In language function, they showed disabilities similar to the autistic group, though to a lesser extent. Unlike autistic children, they were not perseverative. On 2 tests of affect, the schizoid group used even fewer emotional constructs when describing people than did the autistics. (41 ref)
Wolff, Sula & Barlow, Anne. (Royal Hosp for Sick Children, Edinburgh, Scotland) Journal of Child Psychology & Psychiatry & Allied Disciplines, 1979(Jan), Vol 20(1), 29–46. [PA, Vol 64:05840]

261.   Decreased 24-hour urinary MHPG in childhood autism.
Compared a group of 5 boys (mean age 10.2 yrs) with childhood autism and a group of 9 normal boys of similar age and found a decrease in urinary 3-methoxy-4-hydroxy-phenethylene glycol (MHPG) in the autistic group. It is hypothesized that autistic children might have an alteration in central and peripheral noradrenergic function, which might be related to impaired regulation of attention, arousal, and anxiety. (10 ref)
Young, J. Gerald et al. (Yale U Child Study Ctr) American Journal of Psychiatry, 1979(Aug), Vol 136(8), 1055–1057. [PA, Vol 62:11166]

262.   Effects of environmental stimulation on behavior as a function of type of behavior disorder.
Maintains that the study of antecedent stimuli (e.g., environmental stimulation) may provide not only a behavioral means of investigating the biological basis of disordered behavior, but also an understanding of children's attempts to mediate biological differences (e.g., in arousal) with environmental conditions, through the use of specific "disordered" behavior patterns. A heightened readiness to approach environmental stimulation (seen in hyperactive and aggressive children) or avoid it (seen in autistic, anxious, or withdrawn children) appears to (1) directly control the amount of stimulus input, (2) moderate the effectiveness of behavioral consequences, and (3) facilitate the development of different attentional, perceptual-motor, and cognitive skills in these 2 groups of children. Behavioral and learning characteristics and treatment findings are reviewed and related to a theoretical model of optimal stimulation. (57 ref)
Zentall, Sydney S. (Eastern Kentucky U) Behavioral Disorders, 1979(Nov), Vol 5(1), 19–29. [PA, Vol 65:03369]

263.   Effects of age on adaptive behavior levels and academic skill levels in autistic and mentally retarded children.
For 47 autistic (A) and 128 mentally retarded (MR) children (IQs below 50 to 70 or above) cross-sectional comparisons were made between junior (ages 6–9 yrs) and senior (ages 11–14 yrs) groups using ratings obtained from teachers on adaptive behaviors and academic skills. Results show that the levels of toilet training, eating skills, participation in group activities, and self-control in the As improved significantly with age. Number concepts skills also improved significantly with age in this group. However, these adaptive and academic levels were in general significantly lower than those of the MRs. The levels of initiative did not improve significantly in either As or MRs, and they were significantly lower in the As. (23 ref)
Ando, Haruhiko; Yoshimura, Ikuko & Wakabayashi, Shinichiro. (Aichi Prefectural Colony Central Hosp, Kasugai, Japan) Journal of Autism & Developmental Disorders, 1980(Jun), Vol 10(2), 173–184. [PA, Vol 64:12570]

264.   Cross-sectional studies of grammatical morphemes in autistic and mentally retarded children.
Studied the frequency of occurrence of functors in obligatory contexts in 10 verbal autistic and 10 mentally retarded children matched for nonverbal MA (approximately 6–6½ yrs) and rank ordered the percentages of correct use of functors. The grammatical complexity of Ss' language was also described using a transformational grammar. The data were compared to those obtained in a normal group of 10 matched for MA and to the data presented by R. W. Brown (1973) and J. G. deVilliers and P. A. deVilliers (1973) in younger children. Autistic Ss omitted functors frequently and independently of the grammatical complexity of their language. The rank ordering of morphemes was consistent within both the autistic and mentally retarded groups but showed no correlation between the 2 groups or to the rank ordering described by deVilliers and deVilliers. It is suggested that functors in autistic Ss may develop in an atypical but consistent order and that this may be due to specific semantic deficits, particularly in person and time deixis. (30 ref)
Bartolucci, Giampiero; Pierce, Sandra J. & Streiner, David L. (McMaster U School of Medicine, Hamilton, Canada) Journal of Autism & Developmental Disorders, 1980(Mar), Vol 10(1), 39–50. [PA, Vol 64:03395]

265.   [A comparative study of psycho-motor test performances by autistic, mentally and educationally handicapped schoolchildren with the help of the LOS method from the Test Battery for the Mentally Handicapped.] (Germ)
Established a statistically assured difference in the motor performances of autistic, mentally handicapped (MH), and educationally handicapped (EH) children. EH children achieved the best results; their overall retardation was slight, and there were partial failures. Autistic children achieved the 2nd-best results; complete and partial retardations occurred. MH children had the lowest results in the overall performance, with complete motor weaknesses and partial retardations. It is noted that autistic children had the same order of completion of the motor components as the EH, but at a lower level. It is concluded that autistic children should not be classified as MH. (31 ref)
Bodenstein-Jenke, Regina. Praxis der Kinderpsychologie und Kinderpsychiatrie, 1980(Jan), Vol 29(1), 24–31. [PA, Vol 65:03340]

266.   Pronoun errors in autistic children: Support for a social explanation.
Several authors have proposed that cognitive or linguistic rather than social deficits underlie pronoun reversals in autistic children. However, such deficit are not considered sufficient to account directly for reversals. Since young normal children have these same limitations and still do not reverse pronouns, it is

suggested that a social impairment is more likely responsible for the fact that autistic children reverse pronouns. (18 ref)
Charney, Rosalind. (Michael Reese Hosp, Chicago, IL) British Journal of Disorders of Communication, 1980(May), Vol 15(1), 39–43. [PA, Vol 66:08139]

267.   Thyroid hormone in autistic children.
Thyroid hormone plays an important role in the pre- and postnatal development and function of the CNS. Disturbances in thyroid hormone regulation have been hypothesized in childhood autism. The present study evaluated blood indices of thyroid function, including serum thyroxine, triiodothyronine, and thyroid-stimulating hormone, in 58 autistic children. No differences were found between autistic and 75 normal children. (26 ref)
Cohen, Donald J.; Young, J. Gerald; Lowe, Thomas L. & Harcherik, Diane. (Yale U, Child Study Ctr) Journal of Autism & Developmental Disorders, 1980(Dec), Vol 10(4), 445–450. [PA, Vol 65:05505]

268.   The responsiveness of autistic children to the predictability of social and nonsocial toys.
Explored autistic children's ability to develop an expectancy from environmental events. Social and nonsocial toys were presented to 10 3–12 yr old autistic and 10 2 yr 11 mo–3 yr 10 mo old control Ss in situations that either allowed or prevented them from predicting their appearance. Autistic Ss' behavior was seriously disrupted if they could not predict the sequence of environmental stimuli, but their responsiveness to environmental stimuli increased when events were predictable. They approached social objects more readily than nonsocial objects when both were simple in appearance. Findings suggest that an appropriate starting point for therapeutic intervention with autistic children might be to focus on shaping social play in highly structured and predictable environments. (20 ref)
Ferrara, Cindy & Hill, Suzanne D. (U New Orleans) Journal of Autism & Developmental Disorders, 1980(Mar), Vol 10(1), 51–57. [PA, Vol 64:03425]

269.   Comparisons of the Peabody Picture Vocabulary Test and the McCarthy Scales of Children's Abilities with a sample of autistic children.
Administered to 8 autistic children (mean age 7 yrs, 6 mo) the Peabody Picture Vocabulary Test and the McCarthy Scales of Children's Abilities. A correlated *t*-test and Pearson product correlations revealed that the Peabody correlated significantly with the McCarthy General Cognitive Index and Verbal, Perceptual, and Memory scales. A significant difference between the means of the 2 tests was found with the Peabody yielding lower scores. (14 ref)
Ferrari, Michael. (Rutgers U, New Brunswick) Psychology in the Schools, 1980(Oct), Vol 17(4), 466–469. [PA, Vol 66:07043]

270.   The Behavior Observation Scale for autism (BOS): Initial results of factor analyses.
Attempted to define groups of behaviors that empirically described 36 autistic, 30 mentally retarded, and 23 normal children. Ss were examined for 3 sessions on the Behavior Observation Scale. Data indicate that the importance assigned to any one behavior or symptom can vary with the MA or CA of the child studied. To develop objective behavioral diagnostic criteria, it is necessary to establish age-specific norms for the frequencies of behaviors exhibited by autistic children. (4 ref)
Freeman, B. J. et al. (U California, Neuropsychiatric Inst, Los Angeles) Journal of Autism & Developmental Disorders, 1980(Sep), Vol 10(3), 343–346. [PA, Vol 65:02462]

271.   Perceptual-motor deficiency in autistic children.
15 autistic children were matched with 30 normals on the Developmental Test of Visual-Motor Integration (DTVMI). The 2 groups were subsequently compared on ability to (a) increase geometric figure-copying performance using additional information provided during subsequent trials, (b) make figure-ground resolutions, (c) perform a fine motor integration task, and (d) cope with background interference while responding on the DTVMI. The primary deficit observed in the autistic Ss was defective monitoring of the motor response. (9 ref)

Fulkerson, Samuel C. & Freeman, William M. (U Louisville) Perceptual & Motor Skills, 1980(Feb), Vol 50(1), 331–336. [PA, Vol 65:10561]

272.   In search of the cognitive deficit in autism: Beyond the stimulus overselectivity model.
Reviews research on overselective attention in autistic children and explores the information-processing paradigm of B. Hermelin (1976) and her works with N. O'Connor (1970) and D. H. Barlow (1976) as an alternative conception. Methodological flaws and uncertainties in both groups of research are detailed—particularly the use of matching, imprecise definitions of autism, and reliance on the dubious construct of MA. The literature is seen to indicate that overselective attention (a) is not limited to autistic children, (b) may be only one of several developmental lags these children display, and (c) may or may not be strongly correlated with children's language abilities and general intellectual abilities. It is concluded that there is no clear evidence that overselective attention is a productive way of analyzing children's learning in a natural setting when educationally relevant materials are presented to the child. (47 ref)
Gersten, Russell M. (U Oregon) Journal of Special Education, 1980(Spr), Vol 14(1), 47–65. [PA, Vol 66:05951]

273.   Maternal age and infantile autism.
In a total population survey of childhood psychosis in Göteborg, Sweden, 15 boys and 5 girls (2 in every 10,000) fulfilled the diagnostic criteria for infantile autism formulated by M. Rutter (1978). 85% of the mothers were older than average. Mean maternal age in the autistic sample was 30.7 yrs, compared with 26.0 yrs in the general population—a significant difference. Fathers were also older than average (mean age 34 yrs). A tendency toward increasing risks with increasing maternal age is noted. It is suggested that potentially CNS-damaging factors are associated with the increased maternal age and thus responsible for the negative effect on the child. (14 ref)
Gillberg, Christopher. (U Göteborg, Sweden) Journal of Autism & Developmental Disorders, 1980(Sep), Vol 10(3), 293–297. [PA, Vol 65:03398]

274.   Obtaining color discriminations in developmentally disabled children by disrupting response stereotyping.
Four experiments examined response stereotyping as a form of stimulus overselectivity. Stimulus control was limited to response-produced feedback and maintained by intermittent reinforcement in a 2-choice simultaneous discrimination task. Three training techniques were examined to determine their role in establishing and disrupting position stereotyping during discrimination training. Three nonverbal children (aged 6 yrs 3 mo–7 yrs 2 mo) diagnosed as autistic served as Ss. In Exps I and II, the procedure of precluding reinforceable responses to the negative stimulus was examined to determine if it could establish color discrimination where standard procedures had failed. Exps III and IV compared the preclusion technique with timeout contingent on responding to the negative stimulus. In all of the studies, reinforcement for choosing the positive stimulus resulted in a position stereotype. In every case, response preclusion served to disrupt the stereotype and establish the discrimination. Timeout appeared effective in one instance, but experimental manipulation led to the interpretation that discrimination learning in that instance was a function of stimulus generalization. (9 ref)
Glenn, Sigrid S.; Whaley, Donald L.; Ward, Rocky & Buck, R. W. (North Texas State U, Ctr for Behavioral Studies, Denton) Behavior Research of Severe Developmental Disabilities, 1980(Nov), Vol 1(3), 175–189. [PA, Vol 66:08149]

275.   [An epidemiological study of autistic children in Fukushima-ken.] (Japn)
Surveyed 2,233 institutions to determine the prevalence of autism and to examine the regional distribution, family background, medical histories, school conditions, and medical treatment of autistic children under 18 yrs of age. Identified autistic children were given a preliminary examination and interviewed by child psychiatrists. Autism was diagnosed following L. Kanner's (1944) criteria. Results show that 142 children had autism,

autistic males outnumbered autistic females by a ratio of 9:1, and there was a larger number of younger and older autistic children than of those in the middle age range. Parents of autistic Ss had significantly higher levels of education than parents of the normal control group, and 60% of the Ss' mothers had incidences of prenatal and perinatal complications (asphyxia neonatorum, toxemia, and prolonged labor). (23 ref)
Hoshino, Yoshihiko et al. (Fukushima Medical Coll, Japan) Japanese Journal of Child & Adolescent Psychiatry, 1980, Vol 21(2), 111–128. [PA, Vol 65:12915]

276.   Respiratory and vascular responses to simple visual stimuli in autistics, retardates and normals.
The 1st of 2 experiments examined changes in respiratory period, peripheral pulse amplitude (PPA), and cephalic pulse amplitude (CPA) in 3 groups of 4–17 yr olds: 20 autistic (AU), 20 mentally retarded (MR), and 20 normals (NO), matched for CA, sex, and (for AU and MR only) IQ. A respiratory response (RR) measure showed habituation in MR and NO but not in AU. Measures of peripheral and cephalic PPA and CPA showed no habituation in any group, but a higher mean response level for AU. AU thus differed from the other 2 groups in 2 respects—a failure to habituate phasic RRs, and enhanced response magnitude in the vascular systems. Exp II replicated Exp I using 20 preschoolers and 20 university students. Results show significant age effects in the vascular systems, with preschoolers showing enhanced response magnitude. It is argued that AU may display a general developmental lag in phasic vascular response measures and a specific deficit indicated by failure to habituate RRs. (52 ref)
James, Angela L. & Barry, Robert J. (U New South Wales, School of Education, Kensington, Australia) Psychophysiology, 1980(Nov), Vol 17(6), 541–547. [PA, Vol 66:08102]

277.   [20th Congress of the Society of Child and Adolescent Psychiatry.] (Japn)
A meeting of the 20th Congress of the Society of Child and Adolescent Psychiatry included reports, lectures, and/or symposia on the development of speech and its disorder and childhood autism and language. Specific topics included language characteristics and developmental neuropsychology of autism, behavioral evaluation of communication in autistic children, and behavior therapy for language acquisition in autism.
Japanese Society of Child & Adolescent Psychiatry. (Marugame, Japan) Japanese Journal of Child & Adolescent Psychiatry, 1980, Vol 21(1), 68 p. [PA, Vol 66:01442]

278.   Sensory preference and overselective responding in autistic children.
Five autistic and 5 normal children (mean age 6.1 yrs) registered a sensory modality preference by barpressing to select either a visual (slides) or auditory (music) stimulus. Ss were then taught a discrimination between the presence or absence of a compound auditory–visual stimulus (white noise and light). Testing for stimulus overselectivity revealed that autistic Ss attended to only one aspect of the compound stimulus. In all cases this was the sensory modality selected during the preference test. Significant correlations were obtained between Gesell Developmental Schedules scores and degree of overselectivity. Normal Ss registered an equal preference for music and slides and displayed no overselectivity. (33 ref)
Kolko, David J.; Anderson, Lowell & Campbell, Magda. (Georgia State U, Atlanta) Journal of Autism & Developmental Disorders, 1980(Sep), Vol 10(3), 259–271. [PA, Vol 65:03408]

279.   Behavior checklist for identifying severely handicapped individuals with high levels of autistic behavior.
An autism checklist was developed with behaviors selected from a variety of checklists and instruments used to identify autism. Content validity of the behaviors was established, and 3,000 of the checklists were sent throughout the US and Canada to professionals acquainted with handicapped children. 1,049 checklists completed on individuals 18 mo–35 yrs of age were returned. Chi-square analysis indicated that 55 of the 57 behaviors listed were significant predictors of autism when compared to severe mental retardation. A weighted score,

determined by statistics (4 indicating the highest predictor of autism, 1 the lowest), was assigned to each behavior. (21 ref)
Krug, David A.; Arick, Joel & Almond, Patricia. (Portland State U) Journal of Child Psychology & Psychiatry & Allied Disciplines, 1980(Jul), Vol 21(3), 221–229. [PA, Vol 64:11514]

280.   [A developmental study of the language behavior of autistic children: An approach from the cross-sectional study.] (Japn)
Investigated the developmental course of language in 41 autistic children by studying language and communication abilities. Results show that autistic Ss acquired nonverbal gestural communications more easily than verbal communication. Imaginary play and the understanding of rules in games appeared to develop along with language and communication abilities. 23 Ss had learned to speak, and there were no syntactic rules that could not be mastered by any S. Deficiency and misuse of pronouns were observed only in Ss with low syntactic abilities. With the development of syntactic abilities, Ss acquired the correct usage of pronouns. The similarities between autistic and normal children in the course of language development are discussed. (26 ref)
Kurokawa, Shinji; Shirataki, Sadaaki; Shimada, Shozo & Sugiura, Yasuo. (Kobe U School of Medicine, Japan) Japanese Journal of Child & Adolescent Psychiatry, 1980, Vol 21(2), 129–140. [PA, Vol 65:12923]

281.   The Blueberry syndrome.
Too-inclusive and too-rigid classifications of childhood emotional disorders have led diagnosticians to overlook conditions that do not fit under accepted labels. An unnamed disorder that the present author calls the Blueberry syndrome and that shares some features with autism, childhood psychosis, and mental retardation, but also differs significantly from all of these, is discussed. Its principal manifestations are lack of speech, low frustration tolerance, and aggressive response to invasion of personal space. Onset follows a normal pre- and perinatal period, with no evidence of brain damage or emotional disorder. There is mental retardation secondary to language deficits, but no social withdrawal, overwhelming anxiety, or obsessive need for sameness. The children come from the lower socioeconomic strata and from either intact or broken families. Etiology is unknown but may involve genetic mutations affecting development of the cerebral speech area. Treatment focuses on improving present satisfactions and functioning. (14 ref)
Levinson, Boris M. (Blueberry Treatment Ctr, Inc, Brooklyn, NY) Psychological Reports, 1980(Feb), Vol 46(1), 47–52. [PA, Vol 65:10524]

282.   Minor physical anomalies in childhood autism: II. Their relationship to maternal age.
45 autistic children were found by the author et al (see PA, Vol 65:3414) to have an excess of minor physical anomalies (MPA) and birth and pregnancy complications. However, there was no significant positive correlation between birth and pregnancy complications and MPA. The relationship between MPA and maternal age at birth in the same autistic population was investigated in the present study, and a significant positive correlation was found. It is suggested that the examination of autistic children for MPA may provide an effective means of determining a subgroup characterized by a relatively clear family history, low IQ, and severe course. (12 ref)
Links, Paul S. (St Joseph Hosp, Hamilton, Canada) Journal of Autism & Developmental Disorders, 1980(Sep), Vol 10(3), 287–292. [PA, Vol 65:03413]

283.   Minor physical anomalies in childhood autism: I. Their relationship to pre- and perinatal complications.
Investigated 45 autistic children (mean age 13.5 yrs) and 52 of their siblings (mean age 13.9 yrs). While there was a significant association between autism and minor physical anomalies and pregnancy complications, no association was found between physical anomalies and pregnancy and birth complications. Further, autistic Ss with higher anomaly scores had lower IQs, more frequent hospitalizations, and more normal family history

compared to autistic Ss with lower physical anomaly scores. (20 ref)

Links, Paul S.; Stockwell, Michelle; Abichandani, Florinda & Simeon, Jovan. (St Joseph Hosp, Hamilton, Canada) Journal of Autism & Developmental Disorders, 1980(Sep), Vol 10(3), 273–285. [PA, Vol 65:03414]

284.　Effects of interaction on nonhandicapped children's attitudes toward autistic children.
Interviewed 28 2nd and 3rd graders concerning their attitudes toward and understanding of children exhibiting childhood autism confounded by mental retardation. The interviews took place before and after Ss had participated in a week of daily, half-hour play sessions with a class of 6 autistic children. Comparisons of Ss' attitudes at each time indicated that they were overwhelmingly positive on both occasions. Contrary to earlier findings, Ss did not express more negative attitudes as a result of contact with autistic children; they displayed an increase in their understanding of autistic children after contact. Ss' understanding of autism was positively related to the frequency of their communication with the autistic children on the first day of interaction, and their positive attitudes and frequency of solitary play were negatively correlated. (14 ref)

McHale, Susan M. & Simeonsson, Rune J. (U North Carolina, Frank Porter Graham Child Development Ctr, Chapel Hill) American Journal of Mental Deficiency, 1980(Jul), Vol 85(1), 18–24. [PA, Vol 64:08191]

285.　The social and symbolic quality of autistic children's communication.
Observed the developmental status of the communicatory behavior of 11 autistic children (4–9 yrs old) during free play sessions under 2 conditions: (a) when teachers were present to direct Ss' behavior and (b) when teachers were absent and Ss played among themselves. Mean changes in communicatory behavior were measured over 8 mo using a behavior scale designed for this study. The relationship between the developmental status of Ss' communicatory behavior and standardized measures of social and cognitive functioning (e.g., IQ, Vineland Social Maturity Scale) was also assessed. Results reveal that the quantity and social quality of autistic Ss' communicatory behaviors were greater in the teachers' presence than absence and that the symbolic and social quality of Ss' communicatory behavior increased over 8 mo. Also, positive correlations were found between social and symbolic levels of communication and social and cognitive functioning. (13 ref)

McHale, Susan M.; Simeonsson, Rune J.; Marcus, Lee M. & Olley, J. Gregory. (U North Carolina, Chapel Hill) Journal of Autism & Developmental Disorders, 1980(Sep), Vol 10(3), 299–310. [PA, Vol 65:04169]

286.　Objectively defined linguistic parameters in children with autism and other developmental disabilities.
Examined the language of 84 children with autism and other developmental disabilities according to a set of objectively defined linguistic parameters. These criteria were drawn from clinical observations reported in the literature and from developmental norms of language acquisition. Data analysis identified sets of parameters that were correlated with psychiatrists' clinical diagnoses but failed to isolate individual parameters (such as echolalia or noncommunicativeness) that have been suggested to be pathonomic. (22 ref)

Needleman, Rosa; Ritvo, Edward R. & Freeman, B. J. (Neuropsychiatric Inst, Div of Mental Retardation & Child Psychiatry, Los Angeles, CA) Journal of Autism & Developmental Disorders, 1980(Dec), Vol 10(4), 389–398. [PA, Vol 65:05517]

287.　Extra prompts versus no extra prompts in self-care training of autistic children and adolescents.
10 autistic Ss (mean age 13.1 yrs) learned to lace shoes whose laces and eyelets were color-coded and then were exposed to a no-extra-prompt condition in which color codes could not be utilized to solve the position discriminations required to lace properly. 10 other autistic Ss (mean age 11.5 yrs) reached

criterion on a non-color-coded shoe before the extra-prompt condition. Analyses suggested that Ss who first learned under the color-coded extra-prompt condition encountered difficulty in transferring their newly acquired skill to the non-color-coded condition, whereas Ss who learned initially without the extra prompts had little difficulty with the subsequent color-coded condition. A follow-up procedure requiring all Ss to choose between the color prompt and the position cue revealed that 11 of 20 Ss consistently chose the color cue, even though it resulted in improper lacing. It is recommended that clinicians avoid the use of highly salient, non-criterion-related prompts in teaching certain types of adaptive skills to autistic children. (15 ref)

Nelson, David L.; Gergenti, Edward & Hollander, Anthony C. (Boston U, Sargent Coll of Allied Health Professions) Journal of Autism & Developmental Disorders, 1980(Sep), Vol 10(3), 311–321. [PA, Vol 65:03430]

288.　Differential autonomic responses of autistic and normal children.
Compared the autonomic responses of 10 autistic and 10 normal children (mean age 7.63 yrs) using auditory stimuli varying in social relevance. Consistent differences in heart rate and skin conductance level were found between the groups. Results suggest that autistic Ss exhibited deficits in psychophysiological reactivity to a range of environmental stimuli. Findings are discussed in terms of information-processing capabilities of autistic children and probable physiological correlates. (25 ref)

Palkovitz, Robin J. & Wiesenfeld, Alan R. (Rutgers U, Douglass Coll, New Brunswick) Journal of Autism & Developmental Disorders, 1980(Sep), Vol 10(3), 347–360. [PA, Vol 65:03431]

289.　The performance of autistic children on three learning set tasks.
Learning set, matching learning set, and conditional matching learning set tasks were presented to 36 autistic, retarded, and normal children (mean MA about 6 yrs). The majority of autistic Ss were able to solve these problems and to acquire set, and their performance was similar to that of controls. It is suggested that (a) performance was directly related to developmental level rather than to autism per se; (b) learning was enhanced by the use of concrete stimuli, since conditional cues were successfully used here, in contrast to failure in an earlier experiment using abstract cues; and (c) overselectivity was not characteristic of the performance of autistic Ss. (23 ref)

Prior, Margot R. & McGillivray, Jane. (La Trobe U, Bundoora, Australia) Journal of Child Psychology & Psychiatry & Allied Disciplines, 1980(Oct), Vol 21(4), 313–323. [PA, Vol 65:01384]

290.　Auditory brainstem evoked responses in autistic children.
Previous studies have implicated a brainstem dysfunction in autism. The present study matched 6 5–15 yr old autistic (A) children with 6 normal children (controls) by age and sex to evaluate brainstem evoked response (BSER) to auditory stimuli. An evaluation of pure tone audiometric threshold showed no evidence of impairment; however, the electrophysiologic responses differed for the 2 groups. The BSER of the As was remarkable for showing increased latency and markedly increased variability. Findings from the present study give additional evidence of a brainstem dysfunction in autistic children, while the electrophysiologic variability supports the hypothesis of perceptual inconstancy. (22 ref)

Rosenblum, Stuart M. et al. (U Virginia School of Medicine, Charlottesville) Journal of Autism & Developmental Disorders, 1980(Jun), Vol 10(2), 215–225. [PA, Vol 64:12591]

291.　Toward objective classification of childhood autism: Childhood Autism Rating Scale (CARS).
Describes the creation of a scale for rating autistic children, based on direct behavioral observation. The CARS has been used to rate 537 children in a statewide program over a 10-yr period. It consists of 15 scales listed along with a description of the rationale used in their inclusion. Internal consistency of the scale was found to be .94, and an interrater reliability of .71 was obtained by 2 observers rating 280 cases. CARS scores correlated .84 with an overall clinical rating of psychosis indicating

acceptable validity. The categories of individuals that result from the scales' use are compared, and the operational definition of autism reflected by the CARS is compared to those used in other scales. (21 ref)
Schopler, Eric; Reichler, Robert J.; DeVellis, Robert F. & Daly, Kenneth. (U North Carolina School of Medicine, Chapel Hill) Journal of Autism & Developmental Disorders, 1980(Mar), Vol 10(1), 91–103. [PA, Vol 64:02500]

292. HLA and autism.
Studied human leukocyte antigens (HLA) in autism to determine whether a relationship could be established. 20 autistic children and their parents were HLA typed. The control group consisted of 575 potential donors for renal transplantation, 134 healthy Ss, and 48 persons of different families who married into 1 large family that had been HLA typed. Control Ss were from the same geographical area as the experimental Ss. Ss were typed by a modification of the microlymphocytotoxicity tests of P. O. Terasaki and J. D. McCleland (1964). HLA-A2 was significantly increased when compared to geographical controls and when compared to controls from the literature. However, when chi square was corrected for the number of antigen specificities, significance was lost. No antigen was significantly increased in the mothers. HLA-A10 was significantly increased in the fathers, but significance did not remain after correction for the number of antigen specificities. These negative findings do not disprove an association because the numbers are so small. This small sample needs to be enlarged and replicated locally as well as in other geographical areas. (6 ref)
Stubbs, E. Gene & Magenis, R. Ellen. (U Oregon Health Sciences Ctr, School of Medicine, Portland) Journal of Autism & Developmental Disorders, 1980(Mar), Vol 10(1), 15–19. [PA, Vol 64:03473]

293. A proposed reinforcement survey schedule for special needs children.
Describes the development of the Special Needs Reinforcement Survey Schedule for autistic, behaviorally disturbed, learning disabled, and mentally retarded, and/or developmentally delayed children. A reliability study of the 2-part scale is presented. Results of the test–retest procedure with 96 5–12 yr old children with special needs indicate that the scale was reliable over a period of 17 days, with a Kendall correlation of 0.8825 on the Food Reinforcer scale and 0.8623 on the Nonfood Reinforcer scale (both $p < .001$). Suggested uses of the scale include assessment, clinical settings, home programs and research. (6 ref)
Tourigny Dewhurst, Denise L. & Cautela, Joseph R. (Maryview Community Mental Health Ctr, Portsmouth, VA) Journal of Behavior Therapy & Experimental Psychiatry, 1980(Jun), Vol 11(2), 109–112. [PA, Vol 66:04838]

294. Gorky's "Nilushka": Autism case report?
Suggests that M. Gorky's (1921, 1964) description of the child Nilushka resembles more recent scientific accounts of autism (e.g., L. Kanner, 1943; E. Ritvo and B. Freeman, 1978; and M. Rutter, 1978). By contrasting the townspeople with the boy, the author provides an unusual perspective on autism, one that may help explain the special attraction these children hold for parents, researchers, and teachers. (4 ref)
Webster, C. D. (Metropolitan Toronto Forensic Service, Clarke Inst of Psychiatry, Canada) Journal of Autism & Developmental Disorders, 1980(Jun), Vol 10(2), 227–229. [PA, Vol 64:12686]

295. Acute onset of autistic features following brain damage in a ten-year-old.
Presents the case of a boy who, following a prolonged period of unconsciousness, displayed severe eye-to-eye gaze avoidance, sensory inattention, and some other behavioral symptoms normally associated with the syndrome of infantile autism. The symptoms lasted only a few months and were associated with the more permanent behavioral changes of postencephalitic psychosis. (14 ref)
Weir, Kirk & Salisbury, David M. (U London Inst of Child Health, Dept of Child Psychiatry, England) Journal of Autism & Developmental Disorders, 1980(Jun), Vol 10(2), 185–191. [PA, Vol 64:12604]

296. Childhood autism and social class: A question of selection?
132 children with typical autism, other early childhood psychoses, and severe mental retardation without autistic behavior were identified in an epidemiological study in an area of southeast London. The social class distribution of their fathers was examined, and no significant differences were found between the groups or in a comparison with the general population of the area. Fathers of children with autism and related conditions referred to an outpatient autism clinic and fathers joining the National Society for Autistic Children (NSAC) were of higher social class than both the average for England and Wales and the fathers of the study children. Joining the NSAC during its early years and keeping up membership were also linked with higher social class. Findings support the view that reports of a social class bias in autism may be explained by factors affecting referral and diagnosis. (18 ref)
Wing, Lorna. (MRC Social Psychiatry Unit, U London Inst of Psychiatry, England) British Journal of Psychiatry, 1980(Nov), Vol 137, 410–417. [PA, Vol 66:08184]

297. Sign language and autism.
Reviews research findings and issues in teaching sign language to nonspeaking autistic children. Data on over 100 children indicate that nearly all autistic children learn receptive and expressive signs, and many learn to combine signs. These children also exhibit marked improvement in adaptive behaviors. Speech skills are acquired by fewer children and may be developed through simultaneous speech and sign training. Possible explanations for these results are given, together with suggestions for future research. Recommended innovations include exposure to fluent signers and training in discourse and code-switching. Different sign language teaching methods need to be investigated more fully, including emphasis on training sign language within the children's total environment and with greater staff and parental participation. (38 ref)
Bonvillian, John D.; Nelson, Keith E. & Rhyne, Jane M. (U Virginia) Journal of Autism & Developmental Disorders, 1981(Mar), Vol 11(1), 125–137. [PA, Vol 66:06189]

298. Autistic children's responses to structure and to interpersonal demands.
Exposed 10 autistic children aged 8–15 yrs to 4 styles of approach by an adult in which the common context was the child's involvement in the completion of a model-building task. These styles varied in the extent to which they made interpersonal demands of the child and in the amount of task-directed structure that was imposed. Results indicate that the styles applied were reliably discriminable and that Ss' responses, both social and task-directed, were positively related to the interpersonal and task-oriented demands that were made of them. Discussed some individual differences in the responses to the styles that may be relevant to the diagnosis of autism. (23 ref)
Clark, Peter & Rutter, Michael. (U London Inst of Psychiatry, England) Journal of Autism & Developmental Disorders, 1981(Jun), Vol 11(2), 201–217. [PA, Vol 66:10468]

299. Developmental language disorders: Cognitive processes, semantics, pragmatics, phonology, and syntax.
Reviews the research and discusses 2 views of cognitive processes. One of these, emphasizing cognitive mechanisms such as short-term memory, is seen as providing possible explanations for some types of language deficits. The other, a concern with conceptual knowledge, is subjected to a critical analysis questioning how complete an explanation it is able to offer for some aspects of language acquisition. Problems of definition are also discussed when semantic aspects of language are considered. Problems in the pragmatic component of language are seen as providing an explanation for particular aspects of language disorder in some autistic children. The importance of focusing on phonology as a central grammatical process is discussed and linked to dyslexia and to spelling disorders. It is argued that the

acquisition of syntactic structure is not yet understood. Impairments such as a hierarchical planning order deficit may affect syntactic ability and lead to disordered language, as found in some types of developmentally aphasic children. It is concluded that it is important to study all 5 areas and their interrelationships. (67 ref)

Cromer, Richard F. (MRC Developmental Psychology Unit, London, England) Journal of Autism & Developmental Disorders, 1981(Mar), Vol 11(1), 57–74. [PA, Vol 66:06097]

300. Behavioral characteristics of high- and low-IQ autistic children.
Developed the Behavior Observation Scale to objectively differentiate autistic, normal, and mentally retarded children aged 30–60 mo. Operational definitions and procedures are described and data are reported on the frequency of selected behaviors among 114 Ss. Prior studies have revealed that to assess the clinical significance of behaviors in autistic children, both frequency of occurrence per child and the number of children exhibiting the behaviors must be considered concurrently. This study confirms the hypothesis that it is critical to consider IQ when assessing the clinical significance of individual behaviors and groups of behaviors. (7 ref)

Freeman, B. J. et al. (U California Neuropsychiatric Inst, Div of Mental Retardation & Child Psychiatry, Los Angeles) American Journal of Psychiatry, 1981(Jan), Vol 138(1), 25–29. [PA, Vol 65:06823]

301. Transfer of verbal responses across instructional settings by autistic-type children.
Six 5–12 yr olds who learned responses to common questions under 2 different training conditions at school were probed to determine transfer of learning to a novel instructional environment. Four Ss demonstrated only low rates of generalization to a novel environment regardless of the type of training. The other two Ss generalized most responses across settings irrespective of the original training conditions. (24 ref)

Handleman, Jan S. (Rutgers U, Douglass Coll, New Brunswick) Journal of Speech & Hearing Disorders, 1981(Feb), Vol 46(1), 69–76. [PA, Vol 66:10878]

302. Sensory receptor sensitivity in autistic children: Response times to proximal and distal stimulation.
On the basis of behavioral observation, it has been postulated that autistic children prefer proximal (touch, taste) to distal (sight, hearing) sensory modalities. To assess this systematically, 16 autistic children's (aged 11–20 yrs) simple response times (RTs) were measured with auditory, visual, and tactile stimulation. Ss were studied for up to 25 sessions of 40 trials with each modality. RTs were significantly related to MA (Peabody Picture Vocabulary Test). Autistic Ss' responses were significantly slower than normal children's. However, autistic and normal Ss had the same pattern: fastest responding to auditory stimuli and slowest responding to tactile stimulation. Autistic Ss' preference for proximal stimuli probably reflects a continuation of immature behavior rather than a basic disturbance in sensory receptor sensitivity. (11 ref)

Kootz, John P.; Marinelli, Beth & Cohen, Donald J. (Yale U, Child Study Ctr) Archives of General Psychiatry, 1981(Mar), Vol 38(3), 271–273. [PA, Vol 65:12921]

303. Comparison of auditory stimulus processing in normal and autistic adolescents.
Investigated the possibility that autistic adolescents may avoid speech communication with the world around them by "tuning out" or perceptually suppressing auditory speech stimuli. 11 14–21 yr old males with normal pure-tone hearing sensitivity and 5 autistic males with IQs of 70–109 served as Ss. The tune-out auditory suppression hypothesis was examined with each S's own speech as the stimulus under 3 perceptual-motor conditions: (1) speech in a delayed auditory feedback (DAF) mode; (2) a white noise masking speech mode; and (3) speech in a normal, quiet listening mode. Autistic Ss were compared with 6 normal controls on speech time duration and sound level. DAF increased

the speech sound pressure level and increased speech time duration for both groups. (63 ref)

Nober, E. Harris & Simmons, James Q. (U Massachusetts, Amherst) Journal of Autism & Developmental Disorders, 1981(Jun), Vol 11(2), 175–189. [PA, Vol 66:10507]

304. The functions of immediate echolalia in autistic children.
Investigated how immediate echolalia functions for autistic children in interactions with familiar adults. Four echolalic males aged 4–9 yrs were videotaped at school and at home, in both group and dyadic interactions in natural situations such as lunchtime, family activities, and play activities in school. After conducting a multilevel analysis of over 1,000 utterances of verbal and nonverbal factors, response latency, and intonation, it was discovered that immediate echolalia is far from being a meaningless behavior, as has been previously reported. Seven functional categories of echolalia (e.g., nonfocused, self-regulatory, and turn-taking) were discovered and are discussed with reference to behavioral and linguistic features of each category. It is argued that researchers who propose intervention programs of echo-abatement may be overlooking the important communicative and cognitive functions echolalia may serve for the autistic child. (26 ref)

Prizant, Barry M. & Duchan, Judith F. (Southern Illinois U, Carbondale) Journal of Speech & Hearing Disorders, 1981(Aug), Vol 46(3), 241–249. [PA, Vol 66:10515]

305. S+ versus S− fading in prompting procedures with autistic children.
Investigated the relative effectiveness of 2 prompt-fading procedures for teaching difficult visual discriminations to autistic children. Both prompt procedures involved within-stimulus fading where manipulation occurred on the relevant component of the discrimination. One procedure involved fading first along the positive stimulus (S+), while holding the negative stimulus (S−) constant. The other procedure involved fading first along the S−, while holding the S+ constant. Eight autistic children (mean age 8.2 yrs) were each taught 2 discriminations, one by each of the prompt procedures. Results indicate that for all but 1 S, the discriminations were acquired significantly faster with fewer errors when the S+ was faded first. (38 ref)

Schreibman, Laura & Charlop, Marjorie H. (Claremont Men's Coll) Journal of Experimental Child Psychology, 1981(Jun), Vol 31(3), 508–520. [PA, Vol 66:04068]

306. Language disabilities in infantile autism: A brief review and comment.
Studies of autistic children's memory for linguistic materials have yielded what appear to be conflicting results. A review of these studies reveals a pattern of findings consistent with the hypothesis that autistics do, in fact, have a special linguistic coding difficulty. The apparent discrepancies are the result of the use of low-power statistical tests in some experiments. Because the autistic deficit may arise from a failure to use semantic or syntactic knowledge or even from a failure to acquire such knowledge in the first place, future research should be aimed at explicating the precise mechanisms underlying the autistic deficit. (12 ref)

Schwartz, Steven. (U Queensland, Brisbane, Australia) Applied Psycholinguistics, 1981(Feb), Vol 2(1), 25–31. [PA, Vol 66:06002]

307. Sensorimotor skills and language comprehension in autistic children.
Examined the level of sensorimotor concepts of young autistic children in relation to language comprehension. 16 autistic children (mean MA 24.8 mo; mean CA 51.7 mo) were administered a standardized scale of sensorimotor intelligence and receptive language. Ss demonstrated sophisticated sensorimotor skills, particularly object permanence. While their initial performance was inferior to that of 16 normal controls matched for MA, particularly in their use of objects in combination, the difference between groups diminished on the 2nd test administration. On the receptive language measure, autistic Ss were less able to identify words correctly. The sensorimotor behavior of autistic

Ss who demonstrated language comprehension did not differ from those who showed no comprehension, except that the former group tended to use an object as an instrument more frequently. The fact that the autistic Ss were so impaired in language even with fairly good sensorimotor skills suggests that these skills, particularly object permanence, play a minor role in their language acquisition. (25 ref)
Sigman, Marian & Ungerer, Judy. (U California School of Medicine, Los Angeles) Journal of Abnormal Child Psychology, 1981(Jun), Vol 9(2), 149–165. [PA, Vol 66:10524]

308.   Differences in cognitive functioning of retarded children and retarded autistic children: A response to Ahmad Baker.
Argues that A. M. Baker (see PA, Vol 62:6121) implied that the cognitive functioning of autistic children and that of mentally retarded children is the same. The present paper challenges the validity of this implication. Differences between the 2 groups have been demonstrated in subtest profiles from standardized intelligence tests, the use of syntax and interrelatedness in facilitating recall, and language rules. Taken together, these lines of research suggest that there is a cognitive deficit unique to autism that is manifested in impaired language development and use of abstraction. (16 ref)
Sindelar, Paul T.; Meisel, C. Julius; Buy, Mary J. & Klein, Edward S. (Pennsylvania State U, University Park) Exceptional Children, 1981(Mar), Vol 47(6), 406–411. [PA, Vol 65:10533]

309.   Some findings on the use of the adaptive behavior scale with autistic children.
Conducted 2 studies on the use of the Adaptive Behavior Scales (ABS) with 53 autistic children aged 4–13 yrs. Exp I compared ratings by parents and teachers on the same child. For Part I (Adaptive), significant correlations were found on total score and on 7/10 individual scales. For Part II (Behavior), significant correlations were found on only 3/14 scales and not on total score. Exp II examined change measured by the ABS across an academic year. For Part I, significant change occurred on 5/10 scales and on total score; for Part II, significant differences were found on 2/14 scales and not on total score. Correlations with IQ, social quotient, and degree of autism revealed a similar pattern. (12 ref)
Sloan, Jerry L. & Marcus, Lee. (U North Carolina, Div TEACCH, Chapel Hill) Journal of Autism & Developmental Disorders, 1981(Jun), Vol 11(2), 191–199. [PA, Vol 66:10525]

310.   On the nature of linguistic functioning in early infantile autism.
Reviews studies conducted on linguistic functioning in autistic children, within the framework developed in normal language acquisition research. Despite certain methodological weaknesses, the research consistently shows that phonological and syntactic development follow the same course as in normal children and in other disordered groups, though at a slowed rate, while semantic and pragmatic functioning may be especially deficient in autism. These findings are related to other recent studies on the relative independence of different aspects of language. (49 ref)
Tager-Flusberg, Helen. (U Massachusetts, Boston) Journal of Autism & Developmental Disorders, 1981(Mar), Vol 11(1), 45–56. [PA, Vol 66:06007]

311.   Sentence comprehension in autistic children.
Comprehension and strategy use by autistic children were tested in 2 experiments. 18 autistic Ss were compared with 30 normal 3- and 4-yr-olds, matched on the Peabody Picture Vocabulary Test and Raven Colored Progressive Matrices. In Exp I, Ss were asked to act out active and passive, biased, and reversible sentences. The autistic group's overall comprehension was lower than that of the normal controls: Although the autistic Ss did use a word-order strategy, they did not generally use a probable-event strategy. These findings were confirmed in Exp II, in which the same procedure with anomalous 3-word items was used. The results are interpreted as evidence that in autism there is a semantic-cognitive deficit in utilizing conceptual knowledge about relational aspects of the environment and that this deficit

underlies the comprehension difficulties of autistic persons. (37 ref)
Tager-Flusberg, Helen. (U Massachusetts, Boston) Applied Psycholinguistics, 1981(Feb), Vol 2(1), 5–24. [PA, Vol 66:06008]

312.   Implication of sex differences in the familial transmission of infantile autism.
Data on 102 autistic children, 78 boys and 24 girls whose mean age was 6 yrs 7 mo, show that there was a significantly greater proportion of autistic girls than boys with IQs under 50 and with evidence of brain damage. The girls also had a greater proportion of relatives affected with autism or cognitive-language deficit than did the boys. Findings are seen to suggest that if autism is inherited, the specific mechanism may involve multifactorial transmission. (34 ref)
Tsai, Luke; Stewart, Mark A. & August, Gerald. (U Iowa Coll of Medicine, Iowa City) Journal of Autism & Developmental Disorders, 1981(Jun), Vol 11(2), 165–173. [PA, Vol 66:10533]

313.   Asperger's syndrome: A clinical account.
Describes the clinical features, course, etiology, epidemiology, differential diagnosis, and management of Asperger's syndrome. Classification is discussed, and reasons are given for including the syndrome, together with early childhood autism, in a wider group of conditions that have in common the impairment of development of social interaction, communication, and imagination. (34 ref)
Wing, Lorna. (MRC Social Psychiatry Unit, U London Inst of Psychiatry, England) Psychological Medicine, 1981(Feb), Vol 11(1), 115–129. [PA, Vol 66:10537]

314.   Language, social, and cognitive impairments in autism and severe mental retardation.
Outlines an epidemiological stud reported by the present author and J. Gould (see PA, Vol 62:11097) that shows that those with L. Kanner's (1943, 1946) syndrome are one group among a wider range of children, all with impairment of social interaction, communication, and imagination. Most, but not all, children with this triad of impairments are severely mentally retarded, although severe retardation also occurs in those who are sociable and communicative. It is hypothesized that the socially impaired lack certain abilities that are inborn in normal children and the sociable mentally retarded: the capacity to produce and monitor the normal species-specific preverbal sounds, the drive to explore the environment and form concepts to explain experiences, and the ability to recognize that other human beings are of special interest and importance. A possible neurological basis for these problems is considered. (25 ref)
Wing, Lorna. (U London, Inst of Psychiatry, England) Journal of Autism & Developmental Disorders, 1981(Mar), Vol 11(1), 31–44. [PA, Vol 66:05929]

Mental Retardation

315.   Canter Background Interference Procedure applied to the diagnosis of brain damage in mentally retarded children.
Evaluated the efficacy of Task-Central and Task-Peripheral forms of the Canter Background Interference Procedure for the diagnosis of brain damage in mentally retarded children. 30 brain-damaged and 30 non-brain-damaged 6-16 yr. old children were tested on both forms, several days apart, with counterbalanced presentation. A Type IV ANOVA revealed no sequence or order effect and a significant difference between the 2 groups only on the Bender Error score. The 2 forms differed significantly on the difference score and the Number Positive, but not as a function of diagnostic category. Discriminant analyses revealed significant multiple correlations with diagnosis for each form, although the accuracy of prediction was low. Because the comparison of the 2 forms was difficult to interpret, a conceptual link to the present literature remains to be clarified. Results indicate that the performance of older children of average intelligence would be more like that of adults, and several avenues of further research are suggested. (18 ref.)

Adams, Jerry. (William S. Hall Psychiatric Inst., Columbia, S.C.) American Journal of Mental Deficiency, 1970(Jul), Vol. 75(1), 57-64. [PA, Vol 45:02616]

316. Objective measures and occupational success.
The vocational, intellectual, social, and emotional adjustment of 29 adolescent and adult retardates as judged by a significantly interreliable group of judges was statistically analyzed in relation to selected biographical and objective test data. Positive significant relationships were found between certain subtests of the Illinois Test of Psycholinguistic Ability and Picture Arrangement of the WAIS, and several of the categories of adjustment. Negative significant relationship was found between age and all categories of adjustment. Results are discussed in terms of previous findings, theoretical implications, and suggested further research.
Clark, Alice & Foster, James. (U. North Dakota) Mental Retardation, 1970(Aug), Vol. 8(4), 41-44. [PA, Vol 48:01507]

317. Vigilance and verbal conditioning in the mildly and severely retarded.
Administered to 34 mildly and 27 severely retarded adolescent institutionalized Ss a verbal conditioning task consisting of acquisition and reversal phases, and a simple and a complex vigilance task. Severely retarded Ss were slower in response speed than mildly retarded Ss in conditioning. They required a larger number of trials to change from acquisition to reversal phase, and from reversal to a reacquisition and rereversal phase; this was attributed to their relative immobility of nervous processes. In vigilance, both groups showed similar trends in decrement as a function of time at task. Severely retarded Ss were inferior to mildly retarded Ss in their performance in complex vigilance. False detections did not follow any consistent pattern of decrement in complex vigilance, which required some theoretical explanation. The most remarkable result was obtained by comparing good and poor performers in 1 vigilance task, on performance in the other vigilance task, and in conditioning. A direct variation between proficiency in vigilance and conditioning performances was noticed, as also between the 2 vigilance tasks. These relations are explained in terms of orienting response, which provided a basic link between vigilance and conditioning. (22 ref.)
Das, J. P. (U. Alberta, Edmonton, Canada) American Journal of Mental Deficiency, 1970(Nov), Vol. 75(3), 253-259. [PA, Vol 46:03597]

318. Relationships among scores on infant tests for children with developmental problems.
30 preschool children referred for diagnosis of developmental problems were administered the Bayley Scale of Mental Development, the Cattell Infant Intelligence Scale, and the Vineland Social Maturity Scale. Results indicate that the scores on the 2 infant tests are so similar and highly correlated that they might be considered interchangeable in diagnostic settings. Clinically, the Bayley presented advantages of a greater variety of items and separate mental and motor scales, while the Cattell took less time to administer and could be combined with the Stanford-Binet. Although significantly correlated with the 2 infant tests, the Vineland consistently yielded higher scores.
Erickson, Marilyn T.; Johnson, Nancy M. & Campbell, Frances A. (U. North Carolina) American Journal of Mental Deficiency, 1970(Jul), Vol 75(1), 102-104. [PA, Vol 45:00926]

319. Response familiarization and the paired-associate performance of noninstitutionalized retarded and normal children.
Following relevant, irrelevant, or no pretraining with the response terms of a paired-associate (PA) task, 46 normal and 46 retarded children were compared on PA performance. Analyses of free-learning, PA correct responses, type of errors committed, and stage analysis all indicate that the PA deficit results partly from a decreased ability to learn the response terms of a PA task. The superiority of normal children was related to the earlier beginning point for the associative learning phase. Results are discussed in relation to previous research with normal adults and research within the retarded population.

Kellas, George & Butterfield, Earl C. (U. Kansas) American Journal of Mental Deficiency, 1970(Jul), Vol. 75(1), 81-87. [PA, Vol 45:01225]

320. Retention in retarded and nonretarded children as a function of learning method.
Studied rote learning and retention performance as a function of method used in original learning and intellectual level. 60 retarded and 60 nonretarded junior-high and high-school students were randomly assigned to 1 of 3 treatment groups to learn a paired-associate task. Retention was assessed by immediate recall, 24-hr recall, and relearning scores. Data analysis indicates inferior learning performance and a 24-hr retention deficit for retarded Ss. The analysis also indicates that learning method influences results of comparisons of rote learning and retention in retarded and nonretarded Ss.
Stinnett, Ray D. & Prehm, Herbert J. (Eastern Oregon Coll.) American Journal of Mental Deficiency, 1970(Jul), Vol. 75(1), 39-46. [PA, Vol 45:01229]

321. Distractibility in the mentally retarded: Negative evidence for an orienting inadequacy.
Describes 3 studies in which the orienting behavior of normal and mentally retarded children was investigated under a variety of conditions. An initial study found that, in many cases, normal Ss showed nontask orientations to a greater extent than did retarded Ss. An examination of those circumstances wherein the retarded had been found to glance more indicates that such circumstances, often observed in the classroom, are inappropriate for adjudging retarded children to be distractible. Further research involving only retarded Ss shows that the inclusion of an adult in the learning situation greatly increased retarded Ss' nontask orientations. However, it was also shown that if cues were provided by the adult they would be utilized by the Ss; the retarded Ss glancing apparently represented information seeking and not merely vacuous orientations to a salient social stimulus. A new conception of children's attending behaviors is suggested to account for the findings.
Turnure, James E. (U. Minnesota, Inst. of Child Development) Exceptional Children, 1970(Nov), Vol. 37(3), 181-186. [PA, Vol 46:05358]

322. The use of the Draw-A-Man Test with borderline retarded children without pronounced pathology.
Emotional or organic problems in children contributed to an underestimation of intellectual functioning when using the Draw-A-Man Test (DAM). With children of borderline intellectual functioning, who demonstrate no evidence of emotional or organic problems, the DAM closely approximated the Stanford-Binet or WISC results. Results suggest the usefulness of the DAM as a brief screening device for children with borderline intelligence.
Ables, Billie S. (U. Kentucky, Medical School) Journal of Clinical Psychology, 1971(Apr), Vol. 27(2), 262-263. [PA, Vol 46:07068]

323. The influence of brief social deprivation on activity of mentally retarded children.
A plethora of research has demonstrated the facilitative effects of brief periods of social deprivation on children's performance of simple perceptual-motor tasks. Characteristically, these studies have focused on the enhanced effectiveness of social reinforcement consequent to social deprivation, and the ensuing dialectic has concentrated on delineating the theoretical basis for this phenomenon—social drive vs. anxiety arousal. The theoretical issue has tended to obfuscate the potentially salutary nature of social deprivation as an impetus to heightened activity in otherwise lethargic populations. Social deprivation is viewed as a potent therapeutic technique capable of elevating the depressed activity of a large segment of the institutionalized mentally retarded population. (16 ref.)
Altman, Reuben. (U. Missouri) Training School Bulletin, 1971(Nov), Vol. 68(3), 165-169. [PA, Vol 47:11460]

324. [The development of thought structure among normal and mentally retarded children.] (Duth)
In keeping with Piaget's developmental levels, 13 tests were administered to 30 elementary school children and 20 mentally retarded boys. For the mentally retarded Ss, WISC IQ ranged between 52-85 (M = 74). The 8 tests that indicated a difference in the results between the 2 S groups at at least the .01 level were: (a) estimating changes in volume by changing the shape of a clay pellet; (b) determining the equality of weights of 2 sticks, each of which had been equal to a 3rd stick; (c) appraising the changes in the amount of water after it had been poured into varied-shaped glasses; (d) identifying the essential parts of a bicycle; (e) determining the origin of air in a balloon; (f) comprehending a simple question when the description of objects involved perceptual shifting from color of objects to their material; (g) describing a right angle reduced to its smallest size; and (h) drawing an extended railroad track in perspective. The r between the results of the testing and scores on Raven's Progressive Matrices was about +.15.
Angenent, H. L. (U. Groningen, Inst. of Criminology, Netherlands) Nederlands Tijdschrift voor de Psychologie en haar Grensgebieden, 1971(Apr), Vol. 26(4), 215-232. [PA, Vol 47:03529]

325. [An extra small metacentric chromosome found in a mentally retarded child.] (Span)
Describes a case of mental retardation and physical abnormalities associated with an abnormal chromosome profile. A 9-yr-old male was studied at the University of Barcelona clinic. His karyotype showed 47 chromosomes, the extra small (fragment?) chromosome appearing in 15 repeated tests. Physical abnormalities of ears, eyes, and extremities were present. Metabolic tests of S and his parents' karyotypes were normal. 3 of 7 siblings, however, did not survive (2 abortions, 1 early death from leukemia). Possible origins of this metacentric 47th chromosome are discussed as well as its possible coincidental and noncausative appearance in the mentally retarded child. (French & English summaries)
Antich, Jaime & Sabater, Juan. (Autonomous U. Barcelona, Provincial Inst. of Clinical Biochemistry, Spain) Archivos de Neurobiología, 1971(Jul), Vol. 34(4), 315-324. [PA, Vol 49:09276]

326. Analysis of word frequencies in the spoken language of diverse groups.
Bakewell, Helene; Beier, Ernst G.; Lambert, Michael J. & Starkweather, John A. (U. Utah) Catalog of Selected Documents in Psychology, 1971(Fal), Vol. 1, 13. [PA, Vol 48:01026]

327. Use of the opposition concept and outerdirectedness in intellectually-average, familial retarded, and organically retarded children.
Assessed 288 intellectually-average, familial retarded, and organically retarded children of 4 MA levels for their ability to utilize the opposition concept in 1 of 3 experimental conditions. The retarded were found to be deficient in initial possession of the concept and in opposition concept usage, and to be more outerdirected. Organically retarded groups exhibited the most striking deficits on the concept measures and were most outerdirected. Initial possession of the concept was positively related to MA. Use of the opposition concept was related to experimental condition. The retarded Ss were found to be less efficient than the intellectually-average Ss in the transfer of the concept to other instances of opposites. (21 ref.)
Balla, David; Styfco, Sally J. & Zigler, Edward. (Yale U.) American Journal of Mental Deficiency, 1971(May), Vol. 75(6), 663-680. [PA, Vol 47:01451]

328. Formation of backward associations in paired-associates learning by normal children and retardates.
Compared the performances of normal and retarded children matched for MA on paired-associate (PA) learning tasks. In Exp. I, 128 Ss were stopped at different points in forward PA learning and tested for backward associations. Exp. II with 72 Ss compared unidirectional (A-B) and bidirectional (both A-B and

B-A) PA learning. Results indicate that forward learning was only slightly stronger than backward learning for both S groups, and backward association strength remained fairly constant over the course of PA learning. Conditional probability analysis revealed that complete associative symmetry did not characterize the PA learning of normal Ss and retardates. Both normal children and retardates appeared to learn as well spontaneously in the backward direction as they did when they were required to form bidirectional associations.
Baumeister, Alfred A. & Campbell, Cecil. (U. Alabama) Journal of Experimental Psychology, 1971(Aug), Vol. 89(2), 298-305. [PA, Vol 46:11392]

329. What the development of short-term memory is.
Development of memory depends upon changes in several mnemonic processes, which are illustrated in experiments with normal and mentally retarded adults and children, 16-30 and 9-14 yr. old, respectively. The principal focus is upon spontaneous learning strategies, including active rehearsal and specialized nonrehearsal, both of which are found to change systematically with age. There are developments in the relation of learning strategy to changing recall task demands. Finally, it appears that retrieval of rehearsed material is more rapid in older and more intelligent people, but this is not true for retrieval of nonrehearsed material.
Belmont, J. M. & Butterfield, E. C. (Yale U.) Human Development, 1971, Vol. 14(4), 236-248. [PA, Vol 47:10528]

330. Effects of pairing stimuli with reinforcement on multiple schedule performance of children.
Describes 2 experiments with 4 10-12 yr. old mentally retarded boys and 2 additional Ss chosen because their behavior in test components was similar. A nonsense word was paired with reinforcement to determine if pairing affected emission of a response that produced the word in the signalled absence of reinforcement. Ss were trained on a multiple schedule that consisted of a reinforcement component, conditioned reinforcement component, and control component, each set of contingencies being signalled by a different colored light. In the primary reinforcement component, lever presses produced reinforcers which, in some phases, were paired with a word. In the other 2 components, lever presses were not reinforced and a button was made accessible. Button presses in the conditioned reinforcement component produced the word to be (or being) paired, e.g., "yafeh," while button presses in the control component produced another word, e.g., "grunch." Button pressing increased when 1 of the words was being paired and decreased when pairing was discontinued, but directly related rate changes occurred also in the control component. The order of components was shown to be a contributing variable. (27 ref.)
Birnbrauger, J. S. (U. North Carolina, Chapel Hill) Journal of the Experimental Analysis of Behavior, 1971(Nov), Vol. 16(3), 355-365. [PA, Vol 47:11502]

331. Receptive vocabulary as a factor in the discrimination performance of low-functioning children.
3 groups of low-functioning children 1 receiving name training, 1 receiving no-name discrimination training, and the 3rd receiving no training were compared on a series of discrimination problems to determine the effects of denotative naming. A pretest, intervention, posttest design was used with random assignment of 30 institutionalized retardates to the 3 conditions. In Treatment 1, the color-form stimulus name served as a cue for choice; in Treatment 2, problem presentation occurred without naming; in Treatment 3, no intervening training was given. Although the training groups did not differ significantly on training and posttesting, both groups showed reliable improvement across training blocks and performed significantly better on the posttest than did the control Ss. Generalization testing also revealed a statistically reliable difference in favor of the trained groups.
Bricker, William A. & Bricker, Diane D. (George Peabody Coll. for Teachers, John F. Kennedy Center) American Journal of Mental Deficiency, 1971(Mar), Vol. 75(5), 599-605. [PA, Vol 46:05361]

332.   Self-mutilative behavior in the Cornelia de Lange syndrome.
Describes 3 female and 1 male adolescent patients with the Cornelia de Lange syndrome (Type II) in whom compulsive self-mutilation was a major feature. Each patient had a stereotyped pattern of abusive behavior in which there was repeated trauma to the same area. Together with data from 2 additional patients, results indicate that self-mutilation may represent a distinctive feature of this disorder. A relationship between organic disease and the expression of human behavior is suggested.
Bryson, Yvonne; Sakati, Nadia; Nyhan, William L. & Fish, Charles H. (U. California, San Diego) American Journal of Mental Deficiency, 1971(Nov), Vol. 76(3), 319-324. [PA, Vol 48:01506]

333.   [Epidemiologic investigation of metabolic oligophrenias in Cadiz.] (Span)
Describes an epidemiologic study in the province of Cadiz, Spain, conducted to determine the incidence of selected metabolic disorders among mentally-retarded children. Urine analyses for 1,310 children, aged 0-20, previously classified as subnormals, revealed 11 cases of metabolic dysfunction: 6 of phenylketonuria, 2 (brothers) of homocystinuria, and 3 of mucopolysaccharidosis. In 8 of these cases, IQ was 50 or below, with 4 of the 8 cases below 30. It is suggested that similar or more complete tests should be performed on newborns. (French & English summaries)
Calcedo Ordoñez, Alfredo & Fornell Forcades, Josefina. (Marina Hosp., Cadiz, Spain) Archivos de Neurobiología, 1971(May), Vol. 34(3), 209-218. [PA, Vol 49:00935]

334.   Use of the Queensland Test in the subnormal population.
Evaluates the Queensland Test (QT), a performance test in which neither examiner nor subject is required to speak, with subtests Knox cube, imitation test, beads test, passalong test, form assembly test, and pattern matching test. Usefulness of the QT for the subnormal population was investigated for both children and adults. Correlations between the QT and other well known tests of cognitive abilities (WAIS, WISC, Stanford-Binet Form L-M) are discussed with special emphasis on the intercorrelations of the QT subtests. Correlations between tests scores and teacher ratings also are discussed. Nonsignificant relationships for certain of the QT subtests, and the subnormal's poor performance in a situation in which there are reduced cues, suggest that the QT usefulness in this population may be mostly in predicting classroom performance. Correlations were highest with the WISC full scale and WISC performance scale.
Cartan, Sue. (Basil Stafford Training Centre, Wacol, Queensland, Australia) Australian Journal of Mental Retardation, 1971(Dec), Vol. 1(8), 231-234. [PA, Vol 48:09546]

335.   Structural aberrations of autosomes in a mentally retarded population.
Discovered structural autosomal aberrations in 9 of 217 children in a school for the mentally retarded. These include 1 balanced Robertsonian translocation (involving 2 D group chromosomes); 1 translocation Down's syndrome; 2 ring G chromosomes; deletion of the short arms of a B chromosome; deletion of both short and long arms of an E chromosome; elongated short arms on a D chromosome (B-D translocation); elongated long arms of a B chromosome; and a complex rearrangement apparently involving deletions of both long and short arms of a B and elongated short arms on an E chromosome. Familial transmission was observed in 2 of 6 cases in which both parents were studied. All Ss had rare deviant dermatoglyphic patterns. With the exception of the balanced carrier, all had at least 3 clinical anomalies in addition to the mental retardation, although the number and severity of the defects varied.
Corey, Margaret J.; Tischler, Bluma & Sandercock, Joyce. (P. O. Box 111, Nackawick, New Brunswick, Canada) American Journal of Mental Deficiency, 1971(Jan), Vol. 75(4), 487-498. [PA, Vol 46:03596]

336.   Color vision deficiency in the mentally retarded: Prevalence and a method of evaluation.
Recent studies have revealed a much higher prevalence of color vision deficiency in mentally retarded children than found in the nonretarded population. The AO-HRR Color Vision Test was administered to 39 trainable mentally retarded, 71 educable mentally retarded, and 107 emotionally disturbed children. The order of test-plate presentation was modified and a simple conditioning procedure was used as a teaching device where necessary. Using this method, prevalence rates and male-female ratios were no different than those found in the nonretarded population.
Courtney, G. R. & Heath, G. G. (Central State Hosp., Milledgeville, Ga.) American Journal of Mental Deficiency, 1971(Jul), Vol. 76(1), 48-52. [PA, Vol 47:07407]

337.   Amniocentesis: A means of pre-natal diagnosis of conditions associated with severe mental subnormality.
If fetal cells are obtained from the amniotic fluid in the 10th-18th wk. of pregnancy of a woman with high risk of bearing a subnormal child, diagnosis can lead to reassurance or the recommendation of therapeutic abortion. With amniocentesis, genetic counseling can move from quoting risk of recessive defects of 1 in 4 to positive prediction. This can result in relief from months of anxiety, and it is significant that mothers who have borne mongols are beginning to ask for amniocentesis when they become pregnant again.
Cowie, Valerie. (Queen Mary's Hosp. for Children, Carshalton, England) British Journal of Psychiatry, 1971(Jan), Vol. 118(542), 83-86. [PA, Vol 46:11373]

338.   Orientating responses of mentally retarded and normal subjects to word-signals.
Recorded the GSRs of 26 normal and 25 retarded children of comparable CA during a 30-min vigilance task, which consisted of 2 signal and 4 nonsignal words. 1 signal word served as a warning signal, preceding the other, which was an imperative signal for button-pressing. The warning signal evoked a greater number of GSRs in the normals than the imperative one; this was reversed for the retardates. GSR adaptation to signal words occurred at the same rate and level for both groups; but in adaptation to the nonsignal words the retardates maintained a higher level of GSR frequencies than the normals. The attentional deficit model of retardation is not supported by the findings. (15 ref.)
Das, J. P. & Bower, A. C. (U. Alberta, Centre for the Study of Mental Retardation, Edmonton, Canada) British Journal of Psychology, 1971(Feb), Vol. 62(1), 89-96. [PA, Vol 46:01705]

339.   The orienting reflex in intellectually average and retarded children to a relevant and an irrelevant stimulus.
Compared 15 intellectually average and 15 retarded males matched for CA on the digital blood volume component of the orienting reflex (OR) to 2 types of stimuli. In Phase 1, a relevant tone stimulus was presented alone 10 times. Significant orienting occurred in both groups, but there was no reliable evidence of habituation. In Phase 2, an irrelevant light stimulus was presented 10 times during the performance of a task. In accordance with the theorized filtering aspects of the OR, neither group oriented to the irrelevant stimulus. No differences between groups were found in the magnitude of the OR to the tone stimulus, a finding which fails to support the hypothesized weaker OR in retarded Ss. Results are discussed in terms of E. N. Sokolov's theory of the OR.
Elliot, Luke S. & Johnson, John T. (Memphis State U.) American Journal of Mental Deficiency, 1971(Nov), Vol. 76(3), 332-336. [PA, Vol 48:03541]

340.   Social competence of subnormal and normal children living under different types of residential care.
Compared 37 mentally subnormal 12-18 yr. olds, living under different types of hospital care or in the community, with 20 normal 5-6 yr. olds, living in an orphanage or in their own homes, to determine possible differences in social competence. Ss completed the Stanford-Binet Intelligence Scale, Peabody Picture

Vocabulary Test, Vineland Social Maturity Scale, and the Progress Assessment Chart. Results indicate that subnormals living in the community had more social skills and higher verbal abilities than those under different types of residential care, and that long-stay inpatients were inferior to short-stay patients. There was no significant difference in the social efficiency of the 2 groups of normals. (22 ref.)
Elliott, R. & MacKay, D. N. (Muckamore Abbey Hosp., Ireland) British Journal of Mental Subnormality, 1971(Jun), Vol. 17(32, Pt. 1), 48-53. [PA, Vol 47:11471]

341.   Attitudes towards a photograph of a mildly and severely mentally retarded child.
Examined the attitudes of the general public towards the phenotype of a severely and mildly mentally retarded child. Ss were 80 female clerical office workers. The severely retarded child was viewed far more negatively on the Overall scale of the Osgood Semantic Differential than the mildly retarded child. Results are discussed and recommendations are made for professional personnel who work with retarded children. (18 ref.)
English, R. William & Palla, David A. (Syracuse U., Clinical Activities in Rehabilitation Counselor Education) Training School Bulletin, 1971(May), Vol. 68(1), 55-63. [PA, Vol 47:05470]

342.   An objective approach to measurement of interpersonal behavior in phenylketonuria.
Evaluated 43 children with phenylketonuria (PKU) by a structured interaction procedure, and compared results with those obtained from 2 control samples (n = 26). PKU children, judged to be emotionally disturbed and inadequate in communication from independent impressions during psychological testing, performed more poorly than those judged nondisturbed and more adequate in communication under 2 of the 3 social stimulus interaction conditions. PKU Ss who manifested extreme patterns of activity were not significantly different in their interactional behavior from PKU Ss who demonstrated normal activity levels. Differences in interaction behavior were obtained between PKU Ss and normal controls similar on socioeconomic variables.
Friedman, C. J.; Sibinga, M. S.; Steisel, I. M. & Baker, E. C. (Temple U., Medical School) Journal of Consulting & Clinical Psychology, 1971(Oct), Vol. 37(2), 224-227. [PA, Vol 47:09502]

343.   The use of a rating scale for oral behavior in children.
Utilized an oral scale based on B. A. Ruttenberg, M. D. Dratman, J. Fraknoi, and C. Wenar's (see PA, Vol. 40:12457) Behavioral Rating Inventory for Autistic Children, to study 4 categories of oral behavior: pre-oral, oral sucking, oral biting, and oral traits. Observations were made of 32 latency-age male inpatients in a large psychiatric hospital. Ss fell into 4 diagnostic groups: psychotic, retarded and brain damaged, character disordered, and neurotic. Observations were made of all Ss on a monthly basis by nurses and child care workers, over a period of 1 yr. by simply rating the presence or absence of behavior itemized on a checklist. By using rating scales, quantitative measures of behavior of large groups of children can be obtained over a protracted period by untrained Os. This study has demonstrated the presence of primitive oral behavior along with more mature oral behavior in psychotic Ss. It is suggested that scales for measurement of other types of behavior, both libidinal and aggressive, can be developed in a similar fashion.
Graff, Harold & Areonowitz, Albert. (Eastern Pennsylvania Psychiatric Inst., Philadelphia) Child Psychiatry & Human Development, 1971(Sum), Vol. 1(4), 233-242. [PA, Vol 49:04702]

344.   Language behavior of the mentally retarded: Syntactic characteristics.
Language samples from 9 mentally retarded Ss with CAs ranging from 10-18 yr. and MAs ranging from 3.6-10 yr. were analyzed syntactically. Results indicate that certain indices of linguistic sophistication and Ss' MAs were correlated. It was tentatively hypothesized that nonmongoloid retardates develop rules of their language at a different rate but in much the same way as intellectually-average children.

Graham, James T. & Graham, Louella W. (Emory U.) American Journal of Mental Deficiency, 1971(Mar), Vol. 75(5), 623-629. [PA, Vol 46:05348]

345.   [Meaning troubles in mentally deficient children.] (Fren)
Describes a follow-up study in which problems of understanding symbols and meanings were considered in mentally retarded children. Ss in the previous study were 21 11-12 yr. old children whose retardation could not be assigned to an organic origin. In the present study, 6 male and 4 female 11-12 yr. olds whose retardation was due to organic lesions were chosen. Elaborating clinical and theoretical frameworks, the importance of familial data, including anamnestic, socioeconomic, and cultural information, as well as personal histories, was stressed. Analyses and interpretations are made of both S groups with regard to (a) intelligence tests (WISC); (b) operational processes; (c) perception, spatial organization, and mental images; (d) language; and (e) symbolic functioning and projective test performance (Rorschach, TAT). Emphasis is on structural organization, biological and symbolic, and several hypotheses are presented based on clinical data and recent literature. Although no definite explanation of etiology is formed, functioning problems of the Ss' secondary processes are studied in relation to biological dynamics and fantasy elaboration. (29 ref.)
Guignard, Florence, et al.   Psychiatrie de l'Enfant, 1971, Vol. 14(1), 125-231. [PA, Vol 50:05069]

346.   The discrimination learning of normal and retarded children as a function of penalty conditions and etiology of the retarded.
Administered a size-discrimination task to MA-matched normal, familial retarded, and organically retarded children under 2 conditions: (a) reward only, where Ss were reinforced for correct choices; and (b) reward + penalty, where ss were reinforced for correct responses and penalized for incorrect responses. Results indicate that both normal and familial retarded ss showed better learning in the reward + penalty than in the reward only condition, whereas organic retarded Ss did not. In the reward + penalty condition there were significantly fewer learners among the organics than among either the normals or familials. An analysis of the underlying response strategies reveals that normals and familials engaged in more strategy behavior in the reward + penalty than in the reward only condition. No such condition difference was found for the organics. Organic nonlearners employed position preference response sets to a significantly greater degree than either normals or familials who did not differ from each other. (32 ref.)
Harter, Susan; Brown, Lynn & Zigler, Edward. (Yale U.) Child Development, 1971(Jun), Vol. 42(2), 517-536. [PA, Vol 47:01472]

347.   [The serotonin blood content in different forms of mental retardation.] (Russ)
Measured the content of serotonin in the blood plasma of 59 7-17 yr old children with sthenic, asthenic (including cases with congenital cataracts), and atonic forms of oligophrenia. A significant rise in the content of serotonin was found in the asthenic form of oligophrenia. Research on the content of serotonin after the introduction of reserpine into the blood gives reason to suppose that an increase in the level of serotonin in the peripheral blood in cases of oligophrenia is related to the decrease in the activity of MAO.
Isaev, D. N. & Mikirtumov, B. E. (Leningrad Medical Pediatrics Inst., Central Scientific Research Lab., Ussr) Zhurnal Nevropatologii i Psikhiatrii, 1971, Vol. 71(5), 741-744. [PA, Vol 47:07411]

348.   Use of the von Restorff effect to condition rehearsal in retarded children.
Assessed the feasibility of using the von Restorff effect to condition rehearsal in 50 retarded 7-14 yr. olds. It was hypothesized that isolation would have a significant facilitatory effect on the primacy and middle segments of a serial task for retarded Ss. Further, it was predicted that this facilitative effect would generalize to a transfer task containing no isolated items.

Findings support the hypotheses and suggest that a fruitful way of approaching the behavioral inadequacy of the retarded individual might be the systematic training of rehearsal. (15 ref.)
Jacobs, J. Walter & Foshee, Donald P. (U. Alabama) American Journal of Mental Deficiency, 1971(Nov), Vol. 76(3), 313-318. [PA, Vol 48:03569]

349. Special characteristics of retarded children rated as severely hyperactive.
Matched 94 pairs of retarded children (mean age 11.3 yr.) for age and year of examination. Hyperactivity was rated as no problem in 1 S in each pair and as a severe problem in the other S. Findings indicate a higher incidence of CNS damage and/or dysfunction in Ss who were hyperactive than in those who were not. Of 6 cases of hemiplegia, all were in the hyperactive group as were 7 of 8 cases of diplegia. A significantly larger proportion of the hyperactives had a history of convulsive seizures, and significantly more had a residual speech defect.
Jenkins, Richard L. & Stable, Galen. (U. Iowa) Child Psychiatry & Human Development, 1971(Fal), Vol. 2(1), 26-31. [PA, Vol 49:07184]

350. [The clinico-roentgenological diagnosis of microcephaly.] (Russ)
Presents a clinico-roentgenological investigation of 34 children with microcephalic conditions. It was established that primary microcephaly (i.e., hereditary) is characterized by a significant diminution in the proportions of the cranium and the presence of hypertension in some cases. In secondary microcephaly the clinico-roentgenological changes are very polymorphic. 4 types of secondary microcephaly are described: (a) microcephaly with fine bones of the cranial vault, (b) microcephaly with a thickening of the cranial vault, (c) microcephaly with hydrocephaly, and (d) microcephaly in combination with craniostosis and brain atrophy. This type of clinico-roentgenological differentiation permits a more accurate diagnosis of microcephaly in its various forms and permits a more individualized clinical evaluation for each case of the disorder.
Knyazeva, M. P. & Malakhovskaya, M. S. Zhurnal Nevropatologii i Psikhiatrii, 1971, Vol. 71(5), 744-748. [PA, Vol 47:07366]

351. Oral and limb apraxia in mentally retarded children with deviant articulation.
Developed and administered a children's version of the De Renzi, Pieczuro, and Vignolo Test for Oral and Limb Apraxia to 33 children of normal intelligence with articulatory disorders, and 30 retarded children and adults with defective articulation matched in MA with the nonretardates. The retarded group was also divided into 2 etiological categories, organic and nonorganic, based on diagnosis of the residential institution. Results indicate significant between-group differences, with the organic retardates exhibiting significant degrees of apraxia as defined by the test. Nonorganic retardates exhibited significant, but less, apraxic involvement. Correlational techniques revealed no significant association of apraxia with defective articulation, but an association of apraxia with vocabulary MA and intelligence.
Kools, Joseph A.; Williams, Amanda F.; Vickers, Marjorie J. & Caell, Ann. (U. Georgia) Cortex, 1971(Dec), Vol. 7(4), 387-400. [PA, Vol 49:11425]

352. Association and abstraction as mechanisms of imitative learning.
Examined children's ability to recall the commodity preferences of an adult model in a 2 (common dimension vs. no common dimension of the modeled responses) × 2 (number of modeled responses: 6 or 18) × 2 (sex of an S) factorial design. The presence of a common dimension did not increase the number of items recalled by Ss who had observed only 6 responses, but clearly facilitated the recall of those for whom 18 responses had been modeled. 96 boys and 96 girls, both normal and retarded, were Ss. Response latencies were shorter for the common dimension groups than for their no common dimension counterparts regardless of the number of modeled responses that were to be recalled. Results are consistent with the view that, under specifiable circumstances, children's imitative recall may be

mediated by an abstraction process rather than exclusively by associative learning. (15 ref.)
Liebert, Robert M. & Swenson, Sharon A. (State U. New York, Stony Brook) Developmental Psychology, 1971(Mar), Vol. 4(2), 289-294. [PA, Vol 45:10543]

353. [Visual deficiency and mental deficiency.] (Fren)
Analyzes elements common to children who suffer both visual and mental defects. Those with relatively high intelligence generally have a visual acuity of less than 1-10. These Ss display obvious difficulty in motor tests, and are usually of calm, passive, and introverted character. It is noted that differences exist between those who are blind from birth and those who later become blind, the former being better able to cope with their handicap. Parents' attitudes play a primary role in this context, because serious relational difficulties are present in these doubly handicapped children. A concrete adaptation of L. Corman's "Patte Noir" test is demonstrated, suggesting new perspectives in the exploration of blind children's personalities. (German & Spanish summaries)(26 ref.)
Lissonde, B. & Porot, M. (U. Clermont-Ferrand, Neurological & Psychiatric Clinic, France) Revue de Neuropsychiatrie Infantile et d'Hygiene Mentale de l'Enfance, 1971(Jan), Vol. 19(1-2), 1-19. [PA, Vol 49:07221]

354. Early detection of the apparently retarded child: Psychological and behavioural aspects.
Deals with the issue of early detection of the mentally retarded, from the developmental diagnosis viewpoint. Studies have indicated that generally, correlations are low between results of infant scales and those administered later. However, many studies have shown that those individuals identified as mentally retarded by infant scales tend to show retardation on scales administered later. A research study was made with a small group of children referred to an outpatient clinic for the intellectually handicapped before age of 2 yr. old, and subsequently reassessed. Again the findings of the infant scales tended to be reaffirmed by the later assessment. Only 1 case was "badly overestimated," and 8 cases "overestimated" and 1 "underestimated" by the infant scales. It is concluded that there is utility in these infant scales for early identification of the mentally retarded. Sources of probable error in the results of the infant scales are to be found in the variables surrounding the "testing" session itself strange examiner and surroundings as well as problems in the instrument itself.
Macbeth, Neil J. (Gosvenor Hosp., Summer Hill, New South Wales, Australia) Australian Journal of Mental Retardation, 1971(Sep), Vol. 1(7), 224-228. [PA, Vol 48:01516]

355. Operant measurement of subjective visual acuity in nonverbal children.
Examined 5 nonverbal retarded children and 2 literate adults to develop a reliable procedure for measuring visual acuity in nonverbal retarded children. The adults were included in the experiment so that verbal communication with them could validate certain assumptions regarding the experimental procedures. By utilizing a lever press as the criterion response signifying a visual discrimination and employing the Snellen "E" discriminanda, a reliable subjective measure was obtained, not unlike those measures taken from verbal adults. Contrary to several antecedent procedures, a relatively precise measurement of subjective acuity was obtainable from the nonverbal Ss. Additionally, the procedure was successful in evaluating the effectiveness of prosthetic lenses previously prescribed for 2 of the children. (24 ref.)
Macht, Joel. (U. Denver) Journal of Applied Behavior Analysis, 1971(Spr), Vol. 4(1), 23-36. [PA, Vol 47:01460]

356. Normal and retarded children's expectancy for failure.
Administered a series of block designs, ½ of which were interrupted prior to completion to 60 normal and 60 retarded children. Ss were divided among 3 instructional conditions which defined interruption as success, failure, or neutral. Repetition choice was noted and Ss were asked why certain tasks had not been finished. Interruption was perceived differently by normals

and retardates. Retardates perceived interruption as personal failure, normals did not. Although retardates exhibited a success orientation on repetition choice under the success condition, interruption was still seen as due to personal inadequacies.
MacMillan, Donald L. & Keogh, Barbara K. (U. California, School of Education, Riverside) Developmental Psychology, 1971(May), Vol. 4(3), 343-348. [PA, Vol 46:07328]

357.   Oddity learning following object-discrimination learning in mentally retarded children.
Presented 48 mentally retarded children with a 3-choice object-discrimination problem in which color or form was the relevant dimension. Ss were transferred to a 2nd object-discrimination problem or an oddity problem. The relevant dimension in the 2nd object discrimination was either the same as in training (intradimensional shift) or was that which was irrelevant during training (extradimensional shift). Similarly, the relevant vehicle dimension of the oddity problem was either relevant (intradimensional-oddity shift) or irrelevant (extradimensional-oddity shift) in training. The typical dimensional transfer effects were present in both the discrimination problem (intradimensional easier than extradimensional) and in the oddity problem (intradimensional-oddity easier than extradimensional-oddity). The latter findings are related to an extension of the D. Zeaman and B. J. House attention theory of discrimination learning.
Martin, Andrew S. & Tyrrell, Donald J. (U. Connecticut) American Journal of Mental Deficiency, 1971(Jan), Vol. 75(4), 504-509. [PA, Vol 46:03634]

358.   Comparability of WISC and PPVT scores among young children.
Administered the WISC and the Peabody Picture Vocabulary Test (PPVT) to 78 preschoolers. Despite significant correlations between the WISC and PPVT IQ scores, comparison of the scores for each child showed little agreement on gross classifications of intelligence. In general, the PPVT IQ scores tended to underestimate the Verbal, Performance, and Full Scale IQ scores of the WISC and to overestimate the incidence of mental retardation. It is concluded that testing young children with the PPVT as the measure of intelligence is of dubious value for research and clinical applications.
Matheny, Adam P. (U. Louisville, Medical School) Exceptional Children, 1971(Oct), Vol. 38(2), 147-150. [PA, Vol 48:03673]

359.   Sex and the mentally retarded.
Presents a selective review of the literature on sexuality among persons labeled as mentally retarded (MR). Topics covered include maturation, role behavior, contraception, marriage and parenthood, family, and sex education. It is noted that MR children take longer to mature sexually as well as in other ways. They are handicapped by limited coping, conceptual, and adaptive skills, and by isolation from normal peers. It is suggested that reports of "abnormal" sexuality result from MRs getting caught openly doing what others do, and condone, in private. Suggestions are given for sex education and other guidance appropriate for MR children. (46 ref.)
Meyerowitz, Joseph H. (Baylor Coll. of Medicine, Houston, Tex.) Medical Aspects of Human Sexuality, 1971(Nov), Vol. 5(11), 94-118. [PA, Vol 49:04790]

360.   [Tentative psychopathological approach to intellectual deficiency: Dysharmonic deficiencies.] (Fren)
Studies evolutive structures to gain insight into the dimension of deficiency spanning diverse modalities of mental functioning and relational activity. Under the term "dysharmonic deficiencies," morbid types are described, e.g., intellectual weakness, relational disturbances, instrumental problems. The theory of an evolutive structuration possessing an essential trait, common to all varieties of mental deficiency, is proposed. Previously established methodological principles used in the treatment of mentally deficient children are questioned. The individualization of dysharmonic deficiencies is attributed to evolutive dysharmony and to those corresponding to nonevolutive, classical origins. Based on observations of 3 mentally deficient children, suggestions are made for a new battery of tests, designed to uncover a variety of efficiency levels in intellectual functioning and concentrate on specificity. (35 ref.)
Mises, R. & Perron-Borelli, M. Psychiatrie de l'Enfant, 1971, Vol. 14(2), 341-464. [PA, Vol 50:07057]

361.   Development of time concepts in normal and retarded children.
Tested 18 normal and 18 retarded children, matched for MA at 3 levels (6, 9, and 11), for understanding of the time concepts of (a) simultaneity, (b) equality of synchronous intervals, and (c) order of events. For both groups, active ordering of observed events was more difficult than understanding of simultaneity or of equality of synchronous intervals. Understanding increased steadily with increases in MA, and a sequential order of development in time concepts was indicated. Ss at lower MAs understood simultaneity and equality of synchronous intervals better than active ordering of events, whereas at higher MAs these concepts were understood essentially equally. Results suggest a slower rate of development by retardates than by normals. Unequivocal acceptance of this finding was cautioned against due to confounding of IQ with MA level in the retarded Ss.
Montroy, Pheryl; McManis, Donald & Bell, Donald. (Eastern Washington State Coll.) Psychological Reports, 1971(Jun), Vol. 28(3), 895-902. [PA, Vol 46:11396]

362.   Perceptual-motor attributes of mental retardates: A factor analytic study.
Administered 19 items of the Purdue Perceptual-Motor Survey to 99 mentally retarded Ss (mean CA 17.4 yr. and mean IQ 52.3). Factor analyses of the item scores of the total sample, and of a subgroup of 66 nonmongoloid Ss, led to the definition of 7 factors: (a) postural dimensionality, (b) shoulder-arm movement, (c) laterality, (d) ocular control, (e) intelligence, (f) developmental, and (g) possibly cultural sex bias. Similar factor structures emerged for the total sample, and for the nonmongoloid subgroup, with the exception of Factor (e), intelligence. Results generally agree with previous correlational analyses of comparable samples and tend to support the construct validity of the Purdue Perceptual-Motor Survey methodology as applied to the mentally retarded. (25 ref.)
Neeman, Renate L. (State U. New York, Buffalo) Perceptual & Motor Skills, 1971(Dec), Vol. 33(3, Pt. 1), 927-934. [PA, Vol 48:01519]

363.   Perceptual-motor attributes of mental retardates: II. Manipulative dexterity and perceptual-motor abilities of mentally retarded adolescents and young adults.
Administered the Purdue Perceptual-Motor Survey (PP-MS), the O'Connor Finger Dexterity Test, and the Purdue Pegboard to 53 15-32 yr. old retardates. Results support the hypothesis of pronounced interrelations between all manipulative dexterity test variables and 13 of the 19 PP-MS items applied. With the exception of 2 PP-MS items, these results cannot be interpreted as the sole reflection of direct associations between perceptual-motor abilities and dexterity, because of significant interrelations of item variables with the background variables IQ and sex. (19 ref.)
Neeman, Renate L. (Cantalician Center Workshop, Buffalo, N.Y.) American Journal of Occupational Therapy, 1971(Sep), Vol. 25(6), 309-312. [PA, Vol 49:10347]

364.   The cat cry syndrome (5p-) in adolescents and adults.
Presents clinical findings for 5 females and 3 males, all over 15 yr. old. The cat cry was described as a weak, monotonous and plaintive cry accompanied by stridor. Autoradiographic chromosome investigations revealed a partial deletion of the short arm of a B-group chromosome in all Ss. The deleted chromosome belonged to pair no. 5. An unsteady, broad-based gait, malocclusion of the overbite type with forward slanting of the upper incisors and thoraco-lumbar scoliosis was observed. Radiographic examination revealed large and prominent frontal sinuses and shortness of some meta carpals or metatarsals. (31 ref.)

Niebuhr, E. (John F. Kennedy Inst., Glostrup, Denmark) Journal of Mental Deficiency Research, 1971(Dec), Vol. 15(4), 277-291. [PA, Vol 50:11565]

365.   Information-processing limitations of mentally retarded children.
Attempted to measure the channel capacity, i.e., the amount of visual information that could be apprehended and used by 10 nonretarded, 20 educable mentally retarded, and 20 trainable mentally retarded children. This value, which reached an asymptote and 2.5 bits, was found to be a function of the degree of retardation when CA was held constant (CAS ≅ 5 yr.), but not when MA was held constant (MAS ≅ 5 yr.). Analysis of the error matrix showed that shape cues tended to be the most easily processed, while processing of color and size cues was more difficult. Suggestions are made for finding the "bottlenecks" in information processing by tracing the flow of information as Ss attempt to solve a cognitive problem. (18 ref.)
Olson, David R. (Ontario Inst. for Studies in Education, Toronto, Canada) American Journal of Mental Deficiency, 1971(Jan), Vol. 75(4), 478-486. [PA, Vol 46:03616]

366.   The future of the cerebral palsied child.
A typical population of cerebral palsied children in the United States included 33% who were mentally normal and nearly self-sufficient, 25% who showed mainly mental retardation with minimal physical handicaps, 25% with serious physical or mental handicaps who required custodial care, and 5% who were mentally bright but with marked physical defects.
O'Reilly, D. Elliott. (St. Louis U., Medical School) Developmental Medicine & Child Neurology, 1971(Oct), Vol. 13(5), 635-640. [PA, Vol 48:07615]

367.   Subclinical "electrical status epilepticus" induced by sleep in children.
6 7-12 yr old Ss showed dramatic modification of EEG patterns involving continuous generalized spike and wave discharges that continued throughout sleep and that subsided in waking. The subclinical condition, termed electrical status epilepticus, did not disturb the biological cycles of sleep. For 5 of 6 Ss, the condition subsided during REM periods. All Ss were mentally retarded, with degree of retardation directly proportional to age of seizure onset. A striking feature of the condition was total lack of speech in 2 Ss and severe delay in 2 others. Absence or rarity of nocturnal seizures in the reported cases suggests no relationship occurring between nocturnal seizures and the degree of activation of spike and wave discharges. While just 1 S had a family history of seizures, consanguinity was present in 2, and evidence of probable birth trauma appeared in 3 Ss. The condition is believed to be a form of encephalopathy secondary to a focal or multifocal brain lesion. (25 ref.)
Patry, George; Lyagoubi, Souad & Tassinari, C. Alberto. (Hôtel-Dieu du Sacré-Coeur, Quebec, Canada) Archives of Neurology, 1971(Mar), Vol. 24(3), 242-252. [PA, Vol 47:03542]

368.   Pseudostoicism in mothers of the retarded.
Studied the nature of Parent × Child interactions as they affect the retarded child. 3 groups of mothers were identified: (a) those who experience little pain having been immunized by intellectual constriction or emotional limitations; (b) those in whom anxieties and conflicts are stirred, but who handle them with a variety of well-known defenses; and (c) the pseudostoical mothers who fuse the fact of having a retarded child into other intrapsychic mechanisms so that it operates, as it were, in the service of the ego.
Polansky, Norman A.; Boone, Donald R.; DeSaix, Christine & Sharlin, Shlomo A. (U. Georgia) Social Casework, 1971(Dec), Vol. 52(10), 643-650. [PA, Vol 48:01521]

369.   Responding of retarded children on a backscratch schedule of reinforcement.
"In the Backscratch Fixed Ratio (FR) 15 (1 token was dispensed for each 15 lever-presses), the rate of responding for 3 of the 4 Ss declined rapidly; and, eventually, they virtually stopped responding. When the Ss were returned to the Independent FR 15 condition (in the presence of another child rather than alone),

their rates recovered to their former levels. The Ss were then re-exposed to the Backscratch FR 15 condition. During re-exposure, responding was maintained and Ss received about as many reinforcers as they gave. Recovery of responding during the 2nd exposure of the Backscratch FR 15 schedule may be related to the communication that developed between Ss during the course of the experiment and to the carry-over effects of re-exposure to the Independent FR 15 schedule."
Powers, Richard B. & Powers, Elki. (Utah State U.) Psychological Aspects of Disability, 1971(Mar), Vol. 18(1), 27-34. [PA, Vol 47:01478]

370.   Growth hormone investigation in patients with mental dysfunction.
Determined human growth hormone (HGH) responses in 73 Ss affected with various forms of mental retardation, or with emotional disturbance with normal intelligence and abnormal growth. Ss were stimulated by insulin hypoglycemia and arginine infusion. 4 Ss exhibited absent or impaired pituitary hormone secretion and 1 of the 4 presented a unique syndrome of panhypopituitarism associated with intrauterine growth retardation, long eyelashes and eyebrows, sparse hair, and degeneration of the retina. Statistical analysis indicated no significant HGH peak concentrations in groups of either tall males or stunted females who possessed various sex chromosome abnormalities, nor did these groups differ in a variety of clinical parameters including age, physical growth, birth weight, and intelligence. (French summary) (17 ref.)
Pozsonyi, J. & Friesen, H. (Children's Psychiatric Research Inst., London, Ontario, Canada) Canadian Medical Association Journal, 1971(Jan), Vol. 104(1), 26-29. [PA, Vol 45:10022]

371.   Interhemispheric asymmetries of evoked cortical responses in retarded and normal children.
Visual and auditory evoked cortical responses (VECRs and AECRs) were measured in 8 mentally retarded and 6 normal children at 3 interstimulus intervals (ISIs): .5, 1, and 2 sec. VECR amplitudes were greater in the right than in the left hemisphere for the normals, while the opposite relationship between hemispheres was found for the retardates. The maximum positive deflection of the VECR had a longer latency in the left than in the right hemisphere for normals, an asymmetry not found for retardates. Neither AECR amplitudes nor latencies differed for normals and retardates. AECR amplitudes increased with increasing ISIs. The present results, in conjunction with data of previous studies, further demonstrate the relevance of investigating amplitude and latency relations of the evoked cortical response as a function of cerebral hemisphere, as well as the variables of modality, ISI, and degree of verbal content, in the efforts to elucidate the mechanisms of mental retardation.
Richlin, Milton, et al. (New York Medical Coll., Neuropsychological Lab. & Center for Mental Retardation, New York) Cortex, 1971(Mar), Vol. 7(1), 98-105. [PA, Vol 47:07419]

372.   An analysis of right hemispheric deficits in the moderately retarded child as measured by the WISC and Leiter.
Administered the WISC and the Leiter International Performance Scale (LIPS) to 4 groups of 10 Ss: (a) no brain damage, (b) diffuse brain damage, (c) right hemispherical damage, and (d) left hemispherical damage. Abnormalities dated from birth or infancy. Results indicate that the LIPS was as sensitive to right hemisphere damage as the WISC and was especially sensitive to right temporal lobe damage. (17 ref.)
Rubino, C. A.; Krocco, D. & Shea, M. (Mental Retardation Center, Toronto, Ontario, Canada) Ontario Psychologist, 1971, Vol. 3(2), 85-95. [PA, Vol 47:09488]

373.   Reinforcement and generalization of productive plural allomorphs in two retarded children.
Examined the extent to which differential reinforcement can control the acquisition of plural allomorphs in 2 retarded females. In Condition 1, 1 S was trained with reinforcement procedures on a list of words calling for the /-s/ allomorph. She was then given unreinforced probe items to determine the extent of generalization to words calling for the /-z/ allomorph. In

Condition 2, the procedures were reversed and S was trained on /-z/ list and probed for generalization of /-z/ to words calling for /-s/. A 2nd S was exposed to the same conditions in the opposite order. Results lend unequivocal support for the hypothesis of generalized training effects. It is concluded that appropriate usage of the linguistic response class "plurals" is susceptible to generalized training effects of differential reinforcement.
Sailor, Wayne. (Kansas Neurological Inst., Topeka) Journal of Applied Behavior Analysis, 1971(Win), Vol. 4(4), 305-310. [PA, Vol 48:05487]

374.   [Study on adaptive behavior of mentally subnormal.] (Japn)
Examines the nature of adaptive behavior (consisting of social maturity and human relationship) as it applies to mentally and physically handicapped children with respect to their prospects for being accepted as members of their community and participating in its social life. Noting that the social maturity of mental subnormal (MS) adults is more developed than that of MS children, the role of environmental influence is considered. Expert guidance stressing behavioral therapy is seen as a very influential factor in helping MS children to adjust. Moreover, it is suggested that intelligence should not be the standard for community acceptability. Changes in the community value system as well as in the methods of educating and training MS children are considered necessary.
Sakurai, Yoshiro. (National Inst. of Mental Health, Chiba, Japan) Journal of Mental Health, 1971(Mar), No. 19, 71-91. [PA, Vol 48:03557]

375.   Helping behavior among normal and retarded children.
Developed a framework applicable to prosocial behavior. Distinctions between psychological vs. task helping and attempted vs. achieved help were applied to the helping behaviors of 3-5 and 8-10 yr. old normal ($n = 30$) and retarded ($n = 25$) Ss observed in natural settings. Contrary to expectation, older normals were not more helpful than younger normals or retardates. Raw frequencies of helping behavior were greater for younger normals and older retardates who had many opportunities for helping. When opportunities were controlled, older retardates attempted to help more than any other group and succeeded in helping as often. (16 ref.)
Severy, Lawrence J. & Davis, Keith E. (U. Colorado) Child Development, 1971(Oct), Vol. 42(4), 1017-1031. [PA, Vol 48:03559]

376.   Analysis of performances by normals and retardates on Piagetian reasoning assessments as a function of verbal ability.
Administered a battery of 29 reasoning assessments and the WISC or WAIS vocabulary subtest and verbal IQ to 75 normals and 75 retardates, 6-18 yr. old. Analyses of covariance were performed to determine the effect of language development on cognitive development. In general, results support Piaget's contention that cognitive development is not totally dependent on concurrent language development.
Stephens, Beth & McLaughlin, John A. (Temple U.) Perceptual & Motor Skills, 1971(Jun), Vol. 32(3), 868-870. [PA, Vol 47:03556]

377.   Equivalence formation by mentally retarded and nonretarded children using pictorial and printed word stimulus items.
Compared 24 mentally retarded and 24 equal-MA normal children to determine the relative effects of pictorial and printed-word stimulus items on the use of (a) perceptible, (b) functional, and (c) quasi-equivalence groupings in an equivalence-formation task. Results indicate that both groups used perceptible groupings more frequently with pictorial than with word stimulus items. Functional groupings were used less frequently by mentally retarded Ss for both stimulus items. Although all Ss used more quasi-equivalence groupings for word stimulus items, mentally retarded Ss exhibited a disproportionately high frequency of these groupings. Based on J. Bruner's ideas concerning cognitive development, findings suggest that mentally retarded Ss are below MA expectancy in conceptualizing the action qualities of the stimulus environment.

Stephens, Wyatt E.; Nopar, Richard A. & Gillam, Lynn D. (Southern Illinois U.) American Journal of Mental Deficiency, 1971(Sep), Vol. 76(2), 252-256. [PA, Vol 47:09521]

378.   Chromosome studies in a mental deficiency hospital: Total ascertainment.
Conducted a chromosome study of the total population of a hospital for mental deficiency. Most children were severely or profoundly retarded. Results show that apart from Down's syndrome, chromosome abnormalities do not play a significant role in the etiology of mental defect. No sex chromosome abnormalities were detected. These results constrast markedly with a total ascertainment study of a male mental deficient security ward in which the patients ranged from borderline to moderately retarded.
Sutherland, Grant R. & Wiener, Saul. (Royal Hosp. for Sick Children, Edinburgh, Scotland) Australian Journal of Mental Retardation, 1971(Dec), Vol. 1(8), 246-247. [PA, Vol 48:09562]

379.   The language characteristics of hyperverbal hydrocephalic children.
Tested 11 2½-9 yr. old children with spina bifida and a history of hydrocephalus, using the Illinois Test of Psycholinguistic Abilities (ITPA). All Ss were considered clinically to be hyperverbal and had undergone a shunting procedure for hydrocephalus. Through matching with nonhydrocephalic children of similar age and histories of hospitalization, the hydrocephalic Ss showed 1 or more of the following: (a) hyperverbality, (b) inappropriate language use, or (c) an ITPA profile indicating superficiality of language output.
Swisher, Linda P. & Pinsker, Esther J. (Central Inst. for the Deaf, St. Louis, Mo.) Developmental Medicine & Child Neurology, 1971(Dec), Vol. 13(6), 746-755. [PA, Vol 48:07620]

380.   Mental retardation and dyslexia.
Exceptional children may not be immune to dyslexia. Dyslexia may be an important factor in any grouping of exceptionality.
Thompson, Lloyd J. (U. North Carolina, Chapel Hill) Academic Therapy, 1971(Sum), Vol. 6(4), 405-406. [PA, Vol 46:11552]

381.   [Tolerance and stability of parents of the backward child.] (Fren)
Discusses 2 ideas of critical importance in working with parents of backward children, especially in cases where the parents are rejecting or hyperprotective: tolerance or the attitude which maximizes the integration of the backward child into the family, and family stability or the quality which protects the needs and desires of all members of the family. The concept of levels of tolerance and stability are elaborated and the difficulty of estimating these levels are discussed. Ways of communicating with parents, including working through levels of tolerance and stability, to help them accept and nurture backward children are emphasized.
Tomkiewicz, S. Bulletin de Psychologie, 1971, Vol. 25(18), 1040-1047. [PA, Vol 49:09481]

382.   Discrimination learning in mentally retarded and nonretarded children as a function of the number of relevant dimensions.
Reports an experiment with 48 retarded children (mean IQ = 58.8) and 48 nonretarded children (mean IQ = 98) of equal MA (6 yr.). 12 Ss from each IQ group had either 1, 2, 4, or 8 relevant dimensions in a 2-choice visual discrimination task. Results indicate an inverse relationship between the number of relevant dimensions and the number of errors made by both nonretarded and retarded Ss. Retarded Ss made more errors overall. However, no support was found for the hypothesis that observed facilitation would be relatively greater for retarded Ss. Results are discussed in terms of the Zeaman and House attention theory.
Ullman, Douglas G. & Routh, Donald K. (U. Iowa) American Journal of Mental Deficiency, 1971(Sep), Vol. 76(2), 176-180. [PA, Vol 47:09524]

383. [A study on the concept attainment processes of mentally retarded children: Effects of abstractness of learning materials.] (Japn)
Studied the process of abstract concept attainment (Exp I) and the proactive effects of previously attained concepts on later discrimination reversal shift (Exp II) in mentally retarded and normal children. In Exp I, 11 retarded Ss (IQ 60-78) and 10 normal Ss (IQ 95-104) were matched in terms of mental age (MA) (mean = 8.5 yrs). 6 concepts of 15 sets of 3 categories (concrete objects, forms, and numbers) were named by 6 nonsense syllables. Concept attainment was evaluated through 15 series of trials. Results indicate that the retarded required more trials to attain concepts, especially forms and numbers ($p < .01$). In Exp II, 30 retarded (IQ 50-80) and 30 normal (IQ 97-125) Ss were matched in terms of MA (mean = 6.1 yrs). The concept of size was added to the 3 previously used concepts, and these 4 levels were combined with 2 dimensions of equal value. Results indicate that the retarded required more trials in reversal shift. (English summary) (23 ref)
Umetani, Tadao. (Tokyo U. of Education, Japan) Japanese Journal of Educational Psychology, 1971(Dec), Vol. 19(4), 221-231. [PA, Vol 52:05708]

384. Defective thyroid biosynthesis: A case of mental and physical retardation.
Discusses causes of defective thyroid biosynthesis which may lead to mental retardation. Inherited factors are presented, with a study of 1 family. Screening for these defects can be a normal part of routine tests in clinics. Many thyroid defects are overlooked. Intensive screening of infants of families with a history of thyroid conditions should be instituted.
Wellby, Maurice L. (Queen Elizabeth Hosp., Woodville, S. Australia) Australian Journal of Mental Retardation, 1971(Jun), Vol. 1(6), 191-195. [PA, Vol 47:09560]

385. Word-association norms: A comparison of adolescent mental retardates and normals.
Computed correlations between the responses of 4 CA subgroups of retardates and 8 subgroups of normal children to each of 200 stimulus words. 997 retardates, approximately 100 males and 100 females were tested individually. 5 most frequent responses of 4 CA levels of retardates, 136.43, 168.69, 193.20, and 224.61 mo., were compared with 8 CA levels of normals, 108, 120, 132, 144, 156, 180, 204, and 228 mo., respectively. Confidence limits, sigmas, medians, and quartiles for each intergroup comparison were also derived. The 5 most frequent responses by normals and retardates were diverse, but many correlations were extremely high. Thus, comparisons between S groups can be made utilizing stimulus words of the same or varying levels of association values. Word-association strength may thus be controlled in verbal learning experiments involving comparisons of normals and retardates when the S samples comply with the population parameters described.
Winters, John J. & Kahn, Harris. (Edward R. Johnstone Training & Research Center, Bordentown, N.J.) Psychonomic Monograph Supplements, 1971, Vol. 4(8), 129-163. [PA, Vol 47:09525]

386. Measurement of parents' perceptions of their children's development.
2 instruments were developed which assess the degree of realism with which parents perceive their child's current as well as likely future developmental attainments. These instruments were applied to 190 parents of retarded children. While most of these parents were very accurate in estimating their children's current abilities, they expected unrealistically high future attainments. Thus, concurrent and predictive realism were found to be separate constructs, and their relationships to 15 parent and/or child variables were explored. (97 ref.)
Wolfensberger, Wolf & Kurtz, Richard A. (U. Nebraska, Medical Center) Genetic Psychology Monographs, 1971(Feb), Vol. 83(1), 3-92. [PA, Vol 46:01703]

387. Outerdirectedness in the problem-solving of institutionalized and noninstitutionalized normal and retarded children.
8 groups of 24 children, institutionalized and noninstitutionalized, familial and organic retarded, and younger and older normal children, were given 2 measures of outerdirectedness. One was a 3-choice discrimination learning task in which a light was presented above 1 of the 2 incorrect stimuli; the 2nd was a task in which the child could imitate designs made by an adult or presented by a machine. The 4 retarded groups were found to be more outerdirected (i.e., selected the erroneous cued stimulus and imitated more often) than the 4 normal groups. The younger noninstitutionalized normal Ss were found to be more imitative than the older normal Ss. Institutionalization for both normal and retarded Ss and the etiology of retardation were also found to be related to degree of outerdirectedness.
Yando, Regina & Zigler, Edward. (Harvard U.) Developmental Psychology, 1971(Mar), Vol. 4(2), 277-288. [PA, Vol 45:10546]

388. Cross-modal matching among normal and retarded children.
Conducted 2 experiments in which 30 normal 6-10 yr. olds and 20 retarded Ss (6–12 yr. MA) matched 3-dimensional forms cross-modally and intramodally, using vision and active touch. Both groups matched better using vision than touch, committing orientation errors most frequently and shape errors least frequently. MA was negatively correlated with error scores among the retardates.
Zung, Burton J. (Baylor Coll. of Medicine, Houston, Tex.) Child Development, 1971(Nov), Vol. 42(5), 1614-1618. [PA, Vol 48:05480]

389. [Aggression, mental deficiency and epilepsy in a subject of karyotype 47 XYY/48 XXYY.] (Fren)
Reports the case of a 14-yr-old boy admitted to hospital as an emergency for an episode of acute excitation threatening life. In his previous history were convulsions in early infancy, epilepsy of grand mal type, educational retardation, and severe behavioral disturbances. Clinical examination showed mental deficiency (WISC IQ-70) together with congenital malformations and an exaggerated development of the secondary sexual characteristics. Determination of the karyotype showed a mosaic of 47, XXY (23 cells) and 48, XXYY (33 cells). Sex chromatin in the buccal smear was positive. The possible connections between epilepsy, mental deficiency, aggression, and genetic aberration are emphasized. The criminological problems presented by excesses of sex chromosomes are outlined. (German & Spanish summaries)
Benezech, M., et al. (Psychiatric Hosp., Cadillac, France) Revue de Neuropsychiatrie Infantile et d'Hygiene Mentale de l'Enfance, 1972(Oct), Vol. 20(10), 773-775. [PA, Vol 50:11431]

390. Psychiatric consultation in a school for the retarded.
Reviewed 301 consultations by child psychiatrists in a training program. 178 outpatients were seen in a community evaluation and rehabilitation center and 123 patients were seen as inpatient consultations. In the outpatient group the diagnoses included over-anxious reactions of childhood, learning disorders, adjustment reactions, phobic neuroses, and psychosis. 8 patients were not retarded, 9 had no mental disorder. In the inpatient group the diagnosis included anxiety neurosis, schizophrenic reactions, schizoid personality, toxic psychosis, neurotic depression, obsessive-compulsive, adjustment reaction, passive-aggressive personality, hysterical neurosis, antisocial personality, inadequate personality, sexual deviation, and withdrawing reaction. The usefulness of this clinical experience and its augmentation of interdisciplinary care became evident as consultations progressed, and the need to develop systems for combining intellectual and psychiatric categories in more systematic ways is discussed.
Bernstein, Norman R. & Rice, Jack O. (Walter E. Fernald State School, Waverly, Mass) American Journal of Mental Deficiency, 1972(May), Vol. 76(6), 718-725. [PA, Vol 48:11816]

391. Comprehension of possessive and present continuous sentences by nonretarded, mildly retarded, and severely retarded children.
In a task involving comprehension of singular and plural sentences differing in grammatical complexity, 72 severely, mildly, and nonretarded children all found the possessive sentences more difficult to understand. No other statistically significant effects were found, and in particular no differences between the 3 groups or between singular and plural forms.
Berry, Paul B. (U. Manchester, Hester Adrian Research Centre, England) American Journal of Mental Deficiency, 1972(Mar), Vol. 76(5), 540-544. [PA, Vol 48:12035]

392. Generalization of associative clustering tendencies in mentally retarded adolescents: Effects of novel stimuli.
Asked 96 retarded 15-19 yr. olds (mean MA = 10 yr.) to recall 16 words from 4 conceptual categories on 4 consecutive trials. On the 1st 2 trials, equal numbers of Ss received either a randomly organized list or a list organized into categories. On the last 2 trials, 1/3 of each group received either the same list, new words from the same categories, or new words from new categories. On the last 2 trials, all lists were randomly organized. Results indicate that experience with organized lists facilitated clustering on later trials only when the same verbal materials were used for all trials.
Bilsky, Linda; Evans, Ross A. & Gilbert, Lucy. (Columbia U., Teachers Coll.) American Journal of Mental Deficiency, 1972(Jul), Vol. 77(1), 77-84. [PA, Vol 49:04622]

393. [The intellectual defect in phenylketonuria, its dynamics and structure.] (Russ)
Studied the different degrees of retardation in 189 untreated children with phenylketonuria. Most had severe retardation (89.4 +/- 2.2%); mild forms of intellectual insufficiency were revealed in only 10.6 +/- 2.2%. During the 1st 2-3 yrs of life there was a progressive development of mental disorders. A comparison of the intellectual defect in Ss with phenylketonuria and complicated forms of oligophrenia with a similar degree of retardation showed significant qualitative differences in the structure of separate intellectual functions and syndromes. Ss with light forms of phenylketonuria had a higher level of general personality development than oligophrenic children. It is proposed that phenylketonuria be considered an independent form of neuropsychiatric pathology.
Blyumina, M. G. (USSR Academy of Medical Sciences, Inst. of Medical Genetics, Moscow) Zhurnal Nevropatologii i Psikhiatrii, 1972, Vol. 72(2), 276-280. [PA, Vol 51:09436]

394. [On two new cases of microcephalic infants with slowed intrauterine growth born of phenylketonuric mothers.] (Fren)
Reports 2 cases of microcephalism in children born to mothers whose phenylketonuria had been undiagnosed. If phenylketonuria is widely known today, and its influence on the affected children well-described, the same cannot be said for the 2nd generation, i.e., children born to mothers identified and treated for this disorder. Despite the best efforts to diagnose phenylketonuria early in life, it sometimes happens that the condition is identified only retrospectively, following the birth of a microcephalic child. To the small but important collection of such cases in the world's medical literature are added these 2 children, heterozygous for phenylketonuria (both fathers were free of the disorder). The need for more complete early identification of this metabolic error, especially among females, is self-evident.
Boucharlat, J. et al. (University Hosp. Center, Child Neuropsychiatric Service, Grenoble, France) Annales Médico-Psychologiques, 1972(Nov), Vol. 2(4), 542-550. [PA, Vol 50:03167]

395. Responses to action pictures of two groups of mentally retarded subjects.
Analyzed 60 mentally retarded children on discrimination of colored action pictures. Ss were divided into 2 groups paired on perceptual functioning in relation to visual motor tasks. The groups were matched on CA, MA, and IQ. 116 colored pictures illustrating actions were presented. Results show that Ss with visual-motor perceptual disabilities scored significantly lower on the identification of colored action pictures than did those who had minimal visual-motor handicaps. Implications of these data in terms of the Gellner theory and curriculum planning are discussed.
Bradley, Betty H. (Columbus State Inst., O.) Rehabilitation Literature, 1972(Dec), Vol. 33(12), 362-365. [PA, Vol 50:03169]

396. Context and recency cues in the recognition memory of retarded children and adolescents.
Investigated recognition memory for pictures in 24 11-18 yr. old retardates (mean MA = 9 yr.) with novelty either present as a cue or absent. With novelty present, accurate identification of old and new item occurred. When the novelty cue was removed by the repetition of Day 1 items on Day 2, the efficient level of performance was maintained, suggesting that retarded persons are able to use context or recency cues in recognition memory tasks. This ability to distinguish not only that an item has appeared before, but also where or when it occurred, was very efficient in retarded Ss. (16 ref.)
Brown, Ann L. (U. Illinois, Children's Research Center) American Journal of Mental Deficiency, 1972(Jul), Vol. 77(1), 54-58. [PA, Vol 49:00932]

397. Auditory and visual paired-associate learning in first-grade retarded and nonretarded children.
Tested 36 6.3-7.3 yr. old disadvantaged retarded and nonretarded, and advantaged nonretarded 1st graders on lists of noun pairs to determine the efficacy of auditory, visual, and combined auditory-visual modes of presenting paired-associates verbal material. Overall learning scores of the disadvantaged nonretarded Ss were higher than those of disadvantaged retarded. Performance of all Ss under visual and auditory-visual conditions was significantly higher than under auditory. The imagery-inducing quality of pictures was offered as a possible explanation for superior learning under visual and auditory-visual conditions. Differences with previous findings were ascribed to poor control of effects of reading skill in visual learning conditions. (22 ref.)
Bruininks, Robert H. & Clark, Charlotte R. (U. Minnesota) American Journal of Mental Deficiency, 1972(Mar), Vol. 76(5), 561-567. [PA, Vol 48:12060]

398. Incidental learning in nonretarded and retarded children.
Obtained incidental learning scores for 30 nonretarded and 30 retarded children under 2 experimental conditions differing primarily in the degree of externally imposed structure on the learning task. A significant difference was found in favor of the nonretarded Ss, suggesting that this reflected their superiority in employing verbal labels in the absence of instructions which tended to establish verbal learning sets. (20 ref.)
Cegelka, Patricia T. (U. Kansas) American Journal of Mental Deficiency, 1972(Mar), Vol. 76(5), 581-585. [PA, Vol 48:12062]

399. The body schema of normal and mentally retarded children.
Investigated the body schema and its 2 subdivisions, the postural model and surface schemata, in 15 organically impaired retardates, 15 nonorganically impaired retardates, and 30 normal children of preschool MA. The Finger Localization and Localization of Tactile Stimulation subtests of the Southern California Kinesthesia and Tactile Perception Tests were used to measure surface schemata. Postural model was measured by imitation of gestures. Results indicate that organic retardates had a deficit in overall schema, surface, and postural model in comparison to nonorganic retardates. Nonorganics exhibited similar deficits in relation to normals. Findings also demonstrate the importance of controlling for body area when measuring body schemata. (15 ref.)
Clapp, Robert K. (Children's Medical Center, Tulsa, Okla.) Journal of Psychology, 1972(Jan), Vol. 80(1), 37-44. [PA, Vol 47:11464]

400. Effects of between-trials variability and initial response outcome on the alternation discrimination learning of retarded adolescents.
Investigated the effects of between-trials variablity in irrelevant brightness and size, initial response outcome, and MA on the

alternation discrimination of 60 12-17 yr. old retardates. Results indicate that only the main effect of initial response outcome was significant. Nonreinforcement of the 1st response was associated with significantly more nonalternation responses than reinforcement. Results are discussed in terms of the Zeaman-House attention theory and S response predispositions.
Clinton, LeRoy. (Teachers Coll., Columbia U.) American Journal of Mental Deficiency, 1972(Jan), Vol. 76(4), 440-445. [PA, Vol 48:03566]

401.   Single alternation discrimination learning in retarded adolescents as a function of within-trials variability.
Investigated the influence of task complexity, MA, and initial response outcome on the alternation discrimination learning performance of 60 retarded adolescents (mean CA = 15.9 yr.), in a 3 × 2 × 2 design. Results reveal a significant task complexity main effect. In addition, there was a statistically reliable Complexity × Initial Response Outcome interaction which resulted from disproportional complexity effects under the initial response reinforcement condition. Results are discussed in terms of the Zeaman-House attention theory and response predisposition tendencies. (17 ref.)
Clinton, LeRoy & Evans, Ross A. (Teachers Coll., Columbia U.) American Journal of Mental Deficiency, 1972(Jan), Vol. 76(4), 434-439. [PA, Vol 48:05481]

402.   Rigidity in the retarded: A brief review and some recent data.
Discusses major developments in the literature pertaining to the Lewin-Kounin rigidity formulation. Some recent studies comparing 8-16 yr. old mentally retarded children with 40 4-5 yr. old normal children on a variety of discrimination transfer tasks were found to support a rigidity characterization of retardate behavior. In 4 experiments, the mentally retarded Ss were consistently inferior to their normal peers when required to change set and overcome the interfering effects of previous learning. The groups usually showed no differences in performance in the initial acquisition of the discriminations and performed similarly on a positive transfer shift. It appears that the mentally retarded Ss were deficient in some important learning process measured by switching tasks.
Clunies-Ross, G. G. (U. Queensland, St. Lucia, Australia) Australian Journal of Mental Retardation, 1972(Dec), Vol. 2(4), 106-110. [PA, Vol 50:05019]

403.   The mentally sub-normal child in hospital.
Discusses the child's response to hospitalization which, depending upon his emotional and intellectual development, follows a pattern throughout childhood. The mentally subnormal follows this sequence, but is delayed in proportion to the degree of handicap. Possible responses to the stress of hospitalization include: dependency relationships with parents; communication difficulties; dependency on emotional climate due to lack of reasoning ability to work things out for himself; regressive behavior; conversion reactions; loneliness, dejection, and withdrawal. Teaching methods for hospital staff on how to handle these situations are discussed. Segregation of the mentally subnormal in a pediatric hospital is considered wrong; it is noted that prevention of emotional trauma is as important for the retardate as for the normal.
Connell, Helen M. (Children's Hosp., Herston, Queensland, Australia) Australian Journal of Mental Retardation, 1972(Jun), Vol. 2(2), 47-50. [PA, Vol 49:07413]

404.   Biasing effect of pretest referral information on WISC scores of mentally retarded children.
Studied the influence of examiner bias on the WISC scores of 54 8-12 yr. old mentally retarded children by having 3 graduate student examiners test Ss under differential referral conditions: positive, neutral, and negative referral information. Testing was conducted under double-blind conditions in the Ss' schools. WISC IQs, S responses on posttest questionnaires, scoring errors, questioning of Ss, and computational errors did not differ across conditions. (15 ref.)

Dangel, Harry L. (Georgia State U.) American Journal of Mental Deficiency, 1972(Nov), Vol. 77(3), 354-359. [PA, Vol 50:03726]

405.   Mental retardation and neurologic involvement in patients with congenital retinal blindness.
About 10% of blind children have congenital retinal blindness (a recessively inherited disorder producing absence of cones and rods). Of 13 patients studied 10 were mentally retarded, 8 of whom had neurological symptoms (epilepsy, microcephaly, meningocele, etc.). Of 48 unselected case reports, 18 patients were mentally retarded. (French, German, & Spanish summaries) (26 ref.)
Dekaban, Anatole S. (National Inst. of Health, Sec. on Child Neurology, Bethesda, Md.) Developmental Medicine & Child Neurology, 1972(Aug), Vol. 14(4), 436-444. [PA, Vol 49:07121]

406.   Megalencephaly in children: Clinical syndromes, genetic patterns, and differential diagnosis from other causes of megalocephaly.
Studied a residual group of 18 patients with anatomic megalencephaly after those with the known diagnosable types had been excluded. A diversity of clinical and neurologic findings occurred, but none of the Ss had clinical or radiographic signs of increased intracranial pressure. ½ of the Ss were mentally retarded, and none were known to have superior intelligence. Clinical conditions associated with megalencephaly were gigantism, dwarfism, ganglioneuroma, muscular dystrophy, male pseudohermaphroditism, and hypoparathyroidism-hypoadrenocorticism. Males predominated over females 4:1, and at least ½ of the Ss appeared to have a familial basis for their megalencephaly.
DeMeyer, William. (Indiana U., Medical Center) Neurology, 1972(Jun), Vol. 22(6), 634-643. [PA, Vol 48:12005]

407.   [Influence of temporal interval between the stimulus and response presentation in paired-associate learning: Experimentation with feeble-minded children.] (Fren)
Studied paired-associate learning in a 2 * 2 * 2 factorial design experiment with 84 mentally retarded boys and girls (mean IQ = 70; mean CA = 161 mo.). The interval between the visual presentation of stimuli and the oral presentation of letters of the alphabet to be associated with them was 2 or 8 sec. The visual stimuli consisted of 1-7 cm. lines or 1-10 cm. lines, the 2nd set having less similar elements. The letters A through G were presented with lines of increasing length or the reverse. In every instance, learning was best with the longer interval, but the difference was not significant. Stimulus similarity had no significant effect, but the A through G order produced better results than the G through A order (p < .01). Interactions were not significant. (30 ref.)
Denhiere, Guy. (U. Paris, France) Enfance, 1972(Sep), No. 5, 379-396. [PA, Vol 50:09147]

408.   The significance of affect in verbal learning by subnormal children: An exploratory study.
Trained 2 matched groups of 8 subnormal (IQ 40-60) Ss each to associate pictures with unfamiliar printed words. The pictures used for Group A were less affective than those used for Group B (degree of affect was determined by Ss' own preferences). Correct recognition was later tested by the presentation of the printed words without pictures. Group B was significantly more successful than Group A. It is suggested that an increase in the affective connotation of verbal stimuli facilitates correct recognition of those stimuli for Ss of the 40-60 IQ range.
Drinkwater, Betty A. (James Cook U. of North Queensland, Townsville, Australia) Australian Journal of Psychology, 1972(Dec), Vol. 24(3), 327-329. [PA, Vol 50:08231]

409.   [Aspects of verbal memory in students of special auxiliary school.] (Romn)
Carried out a study with 102 mentally retarded children. Each was asked to memorize a series of 15 words repeated 5 times. Characteristics of performance by these Ss are described. Results indicate that variations in verbal memory were directly related to degrees of mental retardation. (Russian & French summaries)
Drutu, Ioan. Studia Universitatis Babes-Bolyai, 1972, Vol 17, 31-39. [PA, Vol 53:03428]

410. **Some aspects of object relationships in borderline children.**

Argues that in borderline children neither self-representations nor object-representations have been integrated into coherent and relatively stable wholes. The child interacts with others largely in terms of his own projection rather than in terms of the other person's actual characteristics. This is seen as a failure to complete the transition out of narcissism into a firm commitment to external reality. Case examples are presented, and the relevant literature is reviewed.

Fast, Irene & Chethik, Morton. (Children's Psychiatric Hosp, Ann Arbor, MI) International Journal of Psycho-Analysis, 1972, Vol 53(4), 479-485. [PA, Vol 53:01472]

411. **Comparison of the self-concept of nonretarded and retarded children matched for chronological age and environmental background.**

Compared children from primary and intermediate special classes (n = 100) with a random selection of children of regular elementary classes (n = 100) from common environments of limited socioeconomic background. Comparison of scores of the California Test of Personality (CTP) with scores from the test developed for this study reveals that Ss from the regular grades scored higher in the CTP than Ss from the special classes. There was a consistency in relative positions for both groups of Ss on the test developed for this research. Those scoring high or low on the CTP replicated their performance by scoring high or low on the test developed for this study. A significant finding was that Ss in the special class scored high in social standards and low in antisocial tendencies.

Goldman, William J. & May, Anne. (Fitchburg State Coll., Mass.) Training School Bulletin, 1972(Nov), Vol. 69(3), 136-140. [PA, Vol 50:01778]

412. **The effects of rehearsal instructions upon the paired-associate learning of normal and retarded subjects.**

Instructed 64 mental retardates (mean CA = 21 yr.) and 64 normal 2nd-6th graders to repeat paired-associates aloud, silently, or to count aloud during the interitem interval (3 or 8 sec.). A 4th group received standard paired-associates instructions. A significant instruction effect and Instruction × Intelligence interaction were observed. Results suggest that retardates were relatively deficient in the spontaneous use of effective rehearsal mechanisms, but could perform as well as normals when instructed to employ a specific strategy.

Gordon, Donald A. & Baumeister, Alfred A. (U. Alabama, Center for Developmental & Learning Disorders) Journal of Genetic Psychology, 1972(Sep), Vol. 121(1), 31-39. [PA, Vol 49:02631]

413. **[Several operant conditioning experiments with mentally retarded children.]** (Germ)

Conducted series of operant conditioning experiments with 8 4-7 yr old children with severely retarded speech development to study learning processes and therapeutic techniques. 3 Ss suffered from Kanner's syndrome, 1 from severe mental retardation with autistic traits, 3 from deaf-mutism, and 1 from congenital acoustic agnosia. In a sequence of fully automated, programed and recorded tests and pretests, Es examined the acquisition and establishment of positive conditioned reinforcers, the learning of correct performance in matching-to-sample discrimination tasks with pictures of food and toys as stimuli, the generalization to newly introduced visual stimuli, extinction, recovery and transfer to audiovisual stimuli matching tasks. All Ss were able to learn and solve the original matching tasks correctly. Ss presented strongly differing reactions to the secondary reinforcers introduced and built up during the tests and some parameters had to be changed before all Ss managed to perform correctly. A quick generalization to new visual stimuli was evident in all Ss, but of the 3 Ss who had not previously comprehended the meaning of words, only one learned to execute audiovisual matching correctly after a process of visual fading-out in combination with the voiced naming of the object to be matched. (English summary) (27 ref)

Gottwald, Peter. (Max Planck Inst for Psychiatry, Munich, W Germany) Zeitschrift für Klinische Psychologie. Forschung und Praxis, 1972, Vol 1(1), 21-47. [PA, Vol 53:03437]

414. **[Children with brain injuries and disability: Life situation and personality.]** (Norg)

Investigated how brain injuries and growing up as seriously disabled can affect children's personality. The following groups of normal or slightly intellectually retarded 9-13 yr. old children were compared: (a) 18 with spastic cerebral palsy (CP), both brain injury and disability; (b) 12 with epilepsy (E), brain injury but without motoric disability; (c) 12 without brain injuries but grown up in a situation similar to the CP Ss (e.g., polio, hemophilia, and deformations) (V), and (d) a randomly chosen normal group of 8 yr. olds from a school. Although similar in intelligence the CP group had the weakest results but the largest spread, the V group fared best, while the E group and controls fell in between, in general, on various clinical tests. Conclusions are based on analysis of so-called emotional and organic signs. The question is raised as to whether the somewhat different personality characteristics are related to organic factors or factors in the situation in which the groups grew up. (English summary) (5 p. ref.)

Grinde, Turid V. (Office of Health, Dept. of Social Affairs, Oslo, Norway) Nordisk Psykologi, 1972, Vol. 24(1), 1-144. [PA, Vol 50:09183]

415. **Development of conservation in normal and retarded children.**

Selected 10 familially retarded children from each of 3 different MA levels: 5, 7, and 9 yr. Ss were matched for MA, CA, and sex with 60 normal children and given 3 kinds of tasks: (a) conservation of number, (b) continuous quantity (water), and (c) weight. Differences in performance on these tasks were primarily attributable to MA but not IQ. As expected, conservation of weight was generally more difficult than conservation of water, and the latter was more difficult than conservation of number for both retarded and normal Ss. However, some exceptions to this order were found. Conservation of inequality was typically less difficult than conservation of equality for all concepts. Implications for developmental theory are discussed. (28 ref.)

Gruen, Gerald E. & Vore, David A. (Purdue U.) Developmental Psychology, 1972(Jan), Vol. 6(1), 146-157. [PA, Vol 48:01510]

416. **An attempt to assess eidetic imagery objectively.**

Investigated the incidence of persons possessing eidetic imagery for 86 normal adult undergraduates, 144 normal children in Grades 1-6, 16 brain-injured children (mean CA = 12 yr.), and 19 familial retardates (mean CA = 12 yr.). 3 methods of evaluation were used for all Ss: (a) the "standard" method, in which S describes a complex scene after viewing it for 30 sec.; (b) a task which requires superimposing the eidetic image of 1 stimulus upon a 2nd stimulus, thus producing an unexpected 3rd pattern; and (c) the C. Stromeyer and J. Psotka task of binocularly fusing 2 Julesz patterns, 1 of which is an eidetic image. The latter 2 methods were considered to be more objective than the 1st and less likely to classify a person incorrectly as an eidetiker. According to the 1st method, eidetikers were found only among the familial retardates (2 of 19 Ss). By the other 2 methods, none of the Ss possessed eidetic ability. (16 ref.)

Gummerman, Kent; Gray, Cynthia R. & Wilson, J. M. (U. Texas) Psychonomic Science, 1972(Jul), Vol. 28(2), 115-118. [PA, Vol 50:02270]

417. **Comparative parental perceptions of a mentally retarded child.**

Used T. Parson and R. Bales' instrumental-expressive role framework to compare the retarded child perceptions of 50 mothers and fathers from the same families. Although not consistently statistically significant, evidence shows that there was a tendency for fathers to perceive their child more instrumentally than mothers, the latters' perceptions being more expressive. Related research questions are discussed.

Gumz, Edward & Gubrium, Jaber F. (Kiwanis Children's Center, Milwaukee, Wis.) American Journal of Mental Deficiency, 1972(Sep), Vol. 77(2), 175-180. [PA, Vol 49:07161]

418.   Late infantile amaurotic idiocy (LIAI).
Clinical, histopathological, and biochemical findings were reported in a 10-yr-old boy with the Jansky-Bielschowsky type of LIAI. Absence of quantitative increase in total amount of gangliosides and an essentially normal pattern of ganglioside distribution were the significant biochemical characteristics. The cerebroside content in the gray and white matter was low for this age, and there was a total loss of N-acetylneuraminate-free glycopeptides of smaller molecular size. A survey of LIAI in the literature indicated histopathological, biochemical and ultrastructural differences among the cases. The present case differed in chemical composition from the ganglioside storage variants of LIAI. It is suggested that this case, and chemically similar ones, may constitute a nosologically distinct variant of LIAI. This hypothesis, however, needs to be confirmed by further case studies.
Haberland, Catherine; Brunngraber, E. G.; Witting, L. A. & Hof, H. (Illinois State Psychiatric Inst., Chicago) Neurology, 1972(Mar), Vol. 22(3), 305-311. [PA, Vol 49:00978]

419.   A comparison of retarded and nonretarded children on the ability to use context in reading.
Compared 15 mentally retarded and 15 nonretarded 10-12 yr. olds on their ability to use context in reading. All Ss received 200-word cloze-treated passages (every 5th word deleted and replaced with a standard sized blank). Each of the passages was at the instructional reading level of each S which had been identified by means of an informal reading inventory. The cloze tests were scored by counting the number of appropriate words the Ss were able to supply for those deleted. The nonretarded Ss showed significantly greater ability to use context in reading.
Hargis, Charles. (U. Tennessee) American Journal of Mental Deficiency, 1972(May), Vol. 76(6), 726-728. [PA, Vol 48:12067]

420.   An application of Guttman facet theory to the study of attitudes toward the mentally retarded in Germany.
Developed a 6 level instrument from facet theory, the Attitude-Behavior Scale: Mental Retardation, to measure attitudes on an abstract-impersonal to concrete-behavioral continuum. The instrument was used to assess the attitude-behaviors of 74 regular teachers, 148 teachers of the retarded, 83 manager-executives, 144 parents of retarded children, and 70 parents of normal children. Relationships between attitude-behaviors and demographic variables, contact with the retarded, knowledge of retardation, and belief in man's ability to control his natural and social environment were examined at the 6 levels. Results indicate that the scale levels discriminate among "known" groups, and that attitudes at the action-behavioral levels have an affective-value-contactual base rather than a cognitive-knowledge one. (36 ref.)
Harrelson, Lawrence E.; Jordan, John E. & Horn, Hartmut. (Bay-Arenac Community Mental Health Services Board, Adult Clinic, Bay City, Mich.) Journal of Psychology, 1972(Mar), Vol. 80(2), 323-335. [PA, Vol 48:03543]

421.   Input and output organization in short-term serial recall by retarded and nonretarded children.
Presented sequences of 6 digits for written ordered recall to 3 groups of 24 Ss: institutionalized cultural-familial retarded adolescents (mean CA = 16 yr.), and nonretarded children in Grades 2 or 3. Input organization was imposed by temporal division into 3-digit groups, while output organization was provided spatially on the answer sheets. It was found that 2nd graders with lower MAs than retarded adolescents showed superior performance only when input organization was imposed. Recall data as a function of serial position (SP) indicated that for retarded Ss, performance gains from the imposed input organization of some SPs were counterbalanced by losses at others. The effects of output organization were negligible.
Harris, Gilbert J. (Inst. of Basic Research in Mental Retardation, Staten Island, N.Y.) American Journal of Mental Deficiency, 1972(Jan), Vol. 76(4), 423-426. [PA, Vol 48:05483]

422.   Recognition memory for faces by retardates and normals.
Showed sequences of 10 faces and sequences of 10 half faces to 12 male and 12 female adolescent familial retardates and 12 male and 12 female 3rd graders of equal MA. Recognition memory was tested by asking S to discriminate the 10 stimuli that had been seen from 10 distractors. The retardates' performance was equal to that of the normals when whole faces were to be remembered, but the normals were superior when half faces were employed. Results suggest that the symmetry of the human face may provide redundancy which aids the retardates' performance.
Harris, Gilbert J. & Fleer, Robert E. (New York State Inst. for Research in Mental Retardation, Staten Island) Perceptual & Motor Skills, 1972(Jun), Vol. 34(3), 755-758. [PA, Vol 48:12068]

423.   A factor analysis of the Laurelton Self-Concept Scale.
Describes an attempt to develop some internally consistent self-report personality scales for mentally retarded persons. 137 items of the Laurelton Self-Concept Scale and the 23-item Locus of Control Scale for Children were administered to 172 special class and institutionalized educable mentally retarded children (mean CA = 14.9 yr.). Responses to the 160 items were intercorrelated and then factor analyzed by the principal components method. 3 different varimax rotations, for 11, 29, and 38 factors, were interpreted. The 3 sets of rotated factor scores were then correlated. It was found that the factor structure of the 29 and 38 factor rotations was quite similar, and factors from these rotations clustered into the broader factors from the 11-factor rotation in psychologically meaningful ways.
Harrison, Robert H. & Budoff, Milton. (Research Inst. for Education Problems, Cambridge, Mass.) American Journal of Mental Deficiency, 1972(Jan), Vol. 76(4), 446-459. [PA, Vol 48:05465]

424.   Effects of rate of stimulus presentation and penalty conditions on the discrimination learning of normal and retarded children.
Examined the effects of rate of stimulus presentation and reinforcement conditions on the 2-choice discrimination learning performance of 80 MA matched normal and familial retarded children. 2 rates of presentation, ½ and 6 sec., and 2 reinforcement conditions, reward only and reward plus penalty, were compared. Normal Ss made relatively few errors under all conditions. For the retarded, learning was significantly better in the 6-sec than the ½-sec condition; and at the ½-sec interval, performance was better in the reward plus penalty than the reward only condition. The effects of these manipulations on the discrimination learning of the retarded are discussed within the context of those approaches which emphasize motivational vs. cognitive differences between MA matched normal and retarded children. (15 ref.)
Harter, Susan & Zigler, Edward. (Yale U.) Developmental Psychology, 1972(Jan), Vol. 6(1), 85-91. [PA, Vol 48:01535]

425.   Short-term memory in normals and retardates as a function of stimulus intensity and recall interval: A test of Ellis's s_t theory.
Tested 2 predictions derived from N. Ellis's (see PA, Vol. 38:6426) stimulus trace (s_t) deficit theory with equal CA (approximately 9 yr.) normal and retarded Ss in a digit recall task. Length of recall interval (0 vs. 8 sec.) and intensity level of the aurally presented items (55 vs. 90 db.) were varied factorially. All of the material was taped and received by Ss through earphones. Contrary to Ellis's theoretical predictions, the 2 IQ groups demonstrated parallel retention functions, and the performance of neither group was affected by the intensity manipulation.
Hayes, Charles S. & Routh, Donald K. (University Hosp. School, Child Development Clinic, Iowa City, Ia.) Psychological Reports, 1972(Jun), Vol. 30(3), 831-836. [PA, Vol 49:02635]

426.   Prediction of mental retardation in infancy.
Out of a population of 2,875 infants in the Child Development Study at Brown University, 230 Ss were followed to age 4 and 115 to age 7. Each S was 1 mo. or more below average on the Bayley Scales of Mental or Motor Development at 8 mo. of age.

At both ages 4 and 7, mean IQ scores were significantly lower than a control group of 150 children.
Holden, Raymond H. (Rhode Island Coll., Learning Center) Mental Retardation, 1972(Feb), Vol. 10(1), 28-30. [PA, Vol 48:03544]

427. The back projection of kaleidoscopic patterns as a technique for eliciting verbalizations in an autistic child: A preliminary note.
Outlines the problems presented by the use of operant conditioning of verbal responses in the case of a 4-yr-old boy diagnosed as autistic. A piece of technical apparatus designed to overcome these problems is described. Results are encouraging in that (a) the reinforcement given by the apparatus proved to be durable, and (b) there was some evidence to suggest that the effects produced in the experimental room had generalized to other situations.
Jellis, Trevor. (Worcestershire Schools Psychological Service, England) British Journal of Disorders of Communication, 1972(Oct), Vol. 7(2), 157-162. [PA, Vol 50:01507]

428. Limits on the measurement of activity level in children using ultrasound and photoelectric cells.
Investigated the use of an ultrasonic motion detection device as a substitute for the O in studying gross and fine motor activity in retarded children. Simultaneous photoelectric cell movement detection recordings were made of normal adult Ss' walking and sitting activity. Peculiarities of the ultrasonic device made it unsuitable for application when there was a need to differentiate and measure fine and gross motor activity. Activity measurement by photoelectric cells was limited to movement which interrupted the light beams. Observation of activity may differ from activity detected by various machines, causing disagreement in the conclusions reached by the different methodologies. The investigator must be aware of the idiosyncracies of activity measuring devices and tailor studies of activity to function within the limitations of the apparatus. (30 ref.)
Johnson, Charles F. (U. Iowa Hosp. School, Child Development Clinic) American Journal of Mental Deficiency, 1972(Nov), Vol. 77(3), 301-310. [PA, Vol 50:07019]

429. Malnutrition and mental deficiency.
Indicates that inadequate nutrition can affect both physiological and psychological development in humans. The 9 mo. of gestation and the 1st few yr. of life are the most critical in the growth of brain tissue and are also the periods of greatest vulnerability to malnutrition. Variables that mediate the effect of nutrition on mental development include prematurity, birth weight, and the nutritional status of the mother during her childhood. A model for thorough research is suggested and is used to evaluate the major studies of the relationship between malnutrition and mental deficiency. (71 ref.)
Kaplan, Bonnie J. (Brandeis U.) Psychological Bulletin, 1972(Nov), Vol. 78(5), 321-334. [PA, Vol 49:07192]

430. The XYY syndrome in children: A review.
Summarizes available data on XYY chromosome pattern appearing in 11 boys 13 yr. old and younger, and reports 2 new cases. Some tendency toward mental subnormality, genital abnormalities, and behavioral disorders is noted. However, it is observed that because of the small sample size and selective effects in referral of Ss, no general conclusions can be drawn. Because of these uncertainties, it is recommended that Ss and their parents not be informed of the presence of the pattern for the time being. (20 ref.)
Kivowitz, Julian. (U. California, Center for the Health Sciences, Los Angeles) Child Psychiatry & Human Development, 1972(Sum), Vol. 2(4), 186-194. [PA, Vol 49:11417]

431. Color distractors in discrimination with retarded and nonretarded children.
Gave 9 6-10 yr. old retarded and 9 6-7 yr. old nonretarded children a series of discrimination trials while central and peripheral vasomotor reactions were monitored. The key discrimination dimension was form, but color distractors were included as an extraneous dimension on ½ of the trials. The experiment examined the behavioral and physiological characteristics of discrimination with color distractors. Retarded Ss made significantly more errors overall than did the nonretarded. In addition, color distractors produced a significant performance decrement with the retarded Ss, but only a minimal decrement with the nonretarded. The physiological measure of orienting did not discriminate significantly between the 2 groups or between distractor and nondistractor conditions. (16 ref.)
Klein, Helen A.; Klein, Gary A.; Oskamp, Linda & Patnode, Camilla. (Wayne State U.) American Journal of Mental Deficiency, 1972(Nov), Vol. 77(3), 328-331. [PA, Vol 50:03250]

432. Motor characteristics and development of retarded children: Success experience.
Reviews some of the motor development literature of the retarded and answers questions fundamental to its accurate conception: (a) comparison of the retarded with intellectually normal children on tests of motor ability, (b) relationship between intellectual and physical development, (c) possibility of remediation of motor disabilities in the retarded, and (d) the effect of motor remediation on intelligence. The study indicates that physical development is an area where the retarded child can achieve a degree of normalcy that could generalize widely in the form of increased motivation and self-confidence. (26 ref.)
Kral, Paul A. (Parsons State Hosp. & Training Center, Kan.) Education & Training of the Mentally Retarded, 1972(Feb), Vol. 7(1), 14-21. [PA, Vol 49:07203]

433. [A "cat cry" syndrome discovered late in the course of a systematic examination.] (Fren)
Presents the case history of a mentally retarded boy of 3 with the chromosomal irregularity associated with the "cri du chat" syndrome, not so identified during infancy. The typical "cat cry" was absent and the genetic defect discovered only fortuitously in the course of a postinfancy neuropsychiatric evaluation prompted by his mental defect. The defining karyotype of breakage in the shorter arm of the 5th chromosome is demonstrated, together with a description of accompanying developmental irregularities in the EEG and dermatoglyph patterns.
Lafon, R.; Emberger, J. M.; Pouget, R. & Chiariny, J. F. Annales Médico-Psychologiques, 1972(Sep), Vol. 2(3), 431-438. [PA, Vol 50:03510]

434. Performance of retarded children on a liquid conservation task: Protocol objectivity and visual screening.
Studied the liquid conservation performance of 48 mentally retarded Ss (MAs 4-9 to 8-4). The effects of visual screening were examined using 2 levels of protocol objectivity. Results indicate no significant differences in conservation performance as a function of either experimental variable. MA was the sole significant predictor of S performance in this study.
Langley, Jan; Drew, Clifford J. & Watson, Carrie M. (U. Utah) American Journal of Mental Deficiency, 1972(May), Vol. 76(6), 729-732. [PA, Vol 48:12073]

435. Family socio-cultural background and the behavioral retardation of children.
Examined hypotheses relating family sociocultural background to behavioral retardation of children. Data obtained from a stratified random sample of all Anglo and Mexican-American households in a southern California city of about 100,000 population, on 2,641 children, are analyzed. The data support the existence of a relationship between family sociocultural factors of ethnicity, social status, community of origin, and residential mobility and the behavioral retardation of children. When ethnic groups are considered separately, more variance is explained by sociocultural factors for Mexican-Americans than for Anglos. For both Mexican-Americans and Anglos, the single most important variable explaining families with and without a behaviorally retarded child is mother's education. (21 ref.)
Lei, Tzuen-Jen; Butler, Edgar W. & Sabagh, Georges. (Pacific State Hosp., Pomona, Calif.) Journal of Health & Social Behavior, 1972(Sep), Vol. 13(3), 318-326. [PA, Vol 49:07212]

436.   Poggendorf illusion among mental retardates.
Measured the Poggendorf illusion in 2 groups of 15 normal and
mentally retarded children of the same CA and 15 undergraduates. A significant difference existed between the 2 groups of
children (p < .01) but none between the normal children and
adults.
Letourneau, Jacques E. (U. Montreal, Quebec, Canada) Perceptual & Motor Skills, 1972(Oct), Vol. 35(2), 535-538. [PA, Vol
49:07216]

**437.   Word frequency and pronunciation and the verbal-
discrimination learning of nonretarded and retarded children.**
Tested an extended version of frequency theory using a sample of
64 retarded and 64 nonretarded children matched for average
MA of 9 yr. Predictions were based on the variables of
pronunciation and word frequency as applied in a verbal
discrimination task. Frequency theory suggests that increasing
word frequency would decrease the retarded child's performance
relative to nonretarded children and that pronunciation would
have no differential effect. In addition, the validity of a rehearsal
and incidental learning deficit in the retarded child was assessed
using an associative matching task. Results provide some support
for frequency theory in that pronunciation had no differential
effect upon intelligence. However, the Frequen-
cy × Intelligence interaction failed to support frequency theory: increasing word frequency had an equally adverse effect on
both nonretarded and retarded Ss. No support for a rehearsal or
incidental learning deficit in the retarded child was found. (17
ref.)
Libkuman, Terry M. (Central Michigan U.) American Journal of
Mental Deficiency, 1972(Nov), Vol. 77(3), 322-327. [PA, Vol
50:03262]

**438.   The development of ESN children's understanding of
conservation in a range of attribute situations.**
Pretested 115 8-16 yr. olds from a school for the educationally
subnormal (ESN) on Piaget-type conservation tasks involving
number, substance, length, distance, area, weight, and volume.
51 Ss who failed to conserve in relation to 2 or more attributes,
were studied further. Ss were divided into 3 groups matched for
age, IQ, and level of initial understanding of conservation. 1
group was instructed on conservation of a variety of attributes, a
2nd group on conservation of area only, and the 3rd group was
given practice in reading. After 1 wk. and 2 mo., 30 of the 34
instructed Ss consistently recognized, generalized, and gave
reasons for conservation. No control S improved in understanding of conservation by the time of the 2nd test.
Lister, Caroline M. (U. Keele, England) British Journal of
Educational Psychology, 1972(Feb), Vol. 42(1), 14-22. [PA, Vol
48:05675]

**439.   Observational learning in retarded and normal children as
a function of delay between observation and opportunity to
perform.**
Divided 24 retarded (mean IQ = 60) and 24 normal (mean
IQ = 104) males into 3 groups each equated (mean and
standard deviation) by stratified assignment on MA. 1 retarded
and 1 normal group were randomly picked to (a) watch a control
film, (b) watch an experimental film and perform immediately,
and (c) watch an experimental film and perform after a 30-min
delay. The number of behaviors matched by each S was subjected
to an analysis of variance. No IQ main effect or interaction with
IQ was found while a significant treatment effect emerged.
Experimental groups performed significantly more modeled
behaviors, and a significant decrement was found when a 30-min
delay was experienced.
Litrownik, Alan J. (San Diego State Coll.) Journal of Experimental Child Psychology, 1972(Aug), Vol. 14(1), 117-125. [PA, Vol
49:02677]

**440.   Pretraining retarded and intellectually average children
for visual discrimination: Nonreward vs. reward.**
Conducted 3 experiments to investigate 2-choice discrimination
learning in a total of 327 retarded and nonretarded children with
MAs ranging from about 2-4.5 yr. The main pretraining

conditions involved nonrewarded or rewarded trials with negative or positive cues before regular discrimination trials. Nonrewarded pretraining with negative cues proved the most effective
method of facilitating correct performance for both levels of
intelligence, although this treatment occasionally accentuated the
"equal-MA" deficit of retarded Ss in rate of attaining the
learning criterion. The facilitation effect was attributable to
inhibitory properties of nonrewarded pretraining, since novelty
influences were found to be transitory and inconsequential with
respect to discrimination learning.
Lobb, Harold. (U. Western Ontario, London, Canada) American
Journal of Mental Deficiency, 1972(Jul), Vol. 77(1), 59-68. [PA,
Vol 49:01013]

**441.   [Special psychology at the 4th All-Union Congress of
Psychologists.] (Russ)**
Describes contributions made to the field of special psychology at
the congress held in June 1971 in Tbilisi. Papers on mental
retardation and on children who show a delay in development
presented by Zh. I. Shif, N. M. Stadnenko, E. A. Gersmia, M. G.
Kolbaya, V. I. Lubovskii, V. G. Petrova, and M. S. Pevzner are
summarized as are papers on disturbances of specific sensory
modalities by T. V. Rozanova, Yu. Daulenskene, L. I. Tigranova,
L. S. Lebedeva, Z. K. Gabashili, and Yu. A. Kulagin. It is noted
that a symposium was devoted to the problems of psychological
diagnosis for the 1st time in the history of the congress.
Lubovskiy, V.; Shif, Zh.; Petrova, V. & Pevzner, M.
Defektologiya, 1972, Vol. 3, 92-96. [PA, Vol 52:01276]

442.   Intellectual subnormalities.
Outlines diagnostic considerations in the evaluation of a child
with an impaired intellectual status. Evaluation includes a
complete medical history and thorough physical examination.
Serial measurements of head circumference, plain head radio-
graphs, EEGs, urine analysis, test reagent studies, cytogenetic
studies or karyotyping, examination of the cerebrospinal fluid,
and psychometric testing are discussed. Etiological considerations include fetal injuries; bacterial, viral or fungal infections;
neoplastic conditions; vascular diseases; metabolic conditions;
toxic substances; and childhood psychoses. Charts are presented
which indicate some treatable causes of intellectual impairment,
screening tests for inborn metabolic disorders, and substances
which may give positive reactions in the urine. For those whose
deficits are not reversible by any specific therapy, management is
discussed. Problems of parental guilt feelings, the daily care
needs of the severely retarded infant, special education, genetic
counseling, and questions of institutionalization are considered.
(22 ref.)
Mellinger, James F. (Mayo Clinic, Rochester, Minn.) Psychiatric
Annals, 1972(Jan), Vol. 2(1), 62-71. [PA, Vol 49:04787]

443.   Progressive matrices and the educationally disadvantaged.
Reports a study suggesting that mentally retarded children score
higher IQs on the nonverbal Raven's Progressive Matrices than
on the Stanford-Binet Intelligence Scale. However, a higher MA
results in a wider discrepancy between attainments and mental
capacity by this measure.
Morán, Roberto E. (U. Puerto Rico, Coll. of Education) Mental
Retardation, 1972(Jun), Vol. 10(3), 9. [PA, Vol 49:01029]

444.   Repeat evaluations of retarded children.
Based on material obtained from a review of records and
interviews of 264 mentally retarded children, a qualitative study
of families who sought multiple evaluations of their children
revealed 6 types of parental motivation. 2 reflect parents' use of
evaluations to deny a defect in the child. The remainder represent
inability of professionals to meet the needs of parent and child.
Suggestions are presented for the adaptation of more effective
services.
Murphy, Ann & Pounds, Lois. (Children's Hosp. Medical
Center, Boston, Mass.) American Journal of Orthopsychiatry,
1972(Jan), Vol. 42(1), 103-109. [PA, Vol 48:01518]

445.   [Filtered speech audiometry in normal children and the mentally retarded.] (Japn)
Found large inter-S variations in ability to discriminate Japanese monosyllables when testing 68 mentally retarded and 25 normal Japanese children and young adults on standard speech audiometry. Developmental stages in discrimination ability were clearly distinquishable in the normal but not in the retarded sample. (17 ref)
Nagafuchi, Masaaki & Watanabe, Takeo. (Tohoku U., Faculty of Education, Sendai, Japan) Japanese Journal of Special Education, 1972(Dec), Vol. 10(2), 36-45. [PA, Vol 52:01282]

446.   "A review of an occupational therapist's research on perceptual-motor attributes of mental retardates": Can perceptual-motor theory be experimentally proved?
Studied the Roach and Kephart Purdue Perceptual-Motor Survey (PP-MS) with respect to validating its results for mentally retarded (MR) young adults. From 3 S populations with mean ages of 23.3, 21.3, and 17.4 yr., respectively, ranging from 36-99 Ss per group, it was found necessary to omit 3 of the 22 PP-MS items because the MR young adults (in contrast to MR children) found these items too difficult. Results of the 1st 2 studies support the construct validity of the PP-MS methodology as applied to MR adolescents and young adults, implying that it measures the same kind of perceptual-motor attributes that have been measured in non-MR schoolchildren. A factor analysis on PP-MS item scores from the 3rd group of Ss resulted in 7 factors. Results support the construct validity of the PP-MS methodology as applied to the MR because it reflects a number of distinct perceptual-motor attributes, as was intended by Kephart. (47 ref.)
Neeman, Renate L. (Cantalician Center for Learning, Buffalo, N.Y.) Australian Occupational Therapy Journal, 1972(Jan), Vol. 19(1), 35-40. [PA, Vol 49:04804]

447.   [Questions about genetic development at the Fourth International Congress on Human Genetics.] (Russ)
Summarizes under the following headings 24 of the papers read at the Congress held in France, September 6-11, 1971: (a) chromosomal aberrations and development, (b) cytological mechanisms of underdevelopment, (c) familial factors favoring the birth of mentally retarded children, and (d) the development of twins. Also described are 12 papers by members of the Soviet delegation not included in the above categories, e.g., a report by M. E. Vartanyan and his coauthors on genetic models and inheritance in schizophrenia.
Nikituk, B. Defektologiya, 1972, Vol. 4(1), 93-96. [PA, Vol 50:08348]

448.   [The effect of coding on memory in mental retardates.] (Japn)
Paired 40 mentally retarded middle-school Ss (IQ 50-70) for chronological age, mental age, and IQ, and assigned them to Like Modality (LM) and Cross Modality (CM) groups. Using lists of 13 stimulus words and 26 conceptually corresponding words for recognition, the coding effect of 2 LMs (visual and auditory) and CM on recognition were compared. CM was significantly more effective than LM ($p < .01$); visual stimulus was more effective than auditory stimulus within CM ($p < .05$); and visual stimulus under the conditions of either modality was more effective than auditory stimulus ($p < .01$). It is concluded that the effect of coding on recognition depends on verbal identification of stimulus and intrusion between stimuli in the process of encoding. (English summary) (18 ref)
Obinata, Shigetoshi. Japanese Journal of Educational Psychology, 1972(Jun), Vol. 20(2), 101-108. [PA, Vol 52:12735]

449.   [Qualities and limitations of the Kohs-Goldstein tests as a means of diagnosing mental retardation.] (Romn)
Administered the Kohs-Goldstein test to 200 mentally retarded children 9-14 yrs old and to 80 normal children 6-14 yrs old. Results were compared for diagnostic value with those of the Binet-Simon test (correlation .54) and the Bender Gestalt test (correlation .78). Since the Kohs-Goldstein test is directed toward the diagnosis of serious mental disorders, it should be used only as part of a larger diagnostic battery in the assessment of mildly retarded children. (Russian & English summaries)
Preda, Vasile. Studia Universitatis Babes-Bolyai, 1972, Vol 17, 41-53. [PA, Vol 53:03445]

450.   [The relation between the figurative and operative aspects in spatial representation and structuring.] (Romn)
Results of a study revealed that within the spatial representation and structuring, the "evoked figurative," the "anticipated figurative," and the operative aspect of cognitive activity are forming a functional unity, within which the operative aspect has the main role. Mentally retarded and normal children were studied. The mentally retarded children had some trouble in (a) the process of passing from "evoked figurative" to "anticipated figurative," from "global anticipation" to "analytic anticipation" and (b) the interaction between figurative and operative. (French summary) (18 ref)
Preda, Vasile. (Babes-Bolyai U., Cluj, Romania) Revista de Psihologie, 1972, Vol. 18(2), 181-190. [PA, Vol 51:11409]

451.   The effect of warm-up on rote learning performance.
Randomly assigned 90 mentally retarded and 90 nonretarded 11-13 yr. olds to 3 pretraining groups. The pretraining task was a list of 4 nonmeaningful paired associates. One group received no pretraining, the 2nd received 3 trials on the pretraining list, and the 3rd, 9 trials. The experimental task consisted of 6 nonmeaningful paired associates. Analysis of the data indicate that the retarded Ss exhibited a pronounced deficit in the early stage of learning and that pretraining had no effect on performance.
Prehm, Herbert J.; Logan, Donald R. & Towle, Maxine. (U. Oregon) Exceptional Children, 1972(Apr), Vol. 38(8), 623-627. [PA, Vol 50:07085]

452.   Structural models and embedded-figure difficulty for normal and retarded children.
Tested 60 normal 6-12 yr. olds and 20 mentally retarded 11-16 yr. olds on an embedded-figures task to determine what stimulus variables correlate with the difficulty of finding a figure hidden in a larger pattern. The number of shared contours, the complexity of the ground, and analysis complexity (defined as the amount by which the total complexity of the parts exceeds the complexity of the whole pattern) resulted in significant, positive correlations with the difficulty of finding an embedded figure. The complexity of the figure, the complexity of the complete pattern, and the number of overlapping lines resulted in nonsignificant, positive correlations with the difficulty in finding the figure. The task is discussed within the theoretical framework of the structural model advocated by R. Narasimhan and N. Sutherland. Results suggest how a pattern might be analyzed into a hierarchy of articulations with each articulation consisting of a hierarchy of component parts.
Reed, Stephen K. & Angaran, A. J. (Case Western Reserve U.) Perceptual & Motor Skills, 1972(Aug), Vol. 35(1), 155-164. [PA, Vol 49:04825]

453.   Curiosity behavior in normal and mentally retarded children.
Tested 13 normal and 9 mentally retarded preschool children (mean CA = 4 yr. 8 mo.) for curiosity behavior and general activity. Although general activity was not found to be related to IQ scores, the results indicate that the normal Ss' level of curiosity behavior was greater than that of the mentally retarded. It is suggested that previous investigators have not reported a relationship between curiosity behavior and intelligence because of their use of Ss having a restricted range of IQ scores.
Richman, Charles L.; Kahle, Douglas & Rutland, Sam. (Wake Forest U.) Psychonomic Science, 1972(Nov), Vol. 29(4-A), 212. [PA, Vol 49:11472]

454.   Language acquisition and the blind retarded child: A study of impaired communication.
Discusses the inadequacy of educational provisions for the blind retarded child. Ordinarily, normally developing blind children do not differ from the nonvisually handicapped child in the manner and rate of language acquisition. If a blind child hears little speech, or if his speech is not attended to, he is denied primary

experiences of speech development. A 3-yr study of the emerging speech patterns of a 9-yr-old nonverbal blind girl is reported. At first she used language to refuse by shouting "No." Her speech centered around nonsense syllables. Although her language became more fluent, in storytelling she narrated only single events related to her own feelings. Her greatest distortions in language usage were in expressing her feelings. Language is communication and the basic system of human interaction, but children who live as isolates in home or in residential institutions do not experience this interaction.
Rogow, Sally M. (U British Columbia, Vancouver, Canada) Education of the Visually Handicapped, 1972(May), Vol 4(2), 36-40. [PA, Vol 53:05678]

455. [Development of several motor activities between the ages of 4 and 6.] (Fren)
Defines a method of evaluating aspects of motor development in children, using a system inspired by that of S. Naville and called total motion. The technique, tested with 123 4-10 yr. old normal and 23 8-13 yr. old retarded children, consists of more or less complicated jumping exercises and play patterns with a ball. This method of observation, which is described in detail, enables purely motor aspects to be distinguished from others more closely connected with space-time organization. (German summary)
Roth, Sylvia. (Service Medico-Pedagogique, Geneva, Switzerland) Psychologie - Schweizerische Zeitschrift für Psychologie und ihre Anwendungen, 1972, Vol. 31(3), 224-253. [PA, Vol 50:00743]

456. Concurrent validity of the Quick Test.
Administered the Quick Test (QT) and the WISC to 27 Ss in a diagnostic clinic for mental retardation. The intercorrelations between the QT individual and combination forms were extremely high. Significant rs were obtained between the QT and Picture Arrangement, Coding, Performance Scale, and Full Scale scores. The magnitude of the rs and the speed and ease of administration suggests the QT can be used for deriving an IQ and screening patients in mental retardation facilities.
Sawyer, R. N. & Whitten, James R. (U. Missouri, Rolla) Psychological Reports, 1972(Feb), Vol. 30(1), 64-66. [PA, Vol 48:07643]

457. [Study of acute psychotic episodes in mentally retarded adolescents and the idea of "decompensation" in child psychiatry.] (Fren)
Describes sudden psychotic interludes in 7 adolescent patients followed systematically over many years because of their mental deficiency. It is noted that cyclic (manic-depressive) disorder is rarely reported, but schizophrenia and mental deficiency occur in the same individual with much greater frequency. Although a number of studies has been concerned with coexistence of the chronic states of these 2 conditions, little attention has been directed toward acute psychotic episodes that may emerge among the mentally subnormal. Longitudinal psychiatric histories, complemented by repeated psychometric and neurologic examinations (including EEG) defined a recurring syndrome. Ss of both sexes, of definitely limited intelligence (IQ circa 50), although friendly and affectionate throughout childhood, suddenly presented bizarre behaviors and delusional or paranoid states postpubertally. Psychopathologic elaborations were primitive, owing to the limited mental ability of the patients, but were unmistakable in basic form (hallucinations, confusions, delusions). Most Ss responded well to treatment with mild neuroleptic drugs, returning to the former state. Single and repeated episodes were observed. The clinical phenomena seem best explained by the notion of decompensation. It is concluded that stress, either physiological or psychological, may trigger the emergence of latent or infraclinical psychopathy. Oligophrenic emotional lability may predispose the patient to an unknown degree.
Schachter, M. (24 Castellane Place, Marseille, France) Annales Médico-Psychologiques, 1972(Apr), Vol 1(4), 507-528. [PA, Vol 49:07292]

458. [Psychological abnormalities in the children of mentally retarded parents.] (Russ)
Assessed the influence of the etiology of parental mental retardation on the incidence of mental retardation among the progeny of retarded adults. Clinical data on the children of former students of a special education school were analyzed. One of 23 children born to 16 probands whose mental retardation was of exogenous origin was mentally retarded. 25 of 49 children born to 34 probands whose mental retardation was due to hereditary factors were mentally retarded. The mentally retarded child of the proband whose retardation was of exogenous origin was the product of a marriage between 2 retarded individuals. Where the proband's retardation was hereditary in nature, if his mate was normal 30% of their children were mentally retarded; if his mate exhibited some psychological illness 47% of their children were mentally retarded; if his mate was mentally retarded 92% of their children were mentally retarded. It is concluded that heredity can be important in the etiology of mental retardation.
Shalimov, V. F. (USSR Academy of Pedagogical Sciences, Scientific Research Inst. of Defectology, Moscow) Defektologiya, 1972, Vol. 3, 42-45. [PA, Vol 52:01292]

459. The process of infantilization.
Discusses D. Levy's (see PA, Vol. 40:9098) identification of infantilization as 1 form of maternal overprotection. It is hypothesized that the child obliges his mother's deviant role by failing to develop to his fullest. Recent research on child neglect in rural Appalachia suggested an intergenerational "cycle of infantilization" among mothers. A study was made of 52 mother-child pairs in which the 7-12 yr. old children were borderline or mentally retarded. Results of studying mother-child communications and interactions and an estimate of the S's gross motor coordination linked IQ decrement among Ss to specific child-rearing practices of their mothers. Results clarify the development of the infantile personality, especially among handicapped children. The role of separation anxiety is considered important. (15 ref.)
Sharlin, Shlomo A. & Polansky, Norman A. (U. Georgia, School of Social Work) American Journal of Orthopsychiatry, 1972(Jan), Vol. 42(1), 92-102. [PA, Vol 48:03560]

460. Performance testing of personality with the mentally retarded.
Administered an abbreviated version of Santostefano's Miniature Situations Test to 92 retarded adolescents. A factor analysis of the items yielded 4 interpretable factors, only 2 of which resembled those found in a previous study with normal adolescents. Factor scores were not generally related to age, sex, IQ, or length of hospitalization. Situational tests are suggested as 1 alternative to conventional personality tests for use with retarded Ss.
Silverstein, A. B. (Pacific State Hosp., Pomona, Calif.) Training School Bulletin, 1972(Aug), Vol. 69(2), 78-82. [PA, Vol 49:04863]

461. The incidence of cytomegalovirus among mentally retarded and microcephalic children in a state institution.
Observed the cytomegalovirus (CMV) complement-fixing antibody in 6 out of 89 (6.7%) mentally retarded children resident in a state institution, selected on the basis of unknown etiology and possible infectious origin. 3 of 6 seropositive Ss were microcephalic. Serological results also indicate that only 7 out of 83 (8.4%) were C-F positive during their full-time stay in the institution. Paired serum samples obtained from microcephalic Ss under 5 yr. of age and of their respective mothers were positive to CMV (7 and 44.5%, respectively). 6 of 16 microcephalic Ss under 5 yr. of age were positive to CMV C-F test, and 2 of these demonstrated viruria. (17 ref.)
Sinha, S. K.; Kaveggia, E. & Gordon, M. C. (Central Wisconsin Colony & Training School, Madison) Journal of Mental Deficiency Research, 1972(Jun), Vol. 16(2), 90-96. [PA, Vol 50:05177]

462. Identification capacities of retarded and normal children.
Examined the effects of information load, delay of response, and number and type of dimension of stimulus variation upon the identification capacity of 3 groups of 6 children: retardates (mean CA = 12 yr.), normal 1st graders, and normal 6th graders. A retardate deficit was found, characterized by a generally lower level of information transmission and increasing retardate-normal differences as task demands increased.
Smith, Jerome & Kaufman, Herbert. (U. Connecticut) Psychonomic Science, 1972(Sep), Vol. 28(6), 321-325. [PA, Vol 49:04866]

463. Concurrent validity of the Peabody Individual Achievement Test.
Administered the Peabody Individual Achievement Test (PIAT), the Wide Range Achievement Test (WRAT), and the WISC to 40 7.9-16.1 yr. old children divided into groups of normal, reading disabled, and mentally retarded Ss. Pearsonian correlations between the tests are presented, as well as means and standard deviations for the WISC. Higher correlations were found between the reading subtests while only moderate correlations were found for the spelling and mathematics subtests. It is concluded that the PIAT may be used with the WRAT and WISC to facilitate differential diagnosis.
Soethe, James W. (2925 Glenwood Dr., Boulder, Co.) Journal of Learning Disabilities, 1972(Nov), Vol. 5(9), 560-562. [PA, Vol 49:07985]

464. Effects of spontaneous vs. externally-cued learning on the permanent storage of a schema of retardates.
Presented a visual digit span test to 70 mentally retarded adolescents, with 50% repetition (e.g., 5 3 1 8 5 3 1 8) embedded in sets of 6, 8, and 10-length digits. Discovery and use of the redundancy was conceptualized as equivalent to the learning of a schema or rule. Ss exposed to this task at 2 sessions on 2 separate days continually increased their capacity to learn the schema. Externally cueing the presence of redundancy improved initial performance but had no greater facilitative effect on permanent storage of the schema than did spontaneous discovery. Comparisons with studies of free recall and paired-associate learning suggest that level of constraint redundancy is a crucial factor in retardates' capacity to permanently store a schema. (15 ref.)
Spitz, Herman H. & Webreck, Cindy A. (E. R. Johnstone Training & Research Center, Bordentown, N.J.) American Journal of Mental Deficiency, 1972(Sep), Vol. 77(2), 163-168. [PA, Vol 49:07990]

465. Mental ages for achievement of Piagetian reasoning assessments.
Describes a study of 75 normal and 75 retarded 6-20 yr. old children, screened for inclusion by the WISC or WAIS, which was conducted to determine mental ages of achievement for 21 Piagetian reasoning measures. Ss continue to be reassessed every 2 yr. Preliminary results in the 4th yr. suggest that (a) transition from concrete to formal thought is not accomplished by normal Ss as early or as completely as previously indicated, (b) retarded Ss achieve success on measures of concrete thought but not of formal or abstract thought, (c) criterion performance on reasoning tasks generally is achieved by retarded Ss at a later mental age than that of normal Ss, and (d) the sequence of task accomplishments established is essentially the same as that reported in Swiss studies by Vinh-Bang.
Stephens, Beth; Mahaney, Edward J. & McLaughlin, John A. (Temple U.) Education & Training of the Mentally Retarded, 1972(Oct), Vol. 7(3), 124-128. [PA, Vol 49:09469]

466. Equivalence formation by retarded and nonretarded children at different mental ages.
Compared 42 retarded and 42 nonretarded children, matched at 3 MA levels (6, 8, and 10 yr.), for performance in equivalence-formation tasks. Differences in the frequency with which perceptibly based, functionally based, and sententially based concepts were used for grouping strategies were studied. The performance of retarded and nonretarded Ss of the same MA was quite similar. Both groups showed MA differences in perfor-

mance. The 3 types of groupings were used with unequal frequency depending upon MA level.
Stephens, Wyatt E. (Southern Illinois U.) American Journal of Mental Deficiency, 1972(Nov), Vol. 77(3), 311-313. [PA, Vol 50:03331]

467. The problem of the classification of mental retardation.
Proposes a new system of classifying the various forms of mental retardation. Using the time of exposure to a pathogenic agent and its etiology as a basis, the forms of mental retardation are classified into 3 groups: (a) those caused by a pathological condition of the reproductive cells of the parents; (b) those caused by harmful factors that act during the intrauterine period; and (c) those caused by damage to the CNS in the perinatal period or in the 1st 3 yr. of life.
Suhareva, G. E. (Ministry of Health, Moscow Research Inst. of Psychiatry, USSR) American Journal of Psychiatry, 1972(May), Vol. 128(11, Suppl.), 29-33. [PA, Vol 48:12052]

468. Classification and mental retardation: Issues arising in the fifth WHO seminar on psychiatric diagnosis, classification, and statistics.
Discusses in detail some of the chief issues considered at the seminar and outlines the reasoning behind the recommendations made. The issues considered include the integration of child psychiatry and mental retardation, multiaxial classification, choice of axes, assessment of intellectual retardation, values and limitations of IQ tests, assessment of social competence, classification of biological factors, application of the multiaxial scheme to adult patients, and field trials to test new schemes of classification. (30 ref.)
Tarjan, G., et al. (U. California, Medical School, Los Angeles) American Journal of Psychiatry, 1972(May), Vol. 128(11, Suppl.), 34-45. [PA, Vol 48:09563]

469. [Cognitive interference and intelligence: Reexamination of the measures of SCWT.] (Japn)
Studied the reliability of the modified Stroop Color-Word Test (SCWT), and the correlation between cognitive interference (as measured by the modified SCWT) and intelligence (as measured by 2 intelligence tests) of 38 normal and 48 mentally retarded children. Test-retest (1 yr interval) reliability coefficients ranged from .60 to .89. Cognitive interference was negatively correlated with intelligence for both normal and mentally retarded Ss. ($p < .01; p < .05$). (English summary)
Uechi, Yasuaki. Japanese Journal of Educational Psychology, 1972(Jun), Vol. 20(2), 92-100. [PA, Vol 52:12745]

470. A word of caution on the use of the WAIS.
Analyzed WISC-WAIS differences with regard to length of test interval and sex. Ss were 50 mentally retarded adolescents from 12 different school districts. Analysis of variance showed that the main effects for sex and test instrument were significant. The girls' WISC mean was approximately 6 points lower than that of the boys. There was a significant gain of 10 points from the WISC to the WAIS.
Walker, Kenneth P. & Walker, Carol A. (Indiana State U.) Psychology in the Schools, 1972(Oct), Vol. 9(4), 374-378. [PA, Vol 49:10100]

471. Body image of handicapped children.
Individually administered a "make-a-person" task to (a) 8 institutionalized children with spina bifida, (b) 8 similarly-afflicted Ss residing at home and attending a special day-school for handicapped children, and (c) 8 normal controls. Ss were matched for sex and age (11-17 yr.) and all were within the normal range of intelligence. The 3-dimensional figures created by Ss were duplicated in exact proportion on graph paper to facilitate measurement and to obtain pertinent data. Results indicate that the institutionalized group had a more distorted body image than the other 2 groups.
Weininger, Otto; Rotenberg, G. & Henry, A. (Ontario Inst. for Studies in Education, Toronto, Canada) Journal of Personality Assessment, 1972(Jun), Vol. 36(3), 248-253. [PA, Vol 48:12018]

472.   [The recessive inheritance of mental retardation in one family.] (Russ)
Describes what the author believes to be a recessively inherited form of mental retardation. The case history, physical state, psychological condition, and neurological status of each of 3 siblings are presented. All these children show underdevelopment of complex forms of psychological activity to the same degree, subcortical degeneration primarily in the hypothalamic area, speech disturbances, and an absence of gross emotional problems. It is concluded that, since 3 siblings with the same clinical picture were born to normal parents in the absence of a similar abnormality among their relatives, they exhibit a form of mental retardation which is recessively inherited.
Yavkin, V. M. (USSR Academy of Pedagogical Sciences, Scientific Research Inst. of Defectology, Moscow) Defektologiya, 1972, Vol. 3, 35-41. [PA, Vol 52:01301]

473.   [Some developmental abnormalities of specific origin.] (Russ)
Discusses mental retardation and emotional disturbances in children whose mother and/or father contracted syphilis prior to their conception and whose serological tests are negative for syphilis. These "parasyphilitic illnesses" are distinguished from congenital syphilis. Results of several surveys are presented. In 7 families where 1 or both parents had syphilis, all 18 children showed no specific manifestations of congenital syphilis, but 17 were mentally retarded. A careful examination of the 97 patients being treated for congenital syphilis at a city dispensary between 1957-1962 showed that only 12 actually had a positive serological reaction; however, a variety of problems (e.g., mental retardation, seizures, psychosis) were found among the remaining 85. 3 case histories are reported to illustrate different "parasyphilitic illnesses."
Yavkin, V. M.; Milich, M. V. & Sazonova, L. V. (Academy of Pedagogical Sciences, Inst. of Defectology, Moscow, USSR) Defektologiya, 1972, Vol. 2, 32-39. [PA, Vol 50:11644]

474.   [Performance of children with a delay in psychological development on tasks which include visual models and verbal instruction.] (Russ)
Studied the performance of 20 1st and 2nd graders with a delay in psychological development (minimal brain damage) on 3 groups of tasks: (a) A visual model was presented which displayed all information necessary to perform the task; (b) A visual model was present which displayed some of the information necessary to perform the task, with verbal instructions supplementing the model; (c) All instructions were verbal. 20 mentally retarded and 20 normal 1st and 2nd graders also participated. Unlike the normal Ss, Ss with a delay in development (a) made an abundance of spontaneously corrected errors, (b) did not improve their performance over trials, and (c) had difficulty in fulfilling several requirements simultaneously. The greatest differences between the 3 groups appeared on tasks with only verbal instructions. While the normal Ss made practically no errors, Ss with a delay in development had difficulties in completing the tasks and the mentally retarded children were unable to complete them.
Zharyenkova, G. I. (USSR Academy of Pedagogical Sciences, Inst of Defectology, Moscow) Defektologiya, 1972, No 4, 29-35. [PA, Vol 53:07782]

475.   Effects of semantic and acoustic relatedness on free recall in normal children and retardates.
Assigned 36 3rd graders (mean age 9.39 yr.) and 36 matched-MA retardates (mean age 15.54 yr.) equally to 3 groups presented with lists of semantically related, acoustically related, or unrelated words for free recall. Results show the normals recalled and clustered significantly more than the retardates. Although all Ss showed significantly greater tendency to cluster semantically than acoustically, only the normals given the semantic list clustered in amounts significantly above chance levels. Significant list differences in terms of amount recalled indicated an inhibitory effect of acoustic relatedness.

Zupnick, Jack J. & Forrester, William E. (U. South Dakota) Psychonomic Science, 1972(Feb), Vol. 26(4), 188-190. [PA, Vol 48:12081]

476.   Surprise and memory as indices of concrete operational development.
Assessed 72 normal and 61 retarded children's use of color, number, length, and continuous quantity as attributes of identity by presenting the Ss with contrived changes in these properties. Mean Binet MAs were 6.3 for normals and 6.2 for retardates. Surprise to the change of color occurred at lower MAs than surprise to all quantitative properties among normals and to continuous quantity and (nonsignificantly) to length among retardates. More retardates than MA-matched normals were surprised at the change of quantity ($p = .058$), but there were no other significant group differences. Study II employed 64 normal children (mean MA = 5.2). Significant relations between surprise and both recognition and reconstruction memory were found for color and number. Surprise and correct memory responses for color preceded those to number, which preceded logical verbal responses to a conventional number-conservation task. (15 ref.)
Achenbach, Thomas M. (Yale U.) Psychological Reports, 1973(Aug), Vol. 33(1), 47-57. [PA, Vol 51:06835]

477.   Ethnic background, measured intelligence, and adaptive behavior scores in mentally retarded children.
Assessed the degree to which classification of levels of mental retardation based on the Vineland Social Maturity Scale differed from the classification based on IQ, for 50 Black and 59 White 4-17 yr old children. The Black group scored lower on IQ, but the groups did not differ on deviation social quotient (DSQ). The distributions of levels of impairment differed as a function of race for classification based on IQ but not for that based on DSQ. On the basis of IQ, more Black than White Ss were classified as very impaired. Similarly fewer Black than White Ss were classified as borderline or above. This effect was not found for DSQ. (16 ref.)
Adams, Jerry; McIntosh, Eranell I. & Weade, Barbara L. (Illinois State Pediatric Inst., Chicago) American Journal of Mental Deficiency, 1973(Jul), Vol. 78(1), 1-6. [PA, Vol 51:05456]

478.   [A method for the psychometric determination of behavioral properties for the documentation of case files in neuropsychiatry in childhood and adolescence.] (Germ)
Presents original questionnaires for measuring traits of independence, industriousness, and social adaptation in mentally retarded juveniles. Test-retest reliability is reportedly high. Examples of the 3 questionnaires are presented.
Altdorff, Volker. (District Hosp. for Psychiatry & Neurology, Bernburg, E. Germany) Psychiatrie, Neurologie und medizinische Psychologie, 1973(Jan), Vol. 25(1), 27-37. [PA, Vol 50:08094]

479.   Cognitive deficits in children with spina bifida and hydrocephalus: A review of the literature.
Anderson, Elizabeth M. (U. London, Inst. of Education, Child Development Research Unit, England) British Journal of Educational Psychology, 1973(Nov), Vol. 43(3), 257-268. [PA, Vol 52:03410]

480.   Social and emotional adjustment of retarded CP infants.
Reported the development of social and emotional adjustment measures for retarded cerebral palsied preschool children and infants under 2 yrs. Fairly consistent relationships between age and intelligence and scores on the scales and between scores on both scales were found for both handicapped and nonhandicapped children.
Banham, Katharine M. (Duke U.) Exceptional Children, 1973(Oct), Vol. 40(2), 107. [PA, Vol 51:03504]

481.   Paired-associate learning by normal children and retardates with relevant redundant compound stimuli.
Compared 96 mental retardates (mean CA = 21 yr., mean MA = 9½ yr.) with 96 normal 3rd-6th graders on a redundant-stimulus paired-associate (PA) task in which the stimulus components differed in meaningfulness (M). The M values of the

colors and trigrams were established preexperimentally for both populations. Various procedural refinements distinguished the present research from previous studies: (a) response pretraining, (b) instructions designed to provide equal emphasis to lower M trigrams and higher M colors, and (c) recognition tests for the measurement of stimulus selection. In contrast to earlier comparative research which suggested that M affects stimulus selection behaviors of normal children only, results indicate that both groups selected the higher M colors as their functional stimuli for stimulus-response associative learning and that both formed a small number of intercue associations.
Berry, Franklin M. & Baumeister, Alfred A. (Columbus Coll.) Journal of Experimental Child Psychology, 1973(Feb), Vol. 15(1), 63-76. [PA, Vol 50:09102]

482.   Reversal and rotation errors by normal and retarded readers.
Investigated the incidence of and relationships among word and letter reversals in writing and Bender Gestalt rotation errors in matched samples of 100 normal and 100 retarded 6-9 yr old readers. No significant differences in the incidence of reversal and rotation errors were found in the 2 groups. Word reversal was an isolated finding with low frequency, while letter reversal and Bender rotation were less isolated and more frequent. The significance of examining for such errors by elementary school children to predict reading retardation is discussed.
Black, F. William. (Fitzsimons General Hosp., Denver, Colo.) Perceptual & Motor Skills, 1973(Jun), Vol. 36(3, Pt. 1), 895-898. [PA, Vol 51:03468]

483.   Conservation tasks with retarded and nonretarded children.
Attempted to determine the best predictors of behavior, explanation, and scores for conservation of (a) two dimensional space, (b) substance, (c) continuous quantity, and (d) weight for nonretarded and retarded children. Results support Piaget's findings about conservation.
Boland, Sandra K. (U. Northern Colorado, Rocky Mountain Special Education Instructional Materials Center) Exceptional Children, 1973(Nov), Vol. 40(3), 209-211. [PA, Vol 51:09437]

484.   The influence of stimulus dimension predisposition in discrimination learning by retarded children.
Investigated the importance of dimensional predisposition in discrimination learning by 80 retarded children at 2 MA levels (4.0-5.9 or 5.10-9.0 yrs). Ss at both MA levels who displayed a preference for color (as indicated by a matching on the color dimension in a pretask) were given match-to-sample procedure in both an original learning and a transfer task in which color or angular rotation was relevant. Results indicate that those Ss given a task with the color dimension as relevant learned more easily than Ss for whom rotation was correct. Original learning on either dimension interfered with a transfer to the other dimension; the interference effect was greater for higher than for lower MA Ss.
Bond, John B.; Black, Kathryn N. & Raskin, Larry M. (Indiana U.) Training School Bulletin, 1973(Nov), Vol. 70(3), 167-171. [PA, Vol 52:05683]

485.   Controlled forgetting in the retarded.
Conducted 3 experiments which investigated selective rehearsal by retarded adolescents in a serial memory task involving instructions to forget a subset of the material presented. Since previous research indicates that retarded children do not selectively rehearse, it was believed that Ss would fail in this task. Exp I ($n = 10$) showed that retardates could perform this task, and there was substantial evidence for cumulative rehearsal. The possibility of an averaging artifact in Exp I was eliminated in Exp II ($n = 10$) by showing evidence of primacy and facilitation due to the forget instruction for individual Ss. Exp III ($n = 20$) indicated that the facilitation due to the forget instruction was due to the effective use of a selective rehearsal strategy. It is suggested that response biases may be involved in previous studies of rehearsal. (31 ref)

Bray, Norman W. (U. Cincinnati) Cognitive Psychology, 1973(Nov), Vol. 5(3), 288-309. [PA, Vol 51:11398]

486.   Conservation of number and continuous quantity in normal, bright, and retarded children.
Examined the relation of chronological age (CA), mental age (MA), and IQ to conservation of number and of continuous quantity by comparing performance of 60 bright (CA = 4 yrs; MA = 6 yrs), normal (CA and MA = 6 yrs), and retarded (CA = 8 yrs; MA = 6 yrs) children. 2 additional groups of 20 Ss were used-normal children matched for CA with the bright children (CA and MA = 4 yrs) and normal children matched for CA with the retarded children (CA and MA = 8 yrs). MA was measured by the Stanford-Binet Intelligence Scale. Retarded Ss performed like normal Ss of the same MA but less well than their normal CA peers. However, bright children did not perform as efficiently as their normal MA peers but more like their normal CA peers. Experiential and intellectual factors appear to be involved in both the MA score itself and conservation performance.
Brown, Ann L. (U. Illinois, Children's Research Center) Child Development, 1973(Jun), Vol. 44(2), 376-379. [PA, Vol 52:12010]

487.   Keeping track of changing variables: Effects of rehearsal training and rehearsal prevention in normal and retarded adolescents.
Reports 2 experiments investigating keeping-track performance in normal and retarded children. Exp I included 2 groups of retarded 11-19 yr old Ss, one trained to rehearse ($n = 10$) and the other given no rehearsal training ($n = 13$). For the latter Ss both accuracy and latency of recall were related to the number of states of the probed variable. The rehearsal Ss were not influenced by this variable. In Exp II, 2 groups of 58 9th graders were Ss, 1 group serving as untreated controls. In the 2nd group, cumulative rehearsal was prevented. The control group showed patterns identical to those of the (rehearsal) trained retardates, whereas the group prevented from rehearsing cumulatively showed patterns typical of noninstructed retardates. Results are discussed in terms of the role of rehearsal strategies in this task and of developmental changes in the spontaneous use of mnemonic strategies.
Brown, Ann L.; Campione, Joseph C.; Bray, Norman W. & Wilcox, Barbara L. (U. Illinois, Children's Research Center) Journal of Experimental Psychology, 1973(Nov), Vol. 101(1), 123-131. [PA, Vol 52:03351]

488.   On the theory and practice of improving short-term memory.
Reviews (a) a series of basic studies that have analyzed the learning and retrieval processes used by nonretarded adults to perform well on a probe-type, short-term memory task; and (b) a series of comparative studies which show that neither nonretarded children nor the retarded spontaneously use certain of these processes. Results of the present 3 applied experiments with mildly retarded 13-21 yr olds ($N = 40$) are also reported. The experiments were designed to determine whether training in the use and sequencing of these memory processes would substantially improve Ss' short-term memory performance. Results indicate that retarded adolescents can use competently all of the component processes sufficient for highly accurate recall but do not recall accurately unless they are taught how to sequence the processes properly. (15 ref)
Butterfield, Earl C.; Wambold, Clark & Belmont, John M. (U. Kansas) American Journal of Mental Deficiency, 1973(Mar), Vol. 77(5), 654-669. [PA, Vol 51:07431]

489.   Scaling meaningfulness (M) of trigrams with children and retardates.
Used the production method and paired-comparisons procedures to scale 25 trigrams for meaningfulness with 72 normal children (mean CA = 9 yrs) and 72 retardates (CA = less than 30 yrs, mean MA = 9 yrs). Reliabilities of scale values derived from subgroup comparisons were moderate. Test-retest reliabilities were somewhat higher. Ratings of these scale values with values

previously obtained from normal adults ranged from .60 to .75. Adult meaningfulness values predicted paired-associate learning for both children and retardates better than did production and paired-comparison values. Results support the assumption that meaningfulness norms obtained from adults are, under some conditions, appropriate for use in learning experiments with children and retardates. (19 ref)
Campbell, Cecil O. & Baumeister, Alfred A. (U. Alabama, Center for Developmental & Learning Disorders) Journal of Psychology, 1973(Jul), Vol. 84(2), 267-277. [PA, Vol 51:07432]

490. Psychological assessment of the handicapped child in a hospital unit.
Describes the medical and psychological evaluations made of children admitted to a hospital for the subnormal. Background data, results of clinical investigations (e.g., hearing assessment, speech therapy, and IQ testing), and treatment provided for 102 children are presented. Results show the need for earlier assessment, development of preschool facilities for the handicapped, increases in speech therapy facilities, and the provision of training programs for families whose children have behavior problems associated with retardation. It is suggested that adequate follow-up care and community services should be developed if the assessment procedures are to have any real value.
Capie, A. C. (Lea Castle Hosp., Psychological Services, Wolverley, England) British Journal of Mental Subnormality, 1973(Jun), Vol. 19(36, Pt. 1), 38-47. [PA, Vol 52:01658]

491. Chromosome survey of moderately to profoundly retarded patients.
Performed chromosome analyses on 130 patients (mean age = 9.7 yrs) selected for study because of moderate to profound mental retardation and multiple congenital anomalies. 28 Ss (21.2%) had a significant chromosome abnormality, including 9 in whom there was a clinical suspicion that a specific chromosomal syndrome was present. Of the 121 Ss without a suspected diagnosis prior to chromosome study, 19 (15.7%) had a chromosome abnormality. Results suggest that chromosome analysis in infants or children with moderate to profound retardation and congenital malformations can provide the physician with information of diagnostic and prognostic value and have implications for genetic counseling of families. (18 ref.)
Carrel, Robert E.; Sparkes, Robert S. & Wright, Stanley W. (Tri-Counties Regional Center, Santa Barbara, Calif.) American Journal of Mental Deficiency, 1973(Mar), Vol. 77(5), 616-622. [PA, Vol 51:07433]

492. Human figure drawing of mentally retarded, brain injured, and normal children.
3 groups of 18 children each, similar in mental age, were given the Harris-Goodenough version of the Draw-A-Man test. Mentally retarded Ss scored higher by presenting more details than either normal or brain-injured Ss. Qualitatively, the drawings of the retarded were better proportioned and organized than those of the brain-injured, and were not inferior to those of the normals. The brain-injured showed fewer details and body parts than the normals, and organization was less good. It is concluded that brain-injured children in particular need art activity to enhance visualization of detail, visual memory, organization, spatial relations, and coordination.
Carter, John L. (U Houston, Clear Lake) Art Psychotherapy, 1973(Win), Vol 1(3-4), 307-308. [PA, Vol 54:09959]

493. Human figure drawing of mentally retarded, brain injured, and normal children.
Administered the Goodenough Draw-A-Man test to 18 mentally retarded (R) boys, 18 brain-damaged (BD) boys, and 18 normal (N) children. The IQ and CA of the groups differed widely, but the MA of all groups was the same (approximately 8½ yrs). Drawings were scored quantitatively by the Harris-Goodenough (HG) criteria and qualitatively by 2 judges on the basis of proportion of parts, inclusion of detail, organization, and inclusion of body parts. The Rs scored higher (showed more detail) on the HG scale, followed by the Ns and BDs.

Qualitatively, the Rs scored higher than Ns only in detail, but higher than the BDs in all respects. Results emphasize the needs of these types of children for different instruction in terms of body image, and the special needs of the BDs for creative art.
Carter, John L. (U Houston at Clear Lake) Art Psychotherapy, 1973(Win), Vol 1(3-4), 307-308. [PA, Vol 59:05770]

494. Sleep patterns and intelligence in functional mental retardation.
Made electrooculograph, EMG, and EEG recordings for 4 consecutive nights in 7 male adolescents with a diagnosis of functional mental retardation. The sleep pattern of this group of Ss was determined, and the various sleep measures were correlated with the IQ and social quotient (SQ). A positive correlation was obtained between REM sleep and the IQ-SQ. Results are discussed with reference to the sleep-cognition hypothesis.
Castaldo, V. & Krynicki, V. (Albany Medical Coll., N.Y.) Journal of Mental Deficiency Research, 1973(Sep), Vol. 17(3-4), 231-235. [PA, Vol 52:08001]

495. L-dopa and REM sleep in normal and mentally retarded subjects.
14 normal adult males and females and 2 12-yr-old males diagnosed as mentally retarded received doses of 500, 200, or 125 mg of levodopa. A lengthened first REM period occurred for Ss receiving 200 mg. No other significant effects were found.
Castaldo, Vincenzo; Krynicki, Victor E. & Crade, Michael. (Union U., Albany Medical Coll.) Biological Psychiatry, 1973(Jun), Vol. 6(3), 295-299. [PA, Vol 51:05459]

496. A survey on the distribution of psychiatric syndromes seen in children in three major groups of changing Turkish culture.
Considers changing Turkish society in 3 main groups: traditional, transitional, and modern. The traditional has the highest frequency of organic and mental retardation problems; in the transitional, psychotic cases exceed expectation; in the modern, neurotic cases are predominant. Organic and hereditary factors appear in the traditional, environmental in the modern. Immigrant groups, faced with social and economic stress, show an increase in both prevalence and severity of psychiatric disorder requiring intensive treatment. The concept of mental illness is more influenced by superstition than by Moslem teachings, the physician is considered the last resort. It is concluded that parent and child guidance are imperative for the transition from traditional to modern life.
Cebiroglu, Ridvan, et al. (U. Istanbul, Turkey) Acta Paedopsychiatrica, 1973, Vol. 39(6), 155-161. [PA, Vol 50:03180]

497. The relationship between pneumoencephalographic measurements and intellectual outcome in children with epileptic seizures.
Reports that in 101 children under 4 yrs old with a history of epilepsy, the size of the cella media did not differ significantly between 68 severely retarded, 18 moderately or mildly retarded, and 15 normal children. The lateral ventricles of the severely retarded were significantly larger than in the other groups. Cases with intracranial hypertension and grossly distorted ventricles were excluded. (19 ref)
Chevrie, J. J. & Aicardi, J. (National Inst. of Health and Medical Research, Saint-Vincent-de-Paul Hosp., Paris, France) Developmental Medicine & Child Neurology, 1973(Oct), Vol. 15(5), 576-583. [PA, Vol 52:01313]

498. Interpretation of psychological test data to children.
Describes a policy introduced at the Child Evaluation Center in Louisville, Kentucky, of interpreting psychological test data to all children capable of profiting by such interpretation. This included retarded, emotionally disturbed, learning disabled, and physically handicapped children. Excerpts from the transcript of a tape-recorded session with a brain-impaired 8-yr-old boy are included as an illustration.
Colley, Thomas E. (U. Louisville, Medical School, Child Evaluation Center) Mental Retardation, 1973(Feb), Vol. 11(1), 28-30. [PA, Vol 50:03413]

499. Autonomic responses of retarded adolescents during anticipation and feedback in probability learning.
Examined cognitive processes involved in probability guessing in terms of autonomic changes. 48 retarded adolescents were required to guess which of the 2 events, *x* or *y*, would follow a cue stimulus. The probabilities of *x d y* were .90:.10 for one group and .70:.30 for the other. Heart rate acceleration was noted during the anticipation period when the S was waiting a confirmation or contradiction of his prediction, but there was a marked deceleration following the positive as well as negative feedback. Acceleration is interpreted as a sign of internal reflection, and deceleration as that of attention to external events. *Das, J. P. & Bower, A. C.* (U. Alberta, Centre for the Study of Mental Retardation, Edmonton, Canada) Journal of Mental Deficiency Research, 1973(Sep), Vol. 17(3-4), 171-175. [PA, Vol 52:08004]

500. Shifts in conceptual thinking by organically and familial retarded adolescents and adults.
Administered the Wisconsin card sort task, involving concept shifts, and the Block Design subtest of the WAIS to samples of organically retarded (*n* = 18) and cultural-familial retarded (*n* = 18) adolescents and adults. One-half of the Ss were told when they were wrong; the other half when right or wrong. The 2 types of cues had no differential effects, except in interaction with number of responses. The organically retarded Ss made significantly more responses before reaching criterion than did the cultural-familial retarded Ss. However, there were no significant differences between groups on perseveration or solution time. There were significant differences among stimulus dimensions, with number being the most difficult, and form and color less so. Organically retarded persons appear to have less facility in hypothesis formation during concept acquisition than cultural-familial retarded persons who have no apparent brain pathology. (20 ref.)
Deich, Ruth F. (Pacific State Hosp., Pomona, Calif.) American Journal of Mental Deficiency, 1973(Jul), Vol. 78(1), 59-62. [PA, Vol 51:05462]

501. Test of Social Inference for retarded adolescents: Measuring social-cue perception.
Administered the Test of Social Inference to 1,335 retardates from 9 geographically diverse locations to test their ability to interpret social cues appropriately. Results show the test to be unbiased with respect to race and place of residence and uncorrelated with chronological age. Slight sex differences were found favoring males. Discrimination between public school retardates, institutionalized retardates, and nonretarded Ss on the basis of test scores was evident. The test correlated moderately with IQ but proved somewhat more highly related to a variety of social behavioral and psychological criteria than to IQ. (19 ref.)
deJung, John E.; Holen, Michael C. & Edmonson, Barbara. (U. Oregon) Psychological Reports, 1973(Apr), Vol. 32(2), 603-618. [PA, Vol 51:01378]

502. Language assessment of mental retardates.
Administered the Assessment of Children's Language Comprehension test to 58 institutionalized mental retardates. Results indicate that (a) the test's cut-off point was too high; (b) verbs and prepositions were better understood in multielement presentations than in isolation, while the reverse was true for modifiers and nouns; and (c) the correct or incorrect interpretation of nouns, verbs, modifiers, and prepositions in isolation was of low predictive value for its understanding in multielement presentations.
Delp, Harold A. & Smeets, Paul M. (Temple U.) Training School Bulletin, 1973(May), Vol. 70(1), 30-32. [PA, Vol 51:03474]

503. Cerebral haemodynamic factors in mentally retarded children.
Compared EEG and rheoencephalographic (REG) findings and performance on Steer's Figure-Ground Test, Steer's-Beatty Closure Test, the House-Tree-Person Test, and the Benton Visual Retention Test of 18 7-18 yr old mentally retarded children and 14 7-18 yr old normal children. Results show that only 7 of the 18 retarded Ss had normal EEG records. Retarded Ss also had a 5% impairment in REG measurements and performed significantly worse on the 4 psychological tests than the normal Ss. (26 ref.)
Doust, J. W. & Podnieks, I. (U. Toronto, Clarke Inst. of Psychiatry, Ontario, Canada) Journal of Mental Deficiency Research, 1973(Jun), Vol. 17(2), 123-128. [PA, Vol 51:07437]

504. WISC short forms with mentally retarded children.
Rescored the complete WISC protocols of 100 mentally retarded children according to 2 selected subtests and 2 selected item short-form methodologies and then compared them for their correspondence to the standard form. High correlations between all short and standard forms were obtained. However, when mean differences between the standard and short-form IQs were examined, less encouraging results were found. A relatively high percentage of individuals changed IQ classification level when the abbreviated forms were used. Results indicate that reliance on short forms for the educational disposition of mentally retarded individuals is questionable. A new short form, the Devereux Short Form, was then derived and cross-validated. It not only satisfied the criteria, but also provided a 40% saving in administration time and allowed for scatter analysis. (16 ref)
Finch, A. J.; Ollendick, T. H. & Ginn, F. W. (Virginia Treatment Center for Children, Richmond) American Journal of Mental Deficiency, 1973(Sep), Vol. 78(2), 144-149. [PA, Vol 52:01258]

505. Theory and data on developmental changes in novelty preference.
Notes that as children mature, their preference for novel stimuli changes to a preference for familiar ones in discriminative situations featuring differential reinforcement. This change, observed before, takes place between 4 and 5 yrs of age. The effect was replicated with 13 retarded adolescents and was found to be largely under the control of MA rather than CA. Stimulus factors also exerted some influence on this developmental change, with novelty-preference being stronger for objects than pictures. A theoretical model is offered which provides separate assessments of learning and novelty-familiarity preferences in experiments using E. Moss and H. F. Harlow's 1947 design typically employed in this area. This model is applied to the present data as well as those of previous studies. Results support the conclusion of a developmental change in novelty-familiarity preference between MA 4 and 5 yrs.
Fisher, Mary A.; Sperber, Richard & Zeaman, David. (State U. New York, Stony Brook) Journal of Experimental Child Psychology, 1973(Jun), Vol. 15(3), 509-520. [PA, Vol 51:03476]

506. The effects of intelligence quotient and extraneous stimulation on incidental learning.
Examined the effect of extraneous auditory stimulation on incidental learning in 27 normal and 27 noninstitutionalized retarded children matched for MA of 6 yrs, 10 mo to 7 yrs. Both groups were assigned to either a no noise, white noise, or varied noise condition. Results indicate that neither IQ level nor noise condition significantly affected correct incidentally learned responses. However, the mentally retarded gave both more total and more incorrect responses than normals.
Forehand, R.; Calhoun, Karen; Peed, S. & Yoder, Pam. (U. Georgia) Journal of Mental Deficiency Research, 1973(Mar), Vol. 17(1), 24-27. [PA, Vol 51:09442]

507. Effects of IQ and mental age on verbal imitative performance of children.
Examined the verbal imitative performance of 32 normal 5-8 yr olds and 32 retarded 8-13 yr olds at 4 MAs (5, 6, 7, and 8 yrs). 3 dependent measures of imitation were taken: total, mimical, and conceptual. Results indicate that both IQ and MA were significant factors in imitative performance. Retardates primarily demonstrated mimical imitation at the MA-5 level and conceptual imitation at the MA-7 level, while normals emitted primarily mimical responses at MA 7. Retardates and normals differed in total imitation only at MA 5.

Forehand, Rex; Robbins, Bruce & Brady, Charles P. (U. Georgia) Journal of Psychology, 1973(Jul), Vol. 84(2), 353-358. [PA, Vol 51:09443]

508. Intentional and incidental learning: A developmental and comparative approach.
Administered a paired-associate learning task to 49 10-, 13-, and 16-yr-old retarded and normal children who were matched for MA and CA. The learning task consisted of 5 pairs administered under 2 conditions: either 5 stimulus designs paired with 5 objects or the same pairs bordered by a different color. Results suggest that older Ss perform better on an intentional learning task than do younger Ss, and that retardates have more difficulty than their CA controls. Retardates and controls did not differ significantly on incidental learning measures. Stimulus designs, not colors, were used as functional stimuli. (18 ref.)
Fraas, Louis A. (Veterans Administration Hosp., Topeka, Kan.) Journal of Mental Deficiency Research, 1973(Jun), Vol. 17(2), 129-137. [PA, Vol 51:07438]

509. Brightness sensitivity and preference in deaf-blind retarded children.
Tested 16 deaf-blind, retarded, preschool, postrubella children in an operant procedure which allowed them to select preferred illumination feedback as reinforcement for operating a simple 2-choice lever switch. The purpose of the program was to evaluate systematically light sensitivity in children for whom such evaluations are not considered possible due to imputed blindness and disorganized behavior. All Ss remaining in the program showed light sensitivity down to the 5 ft-c level. The need to assess boundary conditions of children's visual competence and disability as a prerequisite for planning educational procedures to take maximum advantage of their residual vision is discussed. (16 ref)
Friedlander, Bernard Z. & Knight, Marcia S. (U. Hartford, Infant/Child Language Research Lab.) American Journal of Mental Deficiency, 1973(Nov), Vol. 78(3), 323-330. [PA, Vol 52:03433]

510. Types of mixed lists and paired-associate learning.
Examined the performance of 72 intellectually average children (mean CA = 7.8 yrs) and 72 retardates (IQ range 45-65) on target subsets of word pairs when employed in mixed lists. Results show that the performance of the retarded Ss on a nonassociated subset of word pairs was influenced by the associative strength of the other subsets that made up the entire list. This was not found with the MA-matched average Ss. Results are discussed in terms of learning processes and experimental designs.
Gallagher, Joseph W.; Kistler, Doris & Blouke, Peter. (U. Alabama) American Journal of Mental Deficiency, 1973(Nov), Vol. 78(3), 268-271. [PA, Vol 52:03362]

511. Memory, IQ, and transitive inference in normals and retardates.
Replicated a study by M. L. Roodin and G. E. Gruen (see PA, Vol. 45:6054) to clarify the relationship between IQ, MA, and performance on Piagetian tasks, and to determine whether retarded children have memory deficits. 24 familially retarded children were matched with 24 normal 6-yr-olds on MA (6.5 yrs). 6 males and 6 females from each group were assigned randomly to 1 of 2 conditions in which memory aids were present or absent. The Mueller-Lyer illusion was employed to create a perceptual illusion which reversed the size relationship between the 1st and 3rd sticks of a 3-term series. Significant ($p < .002$) differences were found between groups in the memory aid condition. No differences were found between groups when memory aids were absent or between sexes in either condition.
Gruen, Gerald E. (Purdue U.) Developmental Psychology, 1973(Nov), Vol. 9(3), 436. [PA, Vol 51:05469]

512. Visual discrimination learning in familial retarded and nonretarded children.
36 retarded and 36 nonretarded children, individually matched for MA, were given discrimination problems at 2 levels of stimulus complexity to test the hypothesis that retarded persons require more trials to reach criterion on the more complex problems. The procedure consisted of intellectual assessment, pretesting-pretraining, and concept attainment. The hypothesis was only marginally supported, and results were not consistent across different concepts. However, the method of varying stimulus complexity to manipulate task difficulty was quite successful, Ss taking more trials to reach criterion on the more complex tasks. The need to extend this approach, comparing nonretarded and retarded children of the same MA along this same dimension of complexity while increasing the degree of complexity, is discussed. (26 ref.)
Gruen, Gerald E. & Berg, Berthold. (Purdue U.) American Journal of Mental Deficiency, 1973(Jul), Vol. 78(1), 63-69. [PA, Vol 51:05467]

513. Information processing in familially retarded and nonretarded children.
Presented 25 retarded and 25 nonretarded children, matched for MA, with both 2-bit (4-choice) and 3-bit (8-choice) problem-solving tasks. The hypothesis tested was that differences in the performance of these 2 groups would increase as task complexity increased, with retarded Ss performing more poorly. Generally, results did not support the hypothesis, but nonretarded Ss did obtain higher strategy scores than retarded. Reaction times to 1st move suggested that retarded Ss were overwhelmed by the information in the 3-bit problem and responded quickly as well as randomly.
Gruen, Gerald E. & Korte, John. (Purdue U.) American Journal of Mental Deficiency, 1973(Jul), Vol. 78(1), 82-88. [PA, Vol 51:05468]

514. An analysis of individual differences in generalization between receptive and productive language in retarded children.
Describes 2 experiments in which 4 mentally retarded males (CAs = 11, 13, 20, and 21 yr) were taught generative pluralization rules concurrently in both the receptive and productive modalities of language. Receptive training established correct pointing to either 1 or a pair of objects, in response to a spoken singular or plural label of the object(s). Productive training established correct spoken labels of 1 or a pair of objects presented visually. However, these pluralization rules were established in each modality only for a specific class of plurals, those ending in -s for 1 modality, those ending in -es for the other modality. This training was successful in establishing generative, or rule-governed behaviors, such that untrained examples of singulars and plurals were usually responded to correctly. Despite this concurrent generative behavior, probes revealed little generalization between modalities, 3 Ss did not generalize clearly from receptive training with 1 class of plurals to correct productive use of that class, nor did they generalize from productive training of the other class of plurals to correct receptive response to that class. The 4th S, however, did show strong generalization of both these types. It is concluded that automatic generalization between receptive and productive language is not necessarily an inevitable result of language training, and therefore may require explicit, if temporary, programing, e.g., by direct reinforcement. (15 ref.)
Guess, Doug & Baer, Donald M. (Kansas Neurological Inst., Topeka) Journal of Applied Behavior Analysis, 1973(Sum), Vol. 6(2), 311-329. [PA, Vol 51:01382]

515. Sexual knowledge and attitudes of mentally retarded adolescents.
Assessed 61 noninstitutionalized mildly and moderately retarded adolescents in reference to self-concept, sexual ethics, and knowledge of sex. In addition, parents tried to predict their retarded adolescents' responses in these areas. Parents and teachers provided additional information through, respectively, a social history form and a behavior rating scale. Analysis included (a) normalization of scores, evaluation for internal consistency, and tests for significant differences between means; and (b) intercorrelation of 32 variables on each subject (e.g., sex, IQ, self-concept score). Of 496 possible correlations, 111 were significant. Internal reliability ranged from .46-.94 (adolescent) and from .81-.94 (parent). Retarded respondents were significantly more

liberal in sexual ethics than their parents predicted, but parents accurately predicted the scores of the adolescents on knowledge and self-concept.
Hall, Judy E.; Morris, Helen L. & Barker, Harry R. (U. Alabama, Birmingham) American Journal of Mental Deficiency, 1973(May), Vol. 77(6), 706-709. [PA, Vol 51:07442]

516. [Studies of discrimination learning in mentally retarded children: Effects of reinforcement rates on the learning rate.] (Japn)
Conducted 2 experiments with normal and mentally retarded Ss matched for MA to study the effects of various reinforcement rates on simple discrimination learning. In Exp I, Ss viewed a series of pictures with various numbers of circles in each and were asked to select the correct number of circles. Responses were reinforced at 100, 75, 50, and 25% rates until 8 successive correct responses had been made. Extinction procedures were then instituted. In both normal and retarded Ss, there was a significant effect of reinforcement on acquisition rates and the number of extinction responses increased with decreased reinforcement rates. Retarded Ss required more responses than normal Ss. Exp II was similar to Exp I, except that the stimuli were varied along shape and size dimensions, and correct responses were reinforced at 100, 66, and 33% rates. Normal Ss who learned relatively fast in Exp I were not influenced by the various reinforcement rates. Extinction responses were similar to those found in Exp I.
Hamashige, Tamie. (Tokyo U. of Education, Japan) Japanese Journal of Special Education, 1973(Jun), Vol. 11(1), 14-21. [PA, Vol 52:03364]

517.   Discrimination learning of retarded children as a function of positive reinforcement and response cost.
Studied the relative effectiveness of positive reinforcement, response cost, and a combination condition via a balanced design in which 12 borderline retarded and 12 moderately retarded children performed under each of the 3 conditions. For the borderline retarded group, both response cost and the combination condition were sigificantly more effective than positive reinforcement alone, and there was no significant difference between response cost and combination. For the moderately retarded group, the treatment effect was not significant, although differences were in the same direction as in the borderline group. Findings suggest that intellectual level is an important factor in determining which reinforcement contingency is more effective. (16 ref)
Harris, Lawrence M. & Tramontana, Joseph. (Family & Child Guidance Center, Smethport, Pa.) American Journal of Mental Deficiency, 1973(Sep), Vol. 78(2), 216-219. [PA, Vol 52:01264]

518.   Effects of rewarded pretraining and partial reinforcement on lever pulling by retarded and nonretarded children.
Gave the task of pulling 2 levers for marble rewards to 72 retarded and 72 nonretarded children, matched for MA of about 7 yrs. Half the Ss were given a pretraining task on which they experienced success and half a control pretraining procedure. On the lever-pulling task, half the Ss received 50% reward on the 1st lever and the other half 100% reward; both groups were always rewarded after pulling the 2nd lever. Rewarded pretraining led to slower starting speeds on both levers which was more marked in retarded than in nonretarded Ss. For nonretarded Ss the 50% reinforcement condition led to consistently faster responding on both levers, but this partial reward superiority was seen in retarded Ss only on the early trials. Interpretations of these effects are offered in terms of A. Amsel's theory of frustrative nonreward and E. Zigler's concept of a retardate negative reaction tendency. (24 ref)
Hayes, Charles S. & Routh, Donald K. (U. Iowa, Child Development Clinic) Perceptual & Motor Skills, 1973(Jun), Vol. 36(3, Pt. 2), 1295-1307. [PA, Vol 51:09447]

519.   Problem length and multiple discrimination learning in retarded children.
Presented 26 retarded children in 2 groups (mean MA = 2.6 or 5.3 yrs) with a series of form discrimination problems with either 3 or 10 trials per problem. Learning was faster (on the 1st 3 trials) if each problem lasted for 10 trials. The effect was attributed to a higher reward ratio for the attention response during the longer problems. No significant MA effects were found. Results suggest the importance of providing thorough training on old material before introducing new material. (17 ref)
House, Betty J. (U. Connecticut) American Journal of Mental Deficiency, 1973(Nov), Vol. 78(3), 255-261. [PA, Vol 52:03369]

520.   Sensory integration in normal and retarded children.
Compared 10 retarded (mean IQ = 47, mean age = 12 yrs 7 mo) and 20 normal children matched for MA (mean IQ = 102, mean age = 5 yrs 3 mo) and for CA (mean age = 12 yrs 7 mo) in visual and tactual within- and cross-modal matching of random forms. Results indicate that visual-visual matching was superior for all 3 groups whether or not the task made memory demands. Cross-modal matching was superior to tactual-tactual for normals but not for retardates, and there was an Age × Modalities interaction for normal Ss. Data indicate a failure of intersensory integration in retarded Ss. It is suggested that movement-training programs might improve performance by retardates. (22 ref.)
Jones, Bill & Robinson, Tony. (U. Queensland, St. Lucia, Australia) Developmental Psychology, 1973(Sep), Vol. 9(2), 178-182. [PA, Vol 51:07445]

521.   Delivery of special services to young black children.
Argues that in planning special services for retarded, disadvantaged, or deprived black children, little attention has been given to the effects of these labels on the self-concepts and expectations of the children, and that many positive aspects of young black children's cognitive, affective, and life circumstances have not been fully recognized. Data on these issues are presented and the need to adjust the current deficiency-oriented view of black children is emphasized. (19 ref)
Jones, Reginald L. (U California, Coll of Education, Riverside) Journal of Non-White Concerns in Personnel & Guidance, 1973(Jan), Vol 1(2), 61-68. [PA, Vol 53:01318]

522.   [Physio-psychological study on the development of mentally retarded children by electroencephalogram.] (Japn)
Selected 108 3-15 yr old normal children and 112 7-18 yr old mentally retarded children without exogenous history, motor disorders, and EEG abnormalities. EEGs were recorded monopolarly from 6 regions along the middle line and the bilateral temporal regions during the resting state. The EEGs were analyzed by the band pass filter EEG analyzer. Results show lower frequency in the retarded Ss' EEGs than in those of normals and may suggest retarded brain development. Little difference was found between groups, however, in the EEG developmental process. (25 ref.)
Katada, Akiyoshi. (Tokyo Gakugei U., Japan) Japanese Journal of Psychology, 1973(Jun), Vol. 44(2), 59-67. [PA, Vol 51:05471]

523.   [Physio-psychological study of the development of mentally retarded children: Auto-power spectrum analysis of electroencephalogram.] (Japn)
Examined the development of mentally retarded children's EEGs. Ss were 36 3-15 yr old normal and 39 7-18 yr old mentally retarded children. EEGs were recorded monopolarly from the frontal, the central, the parietal, and the occipital regions along the middle line and the bilateral temporal regions. Autopower spectrum analysis by the general purpose digital computer was conducted. When a dominant component in the spectrum appeared at frequencies lower than 8 Hz, subordinate components were manifest at frequencies higher than 8 Hz. However, when a dominant component appeared at frequencies higher than 8 Hz, subordinate components appeared at lower frequencies. These results were observed in both the normal and retarded Ss. The importance of examining both the dominant and subordinate frequencies in the developmental study of components of EEG by autopower spectrum analysis is noted.
Katada, Akiyoshi. (Tokyo Gakugei U., Japan) Japanese Journal of Psychology, 1973(Oct), Vol. 44(4), 186-194. [PA, Vol 52:09315]

524. Aversive and nonaversive responses to sensory stimulation in mentally retarded children.
Divided 20 mentally retarded children suspected of having sensory problems by virtue of abnormal responses to environmental stimuli into 2 groups. Ss' aversive reactions to 24 sensory stimuli were rated on a scale by 3 raters (a professional retailer of womens clothes, a physical therapy graduate student, and an occupational therapy educator). The trend of the mean scores of responses to the stimuli indicate that there were 2 distinct groups that differed in their reaction to sensory stimulation. The correlations of aversive reaction among sensory modalities differed between the groups. Recognition of these 2 groups and their varying responses to sensory stimulation has significance for understanding the functional problems observed in retarded children and may have implications for the development of more effective treatment. (21 ref.)
Kinnealey, Moya.   American Journal of Occupational Therapy, 1973(Nov), Vol. 27(8), 464-471. [PA, Vol 51:07451]

525.   Automated vs clinical administration of the Peabody Picture Vocabulary Test and the Coloured Progressive Matrices.
Examined the feasibility and reliability of automated administration of the Peabody Picture Vocabulary Test and Coloured Progressive Matrices to retarded adolescents. The automated and normal versions of the tests were compared in a design counterbalanced for order of administration. The children enjoyed interacting with the terminal although lower scores were obtained when the automated version was given first. Test-retest reliability coefficients were similar to those reported in the test manuals. It is suggested that changes in the instructions for the automated versions of these tests will improve reliability and facilitate the collection of data on many additional variables.
Knights, Robert M.; Richardson, Donald H. & McNarry, L. Robert. (Carleton U., Ottawa, Ontario, Canada) American Journal of Mental Deficiency, 1973(Sep), Vol. 78(2), 223-225. [PA, Vol 52:01270]

526.   [Birth weight of reading-class pupils, mentally retarded, and mentally deficient.] (Danh)
Investigated the birth weight of (a) 115 reading-class pupils, (b) 93 mentally retarded pupils, (c) 40 referred mentally deficient, and (d) 203 randomly sampled pupils from normal classrooms in the community. Children with extreme low (premature or dysmature) or high birth weight were found to be risk-groups. The frequencies at or below 2,500 gm were: (a) 8.7%, (b) 22.6%, (c) 22.5%, and (d) 4.4%. Above or at 4,500 gm frequencies were: (a) 9.6%, (b) 7.5%, (c) 2.5%, and (d) 2.5%. The deviation with both extremes combined for the 3 groups from the normal sample was significant.
Kruuse, Emil. (Office of School Psychology, Herstederne, Denmark) Skolepsykologi, 1973, Vol. 10(6), 489-496. [PA, Vol 52:08020]

527.   [Relationships between musical sensitivity and four other psychological factors (CA, MA, IQ and intelligence structure) in mentally retarded children.] (Japn)
Administered the Musical Aptitude Test to groups of normal and mentally retarded children. In normal Ss, correlations between musical sensitivity and CA, MA, and IQ were low. In retarded Ss, however, correlations between musical sensitivity and MA and IQ were high. Modalities of relationships between musical aptitude and CA, MA, IQ, and intelligence structure appeared to be different in brain-injured and non-brain-injured mentally retarded Ss.
Kurihara, Teruo. (Mie U., Faculty of Education, Tsu, Japan) Japanese Journal of Special Education, 1973(Jun), Vol. 11(1), 7-13. [PA, Vol 52:03376]

528.   Maximal oxygen intake of mentally retarded boys.
Found poor maximal oxygen intake, lowered heart rate at maximal work, and lowered work capacity in 44 mentally retarded boys (IQ range 30-70). Findings are attributed to insufficient physical training for children of low intelligence and to psychological limitations preventing stress under conditions of maximal and submaximal exertion.
Kusano, Katsuhiko. (Miyazaki U., Lab. for Handicapped Children, Japan) Journal of Human Ergology, 1973(Sep), Vol. 2(1), 13-19. [PA, Vol 52:05694]

529.   Self concept and the retarded: Research and issues.
Considers that education and psychology have not adequately scrutinized the belief that retarded individuals are inevitably the victims of negative self-concepts. Research in this area is reviewed, focusing specifically on the use of self-report instruments with retarded children. Of significance to the current debate in education is the inability of such research to generate support for the segregated placement of children. The validity and standardization of most self-concept scales is considered open to question and the findings which emanate from their use inconclusive. (58 ref.)
Lawrence, Elizabeth A. & Winschel, James F. (Western Michigan U.) Exceptional Children, 1973(Jan), Vol. 39(4), 310-319. [PA, Vol 50:05106]

530.   Direction following of retarded and nonretarded adolescents.
Presented 18 retarded and 18 nonretarded 14-17 yr olds with sets of directions containing 1, 2, 3, 4, or 5 separate directions (imperative sentences). Ss were required to carry out performances demanded by the directions. Results indicate that the retarded Ss had behavioral deficits in direction-following behavior when the directions were distributed into sets of 2, 3, and 4. Performances of single directions and sets of 5 were not significantly different for the 2 groups. The retarded Ss also demonstrated deficiencies in performances of sets of 2, 3, and 4 directions in the sequence (order) in which they were presented. Sequence performances of the 2 groups for sets of 5 directions did not differ significantly. (20 ref)
Lent, James R., et al. (Parsons Research Center, Kan.) American Journal of Mental Deficiency, 1973(Nov), Vol. 78(3), 316-322. [PA, Vol 52:03379]

531.   Behavioral variability among retardates, children, and college students.
Reports 2 investigations that deal with developmental implications of intraindividual variability among the mentally retarded. In Exp. I, 30 retardates (median CA = 18.1 yr., median MA = 8.9 yr.) were given reaction-time (RT), digit-span, and time-estimation tasks. Results demonstrate that individual differences in response variability were reliable and generalized across tasks. In Exp. II, 27 normal children in Grades 1, 3, or 5 and 9 college students completed the RT task. Developmental changes in variability (efficiency) of performance were found.
Liebert, Ann M. & Baumeister, Alfred A. (U. Alabama, Center for Developmental and Learning Disorders) Journal of Psychology, 1973(Jan), Vol. 83(1), 57-65. [PA, Vol 49:10870]

532.   [Experimental method of sign concept identification.] (Czec)
Studied sign concept identification in 300 normal and 80 retarded or mentally defective 5-15 yr old children. Successive and simultaneous methods of stimulus presentation—the 1st individually and the 2nd for groups—were used. In the successive type, Ss were exposed to stimuli in the form of geometric figures and, after a pretest instruction period with positive and negative feedback, were asked to discriminate among relevant positive, relevant negative, and irrelevant stimuli and to identify and classify them according to these conceptual categories. In the simultaneous-collective method, stimuli were presented to small groups of Ss. No pretest instruction with feedback was used. Ss were exposed to several printed cards containing stimuli in the form of geometric patterns or letters of increasingly difficult type and variety and were asked to identify on each card those 5 items which belonged to the same category. The 2 methods are discussed and their merits compared. Results of data analysis will be published in the near future. (Russian & English summaries)
Linhart, J. & Rejthar, S. (Czechoslovak Academy of Sciences, Psychological Inst., Prague) Československá Psychologie, 1973, Vol. 17(4), 340-346. [PA, Vol 52:08024]

533. Verbal control and intradimensional transfer of discrimination learning in mentally retarded vs intellectually average subjects.

Equal-MA comparisons of low-IQ and kindergarten children during an intradimensional shift after initial training with 2-choice color discrimination showed a performance deficit of mentally retarded groups in 2 experiments. 40 8-17 yr old retarded children and 5-6 yr old intellectually average children were presented object cues via the Wisconsin General Test Apparatus. The disability was so stable across various conditions and levels of original learning that the findings were regarded as incompatible with a theoretical explanation of the deficit based on the probability of dimensional observing responses. Appropriate verbal training greatly facilitated discrimination learning in both phases of the task. Retarded groups showed no disadvantage in using verbalization procedures that were sufficiently simple and meaningful to them. (21 ref)
Lobb, Harold & Childs, Rosemary. (Children's Psychiatric Research Inst., London, Ontario, Canada) American Journal of Mental Deficiency, 1973(Sep), Vol. 78(2), 182-192. [PA, Vol 52:01275]

534. Socio-cultural deprivation or difference?

Contends that since the majority of those classified as mentally retarded are poor, much of this retardation is due to socioeconomic conditions. An examination of the family life of the poor shows many factors which are detrimental to the verbal learning of the child. Such a child in such an environment has few positive influences to help him intellectually. He comes to school ill-prepared, and is labeled as retarded. He has a high expectancy of failure which further retards educability. Teacher expectations have an effect on the measured IQ.
Loquet, C. A. (Warrnambool Inst. of Advanced Education, Victoria, Australia) Australian Journal of Mental Retardation, 1973(Dec), Vol. 2(8), 228-231. [PA, Vol 52:10434]

535. A clinical and psychological investigation into juvenile amaurotic idiocy in Denmark.

Studied 28 cases of juvenile amaurotic idiocy. Seizures started at widely varied age; onset of menarche in 9 girls was 1.75 yrs earlier than in normal Danish girls. Memory span was found to be the earliest affected function. Nearly all patients had symptoms of mental disturbance. (French, German, & Spanish summaries) (17 ref.)
Lou, Hans C. & Kristensen, Kirsten. (National Boarding School for Blind & Partially Sighted Children, Kalundborg, Denmark) Developmental Medicine & Child Neurology, 1973(Jun), Vol. 15(3), 313-323. [PA, Vol 51:01438]

536. Cooperative and competitive behavior of retarded and nonretarded children at two ages.

Assessed cooperative-competitive interaction between 18 pairs of retarded and 16 pairs of nonretarded children aged 6-7 or 11-12 yr. in a situation in which competitive interaction was nonadaptive in terms of reward attainment. The retarded group was significantly more cooperative than the nonretarded group, and the 6-7 yr. old retarded group was more cooperative than the 11-12-yr-old retarded group. Results are discussed in relation to previous developmental studies of cooperation-competition and placed in the context of cognitive and reinforcement theories of social development.
Madsen, Millard C. & Connor, Catherine. (U. California, Los Angeles) Child Development, 1973(Mar), Vol. 44(1), 175-178. [PA, Vol 50:03265]

537. Verbal interactions: Mothers and their retarded children vs. mothers and their nonretarded children.

Compared 20 mentally retarded and 20 nonretarded 3-5 yr. olds and their mothers on frequency of 4 verbal operants, which were obtained from a tape recorded 15-min play session involving each mother and her child. Nonretarded and retarded children differed quantitatively with regard to verbal operants; tacts, mands, and intraverbals occurred with greater frequency with nonretarded children. The only difference between mothers was a higher mand rate for mothers of retarded children. With the exception of echoics by the retarded children, the order of usage of verbal operants was the same between mothers and between children.
Marshall, Nancy R.; Hegrenes, Jack R. & Goldstein, Steven. (U. Oregon, Medical School) American Journal of Mental Deficiency, 1973(Jan), Vol. 77(4), 415-419. [PA, Vol 50:03270]

538. Nutrition and mental development: Food for thought.

Animal studies have shown that deprivation of food early in life results in retarded brain growth from which the animal never recovers. Moreover, studies in human infants have demonstrated that malnutrition in the first 6 mo of life leads to a smaller brain. There are data which show that infants who have severe malnutrition in the first 6 mo of life have decreased mental performance compared with children from the same area who have not been malnourished; however, the presence of other contributing factors has prevented conclusive findings. Current studies in progress in a number of world centers are examining the effects of malnutrition on the young infant. Attempts must be made to ensure adequate calories are received to optimize brain growth and prevent mental retardation in a susceptible population.
McCoy, E. E. (U Alberta, Edmonton, Canada) Mental Retardation Bulletin, 1972–73, Vol 1(3), 65-67. [PA, Vol 58:03110]

539. A developmental diagnosis for 3-year-old children in Japan: I. Tests and methods.

Describes the development of an 11-item test designed to assess the physical and mental phases through which the 3-yr-old passes and to diagnose mentally or physically handicapped children so that appropriate steps can be taken to ensure their proper care. The test items include form board, formation, imitation, judgment, cooperation, arrangement, coordination, classification, reward, connection, and memory. The method of scoring the test is described.
Mishima, Jiro; Azuma, Kiyohazu & Moriya, Kunimitsu. (Waseda U, Tokyo, Japan) Journal of Child Development, 1973(Jan), Vol 9, 32-42. [PA, Vol 57:02237]

540. [On the formation of the concept of conservation in children.] (Japn)

From a population of 165 kindergartners, 1st graders, and mentally retarded children, an experimental sample was given training in conservation of substance. Results show significant training effect ($p < .01$) for the experimental Ss compared with controls. In Exp II the experimental group of kindergartners was trained in conservation of weight, volume, and atomism, with similar results. It is concluded that these concepts can be acquired by synthetic judgment, and that the sequence of acquisition of these concepts is reversible. (English summary)
Mori, Ichio. (Osaka Teacher's Coll, Scientific Educational Research Div, Japan) Japanese Journal of Educational Psychology, 1973(Mar), Vol 21(1), 32-42. [PA, Vol 53:02869]

541. [Speech training of a mentally retarded child with operant procedures: I.] (Japn)

Describes the use of operant conditioning procedures in the remedial speech training of a 3-yr-old mentally retarded and autistic boy. Training procedures included making puzzles, motor and speech imitation activities, and word imitation. Appropriate vocalizations and some forms of imitative and responsive speech were successfully trained. (16 ref)
Nakayama, Osamu & Nakayama, Tomie. (Kawasaki City Rehabilitation Center, Japan) Japanese Journal of Special Education, 1973(Jun), Vol. 11(1), 22-30. [PA, Vol 52:03520]

542. Decoding as a result of synthetic and analytic presentation for retarded and nonretarded children.

Synthetically and analytically taught 2 lists of high frequency words written in a contrived alphabet to 30 mental retardates (mean age = 129 mo) and 30 nonretarded children (mean age = 83 mo) matched on MA. Ss were tested immediately on the taught words and on words that had not been taught but that were composed of previously introduced letters. Both groups learned more words and showed greater transfer when the words were taught synthetically ($p < .05$). There was no difference

between retarded and nonretarded Ss, either in the number of taught words recognized or in transfer words recognized.
Neville, Donald & Vandever, Thomas R. (George Peabody Coll. for Teachers) American Journal of Mental Deficiency, 1973(Mar), Vol. 77(5), 533-537. [PA, Vol 51:07460]

543.　Preference for vibratory and visual stimulation in mentally retarded children.
Investigated relative preference for a vibratory and a visual stimulus in 30 5-12 yr old children with MA 15-47 mo and IQ 15-65. Ss were divided into 3 MA groups with CA constant. 5 forced-choice exposures to each stimulus were followed by 10 free-choice trials during which preferences and other relevant responses were recorded. Results of a significantly greater vibratory preference in the low-MA group than in the middle- and high-MA groups support the assumption of an earlier development of lower senses than higher senses and provide a basis for the reinforcing effect of vibration on behavior shaping in profoundly retarded individuals. (20 ref.)
Ohwaki, Sonoko; Brahlek, James & Stayton, Samuel E. (Rosewood State Hosp., Owings Mills, Md.) American Journal of Mental Deficiency, 1973(May), Vol. 77(6), 733-736. [PA, Vol 51:07463]

544.　Simple device for enhancing feedback in the acquisition of visual motor skills of slow learning children.
Discusses 2 aspects of a conceptual approach to feedback for perceptual learning: (a) the notion of goal-directed behavior (a performance standard to be aimed for by the S) and (b) the need for the S to be informed as to corrections necessary for the goal to be achieved. A behavioristic conception of this task might be that for tracing a line, if tracing response is on track, there will be an increase in the probability that immediately preceding responses will be accurate. If the response is off the track, there will be a decrease in the probability of immediately preceding inaccurate responses. A mechanical lighting device, or light box, was developed to augment visual feedback which normally accompanies the simple visual motor tasks of writing and drawing. 2 case examples are provided illustrating the use of the light box as a teaching device.
Parker, J. L.; Rosenfeld, Susan & Todd, Gillian. (James Cook U. North Queensland, Townsville, Australia) Slow Learning Child, 1973(Nov), Vol. 20(3), 164-169. [PA, Vol 52:06357]

545.　Neuroticism scores of mothers of mentally retarded and of neurotic children.
Administered a 38-item Hindi Health Questionnaire to the mothers of 25 mentally retarded children and of 21 emotionally disturbed children attending a child guidance clinic. The mothers of mentally retarded children were found to be more emotionally disturbed-i.e., more neurotic-than the mothers of emotionally disturbed children ($p < .05$).
Pershad, D.; Kaushal, P. & Verma, S. K. (Postgraduate Inst of Medical Education & Research, Chandigarh, India) Indian Journal of Mental Retardation, 1973(Jan), Vol 6(1), 24-27. [PA, Vol 53:09803]

546.　Heart rate response to novel and signal stimuli in nonretarded and retarded subjects.
Compared the heart rate component of the orienting reflex to novel and signal stimuli in 32 nonretarded and 32 retarded Ss matched on CA (6.6-12.67 yrs). All Ss received 32 trials of 1,000 cps tone presented at 73 dB. Nonretarded and retarded Ss did not differ in their response to a novel stimulus, but did differ in their response to the signal stimulus. Results provide support for the theory that retarded individuals may suffer from a defect in attaching signal value to stimulus events, rather than a defect in orienting to simple novel stimuli.
Powazek, Morris & Johnson, John T. (Memphis State U.) American Journal of Mental Deficiency, 1973(Nov), Vol. 78(3), 286-291. [PA, Vol 52:03388]

547.　A comparative study of short term memory span.
Divided 167 5-15 yr old children who were attending the child guidance clinic of a psychiatric outpatient department into Group A (97 children whose IQ was 84 or lower, mean MA 6.58)

and Group B (70 children whose IQ was above 84, mean MA 9.02). Three null hypotheses were tested: (a) Correlations between short-term memory span (STMS) and CA would show no difference in Groups A and B. (b) Correlations between STMS and MA would show no difference in Groups A and B. (c) There would be no correlation between STMS and IQ. Ss were administered a digit span test and various intelligence tests based on age scales and point scales. In Group A, STMS correlated slightly but significantly with CA, and in Group B it correlated highly. STMS correlated strongly with MA in both groups. Moderate correlation was obtained between STMS and IQ. Thus the 2nd null hypothesis was confirmed, but the 1st and 3rd were not. (16 ref)
Prasad, Mata & Pershad, Dwarka. (Postgraduate Inst of Medical Education & Research, Chandigarh, India) Indian Journal of Mental Retardation, 1973(Jul), Vol 6(2), 102–107. [PA, Vol 60:00768]

548.　Illegitimacy and mental retardation.
Investigated the rate of illegitimacy in 1,400 retarded individuals in a residential institution. The rate was found to be similar to that in the general population. It was found that illegitimate children tended to have lower birth weights and to be a little brighter than legitimate children. Different syndromes of retardation had different incidences of illegitimacy, with Down's syndrome having the lowest rate and the cultural-familial having the highest incidence. Illegitimacy seems to be a factor in placement in a residential institution. The incidence was also high in a group with congenital malformations. Some theories are advanced to explain the findings.
Roboz, Paul & Pitt, David. (Children's Cottages Training Centre, Kew, Victoria, Australia) Australian Journal of Mental Retardation, 1973(Sep), Vol. 2(7), 197-199. [PA, Vol 51:09460]

549.　Psychological characteristics of problem children at the borderline of mental retardation.
8-14 yr. old borderline mentally retarded children who present serious behavior problems have been described as impulsive, lacking facility with time concepts, overinvolved with fantasy, depressed, and hyperactive. A battery of psychological tests (including the WISC, TAT, and Bender Gestalt) was administered to 2 groups of problem behavior borderline-IQ children, 1 adjusted borderline-IQ group and 1 normal-IQ group (n = 15) to test the appropriateness of this description. The measures of impulsiveness and facility with time concepts did not discriminate Ss with problem behavior from adjusted Ss, possibly because the development of anticipation and planning abilities is incomplete in most preadolescent children. The data support the view that behavior-problem children are more involved in fantasy, particularly fantasy with depressive and aggressive content, than adjusted children and are relatively lacking perceptual-motor skills, especially in areas where deficits are often associated with minimal brain damage. (36 ref.)
Rourke, Philip G. & Quinlan, Donald M. (Yale U.) Journal of Consulting & Clinical Psychology, 1973(Feb), Vol. 40(1), 59-68. [PA, Vol 50:01339]

550.　[Facilitative effect of syntactical mediation on paired-associate learning by mentally retarded children.] (Japn)
Gave paired-associate learning tasks to 3 groups of 30 mentally retarded children. Syntactical mediations, one in the form of sentences, the other in the form of required compositions, were given to 2 experimental groups. The effects of these 2 levels of verbal mediations were compared with the effect of simple stimulus-response associative learning undertaken by the control group. Results indicate a significant effect of syntactical mediations on paired-associate learning ($p < .01$).
Saito, Shigeru. Japanese Journal of Educational Psychology, 1973(Dec), Vol 21(4), 233-236. [PA, Vol 53:07710]

551.　Piagetian theory and its approach to psychopathology.
Considers that in psychopathology the interest of an analysis of thought processes within the framework of a Piagetian equilibrium model has become clear. Piagetian research in psychopathology of thought has focused on cognitive discordances, instability,

absence of certain concepts, and the problem of the developmental stage hierarchy. Though this approach has proved revealing, it presents a rather static image of cognitive possibilities. By contrast, analysis of the different forms of regulation stresses the dynamic aspect of cognitive activity. Current research carried out with dyspraxic, mentally retarded, dysphasic, and psychotic children and adult schizophrenics can lead to an interpretation of the particularities of their mechanisms of thought. (19 ref.)

Schmid-Kitsikis, Elsa. (U. Geneva, Switzerland) American Journal of Mental Deficiency, 1973(May), Vol. 77(6), 694-705. [PA, Vol 51:07254]

552.   [Operational aspects in child psychopathology.] (Fren) Discusses the relevance of Piaget's epistemological work for psychological research on the development of intelligence. Results of research on children with the pathologies of mental retardation, deaf-mute, dysphasia, blindness, dyspraxia, and psychosis are briefly presented. Such research has generally been descriptive, but Piaget's theory and experiments have provided little as a basis for exploring the self-regulating and reforming mechanisms of the various genetic stages. (38 ref.)

Schmid-Kitsikis, E. & de Ajuriaguerra, J. (School of Psychology & Educational Sciences, Geneva, Switzerland) Revue de Neuropsychiatrie Infantile et d'Hygiene Mentale de l'Enfance, 1973(Jan), Vol. 21(1-2), 7-21. [PA, Vol 50:09288]

553.   Early predictors of mental retardation.
Examined parents' reports of age of onset of smiling and sitting alone for 454 5-mo to 6-yr-old children who were referred for diagnosis of developmental problems. Data indicate that the 2 milestones predicted the same percentage of Ss who were subsequently diagnosed as severely retarded. The onset of smiling, however, was considered to be more useful for purposes of early prediction because of its occurrence in nonretarded Ss by the age of 5 mo.

Schmitt, Ray & Erickson, Marilyn T. (North Carolina Memorial Hosp., Chapel Hill) Mental Retardation, 1973(Apr), Vol. 11(2), 27-29. [PA, Vol 51:01400]

554.   An experimental study of transfer of training in mental retardates.
10 male and 10 female Indian retardates (aged 10-13 yrs, IQ range 45-65) performed 2 card sorting tasks in a cross-over design study. Results show that transfer from 1 task to another is sufficient to alter the 2nd learning situation so that mastery of the transfer task is rapid. (20 ref)

Sen, Arun K. & Patnaik, Rekha. (U Delhi, India) Indian Journal of Psychology, 1973(Jun), Vol 48(2), 11-20. [PA, Vol 54:07907]

555.   Acquisition and retention of a motor skill by normal and retarded students.
Investigated acquisition and retention of pursuit rotor performance of 47 Black and 53 White retarded and an equal number of normal 11-12 yr olds under conditions of equal practice to an equated mean level of performance with and without immediate feedback. Results show (a) feedback had no effect on performance, (b) retarded Ss with additional practice performed as well as normal Ss, (c) retention by retarded Ss having learned to an equated mean level of performance was superior to that of normal Ss, (d) learning of males was superior to females, and (e) there were no race differences.

Simensen, Richard J. (Old Dominion U.) Perceptual & Motor Skills, 1973(Jun), Vol. 36(3, Pt. 1), 791-799. [PA, Vol 51:03488]

556.   The animism controversy revisited: A probability analysis.
Considers the methodological issues surrounding the animism controversy. A probability model, based on the difference between the expected and observed animistic and de-animistic responses, is suggested as an improved technique for the assessment of animism. The probability model was applied to the answers obtained previously from 3 groups of 20 children on a 70-item animism questionnaire. Results indicate that an animistic tendency was prevalent among 11-yr-old normals, while 6-yr-old normals and 11-yr-old retardates had been guessing. Analysis of Ss' responses revealed that the type of response does not necessarily reflect the type of underlying thought process. (16 ref)

Smeets, Paul M. (California School for the Deaf, Riverside) Journal of Genetic Psychology, 1973(Dec), Vol. 123(2), 219-225. [PA, Vol 52:03393]

557.   Reduction of long latency verbal responding in a multiply handicapped adolescent utilizing an avoidance-positive reinforcement procedure.
Utilized an avoidance procedure with a mentally retarded, emotionally disturbed 17-yr-old male, in an attempt to reduce S's long latencies of verbal responding to a set of 5 cards from the Peabody Picture Vocabulary Test. Results indicate that latencies could be shortened appreciably by the avoidance paradigm, and the resultant shortened latencies could be maintained by a reinforcement procedure. Follow-up, conducted 47 days after termination of the experiment, demonstrated durability of the effects. Generalization was shown to occur to cards not previously employed in an experimental manipulation and to a different therapist.

Spiro, Steven H. & Shook, Gerald. (Plymouth State Home & Training Center, Northville, Mich.) Psychological Record, 1973(Sum), Vol. 23(3), 383-389. [PA, Vol 51:09755]

558.   Establishing a conditional discrimination without direct training: A study of transfer with retarded adolescents.
Conducted 3 experiments to study stimulus classes as a mechanism for transfer with retarded 15-18 yr old adolescents ($N = 9$). The experiments were designed to determine the conditions required to establish similar controlling properties by initially unrelated stimuli. Results demonstrate that conditioning 2 CSs to control the same response to a choice stimulus established them as a stimulus class so that when 1 of the CSs was conditioned to control a new choice response, the 2nd stimulus also controlled the response without direct conditioning. It is suggested that a stimulus class analysis may be a useful attack on some of the problems involved in discussion of concepts, language, and reasoning. (16 ref.)

Spradlin, Joseph E.; Cotter, Vance W. & Baxley, Norman. (U. Kansas, Bureau of Child Research Lab.) American Journal of Mental Deficiency, 1973(Mar), Vol. 77(5), 556-566. [PA, Vol 51:07470]

559.   Equivalence formation by retarded and nonretarded children in structured and unstructured tasks.
Determined whether in retarded and normal children the presentation of pictorial and printed word stimulus items in a relatively structured manner would lead to different patterns of equivalence formation groupings than were yielded by an unstructured presentation. Ss were 60 retarded (IQ range 55-75, CA range 139.53-140.91 mo) and 60 normal (IQ range 95-115, CA range 95.33-102.52 mo) children; Ss were matched for MA (± 4 mo). Both groups produced more responses in the structured administration. Nonretarded Ss produced more responses than retarded Ss, and there were more correct responses to pictorial than to printed word stimulus items. In the structured administration there were similar numbers of perceptible intrinsic and perceptible extrinsic responses by retarded and nonretarded Ss. However, as in earlier studies, retarded Ss did not use intrinsic responses as frequently as functional extrinsic responses, although among nonretarded Ss these types of responses were used with equal frequency.

Stephens, Wyatt E. (Southern Illinois U.) American Journal of Mental Deficiency, 1973(Jan), Vol. 77(4), 445-450. [PA, Vol 51:05480]

560.   Short-term intake functions for sucrose in developmentally retarded children.
Determined short-term (5 min) intake functions for sucrose for 11 brain-damaged, developmentally retarded children using the single-stimulus-presentation method. Sucrose intake was a decreasing function of concentration. Water intake was equal to or greater than the greatest intake of any concentration of sucrose. These intake functions lacked the ascending limb of intake functions for water and weak concentrations of sucrose which are found in other animal species and in human adults. Evidence supports the notion that severely developmentally retarded

children are not ageusic but can discriminate between various concentrations of sucrose and water.
Switzky, Harvey N. (George Peabody Coll. for Teachers) Perceptual & Motor Skills, 1973(Feb), Vol. 36(1), 331-337. [PA, Vol 50:11620]

561.   Cue distinctiveness, learning, and transfer in mentally retarded persons.
Investigated the relationship between training history and the distinctiveness of stimulus cues in original learning and in transfer on the learning of intradimensional (ID) and extradimensional (ED) shifts by 2 groups of 48 retarded Ss (mean MA = 9.6 and 5.8 yrs). Ss were trained on a 2-choice simultaneous visual discrimination task with brightness or shape as the relevant dimension. Following original learning, Ss were randomly assigned to ID and ED shift problems. Difference in ID and ED shift performance depended on the distinctiveness of cues on the relevant and irrelevant dimensions in acquisition and in transfer. ID and ED shift performance also depended on the S's MA level and the relative distinctiveness of the relevant dimensions in acquisition. (20 ref)
Switzky, Harvey N. (George Peabody Coll. for Teachers) American Journal of Mental Deficiency, 1973(Nov), Vol. 78(3), 277-285. [PA, Vol 52:03396]

562.   [A study of figure cognition by mentally retarded children: II. In comparison with normal children.] (Japn)
Compared the perception of geometric form by mentally retarded children with perception by normal Ss in order to find perceptual characteristics of the mentally retarded. 93 children with mental ages 4, 5, and 6 yrs performed recognition tasks, identifying forms similar to 6 standard groups. The data were compared with those of previous studies. Results show that the mentally retarded performed better in identifying topology than in identifying shape, and that normal Ss performed better ($p < .01$) than the mentally retarded when mental age was equated.
Tanaka, Toshitaka & Matsuda, Tadahisa. (Osaka U, Lab of Psychology, Japan) Japanese Journal of Educational Psychology, 1973(Jun), Vol 21(2), 111-115. [PA, Vol 53:03456]

563.   The naming-stimulus effect in paired associate learning: A comparison of normal and mentally retarded children.
Tested normal and retarded Ss, both groups with MA of 6–9 yrs, in a paired-associate learning task involving 2 types of stimuli—pictures and ambiguous figures—and 2 conditions: naming, in which Ss were instructed to pay attention to the stimulus to develop the verbal function, and nonnaming, in which the instruction was not given. It is concluded from the results that mentally retarded children, even when their MA is the same as that of normal children, do not learn easily unless they are instructed to name the stimuli, especially with ambiguous stimuli which are difficult to describe.
Terada, Akira. Research Bulletin of the National Institute for Educational Research, Tokyo, 1973(Oct), No. 12, 37-39. [PA, Vol 52:10444]

564.   [A study of discrimination reversal-shift learning in mentally retarded children: Investigation of reaction time.] (Japn)
Studied developmental aspects of the discrimination reversal-shift learning process on the basis of analysis of reaction time and the number of trials. In Exp I, reversal shift of object-size (Task 1) and form-number (Task 2) was given to 22 13-14 yr old mentally retarded children. In Exp II, 4 successive reversal shifts of Task 2 were given to 12 mentally retarded children of the same ages. Results indicate that (a) younger Ss' preoccupation with concrete aspects of Task 1 interfered with the mediational process, (b) reaction time depended on identification of mediational cues relevant to stimulus dimensions, (c) reaction time was longer in the early stage of learning and immediately after reversal shift, and (d) fast learners have wider variability of reaction time in the early stages. (English summary) (16 ref)
Umetani, Tadao. Japanese Journal of Educational Psychology, 1973(Sep), Vol 21(3), 137-147. [PA, Vol 53:05683]

565.   [A study of discrimination reversal-shift learning in mentally retarded children: Investigation by reaction time.] (Japn)
21 mentally retarded and 21 normal children, all of mental age (MA) 6-8, performed discrimination reversal shift learning tasks consisting of 2 dimensions and 2 values. The number of trials and the simple reaction time (RT) for 4 successive reversal shifts were observed and analyzed. Results show that the number of trials decreased with the increase of MA for the normal children but not for the retarded; that the number increased for the retarded with the repetition of reversal shift, whereas the number decreased for the normal S; and that the RT was shorter and the response pattern was uniform for the retarded children in the original learning.
Umetani, Tadao. (Tokyo U of Education, Japan) Japanese Journal of Educational Psychology, 1973(Dec), Vol 21(4), 248-253. [PA, Vol 53:07714]

566.   Resistance to extinction and frustration in retarded and nonretarded children.
Compared the responses of 20 retarded and 20 nonretarded children to social and nonsocial matching-to-sample tasks during the extinction period which followed the use of social and nonsocial rewards. As predicted by the experience of failure hypothesis, retarded Ss exhibited more resistance to extinction and more frustration responses than nonretarded Ss, although nonretarded Ss initially yielded more frustration responses. While these effects were independent of type of task and type of reward, the loss of social reward led to greater resistance to extinction for both groups. Results support a partial reinforcement extinction effect interpretation of the effects of long-term experience of failure by retarded children on behavior during extinction. (33 ref)
Viney, Linda L.; Clarke, Alex M. & Lord, Janice. (Macquarie U., School of Behavioural Sciences, North Ryde, New South Wales, Australia) American Journal of Mental Deficiency, 1973(Nov), Vol. 78(3), 308-315. [PA, Vol 52:03397]

567.   Testing hearing of subnormal children.
Used the traditional puretone test (PT), the Baby Cry Test (BCT), and the Electrodermal Response Test to test the hearing of 40 mentally retarded 4–15 yr olds. The procedure began with the conditioning of Ss to raise their hands or nod their heads as a response to a high intensity tone. If Ss failed to respond or refused to cooperate, motivational devices such as colored cartoons, ring pegs, and various toys were introduced. Ss then were given the standard PT, followed by the BCT. The BCT was more effective than the PT. Whereas 15% of Ss did not respond to the PT, all Ss showed clear-cut and consistent responses to the BCT. Furthermore, hearing thresholds obtained with the BCT were significantly lower than those obtained with the PT. Several conclusions are drawn regarding proper procedures for testing the hearing of both normal and subnormal children.
Waldon, Edgar F. (U District of Columbia, Mt Vernon Square Campus) Journal of the All-India Institute of Speech & Hearing, 1973(Jan), Vol 4, 44–48. [PA, Vol 59:10199]

568.   Malnutrition and mental development.
Reviews retrospective studies of the relationship between malnutrition and mental deficiency and examines the methodological problems involved. Procedural complications (e.g., inadequate controls, the problem of Ss' possible immobilization, and the difficulty in knowing the developmental history of Ss) are pointed out in 4 relevant studies. The ideal design for such research would be prospective (from the prenatal period), experimental (random assignment to level of nutrition and age of malnutrition), and longitudinal (at least to adolescence). Until methodological problems are corrected, the influence of malnutrition on mental development is questionable. (41 ref.)
Warren, Neil. (U. Sussex, Brighton, England) Psychological Bulletin, 1973(Oct), Vol. 80(4), 324-328. [PA, Vol 51:05487]

569. Stereoscopic depth perception in mental retardation: The problem of directional disparity.
Compared 20 retarded and 20 nonretarded 9-12 yr olds in a visual depth recognition task involving retinal disparity coding. Groups were not differentiated by presentation of nasal disparity cues. With temporal disparities, retarded Ss were consistently less capable of obtaining stereopsis. A neural basis is postulated.
Webb, Thomas E.; Kline, Linda E. & Anderson, Walter F. American Journal of Mental Deficiency, 1973(Nov), Vol. 78(3), 363-365. [PA, Vol 52:03399]

570. Some psychological-social correlates of mental retardation.
Gave 64 male and 37 female mentally retarded 11-19 yr olds the Institute for Personality and Ability Testing Children's Personality Questionnaire and a personal data questionnaire. Ss were also rated on a teacher's opinion sheet. Data show significant differences between Ss and 1,476 normal controls. For the male Ss, there were significant correlations between personality factors and mathematics achievement that differed from those described for normals. Since the observed frequency of broken homes was quite high for the retarded children, it is suggested that the more divergent personality structures of these children might be related to familial instability.
Wilcox, Roger & Smith, James L. (Ohio U., Zanesville) Perceptual & Motor Skills, 1973(Jun), Vol. 36(3, Pt. 1), 999-1006. [PA, Vol 51:03492]

571. One-trial learning of intellectually average and retarded children under three methods of presentation: Storage and retrieval.
3 groups of 5-, 7-, and 9-yr-old intellectually average children ($n = 36$ in each group) and 1 group of 36 retarded children viewed 8 pairs of pictures under 3 methods of presentation for 1 trial at 3 different exposure durations. Tests of recall, recognition, and matching were then given. Matching scores were not above chance, and methods of presentation did not differ. Recognition was superior to recall, and performance on both tasks increased as exposure duration and MA increased. Intelligence level affected performance on the recognition task. Analyses of recognition scores indicate that excessive false alarms deleteriously affected the retarded Ss' performance. (23 ref.)
Winters, John J. & Goettler, Diane R. (Edward R. Johnstone Training & Research Center, Bordentown, N.J.) American Journal of Mental Deficiency, 1973(Jul), Vol. 78(1), 51-58. [PA, Vol 51:05492]

572. Double responding as a technique facilitating oddity discrimination under conditions of S-R discontiguity.
Gave a 3-choice discrimination problem in which 2 identical and 1 odd object served as stimuli to 3 groups of 12 13-16 yr. old mental retardates attending special classes in a public school. 2 groups performed with a 15.2-cm spatial gap interposed between the S and the site to which the response was made, and were either required to touch the stimulus block before moving the remote response block (double responding), or were given no such requirement (discontiguity). The 3rd group responded directly to the stimulus (contiguity). While stimulus-response discontiguity severely impaired learning, double responding significantly facilitated learning and resulted in performance indistinguishable from that produced by the contiguity group.
Wunderlich, Richard A. & Lozes, Jewell. (Catholic U. of America) American Journal of Mental Deficiency, 1973(Jan), Vol. 77(4), 435-438. [PA, Vol 50:03357]

573. The body-image of normal and retarded children.
Compared body-image of retarded children with that of normal children, using the Draw-A-Person Test (DAP). 8 DAP aspects were used for comparison: size, erasure, environment, clothing, detail, fingers, symmetry, and arm position. The 2 groups differed significantly in 7 out of 8 aspects, with only environment failing to differentiate between the groups. Retarded Ss revealed (a) larger size and (b) less erasure, clothing, detail, and symmetry. Retarded Ss tended to leave out fingers.

Wysocki, Boleslaw A. & Wysocki, Aydin C. (Newton Coll. of the Sacred Heart) Journal of Clinical Psychology, 1973(Jan), Vol. 29(1), 7-10. [PA, Vol 50:07140]

574. [The dependence of transfer on pattern analysis in mentally retarded schoolchildren.] (Russ)
Studied transfer in mentally retarded children who were required to assemble 2 models from patterns. When 38 retarded 4th graders learned to construct a stool and were then asked to build a chair or an armchair according to a pattern, many of them attempted to assemble the stool and then attached parts to it which would make it resemble the chair pattern more closely. Ss given help in analyzing the pattern of the 2nd model carried out its assembly more successfully than Ss who did not receive help. Ss who were given help in pattern analysis, but who constructed only one model, did not do as well as Ss who received help and constructed 2 models. It is concluded that in assembling a new model by means of skills acquired while assembling another model, the retarded child frequently commits errors due to an inadequate analysis of the pattern of the new model. Help in analyzing this pattern is beneficial to transfer.
Abdurasulov, D. A. (USSR Academy of Pedagogical Sciences, Inst of Defektology, Moscow) Defektologiya, 1974, No 3, 25-31. [PA, Vol 56:10122]

575. Organization in normal and retarded children: Temporal aspects of storage and retrieval.
Studied the flow of information from input through output in a free-recall task by means of S-paced presentation times, externalized rehearsal, and interword response times. In this context, storage and retrieval of categorized material were examined for 40 10-yr-old normal and 40 16-yr-old mentally retarded children of the same mental age. As indicated by the patterns of input and output times, instructions to rehearse according to category membership led to the formation of higher order memory units that were functional during recall. Input and output times under uninstructed conditions revealed little spontaneous use of conceptual categories in either IQ group, although provision of retrieval cues resulted in a marked increase in recall performance for these Ss. Results are discussed in terms of the chunking and recoding of input and the influence of active, organized storage processing on retrieval. (16 ref)
Ashcraft, Mark H. & Kellas, George. (U Kansas) Journal of Experimental Psychology, 1974(Sep), Vol 103(3), 502-508. [PA, Vol 53:05656]

576. The Prader-Willi syndrome.
Observed 15 children with Prader-Willi syndrome who attended an Australian diagnostic and assessment clinic. Ss included 1 child of dull-normal intelligence, 5 mildly retarded children, and others who functioned at the upper part of the moderately retarded range. Some of the characteristics of the disorder, including high-pitched voice, emotional immaturity and obesity, are described, and problems of managing such children are discussed.
Beange, Helen & Caradus, Verne. (Grosvenor Hosp, Summer Hill, New South Wales, Australia) Australian Journal of Mental Retardation, 1974(Mar), Vol 3(1), 9-11. [PA, Vol 53:01463]

577. The major dilemma of mental retardation: Shall we prevent it? (Some social implications of research in mental retardation).
Discusses the progress being made in determining and evaluating the incidence, prevalence, and causes of mental retardation, and how these findings are useful in developing methods to combat its occurrence. Biological and physiological determinants (e.g., prematurity and low birth weight, malnutrition) and social-environmental factors in mental retardation are reviewed, and the state of related knowledge and technology is assessed. Recommendations for needed research are presented; greater physician awareness and early intervention with children from socially disadvantaged families is urged. (23 ref)
Begab, Michael J. (National Inst. of Child Health & Human Development, Bethesda, Md.) American Journal of Mental Deficiency, 1974(Mar), Vol. 78(5), 519-529. [PA, Vol 52:07993]

578. [Some features of the level of self esteem in children with retarded mental development.] (Russ)
Studied the personality traits of children with retarded mental development accompanied by residual brain lesions. Under the influence of difficulties encountered in school, these children experience a lower level of success. This lack of success affects other activities and leads to the formation of such personality traits as feelings of insecurity and fear of being unsuccessful. It is concluded that a child's choice of task and his or her ability to cope with it depend on the conditions under which the new task is presented and how carefully the child has been prepared. Lack of success leads to refusal to complete a task. (6 ref)
Belopol'skaya, N. L. (USSR Academy of Pedagogical Sciences, Research Inst of Child & Juvenile Physiology, Moscow) Zhurnal Nevropatologii i Psikhiatrii, 1974, Vol 74(12), 1866–1870. [PA, Vol 62:13920]

579. Autonomic correlates of anticipation and feedback in retarded adolescents.
Studied heart rate and galvanic skin response changes associated with confirmation or violation of expectancies in a probability learning task. 2 groups of 18 15–16 yr old retardates guessed which of 2 events, a soft or loud tone, would follow a cue light. For ½ of each group the probability of loud and soft was 90 to 10 while for the other ½ it was 70 to 30. During the anticipation period when Ss awaited the outcome of their predictions, heart rate acceleration was observed, while during the feedback period deceleration was noted. More deceleration occurred on violation trials than on confirmation ones. Deceleration was viewed as attention to external events, while heart rate acceleration was interpreted as reflection or attention to internal events. No evidence to support the attentional deficit hypothesis was obtained.
Bower, A. C. (Rideau Regional Hosp. School, Smiths Falls, Ontario, Canada) Journal of Mental Deficiency Research, 1974(Mar), Vol. 18(1), 31-39. [PA, Vol 52:12756]

580. The mentally retarded: Society's Hansels and Gretels.
Considers that mental retardation is a myth that society uses to justify the institutionalization of the mildly retarded. Research shows that these individuals can lower as well as raise their tested IQs when motivated to do so. They also can resist strong institutional pressure to conform. The vast majority of such children come from troubled families. Diagnosis of mental retardation typically comes after it has already been decided that the child must be removed from the family. It is concluded that professionals should concentrate on the real source of the children's problems rather than defending a delusion.
Braginsky, Benjamin M. & Braginsky, Dorothea D. (Wesleyan U.) Psychology Today, 1974(Mar), Vol. 7(10), 18-30. [PA, Vol 52:05684]

581. Effects of recall order, cue placement, and retention interval on short-term memory of normal and retarded children.
Conducted 2 experiments on organizational strategies in the short-term memory of a total of 40 8-11 yr old MA-matched normal and retarded children. Sequences of digits were presented aurally for immediate and delayed recall (0, 6, and 12 sec). During Exp I the retention intervals were silent, and during Exp II they were filled. Recall was either forward or in reverse order. Recall order was determined by a signal that either preceded or followed each digit string. As predicted, both normals and retardates recalled fewer items correctly under the backward and cue-after conditions). No primacy effect for backward recall by normal and retarded Ss was found. Developmental differences in rehearsal efficiency are discussed. (25 ref)
Brown, R. Michael. (Seattle U) Perceptual & Motor Skills, 1974(Aug), Vol 39(1), 167–178. [PA, Vol 56:02505]

582. The effects of a discriminative cue and an incompatible activity on generalized imitation.
Observed 4 noncompliant male 2-9 yr old retardates in a generalized imitation study. 2 variables were studied: provision of a competing reinforced activity, and use of a cue to aid discrimination between reinforced and nonreinforced imitations.

Both variables increased the rate of discrimination between the 2 sets of stimuli. Greatest discrimination occurred when both cue and alternative task were present. Discrimination decreased when the variables were removed. Results imply that imitation of nonreinforced cues in generalized imitation procedures varies with the degree to which reinforcement is available for other activity, as well as with the complexity of the discrimination problem. Results help indicate conditions under which the generalized imitation effect may be observed in more naturalistic settings. (15 ref)
Bucher, Bradley & Bowman, Elizabeth-Ann. (U Western Ontario, London, Canada) Journal of Experimental Child Psychology, 1974(Aug), Vol 18(1), 22-23. [PA, Vol 53:01464]

583. Recurrence risks in severe undiagnosed mental deficiency.
Studied the families of 179 patients with nonspecific mental retardation. The overall recurrence risk for the same type of retardation was 2.7%. Certain categories carried higher risks of recurrence: for siblings of patients with retardation and symmetrical spastic paraplegia not attributable to birth hypoxia; for siblings of patients who were both retarded and epileptic but who were without neurological signs; for severe subnormality in brothers of mentally retarded males, without specific features and with IQs of 35-51; and for any degree of subnormality among the siblings of index patients without specific features. It is suggested that the excess of males among index patients was probably due to male susceptibility to environmental hazards, since the sex ratio was equal once patients with cerebral palsy and infantile spasms were excluded. There was a small contribution to mental retardation by the Martin-Bell syndrome with nonspecific features and X-linked spastic paraplegia. (22 ref)
Bundey, Sarah & Carter, C. O. (Queen Elizabeth Medical Ctr, Infant Development Unit, Birmingham, England) Journal of Mental Deficiency Research, 1974(Jun), Vol 18(2), 115-134. [PA, Vol 54:01266]

584. Social stereotypes: 3 faces of happiness.
Answers to a self-report questionnaire indicate that the old and physically infirm did not think of themselves as less happy than the young and physically able. O ratings also showed that retarded children enjoyed life as much as normal children did. However, in all ages and physical conditions, the more well-to-do felt themselves happier than others.
Cameron, Paul. (St Mary's Coll Maryland) Psychology Today, 1974(Aug), Vol 8(3), 62-64. [PA, Vol 53:05659]

585. Galactosemia: A short communication.
Galactosemia is a metabolic disorder involving a deficiency of galactose-1-phosphate uridyl transferase and making it impossible for the patient to assimilate milk or milk products. It is manifested in infants by listlessness, jaundice, failure to gain weight, and mental retardation. If a diet of atta, and/or other nutrients which do not contain galactose, is substituted for milk in early infancy, intelligence can in many cases develop normally.
Chandrasekaran, R. (Postgraduate Inst of Medical Education & Research, Chandigarh, India) Indian Journal of Mental Retardation, 1974(Jul), Vol 7(2), 98-102. [PA, Vol 53:11984]

586. The WRAT: Grade level differences for various revisions.
Matched the Reading, Spelling, and Arithmetic subtests from each of 3 forms of the Wide Range Achievement Test (WRAT) and compared the grade level scores for a sample of 72 male adolescent and adult retardates. An analysis of variance was performed which showed that the matched WRAT subtests did not differ significantly, though significant differences were found between the overall WRAT forms ($p < .001$). 1965 WRAT Level II grade level scores correlated higher with mental ages from the Stanford-Binet, Form L-M (SB L-M) than with the Peabody Picture Vocabulary Test. The 1946 WRAT showed better agreement with the SB L-M mental age than did the 1965 WRAT grade level scores. Probable reasons for the test differences are discussed.
Cochran, Malcolm L. & Pedrini, Duilio T. (Glenwood State Hosp.-School, Diagnostic & Evaluation Clinic, Ia.) Training

School Bulletin, 1974(Feb), Vol. 70(4), 224-229. [PA, Vol 52:12719]

587. [Obstetric care and infantile subnormality.] (Span)
Presents obstetric data which show that even small departures from normal childbirth time schedules are associated with a statistically elevated incidence of mental deficiency in the neonate. Anecdotal and documentary evidence indicate that early delivery is often induced to suit the convenience of hospitals and/or medical doctors. It is recommended that this practice be undertaken only when there is clear medical justification.
Coello Higueras, Felipe. Actas Luso-Españolas de Neurología y Psiquiatría y Ciencias Afines, 1974(Jan-Feb), Vol 2(1). [PA, Vol 54:12080]

588. WISC subtest patterns of delinquent male retardates.
Compared WISC subtest scores of 70 male retarded delinquents with IQs of 69 or below with those of nondelinquent male retardates reported in a study by A. B. Silverstein (1968). Results indicate a considerable degree of similarity in WISC performance among delinquent and nondelinquent retardates.
Cook, Thomas W. & Solway, Kenneth S. Psychological Reports, 1974(Aug), Vol 35(1, Pt 1), 22. [PA, Vol 56:08206]

589. A comparison between the structures of divergent production abilities of children at two levels of intellectual functioning.
Administered 12 divergent production tests to 46 subnormal adolescents whose average WISC Full Scale IQ was 69.5, and to a similar group of 48 7th, 8th and 9th graders whose average WISC Full Scale IQ was 104.5. 6 divergent production factors were extracted in each group and rotated to a target derived from J. P. Guilford's 1959 structure of intellect model. In general, the subnormal group produced a better fit to the hypothesized structure than the normal group, although results from the normal group are not considered to be unsupportive of Guilford's theory.
Delaney, J. O. & Maguire, T. O. (University Coll., National U. Ireland, Dublin) Multivariate Behavioral Research, 1974(Jan), Vol. 9(1), 37-45. [PA, Vol 52:08006]

590. [Intentional free paced learning: Comparative study of normal and mentally retarded children.] (Fren)
In Exp I Ss were presented with arbitrary pairs of unrelated words, and in Exp II the list consisted of paradigmatic and syntagmatic associated words. Ss were instructed to study each list until they thought they would be able to give a perfect recall. Normal and retarded children differed in their intentional use of learning mechanisms. This difference (called "lack of realism") is interpreted in terms of cognitive and motivational processes. (French & English summaries) (60 ref)
Denhiere, Guy. (CNRS, U Paris, Lab de Psychologie, France) Enfance, 1974(Sep-Dec), No 3-5, 149-174. [PA, Vol 54:07886]

591. Facilitating the acquisition of an "in front" spatial discrimination.
Compared methods for teaching retarded children to discriminate an "in front" spatial relationship. Nine Ss were given a series of programed stimuli which emphasized a proximity cue, after a brief exposure to trial-and-error training. Eight control Ss were given extended trial-and-error training, but none of these acquired the discrimination. All of the 9 experimental Ss acquired the terminal discrimination, and 7 of the 8 controls did so after one presentation of the programed series.
Dixon, Lois S.; Spradlin, Joseph E.; Girardeau, Frederic L. & Etzel, Barbara C. (Parsons State Hosp & Training Ctr, Research Ctr, KS) Acta Symbolica, 1974, Vol 5(4), 1-21. [PA, Vol 55:10972]

592. Effects of intrauterine rubella infection and its consequent physical symptoms on intellectual abilities.
Performed a psychometric test of the common assumption that rubella infection produces mental retardation, using an instrument independent of the frequently deficient hearing and speech abilities of individuals so affected. 88 testable children with evidence of rubella infection earned a mean IQ score of 100.01 on the Arthur adaptation of the Leiter International Performance Scale. It was discovered that the number of physical symptoms found was mildly related to intellectual level ($r = -.20$, $p < .025$). A group of 16 untestable blind-deaf children was also examined briefly. The overall conclusion is that it is not the rubella infection per se that produces the clinical picture commonly seen as one of retardation, but rather the physical symptoms that limit psychological development and expression. (23 ref)
Dodrill, Carl; Macfarlane, David & Boyd, Robert. (U. Washington Hosp.) Journal of Consulting & Clinical Psychology, 1974(Apr), Vol. 42(2), 251-255. [PA, Vol 52:08093]

593. [A contribution to the study of space perception in the mentally deficient child.] (Fren)
Studied the spatial reasoning of 21 retarded boys 10-14 yrs old. Each S was asked to match the perspective of a simple photographic scene with an appropriate camera position, and his stage on the scale of spatial concept development described by J. Piaget was estimated. It was found that only 3 Ss used spatial logic like that used by normal children of comparable ages, and that Ss relied more heavily on direct perceptual cues than on abstract spatial reasoning. It is suggested that intellectual functions of the retarded may be adequate for repetitive daily tasks, but that the retarded lack systematically structured knowledge. (English, German, & Spanish summaries)
Dufoyer, J. P. & Lhuillier, Ch. (U Renè Descartes, Lab of Genetic Psychology, Paris, France) Revue de Neuropsychiatrie Infantile et d'Hygiene Mentale de l'Enfance, 1974(Jan), Vol 22(1-2), 75-84. [PA, Vol 54:07887]

594. Encoding and retrieval processes in normal children and retarded adolescents.
Studied information-processing capabilities of 14 normal and 14 retarded individuals on a modified Sternberg recognition memory task. 14 5th and 6th graders matched for MA (mean = 10.5 yrs) and 14 retarded institutionalized individuals (mean CA = 16.87 yrs) served as Ss. Presentation of items in the memory set was self-paced, and stimulus exposure times and response latencies were recorded. Normal and retarded Ss spent the same amount of time processing subspan lists during input to the memory system; however, the normal Ss spent less time retrieving information from that system than did the retarded Ss. Part of the superiority of normal Ss was attributable to their higher scanning speeds during the stimulus comparison stage of memory retrieval. The scanning strategy of normal and retarded Ss, on the other hand, was the same: serial and exhaustive. The binary decision stage of retrieval was not related to differences in intelligence.
Dugas, Jeanne L. & Kellas, George. (Columbus Coll.) Journal of Experimental Child Psychology, 1974(Feb), Vol. 17(1), 177-185. [PA, Vol 52:05688]

595. Crooked ears and the bad boy syndrome: Asymmetry as an indicator of minimal brain dysfunction.
The author cites his 1965 study of 275 children classified as mental retardates, learning disabled, delinquent, etc. Among these Ss asymmetry of the ears ranged from 67.8% to 96.2% ($p = .005$). In the current study of 22 Ss, including some adults, significant asymmetry of the ears was likewise found ($p = .009$). It is suggested that the described technique of measuring asymmetry may be a method of screening for the possible existence of congenital central nervous system defects.
Durfee, Kent E. (Scottsdale Psychiatric Ctr, AZ) Bulletin of the Menninger Clinic, 1974(Jul), Vol 38(4), 305-316. [PA, Vol 53:07698]

596. Attitudes of adolescent delinquent boys.
It has previously been suggested that the attitudes of juvenile offenders are qualitatively different from those of "normal" male adolescents. The present study attempted to assess quantitative differences in the attitudes of 20 13-15 yr old male offenders and 20 male nondelinquent controls toward disabled, retarded, aged, alcoholic, and mentally ill persons. Juvenile offenders exhibited

significantly less favorable attitudes than did nondelinquent controls.
Evans, Joseph H. (Boys Town, NB) Psychological Reports, 1974(Jun), Vol 34(3, Pt 2), 1175-1178. [PA, Vol 53:01433]

597.   [On the relationship between mental retardation and childhood psychosis.] (Germ)
Psychosis and mental retardation can occur together in the child. Four types of constellations have been observed: (a) mental retardation and endogenous psychosis with no causal connection between the two; (b) a metabolically determined mental retardation with psychotic symptomatology, such as phenylketonuria or hepatolenticular degeneration; (c) episodic psychosis of the mentally retarded, with confusion, excitement or inhibition, and delusions; and (d) reactive psychosis of mental retardation. These types are discussed, and 2 illustrative case reports are presented. (English summary) (21 ref)
Färber, Helga. (Rheinische Landesklinik für Kinder-und Jugendpsychiatrie, Viersen, West Germany) Zeitschrift für Kinder-und Jugendpsychiatrie, 1974, Vol 2(3), 211–220. [PA, Vol 61:03707]

598.   Sexual development of the moderately retarded child: Level of information and parental attitudes.
Conducted structured interviews with 16 mentally retarded adolescents (mean IQ = 46.8) about their sexual knowledge; parents of these children were also interviewed and completed a questionnaire about their concerns about the sexual development of their children. Overall, the children demonstrated a considerable range of awareness, and at times gave unexpected but accurate information. Parents were most concerned about managing their child's sexual development, and some were concerned that their children would become preoccupied with sex. Implications for sex education of the retarded individual are discussed, and recommendations for decreasing the embarrassment and discomfort associated with sexual matters are noted.
Fischer, Henry L. & Krajicek, Marilyn J. (U. Colorado, Medical School, Denver) Mental Retardation, 1974(Jun), Vol. 12(3), 28-30. [PA, Vol 52:12722]

599.   Sex effect on intelligence and mental retardation.
In a sample of 5,049 pairs of individuals from high-risk pedigrees, no evidence could be found for a uterine or socialization maternal effect on IQ or on the incidence of mental retardation. The observed excess of affected males and higher risk for children of affected females were fully consistent with all of 3 multifactorial threshold models.
Freire-Maia, Ademar; Freire-Maia, Dertia V. & Morton, Newton E. (Faculdade de Ciências, Médicas e Biológicas, São Paulo, Brazil) Behavior Genetics, 1974(Sep), Vol 4(3), 269-272. [PA, Vol 53:01473]

600.   Slow-learner, average, and gifted third graders: Strategy analysis and training for learning.
Measured the performance of 48 gifted, average, and slow-learning 3rd graders on a visual-term memory task which involved free recall of objects presented sequentially by a Kodak Carousel. The objects were grouped into conceptual sets, with 4 objects per set. Ss performed better on concrete than on abstract short-term memory concept tasks.
Friedrich, Douglas. (Central Michigan U) Psychology in the Schools, 1974(Jul), Vol 11(3), 344-350. [PA, Vol 53:09262]

601.   Visual-motor performance: Additional delineation of the "perceptual deficit" hypothesis.
Ongoing research with normals and brain-damaged, nonbrain-damaged, and undifferentiated retardates has attempted to delineate the "perceptual deficit" hypothesis, often used to explain poor performance on visual-motor tasks. However, results of a series of studies by the authors indicate that it is inappropriate to characterize poor performance on visual-motor tasks as due to some unitary perceptual problem. The present study with 16 normal and 32 noninstitutionalized retarded children included the manipulation of both integrative and motor execution variables. Results of the present and previous research suggest the importance of assessing the probable, yet "extrane-

ous," contributing factors of motor execution and/or integrative dysfunctions in faulty performance on typical visual-motor tasks. It is concluded that a simple view of unitary perceptual difficulty masks the issue of multiple and related perceptual-cognitive-motor capabilities and may result in inappropriate prognosis and/or ineffective remediation.
Friedrich, Douglas & Fuller, Gerald B. (Central Michigan U.) Journal of Clinical Psychology, 1974(Jan), Vol. 30(1), 30-33. [PA, Vol 52:03360]

602.   Attentional habituation and mental retardation: A theoretical interpretation of MA and IQ differences in problem solving.
Offers a theoretical proposal concerning individual differences in cognitive processes. Mental retardation and the comparative problem-solving performance of normal and retarded children are examined. On the basis of W. E. Jeffrey's analysis of attention and cognitive development (1968, 1969), it is proposed that IQ and MA differences in problem-solving behavior reflect differences in (a) speed of orienting-reflex habituation and (b) ability to inhibit responding sufficiently. (51 ref)
Furby, Lita. (Yale U) Human Development, 1974, Vol 17(2), 118-138. [PA, Vol 53:01476]

603.   Auditory reactions in mentally retarded children by means of psychogalvanic reflexes.
Examined 29 6-15 yr old male retardates and 32 normal children of matched mental age. Results obtained using psychogalvanic responses for acoustical (drum beat) stimuli show the usefulness of this method and its importance as a screening test or in standard audiometry. (French summary)
Galkowski, Tadeusz. Audiology, 1974, Vol 13(6), 501-505. [PA, Vol 53:03431]

604.   Attitudes toward retarded children: Effects of labeling and academic performance.
The influence of the label "mentally retarded" on the attitudes of peers was investigated in 2 experiments-one with a middle-class sample and the other with a low-socioeconomic status (SES) sample. 48 middle-class and 40 low-SES 4th graders were shown 1 of 2 video tapes of 2 children taking a spelling bee. Half of the Ss saw the target actor as being a competent speller while the remaining half saw him as an incompetent speller. Half of each group was told that the target actor was either a 5th-grade pupil or a mentally retarded boy in a special class. Data from the 2 sets of 2 × 2 (Label × Competence) replications indicate that the label did not significantly affect attitude scores. For the middle-class sample, academic performance was a significant influence on expressed attitudes, with incompetent performance resulting in more negative evaluations. Academic performance did not affect attitude scores among the low-SES sample. Data indicate that labels do not adversely influence the attitudes of peers toward labeled children. (23 ref)
Gottlieb, Jay. (Research Inst for Educational Problems, Cambridge, MA) American Journal of Mental Deficiency, 1974(Nov), Vol 79(3), 268-273. [PA, Vol 53:09893]

605.   Factor structure of fears in the mentally retarded.
Obtained parents' ratings on the 81-item Louisville Fear Survey for Children (LFSC) from a mailed survey for 102 6-21 yr olds who had a mean IQ of 43. Data were subjected to a principal-components factor analysis and rotated by varimax method. 4 relatively independent and psychologically meaningful factors emerged: Separation, Natural Events, Injury, and Animals. These factors correspond substantially to those obtained in studies that used the LFSC with nonretarded populations. (15 ref)
Guarnaccia, Vincent J. & Weiss, Robin L. (Hofstra U) Journal of Clinical Psychology, 1974(Oct), Vol 30(4), 540-544. [PA, Vol 53:05667]

606. [A study on the discrimination learning in mentally retarded children: Effects of attention to the stimulus dimension.] (Japn)
Compared rates of discrimination learning of normal and retarded children, particularly with regard to color and form preferences.
Hamashige, Tamie. (Tokyo U of Education, Japan) Japanese Journal of Special Education, 1974(Jun), Vol 12(1), 24-32. [PA, Vol 53:11950]

607. Low socio-economic status and progressive retardation in cognitive skills: A test of cumulative deficit hypothesis.
Studied the effects of low socioeconomic status (SES) on nonverbal reasoning and verbal ability (2 forms of basic cognitive skills). 100 children of high and low SES and from 2 age groups were administered the Raven Standard Progressive Matrices and Stroop Color-Word Test. In both age groups the high-SES Ss performed better than the low-SES Ss. Greater differences between SES groups occurred among the older than the younger Ss. Results show that the cognitive skills of the low-SES child are progressively retarded, whereas those of the high-SES child develop more quickly. The experiential factors that go with SES may be crucial in determining developmental rates; hence the low-SES children suffer from a cummulative deficit in their cognitive competence rather than being able to compensate for the earlier disadvantage. (25 ref)
Jachuck, Kasturi & Mohanty, Ajit K. (Utkal U, Bhubaneshwar, India) Indian Journal of Mental Retardation, 1974(Jan), Vol 7(1), 36–45. [PA, Vol 62:10709]

608. Ontogenetic changes in two forms of the Muller-Lyer illusion in normal and retarded subjects.
Forms A (arrowheads pointing out) and B (arrowheads pointing in) of the Muller-Lyer illusion were administered to normal and retarded Ss to study possible changes in illusion strength in either or both forms. It was found that only Form A changed in strength when (a) age was varied from 8-18 yrs in normal children and (b) when the illusion was presented repeatedly over 8 trials for normal and retarded children. These findings conflict with perceptual theories which assume that both forms of the illusion change with these manipulations. A control condition was also presented and its utility is discussed. (21 ref)
Johnson, Clark & Jackson, Ernest G. (Hastings Coll) Developmental Psychology, 1974(Nov), Vol 10(6), 949-953. [PA, Vol 53:05674]

609. Comparison of Columbia Mental Maturity Scale, Peabody Picture Vocabulary Test, and Slosson Intelligence Test with mentally retarded children.
Administered the Columbia Mental Maturity Scale (CMMS), Peabody Picture Vocabulary Test (PPVT), and the Slosson Intelligence Test (SIT) to 96 6-18 yr old mentally retarded Ss (IQ range, 30-75). High intercorrelations between the PPVT and the SIT were found (.78 and .86). Partial correlation coefficients with the effects of CA removed were as follows: CMMS and PPVT .77, CMMS and SIT .82, and PPVT and SIT .90. Although MAs from the CMMS and SIT correlated well, the correlation between IQs from the 2 tests was only moderately high. It is concluded that the PPVT and the SIT yield very consistent MAs for mentally retarded Ss of school age and, although somewhat lower than for MAs, the correlations between IQs on the PPVT and SIT are also high.
Johnson, D. Lamont & Shinedling, Martin M. Psychological Reports, 1974(Apr), Vol. 34(2), 367-370. [PA, Vol 52:12727]

610. A voiceless home: Severe speech lag.
Presents a case history describing extremely retarded language development in 2 siblings, a 4-yr-old male and a 5-yr-old female. Speech retardation was attributed to lack of verbal stimulation, cultural deprivation, physical isolation, and parental mental retardation. It was observed that specific language training methods and parental instruction resulted in an increase in the Ss' functional vocabulary as well as gains in their awareness of what constitutes socially acceptable behavior. It is concluded that early developmental assessments, parental education, out-reach specialists, educational TV, and early childhood educational experience may serve to counteract the retarding influence of cultural deprivation on language development.
Jose, Tita. Mental Retardation Bulletin, 1973–74, Vol 2(2), 52-57. [PA, Vol 58:03100]

611. A girl with Wolf-Hirschorn syndrome and mosaicism 46,XX/46,XX,4p-.
Chromosomal analysis of an 11-yr-old mentally retarded girl showed 46,XX/46,XX,4p karyotype. Subsequent clinical examination demonstrated that she had features of Wolf-Hirschorn syndrome.
Judge, C. G.; Garson, O. M.; Pitt, D. B. & Sutherland, G. R. (Children's Cottages, Kew, Victoria, Australia) Journal of Mental Deficiency Research, 1974(Mar), Vol. 18(1), 79-85. [PA, Vol 52:12728]

612. The preschool child: Dilemmas of diagnostic labeling.
Considers diagnostic labeling to be necessary, despite its drawbacks. It is noted that preschool children are generally classified as (a) mentally retarded, (b) autistic, or (c) minimally brain damaged ("learning disability"). "Retarded" has come to be a pejorative label, even though it could mean simply "of subaverage mental functioning, associated with social impairment." Controversy rages over whether autistic children were born autistic or were made so by their mothers. The label "minimal brain dysfunction" is welcomed by both teachers and parents, for it absolves them both of responsibility. It is suggested that all labels should be descriptive adjectives; and one should keep in mind that different labels are appropriate at different times in a child's life. (French summary)
Kessler, Jane W. (Case Western Reserve U, Mental Development Ctr) Canadian Psychiatric Association Journal, 1974(Apr), Vol 19(2), 136-140. [PA, Vol 54:09815]

613. [Dynamic approach to mental retardation.] (Fren)
Discusses the psychodynamic mechanisms and structures underlying the personality of the retarded child. It is suggested that past emphasis on neurobiological classifications of retarded children have led to a neglect of the role of psychogenetic factors in their development. A dichotomy between endogenous and exogenous etiologies has been useful in the description of cases of mild retardation. Review of Rorschach protocols of retarded children indicates that they share similar perceptual mechanisms, modes of thought, and processes of elaboration, but that they produce widely varied fantasies. It is suggested that retarded children are different from both psychotic children and normal younger children.
Lang, J. L. et al. Revue de Neuropsychiatrie Infantile et d'Hygiene Mentale de l'Enfance, 1974(Jan), Vol 22(1-2), 1-18. [PA, Vol 54:07896]

614. The efficacy of "right" as a function of its relationship with reinforcement.
Tested the effects of the relationship between the presentation of a verbal stimulus ("right") and an established reinforcer (candy) on the reinforcement efficacy of the verbal stimulus with 3 groups of 20 8-20 yr old retarded boys. Blocks of training and test trials alternated. During training of the discriminative group, "right" reliably preceded candy, and for the random group "right" and candy were programed independently. "Right" promoted learning in the discriminative group but did not in the latter 2 groups. Results support R. B. Cairns's analysis of the often found failure of approval to be an effective reinforcer in laboratory tests.
Lauten, Max H. & Birnbrauer, J. S. (U North Carolina, Chapel Hill) Journal of Experimental Child Psychology, 1974(Aug), Vol 18(1), 159-166. [PA, Vol 53:01484]

615. Communication in retarded adolescents: Sex and intelligence level.
Conducted 4 interpersonal communication studies with a total of 60 11.5-18.2 yr old retarded Ss. In Exp I 30 dyads, divided equally into 2 sex groups at 3 measured intelligence-adaptive behavior levels, solved problems over a microphone-earphone link. Speakers described ambiguous stimuli for listeners visually

separated from them. There were significant behavior differences among the 3 measured intelligence-adaptive behavior level groups, but not between male and female dyads. The contribution of the speaker and listener to success or failure in the task were systematically examined in Exps II, III, and IV. Exp II examined the behavior of the 30 retarded listeners from Exp I when they were read descriptions given by nonretarded adults. In Exp III nonretarded undergraduate listeners were read descriptions given originally by the retarded speakers from Exp I. In Exp IV the E read the descriptions given by retarded speakers in Exp I to the same speakers now in the listener's role. Results show that the speakers' descriptions were idiosyncratic, and failure in the task could be attributed to poor speaker communication skills rather than to poor listener skills. (23 ref)
Longhurst, Thomas M. (Kansas State U.) American Journal of Mental Deficiency, 1974(Mar), Vol. 78(5), 607-618. [PA, Vol 52:08025]

616. WISC scores vs full scale and abbreviated WAIS scores for retarded adolescents.
Investigated differences between WISC Full Scale IQs obtained on 13 16-20 yr old mentally retarded adolescents during their 15th yr of age and WAIS Full Scale IQs obtained after their 16th birthday using both the 11-subtest WAIS and several abbreviated forms of the WAIS. WAIS scores were constantly higher than WISC scores. Implications for the use of these tests with retarded adolescents are discussed.
Lowe, James D.; Roberts, Margaret & Whidden, Michael. (U Southern Mississippi) Southern Journal of Educational Research, 1974(Sum), Vol 8(3), 326-331. [PA, Vol 53:09897]

617. [Pseudo-feeblemindedness.] (Romn)
Discusses the concept of pseudo-feeblemindedness, tries to establish different categories of the disorder, and describes its main characteristics. Published literature and previous research on this topic provide the data. The importance of discriminating between feeblemindedness and pseudo-feeblemindedness is pointed out. The usefulness of this information to teachers and clinical psychologists and in the diagnosis of school-aged children is emphasized. (English summary)
Lungu-Nicolae, Sora. (Inst of Pedagogical & Psychological Research, Bucharest, Romania) Revista de Psihologie, 1974(Dec), Vol 20(4), 451-460. [PA, Vol 57:03407]

618. Transitive inferences by preoperational, retarded adolescents.
Tested 40 retarded adolescents with MAs of 5-7 yrs for transitive inferences in a choice task. The task involved color-coding of sticks of various lengths, pair-wise discrimination training with visual feedback on 4 adjacent pairs from a 5 stick array, and tests on all possible pairs, allowing for a test of memory of the initial comparisons, end-anchoring effects, and transitive inferences. Compared to intellectually average children of similar MAs, retarded Ss took longer to learn the initial discriminations. However, their performance on tests for transitivity was above chance with the majority of the Ss perfect, and overall performance being slightly lower than that of intellectually average Ss. Memory for the initial comparisons was highly correlated with performance on transitivity, suggesting that a failure to make a transitive inference may be a result of a failure to retrieve the initial comparisons and not a failure to reason logically. (16 ref)
Lutkus, Anthony & Trabasso, Tom. (Princeton U.) American Journal of Mental Deficiency, 1974(Mar), Vol. 78(5), 599-606. [PA, Vol 52:08026]

619. Personal space: Projective and direct measures with institutionalized mentally retarded children.
Administered 2 measures of personal space—a projective interaction measure (PIM) and a direct physical interaction measure (DPIM)—to 5 male and 5 female mildly retarded (IQ range = 52-67) and 5 male and 5 female moderately retarded (IQ range = 35-51) 7-14 yr olds to determine whether they were actually unaware of their abnormality or merely denied its existence. Results indicate a marked difference between the PIM, in which a "normal" peer cutout figure was used, and the DPIM,

in which the stimulus was a "normal" person. Mildly retarded girls and moderately retarded boys increased their distances from the PIM to the DPIM, while moderately retarded girls and mildly retarded boys reduced the distances. Frequent attempts to escape the interaction situation with the "normal" person were observed during the DPIM, which often resulted in a "flight reaction." (15 ref)
Mallenby, Terry W. (U. Manitoba, Winnipeg, Canada) Journal of Personality Assessment, 1974(Feb), Vol. 38(1), 28-31. [PA, Vol 52:05695]

620. Performance profiles of matched normal, educationally subnormal and severely subnormal children on the revised ITPA.
Compared the performance of matched groups of 30 normal, 30 educationally subnormal (ESN), and 30 severely subnormal (SSN) children, all of whom had a mental age of 5 yrs, on the revised Illinois Test of Psycholinguistic Abilities (ITPA). Results show that normals scored highest on all subtests, with ESNs next and SSNs scoring lowest. The largest intergroup differences were found on the Visual Sequential Memory subtest, but significant differences were also found between normals and ESNs on Auditory Sequential Memory and between normals and SSNs on both reception subtests, Auditory Association and Auditory Sequential Memory. Both normals and ESNs showed preference for tests in the auditory-vocal channel over those in the visual-motor channel. Results are discussed in the light of previous ITPA findings, the special circumstances of this study, and the characteristics of the test battery. (28 ref)
Marinosson, G. L. (Child Guidance Clinic, Middleton, England) Journal of Child Psychology & Psychiatry & Allied Disciplines, 1974(Apr), Vol 15(2), 139-148. [PA, Vol 53:03442]

621. [The effects of verbal reinforcement combinations on three-alternative discrimination learning in normal and mentally retarded children.] (Japn)
6 groups of 108 2nd graders and 6 groups of mentally retarded children (mean mental age 8½ yrs) performed 3-alternative discrimination and shift learning tasks of 2 dimensions, color and form, under 3 types of verbal reinforcement combinations, RW, RN, and NW. The mentally retarded NW group showed significant inefficiency in the original learning ($p < .05$). No significant differences of the verbal reinforcement combinations were found between groups in the shift learning. Results indicate that mentally retarded children had more difficulty in using the information of W in the 3-alternative tasks than in 2-alternative tasks.
Matsuda, Michihiko & Matsuda, Fumiko. (Chiba U, Japan) Japanese Journal of Educational Psychology, 1974(Mar), Vol 22(1), 40-44. [PA, Vol 53:07707]

622. Full-time medical practitioners in Canadian mental retardation facilities.
Surveyed full-time physicians working in mental retardation institutions in Canada. Data from 78 physicians, perhaps half of all those employed, show that 50% were primary-care physicians and 30% were psychiatrists. Few of the respondents had had training in child psychiatry, genetics, or mental retardation. It is concluded that physicians who work in institutions for retardates should be specifically trained for this work.
McCreary, Bruce D. (Kingston Psychiatric Hosp, Mental Retardation Services, Ontario, Canada) Canadian Psychiatric Association Journal, 1974(Feb), Vol 19(1), 51-53. [PA, Vol 53:03212]

623. A case for role changes for parents of the mentally retarded.
Suggests that because of several current societal phenomena (e.g., the nature of the contemporary community, the bureaucratic quality of service agencies, and the changing distribution of power) compensatory steps must be taken to insure appropriate responses to the needs of the retarded. Greater activity by parents is urged, and actual parent-role functions are discussed.
Meenaghan, Thomas M. (Marywood Coll., Graduate School of Social Work) Mental Retardation, 1974(Jun), Vol. 12(3), 48-49. [PA, Vol 52:12732]

624.   Piagetian tasks and arithmetic achievement in retarded children.
Administered the Arithmetic Concept Screening Test, a 77-item group test measuring readiness concepts in quantitative thinking (e.g., form and size discrimination) and the Arithmetic Concept Individual Test, which assesses Piagetian concepts (e.g., seriation, classification, and conservation of number) to 12 white and 24 black students with mean CA, MA, and IQ of 10.4, 6.8 and 66.26 respectively. Low to moderate correlations were found between arithmetic skills and the Piagetian concepts. Reasons for the depressed correlations (e.g., S's problem-solving strategies) are discussed.
Melnick, Gerald; Bernstein, Jerry & Lehrer, Barry. (Jersey City State Coll.) Exceptional Children, 1974(Feb), Vol. 40(5), 358-361. [PA, Vol 52:03382]

625.   A comparison of reasoning skills and moral judgments in delinquent, retarded, and normal adolescent girls.
Administered a battery of Piagetian reasoning and moral judgment tasks to 30 delinquent girls aged 13-16, and compared the performance of 16 of these Ss with that of 16 female retardates and 16 female normals; all 3 groups were randomly selected. Measures of conservation, classification, and moral judgment were relatively independent of one another. Results indicate that the delinquents showed delays in their cognitive development but demonstrated no gaps in their ability to formulate moral judgment. Findings suggest that Piagetian assessments would be useful in planning habilitation programs for delinquents. (14 ref)
Miller, Charles K.; Zumoff, Larry & Stephens, Beth. (Reading Counseling Center, Cheltenham, Pa.) Journal of Psychology, 1974(Mar), Vol. 86(2), 261-268. [PA, Vol 52:12688]

626.   [The case of a late infantile amaurotic idiocy.] (Srcr)
Reports the case of a 6-yr-old girl suffering from amaurotic idiocy of the Jansky-Bielschowsky type. The clinical picture was defined by histochemical analysis of cells of the CNS, the Meissner plexus, and other organs. (English summary) (16 ref)
Milovanović, Dragoslav D.; Radojičić, Borivoje & Dožić, Slobodan. Anali Zavoda za Mentalno Zdravlje, 1974, Vol 6(1), 93–98. [PA, Vol 61:03971]

627.   [The utility of the Stanford-Binet, the Raven, and the Goodenough in diagnosing child psychopathology.] (Span)
Studied the differences in intelligence scores obtained with the Stanford-Binet Intelligence Scale, Raven's Progressive Matrices, and the Draw-A-Man Test administered to a group of 57 nonnormal children. Ss were divided into 2 age groups (4-8 and 8-12 yrs) and 3 diagnostic groups: subnormal (IQ less than 70 on the Stanford-Binet), educable (IQ 70-84), and neurotic. Each S took all 3 intelligence tests. Correlations among the tests ranged from .43 to .14. Two subnormal children with brain damage scored higher on the Draw-A-Man Test than on the other 2 tests. Ten older children diagnosed as neurotic scored lower on the Draw-A-Man than on the other 2 tests, and scored at normal levels on the Raven. The Stanford-Binet (Form L) gave the most reliable estimate of intelligence for all 6 groups, perhaps because it uses many different types of items. It is concluded that the 3 tests measure different intellectual characteristics, characteristics which develop uniformly in normal children, but nonuniformly in non-normal children.
Monedero, Carmelo & Sanz, Maria J. (U Complutense de Madrid, Spain) Revista de Psicología General y Aplicada, 1974(Nov-Dec), Vol 29(131), 1087-1100. [PA, Vol 58:09631]

628.   Intensity modulation and the reproduction of auditory duration by nonretarded and retarded children.
28 age-matched retarded (IQ range 67-81) and nonretarded children (mean chronological age for both groups = 10.25 yrs) reproduced the durations of acoustic signals of 3, 7, 11, and 15 sec. It was predicted that the availability of structural cues to stimulus duration would benefit the accuracy of the reproductions by the retarded group to a greater extent than those of the nonretarded group. Structural cues were provided by adding a pulsing rhythm to the acoustic signals through periodic modulation of their intensity. Reproductions by the retarded group became progressively shorter and less accurate than those of the nonretarded group with increments in stimulus duration. Reproductions of intensity-modulated signals were longer and more accurate than those of nonmodulated signals, but this effect was unrelated to the intellectual status of the Ss. Results are considered in terms of the effects of stimulus change on the processing of temporal information and a motivationally mediated bias in the responses of the retarded group. (15 ref)
Mulhern, Thomas J.; Warm, Joel S. & Clark, Debbie. (Albert P. Brewer Developmental Center, Mobile, Ala.) American Journal of Mental Deficiency, 1974(May), Vol. 78(6), 721-726. [PA, Vol 52:08030]

629.   Filtered speech audiometry in normal children and in the mentally retarded.
Presented distorted monosyllables to 20 normal 4-5 yr olds, 5 adults (mean age, 22 yrs), and 68 mentally retarded 8-18 yr olds (IQ range, 50-75) so that 20 monosyllables were distorted with low-pass, high-pass, and band-pass filtering. A 50-db sensation level was sufficient for normal children to discriminate monosyllables with unfiltered speech audiometry. 10-20 db above the average level of normal children was necessary for mentally retarded Ss to discriminate correctly. Discrimination was poor for all Ss with low-pass filtering below 1,200 Hz, but was good for both normal and retarded Ss with high-pass filtering above 1,700 Hz. A gap in discrimination was observed between the 2 groups of Ss with band-pass filtering of 1,200-2,400 Hz. Wide variation in individual discrimination scores was found, especially for the mentally retarded. A developmental trend in discrimination ability for the normal Ss was noted. No sex differences were obtained. (French summary)
Nagafuchi, M. (Tohoku U., Faculty of Education, Sendai, Japan) Audiology, 1974(Jan), Vol. 13(1), 66-77. [PA, Vol 52:01281]

630.   [Intelligibility of distorted speech sounds shifted in frequency and time in normal children and the mentally retarded.] (Japn)
20 monosyllabic sounds and 10 trisyllabic words were distorted by means of a speech stretcher; 3 levels of expansion and 3 levels of compression were used both on the frequency and the time. Ss were 160 normal children of chronological age (CA) 6-17, 10 young adults, and 97 retarded children of CA 6-17, mental age (MA) 3-12, and IQ 31-77. Intelligibility decreased with greater frequency distortion. It increased with CA up to 11 yrs in normal Ss, and with MA in retarded Ss. For time-compressed stimuli, the intelligibility was similar for both groups, while for time-expanded stimuli it was better for retarded children than for normals matched in MA. No sex differences were found. The intelligibility of greatly distorted stimuli dropped sharply in retarded Ss and was significantly lower in Ss with IQ 30 than in those with IQ 40. (English summary)
Nagafuchi, Masaaki & Murakami, Teiji. (Tohoku U, Sendai, Japan) Japanese Journal of Special Education, 1974(Jun), Vol 12(1), 43-53. [PA, Vol 53:11956]

631.   Tay-Sachs disease: Neurophysiological studies in 20 children.
Studied 20 children with proven Tay-Sachs disease. EEGs showed mild abnormalities during the 1st yr of life, with rapid progressive deterioration until death, usually before 4 yrs. The electroretinogram remained unaffected; visual evoked responses were present in the early stages, but not after 16 mo. (German & Spanish summaries) (21 ref)
Pampiglione, G.; Privett, G. & Harden, Ann. (Hosp. for Sick Children, London, England) Developmental Medicine & Child Neurology, 1974(Apr), Vol. 16(2), 201-208. [PA, Vol 52:12797]

632.   A process model approach for research into retardate's parental family: Theoretical and methodological considerations.
Attempts to (a) present a brief review of trends in research on parental families of retardates, (b) point out the theoretical gaps and suggest a process model for generating research hypotheses, (c) outline the methodological inadequacies and suggest alternatives for further research, and (d) formulate research problems

based on the model. The emphasis throughout is on the process by which parental attributes influence the a retarded child's behavior, in contrast to previous studies that have followed a jump-correlational approach and suffered from predictive contaminants. The process model described would probably unravel many of the family influences that lead to a cultural etiology of mental retardation and would clarify the relationships between retarded children and their parents and siblings. These provide a base for trying to prevent mild retardation at the family level and for subsequent control of retardates' behavior in family and social settings. (30 ref)
Panda, Kailas C. (SCS Coll, Puri, India) Indian Journal of Mental Retardation, 1974(Jan), Vol 7(1), 14–24. [PA, Vol 62:11243]

633.   [A comparative study of several psycholinguistic abilities of children having normal and retarded intelligence.] (Russ)
Compared 125 mentally retarded and 125 normal Lithuanian schoolchildren on 4 linguistic abilities thought to be important in 2nd language learning. Ability to hear speech was tested by requiring Ss to repeat a sentence in an unfamiliar language (Russian). To measure plasticity of the articulatory apparatus, Ss were asked to pronounce a Lithuanian tongue twister and Russian words. There were 2 tests of verbal memory (learning a Lithuanian poem and a paired associate list) in which stimuli were Lithuanian words and responses. Ability to construct sentences according to the rules of a language was measured by asking Ss to make into sentences groups of 4 Lithuanian words given in their primary form. Performance was evaluated on a 5-point scale. For each ability tested, the percentage of normal Ss attaining good scores and retarded Ss attaining poor scores was higher. Chi-squares were significant for all but the last task. Tests of ability to hear speech and verbal memory produced the largest differences between the 2 groups. (English summary)
Puoshlyenye, E.-P. (USSR Academy of Pedagogical Sciences, Inst of Defektology, Moscow) Defektologiya, 1974, No 2, 9-16. [PA, Vol 54:09972]

634.   [The sexual behavior of mentally retarded adolescents.] (Germ)
Sexual experiences of 682 mental retardates were not significantly different from those of 147 normal juveniles. Heterosexual experiences were common for both sexes and cohabitation was frequently reported by retarded females.
Radlbeck, Kurt G. (Kreiskrankenhaus/Kreispoliklinik, Borna, E Germany) Psychiatrie, Neurologie und medizinische Psychologie, 1974(Jun), Vol 26(6), 344-352. [PA, Vol 53:09900]

635.   Inapparent congenital cytomegalovirus infection with elevated cord IgM levels: Causal relations with auditory and mental deficiency.
A longitudinal clinical, virologic, and immunologic study found 18 patients with inapparent congenital cytomegalovirus infection among 267 neonates with elevated umbilical-cord IgM levels. Virus excretion persisted in most Ss through the 3rd yr of life, and the concomitant antigenic stimulation resulted in an accelerated development of immunoglobulins M and G and in continued complement-fixing antibody production in 14 Ss. Some degree of sensorineural hearing loss occurred in 9 of 16 Ss tested as compared with 2 of 12 controls, and, in 4, an auditory handicap was either proved or considered likely. A trend toward subnormal intelligence was observed in the infected Ss, and 2 manifested definite mental and social disability. Data indicate that cytomegalovirus infection probably has an important causal role in mild to moderate auditory and mental dysfunction in childhood. (17 ref)
Reynolds, David W., et al. (U. Alabama, Medical Center, Birmingham) New England Journal of Medicine, 1974(Feb), Vol. 290(6), 291-296. [PA, Vol 52:03466]

636.   The role of instruction in the acquisition of a concept of space: An exploratory clinical investigation.
Conducted an experiment on the acquisition of a concept of space, according to J. Piaget's theories and levels. Ss were 9 retarded children 3-5 yrs old. The various levels are described.

Results confirm Piaget's observations. The age levels of spatial concept development need not be fixed, although their order may be constant. Instruction tended to improve Ss' performance. All were from culturally advantaged homes and were able to utilize language as a learning mediator in their approach to the task. It is suggested that the mentally retarded child may be capable of attaining higher levels of concept development than is generally assumed, given special instruction emphasizing his abilities.
Robinson, M. R. (U Queensland, Fred & Eleanor Schonell Educational Research Ctr, St Lucia, Australia) Slow Learning Child, 1974(Nov), Vol 21(3), 164-177. [PA, Vol 53:11958]

637.   Social deprivation and "mental retardation."
Proposes that study of the effects of social deprivation may help to understand psychological etiological factors in "mental retardation." Social deprivation, a relative construct, is viewed as resulting from the difference between predeprived and deprived levels of adult social stimulation, and as being greatly affected by the rate of change. A case history illustrates how the relative social deprivation thesis can contribute to a better understanding of the child's emotional and intellectual development and of treatment techniques. (21 ref)
Rosenheim, Harold D. & Ables, Billie S. (US Army Mental Hygiene Consultation Service, Ft Buckner, Okinawa) Child Psychiatry & Human Development, 1974(Sum), Vol 4(4), 216-226. [PA, Vol 53:11959]

638.   Social factors in mental retardation.
A review of the literature suggests that studies of social factors in mental retardation are conducted primarily within epidemiological frameworks and that the research can be classified into 4 perspectives: (a) the East Coast Prevalence Studies which have been epidemiological in nature with a concern for the incidence of retardation in a given area, (b) the social epidemiological perspective of western Europe which emphasizes program planning and evaluation, (c) social-behavioral research which is concerned with social factors in labeling and life-styles of adult retardates, and (d) the crisis research trend which is concerned with how families cope with retarded children. A synthesis of findings from these 4 frameworks is presented, based on the premise that the family should be viewed as the central core of an understanding of the social elements in mental retardation. (43 ref)
Rowitz, Louis. (Illinois State Pediatric Inst, Chicago) Social Science & Medicine, 1974(Jul), Vol 8(7), 405-412. [PA, Vol 53:05679]

639.   Siblings of retarded children: A population at risk.
Discusses guilt as a major factor underlying the symptoms of siblings of retarded children. The process of reparation is viewed as essential to the alleviation of guilt and anxiety and the assessment of the reparation efforts in diagnosis. Parental reaction to a retarded child is important as siblings develop fantasies and behavior as defenses against guilt and anxiety. 4 cases are presented to illustrate the ways families may deal with a retarded child.
San Martino, Mary & Newman, Morton B. (Mystic Valley Mental Health Ctr, Lexington, MA) Child Psychiatry & Human Development, 1974(Spr), Vol 4(3), 168-177. [PA, Vol 53:01494]

640.   Slow viruses and mental retardation.
Recent research has suggested that several diseases associated with mental retardation (subacute sclerosing panencephalitis, SSPE; progressive multifocal leucoencephalopathy, PML; Creutzfeld-Jakob disease, and "kuru") may be the results of slow-virus infections. These diseases are characterized by progressive personality changes, impairment of intellectual ability, and loss of control over physical movements. The difficulty in diagnosing a slow-virus infection in children is described. The most promising theory concerning why only certain children contract SSPE and PML despite the prevalence of the associated viruses hypothesizes that these viruses can cause a slow infection of the brain only when there is a defect in the body's immune defense system. An investigation is underway to determine whether certain new drugs can stimulate an inactive immune system to

combat a viral infection that might otherwise cause SSPE or PML.
Segal, D. J. (U Alberta, Edmonton, Canada) Mental Retardation Bulletin, 1973–74, Vol 2(1), 12-15. [PA, Vol 58:03603]

641. Assessment of social functioning of 56 mentally retarded children.
Assessed the social functioning of 56 mentally retarded schoolchildren (6–13 yrs old) on the basis of 4 criteria: (a) social interaction, (b) levels of communication, (c) self-responsibility, and (d) social behavior and its level of functioning in relation to level of impairment. An IQ evaluation was done by administering the Social Maturity Scale and Vineland Social Maturity Scale. Results show that mildly retarded Ss functioned more in the lower level of social interaction; as the amount of intellectual impairment decreased, an average or satisfactory level of social functioning could be observed. It is concluded that since intellectual impairment affects the basic channels of communication, parents and teachers should be more involved in developing social behavior of retarded children.
Shastri, A. Inam & Misra, A. K. (Postgraduate Inst of Medical Education & Research, Chandigarh, India) Indian Journal of Mental Retardation, 1974(Jan), Vol 7(1), 31–35. [PA, Vol 62:11250]

642. A study of adjustment problems of mentally retarded children.
Investigated the adjustment of mentally retarded children in the areas of emotional and physical health and social and home adjustment. 50 retarded and 50 nonretarded males 12–18 yrs old, all from middle-class families, were administered the Bell Adjustment Inventory (Hindi adaptation). Results show poor adjustment for the retarded Ss in the areas of home, health, social, and emotional life ($p < 0.01$), indicating poor overall adjustment compared to that of the normal group.
Shukla, T. R. & Khoche, V. (Hosp for Mental Diseases, Ranchi, India) Indian Journal of Mental Retardation, 1974(Jan), Vol 7(1), 4–13. [PA, Vol 62:11251]

643. Complex visual discriminations in cultural familial retardates and normal children.
Examined information processing in a visual matching task in a group of 12 cultural familial retardates (mean age = 18 yrs) and a group of 31 normal children in Grades 2, 5, or 8, using digit sequences of varying complexity as the stimuli. Reaction times (RTs) of normal adult Ss making *same* judgments do not fit into a single-process self-terminating feature testing model, while those for *different* judgments do. This study found that (a) the *same-different* relationship was the same for normal Ss and retardates, with *same* judgment RTs deviating from predictions of a self-terminating model; (b) overall RT was a function of Ss' mental age; and (c) differences in RTs between groups were due primarily to "intercept" rather than "slope" effects, although evidence of a possible slope difference was found between the 8th graders and the other groups.
Silverman, Wayne P. (New York State Inst for Research in Mental Retardation, New York) Journal of Experimental Psychology, 1974(Sep), Vol 103(3), 539-545. [PA, Vol 53:05681]

644. High speed scanning of nonalphanumeric symbols in cultural-familially retarded and nonretarded children.
Administered a task similar to that of S. Sternberg (see PA, Vol 40:10810) to 36 2nd, 5th, and 8th graders and 12 retarded Ss (mean mental ages—MAs—9.9 yrs) with meaningless letter-like figures as the stimuli. Results show that performance increased with age for the nonretarded Ss. The retarded Ss performed above the level expected of their MA-matched nonretarded peers but below the level expected of nonretarded children of equal chronological age. Differences in group performance were due to "intercept" rather than "slope" differences in all instances. (16 ref)
Silverman, Wayne P. (New York State Inst for Research in Mental Retardation, Staten Island) American Journal of Mental Deficiency, 1974(Jul), Vol 79(1), 44-51. [PA, Vol 53:01495]

645. Cytogenetic survey of 504 mentally retarded individuals.
Of the 504 children surveyed, 89 had Down's syndrome, 2 had Cri-du-chat syndrome, 2 had Turner's syndrome, 3 were hermaphrodites, and 2 had pseudo-Klinefelter's syndrome. The remaining 408 residents were not suspected of any defined chromosome aberrations, although chromosome analyses revealed cases of partial monosomy of chromosome 18, numerical aberrations of autosomes, sex chromosome aberrations, and heteromorphis variants of an autosome. (27 ref)
Singh, D. N. et al. (Meharry Medical Coll, Nashville, TN) Journal of Mental Deficiency Research, 1974(Dec), Vol 18(4), 293-305. [PA, Vol 54:07746]

646. Some psycho-biological correlates of mental subnormality.
Surveyed 320 mentally retarded children 1–18 yrs old with the objective of serving their needs better than have previous surveys that were based on the medical model. The author attempts to establish psychobiological correlates (e.g., intelligence, age, sex, and birth order) with the needs of these children to help the community determine what services should be provided for them.
Singh, M. V. (Maulana Azad Medical Coll, New Delhi, India) Indian Journal of Mental Retardation, 1974(Jan), Vol 7(1), 25–30. [PA, Vol 62:11253]

647. The influence of MA and CA on the attribution of life and life traits to animate and inanimate objects.
Used a 70-item questionnaire to determine the influence of MA and CA on the attribution of life and life traits to animate and inanimate objects. Ss were 40 normal and 20 retarded children. Results indicate that (a) the attribution of life and life traits was not determined by CA or MA alone; (b) life and life traits attributed by young normal and retarded Ss were highly dependent on perceptual object characteristics; while (c) those of older normals were mostly based on the biological nature of the object and/or the implicit logical consequences. (18 ref)
Smeets, Paul M. (Parsons State Hospital, Research Center, Kan.) Journal of Genetic Psychology, 1974(Mar), Vol. 124(1), 17-27. [PA, Vol 52:12739]

648. Oddity and match-to-sample tasks as the components of a chained schedule with retarded children.
Conducted 2 experiments with 3 10-14 yr old retarded boys to explore the possibility of presenting a contingency-controlled match-to-sample task as a reinforcing event for the performance on an oddity task. The experimental design included a combination of a reversal and a multiple baseline technique. Results indicate that for 2 of the 3 Ss the performance on the oddity task could be successfully controlled by the contingent presentation of the contingency-controlled match-to-sample task. The oddity performance of 1 S, who showed a strong position bias, improved when he was instructed to verbalize the stimuli before making the oddity response.
Smeets, Paul M. & Striefel, Sebastian. (California School for the Deaf, Multi-Handicapped Unit, Riverside) American Journal of Mental Deficiency, 1974(Jan), Vol. 78(4), 462-470. [PA, Vol 52:08044]

649. Varied environmental conditions and task performance by mentally retarded subjects perceived as distractible and nondistractible.
24 12-yr-old mentally retarded children with high distractibility ratings and 24 13-yr-old retardates with low distractibility ratings comprised 2 groups, each serving under 3 conditions: 3-sided cubicles, very high levels of auditory and visual stimulation, and normal conditions. All Ss performed 2 different tasks, 1/day, under each of the 3 stimulus conditions. Distractible Ss had significantly longer completion times than nondistractible Ss. The only significant effect of the 3 conditions was that completion time by distractible Ss on a relatively difficult task was significantly longer under the condition of increased stimulation than under normal conditions. Data are interpreted as offering no support for the use of reduced stimulation as achieved by

cubicles within educational settings for mentally retarded children.
Somervill, John W.; Jacobsen, Linda; Warnberg, Larry & Young, William. (Southern Illinois U) American Journal of Mental Deficiency, 1974(Sep), Vol 79(2), 204-209. [PA, Vol 53:03453]

650.   Performance of mentally retarded children on pre-arithmetic tasks.
Tested 48 8-15 yr old retarded children on a battery of pre-arithmetic tasks to evaluate their skills in counting objects, use of numerals, and matching numerals to sets. Numeral matching was less difficult than selecting numerals indicated by spoken numbers, which was less difficult than numeral naming. Counting total sets was less difficult than counting a subset from a total set. Ss were able to perform more numeral tasks than counting tasks correctly. Results are compared with a 1971 study of intellectually average kindergarten children by M. C. Wang, et al.
Spradlin, Joseph E.; Cotter, Vance W.; Stevens, Crystal & Friedman, Michael. (U. Kansas, Bureau of Child Research Lab., Lawrence) American Journal of Mental Deficiency, 1974(Jan), Vol. 78(4), 397-403. [PA, Vol 52:08048]

651.   A study of the conceptual ability of normal and mentally retarded children.
Studied the performance of normal and mentally retarded children on the Weigel-Goldstein-Scheerer Color Form Sorting Test. Results confirm that retardates are significantly inferior to normals in their ability to abstract, generalize, and verbalize concepts.
Srividya, G. & Kalanidhi, M. S.   Manas, 1974, Vol 21(1), 33–36. [PA, Vol 59:03641]

652.   Symposium: Developmental gains in the reasoning, moral judgment, and moral conduct of retarded and nonretarded persons.
Presents results from a longitudinal study on the development of Piagetian reasoning, moral judgment, and moral conduct. Findings are analyzed and tabulated for 2 2-yr testings of 75 nonretarded (IQ = 90-100) and 75 retarded (IQ = 50-75) 6-20 yr old Ss. Attention is also given to interrelationships which exist among scores on measures of reasoning, moral judgment, and moral conduct. Discussions of and reactions to the findings on reasoning are provided by J. M. Hunt; on moral judgment, by L. Kohlberg; and on moral conduct, by J. Aronfreed.
Stephens, Beth et al. (Temple U) American Journal of Mental Deficiency, 1974(Sep), Vol 79(2), 113-161. [PA, Vol 53:03454]

653.   Effects of competence and nurturance on imitation of nonretarded peers by retarded adolescents.
Investigated the effects of competence and nurturance on imitation of 128 nonretarded peers by 128 retarded adolescents and whether nonretarded peers would imitate retarded Ss. All Ss were 12-20 yrs old and enrolled in junior and senior high school classes. Retarded Ss were paired with nonretarded peers, whom they had previously named as liked (nurturant) or disliked (nonnurturant), on a task manipulated by E so that levels of competence for all participants could be controlled. For both retarded and nonretarded Ss, competent models were imitated more than noncompetent models, and noncompetent observers were more imitative than were competent observers. No significant effects were found for nurturance. Implications concerning various peer tutoring pairings of retarded and nonretarded children are discussed. (32 ref)
Strichart, Stephen S. (Rutgers State U.) American Journal of Mental Deficiency, 1974(May), Vol. 78(6), 665-673. [PA, Vol 52:08049]

654.   Isolating variables which affect TV preferences of retarded children.
Assessed the TV preference of 6 low-level and 6 high-level 9-12 yr old retardates by providing each S with a simultaneous choice of 4 alternatives (3 TV programs and no program) during a baseline period. All Ss spent most of each session responding and preferred TV over no program. Ss were then given 4 simulta-

neous choices between the preferred program in color, in black and white, audio only, or video only. Of 6 high-level Ss, 5 showed a preference for programs in color, 3 low-level Ss showed a preference for black and white presentations, and the other 4 Ss showed about equal preferences for color and black and white.
Striefel, Sebastian. (Parsons Research Ctr, KS) Psychological Reports, 1974(Aug), Vol 35(1, Pt 1), 115-122. [PA, Vol 56:08219]

655.   Motor development and body image: A reply to Ball.
Clarifies the intentions of W. C. Chasey et al (see PA, Vol 52:8002) in their article using body-image scores with mentally retarded children and cites reliability data supporting the use of the measures employed. Criticisms by T. S. Ball (see PA, Vol 53:Issue 2) of Chasey et al are answered, supporting the latter's study.
Swartz, Jon D. (U Texas, Austin) American Journal of Mental Deficiency, 1974(Sep), Vol 79(2), 227-228. [PA, Vol 53:03455]

656.   [Structure of the adaptive behavior of the mentally retarded: I. A factor-analytic study.] (Japn)
Administered the Japanese translation of the Adaptive Behavior Scale to 1,971 retarded children and 6,092 retarded adults. Significant factors in Part I of the scale were Personal Independence (e.g., self-care and motor ability), Social Adjustment (e.g., telephone usage, locomotion, money handling, speaking, and writing), and Personal and Social Responsibility (e.g., initiative, persistence, self-direction, and socialization). In Part II, Antisocial-aggressive Behavior, Self-stimulating Behavior, and Deficient Interpersonal Behavior were 3 significant factors both for children and adults. (English summary)
Tomiyasu, Yoshikazu; Matsuda, Sei; Murakamai, Eiji & Emi, Yoshitoshi. (Inst for Developmental Research, Aichi Prefectural Colony, Japan) Japanese Journal of Special Education, 1974(Jun), Vol 12(1), 10-23. [PA, Vol 53:11966]

657.   Sexual attitudes of mothers of retarded children.
44 mothers were interviewed to assess their attitudes toward sexual behavior, sex education, birth control, marriage, and dating of their mentally retarded adolescents. Religion influenced mothers' attitudes toward masturbation and marriage. Mothers wanted school sex education and desired formation of parent groups for understanding the sexuality of their children.
Turchin, Gary. (Pearl Buck Ctr, Eugene, OR) Journal of School Health, 1974(Nov), 490-492. [PA, Vol 54:05576]

658.   Comparison of Bender error and time scores for groups of epileptic, retarded, and behavior-problem children.
Made Bender Gestalt error and time score comparisons between groups of 16 epileptic, 27 mentally retarded, and 33 school and/or behavior problem 7-17 yr olds. Results indicate that there were significant differences in error scores between the epileptic and the school-behavior problem groups and between retarded and the school-behavior problem groups, but there were no significant differences in time scores for any groups. An attempt was made to assign Ss to their appropriate groups by using error or time scores alone. Although no single cutoff score was better than chance for accurately assigning group membership, a 2-dimensional plot using both error and time scores was significant. The importance of this system for clinical diagnosis is discussed. Correlations between IQ, error and time scores, and age are reported for each diagnostic group.
Tymchuk, Alexander J. (U. California, Medical School, Los Angeles) Perceptual & Motor Skills, 1974(Feb), Vol. 38(1), 71-74. [PA, Vol 52:07807]

659.   Breadth of attention and retention in mentally retarded and intellectually average children.
100 children with a mean MA of approximately 6 yrs from kindergarten classes and educable and trainable mentally retarded (EMR and TMR) special education classes were presented with a multidimensional demonstration object and instructed to find the one exactly like it among a set of multidimensional choice objects, consisting of all 32 possible combinations of the binary cues (attributes) from each of the 5 dimensions. Retention was examined after 0-, 10-, and 30-sec delay intervals. Results

show that (a) the performance of TMR children was inferior to that of the EMR and intellectually average children; (b) this deficit increased with increased demands on retention; (c) there were no differences between EMR and intellectually average children; and (d) all IQ groups appeared capable of attending to several dimensions simultaneously. Implications for D. Zeaman's 1970 theory of attention in retardates and the marked differences between EMR and TMR children are discussed.
Ullman, Douglas G. (Bowling Green State U.) American Journal of Mental Deficiency, 1974(Mar), Vol. 78(5), 640-648. [PA, Vol 52:08051]

660. **Some findings on psychodiagnostic tests with young retarded adults.**
23 14-21 yr old mental retardates, divided into 2 groups according to scores on the Stanford-Binet Intelligence Scale (IQs up to 40 and above 40, respectively) were administered the Bender Gestalt Test (BGT), the Human Figure Drawing Test (HFD), the Thematic Apperception Test (TAT), and the Rorschach Inkblot Test. As compared to higher IQ Ss, lower IQ Ss showed more signs of brain damage (BGT); obtained lower mental age (HFD); showed poor verbal productivity, had less interaction, perceived environment as more threatening, and had preoccupation with primary needs (TAT); and gave fewer shading and color responses, had lower mean range of content, and made fewer popular responses (Rorschach). Findings are discussed in the light of the applicability of these tests in cases of severe and moderate retardation.
Upadhyaya, S. & Sinha, A. K. (B. M. Inst of Mental Health, Ahmedabad, India) Indian Journal of Clinical Psychology, 1974(Sep), Vol 1(2), 73-79. [PA, Vol 54:05577]

661. **Etiologic factors in mental retardation.**
Proposes that the total evaluation of a mentally retarded child should consider 4 dimensions: the intellectual, the psychiatric, the organic, and the psychosocial. Only about 20-25% of all mentally retarded individuals show a definitive biological etiologic factor (e.g., prenatal infections, postnatal cerebral infections, maternal intoxication, and trauma through a physical agent. Impaired metabolism or nutritional deficiencies that can cause mental retardation include neuronal lipid storage diseases, carbohydrate disorders, amino acid disorders, nucleotide disorders, mineral disorders, endocrine disorders, and severe malnutrition. Gross brain diseases (e.g., neurocutaneous dysplasia, tumors, or cerebrovascular problems) and unknown prenatal influences (e.g., cerebral malformations, craniofacial anomalies, status dysraphicus, and hydrocephalus) may also result in retardation. Chromosomal and gestational abnormalities and various sorts of psychosocial disadvantage are also implicated. (20 ref)
Valente, Mario & Tarjan, George. (U. California, Neuropsychiatric Inst., Los Angeles) Psychiatric Annals, 1974(Feb), Vol. 4(2), 22-37. [PA, Vol 52:10446]

662. **Infant assessment: Stability of mental functioning in young retarded children.**
Administered the Bayley Scales of Infant Development to 23 18-30 mo old patients suspected of being mentally retarded. Between 1 and 3 yrs later, these Ss were reevaluated using either the Bayley Scales of Infant Development or the Stanford-Binet Intelligence Scale. Of the 15 Ss initially found to be in the moderately-to-profoundly retarded range, 73% remained in that category at follow-up. None of the Ss initially functioning in any of the retarded ranges were normal at follow-up. Results are discussed in terms of the utility of the Bayley Scales of Infant Development in diagnosing mental retardation and the resistance to change of impaired intellectual ability. (18 ref)
VanderVeer, Beverly & Schweid, Edda. (U Washington) American Journal of Mental Deficiency, 1974(Jul), Vol 79(1), 1-4. [PA, Vol 53:01499]

663. **Letter cues vs. configuration cues as aids to word recognition in retarded and nonretarded children.**
63 mentally retarded and 54 nonretarded 6-7 yr old children were randomly assigned to 3 independent conditions (outline,

contrast, and letter cue) in which they learned to read words written in a contrived orthography. In the outline condition, the words were outlined; in the contrast condition, they were surrounded by a black background; and in the letter-cue condition, the words were presented without configurational aids, and letter cues were stressed. Retarded Ss in the letter-cue group learned significantly more words than those in the other groups. The cues emphasized did not influence the numbers of words learned by the nonretarded Ss. It is suggested that teachers working with mildly mentally retarded beginning readers avoid stressing configuration cues.
Vandever, Thomas R. & Neville, Donald D. (George Peabody Coll for Teachers) American Journal of Mental Deficiency, 1974(Sep), Vol 79(2), 210-213. [PA, Vol 53:03458]

664. **[The young backward child and his family: The persistence of ties between the parents and the child even when the child has been removed from the home.]** (Fren)
Discusses patterns of interpersonal relations in the families of retarded children. The presence of a severely retarded child is a traumatic situation for the family, and can lead to conflicts between parents, conflicts in the retarded child's siblings, and loss of social status for the family. It is suggested that the ties between a retarded child and his family continue to be strong even if he is removed from the family and institutionalized. It is concluded that the institutionalized retarded child can make real progress only when his teachers are convinced that the parents desire his progress. (English, German, & Spanish summaries)
Villechenoux-Bonnafe, Marie Y. Revue de Neuropsychiatrie Infantile et d'Hygiene Mentale de l'Enfance, 1974(Jan), Vol 22(1-2), 41-51. [PA, Vol 54:07913]

665. **Development and transfer of mediational strategies by retarded children in paired-associate learning.**
Evaluated the ability of 56 retarded children (mean CA = 12.6 yrs; mean MA = 4.9 yrs) to develop and transfer a mediational strategy. More specifically, 3 successive paired associates lists were learned, with prepositional mediators (presented visually, verbally, or in combination) provided for all pairs (100% aid), ½ of the pairs (50% aid), or no pairs (control). During the 3 training tasks, the 100% aid group made significantly fewer errors than the 50% aid or control groups, which did not differ from each other. The 50% aid group employed mediators as effectively as the 100% aid group, but failed to transfer the strategy to unaided pairs. No effect of type of mediator was found. Transfer of the mediational strategy was evaluated on a nonmediated test list 2 wks following training, with Ss in the 100% aid condition performing with significantly fewer errors than control Ss. However, extensive use of the mediational strategy on the nonmediated test list declined considerably over the 2-wk interval even for the 100% aid condition. (17 ref)
Wanschura, Patricia B. & Borkowski, John G. (U. Notre Dame) American Journal of Mental Deficiency, 1974(Mar), Vol. 78(5), 631-639. [PA, Vol 52:08053]

666. **Differentiation of retarded and normal children through toy-play analysis.**
Individually videotaped 3 groups of Ss (20 6-yr-old retardates and 40 normal children matched with the retardates on CA or MA) during an 18-min period in which each S was free to play with any toys he chose. This period was divided into 54 20-sec intervals with 2 independent Os recording all toy usages in 1 of 10 predetermined categories of toy play. Discriminant function analyses were computed comparing the 3 possible pairs of groups. Significant differences were found between (a) retardates and normal 6-yr-olds, (b) normal 6-yr-olds and normal 3-yr-olds, and (c) retardates and normal 3-yr-olds. The "combinations" category of toy play was the most important predictor in differentiating both normal groups from the retarded group.
Weiner, Elliot A. & Weiner, Barbara J. (Oklahoma State U.) Multivariate Behavioral Research, 1974(Apr), Vol. 9(2), 245-252. [PA, Vol 52:08054]

667.   Social variables in the perception and acceptance of retardation.

In Israel, the effects of country of origin (Jews of European or Eastern descent), social class of the parents, and level of retardation of the child on parental guilt feelings, perception of the retardation, and acceptance of the child were studied. 76 mothers of retarded children were interviewed. Results show no effect for country of origin. Middle-class parents and parents of severely retarded children more accurately perceived the retardation than lower-class parents or parents whose children were less severely retarded. There were no differences by social class or level of retardation for parental guilt feelings or acceptance of the child. (24 ref)
Weller, Leonard; Costeff, Chanan; Cohen, Bernard & Rahman, Dalyah. (Bar-Ilan U, Ramat-Gan, Israel) American Journal of Mental Deficiency, 1974(Nov), Vol 79(3), 274-278. [PA, Vol 53:09911]

668.   Criticisms: Regarding the use of the E.P.V.T. in subnormality research.

Argues against the common practice of estimating mental age on the basis of a score on a test of a specific ability, usually receptive vocabulary. It is shown how a relatively high vocabulary age may be achieved on the English Picture Vocabulary Test by subnormal children. The danger of using this as a mental age estimate is stressed, especially in subnormality research where a mental age matching paradigm is employed using normal and subnormal children.
Wheldall, Kevin & Jeffree, Dorothy. (U Birmingham, School of Education, England) British Journal of Disorders of Communication, 1974(Oct), Vol 9(2), 140-143. [PA, Vol 53:07716]

669.   The von Restorff effect and measures of organization in normals and retardates.

32 noninstitutionalized retardates and 32 normals of equal mental age (approximately 8 yrs) heard 10 orders of 10 nouns when the decibel (db) level of the stimuli was the same and when the db level of the 6th item was higher. The von Restorff effect was demonstrated by both groups. The normals' overall recall was superior to that of the retardates' recall. Differences in recall are attributed to the normals' tendency to recall items in the same serial order more consistently. The subjective organization of lists, as measured by order of recall, differed for the normals and retardates; the normal group was more adaptable than the retarded group in adjusting its strategy to different list conditions. (22 ref)
Winters, John J. & Attlee, Leonard C. (E. R. Johnstone Training & Research Center, Bordentown, N.J.) Memory & Cognition, 1974(Apr), Vol 2(2), 301-305. [PA, Vol 52:11522]

670.   Use of retardation-related diagnostic and descriptive labels by parents of retarded children.

105 parents of retarded children completed checklists containing 57 terms used to describe mentally retarded persons, to assess their familiarity with and their reactions to these labels. Data suggest that parents have considerable difficulty in accepting any label for their own children, even terms which are relatively free of negative imagery. While practically all parents were familiar with the term "mental retardation," and while 93% indicated that the term is appropriate for the retarded in general, only 42% thought it appropriate for their own children. Findings also indicate that 2 forces operate in influencing parental reactions to retardation-related terms: the social desirability of a given term and the context in which the parents are asked to judge a label. Contrasting results from previous studies are discussed, and implications for counseling are examined. (43 ref)
Wolfensberger, Wolf & Kurtz, Richard A. (Syracuse U) Journal of Special Education, 1974(Sum), Vol 8(2), 131-142. [PA, Vol 53:01504]

671.   [Discrimination learning in mentally retarded children as a function of rigidity tendency.] (Chin)

Investigated the function of rigidity tendency on the discrimination learning of mentally retarded children and surveyed the effect of original training on shifted learning. Ss were 24 mildly

retarded children, equally divided by sex, with a mean CA of 141.9 mo and a mean MA of 103.8 mo. 2 sets of 2-choice "color-form objects" were presented by way of a discrimination apparatus devised by E. Percentages of stimulus perseveration, number of position preference, and the difference between pre- and post-performance were then calculated for each S. Results show that (a) the stronger the rigidity tendency, the poorer the discrimination work; and (b) it became easier to learn intradimensional-shifted work after finishing original learning. (18 ref)
Wu, Wu-tien.   Bulletin of Educational Psychology, 1974(Jun), Vol 7, 53-62. [PA, Vol 55:00898]

672.   Effect of S-R discontiguity and double responding on two-odd oddity learning by retardates.

36 institutionalized children whose mental age scores were at least 3 yrs below their chronological ages (12-17 yrs) were divided into 3 matched groups of 12 Ss each and presented with a 2-odd oddity discrimination. In 2 groups-stimulus-response (S-R) and double-response-a 6-in spatial gap was imposed between the oddity stimuli and the site response. Group double-response differed from Group S-R only in requiring a double response (i.e., touching a chosen stimulus before making a response). In a 3rd group ($S + R$) no spatial discontinuity between stimulus and response existed; Ss responded directly to the oddity stimulus and not to the remote response block. In contrast to earlier studies there was little effect of discontiguity or of double responding on performance. Most Ss learned the oddity discrimination regardless of their experimental condition and in this regard were unlike retardates of other studies. (15 ref)
Wunderlich, Richard A. (Catholic U of America) Psychological Reports, 1974(Dec), Vol 35(3), 1327-1331. [PA, Vol 53:11969]

673.   The behavior of normal and retarded children in a probability learning task: An attempt to apply a new kind of measure.

117 normal children from 4 age levels (3.1-5.0, 5.1-7.0, 7.1-9.0 and 9.1-12.0) and 42 mentally retarded children (mean CA, 119.8 mo) performed a 3-choice probability learning task. In addition to the measures employed in the early studies, a new kind of measure was used to analyze the children's behavior in the present study. Analyses of the normal Ss' behavior generally confirmed M. W. Wier's (see PA, Vol 39:6842) explanation for the developmental changes of the performances in the task on the whole; however, in the present study the effect of position preference was found at 3.1-5.0 age level rather than at the 6-9 yr level found by Wier.
Abe, Kenichi. (Waseda U, Tokyo, Japan) Journal of Child Development, 1975(Jan), Vol 11, 8-21. [PA, Vol 57:02884]

674.   Role-taking ability and the interpersonal competencies of retarded children.

Studied the relationship between social role-taking ability and competencies of 46 retarded children (mean CA 12.96 yrs) in dyadic interaction. Ss were given M. H. Feffer's role-taking task and assigned to dyads according to rank-order position. A specially designed 2-person game, involving the delivery of differential reinforcements (pennies) to self or other, was used to operationalize the competencies of dyads in maximizing joint profit and in establishing a reciprocal exchange strategy. Results show that high role-taking ability dyads were not only more successful in the interpersonal task, but also demonstrated increasing success across trials. Role taking was also associated with the establishment and maintenance of a reciprocal exchange strategy and with MA and IQ. (17 ref)
Affleck, Glenn G. (U Connecticut, Health Ctr, Farmington) American Journal of Mental Deficiency, 1975(Nov), Vol 80(3), 312-316. [PA, Vol 55:10046]

675.   There is no alternative to the IQ.

Presents data from 3 9-15 yr old boys (IQ range 48-106) to illustrate an approach to understanding the intellectual functioning of the person considered to be retarded from the viewpoint of measured intelligence. The inkblot method was used to differentiate how the individual deals with familiar and unfamiliar problems, emphasizing the language and mode of perceiving, organizing, and responding of the individual to the problems presented to him.

Allen, Robert M. (U Miami, FL) Journal of Personality Assessment, 1975(Aug), Vol 39(4), 377-380. [PA, Vol 54:11767]

676. [Ten years' experience in early detection of epileptic seizures in newborns and infants with natal brain injuries.] (Yugo)

Studied 103 children with neonatal brain injuries from birth through age 3 yrs. At the end of the 3rd yr, 19.4% of the Ss were found to be handicapped: 6.8% with motor retardation, 4.85% with mental retardation, and 7.7% with severe psychomotor retardation.

Barjaktarović-Nikolić, K.; Nikolić, B.; Knežević, L. & Nikolić, P. (Inst of Mental Health, Belgrade, Yugoslavia) Neurologija, 1975, Vol 23(1–4), 47–53. [PA, Vol 59:03644]

677. Retardation in speaking and reading English as a foreign language.

Examines some of the problems of mental retardation in children and defines the mentally retarded child as one who is physically normal but whose short- and long-term intellectual performances fall below the average of his/her peer group. Some of the ways in which mental retardation can be detected are discussed; these include perception, comprehension, and language skills tests and the absence of imaginative thinking. It is argued that some of the "causes" of mental retardation (e.g., rebuking and teacher underrating of student's performance) can be removed by the classroom teacher while others require specialized treatment.

Bhargava, Mahesh & Mathur, Madhu. (National Psychological Corp, Agra, India) Psycho-Lingua, 1975(Jan–Jul), Vol 5(1–2), 33–36. [PA, Vol 63:04167]

678. [Changes in the partition coefficient and interphase potential for calcium and phosphate ions in the erythrocyte plasma system.] (Polh)

The erythrocyte/plasma partition coefficient of calcium and phosphate ions was determined in 50 children with diagnoses of mental retardation, dissociative process, and epileptic seizures. Calcium in the erythrocytes and plasma was determined by the Kramer-Tisdall method, and phosphate content was measured by the technique of Bell-Doisy-Briggs. Interphase potential for these ions was calculated and compared with the values obtained in normal children. The erythrocyte/plasma partition coefficient of calcium ions was markedly lowered in Ss with dissociative process, but was unchanged in the remaining groups. Partition coefficient of phosphate ions was slightly lowered in all of the Ss tested. The interphase potential was lowered in the mentally retarded and epileptic Ss and elevated in Ss with dissociative process. It is concluded that in cases in which variations of the phase boundary between erythrocytes and plasma take place, the electric interphase potential may be a good indicator of such changes. (Russian summary)

Bichoński, Ryszard. (Adam Mickiewicz U, Klinika Psychiatryczna, Krakow, Poland) Psychiatria Polska, 1975, Vol 9(6), 629-634. [PA, Vol 57:05944]

679. Attention in performance of a complex skill by retarded children.

Used "Try" materials to train 9 5-7 yr old retarded children to attend to differences in colors and shapes of objects. Frostig worksheets were used to train the Ss to attend to left-to-right directionality. Evidence suggests Ss' ability to attend to these characteristics was generalized to a complex bead-stringing task. On the latter, significant gains in performance were found immediately after 15 days of practice with training materials and after a 6-mo interval of no further training or practice.

Birchard, Miriam L. & Crowl, Thomas K. (Richmond Coll, City U New York) Perceptual & Motor Skills, 1975(Dec), Vol 41(3), 860-862. [PA, Vol 55:12502]

680. Birth order and mental retardation.

Reports a study of 75 mentally retarded children which found that the largest number of retardates were firstborns, the second largest number were those born second. Together, first- and second-borns made up 60% of this sample.

Biswas, Manju. Indian Journal of Clinical Psychology, 1975(Sep), Vol 2(2), 173-174. [PA, Vol 56:10126]

681. Subcultural mental handicap.

Discusses some conceptual problems in relation to the interaction of genetic influence and social disadvantagement, and some of the results of a study of 144 families with 4-8 yr old mentally handicapped children. The work of R. Heber and H. Garber (1971) in Milwaukee is briefly reviewed, and the data on the 144 families are discussed in relation to the study in Aberdeen by H. G. Birch et al (1970). Possible strategies for intervention are considered.

Blackie, J.; Forrest, A. & Witcher, G. (U Edinburgh, New Coll, Scotland) British Journal of Psychiatry, 1975(Dec), Vol, 535-539. [PA, Vol 55:07384]

682. [A recent investigation of immediate memory among the feebleminded.] (Duth)

Studied the processing of information among undifferentiated retardates (average IQ approximately 70). The memory process includes the pre- and posttraining coding of information, short term memory, long term memory, short term storage, and long term storage. Short term memory scores indicate that adult and child retardates can store new information as long as normals do. The difference between retardates and normals is the amount of information learned and the rate of learning. 2 explanations for this difference are discussed: (a) The retardates show less rehearsal activity. (b) They may have reduced abilities to encode information, as is suggested by the structural trace theory. (44 ref)

Bunt, A. A. (Inst voor Zintuigfysiologie TNO, Soesterberg, Netherlands) Nederlands Tijdschrift voor de Psychologie en haar Grensgebieden, 1975(Mar), Vol 30(2), 93-111. [PA, Vol 54:05563]

683. Rule-governed imitative verbal behavior as a function of modeling procedures.

Investigated the effectiveness of modeling procedures alone, and modeling procedures complemented by the appropriate rule statement, on the production of plurals. 20 7-9 yr old normal and 20 9-14 yr old retarded children were randomly assigned to 1 of 2 learning conditions and to either affective or informative social reinforcement. It was necessary for the S to generate and use a rule in the production of his responses since he was unable to directly copy the model's verbal behavior. Normal and retarded Ss emitted more plurals during the experimental phase when observing a model who complemented his responses by the underlying rule. (27 ref)

Clinton, LeRoy & Boyce, Kathleen D. (U Illinois) Journal of Experimental Child Psychology, 1975(Feb), Vol 19(1), 115-121. [PA, Vol 54:03416]

684. Information producing responses in normal and retarded children.

Gave a total of 30 11-12 yr old normal and retarded children (matched for either MA or CA) trials on several discriminations that varied in difficulty. On standard discrimination trials the retarded Ss did not differ from the MA-control Ss in the number of errors made, but both groups made more errors than the CA-control group. On other trials if Ss were not sure which stimulus was correct they were allowed to press an information key that made the discrimination easier. The retarded Ss made significantly more informational key responses than either of the control groups. Results confirm the findings of prior investigations dealing with outerdirectedness in an experimental situation that did not allow distractibility to be a significant factor.

Cohen, Mark E. & Heller, Tamar. (U Wisconsin, Waisman Ctr, Madison) Journal of Experimental Child Psychology, 1975(Oct), Vol 20(2), 296-306. [PA, Vol 55:07387]

685. Influence of reinforcement on the paired-associate learning of retarded and nonretarded children.

Studied the effect of presence and types of reinforcement (tangible, social, or control) on paired associate (PA) learning performance using 24 retarded and 24 nonretarded 11-14 yr olds. A pictorial PA list (pictures used as stimulus and response items)

was used. Data indicate that the influence of reinforcement on task performance was highly significant. Post-hoc comparisons showed that the use of tangible reinforcement did significantly increase the performance of both retarded and nonretarded Ss. Results also indicate that the nonretarded Ss performed significantly higher than their retarded counterparts.
de Csipkes, Robert A.; Smouse, Albert D. & Hudson, Bobbye A. (US Naval Academy) American Journal of Mental Deficiency, 1975(Nov), Vol 80(3), 357-359. [PA, Vol 55:10053]

686.   Developmental changes in concept utilization among normal and retarded children.
Examined the concepts employed by 100 normal children in kindergarten-Grade 4 (Study 1), and by 48 retarded vs 48 normal children matched for mental ages ranging from 5 to 11 yrs (Study 2). Ss were required to select pairs of pictures from a large array of pictures depicting common objects and to explain the basis for their pairing responses. Factor analysis of the conceptual responses of normal Ss revealed factors for abstraction (nominal and functional concepts as opposed to perceptible concepts) and complementarity ("go together" responses as opposed to similarity responses). Retarded Ss differed from normals primarily in their use of more complementary and fewer similarity concepts. The developmental course of concept utilization for normals was characterized as a change from perceptible to nominal and functional concepts, while that for retarded Ss was characterized as a change from complementary to similarity concepts. (21 ref)
Denney, Douglas R. (U Kansas) Developmental Psychology, 1975(May), Vol 11(3), 359-368. [PA, Vol 54:03417]

687.   Effects of stimulus familiarity on the rehearsal strategies transfer mechanism in retarded and nonretarded individuals.
Investigated the possibility that the familiarity value of stimuli might be a component of the rehearsal strategies mechanism in N. R. Ellis's (1970) multiprocess theory of short-term memory. 40 retarded and nonretarded Ss (undergraduates) of equal CA (18.40 and 19.33 yrs, respectively) were given either paired associate pretraining of nonsense pictures with colors or were presented with nonsense pictures alone. Ss' performance on either an E- or S-paced serial memory task in which the nonsense pictures were employed as stimuli was compared. It was expected that pretraining would increase the familiarity value of nonsense stimuli for nonretarded and, to a lesser extent, retarded Ss, facilitating transfer of information from primary to secondary memory in both groups. Although predictions about the effects of pretraining on retention were not substantiated, results did support the hypothesis that a production deficiency in active encoding can account for the poor secondary memory of mentally retarded Ss.
Dugas, Jeanne. (Columbus Coll) American Journal of Mental Deficiency, 1975(Nov), Vol 80(3), 349-356. [PA, Vol 55:10056]

688.   [Mental deficiency and social cases: A study of the intellectual level of 575 children at the Bouches-du-Rhone departmental children's center.] (Fren)
Made medico-psychological observations which demonstrate the existence of a very large percentage (8-33%) of "deficient" children at the center. Results of the study, based on age, sex, judicial category, and parentage, show that this mental deficiency usually indicates only some blockage in the opportunities for intellectual investment due to a lack of stimuli and to repeated affective traumatism (family separation or pathogenic experiences). This was particularly clear in children who presented serious educational retardation at all levels. Verbal tests penalize these children most; performance tests seem to reflect their capabilities better. It is concluded that children's centers are not at present all they should be; apart from their role as reception and observation centers, they should be places where the situation can be dedramatized, and they should be "deblockage" centers with a human atmosphere appropriate to the child, in the geographical region where the child should live. (German & Spanish summaries)
Dumas-Menguy, Yvonne & Baillon, Jacqueline. (Service unifié de l'enfance DASS, Pédopsychiatre, Marseille, France) Revue de Neuropsychiatrie Infantile et d'Hygiene Mentale de l'Enfance, 1975(Aug-Sep), Vol 23(8-9), 591-618. [PA, Vol 56:08208]

689.   [The psychodiagnosis of mentally retarded: An overview.] (Germ)
Evaluates available diagnostic tests for mentally retarded children. In West Germany, intelligence measurements have an important effect in determining which school will accept a child. It is also important to assess information on social behavior, emotional behavior, organization of perception, motor control, and socialization factors, such as parent upbringing patterns, stimulus milieu, and social class membership. Tests analyzed include the Test Battery for Mentally Retarded Children, Hamburg-Wechsler Intelligence Test for Children, Hannover-Wechsler Intelligence Test for Pre-Schoolers, Columbia Mental Maturity Scale, Raven Coloured Progressive Matrices, Frostig Developmental Test of Visual Perception, Body Coordination Test, Dotting Circles Test, Lincoln-Oseretsky Motor Development Scale, Progress Assessment Chart of Social Development, Psycholinguistic Development Test, Peabody Picture Vocabulary Test, and the Vineland Social Maturity Scale. The strengths and weaknesses of each test are analyzed, and the coordinated application of the tests for obtaining an adequate multidimensional diagnosis is discussed. (41 ref)
Eggert, Dietrich. (Pädagogische Hochschule Niedersachsen, Lehrstuhl für Psychologie, West Germany) Zeitschrift für Kinder- und Jugendpsychiatrie, 1975, Vol 3(3), 312–337. [PA, Vol 62:13927]

690.   Individual differences in the severely retarded child in acquisition, stimulus generalization, and extinction in go-no-go discrimination learning.
Individual differences in 27 institutionalized and noninstitutionalized severely retarded children (mean verbal age, 4.5 yrs) as measured by a questionnaire were related to dependent variables measured in a discrete trial successive go-no-go intradimensional discrimination learning study, followed by stimulus generalization tests on a hue continuum and extinction trials. Significant correlations were found between the number of intersignal responses in learning, responding to and around the nonreinforced stimulus (S-), types of errors in extinction, and the S's position on an excitation-inhibition dimension based on clinical descriptions of the behavior of the retarded given by A. R. Luria (1963). (24 ref)
Evans, P. L. & Hogg, J. H. (U Manchester, Hester Adrian Research Ctr, England) Journal of Experimental Child Psychology, 1975(Dec), Vol 20(3), 377-390. [PA, Vol 55:12505]

691.   A comparison of WISC selected subtest short forms with MR children.
Compared those selected subtest short forms of the WISC which have been used with mental retardates for their effectiveness in meeting 3 criteria suggested by R. Resnick and J. Entin (1971): (a) Correlations between short form and standard form should be highly significant. (b) *t* tests comparing short form and standard form mean IQ should be nonsignificant. (c) The percentage of IQ classification changes should not be so great as to preclude the effective use of the short form. 197 complete WISC protocols with Full Scale IQ equal to or less than 69 were selected for study. Results show that when all 3 criteria were applied, none of the selected subtest methods emerged as acceptable. It is recommended that greater concentration in research be placed on accuracy of individual prediction rather than simple correlation and the saving of time; also, that methodologies other than the selected subtest procedure be investigated.
Finch, A. J. & Childress, W. B. (Virginia Treatment Ctr for Children, Richmond) Mental Retardation, 1975(Feb), Vol 13(1), 20-21. [PA, Vol 54:03419]

692.   Galactosemia: A psycho-social perspective.
Reviews the literature, focusing on psychosocial aspects of galactosemia with emphasis on developmental, intellectual, visual-perceptual, emotional, social, and psychoeducational factors. After a brief biomedical orientation to the disease, several longitudinal studies are reviewed from a psychosocial perspec-

tive. These studies tend to indicate that much can be done for galactosemics in terms of early diagnosis and early diet intervention. The medical and psychosocial problems encountered by these patients require the efforts of a multidisciplinary team.
Gershen, Jay A. (U California, Los Angeles) Mental Retardation, 1975(Aug), Vol 13(4), 20-23. [PA, Vol 55:00911]

693.   [Investigation into the structuration of space in normal and mentally handicapped children.] (Germ)
Mental defectives are varied in behavior and output, maintaining open structures. Contrary to B. Inhelder's opinion, morons are not fixed at given levels. Nor is there closure nor a ceiling which sets bounds to their learning potentialities. They may go beyond their apparent potential and may redevelop. In normal Ss, structures open, close and open again, in the course of development, but they close during a transversal examination as a reaction to the stress situation caused by it, as a strategy dependent on the S's economy. In morons, who continually oscillate, closure does not take place by reason of lack of necessity and reversibility of thinking. There is not dissociation between emotionality and intelligence; hence relational dynamics appear to be essential in the sense that emotionality may open and close the structures.
Guignard, R. (Ctr Clinique de Guidance Infantile, Geneva, Switzerland) Acta Paedopsychiatrica, 1975, Vol 41(2), 70-82. [PA, Vol 54:03425]

694.   Bisecting the Ponzo illusion.
Presented a modification of the Ponzo illusion, in which the judged lines are centered in different sized obliques, to 16 matched normal and mentally retarded 15-18 yr old males with IQs of 51-68 under conditions of equal and unequal retinal sizes. Magnitude of illusion was affected by IQ (WISC) and by physical proximity rather than retinal contour. Results seem to imply a central rather than peripheral explanation for the illusion.
Hill, A. Lewis. (Inst for Basic Research in Mental Retardation, Staten Island, NY) Perceptual & Motor Skills, 1975(Aug), Vol 41(1), 225-226. [PA, Vol 55:04865]

695.   Aetiological factors in mental retardation: A survey of 212 cases.
Attempted to determine the basic cause of the mental handicap in 212 children and adults. The degree of mental handicap was for the most part, within the moderate range, and of the group 114 were recognized cases of Down's syndrome. Among the other 98 cases, an etiological diagnosis could be made in 33 cases; in 11 cases, the handicap was either of genetic origin or had arisen early in pregnancy. In the remaining 54 no cause for the handicap could be determined though 4 were of low birth weight, 5 had cerebral palsy, 2 were psychotic, and 16 had epilepsy.
Hughes, G. C. & Greenman, G.   Australian Journal of Mental Retardation, 1975(Sep), Vol 3(7), 205-207. [PA, Vol 56:00881]

696.   Is the concept of mental retardation apt? A critical discussion.
Scrutinizes the concept of mental retardation. The usual assumptions that mental retardation involves inadequately developed intelligence, derives from an inherited constitutional defect, and is essentially incurable are rejected on the basis of a lack of evidence. The association of social incompetence with mental retardation is dismissed as unacceptably ambiguous. It is proposed, as an alternative, that child retardates be conceived to be unmotivated to learn correct discriminations through the selective scanning of their environments and, as a result, experience reinforcement histories different from normals. The notion of a limited repertoire of behaviors that can be altered should replace that of an inherently limited mentality. (15 ref)
Jayaram, M. (Indian Inst of Science, Bangalore, India) Journal of the All-India Institute of Speech & Hearing, 1974–75(Jan), Vol 5–6, 72–78. [PA, Vol 59:08111]

697.   [What children know about their father's profession.] (Germ)
Found that, contrary to current opinion, most children 11–13 yrs old know the occupation of their fathers. Even among a group of 279 children from classes for the retarded or the learning disabled, 63% knew the correct occupation and another 25% knew at least the kind of work or its location. Statements by 7% disagreed with what their teachers said, and only 5% could not tell at all. Of 103 children from a selective high school, 91% knew their father's occupation, 8% did not, and 1 differed from the teacher. 119 children from intermediate schools gave answers that were approximately half-way between these extremes.
Kerkhoff, Winfried. (Pädagogische Hochschule Ruhr, Abteilung Heilpädagogik, Dortmund, West Germany) Psychologie in Erziehung und Unterricht, 1975, Vol 22(6), 368–372. [PA, Vol 61:03216]

698.   [The rights of mentally handicapped persons in Switzerland.] (Germ)
The head of the section of civil law reports on the revision of Swiss family law, especially laws relating to children, their rights for care, and guardianship. The family of the mentally handicapped child receives special consideration. The child's right to an education and suitable training are emphasized. All discrimination against illegitimate children is removed from the law, and the child's right to an advocate, if the parents prove insufficient, is specified. The law protects the freedom even of mentally ill or mentally handicapped persons as far as they can use freedom responsibly. Institutionalization is legal only if necessary and if the institution is suited to the needs of the patient. Many of the principles of the revision have been formulated on the basis of the United Nations regulations concerning human rights.
Krauskopf, Lutz.   Vierteljahresschrift für Heilpädagogik und ihre Nachbargebiete, 1975(Mar), Vol 44(1), 2–8. [PA, Vol 62:13555]

699.   Mental deficiency and behavioral disorders.
Many mental deficients present behavioral disorders, reflecting either primary conditions or reactions to outside influences. Primary disorders occur in the most affected group and reactive disorders in the mildly deficient. Family dynamics are fundamental in the genesis of the latter group and a complement to primary disorders. The primary group is a high-risk group; the less deficient are vulnerable in terms of reactive or secondary disorders. The child's genome (the sum total of his genetic inheritance) always contains more potential than is expressed phenotypically. Congenital endowment and congenital organization of behavior are patterned by complex biochemical interactions. In turn, early experience leads to enduring patterns of behavior encoded in CNS metabolism. Learning is affected by gene action, but, in a feedback process, gene action is affected by learning.
Krynski, Stanislau. (Habilitation Ctr APAEH, Sao Paulo, Brazil) Acta Paedopsychiatrica, 1975, Vol 41(4-5), 138-161. [PA, Vol 54:12087]

700.   Extinction by retarded children following discrimination learning with and without errors.
Four groups of a total of 16 7.25-13.7 yr old retarded children were trained to respond to a triangle with apex up (S+) and not to a triangle with apex down (S-), with and without errors. A free-operant procedure in which responding to S+ was intermittently reinforced and a trial procedure in which all responses to S+ were reinforced were compared. An extinction procedure in which responses were no longer reinforced was then introduced. Extinction resulted in substantial responding during S- for all groups, except the free-operant errorless group. S- responding during extinction did not differ between the errorless and error-trial groups and was maximum for the free-operant error group.
Lambert, Jean-Luc. (U Liege, Belgium) American Journal of Mental Deficiency, 1975(Nov), Vol 80(3), 286-291. [PA, Vol 55:10065]

701.   The effects of identifying objects on a concept-matching task performed by four preschool groups.
Compared the performance of 20 retarded, 20 brain injured, 20 normal, and 20 disadvantaged children matched for mental age (4 yrs, 10 mo) on a concept-matching task which required Ss to match an index object to one within a multiple choice array on the basis of function or class. Materials were controlled so that

the choice had a conceptual, rather than perceptual, base. Ss were required to identify objects before proceeding to the concept-matching task. Material consisted of 84 common objects and a duplicate set of drawings. 1 set of hypotheses predicted that all groups would be hampered by the 2-dimensional format for both the identification and concept-matching tasks; a 2nd set of hypotheses predicted that there would be a correlation between identification and concept-matching responses. Format hypotheses were confirmed with 2 exceptions: retarded and brain injured Ss did equally well on the concept-matching task in either format. Data concerned with correlations were significant and followed the predicted rank order in the case of 3 groups: the retarded, disadvantaged, and brain injured. Data are interpreted in terms of a mediational pattern theory and a coping response theory. (29 ref)
Levitt, Edith. (Teachers Coll, Columbia U, Research & Demonstration Ctr for Education of Handicapped Children) Genetic Psychology Monographs, 1975(May), Vol 91(2)b, 227-256. [PA, Vol 54:07743]

702.   Possible differential WISC patterns for retarded delinquents.
Under controlled conditions, an attempt was made to assess the generalizability of WAIS hypotheses for the nondefective adolescent sociopath to 80 retarded 13–16 yr old offenders. Groups were separated according to race and sex while IQ, socioeconomic status, and geographic location were controlled. The criteria for selection of Ss were incarceration in a state juvenile correctional facility and a Full Scale WISC IQ below 70. Results suggest that many WAIS signs applicable to nondefective IQ ranges probably are not appropriate for WISC scores of these retarded delinquents. The difficulty in identifying the signs from such a truncated range of scaled scores is discussed. Post hoc analysis, nevertheless, provided some potentially useful WISC signs for combinations of race and sex of retarded delinquents. The need for cross-validation of these signs is stressed.
Lewandowski, Denis G. & Saccuzzo, Dennis P. (Middle Tennessee State U, Ctr for the Study of Crime, Law Enforcement & Corrections) Psychological Reports, 1975(Dec), Vol 37(3, Pt 1), 887–894. [PA, Vol 60:11971]

703.   The prognostic implications of suppression-burst activity in the EEG in infancy.
39 children, seen between 1960 and 1973, showed suppression-burst activity in their original EEG recordings. Follow-up information was available for 19 girls and 10 boys at ages 3-10 yrs. Suppression-burst activity was seen at a mean age of 4 mos. Most of the children (86%) had infantile spasms, and 96% were severely retarded on presentation. 15 died (52%), 9 of them before the age of 2, and all had severe retardation and neurological abnormalities. Of the 14 survivors, only 1 was attending a normal school (she was only mildly retarded on presentation), 71% were severely retarded, 71% had neurological abnormalities, and 60% continued to have fits. It is concluded that although hypsarrhythmia itself is not necessarily associated with a bad prognosis, the finding of suppression-burst activity implies a grave outlook. (French, Spanish, & German summaries) (22 ref)
Maheshwari, M. C. & Jeavons, P. M. (Dudley Road Hosp, Birmingham, England) Epilepsia, 1975(Mar), Vol 16(1), 127-131. [PA, Vol 54:07951]

704.   [The mentally retarded child.] (Fren)
Defines mental deficiency in children and estimates that in France it occurs in 6.75% of the total child population, 4.4% with mild deficiency and 2.35% with average or severe deficiency or profound retardation. The condition may be ascribed to genetic causes, to deficiencies acquired before or around the time of birth, to infections, defective metabolism, traumatic diseases, or convulsive encephalopathies. Environment also has an influence, especially in cases of mild or average deficiency. Mental deficiency is a public health problem and action against it should be taken at the level of the society, the family, and the child himself. The future of the deficient child depends a great deal on his living conditions, the education he receives, and the degree of his acceptance by society.
Manciaux, M. & Deschamps, J. P. (Ctr International de l'Enfance, Paris, France) Vie médicale au Canada français, 1975(Mar), Vol 4(3), 253-259. [PA, Vol 57:06112]

705.   [The factors necessary for a psychopathological approach in a reputedly exogenous mentally deficient child.] (Fren)
Observations on a 9-yr-old illustrate the simplification introduced by the traditional opposition between exogenous and mental deficiency. This child, who had been the victim of an early and severe encephalopathy, evolved, in fact, with a severe progressive dysharmony in which the organic and affective factors appeared in dialectic relation with each other. The profound position taken by the parents, the structure of the family environment, and the attitude of the entourage often play a role in determining the symptomatic expression and evolution of the morbid process. This requires a multidimensional action and the correct understanding of the significance of the symptoms and of the exchanges with the child. (German & Spanish summaries)
Misès, R.; Fortabat, J.-L. & Bréon, S. (Fondation Vallee, Gentilly, France) Revue de Neuropsychiatrie Infantile et d'Hygiene Mentale de l'Enfance, 1975(Feb), Vol 23(2), 129-137. [PA, Vol 56:04156]

706.   [Celebration of Mass with mentally handicapped pupils.] (Germ)
Discusses whether it makes sense to involve mentally handicapped pupils in the celebration of the Mass; i.e., whether they understand its underlying meaning. The question is answered affirmatively. By emphasizing the basic aspects of the shared ceremony and by employing methods developed for the training and education of mentally handicapped children generally, the form of the Mass could be adapted to the level of the pupils to make it possible for them to have a meaningful share in this celebration.
Obholzer, Rudolf. Vierteljahresschrift für Heilpädagogik und ihre Nachbargebiete, 1975(Mar), Vol 44(1), 8–12. [PA, Vol 62:13936]

707.   Efficacy of educational and medical intervention for prevention of mental retardation based on physiological and psychological research.
Presents a 2-part discussion of (a) the learning deficits exhibited by the cultural-familial retarded and (b) the prevention of retardation by early childhood education programs. Physiological evidence is presented for early educational programs by examining the effects of enrichment on the cortical development of infrahumans. A review of the literature indicates that early stimulation does facilitate cognitive development, and both consolidation and early stimulation can be explained at least partially on a physiological basis. The results of existing programs suggest that a remediation program should focus on psychopharmacological intervention while preventive programs should focus on early infant stimulation, both cognitively and nutritionally. Anatomical and chemical changes demonstrated by infrahuman studies suggest that much more can be done to prevent developmental retardation. (49 ref)
O'Connor, P. D. (U North Carolina School of Education, Chapel Hill) Australian Journal of Mental Retardation, 1975(Sep), Vol 3(7), 179-190. [PA, Vol 56:00887]

708.   Extrapolated WISC-R IQs for gifted and mentally retarded children.
Presents extrapolated IQs for the 1974 WISC revised version (WISC-R) for sums of scaled scores that are both below and above the values published in the WISC-R manual. The regression equations on which these extrapolations are based and cautions regarding the clinical use of these IQs are also presented.
Ogdon, Donald P. (Old Dominion U) Journal of Consulting & Clinical Psychology, 1975(Apr), Vol 43(2), 216. [PA, Vol 54:01422]

709. [A factor analysis of the Binet-Simon (revised Stanford, 1937) Form L, using mental retardates.] (Span)
Performed a correlational and factor analytic study using 321 mental retardates (192 males and 129 females, 6–16 yrs old) on the 1937 Form L of the Stanford-Binet. In the factor analysis, 5 factors accounted for 69% of the variance: numerical and arithmetical ability (13%), verbal usage and comprehension (14%), psychomotor skills (14%), perception (17%), and memory (11%). The correlational analysis revealed that verbal and memory categories were positively and significantly correlated with everything else while the remaining 3 factors correlated positively only with one another and negatively with the 1st 2 factors. It is concluded that although different categories are suggested, they are still homogeneous. Furthermore, it is proposed that mental retardation research proceed along the findings of cognitive strategies of mental retardates instead of normals.
Pelechano, V. & Garrido, J. (U de La Laguna, Tenerife, Canary Islands) Análisis y Modificación de Conducta, 1975, Vol 1(0), 85–103. [PA, Vol 59:04745]

710. Infants' home environments: A comparison of high-risk families and families from the general population.
Compared home environments of 30 infants at high-risk for developmental retardation with those of 30 infants from the general population (matched for age, sex, and parity) by means of the Caldwell et al (1968) Home Observation Measurement of the Environment (HOME). 15 high-risk infants attended a day-care intervention program and 15 did not. The HOME showed significant differences between the high-risk groups and the general population, favoring the general population, on all factors (maternal warmth, absence of restriction and punishment, organization of the environment, appropriate toys, maternal involvement, and opportunities for variety) but none between the 2 high-risk groups.
Ramey, Craig T.; Mills, Pamela; Campbell, Frances A. & O'Brien, Carolyn. (U North Carolina, Frank Porter Graham Child Development Ctr, Chapel Hill) American Journal of Mental Deficiency, 1975(Jul), Vol 80(1), 40-42. [PA, Vol 54:09973]

711. Internal consistency of the Northwestern Syntax Screening Test.
Evaluated the usefulness of the 40 receptive and 40 expressive items of the Northwestern Syntax Screening Test (NSST). 20 preschoolers with normal language development, 20 preschoolers functioning within the range of normal intelligence but diagnosed as language impaired, and 20 mentally retarded children comprised the 3 S-groups. Ss were equated for mental age. Stable Hoyt's reliability coefficients indicated that the NSST assessed consistently the syntax and morphology used by Ss with atypical language development. Detailed item analysis revealed the strengths and weaknesses of both receptive and expressive items.
Ratusnik, David L. & Koenigsknecht, Roy A. (Indiana U, Speech & Hearing Ctr) Journal of Speech & Hearing Disorders, 1975(Feb), Vol 40(1), 59-68. [PA, Vol 54:01424]

712. Epidemiology of visual-perceptual dysfunction (HDSA) in mentally retarded and/or learning-disabled children.
Reing, Alvin B. (Brooklyn Coll, City U New York) Catalog of Selected Documents in Psychology, 1975(Fal), Vol 5, 341. [PA, Vol 56:10151]

713. [Language development and mental retardation.] (Fren)
Reviews a set of studies on speech and language development in mentally retarded children. The studies are examined in the light of the controversy surrounding qualitative-quantitative theories of the cognitive and linguistic developments of mentally retarded individuals. (English abstract)
Rondal, Jean A. (U Liège, Belgium) Liaison, 1975, Vol 15(2), 83-95. [PA, Vol 58:01409]

714. [Development of language and mental retardation: A critical review of the English language literature.] (Fren)
Reviews the studies published in English during the last 20 yrs on the phonological, morphological, lexical, syntactical, and com-municative aspects of linguistic development in the mentally retarded child. In each of these areas the relevant data are analyzed and discussed, and the necessity of new or complementary research is suggested. Some of the recurrent themes in the literature in this domain are also discussed. (8 p ref)
Rondal, Jean A. (U Liege Lab de Psychologie Experimentale, Belgium) Année Psychologique, 1975, Vol 75(2), 513-547. [PA, Vol 58:11924]

715. A twofold failure to replicate the results of O'Connor and Hermelin in discriminative learning with reversal in the case of mentally retarded children.
11-yr-old mentally retarded and 5-yr-old normal children (matched for mental age) were tested on form- and size-discrimination and reversal learning tasks. Results reverse the findings of N. O'Connor and B. Hermelin (see PA, Vol 34:6219); retarded Ss learned the discrimination tasks more quickly and the reversal tasks more slowly than the normals.
Rondal, Jean A. & Lambert, Jean-Luc. (U Minnesota, Minneapolis) Journal of Genetic Psychology, 1975(Mar), Vol 126(1), 157-158. [PA, Vol 54:03439]

716. Psychological impact of sterilization on the individual.
Explains the weaknesses in eugenic arguments for forced sterilization of retarded persons. The possible psychological ill effects of involuntary sterilization are elaborated: (a) low self-esteem; (b) reinforcement of sense of helplessness; (c) feelings of failure; (d) increased social isolation and loneliness, interacting with failure to marry and/or become a parent; (e) increased body-damage anxiety; and (f) in the childless person, heightened awareness of mortality. Since retarded persons vary in needs and competence, it is considered that they should be free, when possible, to mature and make decisions as others do. (2 p ref)
Roos, Philip. Law & Psychology Review, 1975(Spr), Vol 1, 45–56. [PA, Vol 60:05478]

717. Relationship between performance in a simple memory task and the level of intellectual abilities.
Tested the hypothesis that short-term memory in slightly mentally retarded children does not differ from that in normal controls and declines only in those mentally retarded children with substantial impairment of intellectual abilities. 60 10-12 yr olds from a regular and a special school were divided into 3 groups according to their scores on the WISC (mean IQs approximately 94, 75, and 63) and were presented 2 simple memory tasks in a visual and an acoustic modality. The difference in performance between the normal and slightly retarded Ss was nonsignificant; statistical significance was achieved only when normal Ss were compared with more severely mentally retarded Ss. Results are discussed in terms of N. R. Ellis's (1963) trace theory. (Czechoslovakian & Russian summaries) (17 ref)
Ruisel, Imrich & Droppová, Zdena. (Slovak Academy of Sciences, Inst of Experimental Psychology, Bratislava, Czechoslovakia) Studia Psychologica, 1975, Vol 17(3), 188-194. [PA, Vol 57:10577]

718. Control strategies in short-term memory and their relationship towards intellectual abilities.
Investigated differences in information processing in short-term memory in 30 8-10 yr olds who were evenly divided into normal and retarded groups according to their scores on the WISC. Sequences of 4-digit numbers were presented which Ss reproduced forwards or backwards depending on instructions given either before or after presentation. Significant differences appeared with the more complex manipulation, backwards reproduction. Significant differences were also noted in the control strategies, and changes in performance in retarded Ss were related to the length of the retention interval. Results are discussed in light of certain memory models and N. B. Ellis's (1970) trace theory. (Russian & Slovak summaries) (31 ref)
Ruisel, Imrich & Droppová, Zdena. (Slovak Academy of Sciences, Inst of Experimental Psychology, Bratislava, Czechoslovakia) Studia Psychologica, 1975, Vol 17(4), 266-274. [PA, Vol 56:06236]

719.   [A study of attitudes of families with mentally deficient members.] (Span)
Assesssed parental attitudes toward mentally deficient sons. It was hypothesized that parental attitudes would be characterized as ambivalent (i.e., rejection and protection) and that family interaction patterns would be similar to those reported in schizophrenic families. Ss were 201 draft age males, 99 of whom had been rejected for military service because of mild to moderate retardation. 54 cases were rejected as schizophrenics and were used as controls. Results generally support the hypotheses. Parents attributed their children's disorders to biological causes, early traumas, or magical causes. There was a distinct tendency to overprotect the child to the point of exclusion from school and social activities. Two family models were found: The majority centered the family and its problems around the retarded child. Others treated the child and his problems as secondary. Parental guilt and overprotectiveness characterized the first; rejection and institutionalization of the retarded characterized the second. (7 ref)
Ruiz Ruiz, M.; Zardón Pérez, J. M.; Quintana, Miró & Serra, Frigola. (Hosp Militar del Generalísimo, Servicios de Psiquiatría y Neurología, Barcelona, Spain) Revista de Psiquiatría y Psicología Médica, 1975(Jan–Mar), Vol 12(1), 19–24. [PA, Vol 65:03532]

720.   [Acquisition of the finger scheme in mentally retarded children.] (Ital)
Investigated 150 mentally retarded Ss 9–14 yrs old, without any neurosensory or neuromotor deficits, as to their acquisition of a finger scheme, using Benton's test of finger agnosia and a verbal test of identification of fingers in a pattern. Motor hand skill, lateral dominance, and dynamic coordination were also tested. Results show that the digital scheme seems to crystallize at 10 yrs. Some correlations exist between proprioceptive and cognitive components necessary for this acquisition and between poor digital identification and deficits in both hand coordination and motor hand skills. A rehabilitation program is proposed. (English & French summaries) (18 ref)
Scarcella, Mario; Marletta, Francesco & Feltri-Faro, Maria L. (U Bari, Italy) Lavoro Neuropsichiatrico, 1975(Jan–Jun), Vol 56(1–3), 127–140. [PA, Vol 60:07694]

721.   Evidence that monoamines influence human evoked potentials.
Measured latency and flash-pattern differentials of the visual evoked potential (VEP) from 4 7-18 yr old retarded phenylketonuric humans, while systematically manipulating rates of amine synthesis in the CNS. Stimulation of monoaminergic activity in the visual processing system, either by lowering inhibitory levels of phenylalanine through dietary restriction or by a properly balanced administration of indole and catecholamine precursors (levodopa and/or levo-5-hydroxytryptophan or levo-tyrosine), shortened VEP latencies and permitted the development of a discriminative brain response to patterned stimuli. The close temporal relationship between these electrophysiological changes and the neurochemical manipulations following treatment initiation or discontinuation suggest that monoamines play a significant role in the mediation of human sensory evoked potentials. (36 ref)
Schafer, Edward W. & McKean, Charles M. (U California, Langley Porter Neuropsychiatric Inst, Brain Behavior Research Ctr, San Francisco) Brain Research, 1975, Vol 99(1), 49-58. [PA, Vol 55:06392]

722.   Perseveration in concurrent performances by the developmentally retarded.
In 4 experiments with a total of 9 21-27 yr old and 2 13-yr-old retarded Ss (IQ range = 40-70), perseveration in choice behavior was defined as failure to match absolute and relative response rates to changes in relative reinforcement rates with concurrent schedules of reinforcement. Overall results show that concurrent performances of Ss varied systematically as a function of type of schedule, schedule value, duration, and symmetry of changeover delays. Relative but not absolute response rates were proportional to relative reinforcement rates with long changeover delays.

Increasing the changeover delay punished changeovers and reduced total reinforcement rates. Contrary to prediction, asymmetrical changeover delays disrupted rather than improved matching. (20 ref)
Schroeder, Stephen R. (Murdoch Ctr, Butner, NC) Psychological Record, 1975(Win), Vol 25(1), 51-64. [PA, Vol 54:01428]

723.   The STYCAR Language Test.
Describes the principles and applications of the STYCAR (Sheridan Tests for Young Children and Retardates) Developmental Language Test. The test is designed to aid in pediatric assessment of language-related functions. (French, German, & Spanish summaries)
Sheridan, Mary D.   Developmental Medicine & Child Neurology, 1975(Apr), Vol 17(2), 164-174. [PA, Vol 54:12093]

724.   [A report of one case of mental deficiency associated with retarded growth and ichthyosis: Review of the literature.] (Fren)
Presents the case of an adolescent in whom 3 congenital afflictions coexisted, a sex-related ichthyosis, mental deficiency, and retarded growth hormone deficiency. The clinical and genetic study showed that in fact 3 family defects were combined. The literature was reviewed in relation to different conditions associated with sex-related ichthyosis and to the conditions associated with other kinds of ichthyosis, specifically "ordinary" ichthyosis and congenital ichthyosiform erythrodermas. (German & Spanish summaries) (20 ref)
Sibertin-Blanc, D.; Ferrari, P. & Duché, D.-J.   Revue de Neuropsychiatrie Infantile et d'Hygiene Mentale de l'Enfance, 1975(Mar-Apr), Vol 23(3-4), 207-215. [PA, Vol 57:03420]

725.   The conservation of number in mental retardates.
Studied the conservation of number in 20 retarded children whose CAs were 8 yrs 11 mo-16 yrs 6 mo and MAs were 2 yrs 9 mo-4 yrs 9 mo. Standard conservation questions, involving the concepts of equivalence, less, and more were used. Ss' conceptual ability was strongly correlated to their MAs. Results are interpreted within the Piagetian framework of intellectual development, and the problems involved in the use of verbal measures with retardates are noted. (18 ref)
Singh, Nirbhay N. & Stott, Grant. (U Auckland, New Zealand) Australian Journal of Mental Retardation, 1975(Dec), Vol 3(8), 215-221. [PA, Vol 56:00891]

726.   Q analysis of the Holtzman Inkblot Technique.
The Q analysis for refinement of the diagnostic effectiveness of projective tests was used and the Holtzman Inkblot Technique was administered to 3 behaviorally distinct groups of Ss: 20 normal, 20 delinquent, and 20 retarded Black male adolescents who resided in socioeconomically depressed neighborhoods. Median and quartile scores were obtained from 19 of the 22 Holtzman variables, and 4 factors were derived from factor analysis. Definable subfactors appeared within the delinquent and retarded groups, but loadings for normal Ss were primarily on 1 factor.
Smith, Patricia M. & Barclay, Allan G. (Madison County Probation Office, Edwardsville, IL) Journal of Clinical Psychology, 1975(Jan), Vol 31(1), 131–134. [PA, Vol 56:03220]

727.   The effects of spatial, temporal, and control variables on the free-recall serial position curve of retardates and equal-MA normals.
In Exp I 7 pictures were sequentially illuminated at a 3-sec rate through 7 translucent windows. A different window provided the starting point for each of 7 tests. 14 retarded and 14 normal children (mean chronological ages = 16.1 and 8.7 yrs, respectively) of equal mental ages (9.6 and 9.5 yrs, respectively) produced equivalent free recall and reliable recency effects. Although groups did not differ significantly at any portion of the curve, only the normals produced a significant primacy effect. The spatial end anchors produced no significant primacy or recency effects. In Exp II with similar numbers and types of Ss, total presentation time remained the same but the pictures were presented at a 1-sec rate. Variations in elapsed time and number of presentations produced a negative primacy effect, a result attributed to the prevention of selective rehearsal and the

resultant interaction of trace decay and order of recall. Superior recall by the normals, particularly in the recency portion of the curve, was attributed to group differences in order of recall strategies. (19 ref)
Spitz, Herman H.; Winters, John J.; Johnson, Shirley J. & Carroll, Janice G. (E. R. Johnstone Training & Research Ctr, Bordentown, NJ) Memory & Cognition, 1975(Jan), Vol 3(1), 107-112. [PA, Vol 53:11964]

728. [Mental retardation as viewed from the literature.] (Polh) Reviews concepts of mental retardation, their use in schools, and criteria for clarifying degrees of retardation. The psychological characteristics of children at various retardation levels are described, particularly the mildly retarded, and possible research designed to help this group is discussed. (Russian & English summaries) (26 ref)
Szurek, Ewa. (U Warsaw Inst of Psychology, Poland) Psychologia Wychowawcza, 1975(Jan-Feb), Vol 18(1), 60-78. [PA, Vol 58:11931]

729. Moral and cognitive development in retarded and nonretarded children.
Studied 30 cultural-familially retarded and 30 nonretarded children matched for MA (assessed with the Peabody Picture Vocabulary Test) within 3 MA levels (64-84, 87-102, and 105-121 mo). Ss were administered measures of moral judgment and cognitive operations hypothesized by L. Kohlberg (1969) to constitute necessary but not sufficient conditions for attainment of specific moral stages. Moral and cognitive performance improved with MA, but there were no differences between the MA-matched retarded and nonretarded children. Moral judgment related more strongly to MA than to any of the specific cognitive operations tested. Findings fail to support the hypothesis of L. Kohlberg and C. Gilligan (1971) that the moral judgment of older individuals should be more advanced than that of younger individuals matched for cognitive level. Findings did offer some support for E. Zigler's (1969) "developmental" concept of cultural-familial retardation. (15 ref)
Taylor, Jonathan J. & Achenbach, Thomas M. (Yale U) American Journal of Mental Deficiency, 1975(Jul), Vol 80(1), 43-50. [PA, Vol 54:09978]

730. [A study on discrimination reversal: Shift learning as a function of MA in mentally retarded children.] (Japn)
Compared discrimination reversal shift in 37 mentally retarded children with 35 normal Ss matched for MA (5-9 yrs), and studied the effect of overlearning on reversal shift relative to the MA variation in the retarded Ss. A significant difference between retardates and normals was found for MA 5-6, but not for MA 7-9 ($p < .05$). The effect of overlearning in the retarded Ss was significant for MA 5-6 ($p < .05$).
Umetani, Tadao. Japanese Journal of Educational Psychology, 1975(Jun), Vol 23(2), 125-129. [PA, Vol 55:02518]

731. Factor analysis of the WISC-R for a group of mentally retarded children and adolescents.
Administered the Wechsler Intelligence Scale for Children--Revised (WISC--R) to 80 retarded youngsters ranging in CA from 6 to 16 yrs. Scaled scores on the 12 tests were correlated, and the matrix was subjected to several factor-analytic techniques. The 3 factors identified for normal children in a previous study of the WISC--R (Verbal Comprehension, Perceptual Organization, and Freedom from Distractibility) also emerged for the retardates, although some differences were observed in the distractibility factor. The WISC--R factor structure for retardates was also similar to the structure of the 1949 WISC that was identified for several groups of institutionalized and noninstitutionalized retardates. Results of the studies involving the 1949 WISC were reviewed critically to help understand the implications of the present findings.
van Hagen, John & Kaufman, Alan S. (San Francisco Boys' Home, CA) Journal of Consulting & Clinical Psychology, 1975(Oct), Vol 43(5), 661-667. [PA, Vol 55:00068]

732. Relationship between linguistic performance and memory deficits in retarded children.
Measured the performance of retarded children on 4 tests of linguistic ability and 2 memory tests (e.g., Northwestern Syntax Screening Test and various subtests of the Illinois Test of Psycholinguistic Abilities). Ss were 50 retarded children, 10 each at mental ages 3, 4, 5, 6, and 7 yrs. The relationship between linguistic performance and memory was assessed by correlational analysis. Multiple and partial correlations were computed using a measure of language comprehension and a measure of memory span as predictor variables and 3 measures of language production as criterion variables. Different patterns of correlation were found with the 3 production measures, suggesting that the relative importance of memory span in language production depends on the specific production task.
Walker, Howard J.; Roodin, Paul A. & Lamb, Mary J. (State U New York, Coll at Oswego) American Journal of Mental Deficiency, 1975(Mar), Vol 79(5), 545-552. [PA, Vol 54:03447]

733. Effects of IQ and mental age on hypothesis behavior in normal and retarded children.
156 mental-age-matched normal and retarded Ss at mental-age (MA) levels of 5.5, 7.5, and 9.5 yrs received blank-trial discrimination problems designed to expose hypothesis behavior. There was evidence that Ss at all MA levels used hypotheses. Use of feedback indicating that a response was wrong increased significantly with MA, while use of feedback indicating that a response was right increased significantly with IQ. On simple problems involving 2 stimulus dimensions, retarded and normal groups used about equal numbers of hypotheses, but on 4-dimensional problems the retarded used fewer hypotheses than normals. It is suggested that this IQ Level $\times$ Problem Complexity interaction may explain contradictions among previous findings regarding IQ effects on learning. (20 ref)
Weisz, John R. & Achenbach, Thomas M. (Yale U) Developmental Psychology, 1975(May), Vol 11(3), 304-310. [PA, Vol 54:03450]

734. Spontaneous and defensive movement in the children's O.R.T. development of the self.
Describes the CORT, an experimental children's version of H. Phillipson's (1955) Object Relations Technique. Scoring and interpretation are based on a system of 5 categories: spontaneous movement, defensive movement, maturity of perception, areas of difficulty and conflict, and analysis of content. Normative data from the CORT records of 408 children—including normals, psychotics, subnormals, delinquents, and phobics—indicate (a) developing perceptual growth and skills in 2-yr age bands from 4 to 16, (b) sex differences in perception and approach, and (c) differences between children from normal and deprived family backgrounds. 2 case studies with complete CORT protocols are used to illustrate scoring procedures and interpretation.
Wilkinson, Norman W. British Journal of Projective Psychology & Personality Study, 1975(Jun), Vol 29(1), 15-27. [PA, Vol 55:01775]

735. Development of lexicon in normal and retarded persons.
24 noninstitutionalized retarded children and 73 kindergartners and 4th and 9th graders labeled chromatic pictures of nouns in a study of the development of their lexicons. Lexical store development was related more to cognitive development (MA) than chronological age. This development was also more highly related with J. B. Carroll and M. N. White's (see PA, Vol 51:9059) measure of age of acquisition of words than to word frequencies in the Thorndike-Lorge word count. The retarded Ss relative efficiency decreased as ease of labeling increased; this led to increasing decrement in performance below expected performance for that MA. This regress in lexical lag is discussed in terms of ages at which words are acquired and the earlier deficiencies of retarded children's lexicons. Comparisons of the several corpora are made in terms of their use in matching normal and retarded groups on experimental tasks in verbal learning. (23 ref)

Winters, John J. & Brzoska, Mary A. (E. R. Johnstone Training & Research Ctr, Bordentown, NJ) Psychological Reports, 1975(Oct), Vol 37(2), 391-402. [PA, Vol 55:04876]

736. Longitudinal development of object permanence in mentally retarded children: An exploratory study.
Monthly testing on a series of Piaget object tasks was carried out on 1-6 yr old profoundly, severely, and moderately retarded children. 49 Ss were followed for 1-5 yrs or to criterion; 18 Ss were followed for shorter periods. 3 general patterns occurred among the noncriterion Ss with approximately equal frequency: (a) little or no change, (b) marked variability, and (c) relatively steady upward change from month to month. Criterion and upward Ss skipped certain substages about 50% of the time. Degree of retardation, chronological age, and diagnostic concomitants of these observations are discussed.
Wohlhueter, M. Judith & Sindberg, Ronald M. (Central Wisconsin Colony & Training School, Madison) American Journal of Mental Deficiency, 1975(Mar), Vol 79(5), 513-518. [PA, Vol 54:03452]

737. Test-retest reliability of the Wide Range Achievement Test.
Administered the Wide Range Achievement Test (WRAT) twice to 106 children attending special education classes for emotionally disturbed or slow-learning children (mean age, 10.6 yrs), using either a 2- or 22-wk inter-test interval. Results show the test-retest reliability coefficients for reading, spelling, and arithmetic subtests are significant for both the 2- and 22-wk interval ($p < .001$). It is concluded that the WRAT was a remarkably consistent and stable measure of academic achievement with this sample of children often seen in the clinic.
Woodward, Christel A.; Santa-Barbara, Jack & Roberts, Robin. (McMaster U, Ontario, Canada) Journal of Clinical Psychology, 1975(Jan), Vol 31(1), 81-84. [PA, Vol 56:03265]

738. Hermaphroditism associated with unusual gonadal finding in a mentally retarded child.
Presents the case of an hermaphrodite, a mentally retarded 13-yr-old male with undifferentiated gonads. Chromosome analysis revealed a 46,XX female karyotype.
Yanagisawa, S. (Yamaguchi U, Medical School, Ube, Japan) Journal of Mental Deficiency Research, 1975(Mar), Vol 19(1), 37-42. [PA, Vol 55:00935]

739. Aerobic work capacity of mentally retarded boys and girls in junior high schools.
Determined the maximal oxygen uptake and ergometer load at heart rate of 170 beats/min (PWC_{170}) in 74 male and 53 female 12-15 yr old mentally retarded Ss (IQ, 36-91) and compared the results with those obtained earlier for normal children of the same age. Retarded Ss showed significantly inferior body height and weight, but no significant difference was found in skinfold thickness. The mean value of PWC_{170} for retarded males and females was 14.34 and 11.31 kpm/kg/min, respectively, significantly less than that of the normal group. Retarded males had mean maximal oxygen uptake per unit body weight of 42.4 ml/kg/min, which was significantly less than the 51.2 ml/kg/min of normal males. Retarded females had a mean of 33.1 ml/kg/min, which was also less than the 41.3 ml/kg/min of normal females. The correlation coefficient between body weight and PWC_{170} was 0.711 and 0.720 for retarded males and females, respectively, while that of body weight and maximal oxygen uptake was 0.641 and 0.656. No significant correlation was found between IQ and PWC_{170}, between IQ and maximal oxygen uptake, or between mental age and maximal oxygen uptake. (15 ref)
Yoshizawa, Shigehiro; Ishizaki, Tadatoshi & Honda, Hiroko. (U Ustunomiya Faculty of Education, Japan) Journal of Human Ergology, 1975(Sep), Vol 4(1), 15-26. [PA, Vol 57:01455]

740. Role-taking ability and the interpersonal tactics of retarded children.
Studied the relationship between social role-taking ability and preferences for interpersonal control tactics in 50 mentally retarded children. Feffer's Role-Taking Task and 2 hypothetical interpersonal control episodes were used as experimental measures. Results were that role-taking proficiency was associated with the development of alter-directed tactics or tactics by which the S appeared to take into account the needs, motivations, or expectations of others. Neither MA nor IQ were significant predictors of interpersonal tactic choice. Controls for IQ and MA did not alter the significance of the association between role-taking and general tactic preferences.
Affleck, Glenn G. (U Connecticut) American Journal of Mental Deficiency, 1976(May), Vol 80(6), 667-670. [PA, Vol 56:04266]

741. Effects of pronounciability on retarded and normal pupils' learning of compound words.
Investigated the effects of 2 levels of pronounciability on 36 14-yr-old retarded, 36 9½-yr-old normal, and 36 14-yr-old normal students' learning of compound words. Results indicate that level of pronounciability did not significantly affect Ss' ability to learn new compound words. Both normal groups exceeded the retarded groups but did not differ significantly from each other.
Allen, Jerry; Williams, Charlotte L. & Dekle, Ocie. (U Georgia) Journal of Research & Development in Education, 1976, Vol 9(Mono), 72–73. [PA, Vol 59:10125]

742. Effects of association value in retarded and normal pupils' learning compound words.
Tested the generalizability of C. L. Williams's (1975) finding that retarded and normal pupils learn high association synonyms more easily than they do low association synonyms. In this study, 36 14-yr-old retarded, 36 9½-yr-old normal, and 36 14-yr-old normal students learned compound words varying in association value. Results show a significant Groups by Trials interaction, but association value did not significantly affect Ss' ability to form new compound words. Both normal groups performed better than the retarded group but did not differ from each other.
Allen, Jerry & Williams, Charlotte L. (U Georgia) Journal of Research & Development in Education, 1976, Vol 9(Mono), 67–69. [PA, Vol 59:10123]

743. Koppitz errors on the Bender-Gestalt for adult retardates: Normative data.
Normative data on the Koppitz developmental scoring system for the Bender Gestalt Test were derived from a sample which included 510 protocols of 15-80 yr old resident retardates. Percentile norms are presented on Koppitz error scorers or 3 American Association on Mental Deficiency (AAMD) ranges of retardation based on WAIS IQs and 2 AAMD ranges of retardation based on Stanford-Binet Intelligence Scale IQs.
Andert, Jeffrey N.; Dinning, W. David & Hustak, Thomas L. (Des Moines Child Guidance Ctr, IA) Perceptual & Motor Skills, 1976(Apr), Vol 42(2), 451-454. [PA, Vol 58:04608]

744. An investigation into the attitudes and sexual behavioral patterns of Black mentally retarded adults.
Investigated the attitudes and sexual behavior patterns of Black mentally retarded adults. Ss were 19–30 yr old educable mentally retarded (EMR), 20 19–30 yr old trainable mentally retarded (TMR), and 17 normal high school students. Group counseling, individual counseling, and an attitudinal questionnaire were used to accumulate data between January and June of 1975. Areas explored were definition of sex, sexual behavior and patterns, sexual fantasy, sexual development, and sexual communication and attitude (discussed individually for each group). Scores obtained from the Sexual Inventory Scale (SIS) Appendix A were computed to give a score for each student and each group. Data were analyzed by computing results from the SIS and ranking them in numerical order. The findings indicate (a) major differences between normals and TMRs; (b) very small differences between normals and EMRs; (c) little, if any, difference between TMRs and EMRs; and (d) areas of significant differences in sexual definitions, attitudes, behavior patterns, and communications of normals and TMRs. Both retardate groups appeared to be selfishly motivated in terms of sex. Logistics presented a problem for the retardates, especially TMRs. Sexual fantasy was most prevalent in the TMRs, with some such tendency demonstrated by EMRS. Age of first sexual experience

was younger in normals, older in TMRs. All groups received counseling, threats, or punishment as a measure of control. Continued research in this area is recommended. (27 ref)
Andrews, James. (U California, Los Angeles) Journal of Black Psychology, 1976(Aug), Vol 3(1), 20–33. [PA, Vol 63:12171]

745. Communication in retarded adolescents: Utilization of known language skills.
Pretested 6 retarded male Ss (mean CA, 14.8 yrs; mean IQ, 50 mo) for comprehension and production of items on a sentence comprehension test and then gave them a referential communication task using these items as stimulus material. Each S acted as speaker and listener with each of the other 5 Ss. The presentation of items was arranged so that the target sentence differed from others of the set equally often in subject, verb, or object. The critical feature was less likely to be communicated successfully when it was the verb. Some Ss were less successful than others in this task but improved with further trials.
Beveridge, M. C. & Tatham, A. (Victoria U of Manchester, Hester Adrian Research Ctr, England) American Journal of Mental Deficiency, 1976(Jul), Vol 81(1), 96-99. [PA, Vol 56:10125]

746. Positive and negative instructions and retarded and normal pupils' performance.
Examined the responses of 36 14-yr-old retarded, 36 9½-yr-old normal, and 36 14-yr-old normal students when dealing with instructions for inclusion (positive) and for exclusion (negative). Results indicate a significant main effect for Groups and a significant Treatments by Trials interaction. Within both treatments the normal groups exceeded the retarded but did not differ from each other. Ss instructed for inclusion exceeded those instructed for exclusion on all trials except Trial 3, where the groups did not differ.
Blake, Kathryn. (U Georgia) Journal of Research & Development in Education, 1976, Vol 9(Mono), 97. [PA, Vol 59:10137]

747. Affirmation and negation in retarded and normal pupils' dealing with binary statements.
Studied how 18 14-yr-old retarded, 18 9½-yr-old normal, and 18 14-yr-old normal students' facility in dealing with positive and negative statements is influenced by the truth value of the statement and the type of response to the task. Results show significant main effects for Groups and Treatments. Within all treatments, older normals exceeded the other 2 groups, which did not differ from each other. Within all groups true affirmatives were easier than true negatives.
Blake, Kathryn. (U Georgia) Journal of Research & Development in Education, 1976, Vol 9(Mono), 95–96. [PA, Vol 59:10132]

748. Types of negation and retarded and normal pupils' drawing inferences from sentences.
Investigated the effects of affirmation and 3 types of negation on the grasp of implications and presuppositions by 72 14-yr-old retarded, 72 9½-yr-old normal, and 72 14-yr-old normal students. With respect to implications, both normal groups did better than the retarded but did not differ from each other. With respect to presuppositions, however, younger normal and retarded Ss did not differ, and both did less well than the older normal Ss. Positives were easier to handle than all 3 types of negatives, and double negatives were easier than explicit and implicit negatives. False presuppositions and false implications were easier to recognize than true ones.
Blake, Kathryn. (U Georgia) Journal of Research & Development in Education, 1976, Vol 9(Mono), 87–88. [PA, Vol 59:10141]

749. Concreteness and abstractness and retarded and normal pupils' learning synonyms.
Investigated how concreteness and abstractness of the material influenced synonym learning by 36 14-yr-old retarded, 36 9½-yr-old normal, and 36 14-yr-old normal students. Results show significant main effects for Treatments and Groups, as well as significant Treatments by Trials and Groups by Trials interac-

tions. Both normal groups learned at a faster rate and to a higher level than the retarded Ss; the normal groups did not differ.
Blake, Kathryn. (U Georgia) Journal of Research & Development in Education, 1976, Vol 9(Mono), 59–60. [PA, Vol 59:10133]

750. Abstractness and concreteness and retarded and normal pupils' sentence comprehension.
Examined the influence of the abstractness/concreteness dimension on the sentence comprehension of 36 14-yr-old retarded, 36 9½-yr-old normal, and 36 14-yr-old normal students. There was a significant Groups by Treatments interaction: For all groups the concrete sentences were easier. On concrete sentences, both normal groups exceeded the retarded Ss but did not differ from each other. On abstract sentences, older normals exceeded the other groups who did not differ from each other.
Blake, Kathryn. (U Georgia) Journal of Research & Development in Education, 1976, Vol 9(Mono), 90–91. [PA, Vol 59:10131]

751. Retarded and normal pupils' comprehension of double-base transformations.
Studied the performance of 108 14-yr-old retarded, 108 9½-yr-old normal, and 108 14-yr-old normal students when dealing with 12 categories of double-base transformations. In the comparison of the subject or object complement with -*ing*, the object complement was slightly easier for the younger normal and retarded groups, and the subject complement was slightly easier for the older normal Ss. Beyond this difference, all Ss responded similarly to the transformations in all comparisons except one.
Blake, Kathryn. (U Georgia) Journal of Research & Development in Education, 1976, Vol 9(Mono), 92–94. [PA, Vol 59:10140]

752. Prompts and retarded and normal pupils' sentence recall.
M. R. Quillian (1969) theorized that any term is a marker for only the immediately superordinate class rather than for all superordinate classes. The present study investigated this relationship for 108 14-yr-old retarded, 108 9½-yr-old normal, and 108 14-yr-old normal students when prompts were present during the learning of sentences and when they were not. All effects were significant, and there was a significant Groups by Treatments by Trials interaction. For all Ss, it did not matter whether prompts were present or absent when those prompts were nouns. For the older normals, the effects of different types of prompt depended on whether they were present or absent during learning. For younger normals and retarded Ss the subject noun was the most effective prompt. The younger normal Ss did not differ from the retarded when dealing with close superordinate prompts that had not been present during learning.
Blake, Kathryn. (U Georgia) Journal of Research & Development in Education, 1976, Vol 9(Mono), 84–86. [PA, Vol 59:10139]

753. Organization of information and retarded and normal pupils' acquisition of ideas.
Compared the effects of 3 organizations of ideas—the complex whole to be remembered, combinations of partial ideas to be integrated and remembered, and separate ideas to be integrated and remembered—on the acquisition of ideas by 54 14-yr-old retarded, 54 9½-yr-old normal, and 54 14-yr-old normal students. In all treatments, the normal groups exceeded the retarded, and the older normals exceeded the younger. There was a significant main effect for Treatments: Ss who studied 4 ideas separately learned as well as Ss who studied the 4 ideas combined. Both groups performed better than Ss who studied sets of 2 ideas combined.
Blake, Kathryn. (U Georgia) Journal of Research & Development in Education, 1976, Vol 9(Mono), 98–99. [PA, Vol 59:10136]

754. Prefixal and sentence negation and retarded and normal pupils' sentence comprehension.
Examined the effects of negation on the sentence comprehension of 72 14-yr-old retarded, 72 9½-yr-old normal, and 72 14-yr-old normal students. Findings show significant main effects for

Groups and Treatments. Older normals exceeded the other groups, who did not differ from each other. For all groups, double negatives were more difficult than the positives or other negatives, and for all Ss in all treatments the reasonable sentences were easier than the unreasonable.
Blake, Kathryn. (U Georgia) Journal of Research & Development in Education, 1976, Vol 9(Mono), 89. [PA, Vol 59:10138]

755.   Context vs paired-associate formats in retarded and normal pupils' learning concept names.
Examined the effects of 2 formats—paired associate and context—on the learning of new concept names by 36 14-yr-old retarded, 36 9½-yr-old normal, and 36 14-yr-old normal students. On both tests the groups differed: Both normal groups exceeded the retarded on the sentences task, and older normals exceeded the younger normals. On the words task, older normals were the fastest, followed by younger normals and then by the retarded Ss. The paired associate and sentence formats were equally effective for all groups.
Blake, Kathryn. (U Georgia) Journal of Research & Development in Education, 1976, Vol 9(Mono), 80–81. [PA, Vol 59:10134]

756.   Massed and distributed practice and retarded and normal pupils' learning synonyms.
Examined the effects of massed and distributed practice on 36 14-yr-old retarded, 36 9½-yr-old normal, and 36 14-yr-old normal students' learning of synonyms. There was a significant Groups by Treatments interaction, with older normals exceeding both other groups, and the younger normal and retarded Ss performing similarly. With the retarded group, massed practice was more effective than distributed. The treatments were similarly effective in the normal groups.
Blake, Kathryn. (U Georgia) Journal of Research & Development in Education, 1976, Vol 9(Mono), 57–58. [PA, Vol 59:10135]

757.   Short-term retention in retarded adolescents as a function of load, delay, and interpolated activity.
40 trainable and 40 educable retarded adolescents (mean IQ, 50.5 and 65.5, respectively) were shown slides containing arrays of 2, 3, 4, or 5 chromatic pictures to be recalled after varying periods (0, 18, 36, and 140 sec) of filled or unfilled activity. Recall in the unfilled condition remained relatively stable over time, while in the filled condition, recall was deleteriously affected by a distractor task. No significant retention slope differences were observed between the 2 IQ groups. As is typically found with nonretarded adults, the curve of forgetting described a negatively accelerated function. With increasing proactive interference there were increasing decrements in short-term recall, with neither IQ group differing from the other. It is suggested that both decay and interference contribute to short-term forgetting in retarded individuals.
Borys, Suzanne V. & Spitz, Herman H. (E. R. Johnstone Training & Research Ctr, Bordentown, NJ) Journal of Psychology, 1976(Nov), Vol 94(2), 207-216. [PA, Vol 58:05605]

758.   Cardiovascular and skin conductance correlates of a fixed-foreperiod reaction time task in retarded and nonretarded youth.
Studied changes in heart rate (HR), digital and cephalic pulse amplitude, and skin conductance during a fixed-foreperiod reaction time (RT) task with 16 male 15-18 yr old mentally retarded Ss (mean MA 9 yrs, 10 mo) and 2 nonretarded groups of 16 Ss each matched on MA and CA. All Ss received 20 RT trials with distractors (music) during the 4-sec preparatory interval (PI) and 20 trials without music in a counterbalanced design. The warning signal was a 1-sec light presentation and the reaction signal was an 82-db tone. Retarded Ss had longer and more variable RTs than controls. Retarded Ss had smaller HR accelerations and decelerations during the PI than the CA group but not the MA group. Further, the retarded group had a marginally lower tonic skin conductance level, smaller skin conductance responses, and smaller constrictions in cephalic pulse amplitude than the CA controls. Results are discussed in terms of attentional and arousal deficits in retarded persons. (35 ref)
Bower, A. C. & Tate, D. L. (Rideau Regional Ctr, Ontario, Canada) Psychophysiology, 1976(Jan), Vol 13(1), 1-9. [PA, Vol 55:10050]

759.   Comparison of nonretarded and mentally retarded children on tasks involving direct and rule-governed imitation.
Examined the influence of intellectual level and social reinforcement on imitation learning. Tasks involving direct and rule-governed imitation of a model were presented to 20 mentally retarded (mean CA 12 yrs 2 mo, mean MA 9 yrs) and 20 nonretarded (mean CA 8 yrs, mean MA 8 yrs 11 mo) children. Ss within each group were randomly assigned to either an affective ("good-fine") or an informative ("correct-right") social reinforcement condition. Reinforcement, administered on an FR-4 schedule, was contingent on the S's imitative behavior. A multivariate ANOVA showed that both the Population × Reinforcement Type interaction and the Reinforcement main effect were significant. Univariate follow-up tests showed that only rule-governed imitation contributed significantly to the multivariate effects. Analysis of simple effects indicated that the retarded Ss performed optimally under affective reinforcement, while the nonretarded performed highest under informative reinforcement. (21 ref)
Boyce, Kathleen D. & Clinton, Leroy. (U Illinois) Perceptual & Motor Skills, 1976(Apr), Vol 42(2), 379-386. [PA, Vol 58:05606]

760.   The prevalence of stuttering among school-age children.
The prevalence of stuttering has generally been reported to be about 1% among school-age children. The present survey of 190,931 school-age children (187,420 in Grades K-12, 3,057 educable mentally retarded, and 454 trainable mentally retarded) indicated a dramatic decrease in this percentage, and confirmed previously reported distributions by age and sex. A higher prevalence of stuttering was found in an urban than in a rural population.
Brady, William A. & Hall, Donald E. (St Elizabeth Hosp, Youngstown, OH) Language, Speech, & Hearing Services in Schools, 1976(Apr), Vol 7(2), 75-81. [PA, Vol 58:09749]

761.   Memory strategies used by young normal and retarded children in a directed forgetting paradigm.
Two experiments investigated the possibility that normal and retarded children equated for immediate memory performance may not use effective strategies to eliminate interference from irrelevant information in memory. In Exp I, Ss were 16 normal children (mean age 7.4 yrs) and 16 retarded children (mean age 9.8 yrs, mean IQ 66.8); in Exp II, Ss were 16 normal children (mean age 6.9 yrs) and 16 retarded children (mean age 10.6 yrs, mean IQ 70.6). In both experiments a directed forgetting paradigm was used in which Ss were presented with 2 sets of 4 pictures, and recalled only 1 set on each trial. On some trials, there was a cue to forget the 1st 4 and to remember only the last 4 pictures. In Exp I both groups adopted a passive-active strategy in which the to-be-remembered items were processed actively only after a forget cue. Exp II replicated this pattern of results. The use of sophisticated directed forgetting strategies seemed to be beyond the immediate abilities of these children. Two possible interpretations of the passive-active strategy are offered: the strategy was an attempt to cope with the presence of occasionally irrelevant information, and the strategy was an attempt to cope with memory overload. (15 ref)
Bray, Norman W. & Ferguson, Robert P. (Cincinnati Ctr for Developmental Disorders, OH) Journal of Experimental Child Psychology, 1976(Oct), Vol 22(2), 200-215. [PA, Vol 57:06095]

762.   Distribution of practice effects on learning retention and relearning by retarded boys.
Used the stabilometer task to study the differences between massed practice and distributed practice on initial acquisition, retention, and relearning of a gross motor skill by mentally retarded boys. 72 Ss (mean age, 137 mo; mean IQ, 38.15) were randomly assigned to either 1 massed practice group or 1 of 3 distributed practice groups with varying intertrial rest intervals.

All Ss were retested for retention and relearning after 8 wks of no practice. Distribution practice was superior to massed practice for initial skill acquisition. Retention was superior, favoring the group given distributed practice, but no significant differences were found between groups for relearning, indicating that the advantage of distributed practice may be temporary and that it is a performance rather than a learning factor. (25 ref)
Chasey, William C. (George Washington U) Perceptual & Motor Skills, 1976(Aug), Vol 43(1), 159-164. [PA, Vol 57:06097]

763. Parents' and teachers' estimates of the social competence of handicapped and normal children.
Assessed the social competence of 60 (a) educable mentally retarded (EMR), (b) trainable mentally retarded (TMR), (c) deaf, (d) cerebral palsied, and (e) normal 6.5–12.5 yr olds by comparing responses of parents and teachers on 3 measures, including the Vineland Social Maturity Scale. Results show that (a) of the handicapped Ss, deaf & EMR Ss were more competent than TMR & cerebral palsied Ss; and (b) parents of normal and handicapped Ss estimated higher social competence than teachers.
Cole, P. G. (U Western Australia, Nedlands) Australian Journal of Mental Retardation, 1976(Dec), Vol 4(4), 1–8. [PA, Vol 59:01156]

764. Differences in attitudes toward sex-typed behavior of nonretarded and retarded children.
Stories about retarded or nonretarded boys or girls were given to 105 classroom teachers (mean age, 28.09 yrs) and 63 caretakers (mean age, 23.52 yrs) of retarded children and 53 teachers (mean age, 30.94 yrs) of nonretarded children. The stories described children in 4 sex-stereotyped activities. Respondents rated each child in the stories on scales of typicality and acceptability. Results indicate that, while nonretarded children were treated as typical when engaging in sex-appropriate, desirable play activities, retarded children were rated as typical when engaging in undesirable activities, regardless of sex appropriateness. Different professional groups appeared to use different criteria when judging the children in the stories. (21 ref)
Copeland, Anne P. & Weissbrod, Carol S. (American U) American Journal of Mental Deficiency, 1976(Nov), Vol 81(3), 280-288. [PA, Vol 58:04164]

765. Suggested criteria for vision classification on the AAMD adaptive behavior scale.
Suggests a supplement to the vision item of the Adaptive Behavior Scale for (retarded) Children and Adults published by the American Association of Mental Deficiency. The expanded new item would involve tests of color vision, depth perception, and oculomotor response, in addition to acuity, and would allow elaborative inference, prognostication, and professional referral to be included in the profile.
Courtney, George R. & Watson, P. Douglas. (Central State Hosp, Milledgeville, GA) Journal of the American Optometric Association, 1976(Apr), Vol 47(4), 469-474. [PA, Vol 58:07726]

766. The validity of the Otis-Lennon Mental Ability Test, Elementary II Level, for suspected mental retardates.
Using Otis-Lennon Mental Ability Test, Elementary II Level, and WISC Verbal, Performance, and Full Scale IQs of 40 4th-6th grade White children, correlations of .71, .57, and .73, respectively, were computed. Results suggest that IQs on the Otis-Lennon are not directly comparable to the WISC IQs and should be interpreted with caution when used as a criterion for identifying mentally retarded White children attending public schools.
Covin, Theron M. Psychology in the Schools, 1976(Jan), Vol 13(1), 25-27. [PA, Vol 56:06838]

767. Comparison of Otis-Lennon Mental Ability Test, Elementary I Level and WISC-R IQs among suspected mental retardates.
Computed correlations of .72, .59, and .76 between the Otis-Lennon I and WISC-R Verbal, Performance, and Full Scale IQs respectively for 119 public school students (mean age 107 mo) suspected to be mentally retarded. On this basis, WISC-R Verbal and Full Scales seem to be more sensitive than the WISC-R

Performance Scale to the mental processes measured by the Otis-Lennon I. Mean differences were not significant for Full Scale IQs. Moderate correlations between the subtest scaled scores were reported. Correlations and *t* tests for stratified samples by race were also computed. Values for Comprehension, Picture Completion scaled scores, and Performance scaled scores were very low for Black Ss.
Covin, Theron M. Psychological Reports, 1976(Apr), Vol 38(2), 403-406. [PA, Vol 56:04946]

768. Comparability of Peabody and WAIS scores among adolescents suspected of being mentally retarded.
Correlations of .91, .87, and .92 were computed between the Peabody Picture Vocabulary Test (PPVT), Form B, and WAIS Verbal, Performance, and Full Scale IQs, respectively, for 14 White and 16 Black 16-yr-old public school students. The PPVT seemed to be more related to the WAIS Verbal and Full Scale IQs than to the WAIS Performance scale. Correlations for stratified samples by race were also computed.
Covin, Theron M. & Covin, June N. Psychological Reports, 1976(Aug), Vol 39(1), 33-34. [PA, Vol 57:02192]

769. [Mental retardation and protein-caloric malnutrition (Ecuadoran studies).] (Span)
Presents the results of a number of studies of the relationship between mental retardation and malnutrition, especially in Equador. Poor rural children with an inadequate diet show a marked inferiority in mental and physical development compared to urban children. The variations in mental capacity are broad and cover almost all the mental categories. Lack of stimulation in the environment of the poor children is another factor contributing to mental retardation. Contrary to previous opinion, some of the studies show that a change to better nutrition and environment can do much to remedy the effects of malnutrition in the early years of life.
Cruz Cueva, José (U Central del Ecuador, Quito) Revista Colombiana de Psiquiatría, 1976(Dec), Vol 5(4), 382–393. [PA, Vol 63:07792]

770. The impact of the child's deficiency on the father: A study of fathers of mentally retarded and of chronically ill children.
Administered the EPPS, a specially developed 46-item sentence completion test on attitudes toward handicapped and normal children and feelings of parental adequacy, the Berger Inventory's Self-Acceptance scale, and Shoben's Parental Attitudes Inventory to 240 fathers of mentally retarded, chronically physically ill, neurotic, and healthy 4-13 yr old children. Results indicate that fathers of children in the 1st 2 groups experience significant stress associated with their fathering a handicapped child. Data from fathers of neurotic children were not included in the present report. Some fathers of mentally retarded children appear subject to a pattern of neurotic-like constriction. Differences in the experiences of fathers and mothers of deficient children are discussed, and suggestions for treatment are offered.
Cummings, S. Thomas. (Menninger Foundation, Topeka, KS) American Journal of Orthopsychiatry, 1976(Apr), Vol 46(2), 246-255. [PA, Vol 56:00765]

771. Metabolic causes of mental retardation: An appreciation of the contribution of the late Dr. Brian Turner.
Discusses inborn errors of metabolism (IEM) with particular reference to the work of B. Turner, a pioneer in the use of mass screening of infants, who developed a testing program that achieved 85-90% coverage of all babies born in New South Wales and made possible the early diagnosis of phenylketonuria. Various other tests and techniques have been developed that identify a number of other diseases very early in life, but financial and administrative problems make it impossible to apply all of them; the author specifies those that he would choose for an optimum mass screening program. Unusual metabolic disturbances revealed by screening are of great importance, as Turner recognized; the study of significant exceptions led to the knowledge that in some individuals an IEM may be vitamin dependent and the disorder may yield to pharmacological therapy. Understanding of the relationship between metabolic

disturbance and clinical manifestations continues to be an urgent topic for research. (15 ref)
Danks, David M. (U Melbourne, Australia) Australian Journal of Mental Retardation, 1976(Mar), Vol 4(1), 1-4. [PA, Vol 57:03626]

772.   Mentally retarded children in hospital and school and home for mentally retarded children in Ghana.
Examination of the case histories of 101 mentally retarded children indicates that about 33% of the retardation was associated with epilepsy, 26% with brain injury, and 10% with infection (postencephalitis). For 60% of the Ss, the age of onset was 1–3 yrs. 44% of the Ss received treatment from medical doctors, and 57% were treated by a herbalist. (French summary) (2 ref)
Danquah, S. A.; Morson, J. & Ghanney, E. (U Ghana Medical School, Accra) Psychopathologie Africaine, 1976, Vol 12(2), 199–205. [PA, Vol 65:03516]

773.   [Influence of the semantic composition of sentences on study time: A comparative study of normal and mentally retarded children.] (Fren)
Tested predictions derived from propositional and componential analysis in 2 experiments using a sentence learning task. Each experiment tested 24 normal and 24 mentally retarded children of the same MAs (9.11 and 10.10 yrs for the 2 experiments, respectively). Mentally retarded Ss were significantly inferior to normal Ss in the progress of learning, showed a greater lack of realism about their own lack of knowledge, and had less ability to discriminate between "neighboring" meanings. Results support the componential analysis of meaning. (35 ref)
Denhière, Guy. (U de Paris VIII, Lab de Psychologie, France) Journal de Psychologie Normale et Pathologique, 1976(Apr–Jun), Vol 73(2), 217–235. [PA, Vol 65:13038]

774.   [Memorization of positions: A comparative study of normal and mentally defective children.] (Fren)
Compared 12 normal children with 12 who were mentally retarded. The Ss' mean CA was 11 yrs 2 mo. The task was to memorize the positions of patterns of 30 points defined by the intersection of 5 columns and 6 rows. During a 5-sec period 5 points were presented, and after the delay of 5 sec, the Ss were to reproduce the positions of the points on the sheet provided them. At intervals of 1 wk the procedure was repeated using a different response sheet each week: a plain white sheet, a sheet ruled in squares, and a sheet with 8 vertical stripes. The mentally retarded did significantly more poorly and showed greater intra-individual variability. The deficit varied depending on the difficulty of the pattern and the nature of response sheet. (French & English summaries) (24 ref)
Denhière, Guy. (U Paris VIII, Lab de Psychologie, France) Enfance, 1976(Oct–Dec), No 4–5, 407–424. [PA, Vol 60:03307]

775.   Pseudo-mental retardation.
Considers the problem of children who possess a normal mental endowment but appear retarded on clinical assessment or psychological testing. This condition, referred to as pseudo-mental retardation (PMR), is regarded primarily as a symptom of emotional disturbances resulting from maternal deprivation. PMR also can occur in lower-class children who have been deprived of normal learning opportunities, or among children with neurotic and psychotic syndromes (e.g., autism or schizophrenia). Children with learning difficulties due to auditory or visual defects constitute a fourth PMR category. (16 ref)
de Sousa, Alan & de Sousa, D. A. (Grant Medical Coll, Bombay, India) Child Psychiatry Quarterly, 1976(Oct), Vol 9(4), 1–5. [PA, Vol 60:05334]

776.   Parental attitude towards retarded children.
Discusses the problems that parents encounter in accepting retardation in their child. Suggestions are given for altering attitudes toward more positiveness, acceptance, affection, approval, and assimilation. The need for increased professional attention to the problem is emphasized.
Devi, A. V. (Niloufer Hosp, Hyderabad, India) Child Psychiatry Quarterly, 1976(Apr), Vol 9(2), 10-12. [PA, Vol 58:05612]

777.   Relationship between the level of intellectual abilities and recognition of meaningless geometrical figures in children.
Compared the performance of mentally retarded children (mean IQs on the WISC of 104 and 74, respectively) in recognizing geometric shapes. Stimulus material was a series of 3 mathematically defined curves of gradually increased difficulty. Ss' recognition of the materials was measured twice, with retention interval of 5 and 20 sec. The types of errors and the possible causes of the lower performance by mentally retarded children are discussed in terms of mechanisms of perception and short-term memory. (Czechoslovakian & Russian summaries) (15 ref)
Droppová, Zdena & Ruisel, Imrich. (Slovak Academy of Sciences, Inst of Experimental Psychology, Bratislava, Czechoslovakia) Studia Psychologica, 1976, Vol 18(3), 191-196. [PA, Vol 57:10567]

778.   Normal and retarded children's understanding of semantic relations in different verbal contexts.
Studied the effect of different semantic relations presented in different verbal contexts to 12 language-disordered (CAs 4.0-7.9 yrs) and 12 normal (CAs 1.6-2.7 yrs) children at the 1- and 2-word stage of development. No significant difference was found between the performance of mentally retarded language-disordered and normal Ss on the verbal comprehension task. Both groups of Ss performed best on the possessive, next on the agent-object, then actor-action, and poorest on the locative relations. Finally, nonsense, telegraphic, and expanded contexts did make a difference in the Ss' understandings with expanded being the best, telegraphic next, and nonsense contexts poorest. Theoretical and clinical implications.are discussed. (29 ref)
Duchan, Judith F. & Erickson, Joan G. (State University Coll New York, Buffalo) Journal of Speech & Hearing Research, 1976(Dec), Vol 19(4), 767-776. [PA, Vol 58:01393]

779.   [Study of the capacity for solving matching problems in mentally retarded children in special classes as a function of the nature of the problems, complexity of the directions, and cues carried by the concrete materials.] (Fren)
Conducted analysis of variance studies of the hypotheses that among mentally retarded children (a) skill in problem solving evolves with age, especially for problems with simply written instructions; (b) problems where a concrete example accompanies the directions are solved more readily than those with directions only, and the problems where directions are accompanied by an example which can be manipulated are solved more readily; (c) results are best for problems whose directions are totally affirmative compared to those with totally negative or both positive and negative directions. Ss were 21 male and 5 female children, some in special classes, ages 10.6-14.6 yrs who were assigned to 2 age groups of 13 Ss each. The Ss completed 25 cartoon-type problems, each presented in 1 or 3 modes: directions only, directions accompanied by concrete examples, or directions accompanied by concrete examples which could be manipulated. Results indicate that the 3rd hypothesis was confirmed and the 1st hypothesis was not. The 2nd hypothesis was partially confirmed: For older Ss presentation of concrete material was a constraint to problem solution; younger Ss solved problems best when directions were accompanied by concrete examples (rather than by concrete examples which could be manipulated).
Dufoyer, J.-P. & Blanchard, M. (U Rene Descartes, Paris, France) Bulletin de Psychologie, 1975-76, Vol 29(16-17), 908-913. [PA, Vol 58:09720]

780.   The concurrent validity of a new intelligence test: The Kahn Intelligence Test (KIT).
The concurrent validity of the KIT was evaluated by correlating it with other tests of intellectual, perceptual, social, linguistic, and psycholinguistic functioning (Stanford-Binet Intelligence Scale, Peabody Picture Vocabulary Test, Illinois Test of Psycholinguistic Abilities, Vineland Social Maturity Scale, Frostig Developmental Test of Visual Perception, and Mecham Language Development Scale), using a sample of 106 intellectually, emotionally, or learning impaired children. Positive correlations

between the KIT and these other measures attest to its potential usefulness as a measure of intelligence.
Fenlon, Whatley & L'Abate, Luciano. (Georgia State U) Psychology in the Schools, 1976(Oct), Vol 13(4), 412-414. [PA, Vol 57:09166]

781.   Teaching styles of mothers and the match-to-sample performance of their retarded preschool-age children.
21 mothers and their preschool-age retarded children (mean IQ, 59.2) were observed during 3 structured teaching sessions. Each session was rated for various forms of maternal preresponse and postresponse activity as well as performance of the children. Results indicate that the most frequent forms of maternal behavior were preresponse verbal directions and instructions; however, the best predictor of children's correct performance was postresponse positive feedback. Patterns of intercorrelations among maternal measures were generally consistent with those reported by R. D. Hess and V. C. Shipman (see PA, Vol 40:4069). The hypothesis is advanced that maternal postresponse feedback may occur as the result of correct responding which, in turn, is more directly affected by other aspects of teaching style.
Filler, John W. & Bricker, William A.   American Journal of Mental Deficiency, 1976(Mar), Vol 80(5), 504-511. [PA, Vol 56:06228]

782.   Use of context and retarded and normal pupils' learning synonyms.
Examined 36 14-yr-old retarded, 36 9½-yr-old normal, and 36 14-yr-old normal students' learning of synonyms out of context, using pictures, and learning the same synonyms in the context of sentences, also using pictures. Results show a significant main effect for Groups and a significant Treatments by Trials interaction. Both normal groups performed better than the retarded group, and Ss using context performed more adequately for the first 3 trials and then leveled off. Ss using word-picture pairs improved across all trials. The 3 groups responded similarly to both treatments.
Frost, Dianne B. (U Georgia) Journal of Research & Development in Education, 1976, Vol 9(Mono), 55–56. [PA, Vol 59:10153]

783.   Type of stimulus and retarded and normal pupils' learning synonyms.
Examined 36 14-yr-old retarded, 36 9½-yr-old normal, and 36 14-yr-old normal students' effectiveness in learning a set of synonyms using 2 methods in the context of a sentence: (a) pairing a known word in context with a paralog, and (b) pairing a picture of the known word with a paralog. There was a significant Groups by Treatments by Trials interaction, with both normal groups obtaining a higher level of learning with the pictures than without them. Retarded Ss obtained higher learning levels on the first 3 trials with pictures, but their scores on the 4th trial were higher without pictures.
Frost, Dianne B. (U Georgia) Journal of Research & Development in Education, 1976, Vol 9(Mono), 53–54. [PA, Vol 59:10152]

784.   The development and generalization of delayed imitation.
Garcia, Eugene E. (U Utah) Journal of Applied Behavior Analysis, 1976(Win), Vol 9(4), 499. [PA, Vol 57:13003]

785.   Frequency of eidetic imagery among hydrocephalic children.
Tested 75 mentally retarded children for eidetic imagery in order to clarify the relationship between eidetic imagery and neuropathology. Ss included 14 with arrested hydrocephalus (mean CA, 12.0 yrs; mean IQ, 55.7); 39 with other diagnoses of brain damage (mean CA, 13.5 yrs; mean IQ, 52.4); and 22 familial cases (mean CA, 13.7 yrs; mean IQ, 56.6). The hypotheses tested were that the frequency of eidetic imagery is higher among hydrocephalics than among other brain-damaged children and higher among hydrocephalics than among familials. The data confirm the hypotheses and are interpreted as supporting a theory in which particular structural impairments in the visual system may delay neural development and result in a persistence of eidetic imagery. (16 ref)

Giray, Erol F.; Altkin, Warren M. & Barclay, Allan G. (State U New York, Oswego) Perceptual & Motor Skills, 1976(Aug), Vol 43(1), 187-194. [PA, Vol 57:08527]

786.   A dynamic approach to disorders in intellectual development.
Gives reasons why the concepts of oligophrenia and dementia should be replaced by the general concept of "disorders in intellectual development." Cross-sectional evaluation of retarded intellectual development is better termed "mental retardation," with etiological attributes added. This term is more in line with the dynamics of child development. It can be subdivided into mild, moderate, severe, and very severe according to international nomenclature of diseases. Mentally deficient children's classification according to old degrees of intelligence can help in determining the kind of education they need; because changes in the intelligence level can occur, the 1st classification of the degree of mental deficiency should not be made before the 6th yr and the final classification should be made after adolescence. IQs are useful, but their reliability is questionable in classifying borderline cases. Dementia is justifiably used in adolescence only after observing conditions and longitudinal studies. Mental retardation should be carefully diagnosed and should not be neglected by physicians, parents, and educators. Intensive medical and pedagogical treatment and other therapeutic measures should be tried before making any definitive prognosis. These efforts should be continued into early adulthood. (28 ref)
Gollnitz, Gerhard & Rosler, Hans-Dieter. (Rostock U Nerve Clinic, W Germany) International Journal of Mental Health, 1975–76(Win), Vol 4(4), 6-18. [PA, Vol 58:03581]

787.   A dynamic approach to disorders in intellectual development.
Gives reasons why the concepts of oligophrenia and dementia should be replaced by the general concept of "disorders in intellectual development." Cross-sectional evaluation of retarded intellectual development is better termed "mental retardation," with etiological attributes added. This term is more in line with the dynamics of child development. It can be subdivided into mild, moderate, severe, and very severe according to international nomenclature of diseases. Mentally deficient childrens' classification according to old degrees of intelligence can help in determining the kind of education they need; because changes in the intelligence level can occur, the 1st classification of the degree of mental deficiency should not be made before the 6th yr and the final classification should be made after adolescence. IQs are useful, but their reliability is questionable in clarifying borderline cases. Dementia is justifiably used in adolescence only after observing conditions and longitudinal studies. Mental retardation should be carefully diagnosed and should not be neglected by physicians, parents, and educators. Intensive medical and pedagogical treatment and other therapeutic measures should be tried before making any definitive prognosis. These efforts should be continued into early adulthood. (28 ref)
Gollnitz, Gerhard & Rösler, Hans-Dieter.   International Journal of Mental Health, 1975–1976(Win), Vol 4(4), 6–18. [PA, Vol 59:12550]

788.   [Analysis of the structure of classification of normal and defective children.] (Germ)
Investigated spontaneous concept-formation processes based on similarity judgments. Results show a shift in preferences for pattern-cues for Ss of different ages. The youngest Ss (4 yrs old) preferred element-cues, while adults used relational cues. Increasing dimensionality was not evident; older Ss only formed more frequently well-defined subjective cue-structures, and many of the younger children answered randomly. Eight-yr-olds with mental deficiency exhibited a distinct weakness in their dimensional cue-integration. Ss of the same age with dyslexia performed at the level of 4-yr-old Ss in cue preference in spite of a very good subjective structure, indicating a weakness in directional and positional cues. (German & Russian summaries)
Grabowski, M. (Humboldt U Berlin, Sektion Psychologie, E Germany) Zeitschrift für Psychologie, 1976, Vol 184(2), 203-214. [PA, Vol 57:12859]

789. Novelty and familiarity as redundant cues in retardate discrimination learning.
Trained 2 groups of a total of 40 retarded 8-19 yr old (CA) Ss--low MA group (mean, 3.3 yrs) and a high MA group (mean, 5.7 yrs)--on 120 different 2-choice visual discrimination problems. For all Ss 60 problems were standard 4-trial problems (standard condition), and the remaining 60 problems were variants of the Moss-Harlow Design--the 1st trial differed from the initial 2-choice trial of the standard condition in that only a single stimulus was present, either positive (positive condition) or negative (negative condition); both cases were followed by 3 trials with both stimuli present. Each S received either positive or negative condition problems, but not both. An analysis of Trial 2 performance revealed that although no interproblem changes in the standard condition occurred, there were large initial performance differences and large interproblem changes in the positive and negative conditions which varied with the MA. Initial performance differences are interpreted as a differential preference for novel and familiar stimuli in the 2 MA groups. Changes in interproblem performance are consistent with the hypothesis that these MA-dependent novelty-familiarity preferences could be influenced by novelty-familiarity redundancy training.
Greenfield, Daryl B. (Massachusetts Inst of Technology) Journal of Experimental Child Psychology, 1976(Apr), Vol 21(2), 289-302. [PA, Vol 56:04278]

790. Relationships between performances of young handicapped children on Peabody Picture Vocabulary test and revised Stanford-Binet scale.
An analysis of the relationship between the Peabody Picture Vocabulary Test (PPVT) and Revised Stanford-Binet Intelligence Scale standard scores for 296 3-, 4-, 5-, and 6-yr-old handicapped children indicated uniform underestimation of the Stanford-Binet scores by the PPVT at the lower performance levels. A regression equation for determining estimates of Stanford-Binet performance from PPVT scores is presented.
Groden, Gerald; Branson, Michael & Mann, Leesa. (Rhode Island Hosp Child Development Ctr, Providence) Perceptual & Motor Skills, 1976(Jun), Vol 42(3, Pt 2), 1227-1232. [PA, Vol 57:04751]

791. The acquisition of prepositional motor responses in handicapped children.
Guralnick, Michael J. (National Children's Ctr, Washington, DC) Journal of Applied Behavior Analysis, 1976(Win), Vol 9(4), 500. [PA, Vol 57:13005]

792. Solving complex perceptual discrimination problems: Techniques for the development of problem-solving strategies.
Investigated techniques for developing problem-solving strategies in handicapped children when they are faced with complex perceptual discriminations, using 32 6-14 yr olds (mean IQ, 63.2). The effectiveness of feedback, modeling, and self-instruction were compared with each other and a control condition on a specially designed matching-to-sample task. The task was designed so that the distinctive features of the stimuli could be identified for instructional purposes. Only the self-instruction technique facilitated performance on the posttest. In addition, these skills generalized to a new set of forms but not to the Matching Familiar Figures Test. Findings are further related to the development of observational skills. (24 ref)
Gurlanick, Michael J. (National Children's Ctr, Washington, DC) American Journal of Mental Deficiency, 1976(Jul), Vol 81(1), 18-25. [PA, Vol 56:10747]

793. [Investigations on motor skills in dyslectic children.] (Germ)
Compared 30 normal 3rd graders, 30 dyslectics, and 30 retarded children on 17 variables. There was no significant difference between normal and dyslectic children on the Raven Coloured Progressive Matrices and only slight inferiority by the dyslectics on the Draw-A-Man Test. Dyslectics were more similar to the retarded in the reproduction of forms and in physical coordination, and intermediate in most other motor tests. It is not certain that motor training will improve general coordination significantly. (English summary) (50 ref)
Gutezeit, Günter & Hampel, Jürgen. (Christian-Albrechts-U Kiel, Kinderklinik, West Germany) Psychologie in Erziehung und Unterricht, 1976, Vol 23(1), 44–51. [PA, Vol 60:07676]

794. Temporal grouping and presentation rate in serial recall by retarded and nonretarded children.
24 retarded male Ss (CA, 16.8 yrs; MA, 8.8 yrs), 24 nonretarded male 2nd graders (CA, 7.6 yrs), and 24 nonretarded male 3rd graders (CA, 8.6 yrs) heard temporally grouped and ungrouped sequences of digits at varying presentation rates in a serial recall task. The facilitatory effect of temporal grouping was not as great for retarded Ss as for nonretarded Ss younger in MA. Several possible explanations for the smaller effect of temporal grouping for the retarded Ss are discussed.
Harris, Gilbert J. & Burke, Deborah. (Herbert H. Lehman Coll, City U New York) Bulletin of the Psychonomic Society, 1976(Aug), Vol 8(2), 91-93. [PA, Vol 57:08492]

795. The predictability of infant intelligence scales: A critical review and evaluation.
Unlike results of other intelligence tests, infant scores have repeatedly demonstrated little relationship to later tests of academic performance. The present article presents a critical review of the relevant research literature dealing with infant test predictability. Although the entire field is reviewed, special attention is given to studies of predictability in mentally retarded populations. It is concluded that (a) studies of reliability have been favorable, with split-half and test-retest correlations rarely falling below .85; (b) infant IQ-stability in normal populations is poor, with correlations between infant tests and school-age tests ranging from −.16 to +.49; (c) infant test scores in subnormal populations are more stable than test scores of other children; (d) other variables used in conjunction with infant scores (e.g., socioeconomic status) might significantly increase the predictability of the infant score alone. (40 ref)
Hatcher, Roger P. (Children's Memorial Hosp, Chicago, IL) Mental Retardation, 1976(Aug), Vol 14(4), 16-20. [PA, Vol 57:02224]

796. Learning concepts: Overlap of dimensions.
Examined whether or not the overlapping of dimensions in 2 out of 3 2-dimensional concepts would influence the concept learning of 36 14-yr-old retarded, 36 9½-yr-old normal, and 36 14-yr-old normal students. Findings show that older normals were superior to Ss in the other 2 groups, who did not differ from each other. There was a significant Groups by Trials interaction, with both normal groups learning faster than the retarded Ss, but there was no difference between treatments for any group.
Hurley, Oliver. (U Georgia) Journal of Research & Development in Education, 1976, Vol 9(Mono), 76–77. [PA, Vol 59:10162]

797. The learning of concepts at three levels of rule complexity.
Compared the performance of 54 14-yr-old retarded, 54 9½-yr-old normal, and 54 14-yr-old normal students in learning concepts at 3 levels of rule complexity: conjunction, inclusive disjunction, and exclusive disjunction. The older normal Ss performed better than Ss in the other groups, who did not differ from each other. There was a significant Groups by Treatments interaction; the younger Ss found exclusive disjunction easier than inclusive. Results indicate, in agreement with other studies, that retarded children perform more like their MA than their CA peers.
Hurley, Oliver. (U Georgia) Journal of Research & Development in Education, 1976, Vol 9(Mono), 78–79. [PA, Vol 59:10163]

798. Moral and cognitive development of moderately retarded, mildly retarded, and nonretarded individuals.
Investigated the relationships of moral maturity, cognitive reasoning, MA, and CA with 3 IQ groups. Ss were 20 moderately retarded (mean MA, 88 mo), 20 mildly retarded (mean MA, 90 mo), and 20 nonretarded (mean MA, 87 mo) individuals. Findings indicate that moderately retarded individuals are at lower levels of cognitive reasoning and moral maturity than MA-matched mildly retarded and nonretarded individuals. The

findings also indicate a stronger relationship between moral maturity and cognitive reasoning than between MA and moral maturity or MA and cognitive reasoning. The findings are discussed in terms of the positions of L. Kohlberg and C. Gilligan (1971) and J. J. Taylor and T. M. Achenbach (see PA, Vol 54:9978). (15 ref)

Kahn, James V. (U Illinois, Chicago Circle) American Journal of Mental Deficiency, 1976(Nov), Vol 81(3), 209-214. [PA, Vol 58:03583]

799.   [Spectral analytical study on the developmental properties of EEG in children: Generalized and localized components of EEG spectra in the normal and the mentally retarded children.] (Japn)

Conducted a study to elucidate the developmental properties of EEG in normal and mentally retarded children through regional differences and regional interrelationships. Ss were 36 3-15 yr old normal and 39 7-18 yr old retarded children. The localized components appearing at 1 or 2 regions tended to show low coherences in relation to the occipital region. The generalized component, observed over all regions, indicated lower coherences in the theta than in the alpha component. It may be inferred that the theta component shown in developing children may be differentiated from the component around 10 Hz.

Katada, Akiyoshi; Ozaki, Hisaki & Yamazaki, Kyoko. (Tokyo Gakugei U, Japan) Japanese Journal of Psychology, 1976(Dec), Vol 47(5), 277-286. [PA, Vol 58:03585]

800.   [Perception and generalization of magnitude in young mentally retarded children.] (Russ)

An investigation of generalization in young mentally retarded children showed that this process is directly connected with the development of perception (i.e., to learn to find a common feature in a set of objects, to unite and generalize them, it is necessary to learn to single out features and to find them in the object). It was discovered that mentally retarded children can differentiate colors but cannot generalize objects by colors. It was hypothesized that this happens because of extremely limited referents for a word (which does not have generalized meaning for a child) and a low level of perception combined with difficulties of transfer. The experiment supported this proposition: those who had difficulties in transfer had difficulties in learning. Their level of generalization directly depended on their level of transfer.

Kataeva, A. A. & Kim, S. G. (USSR Academy of Pedagogical Sciences, Inst of Defectology, Moscow) Defektologiya, 1976(Jun), No 6, 72–78. [PA, Vol 63:07802]

801.   [Several peculiarities of language development in mentally retarded preschool children.] (Russ)

A group of 96 3–5 yr old retarded children diagnosed as having oligophrenia to a debilitating degree were asked to name 275 nouns, 40 verbs, and 10 adjectives. They knew 20% of the nouns, 25% of the verbs, and 50% of the adjectives. When their passive ability to name the words was tested by showing them pictures representing the words, it was shown to be a little more than double their active ability. Their active substitution ability was approximately 50%, but their passive ability was 95%. The use of techniques based on these findings could possibly help correct their retarded speech development. (3 ref)

Kuznetsova, G. V. (USSR Academy of Sciences, Inst of Defectology, Moscow) Defektologiya, 1976(Mar), No 3, 78–82. [PA, Vol 64:10679]

802.   [Several peculiarities of vocabulary and grammar in mentally retarded dyslexic children.] (Russ)

The successful formation of reading habits has been attributed primarily to the level of development of oral speech. Based on this theory, the peculiarities of the lexico-grammar structure of speech of 43 8–12 yr old mentally retarded children with speech defects was investigated. Special attention was paid to vocabulary precision and size and correct use of verbs designating states and actions. Results show that the function of word changing can be more easily corrected than word formation. Grammar structure in mentally retarded children appears to be very poor. It took

much time and effort to make them more attentive, learn not to omit main parts of sentences, and acquire the patterns of grammar commonly used in everyday speech. The slow speech tempo of these children makes their communication with normal children almost impossible, and it is recommended they be prevented from it until they achieve a normal speech tempo.

Lalaeva, R. I. (Pedagogical Inst, Leningrad, USSR) Defektologiya, 1976(Jun), No 6, 9–13. [PA, Vol 63:07806]

803.   [Phonemic development in mentally retarded 1st- and 2nd-grade pupils with reading disorders.] (Russ)

Studied the level of phonemic development, phonemic perception, and phonemic analysis in 43 8–11 yr old mentally retarded pupils with reading disorders, comparing them to 18 normal pupils. Ss were given the following assignments: (a) to compare the same word when it was pronounced correctly and when it was mispronounced; (b) to name similar-sounding words using pictures; (c) to find a picture by its name in a group of items with similar names; and (d) to define the meaning of similar words by their phonemic structure. 34.5% of the pupils with reading disorders failed to differentiate the correct and incorrect pronunciation, although their difficulties had different characters. Pupils with insufficiently developed phonemic perception and analysis had difficulties even in learning letters; they acquired them mechanically and managed to learn only a small number. In a 2nd group of pupils (16%), the insufficient development of phonemic perception had a selective character.

Lalayeva, R. I. (Pedagogical Inst, Leningrad, USSR) Defektologiya, 1976(Feb), No 2, 10–15. [PA, Vol 64:10638]

804.   Dimensions of adaptive behavior of retarded and nonretarded public-school children.

Investigated the psychometric properties of the Adaptive Behavior Scales, Public School Revision, by administering the instrument to 2,618 7-13 yr olds. The sample included White, Black, and Spanish-surname groups from regular and special-education classes. Factor analyses of domain scores indicated 4 dimensions of adaptive behavior: Functional Autonomy, Interpersonal Adjustment, Social Responsibility, and Intrapersonal Adjustment. Comparison of factor structure across school classification and age groups revealed the same 4 dimensions for all groups. Implications for the assessment of adaptive behavior are discussed, and the correspondence between the present behavioral objectives and those defined by investigators studying effective school behavior is noted.

Lambert, Nadine M. & Nicoll, Richard C. (U California, Berkeley) American Journal of Mental Deficiency, 1976(Sep), Vol 81(2), 135-146. [PA, Vol 57:04760]

805.   Psychological diagnosis of mentally retarded children.

Reviews issues and problems related to the assessment of retardates. It is concluded that diagnosis of the mentally handicapped should be an ongoing process involving mini-teaching and learning situations and should take into consideration (a) the maturation and motivation of the child, and (b) the nature, demands, and duration of the task. It is suggested that such procedures contribute more to an understanding of the mentally retarded individual than do test results based on initial or one-shot performance.

Leong, C. K. (U Saskatchewan, Inst of Child Guidance & Development, Saskatoon, Canada) Mental Retardation Bulletin, 1976, Vol 4(1), 10-16. [PA, Vol 58:01400]

806.   Resistance to extinction as a function of IQ and reinforcement ratio among retarded children.

24 children at 3 levels of mental retardation (IQ ranges of 50-60, 30-40, and 20-below, based on scores on the Stanford Binet Intelligence Scale), were trained to barpress on 1 of 2 variable ratio (VR) schedules. Responses were reinforced 25 times on either a VR2 or VR4 schedule. Analysis of the number of responses during extinction indicated an inverse relationship between IQ and resistance to extinction. The partial reinforcement extinction effect was found, but there was no interaction with IQ level. Results support the position that inhibitory control

is an important parameter along which intelligence may be ordered. (18 ref)
Levine, B. A. (Nassau Community Coll) Journal of Mental Deficiency Research, 1976(Mar), Vol 20(1), 25–30. [PA, Vol 56:02512]

807.   Differential reliability and validity of two selected Wechsler Intelligence Scale for Children short forms.
Lombardi, David A. & Cohen, Stanley H.   Catalog of Selected Documents in Psychology, 1976(Feb), Vol 6, 2. [PA, Vol 55:08648]

808.   Failure effects on outerdirectedness: A failure to replicate.
Conducted a replication of part of J. Turnure and E. Zigler's (see PA Vol 39:6841) experiment in which they assessed whether outerdirectedness was a function of failure experiences. 30 nonretarded 2nd graders and 30 retarded 5th and 6th graders, matched on MA, experienced either failure games administered with positive or negative comments followed by an imitative assessment task or received only the imitation task. Results do not support the previous hypothesis concerning the antecedents of outerdirectedness, as no short-term effects of failure were found. Findings refute Turnure and Zigler's hypothesis that outerdirectedness is a function of situational social reinforcement. Differences in tasks presented, methods of analysis, and/or school populations may have contributed to the lack of correspondence with the Turnure and Zigler findings.
Maguire, Marcia. (U Southern California) American Journal of Mental Deficiency, 1976(Nov), Vol 81(3), 256-259. [PA, Vol 58:03591]

809.   Retarded and normal pupils' rule learning, attribute identification and complete learning of an inclusive disjunction concept.
Compared the effect of a rule learning, an attribute identification, and a complete learning problem on 54 14-yr-old retarded, 54 9½-yr-old normal, and 54 14-yr-old normal students' inclusive disjunction concept learning. There was a significant Groups by Treatments by Trials interaction. Within each of the 3 groups, Ss using rule learning attained a higher level and showed a faster rate of learning. Within each of the 3 treatments, older normals performed better and faster than the other 2 groups. When using rule learning and attribute identification, younger normals exceeded retarded Ss, but when using complete learning, these groups performed similarly.
McLaughlin, Phillip. (Virginia Commonwealth U) Journal of Research & Development in Education, 1976, Vol 9(Mono), 41–42. [PA, Vol 59:10173]

810.   Successive and simultaneous presentations and retarded and normal pupils' rule learning, attribute identification, and complete learning of an inclusive disjunction concept.
Compared the effects of successive and simultaneous presentation on 108 14-yr-old retarded, 108 9½-yr-old normal, and 108 14-yr-old normal students' rule learning, attribute identification, and complete learning of an inclusion disjunction concept. The 3 groups responded similarly to the 3 presentation methods. Simultaneous presentation was superior to successive. Within both methods, younger normal and retarded groups responded similarly, while the older normals exceeded both in rule learning and complete learning. Both normal groups exceeded retarded Ss in attribute identification.
McLaughlin, Phillip. (Virginia Commonwealth U) Journal of Research & Development in Education, 1976, Vol 9(Mono), 44–46. [PA, Vol 59:10172]

811.   Retarded and normal pupils' rule learning, attribute identification, and complete learning of a conjunction concept.
Compared the effect of a rule learning, an attribute identification, and a complete learning problem on 54 14-yr-old retarded, 54 9½-yr-old normal, and 54 14-yr-old normal students' learning of a conjunction concept. Results indicate significant main effects for Groups, Treatments, and Trials, and significant Groups by Trials and Treatments by Trials interactions. Older normals exceeded retarded Ss in amount learned and rate of learning. Older normals and younger normals did not differ in these areas,

nor did younger normals and retarded groups. Ss having rule learning exceeded the others in amount learned and rate of learning, while Ss having attribute identification problems and complete learning problems performed similarly.
McLaughlin, Phillip. (Virginia Commonwealth U) Journal of Research & Development in Education, 1976, Vol 9(Mono), 39–40. [PA, Vol 59:10175]

812.   Retarded and normal pupils' rule learning, attribute identification, and complete learning of an exclusion concept.
Compared the effect of a rule learning, an attribute identification, and a complete learning problem on 54 14-yr-old retarded, 54 9½-yr-old normal, and 54 14-yr-old normal students' learning of an exclusion concept. The 3 groups differed in their performance, with older normals exceeding the other groups and the younger normals and retarded Ss performing similarly. All Ss receiving rule learning performed better than those receiving attribute identification. There was no difference between rule learning and complete learning or between complete learning and attribute identification.
McLaughlin, Phillip. (Virginia Commonwealth U) Journal of Research & Development in Education, 1976, Vol 9(Mono), 43. [PA, Vol 59:10174]

813.   IQ, mental age, complexity, and trial blocks and the response latency of retarded and nonretarded children.
Examined the relationship between MA, IQ, complexity, and trial blocks on the processing performance of 20 nonretarded and 20 retarded children. The main effect of Trial Blocks and the MA × Complexity interaction were significant. Results support the conclusion that MA, not IQ, is important for information processing. (21 ref)
Morelan, Steve J. (U Puget Sound, School of Education & Occupational Therapy) American Journal of Mental Deficiency, 1976(Jan), Vol 80(4), 437-441. [PA, Vol 56:00886]

814.   Performance of retarded and nonretarded adolescents when processing relevant and irrelevant information.
Compared the information-processing performance of 12 retarded and 12 nonretarded 13-15 yr olds. Using reaction time (RT) keys each S classified color words, secondary color words, noncolor words, nonsense syllables, and stick figures according to the color of ink in which each stimulus was printed. RTs of the nonretarded Ss were significantly faster than that of retarded Ss; color words and secondary color words significantly interfered with processing performance as measured by correct RTs. Results indicate that the task used here, which was similar to the Stroop Color-Word Test, interfered with response initiation rather than memory retrieval and that the locus of interference for retarded and nonretarded Ss was equivalent.
Morelan, Steve J.; Prehm, Herbert J. & Warrick, Diane B. (U Puget Sound) Perceptual & Motor Skills, 1976(Jun), Vol 42(3, Pt 1), 771-774. [PA, Vol 56:08215]

815.   [Mental retardation and malformation in a child with 5/13 chromosome translocation.] (Port)
Reports a case of mental retardation and physical malformations with chromosome abnormalities in a 9-yr-old boy. Chromosomal analysis showed breakage in some genes to 5p and/or 13q of genetic mutation or an effect of position in readjusted chromosomic segments. (16 ref)
Moura Ribeiro, Valeriana; Ferrari, Iris & Moreira, Lilia M. (Faculdade de Medicina de Ribeirão Preto, Brazil) Arquivos de Neuro-Psiquiatria, 1976(Jun), Vol 34(2), 199–204. [PA, Vol 60:12035]

816.   A comment on the efficiency of the Revised Denver Developmental Screening Test.
The Revised Denver Developmental Screening Test (RDDST) is a short, easily administered test used to measure 4 areas of infant and preschool development. Consideration of the psychometric efficiency of this test using an estimate of the base rate of mental retardation in the screening population of 2,000 children (aged, 1 mo to 6 yrs) reveals that the RDDST is relatively inefficient in the detection of preschool children with IQs below 70.

Nugent, James H. (Central Michigan U) American Journal of Mental Deficiency, 1976(Mar), Vol 80(5), 570-572. [PA, Vol 56:05187]

817.   Preference by the retarded for vibratory and visual stimulation as a function of mental age and psychotic reaction.
Using a vibratory vs visual stimulus choice situation, a shift of modality preference with development was investigated in 60 retarded children and 91 retarded adults with and without psychosis. The overall MA was 8-72 mo. Ss also included 47 normal children (aged 3-5 yrs). In retarded adults and retarded children, the number of vibratory choices was negatively correlated and the number of visual choices positively correlated with MA, while holding constant CA, time in institution, total choices, and mental status. Psychotic adults chose the vibratory stimulus more and the visual stimulus less than did nonpsychotic retardates of corresponding MA. Stimulus alternation was positively correlated with the MA of retarded adults after holding constant other variables. No age trends existed in the normal children. These findings support E. G. Schatel's (1959) theory of development from the autocentric to the allocentric mode of perception. (20 ref)
Ohwaki, Sonoko & Stayton, Samuel E. (Lynchburg Training School & Hosp, VA) Journal of Abnormal Psychology, 1976(Oct), Vol 85(5), 516-522. [PA, Vol 57:03643]

818.   [Habitual rocking in children.] (Czec)
Separated 36 children 3–42 mo old into 3 groups according to the intensity of their automatic rocking. There was no correlation between the intensity of rocking and IQ, but there seemed to be a connection between the stereotypic movements and signs of sadness, tension, and startle reaction. 46 other Ss with rocking movements were selected from 3 groups: young children 6–36 mo old without organic brain damage, young children who were severely retarded, and a group of retardates between 8 and 20 yrs of age. Rocking was found to help the Ss to lower their frustration tension. It is concluded that chronic stress causes disorganization of the higher forms of behavior, which is manifested by the stereotyped activities of automatism.
Olechnowiczová, Hana. (Inst Psychoneurologiczny, Warsaw, Poland) Psychológia a Patopsychológia Dietata, 1976, Vol 11(2), 119–130. [PA, Vol 61:01283]

819.   Retarded and normal pupils' comprehension and recall of chunked and non-chunked connected discourse.
Investigated the manner in which 36 14-yr-old retarded, 36 9½-yr-old normal, and 36 14-yr-old normal students comprehended and recalled chunked and nonchunked connected discourse. For both comprehension and recall there were significant main effects for Groups and Trials. For comprehension, older normals exceeded younger normals, who exceeded retarded Ss. For recall, older normals performed better than Ss in the other groups, who did not differ from each other. Data support the notion that chunking does not facilitate comprehension and indicate that spatial separation of material into meaningful groups does not improve comprehension or exact recall of either normal or retarded students.
Osterhout, Julie.   Journal of Research & Development in Education, 1976, Vol 9(Mono), 104–105. [PA, Vol 59:10180]

820.   [A social habits scale for mental retardates.] (Span)
The factorial structure of the Social Habits Scale, the correlation among its factors, and its test–retest reliability over 6 mo were studied. Ss were 97 male and 70 female mentally deficient children, who were 6–19 yrs old, had IQs from 21 to 70, and exhibited neurological damage. 20 special education teachers answered the questionnaire. The 4 major factors obtained using varimax rotation were (a) personal habits (cleaning, eating, and dressing), (b) reading habits, (c) responsibility and social competence, and (d) personal independence in social interaction. Two strategies were used for applying factorial results in prediction: (a) the conservative model of selecting clear factors and clear-cutting items with high saturation in each factor, and (b) the less rigorous method—selecting numerous overlapping items included in the cumulative scores. Predictive results were not signifi-

cant, but were in the expected direction. Possible interpretations of the results are discussed, and the questionnaire is presented. (15 ref)
Pelechano, Vicente. (Universidad de la Laguna, Tenerife, Spain) Análisis y Modificación de Conducta, 1976, Vol 2(2), 39–56. [PA, Vol 63:00113]

821.   [Some features of probabilistic prediction in normal and exceptional children.] (Russ)
Compared 16 normal 8–9 yr old children, 31 children in special education classes who suffered from retarded development, and 16 mentally retarded children on their ability to predict probabilistic events. Reaction time to vibrotactile stimuli presented either to the right or the left hand was measured as a function of the probability of stimulus presentation, which was .5 for both hands in one experiment and .8 and .2 in another. In normal Ss, reaction time increased with decreasing stimulus probability. Underdeveloped Ss showed high variability in their response to the less frequent stimulus; about one-third of them processed sensory information more slowly and were easily tired. The mentally retarded group showed no differential response to stimuli with different presentation probabilities. (English summary)
Peresleni, L. I. (USSR Academy of Pedagogical Sciences, Scientific Research Inst of Defectology, Moscow) Voprosy Psikhologii, 1976(Mar–Apr), No 2, 115–123. [PA, Vol 60:01324]

822.   Patterns of imitation in mentally retarded children.
Extended the interchange theory of imitation to mentally retarded children in 2 studies in which Ss observed and learned to copy adults using external cues and internal control as aids. In Exp I 24 speaking and 24 nonspeaking 5-20 yr old retardates (having estimated IQs of less than 54) were paired with adults who gave half the children instructions to copy and the other half additional verbal and gestural cues. Nonspeaking retardates receiving frequent cues attended and copied better than those getting initial instructions, gestural cues being equally or more effective than verbal ones. Speaking retardates getting repeated cues finished copying sooner than those getting only instructions, verbal and gestural cues being equally effective. In Exp II 22 retardates from elementary school and kindergarten classes were trained to sit, observe, and copy their teachers in a 2-mo program. Training was evaluated in situations where copying or playing was signalled. Overall, children attended and copied more in the appropriate situation. However, sitting, attention, and copying increased nonspecifically in both situations, and initial situational differences in copying were not observed after treatment. A revision of the interchange theory is presented, implications for attention-deficit and verbal self-control theories are discussed, and notions of "generalized imitation" are criticized. (29 ref)
Quilty, Robert F.; Solowski, Ritva & Maliniemi, Sinikka.
    Scandinavian Journal of Psychology, 1976, Vol 17(2), 104-114. [PA, Vol 56:10150]

823.   Autoshaping and maintenance of a lever-press response in mentally retarded children.
Used 3 autoshaping paradigms to train a leverpress response in 32 9-13 yr old mentally retarded children. Ss undergoing autoshaping (forward stimulus-reinforcement pairings) required fewer acquisition trials than those in a control condition (reverse pairings), indicating that retarded Ss can acquire a leverpress response when only stimulus-reinforcement contingencies are in effect. In addition, the effects of stimulus-reinforcement and response-reinforcement contingencies on the level of maintenance responding were examined by comparing postacquisition performance in the 3 autoshaping conditions. Results indicate that the maintenance level of an autoshaped response in retarded Ss is determined by both the respondent and operant principles.
Ragain, Ronnie D.; Anson, John E. & Sperber, Richard D. (George Peabody Coll for Teachers) Psychological Record, 1976(Win), Vol 26(1), 105–109. [PA, Vol 56:02518]

824.　Ethnicity, geographic locale, age, sex, and urban-rural residence as variables in the prevalence of mild retardation.
Assessed intellectual performance by administering the WISC-R to 950 of a stratified random sample of 1,040 children in Pima County, Arizona. The sample was stratified for ethnicity (Anglo, Black, Mexican-American, and Papago Indian), urban-rural residence, sex, and grade level (1st, 3rd, 5th, 7th, and 9th). The 3 WISC-R IQ scores and cutoff points of 69 and 75 were used in comparisons of prevalence of mild mental retardation. This prevalence was significantly related to ethnicity (with disproportionate representation of all non-Anglo groups occurring at the 75, but not the 69, cutoff) and geographic locale, but not to sex, urban-rural residence, and grade level. In agreement with recent court decisions, it is concluded that manipulation of cutoff points will partially modify disproportionate representation of minority group children in classes for the mildly retarded; the question of optimum education for these children, however, remains unanswered. (27 ref)
Reschly, Daniel J.　& Jipson, Frederick J. (Iowa State U) American Journal of Mental Deficiency, 1976(Sep), Vol 81(2), 154-161. [PA, Vol 57:06116]

825.　Intermittent punishment of key-press responding: Effectiveness during application and extinction.
Examined the resistance of touch-key responses in severely disturbed children to the effects of FR-1 and VR punishment. Subsequent to response suppression, resistance to extinction was examined for the various punishment schedules. A multiple-stimulus design was employed in 3 experiments with a total of 6 5-10 yr olds. The touch-key response was maintained on a VR reinforcement schedule, and the punishing stimulus was a loud (105-db) tone. For the punishment schedules chosen, no difference was seen between the suppressive effects of FR-1 and VR punishment. Subsequent study of resistance to extinction proved impossible, as all Ss ceased responding during punishment application and did not recover the response. It is suggested that responding maintained on a VR schedule is inappropriate for investigating ratio punishment schedules because of its great susceptibility to disruption.
Romanczyk, Raymond G. (State U New York, Binghamton) Psychological Record, 1976(Spr), Vol 26(2), 203-214. [PA, Vol 56:06128]

826.　[Psychiatric aspects of Steinert's disease with neonatal outbreak in children.] (Fren)
Describes 3 cases of atrophic myotonia (Steinert's disease) in neonates that were followed for 6 yrs. These observations, added to those already published, permit a description of the characteristic mental difficulties that accompany this condition: definite mental subnormality, usually borderline between mild and severe mental deficiency, accompanied by a marked retardation of psychomotor development. The outcome is unfavorable and is marked by a gradual intellectual regression.
Rousselot, J.-P.; Martinet, M. & Charlin, A. Annales Médico-Psychologiques, 1976(Jul), Vol 2(2), 256-269. [PA, Vol 60:05516]

827.　Relationship between certain forms of short-term visual memory and intellectual abilities in children.
Studied the effect of varied exposure time on performance by 32 boys and girls aged 8-10 yrs, divided according to WISC scores into an intact (mean IQ, 104) and a mentally retarded group (mean IQ, 74). The material consisted of 15 pictures presented simultaneously in different experimental variants (i.e., position recall and recognition combined with position recall). By varying exposure time and the use of distractors comparable performance was achieved in both the groups, as predicted by N. R. Ellis's (1960) theory. A study of the serial position effect revealed a nontraditional pattern of the U curve with a predominance of the primary effect. (Russian & Slovak summaries) (24 ref)
Ruisel, Imrich　& Droppová, Zdena. (Slovak Academy of Sciences, Inst of Experimental Psychology, Bratislava, Czechoslovakia) Studia Psychologica, 1976, Vol 18(1), 65-75. [PA, Vol 57:10578]

828.　The interference of semantic cues with retarded and normal pupils' learning a syntactic rule for comprehending relative clause transformations.
Tested J. D. Schelly's (1975) theory that, in the study of syntactic structure, semantic clues may enter to interfere with students' use of syntatic cues. Ss in the present study were 36 14-yr-old retarded, 36 9½-yr-old normal, and 36 14-yr-old normal students. Results show significant main effects for Groups, Trials, and Treatments. Older normals exceeded younger normals and retarded Ss, who did not differ from each other. Ss who had neutral sentences performed better than those who had extra semantic clues added.
Schelly, Joan. Journal of Research & Development in Education, 1976, Vol 9(Mono), 100-101. [PA, Vol 59:10189]

829.　Number of embeddings and normal and retarded subjects' comprehension of sentence transformations.
Investigated the performance of 36 14-yr-old retarded, 36 9½-yr-old normal, and 36 14-yr-old normal students when given inductive instruction in comprehending relative clause embeddings, with the variance between treatments being the number of embeddings. Results show significant main effects for Groups and Treatments; there were significant Groups by Treatments and Treatments by Trials interactions. For all groups single embedded sentences were easier, especially for retarded and younger normal Ss. Older normals exceeded the other 2 groups in learning double-embedded sentences; retarded and younger normal Ss performed similarly.
Schelly, Joan. Journal of Research & Development in Education, 1976, Vol 9(Mono), 102-103. [PA, Vol 59:10188]

830.　Learning disabled or slow learner?
Discusses several diagnostic assumptions concerning specific learning disabilities and warns against the misuse of the diagnosis "learning disabled" to describe all children who are slow learners. Differences in learning patterns between the learning-disabled child and the slow learner are presented as a guide for more accurate diagnoses.
Shepherd, Margaret J. (Columbia U, Teachers Coll) School Psychology Digest, 1976(Win), Vol 5(1), 32-35. [PA, Vol 58:05636]

831.　Recall of familiar objects and projected color photographs of objects by mentally retarded individuals of comparable mental age.
Investigated the effects of cue-availability on short- and long-term recall of 40 mentally retarded children. Ss were chosen on the basis of comparable MA (approximately 90 mo) and randomly assigned to either an objects (high cues) group or slides (low cues) group. 52 familiar objects served as stimuli for the objects group, and projected color photographs of the objects were presented to the slides group. In the short-term recall session, Ss were shown stimuli grouped into 8 trials and asked to recall the names of the stimuli in each trial 10 sec after presentation. Delayed recall was obtained 48 hrs later in a free recall session. The objects group scored significantly higher than the slides group on memory span ($p < .01$), short-term recall ($p < .001$), and delayed recall ($p < .025$). The facilitation of recall achieved by using 3-dimensional stimuli was clearly demonstrated, and the relative degree of facilitation was comparable for both short- and long-term recall.
Shotick, Andrew L.; Ray, A. Bartow & Addison, C. Lewis. (Georgia Retardation Ctr, Athens Unit) Perceptual & Motor Skills, 1976(Feb), Vol 42(1), 139-145. [PA, Vol 56:10155]

832.　WISC subtest patterns of delinquent female retardates.
Compared mean WISC subtest ranks of 61 9-17 yr old female delinquent retardates with male delinquent retardates and 10 other previously studied samples of nondelinquent retardates. Only Black female delinquents were unlike the larger population of retardates; they had greater difficulty in the Object Assembly subtest than all other samples. Female delinquent retardates, particularly Blacks, also performed somewhat better on Verbal subtests than either male delinquent or nondelinquent retardates.

Solway, Kenneth S.; Cook, Thomas H. & Hays, J. Ray. Psychological Reports, 1976(Feb), Vol 38(1), 42. [PA, Vol 56:00892]

833. Evidence for dimensional independence in short-term memory of retarded individuals.
Assessed the relative importance of dimensional similarity between test and interpolated problems and absolute difficulty of interpolated material as variables influencing short-term retention in the discrimination learning of retarded persons. 20 14-22 yr old moderate-to-borderline retardates were taught a mixed series of two-trial discriminations consisting of (a) relatively easy, multidimensional ("junk") problems and (b) more difficult, form-relevant dot-pattern discriminations. Test problems and interpolations were either dimensionally similar (both junk or both dot-pattern problems) or dissimilar (train one type of problem, interpolate the other). The major finding is that short-term forgetting occurred only when test and interpolated stimuli were dimensionally similar. Absolute difficulty of interpolations had no effect on retention. These results are interpreted as supporting M. A. Fisher and D. Zeaman's (1973) assumption of dimensional independence of memory processes in retarded persons. A secondary finding is that performance on dot-pattern discrimination varied with intelligence, possibly reflecting intelligence-related differences in the ability to organize perceptually random arrays of dots into discriminative patterns.
Sperber, Richard D. (George Peabody Coll for Teachers, Inst on Mental Retardation & Intellectual Development) American Journal of Mental Deficiency, 1976(Sep), Vol 81(2), 187-193. [PA, Vol 57:06118]

834. The prevalence of language delay in a population of three-year-old children and its association with general retardation.
Using a simple assessment of language and a behavior screening questionnaire, a 1-in-4 random sample of a total population of 3-yr-olds was screened for the presence of language delay and behavior problems. A full psycho-developmental assessment was carried out in 705 children with suspected language delay or a behavior problem, and in 99 control children; the sensitivity and specificity of the language screening-test was examined. Results show the importance of investigating language delay in relation to nonverbal abilities. Of those Ss with a language age less than two-thirds of their chronological age, 37% also had similarly delayed nonverbal mental abilities. 50% of the Ss with a language age of less than 30 mo were generally retarded in their nonverbal abilities. The estimated prevalence of delayed language development is 31/1,000, of specific language delay 5.7/1,000, and of severe retardation 4.2/1,000. Males were more likely than females to have language and general developmental delay. (French, German, & Spanish summaries) (21 ref)
Stevenson, Jim & Richman, Naomi. (Hosp for Sick Children, London, England) Developmental Medicine & Child Neurology, 1976(Aug), Vol 18(4), 431-441. [PA, Vol 57:06133]

835. Effects of sex and ethnic variables on the profiles of the Illinois Test of Psycholinguistics and Wechsler Intelligence Scale for Children.
A study of the effects of sex and ethnicity (Black, Mexican-American, or Anglo-American) variables on the Illinois Test of Psycholinguistic Abilities and WISC profiles of 42 mentally retarded, 42 normal, and 41 children with diagnosed learning or language problems aged 6-10 yrs indicated that while such effects may attain statistical significance, the amount of variance accounted for by the variables is small. Findings question the practical significance of such effects.
Stewart, David W. (Central Louisiana State Hosp, Pineville) Psychological Reports, 1976(Feb), Vol 38(1), 53-54. [PA, Vol 56:00893]

836. Auditory and visual knowledge of results and retarded and normal subjects' learning homonyms.
Investigated the relative effects of 2 types of continuous knowledge of results, visual and auditory, on the learning of homonyms by 36 14-yr-old retarded, 36 9½-yr-old normal, and 36 14-yr-old normal students. Results show that both normal groups exceeded the retarded in amount learned and there was a significant Groups by Treatments by Trials interaction. The normal groups scored higher with visual knowledge of results, but the retarded group scored higher with auditory knowledge of results.
Talley, Diane. (U Georgia) Journal of Research & Development in Education, 1976, Vol 9(Mono), 47-48. [PA, Vol 59:10196]

837. Age trends in parental assessments of the behavior problems of their retarded children.
52 mothers with a retarded child living at home each voluntarily provided a list and description of the 3 most pressing problems she currently faced in the management of her child. Responses were categorized into 12 problem areas and analyzed by age groups (2-4 yrs, 4-6 yrs, 8-12 yrs, and 12-17 yrs). The category of disobedience, stubbornness, and noncompliance was the most pressing issue and occurred with greatest frequency in all age groups except adolescence. There was a trend for most issues to decrease with age. These included (a) eating problems; (b) talking and communication problems; (c) mobility-walking problems; (d) impulsivity, sensitivity, and "temperamental" behavior; (e) aggressiveness toward others; and (f) personal hygiene and dressing problems. In contrast, problems with social interaction peaked in the oldest age group. Concern with toileting and toilet training existed across all age groups and was listed by 45% of the mothers.
Tavormina, J. B.; Henggeler, Scott W. & Gayton, William F. (U Virginia) Mental Retardation, 1976(Feb), Vol 14(1), 38-39. [PA, Vol 56:00895]

838. Knowledge of results and counting of sequential light flashes by retarded and intellectually normal children.
12 adolescent retarded boys (mean age, 19.8 yrs) and 12 3rd-grade boys of equivalent MA observed sequential flashes of light and made judgments of numerosity. Durations of successive flashes were 300, 500, 700, and 900 msec in trains of 1-15 flashes. Over 6 daily sessions, subgroups receiving information about accuracy after each trial made fewer errors, and subgroups receiving none made more errors. The linear trend interaction of knowledge of results with IQ was significant, with performance of the nonretarded Ss decreasing to the level of the retarded Ss in the no-feedback condition. With feedback, the rate of decrease in error over sessions was similar for both levels of IQ. Results indicate a substantial effect of knowledge of results in improving accuracy of counting by retarded and nonretarded children.
Thor, Donald H. & Drous, Juliana. (Edward R. Johnstone Training & Research Ctr, Bordentown, NJ) Perceptual & Motor Skills, 1976(Jun), Vol 42(3, Pt 1), 835-840. [PA, Vol 56:08220]

839. [Medical and genetic problems in mentally retarded children.] (Germ)
Since few methods exist to cure mental retardation, prevention is most important. It is subdivided into (a) prevention of prenatal complications, prenatal diagnosis, and prevention of possible interruption of the pregnancy; and (b) genetic counseling. The biological causes of mental retardation are analyzed, emphasizing prenatal and perinatal complications, and successful methods of prophylaxis are mentioned. Chromosomal abnormalities, their prenatal diagnosis, and the risk that they may be repeated in subsequent pregnancies are described. Genetic counseling, its genetic bases, and its positive effects are discussed. (French summary)
Tönz, Otmar. (Lucerne Children's Hosp, Switzerland) Vierteljahresschrift für Heilpädagogik und ihre Nachbargebiete, 1976(Mar), Vol 45(1), 18-26. [PA, Vol 65:01667]

840. [Comparison of shifting between groups of mentally retarded children, secondary school children and seniors.] (Germ)
Results from the Stroop Color-Word Test indicate that secondary school children worked most accurately and quickly, followed by seniors (accurate but not as quick) and the mentally retarded children. The concepts of color perception and naming were easily shaken for the retarded Ss, and their performance structure differed significantly from that of the seniors. (4 ref)

Tschöpp, Max & Jorswieck, Eduard. (Inst für Sonderpädagogik, Berlin, West Germany) Praxis der Kinderpsychologie und Kinderpsychiatrie, 1976(Jan), Vol 25(1), 22–24. [PA, Vol 65:01524]

841. Scoring system.
Performance on the Bender Visual-Motor Gestalt Test has been repeatedly shown to be sensitive to the effects of brain lesions. However, brain damaged and control populations typically overlap greatly in their error scores. A new Bender scoring system is presented with differential weighting for errors of greater or lesser severity, which permits a profile analysis of different types of error as well. A preliminary report of a validation study is included, with data from 30 epileptic or mentally retarded children and 15 children with school and/or behavior problems; mean ages ranged from 116 to 125 mo. (12 ref)
Tymchuk, Alexander J. & Nishihara, Aline. (U California, Los Angeles) Journal of Pediatric Psychology, 1976, Vol 1(3), 15–17. [PA, Vol 62:00134]

842. Comparison of socio-demographic, treatment and followup variables of mentally retarded and emotionally disturbed children.
110 mentally retarded children and 86 children with emotional disorders who attended the Child Guidance Clinic (Chandigarh, India) were compared on sociodemographic and clinical variables. Both the mentally retarded (MR) group and the emotional disorder (ED) group were found to be composed predominantly of males (64.5% and 59.3%, respectively), and both groups averaged approximately 10 yrs in age. Significant sociodemographic differences were found between the 2 groups. MR Ss, in relation to ED Ss, had (a) a less educated head of household, (b) head of household performing less highly skilled work, (c) nonlocal residence, and (d) rural residence. On clinical variables, the groups differed significantly on reasons for which help was sought, type of treatment received, and type of follow-up received. In relation to ED Ss, MR Ss showed more psychological and physical symptoms, received less drugs and supportive psychotherapy and less intensive psychotherapy/behavior therapy, and had briefer contact with the clinic. (24 ref)
Varma, V. K.; Mangalwedhe, K. P. & Misra, A. K. (Postgraduate Inst of Medical Education & Research, Chandigarh, India) Child Psychiatry Quarterly, 1976(Jul), Vol 9(3), 1–10. [PA, Vol 60:05348]

843. [School and family problems of mentally retarded children.] (Span)
52 children seen for school or school-related problems at a child psychiatry service, all without sensory deficits or specific language or writing difficulties, were tested for intellectual level. Personal history, family history, and data from projective tests were obtained. Of the 28 children aged 4–9 yrs, 15 had IQs between 60 and 85 and 13 between 85 and 105. Of the 24 children aged 10–14, 20 had IQs between 70 and 85, the others between 85 and 105. 40% were firstborns. In 19 cases the mother was overprotective and the father rigid and severe. The need for special facilities for such children is discussed.
Velilla Picazo, J. M.; Miravete Fuertes, P. & Bonals Pi, A. (U de Zaragoza, Facultad de Medicina, Spain) Archivos de Neurobiología, 1976(Mar–Apr), Vol 39(2), 121–142. [PA, Vol 66:01550]

844. Comparisons among two different electro-acoustic impedance measures and otoscopy by an ENT specialist in identifying middle ear anomalies in mental retardates.
Of mental retardates in a residential school, 60 failed initial screening for middle ear abnormalities using a Peters AP-61 impedance bridge. These Ss were retested with that bridge and a Grason-Stadler (GS) 1720 otoadmittance bridge plus otoscopy. Eight middle ear conditions were specifically sought. The 3 measures varied widely: Those conditions nearer the tympanic membrane (TM) were identified readily by otoscopy, those nearer the Eustachian tube by tympanometry. The GS bridge with probe tones of 220 and 660 c/sec appeared more successful than the single probe of the Peters bridge in providing indications

for thin TM or dysarticulation of the ossicular chain. The otolaryngologist classified 49% of the ears as normal, while the Peters and GS bridges classified 37.5 and 22.5% of ears as such. The GS bridge raises the possibility of overreferral in cases of thin TM diagnosed as within normal limits by otoscopy, and in a relatively large number of cases of suspected otitis media not confirmed by the other 2 methods. A 2nd study was conducted with 60 persons with all otologic, audiometric, and tympanometric signs normal but with absence of an acoustic reflex in either ear at 0.5 and/or 2 kc/sec. In these Ss, an American Electromedics Model 83 acoustic bridge was used in stimulus steps of 40–125 db.
Weaver, Ross M.; Arbon, Robert A.; Watkins, Prince L. & Olsen, Robert G. (Brigham Young U) Journal of Auditory Research, 1976, Vol 16(4), 239–246. [PA, Vol 61:06409]

845. Whole and parts methods and retarded and normal pupils' learning compound words.
Investigated 54 14-yr-old retarded, 54 9½-yr-old normal, and 54 14-yr-old normal students' learning of compound words using whole (giving the entire task for practice) and parts (giving parts of the task for practice) learning methods. There was a significant main effect for Groups, with the older normal Ss exceeding the other groups. All groups responded the same way to the whole, pure part, and progressive parts methods.
Williams, Charlotte L.; Allen, Jerry & Dekle, Ocie. (U Georgia) Journal of Research & Development in Education, 1976, Vol 9(Mono), 74–75. [PA, Vol 59:10202]

846. Effects of objective frequency in retarded and normal pupils' learning compound words.
Studied the effects of objective frequency on 36 14-yr-old retarded, 36 9½-yr-old normal, and 36 14-yr-old normal students' learning of compound words. Findings show that level of objective frequency did not significantly affect Ss' ability to learn new compound words. Both normal groups exceeded the retarded but did not differ from each other.
Williams, Charlotte L. & Allen, Jerry. (U Georgia) Journal of Research & Development in Education, 1976, Vol 9(Mono), 70–71. [PA, Vol 59:10201]

847. Development of the formation of categories by normal and retarded persons.
Investigated the development and fragmentation of categories over CA and MA without the requisite of free recall. 26 kindergartners, 26 4th-graders, and 21 9th-graders, and 24 noninstitutionalized retarded pupils (CA, 11.89 yrs; MA, 8.46 yrs) labeled and categorized 480 chromatic slides of picturable objects. As age increased (a) more categories and superordinates congruent with adult criteria were elicited, (b) more superordinates were formed with more items per superordinate, (c) fragmentation of categories increased, and (d) normal Ss were more efficient in the formation of reliable categories than retarded Ss. Results are compared with other developmental and comparative studies in clustering, emphasizing the importance of the availability and accessibility of superordinates in the development of clustering ability. (21 ref)
Winters, John J. & Brzoska, Mary A. (Edward R. Johnstone Training & Research Ctr, Bordentown, NJ) Developmental Psychology, 1976(Mar), Vol 12(2), 125-131. [PA, Vol 55:12526]

848. [Factors modifying the relative value of demonstrational and verbal instruction in learning skills.] (Polh)
Studied the effect of various types of instruction on learning skills of 1,683 Ss aged 4–22 yrs. 333 mentally retarded Ss were included. Skills taught by verbal instruction and demonstration included embroidery, book-binding, assembling puzzles, completing mazes, and making designs out of blocks. Results indicate that the effectiveness of verbal instruction depended on the type of skill to be learned and that the effectiveness of demonstrating a skill depended on the organization of the material. Characteristics of the learner also affected skill acquisition. (English & Russian summaries) (12 ref)
Włodarski, Ziemowit. (U Warsaw, Poland) Psychologia Wychowawcza, 1976(Sep), Vol 19(5), 550–563. [PA, Vol 64:10172]

849. [Peculiarities of grammatical usage in developmentally retarded children.] (Russ)
Studied the ability of retarded children to use some grammatical categories in their active speech. 150 retarded and 30 normal 1st-grade students were given sets of words and pictures and told to construct sentences. To check their ability to understand grammatical structures they were given special sentences with instructions to change them from active to passive voice and explain these changes according to rules of grammar. All assignments were difficult for all children, although normal children performed better. This method can be used along with others to diagnose the level of cognitive development, since it allows one to measure the S's ability to learn and to organize his cognitive activity; these measurements display quantitative and qualitative sides of children's ability to learn. (4 ref)
Yassman, L. V. (USSR Academy of Sciences, Inst of Defectology, Moscow) Defektologiya, 1976(Mar), No 3, 35–43. [PA, Vol 64:10645]

850. Mental retardation, the child and his surroundings: The early detection and stimulation of children in risk of mental retardation caused by socio-cultural factors.
Papers are presented which were delivered at an Extraordinary Session of the International Union for Child Welfare's Advisory Group in the social problems of children and youth in Ostend, Belgium, November 21–25, 1977. Besides introductory and concluding material, 2 studies are given: (1) a psychoanalytic discussion of sociocultural retardation, tracing its causes to privation and loss, anxiety, and the relationship with the Other; and (2) a study of social and educational intervention from infancy to school age for 20 children of retarded mothers (IQ below 80). Much greater intellectual progress was found in the treated children than could be expected from epidemiological data, and comparison with a control group of 20 Ss showed an increase in IQ for the experimental group and a decrease for the control group, especially in the 1st 2 yrs of life.
Advisory Group. (International Union for Child Welfare, Geneva, Switzerland) International Child Welfare Review, 1977, Occ Paper No 1, 56 p. [PA, Vol 63:03493]

851. Television viewing habits of mentally retarded children.
Examined the TV viewing habits of 250 mentally retarded children who were living either in an institution, a hostel for the intellectually handicapped, or at home with their parents. The study attempted to determine whether retarded children watch TV and whether it presents a meaningful learning situation for them. Results indicate that the Ss did watch TV for extended periods of time, especially during the evening meal preparation period. They did not appear either to remember what they had seen for any length of time or to learn much from such activity. The shortcomings of commercially produced programs in relation to the retarded are discussed.
Ahrens, Michael G. & Singh, Nirbhay N. (Mangere Hosp & Training School, Auckland, New Zealand) Australian Journal of Mental Retardation, 1977(Sep), Vol 4(7), 1–3. [PA, Vol 61:08686]

852. Case reports. II: Some interesting case studies of mental subnormality.
Reports on 4 cases of mental retardation in children aged 5, 8, 11, and 14 yrs. Two of the Ss were sibs, an 11-yr-old and a 14-yr-old suspected of having Hunter's syndome. The 4 cases are considered to be of particular interest because they received initial diagnoses, on clinical grounds, of specific disorders until the retardation was revealed by continued close observation. The revised diagnoses were homocystinurias, Hunter's syndrome, and cretinism. The clinical features, laboratory findings, and suggested treatment of each case are described.
Bharucha, M. E. & de Souza, D. A. (Hosp Sion, Bombay, India) Child Psychiatry Quarterly, 1977(Jul), Vol 10(3), 15–18. [PA, Vol 59:10129]

853. A comparison of the Stanford-Binet abbreviated and complete forms for developmentally disabled children.
Three abbreviated versions of the Stanford-Binet Intelligence Scale were reviewed and compared for 50 children with developmental disabilities. Ss' ages were 6 yrs 0 mo to 15 yrs 11 mo. While the IQs obtained from the abbreviated forms correlated highly with the complete Binet IQ, it was felt that the 2-item test yielded too many "misses" both in terms of IQ and classification to be of significant value for use with developmentally disabled children. Although W. A. Terman and M. A. Merrill's (1937) 4-item and C. Wright's (1942) versions both yielded considerable "misses" in classification, they are believed to be of definite value to the time-harried examiner. Caution is advised, however, in the use of abbreviated-form IQs as a basis for important diagnostic decisions.
Bloom, Allan S.; Klee, Steven H. & Raskin, Larry M. (U Louisville Medical School, Child Evaluation Ctr) Journal of Clinical Psychology, 1977(Apr), Vol 33(2), 477–480. [PA, Vol 59:02376]

854. Home Observation for Measurement of the Environment: A validation study of screening efficiency.
Home environments of 91 6-mo-old infants were assessed with the Home Observation for Measurement of the Environment (HOME) Inventory. Multiple discriminant functions composed of the 6 subscale scores from the HOME Inventory were used to predict whether an S would be low IQ (below 70), low average (70 to 89), or average to superior (90 and above) at age 3 yrs. The mean vector of HOME Inventory subscales for the 3 IQ groups was significantly different. Significant univariate effects were observed for 3 HOME Inventory subscales: (a) organization of the physical and temporal environment, (b) provision of appropriate play materials, and (c) maternal involvement with child. The discriminant function of HOME Inventory subscale scores correctly predicted 71% of all Ss who scored below 70 IQ. Results demonstrate the usefulness of the HOME Inventory in a comprehensive program of screening for developmental delay. (15 ref)
Bradley, Robert H. & Caldwell, Bettye M. (U Arkansas, Little Rock) American Journal of Mental Deficiency, 1977(Mar), Vol 81(5), 417–420. [PA, Vol 58:10818]

855. Social competencies in the developmentally disabled: Some suggestions for research and training.
Offers suggestions for the development and instruction of social competencies in developmentally disabled children. The conceptualization of social competencies is based upon the beliefs that (a) effective social functioning involves a complex network of psychological processes, elucidated by cognitive social learning theory; (b) social behaviors occur within a context of frequently changing environmental settings; and (c) effective social functioning requires social behavior patterns to qualitatively change as the child matures. (16 ref)
Brody, Gene H. & Stoneman, Zolinda. (U Georgia) Mental Retardation, 1977(Aug), Vol 15(4), 41–43. [PA, Vol 59:12637]

856. Abuse and neglect as a cause of mental retardation: A study of 140 children admitted to subnormality hospitals in Wiltshire.
A survey of 140 children under age 16 yrs in 2 subnormality hospitals showed that 3% of the children had definitely been rendered mentally handicapped as a consequence of violent abuse, and that a possible maximum of 11% might have been thus rendered mentally handicapped. In 24%, neglect was considered to be a contributory factor in reducing intellectual potential. Impairment of intellect from abuse and neglect, especially in those with "vulnerable" brains due to preexisting abnormality, may be much more common in children than is generally realized. (36 ref)
Buchanan, Ann & Oliver, J. E. (Burderop Hosp, Swindon, England) British Journal of Psychiatry, 1977(Nov), Vol 131, 458–467. [PA, Vol 61:03880]

857.   Effects of preferred stimuli on the free recall of moderately and severely mentally retarded children.
Presented preferred and nonpreferred stimuli to 16 Ss (mean CA 10.84 yrs, mean IQ 39.12) after an empirical determination was made as to whether to classify a particular category of stimuli as preferred or nonpreferred. Preferred stimuli had a significant effect on recall but not on clustering.
Burger, Agnes L. & Erber, Susan C. (New York U) American Journal of Mental Deficiency, 1977(Jan), Vol 81(4), 391-393. [PA, Vol 58:05609]

858.   Performance of retarded adolescents and nonretarded children on the Tower of Hanoi problem.
60 retarded adolescents (MAs 8–11 yrs) and 90 nonretarded children, varying in MA, were presented with 2-disk and 3-disk Tower of Hanoi puzzles, solutions to which require a certain amount of logical foresight. Nonretarded 8–11 yr old Ss performed at close to ceiling on the 2-disk task but had difficulty with the 3-disk task. Retarded groups performed no differently than nonretarded 6- and 7-yr-old Ss. They had some difficulty on the 2-disk task, and very few reached criterion on the 3-disk task. They tended to perseverate in their errors and frequently resorted to game-rule violations. Results supplement a growing body of evidence that retarded people perform many years below MA expectations on tasks requiring foresight and logic.
Byrnes, MaryAnn M. & Spitz, Herman H. (Edward R. Johnstone Training & Research Ctr, Bordentown, NJ) American Journal of Mental Deficiency, 1977(May), Vol 81(6), 561–569. [PA, Vol 59:05890]

859.   Motor skill overlearning effects on retention and relearning by retarded boys.
Used the stabilometer to study the effects that 50, 100, and 150% overlearning had on retention and relearning by 100 mentally retarded boys (mean age 123 mo, mean IQ 47.17) after 8 wks of no practice. All Ss practiced to a learning criterion at which point the learning group stopped. The overlearning groups continued practicing until they attained their designated overlearning levels. 28 Ss were retested for habit strength 24 hrs after reaching criterion. Ss were retested for retention and relearning after 8 wks of no practice. Results show a relationship between overlearning and retention and relearning of a gross-motor skill and support the contention that overlearning is important in retention and relearning by mentally retarded boys. (21 ref)
Chasey, William C. (George Washington U) Research Quarterly, 1977(Mar), Vol 48(1), 41–46. [PA, Vol 61:11156]

860.   The linguistic and cognitive development of mentally retarded children: A review of recent research.
Discusses three approaches to the language behavior and development of retarded children. The first approach is rooted in A. R. Luria's (1961) theory of mental retardation, i.e., that retarded children are characterized by an "inertness" of the verbal system and by a weak connection between this system and the motor system. The second approach represents an extension of Piagetian research to encompass the linguistic and cognitive development of retarded children. Studies employing a third approach, psycholinguistic research, suggest that most mildly and moderately retarded children develop adult-like comprehension of linguistic structures. Advantages of integrating cognitive and linguistic approaches are examined. (40 ref)
Cummins, James. (U Alberta, Ctr for the Study of Mental Retardation, Edmonton, Canada) Mental Retardation Bulletin, 1977, Vol 5(1), 9–29. [PA, Vol 59:12544]

861.   [Study of the physical measurements of mentally handicapped children.] (Fren)
Compared the bodily measurements of 436 retarded children in the Netherlands (300 boys and 136 girls aged 5–16 yrs), who were enrolled in special elementary classes, with norms derived from 12,000 children in regular classes, controlled for age. The retarded group (a) showed greater variability in height and an increased tendency to thinness, especially the boys; (b) were shorter in the upper half of the body; (c) were smaller in thoracic circumference; (d) were markedly smaller in cranial circumfer-

ence; and (e) had less regular pubic development. Thus, the retardates showed consistently more irregularities than the normal group in the measurements taken. (English summary)
de Croock, M. (Inst St-Augustin, École d'Infirmières, Aalst, Belgium) Bulletin de Psychologie Scolaire et d'Orientation, 1977(Jul), Vol 23(3), 139–151. [PA, Vol 60:03305]

862.   Mental abilities of subnormal children.
Used a measure of intelligence (WISC) and divergent production tests and found 2 distinct domains of cognitive functioning for 48 7th–9th grade normal and 46 13–15.9 yr old subnormal (IQs 50–80) children. The emergence of divergent production factors indicates an aspect of intellectual functioning that is not measured by intelligence tests and is independent of the traditional concept of intelligence. A general ability concept was insufficient to describe intellectual functioning in either group. The identification of divergent thinking abilities in the subnormal group suggests a possible narrow approach to the conceptualization of mental abilities in the lower intellectual range. (22 ref)
Delaney, J. O. (National U of Ireland University Coll, Dublin) Irish Journal of Psychology, 1977(Win), Vol 3(3), 181–192. [PA, Vol 62:11226]

863.   [Strategies of learning: A comparative study of normal and mentally retarded children.] (Fren)
In a study with 24 retarded children (average CA, 14.5 yrs; average MA, 10.1 yrs; average IQ, 75.2) and 24 normal children matched for MA with the retarded Ss, it was found that the retarded Ss required significantly longer time to learn simple phrases. (23 ref)
Denhière, Guy. (U Paris VIII, Lab de Psychologie, France) Psychologie Française, 1977(Jan–Jun), Vol 22(1–2), 87–101. [PA, Vol 63:12179]

864.   Classification of reading problems by the Q-technique of factor analysis.
Used the Q-technique of factor analysis to define subtypes of reading problems in terms of performance on 31 tests of rapid reading skills. Ss included a group of 34 children with learning problems, language problems, and mental retardation. Three subgroups were identified within each group by the statistical classification procedure. For the reading group, 1 subgroup was characterized by slow oral word reading, a 2nd by slow auditory–visual letter association, and a 3rd by slow auditory–visual association of words and syllables. The 1st and 2nd subgroups for the mixed group were essentially the same as the 2nd and 3rd subgroups for the reading group, and the 3rd subgroup was characterized by slow visual matching. These results are compared with those of previous investigators, none of whom used multivariate correlational procedures for classifying reading disabilities. It is concluded that the use of statistical classification techniques would greatly facilitate the achievement of a consensus regarding the number and the types of developmental reading disabilities.
Doehring, Donald G. & Hoshko, Irene M. (McGill U, School of Human Communication Disorders, Montreal, Canada) Cortex, 1977(Sep), Vol 13(3), 281–294. [PA, Vol 61:04844]

865.   Sexual interest and activity in adolescents with spina bifida.
Of 63 adolescents with spina bifida, most had had some form of sex education. The source was more often schools and parents than their peers. Sexual interest was almost universally acknowledged and was of a markedly preoccupying nature in about 25% of the cases. Some level of physical intimacy in heterosexual relationships had been established by 18 Ss at some time or another, but males, in particular, were deeply worried about their capacity to establish full sexual relations. A capacity for potency was claimed by about half the males. Worries and uncertainties were very common among the older Ss, and there was a strong need for a program of group and individual counseling to be established.
Dorner, S. (Hosp for Sick Children, London, England) Journal of Child Psychology & Psychiatry & Allied Disciplines, 1977(Aug), Vol 18(3), 229–237. [PA, Vol 60:03348]

866. How does a handicapped child affect the family? Implications for practitioners.

Notes the growing concern for families of the handicapped, with emphasis on the problems of the parents and recognition of the stress created in the family by such a child. The present study was based on data gathered in interviews with 404 families with a developmentally disabled family member. The vast majority of the families interviewed did not perceive the disabled member as having substantial effect on them. Results indicate that the adjustment of family members had been good and indicate no serious consequences to their family. However, the study supports the need for supportive services to ease the demands created by the handicapped person. The types of services perceived by these families as needed are given.
Dunlap, William R. & Hollinsworth, J. Selwyn. (U Alabama Coll of Education) Family Coordinator, 1977(Jul), Vol 26(3), 286–293. [PA, Vol 59:09775]

867. Transfer of associative-clustering tendencies in borderline mentally retarded and nonretarded adolescents.

24 6th graders, 24 7th graders, and 24 borderline mentally retarded special education students (mean CA 165 mo) with MAs roughly equivalent to the 6th graders were randomly assigned to the cells of a 3 (grade level) × 2 (list novelty) × 2 (list organization) factorial design. In the list-novelty condition, Ss were immediately transferred to either a same-categories or a new-categories list on the 3rd and 4th trials. In the list-organization condition, Ss received the lists on the 1st 2 trials in either a random or blocked format. For all Ss, the last 2 trials were presented randomly and contained new words. The results reveal that there was significant negative transfer over trial blocks for the same-categories transfer condition. In addition, the new-categories group clustered significantly more on the 2nd than the 1st trial block. There was no significant interaction between S and treatment factors, suggesting that the processes involved in recall were similar for nonretarded and borderline retarded Ss.
Evans, Ross A. (U Wisconsin, Madison) American Journal of Mental Deficiency, 1977(Mar), Vol 81(5), 482-485. [PA, Vol 58:11910]

868. Use of alternative living plans for developmentally disabled children by minority parents.

Investigated the current use of alternative living plans for developmentally disabled children by various groups of clients eligible for services. The sample consisted of 8,009 Ss, most of whom were mentally retarded, receiving developmental disabilities services in California, Colorado, and Nevada. Results show that the more severe the level of retardation, the more likely the Ss would be found in an institution regardless of race. However, 65% of the moderately and mildly retarded Ss from Black or Spanish-American homes remained with their families in contrast to about 50% of the White Ss. Differences between the groups were even greater for the severely retarded: 60% of the Black or Spanish-American Ss lived at home while only 33% of the White Ss lived at home. Two possible reasons for these findings are presented, and the need for increased communication concerning available community resources is noted.
Eyman, Richard K.; Boroskin, Alan & Hostetter, Sanford. (U California, Neuropsychiatric Inst-Pacific State Hosp Research Group, Pomona) Mental Retardation, 1977(Feb), Vol 15(1), 21-23. [PA, Vol 58:05964]

869. Read-out times from iconic memory in normal and retarded adolescents.

Used the method of limits to obtain an estimate of read-out times for 12 normal and 12 cultural-familial retarded Ss matched for CA (ages 16.73 and 17.27, respectively). The procedure required tachistoscopic presentation of a stimulus array (2, 4, or 6 digits) for a variable duration, followed by a poststimulus cue. The S's task was to recall the digit indicated by the cue. Results indicate that read-out time (a) increased as the number of digits increased, (b) was longer for retardates relative to normals, and (c) decreased with practice for both intelligence groups. The implications of a read-out deficit in retarded individuals are discussed.

Friedrich, Douglas; Libkuman, Terry; Craig, Eugene & Winn, Frank. (Central Michigan U) Perceptual & Motor Skills, 1977(Apr), Vol 44(2), 467–473. [PA, Vol 59:03631]

870. [The use of neuropsychology in genealogical observations of borderline mental retardation.] (Czec)

A neuropsychological study of 3 borderline oligophrenic children and their close family members found in each child and family symptoms of an organic brain syndrome. The view is expressed that borderline mental retardation in families with different organic brain syndromes is due to the mutation of a simple dominant type of heredity. (Russian summary)
Glezerman, T. B. & Frank, V. (Karlova U Medical Faculty, Psychiatric Clinic, Prague, Czechoslovakia) Československá Psychiatrie, 1977(Feb), Vol 73(1), 46–49. [PA, Vol 63:07794]

871. Representational development of the human figure in familial retardates.

Examined representational development of the human figure in 2 groups of Ss matched for MA, socioeconomic status, public school attendance, and intact family structure: (a) 34 3.0–5.10 normal Ss, and (b) 34 4.4–13.1 yr old familially retarded children. Five tasks were employed: drawing a person, figure completion, 2 form puzzles, and drawing on dictation. Results indicate that familial retardates performed as well as normals and at times surpassed them. Performance on these representational tasks was found to be predominantly a function of MA; this finding lends support to a "developmental" theory of familial retardation and refutes the "defect" hypothesis. (28 ref)
Golomb, Claire & Barr-Grossman, Tracy. (U Massachusetts, Boston Harbor Campus) Genetic Psychology Monographs, 1977(May), Vol 95(2), 247–266. [PA, Vol 59:05897]

872. IQ decline in mentally retarded adults: A matter of fact of methodological flaw.

While it has generally been assumed that intelligence in the retarded decreases with age, the institutional research supporting this premise, whether cross-sectional or longitudinal, is methodologically flawed by selective sample attrition. This paper demonstrated that in an institutional population of 284 patients, those leaving, at every age level, were indeed the brightest (as assessed by the WAIS). When the IQ data was viewed cross-sectionally there was the appearance of decline, but when the same population was studied semi-longitudinally, not ony was there no decrease in IQ with age but there were regular increments, particularly in performance scores.
Goodman, Joan F. (U Pennsylvania, Graduate School of Education) Journal of Mental Deficiency Research, 1977(Sep), Vol 21(3), 199–203. [PA, Vol 61:03888]

873. Medical diagnosis and intelligence levels in young mentally retarded children: A follow-up study.

The relationship of diagnosis to initial and subsequent intelligence test levels in 282 young retarded children was investigated through repeated psychometric evaluation on the Bayley Infant Scales of Mental Development or the Stanford-Binet. It was found that although etiology related to 1st test scores (or rate of initial progress), it had no bearing on changes in scores (or course of development). The implications of the surprisingly stable scores for this heterogeneous population are discussed. (28 ref)
Goodman, Joan F. (U Pennsylvania, Graduate School of Education) Journal of Mental Deficiency Research, 1977(Sep), Vol 21(3), 205–212. [PA, Vol 61:03887]

874. Stereotypic attitudes and behavioral intentions toward handicapped children.

56 junior high school pupils were questioned about their attitudes toward mentally retarded and crippled children. Same- and opposite-sex ratings of stereotypes and behavioral intentions were obtained through use of 2 questionnaires—an adjective checklist and a social-distance scale. Results indicate a significant main effect for handicap condition, with stereotypic attitudes toward the crippled child being more favorable than attitudes toward the mentally retarded child. No differences in attitudes toward the 2 handicapping conditions emerged on the measure of behavioral intentions. Sex of S and sex of handicapped child being rated did

not significantly affect attitude scores. The data are discussed in relation to the many methodological difficulties encountered in attitude research toward handicapped populations. (17 ref)
Gottlieb, Jay & Gottlieb, Barbara W. (Nero & Assoc, Rosslyn, VA) American Journal of Mental Deficiency, 1977(Jul), Vol 82(1), 65–71. [PA, Vol 59:11053]

875. **Aspects of auditory and visual attention to narrative material in normal and mentally handicapped children.**
Estimates of auditory and visual attention to narrative material presented on a video system were obtained from 1 group of normal and 2 groups of mentally retarded children (mean CA 4.8, 12.7, and 14.8 yrs, respectively). Visual attention was relatively high, and consistently so across time. In comprehension tests, success was greatest on items that could be answered from visual attention alone, then on items that could be answered from either visual or auditory attention, then on items that could be answered from auditory attention alone. Implications for remedial work with retarded children and for techniques in basic research with normal children are discussed. (29 ref)
Grieve, Robert & Williamson, Kay. (U of St Andrews, Psychological Lab, Scotland) Journal of Child Psychology & Psychiatry & Allied Disciplines, 1977(Aug), Vol 18(3), 251–262. [PA, Vol 60:03314]

876. **Effects of instructional set and self-awareness on task performance of retarded female adults.**
Studied the effects of success, failure, and neutral instructional sets on the task performance of 90 17-36 yr old mentally retarded females (mean IQ 62) under varying conditions of self-awareness. Results show a significant Set × Self Awareness interaction where Ss in the neutral-set condition under high-awareness assembled more pens than Ss under the medium- or low-awareness conditions.
Guarnaccia, Vincent J. & Slis, Vikki. (Hofstra U) American Journal of Mental Deficiency, 1977(Mar), Vol 81(5), 504-507. [PA, Vol 58:11913]

877. **The effects of social reinforcement and task difficulty level on the pleasure derived by normal and retarded children from cognitive challenge and mastery.**
To examine several factors influencing the pleasure derived from mastery, 32 normal 1st graders (mean MA 7.7) and 32 MA-matched familial mentally retarded children were given puzzles representing 4 difficulty levels. Half of the Ss were socially reinforced for their successes, and half performed in an experimenter (E)-absent condition. There was more smiling among normal than retarded Ss, in the social reinforcement than in the E-absent condition, and among girls than boys. The condition effect was greater for girls than boys. In the E-absent condition, normal Ss displayed more pleasure on the difficult than on the easy puzzles, whereas the trend was just the reverse for the retarded Ss. Large within-sex differences were found for normal girls only, revealing that one subgroup derived more pleasure from the more difficult puzzles whereas another subgroup enjoyed the easier puzzles more. Findings are discussed in terms of the author's refinement of R. W. White's (1959) model of effectance motivation. (17 ref)
Harter, Susan. (U Denver) Journal of Experimental Child Psychology, 1977(Dec), Vol 24(3), 476–494. [PA, Vol 60:09574]

878. **Comparability of WISC and Peabody IQs of young children from three heterogeneous groups.**
Peabody Picture Vocabulary Test and WISC IQs of 3 groups of children from differing socioeconomic status (SES) levels and/or intellectual levels were compared. For the total sample of 67, correlations of .88, .88, and .91 were obtained between the Peabody and WISC Verbal, Performance, and Full Scale IQs, respectively. The Peabody IQs correlated .74 with the WISC Full Scale for the middle-range of intelligence (kindergarten). Those of higher SES in a child study center showed the highest correlation .57 between Peabody and WISC Performance Scale IQs. For more deprived children from Headstart, IQs on the Peabody and WISC Verbal Scale correlated .63.

Hatch, Gary L. & Covin, Theron M. (Auburn U) Psychological Reports, 1977(Jun), Vol 40(3, Pt 2), 1345–1346. [PA, Vol 59:10157]

879. **Developmental auditory agnosia in retarded adolescents: A preliminary investigation.**
Four 12–18 yr old mentally retarded adolescents who showed little or no expressive or receptive language were given a series of tests to determine if they could respond to meaningful nonlinguistic sounds. The tests required the Ss to respond to sounds on the basis of meaning by classifying the sounds according to the objects which produced them (i.e., the sound sources). Results show that the Ss could not classify the sounds on the basis of their source, although they could discriminate between them. These results are in contrast to the near perfect classification by another retarded S who lacked speech due to a motor disorder but, nevertheless, showed good understanding of language. The finding that some nonverbal children have difficulty in responding to the meaning of nonlinguistic sounds suggests the possibility that the failure of these children to develop language may have been due to an agnosia not unlike that found in adult stroke patients. (21 ref)
Heffner, Rickye S. (Parsons State Hosp & Research Ctr, KS) Brain & Language, 1977(Oct), Vol 4(4), 521–536. [PA, Vol 60:07677]

880. **The art of the retarded.**
Notes the importance of the quality of expressiveness in children's art, particularly that of the mentally retarded. Relationships between this art and the work of such artists as P. Picasso, J. Pollock, and E. Munch are discussed.
Hilgendorf, Myra. (Art Project for the Mentally Retarded, Melbourne, Australia) Australian Journal of Mental Retardation, 1977(Jun), Vol 4(6), 22–25. [PA, Vol 59:10158]

881. **Communication style and effectiveness in homogeneous and heterogeneous dyads of retarded children.**
Investigated the channels, styles, and successfulness of communication used by retarded children when teaching a simple board game to a listener of similar or dissimilar age and ability to themselves. 40 children, half of high level and half of low level (means MAs 6.6 and 3.7 yrs; mean CAs 15.5 and 11.2 yrs, respectively) instructed a naive listener either at their own or at the other level, after they had been taught the game by the experimenter. Both high- and low-level speakers altered their channels and styles of communication to low-level listeners along the dimensions found by M. Shatz and R. Gelman (see PA, Vol 53:7048) with nonretarded children. However, the communication shifts, particularly those produced by high-level speakers, were ineffective in producing listener understanding. It is concluded that communication-skills training for retarded children must be concentrated not only on the linguistic form, but also on the functional appropriateness of the children's utterances.
Hoy, E. A. & McKnight, J. R. (Queen's U, Belfast, Northern Ireland) American Journal of Mental Deficiency, 1977(May), Vol 81(6), 587–598. [PA, Vol 59:05903]

882. **Assessing social and prevocational awareness in mildly and moderately retarded individuals.**
Revised the Social and Prevocational Information Battery—a series of knowledge tests developed for use with mildly retarded adolescents—to facilitate assessment of moderately retarded persons' knowledge in social and prevocational areas. In addition, the relationship between knowledge and applied performance in these domains was examined. Two samples consisted of 287 group-home residents aged 15–65 yrs, and 200 students (mean CA range 17–19 yrs) in school programs for the trainable mentally retarded. 40% of the IQs obtained for Ss in the group home sample were in the 30–60 range; 80% of obtained IQs in the school sample were in that range. Results indicate that the revised battery demonstrated adequate test, item, and internal-consistency reliability and that mildly and moderately retarded persons' knowledge was substantially related to applied performance in these skill domains.

Irvin, Larry K.; Halpern, Andrew S. & Reynolds, William M. (U Oregon, Rehabilitation Research & Training Ctr in Mental Retardation) American Journal of Mental Deficiency, 1977(Nov), Vol 82(3), 266–272. [PA, Vol 61:02632]

883. The nature and process of development in averaged visually evoked potentials: Discussion on pattern structure.
Reports on trends in research and the results of the authors' recent experiments on the development of averaged visually evoked potential (AVEP) in normal and mentally retarded children. AVEPs with closed eyes and open eyes are discussed separately, because the CNS reacts differently under the 2 conditions; with eyes open, attention is paid to the stimulus. The developmental process of AVEP in both occipital and central areas is examined in Ss 3 yrs and older, including the mentally retarded. As expected, retarded children had an abnormal AVEP pattern development. Assuming that there was no conspicuous obstruction in the visual system itself, the implication is that the functional development of the nonspecific projection system was poor. (37 ref)
Izawa, Shuji & Mizutani, Tohru. (Tokyo Gakugei U, Research Inst for the Education of Exceptional Children, Japan) RIEEC Research Bulletin, 1977(Feb), No 6, 21 p. [PA, Vol 64:01311]

884. Appropriateness of the motor-free visual perception test when used with the mentally retarded.
Investigated the validity and reliability of the Motor-Free Visual Perception Test (MVPT) when used with mentally retarded (MR) Ss. 46 MR 6–8 yr old children's MVPT scores were correlated with CA, IQ, achievement ranking, and the Matching and Copying subtests of the Metropolitan Readiness Tests. Low-magnitude nonsignificant correlations were obtained for CA and achievement, while significant high magnitude correlations were found for IQ, Matching, and Copying. A reliability coefficient of .81 was obtained. Results support the use of the MVPT with MR Ss.
Johnson, D. LaMont; Brekke, Beverly & Harlow, Steven D. (U North Dakota) Education & Training of the Mentally Retarded, 1977(Dec), Vol 12(4), 312–315. [PA, Vol 61:05138]

885. Investigation of the WISC-R for use with retarded children: Correlation with the 1972 Stanford-Binet and comparison of WISC and WISC-R profiles.
Administered the WISC-R to 80 mentally retarded 6–16 yr olds to assess the continuity of measurement between the old and new WISCs. The WISC-R IQs correlated .65–.82 with Stanford-Binet Intelligence Scale IQ for a subsample of 45 Ss, resembling the coefficients between the 1949 WISC and the Binet for retarded groups. In addition, the WISC-R test profiles for the 80 Ss corresponded closely to the WISC test profiles for many retarded samples. Thus, there is evidence to support the continutiy of the WISC-R with its predecessor for retarded populations.
Kaufman, Alan S. & Van Hagen, John. (U Georgia) Psychology in the Schools, 1977(Jan), vol 14(1), 10–14. [PA, Vol 58:04627]

886. The measurement of motor, visual and auditory discrimination skills in mentally retarded children and adults and in young normal chilren.
Investigated the development and dynamics of basic discrimination learning in (a) 117 mildly to profoundly retarded 3–36 yr olds, and (b) 42 physically and mentally intact 13–35 mo old children. The motor, visual, and auditory discrimination skills of all Ss were measured via the AVC Scale—a newly developed behavioral instrument encompassing 6 increasingly difficult nonlanguage tasks. Order analyses of the retarded Ss' performance showed that the order of task difficulty was stable, and that none of those with greater than mild retardation successfully completed a speech discrimination task. Related generalization experiments revealed a positive relationship between AVC performance and the performance of various classroom activities. In the normal Ss, language production was positively associated with AVC performance. These relationships can be partially interpreted within the context of Piagetian theory. Application of the AVC Scale seems to hold potential for the development of educational interventions, training programs for the retarded,

and for the prediction and facilitation of manual sign learning among deaf retarded adults. (50 ref)
Kerr, Nancy et al. (Arizona State U, Tempe) Rehabilitation Psychology, 1977, Vol 24(3, Pt 1–2), 91–206. [PA, Vol 66:03872]

887. Application of Piaget's theory to the study of thinking of the mentally retarded: A review of research.
Notes that the developmental theory of Piaget describes intellectual growth, from sensorimotor intelligence through adult logic, and although Piaget has not dealt with mentally retarded (MR) persons per se, his theory has been applied to that population by many researchers. Results of investigations into this application of Piaget's stage theory of development indicate that the stages of development in the MR parallel those described by Piaget but appear at later chronological periods. Because of the tremendous variability in cognitive MR task performance within IQ categories, it is suggested that identification of specific aspects of concept learning holds promise for enhancing the school performance of MR children through individualized instruction. (3½ p ref)
Klein, Nancy K. & Safford, Philip L. (Cleveland State U) Journal of Special Education, 1977(Sum), Vol 11(2), 201–216. [PA, Vol 59:10164]

888. Adoption agency services for the retarded.
Surveyed current attitudes of adoption agencies on adoption of mentally retarded individuals. Data from 100 replies to a mailed questionnaire sent to a random sample of adoption agencies throughout the US show that the adoption agencies hold exceedingly positive attitudes, indicated by their policies and practices regarding adoption placements for retarded children.
Krisheff, Curtis H. (Florida State U School of Social Work) Mental Retardation, 1977(Feb), Vol 15(1), 38–39. [PA, Vol 58:05997]

889. The Prader-Willi Syndrome.
Cites the Prader-Willi syndrome, which was identified in the mid-1950's by Prader, Lobhart, and Willi, as a case in which it is difficult to determine whether physical or intellectual characteristics are the cause of mental retardation. The syndrome is identified in males through the characteristic of underdeveloped genitalia. Although the children's delayed development is generally complicated by obesity and hypotonia, it is likely that heterogeneity does exist among cases of this syndrome. No real incidence figures have been established, but it is suggested that they lie between 1/100,000 and 1/1,000,000. No final conclusions about the etiology of the syndrome have been reached; however, some evidence suggests that it may result from a disturbance in the hypothalamus or hypothalamic-pituitary unit.
Krywaniuk, L. (U British Columbia, Vancouver, Canada) Mental Retardation Bulletin, 1977, Vol 5(1), 30–33. [PA, Vol 59:12553]

890. [Perseveration responses and discrimination learning among mentally retarded subjects.] (Fren)
Describes perseverative response patterns in the discriminative learning of retarded children. Strategies based on stimulus and position were found to be independent, and dominant error factors observed in an S during a discrimination task were present on initial trials. Response latencies of learners are significantly higher than those of nonlearners (i.e., Ss who exhibited perseverative patterns). In Part 2 of the study the effects of 3 methods of elimination were compared: prolonged exposure on the task, use of a time-out from positive reinforcement, and errorless procedures. Mechanisms that could explain the development of perseverative error patterns in retarded children are discussed. (French & English summaries) (29 ref)
Lambert, J.-L. (U Liège Lab de Psychologie Expérimentale, Belgium) Enfance, 1977(Oct–Dec), No 4–5, 425–446. [PA, Vol 60:03317]

891. Sequential contrast effects with retarded subjects after discrimination learning with and without errors.
In Exp I, 4 retarded adults (CA 25–43 yrs, IQ 30–47) were exposed to a multiple VI-extinction schedule of reinforcement in which the 2-min components were presented in a random order. Two Ss acquired the discrimination with an errorless procedure,

while the 2 other Ss learned the discrimination with errors. The schedule generated sequential contrast effects under both training procedures: response rates during periods of reinforcement were higher when a reinforcement period followed an extinction period than when it followed another reinforcement period. These results were confirmed in Exp II in which 8 male 7-13 yr old retarded children were exposed to a multiple FR-extinction schedule of reinforcement. This study appears to be the first demonstration of sequential contrast effects with human Ss during the acquisition of a discrimination without errors. The results are discussed in terms of H. S. Terrace's theory of errorless learning. (19 ref)
Lambert, Jean-Luc. (Lab of Experimental Psychology, Liege, Belgium) British Journal of Psychology, 1977(Feb), Vol 68(1), 77-83. [PA, Vol 58:11916]

892. **Frequency judgments of nonretarded and retarded individuals.**
Two experiments tested the hypothesis derived from an extended version of frequency theory that retarded individuals, relative to MA-matched normals, are not as accurate in their ability to detect differences in frequency. The method of constant stimuli was used to obtain an estimate of the difference thresholds based on normative word frequency in Exp I and experimentally manipulated trigram frequency in Exp II. Ss were 18 retarded children (mean CA 11.94 yrs, mean MA 8.43 yrs) and 22 MA-matched normals in Exp I, and 18 retarded children (mean CA 12.91 yrs, mean MA 7.93 yrs) and 18 MA-matched normals in Exp II. Results from Exp I support the notion that retarded individuals are not as sensitive to differences in frequency as MA-matched normals. In Exp II, however, the differences in performance between the groups disappeared. Results indicate that the retarded individual can use the frequency cue as effectively as the normal individual and that the differences reported in Exp I simply reflected the inadequacy of the Thorndike and Lorge (1944) word frequency norms for normal and retarded children. Results are also discussed within the context of a frequency theory analysis of discrimination learning by the retarded.
Libkuman, Terry M.; Friedrich, Douglas D.; Holland, Michael K. & Beno, Fred P. (Central Michigan U) Psychological Reports, 1977(Feb), Vol 40(1), 199-206. [PA, Vol 58:05629]

893. **Sources of variation in clinicians' communication to parents about mental retardation.**
Based on data from the authors' previous study (1976), sources of variation in 14 clinicians' diagnostic communication to parents of 37 mentally retarded children were identified and examined. Results demonstrate that the nature of clinicians' communication was related to the severity of the child's diagnosis, clinicians' perception of the parents' level of emotional adjustment, whether the clinicians experienced difficulties in communicating the diagnosis, and their length of clinical experience in the field of developmental disabilities. The dynamics of these relationships are discussed, as are their implications for future research and for needed changes in the current priority structure of medical education. (26 ref)
Lipton, Helene L. & Svarstad, Bonnie. American Journal of Mental Deficiency, 1977(Sep), Vol 82(2), 155-161. [PA, Vol 60:05847]

894. **Delay of gratification: Decisional self-control and experience with delay intervals.**
Obtained actual and verbally reported decisional self-control choices (e.g., 1 penny now or 2 pennies in 1 min) from 40 retarded adolescents who participated in a sheltered workshop. Prior to each of their 8 choices, half of the Ss experienced the same time interval that was included in the choice for that day (e.g., 1 min). Analysis of the number of actual and reported delay choices yielded a significant effect for experience, with the treatment group making more delay choices. In addition to suggesting that decisional self-control can be facilitated by prior exposure to delay intervals, the results indicate that verbally reported choices can be used as a reliable and valid indication of actual choices.

Litrownik, Alan J.; Franzini, Louis R.; Geller, Sanford & Geller, Marilyn. (San Diego State U) American Journal of Mental Deficiency, 1977(Sep), Vol 82(2), 149-154. [PA, Vol 60:05470]

895. **Encoding and high-speed memory scanning of retarded and nonretarded adolescents.**
Conducted a choice RT experiment to assess the encoding and memory-scanning processes of nonretarded and retarded adolescents. Ss were 6 7th graders and 6 special-education students (mean CA 14.2 yrs, mean IQ 72.4). Random forms were used as stimuli, with stimulus-set sizes of 2, 3, and 4. The encoding process was evaluated by means of a stimulus-quality manipulation. Results indicate that both the rate of encoding and memory scanning were related to level of intellectual functioning. In addition, evidence suggesting an interdependence of these memory processes, at least for the retarded Ss, was revealed. (21 ref)
Maisto, Albert A. & Jerome, Margaret A. (U North Carolina, Charlotte) American Journal of Mental Deficiency, 1977(Nov), Vol 82(3), 282-286. [PA, Vol 61:03899]

896. **Rhythmic habit patterns (stereotypies).**
A review of the literature indicates that rhythmic movements, such as head-rolling, head-banging, and body-rocking are seen in normal children in early life, but much more commonly in the mentally handicapped. Emotional disturbance and boredom tend to increase the movements. Various theories have been advanced to account for these stereotyped patterns. They appear to be intentional and may satisfy some inner need or allay frustration, but it is concluded that their true significance is unknown. (French, German & Spanish summaries) (28 ref)
Mitchell, Ross G. & Etches, Philip. (Ninewells Hosp & Medical School, Dundee, Scotland) Developmental Medicine & Child Neurology, 1977(Aug), Vol 19(4), 545-550. [PA, Vol 60:03279]

897. **[The experimental roles of reinforcing agent in adult-child interaction.]** (Finn)
Investigated (a) whether predetermined roles of the reinforcing agent can be produced in adult-child interaction; (b) what phenomena and changes in the child's behavior can be found during role performance; and (c) whether effects of the role on the child could be distinguished in a separate social reinforcement test after interaction. Two types of role, the rewarding agent and the punishing agent, were presented to 2 groups of lower-class children: 4-6 yr old nursery school Ss and 8-13 yr old mildly and moderately mentally retarded children (MA 4-8 yrs). Role performance was observed, and Ss' responses to agents' initiatives were classified as positive or antagonistic. Results indicate that (a) role behavior of adults was relatively stable over several days and across different partners; (b) the regulated behaviors in the role were related to the quality of interaction. The latter was also characterized by the developmental level, previous habits, and skills of the group and individual Ss. When the roles in the group experiments were compared with the reinforcing behavior of teachers in 2 other nurseries and of nurses in the institution, the teachers' behavior was found to be more like that of the rewarding agent than that of the punishing agent. However, the reinforcing behavior of the nurses was seen as more like that of the punishing agent than that of the rewarding agent. Results of the social reinforcement show few changes that could be interpreted as reinforcement effects. (12 p ref)
Nupponen, Ritva. Jyväskylä Studies in Education, Psychology & Social Research, 1977, No 34, 209 p. [PA, Vol 59:13265]

898. **Psychopathology and mental retardation: A statistical study of 100 mentally retarded children treated at a psychiatric clinic: II. Hyperactivity.**
In a study with 100 mentally retarded children referred to a psychiatric clinic, 39 were found to be hyperactive. However, there was no significant relationship between hyperactivity and mental retardation (with or without psychosis) or brain damage. Comparison with a group of 79 nonretarded children revealed no significant difference regarding hyperactivity, thus suggesting

that the disorder is not an inevitable concomitant of mental retardation.

Philips, Irving & Williams, Nancy. (U California Medical School, San Francisco) American Journal of Psychiatry, 1977(Apr), Vol 134(4), 418–419. [PA, Vol 58:11923]

899. Cardiac and respiratory responses during visual search in nonretarded children and retarded adolescents.
Investigated the relationship between physiological response patterns and mental competence by evaluating heart rate and respiratory responses during a sustained visual-search task in 29 nonretarded 5–8 yr olds and retarded 8–26 yr olds. Results support the contention that during tasks demanding sustained attention, retarded individuals, when compared to nonretarded individuals, exhibit physiological responses that parallel their poor performance. Consistent with previous research with nonretarded adults, the nonretarded Ss exhibited a suppression of respiratory and heart-rate variability during attention-demanding tasks. In contrast, the retarded Ss exhibited increases in respiratory and heart-rate variability. These qualitative differences in physiological and behavioral responses, observed during sustained attention, may be viewed as a manifestation of retarded adolescents' defective nervous system. (20 ref)
Porges, Stephen W. & Humphrey, Mary M. (U Illinois) American Journal of Mental Deficiency, 1977(Sep), Vol 82(2), 162–169. [PA, Vol 60:05476]

900. Activity level of mentally retarded individuals: Do they reflect the circadian rhythm?
Examined the effects of circadian variation on the activity level of 69 educable mentally retarded (EMR) and 51 trainable mentally retarded (TMR) 7–16 yr olds in a retardation center. An ultrasonic recording device was used to obtain samples of the general bodily activity level of the Ss. Specifically, activity level as a function of time-of-day (AM vs PM), day-of-week, sex, and educational placement (EMR vs TMR) was examined. Results show significant differences between males and females, with males being more highly active. Findings also show significant differences between EMRs and TMRs, with TMRs being more highly active. PM activity was consistently greater than AM activity for all Ss. Additionally, significant Sex × Time-of-Day interaction was found, indicating that the PM increases in activity were greater for males than females. Substrates for the observed findings are discussed. (18 ref)
Ray, A. Bartow; Shotick, Andrew L. & Peacock, L. J. (State University Coll New York, Brockport) Australian Journal of Mental Retardation, 1977(Mar), Vol 4(5), 18–21. [PA, Vol 60:07690]

901. Reducing responding of retarded persons by DRO schedules following a history of low-rate responding: A comparison of ascending interval sizes.
To assess the reductive effects of stimuli associated with different initial DRO (differential reinforcement of other behavior) values in a program with increasing DRO intervals, a 2-phase experiment was conducted in a laboratory setting with 3 moderately retarded Ss aged 10–18 yrs (IQ range 40–60). In the 1st phase, Ss responded under a 4-ply DRL multiple schedule. In the 2nd phase, they responded under a different multiple schedule [mult (DRO$_1$) (DRO$_2$) (DRO$_3$) (DRL)] in which the initial values of the 3 DRO components were 1, 12, and 20 sec. Upon criterion responding, values were increased along a series of 1, 2, 6, 12, 20, 30, 42, 56, and 72 sec. Results of Phase 2 indicate that (a) there were fewer total responses in the DRO$_1$ component than in the other components for all Ss, and fewer responses in the DRO$_2$ than in the DRO$_3$ component for 2 Ss; (b) the reductive effects of the DRO components transferred to the DRL component; (c) response rates tended to increase initially when the DRO interval was increased for a component; (d) the order of efficiency in establishing schedule control was DRO$_1$-DRO$_2$-DRO$_3$; and (e) a prior history on DRO schedules with small values may have resulted in reduced responding under DRO schedules with higher values. Results are discussed in terms of factors which can affect the success of DRO schedules in reducing responding.

Repp, Alan C. & Slack, Daniel J. (Northern Illinois U) Psychological Record, 1977(Sum), Vol 27(3), 581–588. [PA, Vol 60:05646]

902. The relationship between auditory and visual perception on tasks employing Piaget's concept of conservation.
Attempted to develop a cognitive assessment tool using music. Applying Piaget's developmental theory, 2 auditory conservation tasks were designed and tested: conservation of rhythm and conservation of tempo, each requiring the S to maintain simultaneous attention to 2 auditory stimuli under varied temporal conditions. Ss were 40 developmentally disabled children 7–13 yrs old. The 2 tasks were multiply correlated (using the phi coefficient) with the 2 standardized visual conservation tasks: conservation of area and of continuous volume. All correlations between any 2 tasks were positive and significant. The order of acquisition of the tasks was also significant: Conservation of rhythm occurred first, then conservation of area, volume, and tempo.
Rider, Mark S. (Southern Methodist U) Journal of Music Therapy, 1977(Fal), Vol 14(3), 126–138. [PA, Vol 63:01068]

903. [Maternal linguistic environment and mental retardation.] (Fren)
Reinterprets several studies on maternal linguistic environment and the language learning of mentally retarded children, and presents some original data. It is concluded that maternal communication with the retarded child is not impoverished or otherwise deficient, as several authors have claimed on the basis of improper interpretation of their findings. Maternal speech to the retarded child appears to be appropriate in all respects for language development. Nevertheless, it is both possible and desired to improve the efficiency of maternal speech for faster language development of the child. Several recent approaches to such improvement are discussed. (2½ p ref)
Rondal, Jean A. (U Liège, Lab de Psychologie Expérimentale, Belgium) Enfance, 1977(Jan–Apr), No 1, 37–48. [PA, Vol 60:07691]

904. [Language development and mental retardation: A review of the studies that used the Illinois Test of Psycholinguistic Abilities with mentally retarded children.] (Fren)
This review includes a chart summarizing Ss and results of 11 studies conducted from 1964 to 1974 that used the ITPA to assess mentally retarded Ss. Although a proper interpretation of the data remains difficult due to some persistent methodological problems with the ITPA, results suggest the possibility of a specific deficit in the automatic sequencing aspects of the retarded individual's psycholinguistic functioning. (48 ref)
Rondal, Jean A. (U Liège, Lab de Psychologie Expérimentale, Belgium) Psychologica Belgica, 1977, Vol 17(1), 24–34. [PA, Vol 61:02665]

905. [Mental inertia in children as an object of clinical research.] (Polh)
Suggests that the 2 basic problems confronting researchers in the area of psychological functioning are terminology and indicators of deviations from the norm. It is recommended that the term "mental inertia" be used instead of "borderline" or "mental retardation," and that methods other than quantitative be used to determine the degree of deviation. (English & Russian summaries) (21 ref)
Roskiewicz, Iwona. (Adam Mićkiewicz U, Poznań, Poland) Psychologia Wychowawcza, 1977(May–Jun), Vol 20(3), 263–273. [PA, Vol 64:12751]

906. Role of short-term memory in the interaction between the individual and the environment.
Ruisel, Imrich. (Slovak Academy of Sciences, Inst of Experimental Psychology, Bratislava, Czechoslovakia) Activitas Nervosa Superior, 1977, Vol 19(4), 267–268. [PA, Vol 62:11248]

907. Certain variables affecting short-term memory in children.
Studied organizational strategies (e.g., use of cues, rehearsal), the serial position effect of length of exposure on recall, and the correlation between memory performance and item recognition

in 15 normal (mean IQ 102) and 15 retarded (mean IQ 72) 8–10 yr olds (Exps I–III) and in 30 normal (mean IQ 98) and 30 retarded (mean IQ 70) 8–12 yr olds (Exp IV). Findings demonstrate that the normal Ss' higher level of intellectual ability was shown more clearly in the more complex memory tasks. As the tasks were made more difficult (e.g., by enforced retention of information over a longer time span), the performance of the retarded Ss deteriorated considerably, even though their performance on the same tasks in simpler versions was identical to that of the normal Ss. Implications of the results for psychodiagnostic practices are discussed. (Slovak & Russian summaries)
Ruisel, Imrich. (Slovak Academy of Sciences, Inst of Experimental Psychology, Bratislava, Czechoslovakia) Studia Psychologica, 1977, Vol 19(3), 242–247. [PA, Vol 61:03906]

908.   [Correlation between various forms of serial positional effect and short term memory in children.] (Slok)
Series of random digits were presented to 16 mentally retarded and 16 mentally intact 8–10 yr olds at 3 rates: 3 items/sec, 1 item/sec, and 1 item/3 sec. Results show that performance was best at a rate of 3 items/sec in both groups and that it was worst at 1 item/3 sec in the retarded group. In the retarded Ss, the recency effect predominated over the primacy effect at all rates, which indicates an insufficiency in the rehearsal mechanism. (Russian & English summaries) (36 ref)
Ruisel, Imrich   & Droppová, Zdena. (Slovak Academy of Sciences, Inst of Experimental Psychology, Bratislava, Czechoslovakia) Československá Psychologie, 1977, Vol 21(3), 225–234. [PA, Vol 65:03531]

909.   Mothers' and graduate trainees' judgments of children: Some effects of labeling.
20 graduate students in a clinical practicum in mental retardation and 6 mothers randomly chosen from a university community were asked to rate retarded and nonretarded children on characteristics reflecting social competence and interpersonal attractiveness and also on a social distance scale. Mean CA range of the 4 retarded and 2 nonretarded Ss was 18-60 mo. The children were viewed on videotape in free-play interactions with their mothers. Each retarded child was shown once as an unlabeled child and once as a child labeled retarded. Mothers rated the retarded children as different from the nonretarded children on 6 of 9 measures, regardless of label. When the retarded children were labeled, they were rated by mothers as significantly higher on items related to attractiveness than when they were unlabeled. Students' ratings did not discriminate between retarded children as a function of labeling, with one exception: Like mothers, students rated retarded children as more likable when labeled. Both observer groups, however, placed retarded children, regardless of status, significantly farther from themselves on the social distance scale than they placed nonretarded children. Results are interpreted within the theoretical frameworks of E. Zigler (1971) and J. R. Mercer (1973).
Seitz, Sue & Geske, David. (U Wisconsin) American Journal of Mental Deficiency, 1977(Jan), Vol 81(4), 362-370. [PA, Vol 58:05634]

910.   A study of some conditions relating to the retarded adult's stereotyped responding in a binary-choice task.
Examined the effects of certain conditions on alternation and perseveration in a binary-choice task using 8 17–27 yr old retarded Ss. The conditions included lapse of time (stability of the pattern), stimulus dissimilarity, spatial location of the 2 alternatives, timeout (time away from the task), delay between responses, and differential reinforcement of the 2 choices. The Ss were identified as "pure" alternaters or perseveraters. Perseveration was "disrupted" only by differential reinforcement. Alternation was affected by all experimental manipulations except stimulus dissimilarity. (19 ref)
Siegel, Paul S.; Sawczyn, William & Passman, Richard H. (U Alabama, University) Intelligence, 1977(Apr), Vol 1(2), 208–217. [PA, Vol 61:11166]

911.   [Socialization in normal students, slow learners, and mental retardates.] (Span)
Investigated the socialization patterns of 6–12 yr olds, using the Adaptive and Social Skills (AHS-1) and Disruptive Behavior (ETC-1) scales with 940 normal students, 476 slow learners, and 134 mental retardates. Results indicate that differences in both positive and negative socialization patterns existed between mental retardates and the other 2 groups. Mental retardates exhibited higher occurrence of anti-social behaviors. Results are discussed with their implications to educational procedures and policies. (English summary)
Silva, Fernando; Lopez de Silva, M. Cristina & Pelechano, Vicente. (U de La Laguna, Tenerife, Canary Islands) Análisis y Modificación de Conducta, 1977, Vol 3(4), 89–110. [PA, Vol 61:11168]

912.   Physical stigma and academic performance as factors affecting children's first impressions of handicapped peers.
Studied the effects of 4 variables on attitudes toward mentally retarded children: the sex and social status of the rater and the physical appearance and academic competence of the target child being rated. 72 normal 4th and 5th graders rated audiotapes and photographs of normal and retarded children. Results indicate that competent and physically nonstigmatized children were rated more favorably than incompetent and physically stigmatized children. The data also reveal that girls had a significantly more positive stereotype than did boys of a competent male target child but that boys were more willing to be in physical proximity to the male target child as measured by a social distance scale. Finally, the results indicate that popular Ss rated the attractive and competent target child less favorably than Ss who were not so popular. However, the popular Ss rated the attractive and incompetent target child more favorably than the less popular Ss did. The findings are discussed in terms of the salience of physical labels (i.e., stigma) on attitudes toward children. (16 ref)
Siperstein, Gary N. & Gottlieb, Jay. (U Massachusetts, Boston) American Journal of Mental Deficiency, 1977(Mar), Vol 81(5), 455-462. [PA, Vol 58:11926]

913.   Deficient acquisition strategies: A proposed conceptual framework for analyzing severe language deficiency.
Proposes a conceptual framework for analyzing aberrant or retarded language development. Recent developments in psycholinguistics have led to a view of language acquisition as an interactive process involving external interactions between child and environment and internal interactions between cognitive holdings and processes. The child's active participation in these interactions is conceptualized as a system of language-acquisition strategies. These consist of both information-gathering strategies and information-processing strategies and are distinguished from the adult speaker's facilitation strategies. It is suggested that aberrant or retarded language development may be viewed in terms of specific process deficits in one or more of these strategy systems. In the present article, 3 preverbal information-gathering strategies identified as selective listening, establishment of joint reference, and feedback mechanisms are described. Suggestions for future research and implications for intervention are discussed. (48 ref)
Snyder, Lee K. & McLean, James E. (U Kansas) American Journal of Mental Deficiency, 1977(Jan), Vol 81(4), 338-349. [PA, Vol 58:05647]

914.   Brief report on the WISC-R: I. Comparison of the WISC and WISC-R scores of mentally retarded and gifted children.
Administered the WISC and WISC-R to 12 gifted and 12 mentally retarded children, ages 8 yrs 2 mo to 12 yrs 5 mo, who had been randomly selected from special classes. Results show that WISC Full-Scale IQ scores tended to be significantly higher than comparable WISC-R scores. The difference between Verbal and Performance IQ scores was not significant, indicating that these subscales contribute equally to the Full Scale IQ difference.
Solly, David C. (Preston County Schools, Kingwood, WV) Journal of School Psychology, 1977(Fal), Vol 15(3), 255–258. [PA, Vol 60:08629]

915.   Physical fitness of the mentally retarded: A brief survey of the literature.
Briefly reviews selected articles that may provide answers to such questions as what is physical fitness? How do you measure the physical fitness of a mentally retarded child? How do mentally retarded children compare with normal children in physical fitness? Can the fitness level of retarded children be raised? (56 ref)
Speakman, Haddon G. (Metropolitan Hosp, Dept of Physical Therapy, Detroit, MI) Canadian Journal of Applied Sport Sciences, 1977(Sep), Vol 2(3), 171–176. [PA, Vol 63:07814]

916.   A comparison of state Developmental Disabilities Council member characteristics.
Results of an attitude and interest survey of 576 members show the following: (a) Consumers were more likely than nonconsumers to be female, have more children, have lower incomes, have less education, hold nonadministrative positions, and have more highly focused interests. (b) Small federal allotment states reported having more females and non-Whites, younger members, more small town or rural representation, and more members with lower incomes than large allotment states.
Stedman, Donald J. & Baucom, Linda D. (U North Carolina, Frank Porter Graham Child Development Ctr) Mental Retardation, 1977(Feb), Vol 15(1), 3-6. [PA, Vol 58:05639]

917.   The factorial structure of the ITPA and WISC subtests in three diagnostic groups.
Determined (a) the factorial structure of the Illinois Test of Psycholinguistic Abilities (ITPA) subtests; (b) the extent to which ITPA and WISC subtests load different factors and thus measure different skills; and (c) whether differences existed in the factorial structure of the ITPA and WISC across 3 diagnostic groups of 6-10 yr olds. In 2 of the diagnostic groups, a regular classroom group of 42 Ss, a language/learning disabled group of 41 Ss, a general linguistic factor, a visual-motor factor, and a mediation factor appeared to emerge. A general ITPA factor, a general WISC factor, and an expressive factor were extracted from the data of the 42 mentally retarded Ss. Differences among the factors of diagnostic groups after a canonical correlation of factor loading matrices are discussed. (16 ref)
Stewart, David W. (Central Louisiana State Hosp, Pineville) Journal of Clinical Psychology, 1977(Jan), Vol 33(1), 199-204. [PA, Vol 58:06713]

918.   Effect of verbal and nonverbal short-term memory coding with normal and retarded children.
20 retarded children (mean CA 11.7 yrs) matched with 20 normal children were assigned to verbal or nonverbal stimulus conditions in which pairs of 8-point random shapes were presented as styrofoam objects or drawings. Discrimination measures (d') indicated better recall for verbal coding and 3-dimensional objects. Serial position effects were also found, along with an interaction between coding and dimensionality such that verbal coding facilitated all 3-dimensional serial position performances, but there was a marked decline in verbal coding in the middle positions using 2-dimensional stimuli.
Swanson, Lee. (U Northern Colorado, Coll of Education, School of Special Education & Rehabilitation) Perceptual & Motor Skills, 1977(Jun), Vol 44(3, Pt 1), 917–918. [PA, Vol 59:10195]

919.   Marital stability following the birth of a child with spina bifida.
The marital stability of 142 families where a child with neural tube malformation (mostly spina bifida) was born between 1964 and 1966, including 56 families with a surviving spina bifida child, was examined in January 1976. The divorce rate for families with a surviving child was 9 times higher than that for the local population and 3 times higher than for families experiencing bereavement of their spina bifida child. Marriages which followed a prenuptial conception resulting in a spina bifida child were particularly vulnerable and had a divorce or separation risk of 50%. All the divorced fathers had remarried, but only 1 of the mothers. It is concluded that a handicapped child adds greatly to the strain on a marriage, especially when this has not been cemented before the arrival of a child. This strain is diminished by the child's early death.
Tew, B. J.; Laurence, K. M.; Payne, H. & Rawnsley, K. British Journal of Psychiatry, 1977(Jul), Vol 131, 79–82. [PA, Vol 59:10255]

920.   Spina bifida children's scores on the Wechsler Intelligence Scale for Children.
An analysis of the scores of 58 cases of spina bifida assessed on the WISC suggests a differential intellectual prognosis according to type of lesion, the presence of hydrocephalus, and degree of physical disability and sex, with girls having the poorer outcome.
Tew, Brian. Perceptual & Motor Skills, 1977(Apr), Vol 44(2), 381–382. [PA, Vol 59:03708]

921.   A comparison of three intelligence tests for the assessment of mental retardation.
Administered the WISC, Peabody Picture Vocabulary Test (PPVT), and Slosson Intelligence Test (SIT) to 36 mentally retarded adolescents to determine reliability and comparable performance among the 3 intelligence tests. Correlations as a function of IQ and MA, by sex, were computed among the 3 tests. All were significant, but the WISC and SIT had consistently higher relationships than any other comparisons on both IQ and MA. Analyses also indicated that the PPVT produced higher IQ scores than the WISC or SIT and that MA in the PPVT was influenced by the previous administration of the SIT. It is concluded that, as a screening device, the SIT is more reliable and approximates WISC scores more consistently than the PPVT. (20 ref)
Trivedi, A. (Woodbridge State School, NJ) Journal of Mental Deficiency Research, 1977(Dec), Vol 21(4), 289–297. [PA, Vol 61:05187]

922.   [On mental retardation with epilepsy.] (Japn)
Examined 127 mentally retarded children who were admitted to the Sakura-en Hospital and the children's ward of the Chikugo Mental Hospital. Of these children, 59 (46.5%) were found to be epileptics. In 37 of these cases (62.7%) the onset of the seizures began by age 4; in 16 cases (27.1%) the seizures appear to have developed simultaneously or shortly after the recognition of mental retardation, and in the remaining cases the onset of the seizures occurred considerably after the children were diagnosed as mentally retarded. The types of seizure varied widely, but 6 cases showed the complex forms of epilepsy. The interpersonal relationships of these chilren were poor compared with those of mentally retarded children without epilepsy. Adhesiveness, indirectness, slow-wittedness, and explosiveness were fairly common personality characteristics of these children. (English summary)
Ueda, Jiro; Yoshikawa, Hideo & Yoshikawa, Takehito. (Chikugo Mental Hosp, Japan) Kyushu Neuro-psychiatry, 1977, Vol 23(1), 78–81. [PA, Vol 60:03183]

923.   [Study on the developmental changes of cue mechanisms in the discrimination learning of mentally retarded children.] (Japn)
124 normal 4–10 yr olds and 102 mentally retarded (IQ 50–80) children were tested on a discrimination optional task involving 2 discrimination training trials and 2 test trials. Results show that the proportion of Ss selecting the conceptual shift increased with increasing age for both groups; the opposite effect was seen for perceptual shift. In normal Ss, the proportion of Ss selecting conceptual shift became higher than that selecting perceptual shift at ages 5–6 yrs; for retarded Ss, this phenomenon was noticed at MA 7–8 yrs. The proportion of both groups selecting the mediational shift increased with increasing age; however, the proportion of retarded Ss was 20–30% lower than that of normals at the same age level. It is suggested that the development of discrimination learning mechanisms in retarded children is similar to that in normals, with a 2–3 yr developmental lag. (9 ref)
Umetani, Tadao; Narukawa, Yoshio & Katada, Akiyoshi. Japanese Journal of Educational Psychology, 1977(Dec), Vol 25(4), 209–218. [PA, Vol 64:12756]

924. Activational peaking in educable and trainable mentally retarded persons.
Examined the influence of task complexity and intellectual functioning on the GSR of 10 educable (mean CA 191.5 mo) and 10 trainable (mean CA 194.4 mo) mentally retarded adolescents. Concept identification tasks of varying difficulty were presented until a performance criterion was reached. Analyses of GSR magnitude resulted in significant pre–post problem solution and problem complexity effects. Educable and trainable Ss did not differ on learning rate or GSR activation. Results suggest a possible relationship between intelligence and activational peaking.
Uno, Tad & Gargiulo, Richard M. (Bowling Green State U) Perceptual & Motor Skills, 1977(Jun), Vol 44(3, Pt 2), 1186. [PA, Vol 59:12562]

925. Creativity in developmentally disabled adolescents.
Creative behavior of 20 normal adolescents and 20 educable and 20 trainable mentally retarded adolescents of similar CAs was examined using a modified version of the Torrance Tests of Creative Thinking. Results indicate that educable mentally retarded and normal Ss did not differ significantly on any of Torrance's 4 creativity measures. Significant differences were found between the trainable and nonretarded Ss and the trainable and educable retardates. Results are discussed in terms of level of intelligence and other contributing variables. (15 ref)
Uno, Tad et al. (Bowling Green State U) Psychological Reports, 1977(Jun), Vol 40(3, Pt 2), 1207–1212. [PA, Vol 59:10198]

926. A follow-up developmental study of hypothesis behavior among mentally retarded and nonretarded children.
To clarify the roles of IQ and MA in hypothesis behavior, MA-matched Ss at 3 levels of IQ (70, 100, and 130) and 3 levels of MA (5½, 7½, and 9½ yrs) received blank-trial discrimination learning problems using procedures designed to discourage position-oriented responding. With position responding discouraged, earlier findings were contradicted in that no hypothesis measure showed a main effect of IQ. This suggested that previously reported IQ group differences in hypothesis behavior may not reflect cognitive deficits inherently linked to low IQ, but instead may reflect the influence of specific methodological factors. The finding and interpretation are consistent with E. Zigler's (see PA, Vol 43:8608) "developmental" theory of retardation and inconsistent with the general "difference" position. In additional findings, the predictions that (a) Ss at all 3 MA levels would use hypotheses, and (b) retarded children from special education classes would use hypotheses more often than retarded children "mainstreamed" in classes for the nonretarded were confirmed. (22 ref)
Weisz, John R. (Cornell U) Journal of Experimental Child Psychology, 1977(Aug), Vol 24(1), 108–122. [PA, Vol 59:10200]

927. Validity of the Peabody Picture Vocabulary Test as a measure of hearing vocabulary in mentally retarded and normal children.
The Peabody Picture Vocabulary Test (PPVT) and the auditory and visual subtests of the Illinois Test of Psycholinguistic Abilities (ITPA) were administered to 48 normal (mean CA 84 mo) and 48 retarded (mean CA 79 mo) children. Results suggest that the PPVT is not an adequate measure of hearing vocabulary for mentally retarded Ss. Half of each group was given the visual reception subtest of the ITPA in a form which had been modified to control the visual memory variable. No differences were found as a function of that variable. It is concluded that caution should be exercised when using the PPVT as a clinical diagnostic procedure in the assessment of receptive auditory vocabulary. (23 ref)
Williams, Ann M.; Marks, Colleen J. & Bailer, Irv. (Kennedy Child Study Ctr, New York, NY) Journal of Speech & Hearing Research, 1977(Jun), Vol 20(2), 205–211. [PA, Vol 59:11457]

928. Twenty years of mental retardation research.
Presents testimony given to the US Senate and House Appropriations Committee regarding funding of the National Institute of Child Health and Human Development (NICHD). Major improvements in mental retardation research over the past 20 yrs, due in part to federal funding, are discussed, and the role of NICHD in new research and its applications is stressed.
Zigler, Edward. (Yale U) Mental Retardation, 1977(Jun), Vol 15(3), 51–53. [PA, Vol 59:08125]

929. Head Start has little to do with mental retardation: A reply to Clarke and Clarke.
Asserts that A. D. Clarke and A. M. Clarke's (1977) critique of Head Start in an editorial on mental retardation is based on questionable assumptions, a selective review of research, and errors in fact. It is pointed out that eligibility for Head Start is based on family income and that family income cannot be used to determine intellectual level. The group mean IQ of Head Start children, as compared to middle-class children, is lower by 10–15 points; however, this degree of attenuation in mean IQ does not permit the viewing of Head Start as relevant to issues in mental retardation.
Zigler, Edward & Cascione, Rosa. (Yale U) American Journal of Mental Deficiency, 1977(Nov), Vol 82(3), 246–249. [PA, Vol 61:04678]

930. Gender identity in a group of retarded children.
Administered the Michigan Gender Identity Test (MGIT) to 52 3.1–10.6 yr old retarded and 36 2.1–5.6 yr old normal children to assess the acquisition of gender identity. The IQ of the retarded Ss was determined with the Stanford-Binet Intelligence Scale; an intelligence rating of normal Ss was obtained with the Peabody Picture Vocabulary Test. The MGIT required the ability to sort and categorize photographs of boys and girls wearing conventional clothing and with conventional hairstyles. As part of the test, each S was expected to recognize a self-photo and to be able to categorize it as a boy or a girl. In general, a significant correlation was found between MGIT performance and MA for the retarded Ss. The performance of the normal Ss correlated significantly with both CA and MA. (15 ref)
Abelson, Geoffrey & Paluszny, Maria. (Iowa State U) Journal of Autism & Childhood Schizophrenia, 1978(Dec), Vol 8(4), 403–411. [PA, Vol 62:06301]

931. Cross-sectional study on reaction time of mentally retarded children.
The body reaction time (RT) of 43 male mentally retarded children (CAs 7–13 yrs) was measured, dividing the time into the following 2 components: (a) time required to start the motion in response to the stimulus—premotor time, and (b) time during which the muscles were contracting—motor time. The speed of RT of mentally retarded Ss was slower at each age in comparison with that of nonretarded children ($N = 107$). However, even in mentally retarded Ss the speed of RT showed improvement with increasing age. The slower RT in mentally retarded Ss resulted from their slower premotor rather than motor time component. IQ was related to neither the RT nor premotor time of mentally retarded Ss. (15 ref)
Ando, H.; Wakabayashi, S. & Yabe, K. (Central Hosp, Aichi Prefectural Colony, Kasugai, Japan) Journal of Mental Deficiency Research, 1978(Mar), Vol 22(1), 11–17. [PA, Vol 61:13624]

932. Prevalence of maladaptive behavior in retarded children as a function of IQ and age.
128 mentally retarded children aged 6–14 yrs from a special school in Japan were assessed by teachers in terms of 9 maladaptive behaviors: self-injury, attack against others, destruction of property, hyperactivity, withdrawal, no eye-to-eye gaze, stereotyped behavior, tantrum, fear. Results indicate that the prevalence of some maladaptive behaviors changed as a function of IQ and age and that there were splits of such changes as IQ-dependent and as age-dependent by maladaptive behavior. (9 ref)
Ando, Haruhiko & Yoshimura, Ikuko. (Aichi Prefectural Colony, Central Hosp, Kasugai, Japan) Journal of Abnormal Child Psychology, 1978(Sep), Vol 6(3), 345–349. [PA, Vol 64:01104]

933. Behavioral and neurological characteristics of a hydranencephalic infant.
A modified Prechtl neurological examination and the Brazelton Neonatal Assessment Scale were serially administered to a hydranencephalic infant over the 1st 8 wks of life. Clinical, roentgenographic, neurological, and behavioral findings are reported. In contrast to earlier reports, visual tracking of a moving field and auditory and visual habituation were observed. Further, in addition to previously reported reflex automatisms, the S also possessed what are termed "socially relevant behavioral automatisms." (French, German & Spanish summaries)
Aylward, Glen P.; Lazzara, Anthony & Meyer, John. (Emory U Medical School) Developmental Medicine & Child Neurology, 1978(Apr), Vol 20(2), 211–217. [PA, Vol 62:01338]

934. Transfer of compounds and components in the discriminative learning of retardates.
Assessed the discriminative learning and transfer of compound and component problems in 80 retarded Ss at 2 levels of intelligence. It was found that brighter Ss (mean MA 10 yrs) found the component problems relatively easier than the compound problems to a greater extent than did the less developed Ss (mean MA 5 yrs). The learning of compound solutions was shown to transfer positively to other compound problems and negatively to component problems. Component solutions were found to transfer positively to other component solutions and negatively to compound solutions. These dimensional transfer effects are interpreted to mean that both compound and component solutions were mediated and conceptual in nature. The developmental differences in relative usages of compound and component aspects of stimuli are viewed as the result of differences in direction of attention rather than of differences in complexity of processing. (16 ref)
Barnes, Timothy R. (Rosemont Coll) Journal of Experimental Child Psychology, 1978(Feb), Vol 25(1), 71–79. [PA, Vol 60:11953]

935. [Study of the formation of learning sets by the mentally retarded.] (Fren)
The work of K. H. Pribram (See PA, Vol 34:5135) was adapted to study trial-and-error learning in a group of mentally retarded children (mean WISC IQ 61). A control group (mean WISC IQ 99.5) also took part in the experiment. Ss completed a 2-choice discrimination task and reverse-discrimination tasks with 2, 3, or 4 choices using the modified Wisconsin General Test Apparatus. Errors that were related to the degree to which the search was conducted systematically and the degree to which the correct responses were fixed were analyzed, using the Mann-Whitney U-Test and chi-square. It is concluded that the formation of learning sets serves as an index to intelligence level as measured by the WISC. (15 ref)
Battacchi, Marco W.; Crociati, G. Carlo & Codispoti, Olga. Bulletin de Psychologie, 1977–78(Jan–Feb), Vol 31(3–6), 286–292. [PA, Vol 63:01212]

936. Social interactions and communication patterns in mentally retarded children.
Used an observational approach and videotapes to investigate a group of 4 mentally retarded kindergarten children (MAs 1.2, 1.5, 1.6, and 2.4 yrs) with minimal language development. Results show that when a facilitator (teacher) was present, there were more social interactions and vocalizations, but there was no significant increase in meaningful verbal content. Nonverbal communication rose sharply in the presence of the facilitator. Findings indicate that an observational analysis of patterns of interaction is useful in planning intervention programs in the area of social and communication development. (34 ref)
Berry, Paul & Marshall, Bruce. (U Queensland, Schonell Educational Research Ctr, Brisbane, Australia) American Journal of Mental Deficiency, 1978(Jul), Vol 83(1), 44–51. [PA, Vol 62:03875]

937. Effect of shared experience on role-taking performance of retarded children.
31 retarded Ss, homogeneous with respect to CA (6–12 yrs) and MA and IQ (Peabody Picture Vocabulary Test; 6–8 yrs and 71, respectively) were grouped according to their nonegocentric, intermediate, or egocentric performance on a criterion role-taking task. One week later they were given an experimentally manipulated "shared experience" to determine if such intervention would affect subsequent role-taking performance. Results indicate that egocentric Ss did not benefit from the shared experience in that they failed to take into account the role or perspective of another person when it conflicted with their own. Nonegocentric Ss performed equally well both before and after the shared experience. Ss in the intermediate group, however, benefited from the shared experience of occupying another person's role and modified their responses in a nonegocentric direction. Results are interpreted as consistent with the role of experience in social–cognitive development. (25 ref)
Blacher-Dixon, Jan & Simeonsson, Rune J. (U North Carolina, Frank Porter Graham Child Development Ctr, Chapel Hill) American Journal of Mental Deficiency, 1978(Jul), Vol 83(1), 21–28. [PA, Vol 62:03876]

938. Sentence structures of trainable and educable mentally retarded subjects.
15 educable and 15 trainable mentally retarded children (mean ages 10 yrs 3 mo and 10 yrs 7 mo, respectively) were administered a story completion task that elicits 14 grammatical structures. There were more correct responses from educable than from trainable mentally retarded Ss. Both groups found imperatives easiest, and future, embedded, and double-adjectival structures most difficult. Educable Ss produced more correct responses than trainable Ss for declarative, question, and single-adjectival structures. The cognitive and linguistic processing of both groups is discussed as are the implications for language remediation. (18 ref)
Bliss, Lynn S.; Allen, Doris V. & Walker, Georgia. (Wayne State U, Speech & Hearing Ctr) Journal of Speech & Hearing Research, 1978(Dec), Vol 21(4), 722–731. [PA, Vol 63:12175]

939. General or specific learning of figure-ground perception.
Constructed 2 training programs, one for auditory and one for visual figure–ground perception. The training effect for each program was tested in small groups of 8 pupils and the gain compared with a control group. The 24 7–12 yr old Ss were from an institution for brain-damaged children and an institution for mentally retarded. The effect measured was the pretest–posttest difference on tests for auditory and visual figure–ground perception. Both training groups showed higher gain score than the control group on both tests, but the effect was significant only for visual training on visual figure–ground perception. (58 ref)
Bø, Ola O. (U Oslo, Norway) Scandinavian Journal of Educational Research, 1978, Vol 22(4), 129–153. [PA, Vol 63:12006]

940. Stuttering in the retarded: II. Prevalence of stuttering in EMR and TMR children.
Investigated the prevalence of stuttering among 840 educable mentally retarded (EMR) and 439 trainable mentally retarded (TMR) children enrolled in special classes of private and public schools of Edmonton, Alberta, Canada. Ss identified as stutterers by their classroom teachers were interviewed by 2 trained observers (Os). Of the 73 Ss identified by teachers, 66 were interviewed: 23 were considered by both Os to be stutterers, 29 were considered by both Os to be nonstutterers, and 14 were placed in an "undecided" category. The latter category included cases in which (a) an inadequate speech sample was obtained, (b) the Os disagreed with each other's rating (2 cases), or (c) one or both of the Os were unable to differentiate between stuttering and related communication disorders. Overall, 1.8% of the 1,279 Ss were considered by both Os to be stutterers: The prevalence of stuttering was approximately twice as high in the TMR group as in the EMR. The diagnostic difficulties encountered in this study suggest caution in enrolling mentally retarded children in stuttering therapy. (8 ref)

Boberg, Einer et al. (U Alberta Ctr for the Study of Mental Retardation, Edmonton, Canada) Mental Retardation Bulletin, 1978, Vol 6(2), 67–76. [PA, Vol 63:09931]

941. Cognition and gross motor performance in ESN children.
Compared educationally subnormal (ESN) and normal boys from the same locality on gross motor performance. 24 ESN Ss (IQs 48–91) were randomly assigned to ESN practice and control conditions, and 24 Ss with normal IQs were randomly assigned to normal practice and control treatments. The 4 groups showed no significant differences in age (mean age about 13 yrs), height, weight, and physical work capacity. After being pretested on 8 gross motor tests, Ss in the 2 practice conditions participated in 14 1-hr training sessions over a 4-wk period, involving practice of each of the tests. It was hypothesized that practice would improve the performance of ESN Ss only. Physiological changes as a result of training were inhibited by insuring that intensity of practice never exceeded 25% of initial performance. Results show the following: (a) The Practice Treatment main effect was not significant on any of the items. (b)The IQ Level main effect was significant on sit-ups, 50-yd sprint, and shuttle run tests, marginally significant on pull-ups and right-hand grip, and nonsignificant on left-hand grip and standing broad jump. It is suggested that the inferiority of the ESN child is more a function of the intellectual capacity required to complete a test than a lack of motor ability per se. (15 ref)
Burwitz, Les; Daggett, Anne; Harrison, Peter W. & Davies, Bruce. (Crewe & Alsager Coll of Higher Education, England) American Corrective Therapy Journal, 1978(Jul–Aug), Vol 32(4), 123–126. [PA, Vol 65:02144]

942. Social and attentional aspects of echolalia in highly echolalic mentally retarded persons.
Echolalia was examined in a sample of highly echolalic mentally retarded individuals, which consisted of 11 17–64 yr old adults and a 9-yr-old child. All Ss had been diagnosed as low grade mental defectives (IQ 30–44). When presented with a standard set of questions, under conditions differing in appropriateness for exchange of discourse (e.g., questions presented with examiner and patient face-to-face vs questions presented with the examiner's face averted vs questions addressed towards another person sitting silently beside the patient), Ss' frequency of echolalia varied. Besides showing considerable sensitivity to aspects of discourse exchange, Ss exhibited some limited capacity for processing linguistic information.
Campbell, Brian & Grieve, Robert. (VA Hosp Psychology Service, Pittsburgh, PA) American Journal of Mental Deficiency, 1978(Jan), Vol 82(4), 414–416. [PA, Vol 62:06306]

943. Toward a theory of intelligence: Contributions from research with retarded children.
One approach to the understanding of intelligence is through research with retarded children and adults. Any characterization of the way(s) in which they differ from nonretarded persons results in a specification of important components of intelligence. In this paper, 2 general areas of research are discussed. In one, centering on the role of control processes in memory and problem-solving situations, it is argued that research with the retarded has succeeded in identifying a major component of intelligence. The results from a large number of experiments suggest that a hallmark of intelligence is the ability to generalize information from one situation to another and that this ability depends on effective "executive control." In areas where less research with retarded individuals has been done, it is suggested that comparative/developmental work is necessary to gain a better understanding of the processes in question. This point is illustrated by discussing work aimed at locating individual differences in parameters representing basic components of general information-processing systems. (3 p ref)
Campione, Joseph C. & Brown, Ann L. (U Illinois) Intelligence, 1978(Jul–Sep), Vol 2(3), 279–304. [PA, Vol 63:11179]

944. Meanings that professionals attach to labels for children.
Sought to identify relative meanings among professionals of 3 clinical labels for children—mentally retarded, emotionally disturbed, and juvenile delinquent—as well as an average or unlabeled choice. 40 regular classroom teachers of Grades 6–9 and 32 mental health workers responded on 2 questionnaires designed to measure their reactions to these labels with 9 questions concerned with expectations for the child's success in school and work, implications for treatment strategies, and motivation to work with the child. The labels conveyed clearly different relative meanings, and the 2 professional groups differed in a consistent fashion.
Carroll, Charles F. & Reppucci, N. Dickon. (Yale U) Journal of Consulting & Clinical Psychology, 1978(Apr), Vol 46(2), 372–374. [PA, Vol 61:06845]

945. [The effects of story structures and study trials on memory and reasoning in mentally retarded children.] (Chin)
In a study with 84 mentally retarded and 200 normal children, recall and reasoning from a highly structured story were superior to those from a poorly structured story in both groups of Ss. The easy material led to faster improvement over trials by the retarded than by the normal Ss. (English abstract) (23 ref)
Chen, Yung-hwa. Bulletin of Educational Psychology, 1978(Jun), Vol 11, 9–24. [PA, Vol 65:03512]

946. A comparative study of the sensori-motor capacities of normal and intellectually handicapped children.
The role of early sensory experience is considered to be important in the later development of motor abilities. However, while studies have been undertaken of the overt motor capacities of children with intellectual handicap, little information is available regarding their sensory integration. Results of the present study with 18 mentally retarded (CA 10 yrs; MA 5 yrs) and 56 normal (CAs 5 and 10 yrs) children show that the sensorimotor capacities of such children are more correlated to mental development than to physical growth and development. The significance of the tonal abnormalities and poor awareness of body positioning shown by the study to exist in the retarded child are discussed.
Chenoweth, Robyn & Bullock, Margaret I. Australian Journal of Mental Retardation, 1978(Mar), Vol 5(1), 20–26. [PA, Vol 62:03881]

947. Perceptual and intellectual factors affecting number concept development in retarded and nonretarded children.
Examined the role of MA and visual-perceptual ability in number concept development with 48 nonretarded and retarded children from regular school settings. Ss were administered the Peabody Picture Vocabulary Test and the Frostig Developmental Test of Visual Perception. Both groups were matched on MA and divided into high and low perceptual-ability levels. Using the Dodwell Number Concept Test, each S was tested on various Piagetian tasks. Although retarded and nonretarded groups differed in IQ and CA, equivalence in MA resulted in equivalent number concept performance. For both groups, regardless of variation in IQ and CA, perceptual ability exerted a significant influence in number concept, with high perceptual ability resulting in superior number concept performance. (35 ref)
Cohn-Jones, L. & Seim, R. (Texas A&M U) American Journal of Mental Deficiency, 1978(Jul), Vol 83(1), 9–15. [PA, Vol 62:03883]

948. Facilitation of serial recall in retarded children and adolescents: Verbal and kinesthetic strategies.
Explored the nature of the modality-specific effects of rehearsal training for serial recall. 96 retarded children (mean CA 122 mo, mean IQ 70.6) and adolescents (mean CA 163 mo, mean IQ 68.8) were trained in either verbal or kinesthetic "cumulative rehearsal–fast finish" strategies for picture recall. Results indicate that both strategies facilitated recall on training tasks and on a transfer-recall test. No age effects or Age × Rehearsal Condition interaction resulted. These results support a general cross-modality recoding explanation of rehearsal effects and suggest that retarded individuals are capable of mediating picture recall in their sensorimotor system as well as in their verbal-auditory memory system.

Conroy, Robert L. (State University Coll New York, Oswego) American Journal of Mental Deficiency, 1978(Jan), Vol 82(4), 410–413. [PA, Vol 62:06308]

949.   Genetic disorders and mental retardation.
Genetic disorders are responsible for nearly 50% of the half million moderately and severely mentally retarded. These include chromosomal abnormalities, those due to single genes, and others resulting from a combination of genetic and environmental factors. With the exception of specific metabolic diseases, most genetic disorders are not treatable; thus, prevention by genetic counseling and prenatal diagnosis becomes imperative. Neither of these can be accomplished without an accurate diagnosis. (39 ref)
Crandall, Barbara F. (U California School of Medicine, Los Angeles) Annual Progress in Child Psychiatry & Child Development, 1978, 395–416. [PA, Vol 66:13061]

950.   Present possibilities for the prevention of hereditary mental subnormality.
Studied the etiology of mental subnormality in 1,364 7–11 yr old Hungarian children over a 2-yr period. In the 1,104 cases for which the etiology was established, it is suggested that genetic counseling and prenatal diagnosis could have prevented 26.2% of the inborn errors in metabolism, 29.6% of the malformation syndromes, and 9.7% of the chromosomal abnormalities. (French & German summaries) (2 ref)
Czeizel, A. & Métneki-Bajomi, J. (National Inst of Hygiene, Lab of Human Genetics, Budapest, Hungary) International Journal of Rehabilitation Research, 1978(Jul), Vol 1(3), 301–308. [PA, Vol 63:03343]

951.   Intellectual deficit.
Presents an information-processing model, known as simultaneous and successive synthesis, that was first suggested by A. Juria. Use of the model is demonstrated by data from several experiments with mentally retarded and age-matched normal children.
Das, J. P. (U Alberta Ctr for the Study of Mental Retardation, Edmonton, Canada) Mental Retardation Bulletin, 1978, Vol 6(3), 117–128. [PA, Vol 64:04362]

952.   Early profound deafness and mental retardation.
The difficulties of speech and language development for the prelingually profoundly deaf child are explained, and arguments are made for the use of manual communications methods (i.e., finger spelling and sign language) in the education of deaf children. The relationship of prelingual profound deafness to mental retardation is discussed, and 6 case histories are presented demonstrating successful treatment of deaf people, most of whom were found not to be retarded, which was originally suspected in some cases. (6 ref)
Denmark, John C. (Whittingham Hosp, Dept of Psychiatry, Preston, England) British Journal of Mental Subnormality, 1978(Dec), Vol 24(2, No 47), 81–89. [PA, Vol 64:03397]

953.   Factors influencing the response latencies of subnormal children in naming pictures.
The times taken to name 56 drawings of objects on 5 occasions were analyzed for 21 moderately educationally subnormal [ESN(M)] and 21 severely educationally subnormal [ESN(S)] children, matched for picture-naming vocabulary. The ESN(S) group not only had a higher mean response latency but also showed greater inter- and intra-S variance. Nine objects were selected whose names have a Thorndike-Lorge language frequency of 50 words/million or greater, and 9 others were selected with a frequency of less than 50 words/million. Each object was drawn in 2 ways, one giving a 2-dimensional outline with the addition of important detail, the other drawing also incorporating cues indicating the depth of the object. An ANOVA of Ss' latencies in naming the selected 36 pictures of 18 objects over 5 trials indicated that the method of drawing had no effect on naming latencies. Pictures with high-frequency names were named faster than those with lower frequency names, ESN(S) Ss showing a greater rate of increase in naming latency for the lower frequency words than ESN(M) Ss. Results are discussed in terms

of the Oldfield and Lachman models of lexical memory storage and of the search processes required for the retrieval of names. (25 ref)
Elliott, Colin. (Victoria U of Manchester, England) British Journal of Psychology, 1978(Aug), Vol 69(3), 295–303. [PA, Vol 63:05699]

954.   The effect of visual frame of reference on a judgment of plane stimulus orientation by children.
In 3 studies with 56 normal 4½–9½ yr olds and 24 educationally subnormal children (mental age 4½–5½ yrs), it was found that up to about age 7, children's selection of one of a pair of line stimuli as "falling over" was affected by the nature of the visual surround contours provided. Both the form of the stimulus surround and the presence or absence of a baseline tilted 45° relative to the horizontal were found to affect the children's judgments. The plane (horizontal or vertical) in which the stimuli were presented had no effect on the results. It is argued that while the results show the influence of the visual surround on children's comprehension of "falling over," this may not be wholly explicable in terms of surround contour matching, as conventionally correct judgments were obtained in the absence of all straight line contours in the immediate surround. (18 ref)
Elliott, John M. & Connolly, Kevin J. (U Sheffield, England) Perception, 1978, Vol 7(2), 139–149. [PA, Vol 62:03246]

955.   Suitability of the California Abbreviated WISC for WISC-R subtests with mentally retarded and slow learner children.
Assessed the suitability of the California Abbreviated WISC-Form 1 (CAW-1) for use with WISC-R subtests. Ss were 326 previously evaluated students from 2 southern mountain communities. It is concluded that the CAW-1 was suitable for use with WISC-R subtests with minor alterations. (9 ref)
Erikson, Carol L.; Byrd, Steven H. & Milon, Theresa A. (Buchanan County School Board, Grundy, VA) Psychology in the Schools, 1978(Oct), Vol 15(4), 498–502. [PA, Vol 63:04450]

956.   Minor physical anomalies in hyperactive, retarded and normal children and their families.
13 hyperactive, 9 retarded, and 15 normal boys as well as their siblings and parents were examined for the frequency of minor physical anomalies (MPA). Results indicate that the hyperactives, retardates, their siblings, and parents had equal numbers of MPA that were significantly higher than in the normal control children and their families, who did not differ from each other. It is noted that there were more fathers absent due to divorce or separation in the 2 patient groups. (25 ref)
Firestone, Philip; Peters, Susan; Rivier, Marlene & Knights, Robert M. (Children's Hosp of Eastern Ontario, Ottawa, Canada) Journal of Child Psychology & Psychiatry & Allied Disciplines, 1978(Apr), Vol 19(2), 155–160. [PA, Vol 63:01272]

957.   Empirical validity of Ertl's brain-wave analyzer (BWA02).
The empirical validity of J. P. Ertl's (1974, 1975) brain wave analyzer was investigated by the known contrasted groups method. 32 academically talented (mean IQ score = 147) and 16 academically handicapped (mean IQ score = 79) boys and girls aged 12–14 yrs were compared on 4 Primary Mental Abilities (PMA) tests, 2 Sequential Tests of Educational Progress (STEP) measures, and 7 Brain Wave Analyzer (BWA) measures. The PMA and STEP variables alone provided excellent discrimination between academically handicapped and academically gift Ss. The PMA and STEP variables in combination with BWA variables, (e.g., Frenquency Ratio) did afford more accurate discrimination between the 2 groups than did any 1 measure alone, which suggests that BWA variables can make a valuable contribution to the understanding of "learning potential." BWA variables alone did not furnish an adequate level of discrimination between the 2 groups; the BWA connot be used as a substitute for paper-and-pencil measures of learning potential. Significant sex differences in BWA scores did imply a need for separate norms for males and females, and the norms set forth in the BWA manual should be revised. (14 ref)

Fischer, Donald G.; Hunt, Dennis & Randhawa, Bikkar S. (U Saskatchewan, Saskatoon, Canada) Educational & Psychological Measurement, 1978(Win), Vol 38(4), 1017–1030. [PA, Vol 64:00099]

958. Visual recognition in mentally retarded adolescents: Cue value and instruction effects.
Investigated whether differential subjective frequency of positive and negative cues is built up during discrimination trials, and assessed the effect on recognition memory of instructions that may influence the encoding of stimuli in retarded persons. 12 13-yr-olds (MAs 5–8 yrs) and 12 15-yr-olds (MAs 8–11 yrs) were randomly selected and given recognition tests for positive and negative discrimination stimuli after a single trial through a discrimination problem list. Results indicate that the frequency theory shown by B. Ekstrand et al (see PA, Vol 41:212) to account for the verbal discrimination learning of nonretarded adults may also hold for the visual-discrimination learning of mentally retarded persons. In addition, retarded Ss correctly recognized the stimuli more often after a simple inspection trial than after a standard discrimination-learning trial, indicating that they encoded the stimuli differently depending on the instructional set. The encoding difference was mediated by looking patterns. Both MA and serial position of stimuli on presentation and on test affected recognition.
Fisher, Mary A. (U Maryland, Baltimore County) American Journal of Mental Deficiency, 1978(Jan), Vol 82(4), 359–364. [PA, Vol 61:03885]

959. Moral judgment in retarded and nonretarded school age children.
Assessed the moral judgment of 135 normal, educable retarded, and trainable retarded boys and girls (ages 6–10, 11–13, and 14–16) to determine the significance of age and IQ on moral development. Results indicate significant differences in mean moral judgment between the groups and each age level. The findings substantiate Piaget's stage theory of moral development and suggest that within the retarded population, level of intellectual ability is also significantly related to moral judgment.
Gargiulo, Richard M. & Sulick, Janet A. (Bowling Green State U) Journal of Psychology, 1978(May), Vol 99(1), 23–26. [PA, Vol 62:01311]

960. The current status of three major techniques for the assessment of social competence in the diagnosis of the potentially retarded child.
Presents an overview of the forces responsible for the impetus to evaluate social competency as one of the components of mental retardation. A general review of 3 available instruments, the American Association on Mental Deficiency Adaptive Behavior Scale, the Vineland Social Maturity Scale, and the System of Multi-Cultural and Pluralistic Assessment (SOMPA) is included. The advantages of the SOMPA as compared to the other 2 tests are described. It is concluded that the SOMPA, which was based on normative samples of 700 Black, 700 Chicano/Latino, and 700 White children, may overcome some of the racial and cultural biases of the other instruments. (18 ref)
Givens, Thelma. (U Southern Mississippi) Southern Journal of Educational Research, 1978(Spr), Vol 12(2), 75–84. [PA, Vol 62:12635]

961. Parenting an adult mentally retarded offspring.
Studied the feelings, attitudes, views, problems, and practices of 23 parents of 16 mentally retarded adults (10 males, 6 females). Respondents were 46–78 yrs old. They were administered a 62-item questionnaire during interviews. Almost all said they felt uncomfortable leaving their offspring alone, whether supervised or not. More than half felt that the retardate's presence at home had little effect on their social life. As has been found in other studies, most parents reported no current involvement with professionals. All expressed a wish for more job-related programs for the retarded. Almost all said that they got along well with the retarded individual, but certain problems in the relationships were noted. What would happen to the retarded person when the parent(s) died was a major source of anxiety and two-thirds of the respondents said they needed help or guidance in planning their child's future. Findings of the study do not make it clear whether these parents' tendency toward chronic sorrow, fatigue, social insulation, heavy reliance on the family, unremitting involvement with the retarded offspring, and avoidance in dealing with the future represent the erosion of long-term stresses and the full range of possible adaptations to a harsh reality, or whether they reflect unresolved conflicts within the parents about their offspring. (45 ref)
Goodman, David M. Smith College Studies in Social Work, 1978(Jun), Vol 48(3), 209–234. [PA, Vol 63:12181]

962. The meaning of IQ constancy in young retarded children.
In a clinic population of 289 children, aged 9 yrs and under, suspected of developmental delay, it was found that correlations on repeated administrations of the Bayley Infant Development Scales and/or Stanford-Binet were much higher than in normal children; that the magnitude of the correlations was inversely related to IQ level; that children initially tested under 2 yrs of age displayed more IQ change than those tested over the age of 2, with girls more likely than boys to show a drop, and the greatest amount of fluctuation occurring in the 51–80 range. The IQ constancy of this population suggests that they are growing intellectually at a rate proportional to normal children of their own MA rather than CA; that they may well have more years of maturation before reaching a plateau; and that educational programs should take into consideration this lengthened learning period. (34 ref)
Goodman, Joan F. & Cameron, James. (U Pennsylvania Graduate School of Education) Journal of Genetic Psychology, 1978(Mar), Vol 132(1), 109–119. [PA, Vol 61:13630]

963. Precocious cardiac orienting in a human anencephalic infant.
An anencephalic infant, 3–6 wks old, responded to acoustic stimulation with cardiac decelerations typical of the response pattern seen in normal, older infants. Such precocity implied unexpected competence of lower brain structures and suggested that, in the normal infant, feedback from immature higher centers may sometimes interfere with rather than modulate the functioning of lower centers.
Graham, Frances K.; Leavitt, Lewis A.; Strock, Barbara D. & Brown, James W. (U Wisconsin Hosp, Madison) Science, 1978(Jan), Vol 199(4326), 322–324. [PA, Vol 61:11192]

964. Adjustment of intellectually below-average men not identified as mentally retarded.
Studied the adjustment of adult persons who were intellectually below average but had not been labeled as mentally retarded, with the aim of revealing any groups among them at potential risk of being labeled in the future. In connection with enlistment for military service, 128 19-yr-old men of below-average intelligence (mean IQ 76) and a control group of 80 intellectually average men were selected. A cluster analysis of 22 adjustment variables in the intellectually below-average group gave 4 homogeneous clusters with respect to social and personal adjustment: Well-Adjusted, Personal Problem, Crime, and Work Problem. Ss of the Crime cluster had grown up in big towns, and their parents were registered in the files of the social welfare authorities. Work problems had more frequently been preceded by problems at school. Ss in the Crime cluster and the Work Problem cluster are considered to run the greatest risk of being labeled mentally retarded in the future. (26 ref)
Granat, Kristina & Granat, Sven. (Ulleråker Hosp, Psychiatric Research Ctr, Uppsala, Sweden) Scandinavian Journal of Psychology, 1978, Vol 19(1), 41–51. [PA, Vol 61:08700]

965. [Paradoxical sleep in the mentally deficient.] (Fren)
24 mentally retarded and 8 normal children (average age 10.3 and 9.4 yrs respectively) were given the complete WISC, as well as EEG, EKG, EMG, and electro-aculographic records during sleep. Mean IQ for the retardates was 41 and for the normals 102.5. Periods of paradoxical sleep were defined as the simultaneous presence of desynchronized EEG, eye movements, and muscular hypotonicity. Paradoxical sleep was 14% of total sleep

for the retardates, and 22% for the normals; the correlation was .85. The latency period was significantly greater for the retardates, as were the number and duration of intermediate sleep phases. (English summary) (23 ref)
Grubar, J.-C. (U Lille III, Lab de Psychologie des Activités Cognitives & Linguistiques, France) Enfance, 1978(Apr–Sep), No 2–3, 165–172. [PA, Vol 64:05898]

966.   Extrapolated general cognitive indexes on the McCarthy Scales for Gifted and Mentally Retarded Children.
Although extrapolated IQs are available for Wechsler's intelligence scales, extrapolated values for the General Cognitive Index of the McCarthy Scales of Children's Abilities have not been presented. This study derived regression equations from the normative sample data and computed estimated composite raw scores corresponding to the indexes above 150 and below 50. Extrapolated values are useful for estimating a child's present level of functioning; however, because extrapolated values are not based on empirical data, they should be viewed as estimates and used with caution. (7 ref)
Harrison, Patti L. & Naglieri, Jack A. (U Georgia) Psychological Reports, 1978(Dec), Vol 43(3, Pt 2), 1291–1296. [PA, Vol 64:09251]

967.   Visual perseveration in normal and mentally retarded children.
Investigated visual perseveration within mentally retarded and 2nd-, 5th-, and 8th-grade normal children (12 each group). Ss matched an auditorially presented click to the onset and offset of visually presented stimuli. Time differences between visual stimulus offset and the point at which Ss reported simultaneity of the click and the offset were assumed to reflect visual perseveration. Results show (a) no differences between normal Ss as a function of age, (b) no difference between groups for stimuli of 100-msec or longer duration, and (c) retarded Ss judged stimuli of 20 and 50 msec to be of shorter duration than did normal Ss. This highly specific distinction between retarded and normal Ss suggests a difference in an early stage of perceptual processing.
Hill, A. Lewis & Silverman, Wayne P. (Inst for Basic Research in Mental Retardation, Staten Island, NY) Perceptual & Motor Skills, 1978(Feb), Vol 46(1), 55–62. [PA, Vol 61:08703]

968.   A sensitive scoring method to determine the social development of the mentally handicapped.
Describes the development of a 5-point scale for scoring the Progress Assessment Chart of Social and Personal Development when used with mentally handicapped adults aged 16 yrs and over. Examples are presented for the following test items: self-help—table habits,   self-help—mobility, communication—language, and communication—paper and pencil work.
Huurman-Coertzen de Kock, C. W.   British Journal of Mental Subnormality, 1978(Jun), Vol 24(46, Pt 1), 32–34. [PA, Vol 63:04468]

969.   Spina bifida and the WPPSI.
Administered the Wechsler Preschool and Primary Scale of Intelligence (WPPSI) to 30 spina bifida children (ages 4 yrs 2 mo–6 yrs 10 mo). Overall scores, subtest scores, and scores on factors derived from the test were subjected to a stepwise regression analysis with respect to age, sex, site of lesion, physical disability, and possible effects of hydrocephalus. Results show that the group scored below the assumed population means on Total IQ (81.13) and Performance IQ (76.77). Verbal IQ was 88.5, corresponding to a mean of zero. Findings support the view that the WPPSI is a better assessment instrument for spina bifida children than a general test of intelligence (e.g., the Stanford-Binet) because it provides a profile of subtest performance. The largest multiple correlations were those associated with Block Design and the Performance Factor; in each case, the primary independent variables were Shunt and Age. (13 ref)
Jamison, Elizabeth & Fee, F.   Irish Journal of Psychology, 1978(Win), Vol 4(1), 14–21. [PA, Vol 64:08313]

970.   The Peabody Individual Achievement Test with normal and special school populations.
Notes that since the publication of the Peabody Individual Achievement Test, it has become a frequent part of many educational batteries. However, a serious drawback in its evaluation has been the lack of available information on the test's applicability to special populations and its relationship with other standardized tests of achievement. From this review of the literature on the use of the test with normal, retarded, learning disabled, and emotionally disturbed children, it is concluded that the test can add important diagnostic information in the assessment of handicapped children, although there remain significant areas in which research on the Peabody is still necessary. (21 ref)
Kieffer, Donald M. & Golden, Charles J. (U South Dakota) Psychological Reports, 1978(Apr), Vol 42(2), 395–401. [PA, Vol 62:00090]

971.   Taking the role of retarded children: Effects of familiarity and similarity.
Investigated the effects of 2 variables on children's ability to take a retarded child's role: (a) familiarity with the characteristics of retarded children and (b) similarity of experiences to those of retarded youngsters. Ss were 16 siblings (Grades 4–6) of retarded children, 27 children enrolled in integrated 5th-grade classrooms, and 33 children enrolled in segregated 5th-grade classrooms. Integrated classrooms were defined as those in which at least 1 formally diagnosed retarded child was enrolled for part or all of the day; segregated classrooms were those in which no formally diagnosed retarded children were enrolled. Ss were less accurate in their inferences about the effect and motives of a retarded child as compared to their inferences about a nonhandicapped peer. Results also support the notion that children would be better able to take the role of an individual whose characteristics were familiar to them. The hypothesis that similarity of experience to retarded children would contribute to role-taking accuracy was not confirmed. (8 ref)
Kitano, Margie & Chan, Kenyon S. (New Mexico State U) American Journal of Mental Deficiency, 1978(Jul), Vol 83(1), 37–39. [PA, Vol 62:03396]

972.   [The effect of warning signal on reaction times of mentally retarded children.] (Japn)
Conducted 3 experiments with 12 retarded (mean MA 9.4 yrs; mean CA 14 yrs) and 12 CA-matched normal children to investigate Ss' covert behavior during a simple reaction time (RT) task. Several recurring visual stimuli (cues) were introduced during a constant warning interval. Results show that (a) normal Ss used the strategy of decreasing RT in recognizing the last cue, while retarded Ss were unable to do so; (b) the effect of temporal regularity of the presentation of cues was observed in retarded but not in normal Ss; and (c) the optimum condition under which RT in retarded Ss was most minimized was the condition in which cues were given in temporally regular order with added verbal stimuli. (24 ref)
Kondo, Fumisato.   Japanese Journal of Educational Psychology, 1978(Mar), Vol 26(1), 23–31. [PA, Vol 64:12743]

973.   [The effects of cue stimuli on the reaction times of mentally retarded children: An examination of the temporal factor and the spatial factor.] (Japn)
To investigate the covert behavior performed by retardates during the warning intervals of a simple reaction time (RT) task, cue stimuli differing in mode of temporal presentation (regular vs irregular) and mode of spatial presentation (regular vs irregular) were introduced in the warning interval. 12 retarded and 12 normal children, matched for CA with an average of 14.3 yrs, performed under these conditions. For retardates the spatial regularity produced shorter RTs than the temporal regularity. For normals there was little RT difference among the 4 experimental conditions. Retardates had minimized RT under the condition in which cue stimuli were presented regularly in the spatial order. These results may reflect differences in the covert behavior of retardates and normals. (14 ref)

Kondo, Fumisato. (Kyoto U, Japan) Japanese Journal of Psychology, 1978(Aug), Vol 49(3), 123–130. [PA, Vol 63:07805]

974.   [The comprehension of facial expressions in mentally retarded and normal children.] (Germ)
The comprehension of facial expressions was investigated in 30 normal and 30 mentally retarded 8–10 yr olds. The same order of recognition of different emotions was found in both groups (happy, angry, sad, frightened, surprised). Differences between the 2 groups were discovered as to the preferred presentation mode: Retarded Ss were best in recognizing emotions on photographic pictures, whereas normal Ss were better on comic strips. In both groups, MA was in direct relation with the number of correctly recognized facial expressions. (German summary) (8 ref)
Lambert, Jean-Luc & Defays, Daniel. (U Liège, Lab de Psychologie Expérimentale, Belgium) Psychologie - Schweizerische Zeitschrift für Psychologie und ihre Anwendungen, 1978, Vol 37(3), 216–224. [PA, Vol 63:12186]

975.   Comments on the use of the additive factor method with mentally retarded persons: A reply to Silverman.
Replies to W. P. Silverman (see PA, Vol 62:6342), who pointed out a violation in one of the underlying assumptions of the additive factor method in the data reported by A. Maisto and M. Jerome (see PA, Vol 61:3899). The central issue concerns the lack of independence between slope and intercept function relating reaction time to memory-set size. Maisto examines other research that makes a number of studies with retarded Ss suspect to this violation; he also provides possible explanations for this finding.
Maisto, Albert A. (U North Carolina, Charlotte) American Journal of Mental Deficiency, 1978(Sep), Vol 83(2), 191–193. [PA, Vol 62:06333]

976.   [Professional role, social condition and operative image in mentally disadvantaged children.] (Ital)
Investigated the image of the mentally disadvantaged (MD) child as seen by adults to understand how this image is influenced by the professional role of adults and by personal close experience. 30 mothers of normal children, 20 mothers of MD children attending special primary schools, 30 teachers of a normal primary school, and 10 teachers in a special school for the MD were administered the semantic differential with a questionnaire about operational perspectives in educational and social integration of such children. The descriptions of these children given by the special teachers were closer to the descriptions by their mothers than were the descriptions of these children given by teachers and mothers of normal children. Descriptions of handicapped children were influenced by the socioeconomic level of the family and by the mother's level of education. (French, English, & German summaries) (42 ref)
Mantovani, Giuseppe. (U Milano Facoltà Medica, Inst di Psicologia, Italy) Archivio di Psicologia, Neurologia e Psichiatria, 1978(Apr–Jun), Vol 39(2), 199–223. [PA, Vol 63:09944]

977.   Mental subnormality in Northern Ireland.
Conducted a prevalence survey of mental subnormality in Northern Ireland, using a method similar to one used in an earlier investigation by D. N. MacKay (see PA, Vol 49:2680). In a general population of 1.5 million there were 6,854 ascertained subnormal individuals. The male:female ratio was 1.14:1. Approximately 1 in 3 subnormal people were under residential care. The prevalence of severe subnormality (IQ < 50) in the 15–19 yr old group was .481%. Findings do not support the "steady rate" theory of severe subnormality. (15 ref)
McDonald, G. & MacKay, D. N. (Tower Hill Special Care Hosp, Dept of Psychology, Armagh, Northern Ireland) Journal of Mental Deficiency Research, 1978(Jun), Vol 22(2), 83–89. [PA, Vol 63:01228]

978.   Identifying language disorders in retarded children.
With the implementation of Public Law 94-142, individual educational plans must be written incorporating developmental status data with learning and performance descriptions. The author recommends identifying language delay or disorders in mentally retarded children by relating MA to age-related measures of language development (i.e., comprehension, production, and communication). Instruments or procedures useful for each type of measurement are mentioned. Comparison with cognition measures is justified by the central role accorded to cognition by many language theorists. Data on 82 developmentally disabled children (CA 7 mo–16.8 yrs, cognitive level 8 mo–7 yrs) show agreement of mean scores on informal and standardized cognitive measures and those on other measures. For 8 of the Ss, cognitive measures were lower than those of language development, bringing into question whether cognitive development is necessary or sufficient for language development; the relationship may just be correlational. (45 ref)
Miller, Jon F. (U Wisconsin, Madison) School Psychology Digest, 1978(Nov–Dec), Vol 7(4), 27–44. [PA, Vol 62:05116]

979.   Personality measurement in parents of retarded and emotionally disturbed children: A replication.
Replicated M. T. Erickson's (see PA, Vol 43:4040 and 10223) studies that compared MMPI profiles of parents of emotionally and behaviorally disturbed (ED), mentally retarded (MR), and nonclinic (N) children (50 families in each group). In general, Erickson's findings that the MR and ED parents did not differ, but that both showed elevated profiles relative to N, were confirmed. The results are interpreted to provide partial support for Erickson's "stress reaction hypothesis," whereby the well-known clinic parent MMPI elevations presumably reflect the parents' stress as a result of having a disturbed or handicapped child. (7 ref)
Miller, William H. & Keirn, William C. (U California, Neuropsychiatric Inst, Los Angeles) Journal of Clinical Psychology, 1978(Jul), Vol 34(3), 686–690. [PA, Vol 62:03667]

980.   Conservation of illusion-distorted identity tasks.
Four conservation of illusion-distorted identity tasks were presented to 10 boys whose CAs and MAs were 5–12 yrs and 3–10 yrs, respectively. MA was assessed by the Stanford Binet or the WISC. The study attempted to document individual differences among children with delayed development in the acquisition of conservation skills. Results indicate that the time in which conservation of mass and volume is achieved is after MA 7.6. Analysis of errors by CA and MA on at least 3 of the 4 tasks suggested that conservation follows more closely the development of MA than CA. (11 ref)
Mitchell, M. M. & Duncan, P. G. (U North Carolina, Chapel Hill) Perceptual & Motor Skills, 1978(Jun), Vol 46(3, Pt 1), 907–910. [PA, Vol 62:03714]

981.   Analysis of motor disorder in retarded infants and young children.
Conducted a longitudinal study of 53 10–25 mo old mentally retarded infants and young children without evidence of a frank physical disability. All Ss had diagnostic evaluations that included pediatric and neurologic examination, metabolic studies, genetic work-up, psychological assessment, and developmental testing (i.e., Gesell Developmental Schedules, Developmental Screening Inventory, and Denver Screening Test). Analysis of these data suggests that the Ss' delayed motor development was related to a subtle but specific disturbance in the evolution of infantile reflex behavior. The aberration was characterized by a delay in the appearance of postural adjustment reactions that, under normal circumstances, precede the accomplishment of successive gross-motor milestones. Motor development in this group of retarded children was delayed for their CA but was consistent with the maturational level of postural adjustment reactions. (34 ref)
Molnar, Gabriella E. (Yeshiva U, Albert Einstein Coll of Medicine, Rose F. Kennedy Ctr for Research in Mental Retardation & Human Development) American Journal of Mental Deficiency, 1978(Nov), Vol 83(3), 213–222. [PA, Vol 62:03898]

982. Age & sex distribution in institutionalized mentally deficient children.
50 mentally deficient children from 2 schools in India were interviewed, and data show significant age and sex effects on the distribution of retardation. More males and more younger children were at the schools than females or older (17–20 yr old) children. Possible effects of cultural factors on the identification of retardation are mentioned. (8 ref)
Murari, Pushpa & Sinha, V. (Government Postgraduate Coll, Rampur, India) Asian Journal of Psychology & Education, 1978(Nov), Vol 3(3), 9–11. [PA, Vol 64:12745]

983. Some probable factors causing mental retardation.
Conducted an exploratory study of 250 2–18 yr old children diagnosed as mentally subnormal at the Child Guidance Clinic, R.A.K. College of Nursing, New Delhi. The variables studied included parental age, economic condition, sex, birth anoxia, convulsions, ordinal position, family history of mental subnormality, and modes of delivery. It is concluded that biological and external factors have equal effects on mental subnormality. Correction of adverse social, economic, and cultural conditions in India could reduce or prevent much retardation.
Nanda, Shukla. (R.A.K. Coll of Nursing, Child Guidance Clinic, New Delhi, India) Child Psychiatry Quarterly, 1978(Oct–Dec), Vol 11(4), 106–111. [PA, Vol 63:05712]

984. A report of a case of Hallermann-Streiff syndrome.
Patients with stunted growth and a characteristic facial appearance with beaked nose, small mouth, irregular dentition, and microopthalmia are diagnosed as cases of Hallerman-Streiff syndrome (B. Kirman and J. Bicknell, 1975). A case of Hallerman-Streiff syndrome in a 5-yr-old boy, which perhaps is the 1st such case to be reported from India, is described.
Narayanan, H. S. & Rama, B. S. (National Inst of Mental Health & Neurosciences, Bangalore, India) Australian Journal of Mental Retardation, 1978(Jun), Vol 5(2), 68. [PA, Vol 63:01231]

985. A critical analysis of the attention hypothesis of Zeaman and House: Problems of parameter interactions in multiparameter models.
Examined the attention hypothesis of D. Zeaman and B. J. House (1963) through a systematic, computer-simulation analysis of the parameter interactions found in the One-Look model. The hypothesis states that mental retardates and normals differ in their initial attention habits but not in their learning rates in the context of discrimination learning. The analysis showed that possible differences in the learning rates cannot be ruled out. The result is used to suggest how shift designs can unconfound the effect of the attention habits from the effect of the learning rates and maximize chances of observing possible differences in the learning rates between retarded and normal children.
Okada, Yoshio C. (Rockefeller U, New York, NY) Journal of Experimental Child Psychology, 1978(Feb), Vol 25(1), 173–182. [PA, Vol 60:10644]

986. Nondifferential reinforcements and discrimination learning by retardates.
20 retarded 11–19 yr old Ss received 50 trials of nondifferential reinforcement in the presence of cues on the dimension of shape and subsequently learned either a shape discrimination with color irrelevant or a color discrimination with shape irrelevant. 20 control Ss simply learned the shape or color discrimination. Nondifferential reinforcement significantly facilitated learning of the color discrimination and tended only to hinder (nonsignificantly) learning of the shape discrimination. Results are discussed in terms of N. J. Mackintosh's (1965) attentional theory of discrimination learning.
O'Malley, John J. & Golden, Gregory. (U Scranton) Psychological Reports, 1978(Feb), Vol 42(1), 79–82. [PA, Vol 61:08715]

987. Observations of young normal and handicapped children.
Conducted an observational study of 38 9–29 mo old normal children and of 76 mentally handicapped children functioning at a similar level to determine the extent to which they involved themselves in play with toys and other objects and the extent to which their day was "empty." Observations of normal Ss were made in their homes and in day nurseries; observations of mentally handicapped were made at home, in day care centers (i.e., special schools), and in the schools and wards of subnormality hospitals. In no setting were Ss interacting with adults for more than 20% of their nonroutine time. These findings seem to justify concern over independent play with toys and other objects. The handicapped Ss in all settings had "emptier" days than the normal Ss, this being accounted for by greater amounts of inattentive handling of objects and self-stimulation and lesser amounts of social interaction and attentive play. Attentive play scores for the handicapped varied markedly with setting. In appropriate circumstances, there can be as much spontaneous contact with objects in handicapped children as in normal children at a similar development level. Despite current concern over the effects of day care on the development of very young children, normal children in day nurseries did not differ from normal children at home, either in attentive play scores or in the proportion of nonroutine time spent interacting with adults. (15 ref)
Phemister, M. R.; Richardson, A. M. & Thomas, G. V. (U Stirling, Scotland) Child Care, Health & Development, 1978(Jul–Aug), Vol 4(4), 247–259. [PA, Vol 62:13937]

988. Abbreviated forms of the WISC-R.
Validated the effectiveness of 3 forms of abbreviated WISC-Rs (those of L. W. Yudin, 1966; P. Satz et al, 1967; and A. J. Finch et al, 1973). 100 protocols from 100 6–16 yr old mentally retarded and language/learning impaired children were rescored according to 3 methods of abbreviation previously used with the WISC. Part–whole correlations, correlations of IQs from the original and short forms, were quite high for each of the short-form methods, ranging from .92 to .93 for the Full Scale IQ. Although tests for significance between correlations demonstrated no statistically significant differences, the accuracy of the Finch et al method was superior in estimating IQ. All 3 methods are derived from complete administration of the WISC-R. (18 ref)
Preston, John. (Baylor U) Psychological Reports, 1978(Jun), Vol 42(3, Pt 1), 883–887. [PA, Vol 62:10140]

989. Families and mentally retarded children: Emphasis on the father.
In this review, literature is summarized that is relevant to persons who work with mentally retarded (MR) children and their families. However, the major emphasis is on the relationship between fathers and their MR children. It is suggested that fathers should be more involved with their MR child, and this can be achieved through education, counseling, and various programs. (76 ref)
Price-Bonham, Sharon & Addison, Susan. (U Georgia) Family Coordinator, 1978(Jul), Vol 27(3), 221–230. [PA, Vol 63:01232]

990. Comparisons between mothers' and teachers' evaluations of developmental status.
Examined the relationship between mothers' and teachers' estimates of the developmental level of mentally retarded children. Ratings were obtained from 8 teachers and from the mothers of 35 6–21 yr old individuals (mean IQ 39.74) to determine the extent of agreement in the 5 skill areas assessed by the Developmental Profile. Estimates were also compared to the child's developmental level as measured by an individual intelligence test. Correlations between mothers' and teachers' estimates on each scale of the Developmental Profile ranged from .63 to .81. Significant differences between mothers' and teachers' ratings on the Developmental Profile were found on the Physical, Self-Help, and Communication scales. Correlations between the Stanford-Binet Intelligence Scale and the Developmental Profile IQ equivalent (IQE) were .51 and .63 for mothers and teachers, respectively, and the difference between these correlations was nonsignificant. Mothers' ratings on the Developmental Profile IQE were within 10 points of the Stanford-Binet IQ for 57% of the sample, while the teachers' ratings were within 10 points of the Stanford-Binet for 83% of the children. The utility of the Developmental Profile in evaluating the developmentally disabled child is discussed. (8 ref)

Prout, H. Thompson; Harper, Dennis C.; Snider, Bill & Lindgren, Scott. (U Wisconsin) Journal of Pediatric Psychology, 1978, Vol 3(2), 57–61. [PA, Vol 62:06337]

991. Metamemory development and the mentally retarded children: A review of recent research.
Several investigators suggest that normal and retarded individuals follow roughly the same patterns in development of metamemory. Documented evidence indicates that (a) a child becomes more realistic and accurate in assessing his or her memory capacities with increase in age, and (b) a child is increasingly able to monitor and introspect this memory performance with increase in age and mental ability. A few studies have attempted to show that metamemorial awareness is related to efficient performance on memory; this area has not been fully conceptualized. It is argued that metamemorial knowledge should guide one to adopt strategies in memory performance. Several questions remain to be explored with regard to strategy utilization, changing strategies in the face of failure on a task, and awareness that these behaviors are at the control of an individual. J. H. Flavell (1977) observed that repeated informational feedback in various memory situations might be a source of a child's knowledge of memory. Future research should focus on life experiences of retarded persons in assessing metamemorial awareness. (33 ref)
Ramayya, P. D. & Mulcahy, R. F. (U Alberta, Edmonton, Canada) Mental Retardation Bulletin, 1978, Vol 6(2), 77–91. [PA, Vol 63:09948]

992. The assessment of developmentally disabled children with the WISC-R, Binet and other tests.
Administered the WISC-R, Revised Stanford-Binet Intelligence Scale, Bender Visual Motor Gestalt Test, Developmental Test of Visual-Motor Integration, and Wide Range Achievement Test to 50 children aged 6 yrs 1 mo to 10 yrs 11 mo referred for multidisciplinary evaluation of developmental disabilities. Correlations among the various WISC-R measures (Standard Scores and IQs) and Binet IQ were significant, with relatively strong relationships among the Binet IQ and those WISC-R subtests that require concentration, short-term auditory memory, visual-motor integration, and the acquisition of new learning. The data show that the Binet MA correlated as well or better with the other tests than did the various scores from the WISC-R.
Raskin, L. M.; Bloom, A. S.; Klee, S. H. & Reese, A. (U Louisville Medical School, Child Evaluation Ctr) Journal of Clinical Psychology, 1978(Jan), Vol 34(1), 111–114. [PA, Vol 61:06268]

993. Effects of clustering instructions and category size on free recall of nonretarded and retarded children.
Studied the effects of category size and instructions to cluster on the free-recall learning of 112 nonretarded and retarded children. Mean CAs were 7 yrs 4 mo and 10 yrs 8 mo, respectively; mean MA for the retarded Ss was 7 yrs 4 mo (Stanford-Binet Intelligence Scale and the WISC). Simultaneously presented lists of 12 pictures composed of 2, 3, or 6 categories were shown for 3 study–test trials. Instructions to cluster significantly increased recall and cluster scores on a new list for both nonretarded and retarded Ss. The category-size effect was weak, although it was related to the magnitude of the correlations between organization and recall scores. (18 ref)
Reichhart, Gregory J. & Borkowski, John G. (State University Coll New York, Potsdam) American Journal of Mental Deficiency, 1978(Jul), Vol 83(1), 73–76. [PA, Vol 62:03901]

994. [A standard recording form for basic data on children and youth seen in child guidance clinics: Results of first use.] (Germ)
Presents preliminary results from the application of a questionnaire to measure behavior disturbances, poor school performance, and intellectual deficits in school children, which was developed by the Questionnaire Committee of the German Federal Conference on Child Guidance. Data collected in 1976 from 20 child guidance clinics are analyzed. Frequency distributions found for several items in the data base replicate well-known facts; for other items they bring new information to light.

Statistical analysis of 2 multivariate frequency distributions using an analysis of configuration frequency showed that certain subgroups were significantly larger than expected. Such subsamples were defined as high-risk groups. (7 ref)
Rey, Eibe-Rudolf; Aba, O. & Pfeifer, W. K. (Zentralinstitut für Seelische Gesundheit, Mannheim, West Germany) Zeitschrift für Kinder- und Jugendpsychiatrie, 1978, Vol 6(1), 40–55. [PA, Vol 65:01872]

995. Careers of mentally retarded young persons: Services, jobs and interpersonal relations.
Life histories and follow-up data at age 22 yrs were obtained for a United Kingdom total city population of children who were administratively defined in childhood as mentally retarded (index cases). Histories were also obtained from 76 matched comparisons who at no time had been classified as retarded. Matching was on age, sex, and social background. Placement at school-leaving age and major occupation were reported for the index population. Those index cases not receiving mental retardation services and their matched comparisons were examined on objective and subjective measures of the jobs they held and on selected indicators of interpersonal relationships.
Richardson, Stephen A. (Yeshiva U, Albert Einstein Coll of Medicine) American Journal of Mental Deficiency, 1978(Jan), Vol 82(4), 349–358. [PA, Vol 61:03905]

996. Performance of MA-matched nonretarded and retarded children on discrimination learning and transfer-shift tasks.
Examined the effects of the nature of the relevant dimension, response mode, imagery, and age on discrimination learning and shift performance. Three age groups were used: (a) Group 1—CA 8 yrs, MA 8 yrs; (b) Group 2—CA 5 yrs, MA 5 yrs; and (c) Group 3—CA 8 yrs, MA 5 yrs. The latter group learned both intradimensional and extradimensional shifts slower than did the former 2 groups. Subsequent analyses suggested that the reason for the slower learning in the retarded group was their greater frequency of control by dominant dimensions and/or the initial control by novel stimuli. A 2nd finding was related to the particular procedure employed. Ss were required either to press a button to indicate which of 2 stimuli was correct or to pick up the correct stimulus. Form-relevant but not color-relevant problems were facilitated by the pick-up procedure. These findings suggest that dimensional dominance may be a consequence of the procedures employed in previous reports where children were or were not permitted to manipulate the stimuli. (35 ref)
Richman, Charles L.; Adams, Kathrynn A.; Nida, Steve A. & Richman, Joyce. (Wake Forest U) American Journal of Mental Deficiency, 1978(Nov), Vol 83(3), 262–269. [PA, Vol 62:03902]

997. Parental attitudes of retarded young mothers.
32 retarded mothers (CAs 17–34 yrs; IQs 54–79) were found to have significantly more protective, controlling, and punitive attitudes toward their children than a control group of 32 mothers who had completed 2 or more years of college work. The retarded mothers regarded their own mothers as even more controlling, protective, and punitive than they themselves were. These findings are compatible with the hypothesis that increases in IQ scores of the children of retarded parents could be due to somewhat better parenting. If so, programs for retarded youngsters should place more emphasis on childrearing and family life in order to help counteract inappropriate parental attitudes that retarded children learn from their own parents. (25 ref)
Robinson, Lillian H. (Tulane U Medical School) Child Psychiatry & Human Development, 1978(Spr), Vol 8(3), 131–144. [PA, Vol 62:03903]

998. Considerations in the assessment of blind children who function as severely or profoundly retarded.
Suggests that unevenness in development of blind children who function as severely or profoundly retarded, particularly in language and communication, needs to be considered as a feature of the child's ability to learn rather than as characteristics of his or her retardation. The impact of blindness on early development, environment, and previous opportunities for learning

should be taken into account in assessment, education, and treatment of blind children who function as severely or profoundly retarded. (14 ref)

Rogow, Sally M. (U British Columbia, Vancouver, Canada) Child Care, Health & Development, 1978(Sep–Oct), Vol 4(5), 327–335. [PA, Vol 62:14008]

999. Etiological differences in patterns of psycholinguistic development of children of IQ 30 to 60.
Compared the psycholinguistic abilities of 131 mentally retarded children (CA 4 yrs 9 mo to 19 yrs 6 mo; IQ 30–60) of different etiological classifications (Down's syndrome, biologically brain damaged, environmentally caused retardation, unknown cause) and characterized each etiology according to the different patterns of psycholinguistic skills exhibited by the Ss. Level of skills was determined by the ITPA. Down's syndrome Ss exhibited significantly lower verbal–auditory skills than visual–motor skills. The environmentally caused retardation group showed no significant differences in development of psycholinguistic channels. Down's syndrome Ss had significantly lower verbal–auditory abilities than did the other etiological groups of severely retarded Ss. Etiological differences in the visual–motor channel were less pronounced (e.g., there were no significant differences for 3 of the 5 visual–motor abilities).

Rohr, Art & Burr, David B. (U Colorado) American Journal of Mental Deficiency, 1978(May), Vol 82(6), 549–553. [PA, Vol 61:13639]

1000. Religious views of parents of retarded children.
Enumerates 3 religious attitudes encountered by a physician in parents of mentally retarded children: (a) Religious faith has been a comfort, (b) the retardation is perceived as a punishment from God, and (c) anger toward God.

Schmitt, Raymond. (U North Carolina Medical School, North Carolina Memorial Hosp) Journal of Religion & Health, 1978(Jan), Vol 17(1), 80–87. [PA, Vol 62:03906]

1001. Effects of IQ and mental age on hypothesis testing in normal and retarded children: A methodological analysis.
Assessed the effects of 2 kinds of blank-trial probes for hypotheses upon performance of 200 normal and retarded children of MA levels 5½ and 7½. One kind of probe incorporated position-oriented response sets as legitimate hypotheses; the other measured response sets and hypotheses independently. The probe that incorporated response sets was shown to mask developmental differences and lead to erroneous conclusions. MA produced several effects upon performance, but IQ did not.

Schuepfer, Therese & Gholson, Barry. (Memphis State U) Developmental Psychology, 1978(Jul), Vol 14(4), 423–424. [PA, Vol 62:06341]

1002. Parents' initial reactions to having a mentally retarded child: A concept and model for social workers.
Motivated by the knowledge that the initial reaction experience to having a mentally retarded child is a critical determinant of parental responses for years to come, this paper attempts a close look at and a detailed conceptualization of that experience. In so doing, it has taken into account the available information and understanding and has particularly striven to integrate the psychoanalytic and crisis views. The hoped-for result is a concept that is realistic and a model that is specific, comprehensive, and affirmative enough to be readily usable by social workers. Case material is presented, and a diagram of "the normal coping process" (parents' responses to having a defective child) is included.

Sieffert, Allan. Clinical Social Work Journal, 1978(Spr), Vol 6(1), 33–43. [PA, Vol 61:13640]

1003. Multihandicapped children's preferences for pure tones and speech stimuli as a method of assessing auditory capabilities.
Residual hearing capabilities of 9 severely and profoundly retarded multihandicapped deaf-blind children (mean age 9 yrs, 1 mo) were determined with an operant procedure that allowed the Ss to respond by making a selection between 2 alternative responses. One response option resulted in the presentation of auditory reinforcement (pure tones and speech stimuli of various frequencies); the other option resulted in no reinforcement. Levels of the sound intensity were varied systematically to obtain a "threshold" for selective responding. Each of the severely damaged "untestable" Ss made numerous meaningful responses throughout the testing sessions, thereby revealing the levels of intensity that could be heard and those that were not high enough to elicit preferential responding. Ss responded comparably in conditions employing pure tones and speech. The responses of most of the Ss were comparable across frequency conditions, although some of the Ss' records showed selective responding at lower levels of intensity for certain frequencies than for others. It was also found that varying the level of intensity of the stimuli affected not only the Ss' selective behavior but also their time of task measures and their individual patterns of responding. (26 ref)

Silva, Dennis A.; Friedlander, Bernard Z. & Knight, Marcia S. (U Detroit) American Journal of Mental Deficiency, 1978(Jul), Vol 83(1), 29–36. [PA, Vol 62:03716]

1004. Comments on "Encoding and high-speed memory scanning . . ." by Maisto and Jerome.
Comments on A. Maisto and M. Jerome's (see PA, Vol 61:3899) reported differences in reaction-time performance between retarded and nonretarded adolescents. It is pointed out that when using the additive factor method, Maisto and Jerome violated a critical assumption underlying interpretation of the results and that this departure from theoretically acceptable conditions makes their data difficult to interpret.

Silverman, Wayne P. (New York State Inst for Basic Research in Mental Retardation, Staten Island) American Journal of Mental Deficiency, 1978(Sep), Vol 83(2), 188–190. [PA, Vol 62:06342]

1005. Parents' and teachers' attitudes toward mildly and severely retarded children.
Assessed the attitudes of 74 26–50 yr women toward the community and school integration of mildly and severely retarded children and found them less favorably inclined toward the school integration of the severely retarded. (1 ref)

Siperstein, Gary N. & Gottlieb, Jay. (U Massachusetts, Human Growth & Development Ctr, Boston) Mental Retardation, 1978(Aug), Vol 16(4), 321–322. [PA, Vol 63:01907]

1006. Current issues in mental retardation and cultural disadvantage.
Discusses developments in the overlapping areas of mental retardation and cultural disadvantage reported at the Fourth International Congress of the International Association for the Scientific Study of Mental Deficiency, held in Washington, D.C., during August 1976. Topics covered include innovations in educational approaches, progress in preventing and remediating retardation, and the increased availability of appropriate assessment tools and educational opportunities for cultural minorities. A series of questions are presented for investigation concerning the application of these findings to South Africa: (a) Would a mainstreaming policy in schools be appropriate? (b) What provisions are being made in teacher training to acquaint them with the needs and nature of retarded children? (c) How can community resources be mobilized to deal with the problems? (d) What steps are being taken (e.g., health care, nutrition, sex education, compensatory education, adolescent programs) to prevent and treat retardation? (e) How can a pluralistic model be applied in South Africa to create a more positive attitude toward nondominant cultures, while still providing them with the aspects of Western culture which they desire? (French, German, & Afrikaans summaries) (17 ref)

Skuy, Mervyn. (U of the Witwatersrand, Johannesburg, South Africa) Humanitas: Journal for Research in the Human Sciences, 1978, Vol 4(3), 307–311. [PA, Vol 64:08278]

1007. Visual motor short term memory in educationally subnormal boys.
Examined 45 educationally subnormal (ESN) boys in 3 MA groups of 6, 9, and 12 yrs for developmental trends and rehearsal strategies on a visual motor short-term memory task. Comparisons were made with 45 normal boys aged 6, 9, and 12 yrs.

Developmental trends and rehearsal strategies were almost totally absent in ESN Ss. Normal Ss were superior to ESN Ss when central processing space was available during a condition of rest. No differences were evident when central processing was prevented during an interpolated activity condition. It is concluded that normal–ESN differences could be attributed to lack of mnemonic strategies in the ESN Ss. (24 ref)

Sugden, D. A. (U Leeds, England) British Journal of Educational Psychology, 1978(Nov), Vol 48(3), 330–339. [PA, Vol 64:01329]

1008.   Primacy performance of normal and retarded children: Stimulus familiarity or spatial memory?
On the assumption that serial recall tasks reflect spatial memory rather than verbal rehearsal (e.g., A. Siegal et al; see PA, Vol 56:7676), the purpose of this experiment was to determine the effect of stimulus familiarity on 20 normal and 20 retarded 10–13 yr olds' spatial primacy performance. Linear presentation effects of familiar and nonfamiliar pictures on serial position curve performance when overt verbalization was suppressed were investigated. Results indicate that stimulus familiarity rather than spatial memory is responsible for the primacy effect found in serial position curves. No primacy effect for either the normal or the retardate group was found in the nonfamiliar stimulus condition. Stimulus familiarity also facilitated recall for both groups in the recency position. No overall developmental effects were found between groups of children on serial position performance. Consistent with F. Craik and R. Lockhart's (see PA, Vol 50:189) memory processing model, the present results indicate that stimulus familiarity provided deeper levels of processing, thereby facilitating primacy effects. (13 ref)

Swanson, Lee. (U Northern Colorado) Child Study Journal, 1978, Vol 8(2), 101–110. [PA, Vol 62:03911]

1009.   [Probabilistic prognosis in the speech activity of mentally retarded children.] (Slok)
Probabilistic prognosis can be considered a part of speech automatism and sequential mechanisms. It is responsible, on the one hand, for the adequate choice of language units and on the other hand, for the anticipation of language units. Research suggests that adequate anticipation of the completion of the verbal stimulus is on a lower level in mentally retarded children. Children without mental deficiency complete statements on a wider semantic level involving a broader activity field. The theory that in the mentally retarded child the prognostic process is present only at the lowest levels (i.e., on the associative level) is rejected. The variation of replies is the same in all children. A mechanistic concept of the probabilistic prognosis is also rejected. The child accomplishes the choice of the subsequent text on the basis of an analysis of the whole stimulus configuration. (Russian summary)

Učeň, Ivan. (Výskumný Ústav Detskej Psychológie a Patopsychológie, Bratislava, Czechoslovakia) Psychológia a Patopsychológia Dietata, 1978, Vol 13(4), 301–314. [PA, Vol 63:09951]

1010.   Analysis of cognitive abilities for mentally retarded children on the WISC-R.
Investigated the cognitive abilities of 238 retarded Ss on the WISC-R. The sample consisted of 238 children (135 boys and 103 girls) ranging in ages from 5 yrs 7 mo to 16 yrs 7 mo, with a mean age of 10 yrs, 9 mo. The variation in subtest scores was analyzed by an ANOVA for correlated data of the sample's subtest scores. On the WISC-R Verbal scale, the boys scored slightly higher than the girls on each of the subtests. The girls excelled on the Coding subtest. Greatest variation in subtest scores occurred in the Object Assembly subtest, while the lowest variation occurred in Picture Arrangement. Results indicate that the relative strength and/or weakness of this sample is not restricted to either the Verbal or Performance area. Differences among the WISC-R subtests for retarded Ss seem to be as great within the Verbal–Performance areas as they are between them. (16 ref)

Vance, Hubert B. et al. (James Madison U, Child Study Ctr) Psychological Record, 1978(Sum), Vol 28(3), 391–397. [PA, Vol 63:03515]

1011.   The abilities of retarded students: Further evidence concerning the stimulus trace factor.
Obtained a Wherry-Wherry hierarchical factor solution on the correlations among 11 WISC-R subtests for a sample of 79 mentally retarded boys and girls. Findings are not only congruent with P. E. Vernon's (1950) ability paradigm but also suggest that the ability structure for retardates may well be more complex than the structure for normals. The ability hierarchy for the present sample included a general (*g*) factor defined by positive loadings from all 11 subtests and factors corresponding to the verbal-educational (*v:ed*) and spatial-perceptual (*k:m*) parameters. In addition, a stimulus trace (*ST*) factor corresponding to the ability dimension described by A. Baumeister and C. Bartlett (1962) was obtained. (16 ref)

Vance, Hubert B.; Wallbrown, Fred H. & Fremont, Theodore S. (James Madison U) Journal of Psychology, 1978(Sep), Vol 100(1), 77–82. [PA, Vol 63:05725]

1012.   A study of the play behavior of retarded children.
Used 10 observation categories to classify the toy selection and play activities of 38 mentally retarded children (CAs 7–11 yrs, IQs 61–80). The play of all Ss was videotaped for 2 30-min periods at an interval of 3–6 wks. Ss' teachers completed questionnaires regarding the children's social and emotional behavior. Results of the play behavior inventory show that the Ss spent 28.4% of the 1st observation period and 21.8% of the 2nd observation period cleaning up; this activity represented the largest percentage of time spent in any single activity. Over the 2 observation periods, both boys and girls spent about 22% of their time in repetitive, exploratory, and experimental movements. Toy choice data indicate that the environmental material and the vehicles were the most interesting, and the classroom material and wild animals received the least attention. The hypothesis that the Ss' level of intellectual functioning, which was measured by the HAWIK, would show a significant relationship to the frequency of variance in play behavior was also confirmed. Rank correlations of .06 for the 1st observation period and .48 for the 2nd were found between the final score of the questionnaire and an imitation play index; thus a significant relationship between emotional and social behavior and play was only found for the 2nd observation period. (French & German summaries) (32 ref)

Van der Kooij, Rimmert. (State U of Groningen, Netherlands) International Journal of Rehabilitation Research, 1978(Jul), Vol 1(3), 329–341. [PA, Vol 63:03516]

1013.   Adaptive behavior and Uzgiris-Hunt scale performance of young, developmentally disabled children.
Assessed the relationship between performance on a Piaget-based infant scale and adaptive behavior for 25 developmentally disabled infants and preschoolers. Instruments were the Uzgiris-Hunt Infant Psychological Development Scale and the Alpern-Boll Developmental Profile. Results indicate a significant relationship between these measures. Canonical analysis suggested the relevance of the Piagetian abilities of object permanence and foresight and the adaptive behavior skills of self-help and social behavior for this relationship. (19 ref)

Wachs, Theodore D. & de Remer, Paula A. (Purdue U) American Journal of Mental Deficiency, 1978(Sep), Vol 83(2), 171–176. [PA, Vol 62:06347]

1014.   [On the formation of putting speech sounds into letters in terms of two-syllable words.] (Japn)
Five experiments with an 11-yr-old mentally retarded boy investigated how S learned to put given speech sounds into Japaneses phonemic letters (hiragana). Results show that the most useful learning procedure was when S was required to read 2 letters (a word) on a card, then to choose a picture card equivalent to them, and in addition, to determine the correspondence between the picture card and the letter card. (6 ref)

Wakabayashi, Setsuki & Kitahara, Mieko. Japanese Journal of Educational Psychology, 1978(Dec), Vol 26(4), 239–246. [PA, Vol 64:12757]

1015. Category structure and semantic priming in retarded adolescents.
Investigated the internal structure of semantic categories in 15 mentally retarded adolescents (mean CA 17 yrs, mean MA 9 yrs) as reflected in naming times to pictures of common objects. Pictures were presented in pairs of either categorically related or unrelated items. For related pairs, both the primes (1st pictures) and targets (2nd pictures) varied in rated "typicality," being either typical or relatively atypical members of their primary superordinate category. An analysis of naming times to targets revealed a semantic-priming effect; targets in related pairs were named faster than those in unrelated pairs. Of major importance was the finding that naming times varied as a function of both prime typicality and target typicality. The data suggest that the semantic categories of retarded persons have an internal structure generally similar to that of the nonretarded persons from whom the typicality ratings were obtained and that even relatively atypical exemplars are functional category members for retarded persons.
Weil, Carolyne M.; McCauley, Charley & Sperber, Richard D. (State University Coll New York, Cortland) American Journal of Mental Deficiency, 1978(Sep), Vol 83(2), 110–115. [PA, Vol 62:03915]

1016. The Rorschach and structured tests of perception as indices of intellectual development in mentally retarded and nonretarded children.
In a study of the developmental significance of certain perceptual activities, the Rorschach and 4 structured tests of perception (the Children's Embedded Figures Test, Gestalt Completion Test, Closure Speed Test, and Visual Recognition and Incomplete Objects) were administered to 5 groups of children (CAs 6–12 yrs, MAs 6–12 yrs, IQs 99.92–123.67). All 3 Rorschach measures were significantly related to MA, as were all 4 of the structured tests. The Children's Embedded Figures Test was the best predictor of MA; it accounted for 52% of the variance, while the 6 remaining measures yielded nonsignificant increments to a multiple regression equation. In a factor analysis, the 4 structured tests loaded on 1 factor (51% of total variance), while the 3 Rorschach variables loaded on a 2nd (17%); MA loaded on both (.669 and .447, respectively). In an additional finding, E. Zigler's (see PA, Vol 43:8608) "developmental" hypothesis that level of development and not IQ determines cognitive competence received partial support from 13 of 14 statistical tests. (28 ref)
Weisz, John R.; Quinlan, Donald M.; O'Neill, Patrick & O'Neill, Pamela C. (Cornell U) Journal of Experimental Child Psychology, 1978(Apr), Vol 25(2), 326–336. [PA, Vol 61:08731]

1017. Associative symmetry in the PA learning of retarded and nonretarded children.
Two experiments each studied 20 mentally retarded children (mean CA range 10 yrs 10 mo–11 yrs; mean MA range 7 yrs 5 mo–7 yrs 10 mo) and 20 each of nonretarded 2nd and 5th graders. Ss learned pairs of pictures in a single-function or a double-function order. Associative symmetry was demonstrated by all groups when the lists were presented single-function; forward asymmetry was demonstrated when the list was presented double-function. When categorized pairs were presented double-function, items that were correctly associated by category produced symmetry; items that were correctly associated but not by category produced forward asymmetry. The possible influence of single vs multiple associations on associative symmetry is discussed.
Winters, John J.; Daggett, Susan Z. & Kologinsky, Eileen F. (Edward R. Johnstone Training & Research Ctr, Bordentown, NJ) American Journal of Mental Deficiency, 1978(Sep), Vol 83(2), 122–128. [PA, Vol 62:06352]

1018. Inexpensive apparatuses for use with young children: A WGTA variant.
Details steps for constructing devices adapted from the WGTA (Wisconsin General Training Apparatus) and for use with young children in discrimination tasks. The devices are specially made jack-in-the-boxes to which various discrimination forms can be attached. The units have been used successfully with normal and retarded children and with children (15–60 mo old) with motor difficulties and/or muscle weaknesses.
Wyrick, Michael E. & Sherrod, Kathryn B. (George Peabody Coll for Teachers) Behavior Research Methods & Instrumentation, 1978(Jun), Vol 10(3), 409–410. [PA, Vol 62:12597]

1019. National crisis in mental retardation research.
Argues that the incidence of mental retardation will be significantly reduced only when there is a greater understanding of the nonorganic form of mental retardation, the type that afflicts approximately 75% of persons labeled mentally retarded. Such an understanding requires an interdisciplinary research effort that includes a major contribution from the behavioral sciences. The current level of support of mental retardation and behavioral-science research by the National Institute of Child Health and Human Development limits the nation's capability of achieving the goals of preventing and ameliorating mental retardation. (17 ref)
Zigler, Edward. (Yale U) American Journal of Mental Deficiency, 1978(Jul), Vol 83(1), 1–8. [PA, Vol 62:03918]

1020. Posture, constitution, muscular strength, gross motor function and fine motor function in mentally retarded children.
Data on height, weight, posture (vertical stability, sitting stability, vertical balance), muscular strength (back strength, trunk extension, leg strength), gross motor function (vertical jump, 25-m run), and fine motor function (dropping beads task, transfering soybeans task, pulp pinching task) of 22 mentally retarded children (MA 4.0–9.0 yrs; CA 9.9–16.11 yrs) were analyzed. Vertical stability (static balance) had no relation to other items. Vertical balance (dynamic balance) was related not only to gross motor function but also to back strength and MA. Static balance (vertical stability, sitting stability) had no close relations to fine motor function. Height had a significant relationship to back and leg strength. Just as MA correlated with items of posture, muscular strength, and gross and fine motor functions, CA correlated closely with height, weight, and leg strength. (3 ref)
Abe, Kenichi. Journal of Child Development, 1979(Jan), Vol 15, 22–27. [PA, Vol 64:05887]

1021. Development of psychosexual concepts in relation to expressive language performance.
Cognitive-developmental theory suggests that the learning of gender identity concepts is a sequential process, beginning with the learning of one's own gender and moving to recognition of the invariance of gender as a human characteristic. Neither clinical nor theoretical literature can fully explain the steps involved. In this study, 51 30–84 mo old retarded (mean IQ 64) and 36 25–66 mo old nonretarded (mean IQ 108) children were asked to respond to tasks requiring knowledge of core gender identity (Michigan Gender Identity Test) and gender constancy. When data from both groups were pooled, a significant interaction was found across all ages between expressive language performance (rated by Ss' teachers, speech therapists, and the experimenter) and the development of core gender identity and gender constancy. (20 ref)
Abelson, A. Geoffrey. (Iowa State U, Coll of Education, Ames) Psychiatry, 1979(Aug), Vol 42(3), 274–279. [PA, Vol 65:03505]

1022. Television programs about retarded children and parental attitudes toward their own retarded children.
133 parents and/or their mentally retarded (MR) children viewed 4 30-min TV dramas depicting MR adults and children in everyday situations. Interview data show that the shows were not as effective as expected in favorably altering parental attitudes toward their MR children. (3 ref)
Baran, Stanley J. (U Texas, Austin) Mental Retardation, 1979(Aug), Vol 17(4), 193–194. [PA, Vol 66:07710]

1023. Analysis of the AAMD adaptive behavior scale: Public school version.
Many state agencies have ruled that assignment of students to special education classes for the mentally retarded must be determined by assessment of verbal, performance, and adaptive behaviors. The American Association for Mental Deficiency Adaptive Behavior Scale—Public School Version was subjected

to a normative and validation study using 291 Ss from south-central Texas. Data were collected from groups of regular and special education students, both White and non-White at 8, 10, and 12 yrs of age. Compared to the original normative data, results indicate that (a) the instrument was effective in discriminating between regular and special education groups, (b) a shortened version may be feasible and more practical, and (c) the derived total score may be useful and effective when used as a cutoff score for placement in special education for the mentally retarded. (6 ref)

Boyd, Lenore A. & Chissom, Brad S. (Texas A&M U) Perceptual & Motor Skills, 1979(Oct), Vol 49(2), 595–600. [PA, Vol 65:06413]

1024.   Cardiac change of retarded and nonretarded infants to an auditory signal.
Five mentally retarded infants (mean age 16.5 mo) and 5 nonretarded infants (mean age 16 mo) were presented a tone for 15 trials. Heart-rate change from prestimulus level showed a deceleration on 4 1-sec intervals for the nonretarded Ss and no change for the retarded Ss. Comparison of the 2 groups showed a difference on 5 of the 1-sec intervals following stimulus onset. When the total heart-rate change scores were examined for each S, no overlap of the scores was evident for the Ss in the nonretarded group with the individual scores of the retarded Ss. (19 ref)

Bradley-Johnson, Sharon & Travers, Robert M. (Central Michigan U) American Journal of Mental Deficiency, 1979(May), Vol 83(6), 631–636. [PA, Vol 62:08854]

1025.   Impedance and otoscopy screening of multiply handicapped children in school.
79 physically handicapped, mentally retarded 4–14 yr olds were screened with impedance audiometry, followed by otoscopy. Results indicate that the presence of middle-ear abnormalities increased as the degree of retardation increased and age decreased. As the degree of physical involvement increased, the presence of suspected middle-ear pathology increased. (12 ref)

Bruns, Janet M.; Cram, Janis T. & Rogers, Gayle J. (Michael Dowling School, Minneapolis, MN) Language, Speech, & Hearing Services in Schools, 1979(Jan), Vol 10(1), 54–58. [PA, Vol 64:01109]

1026.   An ethological approach to studying intelligence.
As an alternative to the psychometric approach to studying intelligence, an empirical, observational method is proposed in which the S's problem-solving behavior in everyday situations is analyzed. The results of pilot studies of normal and retarded children are summarized, and other current applications of the method are mentioned. Problems with the method include the following: (a) It is costly, inconvenient, and time-consuming. (b) It is complex, and observer training is not easy. (c) It does not provide direct access to the cognitive processes involved in behavior. However, it supplies valuable and needed information about the individual's interaction with the environment. (9 ref)

Charlesworth, William R. (U Minnesota Inst of Child Development, Minneapolis) Human Development, 1979, Vol 22(3), 212–216. [PA, Vol 63:01216]

1027.   Developmental theory revisited: Findings of longitudinal study.
Reexamines developmental theory in terms of data from longitudinal studies of 4 cohorts of children: (a) the New York Longitudinal Study (A. Thomas and the author; 1977), which examined the significance of temperament for development; (b) a longitudinal study of working class Puerto Rican children; (c) a 6-yr study of middle-class, mildly mentally retarded children; and (d) a longitudinal study of multihandicapped children with congenital rubella. Case vignettes are presented that illustrate the theme that the behavioral development of any individual child includes consistencies and inconsistencies—continuity and change. It is concluded that neither heredity nor environment alone determine development; an interactionist theoretical framework is advocated. (15 ref)

Chess, Stella. (New York U Medical Ctr) Canadian Journal of Psychiatry, 1979(Mar), Vol 24(2), 101–112. [PA, Vol 66:03410]

1028.   Definition of severe mental retardation in school-age children: Findings of an epidemiological study.
Data from a survey of German school-age children were used to test the hypothesis that 2 forms of mental retardation—pathological and subcultural—can be differentiated on the basis of intelligence tests (Columbia Mental Maturity Scale, Peabody Picture Vocabulary Test, a fine motor function test, and a short form of the Vineland Social Maturity Scale). Findings based on the 323 mentally retarded children who were identified indicate that this dichotomy is an oversimplification, since frequency of neurological and other organic impairments was inversely related to intelligence over a fairly wide range. The best cutoff point for screening purposes, in discriminating between severe or moderately severe retardation (usually pathological) on the one hand and mild retardation (usually subcultural) on the other, corresponded roughly to IQ 50. Use of higher thresholds tended to increase misclassification and yield less reliable prevalence rates. Classification of children in the IQ range 50–70 as mentally handicapped (severely or moderately mentally retarded) appeared to be subject to social-class bias and hence could be selectively disadvantageous for children from lower social status families. (22 ref)

Cooper, B.; Liepmann, M. C.; Marker, K. R. & Schieber, P. M. (Zentralinstitut für Seelische Gesundheit, Mannheim, West Germany) Social Psychiatry, 1979, Vol 14(4), 197–205. [PA, Vol 65:02454]

1029.   The interpretation of pronominal reference by retarded and normal readers.
Required 25 retarded and 50 normal readers (8–12 yrs of age) to interpret 2-clause sentences in which the pronominal subject of one clause agreed with the named subject of the other. Some sentences followed an indirect speech format in which the subordinate clause was usually preceded by the main clause; others contained subordinate clauses headed by an adverb, which were not fixed in relation to the main clause. A simple order-based solution sometimes adopted by young children avoids the main and subordinate distinction: If the pronominal subject precedes the named subject its reference is restricted to a different identity (ID2). Retarded Ss produced significantly fewer ID2 interpretations when these were obligatory, confirming that syntactic problems may be implicated in reading retardation. Since retarded Ss did not spontaneously apply the order strategy, the possibility of teaching it where the main–subordinate distinction is too difficult to operationalize is raised. (17 ref)

Dalgleish, B. W. & Enkelmann, Susan. (U Queensland, Brisbane, Australia) British Journal of Educational Psychology, 1979(Nov), Vol 49(3), 290–296. [PA, Vol 65:08206]

1030.   Children's fears: A developmental comparison of normal and exceptional children.
The fears of 82 7–19 yr old boys and girls classified as educable mentally retarded (EMR), 32 as trainable mentally retarded (TMR), and 19 as specific learning disabled, were ascertained through self-report data and compared with those of 106 normal children aged 6–12 yrs. Similar developmental trends were found in all groups, with younger Ss reporting more unrealistic fears than older Ss. When MA was calculated for the EMR and TMR Ss, their developmental trends closely approximated those of the normal Ss. In general, exceptional Ss had a much wider range and a greater number of fears than normal Ss. Most fears were found to be realistic, learned, and dependent upon the S's intellectual and maturational level. (15 ref)

Derevensky, Jeffrey L. (McGill U, Montreal, Canada) Journal of Genetic Psychology, 1979(Sep), Vol 135(1), 11–21. [PA, Vol 63:05698]

1031.   Attitudes of parents of mentally retarded children toward normalization activities.
Parents of mentally retarded children were surveyed via a 5-point Likert scale to determine their attitudes toward normalization activities in general and in relation to their child. All parents

were members of organized groups focusing on the provision and advocacy of services to the retarded. Two questionnaires, one with a general referent and the other with a child-specific referent, were administered to 250 Ss; 217 responses were received. Results indicate significant differences in response, with the more positive attitudes being those associated with a general (the mentally retarded population) rather than specific (my child) referent. Within the general-referent group, parents of teachable mentally retarded children displayed the most positive attitudes. Age, sex, and level of retardation had no effect on child-specific responses. (19 ref)

Ferrara, Dianne M. (U Texas School of Human Development, Special Education Program, Dallas) American Journal of Mental Deficiency, 1979(Sep), Vol 84(2), 145–151. [PA, Vol 63:00089]

1032. Children with supernumerary X-chromosome: A ten-year follow-up study of schoolchildren in special classes.

Describes a 10-yr follow-up study on 8 girls and 18 boys affected by supernumerary X-chromosomes. 26 controls were also studied. The risks of social behavior disturbances, criminality, and alcohol abuse were studied, together with that of mental disorder. No statistically significant differences were found in girls. For the boys, the only difference of statistical significance was that the Klinefelter boys showed a lower frequency of social behavior disturbances than their controls. (9 ref)

Forssman, H.; Thuwe, Inga & Eriksson, B. (St Jorgen's Hosp, Psychiatric Research Ctr, Hisings Backa, Sweden) Journal of Mental Deficiency Research, 1979(Sep), Vol 23(3), 189–193. [PA, Vol 66:06070]

1033. Quantitative and qualitative analyses of moral reasoning in children, adolescents, and adults of similar mental age.

60 mentally retarded adolescents and adults and nonretarded 1st graders, all of comparable MAs (87.95, 92.85, and 85.65 mo, respectively), were administered moral judgment tasks. Although the overall pattern of response was generally similar across groups in dealing with actor size, intent, and consequence of portrayed vignettes, retarded adults did give more positive ratings to smaller than larger actors and gave significantly more positive ratings to situations involving negative intent than retarded adolescents and 1st graders. The 3 groups were also comparable in their resolutions of dilemmas involving authority, peer, and altruism choices. The importance of considering variables other than IQ or MA in research is discussed. The findings are presented as a basis for an alternative way to approach assessing the social cognitive development of retarded populations. (19 ref)

Foye, Howard & Simeonsson, Rune J. (Children's Hosp Medical Ctr, Child Development Unit, Boston, MA) Journal of Pediatric Psychology, 1979(Jun), Vol 4(2), 197–209. [PA, Vol 63:01220]

1034. Mental retardation research, ecological validity, and the delivery of longitudinal education programs.

Discusses the schism that has developed between mental retardation research and the programmatic reform activities taking place in the educational and residential sectors. Principles for conducting more ecologically valid research are advanced to end this separation between fields and to improve the scientific status of mental retardation research. (41 ref)

Gaylord-Ross, Robert J. (San Francisco State U) Journal of Special Education, 1979(Spr), Vol 13(1), 69–80. [PA, Vol 66:08234]

1035. The Lock Box: An instrument to evaluate mental organization in preschool children.

The Lock Box, a large rectangular container with 10 latched doors, each housing a different toy, is designed to investigate mental organization in young children. It differs from general intelligence and special ability tests by emphasizing how a child approaches a problematic situation, rather than how much he/she knows. The Box received preliminary validation as a diagnostic instrument in the present study of 57 retarded and 57 normal children (mean CAs 53 and 51 mo, respectively). In addition to its use as a screening instrument for mental retardation, the Box may identify mental disorganization in

normal children (the cognitively hyperactive/distractible group) as well as good mental organization in retarded children (the delayed but not deviant retarded group). (22 ref)

Goodman, Joan F. (U Pennsylvania Graduate School of Education) Journal of Child Psychology & Psychiatry & Allied Disciplines, 1979(Oct), Vol 20(4), 313–324. [PA, Vol 65:02394]

1036. Neurological processes concerned with communication and their analysis.

Discusses reasons for the failure of language skills and communication to develop in mentally handicapped children. Variables related to the development of such skills are examined, including sensory input and perception, intelligence, concept formation, emotional disturbance and/or psychosis, attention and overactivity, memory and imagery, and intersensory association. The nature of acquired dysphasia in later childhood is contrasted with infant- and adult-onset dysphasia. Genetic, environmental, and physical causes of dyslexia are also considered, and the need to carefully identify the child's language strengths and weaknesses is emphasized. (18 ref)

Gordon, N. S. (Booth Hall Children's Hosp, Manchester, England) Child Care, Health & Development, 1979(Jan–Feb), Vol 5(1), 29–40. [PA, Vol 62:03708]

1037. Adaptive behavior scale: Development as a diagnostic tool via discriminant analysis.

The multidimensional nature of behavior often causes a dilemma for the diagnostician who must interpret inconsistent behavior. Three classifications of 6–12 yr old children were evaluated on the public school version of the Adaptive Behavior Scale by their teachers. Of the 388 nonretarded, 115 educable mentally retarded, and 85 trainable mentally retarded children, 86% were correctly identified via 12-variable classification functions. Results indicate that further development of an adaptive behavior instrument would be desirable as a cost-efficient and powerful diagnostic tool. (17 ref)

Gully, Kevin J. & Hosch, Harmon M. (Washington State U) American Journal of Mental Deficiency, 1979(Mar), Vol 83(5), 518–523. [PA, Vol 62:05091]

1038. Bender visual-motor abilities of slow learners.

Compared the Bender Gestalt Test protocols of 134 rural and 140 urban slow learners (IQ 70–84). Rural Ss performed significantly below their MAs more frequently than urban Ss. Both rural and urban Ss performed developmentally below CAs but as expected for MAs until CA 10 (MA 8). At this point urban Ss appeared to perform as expected from MAs, but a significant number of rural Ss performed below expectations. After CA 14 (MA 11), the differences between the urban and rural groups were not significant. (6 ref)

Hetrick, Ethel W. (Northwestern State U) Perceptual & Motor Skills, 1979(Aug), Vol 49(1), 31–34. [PA, Vol 65:03523]

1039. Sequencing of visual and auditory stimuli in teaching words and Bliss symbols to the mentally retarded.

Compared the relative ease of learning with words and Bliss symbols (B) by 4 trainable (CA 6–9 yrs; IQ 40–61) and 4 profoundly (CA 14–17 yrs; IQ not scored to 30) mentally retarded Ss. Results show that B were the more easily learned, particularly with the profoundly retarded Ss. (7 ref)

Hughes, M. J. (U Manitoba, Winnipeg, Canada) Australian Journal of Mental Retardation, 1979(Dec), Vol 5(8), 298–302. [PA, Vol 66:08238]

1040. Anorexia nervosa and mental retardation: A case report.

Presents the case of a 15-yr-old female to illustrate the interaction between subnormal intelligence and anorexic symptomatology and the relationship between anorexia nervosa and depression. (13 ref)

Hurley, Anne D. & Sovner, Robert. (Dorchester Mental Health Ctr, MA) Journal of Clinical Psychiatry, 1979(Nov), Vol 40(11), 480–481. [PA, Vol 65:03348]

1041.   Census-based prevalence estimates for mental retardation.
Bureau of Census 1976 Survey of Income and Education data from informants in 150,000 representative US households indicate that the estimated national prevalence of mental retardation is .43%; this figure excludes institutionalized persons, unrelated persons in the same households under age 14, and persons under age 3. The figure is lower than (a) the 3% who theoretically have IQs below 70 and (b) the 1% frequently cited prevalence rate derived from persons officially identified as mentally retarded by agencies. (7 ref)
Jones, Larry A. (St Martin's Coll) Mental Retardation, 1979(Aug), Vol 17(4), 199–201. [PA, Vol 66:08240]

1042.   [Spectral analytical study on the developmental properties of EEG in children: Variability of EEG in normal and mentally retarded children.] (Japn)
Studied the variability of the resting arousal EEG in 58 normal and 63 mentally retarded children (ages 3–15 and 7–18 yrs, respectively). EEGs were recorded monopolarly from 6 regions of the scalp, providing autopower spectra and a coefficient of variation of power at each frequency. The variability of power at peak within the theta frequency band in both groups showed a notably higher value as compared with other frequency bands in all regions. Some of the problems of treating this variability of power as a general characteristic of theta waves or as a developmental characteristic are discussed. (32 ref)
Katada, Akiyoshi; Suzuki, Hiroya & Suhara, Kenkichi. (Tokyo Gakugei U, Japan) Japanese Journal of Psychology, 1979(Feb), Vol 49(6), 318–325. [PA, Vol 64:05247]

1043.   Cognitive rigidity in the aged and the mentally retarded.
Three groups of Ss were compared on a visual recognition task that involved changing from one category of identification to another. Ss were 13 noninstitutionalized elderly persons (CA 60–79 yrs, IQ 65–98), 18 students (CA 15–18 yrs, IQ 94–141) and 20 mentally retarded Ss (CA 14–19 yrs, reading ages 0–11 yrs 1 mo). Results show that the mentally retarded Ss had greater difficulty in changing categories than did the nonretarded Ss. Results for the elderly were similar but may have been partly due to the choice of stimulus material. In a 2nd task, the same elderly and nonretarded young Ss named as many objects as possible in 1 min. The elderly group produced fewer responses on average than the young group and fewer categories of such responses. Results suggest that older persons find it more difficult to change between different categories of identification. (7 ref)
Kirby, N. H.; Nettelbeck, T. & Goodenough, S. (U Adelaide, Australia) International Journal of Aging & Human Development, 1978–79, Vol 9(3), 263–272. [PA, Vol 63:11711]

1044.   [The need for a measure of adaptive behavior in mentally retarded children and adolescents.] (Polh)
Describes a series of reliability and validity studies of a Polish modification of the Adaptive Behavior Scale for Children and Adults developed by K. Nihira et al (1974). This test is considered useful in selecting individuals who need educational rehabilitation or psychotherapy. (Russian & English abstracts) (14 ref)
Kostrzewski, Janusz. (Higher School of Special Pedagogy, Warsaw, Poland) Psychologia Wychowawcza, 1979(May–Jun), Vol 22(3), 329–336. [PA, Vol 65:11668]

1045.   Lexical usage of retarded children: An examination of informativeness.
Two experiments studied 28 retarded preschoolers (CAs 27–46 mo, MAs 14–24 mo). Ss were most likely to both label and imitate when the referent objects were informative in the presentation sequence. The frequency of labeling and imitation was particularly high when the informative element was an object exemplar that had not been seen before. Results are discussed in terms of the presuppositional abilities seemingly demonstrated by the children and the implications these abilities have for intervention programs. (12 ref)

Leonard, Laurence B.; Cole, Brenda & Steckol, Karen F. (Purdue U) American Journal of Mental Deficiency, 1979(Jul), Vol 84(1), 49–54. [PA, Vol 62:11236]

1046.   Assessment of cognitive deficiency with the McCarthy scales and Stanford-Binet: A correlational analysis.
Tested matched samples of 15 retarded and 15 normal 4–8 yr old children on the Stanford-Binet Intelligence Scale and McCarthy Scales of Children's Abilities. Pearson correlations between Stanford-Binet IQs and the 6 McCarthy Scale Indexes for retarded Ss were lower than coefficients obtained from the normal Ss and from previous research. While the General Cognitive Index may be interchangeable with IQ in the normal range of intellectual functioning, this relationship was not found for retarded Ss. The "venerable" Stanford-Binet retains its position as the most broadly applicable measure of intellectual functioning. (12 ref)
Levenson, Richard L. & Zino, Thomas C. (Fairleigh Dickinson U) Perceptual & Motor Skills, 1979(Feb), Vol 48(1), 291–295. [PA, Vol 64:02469]

1047.   Using McCarthy scales extrapolated general cognitive indexes below 50: Some words of caution.
Used extrapolated General Cognitive Indexes to determine the relationship between the McCarthy Scales of Children's Abilities and the Stanford-Binet Intelligence Scale for assessing the functioning level of 15 retarded children. A comparison of means for the extrapolated Indexes and Binet IQs (via the *t* test) was significant. Results are interpreted as being due to the error variance associated with extrapolated scores and the absence of data on retarded Ss from the standardization sample of the McCarthy scales. (3 ref)
Levenson, Richard L. & Zino, Thomas C.
(Eds). Psychological Reports, 1979(Oct), Vol 45(2), 350. [PA, Vol 65:06842]

1048.   Visceral larva migrans and eosinophilia in an emotionally disturbed child.
Visceral larva migrans, *Entamoeba coli,* evidence of latent toxoplasmosis, and a history of plumbism were found in an emotionally disturbed, retarded 7½-yr-old boy. Patients with pica should be screened for parasitism and other diseases transmitted orally. (9 ref)
Marcus, Leonard C. & Stambler, Morris. (Tufts U School of Medicine) Journal of Clinical Psychiatry, 1979(Mar), Vol 40(3), 139–140. [PA, Vol 64:03639]

1049.   Correlates of social competence in retarded children.
Tested the hypotheses that (a) significant associations would occur between teacher-based measures of social competence and measures obtained directly from Ss, and (b) the social competence measures would be significantly related to role-taking and referential communication skills. Ss were 32 retarded children (mean IQ 56.4; mean CA 13 yrs 7 mo). Significant associations occurred between 2 types of teacher measures of children's social competence, between measures made by teachers and children themselves, and among scores of social competence and the skills of role-taking and referential communication. Findings suggest ways of assessing social adaptation more directly, which may be extended to specific interventions. (8 ref)
Monson, Lynne B.; Greenspan, Stephen & Simeonsson, Rune J. (U North Carolina) American Journal of Mental Deficiency, 1979(May), Vol 83(6), 627–630. [PA, Vol 62:08875]

1050.   Memory deficit in the mentally retarded: Is this the real problem?
Suggests that the "real problem" that the mentally retarded have in memory deficit is not less capacity for recall but a lack of spontaneous use of strategies to organize and maintain the material for recall. The failure of retarded children to demonstrate generalization of successfully trained memory strategies emphasizes the importance of the use of the information rather than just its availability. Therefore, it may be possible to train the retarded to be more "planful" in their approach to memory tasks. (8 ref)

Mulcahy, Robert F. (U Alberta, Edmonton, Canada) Mental Retardation Bulletin, 1979, Vol 7(3), 123–131. [PA, Vol 66:08255]

1051. Schedule-induced locomotor activity in humans.
In 2 experiments, 4 undergraduates and 2 moderately retarded male adolescents received tokens on either an FI schedule for plunger pulling or various response-nondependent FT schedules ranging from 16 to 140 sec. Locomotor activity such as walking, shifting weight, or pacing was recorded in quarters of the interreinforcement interval to examine the induced characteristics of that behavior in humans. While performance was variable, several characteristics were present that have counterparts in experiments with nonhumans during periodic schedules of food reinforcement: (a) first-quarter rates, and sometimes overall rates, of locomotor activity were greater during intervals that terminated in a visual stimulus and token delivery than those without; (b) overall rates of locomotor activity were greater during FT 16-sec schedules than during FT 80- or 140-sec schedules; (c) rates of locomotor activity decreased during the interreinforcement intervals; (d) locomotor activity was induced by response-dependent and response-nondependent token delivery. Results show that the rate and temporal pattern of locomotor activity can be schedule-induced in humans. (17 ref)
Muller, Philip G.; Crow, Robert E. & Cheney, Carl D. (Oakdale Regional Ctr, Lapeer, MI) Journal of the Experimental Analysis of Behavior, 1979(Jan), Vol 31(1), 83–90. [PA, Vol 63:12190]

1052. Age, intelligence, and inspection time.
10 young retarded males (IQs 51–71) were compared on a simple discrimination task with 10 male university students of the same CA and 28 nonretarded male 7–10 yr olds. Estimates of inspection t;me (λ) were obtained from the pattern of errors made by each S; λ is assumed to reflect the rate at which sensory imput is accumulated and processed. Average estimates of λ from 4 groups of Ss (7, 8, 9, and 10 yrs) were 147, 142, 137, and 139 msec, respectively. The mean for university students was 130 msec, whereas that for retarded adults was 256 msec. Mean RT for all nonretarded Ss increased as stimulus-exposure duration decreased, children being slower than adults. Retarded Ss' RT was less influenced by stimulus-exposure duration and was faster than that of nonretarded Ss at the shortest exposure. Results suggest that slower perceptual speed among retarded persons is a consequence of a permanent deficiency; differences in response strategy may explain the differences in RT. (5 ref)
Nettlebeck, T. & Lally, M. (U Adelaide, Australia) American Journal of Mental Deficiency, 1979(Jan), Vol 83(4), 398–401. [PA, Vol 62:11241]

1053. Sex effect on the risk of mental retardation.
Risks of mental retardation were computed separately for the relatives of male and female probands using data on 1,450 persons collected by E. W. Reed and S. C. Reed (1965). When compared, the risks for the relatives of females were always significantly higher than the risks for the relatives of males. These findings are consistent with the hypothesis of a differential genetic loading for males and females. (12 ref)
Pauls, David L. (U Iowa Coll of Medicine) Behavior Genetics, 1979(Jul), Vol 9(4), 289–295. [PA, Vol 65:01518]

1054. Factor structure of the WISC-R for a clinic-referred population and specific subgroups.
Compared the factor structure of the WISC-R for a clinic-referred population of 594 2nd–6th graders and specific subgroups (emotionally handicapped, learning disabled and slow learner combined, and no significant problem) with that obtained by A. S. Kaufman on the WISC-R (1975) standardization sample. Similar factor-analytic procedures were used, and 3 factors were extracted from each group. The first 2 factors, Verbal Comprehension and Perceptual Organization, which were identified on the standardization sample, were consistently in evidence. However, Factor 3 was much less stable, and it is concluded that there may be some genuine differences between normal and clinical populations on that factor. (3 ref)

Petersen, Calvin R. & Hart, Darrell H. (Educational Support Systems Inc, Salt Lake City, UT) Journal of Consulting & Clinical Psychology, 1979(Jun), Vol 47(3), 643–645. [PA, Vol 62:09878]

1055. A caution against the use of the Slosson Intelligence Test in the diagnosis of mental retardation.
The Slosson Intelligence Test, unlike most current measures of intelligence, uses a ratio method (MA divided by CA) to obtain an IQ score. Due to this, standard deviations are not stable across age levels and present a problem in diagnosing mental retardation. Current criteria for the classification of mental retardation are reviewed, and it is concluded that the Slosson is inappropriate for use in its diagnosis. (15 ref)
Reynolds, William M. (State U New York, Albany) Psychology in the Schools, 1979(Jan), Vol 16(1), 77–79. [PA, Vol 65:11693]

1056. Some characteristics of a population of mentally retarded young adults in a British city: A basis for estimating some service needs.
Describes a population of mentally retarded young people (born in 1951–1955) in terms of the frequency of various kinds and degrees of impairment—intellectual, physical, and behavioral. Ss were resident in a city in 1962 and had at some time been placed in a mental retardation service. The prevalence of the mentally retarded was 16/1,000. Age specific prevalence rates for the same population rose from age 5, reached a plateau of 14/1,000 from ages 10–15 and then dropped for the postschool period to a rate of 5–6/1,000. Classifications of physical impairment, seizure histories, and behavior disturbances are described. (4 ref)
Richardson, Stephen A. (Yeshiva U, Albert Einstein Coll of Medicine) Journal of Mental Deficiency Research, 1979(Dec), Vol 23(4), 275–285. [PA, Vol 66:08267]

1057. [Pathology of intelligence: Deficiencies of chromosomal and genetic origin.] (Fren)
Of the 3 general groups of factors described as responsible for different forms of intellectual deficiency—postnatal and perinatal factors, genetic factors, and chromosomal aberrations—the literature pertaining to the latter 2 is reviewed. Data provide information about chromosomal aberrations among individuals, the most frequently occurring autosomal aberrations, and aberrations of heterochromosomes. Data from the literature on deficiencies associated with genetically based dysfunction are presented in narrative and table form under these categories: name of the dysfunction, nature of the defect, mode of transmission, and behavioral manifestations of the dysfunction. (22 ref)
Roubertoux, Pierre & Carlier, Michèle. (U Paris V, Lab de Psychologie Différentielle, France) Bulletin de Psychologie, 1978–79(Mar–Jun), Vol 32(8–14), 434–442. [PA, Vol 65:01385]

1058. A new syndrome of elevated blood lead and microcephaly.
Determined the blood lead levels of 100 children seen at an outpatient clinic for developmental and learning disabilities in a rural Southern state. One child with moderately elevated blood lead and 9 with minimally elevated blood lead were identified; 7 of these 10 children were microcephalic, a markedly and significantly higher rate of microcephaly than in the remainder of the clinic sample. Most of the children suffering from the lead-microcephaly syndrome were Black, and a majority had birth weights under 2,500 gm, suggesting the possibility that prenatal exposure to lead might have caused their microcephaly and developmental handicaps. (29 ref)
Routh, Donald K.; Mushak, Paul & Boone, Lois. (U Iowa) Journal of Pediatric Psychology, 1979(Mar), Vol 4(1), 67–76. [PA, Vol 62:06418]

1059. A new syndrome of elevated blood lead and microcephaly.
Blood lead level determinations were carried out on 100 children (aged 8 mo to 23 yrs) seen at an outpatient clinic for developmental and learning disabilities in a rural Southern state. One child with moderately elevated blood lead and 9 with minimally elevated blood lead were identified; 7 of these 10 children were microcephalic, a markedly and significantly higher rate of

microcephaly than in the remainder of the clinic sample. Most of the children suffering from the lead-microcephaly syndrome were Black, and a majority had birth weights under 2,500 g, suggesting the possibility that prenatal exposure to lead might have caused their microcephaly and developmental handicaps. (29 ref)
Routh, Donald K.; Mushak, Paul & Boone, Lois. (U Iowa) Journal of Pediatric Psychology, 1979(Mar), Vol 4(1), 67–76. [PA, Vol 62:14010]

1060. Measurement of intelligence by means of children's drawings.
Investigated whether drawing behavior is a good indicator of intelligence. 43 intellectually handicapped children (6–17 yrs old) were administered the WISC, Wechsler Preschool and Primary Scale of Intelligence, Peabody Picture Vocabulary Test, or Stanford-Binet Intelligence Scale. Ss' MAs showed a high correlation with their drawing age (as determined by drawing characteristics defined by V. Lowenfeld and W. Brittain, 1968). Characteristics of Ss' pencil and crayon drawings are described for the following developmental levels: Scribbling (2–3 yrs 6 mo); Preschematic (4–6 yrs 6 mo); Schematic (7–8 yrs 6 mo); and Increasing Realism (9–12 yrs). It is suggested that spontaneous drawings be used when Ss' intellectual level is uncertain (because standardized tests have not or cannot be administered). It is also proposed that examination of drawing behavior may point up instances where intelligence tests may not have accurately reflected an S's intellectual capacity. (6 ref)
Russell, Eleanor R. American Journal of Art Therapy, 1979(Jul), Vol 18(4), 107–117. [PA, Vol 65:13050]

1061. Pathological left-handedness: Cross-cultural tests of a model.
Tested a model that attempts to account for the raised incidence of manifest left-handedness (MLH) reported in epileptic and mentally retarded populations. Data from 673 adult and 192 child (mean age 10.2 yrs) epileptics and 1,230 mentally retarded Ss from 4 cross-cultural studies were analyzed. EEG data provide support for the model that predicts that this raised incidence of MLH is due largely to unilateral (left) rather than bilateral hemispheric dysfunction. (French & German abstracts) (11 ref)
Satz, Paul; Baymur, Lale & Van der Vlugt, Harry. (U Florida, Neuropsychology Lab, Gainesville) Neuropsychologia, 1979, Vol 17(1), 77–81. [PA, Vol 66:06168]

1062. Problem children—handicapped, maladjusted and mentally retarded.
Discusses the causes of handicapped, maladjusted, and mentally retarded children. Factors that may contribute to these problems are divorce, marital conflicts, parental domination or submissiveness, poverty, and immorality. The influence of the community can also be significant, as can the social and educational atmospheres in schools. It is noted that adverse social, economic, and cultural factors appear to play a major role in the etiology of mental retardation. (22 ref)
Singh, Vinod K. (National Inst of Health & Family Welfare, New Delhi, India) , 1979, Vol 18(1–4, Spec Iss), 122–128. [PA, Vol 65:08056]

1063. Measuring the use of a principle by retarded adolescents and nonretarded children on a redundancy series test.
A series test composed of geometric figures placed in redundant patterns was designed to measure the ability of retarded adolescents to use a principle. The test was administered to 20 institutionalized and 17 noninstitutionalized retarded adolescents and to 170 nonretarded children from nursery school through Grade 4. Results show that 4 of the items accounted for most of the errors and that these items were particularly sensitive to an inadequate scanning strategy. The retarded groups showed a mental age lag of at least 1 yr 6 mo and did not perform above chance on the critical items. (13 ref)
Spitz, Herman H. & Semchuk, Maria T. (E. R. Johnstone Training & Research Ctr, Bordentown, NJ) American Journal of

Mental Deficiency, 1979(May), Vol 83(6), 556–560. [PA, Vol 62:07708]

1064. Reinforcement effects on the intelligence test performance of Coloured and White mentally retarded children.
Investigated the effects of contingent social and material reinforcement on the intelligence test performance of 27 White (mean age 10.5 yrs) and 23 Coloured (mean age 13.3 yrs) mentally retarded children. Form A of the Peabody Picture Vocabulary Test (the baseline measure) was administered to all Ss. Based on these scores a randomized block design was used to assign these Ss to 1 of 3 reinforcement conditions (social reinforcement, material reinforcement, or no reinforcement) that were operative during the administration of Form B (the dependent variable). A 2 × 3 (race × reinforcement) factorial analysis of covariance, with the pretest scores as the covariate, yielded a significant reinforcement main effect but a nonsignificant race effect and a non-significant race × reinforcement interaction. On the basis of these results, the practical implications of delivering praise in the standardized test situation is questioned, while the need for further research investigating the importance of the informative component of reinforcers is emphasized. (French, German, & Afrikaans summaries)
Steel, K. & Barling, Julian. (U Witwatersrand, Johannesburg, South Africa) Humanitas: Journal for Research in the Human Sciences, 1979, Vol 5(2), 107–111. [PA, Vol 64:07722]

1065. Occupational interests and mentally retarded people: Review and recommendations.
Reviews several studies on the choice of occupational interests for the mentally retarded adolescent. Several concerns about current evaluation practices (e.g., they have strong occupational, sex, race, and regional biases that discriminate against the choices of many retarded adolescents) are discussed. Recommendations are offered for a client-centered developmental model making the evaluation of occupational interests a viable part of the clients' career/vocational development process. (24 ref)
Stodden, Robert A.; Ianacone, Robert N. & Lazar, Alfred L. (Boston Coll) Mental Retardation, 1979(Dec), Vol 17(6), 294–298. [PA, Vol 66:08273]

1066. A hierarchical analysis of the WAIS performance of adolescent retardates.
A Wherry-Wherry hierarchical factor solution was obtained on the WAIS subtest performance of 100 retardates (mean CA 19.45 yrs). A hierarchical arrangement of abilities consistent with P. E. Vernon's (1950) model of cognitive structure, and consistent with previous reports, was obtained. A g-factor and 2 major group factors were evident. The g-factor was defined by loadings from all subtests. Verbal subtests defined v:ed; performance subtests defined k:m. Bifurcation of the Verbal and Performance subtests was produced when the variance attributable to g was removed. Comparison of the data of this study with those of F. Wallbrown et al (see PA, Vol 52:9854) showed the following differences: The g-factor loadings were lower and more overlap of abilities was identified. Picture Completion was found to be a better measure of k:m than Object Assembly. (12 ref)
Swassing, Ray. (Ohio State U) Journal of Experimental Education, 1978–79(Win), Vol 47(2), 179–181. [PA, Vol 64:08280]

1067. A comparison of posture and gross motor functions between normal children and mentally retarded children.
Compared measurements on postural stability and gross motor functions that need the extensor muscles in 17 normal and 17 retarded children and studied the relationships among the tasks. Ss of each group were matched in MA (6.6 yrs). Vertical stability, sitting stability, and vertical balance were measured as postural stability. Back strength, trunk extension, leg strength, vertical jump, and 25-m run were measured as gross motor function. The retarded group was superior to the normal group in sitting ability, but in vertical balance the normal group was superior. Retarded Ss were superior to normal Ss in 2 muscular strength tasks. In the relationship between posture and gross motor function, a significant correlation was found between vertical stability and gross motor functions in the normal group,

whereas vertical balance correlated significantly only with a few gross motor functions in the retarded group. (2 ref)
Tachi, Akio. (Waseda U, Tokyo, Japan) Journal of Child Development, 1979(Jan), Vol 15, 28–32. [PA, Vol 64:05907]

1068.   [A study on motivation in mentally retarded children: An experimental examination of the motivational hypothesis on an expectancy of success.] (Japn)
Two experiments investigated the motivational effects of expectancy of success in 48 normal and 48 mentally retarded children matched on MA (7–8 yrs). Ss were given a 3-choice discrimination task in which the degree of success/failure was manipulated. Results support the findings of T. H. Ollendick et al (1971) suggesting that mentally retarded children are experienced in failure and thus have a lower expectancy of reinforcement than do normal children. (11 ref)
Tanaka, Michiharu.   Japanese Journal of Educational Psychology, 1979(Jun), Vol 27(2), 121–130. [PA, Vol 64:12755]

1069.   The "cocktail party syndrome" in children with hydrocephalus and spina bifida.
Reviews the literature on the "cocktail party" syndrome (CPS), a language disorder apparently specific to children with hydrocephalus. Results of detailed psychological testing at 5 yrs of age show that children (N = 49) with CPS can be distinguished from other cases of spina bifida, because of significantly lower Wechsler Preschool and Primary Scale of Intelligence scores and very retarded social skills. Visual perceptual abilities were also significantly poorer. The reported verbal fluency of Ss with CPS did not, however, lead to superior scores on the Reynell Expressive Language Scales, for these Ss had difficulty in using language creatively in spite of good syntax. Further assessment at the age of 7 revealed that these Ss were significantly poorer than other cases of spina bifida in reading, spelling, and arithmetic and that they had shorter concentration spans and slightly more behavior problems in school. There was evidence that CPS declined with age and its presence at the age of 10 was diagnostically significant of a subnormal level of intelligence. Children with this are more likely to be female and to have more severe physical handicaps. (51 ref)
Tew, Brian. (School Psychological Ctr, Rhondda, Wales) British Journal of Disorders of Communication, 1979(Sep), Vol 14(2), 89–101. [PA, Vol 66:08377]

1070.   Application of visual reinforcement audiometry (VRA) to low-functioning children.
Assessed visual reinforcement audiometry (VRA) in 21 low-functioning children (aged 10 mo–6 yrs) in an ongoing clinical program. After establishing the specific reinforcing value of the visual stimulus, threshold assessments were made. VRA was an effective test procedure for most of the Ss, providing their developmental ages reached approximately the 10-mo level or higher. On the basis of VRA thresholds and tympanometry, 52% of the Ss seen were referred for medical evaluation. A variation of VRA was used to assess syllable-discrimination performance on a pilot basis. Results are discussed in terms of the potential use of VRA to assess infant speech-sound discrimination in addition to its current use as an indicator of hearing sensitivity. (22 ref)
Thompson, Gary; Wilson, Wesley R. & Moore, John M. (U Washington Child Development & Mental Retardation Ctr) Journal of Speech & Hearing Disorders, 1979(Feb), Vol 44(1), 80–90. [PA, Vol 64:01154]

1071.   Sensorially impaired adolescents.
Discusses the changes occurring in adolescence (physical, social, cognitive development, and ego development) and how these develop in the mentally impaired adolescent. A mentally retarded child requires more time to advance from one stage to another than a typical child and may have an insufficient ego and an inability to interact with the environment. In the age of latency (6–12 yrs), the mentally retarded child may not have the normal experiences of new ideas, perfecting skills, or sexual investigation. At puberty and adolescence, this child may not go to mixed parties or share with peers. (7 ref)

Torrie, Carolyn C. (U Texas, South Central Regional Ctr for Services to Deaf-Blind Children, Dallas) Sexuality & Disability, 1979(Fal), Vol 2(3), 231–237. [PA, Vol 64:10641]

1072.   Sex differences on the WISC-R for retarded children and youth.
Investigated sex differences on the WISC-R subtests for retarded males and females who were matched in terms of WISC-R Full Scale IQs. The sample consisted of 63 females and 63 males ranging in age from 7.3 to 8.3 yrs. Each S was matched in terms of Full Scale IQ. A 2 × 10 ANOVA with repeated measures on a single factor was used to analyze the data. Student's T and Fisher's F ratios were calculated, and differences between subtest means were analyzed by Newman-Keuls test for sample effects. Results show a significant Sex by Subtest interaction. (10 ref)
Vance, Hubert B. (James Madison U, Child Study Ctr) Psychology in the Schools, 1979(Jan), Vol 16(1), 27–31. [PA, Vol 65:11708]

1073.   [A study of the play behavior of retarded children.] (Germ)
Observed 38 retarded children (17 female and 21 male 7–11 yr olds) and recorded their behavior in 10 categories (e.g., choice of toys and use of toy). Findings suggest that the play behavior of retarded children is predominated by a great need to explore, experiment, and move so that they have little opportunity to use toys in a creative way. Males had a particular interest in vehicles and environmental material, females in dolls. Level of play behavior and scores on the HAWIK were positively correlated with each other. This was also true for the correlations between the subtest scores and play behavior, with the exception of Similarities and Block Design. Also, variation in play behavior correlated positively with measured IQs. The correlations indicated that imitation play is important for emotional and social behavior and indicate the advantages of bringing the retarded child into contact with as many toys as possible. (French & Spanish abstracts) (30 ref)
Van der Kooij, R. (Rijksuniversiteit te Groningen, Inst für Heilpädagogik, Netherlands) Acta Paedopsychiatrica, 1979(Oct), Vol 45(1), 25–42. [PA, Vol 65:05695]

1074.   Referential description by children in negative form.
32 5- and 7-yr-old normal primary school children and 32 8- and 11-yr-old mentally retarded children (IQs 50–75) were found to have no difficulty in making negative referential descriptions in natural contexts when their attention was drawn to the context by the experimenter. The degree to which Ss' descriptions reflected awareness of the context was related to their mental maturity, and there was a developmental trend in the form of descriptions. (8 ref)
Watson, Judith M. (Moray House Coll of Education, Edinburgh, Scotland) British Journal of Psychology, 1979(May), Vol 70(2), 199–204. [PA, Vol 64:08281]

1075.   Reactions of mothers with mentally retarded children: A social perspective.
38 mothers of retarded children (ages 5–19 yrs) and 70 mothers of nonretarded elementary and middle-school children were asked a series of Likert-type questions designed to tap social behaviors and attitudes. The mothers of retarded children were more likely to express positive attitudes toward the retarded and to expect that the "average" person in the community has a negative opinion of the retarded than were the mothers of the nonretarded children. Mothers of retarded children also manifested different patterns of social behavior regarding employment and utilization of babysitters in comparison with mothers of nonretarded children. (7 ref)
Watson, Robert L. & Midlarsky, Elizabeth. (Metropolitan State Coll) Psychological Reports, 1979(Aug), Vol 45(1), 309–310. [PA, Vol 65:03539]

1076.   Comparison of tangibly reinforced speech-reception and pure-tone thresholds of mentally retarded children.
16 mentally retarded children (mean CA 8 yrs 6 mo, mean IQ 52) who had normal hearing were examined with 2 tests of auditory sensitivity. One procedure employed a tangibly rein-

forced operant-conditioning paradigm for pure tones, and the other test was based on a modification of operant conditioning for obtaining speech-reception thresholds. The speech procedure, utilizing an attractive mechanical device in the form of a clown, proved to be effective and efficient for use with retarded children. (6 ref)
Weaver, Nancy J.; Wardell, Ferman N. & Martin, Frederick N. (Gallaudet Coll) American Journal of Mental Deficiency, 1979(Mar), Vol 83(5), 512–517. [PA, Vol 62:06349]

1077.　Retardation amongst Aboriginal children in North Australia.
Established a register of 62 retarded children (aged under 19 yrs) from tribally oriented Aboriginal communities in the Northern Territory of Australia and conducted an investigation of the age, sex, and main conditions of each child. The incidence and characteristics of retarded Aboriginals were found to be generally the same as those of retarded Europeans. (13 ref)
Webber, D. L. Australian Journal of Mental Retardation, 1979(Mar), Vol 5(5), 1–4. [PA, Vol 66:08281]

1078.　Severe impairments of social interaction and associated abnormalities in children: Epidemiology and classification.
Investigated the prevalence of severe impairments of social interaction, language abnormalities, and repetitive stereotyped behaviors in children under 15 yrs of age living in an area of London. A "socially impaired" group (more than half of whom were severely retarded) and a comparison group of "sociable severely mentally retarded" were identified in 132 children. Mutism or echolalia, and repetitive stereotyped behaviors were found in almost all the socially impaired Ss, but to a less marked extent in a minority of the sociable severely retarded. Certain organic conditions were found more often in the socially impaired group. A subgroup with a history of L. Kanner's (1956) early childhood autism could be identified reliably but shared many abnormalities with other socially impaired children. The relationships between mental retardation, typical autism, and other conditions involving social impairment are discussed, and a system of classification based on quality of social interaction is considered. (48 ref)
Wing, Lorna & Gould, Judith. (MRC Social Psychiatry Unit, London, England) Journal of Autism & Developmental Disorders, 1979(Mar), Vol 9(1), 11–29. [PA, Vol 62:11097]

1079.　Speed of retrieving information from the lexicon of mentally retarded adolescents.
36 institutionalized retarded adolescents named 48 colored pictures of objects. J. J. Winters et al (1978) established that for nonretarded adults the estimated age-of-acquisition of the names of these 48 objects ranged from 2 yrs 6 mo to 7 yrs of age. The present findings show that pictures whose names had been estimated by nonretarded adults to have been acquired earlier were named more accurately and faster by retarded adolescents than were pictures whose names were estimated to have been acquired later. (10 ref)
Winters, John J. & Cundari, Leigh. (E. R. Johnstone Training & Research Ctr, Bordentown, NJ) American Journal of Mental Deficiency, 1979(May), Vol 83(6), 566–570. [PA, Vol 62:08888]

1080.　Induction, emergence, and generalization of logical operations in retarded children: A training-to-criterion procedure.
Describes a study in which 24 mildly retarded Ss (CA 6–14 yrs; MA 4–6 yrs) were trained to a prespecified criterion on 1 of 3 logical operations tasks involving length; identity conservation, equivalence conservation, or transitivity. The ease with which the concepts were learned suggested that the natural order of emergence was transitive inference, equivalence conservation, and then identity conservation. Significant amounts of generalization to untrained concepts (interconceptual) were evident, as well as generalization to the untrained dimension of weight (intraconceptual). It is concluded that intensive training to a prespecified criterion is capable of producing generalization to concepts dealing with logicomathematical reasoning in mentally retarded children. (22 ref)

Abramson, Marty; Cooney, John B. & Vincent, Lisbeth. (Texas A&M U) Journal of Special Education, 1980(Sum), Vol 14(2), 189–198. [PA, Vol 66:06060]

1081.　A critique of a proposed set of neuropsychodiagnostic rules.
M. Selz and R. Reitan (see PA, Vol 62:8716) presented a system of diagnostic rules involving neuropsychological test data designed to separate normal, learning disabled, and brain damaged children, ages 9–14 yrs, by diagnostic group. The present author criticizes the study on methodological and theoretical grounds. (18 ref)
Amante, Dominic. Journal of Consulting & Clinical Psychology, 1980(Aug), Vol 48(4), 525–527. [PA, Vol 65:00161]

1082.　Test–retest reliability of the Test for Auditory Comprehension of Language when it is used with mentally retarded children.
44 retarded children (CAs 6–15 yrs; average MA 5 yrs 5 mo/Peabody Picture Vocabulary Test) were administered the Test for Auditory Comprehension of Language (TACL) and then retested after a 5-wk interval. A reliability coefficient of 0.91 was obtained between pre- and posttest administrations of TACL. Internal stability was highest for total score, the subtests measuring form class and function words, and grammatical categories. The low coefficients obtained for the subtests of morphological construction and syntactic structure suggest that these should be viewed with considerable caution when considered separately from the total test results. (8 ref)
Anderson, Jack D.; Hess, Robert & Richardson, Kathleen. (U Tulsa) Journal of Speech & Hearing Disorders, 1980(May), Vol 45(2), 195–199. [PA, Vol 65:11627]

1083.　Observational studies of retarded children with multiple stereotyped movements.
Conducted 3 long-term observational studies, involving 7 preschoolers, each of whom exhibited multiple stereotypies, to determine the extent to which the type of activity or setting affected the rates of these responses. Repeated observations were made of each S during a variety of school activities. In Exps I and II, adult–child interactions were also recorded. Results show that, in general, the particular activity greatly affected rates of stereotyped behavior, although some individual differences were evident. Moreover, in Exps I and II, variability was apparent across sessions within a particular setting. For some Ss, there was evidence that their multiple stereotypies were functionally interrelated. Adult interactions, as recorded in Exp II, were both quantitatively and qualitatively different for stereotyping as contrasted with nonstereotyping Ss. An environmental analysis employing a sequential model indicated that there were teacher behaviors that affected the frequency and/or conditional probability of the S's aberrant behavior. (9 ref)
Baumeister, Alfred A.; MacLean, William E.; Kelly, Jeff & Kasari, Connie. (Vanderbilt U) Journal of Abnormal Child Psychology, 1980(Dec), Vol 8(4), 501–521. [PA, Vol 65:08199]

1084.　Is the slow learner in the classroom learning disabled?
Addresses the issue of identifying learning-disabled children and suggests approaches for delineating subgroups of slow-learning children. Findings from the present authors' previous studies, which are reviewed, suggest that only the consistently slow-learning children of normal IQ seen in the clinic and in school can be termed developmentally abnormal and learning disabled. It is also suggested that a developmental view is essential if the understanding of who may be termed learning disabled is to be advanced. Two major strategies have been developed that show promise of providing critical information for defining subgroups of failing children: (a) identification of subgroups of different kinds of learning-disabled children based on common psychological deficiencies and (b) the developmental approach of P. Satz et al (1979), who are systematically searching for psychological precursors to reading failure. It is concluded that procedures for the differentiation and early identification of at least 4 kinds of slow learners (e.g., learning disabled, late bloomers) should be developed. Other suggestions include an approach that can

utilize the knowledge of teachers and other school personnel. (26 ref)

Belmont, Ira & Belmont, Lillian. (Yeshiva U) Journal of Learning Disabilities, 1980(Nov), Vol 13(9), 496–499. [PA, Vol 65:03509]

1085.   Intent and outcome in the moral judgment of mentally retarded and nonretarded children.
Results with 14 2nd graders, 14 educable mentally retarded (mean CA 117.7 mo; mean IQ 62), and 14 trainable mentally retarded (mean CA 192.4 mo; mean IQ 40.7) children show that negative events, whether intent or consequences, were more influential in affecting judgments about rewarding than were positive events. (4 ref)
Bender, Nila N. (U California, Riverside) Mental Retardation, 1980(Feb), Vol 18(1), 39–40. [PA, Vol 66:08224]

1086.   Idiot savant with unusual mechanical ability: An organic explanation.
Suggests that an explanation of idiot savant phenomenon may lie outside of environmental factors, perhaps in the division of functions between the cerebral hemispheres. Frequently, mental retardation is due to congenital or early childhood organic brain syndrome that affects both hemispheres and impairs the development of both kinds of mental abilities. If these organic factors are used to explain the idiot savant phenomenon, then it can be inferred that organic brain syndrome has affected the left hemisphere but has permitted the development of the right hemisphere. A case report is presented to support this argument. (10 ref)
Brink, T. L. (Palo Alto School of Professional Psychology, CA) American Journal of Psychiatry, 1980(Feb), Vol 137(2), 250–251. [PA, Vol 63:09932]

1087.   A comparison of laterality indices in college and retarded subjects.
Assessed the relation of laterality to intelligence by administration of A. Berman's (1971) ICD (Index of Cerebral Dominance) to 20 undergraduates and 20 retarded Ss (IQs 32–75) of comparable age and sex. The college Ss were more lateralized in hand, foot, ear, and eye, but it was primarily foot lateralization that distinguished the groups, despite the fact that hand was the most lateralized subsystem in both groups. While these results are not entirely consistent with Berman's, they generally confirm a positive relation of laterality and intelligence. (10 ref)
Burns, Barbara & Zeaman, David. (Clark U) Journal of Psychology, 1980(Mar), Vol 104(2), 241–247. [PA, Vol 65:07300]

1088.   Escape as a factor in the aggressive behavior of two retarded children.
Four experiments examined the variables controlling the severely aggressive behavior of 2 retarded children (CAs 9 and 14 yrs, Vineland Social Maturity Scale scores 2.3 and 3.3 yrs). In Exp I, each S was presented several demand and non-demand situations. Aggression (A) was frequent in the demand situations and rare in the non-demand situations. When a stimulus correlated with the termination of demands was introduced, A fell to a near zero level. In Exp II, for the 9-yr-old, a variety of preferred reinforcers was introduced into the demand situation contingent on correct responding. A abruptly decreased to a low level. Exps III and IV involved the 14-yr-old. In Exp III, this S was permitted, in one condition, to leave the demand situation if he emitted a nonaggressive response; A decreased to a low level. In Exp IV when S was prevented, in one condition, from leaving the demand situation in spite of high levels of A, A fell to a near zero level. In Exps III and IV, S was permitted, in several conditions, to leave the demand situation following A; A increased to a high level. Results suggest that A can be controlled by introducing strongly preferred reinforcers to attenuate the aversiveness of the demand situation; strengthening an alternative, nonaggressive escape response; or using an escape-extinction procedure. (23 ref)
Carr, Edward G.; Newsom, Crighton D. & Binkoff, Jody A. (State U New York, Stony Brook) Journal of Applied Behavior Analysis, 1980(Spr), Vol 13(1), 101–117. [PA, Vol 65:08203]

1089.   Skin conductance recovery limb in severely mentally retarded children.
Examined the nature of skin conductance response recovery time (RRT), onset angle, and offset angle for 10 mentally retarded (MR) Ss (mean age 15 yrs) and 10 normal Ss (mean age 14 yrs). MR Ss showed significantly shorter RRT, sluggish response onset, and abrupt offset of responses, indicating higher arousal in them than in normal Ss. Response trend over time followed an exponential form for normals, but no definite trend was evident in MR Ss. Analysis of response trend over time appeared to be a better measure than the traditional averaging technique. (19 ref)
Chattopadhyay, Prabal K.; Roy, Arup R.; Bhattacharyya, Amiya K. & Biswas, Prabir K. (U Calcutta Coll of Science, India) Indian Journal of Clinical Psychology, 1980(Mar), Vol 7(1), 53–58. [PA, Vol 66:08229]

1090.   IQs and etiologies: The two-group approach to mental retardation.
A review of the mental retardation literature failed to reveal any empirical studies supporting the assumption that "the retardate having an extremely low I.Q. (below 40) is almost invariably of the physiologically defective type . . . (while familial retardates . . . are almost invariably mildly retarded)" (E. Zigler, 1967). 20,218 institutionalized retardates on whom both IQ and etiologies were available are reported. For institutionalized retardates, the criterion of "invariability" was not met. Since the sample was small relative to the total estimated retarded population, it is concluded that the 2-group theory still retains research and practical merit, and suggestions for increasing its heuristic value are provided. (10 ref)
Cleland, Charles C.; Case, Jan & Manaster, Guy J. (U Texas, Austin) Bulletin of the Psychonomic Society, 1980(Jun), Vol 15(6), 413–415. [PA, Vol 66:01535]

1091.   Injury and insult—considerations of the neuropathological aetiology of mental subnormality.
Reports that the timing of insult or injury to the CNS is of primary importance in mental disabilities. It determines to a large extent the neuropathological lesion, both qualitatively and quantitatively. Disturbances that occur very early in morphogenesis are usually incompatible with survival. Most gross neuropathological lesions arise between the 23rd day of gestation and the end of the 1st trimester, which is a period of rapid organogenesis. The later stages of gestation and the 1st few months of life may see another type of pathology originating, which leaves no traces for the neurologist or neuropathologist. It is possible that irrevocable damage could result if sensory deprivation (or other insult) was inflicted during the periods of maximal dendritic arborization, establishment of synaptic connections, or myelination. Such damage might take the form of mental disability or possibly of a more circumscribed disability such as reading or writing dysfunction. (26 ref)
Cowie, Valerie. (Queen Mary's Hosp for Children, Carshalton, England) British Journal of Psychiatry, 1980(Oct), Vol 137, 305–312. [PA, Vol 66:08230]

1092.   Haptic-visual shape matching by mentally retarded children: Exploratory activity and complexity effects.
Compared haptic and visual matching of 17 retarded (6 with a mean MA of 8.5 yrs and 11 with a mean MA of 5.5 yrs) and 23 nonretarded children at different developmental levels (e.g., nursery, elementary, and junior high school levels), while systematically observing variables known to have developmentally linked effects on task accuracy, including stimulus complexity and haptic exploratory search style. Results show that accuracy depended on both stimulus complexity, modality, and MA, regardless of whether or not Ss were retarded. The selection of haptic search styles also depended on these factors but, in addition, was influenced by intellectual status of the Ss. (17 ref)
Davidson, Philip W.; Pine, Rena; Wiles-Kettenmann, Marilyn & Appelle, Stuart. (U Rochester School of Medicine) American Journal of Mental Deficiency, 1980(Mar), Vol 84(5), 526–533. [PA, Vol 63:12177]

1093. Can memory be educated?
Traditionally, memory has been thought of as a single entity stocked with traces and fragments of the original experience that stayed with the person after the event. Today, memories are seen as the result of dynamic acts in which experience is deliberately internalized through the exercise of strategies (A. L. Brown, 1975). Like the computer, the human memory seems to have a central working memory that is in turn linked to a form of peripheral store—long-term memory. Psychologists have strategies that lead to effective long-term remembering: rehearsal and organization. This strategic model has important implications of memory development; it appears to involve not so much a growth capacity as a refinement in the efficiency with which subskills are orchestrated and applied to memory tasks. The development of memory in children, "metamemory," and implications for the mentally handicapped are discussed. (25 ref)
Davies, G. M. (U Aberdeen, King's Coll, Scotland) Educational Studies, 1980(Jun), Vol 6(2), 155–161. [PA, Vol 66:06067]

1094. A comparison of aspects of the maternal speech environment of retarded and non-retarded children.
Eight mothers were observed in interaction with their retarded children (average age 3 yrs 5 mo) and compared with 8 mothers of nonretarded infants (average age 12 mo). Ss had been matched in terms of various socioeconomic indices (e.g., nationality, marital status, and type of housing) and language behavior. The mothers of retarded children were found significantly more stimulating vocally, more responsive, and less directive than controls. Findings are discussed in terms of possible reasons for such differences and the implications for the child. (19 ref)
Davis, Hilton & Oliver, Barley. (U London Hosp Medical Coll, England) Child Care, Health & Development, 1980(May–Jun), Vol 6(3), 135–145. [PA, Vol 64:05893]

1095. Classification of abnormal children: Discrimination learning ability.
Describes a procedure designed to assess the discrimination learning thresholds of 21 low-functioning children. A performance index that reflected accuracy of discriminative responding, difficulty of the discriminations attained, and learning rate was found to correlate significantly with MA, IQ, Vineland Social Age Social Quotient (Vineland Social Maturity Scale), and language functioning, but not with CA. The question of the optimal magnitude of correlation between a new measure and existing measures is discussed. (13 ref)
Deckner, C. William & Blanton, Richard L. (Vanderbilt U) Journal of Autism & Developmental Disorders, 1980(Dec), Vol 10(4), 405–415. [PA, Vol 65:04501]

1096. [The Rorschach technique as an instrument for investigating the personality in order to evaluate the resources of the exceptional mentally deficient child.] (Port)
Administered the Rorschach to 90 7–16 yr old mentally "deficient" Ss who participated in a program designed to improve their resources. Results demonstrate that the Rorschach test is an effective way of differentiating patients with a real deficiency from those whose intellectual repression is caused by other problems. (English abstract) (31 ref)
Deiss de Farias, Diva; Adrados Ruiz, Isabel & Chagas Nogueira, Ivette T.   Arquivos Brasileiros de Psicologia, 1980(Apr–Jun), Vol 32(2), 73–92. [PA, Vol 66:06495]

1097. [Human figure drawing in special school children.] (Slok)
Analyzed the drawings of 108 male and 106 female mentally retarded Ss. Results show that the "cephalopod" persisted for a long time, drawings in a side view seldom occurred, and depictions of movement were also rare. Differences between age groups and between sexes were not great. Females had a tendency for details (especially eyes), while males tended to draw profiles and movement. (Russian & English abstracts) (7 ref)
Dudášová, Milina. (Comenius U of Bratislava, Medical Faculty, Czechoslovakia) Psychológia a Patopsychológia Dietata, 1980, Vol 15(4), 363–369. [PA, Vol 66:08233]

1098. Attentiveness and responsiveness to auditory stimuli of children at risk for mental retardation.
Tested the hypothesis that differences between 82 high- and low-risk 3–4 yr olds in performance on 4 subtests (e.g., Auditory Reception) of the Illinois Test of Psycholinguistic Abilities would be explained, in part, by differences in attentiveness to auditory stimuli and differences in task orientation. Data revealed the anticipated higher standardized test scores for low-risk Ss. Within the high-risk sample, few differences were found between Ss who attended an intervention day-care program and those who did not. Measures from a laboratory task and a free-play observation suggested that attention is a key factor in understanding the high-risk S's development and also that differences in attention between high- and low-risk Ss can be reliably obtained as early as 3 yrs of age. A lessened attention span was demonstrated by high-risk Ss to both auditory and visual stimuli if either were complex or demanding. (22 ref)
Finkelstein, Neal W.; Gallagher, James J. & Farran, Dale C. (Frank Porter Graham Child Development Ctr, Chapel Hill, NC) American Journal of Mental Deficiency, 1980(Sep), Vol 85(2), 135–144. [PA, Vol 64:12735]

1099. Point of view: A chair at St. George's.
Discusses the practice of psychiatry of the "mentally handicapped" and suggests that such classification labels as psychosis, dementia, neurosis, and personality disorders are inadequate with this population. Rather, further study of the mentally handicapped person's biological and social needs is considered necessary. (21 ref)
Fraser, Bill. (Gogarburn Hosp, Edinburgh, Scotland) British Journal of Mental Subnormality, 1980(Jun), Vol 26(50, Pt 1), 3–8. [PA, Vol 66:06071]

1100. Social acceptability as a function of labels and assigned attributes.
Investigated the effects of categorical labels and assigned attributes on children's social acceptability ratings of another child. 96 4th graders were randomly assigned to 1 of 8 conditions in which they viewed tapes of a normal little boy (labeled either learning-disabled, retarded, emotionally disturbed, or normal) engaged in task-oriented or free-play activity. Ss were given additional positive or neutral information about the boy and were asked several questions after each of 2 tapes about the desirability of the boy (e.g., their own liking for him, their teacher's probable liking, his potential as a football team member). No differences were obtained in ratings as a function of label assigned. Positive information was significantly associated with more favorable ratings of the child, even to questions asked after the less favorably viewed play situation. (33 ref)
Freeman, Sheryl & Algozzine, Bob. (Boulder Public Schools, CO) American Journal of Mental Deficiency, 1980(May), Vol 84(6), 589–595. [PA, Vol 64:01120]

1101. The consequences of adolescent childbearing on postnatal development.
Presents data concerning intellectual development; mental retardation; physical, motor, and neurological development; academic achievement; and social and emotional development as a function of maternal age. It is concluded that the existing data on the developmental sequelae of adolescent childbearing lends only minimal support to the hypothesis that maternal immaturity places the newborn infant at increased developmental risk. Nevertheless, because of the socioeconomic characteristics of adolescent mothers, the outlook for infants of such mothers is dismal primarily because of postnatal environmental factors. (48 ref)
Gunter, Nancy C. & LaBarba, Richard C. (Florida Mental Health Inst, Tampa) International Journal of Behavioral Development, 1980(Jul), Vol 3(2), 191–214. [PA, Vol 66:03278]

1102. [Discrimination shift learning and dimensional dominance in mentally retarded children.] (Japn)
Dimensional dominance (either form or color) among retarded and normal children was assessed prior to their being presented with reversal or nonreversal shift task. During the initial

learning, the dominant dimension was either relevant or irrelevant to the solution. Both rate of criterion attainment during the initial learning and subsequent shift performance were related to dimensional dominance. If the dominant dimension was relevant, retarded Ss learned the task as fast as controls; if the dominant dimension was irrelevant, retarded Ss learned it with more difficulty than controls. This result is discussed in relation to the tendency of the retardates to be bound to one dimension and not switching to another. (12 ref)
Hamashige, Tamie. (Ibaraki U, Mito, Japan) Japanese Journal of Psychology, 1980(Feb), Vol 50(6), 337–340. [PA, Vol 65:10652]

1103.   The relationship between structured and free play in the development of a mentally handicapped child: A case study.
Describes a case study of a mentally and physically handicapped child (CA, 5 yrs 5 mo; developmental age, 1 yr). The S participated in a project in which professionals helped parents to promote the development of their mentally handicapped children, by utilizing both structured play and an individual approach. The study demonstrates the role of structured play, and its relation to free play, in the S's development. (8 ref)
Hewson, Simon; McConkey, Roy & Jeffree, Dorothy. (Rochdale Children's Hosp, England) Child Care, Health & Development, 1980(Mar–Apr), Vol 6(2), 73–82. [PA, Vol 63:12017]

1104.   Learning disorders and sex chromosome aberrations.
No sex chromosome aberrations were detected in a prospective study of 20 18–45 yr old dyslexic men (mean IQ 97.7). A retrospective study of 89 Ss with known sex chromosome aberrations revealed 20 of them to be mentally retarded (IQ $\leq$ 69). Among the 69 Ss of normal intelligence, learning, speech, and attention disorders were frequent. Children with 47,XYY, 47,XXY, and 47,XXX karyotypes appeared particularly prone to experience delays in speech development as well as later academic underachievement in language-related subjects. In contrast, speech development was normal in all of the girls with Turner's syndrome, and later academic difficulties were usually confined to mathematics or science. Hyperactivity was noted with considerable frequency among 47,XYY and Turner's syndrome Ss, but not among Ss with a 47,XXX or 47,XXY karyotype. (41 ref)
Hier, Daniel B.; Atkins, L. & Perlo, V. P. (Michael Reese Hosp, Dept of Neurology, Chicago, IL) Journal of Mental Deficiency Research, 1980(Mar), Vol 24(1), 17–26. [PA, Vol 66:05910]

1105.   Evaluation of adoption of the intellectually handicapped: A retrospective analysis of 137 cases.
An analysis of 137 infants adopted over 30 yrs who suffered from some intellectual handicap provided data on the outcome of this type of adoption. An objective rating scale was used to examine the relationship of the child in the adoptive family. It was found that a third of the adoptees had a good family relationship. In less than a quarter the relationship had failed. The remainder had problems that were being handled satisfactorily. The measured variables that worsened the outcome were severe or profound degree of retardation, presence of a genetic disorder in the child, increasing age, and difficult behavior, particularly when a child of borderline or dull normal intelligence was placed with an "intellectual" family. The knowledge of the natural parents' family medical history, even in the presence of a genetic disorder, favored the adoptive relationship. The presence of a congenital anomaly in the child led to deferral of adoption but did not increase the likelihood of institutionalization. All the families required continuation of support and suitable facilities for the care and education of the child. (9 ref)
Hockey, Athel. (King Edward Memorial Hosp for Women, Subiaco, Australia) Journal of Mental Deficiency Research, 1980(Sep), Vol 24(3), 187–202. [PA, Vol 66:08237]

1106.   Correlation of the PPVT and WISC-R: A function of diagnostic category.
Compared Peabody Picture Vocabulary Test (PPVT) and WISC-R scores for 259 6–16 yr old students. In descending order, Pearson product correlations ranked best for the total sample, emotionally disabled, regular class, mentally retarded, and learning disabled. In all groups, the PPVT overestimated ability, and its scores were significantly different from WISC-R scores as measured by correlated *t*-tests. (10 ref)
Hodapp, Albert F. & Hodapp, Joan B. (Northern Trails Area Education Agency, Clear Lake, IA) Psychology in the Schools, 1980(Jan), Vol 17(1), 33–36. [PA, Vol 65:06422]

1107.   Effects of auditory feedback on velocity extrapolation by mentally retarded and nonretarded groups during rotary pursuit tracking.
18 retarded adolescents (mean CA 16.2 yrs; mean IQ 65.2), 18 CA-matched nonretarded adolescents, and 18 MA-matched nonretarded children stylus-tracked an intermittently disappearing rotary pursuit target with and without auditory feedback. Under the no-feedback condition, all groups demonstrated an almost linear increase in deviation errors over 5 successive 2-sec intervals following disappearance of the target, with the retarded group showing a greater increase than did the CA- and MA-matched groups. Under the feedback condition, the CA-matched group reached an asymptote of target proximity 4 sec after the target disappeared, whereas errors for the retarded and MA-matched groups continued to increase throughout the 10-sec sample period. Performance of the retarded group with no feedback is interpreted as evidence for deficient velocity extrapolation, and failure of the retarded and MA-matched groups to stabilize proximity under the feedback condition is attributed to delayed response to the feedback. (7 ref)
Holden, Edward A. & Corrigan, James G. (Edward R. Johnstone Training & Research Ctr, Bordentown, NJ) American Journal of Mental Deficiency, 1980(Jan), Vol 84(4), 381–386. [PA, Vol 63:07797]

1108.   Self-paced vs. externally paced motor tracking by retarded and nonretarded persons.
Tested an expectancy hypothesis of the psychological refractory period (PRP) as an alternative to an arousal hypothesis to explain retarded persons' longer reaction times. 24 retarded adolescents (mean CA 16.07 yrs; mean IQ 61.79), 24 CA-matched nonretarded adolescents, and 24 MA-matched nonretarded children tracked light stimuli presented under self-paced and externally paced conditions. Response latencies under both conditions were longer for the retarded and MA-matched groups, and all groups decreased latencies from the self-paced to externally paced conditions. Neither hypothesis was supported. It is suggested that group differences were due to differences in the central delay effect of the PRP. (14 ref)
Holden, Edward A. & Corrigan, James G. (Edward R. Johnstone Training & Research Ctr, Bordentown, NJ) American Journal of Mental Deficiency, 1980(Jan), Vol 84(4), 387–392. [PA, Vol 63:07798]

1109.   Agency mandates and norms: Their influence on who receives the label mentally retarded.
Examined J. R. Mercer's (1965–1975) proposal for a social system perspective on mental retardation, in which retardation is viewed as an achieved status in a social system due to the different norms used when defining persons as mentally retarded. A survey of several hundred Manitoba agencies and schools—grouped into 7 types of programs—was made to discover the levels of intellectual, physical, and behavioral disabilities and the demographic characteristics of the 5,519 individuals they had classified as retarded. Results show that social agencies, depending on their functions, differed in the nature of the norms employed in the definition of mental retardation and in the stringency with which the norms were applied. (6 ref)
Hull, John T. & Fishbach, Murray. Psychosocial Rehabilitation Journal, 1980(Fal), Vol 4(3), 29–39. [PA, Vol 66:13436]

1110.   Predicting adaptive functioning of mentally retarded persons in community settings.
Examined the impact of individual, residential, and community variables on adaptive functioning of 369 18–73 yr old retarded persons (median IQ 54) using multiple-regression to analyze scores on the Adaptive Functioning Index (N. J. Marlett, 1977).

Individual characteristics (especially IQ) accounted for 21% of the variance, while environmental variables, primarily those related to normalization, accounted for 35%. The data suggest that environmental normalization may be an effective technology for the promotion of independent functioning of retarded people as well as an ideology. (11 ref)
Hull, John T. & Thompson, Joy C. (Ministry of Community & Social Services, Toronto, Canada) American Journal of Mental Deficiency, 1980(Nov), Vol 85(3), 253–261. [PA, Vol 65:03865]

1111.   Inspection time, intelligence, and response strategy.
Compared 20 17–25 yr old male retarded adults (IQs 51–83) on a simple discrimination task with 10 nonretarded students of the same CA. Estimates of inspection time (λ), a measure assumed to reflect the rate at which sensory input is processed, were obtained from the patterns of errors generated under 2 conditions of response organization. For retarded Ss estimates obtained using a more complex response procedure were significantly longer than those resulting with a simpler procedure, although reaction time (RT) to stimuli remained relatively constant for both procedures. For nonretarded Ss, λ estimates remained approximately the same, although RT slowed significantly when the response required was more complex. Patterns of RT were interpreted as indicating differences between groups in response strategy, with retarded Ss responding on the basis of little stimulus evidence. Exp II attempted to reduce estimates of λ among 14 retarded adult males (IQs 51–79) by encouraging them to accumulate more evidence before responding. In 1 condition Ss were required to wait 5 sec after stimulus onset before responding; in the other, they responded as quickly and as accurately as possible. Delayed responding did reduce estimates of λ obtained but could not account for more than a small part of the difference between the performance of retarded and nonretarded Ss. (8 ref)
Lally, M. & Nettelbeck, T. (Australian National U, Information Sciences Lab, Canberra) American Journal of Mental Deficiency, 1980(May), Vol 84(6), 553–560. [PA, Vol 64:01313]

1112.   Developmental auditory agnosia in the severely retarded: A further investigation.
Investigated hypotheses that (a) ability to recognize the auditory perceptual stimuli for familiar events is a developmental correlate to language acquisition and (b) the low functioning mentally handicapped suffer from auditory agnosia and are impaired in this ability. Ss were 95 nonretarded children (mean CA 4 yrs) and retarded children (mean MA 4 yrs, CA 3–6 yrs). The stimuli were 49 environmental sounds; the task consisted of sound-and-picture matching-to-sample. Results revealed a strong effect of developmental age. The effect of group was not significant, indicating that auditory agnosia may not be common among the lower functioning retarded. The assumption that agnosia may be a major factor underlying the language disability of the severely retarded was reexamined. It is suggested that the severely retarded achieve the requisite perceptual-semantic knowledge base for language too late, after the critical age for spontaneous and efficient language learning has passed. (30 ref)
Lamberts, Frances. (East Tennessee State U, Johnson City) Brain & Language, 1980(Sep), Vol 11(1), 106–118. [PA, Vol 66:08248]

1113.   Effects of stimulus probability on encoding by mentally retarded and nonretarded persons.
Performed a choice reaction-time experiment in which probe stimulus probability and probe stimulus quality were orthogonally manipulated. Ss were 9 14-yr-old retarded (mean IQ 62.15) students and 9 nonretarded 8th graders. The stimuli were random forms presented at 4 probability levels to assess the effect of stimulus probability on the encoding process. The results indicate that the retarded Ss appeared to be less sensitive than did the nonretarded Ss to stimulus-probability information, particularly under degraded stimulus conditions. The relative sensitivity of retarded and nonretarded persons to stimulus-probability information and the effect of such information on the encoding process are discussed. (16 ref)
Maisto, Albert A. & Sipe, Suzanne. (U North Carolina, Charlotte) American Journal of Mental Deficiency, 1980(May), Vol 84(6), 577–581. [PA, Vol 64:01314]

1114.   Validity of the Vocational Adaptation Rating Scale: Prediction of mentally retarded workers' placement in sheltered workshops.
Investigated the validity of the Vocational Adaptation Rating Scale (VARS) for predicting placement of mentally retarded workers in sheltered-workshop settings. The VARS was administered by workshop supervisors to 125 noninstitutionalized adolescents and adults, ranging from severely to mildly retarded (mean CA 22.3; mean IQ 53.4). Frequency and severity of maladaptive behavior in 6 domains predicted the concurrent placement of retarded workers in workshops and their placement 1 yr later. Low to moderate significant partial correlations were found with concurrent placement and 1-yr follow-up placement (controlling IQ, age, and sex). Multiple-correlation analyses indicated that the VARS provided significant increments in predictable variance in workshop placements (13.8–16.1%) relative to predictions based on IQ, age, and sex. Results support the instrument's incremental validity as a measure of maladaptive behavior in vocational settings. (25 ref)
Malgady, Robert G.; Barcher, Peter R.; Davis, John & Towner, George. (New York U) American Journal of Mental Deficiency, 1980(May), Vol 84(6), 633–640. [PA, Vol 64:00216]

1115.   The distribution of the mentally handicapped between districts of a large city.
Compared the rates of psychiatric referrals in various districts in Sheffield, England. Results indicate that poorer residential districts had significantly higher referral rates among 2–24 yr olds when compared with the prime residential sections. Although the differences were most marked for the mildly mentally handicapped, the severely mentally handicapped were also unevenly distributed among districts. (17 ref)
Martindale, A. (Ryegate Ctr, Development Project Case Register, Sheffield, England) British Journal of Mental Subnormality, 1980(Jun), Vol 26(50, Pt 1), 9–20. [PA, Vol 66:06080]

1116.   A computerized system for the classification of developmental, learning, and adjustment disorders in school children.
Presents Program MAC, a FORTRAN IV program that applies series of statistical decision rules for the differential diagnosis and classification of mental retardation, academic under- and over-achievement, social maladjustment, learning disabilities, and other problems found in school-age children. (14 ref)
McDermott, Paul A. (U Pennsylvania) Educational & Psychological Measurement, 1980(Fal), Vol 40(3), 761–768. [PA, Vol 64:12586]

1117.   Adaptive behavior: Teachers and parents disagree.
Examined the bias that may exist in reports of adaptive behavior from informed sources by comparing the perceptions of parents and teachers of mentally retarded children regarding adaptive behavior of selected moderately or severely retarded Ss. Ss were 30 White and 30 Black students (CAs 7–13 yrs; IQs 25–50). Ss were tested on Part 1 of the Adaptive Behavior Scale and on the Cain-Levine Social Competency Scale. Parents rated their children significantly higher than did teachers on the Self-Help dimension of the Social Competency Scale and on the Independent Functioning, Physical Development, Economic Activity, Domestic Activity, and Vocational Activity dimensions of the Adaptive Behavior Scale. Teachers did not rate the children higher than the parents did on any subtests of either of the 2 tests. It is suggested that although test findings may result from more positive perception by parents than teachers, they may also result from the parents' greater information base. (9 ref)
Mealor, David J. & Richmond, Bert O. (Ogeechee Educational Ctr, Midville, GA) Exceptional Children, 1980(Feb), Vol 46(5), 386–389. [PA, Vol 63:09946]

1118.   Coding, planning and mental retardation: Theory, evidence and implications.
The frontal lobes of the human brain represent a functional unit for projecting all aspects of a person's thinking into the future. In contrast, the temporal and occipital-parietal brain divisions are concerned with the processing of information about present and past events. These differences in role distinguish the frontal lobes

from the remaining posterior cortex, and in this view, brain functions are split latitudinally rather than hemispherically. The authors trace the development of an integrated model of cognition stemming from Soviet neuropsychology and review recent research on simultaneous and successive syntheses. Some implications for mental retardation are given. (33 ref)
Molloy, Geoffrey N. & Das, J. P. (Monash U, Faculty of Education, Clayton, Australia) Australian Journal of Developmental Disabilities, 1980(Sep), Vol 6(3), 111–117. [PA, Vol 66:07478]

1119.   Exposure to lead in childhood: The persisting effects.
Discusses the effects of environmental lead exposure on children. In the earliest studies of childhood overexposure to lead, it was found that classroom performance was poorer than in children who had not been exposed. Thereafter, studies showed that mental retardation could be linked with overexposure to lead in drinking water and with high concentrations of blood lead at about the time of birth. In the most recent studies (e.g., H. L. Needleman et al, 1979), a diminished learning ability (IQ drop of 4–7 points) and behavioral changes (e.g., diminished attention span) have been associated with increased concentrations of lead in teeth. (11 ref)
Moore, M. R. (Western Infirmary, Dept of Medicine, Glasgow, Scotland) Nature, 1980(Jan), Vol 283(5745), 334–335. [PA, Vol 65:05766]

1120.   Current issues in applied research with mentally retarded persons.
Examines some of the issues raised by (a) the research guidelines developed by various professional organizations (e.g., American Psychological Association, American Association on Mental Deficiency) and the federal government and (b) the research review procedures mandated by the courts. (20 ref)
Morris, Richard J. & Hoschouer, Ronald L. (U Arizona, Coll of Education, Tucson) Applied Research in Mental Retardation, 1980, Vol 1(1–2), 85–93. [PA, Vol 66:06984]

1121.   WISC-R subtest patterns for learning disabled and mentally retarded children.
WISC-R subtest profiles were examined for 20 learning disabled and 20 mentally retarded children aged 7–8 yrs. The rank order of the WISC-R subtests supports the concept of distinct patterns for these exceptional children. Correlations between the present samples' subtests patterns and previous findings are also reported. (3 ref)
Naglieri, Jack A. (Northern Arizona U, Flagstaff) Perceptual & Motor Skills, 1980(Oct), Vol 51(2), 605–606. [PA, Vol 66:12921]

1122.   A longitudinal study of the psychological aspects of myelomeningocele.
Examination of 30 unselected myelomeningocele children tested regularly from age 18 mo until 6 yrs showed that the condition is often associated with psychomotor retardation in various degrees, depending on the seriousness of neurological complications. Performance level tended to improve with increasing age, mean IQ being lowest in the 1st 2 yrs but approaching normal levels in the preschool years. (16 ref)
Nielsen, Helle H. (U Aarhus, Denmark) Scandinavian Journal of Psychology, 1980, Vol 21(1), 45–54. [PA, Vol 65:10714]

1123.   Home environment, family adjustment, and the development of mentally retarded children.
Examined the longitudinal effect of educational and residential environments on personal, social, and cognitive development of 114 trainable (TMR) and 152 educable (EMR) mentally retarded children (mean IQs 42.4 and 66.4, respectively) and their families. All Ss resided in their natural homes with married parents. Home environmental variables included parental behavior and attitude, psychosocial climate, and demographic and structural characteristics. Measures of family adjustment included the S's effect on the family and the family's capacity to cope with mental retardation. Child characteristics were described in terms of adaptive and maladaptive behavior, psychological and social adjustment, and self-concept, using the Adaptive Behavior Scales. Canonical correlation analyses indicated conceptual and

statistical linkages between home environment, family adjustment, and competency of mentally retarded children. (34 ref)
Nihira, Kazuo; Meyers, C. Edward & Mink, Iris T. (U California School of Medicine, Ctr for the Health Sciences, Los Angeles) Applied Research in Mental Retardation, 1980, Vol 1(1–2), 5–24. [PA, Vol 66:08257]

1124.   Human intelligence and power spectral analysis of visual evoked potentials.
The relationship between intelligence and power spectra of visual evoked potential was investigated, using 8 normal and 8 mentally retarded children (mean Suzuki-Binet IQs 118 and 65.5, respectively). The power spectrum of mentally retarded had a peak at 4–6 Hz, whereas that of normal had 2 peaks at 4 and 12 Hz. It appears the peak at 12 Hz reflects the difference of intelligence. (9 ref)
Osaka, Mariko & Osaka, Naoyuki. (Kyoto U, Japan) Perceptual & Motor Skills, 1980(Feb), Vol 50(1), 192–194. [PA, Vol 65:09825]

1125.   [The use of the Rorschach in the diagnosis of mental deficiency.] (Port)
Reviews literature on the diagnosis of mental deficiency with psychological tests and raises criticisms concerning conventional measures of mental level and IQ. The usefulness of the Rorschach test to detect not only mental level but also intellectual potential is discussed and the influence of emotional life upon the inhibition of intellectual functions is noted. (23 ref)
Prado, Regina L. Arquivos Brasileiros de Psicologia, 1980(Apr–Jun), Vol 32(2), 111–120. [PA, Vol 66:06084]

1126.   The effects of antecedent vestibular stimulation on the receptive language learning of retarded toddlers.
Monitored the receptive language learning of 3 mentally handicapped (as determined by Bayley Scales of Infant Development) 33–34 mo olds. During intervention Ss were exposed to 90 sec of intense vestibular stimulation immediately prior to the language tasks. Results indicate that vestibular stimulation, when applied systematically as an antecedent to the receptive language tasks, decreased the total trials needed to reach criterion for each S. Additionally, it was found that although Ss displayed varied reactions to the vestibular activities, a negative reaction had no effect on the concomitant change in rate of learning. (20 ref)
Raver, Sharon A. Child Study Journal, 1980, Vol 10(2), 77–86. [PA, Vol 65:01520]

1127.   Psychiatric disorders in mentally handicapped children: A clinical and follow-up study.
Describes the clinical psychiatric syndromes encountered in 60 mentally retarded children (mean age 13.5 yrs) treated in a child psychiatric outpatient clinic setting. It was possible to classify these syndromes according to the multi-axial classification scheme for psychiatric disorders in childhood and adolescence. Ss were followed up for some years in many cases, and the natural history of these disorders was generally comparable to that of similar disorders in Ss of normal intelligence, although there was a tendency for some of the disorders to be unusually persistent. Sometimes this persistence was related to the Ss' continuing dependency needs arising from the retardation and to stresses within the family. The disorders responded satisfactorily to standard child psychiatric treatment techniques. It is concluded that child psychiatric services should include assessment and treatment of psychiatric disorders in mentally handicapped children. (19 ref)
Reid, Andrew H. (Strathmartine Hosp, Dundee Psychiatric Services, Scotland) Journal of Mental Deficiency Research, 1980(Dec), Vol 24(4), 287–298. [PA, Vol 66:08112]

1128.   Overt and covert rehearsal in short-term motor memory of mentally retarded and nonretarded persons.
Investigated overt rehearsal and the presence of covert rehearsal in short-term motor memory of 100 retarded Ss (mean MA 10.6 yrs), 100 nonretarded 10-yr-olds, and 100 nonretarded 16-yr-olds. Ss were randomly assigned to 5 retention conditions: immediate recall, a 20-sec unfilled interval, a 20-sec interval filled with interpolated mental activity, a 20-sec interval of overt

rehearsal, and a 20-sec interval filled with simultaneous overt rehearsal and interpolated mental activity. Results indicate that retarded Ss did not engage in spontaneous covert rehearsal of motor information, while nonretarded Ss did. The short-term motor memory of retarded and nonretarded Ss was not different when covert rehearsal was not possible and during overt rehearsal. In general, however, overt rehearsal did not facilitate motor memory. (29 ref)
Reid, Greg. (McGill U, Montreal, Canada) American Journal of Mental Deficiency, 1980(Jul), Vol 85(1), 69–77. [PA, Vol 64:08273]

1129.   [Comments on Edward Zigler's cognitive-motivational theory concerning cultural-familial mental retardation.] (Fren) Comments on E. Zigler's theory of mental retardation, which emphasizes the distinction between difference and developmental theories of mental retardation, and hypothesizes that retardates do not perform on the same level as their normal peers. An analysis of the data finds this distinction to be subtle, cites lack of empirical evidence for the thesis, and questions Zigler's exclusive focus on motivational factors in explaining the differences found in cognitive tasks between normal and retarded children. (English abstract) (3 p ref)
Rondal, Jean A. (U Liège, Lab de Psychologie Expérimentale, Belgium) Psychologica Belgica, 1980, Vol 20(1), 61–82. [PA, Vol 65:11493]

1130.   Season of birth and degree of mental retardation: Failure to confirm a relationship.
No support was found for an association between season of birth and the incidence or degree of mental deficiency among the 419 clients (mean age 24 yrs) of a residential facility for the mentally retarded. (12 ref)
Roszkowski, Michael J. (Woodhaven Ctr, Philadelphia, PA) Psychological Reports, 1980(Aug), Vol 47(1), 100–102. [PA, Vol 66:10610]

1131.   The Adaptive Behavior Scale (ABS) and IQ: How much unshared variance is there?
Investigated the nature of the correlations between IQ and the domain scores of the Adaptive Behavior Scale (ABS) for 224 7–43 yr old (mean IQ of 36) mentally retarded individuals. The adaptive behaviors measured by Part I of the ABS showed relatively large associations with IQ. ABS domain scores that correlated .7 or above with IQ included Independent Functioning, Economic Activity, Language Development, Numbers and Time, and Domestic Activity. In contrast, Part II domains, which deal primarily with conduct disorders, showed low to negligible associations with IQ. (32 ref)
Roszkowski, Michael J. & Bean, Andrew G. (Temple U, Woodhaven Program) Psychology in the Schools, 1980(Oct), Vol 17(4), 452–459. [PA, Vol 66:07088]

1132.   Reply to Amante.
Suggests that most of D. Amante's (see PA, Vol 65:161) questions regarding the present authors' (see PA, Vol 62:8716) study represented Amante's interests rather than the interests addressed by the present authors. Brief answers to the criticisms are offered. (1 ref)
Selz, Marion & Reitan, Ralph M. (U Arizona, Tucson) Journal of Consulting & Clinical Psychology, 1980(Aug), Vol 48(4), 528–529. [PA, Vol 65:00230]

1133.   Extrapolated Stanford-Binet IQs for mentally retarded and mentally gifted individuals.
Presents a procedure for estimating the Stanford-Binet IQs of Ss whose performance places them outside the limits of the 1972 revised IQ tables. A formula is given for converting ratio IQs into deviation IQs, along with a table of the constants required to apply the formula. The method by which these constants were determined is described, and some indication is given of the error involved in the use of the procedure. (6 ref)
Silverstein, A. B. (U California School of Medicine, Neuropsychiatric Inst-Lanterman State Hosp Research Group, Los Angeles) Psychological Reports, 1980(Jun), Vol 46(3, Pt 1), 900–902. [PA, Vol 66:02533]

1134.   Effects of the labels "mentally retarded" and "retard" on the social acceptability of mentally retarded children.
Studied the effects of the labels "mentally retarded" and "retard" on 138 5th and 6th graders' attitudes toward peers. Results indicate that Ss' attitudes (feelings and behavioral intentions) were more positive toward the target child labeled "mentally retarded" than labeled "retard." The data also show that Ss' reactions to the 2 labels were, in part, a function of the physical appearance and academic competence of the peer being rated. Ss had the most negative attitudes toward a child labeled "retard" who appeared to be "normal." In contrast, Ss reacted favorably to the target child labeled "mentally retarded," even when he or she was academically incompetent. Boys were more negative than were girls toward the target child, especially when the child was labeled "retard." Implications for the movement to abandon the use of labels are discussed. (10 ref)
Siperstein, Gary N.; Budoff, Milton & Bak, John J. (U Massachusetts, Coll of Public & Community Service, Boston) American Journal of Mental Deficiency, 1980(May), Vol 84(6), 596–601. [PA, Vol 64:01327]

1135.   Cri du Chat: Report of a case.
Since J. Lejeune et al (1963) first described the syndrome of *Cri du Chat* (Cry of the Cat), cases have been described in the literature in terms of genetic abnormalities. All cases were severely retarded and the mental impairment has been believed to be progressive, although no longitudinal studies have been reported. The present paper presents a case of a 7½-yr-old girl with *Cri du Chat* who has received speech and language therapy for 5 yrs. Her speech, language, and mental development are noted and are not consistent with cases reported previously. (12 ref)
Sparks, Shirley N. & Hutchinson, Barbara. (Western Michigan U, Kalamazoo) Journal of Communication Disorders, 1980(Jan), Vol 13(1), 9–13. [PA, Vol 66:08374]

1136.   The concept of death in preoperational retarded children.
Interviewed 14 preoperational retarded boys and girls (mean age 6.4 yrs), as classified by their failure to pass 3 conservation tasks, for their concepts of death; G. P. Koocher's (see PA, Vol 51:4855) study was used as a model. Each S was asked "What makes things die?"; "How can you make dead things come back to life?"; "When will you die?"; and "What will happen then?" These preoperational retarded Ss did not have realistic concepts of when they will die or of the permanence of death. They did, however, have realistic notions of how things die. It was also found that the types of replies made to these questions were related to their cognitive level. (13 ref)
Sternlicht, Manny. (Yeshiva U) Journal of Genetic Psychology, 1980(Dec), Vol 137(2), 157–164. [PA, Vol 65:08218]

1137.   [Developmental changes of problem-solving processes on probability learning in mentally retarded children.] (Japn)
Investigated the development of problem-solving processes in 48 mentally retarded (MR) and 48 normal (NOR) children using the probability learning task. Ss were 4-, 7-, and 10-yr-olds. Results indicate that (1) younger children of NOR and MR groups could attend to the dominant cue set associated with reinforcement, but neglect the other cues; (2) 7-yr-old Ss of NOR groups could attend to these cue sets, and ones of MR groups could attend to these cue sets in initial blocks of the session but attend to only the dominant cue set associated with reinforcement from the middle blocks to the final blocks; and (3) 10-yr-olds in NOR groups could logically operate these cue sets, and ones of MR groups could not. (18 ref)
Tanaka, Michiharu. Japanese Journal of Educational Psychology, 1980(Mar), Vol 28(1), 48–56. [PA, Vol 66:01548]

1138.   The diagnostic utility of WISC-R measures with children referred to a developmental evaluation center.
Various methods of WISC-R profile analysis were assessed to determine whether diagnostically characteristic differences exist among clinically meaningful groups of children. Although differences in composite WISC-R measures were exhibited by the 14 mentally retarded Ss, the 28 learning disabled Ss, and the 51

Ss with psychological or behavioral disorders, few significant group differences were exhibited on the subtest scatter measures. Results are discussed in terms of caution necessary in making any diagnostic statements based on WISC-R profile scatter because of the similarity of the clinical groups to each other and to the normative sample. (20 ref)
Thompson, Robert J. (Duke U Medical Ctr, Div of Medical Psychology) Journal of Consulting & Clinical Psychology, 1980(Aug), Vol 48(4), 440–447. [PA, Vol 65:00238]

1139. Associative learning in premature hydranencephalic and normal twins.
Tested a 2-mo premature female hydranencephalic infant lacking cerebral hemispheres and her normal male twin for associative learning. After repeated trials in which 2 stimuli were temporally paired, test trials were given in which the 2nd stimulus was omitted. Cardiac orienting responses to stimulus omission indicated that learning had taken place in both infants.
Tuber, David S.; Berntson, Gary G.; Bachman, David S. & Allen, J. Norman. (Ohio State U, Lab of Comparative & Physiological Psychology, Columbus) Science, 1980(Nov), Vol 210(4473), 1035–1037. [PA, Vol 66:08381]

1140. Coincidence anticipation of young normal and handicapped children.
Two coincident-timing experiments examined the role of 3 different target velocities (5, 3, or 1 ft/sec), display extents (67 or 33% of target exposed), and age levels (means 100, 130, and 155 mo) of 41 normal (NM) and 41 mentally retarded (MR) (IQ 54–86) children. Ss made a ballistic response to a target moving horizontally across their visual field. Results of Exp I show no differences between NMs and MRs; Ss had difficulty for both the slow and fast target speeds. In Exp II, with target velocity held constant, no significant differences were reported between NM and MR children, although the longer the Ss were allowed to view the target, the more accurate they were. Results are discussed in terms of the response strategies needed to perform anticipatory ballistic movements. It is suggested that children and adults make their most accurate anticipations when confronted with velocity problems that they have experienced in their daily lives. (24 ref)
Wade, Michael G. (U Illinois Inst for Child Behavior & Development, Champaign) Journal of Motor Behavior, 1980(Jun), Vol 12(2), 103–112. [PA, Vol 66:01551]

1141. A semantic differential investigation of children's attitudes toward three stigmatized groups.
To test the assumption that negative attitudes toward various stigmatized groups are learned in early childhood, 4 semantic differential scales were used to assess children's attitudes toward 4 groups: normals (NOs), crippled (CR), mentally retarded (MR), and mentally ill (MI). Ss were 10 girls and 10 boys from each of Grades 3 and 6. The MI were rated most negatively on both the Evaluation and the Understandability Scales, but were rated comparably to NOs on Activity and Potency. Both MR and CRs were rated less positively than NOs on the E Scale, but not as negatively as MI. No differences were found between the 2 grade levels on attitudes toward the 3 stigmatized groups. Implications for the social labeling theory of mental disorders are discussed. (26 ref)
Wilkins, Joan E. & Velicer, Wayne F. (U Rhode Island, Kingston) Psychology in the Schools, 1980(Jul), Vol 17(3), 364–371. [PA, Vol 66:01099]

1142. Theory, practice, and the zone of proximal development in Soviet psychoeducational research.
Illustrates the integration of theory and practice in Soviet psychoeducational research. Learning disability, mental retardation, width of the zone of proximal development, and research employing this zone are discussed. (8 ref)
Wozniak, R. H. (Columbia U Teachers Coll) Contemporary Educational Psychology, 1980(Apr), Vol 5(2), 175–183. [PA, Vol 65:10664]

1143. Visual-motor localizations in normal and subnormal development.
18 subnormal 12–17 yr olds and 18 normal children, matched for MA (4–6 yrs) on the Columbia Mental Maturity Scale, were compared on a visual target localization task. Severely subnormal Ss were less accurate than normal Ss in conditions where they visually directed or visually guided their hand to the target and received visual knowledge of results. On visually directed localizations without knowledge of results or with proprioceptive knowledge of results (same hand), no significant difference was found between the 2 groups. Another experiment with 43 moderately subnormal children revealed that developmental changes on visually directed and visually guided localizations were a function of MA rather than CA. (11 ref)
Anwar, Feriha. (MRC Developmental Psychology Unit, London, England) British Journal of Psychology, 1981(Feb), Vol 72(1), 43–57. [PA, Vol 66:13057]

1144. Organicity and mental retardation: Analysis of eye and head movements.
Recorded the eye and head movements of 10 mentally retarded (MR) and 10 normal children as each S looked to one side or the other in response to verbal commands, gestural directions, or the appearances of illuminated fixation targets. Results show that large gaze movements of MR Ss were accompanied by head movements more frequently than those of normal Ss. For similar gaze deviations, head movements of MR Ss tended to be larger than those of normal Ss. In addition, head movements of normal Ss rarely began before eye movement, but those of MR Ss often did so. This abnormal MR eye–head movement pattern was more frequent in response to verbal or gestural commands than in responses elicited by illumination of fixation targets. (9 ref)
Atkin, A.; Bala, S.; Herman, P. & Rogowitz, Bernice. (City U New York, Mt Sinai School of Medicine) Journal of Mental Deficiency Research, 1981(Mar), Vol 25(1), 17–24. [PA, Vol 66:06061]

1145. Mental retardation policy and research: The unfulfilled promise.
Discusses reasons for the failure of research to influence the course of policy formulation for problems relating to mental retardation. The nature of the process itself is such that research is secondary to economic, political, and social considerations. Furthermore, the research enterprise is fragmented and uncoordinated and is not oriented toward the needs of policy makers. (13 ref)
Baumeister, Alfred A. (Vanderbilt U, Peabody Coll for Teachers) American Journal of Mental Deficiency, 1981(Mar), Vol 85(5), 449–456. [PA, Vol 65:13030]

1146. Perspective-taking by mentally retarded children: A one-year follow-up.
Demonstrates the value of repeated measurement in the area of social understanding. In a 1-yr follow-up, a role-taking task was readministered to 27 mentally retarded children to determine the effects of time on perspective-taking task performance and examine the relationship between perspective-taking task performance and verbal justification for the performance. Performance from one year to the next was, in general, consistent with developmental expectations. (9 ref)
Blacher-Dixon, Jan & Simeonsson, Rune J. (U California School of Education, Riverside) American Journal of Mental Deficiency, 1981(May), Vol 85(6), 648–651. [PA, Vol 66:06062]

1147. An investigation of factors contributing to the apparent overselective responding of mentally retarded children.
Conducted 2 experiments in which the performances of younger MA and older MA retarded children were compared. The studies were done in an attempt to explain why younger MA children appear to be overselective on discrimination tasks containing relevant redundant cues. In Exp I, 12 males were divided into 2 MA groups—the older and younger Ss had mean MAs, IQs, and CAs of 78 mo, 50.5, and 168.7 mo, and 49.2 mo, 39.5, and 133.8 mo, respectively. The younger MA Ss were more likely than the older MA Ss to learn the discrimination on a configurational

basis. In Exp II, 8 additional males participated. The MA range for the 20 Ss was 45–108 mo; CA 105–178 mo; and IQ 22–69. Ss experienced either a simultaneous or a successive version of the relevant redundant-cue problem. Only the older MA group who was presented with the simultaneous problem demonstrated learning of the individual relevant dimensions. Findings are consistent with the hypothesis that younger MA children appear to be overselective because they tend to solve discriminations on a configurational, rather than on a dimensional, basis. (35 ref) *Butler, Gordon S. & Rabinowitz, F. Michael.* (Memorial U of Newfoundland, St John's, Canada) Child Development, 1981(Jun), Vol 52(2), 430–442. [PA, Vol 66:10590]

1148.   Mentally handicapped adolescents: Their use of leisure.
Surveyed 214 families with regard to the national provision for leisure activities for severely handicapped adolescents. Although national provision appeared to be reasonably comprehensive, this was not reflected in the restricted use of leisure locally. Potential users of such provisions were found to participate primarily in solitary, passive, family-oriented activities. It is suggested that the following factors contribute to this situation: (1) the attitude of patients who have so fully assumed the role as sole provider of care/recreation that they are unaware of the long-term consequences of such action; (2) the lack of local friendships outside the school environment restricts the development of social activities; and (3) the lack of basic skills limits the choice of activities open to handicapped adolescents. (14 ref) *Cheseldine, Sally E. & Jeffree, Dorothy M.* (Victoria U of Manchester, Hester Adrian Research Ctr, England) Journal of Mental Deficiency Research, 1981(Mar), Vol 25(1), 49–59. [PA, Vol 66:06065]

1149.   Adaptive Behavior Scale, Part Two: Predictive efficiency of severity and frequency scores.
Severity and frequency of occurrence methods of scoring the Adaptive Behavior Scales, Part 2, were compared using ratings for 210 mentally retarded persons (CAs 17–45 yrs). Comparisons involved separately correlating the 2 methods with independently obtained clinical impressions of symptomatology. The severity scoring system predicted approximately 11% more of the variance in the criterion than did frequency scores. Results provide considerable construct and predictive validity for the severity scoring system. (4 ref) *Clements, Paul R.; DuBois, Yvonne; Bost, Loujeania & Bryan, Charles.* (North Carolina Div of Mental Health/Mental Retardation Services, O'Berry Ctr, Goldboro) American Journal of Mental Deficiency, 1981(Jan), Vol 85(4), 433–434. [PA, Vol 65:06808]

1150.   Behavioral and linguistic developments in the interactions of normal and retarded children with their mothers.
Examined verbal and behavioral interactions of 18 normal and 18 retarded children (aged 18–96 mo) with their mothers in 15-min free play and 15-min structured task situations. Groups were equated on the basis of Peabody Picture Vocabulary Test Scores (MA), sex, and socioeconomic status. Retarded Ss initiated fewer social interactions, were less responsive to their mother's interactions, and engaged in more solitary play than normal Ss. Mothers of retarded Ss were more directive during the play and task settings, initiated fewer interactions, and were less likely to respond positively to their child's compliant task-oriented efforts. In the retarded group, mothers of Ss with higher MA scores were less responsive to their children's interactions than those of Ss with lower MA scores. In both the normal and retarded groups, the mean length of utterances of mothers to Ss with higher MAs were longer than those of Ss with lower MAs. A series of correlations suggests that variations in the relative match between the speech complexity of mothers and their children were related to a number of behavioral indices of reciprocity in the mother's interactions with the child. (24 ref) *Cunningham, Charles E.; Reuler, Ellen; Blackwell, Jane & Deck, Jennifer.* (Chedoke-McMaster Hosp, Hamilton, Canada) Child Development, 1981(Mar), Vol 52(1), 62–70. [PA, Vol 65:13035]

1151.   The psychometric attributes of Furth's nonverbal conservation test.
Examined the suitability of H. G. Furth's (see PA, Vol 40:4524) nonverbal conservation test as a psychometric tool for measuring individual differences in Zambia. Ss included 192 normal and 21 mentally deficient Zambian children aged 7–13 yrs. The test was validated against age differentiation, differentiation of different intellectual levels, and school performance. Results show that scores on the test increased significantly with increase in age, correlated positively and significantly with school scores, and differentiated normal from mentally deficient Ss. Within the normal sample the test also differentiated dull from average Ss; within the deficient sample the test did not differentiate the moderately from the severely mentally deficient. Results are explained by reference to the characteristics of the test, performance on which requires learning, memory, and perceptual abilities. (16 ref) *Ezeilo, Bernice N.* (U Nigeria, Nsukka) Journal of Experimental Child Psychology, 1981(Feb), Vol 31(1), 71–80. [PA, Vol 65:09231]

1152.   Can preschool children really learn to conserve?
63 preschoolers were given verbal rule training in a 2^3 factorial design to probe the importance of identity, reversibility, and compensation explanations in training number and length concepts, replicating and extending the author's (1977) earlier study of retarded children. As before, identity was the most significant factor in conservation acquisition; reversibility was important as well, but compensation was of little value. Nursery school Ss performed similarly to older children, both retarded and nonretarded, except that younger groups were not able, on average, to conserve as many quantities. Four-year-olds were able to generalize to untrained quantities far better than 3-yr-olds. In a follow-up posttest 2.5 or 5 mo later, 79% of the Ss who had generalized on the 1st posttest maintained or increased their conservation, but 70% of the 3-yr-olds who had conserved on Posttest 1 reverted to nonconservation. (21 ref) *Field, Dorothy.* (U California Inst of Human Development, Berkeley) Child Development, 1981(Mar), Vol 52(1), 326–334. [PA, Vol 65:13040]

1153.   The Lock Box: A measure of psychomotor competence and organized behavior in retarded and normal preschoolers.
The Lock Box, a large container with 10 latched compartments each housing a different toy, is a standardized method for evaluating the preschool child's approach to an unstructured situation. From the spontaneous behavior, coded over 6½ min, scales were derived measuring psychomotor competence, organization of exploration, and aimlessness. The test was administered to 290 normal (mean IQ 111.4) and 91 retarded (mean IQ 58.1) children between the ages of 2 and 7 yrs. In the normal group, scores were highly correlated with CA but not with sex, socioeconomic status, or IQ. Retarded Ss performed significantly more poorly than normal Ss of similar age on all scales, with the greatest discrepancies apparent on an aimless actions scale. The excessive aimlessness of the retarded was evident when competence and tested intelligence were controlled. Findings are related to the development of orderly exploratory patterns in normal and retarded children. (27 ref) *Goodman, Joan F.* (Children's Hosp of Philadelphia, PA) Journal of Consulting & Clinical Psychology, 1981(Jun), Vol 49(3), 369–378. [PA, Vol 66:06072]

1154.   Developmental vs. difference theories of mental retardation: A new look.
Measured performance of 3 groups of 10 children (retarded, nonretarded, and language-impaired; mean CA 72.3 mo; mean MA 62.4, 61.1, 60.6, respectively) on nonlinguistic symbolic and conceptual cognitive tasks. The performance of the retarded and nonretarded groups was essentially similar, and both of these groups generally performed at higher levels than did the language-impaired group. Several testable implications are suggested. (31 ref) *Kamhi, Alan G.* (Case Western Reserve U) American Journal of Mental Deficiency, 1981(Jul), Vol 86(1), 1–7. [PA, Vol 66:08243]

1155. Development of services for mentally retarded people in the Federal Republic of Germany: A survey of history, empirical research, and current trends.
Reviews areas in which empirical investigations have been conducted recently. They are subdivided into research on assessment instruments, descriptive studies (prevalence studies, research on living conditions), and intervention research (self-help programs, language and communication training, problem behavior). The strong influence of the Anglo-American literature, particularly in applied research and assessment, is emphasized. It is also pointed out that there is a lively discussion of conceptual and theoretical issues in mental retardation in Germany. (4½ p ref)
Kane, John F. & Rojahn, Johannes. (Max-Planck-Inst für Psychiatrie, Munich, West Germany) Applied Research in Mental Retardation, 1981, Vol 2(2), 195–210. [PA, Vol 66:08244]

1156. Issues in mental retardation in Canada: Transitions.
Reviews 3 major areas: (1) diagnostic and assessment processes with a discussion of new emphases in criterion referenced testing, adoptive functioning measurement, screening, and neuropsychological testing; (2) program and service development with special emphasis on forces influencing the scope and breadth of these new programs; (3) selected applied research programs focusing on vocational and daily living skills, communication, language intervention, remediation, motor skills, and play development with mentally retarded children. (73 ref)
Kysela, G. M.; Anderson, D. & Marfo, K. (U Alberta, Edmonton, Canada) Applied Research in Mental Retardation, 1981, Vol 2(2), 145–163. [PA, Vol 66:08620]

1157. Mental handicap in the county of Cornwall: Prevalence and the use of services.
Conducted a prevalence survey of mental handicaps in 0–19 yr old children in Cornwall in 1979. The education category ESNS (severe educational subnormality) was used to identify Ss with a severe degree of mental handicap. The use of this category made it difficult to compare the rate with other surveys. A higher prevalence rate was obtained from the most southwesterly areas of Cornwall. (20 ref)
Lindsey, M. P. & Russell, C. M. (St Lawrence's Hosp, Mental Handicap Dept, Bodmin, England) Journal of Mental Deficiency Research, 1981(Jun), Vol 25(2), 77–87. [PA, Vol 66:10603]

1158. Parentalplegia.
Uses the term "parentalplegia" to focus on the secondary parental problems caused by children's primary handicapping condition. Specific case studies of a mental retardate and 2 cerebral palsied children are used to illustrate how parents' behavior is often clearly modified as a result of their child's condition. With misinformation and distortion of thought serving as precursors of parentalplegia, the present authors suggest ways to remediate the effects of this problem through the use of educational and affective strategies. (27 ref)
Murray, Joseph N. & Cornell, Charles J. (Kent State U) Psychology in the Schools, 1981(Apr), Vol 18(2), 201–207. [PA, Vol 66:10833]

1159. Nonretarded and mentally retarded children's performance on a manual-control task with and without visual feedback.
Examined performance differences between 10 nonretarded (mean CA 4.3 yrs) and 10 retarded Ss (mean CA 13.7 yrs; mean MA 4.9 yrs) on a manual-control task. The focus was on possible relationships between Ss' abilities to control their response forces and the focus of their attention. Ss were required to exert force on a transducer within a selected force bandwidth for 3 sec to obtain a reinforcer. Results suggest that the ability to discriminate internal cues is related to IQ differences. (18 ref)
Nidiffer, F. Don & Fowler, Stephen C. (U Virginia Medical Ctr, Charlottesville) American Journal of Mental Deficiency, 1981(Mar), Vol 85(5), 521–529. [PA, Vol 65:13047]

1160. British applied psychology of subnormality.
Topics discussed are the philosophy of care, assessment, types of treatment, and social and educational intervention. Critical areas for future work such as prenatal and perinatal care, parental teaching of the handicapped, and the study of learning strategies are addressed. (109 ref)
O'Connor, N. (MRC Developmental Psychology Unit, London, England) Applied Research in Mental Retardation, 1981, Vol 2(2), 97–113. [PA, Vol 66:08624]

1161. The relationship of play to developmental level in mentally retarded, preschool children.
Observed 21 preschool, mentally retarded children (mean CA of 79.8 mo and mean developmental age of 40.33 mo) during free play periods to investigate the relationship between developmental level and level of play. The Parten Scale of Social Participation, the Smilansky Scale of Cognitive Play, and a combined form of the two scales were used to measure the level of play; the Denver Developmental Screening Test was used to establish Ss' developmental levels. Significant correlations were found between mean play scores obtained on each play scale and the developmental level of the children. Results indicate that the collateral relationship of play to mental development found in preschool nonretarded children may also be seen in young mentally retarded children. (29 ref)
Odom, Samuel L. (U Washington, Seattle) Education & Training of the Mentally Retarded, 1981(Apr), Vol 16(2), 136–141. [PA, Vol 66:08259]

1162. An investigation of self-concept and body image in the mentally retarded.
Explored the relationship of self-drawings (Draw-A-Person test; DAP) to scores on a measure of self-concept (Piers-Harris Self-Concept Scale) in 31 mentally retarded 11–22 yr olds. Five variables hypothesized to be related to self-concept—self-drawing score, size of self-drawing, age, sex, and IQ—were subjected to forward (stepwise) multiple regression analysis. Data analysis revealed that 4 of the 5 variables—sex, size, overall DAP score, and age—shared significant variance with self-concept scores. It is suggested that these variables can provide additional information in evaluating the self-concept of the mentally retarded. (20 ref)
Ottenbacher, Kenneth. (U Central Arkansas School of Health Sciences) Journal of Clinical Psychology, 1981(Apr), Vol 37(2), 415–418. [PA, Vol 66:01544]

1163. Improving the identification of high-risk infants.
Selected 52 Black infants whose families were characterized by low levels of formal education, a fairly low level of maternal intelligence, and very low incomes. By focusing on a group at relatively high risk, the authors hoped to increase the precision and economy of early identification by using more process-oriented information about Ss' early development and environment. As Ss attained 6 mo of age, characteristics of the mother, child, and home were assessed through such measures as the WAIS. At 2 yrs of age, Ss were given the Stanford-Binet Intelligence Scale and divided into a nonretarded group and a high-risk group. A step-wise discriminant analysis was used to derive a predictor set consisting of mother's democratic attitudes, S's temperament, and the amount of time the S spent outside the home that allowed for the correct prediction of 75% of the Ss, with an overall miss rate of 20% and a false positive rate of 29.6%. (32 ref)
Ramey, Craig T. & Brownlee, John R. (U North Carolina, Frank Porter Graham Child Development Ctr, Chapel Hill) American Journal of Mental Deficiency, 1981(Mar), Vol 85(5), 504–511. [PA, Vol 65:13361]

1164. Scatter on the WISC as an indicator of intellectual potential.
Investigated the relationship between subtest scatter on the WISC and higher intellectual potential. All Ss (125 8–17 yr olds) at one time obtained Full Scale IQ scores within the retarded range. Group I consisted of those Ss who upon reexamination with the WISC obtained Full Scale IQ Scores of 75 or below,

while Group II consisted of those Ss whose Full Scale IQ scores were now found to be nonretarded upon reexamination. Results indicate that the scatter on the initial examinations failed to predict the future group membership. Irrespective of group membership, scatter was found not to be related to change in Full Scale IQ scores. It is concluded that subtest scatter is a poor indicator of the presence of higher intellectual potential. It is also suggested that these findings are relevant to the WISC-R. (14 ref)
Ribner, Sol & Kahn, Paul. (New York City Board of Education, Committee on the Handicapped, NY) Psychology in the Schools, 1981(Jan), Vol 18(1), 39–42. [PA, Vol 66:11388]

1165.   A functional classification of seizures and its distribution in a mentally retarded population.
Describes a functional classification of seizure impairment and examines its distribution in 78 females and 107 males classified as mentally retarded in childhood and followed to age 22 yrs. 25% had some history of seizures up to age 22. Seizure histories were found for 19% in the preschool years and 13% in each period of early, late, and postschool years. A drop in minor seizure impairment occurred after age 5. A slightly higher frequency of seizure histories among males was found, largely due to Ss whose IQs were 50–59, where 44% of the males and 5% of the females had seizure histories. No significant association was found between degree of seizure impairment and severity of mental retardation. (14 ref)
Richardson, Stephen A.; Koller, Helene; Katz, Mindy & McLaren, Janice. (Yeshiva U, Albert Einstein Coll of Medicine) American Journal of Mental Deficiency, 1981(Mar), Vol 85(5), 457–466. [PA, Vol 65:13049]

1166.   A sociological perspective on labeling in mental retardation.
Presents a conceptual scheme based on T. J. Scheff's (1966, 1975) labeling theory of mental illness. The framework is condensed into several hypotheses: (a) Residual rule breaking arises from fundamentally diverse sources. (b) Most residual rule breaking is denied and is of transitory significance. (c) Stereotyped imagery of mental retardation (MR) is learned in early childhood. (d) The stereotypes of MR are continually reaffirmed inadvertently, in ordinary social interaction. (e) Labeled MR individuals may be rewarded for playing the stereotyped deviant role and are punished when they attempt to return to conventional roles. (f) When a rule breaker is publicly labeled MR, he/she is highly suggestible and may accept the proffered role as the only alternative. The issue of the medicalization of social problems is discussed, and it is noted that the issue of social and political control of mentally retarded persons is yet to be resolved. (21 ref)
Rowitz, Louis. (U Illinois Medical Ctr, School of Public Health, Chicago) Mental Retardation, 1981(Apr), Vol 19(2), 47–51. [PA, Vol 66:08268]

1167.   Mental illness and mental retardation: Cause or coincidence?
93 patients (aged 6–22 yrs) admitted to an inpatient psychiatric unit for emotionally disturbed, developmentally disabled adolescents were studied in an attempt to clarify the relationship between intellectual functioning and psychoses occurring in the developmental period. The severity and duration of the psychosis, the presence of hallucinations, and the degree of isolation of the S from his or her environment appear to be important factors influencing the occurrence of decreased psychometric test scores. (10 ref)
Russell, Andrew T. & Tanguay, Peter E. (U California, Neuropsychiatric Inst, Los Angeles) American Journal of Mental Deficiency, 1981(May), Vol 85(6), 570–574. [PA, Vol 66:05922]

1168.   "Input capability and speed of processing in mental retardation": A reply to Stanovich and Purcell.
Contrary to the claims of K. E. Stanovich and D. G. Purcell (see PA, Vol 66:1547), the present author argues that he and his colleagues (see PA, Vol 62:13941) did not claim to have demonstrated specific deficits in iconic storage in mental retardation but specifically noted that the precise nature of the input

limitation could not be specified. Stanovich and Purcell's basic criticism is that the Saccuzzo et al design does not rule out nonspecific factors that might have contributed to performance differences. Their specific criticisms of the experimental method are discussed; some are shown to be speculative and others incorrect. (17 ref)
Saccuzzo, Dennis P. (San Diego State U, Psychology Clinic) Journal of Abnormal Psychology, 1981(Apr), Vol 90(2), 172–174. [PA, Vol 66:01546]

1169.   Mental retardation in the United States: Assessment, program development, and applied research.
Discusses the recent history of mental retardation in the US thus revealing a growth in establishing the right to education, treatment, work, due process, and fair wage. New public laws guarantee a right to a free, appropriate, individualized education. Trends in applied biomedical research show new data in medical and biochemical genetics, neurotoxicology of environmental pollutants, neurobiology of developmental behavior disorders, nutrition, and the developmental psychophysiology of mental retardation. New data have emerged with early intervention programs for high risk infants, in sociobehavioral studies of mental retardation, and in research on the quality of life of severely and profoundly retarded persons. Behavior modification has had a major influence on instructional technology in mental retardation. (43 ref)
Schroeder, Carolyn S. & Schroeder, Stephen R. (U North Carolina, Child Development Research Inst, Chapel Hill) Applied Research in Mental Retardation, 1981, Vol 2(2), 181–194. [PA, Vol 66:08269]

1170.   [Psycho-social aspects of coping with diagnosis and of related family dynamics in families having children afflicted with spina bifida and hydrocephalus.] (Germ)
Reports on the psychosocial process of assimilation of the "hydrocephalus" stigma and visible physical handicaps in 46 adolescents—all of whom had undergone a fluid drainage operation within the 1st days or weeks of their lives. In addition, half the Ss were born with a deformity generally classified with the congenital spina bifida defects that also required surgical closure shorly after birth. Interviews with Ss and their families were conducted with respect to the following topics: human interaction upon confrontation with the diagnosis, self-image and self-experience of the handicapped adolescent, and the effect on the parents' marriage after the birth of the handicapped child. The dynamics of these issues and the therapeutic process for families with a handicapped child are discussed.
Seidler, Günter H. (Georg-August-U Göttingen, West Germany) Praxis der Kinderpsychologie und Kinderpsychiatrie, 1981(Feb–Mar), Vol 30(2), 39–47. [PA, Vol 66:13150]

1171.   Care, prevention, and assessment of mental retardation in India.
Reviews the status of mental retardation care and treatment in India. Particular emphasis is placed on recent expansion of physical care, and government and private sector attempts to educate persons to the necessity of having small families due to gross overcrowding. Also, the need to maintain a well-balanced diet, obtain vaccinations against disease, and receive proper medical supervision during pregnancy is stressed. Psychological tests currently in use and areas for future research in mental retardation are reviewed. (10 ref)
Sen, Arun K. (U Delhi, India) Applied Research in Mental Retardation, 1981, Vol 2(2), 129–137. [PA, Vol 66:08627]

1172.   Mental retardation: State of the field in New Zealand.
Emphasizes major institutions affecting the mentally retarded, namely medicine, education, parent advocacy, and legislation. These institutions are examined, with emphasis on factors that are unique to this country. Applied research, particularly that concerned with community intervention and behavioral techniques, is reviewed. Finally, major areas in need of attention such as the education legislation and evaluation of new trends in treatment are identified. (47 ref)

Singh, Nirbhay N. & Aman, Michael G. (U Canterbury, Christchurch, New Zealand) Applied Research in Mental Retardation, 1981, Vol 2(2), 115–127. [PA, Vol 66:08271]

1173. Comment on "Input capability and speed of processing in mental retardation" by Saccuzzo, Kerr, Marcus, and Brown.
In a recent article, D. P. Saccuzzo et al (see PA, Vol 62:13941) claimed to have demonstrated that retarded individuals have specific deficits in iconic storage duration and encoding speed. It is argued that problems with the logic and methodology of their experiment preclude the conclusions that were drawn. The present authors elucidate some of the methodological pitfalls in this research area. (22 ref)
Stanovich, Keith E. & Purcell, Dean G. (Oakland U) Journal of Abnormal Psychology, 1981(Apr), Vol 90(2), 168–171. [PA, Vol 66:01547]

1174. On Saccuzzo's reply.
Comments that D. P. Saccuzzo's (1981) reply to a comment by the present authors (1981) on the article by Saccuzzo et al (see PA, Vol 62:13941) displays considerable misunderstanding regarding several points raised in that comment. (7 ref)
Stanovich, Keith E. & Purcell, Dean G. (Oakland U) Journal of Abnormal Psychology, 1981(Jun), Vol 90(3), 261–262. [PA, Vol 66:06089]

1175. Assessment and management of mental retardation in Hungary.
The incidence of mental retardation in Hungary is estimated at 3% of live-born children. Mental handicap is defined by the combination of 3 criteria: intelligence, as defined by IQ test; social maturity; and structural nervous system defects. Mildly handicapped children receive special education in various educational institutions. Severely mentally retarded persons are taken care of in 30 health institutions with governmental support. Similar institutions are sponsored by the Protestant churches with government aid. They serve one-sixth of the population. Since 1970 the Ministry of Health organized the National Methodological Center and Home for Health Care of Mentally Retarded Children, thus providing interdisciplinary training to mental retardation professionals. A national registry permits long-term computerized follow-up of the mentally handicapped. (12 ref)
Szondy, Mária & Szentágothai, Klára R. Applied Research in Mental Retardation, 1981, Vol 2(2), 139–144. [PA, Vol 66:08629]

1176. Some conditions affecting manipulative play with objects in severely mentally handicapped children.
Four experiments investigated contact and manipulative activity with play materials in a total of 27 normal (NL) children (CA 12–23 mo) and 74 mentally retarded (MR) children (CA 3–16 yrs) functioning at the 1–2 yr old stage of normal development. Exp I found that many MRs were as quick to contact and manipulate a novel object as NLs and that auditory (or visual) feedback seemed to be effective in sustaining attentive activity with an object. Two MRs, however, were slow to contact either familiar conventional toys or a novel object. Exps II and III found that adding stimulus features (e.g., sounds, lights, bright colors) to an object had no consistent effect on the latencies of these slow responders to contact the object. Exp IV found that the amount and kinds of manipulative play of MRs with a range of conventional toys was similar to that of comparable NLs. MRs differed from NLs only in that they interacted less with an attendant adult and displayed less frequent representational use of toys in pretend play. The play of both groups was relatively unaffected by whether only a few (4) or many (15) toys were provided. (14 ref)
Thomas, G. V.; Phemister, M. R. & Richardson, A. M. (U Birmingham, England) Child Care, Health & Development, 1981(Jan–Feb), Vol 7(1), 1–20. [PA, Vol 66:01549]

1177. Stability of the WISC-R for a sample of exceptional children.
Compared the subtest and IQ scores of 75 learning disabled and retarded children on the WISC-R after 2 yrs (CAs at 1st testing 8–14 yrs). Data indicate that the WISC-R provides stable Full Scale IQs. (5 ref)
Vance, H. Booney; Blixt, Sonya; Ellis, Rick & Debell, Susan. (Kent State U) Journal of Clinical Psychology, 1981(Apr), Vol 37(2), 397–399. [PA, Vol 66:00237]

1178. Learned helplessness in Black and White children identified by their schools as retarded and nonretarded: Performance deterioration in response to failure.
20 Black and 20 White children who had been identified as retarded and nonretarded but were similar in MA (110.2–114.3 mo) were administered concept formation problems designed to reveal use of strategies. When feedback was veridical the groups did not differ in their use of effective strategies, but when feedback became consistently negative the groups diverged markedly. Under negative feedback, retarded Ss showed striking deterioration in strategy usage, but nonretarded Ss showed no deterioration. Consistent with these findings, teachers rated retarded Ss as significantly more helpless than their nonretarded peers on a checklist of relevant school behavior. Additional findings suggest that Black retarded Ss may be more susceptible to helplessness than are their White counterparts. Finally, group differences in verbalizations during problem solving bore little relation to group differences in actual performance. Findings point to helplessness deficits in retarded children that may interfere significantly with expression of their actual abilities. (31 ref)
Weisz, John R. (U North Carolina, Chapel Hill) Developmental Psychology, 1981(Jul), Vol 17(4), 499–508. [PA, Vol 66:08283]

1179. Chronic sorrow revisited: Parent vs. professional depiction of the adjustment of parents of mentally retarded children.
In response to a questionnaire mailing, 32 parents of mentally retarded children and 32 social workers essentially agreed that such parents experience periodic crises during the child's development (e.g., diagnosis, siblings surpass child, and entry into school), rather than time-bound adjustment. Social workers tended to underestimate the impact of later developmental periods on parents. Findings suggest that chronic sorrow does not seem to be an abnormal response, but rather a normal reaction to an abnormal situation. Implications for clinical practitioner as they plan programs for and work with families of older retarded persons are discussed. (15 ref)
Wikler, Lynn; Wasow, Mona & Hatfield, Elaine. (U Wisconsin School of Social Work, Madison) American Journal of Orthopsychiatry, 1981(Jan), Vol 51(1), 63–70. [PA, Vol 66:08285]

Downs Syndrome

1180. Short intelligence test ranging from infancy levels through childhood levels for use with the retarded.
Developed a short, general intelligence test for retarded children whose abilities ranged from infancy levels through childhood levels. Standard administration of Cattell and Stanford-Binet tests to 28 mongoloid children provided data statistically used to develop a ⅔ shorter test. The short and standard versions were then administered to a new sample of 31 retarded children. Correlation between the short and standard tests was .97. The average administration time for standard testing was 60 min compared to 16 min for the short form. Vineland scores and standardized psychiatric ratings developed correlations beyond the .001 level of confidence with the short form. The theory and techniques for intellectual evaluations of retarded children are discussed. (26 ref)
Alpern, Gerald D. & Kimberlin, Carolyn C. (Indiana U., Medical School, Indianapolis) American Journal of Mental Deficiency, 1970(Jul), Vol. 75(1), 65–71. [PA, Vol 45:01185]

1181. EEG evoked responses to repetitive auditory stimulation in normal and Down's syndrome infants.
Normal 6- and 12-mo-old infants, exposed to repetitive auditory stimuli, showed a progressive decrement in amplitude of EEG

auditory evoked responses; 6- and 12-mo-old infants with Down's syndrome showed no response decrement. The mental deficit in the latter group may be related to sensory abnormalities. (33 ref.)
Barnet, Ann B.; Ohlrich, Elizabeth S. & Shanks, Betty L. (Children's Hosp., Research Lab., Washington) Developmental Medicine & Child Neurology, 1971(Jun), Vol. 13(3), 321-329. [PA, Vol 47:07404]

1182.   [The language of the mongoloid child.] (Germ)
Analyzed the language development of mongoloid children (42 male and 17 female). Data was obtained by questionnaire from teachers and physicians. Language is strongly retarded, with no increment of improvement beginning at Age 7. Language structure is very primitive usually 1-word utterances or sentence fractions. Speech is inarticulate and halting, with stuttering also noted. However, these children are not "language lazy" but try frequently to reach communication levels. Help is required from the speech therapist.
Buchka, Maximilian. (162 Eintrachtstr., Cologne, W. Germany) Vierteljahresschrift für Heilpädagogik und ihre Nachbargebiete, 1971(Dec), Vol. 40(4), 308-312. [PA, Vol 48:09545]

1183.   Subjective organization and clustering in the free recall of intellectually-subnormal children.
Simultaneous presentation of 6 pictorially presented items to 24 mongoloid and 24 nonmongoloid intellectually-subnormal children resulted in organization in recall. Clustering was found in the recall of categorically related items, and subjective organization in the recall of apparently unrelated items. Significant correlations between clustering and recall were obtained, but not between subjective organization and recall. The clustering condition resulted in higher recall scores than the subjective organization condition. Degree of rehearsal was negatively correlated with subjective organization in the case of mongoloid Ss, whereas number of repetitions was positively correlated with recall. It is concluded that (a) subjective organization was sequential in nature, while clustering was mainly hierarchical, (b) failure to internalize language leads to sequential strategies, and (c) mongoloid Ss, in particular, were retarded in internalization. (24 ref.)
Herriot, Peter & Cox, A. M. (Manchester U., England) American Journal of Mental Deficiency, 1971(May), Vol. 75(6), 702-711. [PA, Vol 47:01473]

1184.   Visibility of the nailfold capillaries in retarded adolescents.
Examined 141 normal and 180 retarded adolescents for a visible, subpapillary capillary plexus in the nailfold; all Ss were white, born in 1954, and tested in the fall of 1969. The 180 retarded children constituted the total population of white patients born in 1954 at 3 state institutions in Pennsylvania. Visibility of the subpapillary plexus was rated for the 4th and 5th fingers of both hands. IQs were available for most Ss, both normal and retarded. Ratings of plexus visibility were found to be much higher for retarded than normal Ss. A significant negative correlation was obtained between IQ and plexus rating among retarded males but not elsewhere. No differences were found between 28 Mongoloid children and age-matched normal controls. There was no association between plexus visibility and length of hospitalization or, by implication, age at 1st hospitalization among the retarded Ss. These findings are interpreted under the hypothesis that plexus visibility is linked on a genetic basis with vulnerability to brain damage in intrauterine life. (20 ref.)
Jones, Marshall B. & Whitson, David W. (Pennsylvania State U., Milton S. Hershey Medical Center) Biological Psychiatry, 1971, Vol. 3(4), 331-337. [PA, Vol 48:03547]

1185.   Immunoelectrophoretic serum patterns associated with mothers of children affected with the G_1-trisomy syndrome (Down's syndrome).
Peripheral-blood sera from 46 of 48 mothers affected with G_1 trisomy showed an extra precipitant line in the gamma-A region of their immunoelectrophoretic patterns. By comparison, only 10 of 48 age-matched control mothers were positive for the same parameter. The incidence of this high-molecular-weight protein-based antigen in mothers of G_1-trisomy-affected children exceeded the incidence of any of the several other immunological parameters previously investigated. The incidence of the extra precipitant line in controls was lower than for any of the several other parameters.
Kerkay, Julius; Zsako, Steven & Kaplan, Arnold R. (Cleveland State U.) American Journal of Mental Deficiency, 1971(May), Vol. 75(6), 729-732. [PA, Vol 47:01459]

1186.   Rhythmic habit patterns in infancy: Their sequence, age of onset, and frequency.
Studied the onset of hand to mouth sucking in (a) 140 normal newborn infants, and (b) 79 abnormal newborn infants of normal and low birth weight, with low Apgar scores and neonatal disease. Results indicate a significant delay in hand sucking in abnormal Ss. The sequence, age of onset, and frequency of other common rhythmic habit patterns, e.g., foot kicking, lip sucking and biting, body rocking, toe sucking, head rolling and banging, and teeth grinding, were also recorded in 200 older infants. The marked delay in the onset of the common rhythmic habit patterns in infants with Down's syndrome and cerebral palsy is also discussed. It is concluded that rhythmic habit patterns may be of value in the diagnosis of developmental retardation in infants. (38 ref.)
Kravitz, Harvey & Boehm, John J. (Northwestern U., Medical School, Chicago) Child Development, 1971(Jun), Vol. 42(2), 399-413. [PA, Vol 47:00588]

1187.   Leukaemia and twinning tendency in families of children with Down's syndrome.
Found 21 leukemic Ss in 801 families of children with Down's syndrome, appreciably more frequently in the families of mothers than of fathers (16.5 and 7.8/1,000 respectively). This observation suggests a tendency to abnormal cell division within mothers' families and is further supported by almost twice the frequency of twins in mothers' families when compared with that of fathers' families. Nearly half the cases of leukemia occurred in families in which twinning also occurred.
Kučera, J. (Inst. of Care for Mother & Child, Prague, Czechoslovakia) Journal of Mental Deficiency Research, 1971(Jun), Vol. 15(2), 77-80. [PA, Vol 52:01272]

1188.   Cytogenetic survey of Down's syndrome in Serbia (Yugoslavia): Incidence of numerical and structural abnormalities.
Cytogenetically examined 180 Ss with Down's syndrome and their families (164 mothers, 132 fathers, and 45 other close relatives). Translocations and mosaics were found in proportions within the range of findings in other surveys. Other major and minor chromosomal anomalies in the Ss surveyed included a triple X mother, a transmitted C/G translocation, an enlarged short arm of a G-group chromosome in 5 families (usually transmitted), a double satellite on a D-group chromosome in 1 S, and satellite-like formations on an E-group chromosome in 5 Ss. One female mongol in the sample gave birth to a normal male child. The possible significance of the various aberrations in relation to the occurrence of mongolism is discussed. (16 ref)
Morić-Petrović, Slavka, et al. (Inst. of Mental Health, Belgrade, Yugoslavia) Journal of Mental Deficiency Research, 1971(Jun), Vol. 15(2), 102-114. [PA, Vol 52:01280]

1189.   A longitudinal study of exceptional cognitive development in a partial translocation Down's syndrome child.
Reports on a 5-yr follow-up of a Down's syndrome boy with exceptional intelligence from a family with a D/partial G translocation [46, XY, $t(D_{p+})$]. S maintained his average verbal-vocabulary intelligence over a period of 6 yr. but now displays perceptual-motor deficit, behavioral distractibility, and performance IQ depression quite similar to children diagnosed as chronic brain syndrome. The longitudinal study of this "partial" Down's syndrome S revealed marked differences among abilities that are generally "masked" by the overall behavioral deficit of the typical Down's trisomy. Some hypotheses concerning degree

of excessive chromosomal material and its relationship to specific areas of stigmata expression are offered.

Rosencrans, C. J. (U. Alabama Medical Center, Birmingham) American Journal of Mental Deficiency, 1971(Nov), Vol. 76(3), 291-294. [PA, Vol 48:03554]

1190. Comprehension and imitation of sentences by Down's syndrome children as a function of transformational complexity.
Describes 2 studies examining the effect of sentence complexity on the ability of 40 6-14 yr old trainable mentally retarded Down's syndrome children, with a mean IQ of 34.3, to comprehend and imitate verbally presented sentences. Ss correctly comprehended simple declarative (kernel) sentences significantly more often than chance expectancy, but comprehended negative sentences less often than would be expected by chance. Imitation of kernel sentences (obligatory transformations only) was significantly better than imitation of sentences in which optional transformations had been applied. No significant differences in accuracy of imitation were observed among the strings with optional transformations.

Semmel, Melvyn I. & Dolley, Diane G. (Indiana U.) American Journal of Mental Deficiency, 1971(May), Vol. 75(6), 739-745. [PA, Vol 47:01480]

1191. Tongue size in Down's syndrome.
Radiographically assessed tongue size relative to mouth cavity in 8 5-15 yr old children with Down's syndrome. In no S was the tongue enlarged, but 5 had localized enlargement of the lingual tonsil resulting in narrowing of the lower pharynx and superior laryngeal aperture. All Ss had enlarged adenoids and tonsils or evidence of such. 3 Ss showed inferior overjet, and 2 had edge-to-edge apposition of the anterior incisor teeth due to a forward position of the mandible relative to the spine. It is suggested that the gaping mouth and protrusion of the tongue seen in many Down's syndrome patients relates to the need to provide an airway. Removal of obstructions such as adenoids, pharyngeal tonsils, and the lingual tonsil would help many of them to close their mouths and would favorably influence jaw development.

Ardran, G. M.; Harker, P. & Kemp, F. H. (U. Oxford, Nuffield Inst. for Medical Research, England) Journal of Mental Deficiency Research, 1972(Sep), Vol. 16(3), 160-166. [PA, Vol 51:03466]

1192. The ITPA and Negro children with Down's syndrome.
Administered the Illinois Test of Psycholinguistic Abilities (ITPA) to a sample of Negro children with Down's syndrome and compared results with those previously reported for Caucasian children with Down's syndrome. The superiority of normal Negro Ss in auditory sequential memory was not shown by the Negro Ss with Down's syndrome. The Negro and Caucasian Down's syndrome Ss did not differ significantly on ITPA profiles.

Caccamo, James M. & Yater, Allen C. (Kansas City Regional Diagnostic Clinic, Mo.) Exceptional Children, 1972(Apr), Vol. 38(8), 642-643. [PA, Vol 50:06961]

1193. [The influence of sex on the phenotypic characteristics of Down's syndrome.] (Russ)
Studied 312 males and 225 females (newborn to 3 yr. olds) with Down's syndrome. While a significantly greater proportion of the girls (16 vs. 3.61%) showed mildly retarded intelligence (p < .01), a significantly larger proportion of the boys (11.91 vs. 2%) were profoundly retarded (p < .01). Congenital defects of the thorax and spine, anomalies of the skeletal-motor apparatus, and stomach hernias were diagnosed significantly more often in boys (p < .01). Boys were also more susceptible to infectious diseases of the respiratory system (p < .05). It is suggested that the more severe clinical manifestation of Down's syndrome in males is due to the male fetus's greater sensitivity to all intrauterine abnormalities, including those caused by trisomy of autosome 21.

Demeedov, A. U. (First Moscow Medical Inst., USSR) Defektologiya, 1972, Vol. 1, 33-37. [PA, Vol 49:04659]

1194. [The influence of sex on the phenotypic characteristics of Down's syndrome.] (Russ)
Studied 312 boys and 225 girls, ranging from newborn to 3 yr. old, with Down's syndrome. A significantly greater proportion of the girls (16% vs. 3.61%) showed mildly retarded intelligence (p < .01), but a significantly larger proportion of the boys (11.91% vs. 2%) were found to be profoundly retarded (p < 01). Congenital defects of the thorax and spine, congenital anomalies of the skeletal-motor apparatus, and congenital stomach hernias were diagnosed in boys significantly more often (p < .01). Boys were more susceptible to infectious diseases of the respiratory system (p < 05). It is suggested that the more severe clinical manifestations of Down's syndrome in males are due to the male fetus' greater sensitivity to all intrauterine abnormalities, including those caused by trisomy of autosome 21.

Demidov, A. U. (First Moscow Medical Institute, USSR) Defektologiya, 1972, Vol. 4(1), 33-37. [PA, Vol 50:09146]

1195. Mental development of infants with Down's syndrome.
Administered the Gesell Developmental Schedules 5 times to 21 Down's syndrome infants and 20 normal controls between the ages of 16 wk. and 18 mo. In each of the 3 areas of the test (motor, adaptive, and social) the Down's syndrome group showed a developmental quotient (DQ) significantly lower than controls at the age of 16 wk. Further analysis in terms of CA and MA, rather than the DQ, showed that whereas the controls conformed to the expected pattern of development, the Down's syndrome group showed a rate of development which was not only slower than normal but progressively deteriorated between the ages considered.

Dicks-Mireaux, M. J. (Guy's Hosp., Pediatric Research Unit, London, England) American Journal of Mental Deficiency, 1972(Jul), Vol. 77(1), 26-32. [PA, Vol 49:00957]

1196. [The spontaneous cerebral electroactivity faster than 14 c/s: EEG findings among mongoloids.] (Ital)
In abnormal EEG records of Mongoloids, at times only sporadic and with low statistical incidence, the presence of rapid spontaneous frequency has been observed. Because of a previous study by the authors concerning fast cerebral electroactivity and because of the opportunity to observe numerous Mongoloids with extreme age variability, it was decided to verify the presence of "rapid rhythms" in a group of male and female patients (N = 62) from 11 mo. to 44 yr., with the greater number of Ss in their 1st and 2nd infancy. In some patients, EEGs were taken in various intervals and in 5 cases also during spontaneous sleep. In 35% of the Ss older than 2 yr., the records showed the presence of high frequency rhythms faster than 14 c/s. Since these activities have also been found in other cases associated with mental deficiency, it is not possible to consider the "fast rhythm" as typical of Mongoloids. (English summary) (19 ref.)

Rinaldi, F., et al. (U. Bari, Psychiatric Clinic, Italy) Acta Neurologica, 1972(May), Vol. 27(3), 291-304. [PA, Vol 50:01337]

1197. The early maternal linguistic environment of normal and nonnormal language learning children.
The language learning child constructs his theory of language on the basis of the linguistic data made available to him. 11 mother-child pairs were selected for the study. 21 language parameters of the early maternal linguistic environment of normal and non-normal language learning children were investigated. Data suggest that 1 factor determining the order in which grammatical structures emerge in the child's language is their frequency of occurrence in the linguistic data made available to him. In particular, mothers of non-normal language learning children expose their children to a different linguistic environment in terms of frequency of occurrence of certain language forms.

Buium, Nissan; Rynders, John; Wolf, Judith & Turnure, James. (U. Minnesota) Proceedings of the 81st Annual Convention of the American Psychological Association, 1973, Vol 8, 79-80. [PA, Vol 50:05012]

1198. MA intellectual assessment by operant conditioning of Down's syndrome children.
Determined whether a systematic relationship exists between mental ability (measured by the Stanford-Binet) and individual operant discrimination measures. 14 Down's syndrome children with a mean CA of 14 yrs and a mean MA of 3 yrs 8 mo were required to discriminate a multiple fixed ratio-external schedule. The operant measure was the number of sessions required to discriminate; criterion was 84% responding during the fixed ratio components. Results show that a systematic relationship exists—faster discrimination is associated with higher MA. Implications were that operant tasks of varying complexity could be used to assess the learning potential of nonverbal children. *Carter, Dianne & Clark, Lincoln.* (U. Iowa) Mental Retardation, 1973(Jun), Vol. 11(3), 39-41. [PA, Vol 51:01377]

1199. Acrocentric chromosomes in cultured leukocytes from mothers of children affected with the G_1-trisomy syndrome.
Studied metaphase plates of cultured peripheral-blood leukocytes from 24 mothers of G_1-trisomy-affected (Down's syndrome) children and from 23 other mothers. The associations of acrocentric satellited chromosomes were examined. The mothers of G_1-trisomy-affected children deviated significantly from the other mothers regarding their relatively high involvement of G-group chromosomes in such associations. (31 ref) *Cotton, James E.; Kaplan, Arnold R. & Zsako, Steven.* (Cleveland Psychiatric Inst., O.) American Journal of Mental Deficiency, 1973(Nov), Vol. 78(3), 249-254. [PA, Vol 52:03356]

1200. Clinical electroencephalographic observations on institutionalized mongoloids confirmed by karyotype.
Recorded 279 EEGs on 202 institutionalized mongoloid patients, ages 1 mo. to 63 yr. whose diagnoses had been confirmed by karyotype. The EEGs were analyzed by conventional impressionistic clinical interpretation. The rate of EEG abnormality was greater (20-25%) than that in the general population. The highest rates of EEG abnormality were found during childhood (prior to 14 yr. of age). Abnormality rates during young adulthood were no higher than those for the general population. They appear to rise prematurely in the 5th and 6th decades, consistent with clinical and pathological observations of acceleration of aging processes in mongoloids. The rate of so-called seizure activity was elevated (9%). 90% of records with "seizure activity" were obtained on Ss under 14 yr. of age. They were usually not associated with a history of seizures. In general, EEG abnormalities were not well correlated with specific behavioral or neurological signs and symptoms. There was no conclusive evidence that rates or types of EEG abnormality were different in Ss with the rarer trisomy 21 mosaic and D/G translocation karyotypes than in Ss with the trisomy 21 karyotype. (French summary) *Ellingson, Robert J.; Eisen, James D. & Ottersberg, Gloria.* (U. Nebraska, Medical Center, Psychiatric Inst., Omaha) Electroencephalography & Clinical Neurophysiology, 1973(Feb), Vol. 34(2), 193-196. [PA, Vol 50:05039]

1201. The school-age siblings of mongol children.
School children with mongol siblings living at home were rated more deviant than controls with a particularly high incidence of antisocial disorders in girls. Children most at risk were those with mother over 40 yrs old at the birth of the mongol, those from large families, and those from the lowest social classes. *Gath, Ann.* (Warneford Hosp., Oxford U., England) British Journal of Psychiatry, 1973(Aug), Vol. 123(573), 161-167. [PA, Vol 51:11405]

1202. Mongolism, parental desires, and the right to life.
Describes the case of a woman who, upon giving birth to a Down's syndrome child, refused to authorize routine corrective surgery for an intestinal blockage. The child was allowed to die. Her husband and the attending physicians and nurses allowed her decision to stand. This case is discussed in depth in an attempt to examine all possible contributing value judgments, ethical/moral decisions, desires, and motives of all the participants in the decision. Analysis demonstrates how giving different

weights to the same considerations can alter the conclusion called for by this situation. It is concluded that the obligation of parents and doctors to serve others' interests, and the right of any infant to live, should have resulted in a decision to save the infant's life. *Gustafson, James M.* (U. Chicago) Perspectives in Biology & Medicine, 1973(Sum), Vol. 16(4), 529-557. [PA, Vol 51:07245]

1203. [A clinical statistical, biochemical and developmental psychological research on children with Down's syndrome.] (Japn)
Reviews physiological and psychological factors in the etiology and symptomatology of Down's syndrome, and compares results of previous studies with a study of mothers and children with Down's syndrome. A previous study found that the age of mothers who have children with Down's syndrome show peaks at 27 and 37 yrs; the present study found only 1 peak at age 27. Complications during pregnancy are discussed; the mothers often showed histories of spontaneous abortion. A prevalence of right-handedness in the children was observed, along with retarded speech development. Cerebrospinal fluid activity in children with Down's syndrome was markedly higher when compared to children with other types of mental deficiency. *Iida, Makoto.* Journal of Mental Health, 1973(Mar), No. 21, 211-248. [PA, Vol 52:03371]

1204. [Intellectual development of chromosomal mosaic children with Down's syndrome.] (Japn)
Determined the intellectual characteristics of children with 46/47 mosaic Down's syndrome. 8 cases were diagnosed as 46/47 mosaicism by chromosomal analysis using peripheral leucocyte cultures and compared with 8 trisomic Down's syndrome children on Tsumori's Infant Mental Development Test. Results show that developmental quotients (DQ) of mosaic Ss were significantly higher than trisomic Ss and that the majority of mosaic Ss belonged to an intellectually borderline or mildly retarded group. Developmental profiles of the mosaic Ss were nearer to normal than those of the trisomic Ss. An analysis of the relationship between IQ and the proportions of cells with trisomic chromosome characteristics in 43 previously reported cases of 46/47 mosaicism shows that mosaic children with higher percentages of trisomic cells are more severely retarded. (47 ref) *Ikeda, Yukie.* (Tokyo U. Education, Japan) Japanese Journal of Special Education, 1973(Mar), Vol. 10(3), 44-59. [PA, Vol 52:01265]

1205. Facilitating two-word utterances in two Down's syndrome boys.
2 young Down's syndrome boys, equated developmentally, served as Ss in a design involving both between- and within-S control procedures with the aim of demonstrating that early 2-word utterances of the pivot-open type could be taught to mentally retarded children. After both of the Ss had been taught the appropriate 10 nouns and 1 participle, the experimental S was trained to structure pivot-open utterances with 5 of the original 10 nouns plus the pivot "gone" in a play situation. The Pivot-Open Practice Instrument was employed to reinforce appropriate responses. The control S's treatment paralleled that of the experimental S except that no pivot-open models were provided. When criterion level was reached for the experimental S, using the 1st 5 nouns, he was exposed to the 2nd 5 nouns. Generalization of the learned structure to these 5 nouns then occurred. The control S was then switched to the experimental condition, whereupon he learned to imitate, produce, and generalize the pivot-open construction. *Jeffree, Dorothy; Wheldall, Kevin & Mittler, Peter.* (U. Manchester, England) American Journal of Mental Deficiency, 1973(Sep), Vol. 78(2), 117-122. [PA, Vol 52:01267]

1206. Down's syndrome and diabetes.
Conducted a survey to determine the prevalence of diabetes in people with Down's syndrome at training centers in England. Out of a total of 914 Ss known to the County Health Department as having this condition, 456 attended either junior or adult training centers and, of these, 404 provided urine specimens on 2 separate occasions. There were 7 cases of diabetes: a prevalence

of 17/1,000. The rate among children aged 0-14 yrs was 20.6/1,000, which is considerably higher than expected in a population of this age group. It is postulated that there is an underlying defect of carbohydrate metabolism in people with Down's syndrome.
Jeremiah, D. E., et al. (West Riding County Health Dept., Wakefield, England) Psychological Medicine, 1973(Nov), Vol. 3(4), 455-457. [PA, Vol 52:03440]

1207.   Tactile-visual equivalence of shape and slant in brain-damaged and mongoloid children.
Administered 2-choice tasks involving discrimination between mirror-image oblique lines, oriented 45° to the right vs left or between a triangle vs a circle, to 8 brain-damaged 12-13 yr olds, 3 mongoloid 11-14 yr olds, and normal 7-13 yr olds. The stimulus chosen for a given pair was presented either visually or by tactile drawing, and order of presentation of slant and shape tasks was varied randomly. Results show that normals readily matched to sample regardless of modality, stimulus type, or locus of tactile stimuli. Mongoloids performed essentially at chance levels on all conditions except the visual-to-visual matching with triangle vs circle stimuli, for which the mean performance was 97%. Mean scores for brain-damaged Ss were higher than those for mongoloids on all conditions except the visual-to-visual triangle vs circle and the guess-rate conditions. All Ss showed their worst performance when slant stimuli were presented to the left of the back.
Kennedy, Marita & Sheridan, Charles. (U. Missouri) Perceptual & Motor Skills, 1973(Apr), Vol. 36(2), 632. [PA, Vol 51:03536]

1208.   [Comparative studies of Down's syndrome and physiologically mentally retarded children on figure-copying ability.] (Japn)
Compared the figure copying performances of 17 Down's syndrome children (mean MA = 5.1 yrs, mean CA = 11.1 yrs) and 12 physiologically mentally retarded children (mean MA = 5.7 yrs, mean CA = 12.1 yrs). There were no significant differences between groups in CA, MA, or IQ. Ss were required to copy 6 figures without a time limit. No differences were found in mean copying scores of either group. Ss with Down's syndrome showed slightly better scores in copying figures composed of oblique lines.
Komiya, Mitsuya.   Japanese Journal of Special Education, 1973(Jun), Vol. 11(1), 31-38. [PA, Vol 52:03374]

1209.   Visual preferences of Down's syndrome and normal infants.
Compared the differential visual responses of 20 Down's syndrome (DS) and 20 normal infants (mean age = 8 mo) to 13 pairs of visual targets. Although DS Ss overall looked longer at the stimuli than normal Ss, they showed a response differential in only 3 stimulus pairs compared with 11 for the normals. 6 of the stimulus pairs elicited significant DS-normal differences, differences related to type of stimulus variation. Form of contour, the variation least attributable to inferior vision in DS infants, elicited the most marked group difference. Results suggest the value of this approach for studying early perceptual-cognitive development in defective infants and point to an early relationship between visual-attentional responses and intellectual potential. (29 ref)
Miranda, Simon B. & Fantz, Robert L. (Case Western Reserve U) Child Development, 1973(Sep), Vol 44(3), 555-561. [PA, Vol 54:01419]

1210.   Perceived voice quality disorders in Down's syndrome children.
Investigated voice quality deviations (e.g., breathiness and roughness) and resonance disability (e.g., nasality) in 20 institutionalized mongoloid children (mean age 10.4 yrs) and 20 normal children (mean age 10.4 yrs). Matched verbal samples were played backwards to 4 groups of judges: 2 groups of naive listeners ($N = 31$), 7 speech pathologists, and 10 school speech therapists. Results show that the mongoloid Ss exhibited significantly more breathiness and roughness than the normal Ss. More nasality was also observed in the mongoloid group. (17 ref.)
Montague, James C. & Hollien, Harry. (U. Arkansas, Little Rock) Journal of Communication Disorders, 1973(Jun), Vol. 6(2), 76-87. [PA, Vol 51:07487]

1211.   Social and play behavior of children with Down's syndrome in sexually homogeneous and heterogeneous dyads.
6 male and 6 female 7-12 yr old children with Down's syndrome interacted in dyads in sexually homogeneous and heterogeneous free-play situations. Actual, observable behaviors were recorded to investigate sex differences in, and the influence of sex of peer on, social and play behavior. Girls engaged in more sedentary activities than boys, and sexual homogeneity resulted in less sedentary activity than sexual heterogeneity. Peer-sex seemed to influence the type rather than the amount of social interaction, with male mongoloids being more influenced by peer-sex than girls. Implications of the results for future studies of mental retardate social behavior and studies of the stereotypic conception of mongoloids as cheerful, friendly, and so forth are discussed.
Schlottmann, Robert S. & Anderson, Victor H. (Oklahoma State U.) Psychological Reports, 1973(Oct), Vol. 33(2), 595-600. [PA, Vol 51:09461]

1212.   Early maternal linguistic environment of normal and Down's syndrome language-learning children.
Investigated the influence of linguistic data in the maternal environments of 6 Down's syndrome and 5 normal language-learning 24-mo-old children. It was found that the Down's syndrome children received a different linguistic input than the "normal" children. The possibility of a relationship between the Down's syndrome children's different early maternal linguistic environment and later characteristics of their deviant-delayed language is considered. Various aspects of language development in general are discussed. (23 ref)
Buiun, Nissan; Rynders, John & Turnure, James. (U Minnesota) American Journal of Mental Deficiency, 1974(Jul), Vol 79(1), 52-58. [PA, Vol 53:01465]

1213.   Development of language, abstraction, and numerical concept formation in Down's syndrome children.
Findings of A. C. Cornwell and H. G. Birch (see PA, Vol 44:5539) suggested the hypothesis that a marked discrepancy between verbal receptive and performance abilities exists in home-reared children with Down's syndrome. This was tested developmentally in 38 5-19 yr old Down's syndrome children. The data show differences between verbal items requiring extensive language expression (designation) and recognition of visually presented objects. Language expression was assessed in numerical concepts and skills and concept formation. Developmentally, this population revealed a slow accretion of certain rote skills and progressive improvement in other abilities, but severe limitations in concept formation, abstraction, and higher level integrative abilities regardless of age. (27 ref)
Cornwell, Anne C. (Albert Einstein Coll of Medicine, Yeshiva U) American Journal of Mental Deficiency, 1974(Sep), Vol 79(2), 179-190. [PA, Vol 53:03426]

1214.   [The incidence of children with Down's syndrome in state schools for mentally retarded trainable classes.] (Germ)
Investigated the incidence of mongoloid children in the 602 state schools for the mentally retarded (trainable classes) in the West German Federal Republic. 21% of all children in these schools suffered from Down's syndrome; 53% were girls and 47% boys. (50 ref)
Dittmann, Werner.   Praxis der Kinderpsychologie und Kinderpsychiatrie, 1974(May-Jun), Vol 23(4), 144-149. [PA, Vol 53:07697]

1215.   Sibling reactions to mental handicap: A comparison of the brothers and sisters of mongol children.
Parents and teachers completed behavioral rating scales on 89 sisters and 85 brothers of 104 mongol children living at home. Disturbance in the boys, known to be not significantly more frequent than in controls, was related to family size and social class. Disturbance in the girls, known to be more frequent than in controls, was related to type of school, birth order, and age in

relation to the mongol child. It is concluded that the presence of a mongol child in the home is associated with deviant behavior as assessed by parents and teachers, and with educational failure in elder sisters, who are probably carrying a large share of the burden of care. (25 ref)
Gath, Ann. (U Oxford, England) Journal of Child Psychology & Psychiatry & Allied Disciplines, 1974(Jul), Vol 15(3), 187-198. [PA, Vol 53:01435]

1216. **[Psychology and psychopathology of the child with Down's syndrome: Structural features.]** (Fren)
Describes psychopathological traits specific to Mongolism observed in 27 institutionalized Mongoloid children between the ages of 6 and 14 yrs. Prominent behaviors and affective reactions observed included conformity, passivity, stubbornness, and clinging affection. Mongoloid children exhibit fixations on oral modes of relating and desires for gratifying maternal type relationships. It is suggested that the affective characteristics of mongoloid children are due to their initial acceptance by their parents, and that psychodynamic analyses of mongoloid children in later life can only be performed on a case-by-case basis. (English, German, & Spanish summaries) (19 ref)
Lang, J. L. Revue de Neuropsychiatrie Infantile et d'Hygiene Mentale de l'Enfance, 1974(Jan), Vol 22(1-2)c, 19-39. [PA, Vol 54:07897]

1217. **The palmo-mental reflex in normal and mentally retarded subjects.**
Compared the palmo-mental reflex (contraction of the mentalis and orbicularis oris muscles in response to a scratch to the thenar eminence of the ipsilateral hand) in (a) 611 normal children and adults, (b) 102 severely retarded children, and (c) 82 retarded adults, including 48 with Down's syndrome. The reflex was present in 66% of normal children under 3 yrs old and in 9% of normal adults, in 81% of retarded children under 3 yrs old, and in 44% of retarded adults, with highest frequency in Down's syndrome patients. It appears to be a primitive reflex which persists in cases of developmental delay or may re-emerge in acquired brain disease. (French, German & Spanish summaries)
Little, T. M. & Masotti, R. E. (Queen's U., Kingston, Ontario, Canada) Developmental Medicine & Child Neurology, 1974(Feb), Vol. 16(1), 59-63. [PA, Vol 52:12785]

1218. **Vocal fundamental frequency characteristics of institutionalized Down's syndrome children.**
Analyzed for mean speaking fundamental frequency matched word samples of "boy," "baby," and "doctor," obtained from 20 institutionalized Down's syndrome children and 20 intellectually average children. While isolated Down's syndrome Ss had relatively high fundamental frequencies, as a group no difference was found between Down's syndrome and intellectually average Ss for that vocal parameter, at least based on the matched verbal samples utilized in this research. Further, no relationship was found within the Down's syndrome group between speaking fundamental frequency and IQ. Clinically noted deviate voices of Down's syndrome persons are possibly related to vocal parameters other than fundamental frequency.
Montague, James C.; Brown, W. S. & Hollien, Harry. (U. Arkansas, Little Rock) American Journal of Mental Deficiency, 1974(Jan), Vol. 78(4), 414-418. [PA, Vol 52:08028]

1219. **Observations from longitudinal data on growth in stature and sitting height of children with Down's syndrome.**
Measured annual growth for a 12-yr period in children with Down's syndrome and for normal children between the ages of 7 and 18 yrs. Although Down's Ss were markedly inferior in both stature and sitting height, their growth during the circumpubertal years, age of maximum growth, and predictability of growth after age 10 did not differ appreciably from that of normals. (15 ref)
Rarick, G. L. & Seefeldt, V. (U. California, Berkeley) Journal of Mental Deficiency Research, 1974(Mar), Vol. 18(1), 63-78. [PA, Vol 52:12736]

1220. **[Long-term psychological and social prognosis in cases of mongolian retardation followed for more than 10 years.]** (Fren)
Re-examines the unresolved problems of social adjustment presented by mongoloid children, and underscores the growing importance of this problem as a consequence of their improved survival rate over the past 30 yrs. 7 individual cases are reported of mongolian children placed in a setting that was optimal from a combined medical, familial, and pedagogic viewpoint. Their development is traced over a 10-yr period, including adolescence and (for some) young adulthood. Contrary to the findings reported by some optimistic writers, the social and economic development of these children was minimal, despite optimal conditions for growth. Although they can learn more than was realized formerly, which grants them a degree of independence in everyday life, they were found, without exception, to be dependent for the rest on the guidance and protection provided by their parents and by society.
Schachter, M. (Comite de l'Enfance Deficiente de Marseille, France) Annales Médico-Psychologiques, 1974(Feb), Vol 1(2), 195-224. [PA, Vol 53:07711]

1221. **Acquisition of matching to sample via mediated transfer.**
2 severely retarded Down's-syndrome males (14 and 18 yrs old, respectively) learned a matching-to-sample performance through mediated transfer. The transfer paradigm involved 3 sets of stimuli, 1 auditory set (A) and 2 visual sets (B and C). Ss were taught directly to do B-A and C-B matching but experienced no direct association between C and A. They acquired the ability to do C-A matching without having been taught that performance directly. They also learned indirectly to name some of the visual stimuli, but naming was apparently not the mediator in the emergent C-A matching. The use of words and letters as stimuli highlighted the possible relevance of mediated associations in the indirect acquisition of elementary reading comprehension and oral reading. The acquisition of matching via mediated transfer also raised some new considerations concerning the role of coding responses in arbitrary matching to sample. (17 ref)
Sidman, Murray; Cresson, Osborne & Willson-Morris, Martha. (Northeastern U) Journal of the Experimental Analysis of Behavior, 1974(Sep), Vol 22(2), 261-273. [PA, Vol 53:03449]

1222. **Auditory-motor channeling in Down's syndrome subjects.**
Administered a pegboard task to 10 children with Down's syndrome (CA range 71-114 mo, MA range 28-41 mo), 10 retarded children with other than Down's syndrome diagnoses (CA range 71-109 mo, MA range 29-43 mo), and 10 nonretarded children (CA range 29-42 mo). During the task, Ss were exposed to 5 2-min periods of controlled auditory and visual extraneous stimulation (auditory patterned, auditory nonpatterned, visual patterned, visual nonpatterned, and no stimulation). Findings do not support the hypothesized auditory-motor channeling difficulty in Down's syndrome Ss since the data revealed no significant between-group differences in the task performances under the experimental stimulation conditions. Support for the greater distraction susceptibility of the auditory modality for Down's syndrome Ss was found (i.e., these Ss had, decreased performance in the auditory nonpatterned condition relative to the no stimulation condition). An inhibitory deficit rather than a general deficiency in auditory-motor channeling of Down's syndrome children is suggested. (28 ref)
Zekulin, Xenia Y.; Gibson, David; Mosley, James L. & Brown, Roy I. (U. Calgary, Alberta, Canada) American Journal of Mental Deficiency, 1974(Mar), Vol. 78(5), 571-577. [PA, Vol 52:08057]

1223. **[The nature, frequency, causes, and varieties of mental handicaps.]** (Germ)
Discusses the various definitions of mental handicaps, emphasizing a medium range of subnormality (i.e., an IQ range of 60–65) and the need for lifelong support of the persons involved. Due to higher survival rates of handicapped infants and especially of children with Down's syndrome, the frequency of mental handicaps in the population has probably increased, although exact statistics are lacking. A large variety of prenatal, perinatal,

and postnatal causes are described, including phenylketonuria, Down's syndrome, and the *cri-du-chat* syndrome. Prenatal plastopathologies, embryopathologies, and fetopathologies are differentiated. Perinatal damage is mainly attributed to asphyxia and other forms of brain damage. The main postnatal causes are disturbances in the diet, encephalitis, and meningitis.
Kramer, Josefine. Vierteljahresschrift für Heilpädagogik und ihre Nachbargebiete, 1975, Vol 44(4), 290–301. [PA, Vol 63:05705]

1224. [The maternal linguistic input of Down's syndrome and of normal Spanish-speaking Cuban-American children.] (Span) Outlines a proposed research project designed to evaluate the role of the maternal linguistic input in the linguistic development of Spanish-speaking Mongoloid and of normal children.
Nathanson, David & López, Gil. (Florida International U) Revista Latinoamericana de Psicología, 1975, Vol 7(2), 321-326. [PA, Vol 54:12090]

1225. The use of IQ as a measure of problem solving ability with mongoloid and nonmongoloid retarded children.
Attempted to determine the relationship of MA and IQ to retardates' learning a task involving conceptualization. Such tasks are considered by A. R. Jensen (1965, 1968, 1973, 1974), in his theory on mental abilities, to test Level II abilities as opposed to Level I abilities which involve rote learning and primary memory. The opposing hypotheses of E. F. Zigler (1967) and M. W. Weir (1967) concerning the use of MA or IQ, respectively, as the best measure of learning rate were examined. A dimension-abstracted oddity task was presented to 40 mongoloid and 40 nonmongoloid White 7-20 yr olds (mean MA, 42.63 mo; IQ range, 24-40). Results support Weir's hypotheses, as IQ was found to determine the rate of learning the task. A major finding shows that nonmongoloids learned the task faster than mongoloid Ss. (17 ref)
Schroth, Marvin L. (U Santa Clara) Journal of Psychology, 1975(Sep), Vol 91(1), 49-56. [PA, Vol 55:04870]

1226. The nature of the colour retention deficit in Down's syndrome.
Discusses an earlier author-conducted study (see PA, Vol 50:5179) where it was shown that Down's syndrome children showed a deficit in short-term retention of color information not shown by matched controls; the experiments were conducted in good daylight illumination. In a replication of that study, using 148 Ss from the original study in blue weak artificial light, retention of green, red, and purple was much improved but the other colors were not affected. Implications of the finding are considered for theories of color vision, short-term retention, and educational technology.
Sinson, Janice C. & Wetherlick, N. E. (Mencap House, Leeds, England) Journal of Mental Deficiency Research, 1975(Jun), Vol 19(2), 97-100. [PA, Vol 56:06288]

1227. A comparison of musical and verbal responses of mentally retarded children.
Conducted a study (a) to determine whether mentally retarded children had a better echoic response to a music series than to an alphabetical series of the same length, and (b) to compare children who manifest symptoms of brain damage with children with Down's syndrome on the number of correct echoic responses. 20 Down's syndrome children and 24 brain-damaged children, ages 10–17 yrs, were tested; all were in the trainable range. The approximate vocal range of each S was determined. Two to 5 notes of an ascending major scale were paired with 2 to 5 letters of the alphabet. These were presented to each S, who was asked to repeat them. There were no differences in the number of correct musical and verbal responses. The brain-damaged Ss performed significantly better than the Down's syndrome Ss on both the musical and verbal tests.
Bokor, Clark R. (Incarnation School, Tampa, FL) Journal of Music Therapy, 1976(Sum), Vol 13(2), 101–108. [PA, Vol 60:03301]

1228. The relationship between affective and cognitive development in Down's syndrome infants.
A close association between affective expression and cognitive development was demonstrated in a longitudinal study of 14 Down's syndrome infants. It was found that the Ss laughed to groups of stimulus items in the same order as did normal infants in previous studies. Although the process was delayed by several months, the retarded babies also laughed first at physically intrusive items and only later to items calling for greater cognitive sophistication. In addition, cognitive developmental status, assessed by the Bayley Scales of Infant Development and the Uzgiris-Hunt scales of cognitive development, paralleled and was predicted by the level of affective development. Predictive and concurrent correlations between Bayley mental scores and various indices of affectivity ranged from .68 to .92. There was striking individual consistency across affective, mental, and motor measures, suggesting the organized nature of retarded development. Finally, since Down's syndrome infants frequently smiled under conditions when normal babies would laugh, a role for tension production, in addition to cognitive factors, is suggested in accounting for the behavior of these infants. (30 ref)
Cicchetti, Dante & Sroufe, L. Alan. (U Minnesota Inst of Child Development) Child Development, 1976(Dec), Vol 47(4), 920-929. [PA, Vol 58:01391]

1229. Variability within Down's Syndrome (Trisomy-21): Empirically observed sex differences in IQs.
Studied the relationship between sex and IQ decline in individuals with Down's syndrome. 104 female and 90 male outpatients from 36 to 155 mo of age were selected from a large pediatric mental retardation clinic on the basis of 2 criteria. Each individual had had a cytogenetic analysis that revealed a karyotype of Trisomy-21, and at least one Stanford Binet (SB) form L-M IQ score was in his/her clinical record. SB IQ scores were investigated using a 2×5 unweighted means ANOVA with sex as one factor and age the other (36-59 mo, 60-83 mo, 84-107 mo, 108-131 mo, and 132-155 mo). Results show several significant effects: (a) As age increased, IQ scores decreased. (b) Females scored higher than males over each group except 84-107 mo. (c) Each age group differed from each other age group except 108-131 mo and 132-155 mo. It is suggested that the presence of the XX (female) sex chromosomes may have reduced the severity of measured mental retardation in this group of Down's syndrome children.
Clements, Paul R.; Bates, Mary V. & Hafer, Marilyn. (Levinson Ctr for Mentally Handicapped Children, Chicago, IL) Mental Retardation, 1976(Feb), Vol 14(1), 30-31. [PA, Vol 56:00913]

1230. Eye-movement density during sleep in normal and pathological neonates and infants.
Analyzed eye-movement frequencies in mongoloid and small-for-age neonates and infants. Correlations with normal babies of corresponding ages showed that the eye-movement intervals shorter than 1 sec were the only discriminative criterion. Statistically significant differences were found between the normal and the abnormal group of neonates and infants. Tentative findings on the effects of 5-hydroxytryptophan on eye-movement intervals are included. (French abstract) (16 ref)
de Lee, C. & Petre-Quadens, O. (U Antwerp, Belgium) Waking & Sleeping, 1976, No 1, 45-48. [PA, Vol 58:11908]

1231. Correlation of IQ in subjects with Down syndrome and their parents and sibs.
WISC or Wechsler Preschool and Primary Scale of Intelligence scores for 23 children (median age 10 yrs) with Down's syndrome and IQ scores obtained from 61 of their normal 1st-degree relatives (adults were tested with the WAIS or the Épreuve Individuelle D'Intellegence Générale) were found to be positively correlated. Although this finding does not explain how much of the relationship results from the genes determining intellectual functions that the Ss share with their relatives, and how much from familial environment influences that affect such factors, it is suggested that the correlation, if upheld in subsequent studies, may have predictive value.

Fraser, F. C. & Sadovnick, A. D. (McGill U, Montreal, Canada) Journal of Mental Deficiency Research, 1976(Sep), Vol 20(3), 179-182. [PA, Vol 57:10569]

1232. **Developmental transformational capacity of children with Down's Syndrome.**
Examined the generative-transformational capacities of 2 groups of 7-19 yr olds with Down's syndrome (mean MAs, 3.6 and 4.6 yrs, respectively). A sentence repetition task was used to assess their knowledge of selected transformational types (simple-active-affirmative-declarative, question, negative, passive, and negative-passive). There were significant effects of Groups and Sentence Types but a nonsignificant interaction of groups by sentence types. Results are taken as support for E. H. Lenenberg's (1967) "slow motion" hypothesis of language development in mentally retarded children. Children with Down's syndrome appear to follow the same patterns of grammatical acquisition as normal children but at a reduced rate associated with the severity of their retardation.
Gordan, Wenda L. & Panagos, John M.   Perceptual & Motor Skills, 1976(Dec), Vol 43(3, Pt 1), 967-973. [PA, Vol 58:01395]

1233. **[Imitation responses in mongoloid children.]** (Germ)
Constructed a test consisting of 20 imitation items to test the frequency of imitative responses. Three groups of 4.4–8.9 yr old children were compared: mongoloids, nonmongoloid retardates, and normal children. The main hypotheses were confirmed: Mongoloids imitated more frequently than a group of normals matched on sex and age; mongoloids tended also to imitate more frequently when compared with nonmongoloid retardates, matched for sex, age, and intelligence. The tendency to imitate seemed to be independent of intelligence. (34 ref)
Hüffner, Ute & Redlin, Wiltraud. (Max-Planck-Inst für Psychiatrie, Munich, West Germany) Zeitschrift für Klinische Psychologie. Forschung und Praxis, 1976, Vol 5(4), 277–286. [PA, Vol 64:01309]

1234. **The temporal and periodic organization of REM eye movements in mental retardation.**
Examined time trends and periodic cycles in REM sleep eye movements in 6 functional and 6 mongoloid adolescent retardates (CAs 14-18 yrs). Both groups of Ss showed approximately equal percentages of linear trends, quadratic trends, linear and quadratic trends, and absence of trend. The eye movement time-series were subjected to an orthogonal spectral analysis. In both groups of Ss, peak spectral estimates generally occurred at 10.6- or 21.3-min periods. Following this, the eye movements of the longest REM periods (and 1 long period of presleep wakefulness) were subjected to a least-squares spectral analysis. This analysis yielded estimates ranging from 22 to 44 min. Eye movements lacked the ultradian organization previously reported for eye movements of normal Ss. These results imply that the ultradian organization of REM sleep and the ultradian organization of eye movements may be independent.
Krynicki, Victor. (Queens Children's Hosp, Bellrose, NY) Neuropsychobiology, 1976, Vol 2(1), 9-17. [PA, Vol 58:11915]

1235. **Perceived age and sex characteristics of voices of institutionalized children with Down's syndrome.**
Tested the hypothesis that the voices of children with Down's syndrome would be perceived as younger than their true CA and that perceptual auditors would have considerable difficulty in identifying the correct sex of these children by voice alone. Perceived age and sex were investigated in 20 institutional children (mean CA, 10.42 yrs) with Down's syndrome who were matched for sex and age with a control group of 20 normal children (mean CA, 10.41). Randomized matched verbal samples were played backwards to a group of 16 listener/judges who rated the samples as to age and sex. Results indicate that the voices of the Down's syndrome Ss were perceived as being more than 2 yrs younger than their group mean age and that there was a negative correlation between the biological sex of such children and their perceived sex.

Montague, James C. (U Arkansas, Speech & Hearing Clinic) Perceptual & Motor Skills, 1976(Feb), Vol 42(1), 215-219. [PA, Vol 56:10143]

1236. **T and B lymphocytes in patients with Down's syndrome.**
Individuals with Down's syndrome are thought to have abnormalities of immune function. Studies were performed to quantify the number of peripheral blood T and B lymphocytes and serum immunoglobulins in 12 individuals and 12 control Ss matched for sex and age. Hepatitis B antigen and antithyroglobulin antibodies as markers of possible immune dysfunction were determined. The numbers of circulating T and B cells, and the level of serum immunoglobulins in children with Down's syndrome did not differ from those in nonretarded control children. Circulating hepatitis B antigen and antithyroglobulin antibodies were not present. These studies indicate that quantitative abnormalities of T and B cells are not present in children with Down's syndrome. The data do not exclude the existence of qualitative abnormalities. (40 ref)
Reiser, Karen; Whitcomb, Charles; Robinson, Ken & MacKenzie, Malcolm R. (U California Medical School, Davis) American Journal of Mental Deficiency, 1976(May), Vol 80(6), 613-619. [PA, Vol 56:04294]

1237. **Down's syndrome and intellectual development.**
Assessed the development of 9 3.0–23.5 mo old Down's syndrome infants, using the Home Observation for Measurement of the Environment and the Bayley Scales of Infant Development. Findings were very similar to previous evaluations of Down's infants. Since developmental age and CA are negatively correlated, the supposition is that at some point in time the Down's infant is not so retarded. Current and past evaluations support this view. The onset of developmental delay in Down's syndrome seems to occur at 4–6 mo, the age when most infants show a shift from subcortical to cortical control of behavior. (18 ref)
Saxon, Samuel A. & Witriol, Ellen. (U Alabama Medical Ctr, Ctr for Developmental & Learning Disorders, Birmingham) Journal of Pediatric Psychology, 1976, Vol 1(3), 45–47. [PA, Vol 62:03905]

1238. **Down's syndrome children in a strange situation: Attachment and exploration behaviors.**
Compared attachment and exploratory behavior of 24 children (mean age, 33 mo), 12 with Down's syndrome and 12 normals. Eight successive 3-min observation "episodes" were carried out in a room with furniture, toys, and various adults present. Episodes differed by whether the child's mother, an adult stranger, both, or neither were in the room. Normals showed more crying when their mothers left, more approach and contact upon her return, more fine motor manipulation before their mothers first left, and more vocalization during almost all episodes. Down's syndrome children showed more visual exploration when left alone. Results suggest that Down's syndrome children view isolation and novel environments as being less threatening than normals do. (24 ref)
Serafica, Felicisima C. & Cicchetti, Dante. (U Pittsburgh) Merrill-Palmer Quarterly, 1976(Apr), Vol 22(2), 137-150. [PA, Vol 57:10581]

1239. **Evidence for increased mental capacity with age in Down's Syndrome.**
Performed a study with 166 Down's Syndrome children (aged 6-17) to examine the effect of age on the performance of a short-term test of memory for color. Results show that 2/3 of the 15-17 yr old Ss could perform tasks which no 6-8 yr old could, suggesting that they might benefit from educational experiences which were of no value at a younger age.
Sinson, Janice C. & Wetherick, N. E. (City of Leeds Society for Mentally Handicapped Children, England) Journal of Mental Deficiency Research, 1976(Mar), Vol 20(1), 31–34. [PA, Vol 56:02521]

1240. **A study of the spontaneous oral language of Down's syndrome children.**
Analyzed language samples from 39 mentally retarded children (CAs 5.8–17.9 yrs; IQs 31–60) attending a day school. Results

show wide between-S variability, with nouns, pronouns, and verbs predominating. Findings indicate that CA is not a significant factor in determining the oral language performance of Down's syndrome children. (7 ref)
Andrews, R. J. & Andrews, Jeanette G. (U Queensland, Schonell Educational Research Ctr, Brisbane, Australia) Exceptional Child, 1977(Jul), Vol 24(2), 86–94. [PA, Vol 64:08261]

1241. Patterns of interaction between a mother and her Down's syndrome child: A single case ethological study.
Reports one mother's strategies for teaching new and previously learned tasks, as an analysis of the sequence of mother–child interactions. Results indicate that (a) both mother and child were able to maintain a continuous communication sequence; (b) mother structured new tasks more and allowed flexibility in the old tasks; (c) mother's language was restricted; and (d) in responding to her child's behavior, the mother made most use of verbal cues. (22 ref)
Berry, Paul; Mathams, Peter & Middleton, Beulah. (U Queensland, Schonell Educational Research Ctr, Brisbane, Australia) Exceptional Child, 1977(Nov), Vol 24(3), 156–164. [PA, Vol 66:03864]

1242. Sleep patterns in mental retardation: Down's syndrome.
EEG and eye movements during 2 consecutive nights were recorded in 21 normal and 21 Down's syndrome Ss (IQ 18–47) of both sexes in the 14–24 yr age range. Records of most Down's Ss were characterized by longer total sleep time, lack of waking alpha, frequent awakening and movement epochs, and fewer spindle bursts. Significantly longer "awake" and Stage 4 percentages, but less Stage 2, were found in the Down's group. They also had longer REM latency, and lower eye movement density based on number of eye movements. Density based on integrated eye activity correlated positively with IQ in the Down's Ss. Spectrum analysis for EEG frequencies from 1 to 20 c/sec showed significantly greater power in the Down's group below 9 and above 12 c/sec, but no difference in the alpha range. The greater power at low frequencies was more pronounced in "awake," Stage 1, and REM. (French summary) (21 ref)
Clausen, J.; Sersen, E. A. & Lidsky, A. (Inst for Basic Research in Mental Retardation, Staten Island, NY) Electroencephalography & Clinical Neurophysiology, 1977(Aug), Vol 43(2), 183–191. [PA, Vol 60:01313]

1243. Parents of Down's syndrome babies: Their early needs.
Reports the results of detailed interviews with 51 parents of Down's syndrome infants shortly after their being informed of the diagnosis. Previous studies are reviewed, and the results confirm several findings of earlier studies. Specifically: (a) The majority of parents wish to be told of the diagnosis as soon as possible and with the spouse present. (b) They do not automatically resent the "teller." (c) They wish to be told directly but sympathetically, in private, and have access to the baby. (d) Several interviews are needed at short intervals following the initial telling for parents to ask further questions and to assimilate more information about their child's condition. (26 ref)
Cunningham, Cliff C. & Sloper, Tricia. (U Manchester, Hester Adrian Research Ctr, England) Child Care, Health & Development, 1977(Sep–Oct), Vol 3(5), 325–347. [PA, Vol 60:11960]

1244. The development of language abilities in mongols: A correlational study.
Administered a battery of language and related measures to 101 8.3–31.1 yr old Down's syndrome individuals. Some of these measures were the Illinois Test of Psycholinguistic Abilities (ITPA), the English Picture Vocabulary Test I, the Stanford-Binet Intelligence Scale, and the Draw-A-Man Test. Ss' spontaneous speech was analyzed using techniques based on those of L. Lassers and G. Low (1960). Results were intercorrelated, and the resulting matrix was factor-analyzed using chronological age as a variable. 28.9% of the variance was accounted for by a General Verbal Ability factor, which loaded highly on all the psycholinguistic tests and the intelligence tests, with moderate loadings on the speech level scores; 8.3% of the variance was accounted for

by a Disfluent Speech factor, which loaded strongly on disfluency scores and moderately on intelligence scores. A structure of speech factor accounted for 24.3% of the variance, and loaded highly on the grammatic closure and vocal encoding subtests of the ITPA, and moderately on the Stanford-Binet. In addition, chronological age loaded strongly on this factor. Patterns of language were also examined.
Evans, D. (U Exeter School of Education, England) Journal of Mental Deficiency Research, 1977(Jun), Vol 21(2), 103–117. [PA, Vol 60:01315]

1245. The impact of an abnormal child upon the parents.
30 families with a newborn baby with Down's syndrome were matched with 30 families with a normal baby. Both groups were followed for 18 mo to 2 yrs and interviewed 6 times. Few differences could be found in the mental or physical health (as assessed by the Eysenck Personality Inventory and the Malaise Inventory, respectively) of the 2 groups of parents, but marital breakdown or severe marital disharmony was found in 9 of the families with Mongoloid babies and in none of the controls. (23 ref)
Gath, Ann. (Borocourt Hosp, Reading, England) British Journal of Psychiatry, 1977(Apr), Vol 130, 405–410. [PA, Vol 59:03633]

1246. Static and dynamic balance skills of trainable children with Down's syndrome.
Compared static and dynamic balance performance of 25 children (mean CA 147.8 mo; mean IQ 39.72) with Down's syndrome and 25 CA- and IQ-matched Ss without Down's syndrome. No significant difference between the 2 samples' static balance performance was noted; Ss with Down's syndrome had significantly superior dynamic balance performance.
le Blanc, Dave; French, Ronald & Shultz, Barry. (El Camino School, Pomona, CA) Perceptual & Motor Skills, 1977(Oct), Vol 45(2), 641–642. [PA, Vol 60:07683]

1247. Assessment of counseling practices at the birth of a child with Down's syndrome.
Attempted to analyze 414 parents' perceptions of their experiences at the birth of their child with Down's syndrome. Ss responded to a detailed questionnaire, results of which suggest that the counseling of parents with a newborn Down's syndrome child demands tact, truthfulness, and empathetic guidance. The parents should be informed of the child's condition in a kind and sensitive manner as soon as the diagnosis of Down's syndrome has been made. Appropriate terminology should be employed, and both parents should be present when the physician reveals their child's condition. Unconditional recommendations of institutionalization of the child with Down's syndrome should be practices of the past. The professionals' thoughtful considerations and mature counsel should assist constructively in shaping the child's future.
Pueschel, Siegfried M. & Murphy, Ann. (Rhode Island Hosp, Child Development Ctr, Providence) American Journal of Mental Deficiency, 1977(Jan), Vol 81(4), 300–324. [PA, Vol 58:05999]

1248. Transposition of intermediate size under immediate and delayed testing conditions by normal, familially retarded, and Down's syndrome children.
Results of a study with 20 normal, 18 familially retarded, and 14 Down's syndrome children show that there was no significant difference in familially retarded Ss' choices elicited immediately or 3 hrs after training. These Ss generally responded to the absolute stimulus. Relational responses did not necessarily depend on the ability of the S to verbalize the problem. Results lend no support to the mediational deficiency hypothesis (i.e., that children's ability to use verbal responses as mediators is a function of age level) and could not be understood in terms of the traditional dichotomy of absolute and relative responses in transposition. (19 ref)
Saito, Shigeru. (Hirosaki U Faculty of Education, Japan) Tohoku Psychologica Folia, 1977, Vol 36(1–4), 32–38. [PA, Vol 62:01328]

1249.　Dichotic verbal processing in Down's syndrome children having qualitatively different speech and language skills.
Used a dichotic word task to contrast the speech-perceptual functioning of 2 groups of Down's syndrome children having qualitatively different speech and language skills to that of nonretarded Ss. Assessment measures included the Test for Auditory Comprehension of Language and the Diagnostic Test of Linguistic Abilities. Although the 20 nonretarded Ss (mean CA 4.3 yrs) showed an average 23% right-ear effect on the task, the average ear effect for 29 Down's syndrome Ss was essentially zero. The pattern of phonemic processing of 14 Down's syndrome Ss (mean CA 13.2 yrs, mean IQ 46) having better speech and language resembled that of nonretarded Ss; however, the pattern of 15 Down's syndrome Ss (mean CA 14.5 yrs, mean IQ 39) having poorer speech and language was atypical. Place of articulation and voicing of phonemes appeared frequently to have different effects in the latter group in the determination of which dichotic words were reported. Although the group having better speech and language had sightly higher MAs and IQs than the poorer group, MAs and IQs were not related to ear-preference scores. (29 ref)
Sommers, Ronald K. & Starkey, Karen L. (Kent State U Speech & Hearing Clinic) American Journal of Mental Deficiency, 1977(Jul), Vol 82(1), 44–53. [PA, Vol 59:10193]

1250.　[The receiving process of speech sounds by a hard-of-hearing child with Down's syndrome.] (Japn)
Analyzed difficulties in receiving speech sounds and the effect of hearing loss on discrimination between them in 4 experiments with a hard-of-hearing 11-yr-old boy with Down's syndrome. Results show that (a) when the task consisted of pairs of speech sounds containing different-vowel-combinations (e.g., *hanatori*) he could learn to discriminate between them easily by learning to match them with the corresponding picture cards, (b) when the task consisted of pairs of speech sounds containing the same-vowel combination, he could not discriminate between them, and (c) although it was difficult for him to acquire the acoustic cues to discriminate among consonants, he could learn to discriminate between some of the difficult pairs by repeated practice.
Wakabayashi, Setsuko. (Tokyo Metropolitan Inst for Neurosciences, Japan) Japanese Journal of Psychology, 1977(Apr), Vol 48(1), 42–48. [PA, Vol 59:07998]

1251.　[The mental and social development of mongoloid children.] (Slok)
Administered the Terman-McNemar Test of Mental Ability, the Brunet-Lezine Developmental Scale, and the Vineland Social Maturity Scale to 105 children with Down's syndrome. Results show that there were no statistically significant intersexual differences in Ss' mental and social development; Ss' development in these areas tended to show a positive trend up to the 10th yr, after which there was a decline. Ss showed relatively higher levels of social maturity than mental maturity. (Russian summary) (15 ref)
Antalová, Jana. (Výskumný Ústav Detskej Psychológie a Patopsychológie, Bratislava, Czechoslovakia) Psychológia a Patopsychológia Dietata, 1978, Vol 13(4), 291–299. [PA, Vol 63:09929]

1252.　Verbal and nonverbal interaction of mothers with their Down's syndrome and nonretarded infants.
Investigated the effects of parental expectancies due to early knowledge of the condition of Down's syndrome in infants on parent–child interactions by comparing verbal and nonverbal interactions between 10 mothers and their Down's syndrome infants (Group A) and 10 mothers and their nonretarded infants (Group B). Mothers in Group A ranged in age from 23 to 43 yrs and their infants ranged from 9.5 to 17.0 mo; Mothers in Group B were 18–39 yrs of age and their infants were 9.1–18.7 mo. Although there was no difference between the groups in mothers' language complexity, mothers of Down's syndrome children spoke at a significantly faster rate. Observational measures of infants show that Down's syndrome babies smiled and vocalized less, but mothers in the 2 groups did not differ significantly on nonverbal interactional behavior. Results are discussed in relation to the conclusions of other investigators who have speculat-

ed that language delays in Down's syndrome children may be due in part to differences in the environment provided by caregivers.
Buckhalt, Joseph A.; Rutherford, Robert B. & Goldberg, Kay E. (East Alabama Mental Health/Mental Retardation Ctr, Opelika) American Journal of Mental Deficiency, 1978(Jan), Vol 82(4), 337–343. [PA, Vol 61:03881]

1253.　Visual calibration of posture in normal and motor retarded Down's syndrome infants.
Two experiments were conducted comparing the effects of discrepant visual feedback on control of standing (Exp I) and sitting (Exp II) in 67 Down's syndrome (DS) and 86 normal infants. Mean ages of the groups of normal Ss in Exp I were 14.0–34.1 mo, and of the DS Ss, 26.6–41.8 mo; in Exp II, normal Ss were 6.9–12.6 mo, and DS Ss were 11.5–21.3 mo. Results show that DS Ss were delayed in achieving motor milestones. When they first sat unsupported a discrepancy between visual and mechanical–vestibular indices of postural stability was less disruptive of their balance than in normal Ss. Yet when they first stood unsupported, the same discrepancy disrupted balance more in these Ss than in the normal ones. The effect of discrepant visual feedback also differed systematically as a function of the Ss' experience of the posture. It is concluded that monitoring posture in relation to a stable visual surround appears to be fundamental to the normal development of motor control. (21 ref)
Butterworth, George & Cicchetti, Dante. (U Southampton, England) Perception, 1978, Vol 7(5), 513–525. [PA, Vol 63:09935]

1254.　Life span changes in the averaged evoked responses of Down's syndrome and nonretarded persons.
Visual, auditory, and somatosensory evoked responses were recorded from 66 Down's syndrome persons in 6 age groups, and from age- and sex-matched nonretarded individuals 5–62 yrs old; Ss were assigned to groups on the basis of observable signs of development and aging. Results indicate that, regardless of stimulus modality, the amplitude of late wave components was dramatically larger for Down's syndrome Ss than for nonretarded Ss. Where obvious amplitude reduction occurred with maturation and aging among nonretarded Ss, amplitude changes were generally absent among Down's syndrome Ss. Findings for Down's syndrome persons are discussed in terms of deficits in central inhibition and abnormalities in neuronal excitability to different levels of stimulus intensity. (31 ref)
Callner, D. A. et al. (VA Hosp, Neuropsychology Lab, Salt Lake City, UT) American Journal of Mental Deficiency, 1978(Jan), Vol 82(4), 398–405. [PA, Vol 62:06305]

1255.　Intelligence levels of Down's syndrome children.
An investigation of the intelligence levels of 180 Down's syndrome children aged 6 mo–18 yrs indicates that their abilities are not as limited as previously thought. Mean IQ was 44.3, based on the Stanford-Binet Intelligence Scale, with 10% of Ss tested on the WISC or Cattell Infant Intelligence Scale. It is suggested that the introduction of special developmental programs from birth onwards has promoted an increase in intellectual development. (27 ref)
Connolly, John A. (Irish Foundation for Human Development, Health Care & Psychosomatic Unit, Dublin) American Journal of Mental Deficiency, 1978(Sep), Vol 83(2), 193–196. [PA, Vol 62:06307]

1256.　Down's syndrome and leukemia: Mechanism of additional chromosomal abnormalities.
Suggests that since Down's syndrome patients have a trisomy-21 chromosomal pattern, and chromosomal abnormalities can be seen in acute leukemia, it is possible that the increased incidence of acute leukemia in Down's syndrome persons may be due in part to their chromosomal abnormalities. Such abnormalities, some appearing in a stepwise clonal evolution, were observed in 5 Down's patients, 4 with acute leukemia and 1 with abnormal regulation of leukopoiesis. The Ss ranged in age from 35-wk gestation premature newborn to 12 yrs. Morphological abnormal

chromosomes were also found in 3 of the Ss. These chromosomal abnormalities are similar to those seen in non-Down's syndrome leukemic patients. Some evidence exists to support a clonal evolution hypothesis of leukemogenesis in non-Down's syndrome patients. The abnormal chromosomal pattern reported in the present sample of Down's syndrome patients could be the result of nondisjunction in mitosis, and leukemia may be the phenotypical expression of this nondisjunction. (21 ref)
Goh, Kong-oo; Lee, Hahng & Miller, Gerald. (U Rochester School of Medicine & Dentistry) American Journal of Mental Deficiency, 1978(May), Vol 82(6), 542–548. [PA, Vol 61:13508]

1257.   Visual Reinforcement Audiometry (VRA) with young Down's syndrome children.
Investigated VRA with 41 Down's syndrome Ss, aged 6 mo–6 yrs. The procedure involved monitoring a head-turn response to a complex noise signal presented in a sound field with an ascending presentation paradigm and reinforced by a complex visual reinforcer. 24 of the Ss were also evaluated with the Bayley Scales of Infant Development (BSID). 68% of the Ss initially oriented towards the source of the auditory stimulus; only a few of the Ss who did not initially orient could be taught to respond. Of the Ss who initially oriented or were taught to respond, thresholds were obtained on 81% in one visit. A systematic relationship was demonstrated between consistency of S response using the VRA technique and BSID Mental Age Equivalent, with 10 mo being the critical age for determining the potential success of the procedure. Findings imply a higher incidence of hearing loss in the Down's syndrome Ss than in the normal pediatric population. (24 ref)
Greenberg, Douglas B.; Wilson, Wesley R.; Moore, John M. & Thompson, Gary.   Journal of Speech & Hearing Disorders, 1978(Nov), Vol 43(4), 448–458. [PA, Vol 63:08635]

1258.   The effect of sign language on picture naming in two retarded girls possessing normal hearing.
Used a multiple baseline design to investigate the effects of simultaneous sign/verbal (SV) presentation on the acquisition of verbal labeling of 2 Down's syndrome girls, ages 6 and 7 yrs. Results show that the simultaneous sign/verbal presentation was more effective than verbal training alone in facilitating the retarded child's ability to verbally label pictures. In addition, the Ss were able to retain the verbal labels 1 wk later with no interim training. It is suggested that a sign/verbal presentation of new vocabulary may decrease the time spent in training through verbal presentation alone. Further research with a larger population of language impaired children is suggested. (16 ref)
Kotkin, R. A.; Simpson, S. B. & Desanto, Debbie. (U Southern California) Journal of Mental Deficiency Research, 1978(Mar), Vol 22(1), 19–25. [PA, Vol 61:13634]

1259.   Mirror reactions of Down's syndrome infants and toddlers: Cognitive underpinnings of self-recognition.
To examine the developmental significance of mirror self-recognition in early childhood, a cross-sectional study with 55 1.3–4.0 yr old Down's syndrome children was conducted. When their image is altered by rouge on the nose, normal infants by 22 mo indicate self-recognition by touching their noses while looking in the mirror. Only a small percentage of Down's syndrome children touched their noses by this age, confirming the expected lag in this development. However, those young Down's syndrome infants with near-normal development quotient (Bayley Scales of Infant Development or Stanford-Binet Intelligence Scale) did manifest the reaction. In general, when developmental age was equated, the Down's syndrome children showed parallel development to normal children. (11 ref)
Mans, Linda; Cicchetti, Dante & Sroufe, L. Alan. (Clark U) Child Development, 1978(Dec), Vol 49(4), 1247–1250. [PA, Vol 62:08870]

1260.   Maternal linguistic environment of Down's syndrome children.
Explored the differences between the maternal linguistic environment of Down's syndrome (DS) and normal children in the hope of finding environmental factors that might retard the acquisition of verbal communication in DS children; 12 mother–child pairs were Ss. Using univariate methods of analysis only 4 of 38 factors measured differentiated the 2 groups. Two of these differences could be interpreted as potentially facilitating the DS child's language development. These results do not support the contention that linguistic input to DS children is different from that of normal children but instead suggest that mothers of DS children are similar to mothers of normal children in sensitively adjusting their maternal speech register to their child's level of functioning. The deficit in verbal communication in DS does not result from impoverished linguistic stimulation. This does not mean that DS children will not benefit from an enriched environment similar to that provided in early intervention programs. (36 ref)
O'Kelly-Collard, Monica. (St Nicholas Hosp, Psychology Dept, Carlton, Australia) Australian Journal of Mental Retardation, 1978(Dec), Vol 5(4), 121–126. [PA, Vol 64:01319]

1261.   A survey of the visual and developmental-perceptual abilities of the Down's syndrome child.
Provides a detailed description of symptoms and incidence of the syndrome called mongolism, a retardive disease involving a triploidy of the 21st chromosome. The results of a survey and test battery of 41 Down's syndrome persons, in 5 age groups from 3 mo to 23 yrs, are included. All patients showed maturational lag, which began as early as 8 mo. Several individuals performed well, however. Visual examinations revealed 24 hyperopes, 10 myopes, and 7 emmetropes. Spherical correction estimated for 9 of the myopes was 4 diopters or more, often with evidence of retinal pathology. Similar correction for the hyperopes ranged from 0 to 4 diopters (20 persons), with 5 persons needing more than 4 diopters. 23 of those examined had strabismus, and 14 had either nystagmus or paresis of an extraocular muscle. Gross and fine motor skills, stereopsis, and eye-hand coordination were also tested, as were laterality and directionality recognition, auditory and visual memory, body awareness, and other faculties. Test scores are presented by age group. (39 ref)
Pesch, Robin S.; Nagy, D. Keith & Caden, Brian W.   Journal of the American Optometric Association, 1978(Sep), Vol 49(9), 1031–1037. [PA, Vol 63:05715]

1262.   Sexual behavior in three Down's syndrome males.
Describes 3 12–19 yr old males with Down's syndrome (DS) who exhibited masturbatory behavior and showed sexual interest in adult women or other children. All Ss had classical signs of DS, showed good language and speech development, and functioned at the upper range of DS in intellectual ability and performance. It is suggested that the sexual behavior exhibited by these Ss is essentially normal, although the social expression of this behavior caused problems. It is also suggested that the stereotype of DS children as asexual is unrealistic. (4 ref)
Peters, Michael. (U Guelph, Canada) Mental Retardation Bulletin, 1978(Sum), Vol 6(1), 26–29. [PA, Vol 62:11244]

1263.   Patterns of correlations for various language measures in mother–child interactions for normal and Down's syndrome children.
Observed 42 normal and Down's syndrome children and their mothers while interacting at home in a free-play situation. The linguistic level of the children as assessed by mean length of utterance (MLU) ranged from 1.00 to 3.00. Quantitative aspects of the verbal interaction were analyzed. They were found to vary with the language level of the children. Correlational analyses confirmed the validity of MLU as a reflection of formal complexity in children's speech and in mothers' speech directed to their children. The data are related to other recent studies on this topic. (17 ref)
Rondal, J. A. (U Laval, Canada) Language & Speech, 1978(Jul–Sep), Vol 21(3), 242–252. [PA, Vol 63:11876]

1264.   Relational meaning encoded in the two-word utterances of Stage 1 Down's syndrome children.
Examined the early 2-word utterances of 4 Down's syndrome children to determine whether they encoded the same relational meanings as children developing language normally. Nine semantic categories were established to classify the Ss' 2-word

constructions. Absolute and proportional frequencies of relational types were then used to analyze the relational meanings. Results reveal that this classification system accounted for a combined 79% of the 2-word utterances expressed by Ss. It is suggested that Down's children demonstrate as much diversity in their use of relational meanings as normals at the same linguistic stage. Findings are discussed with respect to what Down's children know about the world as they begin to produce 2-word combinations. (22 ref)

Coggins, Truman E. (U Washington) Journal of Speech & Hearing Research, 1979(Mar), Vol 22(1), 166–178. [PA, Vol 64:05891]

1265. Communicative and sensorimotor development of Down's syndrome children.

Imperative and declarative performative behavior was examined in nonretarded and Down's syndrome children operating at 2 stages of sensorimotor intelligence. 20 nonretarded Ss ages 7–13 mo, were selected from a pool of 38 normally developing children with IQs of 90 or above. 10 operated at Stage 4 and 10 operated at Stage 5, as measured by the Ordinal Scales of Psychological Development. The Down's syndrome Ss included 3 groups: 6 10–19 mo old Ss operating at Stage 4, 9 16–26 mo old Ss operating at Stage 5, and 5 31–54 mo old Ss operating at Stage 5. In both groups, more advanced types of performative behavior were generally associated with a higher sensorimotor stage. Relative to the nonretarded Ss of the same sensorimotor stages, the Down's syndrome Ss relied more heavily on gestures in their imperative and declarative usage. Evidence was also obtained suggesting that the correspondence between sensorimotor stage and performative behavior is closer at younger than at older ages. (12 ref)

Greenwald, Carol A. & Leonard, Laurence B. (Memphis State U) American Journal of Mental Deficiency, 1979(Nov), Vol 84(3), 296–303. [PA, Vol 63:05702]

1266. Vocalization and looking behaviour of Down's syndrome infants.

Explored the effect of contingent and noncontingent vocal stimulation on vocalization and looking behavior in 10 Down's syndrome infants (aged 7–19 mo). There were 2 experimental sessions consisting of 4 stages: 1-min baseline (B), 1-min experimental condition (E), a further 1-min B, and a final 2-min E. Maternal vocal stimulation was contingent on infant vocalization for the Es of one session and was presented every 10 sec independent of infant vocalization for the Es of the other session. Neither condition increased infant vocalization, but there was a significant decrease in looking at mother during the Bs, which followed maternal vocalization. It is suggested that looking behavior may be an important indication of competence in prelinguistic social communication for developmentally delayed infants. (9 ref)

Gunn, P.; Berry, Paul & Andrews, R. (U Queensland, Schonell Educational Research Ctr, Brisbane, Australia) British Journal of Psychology, 1979(May), Vol 70(2), 259–263. [PA, Vol 64:08269]

1267. Verbal operants in mothers' speech to nonretarded and Down's syndrome children matched for linguistic level.

Verbal response classes produced by mothers speaking to 21 20–32 mo old nonretarded children were compared with those of mothers speaking to 21 38–144 mo old Down's syndrome children matched with them on mean length of utterance. As mean length of utterance increased, total verbal response classes increased for both groups of mothers and children. Nonretarded children and their mothers produced more echoics; retarded children and their mothers produced more intraverbals. The implications of these findings are discussed in relation to previous research and the teaching of language. (16 ref)

Gutmann, Arlyne J. & Rondal, Jean A. (U Minnesota Medical School) American Journal of Mental Deficiency, 1979(Mar), Vol 83(5), 446–452. [PA, Vol 62:06318]

1268. Meaning and structure of Down's syndrome and nonretarded children's spontaneous speech.

Compared the structure of the spontaneous language samples of 9 Down's syndrome children to that of 9 nonretarded children (CAs 7–12 and 2–5 yrs, respectively; mean Peabody Picture Vocabulary Test IQs 55 and 53, respectively) using the generative semantic model proposed by W. L. Chafe (1970). Results show that all Ss used the 4 basic semantic categories (state, process, action, and process–action) as well as certain other selectional and inflectional features. No qualitative differences were found, but specific quantitative variations were noted. (12 ref)

Layton, Thomas L. & Sharifi, Hassan. (U North Carolina, Chapel Hill) American Journal of Mental Deficiency, 1979(Mar), Vol 83(5), 439–445. [PA, Vol 62:06329]

1269. Development and distribution of intellectual and adaptive skills in Down syndrome children: Implications for early intervention.

Presents data on the systematic decline in IQs and Social Quotients in 217 3-mo to 15-yr-old Down's syndrome children. An analysis of the distribution of IQs within different age ranges is also presented. Implications are discussed in terms of factors that might contribute to this decline and variability in functioning, and the need for further studies assessing effects of early intervention on later functioning is stressed. (8 ref)

Morgan, Sam B. (Memphis State U) Mental Retardation, 1979(Oct), Vol 17(5), 247–249. [PA, Vol 66:08253]

1270. Down's syndrome in Fiji and Tonga.

Describes a survey of 42 individuals in Fiji and Tonga with Down's syndrome. Described are Ss' physical characteristics including complications, chromosome analysis (in most cases), and, in Fiji only, the social consequences for the family. It is suggested that diagnosis presents special difficulty among the Melanesian Fijians and that this factor accounts for the observed deficit in the number seen who belonged to this racial group. The study of social consequences did not suggest any pressing need for residential accommodation to be provided for individuals with Down's syndrome, but did show that programs provided by schools for the intellectually handicapped in Fiji are much appreciated by parents. (7 ref)

Price, John; Parslow, Malcolm & Chambers, Diana. (Royal Brisbane Hosp, Australia) Australian Journal of Mental Retardation, 1979(Mar), Vol 5(5), 4–8. [PA, Vol 66:08264]

1271. Two-plated tapping performance by Down's syndrome and non-Down's-syndrome retardates.

18 16-yr-old Down's syndrome males were compared with age- and IQ-matched (range, 36–55) non-Down's-syndrome retardates on a 2-point finger tapping task. No difference was demonstrated in overall tapping rate between the groups over a 60-sec trial; however, Down's-syndrome Ss made significantly more errors as measured by same-plate tapping. Further, a significant correlation was found between rate of tapping and failure to alternate from one plate to the other in the Down's syndrome, but not in the non-Down's-syndrome group. These rates are interpreted as supportive of a hypothesis presented by U. Frith and C. D. Frith (1974), which suggested that Down's-syndrome retardates show a deficit in developing and utilizing pre-programmed motor sequences. (15 ref)

Seyfort, B. & Spreen, O. (Glendale Lodge Psychology Dept, Victoria, Canada) Journal of Child Psychology & Psychiatry & Allied Disciplines, 1979(Oct), Vol 20(4), 351–355. [PA, Vol 65:03534]

1272. Down's syndrome cases from Madras City: Their socio-economic status.

Investigated the incidence of Down's syndrome among the mentally retarded and the socioeconomic status of such children in Madras City, India. Of the 1,773 children seen at the Child Guidance Clinic and Hospital for Children at Egmore, Madras, from January 1973 to December 1975, 1,087 were mentally retarded, 83 had Down's syndrome. The socioeconomic status of the mothers of this group was assessed on the scale of Kuppuswamy, and was compared with the status of every 5th

patient waiting at the outpatient services of the Children's Hospital. To estimate the distribution of the various social classes in the general population, a sample of 100 parents coming to the Hospital on one day was collected. Despite limitation in sample sizes, results suggest that Down's syndrome, as well as other forms of severe mental retardation, is more prevalent in the upper and middle classes than in the more disadvantaged families. (11 ref)
Somasundaram, O. & Papakumari, M. (Inst of Mental Health, Madras, India) Child Psychiatry Quarterly, 1979(Apr–Jun), Vol 12(2), 43–47. [PA, Vol 63:09950]

1273. Discrimination of size, form and order in mongol and other mentally handicapped children.
Tested 136 (MA 2–10.7 yrs) Mongoloid, 129 non-Mongoloid subnormal (MA 2.1–10.4 yrs), and 152 normal children (MA 2.1–11.7 yrs) in a series of experiments to determine visual discrimination and perceptual skills in size, form, and order. An attempt was made to demonstrate possible differences in strategies and behavior in the groups, particularly in the Mongoloid Ss. It was shown that, in spite of contrary impressions arising from results of normal standardized tests, there was no significant difference in performance when extraneous developmental factors were eliminated. There was further support for the existing experimental evidence that poor short-term memory for visual stimuli in terms of size, form, and order is a characteristic weakness of subnormal groups. No relationship was found between MA and visual perceptual tasks in any group, supporting the theory that perceptual skills develop independently. A peculiar phenomenon was discovered in the Mongoloid Ss, significant enough to warrant further investigation—a distinctive form of perseveration and a related and clearly marked tendency to order reversal. (27 ref)
Stratford, B. (U Leeds, Trinity & All Saints' Coll, Horsforth, England) Journal of Mental Deficiency Research, 1979(Mar), Vol 23(1), 45–53. [PA, Vol 66:06091]

1274. Attraction to "good form" in Down's syndrome.
Examined 75 children's performance in tasks involving matching figures to establish whether there is a specific attraction to symmetrical or Gestalt-type "good form" displays in mentally handicapped children, particularly those with Down's syndrome, or if the tendency is toward image reversal. 25 Ss (mean age 10.9 yrs) with Down's syndrome were matched on MA with 25 non-Down's syndrome subnormals (mean age 9.5 yrs) and 25 normals (mean age 4.1 yrs). Symmetrical and asymmetrical displays were presented for reproduction and reproduction from memory. Results support the hypothesis that mentally handicapped children have a significant attraction to symmetrical arrangements and that Down's syndrome children are more significantly attracted than other handicapped children. Evidence is presented to show that what often is mistaken for a tendency to image reversal is in fact an attraction to "monotonicity" and is more related to "good form" than to reversal. (9 ref)
Stratford, B. (U Leeds, Trinity & All Saints Coll, Horsforth, England) Journal of Mental Deficiency Research, 1979(Dec), Vol 23(4), 243–251. [PA, Vol 66:08274]

1275. Effects of rate of repetitive stimulus presentation on the visual evoked brain potentials of young adults with Down's syndrome.
Visual evoked brain potentials (VEP) to repeated stimuli of several interstimulus intervals (ISI) were recorded from 4 19–25 yr old males with Down's syndrome (DS) and 4 normal male controls. VEP amplitudes increased with increase in ISI, and some ISI effect on latency was observed. VEP amplitudes were larger and VEP peak latencies of DS Ss were longer than those of normals. ISI had a more pronounced effect on VEP amplitudes of DS than normal Ss. CNS differences and issues of attention and information processing are discussed. (60 ref)
Yellin, A. M.; Lodwig, A. K. & Jerison, H. J. (U Minnesota, Minneapolis) Biological Psychiatry, 1979(Dec), Vol 14(6), 913–924. [PA, Vol 65:10665]

1276. Behavior of Down syndrome infants in a strange situation.
Recorded the responses of 18 Down's syndrome infants (mean CA 24 mo) in a modified "strange" situation. Results indicate that Ss were aware of the exits and entrances of both mother and stranger. They cried and showed noncrying distress significantly more when their mothers were absent and showed awareness of the focal point of the room by looking at the door more in appropriate experimental episodes. They also showed increased looking at mother and physical contact on reunion with her. It is concluded that the behavior of Down's syndrome infants is qualitatively similar to that of nonretarded children. (10 ref)
Berry, Paul; Gunn, P. & Andrews, R. (U Queensland, Schonell Educational Research Ctr, Brisbane, Australia) American Journal of Mental Deficiency, 1980(Nov), Vol 85(3), 213–218. [PA, Vol 65:03510]

1277. Maternal speech during play with a Down's syndrome infant.
Video recordings of a mother playing with her Down's syndrome infant—a firstborn male—were made by the father when the child was 3.7, 4.1, 8.3, 12.3, and 17 mo old. An analysis of the mother's speech suggested that her mean length of utterance was unrelated to the infant's age. Other characteristics of maternal speech, however, did change with the infant's age and varied with the context of play. More object referencing and more directions were given as the child grew older. The relevance of these features to the child's language development is discussed. (7 ref)
Gunn, Patricia; Clark, Debbie & Berry, Paul. (U Queensland, Fred & Eleanor Schonell Education Research Ctr, Brisbane, Australia) Mental Retardation, 1980(Feb), Vol 18(1), 15–18. [PA, Vol 66:08236]

1278. Down's syndrome: Telling the parents.
Based on surveys, including one conducted with the parents of 79 Down's syndrome infants, suggestions are offered regarding the physician's responsibility to inform parents of their baby's disease. It is concluded that parents should be told together within 3 days of their child's birth and be gently given a careful and reasonable description of the diagnosis. Genetic counseling and sympathetic but informative advice should also be provided. (16 ref)
Lucas, Peter J. & Lucas, Angela M. (Down's Syndrome Assn of Ireland, Dublin) British Journal of Mental Subnormality, 1980(Jun), Vol 26(50, Pt 1), 21–31. [PA, Vol 66:06582]

1279. Down syndrome and short-term memory impairment: A storage or retrieval deficit?
The majority of researchers investigating the memory skills of retarded individuals have used heterogeneous samples of Ss whose sole criteria for grouping was either IQ or MA. The present experiment was designed to evaluate the short-term memory performance of Ss representing a specific type of retardation. Three groups of Ss (8 Down's syndrome; 8 CA control, 6–13 yrs of age; and 8 MA control, 3.5–5.7 yrs) received tests designed to assess recall and recognition memory utilizing either auditory or visual input with verbal and nonverbal responses. Results indicate that the Down's syndrome group possessed deficits in both storage and retrieval abilities, with storage of visually presented stimuli being particularly impaired. (37 ref)
McDade, Hiram L. & Adler, Sol. (U Texas Medical Branch, Child Development Div, Galveston) American Journal of Mental Deficiency, 1980(May), Vol 84(6), 561–567. [PA, Vol 64:01315]

1280. Interrelationships of biological, environmental and competency variables in young children with Down's syndrome.
89 children with Down's syndrome were followed from birth to 36 mo of age. Means and standard deviations of measures on the Bayley Scales of Infant Development and the Vineland Social Maturity Scale indicate that the average child with Down's syndrome functions at the lower end of the mildly retarded range, while the language development is more delayed. Evaluation of correlation coefficients for the same scales (not interscale correlations) revealed the correlations increased with advancing

age. It was also found that the presence of significant congenital heart disease adversely influences the muscle tone and the parents' ability to follow through with the provided guidance. Muscle tone in turn is a powerful predictor of all the outcome variables—including language acquisition, motor and social development, and mental functioning. The general development at 6 mo was noted to influence future language acquisition as well as mental development in subsequent years. The ability to follow through is affected by muscle tone and by the parents' ability to cope. In turn, follow-through had a significant influence on Ss' mental development between 12 and 36 mo. (11 ref)
Reed, Robert B.; Pueschel, Siegfried M.; Schnell, Richard R. & Cronk, Christine E. (Harvard School of Public Health, Boston) Applied Research in Mental Retardation, 1980, Vol 1(3–4), 161–174. [PA, Vol 66:08265]

1281.   Verbal imitation by Down syndrome and nonretarded children.
Investigated grammatical aspects of the spontaneous repetitions of maternal speech by 21 38–144 mo old Down's syndrome and 21 20–32 mo old nonretarded children. Verbal imitations were found to be very similar in grammatical structure for the 2 groups of Ss at comparable levels of language development. (18 ref)
Rondal, Jean A. (U Liège, Belgium) American Journal of Mental Deficiency, 1980(Nov), Vol 85(3), 318–321. [PA, Vol 65:03529]

1282.   Producing positive interaction among Down syndrome and nonhandicapped teenagers through cooperative goal structuring.
Compared the effects of cooperative, competitive, and individualistic goal structures on the dimensions of interpersonal interaction and attraction. Ss were 18 nonhandicapped and 12 Down's syndrome 13–15 yr olds who participated in 8 weekly sessions of bowling. Results indicate that significantly more positive interactions and evidence of greater interpersonal attraction (sociometric measure) took place between nonhandicapped Ss and Down's syndrome Ss in the cooperative condition than in the competitive and individualistic conditions. (16 ref)
Rynders, John E.; Johnson, Roger T.; Johnson, David W. & Schmidt, Bernie. (U Minnesota, Special Education Programs, Minneapolis) American Journal of Mental Deficiency, 1980(Nov), Vol 85(3), 268–273. [PA, Vol 65:03533]

1283.   Phonological analysis of four Down's syndrome children.
Several studies have reported that the articulatory abilities of Down's syndrome children are poor, but the studies have provided little detail on the nature of the articulation problem. This paper presents a phonological analysis of the spontaneous speech of 4 Down's syndrome children, ages 3 yrs 10 mo–6 yrs 3 mo, including (a) the phonetic inventory of each S, (b) a comparison of target consonant phonemes and Ss' renditions of these phonemes, and (c) a characterization of Ss' errors in terms of phonological processes. The findings indicate that (1) although Ss were capable of producing nearly all the consonant phonemes, correct production was often limited to a particular position within the word; (2) the phonological processes that accounted for Ss' errors were similar to those reported for young normal children; and (3) the phonological abilities of the 4 Ss were comparable to, or better than, their general language ability as measured by mean length of utterances in morphemes. (19 ref)
Stoel-Gammon, Carol. (U Washington, Seattle) Applied Psycholinguistics, 1980(Feb), Vol 1(1), 31–48. [PA, Vol 66:06090]

1284.   Preferences in attention to visual cues in Down's syndrome and normal children.
17 8–16 yr old Down's syndrome children were matched on MA (6 yrs) with 17 4–6 yr old normal Ss; all Ss had reached a criterion on a matching task (MT). All Ss were tested twice on 2 MTs—increasing pattern density and increasing density plus size. Both groups preferred the dimension of size over density of pattern. (15 ref)

Stratford, B. (U Leeds, Trinity & All Saints' Coll, Horsforth, England) Journal of Mental Deficiency Research, 1980(Mar), Vol 24(1), 57–64. [PA, Vol 66:06092]

1285.   Perception and perceptual-motor processes in children with Down's syndrome.
Controversy exists regarding visual discrimination of form and its execution. The hypothesis that an inability to reproduce a display is not necessarily an indication that the display has been incorrectly perceived was examined in 34 children with Down's syndrome (DS [mean CA 11.9 yrs]) matched for MA with a control group of 25 normal children (mean CA 4.2 yrs). 15 DS Ss were identified who revealed perceptual deficits on block construction tests, and experimental work was conducted to determine the extent and nature of this impairment. The construction tests consisted of various displays made from 5 equal sized blocks. This was followed by an identification test consisting of 2-dimensional representations of the block designs printed on cards. All 15 DS Ss were able to recognize and identify correctly a display from a selection that corresponded to a stimulus display, and 11 were able to go further and recognize a 2-dimensional representation of the stimulus. These findings support the hypothesis. (17 ref)
Stratford, Brian. (Trinity & All Saints' Colls, Leeds, England) Journal of Psychology, 1980(Jan), Vol 104(1), 139–145. [PA, Vol 65:08219]

1286.   Parental responses to their developmentally delayed children and the South Glamorgan Home Advisory Service.
Examined (a) how parents with a handicapped child describe their child's behavior and (b) to what extent their description is a function of the child's degree of handicap. The sample included 4 groups: 61 families of 4–90 mo old handicapped children—27 with Down's Syndrome (Group 1); 13 with nonspecific developmental delay with a developmental quotient (DQ) above 65 (Group 2); and 21 with a DQ under 65, some of whom also had a limb dysfunction (Group 3)—and 25 families of similar aged controls (Group 4). Parents completed a semantic differential containing 17 attitudinal and 15 child descriptive scales. Parents of handicapped children also indicated their preferences for possible services. Results show a consistent trend for parents to view their child increasingly favorably over time. Significant differences were found between parents of controls and parents of Group 3. The majority of parents favored the home advisory service first and part-time day care second. (34 ref)
Wishart, M. C.; Bidder, R. T. & Gray, O. P. (U Wales Hosp, Dept of Child Health, Cardiff) Child Care, Health & Development, 1980(Nov–Dec), Vol 6(6), 361–376. [PA, Vol 65:10536]

1287.   Auditory evoked brain potentials as a function of interstimulus interval in adults with Down's syndrome.
Auditory evoked potentials (AEPs) to repeated binaural tone pips of several interstimulus intervals (ISIs) greater than/equal to 1 sec were recorded from the vertex of 8 males (aged 19–25 yrs) who were either normal or had Down's syndrome (DS; trisomy 21). AEP amplitudes, as well as 1 latency measure, of both experimental groups increased with the lengthening of ISI. AEP peak latencies of the DS group were longer than AEP peak latencies of the normal group for all the ISIs employed. AEP amplitudes of the DS group tended to be larger than those of the normal group. Findings are discussed in relationship to issues of attention. (French summary) (19 ref)
Yellin, A. M.; Lodwig, A. K. & Jerison, H. J. (U Minnesota, Div of Child & Adolescent Psychiatry, Minneapolis) Audiology, 1980(May–Jun), Vol 19(3), 255–262. [PA, Vol 65:13056]

1288.   The development of eye contact between mothers and normal versus Down's syndrome infants.
Eye contact between mothers and 7 normal as well as 5 Down's syndrome infants was recorded over Ss' 1st 6 mo of life, both during naturalistic face-to-face interactions (mobile condition) and when mothers were silent and kept their faces still (immobile condition). Mental Development Index scores from the Bayley Scales of Infant Development were 66–102 for Down's syndrome Ss and 99–120 for normals. In the mobile condition normals

consistently showed double peak patterns in the development of eye contact at 7 and 14 wks of age. Analysis of temporal and discriminative aspects of the eye contact revealed qualitative differences between the 2 peaks. Down's syndrome Ss showed delays in the onset of eye contact and in the establishment of high levels of this behavior. Once these levels were attained during the 3rd mo, high overall levels as well as long episodes of eye contact were maintained for much longer than in the normals. Although this appeared to be beneficial for the formation of the mother–infant bond, it also indicated increasing delays in the development of new functional uses of eye contact. Impairments in both maturational and psychological processes were thus implied. (39 ref)
Berger, Jiri & Cunningham, C. C. (Victoria U of Manchester, Hester Adrian Research Ctr, England) Developmental Psychology, 1981(Sep), Vol 17(5), 678–689. [PA, Vol 66:13058]

1289. Interplay among behavioral systems: Illustrations from the study of attachment, affiliation, and wariness in young children with Down's syndrome.
42 Down's syndrome (DS) children, aged 30–42 mo, were seen in M. D. Ainsworth and B. A. Wittig's (1969) "strange situation" to assess the interrelationships among the affiliative, attachment, and fear/wariness behavioral systems. A stranger evoked affiliative behaviors in Ss but also elicited wariness and attachment behaviors. The emergence, sequence, and intensity of these behavioral systems varied with the context and the behaviors of both stranger and mother. The finding that more than one behavioral system was activated suggests that an explanation of social responsiveness must be sufficiently broad and integrative to encompass different but interrelated behavioral systems, with their respective functions and determinants. Despite certain quantitative and qualitative differences, behavioral systems appear to be organized similarly in DS and normal children. It is argued that the behavioral organization manifested by the retarded children supports and extends E. Zigler's (see PA, Vol 43:8608) "developmental" position. These findings suggest that the DS group constitutes a legitimate target of research for elucidating the processes of normal and deviant development. (43 ref)
Cicchetti, Dante & Serafica, Felicisima C. (Harvard U) Developmental Psychology, 1981(Jan), Vol 17(1), 36–49. [PA, Vol 65:08204]

1290. Spontaneous imitations of Down's syndrome children: A lexical analysis.
Describes the spontaneous imitations produced by 4 Stage 1 Down's syndrome children (CA 3 yrs 10 mo to 6 yrs 3 mo). The imitative speech of Ss was compared to their spontaneous productions to determine whether words imitated were different from those produced spontaneously. Findings suggest that Down's children are similar to normal-language learners in that they selectively imitate model utterances during this linguistic stage. (21 ref)
Coggins, Truman E. & Morrison, Judith A. (U Washington, Child Development & Mental Retardation Ctr, Seattle) Journal of Speech & Hearing Research, 1981(Jan), Vol 24(2), 303–308. [PA, Vol 66:10592]

1291. Social development and feeding milestones of young Down syndrome children.
During an interdisciplinary longitudinal study, the social development and mastery of feeding skills of 89 Down's syndrome children were investigated at 6-mo intervals between 6 and 36 mo of age. Sex, cardiac status, and muscle tone of Ss and parental follow-through data were examined for potential influence on Vineland Social Maturity Scale scores and on a selected subset of feeding milestones. The Bayley Scales of Infant Development were also completed. Ss attained significantly higher scores on the Vineland and achieved most feeding milestones much earlier if they had no or only mild congenital heart disease, if their parents followed-through appropriately with furnished guidance, and if they had "good" muscle tone. (22 ref)
Cullen, Susan M. et al. (Children's Hosp Medical Ctr, Developmental Evaluation Clinic, Providence, RI) American Journal of

Mental Deficiency, 1981(Jan), Vol 85(4), 410–415. [PA, Vol 65:08205]

1292. The temperament of Down's syndrome infants: A research note.
The mothers of 28 Down's syndrome infants (6–18 mo old) completed the Carey Survey of Temperamental Characteristics. Only 2 Ss were found to fit the amiable, mild stereotype while 5 exhibited signs of having difficult temperaments. Further, ratings of Ss' temperament revealed that mothers held a more positive impression than was reflected in the questionnaire's characteristics, indicating the existence of successful coping skills. (12 ref)
Gunn, P.; Berry, P. & Andrews, R. J. (U Queensland, Schonell Educational Research Ctr, Brisbane, Australia) Journal of Child Psychology & Psychiatry & Allied Disciplines, 1981(Apr), Vol 22(2), 189–194. [PA, Vol 66:01541]

1293. The affective response of Down's syndrome infants to a repeated event.
In a study with 17 Down's syndrome infants, the older Ss (mean age 20 mo 6 days) responded to the regular reappearance of a squeaky doll with significantly more affective behavior than did younger Ss (mean age 9 mo 24 days). When the younger Ss were included in a longitudinal study of their responses to this same event, the onset of affective behavior was significantly correlated with the mental development index of the Bayley Scales of Infant Development. (7 ref)
Gunn, P.; Berry, Paul & Andrews, R. J. (U Queensland, Schonell Educational Research Ctr, Brisbane, Australia) Child Development, 1981(Jun), Vol 52(2), 745–751. [PA, Vol 66:10596]

1294. The motor deficit in Down's Syndrome children: A problem of timing?
17 Down's syndrome (DS) children and 17 retarded non-DS, matched on MA (mean of 61.92 mo) and CA (mean of 121.97 mo), performed continuous tracking and drawing tasks. 12 normal Ss performed the main tracking task. There were no differences between the groups on the spatial aspects of the tasks. On temporal components, normals were better on all measures. DS Ss were also poorer than retarded controls, showing more undershooting at corners, more problems in keeping up with the moving pattern, and inability to continue the pattern without a model on the still-moving paper following a 5-min practice session. Results are discussed in terms of a specific motor programing deficit in DS children. (17 ref)
Henderson, Sheila E. & Morris, Janet. (U London, Inst of Education, England) Journal of Child Psychology & Psychiatry & Allied Disciplines, 1981(Jul), Vol 22(3), 233–245. [PA, Vol 66:10598]

1295. Performance of Down syndrome and other retarded children on the Cratty Gross-Motor Test.
Administered the Cratty Test of Gross-Motor Performance to 18 Down's syndrome and 18 other mentally retarded children (CAs 7–14 yrs; mean MA 5 yrs). Examination of their test profiles showed that the Down's syndrome Ss had consistently lower scores than did matched controls, but only 2 of the differences were significant. Findings provide tentative support for the notion that Down's syndrome children suffer a specific deficit in some areas of motor coordination. A number of criticisms of the internal consistency of the test are discussed in terms of their theoretical and practical implications. (18 ref)
Henderson, Sheila E.; Morris, Janet & Ray, Sheila. (U London Inst of Education, England) American Journal of Mental Deficiency, 1981(Jan), Vol 85(4), 416–424. [PA, Vol 65:06829]

1296. Pretend play and patterns of cognition in Down's syndrome children.
Examined the relationship between cognitive functioning of 30 Down's syndrome Ss as measured by the Bayley Scales of Infant Development and their symbolic play level. Ss' CAs ranged from 20 to 53 mo and MAs were 12–26 mo. Each S was seen at home with the mother or primary caretaker present. A ½-hr play session was videotaped, followed by administration of the Bayley Infant Behavior Record. Analysis of play behavior supported a 4-

level scale. Symbolic play level was more highly correlated with MA than with CA. Performance on the Infant Behavior Record was also highly correlated with symbolic play level. (35 ref)
Hill, Patricia M. & McCune-Nicolich, Lorraine. (New Jersey Dept of Education, Branch of Special Education, Trenton) Child Development, 1981(Jun), Vol 52(2), 611–617. [PA, Vol 66:10599]

1297.   Self-recognition in retarded children.
Investigated the relationship between cognitive and affective development in 24 Down's syndrome and multihandicapped Ss (MAs 7–36 mo; mean CAs 34.8–45.6 mo). Ss watched TV images of themselves with faces marked or unmarked and of a peer whose face was marked. The objective technique of increased mark-directed responses was used as evidence of self-recognition, and Ss' reactions as they watched these images were rated. The emergence of self-recognition was closely tied to the maturity of Ss' general responsiveness to their reflections. The Down's syndrome Ss made a broad range of responses, including the curiosity and self-conscious behaviors characteristic of normal children during the 2nd yr of life, and all except one of these Ss show evidence that they recognized their images. In contrast, the range of behaviors displayed by multihandicapped Ss was greatly restricted and similar to children in the 1st yr of life. Less than half of these Ss showed an emergence of self-recognition. (20 ref)
Hill, Suzanne D. & Tomlin, Cynthia. (U New Orleans, Lakefront) Child Development, 1981(Mar), Vol 52(1), 145–150. [PA, Vol 65:12857]

1298.   Hearing loss of Down syndrome adults.
Obtained audiological hearing-test data for 51 Down's syndrome Ss (CAs 15–51 yrs). Depending on hearing-loss criteria, 51–74% of Ss had some degree of hearing impairment. Correlation coefficients between these hearing-acuity measurements and receptive hearing vocabulary scores suggest a moderate relationship. Data indicate that Ss were prone to a wide variety of hearing difficulties that reflected a variety of ear pathologies. These data and other studies have shown that Down's syndrome adults and children need frequent hearing screening and, when indicated, otological and/or audiological management. When otological treatment will be of long duration, aural rehabilitation, including prescription amplification, may be indicated as an adjunctive therapeutic procedure. (10 ref)
Keiser, Hope et al. (U Arkansas, Speech & Hearing Clinic, Little Rock) American Journal of Mental Deficiency, 1981(Mar), Vol 85(5), 467–472. [PA, Vol 65:12858]

1299.   Social familiarity and communication in Down syndrome.
Analyzed the communication of 8 Down's syndrome (DS) individuals (mean CA 25 yrs and mean MA 5.08 yrs) with strangers and with acquaintances. The spontaneity of their speech and the communicative demands they made on their audiences were low. Some Ss broke rules of conversation by not answering questions. Surprisingly, their speech was not more spontaneous with acquaintances. It was further observed that DS Ss' conversations were mainly restricted to comments on current actions. However, different postures were adopted and different body mobility exhibited depending on partner familiarity. It is concluded that DS persons prefer to express intimacy/social distance in nonverbal modalities. (15 ref)
Leudar, I.; Fraser, W. I. & Jeeves, M. A. (U St Andrews, Psychology Lab, Scotland) Journal of Mental Deficiency Research, 1981(Jun), Vol 25(2), 133–142. [PA, Vol 66:10602]

1300.   Relationship between language and sensorimotor development of Down syndrome and nonretarded children.
Investigated the relationship between sensorimotor and language development of Down's syndrome (DS) and nonretarded (NR) children. The Ordinal Scales of Psychological Development (OSPD) and the Receptive and Expressive Emergent Language (REEL) scale were administered to 18 DS and 18 NR Ss with developmental ages of approximately 17-mo. Comparison of the resulting scores indicated that although there were no differences between the groups on 4 subscales of the OSPD, there were

significant differences in favor of the NR Ss on the Vocal Imitation subscale of the OSPD and on Receptive and Expressive measures of the REEL. Results indicate that DS children are delayed in their language development compared to NR children of the same developmental age. This language delay appears to be related to deficiencies in vocal imitation skills but not related to general sensorimotor functioning. (29 ref)
Mahoney, Gerald; Glover, Anne & Finger, Iris. (U California, Los Angeles) American Journal of Mental Deficiency, 1981(Jul), Vol 86(1), 21–27. [PA, Vol 66:08251]

1301.   The behaviour of children with Down syndrome in normal playgroups.
Observed 7 Down's syndrome (DS) children (CA 3–4½ yrs) on their 1st day in a normal playgroup or after regular attendance at a playgroup. The observations were recorded by video cameras fitted with telescopic lenses and placed at opposite ends of the room, far enough away to be ignored by Ss. It appears that the normal children made unsuccessful attempts to establish contact with DS Ss and eventually gave up, with the result that DS Ss became isolates in the group, interacting with no one except adult helpers. (DS Ss had been well prepared and were capable of all the activities engaged in by the normal children.) It is suggested that their failure may be interpreted by the other children as gaze aversion—evidence of a desire to avoid interaction. (12 ref)
Sinson, Janice C. & Wetherick, N. E. Journal of Mental Deficiency Research, 1981(Jun), Vol 25(2), 113–120. [PA, Vol 66:10612]

1302.   A comparative study of pre-meaningful vocalizations produced by normally developing and Down's syndrome infants.
Pre-meaningful vocalizations produced by 9 normal and 10 Down's syndrome infants were recorded as part of a longitudinal study of language development. The recordings were phonetically transcribed using a modified version of the International Phonetic Alphabet. Data were analyzed in terms of age at onset of reduplicated babbling, developmental trends for place of consonant articulation, and developmental aspects of vocalic productions. In general, substantial similarities between the 2 groups were observed with regard to the selected parameters. Both groups began to produce canonical, reduplicated babbling at 8–8½ mo of age, and trends regarding consonantal and vocalic development for the 2 groups were similar during the 1st 15 mo of life. (20 ref)
Smith, Bruce L. & Oller, D. Kimbrough. (U Washington, Seattle) Journal of Speech & Hearing Disorders, 1981(Feb), Vol 46(1), 46–51. [PA, Vol 66:10613]

1303.   Position cues in discrimination behaviour of normal, Down syndrome and other mentally handicapped children.
12 Down's syndrome (DS), 12 other mentally handicapped, and 12 normal children matched for MA (mean of 5.8 yrs) were tested on a visual discrimination task. There was some evidence to support the suggestion that certain types of mentally handicapped children attend to single cues rather than to total configuration. There was also evidence of perceptual distortion resulting in reversal and attraction to "good form." Differences were detected between DS and non-DS handicapped Ss that were consistent with the suggestion that DS children characteristically show flexibility in approach to perceptual discrimination tasks. Results are not inconsistent with interpreting perceptual processes in handicapped and normal children as essentially similar. (13 ref)
Stratford, B. & Metcalfe, J. Alban. (U Nottingham, School of Education, England) Journal of Mental Deficiency Research, 1981(Jun), Vol 25(2), 89–103. [PA, Vol 66:10615]

1304.   The development of grammar in Down's syndrome children between the mental ages of 2–0 and 6–11 years.
Compared syntactic usage of institutionalized and home-reared Down's syndrome children with that of normally developing children of equivalent MA, using the Developmental Sentence Scoring (DSS) procedure (L. Lee, 1974). Compared with normal Ss, the Down's syndrome Ss evidenced a more homogeneous pattern of syntactic usage and tended to acquire only low-level

syntactic structures, as identified by DSS. Results indicate no significant differences in syntactic usage between males and females or institutionalized and home-reared Ss. (5 ref)
Wiegel-Crump, Carole A. (Louisiana State U, Baton Rouge) Education & Training of the Mentally Retarded, 1981(Feb), Vol 16(1), 24–30. [PA, Vol 66:08284]

Institutionalized Mentally Retarded

1305. Effect of meaningfulness on learning syntactic units.
Examined the influence of meaningfulness (semantic consistency) and nonmeaningfulness (anomaly) on the learning of syntactic word pairs with 36 3rd-grade normal and 36 institutionalized retarded children. Using a paired-associate technique, Ss were presented with either a list of meaningful word pairs or nonmeaningful pairs. Results show that meaningful pairs were learned more readily than nonmeaningful pairs at both ability levels. No differences were found between normals and retardates for the meaningful pairs. Normals learned the nonmeaningful pairs with fewer errors than the retarded Ss. This latter finding is discussed in terms of types of overt errors made and presentation rate.
Gallagher, Joseph W. (U. Alabama) American Journal of Mental Deficiency, 1970(Jul), Vol 75(1), 27-32. [PA, Vol 45:01219]

1306. Effect of five free association strength values on paired-associate learning.
Examined the influence of free association strength (FAS) on paired-associate learning with 75 1st- and 75 3rd-grade nonretarded children and 75 institutionalized retarded children matched for MA with the 3rd-grade Ss. Results indicate that the mean number of errors decreases as FAS increases. Performance of the retarded Ss was similar to that of the 3rd-grade group for the highly associated pairs, but for weakly associated pairs the retarded group's performance was more like that of the 1st-grade Ss.
Gallagher, Joseph W. & Reid, Donald R. (U. Alabama) American Journal of Mental Deficiency, 1970(Jul), Vol. 75(1), 33-38. [PA, Vol 45:01220]

1307. Refractive errors in institutionalized mentally retarded and emotionally disturbed children.
Screened 106 institutionalized emotionally disturbed (ED), 40 trainable mentally retarded (TMR), and 69 educable mentally retarded (EMR) children in a school of special education for refractive errors. As individual classes and as a single retarded group, TMR and EMR Ss showed significantly more hyperopia than ED Ss and Ss of comparable age from the normal classroom. TMR Ss did not differ significantly from EMR Ss.
Courtney, G. R. (Central State Hosp., Milledgeville, Ga.) American Journal of Optometry & Archives of American Academy of Optometry, 1971(Jun), Vol. 48(6), 492-496. [PA, Vol 46:10905]

1308. Habituation of the GSR to tones in retarded children and nonretarded subjects.
Studied habituation patterns of the GSR to auditory stimuli in 30 institutionalized retarded children and 30 8th grade nonretarded Ss. All children habituated to the 100- and 70-db tones, but showed little change in response to the 35-db tones. At the 70-db intensity, control Ss had a greater initial response and responded throughout more strongly than retardates; the response to the 100-db tones was greater for the retardates.
Fenz, Walter D. & McCabe, Michael W. (U. Waterloo, Ontario, Canada) American Journal of Mental Deficiency, 1971(Jan), Vol. 75(4), 470-473. [PA, Vol 46:03601]

1309. Discrimination learning in retarded and nonretarded children as a function of task difficulty and social reinforcement.
Compared the learning performances of 33 nonretarded, 37 noninstitutionalized retarded, and 38 institutionalized retarded 6-16 yr. olds matched for MA on an oddity problem and a simple 3-choice discrimination task, with or without social reinforcement. The oddity problem was more difficult than the 3-choice task for all 3 groups. On both learning tasks, nonretarded Ss made significantly more correct responses than either retarded group. Although more nonretarded than retarded Ss learned the oddity problem, there were no group differences in the frequency of learners on the 3-choice task. On this latter task, the institutionalized retarded Ss made more correct responses in the nonsocial condition, while the pattern was just the reverse for the noninstitutionalized retarded Ss. Findings are discussed in terms of the need to consider more than 1 learning measure and the effects of motivational variables in the assessment of nonretarded-retarded differences. (21 ref.)
Harter, Susan; Brown, Lynn & Zigler, Edward. (Yale U.) American Journal of Mental Deficiency, 1971(Nov), Vol. 76(3), 275-283. [PA, Vol 48:03567]

1310. Measure of activity level in mentally retarded children and adolescents.
Reports the adaptation of a relatively inexpensive calendar watch as a motion recorder to investigate the activity level of 33 institutionalized mentally retarded 6-15 yr olds. Results indicate that such a motion recorder is a reliable measure of activity in this population. Results are discussed in terms of the practical application of this recorder both in research efforts and in the treatment of the hyperactive child.
Massey, Philip S.; Lieberman, Allan & Batarseh, Gabriel. (South Carolina Dept. of Mental Retardation, Ladson) American Journal of Mental Deficiency, 1971(Sep), Vol. 76(2), 259-261. [PA, Vol 47:09510]

1311. Expectancy of success and the probability learning of retarded children.
Tested 23 male and 22 female institutionalized retarded children who had previously experienced either a success, failure, or control precondition on a probability learning task designed to assess expectancy of success. Ss were matched for CA, MA, IQ, and length of institutionalization. The following measures were also collected as S variables: Locus-of-Control Scale, Cottage Rating Scales, school rating, and Reading and Arithmetic subscales from the Metropolitan Achievement Test. The preconditions were found to have many of the expected effects on the cognitive strategies employed in the learning task. Ss in the failure condition showed the greatest avoidance of failure (maximizing strategy), while Ss in the success condition tended to show more success striving (lose-shift strategy). Males were found to exhibit more failure-avoiding strategies than females. The overall pattern of results is interpreted as providing support for the hypothesis that a low expectancy of success in retarded children can be modified. (19 ref.)
Ollendick, Thomas; Balla, David & Zigler, Edward. (Purdue U.) Journal of Abnormal Psychology, 1971(Jun), Vol. 77(3), 275-281. [PA, Vol 46:06165]

1312. The Purdue Perceptual Motor Survey and the Bender Gestalt as measures of perceptual motor abilities in children.
Administered the Purdue Perceptual Motor Survey and the Bender-Gestalt Test to 38 normal, 38 perceptually handicapped, 58 emotionally disturbed, and 20 retarded children from various institutions. Both tests (a) differentiated between normals and exceptionals at about the same rate of accuracy, but (b) fell short of having meaningful diagnostic utility.
Richardson, Wayne & Rubino, Carl. (Mental Retardation Center, Toronto, Ontario, Canada) Ontario Psychologist, 1971, Vol. 3(4), 243-247. [PA, Vol 48:01035]

1313. Validity and reliability of the red-green AO H-R-R Pseudoisochromatic Plates with mentally retarded children.
Examined 69 institutionalized mentally retarded children to determine the reliability and validity of the 14 red-green plates of the AO H-R-R Pseudoisochromatic Plates. The stability of the raw score and diagnosis, and the internal consistency were evaluated in addition to the validity of the diagnosis and the validity of the individual plates. Results indicate high internal consistency but low stability and validity. Use of the H-R-R plates with mentally retarded children is not recommended.

Salvia, John A. & Ysseldyke, James E. (U. Illinois) Perceptual & Motor Skills, 1971(Dec), Vol. 33(3, Pt. 2), 1071-1074. [PA, Vol 48:01523]

1314. Some characteristics of mental defectives displaying self-mutilative behaviors.
Evaluated 400 institutionalized mentally defective Ss for the occurrence of self-mutilative behaviors (SMB). Within the group of 35 identified Ss with an average age of 19.9 yr., there appeared to be no overall relationship between age and sex and the severity of the SMBs displayed. Results indicate that there is a relationship between IQ, the number of other demonstrated undesirable behaviors, and the severity of SMB. Results further suggest that, relative to the onset of SMBs the period of the 1st 4 yrs of life may be no more critical than any later childhood period.
Smeets, Paul M. (Woods Schools, Langhorne, Pa.) Training School Bulletin, 1971(Aug), Vol. 68(2), 131-135. [PA, Vol 47:05485]

1315. Social approach and avoidance tendencies of institutionalized retarded and noninstitutionalized retarded and normal children.
36 institutionalized retarded, noninstitutionalized retarded, and normal children of comparable MA performed on a 2-task interpersonal distance measure which assessed positive (approach) and negative (avoidance) reaction tendencies. A free-play period was interpolated between the 2 tasks. ⅓ of each group performed under a support, punishment, or neutral condition. The institutionalized retarded Ss were found to be more motivated to approach an adult, but more wary of doing so, than either of the other groups. Experimental condition effects were found for the institutionalized retarded group but not for the other groups. Results found with the social interpersonal distance measure were consistent with those of earlier studies employing time persistence measures. (24 ref.)
Weaver, S. Joseph; Balla, David & Zigler, Edward. (U. Kansas Medical Center, Kansas City) Journal of Experimental Research in Personality, 1971(Jun), Vol. 5(2), 98-110. [PA, Vol 48:01530]

1316. Stability of the Pictorial Test of Intelligence with retarded children.
46 institutionalized retarded 7-12 yr. olds were given the Pictorial Test of Intelligence (PTI) and retested 18 mo. later. The test-retest correlation of .80 provides evidence for long-term reliability for the PTI. When the sample was divided into high- and low-IQ groups, findings indicate greater stability for Ss with IQs from 55-83 than for those from 40-55.
Bonfield, Reggie. (Pennsylvania State U.) American Journal of Mental Deficiency, 1972(Jul), Vol. 77(1), 108-110. [PA, Vol 49:04629]

1317. Imitative sign training as a facilitator of word-object association with low-functioning children.
Administered a 90-item 2-choice discrimination test to 26 institutionalized retardates with mean CA of 12.7 yr. Half were given a sequence of training in which imitative-sign movements were taught and subsequently paired with appropriate words followed by pairing with appropriate objects. Periodic word-object association probe tests were administered to all Ss, with controls exposed to no other training. Following training, a posttest was administered consisting of the 90-item word-object discrimination test using the object's name to indicate correct choice. Results show reliable differences between the experimental and control Ss on the criterion measure suggesting that the imitative-sign training facilitated word-object association.
Bricker, Diane D. (George Peabody Coll. for Teachers, Nashville, Tenn.) American Journal of Mental Deficiency, 1972(Mar), Vol. 76(5), 509-516. [PA, Vol 48:12059]

1318. Acoustic impedance and tympanometry with the retarded: A normative study.
Obtained acoustic impedance and tympanometry data from 100 institutionalized mentally retarded children representing a broad range of ages, etiological classifications, and measured intelligence levels. Ss had no known history of middle ear pathology and were demonstrated to have hearing within the normal range by behavioral pure-tone audiometry. Tests included measures of absolute impedance (expressed in acoustic ohms), relative impedance (stapedius muscle reflex activity), and pressure-compliance relationships. Normative data, including measures of central tendency and inter-S variability, are reported for each of the criterion measures. Acoustic reflex thresholds are presented with reference to the behavioral thresholds, and puretone-reflex threshold differences are discussed. Curves representing alterations in eardrum compliance with artificially induced ear canal pressure changes are illustrated. Measures of absolute impedance are also presented and are discussed with respect to the other tests. All test findings are related to existing data for normal populations. Potential clinical applicability of acoustic impedance measurements and tympanometry with mentally retarded persons is considered. (French summary) (22 ref.)
Fulton, R. T. & Lamb, L. E. (U. Kansas) Audiology, 1972(May), Vol. 11(3-4), 199-208. [PA, Vol 48:07637]

1319. The effects of retinal and physical orientation, physical size and distance, and intelligence on the perceived "meaning" of stimuli.
Conducted a study with 14 institutionalized, mentally retarded, male 17-19 yr. olds, 10 normal male 9th graders, and 18 normal male 2nd graders. The perceived meaning of stimuli in a 45. conflict situation was examined as a function of 2 stimulus variables (stimulus size and viewing distance) and 2 S variables (MA and CA). Results indicate that responses are not determined by these variables, and the Ss are preset to interpret stimuli according to the physical, rather than the retinal, coordinate system.
Hill, A. Lewis. (Inst. for Research in Mental Retardation, Staten Island, N.Y.) Psychonomic Science, 1972(Jul), Vol. 28(2), 113-114. [PA, Vol 50:03233] ·

1320. [Study of chromosomal aberrations in a population of mental defectives.] (Fren)
Conducted a systematic study of 103 institutionalized mentally deficient children. The incidence of chromosomal aberration was 4 times that of the general population. (German & Spanish summaries) (36 ref.)
Jalbert, P., et al. (U. Grenoble, Medical Faculty, Lab. of Histology, France) Revue de Neuropsychiatrie Infantile et d'Hygiene Mentale de l'Enfance, 1972(Oct), Vol. 20(10), 761-772. [PA, Vol 50:11511]

1321. Relationship of "brain damage" to I.Q. variations among mentally retarded institutionalized girls.
Using a sample of 21 "neurologically normal" mentally retarded institutionalized girls and a sample of 9 comparable girls with a diagnosis of "brain damage," it was found that "brain damage" has a highly significant association with "loss" of IQ points during institutionalization. The "loss" was not a reflection of a deteriorated test performance, but of the performance level remaining static or increasing little in relation to the increase in CA. It is concluded that, from the viewpoint of intellectual development, girls with a diagnosis of "brain damage" were unable to benefit from the institutional environment to the same degree as girls who were "neurologically normal." Applying the findings, brain-damaged children residing in institutions generally require an even more intensive activities program to stimulate their mental development than do children in institutions.
Kraus, J. & Judd, L. (Dept. of Child Welfare & Social Welfare, Sydney, New South Wales, Australia) Australian Journal of Mental Retardation, 1972(Mar), Vol. 2(1), 22-24. [PA, Vol 49:01173]

1322. Lexical usage of mentally retarded and nonretarded children.
Compared, individually, the part of speech usage of 27 institutionalized retarded children to that of nonretarded. Most of the retarded Ss diverged in 1 or more part of speech categories from nonretarded Ss of either the same CA or MA. In contrast, when analyzed as a group, retarded Ss did not differ from the nonretarded. It is possible that the differences in individual

lexical usage were due to the institutionalization rather than being a characteristic of retarded speech.
Lozar, Barbara; Wepman, Joseph M. & Hass, Wilbur. (U. Chicago) American Journal of Mental Deficiency, 1972(Mar), Vol. 76(5), 534-539. [PA, Vol 48:12046]

1323.   Ten dimensions of maladaptive behavior in mentally retarded early adolescents.
Administered the Adaptive Behavior Scale to 458 adolescents in residential institutions for mentally retarded. A factor analysis of 44 subscale scores delineated 10 salient dimensions encompassing various forms of extrapunitive maladaptive behavior to intropunitive maladaptive behavior and other forms of inadequate coping behavior. These factors should serve as useful concepts for description and rehabilitation of retarded individuals.
Nihira, Kazuo. (U. California, Neuropsychiatric Inst., Los Angeles) Proceedings of the 80th Annual Convention of the American Psychological Association, 1972, Vol. 7(Pt. 2), 723-724. [PA, Vol 48:05474]

1324.   The psychodynamics of humor, as seen in institutionalized retardates.
Analyzed the jokes told by 30 adolescent and 30 adult institutionalized retardates, using Freud's psychodynamic concepts and following M. Wolfenstein's classification of children's humor. Results support psychoanalytic postulates that humor unconsciously reflects a need for rebellion and desire for infantile narcissistic victory due to feelings of lack of self-possession.
Pustel, Gabriel; Sternlicht, Manny & Siegel, Louis. (Willowbrook State School, Staten Island, N.Y.) Journal of Psychology, 1972(Jan), Vol. 80(1), 69-73. [PA, Vol 47:11488]

1325.   Institutionalized retardates' animal drawings: Their meanings and significance.
Obtained animal drawings from 731 institutionalized adult and adolescent male and female retardates of varying intellectual level. A frequency distribution was composed, the type and sex of the animals drawn were analyzed, and the findings contrasted with those already obtained from a comparable nonretarded population. An image of the retarded emerged from the drawings, which, generally, were convergent on the adult level but divergent for the adolescents. A possible rationale for this is offered.
Pustel, Gabriel; Sternlicht, Manny & DeRespinis, Michael. (Willowbrook State School, Staten Island, N.Y.) Journal of Genetic Psychology, 1972(Mar), Vol. 120(1), 103-109. [PA, Vol 48:03552]

1326.   Verbal mediation and perceptual transfer in nonretarded and retarded children.
Assessed the effects of language training on perception in 162 noninstitutionalized retarded, institutionalized retarded, and nonretarded children matched on MA. Within each group, 3 experimental treatments were employed: the common labels group associated 2 labels to 4 random visual forms, distinctive labels Ss associated 4 different labels to the same 4 forms, and a 3rd group viewed the forms without labels. In the criterion task, all Ss judged tachistoscopically presented pairs of the previously employed forms same or different. Results indicate perceptual responses of the 3 groups were differentially affected by the labeling training. Nonretarded Ss were influenced by both treatments, noninstitutionalized retarded Ss only by distinctive label training, and institutionalized retarded Ss by neither. Differences associated with institutionalization were interpreted as support for the importance of cultural determinants in retardation. (23 ref.)
Rosenberg, Sue; Katz, Phyllis A. & Karp, Barry. (Yeshiva U.) American Journal of Mental Deficiency, 1972(Mar), Vol. 76(5), 527-533. [PA, Vol 48:12079]

1327.   Areas of parental concern about retarded children.
Asked parents of 90 children (from infancy to late teens) admitted to an institution for the retarded, and parents of a contrast group of 38 retarded children who remained at home their prime areas of concern with regard to the retarded child. 7 major problems were identified, identical for both groups, and

seen with the same degree of relative urgency. The problem areas were broadly classified as concern for the welfare of the retarded child, the family, and the community. Some implications for needed community services are noted. Parents who hospitalized their retarded child expressed greater overall concern for the welfare of the family; parents who kept the child at home expressed greater overall concern for the welfare of the child.
Skelton, Mora.   Mental Retardation, 1972(Feb), Vol. 10(1), 38-41. [PA, Vol 48:03562]

1328.   Developmental course of responsiveness to social reinforcement in normal children and institutionalized retarded children.
Tested 39 institutionalized retarded and 39 noninstitutionalized normal children of 3 MA levels on a simple 2-part satiation game which assessed responsiveness to social reinforcement. Younger Ss were found to be more responsive to such reinforcement than older Ss. Retarded Ss were found to be more motivated for social reinforcement than the normals at each age level. Ss with greater preinstitutional deprivation and those who received relatively few visits were found to be especially responsive to social reinforcement. Implications for the programming of institutions for the retarded are discussed. (16 ref.)
Zigler, Edward & Balla, David. (Yale U.) Developmental Psychology, 1972(Jan), Vol. 6(1), 66-73. [PA, Vol 48:01533]

1329.   Developmental and experiential determinants of self-image disparity in institutionalized and noninstitutionalized retarded and normal children.
Gave 118 institutionalized and noninstitutionalized retarded, younger normal, and older normal boys 2 forms of instruments designed to measure real self-image, ideal self-image, and self-image disparity. The older normals had greater disparity, lower real, and higher ideal self-image scores than the younger normals. On the instrument permitting the greatest response differentiation, disparity was greatest and the number of extreme responses declined with increasing development. The retarded had smaller disparity and lower ideal images than the normals. Institutionalized Ss had greater disparity as well as lower real and ideal images than noninstitutionalized Ss. Findings indicate that an understanding of the self-concept requires a consideration of both cognitive-developmental and experiential factors. (24 ref.)
Zigler, Edward; Balla, David & Watson, Neill. (Yale U.) Journal of Personality & Social Psychology, 1972(Jul), Vol. 23(1), 81-87. [PA, Vol 48:12057]

1330.   TV and social learning in the institutionalized MR.
Discusses the importance of television as a medium of social learning. Pertinent research on observational learning is presented and it is suggested that observer variables that are characteristic of retarded children, heightened susceptibility to social reinforcement, high dependency and low self-esteem, create a situation in which these children are highly likely to observationally learn social behavior from television. (40 ref.)
Baran, Stanley J. (U. Massachusetts) Mental Retardation, 1973(Jun), Vol. 11(3), 36-38. [PA, Vol 51:01372]

1331.   Effects of differential reinforcement procedures on discrimination learning by institutionalized mentally retarded children.
Administered a 2-choice discrimination task under 1 of 6 conditions of reward (response-contingent consumable, response-contingent nonconsumable, token-consumable, token-nonconsumable, token, social) to 60 institutionalized mentally retarded children (mean CA = 141 mo, mean MA = 73.5 mo). Results indicate that response-contingent nonconsumable rewards were no more distracting than response-contingent consumable rewards nor was the presentation of material rewards by the token-reinforcement procedure less distracting than the response-contingent reinforcement procedure. Further, social reinforcement was less effective than response-contingent nonconsumable rewards; however, no differences were found between social reinforcement and the other material rewards regardless of reinforcement procedure.

Blair, John R. & Fox, Bruce R. (Eastern Michigan U.) Psychological Reports, 1973(Oct), Vol. 33(2), 447-450. [PA, Vol 51:09435]

1332. The relationship of cognitive and motor response inhibition to age and IQ.
Investigated the relationship of age and IQ to response inhibition in children in 2 experiments. 2 tasks were employed: a "walk slowly" task designed to measure motor inhibition and a simple matching task designed to measure cognitive inhibition. In Exp I, Ss were 20 "normal" 4-7 yr olds. Response inhibition was found to increase with age. In Exp II, Ss were 24 8-12 yr old and 24 13-17 yr old institutionalized retardates. One-half of the Ss in each age group had IQs between 40 and 55 and half had IQs between 56 and 70. Motor response inhibition varied as a function of IQ but not age.
Costantini, Arthur F. & Hoving, Kenneth L. (U. Connecticut) Journal of Genetic Psychology, 1973(Dec), Vol. 123(2), 309-319. [PA, Vol 52:03355]

1333. "Superstition": The effects of independent and contingent events on free operant responses in retarded children.
Describes 3 experiments with institutionalized, developmentally retarded 143-228 mo old females ($N = 6$). In a free-field situation, following free-operant baselines on stereotyped movements (hand-wringing and head-rolling), the response-independent delivery of food was scheduled. The effects of response-independent schedules were studied following VI, fixed-ratio (FR), and extinction baselines for stereotyped (body-rocking) and manipulanda (ball and leg) responding. Results show that a reinforcer delivered independently of behavior accelerated baseline response rates for dominant free-operant behavior and decelerated response rates following VI and FR schedules. Results also show that a stimulus may acquire multiple functions with respect to a reinforcing event. (29 ref.)
Hollis, John H. (Kansas State U., Coll. of Education) American Journal of Mental Deficiency, 1973(Mar), Vol. 77(5), 585-596. [PA, Vol 51:07443]

1334. Syntactic indices of language use of mentally retarded and normal children.
Compared the language usage on responses to TAT cards of 3 groups of 11 yr olds: 10 institutionalized retardates, 10 noninstitutionalized retardates, and 30 normals. The distribution of Ss' words into common, uncommon, and part-of-speech categories was analyzed, as well as the complexity and diversity of sentences, verb phrases, and noun phrases. Retarded Ss did not differ from normals in the use of common and uncommon words, nor in part-of-speech categories. Also, their verb and noun phrases were in many respects comparable to those used by normals. The clearest differences were found in the measures of sentence complexity and diversity: scores were lowest for the institutionalized retardates, intermediate for the noninstitutionalized retardates, and highest for the normals. Additional comparisons of the patterns of scores with those received by younger children showed that the institutionalized retardates were most comparable to normal 5 yr olds, particularly in their sentence usage, whereas the noninstitutionalized retardates were most comparable to normals of the same CA. (15 ref.)
Lozar, Barbara; Wepman, Joseph M. & Hass, Wilbur. (U. Chicago, Early Education Research Center) Language & Speech, 1973(Jan), Vol. 16(1), 22-33. [PA, Vol 51:03484]

1335. A note on perceived self-acceptance of institutionalized mentally retarded (IMR) children.
Administered 3 measures of social interaction with, or acceptance by, a "normal" person to 30 institutionalized mentally retarded 12-14 yr olds. The measures were a questionnaire, a projective cutout referent method, and a direct physical measure of interaction distances. Ss were further divided into 3 groups based on degree of retardation (i.e., mild, moderate, and severe range). Post hoc pairwise comparisons indicate group and sex effects. Results are discussed in relation to previous research.

Mallenby, Terry W. (U. Manitoba, Winnipeg, Canada) Journal of Genetic Psychology, 1973(Sep), Vol. 123(1), 171-172. [PA, Vol 51:07454]

1336. Field dependence and outer-directedness in the problem solving of retardates and normal children.
Studied outer-directedness (as measured by reliance on an external cue in a problem-solving task) in relation to field dependence (measured by the Embedded Figures Test) and mental age (measured by the Slosson Intelligence Test). In Exp I, institutionalized retardates (mean chronological ages = 22–23 yrs) from high and low MA groups (mean MAs = 8.7 and 6.4 yrs, respectively), field dependents (FD) but not field independents (FI), were differentially affected by the presence or absence of an external cue. FD Ss were more outer-directed than FI Ss, but low-MA Ss were not more outer-directed than high-MA Ss. In Exp II, the relationship between outer-directedness and field dependence was replicated in a nonretarded, noninstitutionalized group of 48 black 1st graders. It is suggested that FD Ss have more difficulty than FI Ss in giving up reliance on a formerly relevant cue.
Massari, David J. & Mansfield, Richard S. (Temple U.) Child Development, 1973(Jun), Vol. 44(2), 346-350. [PA, Vol 52:12731]

1337. The use of the Columbia Mental Maturity Scale with institutionalized mentally retarded children.
Evaluated (a) the Columbia Mental Maturity Scale (CMMS) relative to its correlation with the Stanford-Binet (S-B), WISC, Peabody Picture Vocabulary Test (PPVT), and (b) the test-retest reliability of the CMMS in a group of institutionalized mentally retarded children. 82 male and 71 female residents of a training facility for the mentally retarded were administered the 5 instruments over a 9-mo period, including the CMMS twice. Results show reliability coefficients from .93 for the younger group to approximately .87 for the older group for the CMMS. Validity coefficents ranged from .44 for the WISC to .52 for the S-B when they were correlated with the initial administration of the CMMS.
Riviere, Michael S. (Southern Illinois U., Carbondale) Educational & Psychological Measurement, 1973(Win), Vol. 33(4), 993-995. [PA, Vol 52:03389]

1338. Comparison of retarded and non-retarded adolescents on need-approval.
Compared age and sex matched groups of normal, institutionalized and noninstitutionalized mentally retarded adolescents ($n = 50$ in each group) on need-approval as measured by the Marlowe-Crowne Social Desirability scale. All groups appeared significantly different from one another with the strength of need-approval following a noninstitutionalized, institutionalized, and normal order from high to low, respectively. Because previous data would predict a greater need for approval in retarded than normal Ss, the higher scores of noninstitutionalized Ss appeared somewhat inconsistent. A competitive community interpretation is presented and discussed.
Talkington, Larry W. & Riley, Jim. (Fairview Hosp. & Training Center, Ore.) Psychological Reports, 1973(Aug), Vol. 33(1), 39-42. [PA, Vol 51:07475]

1339. Biorhythms and activity level of institutionalized mentally retarded persons diagnosed hyperactive.
Placed 5 profoundly retarded children (2 male and 3 female) in single sex groups of 2, 3, and 4 in a room containing a tubular steel play apparatus designed to elicit play behavior in young children. The free play activity was monitored via a heart rate telemetry system. Data were continuously recorded during play sessions lasting up to 2 hrs. The data were analyzed (a) to ascertain whether average activity level was susceptible to manipulation by variation of selected parameters (group size and sex), and (b) to test for the existence of periodic components (biorhythms) in the Ss' free play. There were no significant differences due to sex or to playgroup size. Power spectra of the play sessions produced a variety of biorhythms with no clear bandwidths indicated. A white noise test supported the hypothe-

sis that frequencies faster than 15 min/cycle were noise. Frequencies slower than 15 min/cycle indicated no clear periodic components with respect to levels of group size or sex. The spectra indicated a great deal of random (noise) behavior. Results are discussed with respect to current diagnosis of hyperactivity. (23 ref)

Wade, Michael G. (U. Illinois, Children's Research Center) American Journal of Mental Deficiency, 1973(Nov), Vol. 78(3), 262-267. [PA, Vol 52:03398]

1340. A search for aspartylglycosaminuria in Poland.
Conducted a survey of 1,792 institutionalized, low-grade mentally retarded children using 2-dimensional paper chromatography for amino acids. No cases of aspartylglycosaminuria were found, but there were 56 cases of phenylketonuria.

Galewicz, Alicja; Gorska, Danuta; Rodo, Maria & Zaremba, J. (Psychoneurological Inst, Warsaw, Poland) Journal of Mental Deficiency Research, 1974(Jun), Vol 18(2), 135-137. [PA, Vol 54:01414]

1341. Complex interactions of an auditory ability and aspiration in predicting specific reading deficits.
Demonstrated the curvilinear interaction of an auditory ability factor and level of aspiration- a personality variable-in the prediction of performance on 9 Spache Diagnostic Reading Scales. Of 49 11-26 yr old institutionalized mentally retarded Ss tested, those scoring high in auditory ability performed best on the reading criteria under the condition of "realistic" aspiration and performed poorest when aspiration scores indicated larger positive and negative discrepancy scores. Low auditory-ability Ss performed better under the conditions of positive discrepancy (aspired performance exceeding attained performance). This form of interaction was observed repeatedly in 8 of the 9 reading diagnostic areas. An interpretation of the interaction effects and a discussion of the findings are included. (20 ref)

Gickling, Edward E. & Joiner, Lee M. (U Tennessee) American Journal of Mental Deficiency, 1974(Sep), Vol 79(2), 162-168. [PA, Vol 53:03435]

1342. Temporal variables in simple reaction times of mentally retarded boys.
The effects of specific temporal factors in simple reaction time (RT) trials-foreperiod lengths of the target trial and of the trial preceding, and intertrial interval-were investigated in 12 nonretarded and 12 institutionalized retarded 14-20 yr old males. For both groups it was found that (a) RTs were shortest when the preliminary interval was equal to or greater than the prior preliminary interval, (b) RTs were impaired when the preliminary interval was less than the prior preliminary interval, and (c) the degree of impairment was directly referable to the differences between the 2 foreperiod values. All effects were significantly greater for the retarded than for the nonretarded Ss. Increasing the intertrial interval had little effect on the nonretarded Ss but tended to accentuate the obtained effects in the retarded Ss. Findings are interpreted as directly opposed to a stimulus-trace deficit theory but consistent with an expectancy model, with greater rigidity characterizing the retarded Ss. (29 ref)

Gosling, Harrington & Jenness, David. (Columbia U) American Journal of Mental Deficiency, 1974(Sep), Vol 79(2), 214-224. [PA, Vol 53:03436]

1343. The assessment of effectance motivation in normal and retarded children.
Constructed several measures of effectance motivation and assessed their validity by administering them to groups of Ss whose motivation was assumed to differ. 37 normal, 32 noninstitutionalized retarded, and 34 institutionalized retarded children matched on MA were employed. For the 4 components of effectance motivation investigated—variation seeking, curiosity, mastery for the sake of competence, and preference for challenging tasks—normals demonstrated more effectance motivation than did either retarded group. The measures also proved sensitive to differences between the noninstitutionalized and institutionalized retarded. Verbal inquiry data resulted in a pattern of findings parallel to that obtained with the task

measures, providing further support for the validity of the measures. Measurement problems and the need for constructing adequate developmental indices of effectance motivation are emphasized. (18 ref)

Harter, Susan & Zigler, Edward. (Yale U.) Developmental Psychology, 1974(Mar), Vol. 10(2), 169-180. [PA, Vol 52:05690]

1344. Examination of Pressey's assimilation theory of the Poggendorff illusion.
Predictions based on A. W. Pressey's (see PA, Vol 48:75) assimilation theory of the Poggendorff illusion were tested on a new form of the illusion. Ss were 10 institutionalized retarded male 13-16 yr olds, 10 normal 9th grade males, and 18 normal 2nd grade males. Results indicate that modifications of the assimilation theory are necessary; a proposed modification is discussed. (16 ref)

Hill, A. Lewis. (New York State Inst. for Research in Mental Retardation, Staten Island) Perceptual & Motor Skills, 1974(Feb), Vol. 38(1), 27-35. [PA, Vol 52:08016]

1345. Clustering in nonretarded and retarded subjects: Some basic determinants.
Tested the possibility that the contradictory results of free-recall clustering studies of retarded and nonretarded Ss may have been caused in part by inadequate attention to the determinants of clustering in stimulus item selection. It was predicted that if list pairs consist of highly familiar members, belong to independent categories, and have well-established direct and indirect associations for both retarded and matched-MA nonretarded Ss, there will be (a) significant clustering for both groups, and (b) no significant differences in clustering between the groups. 9 object pairs meeting these conditions were selected as stimulus items. 30 institutionalized retarded Ss and 30 MA-matched elementary school nonretarded Ss were presented 18 items for 5 free-recall trials. A different random order was used on each trial. Results support the 1st prediction and partially support the 2nd. Normative data were also collected to permit an examination of the relative degrees to which the nonretarded and retarded Ss emitted associative and category responses. The validity of using clustering as a measure of what A. R. Jensen terms the cognitive-conceptual level of intelligence is discussed. (19 ref)

Palmer, Michael. (Mansfield Training School, Mansfield Depot, Conn.) American Journal of Mental Deficiency, 1974(Jan), Vol. 78(4), 454-461. [PA, Vol 52:08035]

1346. Social control by adult preference in operant conditioning with children.
Conducted 2 experiments in which 4 institutionalized female retardates (Exp I) and 4 normal 1st graders (Exp II) played a 2-choice marble dropping game while an adult E watched. When 1 of 2 colored lights was presented, 2 tokens were dispensed as soon as the S dropped a marble, and when the other light was on, 1 token was dispensed. During choice trials that were interspersed among single-color trials S was required to choose 1 of the 2 different colored holes. After S developed a preference for the 2-token color, E stated a preference for the color that earned only 1 token. 6 of the 8 Ss immediately switched to the 1-token response when E stated his preference. Only 2 Ss switched back to the 2-token response when E left the room. Ss complied with E's preference regardless of whether it also included a negative component (i.e., what E did not like). There were no systematic differences between retarded and normal Ss. (23 ref)

Redd, William H. (U. Illinois, Children's Research Center) Journal of Experimental Child Psychology, 1974(Feb), Vol. 17(1), 61-78. [PA, Vol 52:05700]

1347. Structure-of-intellect categories in Stanford-Binet performance.
Scored the Stanford-Binet Intelligence Scale protocols of 80 institutionalized retarded children using the 14 categories in J. P. Guilford's 1967 structure of intellect model. Statistically significant differences were found among the operation and product categories, but several reasons are suggested for not taking these results at face value. (15 ref)

Silverstein, Arthur B. (Neuropsychiatric Inst., Pacific State Hosp. Research Group, Pomona, Calif.) American Journal of Mental Deficiency, 1974(May), Vol. 78(6), 762-764. [PA, Vol 52:10440]

1348. Conditioning history and the imitation of reinforced and nonreinforced behaviors.
Explored the effect of conditioning history on the performance of imitative behaviors when a choice was given between a reinforced and a nonreinforced behavior or between 2 reinforced behaviors. The conditioning history consisted of exposure to a repeatedly demonstrated reinforced behavior (SDC). During subsequent choice presentations the SDC behavior was paired with a reinforced (SDA) or nonreinforced (Sd) alternative behavior. A multiple baseline design was utilized to control for the effect of the length of conditioning history. 6 institutionalized retarded children served as Ss. The 2 Ss with no conditioning history imitated the Sd behaviors as often as the SDA behaviors and consistently more often than the SDC behaviors. In contrast, 3 of the 4 Ss who had the conditioning history imitated the SDC behaviors more often than both other behaviors and eventually stopped imitating the Sd behavior. The 4th S with a conditioning history did not show this response pattern, but showed a preference for imitating the last of 2 modeled behaviors. No systematic differences in imitative performance were observed between the 2 pairs of Ss with a conditioning history as a function of the length of conditioning history. Results suggest that the conditioning history may be largely responsible for the differential imitative performance of reinforced and nonreinforced behaviors. (17 ref)
Smeets, Paul M.; Striefel, Sebastian & Gast, David L. (U. Leiden, Netherlands) Journal of General Psychology, 1974(Apr), Vol. 90(2), 257-270. [PA, Vol 52:08045]

1349. Reliability and reactivity of the videotape technique on a ward for retarded children.
In 2 experiments 4 trained college student observers rated several dimensions of ward aide-resident interaction, using the Interaction Recording System to score behaviors filmed by a remotely controlled videotape camera. Ratings proved to be both reliable and reactive. Agreement among the videotape ratings averaged 82%. Average cross-modal agreement was 79%. Aides were found to systematically interact in a more socially desirable mannner when the camera was present. Cautions and suggestions for future use of the videotaping technique are discussed.
Spencer, Frank W. et al. (U Connecticut) Journal of Community Psychology, 1974(Jan), Vol 2(1), 71-74. [PA, Vol 56:10446]

1350. Effects of external emphasis and redundancy level on the paired-associate learning of retarded adolescents and nonretarded children.
Presented 96 institutionalized adolescents and nonretarded 3rd- and 4th-grade children with sets of paired associates which differed in redundancy level and external emphasis. Redundancy level (33 and 50%) was embedded in a list of paired associates by varying the number of repetitions in the response terms. The redundancy was variously emphasized by being ungrouped, grouped spatially, or grouped perceptually. Presentation was simultaneous, and during testing all stimulus terms were presented simultaneously for the free-ordered recall of the response terms. For both groups performance was better with the 50% redundancy lists. External emphasis reliably improved the performance of the nonretarded children in certain conditions, but not the performance of the retarded adolescents in any condition. Institutionalized retarded adolescents did not recognize and utilize the organizational cue of redundancy as readily as did nonretarded children.
Spitz, Herman H. & Borys, Suzanne V. (Edward R. Johnstone Training & Research Center, Bordentown, N.J.) American Journal of Mental Deficiency, 1974(May), Vol. 78(6), 734-739. [PA, Vol 52:08046]

1351. Imitation of live and videotaped models.
Compared the imitative performance of retarded children when the behaviors were presented by live vs videotaped models. Ss

were 3 male and 3 female institutionalized adolescents with a mean age of 12.10 yrs and a mean IQ of 58.5. Ss were given an opportunity to respond after each behavior was modeled; each S was exposed to a variety of behaviors and to all experimental conditions. Models of different ages were used. Results show that the videotaped models exerted a great deal of control over the imitative behavior of 50% of the Ss. Such a degree of control by videotape models whose behavior was sterile and unreal suggests that, especially when behaviors were not reinforced, videotape models could be used for the economic training of populations deficient in basic social and language skills. (23 ref)
Striefel, Sebastian & Eberl, Dieter. (U Kansas) Education & Training of the Mentally Retarded, 1974(Apr), Vol 9(2), 83-88. [PA, Vol 53:09909]

1352. Paired-associate learning of EMR adolescents and nonretarded children as a function of methods of presentation and training.
32 nonretarded children and 64 noninstitutionalized and institutionalized retarded adolescents of equal mental age (7.9 yrs) learned an 8-pair list of pictures of common objects by the method of anticipation or the study-test method with or without training on each method. Overall, the study-test method was superior to the anticipation method for the 3 groups, and the hierarchy of efficient performance was nonretarded children, noninstitutionalized, and then institutionalized retarded adolescents. Preceiling analyses indicated that training was influential, but only with the institutionalized group. Differences in performance between methods are discussed in terms of relative confusability of the methods; differences among groups are attributed to the influence of training prior to ceiling performance and to differential verbal experiences prior to testing. (21 ref)
Winters, John J.; Attlee, Leonard C. & Harvey, Frank. (Edward R. Johnstone Training & Research Ctr, Bordentown, NJ) American Journal of Mental Deficiency, 1974(Jul), Vol 79(1), 70-76. [PA, Vol 53:01503]

1353. Galvanic skin response orienting response as a measure of tactile discrimination in retarded children.
The galvanic skin response orienting reflex has been successfully applied to the measurement of normal and disordered tactile sensation and perception in nursery-school children, college students, and brain-injured adults. Because the technique eliminates practially all of the cognitive requirements of conventional measurement procedures, it provides a potential approach for measuring somato-perceptual abilities in the younger, language deficient, and more severely retarded child. In the present study the feasibility of the technique was evaluated by applying it to the discrimination of touches to the soles of the feet of 10 institutionalized retarded children and 10 nonretarded children; mean chronological age of all Ss was approximately 9 yrs. In this simple discrimination, retarded Ss performed as well as the nonretarded Ss. (20 ref)
Ball, Thomas S.; Barber, Joseph & Kohler, Hugh. (Neuropsychiatric Inst-Pacific State Hosp Research Group, Pomona, CA) American Journal of Mental Deficiency, 1975(Mar), Vol 79(5), 559-564. [PA, Vol 54:03410]

1354. Recognition memory: Retention interval and information load.
Conducted 2 experiments with a total of 26 institutionalized 14- and 15-yr-old retardates to study the effect of retention interval and information load on short-term recognition memory. The task consisted of an input trial of 1-15 pictures followed by a test trial of 1 picture, with the S having to press different levers to indicate whether the probe picture had been present on the input trial. Retention intervals between input trial and test trial were manipulated over a range of 1-24 sec. Both accuracy and latency of response were measured. Results show that latency increased and accuracy decreased as a function of both retention interval and number of stimuli. In addition, number of stimuli interacted with retention interval such that accuracy was not affected by retention interval when information input was small but decreased quite dramatically at longer retention intervals when

input was larger. Results are discussed in terms of current memory-search models for both normal and retarded Ss. (22 ref) *Glidden, Laraine M. & Scott, Keith G.* (Teachers Coll, Columbia U) Journal of Experimental Child Psychology, 1975(Feb), Vol 19(1), 195-208. [PA, Vol 54:03424]

1355. The Peniston Adaptive Behavior Developmental Inventory for mentally retarded children and adults.
Describes the development and preliminary standardization of the Peniston Adaptive Behavior Developmental Inventory (PABDI) which measures the social competency and adaptive functioning level of institutionalized mental retardates. The PABDI profiles an individual's achievement in 9 areas: eating, dressing, grooming, body awareness, fine motor, gross motor, social, academic, and language. For standardization, the PABDI was administered to 807 5-46 yr old residents of a training center for the mentally retarded and to 36 students in a day school for the retarded. 113 children and 100 adults randomly chosen from the original sample were retested 5 mo later. Linear correlation coefficients derived from the 2 testings indicate that the PABDI is a reliable measure. The inventory is suggested to be a useful tool for developing treatment or behavior modification plans and for use as a structured interviewing device to identify problems in the behavioral repertoire of the retarded person.
Peniston, Eugene. (Southside Virginia Training Ctr, Petersburg) Research & the Retarded, 1975(Sum), Vol 2(3), 29-31. [PA, Vol 58:02567]

1356. A test battery approach to the audiological screening of mentally retarded children.
Conducted an audiological screening of 47 institutionalized moderately to severely retarded children, most of whom were multiply handicapped. Ss were aged 6–19 yrs, their individual intelligence test scores ranged between standard deviations of −3.00 and −5.00, and their communication skills were generally absent or poorly developed. 36 Ss were undergoing some form of drug therapy. A test battery was used to obtain audiological responses in a sound-proofed acoustic decoupled room. Reliable results over the entire test battery were provided by 9 Ss, and useful information was obtained concerning the remaining 38 Ss. Play audiometry proved to be the least effective of the test battery procedures, for the Ss generally exhibited some reduction in sensitivity to sound stimuli with its use, and 12 Ss were unable to meet the conditioning criterion. Maximum static compliance and middle ear pressure measurements indicated the existence of active middle ear pathologies in at least one-third of Ss. Among 10 Ss who evidenced absent stapedius reflexes without evidencing middle ear infection, there was a tendency ($p < .10$) toward involvement in drug therapy. Free-field audiometry tests proved to be effective with all but 3 Ss.
Smyth, Veronica. (U Queensland, Brisbane, Australia) Exceptional Child, 1975(Nov), Vol 22(3), 173–185. [PA, Vol 59:10192]

1357. The effects on induced passive rehearsal and the von Restorff phenomenon on the free recall of normals and retardates.
36 noninstitutionalized retardates (mean CA, 11.9 yrs) and 36 normal children (mean CA, 8.03 yrs) of equal MA (approximately 8 yrs) listened to 11 orders of 20 nouns with no instructions to overtly or covertly rehearse. All Ss were tested in each of 3 list conditions: (a) when all words were at the same decibel (dB) level, (b) when the 11th item was at a higher dB level, and (c) when the items were repeated at the same dB level using the rehearsal protocol of D. Rundus (1971). The normals' overall recall was superior to that of the retardates' recall. Repetition of items had no effect on the performance of either group except in the recency portion of the learning curve and on the initial trial for both groups and the 5th trial for the retarded group. The normal group was more susceptible to the von Restorff effect than was the retarded. Results are discussed in terms of the changing and different recall strategies of the 2 groups. (33 ref)
Winters, John J. & Ward, Thomas B. (E. R. Johnstone Training & Research Ctr, Bordentown, NJ) Memory & Cognition, 1975(Jul), Vol 3(4), 421-426. [PA, Vol 55:02519]

1358. Adult's presence: Effects of an adult as the site and the mediator of reinforcement.
Investigated 2 variables that may control institutionalized, retarded children's behavior under a schedule of contingent reinforcement for a simple motor response. Ss were 40 retardates (mean CA, 17.07 yrs; mean IQ, 51.35). The distance between the adult and the site at which reinforcers were administered (locus of reinforcement) and the extent to which the adult mediated the dispensement of reinforcers (mediation of reinforcement) were varied. A Setting main effect and a Setting $\times$ Time interaction were observed.
Boyce, Kathleen & Clinton, Leroy. (U Illinois) Perceptual & Motor Skills, 1976(Aug), Vol 43(1), 167-172. [PA, Vol 57:06094]

1359. Establishing stimulus equivalences among retarded adolescents.
In 4 experiments with a total of 6 11-15 yr old institutionalized Ss, 2 separate sets of stimuli were established as stimulus classes in a match-to-sample task by using each stimulus as both a sample and choice stimulus for every other member within that set. After classes were established, Ss were taught to select 1 member of each class when an associated auditory stimulus was presented. After this training, 3 of 6 Ss were able to select the remaining members of each stimulus class in response to the appropriate auditory stimuli without direct training. The other 3 Ss also demonstrated transfer after additional members of each stimulus class were brought under the control of the auditory stimuli through direct training. (17 ref)
Dixon, Michael & Spradlin, Joseph. (U Kansas, Bureau of Child Research) Journal of Experimental Child Psychology, 1976(Feb), Vol 21(1), 144-164. [PA, Vol 56:00876]

1360. Aging and IQ change in institutionalized mentally retarded.
Investigated Verbal, Performance, and Full Scale WISC or WAIS IQ change in an institutionalized mentally retarded population. 402 Ss who had received 2 routine administrations of either test and who ranged in age from 11 to 44 yrs were divided into 6 groups (2 WISC and 4 WAIS), and changes in scores were studied. Contrary to the view suggested by previous research, Full Scale IQ did not decrease with age. There were, in fact, slight increments, larger and more consistent in Performance than Verbal IQ. This differential change is discussed in terms of the J. L. Horn-R. B. Cattell (1966) theory of "fluid" and "crystallized" intelligence. (34 ref)
Goodman, Joan F. (U Pennsylvania) Psychological Reports, 1976(Dec), Vol 39(3, Pt 1), 999-1006. [PA, Vol 58:01394]

1361. Relationship among the self-direction, responsibility, and socialization domains of the Adaptive Behavior Scale.
Investigated the relationship among the Socialization, Self-Direction, and Responsibility domains of the Revised Adaptive Behavior Scale. Based upon the scores of 338 mentally retarded institutionalized male and female children and adults, high positive and significant correlations were obtained among these 3 domains. The relationship is explained in terms of a possible motivational link among the 3 domains.
Leva, Richard A. (State University Coll New York, Fredonia) American Journal of Mental Deficiency, 1976(Nov), Vol 81(3), 297-298. [PA, Vol 58:03588]

1362. Factors relevant to the rhythmic perception of a group of mentally retarded children.
Administered a rhythmic perception test individually to 32 male and 22 female institutionalized mentally retarded children (mean CA 16 yrs, mean IQ 46). The test, devised by the author, consisted of 20 pairs of various rhythmic examples, each example being one measure in length with a time signature of 4/4. The increase in the square of the multiple correlation coefficient was used to determine the relationships between the rhythmic perception scores and the 5 independent variables of CA, IQ, social age, social quotient, and sex. Results show that of these variables, IQ, chronological age, and sex—in descending order of importance—were the 3 most influential in determining rhythmic perception scores, each increasing the square of the multiple

correlation coefficient above a 1% increase and together accounting for 15.64% of the total explained percentage variation in measured rhythmic perception.
Lienhard, Marta E. (Loyola U in New Orleans, Coll of Music) Journal of Music Therapy, 1976(Sum), Vol 13(2), 58–65. [PA, Vol 60:03318]

1363. Influence of multiple models on the behavior of institutionalized retarded children: Increased generalization to other models and other behaviors.
After being pretested to determine base levels of imitation, 32 9-14 yr old retarded children were reinforced for imitating a model in 9 training sessions. Ss in a single model condition were reinforced by the same model across all sessions, whereas Ss in a multiple model condition were reinforced by 3 different models (3 sessions per model). A posttest to assess levels of imitation was then conducted by a model with whom the Ss had not had contact and who demonstrated a new set of behaviors. Results during training sessions show that (a) Ss learned to imitate, and this learning was not inhibited by multiple models; and (b) Ss generalized and imitated nonreinforced behaviors, and this response generalization was facilitated by multiple models. Most importantly, pre-posttest comparisons indicated that generalized use of the new response class (imitation) with new models was 8 times greater for Ss trained with multiple as opposed to single models. Implications for the maintenance and generalized effectiveness of social intervention programs are discussed.
Marburg, Carol C.; Houston, B. Kent & Holmes, David S. (U Texas, Austin) Journal of Consulting & Clinical Psychology, 1976(Aug), vol 44(4), 514-519. [PA, Vol 56:10331]

1364. Rehearsal capacity and dimensional independence in retardates.
Retardate use of retention strategies and the independence of color and form retention were compared with predictions of the attention-retention theory of retardate discrimination learning. 16 institutionalized Ss were selected for study, 10 in the high-MA range (MA 10.8 yrs, CA 15.4 yrs) and 8 in the low-MA range (MA 6.2 yrs, CA 13.7 yrs). Lists of 2-choice discrimination problems were increased in length from 1 to capacity, which was defined through criterion retention across a 20-sec interval. It was demonstrated that (a) capacity and rate of adjustment of retentional strategy were directly related to intelligence, (b) at capacity limits the retention of problems in 1 dimension interfered with retention in a 2nd dimension, and (c) results consistent with a capacity allocation strategy were obtained. Results reflect short-term memory capacity constraints on the use of rehearsal. (19 ref)
McBane, Bonnie M. (U Wisconsin, Madison) Journal of Experimental Child Psychology, 1976(Oct), Vol 22(2), 216-228. [PA, Vol 57:06113]

1365. Dimensions of adaptive behavior in institutionalized mentally retarded children and adults: Developmental perspective.
Factor analyses were performed utilizing the subscale scores of the American Association on Mental Deficiency Adaptive Behavior Scale, Part One, for 3,354 institutionalized mentally retarded children and adults. Eight different age groups (4-69 yrs) were studied to determine (a) the underlying dimensions of adaptive behavior measured by the scale, (b) similarity of factor structure across ages, (c) whether there were developmental changes revealed by factor scores, and (d) the extent to which the findings are related to level of retardation. Three salient factorial dimensions—Personal Self-Sufficiency, Community Self-Sufficiency, and Personal-Social Responsibility—appeared across the wide span of age ranges. The implication of these factors is discussed in terms of the critical period of development, rate of growth, and maximum level of growth of Ss grouped by level of retardation. (17 ref)
Nihira, Kazuo. (U California, Los Angeles) American Journal of Mental Deficiency, 1976(Nov), Vol 81(3), 215-226. [PA, Vol 58:03595]

1366. Spontaneous fluctuation in rate of body rocking: A methodological note.
Presents descriptive data on the natural occurrence of stereotyped body rocking in 3 institutionalized, mentally retarded children, ages 10 and 12 yrs. Both ward and test situation observations suggest that there is spontaneous fluctuation in rate of body rocking. These findings raise a serious methodological problem pertinent to the evaluation of experimental data on stereotyped behavior; rate change attributed to experimental manipulation may in fact be an instance of spontaneous fluctuation.
Pohl, P. (Max-Planck Inst fü-5r Psychiatrie Munich, W Germany) Journal of Mental Deficiency Research, 1976(Mar), Vol 20(1), 61–65. [PA, Vol 56:02516]

1367. Effects of a memory aid on three types of conservation in institutionalized retarded children.
Assessed qualitative identity, quantitative identity, and equivalence conservation in 60 retarded children in 3 groups (MAs 5.4, 6.3, and 7.5, as measured by the Peabody Picture Vocabulary Test). Half of the Ss were provided a memory aid while the other half were not. The memory aid did not facilitate conservation on any of the tasks. The order of task difficulty found was qualitative identity, quantitative identity, and equivalence conservation. These data are discussed in terms of memory deficits and factors contributing to conservation and MA.
Roodin, Paul A.; Sullivan, Laraine & Rybash, John M. (State University Coll New York, Oswego) Journal of Genetic Psychology, 1976(Dec), Vol 129(2), 253-259. [PA, Vol 58:03600]

1368. Responses to frustration: Comparison of institutionalized and noninstitutionalized retarded adolescents and nonretarded children and adolescents.
30 adolescents (10 institutionalized retarded, 10 noninstitutionalized retarded, 10 nonretarded CA-matched) and 10 children (nonretarded MA-matched) were individually given the Rosenzweig Picture-Frustration Study (Children's Form); MA was determined by scores on the Peabody Picture Vocabulary Test. Responses were scored for direction of blame and reaction type, yielding 9 frustration response categories. Three of the 9 response categories showed significant group relationships. Retardation, institutionalization, and CA all had an effect on responding, although analysis of response profiles showed all groups to be very similar in response pattern.
TeBeest, Dennis L. & Dickie, Jane R. (Hope Coll) American Journal of Mental Deficiency, 1976(Jan), Vol 80(4), 407-413. [PA, Vol 56:00896]

1369. An assessment of hypothesis testing in mentally retarded adolescents.
Tested 31 educable and 21 trainable institutionalized retarded adolescents (mean CA, 17.02 and 16.67 yrs; mean MA, 10.34 and 7.29 yrs, respectively) on a discrimination learning problem with a modified blank trials procedure to measure their hierarchy of hypotheses. Results indicate that the hierarchy and size of initial hypothesis sets varied as a function of degree of retardation. Trainable retarded Ss had fewer hypotheses, and initially chose position hypotheses predominantly. Under discriminant reinforcement, most of these were readily switched to stimulus dimension hypotheses, which they retained during additional nondiscriminant (100%) reinforcement trials. Educable retarded Ss predominantly chose stimulus dimension hypotheses initially, and most of these switched to position hypotheses during either discriminant or non-discriminant reinforcement trials. Results indicate an IQ effect on the determination of the hypothesis that is originally tested.
Whittemore, C. L. & Spitz, H. H. (Columbia U) Journal of Mental Deficiency Research, 1976(Dec), Vol 20(4), 243-250. [PA, Vol 58:05643]

1370. Attitudes and life commitments of older siblings of mentally retarded adults: An exploratory study.
Administered a questionnaire to 90 25–66 yr old individuals who were siblings of 72 institutionalized mentally retarded adults to investigate their life commitments in career, marriage, and

family, and their recollections of family life in childhood and adolescence. Results show that the majority of Ss felt their adult life commitments were not affected by having a mentally retarded sibling. Results suggest 2 areas of significance for the clinician in a counseling relationship with the family of a mentally retarded child; (a) Most families have adequate personal resources to cope with the problems of having a retarded child, and were able to provide a proper developmental environment for their normal children. (b) The siblings' sex roles are important in their adjustment to having a retarded brother or sister. (15 ref)

Cleveland, Douglas W. & Miller, Nancy. (Regional Ctr of Orange County, Client Services Div, Orange, CA) Mental Retardation, 1977(Jun), Vol 15(3), 38–41. [PA, Vol 59:08104]

1371.   Array properties and conservation of number performance with retarded adolescents and young adults.
Investigated the effects of array transformations, contradictions, and size on same–different judgments in a conservation task. 31 institutionalized retarded adolescents responded to 18 conservation of number tasks. Results show that, within the range of each row containing 4–6 items, there was no significant effect on performance with variations in the total number of items or the numerical difference between rows. Unexpectedly, pre- and posttransformed arrays did not cause significant differences in judgment errors. When significant differences did appear between transformed and untransformed arrays, it seemed to be due to a 1-to-1 correspondence existing in one of the arrays and not to the effect of a transformation. The optimal performance under 1-to-1 correspondence conditions and the observed orderly decrease in correct responding is explained as a function of the number of contradictions in the stimulus array. The explanation of judgment errors being caused by contradictions between numerosity and length and/or density cues was interpreted within C. T. Brainerd's (1973) theory of the development of early number concepts. (24 ref)

Gaylord-Ross, Robert J. (Yeshiva U) American Journal of Mental Deficiency, 1977(Sep), Vol 82(2), 170–177. [PA, Vol 60:05459]

1372.   Being imitated by an adult and the subsequent imitative behavior of retarded children.
Assigned 57 institutionalized retarded 7–20 yr olds (IQs 25–65, MAs 2–12 yrs) to 1 of 3 experimental conditions during a simple 3-choice task in which the Ss and the experimenter (E) took turns feeding colored plastic "cookies" to a "Cookie Monster." In the imitation condition, the E imitated the S's choice, and in the nonimitation condition, the E avoided imitating the S. Following imitation or nonimitation, the S was given opportunities to imitate the E. In the modeling only condition, the S's choice always followed the E's so that the S always had the opportunity to imitate. ANOVA revealed a significant difference among the 3 conditions in the Ss' tendency to imitate the E. Paired comparisons between conditions showed that Ss in the imitation condition imitated significantly more than Ss in either the nonimitation or modeling only condition. The nonimitation and modeling only conditions did not differ significantly. (19 ref)

Hallahan, Daniel P. et al. (U Virginia School of Education) American Journal of Mental Deficiency, 1977(May), Vol 81(6), 556–560. [PA, Vol 59:05898]

1373.   The performance of cultural-familial retardates on conservation tasks.
Data from 29 institutionalized cultural-familial mental retardates given Piagetian tasks of conservation show a lack of significant differences between younger (13–15 yrs) and older (16–19 yrs) Ss. Consistencies between Piaget's results and the current data indicate that retardates' reasoning, while slower, follows the same laws as normal children's. The data indicate that retarded children are characterized by slower progressions through identical sequences of cognitive stages and more limited upper stages of cognition.

Lesser, Harvey; Degnan, Micaela O. & Markey, Noel A. (Rutgers U, Camden Coll of Arts & Sciences) Journal of Genetic Psychology, 1978(Mar), Vol 132(1), 153–154. [PA, Vol 61:13637]

1374.   A study on place of origin of institutionalized mentally deficient children.
Tested the hypothesis that there is a residential relationship between rural and urban mental deficiency. Interview schedules of 50 4–20 yr old mentally deficient children (36 males, 14 females) from a Lucknow school for retardates show that most of these children of both sexes came from urban backgrounds. Rural criteria for mental deficiency may differ from urban criteria. (8 ref)

Murari, Pushpa & Sinha, V. Psycho-Lingua, 1978(Jan), Vol 8(1), 31–33. [PA, Vol 63:12191]

1375.   Behavior rating inventory for moderately, severely, and profoundly retarded persons.
Used the authors' Behavior Rating Inventory for the Retarded to assess the reliability and validity of the behavior of a sample of 45 Caucasian 6–15 yr old institutionalized mentally retarded children (IQs 2–53). The scale measures communication, self-help, physical skills, self-control, and social behavior. Clinically and statistically acceptable levels of interrater agreement were found. With respect to validity (a) several factors loaded very highly on items consistent with the a priori labeling of subscales; (b) 2 of the factors (Cognitive and Psychomotor Development) accounted for about 75% of the explained variance in ward placement levels; and (c) individual items on the inventory correlated highly with independently derived measures of the actual behavior these items represented. The major advantages of this scale over existing ones include its validity and relative ease of administration and scoring. (32 ref)

Sparrow, Sara S. & Cicchetti, Domenic V. (Yale U Child Study Ctr) American Journal of Mental Deficiency, 1978(Jan), Vol 82(4), 365–374. [PA, Vol 61:02672]

1376.   An exploratory study of creativity in mentally retarded youth.
Investigated the creative thinking ability of 40 adolescent students in an institution for the mentally retarded. Ss were divided into 4 groups representing high and low age and IQ combinations. Ss were administered a battery that contained 4 individual tests adapted from the Torrance Tests of Creative Thinking: 2 motor tasks (Incomplete Figures and Circles) and 2 verbal tasks (Unusual Uses and Just Suppose). Findings show that higher ability levels, as indicated by IQ scores, were more consistently related to higher levels of creative performance than lower ability levels. It is suggested that replication of the present study comparing samples of both institutionalized and noninstitutionalized retarded and normal Ss may shed light on the extent and nature of creativity as it relates to ability level and environment. (20 ref)

Talkington, Larry W. & Briggs, Nancy C. (Developmental Ctr, Muskegon, MI) Education & Training of the Mentally Retarded, 1978(Feb), Vol 13(1), 55–59. [PA, Vol 61:08727]

1377.   Performance of institutional retardates on standard and new forms of the Quick Test.
121 institutionalized mentally retarded patients aged 8–59 yrs were tested on Forms 1–3 (published forms) and 4–6 (parallel forms) of the Quick Test; IQs were correlated with other IQs (WISC, WAIS, and Stanford-Binet Intelligence Scale) available from institution records. The forms of the Quick Test correlated significantly with the more traditional and time-consuming tests of intellectual performance. It is concluded that the Quick Test is an excellent tool for experimenters and educators who need an efficient and reliable estimate of intellectual development.

Zimmermann, Robert R. et al. (Central Michigan U) Perceptual & Motor Skills, 1978(Feb), Vol 46(1), 263–266. [PA, Vol 61:07636]

1378.   Factors influencing the interrogative strategies of mentally retarded and nonretarded students.
The interrogative strategies of institutionalized mentally retarded young adults (mean CA 20.34 yrs, mean IQ 62.2) and nonretarded 1st- and 4th-graders were investigated using a 20-questions type task. Ss were presented with 8- and 16-cell matrices consisting of geometric forms, and the items that were eliminated

by their questions were either covered or left uncovered. A variety of dependent measures was obtained, including information efficiency and proportion of redundant and constraint-seeking questions. In contrast to findings in previous research, the present results show that reducing array size and covering eliminated items significantly improved various aspects of children's interrogative strategies, lending support to the idea that reducing cognitive strain can enhance information-processing ability. Despite task simplification, the performance of the 4th graders exceeded that of the 1st graders on most measures, and the performance of the retarded young adults was comparable to, or poorer than, that of the 1st graders, who were of appreciably lower MA. (14 ref)
Borys, Suzanne V. (Edward R. Johnstone Training & Research Ctr, Bordentown, NJ) American Journal of Mental Deficiency, 1979(Nov), Vol 84(3), 280–288. [PA, Vol 63:05694]

1379. A differential diagnosis of organicity in mentally handicapped children.
50 institutionalized (CAs 125–222 mo) and 50 noninstitutionalized (CAs 122–216 mo) retarded children, matched on intelligence (WISC IQs, 50–70), were given the Memory-for-Designs Test (MFD) as a measure of organicity. Results indicate that the error scores of the institutionalized Ss on the MFD were significantly higher than those of the noninstitutionalized Ss. The MFD results are interpreted in terms of the current trends to institutionalize organically impaired retarded children and to accommodate familially retarded children in classes that are part of the regular school system. (11 ref)
Nesbit, Wayne C. & Hartmann, B. D. (Memorial U of Newfoundland, St John's, Canada) British Journal of Mental Subnormality, 1979(Dec), Vol 25(49, Pt 2), 75–78. [PA, Vol 65:13046]

1380. Physiological and psychiatric investigations into a group of mentally handicapped subjects with self-injurious behaviour.
Compared 17 6–50 yr old institutionalized mentally retarded Ss exhibiting self-injurious behavior (SIB; primarily head banging) with 14 9–59 yr old mentally retarded controls without SIB. Ss were rated by ward personnel using a behavior scale developed by the authors. Psychiatric assessment was conducted over an 8-wk period using the Modified Manifest Abnormality Scale for Clinical Interview. Ss' family and school records were examined and compared; physiological tests were also given. Significant differences between the 2 groups were found only for pulse rate, hours of sleep, and frequency of crying. The psychiatric rating on each S was combined to form an overall degree of severity, and the 2 groups were combined to form a median score. The SIB group had a higher proportion of scores above the median than the non-SIB Ss: 12 out of 17 Ss vs 2 out of 14 Ss, respectively. (30 ref)
Matin, M. A. & Rundle, A. T. (St Lawrence's Hosp, Caterham, England) Journal of Mental Deficiency Research, 1980(Jun), Vol 24(2), 77–85. [PA, Vol 66:08252]

1381. Surveying mentally retarded persons: Responsiveness and response validity in three samples.
In an exploration of the feasibility and utility of survey research with retarded populations, interviews were conducted with 52 institutionalized children, 58 institutionalized adults, and 57 community children, as well as with their parents or attendants. Analyses indicated that higher IQ Ss were generally more responsive to questions, more often in agreement with the nonretarded informants, and less acquiescent on yes–no questions than were lower IQ Ss. Although these relationships varied in strength from sample to sample, overall differences among samples were nonsignificant. (26 ref)
Sigelman, Carol K. et al. (Eastern Kentucky U) American Journal of Mental Deficiency, 1980(Mar), Vol 84(5), 479–486. [PA, Vol 63:10983]

1382. The involvement of parents with their intellectually handicapped children in institutions.
Studied the involvement of parents with their intellectually handicapped children living in institutions. Questionnaires were distributed, and replies were received from 10 administrators of residential institutions, 9 staff members of a selected institution, and the parents of 48 of the children living at this institution. The extent of parental involvement varied greatly among institutions and took many forms. A significant relationship was found between distance of parental home from institution and frequency of parent–child contact, but not between frequency of parent–child contact and the variables of child age or level of retardation. Most respondents believed that parental involvement was beneficial to child, parents, and staff and was therefore worthy of encouragement. (6 ref)
Ciddor, Janet S. & Finniecome, Josephine A. (Spastic Ctr, Mosman, Australia) Australian Journal of Developmental Disabilities, 1981(Mar), Vol 7(1), 33–37. [PA, Vol 66:08680]

1383. Trends in maladaptive behavior of mentally retarded persons placed in community and institutional settings.
Results from 426 retarded Ss (average age 12 yrs) demonstrate that no significant time trend was present for either the institutional or community groups, regardless of Ss' age and level of retardation. Placement, level of retardation, and age, however, were related to overall prevalence of maladaptive behavior. (20 ref)
Eyman, R. K.; Borthwick, S. A. & Miller, C. (Lanterman State Hosp, Neuropsychiatric Inst Research Group, Pomona, CA) American Journal of Mental Deficiency, 1981(Mar), Vol 85(5), 473–477. [PA, Vol 65:13039]

1384. The prevalence of peptic ulcer in an institution for the mentally retarded.
Of the 1,700 10–72 yr old residents (IQs 0–100) at risk, 91 were found to have X-ray or endoscopy evidence of peptic ulcers, a prevalence rate of 5.4%. The more severely retarded patients showed a higher ulcer prevalence than those less retarded, and males (n = 1,005) demonstrated higher rates than females. The presence of medical and neurological disabilities, including limitations of vision and communication, was positively associated with ulcer development. (13 ref)
Kim, Mira; Learman, L.; Nada, Nel & Thompson, Karen. (U California, Los Angeles) Journal of Mental Deficiency Research, 1981(Jun), Vol 25(2), 105–111. [PA, Vol 66:10424]

1385. When in doubt, say yes: Acquiescence in interviews with mentally retarded persons.
Conducted 15–20 min interviews with 3 samples of mentally retarded persons: (a) 33 institutionalized children (CA 12–16 yrs, mean IQ 42.08), (b) 36 institutionalized adults (mean IQ 39.76), and (c) 50 community resident children (CA 12–16 yrs, mean IQ 47.53). The main purposes of the study were to establish rates of acquiescence (ACQ) to questions regardless of their content and to assess the relationships between ACQ, residential setting, and IQ. Results show that ACQ was approximately 40% for both groups of institutionalized Ss and approximately 50% for the community Ss. Lower-IQ Ss tended to acquiesce more than higher-IQ Ss. 12-mo follow-up interviews were held using a different schedule with 29 of the institutionalized Ss (7 moderately and 22 severely mentally retarded). This time, however, the range of scores (20–83.3%) indicates that the extent of ACQ factual as well as subjective questions were used. Results show a 55.7% ACQ depended on the specific nature of the question. The danger of relying on yes–no questions to obtain information from this population is discussed as is the need for increased concern with the issue of response validity. (12 ref)
Sigelman, Carol K.; Budd, Edward C.; Spanhel, Cynthia L. & Schoenrock, Carol J. (Eastern Kentucky U, Richmond) Mental Retardation, 1981(Apr), Vol 19(2), 53–58. [PA, Vol 66:08270]

Mild Mental Retardation

1386. Self-concept of EMR and nonretarded adolescents.
Compared the self-concept of 42 educable mentally retarded (EMR) adolescents with 49 nonretarded adolescents attending a public high school. The Tennessee Self-Concept Scale was used

as the measurement instrument. It was hypothesized that EMR adolescents would have significantly more negative self-concepts than nonretarded Ss. Significant differences were found for the variables of self-criticism, identity, social self, family self, and moral-ethical self scales. All differences were in the hypothesized direction.
Collins, Hardin A.; Burger, Gary K. & Doherty, Daniel. (St. Louis U.) American Journal of Mental Deficiency, 1970(Nov), Vol. 75(3), 285-289. [PA, Vol 46:03594]

1387. Performance of mentally handicapped and average-IQ children on two modified cloze tasks for oral language.
Matched 22 public school educable mentally retarded (EMR) and 22 average-IQ children for MA (approximately 9.5 yr.) and reading age (approximately 8.6 yr.). Ss were administered 2 modifications of the cloze procedure that reflect 2 important processes in oral language: production and recognition. It was determined that (a) EMR Ss were significantly poorer than average-IQ Ss in cloze performance, and (b) the recognition cloze task was significantly easier than the production cloze task; no qualitative differences were found in the performance of the 2 samples. Results reflect inefficiencies in the organization and retrieval of linguistic stimuli of low-IQ children. Implications for potential language training programs utilizing cloze procedure are discussed. (15 ref.)
Goodstein, Henry A. (U. Connecticut) American Journal of Mental Deficiency, 1970(Nov), Vol. 75(3), 290-297. [PA, Vol 46:03605]

1388. Effects of learning method on learning stage in retarded and nonretarded adolescents.
Compared the learning performance of 60 educable mentally retarded and 60 intellectually-average adolescent Ss as a function of learning stage using a paired-associate learning task. 20 Ss within each group were randomly assigned to 1 of 3 methods of learning: the equal amount learned (EAL) method; the modified method of adjusted learning; and the method of adjusted learning. Analyses of variance indicate that (a) retarded Ss exhibited a deficit at each stage of learning (response learning and associative stages), and (b) the EAL method prolonged both the response learning stage and the stage of learning wherein the S consistently pairs correct stimulus and response items.
Prehm, Herbert J. & Stinnett, Raymond D. (U. Oregon) American Journal of Mental Deficiency, 1970(Nov), Vol. 75(3), 319-322. [PA, Vol 46:03635]

1389. A study of recognition and reproduction of Bender Gestalt figures by children of average and below intelligence.
Assessed differences in the recognition and reproduction abilities of 40 educable mentally retarded and 40 nonretarded children. Results support the common sense notion that children of both groups are more skillful in recognizing visually presented stimuli than in reproducing them. Retardates were affected by visual perceptual maturation in reproduction and recognition activities, with this influence more marked for the latter activity.
Allen, Robert M.; Adamo, Cynthia; Alker, Leslie N. & Levine, M. N. (U. Miami) Journal of Genetic Psychology, 1971(Sep), Vol. 119(1), 75-78. [PA, Vol 47:03528]

1390. Relationships among visual figure-ground perception, word recognition, IQ, and chronological age.
Administered the Southern California Figure-Ground Visual Perception Test and the Botel Reading Inventory to 118 7-12 yr old educable mentally handicapped children (WISC IQ 45-85). Significant differences in visual figure-ground perception were found between achievers who showed no word recognition and those who showed word recognition. Visual figure-ground perception was related to IQ and CA.
Brooks, Clarence R. & Nat Clair, Theodore. (U. Iowa) Perceptual & Motor Skills, 1971(Aug), Vol. 33(1), 39-62. [PA, Vol 47:03534]

1391. Variability in reaction times of normal and educable mentally retarded children.
The RTs of 10 normal and 10 mentally retarded students (IQ, 45-70) were tested by the Lafayette visual choice RT test. A Wilcoxon matched-pairs signed-ranks test showed significant differences between the RTs of the normals and retardates on both the simple and choice tasks. It is suggested that future research should consider other abnormalities, aside from low IQ, that accompany mental retardation.
Caffrey, Bernard; Jones, Judith D. & Hinkle, Barbara R. (Clemson U.) Perceptual & Motor Skills, 1971(Feb), Vol. 32(1), 255-258. [PA, Vol 46:03749]

1392. Associative learning ability in mentally retarded children under varied stimulus conditions.
Investigated associative learning ability in 32 educable mentally retarded children (mean CA, 127.8 mo.; mean IQ was 69.7). Ss were randomly assigned to 4 independent groups and were exposed to 4 stimulus conditions. Each S received all 4 treatments, with order of stimuli presentation fixed for each group. Results indicate that (a) there were significant differences among trials to criterion under varied stimulus conditions in the paired-associate tasks, (b) there were no significant differences between the groups as a result of the order of stimulus presentation, and (c) visual-visual wordlike stimuli required significantly more trials to criterion than the other 3 stimulus conditions.
Davis, William E. (U. Maine) American Journal of Mental Deficiency, 1971(Sep), Vol. 76(2), 197-200. [PA, Vol 47:09518]

1393. Numerosity discrimination of homogeneous and sub-grouped dot patterns by EMR adolescents and normals.
36 institutionalized educable retarded adolescents, and 2 groups of 36 nonretarded adolescents of equal MA and CA were presented patterns of 4-10 dots at .01-, .1-, and 1-sec exposure times and asked to estimate the number. Half the dot patterns were objectively subgrouped and half were ungrouped (homogeneous). It was found that both nonretarded groups performed significantly better than retarded Ss. Retarded and MA Ss were more adversely affected by increased information load and increased transmission rate. At the shortest exposure times, grouped dot patterns were more difficult than ungrouped, apparently because they subtended a larger visual angle. Differences in the channel capacity of retarded and nonretarded adolescents are discussed.
Hoats, David L. (Edward R. Johnstone Training & Research Center, Bordentown, N.J.) American Journal of Mental Deficiency, 1971(Sep), Vol. 76(2), 200-224. [PA, Vol 47:09503]

1394. Effects of temporal grouping on unimodal and multimodal sequential information processing in nonretarded and retarded subjects.
Compared 26 educable mentally retarded (EMR) adolescents with 26 equal-MA nonretarded 10 yr olds. Ss reported the number of pulses in varying length sequences which were (a) presented to the same modality, (b) alternated between 2 modalities, and (c) alternated among 3 modalities. On half of the trials intrasequence stimuli were temporally equidistant and on half they were grouped into couplets. It was found that (a) EMRs made significantly more errors, and (b) errors increased with increased modality switching rate. The main effect of temporal grouping was not significant. However, when temporal grouping was congruent with modality sequencing, the error increments previously obtained with ungrouped sequences were completely eliminated. This effect supports the hypothesis that congruence between temporal grouping and modality sequence minimizes switching interference for equal-MA nonretarded Ss and EMRs by emphasizing a counting strategy which equal-CA nonretarded Ss presumably use without temporal congruence.
Holden, Edward A. (Edward R. Johnstone Training & Research Center, Bordentown, N.J.) American Journal of Mental Deficiency, 1971(Sep), Vol. 76(2), 181-184. [PA, Vol 47:09504]

1395. Probability judgments by EMR and nonretarded children: II. A replication and extension.
Presents a replication and extension of J. S. Carlson and D. L. MacMillan's (see PA, Vol. 44:15138) study. A group of 20 nonretarded 11-yr-old Ss were cross-matched with 2 groups of 20 educable mentally retarded Ss (ages 11 and 14, respectively) on

the basis of CA and MA. A probability task was administered individually, which required Ss to predict an event outcome, justify the prediction, draw, and follow or resist a countersuggestion. This sequence was repeated on 5 trials. Results suggest that (a) retarded and nonretarded Ss did not substantially differ in the ability to predict, but younger retarded Ss were less able to verbally justify their predictions; and (b) younger retarded Ss were more susceptible to countersuggestion than were nonretarded or older retarded Ss.
MacMillan, Donald L. & Carlson, Jerry S. (U. California, Riverside) American Journal of Mental Deficiency, 1971(Jul), Vol. 76(1), 82-86. [PA, Vol 47:07427]

1396.   Effect of instructional set on perceptions of event outcomes by EMR and nonretarded children.
Matched 48 educable mentally retarded (EMR) children with 48 normal Ss on MA and CA, to determine whether their perceptions of interruption would vary as a result of instructional set. Instructions served to define interruption as success, failure, or neutral. No significant differences were found on placement of credit for completed tasks. Results are interpreted to suggest that retarded Ss perceive interruption as personal failure, whereas normal children do not. Results are discussed in terms of the high expectancy for failure characteristic of the mentally retarded.
MacMillan, Donald L. & Knopf, Eddi D. (U. California, Riverside) American Journal of Mental Deficiency, 1971(Sep), Vol. 76(2), 185-189. [PA, Vol 47:09509]

1397.   Influence of memory strategies upon the learning of new words among educable retarded children.
Attempted to determine whether E-supplied memory strategies could facilitate word recognition learning among educable retarded children. 3 groups were formed. The syntactical group received memory strategies during the word recognition task. The word formation group was given cue word training. The repetition group was instructed to repeat the words during the word recognition task. Relearning trials were administered 48 hr. after the word recognition task. While there were no significant differences in mean correct responses during acquisition, there were significant differences during relearning in favor of the syntactical group.
Martin, Clessen J. & Herndon, Mary A. (Texas A & M U., Human Learning Research Lab.) Proceedings of the 79th Annual Convention of the American Psychological Association, 1971, Vol. 6(Pt. 2), 617-618. [PA, Vol 46:05365]

1398.   Analysis of Welsh Figure Preference Test scores of educable mentally handicapped children.
Administered the Revised Art Scale (RA) of the Welsh Figure Preference Test (WEPT) to 183 intermediate-level special class educable mentally handicapped (EMH) children, to 48 normal 2nd graders, and to 47 normal 6th graders, all enrolled in public schools, to evaluate the responses of the EMH group in terms of sex, CA, MA, and IQ, and to compare these responses with scores of 2nd and 6th grade Ss. EMH children scored significantly lower than 6th graders equal to EMH Ss in mean CA, on both the RA and Don't Like (DL) Scales (p < .001 and p < .01, respectively), but were not significantly different from 2nd graders equal to EMH Ss in mean MA. A significant difference in scores of the EMH boys and girls was found on the RA Scale (p < .05) but not on the DL Scale. No significant differences between scores of the boys and ₉4r
Mitchell, Marlys M. (U. North Carolina, Chapel Hill) Training School Bulletin, 1971(Feb), Vol. 67(4), 214-219. [PA, Vol 46:07513]

1399.   Personality assessment of retarded children.
Administered the Revised Art scale (RA) of the Welsh Figure Preference Test (WFPT) to 183 intermediate-level special class educable mentally handicapped (EMH) children (mean CA was 141.3 mo. for boys and 133.6 mo. for girls), to 48 normal 2nd graders, and to 47 normal 6th graders, all enrolled in public schools, to evaluate both its relationship to teacher's ratings of classroom behavior and its appropriateness as a personality

assessment instrument for use with EMH children. RA scores were significantly different for EMH boys and EMH girls, but not for 2nd grade or 6th grade boys and girls. Sex differences among the EMH group were also noted on test-retest reliability. Analysis of behavior ratings by RA scores provided little basis for pursuing use of this test for personality assessment of EMH children, although the few obtained differences were generally in the expected direction. The number of significant relationships between "don't like" scores and behavioral ratings was seen as holding more promise for future investigations. Significant differences in scale scores and reliability coefficients between EMH boys and EMH girls are observed.
Mitchell, Marlys M. (U. North Carolina, Chapel Hill) Training School Bulletin, 1971(Nov), Vol. 68(3), 186-192. [PA, Vol 48:01712]

1400.   [A study of the reaction of a group of mothers of retarded children using the Parental Attitude Research Instrument (PARI).] (Ital)
Administered the PARI to 2 groups of 30 Ss each. One was composed of mothers of children with no serious physical deficiency but with mild mental deficiency, and the other of mothers with normal children. On some items significant differences were found between the 2 groups. Results are interpreted as signs of maternal maladjustment to extra-familial social environment or as the acceptance of maternal duties.
Pancheri, Paolo. (U. Rome, Inst. of Psychiatry, Italy) Rivista di Psichiatria, 1971(Sep), Vol. 6(5), 394-407. [PA, Vol 50:01323]

1401.   Standardization of the VISA (Vocational Interest and Sophistication Assessment) technique.
Reports the culmination of 8 yr. of data collection and analysis in the development of a reading-free test of vocational interest and sophistication for use with retardates. A sample of over 3000 mildly retarded adolescents and young adults were administered a newly designed picture-inquiry instrument to measure vocational interest and knowledge. Ss were drawn from institutions, schools, and workshops. Reliabilities and norms for both male and female forms of the test were substantially established. Data regarding validity and applicability, while more limited, were promising.
Parnicky, Joseph J.; Kahn, Harris & Burdett, Arthur B. (Ohio State U.) American Journal of Mental Deficiency, 1971(Jan), Vol. 75(4), 442-448. [PA, Vol 46:03618]

1402.   Relationship of Peabody Picture Vocabulary Test and Wechsler Intelligence Scale for Children in an educable retarded group: A cautionary note.
Studied the equivalence and relationship of Peabody Picture Vocabulary Test and WISC scores in a retarded population. 49 7-14 yr. old students in a class for the educable retarded served as Ss. The Peabody IQ consistently overestimated WISC Verbal, Performance, and full scale IQs. Intercorrelations between IQs from the 2 tests were low. A more cautious approach to use of the Peabody as a substitute measure for the WISC is suggested.
Pasewark, Richard A.; Fitzgerald, Bernard J. & Gloeckler, Ted. (U. Wyoming) Psychological Reports, 1971(Apr), Vol. 28(2), 405-406. [PA, Vol 46:07516]

1403.   Perceptual recognition and guessing behavior by normal and educable retarded children.
Studied the recognition of fragmented (or incomplete) stimulus forms by 46 normal and 46 educable-retarded children (EMRs) at 2 MA levels—8 and 5 yr. A series of 12 slides was presented, and the number of brief exposure periods required to make a correct identification was recorded. Analyses of results show that younger MA Ss needed more exposures to identify these forms. While there were no effects of IQ, the EMRs made many more incorrect guesses than did normals, and the younger EMRs guessed more than all other children.
Raskin, Larry M.; Fong, Louella J. & Black, Kathryn N. (Purdue U.) Psychonomic Science, 1971(Mar), Vol. 22(6), 371-372. [PA, Vol 47:03555]

1404. Retention and transfer of mediation set in paired-associate learning of educable retarded children.
Obtained measures of ability to learn paired associates and use mediational links on 6.2-10.6 yr old educable mentally retarded Ss in a laboratory setting. 19 experimental Ss were given long-term mediation training within the context of a special music program which emphasized the principle and utility of mediational links. 19 controls participated in a traditional primary music program. Postexperimental measures show retention and transfer of the mediation training by experimental Ss with marked improvement in their nonverbal ($p < .001$) and verbal ($p < .0005$) paired-associate performance. (18 ref.)
Ross, Dorothea. (Stanford U., Medical School, Palo Alto, Calif.) Journal of Educational Psychology, 1971(Aug), Vol. 62(4), 322-327. [PA, Vol 47:01479]

1405. Success and failure as determinants of the performance predictions of mentally retarded and nonretarded children.
Tested the hypothesis that experimentally-induced success and failure experiences would differentially affect educable mentally retarded (EMR) and nonretarded children. 24 EMR Ss were matched with 24 MA and 24 CA controls. All Ss were given 6 trials on a vocabulary task: 3 success trials (simple words) and 3 failure trials (difficult words). Ss gave a prediction-of-performance estimate for each trial. Findings indicate that success raised performance estimates and failure lowered them for all Ss. EMR Ss and their MA controls set higher estimates across trials than the older CA controls. Results are interpreted as being contrary to the stated hypothesis. (27 ref.)
Schuster, Sheila O. & Gruen, Gerald E. (U. Louisville) American Journal of Mental Deficiency, 1971(Sep), Vol. 76(2), 190-196. [PA, Vol 47:09513]

1406. Effects of stimulus complexity on visual search performance of normals and educable retardates.
32 4th and 32 10th grade nonretarded students and 32 institutionalized and 28 noninstitutionalized adolescent retardates performed a visual search task in which the figures varied in rated complexity. Visual search latency was significantly longer for the lower 3 MA groups. For all groups, figures of low-medium and medium complexity were most difficult to find.
Spitz, Herman H. & Borland, Maureen D. (Edward R. Johnstone Training & Research Center, Bordentown, N.J.) American Journal of Mental Deficiency, 1971(May), Vol. 75(6), 724-728. [PA, Vol 47:01466]

1407. Response-chain learning of mentally retarded adolescents under four conditions of reinforcement.
Presented a sequential response-chain task to 4 matched groups of 16 educable, teenage retarded Ss, each of which was exposed to a different token reinforcement condition. Analysis of variance for treatment effects indicates that a response-cost condition and a combination response-cost/reward condition resulted in more rapid acquisition than the standard reward-for-correct or a nontoken control condition. Implications of the findings are discussed as related to a failure-avoidance hypothesis. (21 ref.)
Talkington, Larry W. (Fairview Hosp. & Training Center, Salem, Ore.) American Journal of Mental Deficiency, 1971(Nov), Vol. 76(3), 337-340. [PA, Vol 48:03570]

1408. Numerosity discrimination of repetitive visual stimuli by mildly retarded adolescents and normal children.
Compared 20 male and 20 female retarded adolescents with 40 younger normals matched for sex and MA on a visual numerosity task. Sequential light flashes of 300, 500, and 700 msec. Occurring in multiple loci were presented in trains of 3-38 flashes. Error frequency and magnitude scores were significantly (p < .001) greater for the retardates and group differences increased with increasing numerosity and decreasing flash duration (p < .001). Retardates reported significantly lower flash counts (p < .001) than did normals with stimulus durations of 300 and 500 msec. Source of count rate discrepancy between groups may be attributed to threshold differences in accuracy of counting and application of appropriate counting strategies.

Thor, Donald H. (Edward R. Johnstone Training & Research Center, Bordentown, N.J.) Journal of Abnormal Psychology, 1971(Aug), Vol. 78(1), 30-34. [PA, Vol 47:03548]

1409. Types of verbal elaboration in the paired-associate performance of educable mentally retarded children.
Investigated the effects of 3 types of verbal elaboration on the learning and reversal of paired-associates by 16 male and 16 female educable mentally retarded children. A standard labeling condition was compared with 3 elaboration conditions: sentence, semantic paragraph, and syntactic paragraph elaboration. Verbal elaboration markedly facilitated acquisition of word pairs over labeling, and provision of either type of paragraph elaboration produced slightly smaller, but statistically significant increments beyond the effect of sentences. Backward associations were also significantly enhanced in all elaboration conditions. Several explanations pertinent to the distinctive effects of verbal elaborations on the learning and reversal of paired-associates are discussed. (24 ref.)
Turnure, James E. (U. Minnesota) American Journal of Mental Deficiency, 1971(Nov), Vol. 76(3), 306-312. [PA, Vol 48:03571]

1410. Extended verbal mediation in the learning and reversal of paired-associates by EMR children.
Extended the effects of syntactic mediation on paired-associate (PA) learning beyond the previous limit of the single sentence by embedding the stimuli to be associated in 2-sentence paragraphs. The effects of paragraph mediation on the PA learning of 30 educable mentally retarded children in 3 groups with mean CAs of 9.5, 9.8, and 9.6, respectively, were compared to the effects of word and sentence mediation in a Latin square for repeated measures design. Results show acquisition to be greatly enhanced for sentence and paragraph mediation over word mediation, and paragraph mediation was found to be slightly, but significantly, superior to sentence mediation. Results of a reversal manipulation indicate that syntactic mediation dramatically facilitates backward associations. This finding was interpreted in relation to certain necessary requirements of transformational grammars. (24 ref.)
Turnure, James E. & Walsh, M. Kateri. (U. Minnesota) American Journal of Mental Deficiency, 1971(Jul), Vol. 76(1), 60-67. [PA, Vol 47:07430]

1411. Acoustic impedance measurements with hard of hearing mentally retarded children.
Assessed a variety of impedance measurements, to identify the presence of ear pathology and to differentiate between pure sensorineural and mixed type hearing losses in mentally retarded children. 23 5-14 yr old deaf educable retardates on whom complete and highly reliable audiograms had been obtained served as Ss. Results demonstrate that use of the acoustic reflex threshold and tympanogram should help in reaching audiological conclusions with difficult-to-test mentally retarded children.
Borus, Judith F. (Ohio State U., Nisonger Center for Mental Retardation) Journal of Mental Deficiency Research, 1972(Sep), Vol. 16(3), 196-202. [PA, Vol 51:03511]

1412. Gross motor performance in minimally brain injured children.
Presents a description of Ss from special education classes as a prerequisite to curriculum development. In general, age changes in mean performance were linear with scores of boys being superior. The level of performance very closely resembled that of comparison groups of educable mentally retarded children from the same school districts. (21 ref.)
Broadhead, Geoffrey D. (Moray House Coll. of Education, Edinburgh, Scotland) Journal of Motor Behavior, 1972(Jun), Vol. 4(2), 103-111. [PA, Vol 50:01213]

1413. A rehearsal deficit in retardates' continuous short-term memory: Keeping track of variables that have few or many states.
Tested 12 institutionalized mildly retarded children (CA = 16, MA = 9) on a continuous short-term memory task that required them to keep the current state of a number of variables updated. Performance was dependent on the number of states of

the probed variables, and there was a marked recency but no primacy effect in the serial position curves. These data are similar to those obtained with preschool children but quite different from those typically found with adults. It is suggested that the developmentally young perform poorly on such tasks because they fail to rehearse the current state of the to-be-remembered variables. (19 ref.)
Brown, Ann L. (U. Illinois, Children's Research Center) Psychonomic Science, 1972(Dec), Vol. 29(6-B), 373-376. [PA, Vol 50:01214]

1414. A visual memory scale (VMS) designed to measure short-term visual recognition memory in 5- and 6-year-old children.
Investigated the relationship between short-term memory and different behavioral characteristics in 3 different groups of 5-6 yr. olds. The groups were normal Ss ($n = 198$), educable mentally retarded ($n = 13$), and educable mentally retarded Ss with CNS impairment ($n = 19$). A significant negative correlation was found between memory errors and tests of reading readiness and reading achievement with 1st-grade children. The VMS differentiated between neurologically impaired retarded children and nonneurologically impaired children.
Carroll, James L. (Central Michigan U.) Psychology in the Schools, 1972(Apr), Vol. 9(2), 152-158. [PA, Vol 48:12036]

1415. Influence of verbal feedback on auditory discrimination test performance of mentally retarded children.
Investigated the performance of 26 5.4-13.9 yr. old educable retardates on the Wepman Auditory Discrimination Test (WADT) when Ss received positive verbal feedback for correct responses. Although some improvement was noted, results indicate verbal feedback did not significantly alter test scores of retarded Ss. Performance on the WADT was significantly correlated with MA and grade level achievement for reading, spelling, and arithmetic.
Dahle, Arthur J. & Daly, David A. (U. Alabama, Birmingham) American Journal of Mental Deficiency, 1972(Mar), Vol. 76(5), 586-590. [PA, Vol 48:12063]

1416. The use of verbal self reports with the educable mentally retarded.
Examined the performance of 40 educable mentally retarded males on the Laurelton Self Attitude Inventory and the Parent-Child Relations Questionnaire for Fathers and Mothers. It is concluded that a social desirability factor in combination with low instrument validity and reliability contributed substantially to the overall results. The tendency of such a population to comply with social expectation is considered to be critically important in the interpretation of personality tests by professionals working in this area. (16 ref.)
Daniels, Lloyd K. & Stewart, James A. (Central Connecticut State Coll.) Training School Bulletin, 1972(Feb), Vol. 68(4), 212-216. [PA, Vol 48:09547]

1417. Patterns of cognitive ability in nonretarded and retarded children.
60 educable mentally retarded (EMR) 13-15 yr. olds and 60 nonretarded 5-6 yr. olds, matched on MA, were given 5 cognitive tasks of reasoning and memory (e.g., the Coloured Progressive Matrices and Memory-For-Designs Test). The performance of nonretarded Ss was superior to EMR Ss in each of the tasks. Test scores were subsequently factor analyzed for each sample, and 2 factors extracted. The factors, essentially similar for both samples, were interpreted to reflect the successive and the simultaneous modes of processing information, as suggested by A. Luria. Nonretarded and EMR Ss had disparate loadings for some tests suggesting that the 2 groups may be using distinct modes of coding information. (16 ref.)
Das, J. P. (U. Alberta, Center for the Study of Mental Retardation, Edmonton, Canada) American Journal of Mental Deficiency, 1972(Jul), Vol. 77(1), 6-12. [PA, Vol 49:00954]

1418. A comparison of the results of a revised version of Berko's test of morphology with the free speech of mentally retarded children.
Presented a revised version of J. Berko's test of morphology to 30 educable mentally retarded public school children, 6 each from the MA groups 6, 7, 8, 9, and 10. Samples of free speech were also elicited. The features tested were compared to the same features in the free speech to see if the test could predict the occurrence or nonoccurrence of errors in the free speech. Correlational analysis suggests that this was not the case. It is concluded that the paradigm itself, whether it uses nonsense syllables or real words as eliciting stimuli, is not useful in testing development of bound morphemes in educable mentally retarded children.
Dever, Richard B. (U. Wisconsin) Journal of Speech & Hearing Research, 1972(Mar), Vol. 15(1), 169-178. [PA, Vol 49:11364]

1419. A methodological analysis of the children's manifest anxiety scale with normal and retarded children.
Administered the CMA scale twice in 10 mo. to 16 educable mentally retarded male 7-11 yr. olds and 19 normal male CA-controls of average intelligence, to examine (a) long-term test-retest reliability of the CMA scale, (b) suitability of the scale with a younger CA-group, and (c) difference in anxiety scores for normal and retarded Ss. Controls were employed for situational variables (e.g., procedural modifications, residential and educational status, and IQ-range). Test-retest correlations indicate that the scale was reliable for normal Ss but not for retarded Ss. CMA scale effects based on age and IQ were found. Older retardates received higher anxiety scores than the younger retardates on Test 2, while Test 1 difference was not significant. Retarded Ss obtained higher anxiety scores than normal Ss on Test 1. It is concluded that reliability over a 10-mo period is poor for retarded Ss and that the instrument is of doubtful utility with younger retarded Ss. (22 ref.)
Flanigan, Patrick J. (U. Wisconsin) Journal of Experimental Education, 1972(Sum), Vol. 40(4), 46-51. [PA, Vol 49:01516]

1420. Motor educability and chronological age as potential estimates of errors in perceptual-motor development of educable mentally retarded children.
Describes a pilot study designed to estimate the degree of accuracy with which performances of educable mental retardates on tests of perceptual-motor skills could be predicted by chronological age. 12 male and 2 female educable mentally retarded students (IQ = 55-70) were studied. The Purdue Perceptual-Motor Survey was administered. Results show that chronological age in months significantly increased the accuracy of prediction. Also, when scores on the Johnson Test of Motor Educability were checked, they were highly correlated with those on the Purdue test. (16 ref)
George, Colleen. (North Texas State U) American Corrective Therapy Journal, 1972(Jul), Vol 26(4), 105-111. [PA, Vol 53:03433]

1421. Demographic, historical, and ability correlates of the Laurelton Self-Concept Scale in an EMR sample.
Presents an extension of a study by the authors (see PA, Vol. 48:Issue 3) on factor scales derived from the Laurelton Self-Concept Scale. The obtained scores of 172 educable mentally retarded (EMR) children were correlated with demographic, historical, and learning competence measures. Results indicate that reported self-concepts of EMRs are related to the objective facts of their role, situation, and behavior. Low significant correlations were obtained in directions suggested by face content of the factors, establishing some concurrent validity for the Laurelton Scale. However, some expected relationships were reversed or obscured, suggesting that denial may have operated for subgroups of Ss. High threat areas evoked more denial than low areas, and low IQ was more associated with denial than high IQ. Kohs' learning potential (LP) scores correlated negatively with maladjustment and friendlessness. The most intellectually disabled, by the LP criterion, reported themselves to be the most socially and emotionally handicapped.

Harrison, Robert H. & Budoff, Milton. (Research Inst. for Education Problems, Cambridge, Mass.) American Journal of Mental Deficiency, 1972(Jan), Vol. 76(4), 460-480. [PA, Vol 48:05466]

1422. Schema learning in retarded children.
Required 30 male mildly retarded (52-67 IQ) 8-17 yr. olds to reproduce checkerboard patterns containing 16, 20, 25, 30, and 36 cells. With increases in pattern complexity there was a decrease in the percent but not the amount of information retained (correcting for guessing). Ss performed significantly above chance even on the 36-cell patterns. In Exp. II, 20 additional Ss abstracted a schema from 36-cell patterns without exposure to the prototype or without knowledge of results. These Ss retained 262% more cells than 20 control Ss who were trained with nonschematic patterns. Results indicate that training retarded children to abstract and use schemata should allow them to process more information despite limited channel capacity.
Jones, Elvis C.; Myers, Donald G. & Cleveland, Donald L. (Frostburg State Coll.) Psychological Reports, 1972(Apr), Vol. 30(2), 447-453. [PA, Vol 50:03244]

1423. Occupational aspirations of the educable mentally retarded.
Investigated whether 40 Negro and 43 Caucasian 12-yr-old educable mentally retarded boys in special classes were realistic in their occupational conceptualization and interest. Results of a simple questionnaire reveal that both groups expressed realistic expectations with respect to future occupations.
Knight, Octavia B. (North Carolina Central U., Durham) Training School Bulletin, 1972(Aug), Vol. 69(2), 54-57. [PA, Vol 49:05460]

1424. [The acquisition and use of similes by mentally retarded school children.] (Russ)
Studied the use of similes by 20 5th graders with mild mental retardation. A text containing 3 similes was read and several questions were discussed which were designed to clarify the comparisons involved in the similes. Ss were then asked to reproduce the text. The reproductions were divided into 3 groups, from Level 1 answers, which showed one-to-one correspondence to the models or had small appropriate semantic-grammatical changes, to Level 3 answers, which showed little or no understanding of the comparisons. Of the 60 possible simile reproductions (3 from each of 20 Ss), a majority were reproduced at Levels 1 and 2. Level 3 answers were given by only 5 Ss, indicating that most of them were able to cope with this task. The 2 similes in which what was being compared (subject) closely resembled that with which it was being compared (object) were easier than the simile in which subject and object were related remotely. In the easiest simile, subject and object had distinct features of difference as well as of likeness, which prevented their relationship from being interpreted as one of identity.
Komskaya, S. N. (Svyerdlovskii Pedagogical Inst, USSR) Defektologiya, 1972, No 6, 17-23. [PA, Vol 54:03433]

1425. Structured vs unstructured visual-motor tests for educable retarded children.
Administered the Beery's Development Test of Visual-Motor Integration, a structured test, and the Bender Visual Motor Gestalt Test, an unstructured one, to 24 6-12 yr. olds with IQs ranging from 50-80. Developmental age scores and/or equivalents were obtained. Both Koppitz and Bender methods were used to score the Bender protocols. Intercorrelations between the Bender (Koppitz and Bender scoring) and Beery were statistically significant ($p < .01$). For this sample, a structured booklet for visual-motor testing (Beery) measures visual-motor skills in a manner comparable to the unstructured Bender.
Krauft, Virginia R. & Krauft, Conrad C. (U. Arkansas) Perceptual & Motor Skills, 1972(Jun), Vol. 34(3), 691-694. [PA, Vol 48:12193]

1426. Digital skin temperature as a physiological correlate of attention in nonretarded and retarded children.
Recorded digital skin temperature (SKT) of 20 9-yr-old nonretarded and mildly retarded Negro males during alternate periods of white noise and a movie to test that decreases in SKT reflect a physiological component of the attentional process, and that attentional differences of nonretarded and retarded Ss are manifested in this hypothesized physiological correlate of attention. Results indicate that: (a) SKT decreases occurred to changes in environment for both nonretarded and retarded Ss, (b) SKT drop durations were longer during the movie than during white noise for all Ss, and (c) SKT changes did not conclusively differentiate between nonretarded and retarded Ss.
Landers, William F.; Ball, Steven E. & Halcomb, Charles G. (Texas Technological U.) American Journal of Mental Deficiency, 1972(Mar), Vol. 76(5), 550-554. [PA, Vol 48:12043]

1427. Facilitative effect of input organization as a function of verbal response to stimuli in EMR and nonretarded children.
Presented a series of digits for recall to 30 educable mentally retarded (EMR) and 30 nonretarded children matched on MA under 3 conditions: (a) digits ungrouped and called as single integers, (b) digits spatially grouped and called as single integers, and (c) digits grouped and called as higher decade numbers. It was found that EMRs improved in recall as the degree of input organization increased, while nonretarded Ss performed best under the least degree of experimental organization. Results support the notion that learning performance is a function of the goodness of fit between the structure of a task and an S's preference for organizational strategy.
MacMillan, Donald L. (U. California, Riverside) American Journal of Mental Deficiency, 1972(Jan), Vol. 76(4), 408-411. [PA, Vol 48:05485]

1428. Paired-associate learning as a function of explicitness of mediational set by EMR and nonretarded children.
Compared 3 methods of presenting paired-associates to 30 pairs of MA-matched educable mentally retarded and nonretarded children. Control Ss simply named the objects of each of 3 9-pair lists; explicit-mediation Ss were provided with a specific sentence mediating the 2 objects on the 1st 2 lists and then simply named the objects on the 3rd list; and self-generated Ss were instructed to generate their own mediating sentences without assistance on the 1st 2 lists and then simply named the objects on the 3rd list. All groups learned the same paired-associates to a criterion of 1 errorless trial or until a total of 18 trials was reached. No main effect for classification (retarded-nonretarded) was found. Both explicit-mediation and self-generated conditions were superior to the control condition on learning (Lists 1 and 2). On the transfer task (List 3), explicit-mediation Ss did better than both control and self-generated Ss. Results question the notion of an inefficiency in the utilization of verbal mediators by retarded Ss.
MacMillan, Donald L. (U. California, Riverside) American Journal of Mental Deficiency, 1972(May), Vol. 76(6), 686-691. [PA, Vol 48:12075]

1429. Evaluation of a strategy-oriented training program on the verbal abstraction performance of EMRs.
Compared the effects of hypothesis testing strategy training and paired-associate training on the verbal abstraction performance of 50 male mentally retarded adolescents. Ss receiving strategy oriented training learned to "test out" associates against nouns that were part of an abstraction set to determine appropriate abstractions. Ss receiving paired-associate training memorized nouns along with associates that would serve as abstractions when the nouns appeared as part of abstraction sets. Strategy oriented training facilitated performance on transfer items and training items, while paired-associate training improved performance on training items only.
McIvor, William B. (Columbia U., Teachers Coll.) American Journal of Mental Deficiency, 1972(May), Vol. 76(6), 652-657. [PA, Vol 48:12077]

1430. Curiosity in retarded children: Sensitivity to intrinsic and extrinsic reinforcement.
Tested 50 educable mentally retarded 7-13 yr. olds for curiosity by a method which involved choosing from among briefly exposed stimulus sets each of which varied along a 3-point complexity continuum. In an attempt to modify subsequent curiosity behavior, Ss were administered a jigsaw puzzle under differing conditions: (a) Ss were interrupted or permitted to finish the puzzle; (b) Ss received a monetary reward, ostensibly for adequate performance; and (c) controls finished the puzzle, performing without reference to money. All Ss then received an additional series of complexity triads. As predicted, Ss who had been interrupted on the puzzle (intrinsic reinforcement) and received money (extrinsic reinforcement) showed the highest curiosity scores, while Ss who were permitted to complete the puzzle but were denied the money showed lowest curiosity. Results are presented for latency to response, duration of response, consistency across items, sex, and age. The utility of distinguishing intrinsic and extrinsic reinforcement as operating under 2 independent systems is discussed. (23 ref.)
Miller, Martin B. & Geller, Daniel. (Yeshiva U.) American Journal of Mental Deficiency, 1972(May), Vol. 76(6), 668-679. [PA, Vol 48:12078]

1431. Projection of affect after task performance by retarded and nonretarded children.
24 9-16 yr. old educable mentally retarded and 24 10-15 yr. old normal children engaged in a 2-person game-like task. Ss were then shown photographed poses of affective expressions by a child they did not know but who was described as having participated in the same task. Ss were told that 1 of the photographs was taken immediately after the task, while the others were taken some time later. They were asked to guess which was taken after the task, which best represented the way they felt after task participation, and which represented the way they wished they had felt. Retarded Ss were likely to attribute negative feelings (frequently anger) to the other child and positive feelings to themselves, while intellectually average Ss showed opposite response tendencies. Both groups were likely to wish they felt positively. For retarded Ss, performance in the task was related to attributions of how the other child felt but not to self-feelings, while the opposite was the case of nonretarded Ss. Results, most of which were contrary to predictions, are considered in terms of differential locus of evaluation in children, retarded or not, and briefly discussed in terms of self-concept literature. (15 ref.)
Miller, Martin B. & Gottlieb, Jay. (Yeshiva U.) American Journal of Mental Deficiency, 1972(Sep), Vol. 77(2), 149-156. [PA, Vol 49:07240]

1432. [Characteristics of attention in children with a delay in development.] (Russ)
Studied attention in children with a delay in development (minimal brain damage) by measuring the latency periods of their motor reactions to tactile stimuli under various distracting conditions. Vibrators were strapped to the wrists of 15 Ss with a delay in development, 12 mildly retarded Ss, and 16 normals. Each S had to respond as quickly as possible with the hand being stimulated while simultaneously hearing noise, music, or a story. Children with a delay in development had a longer mean reaction time (RT) than did the normals, and the variability of their RT was greater. RT did not change as a function of type of distracting sound for normals, but children with a delay in development were hampered more by the simultaneous presentation of a story than by the other distractors. It is concluded that children with a delay in development have deficits in speed of processing information and in ability to concentrate attention. The use of RT as a diagnostic tool is discussed.
Pyeryeslyeni, L. I. (USSR Academy of Pedagogical Sciences, Inst of Defectology, Moscow) Defektologiya, 1972, No 4, 23-28. [PA, Vol 53:07764]

1433. Contextual constraints beyond a sentence on cloze responses of mentally retarded children.
Gave 2 cloze tasks constructed from 2nd-grade readers to 58 educable mentally retarded junior high school students. One task consisted of selections containing sentences in the natural order of discourse (NAT); the other involved materials wherein the sentence order was modified (MOD). The 2 conditions differed in availability of contextual cues beyond a sentence. ANOVA confirmed the hypothesis that significantly more correct cloze responses would be produced in the NAT condition. It is concluded that the Ss were not word calling or responding solely to cues within the immediate context of the deleted word. They were responding to paragraph level cues beyond a sentence. Possibilities for future studies and educational implications are discussed. (36 ref.)
Ramanauskas, Sigita. (U. Connecticut, School of Education) American Journal of Mental Deficiency, 1972(Nov), Vol. 77(3), 338-345. [PA, Vol 50:03297]

1434. Written language abilities of EMR and nonretarded children with the same mental ages.
Compared the written language ability of 22 educable mentally retarded (EMR) junior high students and 22 nonretarded children in Grades 4-6, on: (a) mean sentence length, (b) composition length, (c) type-token ratio, (d) total types, (e) J. Carroll's type-token ratio, (f) spelling correctness ratio, and (g) grammatical correctness ratio. Ss were stratified on IQ, parent's occupation, sex, and MA (9-12 yr.). Consistent with previous studies, nonretarded Ss were superior to EMR Ss on type-token ratio, total types, Carroll type-token ratio, and grammatical correctness ratio. (19 ref.)
Sedlak, Robert A. & Cartwright, G. Phillip. (Pennsylvania State U.) American Journal of Mental Deficiency, 1972(Jul), Vol. 77(1), 95-99. [PA, Vol 49:04851]

1435. [Recognition of simple visual stimuli by children with a delay in psychological development.] (Russ)
Studied recognition thresholds for simple visual stimuli in 19 children with a delay in development (minimal brain damage), 23 mildly retarded children, 20 normal children, and 10 adults. Child Ss were 9-11 yrs old. Stimuli, 1-6 dots, were presented tachistoscopically. Thresholds for normal children were similar to those for adults; thresholds for children with a delay in development were higher, and those for mentally retarded children were even higher. With unsymmetrically arranged stimuli having more than 4 elements, under conditions of increasing exposure, 20 mentally retarded Ss showed "split" thresholds. They began by responding correctly on almost 100% of the trials, but with further increases in exposure the number of errors rose sharply until much longer presentation times were employed. This did not occur in any normals and in only 3 children with a delay in development. The significance of these results for the differential diagnosis of children with a delay in development and for their education is discussed.
Shoshin, P. B. (USSR Academy of Pedagogical Sciences, Inst of Defectology, Moscow) Defektologiya, 1972, No 4, 35-40. [PA, Vol 53:07772]

1436. Speech-hearing measurements in an intellectually average to below average group of children.
Investigated relationships between MA, CA, IQ, physiological age (PA) and speech hearing ability. Ss included 187 6-15 yr. olds with pure tone acuity of at least 25 db. but lowered IQs of 45-94 and MAs of 5.8-11.5. Ss were given the WISC, Threshold by Identification of Pictures (TIP) test, and Discrimination by Identification of Pictures (DIP) test. Results indicate that MA, IQ, PA, institutionalization, and organic bases for retardation were not significantly related to speech reception threshold or speech discrimination. Speech hearing was mostly independent of age and IQ effects. Reliability of the TIP and DIP compared favorably with their use for nonretarded children. (23 ref.)
Siegenthaler, Bruce M.; Sallade, Jacqueline B. & Tardibuono, John S. (Pennsylvania State U.) American Journal of Mental Deficiency, 1972(Jan), Vol. 76(4), 427-433. [PA, Vol 48:03561]

1437. The effect of phrasal cueing on free recall of EMR and non-retarded children.
Presented Ss with 4 types of 9-word strings which differed in the degree of syntactic and associative structure. Each S was presented with 1 of 3 cueing conditions. Findings indicate that educable mentally retarded (EMR) children revealed their best recall performance relative to nonretarded children when pausal cues were provided at phrasal boundaries within sentences containing standard syntax. Recall of EMR children was relatively inferior when Ss were not provided with these cues but were required to impose a structure in recording verbal strings which conformed to standard syntactic rules. (16 ref.)
Sitko, M. C. & Semmel, M. I. (Indiana U.) American Educational Research Journal, 1972(Spr), Vol. 9(2), 217-229. [PA, Vol 49:03320]

1438. Effects of redundancy level and presentation method on the paired-associate learning of educable retardates, third graders, and eighth graders.
Presented 84 retardates, 84 normals of approximately equal CA (8th graders), and 84 normals of equal MA (3rd graders) with sets of paired associates which differed in redundancy level by varying the number of repetitions in the response terms. In Exp. I, presentation and testing were by the standard anticipation method. In Exp. II, presentation was simultaneous, and during testing all stimulus terms were presented simultaneously for free-ordered recall of the response terms. To achieve near perfect performance, the lower MA groups required more redundancy than the higher MA group. Compared to the anticipation method, and particularly on the low redundancy material, simultaneous presentation and free-ordered recall negatively affected the performance of retardates, positively affected the performance of 8th graders, and had no effect on 3rd graders.
Spitz, Herman H. (E. R. Johnstone Training & Research Center, Bordentown, N.J.) Journal of Experimental Psychology, 1972(Sep), Vol. 95(1), 164-170. [PA, Vol 49:04235]

1439. Effects of two types of redundancy on visual digit span performance of retardates and varying aged normals.
Tested 5 groups of normals ($n = 186$; mean ages 10, 13, 18, and 30 yr.) and a group of adolescent educable retardates ($n = 60$, mean age 16 yr.) with digits of varying lengths under 2 types of redundancy conditions. Repetition redundancy (e.g., 5, 2, 8, 5, 2, 8) was more difficult to recognize than couplet redundancy (e.g., 5, 5, 2, 2, 8, 8). However, once recognized, digits containing repetition redundancy were easier to recall than digits containing couplet redundancy. When repetition redundancy was made highly salient, the performance of lower MA groups was greatly improved. The information value of redundant digits was less predictive of performance than knowledge of the type of redundancy. It is concluded that the 2 types of redundancy differentially affect performance because of differences in temporal and recognition factors. (16 ref.)
Spitz, Herman H.; Goettler, Diane R. & Webreck, Cindy A. (Johnstone Training & Research Center, Bordentown, N.J.) Developmental Psychology, 1972(Jan), Vol. 6(1), 92-103. [PA, Vol 48:01540]

1440. Mental elaboration and learning in EMR children.
A. R. Jensen has recently extended his 2-level theory of intelligence (see PA, Vol. 43:9740) to mental retardation. This theory implies that retarded children should be deficient in conceptual abilities, e.g., elaboration of paired associates (PA). Although previous research investigating elaboration has tended to support this implication, insufficient instructional sets and training procedures may have been used. In the present study, 24 educable mentally retarded (EMR) 10-15 yr. olds were randomly assigned to 1 of 3 treatments: repetition (control condition), verbal context, and imagery. The major hypothesis, that instructions to elaborate in the form of either images or verbal contexts would greatly facilitate PA recall, was supported by results from 2 lists. A secondary hypothesis, that the imagery elaboration group would recall significantly more nouns than the verbal-context elaboration group, was not supported. It is concluded

that elaboration training is an effective means of facilitating the recall performance of EMR children. (27 ref.)
Taylor, Arthur M.; Josberger, Marie & Knowlton, James Q. (U. Minnesota) American Journal of Mental Deficiency, 1972(Jul), Vol. 77(1), 69-76. [PA, Vol 49:04876]

1441. Elaboration structure and list length effects on verbal elaboration phenomena.
Investigated the effects of elaboration structure (sentence, semantic paragraph, and syntactic paragraph) and list length (8, 12, or 16 pairs) on paired-associate learning in a 3 * 3 design. 75 educable retardates (mean CA = 10.4 yr.) were tested on acquisition (stimulus-response) and reversal (response-stimulus) tasks. Significant acquisition differences were found in the 8-pair list; semantic paragraph Ss performed better than sentence Ss. In the longer lists, all structures were equally effective in facilitating acquisition (mean correct on the 1st trial = 60%) as well as reversal (mean correct = 95%). Analyses of sentence form indicate that significantly fewer acquisition errors were made on pairs presented in declarative and imperative (as opposed to interrogative) elaborations. Ss in all conditions generally recalled the elaborations as declarative sentences. Further observations at 24 pairs confirmed the 12- and 16-pair findings. (33 ref.)
Thurlow, Martha L. & Turnure, James E. (U. Minnesota) Journal of Experimental Child Psychology, 1972(Oct), Vol. 14(2), 184-195. [PA, Vol 49:04881]

1442. Stereoscopic contour perception in mental retardation.
Showed 30 8-, 11-, and 15-yr-old educable mentally retarded and 40 5-, 8-, 11- and 15-yr-old nonretarded Ss geometric designs whose contours were created from binocular cues (stereoscopic contour) or from monocular cues (line-drawn contours). Both groups showed rapid and highly accurate recognition performance under both presentation conditions, and this performance was relatively stable across age levels. Findings suggest that cortical processing of binocular input is generally not disturbed in mild forms of mental retardation and may be relatively unaffected by developmental factors during childhood.
Webb, Thomas E. (U. Pennsylvania) American Journal of Mental Deficiency, 1972(May), Vol. 76(6), 699-702. [PA, Vol 48:12056]

1443. Functional analysis of intelligence test performance of children with learning problems.
Analyzed the WISC performance of 77 boys with serious school learning problems according to 3 factors hypothesized to reflect functional differences in learning styles. Subsamples identified as learning disordered, learning disordered hyperactive, or educable mentally retarded, differed in patterns of subtest scores, although within groups Verbal and Performance IQs were not significantly different. Attentional difficulties in hyperactive learning disordered children were confirmed. Specification of areas of strength and weakness through the proposed process analysis is suggested as a basis for differentiated remedial program planning.
Wetter, Jack; Keogh, Barbara K.; McGinty, Ann & Donlon, Genevieve. (U. California, Los Angeles) Proceedings of the 80th Annual Convention of the American Psychological Association, 1972, Vol. 7(Pt. 2), 551-552. [PA, Vol 48:05682]

1444. The role of imagery in incidental learning of educable retarded and normal children.
Administered an orientation task to 45 educable retarded and 45 normal 8-13 yr. olds. Noun and picture paired associates were presented 1 or 4 times under 1 of 3 instructional conditions: intentional imagery, incidental imagery, or intentional control (no imagery). An immediate associative recall test showed both imagery conditions to be superior to the intentional control condition. Furthermore, imagery instructions facilitated incidental recall of the retarded Ss equal to the recall of normal Ss in the intentional condition. 4 presentations of pairs improved the learning of both groups. In contrast to normal Ss, the recall of retarded Ss was greater with 4 presentations under imagery instructions than under intentional control instructions. Results are discussed in terms of imagery processes and their educational implications. (16 ref.)

Yarmey, A. Daniel & Bowen, Norma V. (U. Guelph, Ontario Canada) Journal of Experimental Child Psychology, 1972(Oct), Vol. 14(2), 303-312. [PA, Vol 49:04909]

1445.   Miscue language patterns of mildly retarded and nonretarded students.
Investigated the differences and similarities in the language miscues of 10 Black educable mental retardates (EMRs) and 3 nonretarded Black groups: 27 kindergartners, 13 1st graders, and 33 4th-6th graders (CA peers of the EMR groups). Responses to a variation of P. Menyuk's repeated sentence task were analyzed. The sentences employed a wide variety of basic sentence types and syntactic structures. It was found that EMRs were similar to their CA peers on concrete word errors, and similar to kindergartners on function-word errors. These results lend support for the hypothesis that EMRs have a slower rate of language development, and suggest that existing language programs for EMR should concentrate on function words.
Anastasiow, Nicholas J. & Stayrook, Nicholas G. (Inst. for Child Study, Bloomington, Ind.) American Journal of Mental Deficiency, 1973(Jan), Vol. 77(4), 431-434. [PA, Vol 50:03152]

1446.   Comment on Das' "Patterns of cognitive ability in nonretarded and retarded children."
Examines J. P. Das's (see PA, Vol. 49:954) report of findings of less adequate performance and differing cognitive processes in mildly retarded children compared with children of average intelligence. These findings are taken as suggesting a reappraisal of the developmental approach to retardation. It is considered, however, that Das failed to distinguish conceptually between organic and familial retardation, as demanded by the developmental position, and employed an S sample with a high probability of containing many organically impaired children. The experimental measures employed are typically seen as reflecting organic impairment in persons of any IQ level.
Balla, David. (Yale U.) American Journal of Mental Deficiency, 1973(May), Vol. 77(6), 748-749. [PA, Vol 51:07427]

1447.   Socioeconomic traits in mildly retarded children of differential diagnosis.
Investigated the extent to which children diagnosed as minimally brain injured (MBI) or educable mentally retarded (EMR), but in the same IQ range, compared with respect to socioeconomic traits. Traits were assessed from questionnaires returned from the homes of 92 MBI and 110 EMR children in special school classes, whose IQ's ranged from 69-85. The MBI were favored in terms of parental education, occupation, and social position. No differences were found with regard to the sex or number of children in the family, birth order, or month of birth. (17 ref.)
Broadhead, Geoffrey D. (Moray House Coll. of Education, Edinburgh, Scotland) Rehabilitation Literature, 1973(Apr), Vol. 34(4), 104-107. [PA, Vol 50:09108]

1448.   The happiness of retarded children.
Selected 20 male and 20 female educable retardates (average IQ 71, age 13) and an equal number of normal controls (average IQ 98, age 14). Ss were systematically observed at school in class and at recess for 4 1-min periods and rated as appearing happy, neutral, or unhappy. Ss were also rated by their teacher and 1 parent for intelligence, social adjustment, and life-satisfaction. Only the ratings of intelligence significantly differed for the 2 groups. It is concluded that the life-satisfaction of retardates is probably comparable to that of normals.
Cameron, Paul & Titus, Donna. (U. Louisville) Proceedings of the 81st Annual Convention of the American Psychological Association, 1973, Vol. 8, 803-804. [PA, Vol 50:09116]

1449.   Methodological study of conservation in retarded adolescents.
Tested 24 educable mentally retarded 14 yr olds on conservation of substance, weight, and volume. 12 Ss were tested by the prediction and judgment questions always ending in "more" for substance and weight and "higher" for volume. The other Ss were tested by the questions using "same." Explanation and countersuggestion followed the prediction and judgment questions. Results show that (a) prior to countersuggestion the group

tested with "same" scored significantly higher, but (b) after countersuggestion there was no difference between the groups, and (c) countersuggestion elicited more conservation responses in the group tested by "more" questions than prior to countersuggestion. Findings support the hypothesis that differing question formats affect conservation performance. Methods for reducing Type I error are discussed. (23 ref)
Carlson, Jerry S. & Michalson, Linda H. (U. California, School of Education, Riverside) American Journal of Mental Deficiency, 1973(Nov), Vol. 78(3), 348-353. [PA, Vol 52:03352]

1450.   The educable mentally retarded choose their art activities: Two-dimensional or three-dimensional.
28 educable mentally retarded children (mean chronological age 11 yrs, mean mental age 6 yrs) were given the choice of 4 art activities: 3-dimensional (assemblage of colored blocks or paper sculpture) and 2-dimensional (tempera painting or collage of colored papers). Tested individually, 24 Ss chose painting, 2 chose paper cutting, and only 2 chose block assemblage. The choice was related neither to sex nor to IQ. A rigid clinging to familiar objects and techniques may account for the preference for 2-dimensional media.
Carter, John L. (U Houston) Art Psychotherapy, 1973(Fal), Vol 1(2), 141-144. [PA, Vol 53:09889]

1451.   The educable mentally retarded choose their art activities: Two-dimensional or three-dimensional.
Of 28 educable mentally retarded children (12 girls and 16 boys, CA approximately 9-12½ yrs, MA approximately 4½-8½ yrs), who were asked to choose their art activities, 92.8% chose 2-dimensional projects. Possible reasons for differences between these results and those of other studies are discussed.
Carter, John L. (U Houston) Art Psychotherapy, 1973(Fal), Vol 1(2), 141-144. [PA, Vol 57:12994]

1452.   Reply of an eclectic to a developmentalist.
Demonstrates that D. Balla's (see PA, Vol. 51:Issue 4) comment that this author's sample was from an "organically impaired" rather than from a familial retarded population is unfounded. Similarly, the tests used in the study could not be described as typical tests for detecting brain damage; rather, more recent research has reaffirmed that they are subsumed adequately under 2 orthogonal factors, simultaneous and successive integration. It is concluded that a dogmatic adherence to a developmental or defective position could be a handicap in understanding retardation.
Das, J. P. (U. Alberta, Edmonton, Canada) American Journal of Mental Deficiency, 1973(May), Vol. 77(6), 749-750. [PA, Vol 51:07436]

1453.   Risk-taking by retarded and nonretarded children.
Used a switch game to measure risk-taking propensities of 30 male and 30 female mildly retarded children (mean IQ 68) in special education classes and 60 nonretarded children of comparable MAs in 3rd-5th grades. Results indicate that in certain risk situations, retarded children take as many or more risks than do nonretarded children. There were no sex differences.
Hayes, Charles S. (U Iowa, Child Development Clinic) Psychological Reports, 1973(Jun), Vol 32(3, Pt 1), 738. [PA, Vol 56:00880]

1454.   Prognostic significance of performance-verbal ability patterns in predicting employment adjustment of EMR adolescents.
Examined the value of WISC performance-verbal ability patterns in predicting future adjustment for educable mentally retarded Ss. It was hypothesized that performance bias would be a favorable and verbal bias an unfavorable prognostic index of adjustment. On completion of a 3-yr period following special school release, 95 Ss were placed into 1 of 2 categories: (a) those still remaining in open employment (adjusted) and (b) those who had been institutionalized (nonadjusted). Results suggest that both performance and verbal bias have short-term predictive value.

Jackson, R. N. (Aberdeen Coll. of Education, Scotland) American Journal of Mental Deficiency, 1973(Nov), Vol. 78(3), 331-333. [PA, Vol 52:03850]

1455.   Rehearsal processes in the short-term memory performance of mildly retarded adolescents.
Employed a procedure for the direct observation of rehearsal to assess the degree of spontaneous and instructed rehearsal activity in 2 experiments with a total of 80 cultural-familial retardates (mean age = 16 yrs). Ss typically did not spontaneously adopt active acquisition strategies for list learning. Instruction in a cumulative rehearsal strategy resulted in marked facilitation of recall performance. Results are discussed in terms of production vs mediation deficiencies and N. R. Ellis's rehearsal strategy deficit hypothesis.
Kellas, George; Ashcraft, Mark H. & Johnson, Nancy S. (U. Kansas) American Journal of Mental Deficiency, 1973(Mar), Vol. 77(5), 670-679. [PA, Vol 51:07448]

1456.   Modality strengths and aptitude-treatment interaction.
Developed 2 tests to measure auditory and visual memory (AM and VM) in children. The tests contained 20 words, all in the immediate sight vocabulary of the 57 8-12 yr old educationally handicapped Ss (IQ range, 80-129), taken from the Mills Learning Methods Test. In addition, Ss either read or heard 2 7-8 sentence stories and were asked to recall all they could about them. The 2-wk test-retest reliability for the AM and VM tests were .657 and .561, respectively. VM and AM scores were also correlated with Wide Range Achievement Test and WISC scores. 22 Ss were identified as having either visual or auditory strength (VS or AS); VS Ss performed better on the stories presented visually, while AS Ss were superior on the auditory stories. Results suggest that the AM and VM tests were reasonably reliable and that performance on these tests was significantly related to memory of continuous discourse presented in various modes. (23 ref)
Lilly, M. Stephen & Kelleher, John.   Journal of Special Education, 1973(Spr), Vol. 7(1), 5-13. [PA, Vol 52:03380]

1457.   Intra-individual variability of normal and educable mentally retarded children on a coincidence timing task.
Compared the level of performance (constant error) and the intra-individual variability of 100 intellectually normal and 100 educable mentally retarded children, using a visual coincidence timing task. The mean performance of the normal Ss was significantly superior to that of the retarded Ss, and the intra-individual variability of the retarded was significantly greater than that of the normals. The hypothesis that high intra-individual variability and depressed level of performance are closely associated was not supported.
McGown, Carl M.; Dobbins, D. Alan & Rarick, G. Lawrence. (Brigham Young U.) Journal of Motor Behavior, 1973(Dec), Vol. 5(4), 193-198. [PA, Vol 52:03381]

1458.   A mechanism for transition of concrete to abstract cognitive processes.
Proposes an extension of discrimination-learning theory based on the inhibition of stimulus intensity as a mechanism of cognitive development. According to this discrimination-inhibition theory, children experience concrete cues such as form, brightness, etc., with an intensity which captures and holds the orienting response and thereby prevents children from focusing on more abstract stimuli (e.g., cues for number of elements and identity over time). Ss were 48 normal and 37 educable mentally retarded kindergartners and 1st graders. The amount of stimulus distortion in Piaget's conservation-of-number paradigm was varied. Results indicate that the predominant category of transitional children (both normal and retarded) was composed of children who conserved at a low level of stimulus intensity but failed to conserve at a higher level of stimulus intensity ($p < .01$). Data support the discrimination-inhibition theory.
Melnick, Gerald I. (Yeshiva U, Curriculum Research & Development Ctr in Mental Retardation) Child Development, 1973(Sep), Vol 44(3), 599-605. [PA, Vol 53:00876]

1459.   Let's look at children: EMR normative data.
Administered the Written Exercises for First Graders to 141 educable mentally retarded (EMR) children (MA = 6-9 yr). Results of EMR Ss with MA of 6 yrs and of normal 1st graders were similar and suggest the appropriateness of the test for EMR children.
Mitchell, Marlys M. & Brantley, John C. (U. North Carolina, Chapel Hill) Mental Retardation, 1973(Apr), Vol. 11(2), 38-42. [PA, Vol 51:01389]

1460.   Surrogate and natural parent comparisons between institutional and non-institutional children.
Rated the surrogate parents of 20 8-13 yr old institutionalized educable mental retardates (EMRs) and the natural parents of a matched sample of 20 noninstitutionalized EMRs on Hollingshead's Two-Factor Index of Social Position. Results indicate that the institutional surrogate parents had significantly higher socioeconomic status. The present and previous findings suggest that this higher social position may have a positive influence on language habilitation among institutional EMRs.
Montague, James C. (U. Arkansas, Little Rock) Training School Bulletin, 1973(Feb), Vol. 69(4), 185-190. [PA, Vol 51:05475]

1461.   Lexical analysis of institutional versus non-institutional mentally retarded.
Utilizing recorded verbal responses to the TAT, 10 institutionalized and 10 noninstitutionalized 8-13 yr old educable retarded children were compared on a 13-category, part-of-speech system. Results of a contentive-functor analysis, contrasting group, sex, and interaction, indicated that only the preposition category was significantly different between groups (favoring the noninstitutionalized group). Although speculations are made concerning the significance of the preposition category, results are interpreted as indicating that no difference existed between these groups with respect to part-of-speech usage.
Montague, James C.; Jensen, Paul J. & Wepman, Joseph M. (U. Arkansas, Little Rock) Training School Bulletin, 1973(Nov), Vol. 70(3), 160-166. [PA, Vol 52:05697]

1462.   Memory as a key factor in retarded learning: A brief report.
Studied the relationships between intelligence level and the use of logical elimination procedures to solve concept problems under 2 conditions: (a) where clues had to be retained in short-term memory (STM) and (b) where effects of STM deficits were controlled. The relationship was examined in terms of 3 dependent variables. Mildly retarded children were randomly assigned to the 2 treatments. Results indicate that STM was the key factor hindering problem-solving by retarded Ss. These Ss were no different from normal Ss in the use of hypothesis testing in the problem-solving situation, but were unable to apply them in a logical sequence because of STM problems. It is concluded that (a) retarded Ss were capable of solving concept problems when feedback information was available for referral, (b) retarded Ss did indicate considerable hypothesis testing in the problem-solving situation but were unable to string together the hypothesis sets in a logical sequence, (c) memory seemed to be the key factor hampering the problem-solving ability of retarded Ss, and (d) the potential for increasing the learning rate and capacity of retarded children through scientific teaching has yet to be realized.
O'Connor, Peter D. (U. North Carolina, Chapel Hill) Australian Journal of Mental Retardation, 1973(Dec), Vol. 2(8), 236-24l. [PA, Vol 52:10437]

1463.   Intellectual development and the role of salience in intentional and incidental recall.
Gave 2 groups of 60 mildly retarded and average-IQ children in Grades 1, 4, or 6 2 tasks: a salience assessment task involving 4 dimensions from which individual-dimensional salience hierarchies were constructed, and a memory task which provided information on intentional and incidental recall. The memory task was structured according to an individual S's salience hierarchy. All S groups appeared to detect and process perceptual information in a similar fashion. Perceptual salience influenced

recall on both aspects of the memory task; age and IQ were related to intentional recall, but only age predicted incidental recall.

Odom, Penelope B.; Switzky, Harvey N. & Heal, Laird W. (George Peabody Coll. for Teachers) American Journal of Mental Deficiency, 1973(Mar), Vol. 77(5), 607-615. [PA, Vol 51:07462]

1464. Relationships among scores on intellectual achievement responsibility and cognitive style measures in educable mentally retarded children.
Tested 33 Black and 25 White 9–13 yr old intermediate educable mentally retarded children (EMRs), IQ 50–83, on a modified version of the Intellectual Achievement Responsibility Questionnaire (IARQ) and on the Matching Familiar Figures Test (MFFT). This version of the IARQ, modified for use with EMRs, yielded a Spearman-Bowman reliability coefficient of 0.66. The relationship of the IARQ to the 1st response latency or to the total number of errors on the MFFT was low and insignificant for both Black and White retardates. Whites and Blacks performed equally well on both instruments. Study 2 tested junior high school EMRs (157 boys and 92 girls 13–16 yrs old, IQ 50–83) on the modified IARQ, and tested 92 of the boys on the Children's Embedded Figures Test (CEFT). Results on the IARQ indicate that boys were slightly more internal than girls. The reliability coefficient was 0.67 for boys and 0.76 for girls. No significant relationship was found between IARQ and CEFT scores. (20 ref)
Panda, Kailas C. & Lynch, William W. Indian Journal of Mental Retardation, 1973(Jul), Vol 6(2), 55–66. [PA, Vol 60:00136]

1465. Humor products of high grade, institutionalized retardates.
Administered the "Draw-Something-Funny" test to 60 mildly retarded institutionalized Ss, 30 adults and 30 adolescents, half of each sex. Mean adolescent CA was 16.2 yrs, average IQ 57.6; mean adult CA was 28.7 yrs, average IQ 59.6. Results were classified according to Harms's (1943) model of 4 stages of human development. Results indicate that most of these Ss were operating at Stage 2 of the Harms model (age 3-7 yrs, when humor is seen in the unusual, strange, or distorted, or in the misfortunes of others). Male adolescents, however, functioned equally well in Stage 2 and Stage 3 (age 8-13, with an urge to caricature situations environmentally and with predominating feelings of inferiority, revenge, and jealousy). Indicants of social actions were seldom used in the drawings of any of the groups; it is felt that this omission or avoidance of social factors reflects a difficult problem in the social relationships of Ss of this type.
Pustel, Gabriel & Siegel, Louis. (Willowbrook State School, Staten Island, NY) Art Psychotherapy, 1973(Apr), Vol 1(1), 67-68. [PA, Vol 58:09739]

1466. Humor products of high grade, institutionalized retardes.
Studied responses to the Draw-Something-Funny test made by 60 mildly retarded institutionalized adolescents and adults. Results show that these groups avoid social situations as examples of humor but find amusement in others' distress and misery via distortion of bodily features.
Pustel, Gabriel & Siegel, Louis. (Willowbrook State School, Staten Island, N.Y.) Art Psychotherapy, 1973(Apr), Vol. 1(1), 67-68. [PA, Vol 52:05699]

1467. Clustering and subjective organization in a free recall task with retardates: A comparison of two methodologies.
Reiss, Philip & Reiss, Rosalind. (Yeshiva U., Ferkauf Graduate School) Catalog of Selected Documents in Psychology, 1973(Spr), Vol 3, 56. [PA, Vol 52:05701]

1468. Incidental learning of mildly mentally retarded and normal children under two conditions.
Attempted to extend H. Goldstein and C. Kass's (see PA, Vol 36:3CJ45G) findings concerning the incidental learning of retardates by using a normal instead of a gifted comparison sample and including a color modality. In a 2 × 2 design, 42 normal and 42 mildly retarded children, matched on MA of 7

yrs, were shown a colored or black-and-white picture depicting a street scene. Incidental learning was measured by means of naming, detailing, and identification tasks. Retardates and normals showed equal incidental learning ability, supporting Goldstein and Kass's findings. The color modality had no effect on performance.
Rodee, Burton & Sellin, Donald. (U. Wisconsin, Whitewater) Training School Bulletin, 1973(Feb), Vol. 69(4), 180-184. [PA, Vol 51:05478]

1469. Effect of background music on learning.
Investigated the effects of calming background music on task relevant and task irrelevant learning of 64 educable mentally retarded children. Differences were found between music and nonmusic groups on task relevant learning scores but not on task irrelevant scores (p = .026).
Stainback, Susan B.; Stainback, William C. & Hallahan, Daniel P. (U. Virginia) Exceptional Children, 1973(Oct), Vol. 40(2), 109-110. [PA, Vol 51:03489]

1470. Auditory-visual stimuli, spoken-written response mode and task difficulty and activity levels of mildly retarded children.
Studied the effects of auditory vs visual stimulus modes and oral vs written response modes upon activity levels exhibited by 18 mildly retarded 11-15 yr olds in a series of tasks of varied difficulty. Activity was greater during intertrial intervals than during stimulus presentations, and greater during hard than during easy tasks. Ss appeared to perceive tasks which required spoken responses as being more difficult than those requiring written responses.
Stephens, Wyatt E. & Henry, Guy H. (Southern Illinois U.) American Journal of Mental Deficiency, 1973(Jan), Vol. 77(4), 455-459. [PA, Vol 51:05479]

1471. Competition and social stimulation effects on simple motor performance of EMR children.
40 educable mentally retarded (EMR) children, assigned to 1 of 8 groups, were allowed 1 min to complete the simple motor Maze and Dots subtests of the Factored Aptitude Series. The groups differed as to whether the Ss were males or females, received competitive or noncompetitive instructions, and carried out the tasks in the presence or absence of social stimulation. Results include a significant Competition main effect and a significant Sex × Social Stimulation interaction on the efficiency ratings (response rate minus errors) for the maze task. The analysis of the dots task efficiency ratings shows only the effect of Social Stimulation to be significant. Although both Competition and Social Stimulation effects were noted, they were found to be somewhat task dependent. The significant interaction with sex suggests that it is not possible to generalize the effects of these variables across the sex variable at this time.
Stoneman, Zolinda & Keilman, Peggy A. (George Peabody Coll. for Teachers) American Journal of Mental Deficiency, 1973(Jul), Vol. 78(1), 98-100. [PA, Vol 51:05481]

1472. Counting and tracking of sequential visual stimuli by EMR and intellectually average children.
Conducted 2 experiments to examine the nature of the deficit in counting ability of educable mentally retarded (EMR) children. In Exp I 18 adolescent retarded boys performed counting and tracking tasks by responding to successive light flashes with random interflash intervals. No significant differences in accuracy of numerosity discrimination were obtained between task conditions. Exp II compared the tracking performance of 20 EMR boys with 20 younger, intellectually average boys of the same MA. IQ scores of retarded Ss were from individually administered WISC; IQ scores of nonretarded Ss were from the group administered California Test of Mental Maturity. The 2 groups did not differ significantly in mean errors in tracking performance, but the retarded group made errors of greater magnitude than the nonretarded. Magnitude of error increased with flash numerosity and more so by the retarded than by the nonretarded Ss. Data suggest that deficits in counting and tracking performance of the mildly retarded child are primarily related to stimulus input variables.

Thor, Donald H. (Edward R. Johnstone Training & Research Center, Bordentown, N.J.) American Journal of Mental Deficiency, 1973(Jul), Vol. 78(1), 41-46. [PA, Vol 51:05484]

1473.   Outerdirectedness in EMR boys and girls.
21 retarded boys and 21 retarded girls performed on an oddity learning task in 1 of 3 conditions: no E present (Not In), E present with relevant cues (Relevant Cue), and E present with irrelevant cues (Irrelevant Cue). Glancing data confirmed the hypothesis that Ss would generally show greater nontask orienting in the presence of an E. Learning data revealed significant treatment effects only for boys; performance in the relevant cue condition was better than in the irrelevant cue condition. Reversal trials confirm these findings and further reveal a significant positive correlation between learning and glancing in the relevant cue condition and a significant negative correlation in the irrelevant cue condition. Results are in general agreement with expectations arising from an outerdirectedness hypothesis. (17 ref)
Turnure, James E. (U. Minnesota) American Journal of Mental Deficiency, 1973(Sep), Vol. 78(2), 163-170. [PA, Vol 52:01297]

1474.   Effects of brain-injury and other subject characteristics on paired-associate performance under paragraph elaboration.
Investigated the effects of paragraph elaboration on paired-associate learning and reversal in 137 educable mentally retarded children classified as either brain-injured or non-brain-injured. Analyses of the relationship between performance on a 6-pair list and brain-injury classification were significant for acquisition only. Results suggest that the presence or absence of brain-injury may have implications for the choice of response measures in studies of language and learning. Results are also related to current questions regarding the interpretation and implications of A. R. Luria's theory of mental retardation. (18 ref.)
Turnure, James E.; Larsen, Sharon N. & Thurlow, Martha L. (U. Minnesota) American Journal of Mental Deficiency, 1973(Jul), Vol. 78(1), 70-76. [PA, Vol 51:05539]

1475.   Facilitation of class inclusion among mentally retarded children.
Investigated the effect of 3 task variables on the solution of verbal problems requiring quantitative class inclusion among 4 MA levels (7, 8, 9, 10). The task variables were (a) 2 or 3 pictures used in the problem, (b) enactive or iconic representation of the problem, and (c) numerical differences of the disjoint subtests in the problem. Ss were 96 9-20 yr olds enrolled in special classes for the educably mentally retarded. The main effects for number of pictures and mode of representation of the problem were not significant. Interaction effects revealed that the MA 10 group performed statistically better under the 2 picture and iconic conditions. A statistically significant main effect for numerical difference of subsets was obtained with numerically equal subsets resulting in significantly more correct answers. It is concluded that manipulation of the task variables may be more appropriate at a particular level of cognitive development than at another level. (18 ref)
Vitello, Stanley J. (Pennsylvania State U.) American Journal of Mental Deficiency, 1973(Sep), Vol. 78(2), 158-162. [PA, Vol 52:01299]

1476.   Self identification in the Make-A-Picture Story protocols of a group of retarded boys.
Administered the Make A Picture Story test to 24 10-yr-old educable mentally retarded boys and 24 nonretarded boys of similar age and socioeconomic class. Analysis of patterns of identification in the protocols suggests a significantly greater use of self-identification in the stories of the nonretarded group.
Ward, James. (U. Victoria, British Columbia, Canada) American Journal of Mental Deficiency, 1973(Jan), Vol. 77(4), 469-471. [PA, Vol 51:05486]

1477.   The relationship between WISC and WAIS IQs with educable mentally retarded adolescents.
Obtained WISC and WAIS scores from 51 adolescent Ss in an institution for the mentally retarded. Results show significant differences between WISC and WAIS Full Scale IQ. In each case, the WAIS scales yielded higher estimates, but it is also noted that high correlations existed between the 2 tests.
Wesner, Chester E.   Educational & Psychological Measurement, 1973(Sum), Vol. 33(2), 465-467. [PA, Vol 51:05489]

1478.   Social stereotypes for normal, educable mentally retarded, and orthopedically handicapped children.
Analyzed attitudes of 341 children in 12 5th-grade classes (median age = 10 yrs) by asking them to check a list of 46 descriptive words or phrases as they felt the words applied to (a) themselves (i.e., members of their own class), (b) other 5th-grade classes, (c) educable mentally retarded (EMR) pupils, and (d) orthopedically handicapped (OH) pupils. EMRs were asked to rate themselves and the 5th graders. Positive self-perceptions were held equally by normal Ss and EMRs; both groups viewed themselves more favorably than they were viewed by the other group. Normal Ss viewed members of their own class more favorably than they viewed those in other classes. A generally unfavorable stereotype was held for the EMRs, not only as to their academic difficulties but in the social-personal area. EMRs saw 5th graders unfavorably. Positive social stereotypes were held by normal Ss toward OHs; these attitudes were unrealistic and did not appear to be carried over into behavior. The general purport of results is that by age 10 considerable similarity of attitude has developed among both normal and retarded children.
Willey, Norman R. & McCandless, Boyd R. (Indiana Central Coll.) Journal of Special Education, 1973(Fal), Vol. 7(3), 283-288. [PA, Vol 52:03401]

1479.   Convergent and discriminant validity of the Peabody Individual Achievement Test with educable mentally retarded children.
Examined the Peabody Individual Achievement Test, also applying the Wide Range Achievement Test, and Metropolitan Achievement Test, to analyze validity of subtests. Results are discussed in terms of influence of trait or method on the performance of educable mentally retarded children.
Ysseldyke, James E.; Sabatino, David A. & Lamanna, Joseph. (Pennsylvania State U., Center for Educational Diagnosis & Remediation) Psychology in the Schools, 1973(Apr), Vol. 10(2), 200-204. [PA, Vol 50:08140]

1480.   Beam walking in special education.
Obtained data on an experimental beam-walking test from 415 boys and girls diagnosed as minimally brain-injured or educable mentally retarded. In general, analysis of variance indicated acceptable reliability estimates with the higher estimates for the educable retardates. Age changes in mean performance were apparent for all groups, no significant differences being noted between the sexes. The intellectually more able group of brain-injured children did not outperform the educable retardates. (21 ref)
Broadhead, Geoffrey D. (Moray House Coll. of Education, Edinburgh, Scotland) Rehabilitation Literature, 1974(May), Vol. 35(5), 145-147. [PA, Vol 52:07995]

1481.   Social class correlates of gross motor performance in special education.
Seeking to describe the relationship between social class traits and the gross motor performance of children in special education, data were obtained on 415 boys and girls, 8-13 yrs old, in separate classes for the minimally brain injured and for the educable mentally retarded. Most of the correlation coefficients were low, with few reaching statistical significance. Thus, differences in the gross motor performance of these children cannot be explained by the educational or occupational status of their parents, the number of children in the family, or the month of birth of the Ss. Nor were differences noted according to the disability category, sex, or chronological age of the children. (21 ref)
Broadhead, Geoffrey D. (Moray House Coll of Education, Edinburgh, Scotland) Rehabilitation Literature, 1974(Nov), Vol 35(11), 331-335. [PA, Vol 54:01445]

1482.   Effects of auditory reception on auditory and visual learning tasks.
Studied the effect of auditory reception on the learning of auditory and visual paired associate learning tasks in 72 educable retarded 9-13 yr old males. The 1st hypothesis was that high auditory receivers will perform significantly better than low auditory receivers on the auditory paired associate learning task. The 2nd hypothesis was that there will not be a significant difference between high auditory receivers and low auditory receivers on the visual paired associate learning tasks. Results indicate that auditory discrimination, as measured by the Wepman Auditory Discrimination Test, was a significant factor in auditory learning. High auditors performed significantly better than low auditors on the auditory paired associate learning task. There was no significant difference between high auditors and low auditors on the visual paired associate learning task.
Burcham, Temmie et al.   Education & Training of the Mentally Retarded, 1974(Apr), Vol 9(2), 56-61. [PA, Vol 53:09887]

1483.   [The effect of reinforcement and material organization on verbal paired-associate learning in normal and mentally retarded children.] (Chin)
Examined the effects of reinforcement and material organization on verbal paired associate learning in 40 educable mentally nonretarded children. 40 Ss were matched in MA and the others in CA. In each group 20 received reinforcement and 20 received no reinforcement. Results show that all groups performed significantly better on paired words of high associative strength than on those of low associative strength. Significant interactions between IQ level and learning material factors are discussed. The reinforcement variable did not affect the performance of any group on paired associate learning.
Chen, Yung-hwa.   Bulletin of Educational Psychology, 1974(Jun), Vol 7, 15-22. [PA, Vol 54:12079]

1484.   Factor structures of retarded and nonretarded children on Raven's Progressive Matrices.
Item responses of normal and educable mentally retarded children on Raven's Coloured Progressive Matrices were submitted to a principal components analysis and varimax rotation. 4 factors were obtained which corresponded to readily identifiable problem types. The factor structure for both groups of Ss was replicated by an independent sample. Comparability of factor structures of normal and retarded Ss indicate the factorial invariance of this test with children of different IQ levels.
Corman, Louise & Budoff, Milton. (Research Inst for Educational Problems, Cambridge, MA) Educational & Psychological Measurement, 1974(Sum), Vol 34(2), 407-412. [PA, Vol 53:02152]

1485.   Tangible rewards in assessing auditory discrimination performance of mentally retarded children.
Studied the performance of 30 educable mentally retarded 6.75-16.5 yr olds enrolled in special education classes on the Auditory Discrimination Test when Ss received tokens and tangible rewards for correct responses. Although the use of rewards did not affect overall performance, improvement in discrimination ability for word pairs contrasted by differences in the final consonant was observed.
Dahle, Arthur J. & Daly, David A. (U. Alabama, Birmingham) American Journal of Mental Deficiency, 1974(Mar), Vol. 78(5), 625-630. [PA, Vol 52:08003]

1486.   Expectancy in educable subnormal children and their normal mental age controls.
The long reaction times of mentally subnormal children have commonly been attributed to an inability to build up an adequate preparatory set. The present experiment tested this suggestion by comparing the ability of normal and educable subnormal (ESN) children to anticipate a regularly occurring event. The performance of 12 13-yr-old ESN boys was found to be inferior to that of 12 9-yr-old boys matched on mental age (9 yrs) both in terms of the accuracy and the variability of their anticipations. This inferiority disappeared when visual input was restricted to the relevant events. It is concluded that ESN children suffer both in the accuracy and in the variability with which they estimate time intervals. It is suggested that these deficits may be mediated either by a relatively high level of distractability or by a relatively low level of arousal. (19 ref)
Folkard, Simon. (MRC Applied Psychology Unit, U Sussex, Brighton, England) Quarterly Journal of Experimental Psychology, 1974(Aug), Vol 26(3), 495-502. [PA, Vol 53:03429]

1487.   Digit recall of mentally retarded and nonretarded children under three presentation rates.
2 groups of nonretarded children were matched on chronological age (CA) mean of 10 yrs and on Peabody Picture Vocabulary Test mental age (MA) with 27 mildly retarded children. The 3 groups were presented with a serial recall task similar to the forward series of the Digit Span subtest of the WISC. Digit strings of systematically increasing length were presented aurally at each of 3 presentation rates. The maximum length of digits Ss were able to recall correctly was found to be related to IQ, but not to MA or CA. The fastest rate of presentation produced significant increases in the accuracy of recall for all groups. Separate serial position analyses for strings containing different types of errors revealed strikingly different serial position functions for each error type. (38 ref)
Frankel, Fred & Tymchuk, Alexander J. (U California, Medical School, Los Angeles) American Journal of Mental Deficiency, 1974(Nov), Vol 79(3), 311-319. [PA, Vol 53:09892]

1488.   Labeling, rehearsal, and short-term memory in retarded children.
Used a short-term memory task to explore the effects of verbal labeling and rehearsal on serial-position recall in 86 mildly retarded 9-11 yr old children. A stimulus array consisting of 7 cards depicting familiar animals was presented for 7 trials. In Exp I, recall when Ss labeled the pictures as they were shown was compared to recall when no labeling occurred. Total recall was not affected, but for the older age group primacy recall was hindered and recency recall was facilitated by labeling. In Exp II, when prompting accompanied rehearsal, recall improved at both recency and primacy positions. When prompting occurred for the primacy positions only, recall was higher for these positions but not for other positions.
Hagen, John W.; Streeter, Lynn A. & Raker, Richard. (U Michigan) Journal of Experimental Child Psychology, 1974(Oct), Vol 18(2), 259-268. [PA, Vol 53:05668]

1489.   High speed memory scanning in mental retardates: Evidence for a central processing deficit.
Tested groups of 10 male 3rd-grade, high-school, and adult normal Ss and 2 diagnostic categories of educable mental retardates (cultural familials and encephalopathies) in a Sternberg-type memory scanning recognition task. All 5 groups showed the characteristic linear increase in correct reaction time as the number of items in the memorized set increased. The slopes of the linear functions, however, were steeper for the 2 retardate samples than for the normal samples, suggesting a central processing deficit which could not be attributed to a lag in development.
Harris, Gilbert J. & Fleer, Robert E. (Herbert H. Lehman Coll., City U. New York) Journal of Experimental Child Psychology, 1974(Jun), Vol. 17(3), 452-459. [PA, Vol 52:12726]

1490.   Children's verbal abstracting: Effects of enriched input, age, and IQ.
Gave 144 intellectually average (mean IQ = 100) and mildly intellectually subnormal (mean IQ = 82) children in Grades 1, 4, and 6 a verbal similarities task (composed of items from the Similarities subtests of the WAIS and WISC). 10 items were administered under a nonenriched (2 exemplars) condition and the remaining 10 items under 1 of 3 enriched (3, 4, or 5 exemplars) conditions. There was also a baseline control condition in which all items were presented under the nonenriched procedure. The intellectually subnormal children demonstrated higher verbal abstracting scores under the enriched conditions as compared to their baseline control group. The intellectually subnormal group also showed evidence of a learning-set-like

phenomenon: experience with the enriched items raised their verbal abstracting scores on subsequent nonenriched items. (25 ref)

Haywood, H. Carl & Switzky, Harvey N. (George Peabody Coll. for Teachers) American Journal of Mental Deficiency, 1974(Mar), Vol. 78(5), 556-565. [PA, Vol 52:08015]

1491.   Enumeration versus tracking during unimodal and multimodal sequential information processing in normals and retardates.
Presented varying length pulse sequences to 24 16-yr-old educable retardates, 24 equal chronological age (CA) normals, and 24 9-yr-old equal mental age (MA) normals under 3 modality switching conditions and 2 response modes. Error magnitudes were greatest for retardates, less for equal-MA normals, and least for equal-CA normals. Error magnitudes also increased significantly from the no switching to maximum modality switching condition, from the enumeration to motor tracking response mode, and with increasing numerosities. Error increases from enumeration to tracking and from no switching to maximum modality switching rates were predominantly underestimations, confirming previous findings that attention shifting interferes with input or storage of stimulus number.
Holden, Edward A. (Edward R. Johnstone Training & Research Ctr, Bordentown, NJ) Developmental Psychology, 1974(Sep), Vol 10(5), 667-671. [PA, Vol 53:03440]

1492.   Effects of incentive on rotary pursuit performance by normals and retardates.
Based on previous comparative research inconsistency in the rotary pursuit performance of 30 normals (mean age, 12.5 yrs) and 30 educable retardates (mean age, 12.4 yrs; mean IQ, 72.5), the present study manipulated knowledge of results across 2 intellectual levels. Significant effects of IQ, Trials, and Incentive and several interesting significant interactions were found. Normals increased their performance efficiency over retardates' as trials progressed. Ss at both intellectual levels, when provided incentives, increased their performance over that of similar groups without incentive as trials progressed. An IQ × Incentive trend was found, with educable retardates appearing to profit more from incentive than normals.
Holland, Jean M.; Friedrich, Douglas & Hawkins, William F. (Central Michigan U) Perceptual & Motor Skills, 1974(Aug), Vol 39(1, Pt 2), 491-494. [PA, Vol 56:10139]

1493.   WISC subtest patterns of educationally handicapped and educable mentally retarded pupils.
The scaled scores of the WISC for 157 Ss were grouped according to Witkin's 3 factors (e.g., verbal comprehension, attention-concentration, and analytical-field-approach). Significant differences in analytical, attention, and verbal-index scores were obtained. It is concluded that treatment programs should be individualized after diagnosis because standardized approaches designed to help these types of children tend not to be helpful.
Keogh, Barbara K. & Hall, Robert J. (U California, Los Angeles) Psychology in the Schools, 1974(Jul), Vol 11(3), 296-300. [PA, Vol 53:10522]

1494.   Social reinforcement and knowledge of results as determinants of motor performance among EMR children.
Determined the effect of social reinforcement and knowledge of results on the performance of an accuracy motor task by 80 educable mentally retarded children (chronological age range 8-14 yrs; mental age range 5-10.3 yrs). An analysis of variance was performed on the 2 (Knowledge of Results) × 4 (Social Reinforcement) × 6 (Block) factorial design with repeated measures on the last factor. The motor task used was performance on a photoelectric rotary pursuit. Results indicate that motor performance with this population improved in all social reinforcement conditions to a greater degree when knowledge of results was present than when it was absent. (24 ref)
Levy, Joseph. (U. Waterloo, Faculty of Human Kinetics & Leisure Studies, Ontario, Canada) American Journal of Mental Deficiency, 1974(May), Vol. 78(6), 752-758. [PA, Vol 52:08023]

1495.   Factor analysis of gross and fine motor ability in developmentally disabled children.
Performed a factor analysis using scores from a variety of gross and fine motor tests given to 93 educable mentally retarded and/or developmentally disabled children aged 64-174 mo. Results suggest that motor ability be viewed in terms of 8 functioning areas: upper extremity coordination, rhythmic ability, general muscular coordination, gross motor functioning, praxis, dynamic balance, maturation, and sex. It is noted that factor structure findings should be considered in relation to the specific population under study. (35 ref)
Liemohn, Wendell P. & Knapczyk, Dennis R. (Indiana U Developmental Training Ctr) Research Quarterly, 1974(Dec), 45(4), 424-432. [PA, Vol 56:04153]

1496.   The measurement of mental retardation by a culture-specific test.
Gives a number of correlations between the WISC and the Black Intelligence Test for Cultural Homogeneity. Ss were 30 black students in classes for the educable mentally retarded (EMR). It is concluded that EMR students will score poorly on test instruments regardless of cultural specificity built into the instrument.
Long, Peggie A. & Anthony, John J. (School Board of Alachua City, Gainesville, FL) Psychology in the Schools, 1974(Jul), Vol 11(3), 310-312. [PA, Vol 53:10526]

1497.   Physiological responses of EMR children to strenuous exercise.
A battery of physiological tests administered to 62 10-13 yr old black and white educable mentally retarded boys resulted in no statistically significant physiological differences between the 2 racial groups. The maximal oxygen uptake for Ss appeared to be lower than data reported for nonretarded children; some rationale for this lower aerobic power is discussed. (24 ref)
Maksud, Michael G. & Hamilton, Lyle H. (U Wisconsin, Milwaukee) American Journal of Mental Deficiency, 1974(Jul), Vol 79(1), 32-38. [PA, Vol 53:01486]

1498.   Definition of the mentally retarded: Decision time for AAMD.
Discusses the implications of recent court suits and legislative enactments which have provided stricter definitions of the "educable mentally retarded." Areas of responsibility, continuing responsibility, and shared responsibility for the American Association on Mental Deficiency for children with learning problems are noted.
Meyers, C. Edward & Lombardi, Thomas P. (U. Southern California) Mental Retardation, 1974(Apr), Vol. 12(2), 43. [PA, Vol 52:10435]

1499.   Self-concept of institutional and non-institutional educable mentally retarded children.
Compared 20 public school special education and 20 institutionalized educable mentally retarded 8.0–13.6-yr-old children on an experimental I Feel-Me Feel self-perception scale. No significant differences in self-concept were found between the institutional and noninstitutional groups or between sexes. All Ss had generally good self-concepts.
Montague, James C. & Cage, Bob N. (U. Arkansas, Little Rock) Perceptual & Motor Skills, 1974(Jun), Vol. 38(3, Pt. 1), 977-978. [PA, Vol 52:12733]

1500.   Verbal auditory screening with the educable mentally retarded.
Investigated the efficiency of the Verbal Auditory Screening for Children (VASC) compared to a pure-tone threshold test as a technique to identify hearing impairment among 97 6-15 yr old educable mentally retarded children. The VASC correctly identified 72.2% of the total Ss. Of the 36 Ss failed by the pure-tone threshold test, 75% were missed by the VASC. It is concluded that the VASC technique cannot identify all cases of hearing loss identified by a pure-tone threshold test when used with educable mentally retarded children.
Neal, W. R. (U Georgia, Coll of Education) Training School Bulletin, 1974(May), Vol 71(1), 62-66. [PA, Vol 53:01490]

1501.   **Conceptual preference in children: Task-specific findings.**
Administered a forced-choice equivalence formation task to 36 1st, 4th, and 6th graders with average (105-120) and below average (70-90) IQs. Ss' preferences for 4 dimensions (color, form, activity, and function) were compared. There was an increase in symbolic preferences (activity and function) in the 6th graders. In contrast to previous findings, there were no IQ differences. This discrepancy is discussed in terms of capabilities (competencies) vs strategies (performance and task variables).
Odom, Penelope B. (George Peabody Coll. for Teachers) American Journal of Mental Deficiency, 1974(May), Vol. 78(6), 659-664. [PA, Vol 52:08032]

1502.   **Effects of race and sex on attribution of intellectual achievement: Responsibility for success and failure situations among educable mentally retarded children.**
Conducted a locus-of-control study with 249 educable mentally retarded (EMR) children-157 boys (100 black, 57 white) and 92 girls (50 black, 42 white)-from 2 inner-city junior high schools in a midwestern city in the US. The Intellectual Achievement Responsibility test was administered. Ss indicated greater externality in described failure situations than in success situations ($p < .05$), and male Ss appeared to be more internally controlled than females ($p < .05$). Ethnic-group membership did not produce a significant main effect or a significant interaction with sex. Differences between EMR and normal Ss are discussed. (22 ref)
Panda, Kailash C. & Lynch, William W. (SCS Coll, Puri, India) Indian Journal of Mental Retardation, 1974(Jul), Vol 7(2), 72-80. [PA, Vol 53:11957]

1503.   **Facilitation of semantic integration in sentence memory of retarded children.**
Gave 40 children classified in the EMR ability range (chronological age range 89-161 mo) a sentence recognition test following verbal presentation of short paragraph stories. Ss spontaneously generated implied information from the stories and remembered the integrated semantic meanings of the passages rather than the individual sentences. In Task 2, ½ of the Ss were given imagery instructions prior to listening to the paragraphs. The imagery-instructed Ss constructed more inferential relationships and retained more of the semantic information of the stories than Ss not receiving imagery instructions. Results are discussed with regard to the constructive and operative aspects of comprehension. Implications for the study of memory in moderately retarded children are also presented. (20 ref)
Paris, Scott G.; Mahoney, Gerald J. & Buckhalt, Joseph A. (Purdue U.) American Journal of Mental Deficiency, 1974(May), Vol. 78(6), 714-720. [PA, Vol 52:08036]

1504.   **Comparison of retarded and nonretarded children on the dimensions of behavior in recreation groups.**
Placed 70 6-17 yr old educable mentally retarded (EMR) children in adult-led recreation groups of nonretarded children at a community center over a 4-yr period to investigate the extent to which EMR children can participate in such groups. The 2 dimensions usually found in studies of child behavior were descriptive of the behavior of both the EMR and the nonretarded children. The EMR children scored lower on the dimension of Interest-Participation vs Apathy-Withdrawal than did the nonretarded children, but with some overlap of the distributions. No difference was found between EMR and other children on the dimension of Cooperation-Compliance vs Anger-Defiance. Individual differences in behavior of the EMR children on these dimensions were, in part, predictable and consistent over groups.
Peters, Edward N.; Pumphrey, Muriel W. & Flax, Norman. (New York State Dept of Mental Hygiene, Rochester) American Journal of Mental Deficiency, 1974(Jul), Vol 79(1), 87-94. [PA, Vol 53:01491]

1505.   **Comparison of conceptual strategies for grouping and remembering employed by EMR and nonretarded children.**
Compared the kinds of groupings generated in a sorting task by 86 educable mentally retarded children (mean IQ = 70) and 31 nonretarded 2nd graders matched for CA and socioeconomic status. Further comparisons were made of the total recall and organization of recall in each group. As expected, there were significant differences between the samples on indices of grouping strategies generated. These differences were related to highly significant differences in recall scores. Implications of the findings are discussed and it is concluded that an analysis of recall performance and its relationship to sorting performance provides a useful approach to the analysis of learning strategies. (25 ref)
Riegel, R. Hunt & Taylor, Arthur M. (Western Michigan U.) American Journal of Mental Deficiency, 1974(Mar), Vol. 78(5), 592-598. [PA, Vol 52:08037]

1506.   **Comparability of Columbia Mental Maturity Scale and Stanford-Binet, Form L-M, estimates of intelligence.**
Analysis of results of administration of the tests to 45 educable mentally retarded children indicates substantial agreement between these estimates of intelligence. Use of the 1972 revision of the Columbia Scale in screening applicants for special education classes appears defensible, but it is suggested that placement should not be made solely on the basis of Scale results.
Ritter, David; Duffey, James & Fischman, Ronald. (Montgomery County Schools, Pa.) Psychological Reports, 1974(Feb), Vol. 34(1), 174. [PA, Vol 52:08735]

1507.   **Spatial egocentrism in nonretarded and retarded children.**
Examined the relation of chronological (CA) and mental (MA) ages to 2 spatial egocentrism tasks by comparing the performance of MA-matched nonretarded and retarded children, and CA-matched nonretarded and retarded children. 28 2nd graders, 30 6th graders, and 20 retarded children participated. Retarded children performed similarly to nonretarded Ss of the same MA but inferior to their nonretarded CA peers.
Rubin, Kenneth H. & Orr, R. Robert. (U Waterloo, Ontario, Canada) American Journal of Mental Deficiency, 1974(Jul), Vol 79(1), 95-97. [PA, Vol 53:01493]

1508.   **Bender-Gestalt correlates among normal and retarded students: CA, IQ, and pursuit rotor performance.**
Found that among mentally retarded Ss, the best predictor of Bender-Gestalt test performance was rotary pursuit performance. Age also contributed significantly to the regression equation. Among normal Ss, the significant predictors were rotary pursuit performance and intelligence. When intelligence was not held constant, it became the most powerful predictor for both groups. (20 ref)
Simensen, R. J. (Armstrong State Coll.) Journal of Clinical Psychology, 1974(Apr), Vol. 30(2), 172-175. [PA, Vol 52:10441]

1509.   **Logical problem solving by educable retarded adolescents and normal children.**
Gave a simplified version of the logical problem-solving task developed by E. D. Neimark to 20 institutionalized and 18 noninstitutionalized retardates and to 20 children from kindergarten through 3rd grade. The performance of the retardates fell below that of the normals of equal mental age. Although the retardates and the younger children solved the problem when the critical information was supplied to them, most of these Ss could not generate the necessary information by themselves, and continued to make redundant responses. For the normals, performance improved up to 81/2-9 yrs of age, at which point 90% reached criterion. Training improved the performance of 7 yr olds but had little or no effect on the performance of 6 yr olds and institutionalized retarded adolescents. (17 ref)
Spitz, Herman H. & Nadler, Barbara T. (Edward R. Johnstone Training and Research Center, Bordentown, N.J.) Developmental Psychology, 1974(May), Vol. 10(3), 404-412. [PA, Vol 52:10442]

1510.   **Manipulation of numerical presentation in verbal problems and its effect on verbal problem solving among EMH children.**
Examined the effect of numerical presentation, set language, and distractor position on the problem-solving abilities of 24 educable

mentally handicapped children. Results suggest that the use of supraordinate set language and the presence of distractors in the subject position of the extraneous information sentence leads to less efficient verbal problem solving. The results are attributed, in part, to the existence of rote computational habits. Implications for educational interventions are suggested.
Thibodeau, Gerard P. (U. Connecticut) Education & Training of the Mentally Retarded, 1974(Feb), Vol. 9(1), 9-14. [PA, Vol 52:08050]

1511. Modality preference and reading task performance among the mildly retarded.
Randomly placed 22 7–9 yr old mildly retarded Ss with auditory preferences and 22 with visual preferences into instructional groups emphasizing either an auditory (phonic) or visual (look-say) approach to reading. Each S was taught a group of unknown (nonsense) syllables for a 30-min period. Number correct following the training session served as the dependent measure. Results fail to support the assumption that children learn best when taught to their perceptual strengths. Neither approach was superior, irrespective of preferred modality. (24 ref)
Tyler, James L. (U. Mississippi) Training School Bulletin, 1974(Feb), Vol. 70(4), 208-214. [PA, Vol 52:12744]

1512. Visual masking, mental age, and retardation.
In a recognition task involving both forward and backward visual masking, performance of 20 mildly retarded adolescents was less accurate than that of 20 normal Ss matched for chronological age and 20 matched for mental age. It is suggested that the iconic memory impairment of retarded Ss is attributable in part to mental retardation and not simply to low mental age. (17 ref)
Welsandt, Roy F. & Meyer, Philip A. (Wisconsin State U) Journal of Experimental Child Psychology, 1974(Dec), Vol 18(3), 512-519. [PA, Vol 53:09912]

1513. Eye movements and conservation development in mildly retarded and nonretarded children.
Tested 30 nonretarded and 30 mildly retarded elementary-school children (mean ages = 86-123 mo) on 4 Piagetian conservation tasks (number, length, and continuous quantity solid-liquid). Eye movements were recorded during the response period for each task. Comparisons were made between nonretarded conservers and nonconservers and between mildly retarded conservers and nonconservers. Eye movements clearly differentiated conservers and nonconservers in nonretarded and, to a slightly lesser degree, mildly retarded groups. Results indicate that conservation acquisition was accompanied by 2 discernible changes in perceptual activity. Visual exploratory behavior appeared to increase and centration effects to decrease following conservation acquisition. Results are discussed in terms of Piaget's theoretical position and possible cognitive structural differences between nonretarded and mildly retarded children. (19 ref)
Wilton, Keri M. & Boersma, Frederic J. (U Canterbury, Christchurch, New Zealand) American Journal of Mental Deficiency, 1974(Nov), Vol 79(3), 285-291. [PA, Vol 53:09913]

1514. Effects of modeling and verbal cues upon concept acquisition of nonretarded and retarded children.
Administered 9 easy and hard items from the Leiter International Performance Scale under 4 conditions (no modeling, modeling only, modeling and low meaning verbalizations, and modeling plus conceptual verbalizations) to 40 educable mentally retarded children (mean CA range 11.66-12.02 yrs; mean MA range 6.97-7.37) and 40 nonretarded children (mean CA range 6.65-6.69 yrs; mean MA range 7.08-7.57). There were no significant differences in the effects of the various conditions on the number of errors on simple items, while on hard items, the 3 modeling conditions were associated with significantly fewer errors than the no modeling condition. The modeling and conceptual verbalization group performed significantly better than the 2 other modeling groups. Nonretarded Ss spent more time completing the tasks than the retarded Ss.
Yoder, Pam & Forehand, Rex. (U. Georgia) American Journal of Mental Deficiency, 1974(Mar), Vol. 78(5), 566-570. [PA, Vol 52:08056]

1515. Structural similarity of the motor domain of normal and educable retarded boys.
Six derived factor solutions (3 orthogonal and 3 oblique) described factors from the intercorrelation matrices of 47 motor performance and physical growth measures obtained on 71 normal boys and 71 educable retarded boys aged 6-9.9 yrs. Six comparable common factors, labeled (a) Strength/Power/Body Size; (b) Gross Limb Eye Coordination; (c) Fine Visual Motor Coordination; (d) Fat or Dead Weight; (e) Balance; and (f) Leg Power and Coordination were identified in the factor patterns of both groups of Ss. Four comparable specific factors were also recognized for both groups. Application of the H. F. Kaiser et al (1971) technique to quantify the similarity of factor patterns supported the conclusion that the basic components which underlie a major portion of the motor domain of intellectually normal and educable retarded boys are tangibly coincident. (27 ref)
Dobbins, D. Alan & Rarick, G. Lawrence. (U Texas, Austin) Research Quarterly, 1975(Dec), Vol 46(4), 447-456. [PA, Vol 56:04272]

1516. The usefulness of the semantic differential with "mild grade" mental defectives.
Tested the hypotheses that (a) mildly retarded Ss, in comparison with Ss of average intelligence, would show less discrimination in the use of the semantic differential (SD) and (b) such discrimination deficiencies would predispose retarded Ss toward a polarized response bias. 20 retarded males (mean age, 19.1 yrs) in a training center and 15 high school students matched for socioeconomic status and age were administered an SD containing 17 concepts representing 3 areas (personal, love-affection, and environmental). Ss rated the concepts on 7 bipolar scales loading on the evaluative dimension, 4 scales on the potency dimension, and 4 on the activity dimension. A discrimination index was computed for each concept. Results support both hypotheses. The significantly lower discrimination indexes of the retarded Ss were largely attributable to their significant preference for the 1st choice point. Results have implications for the reliability and validity of the SD used with retarded groups. (28 ref)
Dow, M. G.; Ledwith, F; Fraser, W. I. & Bhagat, M. (Gartnavel Royal Hosp, Glasgow, England) British Journal of Psychiatry, 1975(Oct), Vol 127, 386-392. [PA, Vol 55:04861]

1517. Folate-responsive homocystinuria and "schizophrenia": A defect in methylation due to deficient 5,10-methylenetetrahydrofolate reductase activity.
Homocystinuria and homocystinemia without hypermethioninemia, but with recurrent episodes of folate responsive schizophrenic-like behavior, was documented in a mildly retarded adolescent girl who lacked the habitus associated with cystathionine synthase deficiency. Methylenetetrahydrofolate reductase was 18% of control values; a deficiency of this compound could explain the homocystinemia and homocystinuria. (44 ref)
Freeman, John M.; Finkelstein, James D. & Mudd, S. Harvey. (Johns Hopkins U Hosp) New England Journal of Medicine, 1975(Mar), Vol 292(10), 491-496. [PA, Vol 54:01453]

1518. Differences between EMR and nonretarded children in fluency and quality of verbal associations.
An association task, in which an S was asked to give up to 25 associations to each of 10 verbal stimuli, was administered to 32 educable mentally retarded (EMR) and 32 nonretarded Ss, along with the Peabody Picture Vocabulary Test. The associations were scored for quantity and speed of response and categorized by a modification of J. H. Flavell and J. Draguns's (1957) system for response quality. As expected, the 2 groups differed in vocabulary size. When vocabulary size was controlled, relatively few differences between EMR and nonretarded Ss remained: EMR Ss were slower than nonretarded Ss in their 1st and continuing responses to the association stimuli, used fewer logical associations, and used fewer responses with vocational connotations. In light of the fact that after adjustment for vocabulary differences the 2 groups differed on only 6 of the 24 measures examined, the associative networks of the 2 groups were surprisingly compara-

ble. The remaining differences demonstrated a specific deficit in logical connections and in speed of access to the associative net. (22 ref)
Harrison, Robert H.; Budoff, Milton & Greenberg, Gail. (Research Inst for Educational Problems, Cambridge, MA) American Journal of Mental Deficiency, 1975(Mar), Vol 79(5), 583-591. [PA, Vol 54:03429]

1519. The significance of stimuli on conservation of number with educable mentally retarded children.
Studied the differential effects of the significance of stimuli on educable mentally retarded (EMR) children in a conservation of number experiment. Ss were 30 low- and 30 middle-socioeconomic status (SES) children with a mean IQ of 68.9 attending classes for the EMR. The effect of using candies or paperclips was investigated in Piaget's 1-to-1 correspondence task. A significant interaction between SES and the significance of stimuli was found. This is discussed in terms of the possible misdiagnosis of lower-class children, multiple criteria diagnostic procedures, and the relevance of cues. (23 ref)
Kahn, J. V. & Reid, D. K. (U Illinois, Chicago Circle) British Journal of Educational Psychology, 1975(Feb), Vol 45(1), 62-67. [PA, Vol 54:01418]

1520. Motor and perceptual determinants of performance on the Bender-Gestalt and the Beery developmental scale by retarded males.
Administered the Bender Visual Motor Gestalt Test and Beery's Developmental Test of Visual Motor Integration to 51 educable mentally retarded boys aged 72-161 mo. These scores were compared with scores Ss received on 3 gross motor tasks by computing simple correlation coefficients and multiple regression coefficients with the Bender and Beery tests as dependent variables. The simple *rs* were similar, but order of inclusion of independent variables in the regression analysis suggests differences.
Liemohn, Wendell & Wagner, Patrick. (Indiana U) Perceptual & Motor Skills, 1975(Apr), Vol 40(2), 524-526. [PA, Vol 54:09967]

1521. Effect of experimental success and failure on the situational expectancy of EMR and nonretarded children.
Studied the effect of differing histories of success and experimentally induced success and failure on the generalized and situational expectancy of a total of 48 educable mentally retarded (EMR) and nonretarded children; Ss were divided into 3 groups of 16 each. EMR Ss were matched with 1 sample of nonretarded Ss on the basis of CA (12-14 yrs) and another sample of nonretarded Ss on the basis of MA (7-10 yrs). Ss were asked to indicate how well they thought they would do on an experimental task (verbal estimate) and to predict how many out of 8 trials on which they would be successful. Then they were exposed either to experimentally induced success or failure. Ss were then asked to give a verbal estimate and numerical prediction for a subsequent block of trials. Results fail to support the role of history of success on expectancy; however, the experimentally induced success and failure had a significant effect on both verbal estimates and numerical predictions independent of groups. Results are discussed in terms of social-learning theory, and certain methodological problems in this time of research are noted.
MacMillan, Donald L. (Neuropsychiatric Inst, Pacific State Hosp Research Group, Pomona, CA) American Journal of Mental Deficiency, 1975(Jul), Vol 80(1), 90-95. [PA, Vol 54:09969]

1522. Tactile function of educable mentally retarded children.
Studied the tactile perception ability of 29 7- and 8-yr-old educable mentally retarded children using the tactile perception portions of the Southern California Sensory Integration Tests. Ss were also observed for tactile defensive behavior. Compared to normal children of the same age (as reported in normative data), this sample of children was significantly inferior in manual form, finger identification, graphesthesia, and perception of simultaneous stimuli, but not in the localization of single stimuli. During the testing, 62% showed tactile defensive behavior. The role of

tactile perception in the development of symbolic communications is reviewed. (27 ref)
McCracken, Alice. (Southside Virginia Training Ctr, Petersburg) American Journal of Occupational Therapy, 1975(Aug), Vol 29(7), 397-402. [PA, Vol 54:12089]

1523. Language performance of educable mentally retarded and normal children at five age levels.
Analyzed and compared the language performance of 30 educable mentally retarded and 30 normal children at mental age levels of 6-10 yrs. Both syntactic and functional performance variables were investigated during interviews with the Ss. Results indicate language performance differences between the 2 groups, with the primary discriminators being hesitation phenomena (false starts, filled pauses, and repeats) and clausal constructions (relative and subordinate clauses), resulting in a higher sentence elaboration level for normal children.
Naremore, Rita C. & Dever, Richard B. (Indiana U) Journal of Speech & Hearing Research, 1975(Mar), Vol 18(1), 82-95. [PA, Vol 54:01421]

1524. Stimulus persistence in retarded and nonretarded children: A signal detection analysis.
Tested 9 institutionalized educable mentally retarded (mean CA 12.7 yrs) and 9 nonretarded (mean CA 13.01 yrs) males on a visual backward masking task. Signal detection analysis was used to separate the sensory and nonsensory aspects of behavior, and the presentation of stimuli was randomized to minimize the formation of effective strategies. Two sets of instructions, strict and lenient, and 2 stimulus durations, 10 and 30 msec, were used in a repeated measures design. No differences were found between the groups on interstimulus interval threshold or measures of stimulus sensitivity, criterion placement, and false positive rate. Retarded Ss showed significantly greater inter-S variability in criterion placement but failed to raise their criterion in response to strict instructions. Results suggest that (a) stimulus-trace concepts of retardation have been confounded by retarded Ss' inability to compete effectively with nonretarded Ss in the experimental situation, and (b) signal detection procedures are a useful alternative to traditional psychophysical techniques in such comparative research. (26 ref)
Ryan, Mike & Jones, Bill. (Baillie-Henderson Hosp, Toowoomba, Australia) American Journal of Mental Deficiency, 1975(Nov), Vol 80(3), 298-305. [PA, Vol 55:10074]

1525. Imitation of retarded children by their nonretarded peers.
Conducted a study of 60 nonretarded 9-12 yr olds and 20 similar-aged educable mentally retardates (EMR) to determine whether nonretarded children would imitate the behavior of retarded children who were more competent in an experimental task and to determine whether this imitation would generalize to the selection of the retarded children as task partners in another situation. Each nonretarded O was allowed to imitate the task behavior of an EMR model when the model was either more, equally, or less competent than the O in the experimental task. Results indicate that (a) nonretarded Os imitated the behavior of the high competent EMR model significantly more often than the moderately competent model, with the latter in turn being imitated more than the noncompetent model and (b) that females imitated both low and high competent models more than males, who were most apt to imitate the behavior of moderately competent models. Competent EMR models were more likely to be chosen as partners on a future game task. (15 ref)
Strichart, Stephen S. & Gottlieb, Jay. (Rutgers State U, Graduate School of Education, New Brunswick) American Journal of Mental Deficiency, 1975(Mar), Vol 79(5), 506-512. [PA, Vol 54:04134]

1526. Melodic memory tests: A comparison of normal children and mental defectives.
A melodic memory test divided into 2 series, one tonal and the other atonal, was given to 480 children of normal intelligence and 396 mental defectives. The normal group ranged in age between 5 yrs, 6 mo and 16 yrs, 6 mo. The defectives (IQs between 50 and

85) had an age range of 8 yrs, 4 mo to 16 yrs, 6 mo. Results demonstrate that the acuity of perceptive discrimination in the defectives was clearly inferior to that of the normal children of the same CA and approximated that of normal children of the same MA. Tonal acculturation was shown by a significantly easier discrimination in the tonal series, in relation to the MA of the Ss. (15 ref)
Zenatti, Arlette. (U Paris, France) Journal of Research in Music Education, 1975(Spr), Vol 23(1), 41-52. [PA, Vol 54:09982]

1527.   Long-term effectiveness of imagery instruction with retarded persons.
Investigated the effects of imagery instructions on paired-associate learning efficiency and on the retention of 16 picture pairs, using 2 groups with a total of 30 educable mentally retarded Ss with approximate mental ages of 8 and 11 yrs, respectively. While facilitated list mastery was obtained under imagery instructions, no facilitation was found for 1-wk retention performance. However, in learning a new list immediately following the retention task, Ss who had received imagery instructions during original learning continued to exhibit facilitated learning. (28 ref)
Zupnick, Jack J. & Meyer, Philip A. (U South Dakota) American Journal of Mental Deficiency, 1975(Mar), Vol 79(5), 519-525. [PA, Vol 54:03455]

1528.   Transfer of categorical clustering set in mildly retarded adolescents.
Investigated the relative effectiveness of instructions to adopt an organizational strategy vs exposure to category labels. 24 retarded adolescents were assigned to each of 3 conditions (blocking plus instructions, blocking plus labels, and blocking) for pretraining and training. Immediately after training, all Ss received a transfer task consisting of a new randomly organized list containing words from the same (training) categories for half of the Ss and from different categories for the other half. When exposure to category labels accompanied blocking, results indicated increased clustering and recall during the training phase and a trend toward increased clustering during the transfer phase.
Bilsky, Linda H. (Teachers Coll, Columbia U) American Journal of Mental Deficiency, 1976(May), Vol 80(6), 588-594. [PA, Vol 56:04269]

1529.   Cognitive strategy accessibility as a function of task requirement in educable mentally retarded adolescents.
Investigated the accessibility of cognitive strategies in 115 mentally retarded adolescents (CA, 14.81; IQ, 62.44 as measured by the Peabody Picture Vocabulary, the WISC, or the Stanford Binet Intelligence Scale). Three tasks—abstraction, categorical clustering, and sorting—were used. The accessibility of cognitive strategies was found to be related to explicitness of the task requirement. Data are interpreted as supportive of a production deficiency in the mentally retarded. (15 ref)
Blackman, Leonard S. & Burger, Agnes L. (Teachers Coll, Columbia U) Bulletin of the Psychonomic Society, 1976(Sep), Vol 8(3), 221-223. [PA, Vol 57:08483]

1530.   The effects of training specific mnemonics on the metamnemonic efficiency of retarded children.
Investigated the effects of training specific mnemonic skills on recall readiness in 66 educable retarded children in 2 groups (MAs 6 and 8 yrs). Equal numbers of Ss at each age were instructed in an anticipation, rehearsal, or label strategy. On the first posttest (prompted), label training did not affect performance, but anticipation and rehearsal training facilitated recall readiness estimation for both younger and older children. However, on 2 subsequent posttests (unprompted, 2 days and 2 wks after training), the younger Ss returned to their pretraining competency, while the older group maintained high performance. Consideration of observational data suggest that overt activity related to the trained mnemonic correlated with recall readiness efficiency for the older but not the younger group. Even though younger children produced the strategy, they failed to monitor its effectiveness. The implications of training specific mnemonic

skills are discussed in relation to developing metamnemonic efficiency. (20 ref)
Brown, Ann L. & Barclay, Craig R. (U Illinois) Child Development, 1976(Mar), Vol 47(1), 71-80. [PA, Vol 56:10127]

1531.   Efficiency of self-generated elaborations by EMR and nonretarded children.
Gave paired-associates learning tasks to 24 regular class 2nd graders and 24 educable mentally retarded (EMR) class children (mean CA, 102.7 mo). Ss in each group received instructions to elaborate the noun pairs by embedding them in a sentence, and a qualitative analysis of the elaborations generated by the Ss was conducted by comparing levels of recall associated with the different types of elaboration. Elaborations that were conjunctive in nature, especially those which expressed thematic or functional relationships, were most effective overall. EMR Ss generated more inefficient elaborations than did nonretarded Ss.
Buckhalt, Joseph A.; Mahoney, Gerald J. & Paris, Scott G. (East Alabama Mental Health-Mental Retardation Ctr, Opelika, AL) American Journal of Mental Deficiency, 1976(Jul), Vol 81(1), 93-96. [PA, Vol 56:10128]

1532.   The personality characteristics of ESN(M) adolescents: Do teachers' views match reality?
Administered the Eysenck Junior Personality Inventory to mildly educationally subnormal (ESN-M) school children and to a control sample attending remedial classes. Results indicate that the ESN were not more emotionally unstable or socially withdrawn than the remedial sample or the population in general.
Burden, Robert. (Exeter U, England) AEP (Association of Educational Psychologists) Journal, 1976(Xmas), Vol 4(3), 18–20. [PA, Vol 59:05889]

1533.   Utilization of the OVIS with an EMR population.
Evaluated the Ohio Vocational Interest Survey (OVIS) for use with the educable mentally retarded (EMR). 158 EMR 9th graders from 12 of Pittsburgh's 13 high schools were the Ss with 115 mainstream 9th graders as controls. Administration of the test to EMRs was supervised by 12 rehabilitation counselors, one in each school. The controls were tested in a mass program. Ss showed significantly more inconsistent responses and fewer consistent ones than controls. There were 82% usable responses from the EMRs and 92% from controls. Counselors rated Ss' understanding as poor and their attention as inadequate. Of the 12 counselors, 10 did not recommend the use of the OVIS with EMR students because of the time required and the poor results. The 2 who wanted to continue its use felt that it stimulated interest and had other secondary benefits. It is suggested that a shorter, simpler instrument be used.
Cohen, Charles & Drugo, John. (Pittsburgh Board of Education, PA) Vocational Evaluation & Work Adjustment Bulletin, 1976(Mar), Vol 9(1), 22-25. [PA, Vol 56:08777]

1534.   Verbalization in EMR children's observational learning.
Examined the effect of descriptive verbalization during observation of a model on mentally retarded boys' retention for what they had observed. 40 9- to 12-yr-old boys in public-school educable mentally retarded classes were grouped on the basis of relatively high (75 and above) or low (67 and below) IQ scores. One-half of each group observed a videotaped model perform a series of novel acts, while in addition to viewing the tape, the other half described the model's actions. Observational learning was immediately tested through a set of prompts for imitation, with prizes offered commensurate with level of performance. Regardless of IQ group, Ss who were required to verbalize the model's behavior were able to imitate it significantly better than Ss who merely watched the model; high and low IQ groups did not significantly differ in observational learning. (40 ref)
Cullinan, Douglas. (Northern Illinois U) American Journal of Mental Deficiency, 1976(Jul), Vol 81(1), 65-72. [PA, Vol 56:10133]

1535.   Separation potential of educable retarded and intellectually normal boys as a function of motor performance.
Examined the relationship between motor performance and intelligence in terms of the accuracy of discrimination possible (based on motor performance data only) between S groups representing 2 levels of intelligence. 71 males of normal intelligence and 71 educable retarded males (mean ages 100.7 and 102.7 mo, respectively) were administered 47 motor performance and physique measures. Utilizing separate factor analyses, 16 variables emerged as common across the derived factor structures of the 2 groups. A discriminant function analysis showed that better than 94% of the normal Ss were correctly identified, and 84% of the retarded Ss were correctly identified. An unweighted separation analysis involving person clusters showed that the 4 person clusters that accounted for the major percentage of the educable boys (73%) accounted for only 7% of the intellectually normal boys. The 5 person clusters that accounted for 86% of the normal boys accounted for 23% of the educable boys. Results indicate that motor performance data can separate groups of differing intelligence levels with substantial accuracy. (20 ref)
Dobbins, D. Alan & Rarick, G. Lawrence. (U Texas, Austin) Research Quarterly, 1976(Oct), vol 47(3), 346-356. [PA, Vol 58:05614]

1536.   [Factor structure of psycholinguistic abilities in light mental retardation.] (Srcr)
Administered the Illinois Test of Psycholinguistic Abilities (ITPA) to 60 8–9 yr old children with IQs of 55–69 on the Wechsler nonverbal scale. Factor analysis revealed 4 factors: Auditory Linguistic, Visual Memory, Linguistic Closure, and a complex linguistic factor. Similar factor structure had been obtained earlier in a group of normal children of comparable age. In contrast, large differences in mean scores appeared between the 2 groups in all 12 subtests. Such results indicate that ITPA is an excellent diagnostic device for mental retardation. Unexpected similarity in factor structure between 2 groups differing widely in manifest psycholinguistic abilities is explained by the character of the ITPA subtests and factors. The latter are interpreted as germinal psycholinguistic factors, independent of intellectual factors but insufficient for complete psycholinguistic development. For such development to occur, it seems necessary to suppose the existence of other psycholinguistic abilities, not measured by ITPA, or the influence of intellectual factors on such abilities.
Fulgosi, Ante & Marković, Slavica. (Odsjek za psihologiju, Filozofski fakultet, Zagreb, Yugoslavia) Revija za Psihologiju, 1976, Vol 6(1–2), 3–12. [PA, Vol 60:06464]

1537.   Blocking of stimuli and the free recall and subjective organization of EMR adolescents.
Studied number of unrelated stimulus items presented consistently and spatially grouped (1, 3, or 5) in a multitrial free recall experiment with educable mentally retarded Ss (mean CA, 15.9 yrs; mean IQ, 64.4 mo). This blocking was effective in improving recall from recently presented items, increasing subjective organization, and leading to the formation of stable clusterable output groups. Some evidence suggests that overall recall also increased as a result of the consistent and simultaneous presentation. It is emphasized that for a retarded population the relationship between organization and recall may not be strong unless intensive strategy training is employed. (20 ref)
Glidden, Laraine M. (Teachers Coll, Columbia U) American Journal of Mental Deficiency, 1976(Jul), Vol 81(19, 58-64. [PA, Vol 56:10135]

1538.   A comparison between the WISC and WISC-R among educable mentally retarded students.
Compared differences and similarities between WISC and revised WISC (WISC-R) scores for 48 10- and 13-yr-old educable mentally retarded students, who were matched according to sex and race; all Ss were from a rural southeastern US area. The Wisc-R yielded significantly lower Verbal scale (VS), Performance scale (PS), and Full Scale (FS) IQ scores than the WISC for these Ss. The FS IQ scores from the WISC-R averaged 7.5 points lower than the WISC FS IQs, with similar differences noted for VS and PS scores. There was no significant difference in FS IQs between the 2 age groups. Results suggest that many children classified as borderline or slightly above by the WISC will be classified as mentally deficient by the WISC-R.
Hamm, Harry et al. (Waycross Area Program for Exceptional Children, GA) Psychology in the Schools, 1976(Jan), Vol 13(1), 4-8. [PA, Vol 56:04279]

1539.   Affective reactions of retarded and nonretarded children to success and failure.
After performing a simple motor task, 104 mildly retarded and 104 nonretarded 8-16 yr old girls and boys pointed to photographs of modeled affective facial expressions to indicate how they felt, wished to feel, and thought their teachers would feel about their performance. Ss in both IQ groups frequently attributed positive affect to themselves and their teachers after success, although younger retarded Ss were less positive than were nonretarded Ss in teacher affect attributions. Following failure, retarded Ss were generally less frequently negative than were nonretarded Ss in affect attributions to themselves and particularly to their teachers. Emphasis on success and minimization of failure in classrooms for retarded children is offered as one possible explanation for the IQ group affect differences following failure.
Hayes, Charles S. & Prinz, Robert J. (U Iowa Hosp School) American Journal of Mental Deficiency, 1976(Jul), Vol 81(1), 100-102. [PA, Vol 56:10137]

1540.   A factor study of Cratty's Body Perception Test.
Investigated the subtest items included in B. J. Cratty's body perception test using 89 children classified as educable mentally retarded or otherwise developmentally disabled. A factor analysis of the data was conducted and the 3 factor solutions derived suggest reconstituting the sequencing of subtest items.
Knapczyk, Dennis R. & Liemohn, Wendell P. (Indiana U) Research Quarterly, 1976(Dec), Vol 47(4), 678-682. [PA, Vol 58:05626]

1541.   Inference of word meaning from syntax structure by normal children and retarded adolescents.
Tested 136 5-12 yr olds and 30 institutionalized adolescents (CA, 17.11 yrs; MA, 9.18 yrs) on R. W. Brown's (see PA, Vol 33:1141) task developed to assess ability to infer nonsense word meanings from syntactic clues. Response accuracy for the normal Ss was consistently low from 5 to 8 yrs of age, after which it increased steeply. However, accuracy levels were markedly below those reported by Brown and raise questions concerning his finding that young children are largely successful in using the grammatical context of new words to guess their meaning. Performance of retarded Ss did not parallel that of normal Ss and on 2 of the 3 parts of speech their performance fell below MA expectations, a result attributed to their deficient generalization ability.
Lieber, Carolyn W. & Spitz, Herman H. (E. R. Johnstone Training & Research Ctr, Bordentown, NJ) Journal of Psychology, 1976(May), Vol 93(1), 3-12. [PA, Vol 56:04288]

1542.   Response differences on word-naming and WISC vocabulary.
Examined whether the symptom of defective attention and the strength of verbal fluency could be used to differentiate learning-disabled boys from normal and educable mentally retarded (EMR) learners. Using the WISC Vocabulary subtest and a word-naming task, response differences among groups of 10 learning-disabled, 10 EMR, and 15 normal Ss, all aged 7-9 yrs, were examined. Four discriminant function analyses indicated that the normals performed well on both tasks and the EMR Ss performed poorly, whereas the learning-disabled Ss had a strength of verbal fluency that discriminated them from the EMRs and an attentional deficit that discriminated them from the normal controls.
Morgan, Patricia & Caldwell, H. Stephen. (Oklahoma State U) Perceptual & Motor Skills, 1976(Jun), Vol 42(3, Pt 1), 961-962. [PA, Vol 56:10144]

1543. Performance of MA-matched nonretarded and retarded children on measures of field-dependence.
34 nonretarded and 34 educable mentally retarded children, matched on MA, were given the rod and frame test, Children's Embedded Figure Test, and Raven's Coloured Progressive Matrices. Scores of retarded Ss were consistently lower than nonretarded Ss' scores on each test. Nonretarded Ss' performance aligned with an analytical, field-independent cognitive style in contrast to the retarded Ss' performance that was characterized by a more global, field-dependent style.
Nesbit, W. C. & Chambers, J. (Memorial U Newfoundland, St John's, Canada) American Journal of Mental Deficiency, 1976(Jan), Vol 80(4), 469-472. [PA, Vol 56:00811]

1544. A concurrent validity study of the KeyMath Diagnostic Arithmetic Test.
Administration of the KeyMath Diagnostic Arithmetic Test (KeyMath) and the Level I Arithmetic subtest of the Wide Range Achievement Test (WRAT) to 30 educable mentally retarded students (mean CA 10.4 yrs) indicated that, when raw score data is the examiner's primary concern, the KeyMath and WRAT yield highly comparable results with a retarded population. In decision-making efforts which involve choosing one of the two instruments, the lower administration time of the WRAT must be weighted against the additional diagnostic capacities of the KeyMath.
Powers, David A. & Pace, Tommy J. (U Alabama Coll of Education) Mental Retardation, 1976(Dec), Vol 14(6), 48. [PA, Vol 58:00170]

1545. Perceptions of interpersonal communication of EMR adolescents and their mothers.
Views the communication process between parent and child as critical in the complexity of problems faced by the educable mentally retarded (EMR). The present study investigated the communication interaction between 46 13-19 yr old EMR Ss and their mothers to determine whether problems were perceived to exist between them. All Ss were interviewed using a modified version of the Parent-Adolescent Communication Inventory. Results indicate that perceived problems did exist between the parents and adolescents, particularly between EMR males and their mothers. (16 ref)
Sheperd, George & Marshall, Albert H. (U Oregon) Education & Training of the Mentally Retarded, 1976(Apr), Vol 11(2), 106-111. [PA, Vol 56:08217]

1546. Dimensional salience and short-term memory recognition in mentally retarded children.
Tested the a priori assumption that 3-dimensional materials facilitate short-term memory recognition, using 10 educable mentally retarded children. Measures from signal detection theory were used to differentiate between strength of memory and response bias. Significantly better recognition was found with 3-dimensional material than with 2-dimensional representations. Primacy and recency effects, as well as a response bias for middle positions, were found in both treatment conditions. Present findings support C. M. Haltom's (1970) hierarchy of stimulus salience.
Swanson, H. Lee & Watson, Bill. (U South Carolina Coll of Education, Columbia) Perceptual & Motor Skills, 1976(Jun), Vol 42(3, Pt 2), 1163-1166. [PA, Vol 57:06121]

1547. Comparison of nonretarded and mentally retarded children on a perceptual learning task.
Performances of 12 educable mentally retarded (EMR) and 12 nonretarded 6th graders on a perceptual learning task were compared to investigate the information processing of visually presented stimuli in Ss with different intelligence levels. A minicomputer flashed either familiar (lower-case) or unfamiliar letters (Gibson-like figures) in either a simultaneous or successive mode on a same-different matching task. The computer automatically calculated accuracy and latency data for each S. Results show that accuracy was superior in the nonretarded group and that mean latencies for the EMR group were consistently higher. However, when latencies were corrected for differences in basic

reaction time, there were no significant differences between the groups in the speed of processing the information. It is concluded that future studies assessing the latency measures of Ss of differing intellectual levels should secure some estimate of basic response time independent of the latencies obtained during the experimental task.
Terry, Pamela R. & Samuels, S. Jay. (Indiana U, Ctr for Innovation in Teaching the Handicapped, Bloomington) American Journal of Mental Deficiency, 1976(Sep), Vol 81(2), 167-171. [PA, Vol 57:06940]

1548. The effectiveness of interrogatives for promoting verbal elaboration productivity in young children.
36 nonretarded and 60 educable mentally retarded children (mean ages, 5.1 and 7.5 yrs, respectively) were tested to determine whether specific formats of interrogatives would be instrumental in inducing the generation of effective verbal mediators. Six experimental conditions were compared: Labeling, Sentence Generation, Sentence Repetition, Response to What, Response to Why A, and Response to Why B. Analysis of correct responses indicated that Ss in the 3 question conditions performed better than Ss in the nonquestion conditions. No differences existed between the 2 S categories. In addition, analyses of semantic and nonsemantic errors suggested that the question conditions induced greater semantic analysis in the Ss than the nonquestion conditions.
Turnure, James; Buium, Nissan & Thurlow, Martha. (U Minnesota) Child Development, 1976(Sep), Vol 47(3), 851-855. [PA, Vol 57:08006]

1549. Outerdirectedness in retarded children as a function of sex of experimenter and sex of subject.
Effects of same- and cross-sex Es on attentive behavior and learning of 32 male and 32 female educable mentally retarded children were examined in 2 conditions: not present (not in) or present and providing cues relevant to task mastery (relevant cue). A significant Sex of E × Sex of Subject interaction was found in the learning data, with girls performing significantly better than boys when the E was male; the reverse pattern was evident, although not statistically significant, when the E was female. Some effects were also found for individual Es. Although significantly more nontask orienting responses were observed in the relevant-cue condition, Ss in this condition performed as well on the learning task as did Ss in the not-in condition. Reversal trials showed greater glancing and superior performance in the relevant-cue condition. (21 ref)
Turnure, James E.; Larsen, Sharon N. & Thurlow, Martha L. (U Minnesota) American Journal of Mental Deficiency, 1976(Jan), Vol 80(4), 460-468. [PA, Vol 56:00897]

1550. Use of constraint-seeking questions by retarded and nonretarded individuals.
A 20-questions problem-solving task was given to 116 educable mentally retarded adolescents and 65 nonretarded MA-equated 4th graders. Ss' questions were classified as either constraint seeking or nonconstraint seeking, and the problem-solving strategies were evaluated in terms of their efficiency of solution. Nonretarded Ss asked more constraint-seeking questions, and their strategies reflected more efficient problem-solving solutions. The majority of Ss in both groups appeared to be in F. A. Mosher and J. R. Hornsby's (1966) suggested transitional stage, as demonstrated by the fact that their strategies fell between employing only questions that eliminated one item in the stimulus array (hypothesis scanning) and questions that consistently eliminated the maximum number of items (perfect focusing). In addition, nonretarded Ss' strategies reflected a greater awareness of the apparent organizational demands of the task and especially an awareness of the entire range of dimensions in the stimulus array.
Blackman, Leonard S.; Whittemore, Charles L.; Zetlin, Andrea G. & McNamara, Barry. (Columbia U Teachers Coll) American Journal of Mental Deficiency, 1977(Jul), Vol 82(1), 19–25. [PA, Vol 59:10130]

1551. Influence of contextual cues on the choice reaction time of mildly retarded adults.
Compared 8 mildly retarded males (mean IQ 69) aged 17–25 yrs and 8 male college students on an 8-choice reaction-time (RT) task. Removing a midline that divided the stimulus display in halves slowed RTs of retarded Ss to stimuli adjacent to the line. In the absence of this line, retarded Ss were also much more dependent upon the position of the preceding stimulus and response.
Brewer, N. & Nettelbeck, T. (U Adelaide, Australia) American Journal of Mental Deficiency, 1977(Jul), Vol 82(1), 37–43. [PA, Vol 59:10142]

1552. The feeling of knowing experience in educable retarded children.
Required 50 educable retarded children to predict their recognition accuracy when recall failed. Ss were divided into 3 ability levels: (a) old Ss (mean CA 13.25 yrs, mean MA 10.5 yrs), (b) medium Ss (mean CA 11.25 yrs, mean MA 8.75 yrs), and (c) young Ss (mean CA 9 yrs 5 mo, mean MA 6 yrs 9 mo). Results indicate that old and medium Ss could reliably predict their recognition accuracy, suggesting sensitivity to their own feeling of knowing experience, but that the young Ss showed no evidence of this sensitivity. Even though the young Ss had difficulty predicting their recognition accuracy in advance they were able to estimate the success or failure of their responses after they had occurred. Results are discussed in terms of the complexity of the metamemory judgment required, and the advisability of evaluating metamemorial knowledge across several situations is emphasized. (21 ref)
Brown, Ann L. & Lawton, Sallie C. (Ctr for the Study of Reading, Urbana, IL) Developmental Psychology, 1977(Jul), Vol 13(4), 364–370. [PA, Vol 59:08101]

1553. [Causes of mild mental retardation.] (Czec)
Studied a sample of 100 7–15 yr old special-school children (IQs 50–70) who did not manifest any signs or suspicions of CNS damage (77% of the examined children). Their parents (200) and siblings (203) were submitted to anthropological and psychological examinations, and a sociological investigation of the families was carried out. The anthropological findings showed some deviations (brachycephaly, anomalies of dermatoglyphics) in the Ss and their family members, which, however, were not sufficiently marked to attribute a special somatic type to these families. Some measures (mothers' age range and smaller stature) may have resulted in pathology during pregnancy. A social gradient of the occurrence of subnormality was not found, and psychosocial deprivation did not play an etiological role in view of the fact that in 70% of all families only 1 child was mentally retarded. Although 57% of the parents and 18.7% of the siblings were mentally subnormal (IQ < 70), heredity of their children's subnormality could not be proved, and heritability was estimated at .10 only. Mild forms of mental retardation seem to be conditioned by minimal brain damage during the perinatal period. (Russian summary) (27 ref)
Brunecký, Zdeněk; Zahálková, Milada & Vácová, Věra. (Výzkumný Ústav Pediatrický, Brno, Czechoslovakia) Psychológia a Patopsychológia Dieťaťa, 1977, Vol 12(1), 3–14. [PA, Vol 62:11225]

1554. Brief report on the WISC-R: IV. WISC-R vs. WISC: A comparison with educable mentally retarded children.
Administered the WISC to 33 and the WISC-R to 29 educable mentally retarded children, ages 12.5–14.5 yrs, who had previously been shown to be equivalent on earlier WISC and Stanford-Binet Intelligence Scale scores. Results show that all 3 WISC IQ scores were significantly higher than the comparable WISC-R scores.
Catron, David W. & Catron, Sarah S. (Wake Forest U) Journal of School Psychology, 1977(Fal), Vol 15(3), 264–266. [PA, Vol 60:08567]

1555. Proactive interference and its release in short-term memory of mildly retarded adolescents.
Investigated release from proactive interference in mildly retarded adolescents due to taxonomic shifts and rest periods prior to the final, critical-word triad. The 40 Ss had a mean IQ of 59.9. Interference accumulated rapidly across the 1st 3 trials; a shift in a triad's taxonomic class on the final trial produced a substantial release from proactive interference. Although proactive interference dissipated when the interval between Trials 3 and 4 was increased to 120 sec, the extent of recovery from proactive interference for the rest period plus taxonomic shift was no greater than a taxonomic shift alone. Results indicate that taxonomic category is a salient encoding dimension for retarded adolescents.
Cody, William J. & Borkowski, John G. (U Notre Dame) American Journal of Mental Deficiency, 1977(Nov), Vol 82(3), 305–308. [PA, Vol 61:01274]

1556. The nature of control by spoken words over visual stimulus selection.
Trained 8 retarded adolescents to select 1 (a trained positive stimulus, S+) of 2 visual stimuli in response to a spoken word (a trained word). Two different visual stimuli alternated randomly as the negative stimulus (S–). To determine if the spoken word was merely a temporal discriminative stimulus for when to respond, or if it also specified which visual stimulus to select, Ss were given intermittent presentations of untrained (novel) spoken words. All Ss consistently selected the S+ in response to the trained spoken word and selected the previous S– in response to the untrained spoken words. It was hypothesized that the Ss were responding away from the S+ in response to untrained spoken words, and control by untrained spoken words would not be observed when the S+ was not present. The 2 visual S– stimuli selected on trials of untrained spoken words were presented simultaneously. The untrained spoken words presented on these trials no longer controlled stimulus selections for 7 Ss. Results support the hypothesis that previous control by spoken words was due to responding away from the trained S+ in response to untrained spoken words.
Dixon, Lois S. (Parsons State Hosp, Parsons Research Ctr, KS) Journal of the Experimental Analysis of Behavior, 1977(May), Vol 27(3), 433–442. [PA, Vol 59:10148]

1557. The performance of intellectually normal and educable mentally retarded boys on tests of throwing accuracy.
71 educable retarded and 71 intellectually normal boys (mean CAs 102.3 and 100.7 mo, respectively) were measured for both vertical and horizontal errors on an overarm throwing task. Throwing accuracy, in terms of the total variance about the target, of normal Ss was superior to that of retarded Ss. Variable and constant errors (absolute values) of the retarded Ss were greater than those for the normals. The relative contribution of variable error to the total variance of retarded Ss was not substantially greater on either horizontal or vertical measures than were those for the normals. Findings do not support the variability hypothesis of A. A. Baumeister (1968), which states that variable error contributes more to the performance levels of the retarded than of normals. (15 ref)
Dobbins, D. Alan & Rarick, G. Lawrence. (U Wales, Swansea) Journal of Motor Behavior, 1977(Mar), Vol 9(1), 23–28. [PA, Vol 59:01308]

1558. Locus of control and law knowledge: A comparison of normal, retarded and learning disabled adolescents.
Investigated the relationship between knowledge of skills required for coping with community life and locus of control. Comparisons of scores of 45 10th and 11th graders, and 49 educable mentally retarded and learning disabled 15–21 yr olds on the Children's Locus of Control Scale and a test of knowledge of law about such matters as credit, theft, and marriage indicated that (a) normal high school Ss were more likely to see outcomes as determined by their own behaviors than were retarded and learning disabled Ss; (b) normal Ss were better informed about legal matters crucial to community life than were mentally retarded and learning disabled Ss; (c) mentally retarded and

learning disabled Ss did not differ in law knowledge or on locus of control; (d) locus of control was not directly related to IQ within the retarded/learning disabled group; and (e) a moderate positive correlation was found between locus of control and law knowledge for the total group. Findings support J. B. Rotter's (1966) social learning theory. These findings also suggest that educators may need to provide more direct and specific training in critical aspects of layman's law for most retarded and learning disabled adolescents and for average students who manifest external locus of control beliefs. (19 ref)
Gardner, David C.; Warren, Sue A. & Gardner, Paula L. (Boston U School of Education) Adolescence, 1977(Spr), Vol 12(45), 103–109. [PA, Vol 59:03632]

1559. The effect of labels and instruction on concept attainment in the educable mentally retarded.
Examined concept attainment in 80 educable mentally retarded and 80 normal boys of high and low MA (6.21–8.33 yrs). The concept of an equilateral triangle was assessed following random exposure to 1 of 4 experimental conditions assessing the influence of verbal labels and instructions on the labels. A $2 \times 2 \times 4$ multivariate ANOVA revealed a significant effect of MA; however, retarded and normal Ss did not differ in mean performance on any of the 5 dependent measures. The hypothesized treatment effect was significant at the formal level of concept attainment. Findings are discussed in terms of theoretical and educational implications. (24 ref)
Gargiulo, Richard M. (Bowling Green State U) Contemporary Educational Psychology, 1977(Jul), Vol 2(3), 284–291. [PA, Vol 59:10154]

1560. A comparison of WISC and WISC-R results of urban educable mentally retarded students.
Compared the WISC-R scores of 20 educable mentally retarded students with their previously administered WISC scores. The average interval between administrations was approximately 3 yrs, and Ss had a mean age of 11 yrs at the time of the WISC administration. Significant correlation coefficients were obtained between 5 corresponding subtests and between Performance IQs and Full Scale IQs. Results from t tests for correlated data indicated that mean WISC-R Verbal Performance, and Full Scale IQ scores were not significantly lower than their corresponding WISC scores. Results indicate that WISC-R scores in comparison to WISC scores appeared to be more stable in the lower IQ ranges and less vulnerable to cultural bias.
Gironda, Ronald J. (Jersey City Public Schools, NJ) Psychology in the Schools, 1977(Jul), Vol 14(3), 271–275. [PA, Vol 59:11426]

1561. Stimulus relations, blocking, and sorting in the free recall and organization of EMR adolescents.
72 educable mentally retarded adolescents (mean CA 16 yrs 9 mo, mean WISC IQ 67) received a list of either clustered or unrelated words according to 1 of 3 presentation methods. In blocked groups, words were presented both spatially blocked in 4's and consistently ordered from trial-to-trial. In sorting groups, Ss were required to group the stimuli themselves into 4 groups of 4. Ss in the blocked-random conditions received the items spatially grouped in 4's, but they were not consistently ordered (i.e., the groupings changed from trial-to-trial). Clustered items were recalled better than unrelated items, and both consistent blocking and sorting produced better recall than did the blocked-random treatment. The data for organizational measures generally paralleled those for correct recall. Results are discussed in terms of appropriate techniques for remediating input organizational deficits. (26 ref)
Glidden, Laraine M. (St Mary's Coll of Maryland, Div of Human Development) American Journal of Mental Deficiency, 1977(Nov), Vol 82(3), 250–258. [PA, Vol 61:03886]

1562. Sentence mediation and stimulus blocking in free recall.
In a 2-phase training study, 48 educable mentally retarded adolescents were initially provided with sentences linking each pair of 2 words in a 20-word list to be free recalled. In a 2nd phase, Ss were required to create and verbalize their own

sentences. This sentence-mediation condition was compared with (a) one in which items were presented in the same fixed pairs from trial-to-trial, but without sentences, and (b) a group that received items in changing pairs. Results indicate superiority of both sentence-mediation and fixed-pairs treatments in comparison to the changing-pairs condition on both correct recall and subjective organization. Sentences did not facilitate recall more than did consistent ordering. Results are discussed in the context of the growing evidence that providing input structure can remediate organization deficits in retarded persons. (18 ref)
Glidden, Laraine M.; Bilsky, Linda H. & Pawelski, Christine. (St Mary's Coll, Div of Human Development, MD) American Journal of Mental Deficiency, 1977(Jul), Vol 82(1), 84–90. [PA, Vol 59:12548]

1563. Developmental analysis of outerdirectedness in noninstitutionalized EMR children.
Investigated the developmental nature of outer-directedness among 40 high and low MA Black educable mentally retarded elementary and secondary school students using a block-design task equally difficult for both MA groups. Results show that high MA Ss imitated and glanced less than low MA Ss, and support the hypothesis that outer-directedness decreases with increasing MA.
Gordon, Donald A. & MacLean, William E. (Emory U) American Journal of Mental Deficiency, 1977(Mar), Vol 81(5), 507–511. [PA, Vol 58:11912]

1564. Interpersonal distance behavior of mentally retarded and nonretarded children.
Compared 60 mildly retarded 10–14 yr olds with 60 nonretarded 6–10 yr olds of comparable MAs on interpersonal-distance choice behavior to an adult male stranger. Contrary to the original prediction, stemming from E. Zigler's (1973) negative-reaction tendency formulation, interpersonal distance by retarded Ss was not generally different from that of nonretarded Ss. Analysis of the interaction between IQ group and approach condition (S approaching adult or adult approaching S), however, indicated that retarded Ss preferred greater distance fom the approaching adult than did nonretarded Ss. This result raises the possibility that perception of lessened personal control by retarded Ss stimulated a stronger avoidance reaction.
Hayes, Charles S. & Koch, Richard. (U Iowa Hosp School, Child Development Clinic) American Journal of Mental Deficiency, 1977(Sep), Vol 82(2), 207–209. [PA, Vol 60:05229]

1565. Projective assessment of personal space among retarded and nonretarded children.
Used a figure-placement method to examine the personal space usage of 60 mildly retarded (mean CA 12.1 yrs) and 60 nonretarded children (mean CA 8.1 yrs) of comparable MA (mean, 8.1 yrs for each group). Spatial distance between a self-figure and 2nd figure for both groups was least when the 2nd figure was designated with positive affect, greater when designated with neutral affect, and greatest when the designation involved negative affect. Retarded Ss used less spatial distance than nonretarded Ss when the interaction involved a self- and teacher-figure, supporting E. Zigler's (1973) positive- and negative-reaction tendency formulation. More space was used by both groups when the 2nd figure was designated as not smart than when designated as smart. (17 ref)
Hayes, Charles S. & Siders, Cathie. (U Iowa Hosp School, Child Development Clinic) American Journal of Mental Deficiency, 1977(Jul), Vol 82(1), 72–78. [PA, Vol 59:12551]

1566. Temporal extrapolation of unimodal and multimodal stimulus sequences in retarded and nonretarded persons.
24 retarded adolescents (CA 16.1 yrs, IQ 62.4), 24 CA-matched nonretarded adolescents, and 24 MA-matched nonretarded children attempted to match the repetition rate of 10-sec stimulus sequences presented under 4 modality switching conditions (unimodal, trimodal double alteration, trimodal single-alteration periodic, and trimodal single-alteration aperiodic) and at 2 pulse frequencies (12.5/10 sec and 25/10 sec). Error magnitudes were least for the CA-matched Ss and under the faster pulse rate

increased from the no-switching to maximum-switching condition in all groups. Error increases from the no-switching to maximum-switching condition were preponderantly underestimations. No differences between groups were obtained for a switching condition in which the modality-sequence pattern was aperiodic (e.g., ear-eye-skin equals eye-ear-skin). A hypothesis of longer psychological refractory periods in retarded adolescents is rejected in favor of one explaining their inferior performance on sequential enumeration and tracking tasks in terms of inefficient organizational abilities.
Holden, Edward A. & Winters, Emilia A. (Edward R. Johnstone Training & Research Ctr, Bordentown, NJ) American Journal of Mental Deficiency, 1977(May), Vol 81(6), 578–586. [PA, Vol 59:05900]

1567. Reliability and validity of the Social and Prevocational Information Battery for mildly retarded individuals.
The reliability and validity of the Social and Prevocational Information Battery (SPIB) for educable mentally retarded (EMR) individuals was evaluated with samples other than those on whom the battery was developed. The new sample groups included 74 senior-high EMR students from Alaska, 71 senior-high and 73 junior-high EMR students from Kentucky, and 109 postschool mentally retarded individuals from Oregon. Results substantiate the reliability and validity indices reported by A. Halpern et al (1975) and provide encouraging evidence for the general appropriateness of the SPIB for use with mildly retarded adolescents and young adults.
Irvin, Larry K. & Halpern, Andrew S. (U Oregon, Rehabilitation Research & Training Ctr in Mental Retardation) American Journal of Mental Deficiency, 1977(May), Vol 81(6), 603–605. [PA, Vol 59:04736]

1568. Effects of emotions on altruism and social inference in retarded adolescents.
The effects of positive and negative emotions on concern for others (altruism) and awareness of others (social inference) were investigated with 60 male and 61 female public school educable (IQ 50–80) retarded 13-, 14-, and 15-yr-olds. The Test of Social Inference was used. That induced positive affect would increase altruism was supported. A significant, positive correlation (.27 and .25) was found between altruism and social inference.
Karpf, Ronald J. (Camden County Hosp Complex, Div of Skilled Nursing & Intermediate Ctr, Lakeland, NJ) Psychological Reports, 1977(Aug), Vol 41(1), 135–138. [PA, Vol 60:05466]

1569. Role of attention in the reaction-time performance of mentally retarded adolescents.
Explored overt indices of attending behavior during a simple reaction-time (RT) task in order to assess the nature of attention problems that presumably serve to impair efficient RT performance in retarded individuals. To achieve this purpose, RT scores and degree of off-task glancing during the preparatory interval were compared for 10 educable mentally retarded (mean CA 15.6 yrs, mean IQ 64.8) and 10 nonretarded (mean CA 15.4 yrs, mean IQ 120.5) Ss. Retarded Ss were significantly slower in RT performance and exhibited a greater degree of off-task glancing than did nonretarded Ss. The frequent off-task glancing exhibited by retarded Ss is interpreted to be reflective of inattention to task; it is suggested that this form of inattention was at least partially responsible for their slower RT performance. Methodological implications are discussed.
Krupski, Antoinette. (U California, Graduate School of Education, Los Angeles) American Journal of Mental Deficiency, 1977(Jul), Vol 82(1), 79–83. [PA, Vol 59:12552]

1570. Personality characteristics of educable mental retardates.
Used a Hindi version of the Elementary School Personality Questionnaire to study the personality patterns of 200 normal and 100 educable mentally retarded (EMR) 7–12 yr old children matched on age, sex, socioeconomic status, grades, and residential background. The mentally retarded children were generally found to be socially cold (A–), emotionally unstable (C–), depressed (F–), undependable (G–), withdrawn (H–), tough-

minded (I–), simple (N–), and guilt prone (O+). Factors D (excitability), E (dominance), J (internal restraint), and Q4 (ergic tension) did not significantly differentiate the normal and the retarded children.
Lal, J. N. & Krishna, Shyam. (U Gorakhpur, India) Asian Journal of Psychology & Education, 1977(Jul), Vol 2(2), 44–48. [PA, Vol 61:01281]

1571. Semantic and acoustic processing in free and cued recall by educable mentally retarded adolescents.
The abilities of educable mentally retarded adolescents to encode and retrieve words with semantic and acoustic cues were investigated in a free and cued recall task. On each of 3 trial blocks, 98 Ss in 7 groups were presented 20 unrelated stimulus words. Groups received either semantic, acoustic, or no encoding cues along with the stimuli. Free recall was requested from all Ss followed immediately by a 2nd period of either free recall or cued recall with the semantic or acoustic cues. Semantic cues were most effective when presented both at encoding and retrieval. Ss were unable to use acoustic information as effective retrieval aids. Results are discussed in terms of encoding dimension dominance and mediational deficiencies. (23 ref)
Mar, Harvey H. & Glidden, Laraine M. (Columbia U Teachers Coll) Intelligence, 1977(Jul), Vol 1(3), 298–309. [PA, Vol 61:08708]

1572. A comparison between the WISC and WISC-R among a clinical referred population.
Compared the 3 scales of the WISC and the WISC-R for degree of intercorrelation. The differences among scores and among variances were also computed for the 2 tests. 58 children aged 6–14 yrs from a clinical referred population were studied—13 Ss classified as educable mentally retarded (EMR), 31 classified as learning disabled or emotionally disturbed, and 14 children in regular classrooms. Results include significant correlations in all cases, no systematic changes in variance, and significantly lower IQs on the WISC-R for all Ss except the EMRs.
McGonagle, Bonnie. Psychology in the Schools, 1977(Oct), Vol 14(4), 423–426. [PA, Vol 60:07560]

1573. Categorical encoding in short-term memory by retarded and nonretarded children.
Investigated the use of consonants and digits as encoding categories in short-term memory by 32 educable mentally retarded (EMR) children (mean CA, MA, and IQ, 143.41 mo, 95.13 mo, and 71.47, respectively) and 32 nonretarded 5th & 6th graders (mean CA, MA, and IQ, 141.78 mo, 154.13 mo, and 106.78, respectively), matched on CA. The task employed was a modification of the release from proactive inhibition technique similar to that used by D. D. Wickens et al (1963). Results indicate that digits and consonants are significant categories used for encoding in short-term memory by EMR and nonretarded Ss but that nonretarded Ss more effectively utilize consonant material as an encoding dimension than do CA-matched EMR Ss.
Narwicz, Susan & Cunningham, Thomas. (Ohio State U) American Journal of Mental Deficiency, 1977(Mar), Vol 81(5), 463-469. [PA, Vol 58:11921]

1574. Comparability of WISC and WISC-R scores among borderline and mildly retarded children.
Studied the comparability of WISC and Revised WISC (WISC-R) IQ scores in 48 mildly retarded and borderline children. All WISC-R and WISC IQ and subtest scores were significantly related, but not directly comparable. Generally, the WISC-R yielded lower scores with the exceptions of the Performance IQ score and the Picture Completion, Picture Assembly, and Object Assembly subtest scores. Subtest patterning on the WISC-R for this group was similar to previously reported data on the WISC. Caution is suggested in making direct comparisons of WISC and WISC-R scores, at least within the ability range studied.
Reschly, Daniel J. & Davis, Ronald A. (Iowa State U) Journal of Clinical Psychology, 1977(Oct), Vol 33(4), 1045–1048. [PA, Vol 60:09583]

1575.   Ethnicity, geographic locale, age, sex, and urban–rural residence as variables in the prevalence of mild retardation.
Administered the WISC-R to 950 1st–9th graders who were stratified for ethnicity (Anglo, Black, Mexican-American, and Papago Indian), urban–rural residence, sex, and grade level. The 3 WISC-R IQ scores and cutoff points of 69 and 75 were used in comparison of prevalence of mild mental retardation. This prevalence was significantly related only to ethnicity and geographic locale. (27 ref)
Reschly, Daniel J. & Jipson, Frederick J. (Iowa State U) Annual Progress in Child Psychiatry & Child Development, 1977, 612–624. [PA, Vol 66:06087]

1576.   Borderline versus mentally deficient.
Administered, in counterbalanced order, the WISC-R and the WISC to 44 12–16 yr old educable mentally retarded pupils from 2 special schools for the intellectually handicapped in Melbourne, Australia. Results show that WISC-R IQ estimates tended to be considerably lower than WISC IQ estimates, thus supporting the results of previous research concerned with the 2 tests in the US and in Australia. It is suggested that possible disadvantage for EMR children and adolescents could occur as a result of the administration of WISC-R unless the criteria for placement into special schools and for sheltered workshop employment are revised.
Rowe, Helga A. (Australian Council for Educational Research, Hawthorn) Australian Journal of Mental Retardation, 1977(Mar), Vol 4(5), 11–14. [PA, Vol 60:08320]

1577.   Multitrait-multimethod analysis of measures of reflection-impulsivity.
To examine the construct validity of measures of reflection-impulsivity (R-I), multitrait-multimethod matrix procedures suggested by D. T. Campbell and D. W. Fiske (1959) were applied to data collected from 115 6–11 yr old educable mentally retarded Ss. Specifically, the 2 R-I dimensions of time and error were assessed by the Matching Familiar Figures Test, Kansas R-I Scale for Preschoolers, and Test of R-I in Social Content, at 2 different age levels. Although the correlations between the dimensions based on 2 somewhat similar methods were consistent with expectations at the younger age level, the data generally demonstrated minimal and weak construct validity. Results are discussed in terms of the inherent differences between methods and the need to specify the measurement paradigm as well as the nature of the content employed in the instruments.
Smith, I. Leon & Singer, Steven. (Yeshiva U, Curriculum Research & Development Ctr in Mental Retardation.) Educational & Psychological Measurement, 1977(Win), Vol 37(4), 929–937. [PA, Vol 60:10794]

1578.   EMR and nonretarded children's reactions to contradiction.
Sensitivity to logical contradiction, as measured by surprise reaction to the Jastrow illusion, was investigated in 30 nonretarded children, 30 educable mentally retarded (EMR) children equated for CA, and 30 EMR children equated for MA. MA-matched peers (nonretarded and EMR Ss) performed at a similar level and at a significantly higher level than EMR Ss equated with the nonretarded Ss for CA. Results indicate that sensitivity to logical contradiction is more fundamentally related to MA than to CA in EMR children when their performance is compared to that of nonretarded children.
Smith, J. David. (Lynchburg Coll) American Journal of Mental Deficiency, 1977(Jul), Vol 82(1), 94–97. [PA, Vol 59:12560]

1579.   Perceptual decentering in EMR and nonretarded children.
Perceptual decentering was examined in 90 normal children (mean CA 8.5 yrs), educable mentally retarded (EMR) children (mean CA and MA, 8.5 yrs and 5.7 yrs) equated for CA, and EMR children (mean CA and MA, 12.5 yrs and 8.6 yrs) equated for MA. Results indicate that perceptual decentering is more fundamentally related to MA than to CA in EMR Ss.
Smith, J. David. (Lynchburg Coll) American Journal of Mental Deficiency, 1977(Mar), Vol 81(5), 499–501. [PA, Vol 58:11927]

1580.   Performance of retarded adolescents and nonretarded children on one- and two-bit logical problems.
Describes 4 experiments with 213 children. Groups of adolescents of retarded and borderline intelligence, ranging in IQ from 44 to 80 and in mean MA from 8 to 12 yrs, and groups of nonretarded Ss ranging in mean MA from 6 to 12 yrs, were given logical problem solving tasks. In the nonretarded groups, on a 1-bit problem only the kindergartners (mean MA 6 yrs) failed to perform above chance and were not tested further. On a 2-bit problem, only the 1st graders (mean MA 7 yrs) failed to perform above chance. Conversely, in the low IQ groups, only the borderline group (mean MA 12 yrs) performed reliably above chance on the 1-bit problem, and none performed above chance on the 2-bit problem. It is concluded that there is a profound deficiency in low IQ individuals on certain tasks requiring logic and foresight and that MA markedly overestimates their performance relative to the performance of nonretarded individuals.
Spitz, Herman H. & Borys, Suzanne V. (Edward R. Johnstone Training & Research Ctr, Bordentown, NJ) Journal of Experimental Child Psychology, 1977(Jun), Vol 23(3), 415–429. [PA, Vol 59:05914]

1581.   Performance characteristics of retarded and normal students on pattern recognition tasks.
Compared the performance of normal and educable mentally retarded children on pattern recognition tasks. Pattern recognition was assessed by the administration of 96 pattern tasks which measured the ability of children to find (a) duplicate patterns and same elements as presented in model pattern sequences, (b) opposite patterns and same elements as presented in model pattern sequences, and (c) duplicate patterns but different elements than presented in model pattern sequences. 38 normal and 37 mentally retarded Ss were matched on MA (mean range 7.43–9.19 yrs) derived from individual and group intelligence tests (e.g., Slosson Intelligence Test, WISC, and Stanford-Binet Intelligence Scale). Results indicate significant differences in performance measures between groups and various pattern tasks. The data support these suppositions: (a) Mentally retarded and normal children show the same type of progression through the hierarchical arrangement of pattern tasks; (b) mentally retarded children show a slower progression through the hierarchy than normal children when matched on MA. Educational implications are discussed. (21 ref)
Sternberg, Les; Epstein, Michael H. & Adams, Dan. (Northern Illinois U) Contemporary Educational Psychology, 1977(Jul), Vol 2(3), 209–218. [PA, Vol 59:10194]

1582.   Dimensionality and signal detection effects on a short-term memory task with mentally retarded children.
Compared a priori (proportion correct) and d' (unbiased) measures, using data from H. Swanson and B. Watson's (see PA, Vol 57:6121) study with 10 educable mentally retarded children on a serial recognition task. Treatment main effects were similar using both measures. Significant primacy and recency effects were found with d' measures; however, this was not found in a post hoc analysis of proportion correct scores. Results suggest that future investigations of serial recognition performance with emotionally mentally retarded children use an unbiased index of memory strength.
Swanson, H. Lee. (U Northern Colorado, School of Special Education & Rehabilitation) Psychological Reports, 1977(Apr), Vol 40(2), 421–422. [PA, Vol 59:05915]

1583.   An effective use of the public school version of the AAMD Adaptive Behavior Scale.
Suggests ways to administer, score, and interpret the findings of the American Association on Mental Deficiency Adaptive Behavior Scale, in order to plan effective programs for children referred for placement in classes for the mentally retarded. Adaptive behavior as an area of assessment is discussed, together with the use of criteria for placement of children in regular classes or in classes for the educable mentally retarded.
Windmiller, Myra. (U California Pupil Personnel Services & School Psychology Programs, Berkeley) Mental Retardation, 1977(Jun), Vol 15(3), 42–45. [PA, Vol 59:08926]

1584.   Characteristics of the conditional reasoning of educable retardates.
A pictorial conditional reasoning test was administered to 3 cross-sectional groups of educable mentally retarded (EMR) children and adolescents (36 Ss). The test items varied according to principle of inference and type of content. ANOVA of the number of correct judgments showed a significant main effect for principle of inference. On the other hand, the expected differences for age group and type of content were not found. An examination of the explanations associated with correct and incorrect judgments showed that retardates' reasoning strategies were congruent with those reported for younger normals in previous studies. Results are discussed in terms of contemporary conceptions of mental retardation and education for the retarded. (29 ref)
Antonak, Richard F. & Roberge, James J. (U New Hampshire) American Educational Research Journal, 1978(Fal), Vol 15(4), 519–528. [PA, Vol 63:12172]

1585.   Effect of imposed vs. self-generated imagery and sentence mediation on the free recall of retarded adolescents.
Investigated the effectiveness of verbal and imaginal elaborations on the free recall of 50 institutionalized educable mentally retarded adolescents (mean CA 18 yrs, mean IQ 66.2). Ss were assigned to 1 of 5 conditions: experimenter (E)-imposed verbalization, E-imposed imagery, S-generated verbalization, S-generated imagery, and control. Ss saw 15 pictures, presented in sets of 3, for 5 trial blocks and were asked to recall the 15 pictures after each trial block. Over all trials combined, results show that recall in the E-imposed verbalization and the E-imposed imagery conditions was reliably superior to recall in the control and S-generated verbalization conditions. Although Ss were capable of producing verbal or imaginal elaborations, as evidenced by postexperimental inquiry, elaborations facilitated recall only when they were supplied by the E. (9 ref)
Borys, Suzanne V. (Edward J. Johnstone Training & Research Ctr, Bordentown, NJ) American Journal of Mental Deficiency, 1978(Nov), Vol 83(3), 307–310. [PA, Vol 62:03877]

1586.   Reflection–impulsivity in retarded adolescents and nonretarded children of equal MA.
22 educable mentally retarded adolescents (mean CA 18.85 yrs, mean IQ 62.6, mean MA 9.98) and 19 nonretarded children (mean CA 9.98 yrs) of equal MA were given the preschool and elementary forms of the Matching Familiar Figures Test to assess reflection–impulsivity. Results show that the EMR adolescents did not differ significantly in accuracy and had somewhat longer response latencies than did the nonretarded children. In view of these results, it is unlikely that impulsivity contributed to the previously reported performance decrement displayed by retarded individuals on problem-solving tasks.
Borys, Suzanne V. & Spitz, Herman H. (Edward R. Johnstone Training & Research Ctr, Bordentown, NJ) American Journal of Mental Deficiency, 1978(May), Vol 82(6), 601–604. [PA, Vol 62:01307]

1587.   The sufficient conditions for directed forgetting in normal and educable mentally retarded adolescents.
Three studies investigated the conditions under which normal and educable mentally retarded (EMR) adolescents (92 13–15 yr olds) would or would not disregard irrelevant information in memory. A directed forgetting task was used in which the S was required to recall short sequences of picture names. In some sequences there was a cue to forget the first few pictures (irrelevant information) and to remember only the subsequent pictures (relevant information). When the normal Ss were given no explanation of the forget cue, there was interference from the irrelevant information. A minumum explanation of the cue, however, was sufficient to eliminate interference for the normal Ss. The same minimal explanation was not sufficient for EMR Ss. It was clear that irrelevant information in memory interfered with the performance of EMR Ss given only a minimal explanation of the forget cue. The results are viewed as important, since most naturalistic situations do not involve an elaborate explanation of the importance of disregarding irrelevant information previously stored in memory. (16 ref)
Bray, Norman W.; Justice, Elaine M. & Simon, Deborah L. (U Alabama, University) Intelligence, 1978(Apr–Jun), Vol 2(2), 153–167. [PA, Vol 64:02680]

1588.   Motor components in the choice reaction time of mildly retarded adults.
Examined the contributions of specific motor-coordination disabilities and general slowness of motor function to the choice reaction times (RTs) of a total of 22 18–27 yr old mentally retarded males examined in 2 experiments. RTs for the same stimulus–response (S–R) pairs were significantly shorter when presented in 2-choice than in 8-choice RT situations. Furthermore, in an 8-choice task, large RT differences between retarded and nonretarded Ss decreased (i.e., from about 170 msec to 40 msec) when processes of stimulus discrimination and S–R translation were minimized by direct stimulation of the response mechanisms.
Brewer, N. (U Adelaide, Road Accident Research Unit, Australia) American Journal of Mental Deficiency, 1978(May), Vol 82(6), 565–572. [PA, Vol 61:13625]

1589.   Correlations among Frostig visual perception scores and IQs of mildly mentally impaired and intellectually superior primary children.
Administered the Frostig Developmental Test of Visual Perception to 12 primary mildly mentally impaired (mean IQ 71.5) and 18 primary intellectually superior (mean IQ 127.8) children, obtaining IQ scores from Wechsler and Stanford-Binet Intelligence Scales for the handicapped and from Otis Mental Ability Test for the gifted. Significant Spearman rank correlations were obtained between IQ and position in space (.57) and total test scores (.52) for the handicapped. No significant correlations were found among IQ, Frostig subtests, and total test scores for the gifted. Results may indicate that correlations between 2 variables depend on the type of intelligence tests.
Brock, Patricia B.; Hisama, T. & Casey, John P. (Southern Illinois U) Perceptual & Motor Skills, 1978(Feb), Vol 46(1), 262. [PA, Vol 61:07567]

1590.   Use of active sorting and retrieval strategies as a facilitator of recall, clustering, and sorting by EMR and nonretarded children.
Assessed the ability of 60 12-yr-old educable mentally retarded (EMR) children (mean MAs 7.4–7.7 yrs; mean IQ 61.2) and 60 nonretarded 8-yr-olds to acquire and retain a sorting and retrieval strategy designed to be facilitative of recall and clustering. All Ss were given a baseline task and, based on their performance, were assigned to 1 of 3 groups: experimental, practice, and control. The experimental group received a multi-session training procedure that consisted of instructing the Ss to arrange the stimuli in conceptual arrays, to name individual stimuli and the superordinates to which the stimuli belong, and to count the number of stimuli in each superordinate. The practice group was presented with the same stimuli but received no training. The control group received only the baseline and criterion measures. Analyses of data showed significantly superior performance by the experimental group on measures of short- and long-term recall, clustering, and sorting. (21 ref)
Burger, Agnes L.; Blackman, Leonard S.; Holmes, Marilyn & Zetlin, Andrea. (New York U) American Journal of Mental Deficiency, 1978(Nov), Vol 83(3), 253–261. [PA, Vol 62:03880]

1591.   Training visual–spatial ability in EMR children.
42 educable mentally retarded children aged 8–14 yrs were randomly assigned to either a visual–spatial training condition or a control group. Ss who received training showed a gain from pre- to posttest on the Children's Embedded Figures Test that corresponds to approximately 4 yrs of maturation in nonretarded children. The performance of control Ss on the posttest was not significantly different from their performance on the pretest. Correlations between measures of visual–spatial ability and the employment adjustment of retarded persons obtained by other

investigators suggest the potential importance of developing the visual–spatial skills of this population. (15 ref)

Connor, Jane M.; Serbin, Lisa A. & Freeman, Mark. (State U New York, Binghamton) American Journal of Mental Deficiency, 1978(Sep), Vol 83(2), 116–121. [PA, Vol 62:03884]

1592. Academic performance and cognitive processes in EMR children.

Data from 52 educable mentally retarded children (mean CA 14 yrs 1 mo; IQ range 55–80) show the following: Simultaneous processing was significantly related to Wide Range Achievement Test (WRAT) arithmetic and WISC Performance IQ, whereas successive processing was involved in WRAT spelling and WRAT oral reading and negatively related to WISC Performance IQ. Silent reading and WISC Verbal IQ were related to neither processing strategy.

Das, J. P. & Cummins, James. (U Alberta, Ctr for the Study of Mental Retardation, Edmonton, Canada) American Journal of Mental Deficiency, 1978(Sep), Vol 83(2), 197–199. [PA, Vol 62:06310]

1593. Availability and accessibility of information in the semantic memory of retarded and nonretarded adolescents.

Studied the availability of semantic information in storage and the accessibility of that information for retrieval in retarded and nonretarded adolescents. In Exp I, 40 normal and 40 CA-equivalent (mean, 15 yrs) retarded Ss were required to retrieve information from semantic categories and to judge whether specific items were members of a given category. Results showed large IQ group differences on the retrieval task which could not be wholly accounted for by the items available in storage. Exp II attempted to remediate this retrieval deficit by introducing an organized retrieval plan consisting of subcategory cues. This organization facilitated retrieval as long as it was experimentally provided. Retrieval returned to its original level, however, when the cues were withdrawn. Ss were 63 educable mentally retarded adolescents. It is concluded that retarded persons had an accessibility deficit in addition to an availability deficit; one aspect of this accessibility deficit involved the failure to use spontaneously mnemonic strategies that were consistent with the semantic organization. (18 ref)

Glidden, Laraine M. & Mar, Harvey H. (St Mary's Coll of Maryland, Div of Human Development) Journal of Experimental Child Psychology, 1978(Feb), Vol 25(1), 33–40. [PA, Vol 60:11961]

1594. Stimulus generalization following extradimensional and intradimensional training in educable retarded children.

Conducted 5 related experiments with a total of 57 educable mentally retarded Ss (CAs 122–191 mo, verbal ages 75–144 mo) to investigate stimulus generalization following go/no-go discrimination training. Exp I employed an extradimensional paradigm in which generalization testing was on the hue dimension following training on an independent (orientation) dimension. Following true discrimination training only 25% of the Ss showed a decremental stimulus generalization gradient on the hue dimension, although all Ss exhibited flat gradients in pseudodiscrimination and positive stimulus (S+) control groups. An increase in difficulty of the orientation discrimination in Exp II did not increase the number of decremental gradients. In Exp III, Ss who exhibited decremental gradients in Exps I and II underwent further generalization testing with modified stimuli to establish a symmetrical gradient peaked at a hue S+ to be employed in Exps IV and V. In these experiments an intradimensional paradigm was employed with positive and negative stimuli drawn from the hue dimension. Excitatory control by positive and inhibitory control by negative stimuli (S–) were demonstrated, as were inhibitory consequences of S– such as peak and area shift.

Hogg, J. & Evans, P. L. (U Manchester, Hester Adrian Research Ctr, England) Journal of Experimental Child Psychology, 1978(Apr), Vol 25(2), 224–241. [PA, Vol 61:08705]

1595. Patterns of cognitive ability in retarded children: A reexamination.

Conducted a partial replication of J. P. Das's (see PA, Vol 49:954) study of patterns of cognitive abilities in mentally retarded and nonretarded children. 67 educable mentally retarded children were given a set of cognitive tasks shown in previous research to measure simultaneous and successive syntheses. These measures included Raven Coloured Progressive Matrices, Memory-for-Designs Test (MFD), Digit Span test of the WISC, and tests of serial recall and short-term memory. Results of factor analysis were consistent with those of Das except for the loadings on the MFD and the visual short-term memory test, a pattern of cognitive processes similar to patterns found for nonretarded children in other research. Results are discussed in terms of implications for research on strategic behavior in mentally retarded children. (18 ref)

Jarman, Ronald F. (U British Columbia, Vancouver, Canada) American Journal of Mental Deficiency, 1978(Jan), Vol 82(4), 344–348. [PA, Vol 61:03893]

1596. Verification of property statements by retarded and nonretarded adolescents.

14 educable mentally retarded (mean CA 16 yrs 10 mo, mean MA 10 yrs, mean IQ 68.5) and 14 nonretarded 17-yr-old adolescents verified true and false statements about the properties of common objects. For the true sentences, half contained properties rated as highly salient to the given object, and half contained less salient properties. Further, at each level of salience, half of the properties were static (physical) properties (e.g., "Carrots are orange"), and half were action properties (e.g., "Rabbits can hop"). True verification times were more rapid for all Ss when sentences contained highly salient properties. In addition, sentences containing action properties were verified faster than those containing static properties, but only by the retarded Ss (whose response times were slower overall). Additional analyses indicated that the retarded Ss responded particularly rapidly to action properties that designate "what can be done to an object" (extrinsic-action properties) as opposed to "what an object can do" (intrinsic-action properties). These findings are discussed in relation to the organization of semantic knowledge and the apparent group differences in the weighting of semantic features. (17 ref)

McCauley, Charley; Sperber, Richard D. & Roaden, Saundra K. (George Peabody Coll for Teachers) American Journal of Mental Deficiency, 1978(Nov), Vol 83(3), 276–282. [PA, Vol 62:03894]

1597. Subtest order and WISC-R scores of a sample of educable mentally retarded subjects.

All the Verbal subtests of the WISC-R were administered first, then all the Performance subtests, and in standard order to 56 educable mentally retarded children (31 males and 25 females; 43 Blacks and 13 Whites) ranging in age from 6 yrs 9 mo to 16 yrs 8 mo. Verbal, Performance, and Full Scale IQs were slightly but significantly higher when subtests were administered in the standard order. (13 ref)

Morris, John D. et al. (Georgia Southern Coll) Psychological Reports, 1978(Oct), Vol 43(2), 383–386. [PA, Vol 63:08704]

1598. Cognitive training for EMR children: Choosing the best alternative.

28 educable mentally retarded children (mean CA 11.14 yrs, mean IQ 60.93 yrs) participated in an 8-wk training program on choosing the best alternative. The training was presented within the context of small-group discussions of familiar social problems and participation in table games. 28 control Ss (mean CA 10.03 yrs, mean IQ 63.04) engaged in similar activities but without specific cognitive training. The experimental group's posttest scores were significantly superior to those of the control group, a finding that suggests a major experiential component in the deficit in problem-solving skills typical of EMR children and provides support for the efficacy of early intensive cognitive training.

Ross, Dorothea M. & Ross, Sheila A. American Journal of Mental Deficiency, 1978(May), Vol 82(6), 598–601. [PA, Vol 62:01326]

1599.   Cognitive tempo in educable mentally retarded children.
Investigated the relationship of time and errors on the Matching Familiar Figures Test to the MA of 40 Caucasian, male, educable mentally retarded (EMR) children. Ss were aged 6–18 yrs, had IQs of less than 80, were exhibiting problems in adaptive behavior, and were all receiving special education services. An ANOVA revealed that with increasing MA, elapsed time to 1st response increased and errors decreased, thus indicating an MA developmental decrease in impulsivity. For all Ss, time was inversely related to errors. The data suggest that the development of cognitive tempo in EMR children parallels that of nonhandicapped children. (2 ref)
Rotatori, Anthony F.; Cullinan, Douglas; Epstein, Michael H. & Lloyd, John. (Northern Illinois U) Journal of Psychology, 1978(Jul), Vol 99(2), 135–137. [PA, Vol 62:13939]

1600.   Effect of reinforcement of response on internal consistency of selected WISC-R subtests.
Examined the differential effects of 3 types of reinforcers (verbal praise, token, and verbal neutral) and 2 levels of schedule of reinforcement (continuous and FR) on the Arithmetic, Picture Completion, and Block Design subtests from the WISC-R with 120 educable mentally retarded Ss (mean age 11.8 yrs). Although the pattern of coefficients was similar for the 2 schedule conditions, there was a trend for the FR schedule to result in a greater number of attempted items and higher coefficients of internal consistency. The superiority of any type of reinforcer treatment was not demonstrated. (3 ref)
Saigh, Philip A. & Payne, David A. (American U of Beirut, Lebanon) Psychological Reports, 1978(Dec), Vol 43(3, Pt 1), 756–758. [PA, Vol 64:08277]

1601.   Factor analysis of WISC-R scores for children identified as learning disabled, educable mentally impaired, and emotionally impaired.
The WISC-R scores for 799 children identified by school personnel as needing special education services were factor analyzed according to type of classification. WISC-R factor loadings were obtained for the scores of children labeled Learning Disabled, Educable Mentally Impaired, and Emotionally Impaired, as well as groups labeled Other and None. Overall, results show the WISC-R to be factorially similar for all groups, with 2 principal factors emerging which correspond to the Verbal–Performance structure of the test. Significance tests among mean scores and IQ scores yielded few meaningful differences across groups. (14 ref)
Schooler, Douglas L.; Beebe, Michael C. & Koepke, Thomas. (Eastern Michigan U) Psychology in the Schools, 1978(Oct), Vol 15(4), 478–485. [PA, Vol 63:06441]

1602.   Effect of familiarity on primacy performance of normal and retarded children.
On the assumption that serial recall tasks reflect spatial memory rather than verbal rehearsal, an experiment was conducted to determine what effect stimulus familiarity had on the spatial primacy performance of 20 educable retarded and 20 normal 10–13 yr olds. Linear presentation effects of familiar and nonfamiliar pictures upon serial position curve performance when overt verbalization was suppressed were investigated. Results indicate that an interaction of stimulus familiarity and spatial memory is responsible for the primacy effect found in serial position curves. No primacy effect for either S group was found in the nonfamiliar stimulus condition. No overall developmental effects were found between groups on serial position performance. Consistent with F. Craik and R. Lockhart's (1972) memory processing model, results indicate that stimulus familiarity provided deeper levels of processing, thereby facilitating primacy effects. (12 ref)
Swanson, Lee. (U Northern Colorado Coll of Education, School of Special Education & Rehabilitation) Journal of General Psychology, 1978(Oct), Vol 99(2), 173–180. [PA, Vol 63:07816]

1603.   Comparison of the WISC-R and PPVT for a group of mentally retarded students.
Compared the WISC-R and Peabody Picture Vocabulary Test (PPVT) scores of 65 7.5–14.5 yr old students classified as mentally retarded. Correlational data indicate that for this sample of mildly retarded Ss, the PPVT IQ score was significantly higher than the Full Scale IQ from the WISC-R. Findings indicate that the same general pattern exists for the WISC-R and PPVT as for the WISC and PPVT scores. (5 ref)
Vance, Hubert; Prichard, Karen K. & Wallbrown, Fred H. (James Madison U Child Study Ctr) Psychology in the Schools, 1978(Jul), Vol 15(3), 349–351. [PA, Vol 62:07717]

1604.   Diagnostic test pattern differences among LD, ED, EMH, and multi-handicapped students.
Examined diagnostic test data in conjunction with familial and cultural information taken from the case files of children who had been diagnosed as learning disabled (LD), educable mentally handicapped (EMH), or emotionally disturbed (ED), multi-handicapped or other, to determine their discriminative efficacy in differentiating LD children from non-LD children. 1,524 6–17 yr olds with average intelligence, as measured by performance on the WISC-R, were used. Six discriminant functions analyses were performed on variables selected from the above 3 sources of information. Results of the discriminant analyses consistently failed to discriminate LD Ss from the other Ss. A transpose factor analysis performed on these variables showed considerable overlap of variables between factors. A review of research examining the discriminative efficacy of widely used diagnostic tests indicates that these tests have little utility in distinguishing LD from non-LD children. A more appropriate diagnostic model is proposed that accounts for the child's unique processing of information relative to his or her content base and ability to perform a corresponding behavior. (22 ref)
Webster, Raymond E. & Schenck, Susan J. (U Connecticut) Journal of Educational Research, 1978(Nov–Dec), Vol 72(2), 75–80. [PA, Vol 63:11095]

1605.   Use of a relational focus strategy in oddity performance of EMR adolescents.
A series of 5-item oddity tasks was administered to 44 educable mentally retarded adolescents (CAs 12.2–17.1 yrs; IQs 52–75) to determine whether a consistent strategy was used to achieve problem solutions. Such a strategy requires establishing a relational hypothesis for 2 items in a set and retaining that hypothesis in memory while testing subsequent items against it. Evidence for use of a consistent strategy would be found in a particular pattern of response latencies and errors dependent on the position of the odd stimulus in each 5-item set. ANOVA of the mean latency scores and errors for the 5 positions in which the odd item occurred suggested that a consistent strategy was being applied. (4 ref)
Zetlin, Andrea G. & Blackman, Leonard S. (U California, Riverside) American Journal of Mental Deficiency, 1978(Nov), Vol 83(3), 304–306. [PA, Vol 62:03917]

1606.   Sensitivity of retarded children's performance to social psychological influences.
Tested 48 mildly mentally retarded male and female Ss (mean age 171.1 mo) on their ability to complete paper and pencil mazes of low and high levels of difficulty in the presence of (a) the experimenter (E), (b) E and an observer, and (c) E and an observer who, they were told, would be evaluating them. In the simple maze condition, the presence of an evaluative observer significantly lessened the number of trials needed to successfully complete the maze when compared to the other 2 conditions. When the child attempted the complex maze, the presence of an evaluative observer significantly increased the number of trials needed to reach criteria. Results are discussed in the context of the drive theory of social facilitation. Implications for classroom training are examined.
Zucker, Stanley H. (Arizona State U) Education & Training of the Mentally Retarded, 1978(Apr), Vol 13(2), 189–194. [PA, Vol 61:13643]

1607. A comparison of the General Information subtest of the Peabody Individual Achievement Test with the Information subtest of the Wechsler Intelligence Scale for Children-Revised. Administered the WISC-R and the Peabody Individual Achievement Test (PIAT) to 69 males and 31 females ranging in CA from 7 yrs 2 mo to 16 yrs 11 mo. Ss' IQ scores ranged from 44 to 121. A high positive correlation ($r = .73$) between WISC-R and PIAT Information subtest scores substantiated the value of the PIAT Information subtest as a general screening device. Results also indicate that data from Information subtests should be used with caution when mentally retarded students are evaluated. (9 ref)
Beck, Frances W.; Lindsey, Jimmy D. & Facziende, Betty. (Louisiana State U and A&M Coll) Educational & Psychological Measurement, 1979(Win), Vol 39(4), 1073–1077. [PA, Vol 66:04414]

1608. Hierarchical semantic organization in educable mentally retarded children.
Investigated the extent to which educable mentally retarded (EMR) children make functional use of a hierarchical class inclusion system in a memory retrieval task that does not have experimenter-imposed input organization. 54 EMR children from 3 samples—(a) Elementary A (15 Ss; mean CA 131.4 mo; mean MA 84.7 mo, mean IQ 64.8); (b) Elementary B (19 Ss; mean CA 153.6 mo, mean MA 91.9 mo, mean IQ 60.1); and (c) High School (20 Ss; mean CA 189.3 mo, mean MA 116.9 mo, mean IQ 61.6)—looked at 8 familiar pictures. Subsequently they attempted to recall each picture when given as retrieval cues the corresponding noun and four other words that represented a hierarchical class inclusion system for that particular picture. Five predictions based on a model of semantic distance in the structure were tested. Four of the predictions were significantly confirmed. Thus, Ss showed evidence of functional use of a hierarchical class inclusion system in memory retrieval. These results are not suggested by most of the relevant literature in mental retardation. (18 ref)
Bender, Nila N. & Johnson, N. S. (U California School of Education, Riverside) Journal of Experimental Child Psychology, 1979(Apr), Vol 27(2), 277–285. [PA, Vol 62:06304]

1609. Training self-checking routines for estimating test readiness: Generalization from list learning to prose recall.
The 1st and 3rd authors (see PA, Vol 56:10127) trained 66 educable retarded children to use either of 2 memory strategies, anticipation or rehearsal, involving a self-checking component. Following the training, both their free-recall performance and their ability to estimate their readiness for a recall test improved significantly. In the present research, 58 of the same students were tested for maintenance and generalization 1 yr following the original training. The younger children (MA 6 yrs, CA 10 yrs) showed no effects on the training, whereas an older group (MA 8 yrs, CA 13 yrs) both maintained the trained strategies on the original rote-recall task and generalized it effectively to a novel situation involving gist recall of prose passages. In comparison to a pair of control groups, the Ss trained in the use of self-checking routines took more time studying, recalled more idea units from the passages, and further, their recall was more clearly related to the thematic importance of the constituent idea units, a pattern characteristic of developmentally more advanced Ss. (33 ref)
Brown, Ann L.; Campione, Joseph C. & Barclay, Craig R. (Ctr for the Study of Reading, Champaign, IL) Child Development, 1979(Jun), Vol 50(2), 501–512. [PA, Vol 62:13925]

1610. Digit span estimation and the effects of explicit strategy training on recall of EMR individuals.
Assessed accuracy of digit span estimation by educable mentally retarded Ss at 2 different MA levels—8 and 11 yrs. The effects of explicit strategy training, generalized instruction, and no training on recall performance and apportionment of study time were compared. The older group of Ss was more realistic in their digit span estimation than was the younger group. Explicit strategy training facilitated digit recall and evoked longer study times than did the other conditions. (14 ref)
Burger, Agnes L. & Blackman, Leonard S. (New York U) American Journal of Mental Deficiency, 1979(May), Vol 83(6), 621–626. [PA, Vol 62:08856]

1611. Comparability of WISC-R and WAIS IQ scores in educable mentally handicapped adolescents.
Administered the WISC-R and WAIS to 30 16-yr-old educable mentally handicapped students in a test–retest design to distribute practice effects. The average interval between administrations was approximately 37 days. Results from *t*-tests of significance of difference between the means were obtained for the total group and for 2 subgroups (receiving either the WISC-R or WAIS as the 1st test). Data reveal significantly higher WAIS scores on all levels of Verbal, Performance, and Full Scale IQs for all groups. (11 ref)
Craft, Nancy P. & Kronenberger, Earl J. Psychology in the Schools, 1979(Oct), Vol 16(4), 502–504. [PA, Vol 65:02455]

1612. Behavior problems of educationally handicapped and normal pupils.
Male pupils identified as behaviorally disordered, learning disabled, and educable mentally retarded (*N*s = 153, 172, and 176, respectively), as well as 309 nonidentified normal boys, were rated by their teachers on the Behavior Problem Checklist (BPC). Ratings indicated significant differences for pupil category, BPC dimension, and Category-by-Dimension interaction, but no significant differences for age alone or in interaction with other factors. Categories of pupils were best discriminated on the basis of Conduct Disorder and Personality Problem dimensions of the BPC. (21 ref)
Cullinan, Douglas; Epstein, Michael H. & Dembinski, Raymond J. (Northern Illinois U) Journal of Abnormal Child Psychology, 1979(Dec), Vol 7(4), 495–502. [PA, Vol 65:03344]

1613. Strategy training and semantic encoding in mildly retarded children.
Conducted 2 experiments with 78 mildly retarded children. In Exp I, 3 groups of mildly retarded 5th- and 6th-grade preadolescents were matched on the basis of their performance on a free recall test. The groups were then given instruction in the use of a semantic encoding strategy, acoustic encoding strategy, or repetitive rehearsal strategy and practice using the memory strategy on 2 lists of unblocked categorized items. Performance was uniformly higher for Ss using the semantic encoding strategy on both training lists and on unprompted tests up to 7 days later. On a test 7 mo later, however, there were no differences in recall performance for the 3 groups until the appropriate strategy was prompted on the 2nd trial; then, the semantic condition showed greater improvement than the other groups. Clustering data were also analyzed and were superior for the semantic condition on all tests except the 1st trial of the 7-mo delayed test. In Exp II an incidental learning task was used with 3 different orienting questions. Enhanced performance with semantic processing was found in a group of 13-yr-olds but not in a group of 10-yr-olds. (25 ref)
Engle, Randall W. & Nagle, Richard J. (U South Carolina, Columbia) Intelligence, 1979(Jan–Mar), Vol 3(1), 17–30. [PA, Vol 64:05894]

1614. Enhancing the incidental learning of EMR children.
In a study of Type I incidental learning in 112 educable mentally retarded children (CAs 81–167 mo, IQs 44–86), 4 orienting-instruction conditions and 2 tasks (2 and 3 dimensions) were used. One orienting-instruction condition was superior for enhancing incidental learning. This task-specific strategy continued to produce the best incidental learning during a 24-hr follow-up session. Results are discussed in terms of recent memory models. (17 ref)
Fox, Robert & Rotatori, Anthony F. (Western Illinois U) American Journal of Mental Deficiency, 1979(Jul), Vol 84(1), 19–24. [PA, Vol 62:11231]

1615. Educable mentally retarded, learning disabled, emotionally disturbed: Similarities and differences.
Analyzes characteristics, across cognitive, affective, and demographic categories, attributed to 378 children identified as

educable mentally retarded, learning disabled, and emotionally disturbed in order to determine their relevance in defining and identifying exceptional children. (3 ref)
Gajar, Anna H. (Pennsylvania State U, Div of Special Education) Exceptional Children, 1979(Mar), Vol 45(6), 470–472. [PA, Vol 62:06094]

1616. Extended recency effect extended: Blocking, presentation mode, and retention interval.
Examined the effect of blocking of stimulus items on the free recall of 117 educable mentally retarded 12–17 yr olds (IQs 48–77). In Exp I a multitrial free-recall list of 15 pictures was presented either simultaneously in groups of 3 or 1 at a time. Consistent ordering was used in both conditions, so that on each trial, each item in each set of 3 pictures was presented contiguously with the other 2 items from that set. Recall came immediately or after a filled or unfilled delay of 24.5 sec. Simultaneous presentation led to higher recall, subjective organization, and clustering than did sequential presentation; but analysis of serial-position curves showed a much reduced extended recency effect in comparison with previous studies. Exp II determined whether the cause of the reduced extended recency was the use of pictures rather than words as stimuli. Stimuli were presented either as pictures, as pictures with auditory labels, or as words with auditory labels, with both simultaneous and consistent ordering for all conditions. Results indicate a strong extended recency effect for all groups, eliminating presentation mode as a causal factor in the data of Exp I. It is concluded that blocking leads to increased organization and recall over a variety of presentation modes, rates, and block sizes. (11 ref)
Glidden, Laraine M.; Pawelski, Christine E.; Mar, Harvey & Zigman, Warren. (St Mary's Coll of Maryland) American Journal of Mental Deficiency, 1979(Jul), Vol 84(1), 74–81. [PA, Vol 62:11233]

1617. Brief reports on the WISC-R: III. WISC-R scatter indices: Useful information for differential diagnosis?
Analyzed the WISC-R Verbal-Performance, Full Scale IQ, Verbal IQ, and Performance IQ scatter indices of 101 verified special education students. Results indicate that none of these measures discriminated among emotionally disturbed, learning disabled, minimally brain injured, and educable mentally retarded Ss. These scatter indices were also compared with analogous data collected from a nationwide, representative sample of normal children (A. S. Kaufman, 1976). Significant differences were obtained between the 2 groups on Verbal-Performance, Full Scale IQ, and Performance IQ scatter dimensions. Further analyses revealed, however, that 40% of the normal Ss exhibited as much or more scatter than the average special education S on each of these 3 scatter indices. There were no significant differences between the 2 groups on the Verbal IQ scatter index. Results are discussed in terms of the limited utility of WISC-R scatter indices for the purpose of differential diagnosis. (11 ref)
Gutkin, Terry B. (U Nebraska, Lincoln) Journal of School Psychology, 1979(Win), Vol 17(4), 368–371. [PA, Vol 65:02466]

1618. Alternative approaches to the measurement of adaptive behavior.
Examined the relative efficacy of behavior rating and knowledge testing approaches for predicting criterion behavior. Three tests from the Social and Prevocational Information Battery were selected as a foundation for the development of analogous behavior-rating and applied-performance instruments. All 3 types of instruments—Banking, Purchasing, and Job-Seeking Skills—were administered to the same Ss, mildly retarded adolescents (96% of whom were in Grades 9–12), to estimate the validity of testing and rating approaches. Although both approaches were found to be valid, the testing approach appeared to be superior on demonstrated ability to perform a desirable behavior in a relevant context, at least once, in response to the request of a facilitative other person. (6 ref)
Halpern, Andrew S.; Irvin, Larry K. & Landman, Janet T. (U Oregon, Rehabilitation Research & Training Ctr in Mental Retardation) American Journal of Mental Deficiency, 1979(Nov), Vol 84(3), 304–310. [PA, Vol 63:04425]

1619. Effects of music on learning a motor skill by handicapped and non-handicapped boys.
38 educable mentally retarded and 33 normal 10–12 yr old boys were divided into 6 groups to learn a motor skill; 4 groups practiced with classical or popular background music and 2 practiced with no music. Results show no significant main effects for intelligence group or treatment on performance.
Karper, William B. (U North Carolina, Greensboro) Perceptual & Motor Skills, 1979(Dec), Vol 49(3), 734. [PA, Vol 66:03869]

1620. Movement coding and memory in retarded children.
Conducted 3 experiments on the coding and retention of movement-generated information with 2 groups of mildly retarded children varying in MA. The cue to be reproduced was the terminal position of the limb that studies with adults have shown to require central processing activity for maintained performance. In Exp I, although the older MA group was superior, both groups showed similar decrements in performance over a 15-sec interval. In Exp II, procedures were adopted in an attempt to overcome performance deficits. The 3 Ss were allowed to choose (i.e., preselect) their own movements in addition to performing constrained movements. Preselected reproduction was superior to constrained at all 3 retention intervals (0, 7, and 15 sec) but was not statistically different among age groups. Also, performance was maintained for both groups over 7 sec but deteriorated over 15 sec. These results were replicated with 24 Ss in Exp III, which also showed that an interpolated motor task designed to block rehearsal processes interfered with reproduction at the 7- and 15-sec retention-interval conditions. Results indicate that mildly retarded children can maintain motor information over brief time periods and also illustrate the important contribution of the planning component in facilitating the coding of motoric information. (24 ref)
Kelso, J. A.; Goodman, David; Stamm, Carol L. & Hayes, Charles. (Haskins Lab, New Haven, CT) American Journal of Mental Deficiency, 1979(May), Vol 83(6), 601–611. [PA, Vol 62:08867]

1621. Contributions of school classification, sex, and ethnic status to adaptive behavior assessment.
Investigated the contributions of school classification (regular vs educable mentally retarded [EMR]) and sex and ethnic status to domain scores from the Public School Version of the Adaptive Behavior Scale using data from over 1,600 regular and EMR Ss among White, Black, and Spanish-background Ss, ages 7 to 13 yrs. Results replicate earlier findings that domain scores were valid for differentiating among children of different adaptive behavior levels as inferred from school classification status. Ethnic status was not a unique contributor to Part 1 domain scores when the effects of classification were accounted for. On the Part 2 domains, ethnic status and sex were significant contributors to some domain scores, but not at all age levels. It is concluded that the Scale was valid for differentiating among Ss assigned to regular and EMR classes from ages 7 to 12. The failure of sex and ethnic status to make contributions to Part 1 domain scores suggests that there are common expectancies for personal independence and responsibility between boys and girls from different ethnic groups. With respect to the role of sex and ethnic status in Part 2 scores, it is suggested that difference in environmental tolerance for affective or emotional responses to the school or community was a more reasonable explanation than the inference that girls and boys or children from different cultural backgrounds were inherently different with respect to these behaviors. (15 ref)
Lambert, Nadine M. (U California, Berkeley) Journal of School Psychology, 1979(Spr), Vol 17(1), 3–16. [PA, Vol 64:05903]

1622. Free recall of nonretarded and EMR children: Associative and categorical bases of clustering.
A 12-item stimulus list composed of 3 conceptual categories, each with 2 low- and 2 high-associated word pairs, was presented for free recall. 20 educable mentally retarded (EMR) preadolescents, 20 EMR adolescents, and 20 nonretarded 4th graders showed associative clustering in accordance with preexperimental interitem associative strength. Nonretarded Ss showed signifi-

cantly greater recall and categorical clustering than did the EMR groups. No groups benefited from instructions to cluster. Nonretarded children do not appear to need outside help to accomplish clustering of categorizable material, whereas retarded persons seem to require stronger interventions to induce organization in recall. (11 ref)
Lathey, Jonathan W. (Wassaic Developmental Ctr, Chidren's Unit, NY) American Journal of Mental Deficiency, 1979(Jul), Vol 84(1), 96–99. [PA, Vol 62:11235]

1623. Brief reports on the WISC-R: II. The comparability of the WISC-R and WAIS among 16-year-old EMR children.
Administered the WAIS and WISC-R to 30 16-yr-old educable mentally retarded Ss in counterbalanced order. The WAIS yielded significantly higher Verbal, Performance, and Full Scale IQ scores. Comparisons of corresponding subtests indicate that all WAIS subtests were significantly higher than the WISC-R except Picture Completion. Correlations between corresponding WAIS and WISC-R IQ scales and subtests, however, were significant. Results suggest differences between the 2 instruments among children of subnormal intelligence, thus presenting the possibility that a child may be differentially classified based on the selection of the intelligence test. (14 ref)
Nagle, Richard J. & Lazarus, Susan C. (U South Carolina, Columbia) Journal of School Psychology, 1979(Win), Vol 17(4), 362–367. [PA, Vol 65:02488]

1624. Comparison of McCarthy General Cognitive Indexes and Stanford-Binet IQs for educable mentally retarded children.
15 educable mentally retarded children, aged 6½–8½ yrs, were tested on the McCarthy Scales of Children's Abilities and the Stanford-Binet Intelligence Scale (1972 norms). Ss were tested over a 6-mo period in public schools located in northeast Georgia. Since 8 of the 15 Ss obtained General Cognitive Indexes below the norms presented in the McCarthy manual, extrapolated scores were assigned to increase the precision of the comparison. Although the 2 scores correlated significantly, the mean Index with IQ was significantly lower than the mean IQ for this sample. (14 ref)
Naglieri, Jack A. & Harrison, Patti L. (U Georgia) Perceptual & Motor Skills, 1979(Jun), Vol 48(3, Pt 2), 1251–1254. [PA, Vol 64:12747]

1625. Responses to the language of educable mentally retarded and normal children: Stereotypes and judgments.
Investigated whether a group of hearing and speech professionals held stereotypes about the language of mentally retarded and normal children and whether their evaluations of such children's actual language behavior would reflect these stereotypes. 75 graduate students in speech pathology and audiology rated the speech and language of 2 educable mentally retarded and 2 normal boys. Results indicate that the judges held preconceived ideas about language behavior of educable mentally retarded and normal children, which were reflected in their judgments of the children's verbal language. (13 ref)
Naremore, Rita C. & Hipskind, Nicholas M. (Indiana U Speech & Hearing Ctr, Bloomington) Language, Speech, & Hearing Services in Schools, 1979(Jan), Vol 10(1), 27–34. [PA, Vol 64:01318]

1626. Perceived control and learned helplessness among retarded and nonretarded children: A developmental analysis.
Learned helplessness is produced by successive failures and by feedback attributing failure to uncontrollable causes. Retarded children appear to encounter both causal factors frequently and may thus be susceptible to helplessness. To test this possibility, children of low (70), average (100), and high (130) IQ at 3 MA levels (5½, 7½, and 9½ yrs) were administered a response-initiation measure, a puzzle-repetition measure of perseverance after failure, and a questionnaire designed to gauge attributions for failure. Teachers also rated Ss on a helplessness scale. Helplessness, as measured by the 2 questionnaires, declined with MA. On the 3 helplessness measures derived from Ss themselves, there was an IQ by MA interaction: The low-IQ group showed more helplessness relative to nonretarded children at the upper

MA level than to nonretarded children at the 2 lower levels. Results, although qualified in some respects, are consistent with the view that helplessness can be learned over time by children who repeatedly fail to effect the outcomes that they desire and who learn to attribute failure to factors beyond their control. (31 ref)
Weisz, John R. (U North Carolina, Chapel Hill) Developmental Psychology, 1979(May), Vol 15(3), 311–319. [PA, Vol 62:08426]

1627. Accumulation of and release from proactive inhibition in short-term memory by retarded and nonretarded persons.
32 Ss in 4 groups—1 group of educable mentally retarded adolescents and adults and 3 groups of nonretarded children and adolescents—were compared during accumulation of and release from proactive inhibition. All groups demonstrated the effects of and release from proactive inhibition. Analyses of intralist intrusions indicated that these errors did not differentially affect performance by any group during the accumulation of proactive inhibition and did not occur during its release. (16 ref)
Winters, John J. & Cundari, Leigh. (E. R. Johnstone Training & Research Ctr, Bordentown, NJ) American Journal of Mental Deficiency, 1979(May), Vol 83(6), 595–600. [PA, Vol 62:08889]

1628. Structural aspects of maternal speech to infants reared in poverty.
27 mother–infant dyads (infants aged 6 mo; mean maternal age 19 yrs) were seen as part of a longitudinal study of lower-socioeconomic-status infants at high but varying risk for mild mental retardation. A 20-min unstructured interaction session was videotaped in a laboratory setting. Transcriptions were made of mothers' speech to their infants. Measures of maternal language included sentence form, amount of speech, and syntactic complexity. The proportion of imperatives, but not the amount of maternal speech, was positively correlated with composite measure of risk status and negatively correlated with maternal education and WAIS IQ. Similar to previous findings for maternal speech to older infants, syntactic complexity was not significantly related to social risk indices. In terms of descriptive aspects of the data, there was a high degree of variability on the language measures—indicative of wide individual differences in maternal language style. (15 ref)
Adams, Judith L. & Ramey, Craig T. (U North Carolina, School of Public Health, Chapel Hill) Child Development, 1980(Dec), Vol 51(4), 1280–1284. [PA, Vol 65:07845]

1629. Torque, lateral dominance and handedness in normal, disturbed, and learning disabled children.
Compared lateral hand dominance and torque (The Torque Test) between 437 3rd graders selected from 4 special education populations (emotionally disturbed, educable mentally retarded, speech and hearing disabled, and learning disabled) and a general education population of 296 Ss (nonspecial: not classified for any exceptional education classifications). Significant differences were found between the learning disabled group and speech and hearing disabled and the "nonspecial" group. Similarly, emotionally disturbed and educable mentally retarded torque-rates were found to be significantly higher than the torque-rate for the "nonspecial" classification. Findings are discussed in relation to the corpus callosum and its role in hemispheric exchange and to concepts concerning neuropsychological organization. (43 ref)
Alberts, Fred L. & Tocco, Thomas S. (U Southern Mississippi, Hattiesburg) Clinical Neuropsychology, 1980, Vol 2(4), 157–160. [PA, Vol 66:10406]

1630. Word frequency and contextual richness effects on word identification of educable mentally retarded children.
35 educable mentally retarded (EMR) children (CA 8 yrs 6 mo to 11 yrs 2 mo; MA 4 yrs 5 mo to 10 yrs 2 mo) participated in an oral fill-in-the-blank sentence task during which graphemic clues were provided if necessary. ANOVA supported the facilitative effects of contextual information on word identification by EMR Ss. Strong effects were also found for the frequency level of the target word; however, contextual information was of little help in identifying low frequency words. (10 ref)

Allington, Richard L. (State U New York, Albany) Education & Training of the Mentally Retarded, 1980(Apr), Vol 15(2), 118–121. [PA, Vol 66:10587]

1631. Input organization as a mediating factor in memory: A comparison of educable mentally retarded and nonretarded individuals.
Examined the effect of presentation context on the organization and recall of strongly and weakly related words in 56 educable mentally retarded (EMR) adolescents (mean age 14.7 yrs) and 56 normal 5th graders. Ss were matched by their MAs obtained from the WISC-R. Ss sorted words into experimenter-defined groups of 4 in blocked-random or blocked-consistent fashion. In sort-prompt conditions, Ss were free to structure their own relationships among items during presentation, following instructions to form meaning-based groups (i.e., minimum), or were given explicit training in sorting categorization and sorting stability (i.e., maximum). Both S groups found the minimum-sort-prompt method to be as effective as the maximum for improving measures of recall and clustering relative to the blocked-random method. Normal Ss showed higher levels of organization for strongly related items, and better recall and organization for weakly related items. Subsequent analyses suggested that the lower memory performance of the EMR Ss receiving weakly related items was the result of both inconsistent and poorly structured sorting schemes across trials. (13 ref)
August, Gerald J. (U Iowa Hosp & Clinics, Iowa City) Journal of Experimental Child Psychology, 1980(Aug), Vol 30(1), 125–143. [PA, Vol 64:08262]

1632. The psychiatric assessment of a Vietnamese refugee through art.
Presents the case of an 18-yr-old South Vietnamese woman to illustrate the applications of art to the management of patients with cross-cultural language difficulties. A determination was made, based on the woman's art work, that she was mildly mentally retarded. Her art work matured rapidly from that of a 4–7 yr old to that of an adolescent in less than 3 mo. The experience with the interpreter in evaluating the patient for psychopathology resembled that reported by L. R. Marcos (1979). (5 ref)
Burch, Earl A. & Powell, Carolyn H. (William S. Hall Psychiatric Inst, Columbia, SC) American Journal of Psychiatry, 1980(Feb), Vol 137(2), 236–237. [PA, Vol 63:10034]

1633. Maintenance and generalization of a sorting and retrieval strategy by EMR and nonretarded individuals.
Examined the ability of 47 educable mentally retarded and 51 nonretarded individuals to maintain and generalize a sorting and retrieval strategy designed to facilitate recall and clustering. Each of the groups was assigned to 1 of 3 conditions: experimental, practice, or control. Only Ss in the experimental condition received strategy training. The 3 conditions were each further divided into 2 subconditions—superordinate and associative. The experimental task consisted of 2 phases—word elicitation and recall. Data show that after a 6-mo interval, the strategy was still maintained; however, neither the far-generalization data that were provided by the word-elicitation phase nor the near-generalization data, obtained through the recall phase, revealed any significant results. (10 ref)
Burger, Agnes L.; Blackman, Leonard S. & Tan, Norma. (New York U) American Journal of Mental Deficiency, 1980(Jan), Vol 84(4), 373–380. [PA, Vol 63:07789]

1634. A study of arousal in mentally retarded children.
Measured basal skin conductance (SC) and spontaneous autonomic activity (SAA) in 10 mentally retarded children (borderline) and 10 normal children (mean age 13 yrs). Though retarded Ss showed higher SC and greater frequency of SAA than normals, differences were not significant. (12 ref)
Chattopadhyay, Prabal K.; Roy, Arup R.; Biswas, Prabir K. & Bhattacharyya, Amiya K. (U Calcutta Coll of Science, India) Indian Journal of Clinical Psychology, 1980(Mar), Vol 7(1), 47–51. [PA, Vol 66:08228]

1635. Cognitive processing, academic achievement, and WISC-R performance in EMR children.
Investigated the extent to which simultaneous and successive processing were related both to WISC-R performance and academic achievement in 95 educable mentally retarded (EMR) adolescents. The factor structure of the WISC-R was found equivalent to that reported for non-retarded children. Wide Range Achievement Test Arithmetic scores were significantly related to WISC-R freedom from distractibility and perceptual organization factor scores as well as to simultaneous processing. (6 ref)
Cummins, James P. & Das, J. P. (U Toronto, Ontario Inst for Studies in Education, Canada) Journal of Consulting & Clinical Psychology, 1980(Dec), Vol 48(6), 777–779. [PA, Vol 65:03514]

1636. Maintenance and generalization of a semantic rehearsal strategy in educable mentally retarded children.
51 11–12 yr old educable mentally retarded children (mean WISC-R IQ 64.7), equated on the basis of a free recall pretest, were given a series of lists for free recall. Approximately half the Ss were trained in the use of a strategy to induce deeper level semantic encoding and the discovery of categorical relationships, and half constituted a "no-training" control group with standard free recall instructions. Ss received either related or unrelated lists during the training phase and related or unrelated lists during 2 posttests (immediately following and 1 wk after training). Results suggest that the semantic strategy was maintained over the 1-wk delay, and that it also generalized to word lists unlike those used during training. The degree of generalization was greater for those Ss receiving related lists during training. (31 ref)
Engle, Randall W.; Nagle, Richard J. & Dick, Malcolm. (U South Carolina, Columbia) Journal of Experimental Child Psychology, 1980(Dec), Vol 30(3), 438–454. [PA, Vol 65:05685]

1637. Developmental aspects of incidental learning in retarded children.
114 educable mentally retarded children divided equally into 2 groups by MA (older, 102–142 mo vs younger, 49–102 mo) were exposed to 1 of 3 different orienting instructions (incidental-semantic, intentional-control, or incidental-categorize) within an incidental learning paradigm. The experimental task consisted of 18 pictures representing 6 instances of each of 3 common taxonomic categories. Older Ss recalled significantly more pictures with better clustering than younger Ss. Ss receiving incidental-categorize instructions recalled significantly more items and showed significantly more clustering than Ss receiving the other instructions. The superiority of the categorize condition was maintained during a 24-hr follow-up session. (13 ref)
Fox, Robert & Fulkerson, Frank E. (Western Illinois U) Bulletin of the Psychonomic Society, 1980(Jun), Vol 15(6), 395–398. [PA, Vol 66:01539]

1638. Characteristics across exceptional categories: EMR, LD, and ED.
Characteristics, across categories, of 198 students (mean CAs 9–12 yrs; mean MAs 8–10 yrs) previously identified as educable mentally retarded, learning disabled, and emotionally disturbed were analyzed in order to validate their relevance in distinguishing among the 3 groups. Characteristics selected for study were grouped into 3 areas: (a) cognitive (including IQ, reading underachievement, and subtest scatter on the WISC); (b) affective (rated on statistically interrelated patterns of behavior labeled "conduct disorder," "personality problem," and "immaturity–inadequacy"), and (c) demographic (socioeconomic status). Results show wide separation on 2 discriminant functions and reveal the significance of certain measures in classifying exceptional children. IQ, underachievement in reading, test-score scatter, conduct disorder, and the personality-problem measure correctly classified 81.8% of Ss. However, the question of educational relevance remains unanswered. (31 ref)
Gajar, Anna H. (Pennsylvania State U) Journal of Special Education, 1980(Sum), Vol 14(2), 165–173. [PA, Vol 66:05908]

1639. Subtest patterns and recategorized groupings of the McCarthy Scales for EMR children.
Examined scores of 40 educable mentally retarded (EMR) children (aged 6–8.5 yrs) on the McCarthy Scales of Children's Abilities to determine areas of strengths and weaknesses. Subtest profiles were explored, and McCarthy tasks were recategorized in accordance with the approaches of A. Bannatyne (1974) and J. M. Sattler (1974) to investigate EMR persons' performance. Ss showed a strength in memory for common objects and weaknesses in acquired knowledge, numerical reasoning, and conceptual thinking. In addition, Ss' average General Cognitive Index was lower than would be expected for a group of EMR children. (31 ref)
Harrison, Patti L.; Kaufman, Alan S. & Naglieri, Jack A. (American Guidance Service, Circle Pines, MN) American Journal of Mental Deficiency, 1980(Sep), Vol 85(2), 129–134. [PA, Vol 64:11454]

1640. A comparison of the performance of normal, learning disabled, and educable mentally retarded children on Cattell's ability constructs.
Explored the use of R. B. Cattell's (1971) ability traits (fluid and crystallized intelligence, visualization, and fluency) as difference characteristics of the learning disabilities category. Previous research and conceptual differences among the learning disabled (LD), normal, and educable mentally retarded (EMR) populations suggested that LD children would perform better than EMR children but not as well as normal children on measures of the traits. 15 7–8.6 yr old Ss from each category were administered measures of the traits. An analysis of the scores indicated significant differences between LD and normal Ss and between LD and EMR Ss on the visualization and fluency measures. Significant differences between the groups were also found on the crystallized intelligence measure but not in fluid intelligence. (10 ref)
Hill, David S. (Ohio State U) Journal of Learning Disabilities, 1980(Aug–Sep), Vol 13(7), 383–386. [PA, Vol 64:10637]

1641. Pursuit rotor learning of mildly retarded children under supplementary feedback conditions.
A rotary pursuit task was used to study the effects of augmenting, task-inherent information (feedback) in enhancing motor acquisition of 119 mildly retarded Ss (mean CA 141 mo, mean IQ 66). Ss were trained on the task under control and 6 differential applications of supplementary visual, tactile, or auditory feedback. Task acquisition was facilitated by supplementary feedback in specific treatments. Also, acquisition was favored under conditions where the locus of the supplementary feedback was juxtaposed with the "correct" response behavior. Those feedback treatments that were juxtaposed with incorrect or "error" behavior did not serve to facilitate acquisition of the task. A tenable explanation for the consistency of the difference between treatments could be an increase in habit state, created by the locus of the feedback that served to reinforce the elicited response. (15 ref)
Horgan, James S. (U Illinois, Inst for the Study of Developmental Disabilities, Chicago Circle) Perceptual & Motor Skills, 1980(Jun), Vol 50(3, Pt 2), 1219–1228. [PA, Vol 66:03868]

1642. Computational errors of mentally retarded students.
Examined the computational errors made by 370 8–18 yr old educable mentally retarded students (average IQ 62.7) on the Arithmetic subtest of the Wide Range Achievement Test. These retarded Ss had a lower percentage of grouping and inappropriate inversion errors and a higher percentage of incorrect operation errors than did normal Ss reported in a study by J. M. Englehardt (see PA, Vol 60:1851). (5 ref)
Janke, Robert W. (Strongsville City Schools, OH) Psychology in the Schools, 1980(Jan), Vol 17(1), 30–32. [PA, Vol 65:05690]

1643. Metamemory and the transfer of an interrogative strategy by EMR children.
Taught 34 educable mentally retarded children (EMR; mean age 10.2 yrs) to produce an interrogative strategy as an aid to paired-associate learning. Interrogative training was spread over 4 sessions with experimenter guidance gradually faded; training was followed by tests of long-term retention for the trained items, strategy maintenance, and generalization. Metamemory was assessed prior to training and following generalization. Analysis of recall demonstrated successful maintenance and generalization of the interrogative strategy; the quality of elaborations produced by the trained children predicted recall accuracy. Importantly, metamemory pretest measures for the interrogative trained Ss were related to strategy use at generalization. Metamemory posttest reliably predicted recall during training, maintenance, and generalization sessions and strategy use at maintenance. Interrogative training did not noticeably improve general aspects of metamemorial knowledge. (19 ref)
Kendall, Constance R.; Borkowski, John G. & Cavanaugh, John C. (U Notre Dame) Intelligence, 1980(Jul–Sep), Vol 4(3), 255–270. [PA, Vol 66:03871]

1644. Effects of stimulus characteristics on the logical problem solving behavior of retarded adolescents and nonretarded children.
Previous research by H. H. Spitz and B. T. Nadler (see PA, Vol 52:10442) demonstrated that nonretarded 6-yr-olds and educable retarded adolescents were unable to generate the solution to a logical problem-solving task. In this study, an attempt was made to improve this performance by changing the format of a precriterion task. 60 nonretarded 6-yr-olds and 60 retarded 15-yr-olds were asked to indicate the identity of a hidden design by only uncovering 2 of 3 sources of information. Highlighting relevant attributes by reducing extraneous information aided problem solving in the precriterion task (a 1-bit problem), but Ss failed to formulate a rule that would have enabled them to solve the similar but more complex criterion task (a 2-bit problem). (22 ref)
Nadler, Barbara. (Rutgers U) Child Study Journal, 1980, Vol 10(1), 27–40. [PA, Vol 65:01517]

1645. Effects of stimulus characteristics on the logical problem solving behavior of retarded adolescents and nonretarded children.
60 retarded (MA 9.43 yrs) and 60 nonretarded (CA 6.41 yrs) Ss were asked to indicate the identity of a hidden design by only uncovering 2 of 3 sources of information. Highlighting relevant attributes by reducing extraneous information aided problem solving in the pre-criterion task (a 1-bit problem), but Ss failed to formulate a rule that would have enabled them to solve the similar but more complex criterion task (a 2-bit problem). (22 ref)
Nadler, Barbara. (Rutgers U) Child Study Journal, 1980, Vol 10(1), 27–40. [PA, Vol 64:01317]

1646. Comparison of McCarthy General Cognitive Index and WISC-R IQ for educable mentally retarded, learning disabled, and normal children.
Examined the relationship between the McCarthy Scales of Children's Abilities, General Cognitive Index, and the WISC-R Full Scale IQ for 20 educable mentally retarded (MR), 20 learning disabled (LD), and 20 normal children (6 yrs 4 mo–8 yrs 11 mo). Ss were comparable with respect to age, sex, and race. The mean McCarthy Indexes for MR and LD Ss were significantly lower than the mean WISC-R Full Scale IQs. When the Index and Full Scale IQ were converted to a common metric and compared, the mean index for MR and LD Ss remained lower than the Full Scale IQs, although the differences were nonsignificant. The measures correlated significantly for all 3 samples and ranged from .51 to .82. (19 ref)
Naglieri, Jack A. (Northern Arizona U, Flagstaff) Psychological Reports, 1980(Oct), Vol 47(2), 591–596. [PA, Vol 66:06083]

1647. McCarthy and WISC-R correlations with WRAT achievement scores.
Explored the relationships between the McCarthy General Cognitive Index and WISC-R Full Scale IQ with the Wide Range Achievement Test (WRAT) Reading scores with 20 educable mentally retarded and 20 learning disabled 6–8 yr olds. WRAT scores did not correlate significantly with the WISC-R and

McCarthy scores for the retarded sample, while substantial correlations were found for the learning-disabled group. Analysis indicated that the McCarthy and WISC-R were positively and equally related to the WRAT Reading section. (9 ref)
Naglieri, Jack A. (Northern Arizona U, Flagstaff) Perceptual & Motor Skills, 1980(Oct), Vol 51(2), 392–394. [PA, Vol 66:11672]

1648.   A paper-and-pencil inventory for the assessment of Piaget's tasks.
A comprehensive, objective inventory for measuring Piagetian tasks was developed and tested on 542 8–19 yr old Ss to determine its usefulness for normal and retarded students. It was found to be reliable and valid and to have advantages over other Piagetian tests. Improvements are suggested, and its potential as an educational and research tool is discussed. (24 ref)
Patterson, Henry O. & Milakofsky, Louis. (Pennsylvania State U, Berks Campus, Reading) Applied Psychological Measurement, 1980(Sum), Vol 4(3), 341–353. [PA, Vol 65:00220]

1649.   The effects of memory strategy instruction in the short-term memory of the mentally retarded.
Investigated the effectiveness of teaching mnemonic strategies to overcome difficulties of mentally retarded students in retaining the motor short-term memory information of a preselected movement. 40 educable mentally retarded students with a mean CA of 11.6 yrs and a mean IQ of 66.8 participated. The memory strategy was a combination of the "feel" of the movement and the spatial location of the hand relative to the body. The 2×2 factorial design involved an instructional treatment factor that included giving Ss memory strategy vs no memory-strategy instruction and a retention condition factor that included immediate recall and a 15-sec retention interval. Data support the effectiveness of the memory-strategy instruction. (22 ref)
Reid, Greg. (McGill U, Montreal, Canada) Journal of Motor Behavior, 1980(Sep), Vol 12(3), 221–227. [PA, Vol 66:03881]

1650.   Intelligence-related differences in the relative salience of object-property relationships.
Three groups of 19 nonretarded 8–16 yr olds and 10 educable mentally retarded 16-yr-olds (MA 10 yrs) were asked to verify statements about the properties of animate and inanimate objects. Properties were of 4 types: intrinsic action (e.g., "sharks can swim"), extrinsic action (e.g., "horses can be ridden"), static (e.g., "turtles have shells"), and superordinate category (e.g., "dogs are animals"). Retarded Ss, relative to nonretarded Ss of all ages, responded particularly slowly to static property statements when objects were animate and to intrinsic-action properties when objects were inanimate. Data suggest intelligence-related differences in the types of semantic properties that are most strongly associated with particular object concepts and, as such, may be indicative of fundamental differences in the way in which the core meaning of individual concepts is represented in semantic memory. (14 ref)
Roaden, Saundra K.; McCauley, Charley & Sperber, Richard D. (George Peabody Coll) American Journal of Mental Deficiency, 1980(Mar), Vol 84(5), 518–525. [PA, Vol 63:12192]

1651.   Toward operationalizing a psychoeducational definition of learning disabilities.
Presents an operational definition of "learning disabilities" based on the view from the stand that classificatory psychoeducational definitions must ultimately relate to educational processes. Thus, the condition should be described in terms of abilities crucial to educational achievement, and noneducational criteria should not be employed. It is pointed out that the most generally accepted current definition—which identifies children as "learning-disabled" on the basis of behavioral criteria, while excluding etiological and other nonbehavioral factors—overlooks functional similarities among such groups as educable mentally retarded and emotionally disturbed children. These similarities warrant the inclusion under the rubric of "learning-disabled" of some children who may also be grouped within other diagnostic categories. Consequently, the definition provided here is based on a primary concern with day-to-day learning and management

issues. Concepts subtended by the definition are operationally defined, and its relationship to programming is discussed. (45 ref)
Schere, Richard A.; Richardson, Ellis & Bialer, Irv. (City U New York, Brooklyn Coll) Journal of Abnormal Child Psychology, 1980(Mar), Vol 8(1), 5–20. [PA, Vol 65:10660]

1652.   Reliability of the Concept Assessment Kit-Conservation for educable mentally retarded children.
Obtained internal consistency, alternate form, and stability coefficients for the Concept Assessment Kit-Conservation (CAK-C) for a sample of 135 7–14 yr old educable mentally retarded (EMR) children. The internal consistency and alternate form coefficients appeared to be acceptably high, and the stability coefficients, while appreciably lower, still suggested some degree of consistency over a 1-yr period. The reliabilty of the CAK-C is judged to be satisfactory for EMR children. (1 ref)
Silverstein, A. B.; Brownlee, Linda & Legutki, Greg. (U California School of Medicine, Neuropsychiatric Inst, Los Angeles) Psychology in the Schools, 1980(Jan), Vol 17(1), 4–6. [PA, Vol 65:06446]

1653.   Dimensions underlying a hierarchically based assessment of social problem-solving.
The dimensions underlying the THINK procedure (Test of the Hierarchy of Inductive Knowledge) designed to assess 9 levels of social problem-solving among educable mentally retarded (EMR) learners were explored in relation to IQ and MA. Principal-factor solutions followed by oblimin rotations were performed on data collected from 120 EMR children (CAs 9–14 yrs; mean WISC IQ 68.9). Results yielded 3 hierarchical factors, 2 that were moderately related to IQ and MA and 1 that was independent of IQ and MA. (7 ref)
Smith, I. Leon & Greenberg, Sandra. (Professional Examination Service, New York, NY) American Journal of Mental Deficiency, 1980(Jan), Vol 84(4), 411–414. [PA, Vol 63:06653]

1654.   A longitudinal comparison of the WISC and WISC-R with special education pupils.
Investigated the degree of comparability between the WISC and WISC-R over time using 276 8–9 yr old mildly mentally handicapped children who had received a WISC (Trial 1) and a WISC or WISC-R (Trial 2) after an interval of 3 yrs. Ss were grouped on the basis of a test administered in Trial 2. Group 1 contained 183 children who received the WISC on Trial 2, while Group II was composed of 93 children who had been posttested on the WISC-R. Verbal IQ, Performance IQ, and Full Scale IQ for both instruments were transcribed from Ss' special education folders. ANOVA failed to support the hypotheses that the WISC-R yields mean Verbal, Performance, and Full Scale IQ scores greater than or equal to the corresponding mean IQ scores of the WISC. It is concluded that the WISC-R may unfairly penalize special education children who reevaluated with this instrument and that action should be taken to insure that children are evaluated for special class placement on comparable bases. (7 ref)
Thomas, Paulette J. (U New Orleans) Psychology in the Schools, 1980(Oct), Vol 17(4), 437–441. [PA, Vol 66:09128]

1655.   Intellectual and special aptitudes of tenth grade EMH students.
Obtained special aptitude scores of 84 educable mentally handicapped (EMH) 10th graders with the Nonreading Aptitude Test Battery (NATB) while IQ (44–84) was quantified with the WISC-R. It was hypothesized that aptitudes would emerge from the NATB that would have otherwise been overlooked by sole reliance on the WISC-R. Low to moderate correlations between NATB and WISC-R scores prevented immediate extraction of aptitudes independent of intelligence, but cross-tabulations of NATB scores across IQ levels revealed that Ss often scored at average or above levels on such NATB factors as Form Perception, Clerical Perception, Spatial, and Dexterity. It is concluded that EMH students possess a variety of special aptitudes that could broaden their vocational choice and dissipate the myths surrounding their place in the work world. (14 ref)

Watkins, Marley W. (Phoenix Union High School System, AZ) Education & Training of the Mentally Retarded, 1980(Apr), Vol 15(2), 139–142. [PA, Vol 66:11403]

1656.   Distinguishing among three subgroups of handicapped students using Bannatyne's recategorization.
Examined the utility of A. Bannatyne's (1968, 1974) recategorization system. A stepwise discrimination functions analysis was performed on the subtest scaled scores from the WISC-R for 294 learning disabled (LD), 36 educably mentally retarded (EMR), and 71 emotionally disturbed (ED) students. Results show that 100% of the EMR and ED Ss were predicted to be labeled LD on the basis of this recategorization, while 99.7% of the LD Ss were predicted to be LD. (8 ref)
Webster, Raymond E.   & Lafayette, Ann D. (U Connecticut, Storrs) Journal of Educational Research, 1980(Mar–Apr), Vol 73(4), 237–240. [PA, Vol 65:11286]

1657.   Evaluation of auditory sensory memory of mentally retarded and nonretarded persons.
Compared the performance of 24 mentally retarded (mean age 14.45 yrs), 24 equal-MA controls (mean age 10.3 yrs), and 24 equal-CA controls (mean age 14.65 yrs) in 2 experiments designed to identify processes of auditory sensory memory. In the 1st study, backward masking of pure tones occurred for a group of retarded adolescents; however, no differences in masking functions were obtained for the retarded group and control groups of equal CA and MA. In the 2nd study a gap-detection task was used as an apparent index of echoic trace durability. Since retarded persons were hypothesized to have a less durable echoic trace, the unique prediction was made that they would outperform control Ss on the task. The retarded group was significantly more accurate and exhibited a lower threshold than did the nonretarded, CA-matched control group. The applicability of these tasks for investigations of mental development is noted, and suggestions are made concerning improvements and extensions of the present research. A theoretical model is proposed to incorporate the current pattern of results. (28 ref)
Campbell, Edward M. & Meyer, Philip A.   American Journal of Mental Deficiency, 1981(Jul), Vol 86(1), 50–59. [PA, Vol 66:08226]

1658.   Patterns of language performance in educable mentally retarded children.
41 familial educable mentally retarded children (IQs 50–80) were given 12 language tasks measuring comprehension, formulation, and repetition at the semantic, syntactic, and phonologic levels of language. Through the Q technique of factor analysis, 6 language patterns, derived from positive and negative loadings on 3 factors, emerged. The 6 patterns of language performance revealed that Ss did not perform the same across all language dimensions. Their language performance demonstrated different patterns of strengths and weaknesses among the tasks relative to their overall performance. (17 ref)
Chapman, Darwin L. & Nation, James E. (Montgomery County Intermediate Unit, Norristown, PA) Journal of Communication Disorders, 1981(May), Vol 14(3), 245–254. [PA, Vol 66:08227]

1659.   Recategorized WISC-R scores of learning disabled children and differential diagnosis.
Analyzed WISC-R profiles along a 3-factor approach (Spatial, Verbal-Comprehensive, Attention-Concentration) as suggested by A. Bannatyne (1968) for purposes of differential diagnosis. The WISC-R profiles of 278 school-verified learning disabled children were compared to those of 563 Ss (aged 4–19 yrs) in 4 other groups: educable mentally impaired, emotionally impaired, otherwise impaired, and nonimpaired. The total sample was drawn from the State of Michigan public schools. Statistically significant differences were found between the learning disabled group and the other groups on WISC-R subtest scores. Further analysis revealed that 36% of the learning disabled and 32% of normal Ss exhibited this WISC-R profile. Analysis of WISC-R profiles was not useful in differential diagnosis among the 5 groups. (23 ref)

Clarizio, Harvey & Bernard, Robert. (Michigan State U, East Lansing) Psychology in the Schools, 1981(Jan), Vol 18(1), 5–12. [PA, Vol 66:11337]

1660.   Intelligence-related differences in semantic processing speed.
20 educable mentally retarded (mean IQ 67) and 21 nonretarded adolescents verified superordinate and basic level descriptions of common objects. Obtained category decision times, as measured by superordinate–basic level difference scores, were longer for retarded than for nonretarded Ss, indicating fundamental group differences in semantic processing speed. Additional data are interpreted as indicating that retarded adolescents may be slower in making basic level as well as superordinate level decisions, suggesting that they have difficulty in making semantic classification decisions in general. Other results, from a semantic priming task performed by the same Ss, suggest that the obtained group differences in semantic processing speed were related to the active (deliberate) processes required for verification, rather than to category knowledge per se or to more passive processes associated with the activation of stored semantic knowledge. (23 ref)
Davies, Deborah; Sperber, Richard D.   & McCauley, Charley. (Stockton State Coll) Journal of Experimental Child Psychology, 1981(Jun), Vol 31(3), 387–402. [PA, Vol 66:03865]

1661.   Investigation of the norms and concurrent validity for the Adaptive Behavior Inventory for Children (ABIC).
Administered the ABIC to 482 1st–5th graders who were stratified by sociocultural group (White, Black, Hispanic, and Native American Papago). Little evidence of concurrent validity was found in an examination of correlations among the ABIC, standardized achievement test results (Metropolitan Readiness Test), teacher ratings of classroom performance, intelligence (WISC-R), and sociocultural measures. Caution in the use of the ABIC in other regions and with other sociocultural groups is recommended. Implication for the measurement of adaptive behavior, for the issue of bias in assessment, and for the diagnostic construct of mild mental retardation are discussed. (21 ref)
Kazimour, Kimberly K.   & Reschly, Daniel J. (Iowa State U, Ames) American Journal of Mental Deficiency, 1981(Mar), Vol 85(5), 512–520. [PA, Vol 65:11666]

1662.   Iconic store readout of mildly mentally retarded and nonretarded individuals.
Required 12 mildly retarded (mean age 21.36 yrs) and 24 nonretarded Ss (12 equal-CA Ss, mean age 21.86 yrs; 12 equal-MA Ss, mean age 9.45 yrs) to report tachistoscopically presented linear arrays of letters differing with respect to the number of letters per array. On some trials a visual mask appeared coincidentally with or at VIs following the onset of the letter array. By varying information load and stimulus onset asynchrony and by including a no-mask condition, it was possible to assess the iconic store readout for each of the 3 groups. Results reveal that the mask was influential in disrupting the sensory store readout for all groups and that the low-MA Ss demonstrated a slower sensory store readout relative to the equal-CA group. The retarded Ss demonstrated the slowest sensory store readout. (15 ref)
Mosley, James L. (U Calgary, Canada) American Journal of Mental Deficiency, 1981(Jul), Vol 86(1), 60–66. [PA, Vol 66:08254]

1663.   Comparison of the PPVT-R and WISC-R with urban educable mentally retarded students.
Comparisons of the revised Peabody Picture Vocabulary Test (PPVT-R) and the WISC-R were made with 67 educable mentally retarded students (mean CA 11.25 yrs). Significant differences were found between the PPVT-R mean standard scores and Verbal, Performance, and Full Scale IQs. The PPVT-R did not correlate significantly with the WISC-R scales or subtests, suggesting that the tests are measuring different abilities. (7 ref)

Prasse, David P. & Bracken, Bruce A. (U Wisconsin School of Education, Milwaukee) Psychology in the Schools, 1981(Apr), Vol 18(2), 174–177. [PA, Vol 66:09399]

1664. The effects of positive examiner verbal comments on the total WISC-R performance of institutionalized EMR students.
Forty educably mentally retarded (EMR) students (mean CA 11.5 yrs; mean IQ 72) were randomly selected and assigned to 1 of 2 treatment groups. Experimental Ss were verbally praised after their responses to the WISC-R questions, while controls received nonevaluative procedural comments. The scaled scores for 5 of 11 subtests, in addition to the Verbal, Performance, and Full Scale indices, were significantly greater under the experimental procedure. (16 ref)
Saigh, Philip A. (American U of Beirut, Lebanon) Journal of School Psychology, 1981(Spr), Vol 19(1), 86–91. [PA, Vol 66:07092]

1665. Item analyses of the Concept Assessment Kit-Conservation for educable mentally retarded children.
Conducted a series of item analyses of the Concept Assessment Kit—Conservation for 155 educable mentally retarded children (mean CA 10.88 yrs; mean MA 7.19 yrs). The probability of a correct response differed from task to task, and there was evidence that the order of difficulty of the tasks for this sample resembled that for nonretarded children. The probabilities of the 2 incorrect responses were generally not equal, and the choice of one or the other incorrect response showed some relation to CA, MA, and IQ, particularly the last 2 variables. (15 ref)
Silverstein, A. B.; Brownlee, Linda & Legutki, Greg. (MRRC-Lanterman State Hosp Research Group, Pomona, CA) Psychology in the Schools, 1981(Apr), Vol 18(2), 139–143. [PA, Vol 66:09415]

1666. Parents' views on the development of social competencies in their mildly intellectually handicapped adolescents.
Developed and administered an interview schedule to parents of 43 16–21 yr old mildly intellectually handicapped adolescents attending a work preparation center. The schedule provided insights into home background influences and underlying parents' perceptions and expectations. This determined the extent of the need for parental involvement, support, and subsequent directions for programing. The reponses revealed that many Ss were still home-based and family dependent. Some parents were prolonging the dependence of their childen rather than reinforcing the independent living skills training at the center. Parents were aware of important deficiences in Ss' lack of friends and leisure time interests, but needed guidance in helping in these areas. There was a special need for supportive contact with families during Ss' first weeks in employment. (20 ref)
Smith, Helen M. & Sykes, Stewart C. (Monash U Faculty of Education, Clayton, Australia) Australian Journal of Developmental Disabilities, 1981(Mar), Vol 7(1), 17–26. [PA, Vol 66:08272]

1667. Effects of type of reinforcement on the intelligence test performance of retarded Black children.
Examined the effects of reinforcement on 100 Black male 9–11 yr olds who had been diagnosed as being mildly mentally retarded, using the WISC-R. After each correct response, Ss were given no reinforcement, a candy reward, traditional social reinforcement, or culturally relevant social reinforcement. Ss given tangible or culturally relevant rewards obtained significantly higher scores that did Ss given either no reinforcement or traditional social reinforcement. (3 ref)
Terrell, Francis; Terrell, Sandra L. & Taylor, Jerome. (North Texas State U, Denton) Psychology in the Schools, 1981(Apr), Vol 18(2), 225–227. [PA, Vol 66:10616]

Moderate Mental Retardation

1668. Reactions to physical and social distracters by moderately retarded institutionalized children.
Investigated the orienting behavior of mentally retarded children under a variety of conditions, all involving a discrimination learning task. In Exp. I, the data from these Ss were compared with those available from a previous investigation which involved normal Ss of comparable MA and CA. It was found that, in many cases, the normal Ss showed nontask orientations to a greater degree than did the retarded Ss. An examination of those circumstances under which the retarded glanced more often indicated that these circumstances, often observed in the classroom, are inappropriate for adjudging retardates to be distractible. Exp. II added a social agent to the conditions for task performance, using Ss from Exp. I. The presence of an adult in the learning situation greatly increased nontask orientations. However, it was also shown that if cues are provided by the adult, they will be utilized by the Ss so that their glancing apparently represented information-seeking and not merely vacuous orientations to a salient social stimulus. Exp. III, using naive Ss, replicated the pattern of results found in Exp. II.
Turnure, James E. (U. Minnesota) Journal of Special Education, 1970(Sum), Vol. 4(3), 283-294. [PA, Vol 46:07350]

1669. A developmental study of the subject matter choices in the free drawing of trainable mentally retarded subjects.
Analyzes drawings of 25 male and 19 female trainable retarded children with MAs from 2.7-6.6 yr and CAs from 8.3-14.10 yr and compares them to drawings of normal children with respect to choice of subject matter and human body schema. Differences were found in subject matter preferences between Ss and normal children of a comparable MA: Ss drew fewer weapons and instruments and more humans. Age trends were also noted: lower MA Ss drew more humans and fewer plants than higher MA Ss. Sex differences followed cultural expectations. It is concluded that "art samples can be reliably categorized and that their subject matter is significantly related to the intellectual development of the artist."
Israel, Lawrence J. & Heal, Laird W. (George Peabody Coll. for Teachers) Exceptional Children, 1971(Apr), Vol. 37(8), 597-600. [PA, Vol 47:01620]

1670. Parent vs. teacher behavior ratings of TMR pupils.
The Test Behavior Observation Guide (TBOG) was completed by 65 mothers and 28 teachers on 65 trainable mentally retarded 8-19 yr old pupils to permit a comparison of the parent and teacher behavior ratings. Partitioned chi-square was used for a 4-way analysis of high and low ratings. Significant differences between parent and teacher ratings were found in motor activity and amount of speech (for the girls) and in effort and cooperation (for the boys).
Jamison, Colleen B.; Attwell, Arthur A. & Fils, David H. (California State Coll., Los Angeles) American Journal of Mental Deficiency, 1971(May), Vol. 75(6), 746-751. [PA, Vol 47:01621]

1671. Psychophysical scaling of brightness and shape dimensions in mentally retarded persons.
Used a sample of 33 institutionalized moderately retarded adolescents and adults to obtain psychometric functions for stimuli on a brightness and on a shape dimension so as to scale these stimuli in terms of their distinctiveness. Stimuli on the brightness dimension were taken from the Munsell achromatic series. Stimuli on the shape dimension were generated by varying the vertical-horizontal dimensions of a rectangular bar while keeping area and depth constant so as to yield a vertical and horizontal series of stimuli. For all practical purposes the distinctiveness of cues on 1 stimulus dimension was independent of stimulus cues on the other dimension. The obtained psychometric functions were applied successfully in subsequent research to scale stimuli in terms of their discriminability.

Switzky, Harvey N. (George Peabody Coll. for Teachers) American Journal of Mental Deficiency, 1971(Nov), Vol. 76(3), 341-347. [PA, Vol 48:03563]

1672. Recognition memory: The relationship of accuracy and latency of response under different memory loads in retardates.
Studied 10 moderately retarded, well-practiced children in a repeated measures design. The task was the recognition of pictures using a probe procedure. Accuracy decreased as a function of number of pictures (1, 5, 9, or 15) that were present and latency of response increased. Correlational analyses showed high reliabilities and intercorrelations among the accuracy and latency scores but low intercorrelations of accuracy and latency. A varimax factor rotation yielded 2 factors associated, respectively, with latency and accuracy.
Urbano, Richard C.; Scott, Keith G. & McCarthy, Kathleen. (Florida State U.) Journal of Experimental Child Psychology, 1971(Oct), Vol. 12(2), 270-277. [PA, Vol 47:07431]

1673. Lateral preference and ability to conserve multiple spatial relations by mentally retarded children.
Divided 31 8-10 yr. old trainable mentally retarded Ss into lateralized and mixed-dominant groups. Ss were then tested for their ability to perform a spatial task requiring short-term memory and reversible visual imagery. Ss with inconsistent and crossed laterality patterns were better in visual-spatial ability than Ss whose sided preferences were unilateral in eye, hand, ear, and foot modalities. Results support the developmental importance of bilateral sensory and motor functioning.
Kershner, John R. (Ontario Inst. for Studies in Education, Toronto, Canada) Perceptual & Motor Skills, 1972(Aug), Vol. 35(1), 151-152. [PA, Vol 49:04748]

1674. Conservation in trainable mentally retarded children.
Tested 27 trainable mentally retarded children to determine whether they showed conservation of number and volume as found by Piaget in normal children. Complex analyses of various and Pearson product-moment correlations showed that the degree of conservation was significantly correlated with both IQ and MA but was essentially independent of CA.
Klauss, Susan D. & Green, Martha B. Training School Bulletin, 1972(Nov), Vol. 69(3), 108-114. [PA, Vol 50:01280]

1675. The effects of summated stimuli with retarded children.
Conducted a study with 12 moderately retarded males (mean CA = 10 yr.) to test the stimulus summation hypothesis. This hypothesis states that when 2 conditioned stimuli are presented in combination and each stimulus controls a certain degree of response strength, their response strengths summate. Thus, the strength of the response controlled by the compound stimulus is greater than the strength of the responses controlled by the individual stimuli. Ss were given discrimination training under 3 different stimuli, 2 correlated with reinforcement and 1 with extinction. Stimuli were combined in all possible combinations of 2 under extinction and reinforcement conditions. Results support the summation hypothesis. (25 ref.)
Melnick, Joseph. (U. Kentucky) Journal of Experimental Child Psychology, 1972(Oct), Vol. 14(2), 277-286. [PA, Vol 49:04788]

1676. Temporal and contextual cues as discriminative attributes in retardates' recognition memory.
Compared the strength, frequency attribute, and context marker theories of recognition memory in 5 experiments with a total of 19 moderately retarded adolescents. Accuracy at distinguishing target (T) items from distractor (D) items exceeded 90% correct even when all items were equated for frequency of occurrence and recency of last appearance. As long as the 1st occurrence of the items was temporally isolated in an inspection set this level was maintained. However, when both T and D items occurred initially together in the inspection set, performance dropped to 70% correct. Results are inconsistent with strength and frequency attribute theories and consistent with a context marker theory of recognition. The special role of temporal cues is discussed, with particular emphasis on the imporantce of the item's "birthdate," the time tag associated with the item's initial appearance. (22 ref.)

Brown, Ann L. (U. Illinois, Children's Research Center) Journal of Experimental Psychology, 1973(Apr), Vol. 98(1), 1-13. [PA, Vol 50:09109]

1677. Conservation of vertical-horizontal space perception in trainable retarded children.
Assessed the performance of 31 8-10 yr old trainable retarded children on their ability to conserve multiple spatial relations, which is a right cerebral hemisphere function. Ss' pattern of responses suggested, in A. Luria's (1966) terms, a successive rather than a simultaneous mode of processing spatial information. The Ss were deficient, in A. Jensen's (1969) terms, on both Level I and Level II spatial tasks. In contrast to 31 7-yr-old nonretarded children who had little difficulty with static images, the retarded Ss had as much difficulty reproducing perceptual copies (Level I) as they had in adapting to reorientations of the visual field (Level II). The performance of the retarded Ss was characterized by perceptual dominance, inability to decenter, transductive reasoning, and irreversibility—all traits of the child who has not reached Piaget's stage of concrete operations. (26 ref.)
Kershner, John R. (Ontario Inst. for Studies in Education, Toronto, Canada) American Journal of Mental Deficiency, 1973(May), Vol. 77(6), 710-716. [PA, Vol 51:07449]

1678. Factors affecting concept acquisition in institutionalized young adults.
Studied concept acquisition in 30 moderately retarded young adults (mean MA = 6.8 yrs, mean CA = 18.2 yrs) and their matched MA and CA controls under free, cued, or constrained conditions (Phase I) and its transfer to a related task (Phase II). The retarded Ss had the most errors, trials to criterion, and time per trial during Phase I; however, their Phase II performance was comparable to their MA controls. These groups also showed comparable positive transfer, while CA controls showed significant negative transfer. Experimental condition effects generally were not found. Results indicate that retarded Ss may show a production deficiency when performing concept acquisition tasks, although this may be overcome if they are given sufficient opportunity to develop an adequate learning set. (26 ref.)
Miller, Harold R. (Hamilton Psychiatric Hosp., Ontario, Canada) American Journal of Mental Deficiency, 1973(Jan), Vol. 77(4), 460-467. [PA, Vol 51:05474]

1679. Correlates of social competence among trainable mentally retarded children.
Measured the performances of 110 8-16 yr old trainable mentally retarded children, using a Likert scale for social competence. Measures of biological-genetic potential, motivational factors, and situational factors were used as independent variables. Using a multiple step-wise regression, CA, interaction, IQ, and teacher expectation, 65% of the variance in social competence was explained. Results indicate that biological-genetic factors (IQ and age) and experience with the environment (social interaction) were the primary independent variables, suggesting that increased social interaction in an environment of high teacher expectation can increase the performance and adaptability of the trainable mentally retarded child. (25 ref.)
Newman, Helen G. & Doby, John T. (American Dental Assn., Div. of Behavioral Sciences, Chicago, Ill.) American Journal of Mental Deficiency, 1973(May), Vol. 77(6), 722-732. [PA, Vol 51:07461]

1680. A Guttman scalogram analysis of haptic perception for trainable mentally retarded children.
Administered Piaget and B. Inhelder's test of haptic perception to 47 trainable mental retardates (CA = 72-196 mo., MA = 30-96 mo.), and subjected their scores to a Guttman scalogram analysis. Ss' responses were congruent with previous results with nonretarded and blind children; stages scaled almost perfectly in accordance with Piaget and Inhelder's developmental order. One notable exception occurred; the topological figures were the most difficult items rather than among the most easy or most frequently correct. This misplacement may be specific to these Ss or due to their instructional program. (16 ref.)

Yoshida, Roland K. (U. Southern California) American Journal of Mental Deficiency, 1973(Jan), Vol. 77(4), 439-444. [PA, Vol 50:03359]

1681.   Parental views on sexual development and education of the trainable mentally retarded.
Administered to 270 parents of 206 retarded persons a questionnaire on the sexual history of the trainable mentally retarded (TMR) children, attitudes toward sex education, and the possibility of married life for their children. Parents reported little evidence of sexual misbehavior or even interest in sexual matters but generally lacked confidence in their children's future sex behavior. Most believed that they had primary responsibility for sex education, although few felt comfortable about their ability to provide it. Nearly ½ of the parents favored voluntary sterilization of the trainable, but less than 1% of the retardates in the sample had undergone, nor were their parents seriously considering, sterilization. Relationships between the amount of sex information the parents perceived they themselves possessed and their own attitudes toward sex, marriage, and parenthood for the trainable are presented.
Alcorn, Dewaine A. (U Nebraska) Journal of Special Education, 1974(Sum), Vol 8(2), 119-130. [PA, Vol 53:01461]

1682.   Keeping track of changing variables: Long-term retention of a trained rehearsal strategy by retarded adolescents.
Appraised the keeping-track performance of 10 trained-to-rehearse and 10 untrained moderately retarded adolescents 6 mo after the training had terminated. 8 of the trained Ss maintained their rehearsal strategy even in the absence of instructions to do so. Rehearsal Ss responded faster, more accurately, and with a more mature pattern of responses than either the untrained Ss or the 2 trained Ss who abandoned their strategy. The educational implications of developing flexible strategies are discussed in relation to the limitations imposed by the developmental level of the S. (24 ref)
Brown, Ann L.; Campione, Joseph C. & Murphy, Martin D. (U. Illinois, Children's Research Center) American Journal of Mental Deficiency, 1974(Jan), Vol. 78(4), 446-453. [PA, Vol 52:07996]

1683.   Incidental learning and short-range memory in normals and retardates.
Tested and largely confirmed M. R. Denny's hypothesis of an incidental learning deficit in retardates. 18 normal kindergartners and 18 moderately retarded and organically impaired Ss, matched for MA, were given 2 tasks: (a) geometric shapes, requiring sorting according to shape and recalling and recognizing according to color (with color representing incidental learning); and (b) familiar objects, requiring naming the color of common, familiar, pictured objects and recalling and recognizing according to object name (with object name representing incidental learning). Normals showed more incidental learning on the objects task, significantly so for recognition. On the shapes task, retardates gave incorrect responses; normals did not. Thus, retardates learn incidentally but tend to be inferior to normal peers.
Deich, Ruth F.   Perceptual & Motor Skills, 1974(Apr), Vol 38(2), 539-542. [PA, Vol 53:01468]

1684.   [A comparative study on the social competence of trainable mentally retarded children and non-retarded children with the Vineland Social Maturity Scale.] (Germ)
A short German version of the Vineland Social Maturity Scale was tried out on 728 trainable mentally retarded children 7-12 yrs old and on 446 nonretarded children 2-6 yrs old. Psychometric data on reliability and validity were gathered, showing a relatively high usefulness of the scale even for nonretarded children. Problems of the relevance of the concept of social maturity as a classificational device for mental retardation, and the use of intelligence and psychomotor tests, are discussed. Although a 3-dimensional diagnosis (intelligence, motor, social competence) creates more possibilities for therapeutic procedures, it is concluded that the concept of social competence needs further elaboration to become a useful part of a multidimensional

diagnostic and therapeutic system for classifying and treating mental retardation. (27 ref)
Eggert, Dietrich. (Pädagogische Hochschule Niedersachsen, Hannover, W Germany) Praxis der Kinderpsychologie und Kinderpsychiatrie, 1974(May-Jun), Vol 23(4), 139-144. [PA, Vol 53:07699]

1685.   If the model fits: An analysis of the structure of the Revised Illinois Test of Psycholinguistic Abilities for moderately mentally retarded children.
Conducted a factorial study of the revised Illinois Test of Psycholinguistic Abilities with 98 moderately mentally retarded school children to determine the domain mapped by the subtests and whether these fit the theoretical psycholinguistic model of channels, processes, and levels of communication. Raw scores from the 10 alpha factor analyses, image analysis, and principal component analysis were used to obtain "method independent" and more meaningful results. Factor loadings from the alpha factor and image analyses were tested for congruence by the Schonemann method and a factor "reliability" study was carried out with separate principal component analyses on 2 random subsamples of 49 children each. Results support the channel separation postulated by the theoretical model. Implications for language programming for the moderately mentally retarded are discussed. The need for a taxonomic study of psycholinguistic abilities of retarded and nonretarded children within the framework of current views of developmental psycholinguistics is stressed.
Leong, Che Kan. (U Saskatchewan, Inst of Child Guidance & Development, Saskatoon, Canada) Slow Learning Child, 1974(Jul), Vol 21(2), 100-113. [PA, Vol 54:07899]

1686.   Physical fitness and intelligence in TMRs.
Administered the AAHPER Youth Fitness Test, the Fleishman Basic Fitness Test, and the Stanford-Binet Intelligence Scale to 21 undifferentiated trainable mentally retarded males to determine the relationship between physical fitness and intelligence in trainable adolescents. Results show a significant relationship between IQ and physical fitness even though the relationship does not indicate cause. (16 ref)
Liese, James E. & Lerch, Harold R. (Area VI Developmental Disabilities Board, Stockton, CA) Mental Retardation, 1974(Oct), Vol 12(5), 50-51. [PA, Vol 53:05676]

1687.   Retarded children's perceptions of favorite television characters as behavioral models.
Gave various hypothetical situations to 45 male and 25 female trainable mentally retarded 5-20 yr olds and asked them what they would do in those situations, what was the right thing to do, what their parents would want them to do, what their best friends would do, and what their favorite TV characters would do. The strongest relationships existed between how Ss reported they would behave, how their best friends would behave, and how their favorite TV characters would behave. Few sex differences were found, although differences between females in this study and females in studies testing nonretardates are discussed.
Baran, Stanley J. & Meyer, Timothy P. (Cleveland State U) Mental Retardation, 1975(Aug), Vol 13(4), 28-31. [PA, Vol 55:00887]

1688.   The effects of stimulus preference on habituation of looking behavior in normal and retarded children.
Determined picture preferences in terms of looking time for groups of 48 normal and 48 moderately retarded 6-15 yr olds. Categories of highly preferred and nonpreferred pictures were then used with a constant picture stimulus alternated with a continually changing stimulus. For both groups, habituation of looking time was similar, being significant for preferred and nonsignificant for nonpreferred stimuli. Findings support an "attention" interpretation of any differential effects of stimulus satiation or habituation in normal vs retarded individuals.
Hyman, Lester M.; Duffy, Karen; Dickie, Jane R. & Denny, M. Ray. (Michigan State U) Bulletin of the Psychonomic Society, 1975(Oct), Vol 6(4A), 355-357. [PA, Vol 55:07395]

1689. Interrelationships between intellectual, perception, and motor measurements in trainable retardates.
Studied the possible relationship between IQ scores, perception dispersion angles, weight, body power, hand-sight and hand-sound response time, foot-sight and foot-sound response time, 25-yd sprinting time, and 300-yd run-walk time in 50 trainable mentally retarded Ss. Ages were 12-16 yrs, and IQs were 25-49. Results indicate a significant relationship between perception and intelligence of trainable retardates but not between power and intelligence. A relationship was found between hand-sight, hand-sound, foot-sight, and foot-sound response times. Maturation appeared to play a role in the power produced by the Ss and in their weight, but not in IQ, perception response time, sprinting time, or 300-yd run-walk time.
Johnson, Robert E. (U Kentucky, Coll of Education) American Corrective Therapy Journal, 1975(Sep-Oct), Vol 29(5), 151-154. [PA, Vol 55:10063]

1690. Long-term transfer of a mediational strategy by moderately retarded children.
Instructed 60 moderately retarded children (mean CA 12.34 yrs) to produce prepositional mediators by physically manipulating paired associate (PA) objects in learning 3 9-item PA lists. Mediational training, distributed across days or weeks, consisted of 1 or 3 different prepositions supplied for 2/3 or for all of the items. Mediation Ss performed significantly better than control Ss on an unaided test list administered 2 wks after training, regardless of distribution of training, degree of aid, or number of prepositions provided during training sessions. The degree of transfer, which was larger than in previously reported studies, was attributed to the instructional procedures requiring active production of prepositional mediators, coupled with an emphasis on their value. It is suggested that individual variability in mediational transfer should be considered in future research on mediational transfer.
Wanschura, Patricia B. & Borkowski, John G. (State University Coll New York, Cortland) American Journal of Mental Deficiency, 1975(Nov), Vol 80(3), 323-333. [PA, Vol 55:10078]

1691. [Observations on the possibility of using thought strategies in a group of adolescents of moderate intellectual deficit.] (Ital)
A problem-solving situation devised by J. Bruner to study the use of cognitive strategies was administered, together with the WISC, to 46 13-yr-old Ss from a school for moderately retarded children. It has been supposed that failure to use an expected strategic sequence is due not only to the intellectual deficit but also to the mode of utilizing available resources. In fact, however, most of the Ss who failed to follow an expected strategy in solving the problem seemed hampered by an insufficient perceptual recognition and by inability to reconsider and discard hypotheses that first emerge impulsively. (French, English & German summaries)
Ambrosiano, Laura. (U Cattolica del Sacro Cuore, Inst di Psicologia, Milan, Italy) Archivio di Psicologia, Neurologia e Psichiatria, 1976(Jul–Sep), Vol 37(3), 353–366. [PA, Vol 59:08098]

1692. Optimizing test performance of moderately and severely mentally retarded adolescents and adults.
Conducted a study with 38 retarded persons (CA, 12-22 yrs; mean MA, 46.11 mo) which provides further evidence for the validity of a learning potential assessment procedure with institutionalized moderately and severely retarded adolescents and adults. Significant positive correlations were obtained between psychometric and learning scores, attendants' and teachers' ratings of ability, and the posttraining scores on the modified Kohs Extended Learning Potential procedure. In addition, performance on this test-train-test procedure was compared with a train-within-test format for 2 different tasks: training embedded within the administration of the Leiter International Performance Scale and a formboard version of the Raven Coloured Progressive Matrices. Ss responded equally to the 2 formats. Stanford-Binet Intelligence Scale IQs were least predictive of performance on the 3 learning potential measures and were unrelated to teachers' and attendants' ratings of ability. Implications are discussed with particular attention to the potential advantages of the train-within-test model. (27 ref)
Budoff, Milton & Hamilton, James L. (Research Inst for Educational Problems, Cambridge, MA) American Journal of Mental Deficiency, 1976(Jul), Vol 81(1), 49-47. [PA, Vol 56:10129]

1693. TMR children's competence in processing negation.
Reexamined the results of previous research which have suggested that trainable mentally retarded lack the competence to process negation when reversible sentences are used to test comprehension. 65 10-21 yr old institutionalized students with a mean IQ of 30 were asked to evaluate 16 picture pairs, 8 each for nonreversible and reversible sentences. Nonreversible sentences, both positive and negative, were interpreted correctly more often than reversible sentences. There was a significant correlation between comprehension and MA. Results are interpreted as substantiating the adverse effect of sentence reversibility on comprehension and as evidence for the position that retarded children develop basic grammatical structures including negation at a relatively late age, but in normal interrelationship and sequence with other language and cognitive abilities. It is concluded that nonreversible pictures realistically represent that intent and function of negation and that earlier findings may have reflected the inappropriateness of task characteristics and scoring criteria rather than a true comprehension deficit. (15 ref)
Lamberts, Frances & Weener, Paul D. (Pennsylvania State Coll National Learning Resource Ctr) American Journal of Mental Deficiency, 1976(Sep), Vol 81(2), 181-186. [PA, Vol 57:06109]

1694. Acquisition of concepts by TMR children as a function of type of modeling, rule verbalization, and observer gender.
A 4-factor repeated measures design was established to determine (a) whether or not trainable mentally retarded (TMR) children could acquire a novel rule-governed concept via modeling, and (b) the effects of type of modeling demonstration, verbal rule provision, and observer gender on concept matching and transfer by TMR children. 24 male and 24 female TMR children (mean IQ 44 and mean MA 5.67 yrs) were divided into 4 groups, each equated by stratified assignment on IQ and MA. One male and one female group were randomly selected to observe a live female model present (a) massed-demonstration trials while vebalizing the concept, (b) massed trials without the concept being verbalized, (c) distributed-demonstration trials with the conceptual verbalization, and (d) distributed trials without conceptual verbalization. Ss were then presented with 3 transfer tasks, successively requiring a greater degree of generalization from the demonstration task. It was found that TMR children could acquire and transfer the complex concept via modeling. Distributed demonstrations yielded better initial response matching, while massed demonstrations led to better transfer. Rule provision facilitated transfer for massed-demonstration groups and facilitated matching for the male distributed-trials groups. (17 ref)
Litrownik, Alan J.; Franzini, Louis R. & Turner, Glenyth L. (San Diego State U) American Journal of Mental Deficiency, 1976(May), Vol 80(6), 620-628. [PA, Vol 56:04290]

1695. The use of a nonverbal instrument to assess the self-concept of young trainable retarded children.
Administered the Self-Social Symbols Test (SSST) 3 times to 19 7-12 yr old trainable mentally retarded (TMR) Ss (mean IQ 46.6). An evaluation interview form was administered to the teacher of those Ss who attended public school, and to the attendants of those Ss who were in an institution. Correlations between the SSST test-retests scores were determined, and several items were cited for their high reliability. Correlations between SSST scores and teacher/attendant evaluations were also investigated, and 2 items were determined as having high validity. There was a high correlation between subtest scores on self-esteem and teacher/attendant predictions of the adult status that they thought the Ss would achieve. It is concluded that the TMR child has a self-concept as measured by the SSST, and that some, but not all, of the items are measuring it. (19 ref)

Poudrier, Barbara R.; Mercer, Cecil D. & Howard, Douglas P. (U Maine, Farmington) Research & the Retarded, 1976, Vol 3(2), 54-65. [PA, Vol 58:08667]

1696.   Note of an error in "Action concept" usage by nonretarded and retarded children on structured tasks with praise for performance.
Reports an overcalculation of Stanford-Binet MAs as the moderately retarded children in a study by W. E. Stephens et al (1975) and cautions that the inferior performance of these Ss as compared to that of a mildly retarded group may not be explainable in terms of the factors discussed.
Spitz, Herman H. & Stephens, Wyatt E.   American Journal of Mental Deficiency, 1976(Sep), Vol 81(2), 197. [PA, Vol 57:06119]

1697.   Instructional modeling and the development of visual- and verbal-mediation skills by TMR children.
Administered a study-recall paired-associate (PA) learning task to 40 trainable mentally retarded (TMR) children (mean CA 11 yrs, 2 mo; mean IQ 48.86) under 1 of 4 instructional-modeling conditions: imagery, verbal mediation, imagery and verbal mediation, and a control condition. On one-half of the PA-learning study trials, Ss were provided modeled mediating responses (connective pictures and/or sentences), and on the other trials no model was provided. Ss' use of mediating responses on study trials was evaluated as was their recall performance. Each instruction-modeling condition resulted in more effective mediator use and better recall than the control condition. Verbal-mediation training was more effective than instruction in the use of visual imagery. Generation of mediators was most apparent when Ss were first provided with models and then required to generate their own mediating responses. Gains in mediator use and recall were retained over a period of several days.
Greeson, Larry E. & Jens, Ken G. (Miami U, OH) American Journal of Mental Deficiency, 1977(Jul), Vol 82(1), 58–64. [PA, Vol 59:10156]

1698.   The attachment of a retarded child to an inanimate object: Translation into clinical utility.
Describes the relationship of a moderately retarded 9-yr-old boy with autistic features to an inanimate object, relates this relationship to his emotional development, and suggests methods for utilizing observations of his behavior with the object for assessment of cognition. It is suggested that the object differs only qualitatively from a transitional object. Implications for the evaluation of retarded children include (a) the need for approaches identical to those used in evaluating intellectually normal children, and (b) the interdisciplinary assessment of combinations of behavioral and dynamic techniques. Implications for parent counseling, institutional policies, therapeutic practice, psychological assessment, and personality theory are outlined. (18 ref)
Haslett, Nancy R. et al. (Louisiana State U Medical Ctr, Div of Child Psychiatry, New Orleans) Child Psychiatry & Human Development, 1977(Fal), Vol 8(1), 54–60. [PA, Vol 61:01278]

1699.   The validity of the TMR as a measure of achievement in life-adjustment skills.
40 children (mean CA 14.7 yrs, mean IQ 23.7) were tested with the Performance Profile for the Severely and Moderately Retarded (TMR) and the Vineland Social Maturity Scale (VSMS). 120 activity and child care aides administered the TMR. One staff psychologist administered the VSMS. High correlations were found between the social age of the VSMS and the TMR, as well as the 5 areas of social development that the 2 tests are supposed to measure. Interrater reliability between the direct care aides was high, always exceeding .95. A procedure for developing age norms on the TMR is presented. The feasibility of using the TMR as a primary instrument in measuring social behavior is then discussed.
Husted, John & Garland, George. (Warren G. Murray Children's Ctr, Centralia, IL) Journal of Instructional Psychology, 1977(Win), Vol 4(1), 28–32. [PA, Vol 61:10107]

1700.   A review of studies of the socio-familial backgrounds and educational facilities of the homes of moderately educationally subnormal children.
A review of the literature on the home backgrounds of moderately educationally subnormal children (ESN) indicates that the relatively few studies reported were limited in either range or sample size or both. Certain characteristics, however, did emerge consistently: The majority of ESN children come from lower working class families; there are fewer firstborn ESN children than there are firstborn non-ESN children; the mean percentage of ESN children from single parent or disrupted families is greater than for non-ESN children. The information that is available tends to support the notion of a syndrome of familial moderate educational subnormality. Evidence from one investigation points to certain ethnic differences that may be important in any program of intervention. (28 ref)
Saunders, Malcolm. (Bradford Coll, England) Child Care, Health & Development, 1977(Nov–Dec), Vol 3(6), 407–423. [PA, Vol 61:08722]

1701.   Tic-tac-toe performance as a function of maturational level of retarded adolescents and nonretarded children.
Two groups of 37 retarded adolescents, differing from each other primarily in IQ and MA (56 vs 65 and 8.43 vs 10.25, respectively) were compared with 2 groups of 38 nonretarded children, differing from each other in CA (8.85 vs 9.91) and MA on a modified tic-tac-toe game. The MAs of the retarded and nonretarded groups were approximately the same. It was found that the slope of performance improvement with increasing maturational level was the same for both S groups, but the performance of the retarded adolescents was approximately 1.5 yrs behind MA expectations, as derived from the performance levels of the normal children. These findings support previous suggestions of a major retardate deficit in tasks requiring logical foresight.
Spitz, Herman H. & Winters, Emilia A. (Edward R. Johnstone Training & Research Ctr, Bordentown, NJ) Intelligence, 1977(Jan), Vol 1(1), 108–117. [PA, Vol 61:11170]

1702.   Reliability of selected psychomotor measures with mentally retarded adult males.
Reliability estimates were determined for 24 moderately mentally retarded adult males on 3 psychomotor tasks. Ss were aged 18–59 yrs and had a mean IQ of 45.47. For 4 consecutive days, measures were taken on RT, auditory and visual, 15 trials daily for each; grip strength, dominant and nondominant hand, 2 trials daily for each; and standing long jump, 3 trials daily. ANOVAs, adjusted for day-to-day trend, were applied to the data. Intraclass reliability coefficients for both dominant ($R = .96$) and nondominant ($R = .94$) handgrip strength were high. RT scores for both the auditory and visual data were moderately reliable. A low reliability coefficient ($R = .49$) was obtained for the standing long jump. (21 ref)
Dunn, John M. (Oregon State U) Perceptual & Motor Skills, 1978(Feb), Vol 46(1), 295–301. [PA, Vol 61:08695]

1703.   Immediate and delayed reward preferences of TMR adolescents.
35 trainable mentally retarded students (mean CA 18.8 yrs, mean IQ 36.8) were presented with a list of 32 reward options, consisting of primary (food) and secondary (cash equivalent) rewards that were immediately available or delayed 1 day at a ratio of 1:2. The greatest number of delay choices occurred when the decision was between immediate/secondary and delayed/primary rewards. Ss subsequently classified as delayers (34.3%) made the fewest delay choices when presented with immediate/primary vs delayed/secondary options. Nondelayers made the most delay choices when given an immediate/secondary or delayed/primary choice.
Franzini, Louis R.; Litrownik, Alan J. & Magy, Martin A. (San Diego State U) American Journal of Mental Deficiency, 1978(Jan), Vol 82(4), 406–409. [PA, Vol 62:06314]

1704. Developmental priority of identity conservation: Acceleration of identity and equivalence in normal and moderately retarded children.
To clarify the chronological relationship between identity and equivalence conservation, 40 normal, nonconserving 51–69 mo old children (Exp I) were exposed to brief videotape demonstrations of a model conserving identity and equivalence, identity only, equivalence only, or neither. Subsequent performances indicated that identity was easier to accelerate than equivalence, and training in both identity and equivalence appeared to be most effective in accelerating conservation. 20 trainable mentally retarded Ss (MAs 6–8 yrs) were then exposed to either the identity-equivalence-conserving or control model (Exp II). This population, which some have argued remains at a preoperational level of functioning, was more likely to conserve identity than equivalance. In addition, conservation in the training group increased following training, though these gains were not maintained over a 3-wk retention interval. (22 ref)
Litrownik, Alan J.; Franzini, Louis R.; Livingston, M. Kimball & Harvey, Susan. (San Diego State U) Child Development, 1978(Mar), Vol 49(1), 201–208. [PA, Vol 62:01320]

1705. A comparison of two procedures (NSST and Concrete Objects) for measuring receptive and expressive language of mentally retarded children.
Administered the Northwestern Syntax Screening Test and the authors' Concrete Objects Test to 30 trainable mentally retarded children (mean CA 10 yrs, 4 mo; mean IQ 48). Results indicate that the use of concrete objects to measure the receptive language of this population yielded more satisfactory results than a picture-sentence association task. Explanations for this finding are offered, and modifications for testing some syntactic forms are discussed.
Martin, Jane & Engel, Bonnie. (Glassboro State Coll) Language, Speech, & Hearing Services in Schools, 1978(Jul), Vol 9(3), 176–182. [PA, Vol 63:02068]

1706. Attentional changes during discrimination learning by retarded children.
Eight moderately retarded children (CAs 11–17 yrs; MAs 3 yrs 1 mo to 5 yrs; IQs 29–50) were trained on a simultaneous 2-choice discrimination problem and a series of discrimination-shift problems. The procedure required Ss to perform overt observing responses to produce elements of the discriminative stimuli, making it possible to measure directly changes in attention to different aspects of stimuli during learning. The patterns of change in observing responses were generally in line with descriptions of attentional changes derived from 2-process theories of discrimination learning; e.g., the frequency of irrelevant observing responses was high during the presolution period during extradimensional shifts but was low during intradimensional shifts. Contrary to current theories, extradimensional shifts usually caused an increase in relevant observing responses. Ss responded to later shift problems by initially increasing both relevant and irrelevant observing responses, then withholding irrelevant ones.
Singh, N. N. & Beale, I. L. Journal of the Experimental Analysis of Behavior, 1978(May), Vol 29(3), 527–533. [PA, Vol 62:11254]

1707. The effect of dimensional preference on optional shift behavior and concept attainment of retarded adolescents.
63 moderately retarded adolescents of similar CAs and MAs participated in an experiment designed to assess the influence of dimensional dominance and preference on 2 concept learning tasks. After dominance assessment, Ss were randomly assigned to a preferred or nonpreferred condition and received both an optional shift and concept assessment test. Results indicate a significant difference between color- and form-dominant learners and between Ss assigned to preferred and nonpreferred dimensions. No difference was observed on the concept assessment measure. A significantly greater number of Ss solved the optional shift task intradimensionally. Intradimensional shifts were also learned faster than extradimensional shifts. The data are interpreted in terms of developmental and mediation hypotheses and

viewed as consistent with D. Zeaman and B. House's (1963) chaining prediction. (20 ref)
Gargiulo, Richard M.; Uno, Tad; Sears, James D. & Hiszem, Paul. (Bowling Green State U) Bulletin of the Psychonomic Society, 1979(Sep), Vol 14(3), 219–222. [PA, Vol 64:12737]

1708. [Experiments with errorless discrimination learning.] (Fren)
Conducted a series of experiments with 8–16 retarded children (WISC IQs 30–50) divided into experimental and control groups. Two methods were used: (a) The correct stimulus (e.g., a square) was shown by itself first, then the incorrect stimulus (e.g., a circle) was shown in a pale, sketchy form that was gradually made clearer in subsequent trials until it was comparable to the correct choice. (b) A similar method was used to teach discrimination between 2 colors. The circle and square were then superimposed and the colors faded out. Both methods proved superior to trial-and-error methods, but only the 1st method proved superior in resistance to extinction over time. Further experiments showed the optimum kind of reinforcement to be intermittent and the learning to be generalizable only when specifically programmed. Applications to special education and the role of error in human learning are discussed. Further research is recommended to analyze the utility of errorless learning with retarded children of different chronological ages and diagnostic categories. (English summary) (17 ref)
Lambert, Jean-Luc. (U Liège, Belgium) Enfance, 1979(May–Jun), No 2, 107–132. [PA, Vol 66:00085]

1709. Exploration and play in retarded and nonretarded preschool children: Effects of object complexity and age.
Three-dimensional random polygon objects ranging in complexity between 4 and 40 turns were presented to 12 30-mo-old and 12 42-mo-old moderately retarded and nonretarded children. Time spent in exploration and play was measured over 3 successive exposure-time blocks. Exploration time for the combined sample of retarded and nonretarded younger Ss did not vary with object complexity. The older retarded Ss explored objects of low complexity more than did either the combined sample of younger Ss or the older nonretarded Ss. Nonretarded older Ss explored complex objects more than did the combined sample. Exploration time decreased linearly with exposure-time blocks. Play time increased linearly with successive exposure-time blocks and decreased linearly with increasing complexity. (27 ref)
Switzky, Harvey N.; Ludwig, Luther & Haywood, H. Carl. (Northern Illinois U) American Journal of Mental Deficiency, 1979(May), Vol 83(6), 637–644. [PA, Vol 62:08885]

1710. Social interaction amongst young moderately mentally retarded children.
Seven 4–8 yr old moderately mentally retarded children were individually taught gross motor skills during free play. Seven behavior categories were used as a time-sampling observation instrument to code the social interactive behaviors displayed; those categories included solitary, parallel, and initiated interaction, association, cooperation, coordination, and negative social interaction. Analysis of 280 play observations revealed that the social interaction that occurred was of low sophistication: Less than 25% of the play time was spent in social interaction that required mutual participation by 2 or more Ss; 50% of the time was spent mainly in solitary play; and the remaining 27% was involved with maintaining a parallel interaction of responding affirmatively, for the most part, to an initiated interactive behavior. (9 ref)
Wasson, Donna L. & Watkinson, E. Jane. (U Alberta, Edmonton, Canada) Mental Retardation Bulletin, 1979, Vol 7(2), 74–88. [PA, Vol 66:08280]

1711. Differential analysis of selected prompts and neurological variables in motor assessment of moderately mentally retarded children.
Evaluated the specificity of gross-motor assessment strategies presently used with moderately mentally retarded children (CA 5–14 yrs) by measuring voluntary motor performance as a function of level of reflex development, level of orthopedic

functioning, and type of prompts used in test instructions. After 40 Ss' levels of reflex and orthopedic functioning were clinically assessed, Ss were randomly assigned to multisensory-, physical-, modeling-, and verbal-prompt treatment groups. Multisensory prompts and differential use of selected prompts were effective with younger and older Ss, respectively. A significant interrelationship was found between Ss' levels of reflex development and voluntary motor performance. (29 ref)
Ilmer, Steven & Drews, Judith. (U Minnesota, Minneapolis) American Journal of Mental Deficiency, 1980(Mar), Vol 84(5), 508–517. [PA, Vol 63:12991]

1712.   Role-taking, moral development, and mental retardation.
Measured role-taking ability and level of moral development (L. Kohlberg, 1976) in 16 moderately retarded adolescents (mean CA 15 yrs; mean MA 9 yrs), 16 nonretarded adolescents matched for CA, and 16 nonretarded children matched for MA. The mentally retarded Ss scored significantly lower on role-taking ability and moral development than the adolescents matched for CA. They did not differ from Ss of their same MA in role-taking ability, and they tended to score lower in moral development. Results provide qualified support for Kohlberg's (1969) theory of moral development. (26 ref)
Perry, Joan E. & Krebs, Dennis. (Simon Fraser U, Burnaby, Canada) Journal of Genetic Psychology, 1980(Mar), Vol 136(1), 95–108. [PA, Vol 64:01320]

1713.   Referential communication skill levels of moderately mentally retarded adolescents.
Referential communication skills of moderately mentally retarded adolescents (20 speaker–listener dyads) were investigated. In Study 1, S performance on referential communication activities divided into 3 skill levels requiring sampling, comparison, and critical-features analysis was examined. Degree of idiosyncratic messages communicated by retarded speakers was investigated in Study 2. Listening competence of retarded Ss and 20 normal adult listeners was compared in Study 3. Retarded Ss did consistently better on referential communication tasks requiring only sampling than on tasks requiring comparison or critical analysis. Referential communication messages provided by retarded speakers did not have greater meaning to themselves than to others. Finally, retarded listeners and adult listeners did not differ significantly in their ability to utilize the information given by retarded speakers. (16 ref)
Rueda, Robert & Chan, Kenyon S. (Arizona State U) American Journal of Mental Deficiency, 1980(Jul), Vol 85(1), 45–52. [PA, Vol 64:08276]

1714.   Acquisition, generalization, and maintenance of an assembly task by mentally retarded children.
Taught 4 6–9 yr old trainable mentally retarded Ss a 3-piece assembly task. Ss were taught to verbalize the steps in the designated sequence before assembling the objects. Data were collected on their performance in both the training setting and the regular classroom. Maintenance sessions were also recorded. Each S rapidly acquired the target behavior in the treatment setting and was successful in generalizing and maintaining the behavior in an extra-treatment setting. (8 ref)
Wacker, David P.; Carroll, James L. & Moe, Glenn L. (U Iowa) American Journal of Mental Deficiency, 1980(Nov), Vol 85(3), 286–290. [PA, Vol 65:03538]

1715.   Reasoning by trainable mentally retarded and young non-retarded individuals.
54 trainable mentally retarded children (TMR) in 3 age groups (mean CAs 8, 12, and 16 yrs; mean MAs 3, 5, and 7 yrs) and 3 groups of normal Ss matched for MA were presented with 2 problem-solving tasks. The solution for each task required a novel response to be generated from mental manipulations of previously learned experiences and anticipation of possible outcomes. Ss were required to combine relevant parts of the problem and independently arrive at a solution from the combination. Performance of the normals was generally superior to that of the TMRs. Developmental trends were evident only among normals. (23 ref)

Zetlin, Andrea G. & Bilsky, Linda H. (U California, Neuropsychiatric Inst, Los Angeles) Journal of Mental Deficiency Research, 1980(Mar), Vol 24(1), 65–71. [PA, Vol 66:06094]

1716.   Characterizing verbal interaction among moderately mentally retarded peers: Some methodological issues.
Analyzed the peer interaction of 3 moderately mentally retarded adolescents (CAs of 13 yrs 10 mo to 14 yrs 7 mo and IQs of 40–50) using qualitative and quantitative observation techniques. It is concluded (1) that there is a need for a different type of quantitative coding scheme that looks at units of interaction rather than subunits of time and (2) that qualitative analysis should precede the construction of quantitative measures to ensure ecologically valid behavior descriptors. (17 ref)
Zetlin, Andrea G. & Sabsay, Sharon. (U California, Los Angeles Neuropsychiatric Inst) Applied Research in Mental Retardation, 1980, Vol 1(3–4), 209–225. [PA, Vol 66:07002]

1717.   Communication functioning in Trisomy 9p.
Investigated the communication patterns of 4 males (3 children and 1 adult aged 4 yrs 8 mo to 20) diagnosed as moderately mentally retarded because of chromosomal aberration Trisomy 9p. Ss exhibited expressive language deficits in relation to comprehension and general level of functioning. They used approximations of single words and tended to rely on gestures for expression. Unusual acoustic characteristics of speech are also noted. (9 ref)
Owens, Alma & Beatty-DeSana, Jeanne. (Georgia Retardation Ctr, Atlanta) Journal of Communication Disorders, 1981(Mar), Vol 14(2), 113–122. [PA, Vol 66:08260]

1718.   Problem solving in pre-operational youngsters.
Examined the problem-solving behavior of 3 groups of trainable retarded (IQs 37–50) youngsters ($n = 54$) divided according to CA (7.7–9.3, 10.10–13, and 15.2–16.9 yrs, respectively) and 3 groups of intellectually average children ($n = 54$) of comparable MA (3.3–8.3 yrs) to determine (1) individual differences in task performance within and between populations, and (2) the effect of prompting cues on the performance of those students who do not independently generate a solution. Results suggest that the underlying intellectual demands of the task were within the capabilities of youngsters assumed to be at the preoperational level of development. (11 ref)
Zetlin, Andrea G. (U California, Neuropsychiatric Inst, Los Angeles) Journal of Mental Deficiency Research, 1981(Jun), Vol 25(2), 127–132. [PA, Vol 66:10619]

Severe Mental Retardation

1719.   Crib confinement as a factor in repetitive and stereotyped behavior in retardates.
Observed 55 39-167 mo. old severely and profoundly retarded ambulatory children for 20 1-min intervals/child. Repetitive, stereotyped, and object manipulation behaviors were observed under "in-crib" and "out-of-crib" conditions. Results generally support the hypothesis that certain repetitive behaviors occurring more often inside cribs may be partly a function of confinement and the amount of stimulation on the immediate environment. It is suggested that headbanging, which occurred more often outside cribs, may be "operant headbanging," learned as a function of reinforcements provided by staff, and apparently as a device to communicate needs in certain nonverbal retarded children. (18 ref.)
Warren, Sue A. & Burns, Norman R. (Massachusetts Dept. of Mental Health, Region V, Boston) Mental Retardation, 1970(Jun), Vol. 8(3), 25-28. [PA, Vol 47:11499]

1720.   Factors in the verbal and motor learning of imbeciles.
Performed 2 experiments to investigate the effects of age and practice on the verbal and motor performance of imbeciles. In the verbal experiment, 4 groups (old and young) were given different degrees of practice on a vocabulary test. It was found that both age and practice significantly improve the abstract definition of words by imbecile Ss. In the motor experiment, E

demonstrated the task for them (Condition I). This condition seems to significantly improve the Ss' performance. When E performed the demonstration by using a miniature task (Condition II), Ss did not significantly benefit from this experience. However, when Ss were allowed to carry out the miniature task in addition to observing the E (Condition III), their performance was significantly improved. Age did not differentiate between the groups on the motor task.
Al-Issa, Ihsan. (U. Calgary, Alberta, Canada) Journal of Psychology, 1971(Mar), Vol. 77(2), 151-156. [PA, Vol 46:01704]

1721. Conditions governing nonreinforced imitation.
Tested the conditioned reinforcement and the discrimination hypotheses interpretations of imitative responding which is not explicitly reinforced. Measures were obtained of the rate with which 4 severely retarded and 12 normal kindergarten children imitated exemplified activities as a function of whether or not models reinforced imitative responding, and whether the nonreinforceable responses differed topographically from rewarded demonstrations or were highly similar. In accord with the discrimination hypothesis, Ss continued to perform nonrewarded matching responses that were difficult to discriminate from rewarded imitations, but discontinued imitating those that were easily distinguishable. Evidence was obtained that nonreinforced imitations may be maintained in some instances by erroneous anticipated consequences. (16 ref.)
Bandura, Albert & Barab, Peter G. (Stanford U.) Developmental Psychology, 1971(Sep), Vol. 5(2), 244-255. [PA, Vol 47:03550]

1722. Unstable behaviour in severely subnormal children.
Rated the behavior of 293 severely retarded institutionalized children through questionnaired filled out by senior staff members. 33% of Ss showed unstable or disturbed behavior. Of these, ¼ were seen as excessively attention-seeking, ¡5 as overactive and noisy; ¡6 as aggressive or destructive, and a few as wanderers, escapers, or self-mutilators. Nonepileptic Ss showed more of these disturbances than epileptics. (14 ref.)
Donoghue, E. C. & Abbas, K. A. (Queen Mary's Hosp. for Children, Carshalton, England) Developmental Medicine & Child Neurology, 1971(Aug), Vol. 13(4), 512-519. [PA, Vol 47:07409]

1723. Utility of three behavioral indices for studying severely and profoundly retarded children.
Examined the utility of the Vineland Social Maturity Scale (VSMS), the Comprehensive Behavior Checklist (CBCL), and the Cain-Levine Social Competency Scale (CLSCS) for the differential diagnosis, placement, therapeutic programming, and the measurement of change with 58 severely and profoundly retarded 8-17 yr. olds. The VSMS and CBCL were normally distributed and significantly related to clinical judgments of competence. The CLSCS failed to distribute normally due to the large number of Ss with minimal scores. The advantages of these instruments are discussed.
Gardner, James M. & Giampa, Franklyn L. (Orient State Inst., O.) American Journal of Mental Deficiency, 1971(Nov), Vol. 76(3), 352-356. [PA, Vol 48:01509]

1724. The psychological evaluation of profoundly retarded children using concrete reinforcers.
A number of investigators have shown rather conclusively that infant intelligence scales do not predict later intelligence scores if the test is given before the child is 12 mo. old. 2 factors seem to be involved in this lack of predictive validity. 1 of these is that the responses of the very young child are by nature unreliable because of inconsistencies in the child's attentiveness, motivation, and alertness. 40 profoundly retarded 9-14 yr. old children were administered the Cattell Infant Intelligence Scale. 22 received a modified Cattell in which a concrete reinforcer was substituted for the regular test equipment. Ss who were given the modified Cattell scored significantly higher than Ss receiving the standard Cattell in both mental age and IQ.
Husted, J.; Wallin, K. & Wooden, H. (Warren G. Murray Children's Center, Centralia, Ill.) Journal of Psychology, 1971(Mar), Vol. 77(2), 173-179. [PA, Vol 46:01701]

1725. The home background of the severely subnormal child: A second study.
28 severely subnormal children living at home were matched individually with normal children for MA, sex, and socioeconomic background. It was predicted that the subnormal Ss would show a relative deficit on both stimulation and affection measures. On parental interview assessment the groups did differ significantly both overall and in the affection area; the difference in the stimulation area did not reach statistical significance. On 4 objective tests of experiences there were clear differences overall as well as on 3 of them taken individually. (20 ref.)
Jeffree, D. M. & Cashdan, Asher. (Manchester U., Hester Adrian Research Centre, England) British Journal of Medical Psychology, 1971(Mar), Vol. 44(1), 27-33. [PA, Vol 46:11381]

1726. Sex chromatin aberrations among children with severe mental retardation.
Performed a sex chromatin survey by means of buccal smears among 1,000 children with mental retardation. 14 aberrations were found, with a conspicuously high frequency (9/406) in the group of grossly defectives (IQ < 20). IQs ranged from less than 20-75.
Méhes, K. & Sulyok, E. (U. Pecs, Medical School, Hungary) Human Heredity, 1971, Vol. 21(1), 54-56. [PA, Vol 47:09511]

1727. [Severe mental retardation: Study of 200 children admitted to the department for the chronic sick of the Paris Public Assistance.] (Fren)
Examined the etiology and sociofamilial background of 200 2-20 yr. old retardates admitted to a French hospital which has no selective entry procedures. Results indicate an overrepresentation of lower-class children in comparison to previous statistical reports. Hereditary disease was found in 12%, and 1 out of every 3 Ss was premature. There was a very clear discrepancy between length of pregnancy and birth weight (dismaturity). 20% had a difficult birth and/or severe signs of neonatal distress. In 20% illness in infancy seemed to have caused lesions. Signs of psychogenic disturbance suggesting psychosis were found in some Ss with organic abnormalities and in the 20% who had no discernible organic etiology. In addition to mental deficiencies, 75% of the Ss had diminished stature; 15% had a very marked reduction in body weight; 60% had physical or trophic abnormalities; 50% had severe neurological disturbances; 25% had sensory disturbances; and 50% had epilepsy. Results demonstrate that a severely-retarded child nearly always has multiple handicaps. (German & Spanish summaries) (21 ref.)
Rieu, P.; Tomkiewicz, S.; Kafe, H. & Roland, Th. (National Inst. of Health & Medical Research, Paris, France) Revue de Neuropsychiatrie Infantile et d'Hygiène Mentale de l'Enfance, 1971(Mar), Vol. 19(3-4), 115-149. [PA, Vol 49:09436]

1728. Transfer of stimulus control: Measuring the moment of transfer.
3 severely retarded adolescent boys acquired simple form discrimination errorlessly. Each was 1st taught to press a red key vs. a simultaneously present white key. After this discrimination had been established, black figures were superimposed on the red and white keys. Each correct response affected the next trial by delaying the onset of the red stimulus an additional .5 sec. Transfer of stimulus control to the figures was indicated when Ss responded correctly before the onset of the red stimulus. A series of errorless discrimination reversals was accomplished with this technique, during which the number of trials to transfer systematically decreased with successive reversal. (19 ref.)
Touchette, Paul E. (Massachusetts General Hosp., Boston) Journal of the Experimental Analysis of Behavior, 1971(May), Vol. 15(3), 347-354. [PA, Vol 46:07349]

1729. Severely retarded children in a London area: Prevalence and provision of services.
Prevalence of severely retarded children in a Camberwall district in England, as computed in a 1-day census, is presented and compared with other data with a view toward familiarization of the problem and development and organization of the systems of care and treatment.

Wing, Lorna. (Medical Research Council, Social Psychiatry Unit, Inst. of Psychiatry, London, England) Psychological Medicine, 1971(Nov), Vol. 5(1), 405-415. [PA, Vol 48:09565]

1730. Is reinforcement necessary for the development of a generalized imitation operant in severely and profoundly retarded children?
Examined whether a generalized imitation operant can be developed without extrinsic reinforcement, as the stimulus-stimulus (S-S) viewpoint argues, or if it is essential as the stimulus-response (S-R) view asserts. Results with 2 severely retarded male children favor the latter theory, but not without reservations. Replication with 2 profoundly retarded children yielded virtually the same, albeit more pronounced, results supporting the S-R viewpoint.
Bry, Peter M. & Nawas, M. Mike. (Children's Psychiatric Center, Eatontown, N.J.) American Journal of Mental Deficiency, 1972(May), Vol. 76(6), 658-667. [PA, Vol 48:12061]

1731. [The meowing cat syndrome: A multidisciplinary study of a case.] (Port)
Examines the case of a severely retarded 8-yr-old boy from the psychiatric, physiological, genetic, and biological points of view. A detailed profile of this S is compared to 7 others exhibiting the meowing cat vocalization and to various scales of retardation. Specific criteria for diagnosing this syndrome are considered. (24 ref)
Krynski, Stanislau et al. (Ctr de Habilitação do APAE, São Paulo, Brazil) Revista Brasileira de Deficiencia Mental, 1972(Mar), Vol 7(1), 23-24. [PA, Vol 53:01483]

1732. Ikonic imagery in the severely subnormal.
Studied 23 17-52 yr. old severely subnormal (SSN) adults for their ability to reproduce and transpose matrices. Ss could transpose the matrices at an MA equivalent to the CA at which children normally do. Ability to reproduce the same matrices was not in evidence prior to the ability to transpose them, as in normal children. It is suggested that cognitive development in SSNs is qualitatively different from that of normal children.
Mackay, C. K. (U. Aberdeen, Scotland) British Journal of Psychology, 1972(Nov), Vol. 63(4), 597-603. [PA, Vol 49:09402]

1733. [The execution of a practical task by severely retarded children and their verbal account of their performance.] (Russ)
16 10-15 yr. old severely retarded Ss correctly performed a task consisting of 3 elements ("Go to the blackboard, pick up the chalk, and write the letter 'a'"), but immediately afterward only 1 S could give an entirely correct verbal account of what he had done. When, having completed the 3-element task, Ss were asked to execute just its 1st 2 elements, 4 continued to write a letter on the blackboard. Results are interpreted as documenting a discrepancy between motor responses and verbal responses in the severely retarded child and as supporting A. R. Luria's suggestion that, while verbal instructions from an adult can initiate action, they can not modify an ongoing activity. Methods for improving verbal report in children with "balanced," "inhibitory," and "excitatory" types of mental retardation are discussed.
Maller, A. R. (Auxiliary School No. 532, Moscow, USSR) Defektologiya, 1972, Vol. 4(1), 30-33. [PA, Vol 50:09227]

1734. The spectrum of severe mental deficiency: Experiences with 1400 cases.
Reviews 1,400 cases of severely retarded children seen at a clinic. Using R. Heber's classification of retardation, Ss were classified into 8 categories: infection, toxic agents, injury, metabolic disorder, tumor, unknown prenatal influence, unknown cause with neurological signs, and unknown cause without neurological signs. Specific syndromes are also listed and percentages of each category given. It is noted that the sample should not be considered characteristic of mentally retarded children in general. It was found that 16.7% of the total was due to environmental cause, 6.6% due to heredity causes, and 11.7% of mixed origin. The causes of 53% were unknown. There were indications of organic factors in the background. It is suggested that there is a possibility of tissue rejection (mother rejecting baby) being involved in some abnormal individuals. (17 ref.)

Pitt, David; Roboz, Paul & Seidurs, Elvira. (Children's Coll. Training Center, Kew, Victoria, Australia) Australian Journal of Mental Retardation, 1972(Jun), Vol. 2(2), 40-46. [PA, Vol 49:07262]

1735. Preferences in institutionalized severely retarded children for selected visual stimulus material presented as operant reinforcement.
Presented 3 stimulus materials (a color motion picture of attendant-child caretaking interaction, a series of black and white slides of the same caretaking, and a black and white slide projected out-of-focus and designated as neutral) as operant reinforcers to 30 severely and profoundly retarded 2-10.2 yr. old inpatients in order to determine relative preferences for these materials. Ss were presented all paired combinations and permutations of the stimulus materials over a 6-day trial period using an automated learning device called PLAYTEST. Results show a significant and consistent preference for the color motion picture material. Data reported in the experiment offer a convincing demonstration of the validity of J. Piaget, B. F. Skinner, and R. W. White's position concerning the development of orienting and attentional behavior through operant reinforcers.
Rynders, John E. & Friedlander, Bernard Z. (U. Minnesota) American Journal of Mental Deficiency, 1972(Mar), Vol. 76(5), 568-573. [PA, Vol 48:12080]

1736. Comparative behavioral ratings of parents with severe mentally retarded, special learning disability, and normal children.
Examined the perceptual similarities and differences of parents of 56 normal and 30 learning-disabled 5-11 yr. old children and of 23 7-12 yr. old severely mentally retarded Ss. All 3 groups of parents were sent the same 30-item behavioral rating scale and instructions. The scale contained 3 types of items; those indicating behavioral or emotional disturbances, those indicating possible neurological disturbance, and those with little or no diagnostic value. The return was approximately 98%. A specific learning disability syndrome emerged from the parents of learning disabled Ss, as well as several variables indicating possible neurological dysfunction and-or emotional disturbance.
Strag, Gerald A. (Iowa State Dept. of Social Services, Mental Health Inst., Independence) Journal of Learning Disabilities, 1972(Dec), Vol. 5(10), 631-635. [PA, Vol 50:01358]

1737. [Unintended artistic effects in the drawings and paintings of mentally retarded children.] (Polh)
Tyszkiewicz, Magdalena. (Outpatient Mental Health Clinic, Gdynia, Poland) Psychiatria Polska, 1972(May), Vol. 6(3), 267-275. [PA, Vol 51:05485]

1738. Exploratory studies of early cognitive development.
Studied developments in cognitive processes in the early preschool years by observing the actions that young children perform upon objects, while relating them by a spatial relation or attribute. Matching tasks and material for spontaneous handling were given to 31 19-42 mo. olds and to 23 severely subnormal children. It is suggested that 1 aspect of early cognitive development is increasing selectively in sequences of matching actions.
Woodword, Mary W. & Hunt, M. R. (U Wales, University Coll of Swansea) British Journal of Educational Psychology, 1972(Nov), Vol. 42(3), 248-259. [PA, Vol 50:00757]

1739. Parental behaviors in profoundly retarded subjects.
Observed the behavior of 13 male and 16 female profoundly retarded 18-30 yr old adults in response to the visual stimulus of a human infant. Little support was obtained for the ethologically based hypothesis that the infant as a sign-stimulus would release parental (i.e., approach) behavior. However, significantly more active-approach behavior was observed in female than male Ss.
Cleland, C. C.; Hereford, S. McF.; Fellner, M. & Lawrence, W. (U. Texas) Perceptual & Motor Skills, 1973(Feb), Vol. 36(1), 215-218. [PA, Vol 50:11455]

1740. Partial trisomy of chromosome 11: A case report.
Found partial trisomy of the short arms of chromosome 11 in a profoundly retarded child with multiple physical defects by means of fluorescent karyotyping of the chromosomally-balanced carrier father. Despite 4 pregnancies, the parents failed to produce any living normal children, suggesting selection for the unbalanced chromosomal complement.
Falk, Rena E., et al. (U. California, Medical Center, Los Angeles) American Journal of Mental Deficiency, 1973(Jan), Vol. 77(4), 383-388. [PA, Vol 50:03203]

1741. Selective responses to auditory and auditory-vibratory stimuli by severely retarded deaf-blind children.
Evaluated responsiveness to auditory stimulation in 15 severely retarded deaf-blind preschool children (mean age = 7.5 yrs) by measuring their operant choice between no sound at all and musical selections at 80 db SPL. A vibratory assist was employed for those Ss whose responses were inconclusive. This assistance proved to be crucial in helping some of the Ss develop consistent listening response competence. Results obtained from testing with and without hearing aids led to speculations concerning the value of the aids with some of the children. Extensive numerical records document details of individual performance.
Friedlander, Bernard Z.; Silva, Dennis A. & Knight, Marcia S. (U Hartford) Journal of Auditory Research, 1973(Apr), Vol 13(2), 105-111. [PA, Vol 54:11904]

1742. Severely retarded children in Quebec: Prevalence, causes, and care.
McDonald, Alison D. (McGill U., Montreal, Quebec, Canada) American Journal of Mental Deficiency, 1973(Sep), Vol. 78(2), 205-215. [PA, Vol 52:01278]

1743. [Cognitive styles and structures in the normal and the retarded child.] (Fren)
Presents results of a study of differences in cognitive styles between normal and mentally deficient 9-14 yr. old children. 2 groups of institutionalized Ss, microencephalopathic and severely retarded, were examined in depth with a wide variety of instruments. It was found that the Ss performed better than could be explained by neuropsychological operations according to genetic theory. There was also far more heterogeneity of cognitive styles than among normals, with no reliance on language. It is concluded that reeducation should concentrate on the individual and his culture rather than trying to reestablish normal development.
Moretti, G. & Saccomani, L. Revue de Neuropsychiatrie Infantile et d'Hygiene Mentale de l'Enfance, 1973(Jan), Vol. 21(1-2), 23-32. [PA, Vol 50:09243]

1744. The effectiveness of a Peabody Language Development Kit with severely subnormal children.
Studied an experimental group (*n* = 11) and a control group (*n* = 10) of severely subnormal children. The experimental group was given daily instruction with Level P of the Peabody Language Development Kits. Both groups were pre- and post-tested on some subtests of the Illinois Test of Psycholinguistic Abilities (ITPA). After a 10-mo period, the experimental group showed significant gains over the control group on the ITPA subtest scores. Some caution is advised in interpreting these results.
Shiach, G. McG. (Cambridgeshire & Isle of Ely Education Authority, England) British Journal of Educational Psychology, 1973(Nov), Vol. 43(3), 294-297. [PA, Vol 52:04088]

1745. Reading and crossmodal transfer of stimulus equivalences in severe retardation.
Taught 2 severely retarded, Down's syndrome males aged 17 and 18 yrs to match printed words to each other (visual discrimination) and dictated words to their corresponding pictures (auditory comprehension). However, Ss were still unable to match the printed words to their pictures (reading comprehension) or read the printed words orally. Ss were next taught to match the dictated to the printed words and were then able to read the words orally and with comprehension. The learned equivalences of dictated words to pictures and to printed words transferred to the purely visual equivalence of printed words to pictures. The success of the mediated-transfer paradigm suggests that inability to achieve crossmodal transfer of stimulus equivalences is not necessarily the cause of reading deficiency in severe retardation, and provides a technique for introducing severely retarded children to simple reading skills. (16 ref.)
Sidman, Murray & Cresson, Osborne. (Northeastern U.) American Journal of Mental Deficiency, 1973(Mar), Vol. 77(5), 515-523. [PA, Vol 51:07467]

1746. Short-term retention of colour and shape information in mongol and other severely subnormal children.
Tested 2 groups of severely subnormal children (46 mongols and 41 nonmongols) for short-term retention of color and shape information using colors of equal brightness. Both groups could do a simultaneous match on the basis of the color or shape, but the mongol group made many errors in successively matching colors and in pointing to named colors. They experienced no difficulty in successively matching and naming shapes and the nonmongol group had little difficulty with either color or shape. Possible explanations of this deficit are considered.
Sinson, Janice & Wetherick, N. E. (Leeds Polytechnic, England) Journal of Mental Deficiency Research, 1973(Sep), Vol. 17(3-4), 177-182. [PA, Vol 52:08043]

1747. Nonspeech noun usage training with severely and profoundly retarded children.
Used a nonspeech symbol system, consisting of small pieces of masonite cut into various shapes, to investigate the learning of noun usage by 62 nonverbal, severely or profoundly retarded 7-16 yr olds. Results indicate that most such Ss could learn appropriate skills and did so in a short period of time when this nonspeech response mode was employed.
Carrier, Joseph K. (Parsons State Hosp Research Ctr, KS) Journal of Speech & Hearing Research, 1974(Sep), Vol 17(3), 510-517. [PA, Vol 53:05660]

1748. Somatosensory enrichment of deaf, blind, retarded adolescent through vibration.
Examined the effect of vibration to the hand on smiling behavior of a blind, deaf, profoundly retarded adolescent girl. Results show significant differences between observation and experimental periods for the duration of smiling behavior.
Halliday, Gordon W. & Evans, Joseph H. (U. Kansas) Perceptual & Motor Skills, 1974(Jun), Vol. 38(3, Pt. 1), 880. [PA, Vol 52:12725]

1749. The effects of visual cue fading and task complexity on auditory discrimination in severely retarded children.
Investigated 2 procedures—visual cue fading and task complexity—involved in teaching simple auditory discriminations to 20 severely retarded children (mean CA = 9 yrs) were assigned to 1 of 4 treatment groups in a 2 × 2 factorial design. Analysis of variance on the final day's data indicated differences favoring visual cue fading procedures and that a 2-stimulus task was much more difficult than a 1-stimulus task. Another analysis of variance showed only differences in task difficulty. The need for further investigations into the variables affecting auditory discrimination is indicated. (15 ref)
Harvey, Eric & Bornstein, Robert. (Center for Human Development, Mt. Pleasant, Mich.) Psychological Record, 1974(Win), Vol. 24(1), 109-117. [PA, Vol 52:08014]

1750. Dendritic development in neocortex of children with mental defect and infantile spasms.
Analyzed the dendritic spread of pyramidal neurons in the middle frontal gyrus of 11 mentally defective patients. Results suggest that defective growth of cortical dendrites is common in the severely retarded. Limitations of the Golgi method used may account for failure to detect abnormalities in less retarded patients and in older patients.
Huttenlocher, Peter R. (Yale U., Medical School) Neurology, 1974(Mar), Vol. 24(3), 203-210. [PA, Vol 52:08018]

1751. **[Cytogenetic investigations in a severely mentally retarded and a backward group in a school for mentally subnormal children.]** (Fren)
Studied the relationship between mental deficiency and abnormal chromosome patterns. The karyotypes of 115 severely retarded children of both sexes ranging in age from 3 to 16 yrs were examined for possible anomalies. Detailed histories were obtained of mental retardation in the Ss' parents or siblings. Excluding 10 cases of trisomy 21, anomalous karyotypes were found in 11 of the 115 Ss. It is suggested that routine examination of the chromosomes of retarded persons might yield correlations between phenotypic and karyotypic abnormalities. (English, German, & Spanish summaries)
Suerinck, E. et al. (Bethanie Medico-Pedagogical Inst, Largentiere, France) Revue de Neuropsychiatrie Infantile et d'Hygiene Mentale de l'Enfance, 1974(Jan), Vol 22(1-2), 103-119. [PA, Vol 54:07911]

1752. **Epidemiology of severe mental retardation in children: Community studies.**
Reviews 27 community studies of severe mental retardation (defined as IQ less than 50). The prevalence rate of this condition was about 4/1,000 in older children; the rate was somewhat higher in males but did not vary by social class. About ½ of severely retarded children had significant associated handicaps. The cause of most cases of severe mental retardation was not known, but Down's syndrome accounted for ⅟₁₆-⅓ of the cases and a small percentage were due to other chromosomal abnormalities, metabolic diseases, or infection. (39 ref)
Abramowicz, Helen K. & Richardson, Stephen A. (Albert Einstein Coll of Medicine, Rose F. Kennedy Ctr, Yeshiva U) American Journal of Mental Deficiency, 1975(Jul), Vol 80(1), 18-39. [PA, Vol 54:09956]

1753. **Imitation and comprehension of language in severe subnormality.**
In 3 experiments, the ability of 16 severely retarded children (mean CA 172.6 mo, mean Vocabulary Age on the English Picture Vocabulary Test 65.8 mo) to both imitate and comprehend language was investigated. Latencies to response in a picture-choice comprehension situation were also analyzed. The independent linguistic variable for all tasks was syntactic complexity. The types of error and response latencies suggest that as syntactic complexity increased, both imitation and comprehension became more difficult for the Ss. The usefulness of imitation as a psycholinguistic assessment technique is discussed. (27 ref)
Berry, Paul & Foxen, Tom. (U Manchester, England) Language & Speech, 1975(Jul-Sep), Vol 18(3), 15-203. [PA, Vol 56:10124]

1754. **Recognition and reproduction of words by Down's syndrome and non-Down's syndrome retarded children.**
Compared 10 7.75-11.25 yr old children with Down's syndrome with 10 other severely retarded children on tests of recognition and reproduction of real and nonsense words after 0-, 15-, and 30-sec delay. Results indicate that Down's syndrome children performed better on the recognition task, but worse on the reproduction task after delay, as compared with the other retarded children. It is hypothesized that the articulatory deficit in the Down's syndrome group is part of a general motor disability due to a difficulty in preprogramming sequences of movements. (18 ref)
Dodd, Barbara. (MRC Developmental Psychology Unit, London, England) American Journal of Mental Deficiency, 1975(Nov), Vol 80(3), 306-311. [PA, Vol 55:10054]

1755. **Stimulus generalization following extra-dimensional training in educationally subnormal (severely) children.**
Conducted 2 experiments to (a) examine the use of discrimination learning paradigms in the study of attentional transfer and (b) contrast the technique of go-no-go discrimination learning followed by stimulus generalization testing with the more familiar simultaneous learning paradigm followed by a shift in the relevant cues. In Exp I 9 educationally subnormal (severely) (ESN(S)) children were trained in a go-no-go discrimination

involving stimuli differing in orientation, and were tested on generalization on an orthogonal dimension (hue). Of the 6 Ss who learned the discrimination, 5 showed clear decremental gradients on the hue dimension. In contrast a Pseudo-Discrimination group (PD) of 8 Ss matched to those in the True Discrimination (TD) group showed no gradients. These Ss were not trained in the orientation discrimination, but were reinforced for responding on 50% of each of the S+ and S- stimulus presentations. They thus received equal exposure to, but no differential training on, the orientation dimension. An S+ only group of 4 Ss who received no exposure to the orientation stimuli showed no gradients when stimulus generalization testing on the hue continuum was conducted. Results are discussed in terms of transfer deriving from stimulus control by relational aspects of the stimuli, in terms of control by constant irrelevant stimuli, and in terms of the study of stimulus control in ESN(S) children. In Exp II the influence of the codability of the colors on the location of the peak of the stimulus generalization gradients in the TD group was investigated. (24 ref)
Hogg, J. & Evans, P. L. (U Manchester, Hester Adrian Research Ctr, England) British Journal of Psychology, 1975(May), Vol 66(2), 211-224. [PA, Vol 54:05567]

1756. **Stimulus input recruitment and stimulus trace decay factors in the trace conditioning deficit of severely retarded young adults.**
Used trace and delay classical eyelid conditioning procedures to investigate the relative contributions of CS input recruitment and trace decay processes to the trace conditioning deficit of 24 severely 12-18 yr old and profoundly retarded Ss. Both trace and delay conditioning groups were used at interstimulus intervals (ISIs) of 500 and 950 msec. The CS durations were 50 msec for the 500-msec ISI trace group and 500 msec for the 950-msec trace group. The "empty" interval between CS offset and the onset of the UCS was 450 msec for both trace conditioning groups. After 250 conditioning trials, there was no difference between the 2 trace groups, and both were significantly below the delay groups to final level of responding. Results suggest that stimulus trace decay rather than input recruitment, as manipulated by varying CS duration, accounted for the poor trace conditioning performance demonstrated by these Ss.
Ross, Susan M. & Ross, Leonard E. (U Wisconsin, Madison) American Journal of Mental Deficiency, 1975(Jul), Vol 80(1), 109-113. [PA, Vol 54:09976]

1757. **Comparisons of two sets of Piagetian scales with severely and profoundly retarded children.**
Administered H. H. Corman and S. K. Escalona's (1969) scales for object permanence and spatial relationships and the corresponding scales of I. C. Uzgiris and J. Hunt (1975) to 64 severely and profoundly retarded children (mean CA, 14 yrs). Most of the findings applied equally to both sets of scales: the scoring reliability was very high; the total scores did not vary as a function of S characteristics (except IQ) or testing conditions; differences in the difficulty of the items did not correspond closely to those reported for nonretarded infants, and the scalability of the items was much lower. Less time was required to administer the 2 scales constructed by Uzgiris and Hunt, but their object permanence scale showed a pronounced ceiling effect and the internal consistency of their spatial relationships scale was unacceptably low. (18 ref)
Silverstein, A. B.; Brownlee, Linda; Hubbell, Mimi & McLain, Richard E. (Neuropsychiatric Inst--Pacific State Hosp Research Group, Pomona, CA p) American Journal of Mental Deficiency, 1975(Nov), Vol 80(3), 292-297. [PA, Vol 55:10075]

1758. **[Epidemiological survey: Parisian children with multiple handicaps or severely handicapped.]** (Fren)
Conducted a statistical survey of 586 children ranging from newborns to 16-yr-olds who were mentally deficient (IQ < 55) or who had multiple handicaps, whatever their IQ. Detailed analyses were made of the respective incidence of the various handicaps which, when occurring together, fulfill the concept of multiple handicap: motor handicap of cerebral and peripheral origin, orthopedic disorders, sight and hearing defects, epilepsy,

psychotic or nonpsychotic behavior problems, and serious somatic diseases. The various combinations of handicaps were studied statistically and are presented both according to the IQ and to the main handicap. Ss were also investigated from the functional point of view (level of attainment in language and walking). The etiological part includes a detailed study of the course of pregnancy, the birth and postnatal diseases of Ss, and an attempt at synthesis is made by arranging the various etiologies in a logical order. Also studied were the positions of Ss for the purpose of feeding and the extent to which the feeding urge was satisfied. The research attempts, in conclusion, to assess the prevalence of these various handicaps, with the help of a supplementary study of 450 case histories of similar children examined when they were issued a Disabled Person's Identity Card. (German and Spanish summaries)
Tomkiewicz, S. (Inst National de la Santé et de la Recherche Médicale, Montrouge, France) Revue de Neuropsychiatrie Infantile et d'Hygiene Mentale de l'Enfance, 1975(Jul), Vol 23(7), 389-403. [PA, Vol 57:05957]

1759.   Task difficulty and motor performance in severe subnormality.
20 mentally retarded Ss (mean MA 5.4 yrs; mean IQ 33.4), 20 normal adults, and 20 normal children (mean CA, 23.3, 23.4, and 5.4 yrs, respectively) performed on the pursuit rotor apparatus on 2 separate occasions. The 1st involved 10 trials with the rotor revolving at 15 rpm, and the 2nd involved 10 trials at 30 rpm. Results suggest that IQ, and not MA, is the critical factor involved in the intelligence-complexity relationship in pursuit rotor performance, since the retarded Ss were most adversely affected by an increase in task difficulty.
Bankhead, I. (New U of Ulster, Northern Ireland) Journal of Mental Deficiency Research, 1976(Dec), Vol 20(4), 261-165. [PA, Vol 58:05601]

1760.   Elicited imitation and production of language by severely subnormal children.
The relationship between elicited imitation and production of language is confusing in the available psycholinguistic literature. The present study attempted to clarify this relationship. 17 severely mentally handicapped children (mean CA 137.12 mo, mean vocabulary age 43.47 mo) were involved in a series of tests in which they were asked (a) to imitate a wide range of linguistic stimuli, including single words through to complex sentences (taken from the Language Imitation Test), and (b) to talk to the E about a series of picture stimuli. It is concluded that the Ss used linguistic strategies on both tasks, indicating that similar psycholinguistic skills were involved.
Berry, P.   & Taylor, J. (U Queensland, Brisbane, Australia) Language & Speech, 1976, Vol 19(2), 160-172. [PA, Vol 58:05603]

1761.   Elicited imitation and assessment of abilities.
It is possible to regard imitation within at least three theoretical frameworks. First, imitation may be regarded as a special case of another more general form of learning (F. Allport, 1924; B. Skinner, 1953). Second, it is possible to consider imitation as a unique process which may be accounted for in its own right (A. Bandura, 1969). A third theory of imitation has its origin in the work of Piaget (1951) and suggests that imitation is only one aspect of the total functioning of an individual and lies between accommodation and assimilation. The Piagetian account of imitation implies that as an individual develops, his/her imitations undergo a series of transformations, so that the level of organization of the individual directly influences the imitations. There is some evidence that, in the case of the severely subnormal child, the Piagetian theory has implications for the development of learning and the assessment of abilities. In a series of experiments previously conducted by the author (1971, 1973), requiring severely mentally handicapped children to imitate sounds in words, whole words, strings of words, and sentences of varying complexity, an analysis of errors indicated differential levels and strategies of processing the linguistic input. The level of performance correlated significantly with abilities on other tasks of linguistic ability such as receptive vocabulary, compre-

hension of sentences of varying syntactic complexity, and ability to vary syntactic complexity. (23 ref)
Berry, P. B. (U Queensland, Brisbane, Australia) Language & Speech, 1976(Oct–Dec), Vol 19(4), 363–373. [PA, Vol 59:10128]

1762.   A preliminary survey of beliefs about severely retarded children in Ghana.
Data collected from 306 parents of mentally retarded children and from 800 other individuals indicate that both educated and uneducated parents believed that severe retardation is associated with misfortune that is linked to a curse by a supernatural being. Only 5% of the educated urban parents attributed the cause to genetic or biological and metabolic processes and felt that the severely retarded needed hospital treatment. (French summary) (4 ref)
Danquah, S. A. (U Ghana Medical School, Accra) Psychopathologie Africaine, 1976, Vol 12(2), 189–197. [PA, Vol 65:03515]

1763.   A comparison of the phonological systems of mental age matched, normal, severely subnormal and Down's Syndrome children.
Compared the number and type of phonological errors made spontaneously and in imitation by MA-matched normal, severely subnormal, and Down's Syndrome (DS) children. Results indicate that the normal and severely subnormal non-DS children performed equally, while the DS children made more errors, and those errors were more inconsistent than errors by the other 2 groups. The DS children made fewer errors in imitation than they did in spontaneous production. Findings are interpreted as an indication that phonological development is linked to general mental development in severely subnormal non-DS children. The exceptional performance of the DS group was hypothesized to be partly due to a general difficulty in generating predetermined sequences of movements. (23 ref)
Dodd, Barbara. (MRC Developmental Psychology Unit, London, England) British Journal of Disorders of Communication, 1976(Apr), Vol 11(1), 27-42. [PA, Vol 56:04273]

1764.   Testing measures of the quality of residential care: A pilot study.
Summarizes results from a pilot study, designed to test a method of measuring the quality of care provided in 2 residential units for severely mentally handicapped children. The overall aim was to devise general measures of the learning conditions (the quality of care), within residential units, which relate to groups of clients and are equally applicable at different times of the waking day. Such measures will constitute a helpful monitoring instrument only if they are shown to be reliable, to have at least face-validity, to be based on representative and accurate data, and to differentiate between settings which, intuitively, appear to differ in the extent to which appropriate behavior by clients is prompted and reinforced.
Durward, Lyn   & Whatmore, Ron. (Wessex Regional Health Authority, Health Care Evaluation Team, Winchester, England) Behaviour Research & Therapy, 1976, Vol 14(2), 149-157. [PA, Vol 56:04566]

1765.   Language development and non-verbal skills in severely mentally retarded children: An epidemiological study.
Studied 150 children who were identified from a 1-day census of the Camberwell (England) Psychiatric Case Register of all severely mentally retarded children aged 0–14 yrs. Language level and nonverbal intelligence (using such measures as the Bayley Scales of Infant Development and the WISC Performance and Verbal scales) were measured. Nonverbal IQ under 20 was very significantly associated with absence of any comprehension or use of speech or symbolic gesture, but some children with no language had nonverbal IQs above 20 and a few had nonverbal IQs above 50. Statistical analysis showed that defects of hearing and vision and admission to residential care were significantly related to absence of language regardless of the level of nonverbal intelligence. Behavior problems were significantly associated with absence of language but not with level of nonverbal intelligence. The prevalence of and the special problems present-

ed by the children with marked discrepancies between nonverbal skills and language level are discussed. (36 ref)
Gould, Judith. (MRC Social Psychiatry Unit, U London Inst of Psychiatry, England) Journal of Mental Deficiency Research, 1976(Jun), Vol 20(2), 129–146. [PA, Vol 59:10155]

1766. Utility of the Uzgiris and Hunt scales of sensorimotor development with severely and profoundly retarded children.
Examined the reliability and validity of the scales of sensorimotor development by I. C. Uzgiris and J. McV. Hunt (1975). Ss were 63 severely or profoundly retarded children 42-126 mo old. 30 were living in residential facilities, and 33 were living at home and attending day schools. All Ss were assessed on all 6 scales of the Uzgiris and Hunt instrument. Interexaminer and test-retest reliabilities were computed. Scalogram analyses were also computed for all but the Schemes scale. The scales were found to be reliable and, as theorized by Piaget, ordinal wih the present sample. These findings indicate that the scales can be used reliably and validly with severely and profoundly retarded children, and their present and potential application is discussed.
Kahn, James V. (U Illinois, Chicago Circle) American Journal of Mental Deficiency, 1976(May), Vol 80(6), 663-665. [PA, Vol 56:03237]

1767. The effect of intonational emphasis on sentence comprehension in severely subnormal and normal children.
Investigated the effect of intonational emphasis on the sentence comprehension of severely subnormal and normal preschool children by stressing the critical elements of sentences of varying syntactic structure. Results agree with previous work, in that intonational emphasis did not facilitate comprehension. There was, however, some evidence to show that intonational emphasis may have a detrimental effect on the subnormal child's comprehension of negative structures.
Wheldall, Kevin & Swann, William. (U Birmingham, England) Language & Speech, 1976(Jan-Mar), Vol 19(1), 87-99. [PA, Vol 57:01454]

1768. Stimulus overselectivity: A common feature in autism and mental retardation.
Conducted a study with 3 groups of children with different IQ levels: 10 severely retarded Ss (mean IQ, 39.3; mean CA, 15.8 yrs); 10 moderately retarded Ss (mean IQ, 66.1; mean CA, 14.3 yrs); and 10 nonretarded Ss (mean age, 11.1 yrs). Ss were trained to discriminate between stimulus cards containing 2 or more pictures. In subsequent testing the pictures were presented singly to determine how many pictures the S had responded to during discrimination training. The lower the IQ, the fewer pictures the S responded to. It is speculated that intellectually retarded functioning may be related to problems in overselective attention; the lower a person's IQ level, the less of the environment becomes functional in controlling his behavior. (18 ref)
Wilhelm, Hannelore & Lovaas, O. Ivar. (Ludwig-Maximilians-U München, W Germany) American Journal of Mental Deficiency, 1976(Jul), Vol 81(1), 26-31. [PA, Vol 56:10157]

1769. Retardation and twin concordance in infant mental development: A reassessment.
A reappraisal is made of P. L. Nichols and S. H. Broman's (see PA, Vol 52:9841) conclusion that there is no evidence that genetic influences are important in infant mental development if severely retarded twins are excluded from the sample. The reappraisal touches on certain idiosyncrasies of their sample, the test scores reported, and their definition of severe retardation. Data are presented for a sample of 460 White monozygotic and same-sex dizygotic twins who had been followed longitudinally since birth. For Bayley Mental Scale scores at 9 mo of age, the monozygotic within-pair correlation was 0.85 and the dizygotic within-pair correlation was 0.62. With 13 retarded twins excluded, the correlations became 0.81 and 0.64, respectively, with the monozygotic correlation still being significantly larger (p < 0.01). Present results indicated that genetic factors play a role in infant mental development.

Wilson, Ronald S. & Matheny, Adam P. (U Louisville Health Sciences Ctr) Behavior Genetics, 1976(Jul), Vol 6(3), 353-358. [PA, Vol 57:08011]

1770. Feedback, language and listener performance in severely retarded children.
Presents an analytical framework for investigating the relationship between language and action in a dyadic communication task. Three Down's syndrome children were found to improve their performance on the introduction of speaker feedback; when feedback was removed the listeners' performance returned to its previous level. A study was carried out of the relationship between the speaker's message, the listener's choice of stimulus item, and the listener's spontaneous verbalizations. This relationship differed for individual Ss and also changed as their performance improved on the task. This result is interpreted as showing that the Ss learned to eliminate different nonfunctional communication strategies as they improved on the task. The importance of this knowledge for remediation purposes is stressed. (16 ref)
Beveridge, Michael & Mittler, Peter. (U Manchester, Hester Adrian Research Ctr, England) British Journal of Disorders of Communication, 1977(Oct), Vol 12(2), 149–157. [PA, Vol 60:11955]

1771. Effects of auditory stimulation upon the motor test performance of severely retarded children.
Exposed 9 retarded, overactive Ss age 5–14 to successive testing on 2 simple form boards. On the easier of the 2 tasks, mean performance time increased significantly when a controlled "soothing" auditory input could be heard rather than normal playground noises. However, this difference disappeared on the more difficult task. Possible implications regarding attention and learning in retarded children are discussed.
Booth, G. K. & Dunbar, Rhoda. AEP (Association of Educational Psychologists) Journal, 1977(Spr), Vol 4(4), 19–24. [PA, Vol 59:08099]

1772. Recognition memory for colors and faces in profoundly retarded young children.
Examined visual recognition memory in a group of 16 profoundly retarded young children (mean CA 6.1 yrs) whose visual–motor developmental level (Bayley Scales of Infant Development) was estimated to be below 1 yr. Ss were tested for recognition of a previously shown face photo or a previously exposed color either immediately or following a short-term delay by observing the distribution of their visual fixation responses to novel stimuli when paired with previously seen targets. During a study or "familiarization" period the Ss devoted approximately the same amount of attention to photos of faces as they did to colored, abstract patterns; and individual differences in overall looking time proved to be reliable. During the recognition testing phase the Ss demonstrated immediate recognition memory for both faces and colors, preferring a novel to a previously exposed target, but responsiveness to novelty declined abruptly over a short-term delay, providing little evidence for delayed recognition. (20 ref)
Butcher, Marian J. (Case Western Reserve U) Intelligence, 1977(Oct), Vol 1(4), 344–357. [PA, Vol 61:08691]

1773. [Motivation and learning in severely mentally retarded children.] (Germ)
A group of 31 severely retarded, institutionalized children between the ages of 6 yrs 2 mo and 18 yrs 3 mo (average hospitalization 7.4 yrs) were given a preference test, motivation tests, and a discrimination task involving sweets or pastries. In the discrimination task, the child was expected to choose a cylinder of the correct color (either red or blue) to obtain the treat. If children made the correct choice 10 times consecutively, they were considered to have learned the task; if by the 100th attempt the task was still not learned, the observer discontinued the testing. Based on the discrimination task, the Ss were divided into 3 groups: Group A included 5 Ss who made no attempt and 7 Ss who on their own initiative stopped trying. Group B included 10 Ss who made 100 attempts but failed to reach the

learning criterion. Group C included 9 Ss who were both motivated and successful in performing the task. Group C showed the highest participation in the preference test, and Group A the lowest. There was no significant difference among the 3 groups in regard to age or length of hospitalization. (14 ref) *Dirlich-Wilhelm, Hanne; Pohl, Peter & Butollo, W. H.* (Ludwig-Maximilians-U München, Inst für Psychologie, West Germany) Zeitschrift für Kinder- und Jugendpsychiatrie, 1977(Jun), Vol 5(2), 103–114. [PA, Vol 63:03498]

1774. Evaluation of entertainment materials for severely retarded persons.
Research with retarded and nonretarded populations suggests that toys can be an important part of group-care programs. Yet in a review of the literature, P. Wheman (1976) showed that there was a paucity of empirical data on effective toy utilization with retarded populations. In the present study, time-sampling measurements were made of the free-play behavior of 11 11-26 yr old severely retarded females (IQ under 30) with 20 different toys and comparison items. Data analysis revealed that (a) Ss had strong preferences among toys; (b) there was a low, nonsignificant correlation between toy preference and price; and (c) professional staff were unable to make accurate predictions of toy preference. Ss were idle 65% of the time when only the 10 less popular toys were available, but only 25% of the time when only the 10 more popular toys were available. It is concluded that (a) the behavior of retarded individuals is strongly influenced by the toys available to them, (b) empirical data are necessary to make effective and economical use of materials, and (c) the lack of such data for retarded populations makes this an important area for research.
Favell, James E. & Cannon, Preston R. (Western Carolina Ctr, Morganton, NC) American Journal of Mental Deficiency, 1977(Jan), Vol 81(4), 357-361. [PA, Vol 58:05617]

1775. The use of the Vineland Social Maturity Scale, the Merrill-Palmer Scale of Mental Tests (non-verbal items) and the Reynell Develomental Language Scales with children in contact with the services for severe mental retardation.
Psychological tests were administered to a complete population of severely retarded children, aged 0–14 yrs, from 1 area of southeast London. The 56 children selected included all those who had obtained scores on measures of social maturity, visuospatial skills not involving symbolic concepts, and level of language comprehension (Vineland Social Maturity Scale, Reynell Developmental Language Scales, and the Merrill-Palmer Scale). Results show very low correlations between the age-related quotients obtained for each measure. This suggested that, in severely retarded children, marked discrepancies can occur between different areas of cognitive and social development. Some children could be classified as moderately or mildly retarded on one type of test but as profoundly retarded on another. The profiles on the tests were related to diagnosis and behavior pattern. The findings highlight the problems of assessment and educational placement of retarded children. (36 ref)
Gould, Judith. (MRC Social Psychiatry Unit, Inst of Psychiatry, London, England) Journal of Mental Deficiency Research, 1977(Sep), Vol 21(3), 213–226. [PA, Vol 61:03889]

1776. Severe mental retardation in children in a northern Swedish county.
In an unselected series of children with severe mental retardation born in 1959–1970 in a northern Swedish county, an analysis was made of the incidence, prevalence, gestational age, birth weight, associated CNS disorders, and etiological and pathogenetic aspects. The mean annual incidence of severe mental retardation in children alive at the age of 1 yr was 3.9 per 1,000. The prevalence of severe mental retardation at 1–16 yrs of age was 3.5 per 1,000. The mean gestational ages and birth weights were lower than those of an average Swedish population of newborns. The distribution of birth weights in relation to gestational age showed that there were too many small-for-gestational-age children. The dominating etiology of mental retardation was prenatal, which was noted in 68%. In 35% the mental retardation was due to a chromosomal aberration and in 17% to mutant

genes. 8% of the children had associated prenatal stigmata of unknown etiology, and in 8% an acquired etiology was found, mainly fetal deprivation of supply. A perinatal etiology was found in only 8% and a postnatal etiology, as well as psychosis, in 1% of the children. In 22% no obvious etiology was traced. Among the 161 children, 52% had 1 or more associated CNS handicaps—epilepsy (36%) and cerebral palsy (19%) being the most common. Severe impairment of vision was seen in 10% and severe impairment of hearing in 6% of the children. (21 ref)
Gustavson, K. H.; Holmgren, G.; Jonsell, R. & Blomquist, H. K. (U UmeåHosp, Sweden) Journal of Mental Deficiency Research, 1977(Sep), Vol 21(3), 161–180. [PA, Vol 60:09573]

1777. Self-recognition among institutionalized profoundly retarded males: A replication.
Pretested 18 profoundly retarded males (CAs 19.33-28.00 yrs) for the ability to recognize their mirrored and photographic images. Nine Ss were then given mirror training for 10 min daily on 13 consecutive days. Posttest results indicate no improvement in recognition as measured. These findings are similar to those reported by T. F. Pechacek et al (see PA, Vol 51:1393), indicating that (a) profoundly mentally retarded males rank somewhat below adolescent chimpanzees and orangutans in the ability to make "self-directed" responses to their mirrored images; and (b) mirror training does not transfer to self-photograph discrimination for which comparative data are unavailable.
Harris, Larry P. (U Texas, Austin) Bulletin of the Psychonomic Society, 1977(Jan), Vol 9(1), 43-44. [PA, Vol 58:05625]

1778. Toward a curriculum for the profoundly retarded, multiply handicapped child.
Describes an approach to formulating programs for the profoundly retarded child. It is suggested that the basis for programming should be an analysis of the child's ability to operate on and find out about his environment.
Kiernan, Chris. (U London Inst of Education, Thomas Coram Research Unit, England) Child Care, Health & Development, 1977(Jul–Aug), Vol 3(4), 229–239. [PA, Vol 60:11968]

1779. Idiots savants: A review.
Reviews factors advanced to explain the phenomenon of severely retarded persons who possess special talents that exceed the population norm. These factors include (a) genetic conditions, (b) brain damage, (c) reception of special training, (d) special motivation, (e) skill chosen on the basis of inherited abilities or parental identification, (f) sensory hyperacuity, (g) deficit in ability to abstract, (h) eidetic imagery, (i) possible status as psychotics in remission, and (j) environmental influences, such as childrearing practices. It is noted that a plurality of theories may be required by the heterogeneity of the phenomenon and that several of the identified factors may operate together in any individual case. The suggestion is made that multiaxial classification be employed to make possible an estimation of the degree to which psychiatric syndromes are implicated in conjunction with particular patterns of intellectual functioning. (24 ref)
Lester, David. (Richard Stockton State Coll) Psychology: A Quarterly Journal of Human Behavior, 1977(Feb), Vol 14(1), 20–23. [PA, Vol 59:12555]

1780. [Sexuality and procreation among the profoundly retarded.] (Fren)
Although puberty and the accompanying problems of sexuality have been studied for the normal adolescent, far less attention has been given to the parallel problems of the mentally retarded. The complex questions involved require rigorous study and judicious interpretation.
Pasquasy, R. Bulletin de Psychologie Scolaire et d'Orientation, 1977(Jul), Vol 26(3), 141. [PA, Vol 66:01545]

1781. Characteristics of the cognitive development of profoundly retarded children.
Examined the sensorimotor skills of 40 8–14 yr old profoundly retarded institutionalized children (MAs 11–23 mo, IQs 7–19) on a set of Piagetian tasks to determine (a) whether their performance would replicate the invariant sequential pattern found in normal infants, (b) the parallelism of stage attainments into

various domains of sensorimotor functioning, and (c) the role of MA and CA variables in sensorimotor performances. Stage attainments followed Piaget's hypothesized invariant sequences and generally replicated findings made with normal infants but lacked the parallel stage performance across various domains as theorized by Piaget. In addition, MA was significantly correlated with sensorimotor skills. (20 ref)
Rogers, Sally J. (Southwest Missouri State U) Child Development, 1977(Sep), Vol 48(3), 837–843. [PA, Vol 60:01325]

1782.   An approach to the evaluation of early intervention projects with mothers of severely handicapped children: The attitude dimension.
Reviews the literature and describes a research investigation currently being conducted on the changing attitudes of mothers of severely handicapped preschool children. A summary is presented of the most frequently cited emotional reactions following the birth of a handicapped child, followed by a description of a Maternal Attitudes Battery designed to obtain quantitative measures of relevant maternal attitudes. This is presented within the framework of an evaluation model specifically chosen to investigate the effectiveness of a specific home intervention project. Results will include the social and emotional evaluation of mothers of severely handicapped children using both norm- and criterion-referenced measures of both immediate and long term effects of intervention. (30 ref)
Burden, R. L. (U Exeter School of Education, England) Child Care, Health & Development, 1978(May–Jun), Vol 4(3), 171–181. [PA, Vol 62:04273]

1783.   The effectiveness of distorted music versus interrupted music to decrease self-stimulatory behaviors in profoundly retarded adolescents.
Ss were 4 profoundly retarded and multiply handicapped clients, 7–22 yrs old, with high rates of self-stimulatory behavior. There were 2 baseline conditions (silence and noncontingent music) and 2 treatment conditions (contingent music and distorted music, and contingent music and silence). During treatment sessions, music listening was contingent upon appropriate behavior. Whenever specified inappropriate behavior occurred, distorted music or silence was presented. No substantial decrease in the self-stimulatory behavior took place. Data were inconsistent for all Ss across all conditions. Possible reasons for the lack of effect are discussed. (1 ref)
Greenwald, M. Amelia. (Area Residential Care Ctr, Dubuque, IA) Journal of Music Therapy, 1978(Sum), Vol 15(2), 58–66. [PA, Vol 63:10191]

1784.   Sensory reinforcement and contingency awareness of profoundly retarded children.
In 2 experiments, 3 of 4 profoundly retarded and physically handicapped children with MAs below 7 mo (Bayley Scales of Infant Development) demonstrated instrumental learning of a manipulative response that produced either illumination or music. Discrimination of response-dependent from response-independent stimulation was demonstrated by the 3 Ss. Further, change in 2 categories of collateral behavior—vocalizing and smiling—seemed to reflect recognition of changes in stimulus conditions. Results indicate that profoundly retarded children share with normally developing infants and children the capacity to be reinforced by sensory stimulation and to discriminate contingent from noncontingent events. (29 ref)
Haskett, Josh & Hollar, W. David. (Fairview State Hosp, Costa Mesa, CA) American Journal of Mental Deficiency, 1978(Jul), Vol 83(1), 60–68. [PA, Vol 62:03889]

1785.   Communication with the severely and profoundly handicapped: A psycholinguistic approach.
Discusses the early linguistic environment of normal infants and children and applies what is known about the acquisition of language by normal children to children who have severe and profound handicaps. It is suggested that profoundly retarded children could have more chance of acquiring verbal language if educators created a climate that contained the natural reinforcers

that mothers use in helping their children learn to communicate. (18 ref)
Michaelis, Carol T. (George Mason U) Mental Retardation, 1978(Oct), Vol 16(5), 346–349. [PA, Vol 63:05709]

1786.   Behavioral and spatial change in response to an altered behavioral setting.
Used behavioral mapping to record behavior and spatial use by 35 17–25 yr old severely and profoundly retarded males during free time in the day room at a state institution. The 3-wk study used Week 1 for baseline, Week 2 for treatment, and Week 3 for posttreatment. During Week 2, novel materials were placed in the dayroom in 4 conceptually distinct groupings: arts and crafts, games, empty, and lounge. During treatment, Ss engaged in significantly more active and socially involved behaviors, avoided isolated behaviors and empty dayroom areas, and evidenced adaptive behavior to novel environmental objects. This involvement was greatly dissipated during Week 3. Treatment implications of these changes, use of behavioral mapping in future research, and methodological issues are discussed. (24 ref)
Miller, Ted L. (U Tennessee, Chattanooga) Environmental Psychology & Nonverbal Behavior, 1978(Fal), Vol 3(1), 23–42. [PA, Vol 63:09947]

1787.   Rejection of success in two severely retarded children.
The performance of 2 severely retarded boys with low self-esteem (LSE) was compared to that of 2 severely retarded boys with normal self-esteem (NSE) on a ring-stacking task with high and low levels of reward. NSE Ss performed faster for high rewards, but LSE Ss performed faster for low rewards and rejected high rewards. Results indicate that some children should be reinforced with relatively low rewards. (4 ref)
Reiss, Steven; Reiss, Maggi M. & Reppucci, N. Dickon. (U Illinois, Chicago Circle) Cognitive Therapy & Research, 1978(Sep), Vol 2(3), 293–297. [PA, Vol 64:12749]

1788.   The Slosson Intelligence Test as a quick screening test of mental ability with profoundly and severely retarded children.
Investigated the test–retest reliability of the Slosson Intelligence Test when administered and scored by 9 special education teachers who had no experience in psychological testing. Ss were 53 profoundly and severely retarded children, ranging in age from 5 to 16 yrs. Pearson product-moment coefficients were .92 for girls, .96 for boys and .94 for all Ss for scores on 2 occasions. Results support R. L. Slosson's (1963) contention that the test can be reliably administered by personnel with little psychometric knowledge. (6 ref)
Rotatori, Anthony F. & Epstein, Michael H. (Northern Illinois U) Psychological Reports, 1978(Jun), Vol 42(3, Pt 2), 1117–1118. [PA, Vol 63:02436]

1789.   Identification of severe mental handicap.
Parents of 212 7–13 yr old severely educationally handicapped children were asked about the circumstances of the identification of their child's handicap. Findings as a whole were similar to those in other studies but varied significantly according to the clinical group of the child. In the "no specific pathology" group, identification occurred later and was further delayed from the time that parents became anxious than it was for children in other groups. By the end of the 1st yr only 27% and by the end of the 2nd yr less than 50% of the parents had learned of the serious nature of their child's condition. 17% of these children were not recognized until they reached school age. It is concluded that since "no specific pathology" children may benefit as much or perhaps more from early intervention as children in the more easily identifiable groups, attention should be paid to means of recognition and of giving appropriate help and support to their parents. (12 ref)
Smith, Beryl & Phillips, C. J. (U Birmingham Faculty of Education, England) Child Care, Health & Development, 1978(May–Jun), Vol 4(3), 195–203. [PA, Vol 62:03908]

1790.   Systematic recording of behaviors and skills of retarded and psychotic children.
Describes the design, administration, and scoring of the 1st edition of the Children's Handicaps, Behavior and Skills struc-

tured interview schedule, which is intended to elicit information concerning mentally retarded or psychotic children. Ss were 104 children under 15 yrs of age, all of whom were receiving special education. Most of the Ss were receiving services for the severely mentally retarded; the other Ss had at least some behaviors associated with early childhood psychoses. A high level of reliability was achieved with experienced interviewers and good informants. The levels of overall agreement between parent and professional informants on the 62 sections of the schedule were, in general, 70% or above. Agreement was better for rating absence of skills or behavioral abnormalities than for rating their presence. This tendency was particularly marked for the behavioral abnormalities. Parents, when compared with professional workers, tended to describe their children as having higher developmental skills, more social contact but also more repetitive and difficult behavior. (21 ref)
Wing, Lorna & Gould, Judith. (U London Inst of Psychiatry, England) Journal of Autism & Developmental Disorders, 1978(Mar), Vol 8(1), 79–97. [PA, Vol 61:12382]

1791. Tangible and social reinforcers for correct responses in assessing severely retarded school-age children.
To investigate the effect of positive reinforcement on correct responses to P. Hecht's (1975) Developmental Checklist—Reasoning and Problem Solving, 12 male and 12 female severely retarded Ss were divided into 3 equal groups. Each treatment was the presentation by the same examiner of either all tangible or all social reinforcers upon completion of correct responses by the S to the checklist. The difference between the means under social and tangible reinforcements was not significant.
Zumberg, Marshall. (Wayne State U) Psychological Reports, 1978(Feb), Vol 42(1), 106. [PA, Vol 61:08734]

1792. Kinaesthetic movement after-effects in children with Down's syndrome.
Compared matched groups of severely subnormal and Down's syndrome children (*n* = 20; mean age 12.01 yrs) with 20 normal children (mean age 8.15 yrs) matched on either CA or MA. No difference was found between the normal and severely subnormal Ss, but the magnitude of the aftereffect measures in Down's syndrome Ss suggests that asymmetrical pointing produced kinesthetic aftereffects that disrupted these Ss' total frame of spatial reference. (27 ref)
Anwar, Feriha & Hermelin, Beate. (MRC Developmental Psychology Unit, London, England) Journal of Mental Deficiency Research, 1979(Dec), Vol 23(4), 287–297. [PA, Vol 66:08223]

1793. Self-blame and communication failure in retarded adolescents.
Two studies identified 62 severely retarded adolescents who made little use of their relatively high level of linguistic ability in the initiation of social interactions. Ss were compared to a similar group, who did initiate more frequently, on an experimental measure of self-blaming for communication failure. No differences were found between the 2 groups in respect to frequency with which they blamed themselves. However, the low interacting group did improve the clarity of their communicative messages in the failure condition, indicating that their initially lower level of communicative competence could be improved with changes in the eliciting conditions. (18 ref)
Beveridge, Michael; Spencer, Jenny & Mittler, Peter. (U Manchester, England) Journal of Child Psychology & Psychiatry & Allied Disciplines, 1979(Apr), Vol 20(2), 129–138. [PA, Vol 64:10633]

1794. Language comprehension processes of mentally retarded children.
Compared sentence comprehension strategies of 18 severely retarded children (CA 7.33–18.0 yrs; MA 1.83–7.08 yrs) with those of 18 nonretarded children matched on MA. Using toys, the Ss acted out a series of simple active- and passive-voice sentences describing events that were either probable, improbable, or neutral with respect to semantic expectations. The retarded Ss tended to rely more on semantic expectations than

did the nonretarded. Retarded Ss whose MAs were less than 3 yrs did not take word order into account, but those of higher MA did use a word-order strategy. They assumed that the 1st noun in the sentence corresponded to the actor in the external situation. (11 ref)
Dewart, M. Hazel. (Central School of Speech & Drama, London, England) American Journal of Mental Deficiency, 1979(Sep), Vol 84(2), 177–183. [PA, Vol 63:01219]

1795. Applications of the Piagetian literature to severely and profoundly mentally retarded persons.
Recently there has been a large number of published reports dealing with Piaget's theory and mentally retarded individuals. Studies that have included severely and profoundly retarded children as Ss are surveyed as well as studies that have included only higher functioning retarded or nonretarded individuals. Even though Piaget's theory of cognitive development has 4 stages, only the sensorimotor period and the preoperational stage are discussed because severely and profoundly retarded individuals do not achieve a more advanced level of cognitive functioning. Ways in which Piaget's sensorimotor and preoperational periods are relevant to assessment and educational practices for severely and profoundly retarded persons are discussed. (54 ref)
Kahn, James V. (U Illinois, Chicago Circle) Mental Retardation, 1979(Dec), Vol 17(6), 273–280. [PA, Vol 66:08242]

1796. [Cognitive profiles of young profoundly retarded children by means of Uzgiris and Hunt's Scale VI.] (Fren)
The Infant Psychological Development Scale was adapted for use with profoundly mentally retarded children. Scale VI, which assesses Ss' development of schemes for relating to objects, was useful for evaluating Ss when traditional testing was not applicable. (English summary) (5 ref)
Lambert, Jean-Luc & Saint-Remi, Jacqueline. (U Liège, Lab de Psychologie Expérimentale, Belgium) Psychologica Belgica, 1979, Vol 19(1), 99–107. [PA, Vol 64:11516]

1797. Observations on elicited language imitation with the severely retarded.
Examined word, phrase, and sentence imitation responses by 42 institutionalized, severely retarded adolescents (mean age 18.1 yrs) to study (a) the validity of imitation in language assessment with the retarded and (b) the developmental characteristics of language processing by retarded speakers. Ss were administered the Columbia Mental Maturity Scale; MA of Ss ranged from less than 3 yrs to 9 yrs 11 mo. High response consistency in imitation, and semantic and syntactic substitutions are interpreted as evidence of internalized control of grammar by Ss. An MA but not CA correlation with imitation ability was found. One-third of the Ss did not produce good imitations for 3-word, Subject-Verb-Object phrases; Ss who did produce good imitations of such phrases could also imitate longer phrases and sentences. Evidence of metalinguistic awareness is presented, and results and teaching implications are discussed in terms of Ss' ability to process basic semantic relationships. (47 ref)
Lamberts, Frances & Burns, Martha. (Northwestern U) Language & Speech, 1979(Jan–Mar), Vol 22(1), 21–35. [PA, Vol 64:08271]

1798. Spoken words and manual signs as encoding categories in short-term memory of mentally retarded children.
The release-from-proactive-inhibition paradigm was used to test differential encoding of manual signs and spoken words by 6 severely retarded children (IQ 27–68). Scores for shift conditions were significantly different from scores for nonshift conditions on the last trial, indicating that manual signs were encoded differently from spoken words for short-term memory storage. (11 ref)
Reid, Barbara & Kiernan, Chris. (U London Inst of Education, Thomas Coram Research Unit, England) American Journal of Mental Deficiency, 1979(Sep), Vol 84(2), 200–203. [PA, Vol 63:01234]

1799.   Usefulness of the Slosson Intelligence Test with severely and profoundly retarded children.
Investigated the concurrent validity of the Slosson Intelligence Test when administered and scored by 5 special education teachers whose Ss were 40 severely and profoundly mentally retarded schoolchildren 11.3–19.9 yrs of age. A Pearson correlation of .90 was obtained between raw scores on the Slosson and the Stanford-Binet Intelligence Scale. The skewness of the distribution and the similar nature of the tests inflated the obtained validity. (3 ref)
Rotatori, Anthony F.;   Sedlak, Bob   & Freagon, Sharon. (Northern Illinois U) Perceptual & Motor Skills, 1979(Feb), Vol 48(1), 334. [PA, Vol 64:02496]

1800.   The functional significance of complex hand movement stereotypies in the severely retarded.
Examined complex hand movement stereotypies in 3 13–17 yr old severely retarded adolescents. Ss were assigned to each of 3 conditions: a restricted environment (S was alone in a room with an unfamiliar adult and few toys); an enriched environment (with a familiar adult and a wide variety of toys); and an overcorrection condition (the adult did not encourage play and administered a functional movement training procedure each time the S engaged in complex hand movements). Behavioral observations, gross motor behaviors, and psychophysiological (EKG) measures were recorded for each S. Results indicate that complex hand movement stereotypies might serve as a self-stimulatory rather than a "de-arousing" function. The prevention of the complex hand movements resulted in increases of other stereotypies such as rocking. These findings question the concept of stereotyped behaviors as a single class; rather, single behaviors need to be viewed as part of a system. (13 ref)
Young, Roger & Clements, John. (St Cadoc's Hosp, Ty Bryn Adolescents' Unit, Caerleon, Wales) British Journal of Mental Subnormality, 1979(Dec), Vol 25(49, Pt 2), 79–87. [PA, Vol 65:13057]

1801.   An interview technique in assessing retarded children: A comparative study of the reliability of the Children's Handicaps, Behaviour and Skills (HBS) Schedule.
Describes the use of the HBS Schedule with 171 severely retarded children (0–15 yrs). It is concluded that the HBS constitutes a valuable supplement in the evaluation of such children and deserves propagation for routine applications, provided satisfactory instructions to interviewers can be given. (18 ref)
Bernsen, Alice H. (Psychiatric Hosp in Aarhus, Inst of Psychiatric Demography, Denmark) Journal of Mental Deficiency Research, 1980(Sep), Vol 24(3), 167–179. [PA, Vol 66:08225]

1802.   A comparative study of speech perception in young severely retarded children and normally developing infants.
The discrimination of minimally paired sounds by 7 retarded children (mean CA 3 yrs 2 mo; mean IQ 38.4) was compared with the discrimination performance of 8 normally developing 7-mo-olds. Ss were tested using the Visually Reinforced Infant Speech Discrimination paradigm in which they were taught to respond with a head turn to a change in a repeating background auditory stimulus. Responses were reinforced by activation of an animated toy. All Ss proved to be conditionable, and both groups evidenced discrimination of the speech contrasts tested. Data suggest that retarded children have more difficulty processing a contrast cued by rapid spectral changes (often associated with consonant discrimination) than they do a contrast cued by steady-state spectral information (often associated with the perception of slowly articulated vowels). The normally developing Ss did not find rapid spectral cues more difficult than steady-state cues. (15 ref)
Eilers, Rebecca E. & Oller, D. Kimbrough. (U Miami, Mailman Ctr for Child Development, FL) Journal of Speech & Hearing Research, 1980(Jun), Vol 23(2), 419–428. [PA, Vol 66:01537]

1803.   Ape-language controversy flares up.
Presents a news report examining the background of the current controversy about whether apes are capable of true language,

even though they are able to learn large vocabularies of signs. The philosophical, linguistic, and methodological issues involved in the conflict and differences in the procedures used—American Sign Language (Ameslan) vs artificial languages (geometrical symbols or lexigrams)—are described. The current level of conflict is traced to H. Terrace's 1979 study that reported results of an attempt to teach Ameslan to a young chimpanzee, Nim Chimpsky; the views of the study's supporters and debunkers on many disputed points are reported. Although the conflict has now led some people to question the value of any ape-language studies, the chimpanzee work has led to the development of methods for teaching severely retarded humans. (6 ref)
Marx, Jean L.   Science, 1980(Mar), Vol 207(4437), 1330–1333. [PA, Vol 65:07182]

1804.   The relation between choosing and working prevocational tasks in two severely retarded young adults.
Investigated the relation between prevocational preference, as measured by client's selection of a task object, and the work that followed that choice. After selecting a task object, 2 severely retarded Ss, aged 19 and 20 yrs, worked a task previously assessed to be more or less preferred than the one indicated by the object. Results indicate that when the selection represented a task that was less preferred than the one actually worked, choices for that object increased on subsequent trials. Conversely, when the selection represented a task that was more preferred than the task S actually worked, choices for the object decreased on subsequent trials. The work that followed object choices reinforced or punished subsequent selections. Findings indicate that Ss' object choices were valid indicators of their preference for working different tasks. They were also consistent with D. Premack's (1959, 1971) principle that one class of responses may reinforce or punish a different class of responses for the same individual. (6 ref)
Mithaug, Dennis E. & Mar, Deanna K. (U Colorado, Colorado Springs) Journal of Applied Behavior Analysis, 1980(Spr), Vol 13(1), 177–182. [PA, Vol 65:08212]

1805.   Measurement error in direct observations: A comparison of common recording methods.
Analyzed videotapes of 3 brief, 3 medium, and 3 long duration types of stereotyped behavior of 8 severely retarded children to provide a criterion record of the true percentage duration of the behavior. As predicted, the whole-interval method grossly underestimated and the partial-interval methods grossly overestimated the true percentage duration of the behavior, except when the duration of individual responses was much longer than the observation interval. Momentary time-sampling was not an errorless method but was superior to the others. Implications for the detection of treatment effects by direct observations are discussed. (9 ref)
Murphy, Glynis & Goodall, Elizabeth. (U London Inst of Psychiatry, England) Behaviour Research & Therapy, 1980, Vol 18(2), 147–150. [PA, Vol 65:09151]

1806.   Dominance, agonistic and territorial behaviour in institutionalized mentally retarded patients.
Obtained an interactional dominance hierarchy in a group of 20 severely to profoundly retarded females (CA 16–50 yrs; IQs less than 36) by observing the frequency of patient contacts, the duration of contact, and the frequency of contact initiation. A hierarchy based on the initiation and reception of agonistic behavior was also obtained. The interactional dominance hierarchy was positively related to the agonistic hierarchy and to S clinical behavior condition. 17 Ss displayed territorial behavior. The more dominant had the larger territories and those in adjoining positions in the dominance hierarchy had distant territories. (17 ref)
Paslawskyj, Lesia & Ivinskis, A. (U Newcastle, Australia) Australian Journal of Developmental Disabilities, 1980(Mar), Vol 6(1), 17–24. [PA, Vol 66:08262]

1807. **[Communicating with Stevie: Report by a mother.]** (Germ)
Describes the system developed by a mother to communicate with her blind, spastic, and severely retarded son
R. B. Acta Paedopsychiatrica, 1980(Jan), Vol 45(4), 225–229. [PA, Vol 65:10531]

1808. **Mental retardation and unilateral anophthalmia in hemifacial microsomia.**
A 3-yr-old boy with left anophthalmia and hemifacial microsomia was found to be not severely retarded. Previous reports have emphasized concomitant severe mental retardation in patients with this malformation complex. Review of the literature and the present case indicate that mental retardation is a variable feature of this condition. (8 ref)
Starzak, Robert J. & Fujimoto, Atsuko. (Los Angeles County-U Southern California Medical Ctr) American Journal of Mental Deficiency, 1980(Nov), Vol 85(3), 315–317. [PA, Vol 65:03361]

1809. **A note on developmental trends in the symbolic play of hospitalized profoundly retarded children.**
Administered M. Lowe's (1975) Symbolic Play Test to 34 profoundly retarded hospitalized children (CA 7.3–18.6 yrs; Vineland social age below 3.5 yrs). A pattern of behavior similar to that of normal young children was seen in symbolic play, supporting the view that such changes are developmental rather than determined by experience. The need for research into the systematic variation of the scale of Symbolic Play Test items is stressed. The relationship between the emergence of doll-related play and 2-word utterances is discussed in the context of Piagetian theory. (37 ref)
Whittaker, Christopher A. (Newcastle upon Tyne Polytechnic, England) Journal of Child Psychology & Psychiatry & Allied Disciplines, 1980(Jul), Vol 21(3), 253–261. [PA, Vol 64:12758]

1810. **A strategy for research on the use of nonvocal systems of communication.**
Discusses problems with current research on the use of nonvocal communication systems with special reference to the severely and profoundly mentally retarded. A research strategy, designed to provide a method whereby critical practical and theoretical issues can be isolated, is described and illustrated with examples from ongoing research. (32 ref)
Kiernan, Chris. (U London, Inst of Education, England) Journal of Autism & Developmental Disorders, 1981(Mar), Vol 11(1), 139–151. [PA, Vol 66:06198]

1811. **Ultradian rhythms in stereotyped and self-injurious behavior.**
Five institutionalized profoundly mentally retarded persons (CAs 13–21 yrs) who exhibited stereotyped motor movements, including self-injurious behavior, were observed continuously in their typical environments for 8–14 hrs on each of several days. In addition to targeting stereotyped responses, the authors collected data pertaining to activities, settings, other behavioral states and social interactions. Spectral and cross-spectral analyses were conducted on data from each daily session. Power spectra indicated a marked ultradian or less than 24-hr rhythm for each S on each day. Spectral density estimates are thought to reflect the influence of rhythmic changes in the institutional environment and, to a lesser degree, the influence of an endogenous rest–activity rhythm. (24 ref)
Lewis, Mark H.; MacLean, William E.; Johnson, Willard L. & Baumeister, Alfred A. (U North Carolina, Biological Sciences Research Ctr, Chapel Hill) American Journal of Mental Deficiency, 1981(May), Vol 85(6), 601–610. [PA, Vol 66:06078]

1812. **Sensorimotor functioning and prelinguistic communication of severely and profoundly retarded individuals.**
Examined the prelinguistic, nonverbal communicative behavior of 40 institutionalized severely and profoundly retarded Ss (mean age 13 yrs) functioning at various stages of Piaget's sensorimotor period. Five scales of I. Uzgiris and J. McV. Hunt's (1975) sensorimotor assessment were used to determine general level of sensorimotor functioning. A standard set of communication elicitation tasks was employed to examine the gestures used to communicate in both imperative and declarative contexts. More competent sensorimotor performance was associated with higher frequency of more sophisticated and symbolic forms of gestural communication, and Ss generally used more complex gestures to communicate in the imperative than in the declarative tasks. Applicability of the results to the design of language-intervention programs and their implications for general theory concerning the relations between language and cognition and between normal and atypical development are discussed. (14 ref)
Lobato, Debra; Barrera, Ricardo D. & Feldman, Robert S. (U Vermont, Burlington) American Journal of Mental Deficiency, 1981(Mar), Vol 85(5), 489–496. [PA, Vol 65:13044]

1813. **Quality of learning of severely retarded adolescents.**
Employed a modified discrimination-reversal task to assess the quality of learning of 7 severely retarded adolescents (mean MA 2.4 yrs; mean CA 17.7 yrs). Ss initially were trained to criterion on a series of multidimensional object-discrimination problems. Subsequent to 1 reversal trial on each problem, 1 of 3 postreversal conditions was introduced: (a) a standard discrimination-reversal condition, (b) a condition that substituted a novel stimulus for the 1st object, or (c) a condition that replaced the 2nd object with a novel stimulus. Ss' performance on the modified discrimination-reversal task was at the same level for all 3 conditions. In comparison to earlier findings with nonhuman primates, results are interpreted as indicative of mediational learning processes. (23 ref)
Meador, Darlene M. & Rumbaugh, Duane M. (Georgia State U, Atlanta) American Journal of Mental Deficiency, 1981(Jan), Vol 85(4), 404–409. [PA, Vol 65:08211]

1814. **Stability of two Piagetian scales with severely and profoundly retarded children.**
Administered the Scales for Object Permanence and Spatial Relationships to 98 severely and profoundly retarded Ss (mean CA, 13.3 yrs). Correlations between the scores on 3 administrations were .76–.87, and the mean change was less than 1 point on each of the scales. Findings demonstrate the high stability of the scales when environmental conditions are themselves highly stable. (4 ref)
Silverstein, A. B.; Brownlee, Linda; Hubbell, Mimi & McLain, Richard E. (Neuropsychiatric Inst-Pacific State Hosp Research Group, Pomona, CA) Educational & Psychological Measurement, 1981(Sum), Vol 41(2), 263–265. [PA, Vol 66:07099]

1815. **Interrater reliability of the TARC Assessment System.**
11 profoundly retarded residents of an institution for the mentally retarded were rated on the TARC Assessment Inventory for Severely Handicapped Children by 3 independent observers. A correlational analysis and a point-by-point agreement analysis were conducted to determine the extent of observer agreement (interrater reliability). Results indicate low levels of agreement on several sections of the scale. Implications for assessing the profoundly retarded are discussed. (10 ref)
Westling, David L.; Koorland, Mark A. & Tait, Pearl E. (Florida State U, Tallahassee) Education & Training of the Mentally Retarded, 1981(Feb), Vol 16(1), 31–36. [PA, Vol 66:09132]

Treatment & Rehabilitation

Autism

1816. **A group treatment approach to multiple problem behaviors of autistic children.**
Describes a group behavior therapy approach involving social-environment programing with a professional supervisor, but a nonprofessional staff. 4 autistic children were observed individually and in a group to determine their gross behavioral deficits in various response classes. A range of response constituents was identified and techniques to stimulate and reinforce those responses were developed. The severely psychotic Ss with

extreme deficit and surplus behavior were significantly improved in the 3½-yr program of behavior modification.
Graziano, Anthony M. (State U. New York, Buffalo) Exceptional Children, 1970(Sum), Vol. 36(10), 765-770. [PA, Vol 46:05243]

1817. Treatment effects of a total behavior modification program with five autistic children.
Studied 5 autistic children to devise effective treatment procedures with the goal of eventual return to their homes. An experimental-clinical approach was used to design behavior modification programs specifically for each S. All Ss made varying degrees of progress, but their learning deficits continued to interfere with learning all new responses, necessitating continuation of a structured home or institutional existence to maintain the treatment gains. Retardation remained a characteristic of all Ss, retrieval of previously decelerated referral behaviors was problematic at date of discharge, and response acquisition did not appreciable facilitate learning of more complex behavior on the same response hierarchy.
Browning, Robert M. (Wisconsin Children's Treatment Center, Madison) Behaviour Research & Therapy, 1971(Nov), Vol. 9(4), 319-327. [PA, Vol 48:03396]

1818. [Operant conditioning techniques with autistic children.] (Swed)
Mentions good results reported from "operating-technique" therapy used in grave psychotic cases where patients must be treated without their consent because the symptoms are destructive toward the patient or others. The treatment of 3 preschool children diagnosed as autistic is reported. Therapy was focused directly on the symptoms, particularly the linguistic disturbances which are characteristic of autism. Results corroborate the theory of other researchers that improved language functions will reduce or eliminate other types of nonfunctional behavior.
Carlsson, Bengt. (Mjörnhemmet, Göteborg, Sweden) Nordisk Psykologi, 1971, Vol. 23(2), 200-210. [PA, Vol 48:09463]

1819. Initial interventions in psychotherapeutic treatment of autistic children.
Discusses psychoanalytically oriented therapy with autistic children using clinical case material. The main focus is on the principles and actual techniques of the initiation of treatment as the therapist-child relationship is seen as the necessary step in achieving a reversal of the autistic process. An object relations model of development is used to assess the child's functioning, as the information is obtained through detailed anamnesis and group observations. Sensitivity in reading cues in the child's behavior and responding to them in a flexible manner is stressed. Sharing affect responses and discharge behaviors seems to have been particularly effective. The results have shown modest gains in the object relations development of these seriously disturbed children.
Holter, F. Robert & Ruttenberg, Bertram A. (Developmental Center for Autistic Children, Philadelphia, Pa.) Journal of Autism & Childhood Schizophrenia, 1971(Apr), Vol. 1(2), 206-214. [PA, Vol 47:05291]

1820. [Speech treatment by means of behavior therapy of mute autistic children.] (Germ)
2 boys with infantile autism, with no obvious organic etiology in the older but with cerebral damage in the younger, possibly subsequent to a vaccination encephalitis, were treated by operant conditioning during 5 21-day periods. Strengthened capacity for imitation, then simple sounds, to the stage of echolalia, words, and sentences of 2 or 3 appropriate words, proceeded in series. Reinforcers were fruit juice, chocolate, and verbal appraisal. At the end of treatment vocabulary had grown to 41 and 25, respectively, intelligently used words.
Kehrer, H. E. & Körber, H. P. (U. Münster, Child & Juvenile Psychiatric Neuroclinic, W. Germany) Acta Paedopsychiatrica, 1971(Jan), Vol. 38(1), 2-17. [PA, Vol 47:07279]

1821. The physical environment of the mentally handicapped: IV. A playroom for autistic children, and its companion therapy project: A synthesis of ideas from ethology, psychology, nursing and design.
Richer, John M. & Nicoll, Stephen. (Smith Hosp., Henley-on-Thames, England) British Journal of Mental Subnormality, 1971(Dec), Vol. 17(33, Pt. 2), 132-143. [PA, Vol 48:03405]

1822. Effects of L-dopa in autism.
Attempted to determine if the administration of L-dopa to autistic children would lower blood serotonin concentrations, and, if it did, would the lowering be associated with behavioral changes. High levels of blood serotonin concentrations had been reported to be associated with autism. Ss were 4 3-13 yr old boys all possessing perceptual and motor abnormalities associated with autism. 3 other autistic children and 1 normal adult served as controls. Base-line measures were obtained on blood measures, urine, repetitive hand movements, and EEG recordings. While the drug had no basic effect on behavior, it did significantly lower blood serotonin concentrations in 3 of the 4 Ss and tended to increase platelet counts although significantly in only 1 case. The absolute concentration levels were still high when compared with normals. The potential physiological mechanisms are discussed. (25 ref.)
Ritvo, Edward R., et al. (U. California, Center for Health Sciences, Neuropsychiatric Inst., Los Angeles) Journal of Autism & Childhood Schizophrenia, 1971(Apr), Vol. 1(2), 190-205. [PA, Vol 47:05340]

1823. Effect of treatment structure on development in autistic children.
Because of the wide variation of structures used in the treatment of autistic children, a study was designed in which structure was changed from relative structure to relative unstructure over 2 repeated cycles of 2 wk. each. Both children and therapists were rated on their reactions. Ss were 4 boys and 1 girl, 4-8 yrs old, with a mean Social Quotient of 61 on the Vineland Social Maturity Scale. Findings indicate that Ss tend to react more favorably to structure than to unstructure. Individual differences show that Ss on a higher developmental level are better able to utilize relative unstructure than those functioning on a lower developmental level.
Schopler, Eric; Brehm, Sharon S.; Kinsbourne, Marcel & Reichler, Robert J. (U. North Carolina, Memorial Hosp., Child Research Project) Archives of General Psychiatry, 1971(May), Vol. 24(5), 415-421. [PA, Vol 47:09387]

1824. Lithium and chlorpromazine: A controlled crossover study of hyperactive severely disturbed young children.
Conducted a controlled crossover study of lithium and chlorpromazine involving 10 3-6 yr. old severely disturbed children, of whom 6 were schizophrenic and 1 autistic. Ss were matched for motor activity (hyper- and hypoactive) and prognosis. More symptoms diminished on chlorpromazine than on lithium. However, improvements were only slight on both, except in 1 S whose autoaggressiveness and explosiveness practically ceased on lithium (nonblind evaluations). Blind ratings indicated no statistically significant difference between the 2 drugs as well as absence of statistically significant change from base line to treatment with either. Lithium diminished the severity of individual symptoms, though not statistically significant, such as explosiveness, hyperactivity, aggressiveness, and psychotic speech. Its effect in adult schizophrenia is compared to responses of schizophrenic children. The relationship of EEG to clinical improvement and toxicity, and effect of lithium on hyperactivity and aggressiveness are discussed. It is suggested that lithium may prove of some value in treatment of severe psychiatric disorders in childhood involving aggressiveness, explosive affect, and hyperactivity. (54 ref.)
Campbell, Magda, et al. (New York U., Medical Center) Journal of Autism & Childhood Schizophrenia, 1972(Jul), Vol. 2(3), 234-263. [PA, Vol 50:07210]

1825. Reflections on communication and autistic children.
Discusses the significance of the commonly accepted fact that a major defect of autistic children is their inability to communicate. It is noted that noncommunication and resulting misinterpretation can occur when an autistic child fails to comprehend because he lacks understanding of the interrelations of language. It is suggested that study of the nature of human communication and how it gets established in each individual may provide a key to treatment of autism.
Creak, Mildred. Journal of Autism & Childhood Schizophrenia, 1972(Jan), Vol. 2(1), 1-8. [PA, Vol 50:11458]

1826. The elimination of self-stimulatory behavior of autistic and retarded children by overcorrection.
No effective method is in general usage for eliminating the self-stimulation of retardates and autistics. An overcorrection rationale was used to develop such a method. The overcorrection procedures emphasized either correction of the environmental effect resulting from the self-stimulation or a contingent period of practice in the correct mode of the behavior. The procedures were applied to autistic and retarded children who exhibited high rates of self-stimulation. The overcorrection procedures eliminated all the Ss' self-stimulation and were more effective than several alternative inhibitory procedures. Overcorrection procedures are rapid, enduring, and effective methods of eliminating self-stimulation.
Foxx, R. M. & Azrin, N. H. (Anna State Hosp., Ill.) Proceedings of the 80th Annual Convention of the American Psychological Association, 1972, Vol. 7(Pt. 2), 761-762. [PA, Vol 48:05125]

1827. [Social and educational problems during development of autistic children: III. An autistic child seen by us 16 years ago.] (Japn)
Reports excerpts from developmental history and interview records of a boy studied from the ages of 5 to 20 yrs. Based on a review of the treatment process of long-term cases hospitalized for 8-16 yrs, the following basic directions for treating autistic children were proposed: (a) preoccupation with the fixed concept of autism should be avoided; (b) facilitation of the child's development should be the 1st priority; (c) therapists, school, and family should always cooperate in the child-centered treatment; and (d) diagnosis should be made for the client's sake.
Goto, T. Japanese Journal of Child Psychiatry, 1972(Jul), Vol. 13(4), 226-230. [PA, Vol 52:05550]

1828. [Behavior therapy with mentally handicapped children: Basic concepts, results and problems of behavior therapy with retarded, autistic and schizophrenic children.] (Germ)
Discusses the principles of operant conditioning methods and procedures applied in the treatment of mentally retarded, autistic, and schizophrenic children and reviews the literature on the theoretical concepts, research programs, and results of behavior modification methods. The procedures used to develop socialization, language and self-help skills, and to eliminate disruptive, hostile, self-stimulating behavior, self-injurious tendencies, social withdrawal, echolalia, and other behavioral disturbed patterns are discussed. The techniques of prompting, fading, shaping, and timeout, and reinforcement, etc. also are described. Recent attempts to carry out behavioral modification in a natural milieu, mainly in the school and the home, with parents and teachers in a therapeutic role, are evaluated. (English summary) (8 p ref)
Gottwald, Peter & Redlin, Wiltraud. (Max Planck Inst. for Psychiatry, Munich, W. Germany) Zeitschrift für Klinische Psychologie. Forschung und Praxis, 1972, Vol. 2(1), 93-149. [PA, Vol 51:07691]

1829. Use of behavior modification techniques to institute verbal behavior in autistic children.
Green, John E. (Texas A&M U.) Catalog of Selected Documents in Psychology, 1972(Spr), Vol. 2, 69-70. [PA, Vol 49:07470]

1830. The patient, the mother, the therapist: An interactional triangle in the treatment of the autistic child.
Discusses the psychotherapy process of an autistic child from 3½-6 yr. old. Based on the developmental history, and the clinical observations during psychotherapy, an attempt is made to present the patterns of communication and interaction as they developed from the original mother-child interaction through the development and changes in the child-therapist communication patterns. These changes were paralleled by changes in the mother-child interaction and in the mother-therapist interaction. The early unpredictable system of mother-child communication consisted of a mixture of aggression and rejection appearing at random. Through the initiation of psychotherapy, this reverberating pathological interaction changed to an interactional triangle between child-therapist, mother-child, and mother-therapist. Presently the child uses meaningful nonverbal communication, but does not use vocalization to convey messages. The therapy is continuing. The term of "jargon communication" is proposed to define the global expressive disorder in autism. The distorted language (or the lack of it) and other pathological motor manifestations, representing a nonverbal gestural jargon, lead to the "jargon communication." (38 ref.)
Jakab, Irene. (Harvard Medical School, Boston, Mass.) Journal of Communication Disorders, 1972(Jul), Vol. 5(2), 154-182. [PA, Vol 49:02901]

1831. The relationship of self-stimulation to learning in autistic children.
Conducted 3 experiments to study the acquisition of discriminative behavior in 1 5-yr-old and 2 7-yr-old autistic children with high-frequency self-stimulatory behavior. It was found that (a) Ss did not acquire the discrimination while engaged in self-stimulation; (b) suppression of self-stimulation produced an increase in correct responding, with eventual acquisition of the discrimination; and (c) successful discrimination learning was always associated with a reduction in self-stimulatory behavior, even when aversive stimuli were not used for suppression.
Koegel, Robert L. & Covert, Andrea. (U. California, Santa Barbara) Journal of Applied Behavior Analysis, 1972(Win), Vol. 5(4), 381-387. [PA, Vol 49:11422]

1832. The role of shared mastery in therapy with autistic and schizophrenic children.
Discusses the contention that the initial strategic goal of therapy, after establishing favorable contact, will be to initiate and foster some degree of competence so that the child desires further communication with the world. Psychological encounters are aimed at giving the child a sense of mastery, presented in a stratagem of graded levels. This is regarded as a dual task for the therapist: (a) providing a measure of self-esteem in that the child sees that his actions create a favorable effect upon the world, and (b) guiding this rewarding modification so that the child sees that object relations are pleasurable. Excerpts from several psychotherapy sessions with an echolalic autistic boy are included to show that therapist intrusion, without the structure of redirection, can stimulate regression, while the inclusion of a past area of mastery may provide impetus for a greater range of adaptive behavior. Masterful sharing is suggested to enhance the child's ego functioning and rhythm of the therapeutic relationship. (17 ref.)
Needleman, Murray & Ward, Alan J. (Eastern State School & Hosp., Autistic Children's Unit, Trevose, Pa.) Psychotherapy: Theory, Research & Practice, 1972(Spr), Vol. 9(1), 51-53. [PA, Vol 50:05468]

1833. [Pharmacological treatment for handicapped children: I. Handicapped children and drugs.] (Japn)
Replies to a parent of an autistic child who criticized Japanese physicians for selling ineffective drugs and the medical system for permitting such a treatment. It is argued that the income from selling drugs to patients is the largest financial resource for medical service agencies, and that measurement of effectiveness of medication is complex and difficult. Most physicians are little aware of the philosophy in treating severely handicapped children who possess virtually no possibilities of becoming productive citizens. Prescription of anticonvulsion drugs can be made adequately only through close observation and regular laboratory testing of hospitalized patients. There are no clearly defined norms for abnormal behavior for which behavior drugs

are prescribed, and chemotherapy remains auxiliary in treating handicapped children. It is concluded that drugs should be administered as little as possible.
Ozawa, I. Japanese Journal of Child Psychiatry, 1972(Jul), Vol. 13(4), 231-235. [PA, Vol 52:05939]

1834. A psychodynamic model of the mother of the autistic child.
Reports a study of mothers of 25 autistic children showing they were the victims of psychic over-determination. It is suggested that the treatment of the mother should parallel the treatment of the child. Just as the child needs to develop, so the mother needs to build her own identity, her knowledge of herself, her capacities, and her abilities. Insight is a distant goal, and for most mothers it may be neither obtainable nor desirable. Improvements in self-esteem, self-observation, and in relationships with others, including the atypical child, are suggested as feasible goals.
Roth, Edna F. Smith College Studies in Social Work, 1972(Jun), Vol. 42(3), 175-202. [PA, Vol 49:04833]

1835. Stimulus factors in the training of prepositional usage in three autistic children.
Trained 3-, 5-, and 7-yr-old language deficient, autistic children to use the prepositions "in" and "on." Ss were exposed to conditions of training that differed in the method of employment of stimulus objects used to train prepositional usage. 2 Ss were trained 1st with ambiguous stimuli, i.e., the same stimulus objects were used for training both prepositions. The 2 Ss were then switched to a training condition with nonambiguous stimulus objects, i.e., objects used for training "in" were different than those used for training "on." The 2 Ss were then switched to the ambiguous stimulus condition and finally returned again to training with nonambiguous stimuli (4 conditions). A 3rd S began with training on nonambiguous stimuli, was switched to an ambiguous condition, and was then switched back to nonambiguous stimuli (3 conditions). Results for 2 of the 3 Ss indicate that accurate usage of the 2 prepositions was obtained only under training conditions with nonambiguous stimuli. Results for the 3rd S suggest that initial training with nonambiguous stimuli might enhance subsequent accurate responding with ambiguous stimuli.
Sailor, Wayne & Taman, Trudie. (Kansas Neurological Inst., Topeka) Journal of Applied Behavior Analysis, 1972(Sum), Vol. 5(2), 183-190. [PA, Vol 49:02733]

1836. An experimental study of rage-reduction treatment of autistic children.
Tested a new treatment method for autism on each of 2 matched samples of 15 3½-13 yr. old autistic children. Single rage-reduction sessions were compared with comparable periods of therapist contact. Significant positive changes in 17 of the 18 behaviors studied (e.g., behaviors approach to therapist or eye contact) were found only for the rage-reduction group. (15 ref.)
Saposnek, Donald T. (Children's Psychiatric Center, Eatontown, N.J.) Child Psychiatry & Human Development, 1972(Fal), Vol. 3(1), 50-62. [PA, Vol 50:07518]

1837. [Social and educational problems during development of autistic children: I. A case report on an autistic child observed for nine years in residential setting.] (Japn)
The case record of a boy observed between the ages of 10 and 18 yrs reveals the following possible basic traits of the autistic syndrome: difficulties in understanding perceived content as a meaningful whole and in relation to himself; deficit of reading comprehension of words and sentences; response delay; fluctuation of levels of functioning; and changes in stimulus threshold.
Sogame, Shiro & Okunomiya, Yusei. (Mie Prefectural Takachaya Hosp., Japan) Japanese Journal of Child Psychiatry, 1972(Jul), Vol. 13(4), 213-221. [PA, Vol 52:05607]

1838. Language training for the autistic child using operant conditioning procedures.
Describes the nature of behaviors encountered in autistic children. Characteristics of their speech and language behavior are delineated and some principles related to modifying deviant language are discussed. The need to observe and record responses to teaching procedures is cited. The role of consequent and antecedent events is discussed based on the findings in several clinical experimental studies. The relationship of developmental psycholinguistics and behavioral psychology as they apply to the complex problems of improving the linguistic performance of nonverbal autistic children is emphasized. (21 ref.)
Stark, Joel. (Queens Coll., City U. New York) Journal of Communication Disorders, 1972(Jul), Vol. 5(2), 183-194. [PA, Vol 49:03037]

1839. The use of structural therapy in the treatment of autistic children.
Discusses concepts of body ego and behavioral ego and their relation to the etiology of autism. It is proposed that children with the syndrome of early infantile autism are completely lacking in the development of any body ego and that this allows for a deviant type of ego development. Autistic children are believed to have suffered from a deficit of novelty, variation, and patterned stimulation in their early development which can be traced to 3 sources: (a) an organic problem at birth which results in an abnormally high stimulus barrier, (b) hypersensitivity due to some organic problem, or (c) an unstimulating nonnurturent home environment. A set of treatment guidelines is outlined, all phases involving a gradual increase in the level of physical, verbal, olfactory, kinesthetic, and affective stimulation given to the child. The 1st task of breaking down the functioning of the behavioral ego is followed by efforts to stimulate the body ego. (35 ref.)
Ward, Alan J. (Eastern State School & Hosp., Trevose, Pa.) Psychotherapy: Theory, Research & Practice, 1972(Spr), Vol. 9(1), 46-50. [PA, Vol 50:05592]

1840. The rationale for computer-based treatment of language difficulties in nonspeaking autistic children.
Describes principles involved in a computer-based treatment method for language difficulties in 17 nonspeaking autistic children. Ss were assumed to be dissymbolic with a primary difficulty in processing any type of symbols, language being the most important symbolic system used in human communication. The main treatment principle involved the encouragement of exploratory play with a keyboard-controlled audiovisual display on which symbols were made to appear accompanied by human voice and other sounds. Adult interference was minimized so that an S could self-select and self-direct his own play. 13 Ss showed linguistic improvement. The 4 cases of failure to improve were Ss who refused to play with the display device.
Colby, Kenneth M. (Stanford U., Artificial Intelligence Lab.) Journal of Autism & Childhood Schizophrenia, 1973(Jul), Vol. 3(3), 254-260. [PA, Vol 51:07556]

1841. Teaching and generalization of instruction-following in an "autistic" child.
Used operant reinforcement procedures designed to increase instruction-following in a 4-yr-old boy diagnosed as "autistic." The procedures succeeded dramatically, and the behavior generalized across people and novel instructions and persisted when the primary treatment intervention was withdrawn.
Craighead, W. Edward; O'Leary, K. Daniel & Allen, Jon S. (Pennsylvania State U.) Journal of Behavior Therapy & Experimental Psychiatry, 1973(Jun), Vol. 4(2), 171-176. [PA, Vol 51:03684]

1842. Successful treatment of childhood autism.
Treated an autistic 5½-yr-old child successfully by the operant conditioning technique. S had a baseline of zero in speaking relevant words and in appropriate behavior (e.g., following directions). Spontaneous relevant verbalization and appropriate behavior were reinforced by primary and conditioned reinforcers. The method of successive approximation was used to shape more complex skills (e.g., spelling and writing). At the conclusion of the program, S's speech approached relevance 95% of the time and he also learned many of the skills expected of a 5½-yr-old child.

Ferinden, William E. & Cooper, Judith M. (Linden Schools, N.J.) Language, Speech, & Hearing Services in Schools, 1973(Jul), Vol. 4(3), 127-131. [PA, Vol 51:07273]

1843.   The parent as a therapist.
Suggests that courses designed to train parents to be auxiliary therapists for their children be incorporated into community health programs. Such a service would provide long-term contact utilizing short training sessions and periodic refresher courses. A case history involving a 9-yr-old autistic child is outlined.
Fodor, Iris E. (New York U.) MH, 1973(Spr), Vol. 57(2), 16-19. [PA, Vol 52:10685]

1844.   The elimination of autistic self-stimulatory behavior by overcorrection.
Used overcorrection procedures, consisting of a period of practice in the correct mode of the behavior contingent upon self-stimulatory behavior, in a behavioral day-care program. 3 retarded children and 1 autistic child who exhibited object-mouthing, hand-mouthing, head-weaving and hand-clapping were treated. For some behaviors, comparisons were made between the overcorrection procedure and several alternative procedures, such as physical punishment by a slap, reinforcement for non-self-stimulatory behavior, a distasteful solution painted on the hand of a hand-mouther, and free reinforcement. The overcorrection procedures eliminated self-stimulatory behaviors of all 4 Ss in tutorial sessions and during the entire school day and were more effective than the alternative procedures in eliminating self-stimulation. Overcorrection procedures appear to be rapid, enduring, and effective methods of eliminating self-stimulatory behavior. (24 ref.)
Foxx, R. M. & Azrin, N. H. (Anna State Hosp., Behavior Research Lab., Ill.) Journal of Applied Behavior Analysis, 1973(Spr), Vol. 6(1), 1-14. [PA, Vol 50:09470]

1845.   [Therapy of autism.] (Germ)
Considers that methods of therapy with autistic children depend on etiological concepts. Recently, pragmatism has gained in importance, and the use of psychopharmacological drugs has become widespread. Psychotherapy requires special methods, and work with the mother of an autistic child is essential. Psychomotor therapy is a therapeutic advance of great importance; however, results of any kind of treatment are limited.
Haffter, C. (U. Basel, Psychiatric Clinic for Children & Adolescents, Switzerland) Acta Paedopsychiatrica, 1973, Vol. 39(8-10), 224-230. [PA, Vol 50:09501]

1846.   Embracement and enticement: A therapeutic nursery group for autistic children.
Describes the establishment and use of a therapeutic nursery group with 20 2-5 yr old autistic Ss in a residential treatment center for emotionally disturbed and psychotic children. The presence of a surrogate mother and father figure in a simulated family group was used with the hope that involvement of the Ss in such therapy would arrest further withdrawal and stimulate interaction with the environment. The group environment was chosen to provide acceptance and support, and embracement and play therapy were utilized. Emphasis was placed on ego growth and physical integration through acquisition of intellectual and motor skills. Results of the program, despite its limitations, were positive.
Harper, Juliet. (Macquarie U., School of Behavioural Sciences, North Ryde, New South Wales, Australia) Slow Learning Child, 1973(Nov), Vol. 20(3), 173-182. [PA, Vol 52:06002]

1847.   Music: A physiologic language.
Several theoretical considerations contribute to the notion that music therapy is a useful adjunct to psychotherapy, particularly in the treatment of schizophrenia and autism. The advantage of music in therapy is that music can communicate at the more primitive, physiologic level of rhythm, and develop a rapport that may not be attainable with conventional language. Music, becoming more complex as it incorporates melody and harmony, aids the psyche in becoming more complex. Going from simple rhythms to complex music is a progression rather than a regression. In the case of the schizophrenic, the trend toward

complexity will necessitate a reintegration of the ego if the music is to be followed. With the autistic child, the music in its alien complex form may aid in the development of ego boundaries (i.e., self and not-self). Music thus is potentially capable of bridging the gap between the language of physiology and the language of consciousness.
Hudson, Wayne C. (U. Zurich, Switzerland) Journal of Music Therapy, 1973(Fal), Vol. 10(3), 137-140. [PA, Vol 51:11553]

1848.   Scaling the fortress walls: Some ways of working with autistic children.
Lists approaches to severely autistic children under the categories of body image, relationships, materials, and words and feelings. The theoretical approach might be called psychodynamic but eclectic, characterized by relationship therapy. Issues discussed concern the values of (a) stress vs. protectiveness in a child's environment, (b) entering into his fantasies and feelings vs. making reality demands and limitations on him, and (c) reinforcing positive behavior through rewards or relationships.
Jerome, Alice. (Step School, Chicago, Ill.) Acta Paedopsychiatrica, 1973, Vol. 39(8-10), 263-270. [PA, Vol 50:09535]

1849.   [Behaviour therapy of contact disturbances in autismus infantum.] (Germ)
Systematically treated 2 7-yr-old autistic boys by means of behavior therapy during 65 sessions in 4 wks, using operant conditioning with a slot-machine. In the latter part of the program, learning through imitation was reinforced by conditions of competition. Results were reported as excellent in 1 case, moderately good in the other. (18 ref.)
Kehrer, H. E. & Budde, R. (U. Munster, Neuroclinic for Children & Adolescents, W. Germany) Acta Paedopsychiatrica, 1973, Vol. 39(8-10), 253-263. [PA, Vol 50:09539]

1850.   [Countertransference as the deciding factor in establishing communication with a 3-4 yr old girl.] (Port)
Records the unusual case of a World War II orphan abandoned in Berlin in 1945. The child, an autistic mute whose estimated age was 3-4 yrs, received psychotherapy utilizing maternal countertransference. A traumatic incident triggering uninhibited maternal emotions from the therapist brought about a breakthrough in verbal communication. Therapy terminated 10 mo later (total duration 16 mo) with typical age-level behavior. (English summary) (23 ref)
Kemper, Kattrin A. Estudos de Psicanalise, 1973, No 6, 21-32. [PA, Vol 53:01619]

1851.   Some generalization and follow-up measures on autistic children in behavior therapy.
Details the treatment of 20 autistic children. At intake, most of the Ss were severely disturbed, having symptoms indicating an extremely poor prognosis. They were treated in separate groups, and some were treated more than once, allowing for within- and between-S replications of treatment effects. Reliable measures of generalization were employed across situations and behaviors as well as across time (follow-up). Findings can be summarized as follows: (a) Inappropriate behaviors (self-stimulation and echolalia) decreased during treatment, and appropriate behaviors (appropriate speech, appropriate play, and social nonverbal behaviors) increased. (b) Spontaneous social interactions and the spontaneous use of language occurred about 8 mo. into treatment for some of the Ss. (c) IQs and social quotients reflected improvement during treatment. (d) There were no exceptions to the improvement; however, some of the Ss improved more than others. (e) Follow-up measures recorded 1-4 yr. after treatment showed that large differences between groups of Ss depended upon the posttreatment environment (those groups whose parents were trained to carry out behavior therapy continued to improve, while Ss who were institutionalized regressed). (f) A brief reinstatement of behavior therapy could temporarily reestablish some of the original therapeutic gains made by the Ss who were subsequently institutionalized. (33 ref.)
Lovaas, O. Ivar; Koegel, Robert; Simmons, James Q. & Long, Judith S. (U. California, Los Angeles) Journal of Applied

Behavior Analysis, 1973(Spr), Vol. 6(1), 131-166. [PA, Vol 50:09578]

1852. Music therapy in the treatment of an autistic child.
Because of comments in the literature that autistic children show uncommon interest in music, the staff of a children's unit recommended daily music therapy sessions for a 7-yr-old autistic boy in residential treatment. The clinical procedures used in his music therapy are described, and subjective evidence of the effectiveness of these procedures is presented. Although the effectiveness of music therapy in the treatment of autism cannot be fully known at this point, it appears that some positive attributes can be noted.
Mahlberg, Mavis. (Larned State Hosp., Kan.) Journal of Music Therapy, 1973(Win), Vol. 10(4), 189-193. [PA, Vol 52:03582]

1853. An objective evaluation technique for autistic children: An introduction of CLAC scheme.
Describes a series of brief questionnaires devised under the name of the Check List for Autistic Children. The results of evaluation on rating scales were transcribed on radiant psychograms. The size and shape of polygons resulting from the linking of the rating points illustrate quantitative progress and areas of better and worse improvement. The scheme is a by-product of experience with operant conditioning techniques in treating autistic children and is neither final nor perfected.
Makita, K. & Umezu, K. (Keio U., School of Medicine, Tokyo, Japan) Acta Paedopsychiatrica, 1973, Vol. 39(8-10), 237-253. [PA, Vol 50:09582]

1854. Cognitive-developmental training with elevated boards and sign language.
Presented cognitive-developmental training involving use of connected boards elevated 3-6 ft above the ground, together with special language signs, to 19 mute autistic children (median CA = 11 yrs). 13 Ss were in residential treatment and 6 attended day school. Signs were systematically paired with appropriate spoken words which all Ss learned to understand. Also, all Ss learned to initiate signs to achieve desired objects or goals. The day school Ss, who were considerably younger than residential Ss, achieved significantly greater expressive use of signs and words. The case histories of 2 Ss who made the transition from signs to expressive spoken language are summarized. The training program is discussed in detail. (22 ref)
Miller, Arnold & Miller, Eileen E. (Language & Cognitive Development Center, Boston, Mass.) Journal of Autism & Childhood Schizophrenia, 1973(Jan), Vol. 3(1), 65-85. [PA, Vol 51:09306]

1855. Social punishment in the modification of a preschool child's "autistic-like" behavior with a mother as therapist.
Systematically cued the mother of a 3-yr-old girl who showed autistic-like behavior to approve and disapprove of her child's behavior using a wireless microphone. After baselines were taken on 2 categories of problem behavior (pre-academic and social behavior), the social contingencies were applied successively to each category. The pre-academic task was quickly established in the S when the mother applied these social contingencies. This result was replicated with requests for social interaction. In the final phase, cueing was withdrawn from both situations and the mother was able to maintain the S's improved behavior. An analysis of the mother's behavior suggests that her increased use of social punishment for inappropriate behavior was the key factor in the S's increasing responsiveness. Follow-up 7 mo later indicated that the improvements were maintained. (21 ref)
Moore, Benjamin L. & Bailey, Jon S. (West Virginia U., Medical School) Journal of Applied Behavior Analysis, 1973(Fal), Vol. 6(3), 497-507. [PA, Vol 51:09738]

1856. Autism: Beautiful children.
Discusses the general appearance and behavior of the autistic child and outlines the characteristics of autism that indicate a diagnosis of the disorder: (a) gross and sustained impairments in emotional relationships, (b) sustained resistance to change, (c) absent or underdeveloped speech, (d) apparent unawareness of personal identity, (e) pathological preoccupation with particular

objects, and (f) a background of retardation, with isolated phases of normal or exceptional intellectual functioning. All or some of these signs may be present in a case of autism. The question of the etiology of autism is still unanswered, although the 2 principle positions revolve around organic vs environmental deficiencies, and choice of treatment is based on the etiologic theory postulated. Operant conditioning techniques and psychotherapy have both had some success and when used together may have promise. Carefully designed behavior modification programs may be effective in rehabilitating the autistic child in language and social skills.
Mulcahy, R. F. (U Alberta, Edmonton, Canada) Mental Retardation Bulletin, 1972-73, Vol 1(3), 73-77. [PA, Vol 58:03478]

1857. [A group therapy of autistic children: The result of four year Saturday class treatment at Kyushu University Psychiatric Hospital.] (Japn)
Describes a group therapy program for autistic children conducted at a university hospital and staffed by volunteer psychologists, students, and mothers. The program involved both group and individual activities, and play therapy was stressed. Therapy sessions were held weekly; 15 2-12 yr old children were treated during the 1st yr. Problems of organizing the program, frustrations encountered by the mothers and therapists, and the importance of the therapists' attitudes and the mothers' participation are discussed. 2 successful cases are described in detail.
Murata, Toyohisa, et al. (Kyushu U. Hosp., Psychiatric Outpatient Clinic, Fukuoka, Japan) Kyushu Neuro-psychiatry, 1973(Sep), Vol. 19(2), 170-177. [PA, Vol 52:01520]

1858. Effect of contingent and non-contingent reinforcement on the behavior of an autistic child.
Briefly reviews the literature and presents an experimental study designed to determine the effects of noncontingent and contingent reinforcement of eye contact on the behavior of a 4½-yr-old autistic boy. Rate changes in 20 types of behavior comprising a variety of simple responses, contacts, vocalizations, verbalizations, or movements under the 2 reinforcement conditions and during baseline were recorded and compared. Significant changes were found in the frequency of vocalization, eye contact, and when the child placed his hands over ears. It is suggested that when many types of behavior are examined simultaneously there are some that show as marked a change during noncontingent as during contingent reinforcement. Reinforcement could be a setting stimulus changing the child's expectations and prompting many changes in behavior that might be thought to result from the reinforcement procedure. (18 ref)
Ney, Philip G. (U. British Columbia, Vancouver, Canada) Journal of Autism & Childhood Schizophrenia, 1973(Apr), Vol. 3(2), 115-127. [PA, Vol 52:03752]

1859. Naturalistic treatment of an autistic child.
Evaluated a naturalistic treatment program for a 4-yr-old autistic boy administered by the parents over a 2-yr period. Operant reinforcement techniques previously developed and tested in laboratory settings were initially assessed in a clinic and eventually in the family's home. Experimental manipulations were performed in both settings on rituals, crying and whining, compliance, nonverbal imitation, and verbal imitation. Results clearly indicate that parents can effectively treat autistic behaviors provided that they receive adequate training and supervision in operant reinforcement therapy, and provided that sufficiently potent reinforcers are available to maintain behavior. (26 ref.)
Nordquist, Vey M. & Wahler, Robert G. (U. Tennessee) Journal of Applied Behavior Analysis, 1973(Spr), Vol. 6(1), 79-87. [PA, Vol 50:09618]

1860. Some thoughts on childhood psychosis: Self and object.
Presents the case history of a psychotic 3½-yr-old girl who underwent treatment as part of a program studying the separation-individuation phase in normal and psychotic children. Her activity consisted of aimlessly wandering around the playroom and a concentrated repetitive filling and emptying of her baby bottles with dried peas and beads. Her development was aberrant in the 2nd half of the 1st yr. Although the S was exposed to

impressive therapeutic treatment and withdrew from the autistic world she had inhabited, her treatment was unsuccessful in that after 2 yrs her parents decided to institutionalize her. (18 ref) *Roiphe, Herman.* (Albert Einstein Coll. of Medicine, Yeshiva U.) Psychoanalytic Study of the Child, 1973, Vol 28, 131–145. [PA, Vol 52:05866]

1861.   The use of music in establishing communication with an autistic mentally retarded child.
Shows the effectiveness of the use of music in breaking through emotional boundaries and establishing communication with persons who have not as yet appeared to experience communication.
Saperston, Bruce. (Mental Retardation Training Centers, Austin, Tex.) Journal of Music Therapy, 1973(Win), Vol. 10(4), 184-188. [PA, Vol 52:03603]

1862.   Movement therapy with autistic children.
Discusses 4 case histories of autistic children. Ss are (a) a 6-yr-old compliant female who had mastered speech, but had no feeling connected with the tasks she performed, (b) a 4-yr-old boy who spent his time wandering aimlessly, (c) a 6-yr-old girl who played endlessly with little objects, and (d) a 5-yr-old girl who liked to hurtle across a room. Treatment included strongly rhythmic exercises and dances coupled with music and body contact and verbal and nonverbal interpretations. This interaction with the children on the part of the analyst resulted in a limited amount of progress.
Siegel, Elaine V.   Psychoanalytic Review, 1973(Spr), Vol. 60(1), 141-149. [PA, Vol 50:11868]

1863.   An inpatient treatment program and outcome for 57 autistic and schizophrenic children.
Describes the evolution and structure of a treatment program in a psychiatric hospital including a specialized sequential school and task curriculum. Therapeutic outcome is reported for 57 children treated in a specially designed unit over an 11-yr period. One-third of the children ultimately were discharged to their own homes. The rate of discharge showed a positive correlation with late onset, development of speech by age 5, and completion of bowel and bladder training at the time of admission. The 33 patients of the sample with early infantile autism tended to remain chronically hospitalized compared to cases with later onset. A profile of behavioral function is suggested as a useful prognostic indicator and method for classifying populations so that comparative treatment effectiveness in different samples can be meaningfully measured.
Treffert, Darold A.; McAndrew, John B. & Dreifuerst, Paul. (Winnebago State Hosp., Wis.) Journal of Autism & Childhood Schizophrenia, 1973(Apr), Vol. 3(2), 138-153. [PA, Vol 52:03898]

1864.   The joint treatment of an "autistic" child by clinical psychology and speech therapy.
Reports the use of structural therapy in treating a 3½-yr-old autistic girl on an outpatient basis. Focus of the treatment was on the improvement of body image and human relationships. The patient was initially nonrelating, nonverbal, hyperactive, and fearful. The therapy and its progress are described in detail. 16 mo of treatment helped her to develop warm relationships with her immediate family, to start using simple words and short phrases for communication, to become less hyperactive, and to begin establishing peer relationships. The importance of differential diagnosis in early childhood disorders, of the choice of therapeutic strategy, and the relevance of improved body image and human relationships are stressed. (15 ref)
Ward, Alan J. & Leith, Virginia M. (Eastern State School & Hosp, Trevose, PA) International Journal of Child Psychotherapy, 1973(Oct), Vol 2(4), 451-470. [PA, Vol 53:07878]

1865.   "After you hit a child, you can't just get up and leave him; you are hooked to that kid": A conversation with Ivar Lovaas about self-mutilating children and how their parents make it worse.
Presents a discussion of Lovaas's work with autistic children. It is suggested that the best approach to troubled children is to treat them like people and not like patients. Most parents inadvertently reward self-mutilating behavior by feeling that such behavior shows that the child needs love. Immediate painful punishment stops self-mutilating behavior. This empirical fact is more important than any theories about abnormal behavior.
Chance, Paul.   Psychology Today, 1974(Jan), Vol. 7(8), 76-84. [PA, Vol 52:01501]

1866.   Use of a peer model in language training in an echolalic child.
Describes the technique used with a 10-yr-old female diagnosed as autistic with chronic schizophrenic reactions. She was trained to speak in a normal voice volume and acquired a labeling vocabulary, via an imitation learning paradigm which utilized a peer model. Results indicate that the modeling paradigm facilitated both volume training and label acquisition.
Coleman, Sara L. & Stedman, James M. (San Antonio Children's Ctr, TX) Journal of Behavior Therapy & Experimental Psychiatry, 1974(Dec), Vol 5(3-4), 275-279. [PA, Vol 53:12038]

1867.   [The conditioning of evoked potentials in mental retardation.] (Fren)
Evoked potentials were conditioned in 4 groups of 7-13 yr olds: 11 normal children, 11 normals hospitalized with somatic illnesses, and 2 groups of 12 mentally retarded children with IQs of 45-65 and 20-50, respectively. The CS used was a 4-msec sound 25 db above threshold; the UCS was a 0.1 msec light 40 cm from the eyes; and the interstimulus interval was 700 msec. In the normal Ss the evoked potentials were wide and regular. An elective increase in the evoked potential to sound was noted. Generalized slow waves were very rare. Ss with lowest IQ had irregular evoked potentials of low amplitude. Conditioning led to an anticipation of a late generalized slow wave and to a response to sound alone which consisted of a group of responses usually produced only by a combined sound/light stimuli. The hospitalized normals and the retardeds with higher IQs showed heterogeneous results. Findings demonstrate not only the poor learning capacity in mentally retarded children, but also the different forms of learning in children with normal and with deficient mental capacity. (German & Spanish summaries)
Combe, P. et al. (Hôpital Gatien de Clocheville, Clinique Pédiatrique, Tours, France) Revue de Neuropsychiatrie Infantile et d'Hygiene Mentale de l'Enfance, 1974(Dec), Vol 22(12), 753-769. [PA, Vol 57:10566]

1868.   Teaching a symbol language to autistic children.
Used a strict training procedure to advance language in 2 language-deficient autistic males aged 6 and 9 yrs. A "particle language," consisting of English words printed on magnetic particles placed on a magnetic board, was used to map the interaction between S and E, which led to food reinforcement. The domain of this interaction was expanded to include the comprehension and production of simple commands, descriptions, and questions. Each set was introduced by means of a training procedure which gradually admitted multiple choice. The procedure is discussed in terms of its potential advantages for training language.
de Villiers, Jill G. & Naughton, Joseph M. (Harvard U.) Journal of Consulting & Clinical Psychology, 1974(Feb), Vol. 42(1), 111-117. [PA, Vol 52:06347]

1869.   Orff-Schulwerk: An effective treatment tool with autistic children.
Cites autism, also known as Kanner's Syndrome, as the earliest occurring form of mental illness, usually manifesting itself between birth and 2 yrs. It is, in addition, one of the most severe types of disturbances affecting children. The Orff-Schulwerk treatment method for autism is described. The significant element in all group situations is that the child not only learns a certain skill or performs a task appropriately, but also becomes invested in a learning situation. For an autistic population, investment becomes the overriding focus in any activity. The most significant value of the Orff-Schulwerk technique is its ability to help even the most severely autistic child to become invested over a period of time in a meaningful group experience.

A discussion of the inclusion of sign language in the method is presented.
Hollander, Fred M. & Juhrs, Patricia D. (Napa State Hosp., Autistic Children's Program, Imola, Calif.) Journal of Music Therapy, 1974(Spr), Vol. 11(1), 1-12. [PA, Vol 52:12843]

1870. [Group therapy with autistic children and their mothers.] (Japn)
Describes a treatment program for 6 autistic children and their mothers. The sensory-motor, social, and verbal activities of the children were stimulated in 12 2-hr weekly sessions. Mothers attended 12 weekly sessions of 1½ hrs each, in which objective self-evaluations of their attitudes were made possible through group interaction. It is concluded that group therapy combined with individual therapy is effective.
Ikeda, Yoshiko; Narita, Toshie; Katori, Jyunko & Asayama, Takane. (National Inst of Mental Health, Ichikawa, Japan) Journal of Mental Health, 1974(Mar), Vol 48(22), 39-50. [PA, Vol 54:05932]

1871. The back projection of kaleidoscopic patterns as a technique for eliciting verbalizations in an autistic child.
Reports the results of sessions 14-30 using the back projection of kaleidoscopic patterns to elicit verbalizations in a 4-yr-old autistic boy who had previously evidenced problems in the operant conditioning of verbal responses. Sessions 1-13 are reported in PA, Vol 50:1507. The apparent long-term durability of the kaleidoscope's reinforcing properties and its use in increasing S's attention span are discussed. It is suggested that one of the functions of babbling in the child's acquisition of language is to develop the natural rhythms of a normal speech pattern.
Jellis, Trevor & Grainger, Sam. (Worcestershire Schools, Psychological Services, England) British Journal of Disorders of Communication, 1974(Apr), Vol. 9(1), 65-68. [PA, Vol 52:08148]

1872. An extinction procedure for eliminating self-destructive behavior in a 9-year-old autistic girl.
A 24-wk program of 2 daily 2-hr sessions of noncontingent social isolation was successful in eliminating multiple self-destructive behaviors in a 9-yr-old autistic child. A previous program of response-contingent shock met with failure, resulting in (a) increased self-destructive responding, (b) complete suppression of self-feeding, and (c) the necessity for constant physical restraint. Generalization of the extinction program to the ward was inferred on the basis of the S's subsequent cessation of restraint-wearing, a decrease in self-destructive behavior in the dayroom and subsequently in other settings following the removal of restraints, and a renewed interest in food. A brief program based upon elements of the noncontingent social isolation program was sufficient to reinstitute self-feeding. The S was gradually removed from social isolation sessions with no reappearance of self-destruction. However, during Week 72, self-destructive behavior again appeared, at which time a reinstatement of the original program dramatically reduced its rate. (26 ref)
Jones, Fredric H.; Simmons, James Q. & Frankel, Frederick. (U Rochester Medical Ctr) Journal of Autism & Childhood Schizophrenia, 1974(Sep), Vol 4(3), 241-250. [PA, Vol 56:08400]

1873. [Behaviour therapy in childhood autism.] (Germ)
Reviews the literature on behavior therapy in childhood autism. Behavioral symptoms can consist of behavioral deficits (lack of contact, mutism, dependency, and lack of sphincter control) or behavioral excesses (stereotypy, restlessness, self-destructiveness, and aggressiveness). Behavioral deficits are treated by operant conditioning, and behavioral excesses are treated by aversion conditioning. During the last several years, 23 autistic children were treated at the Universität Münster. Treatment lasted from a few weeks to many months. Four of 9 mute children acquired speech. Speech improved in 14 children with disturbed speech, and of 20 children with stereotypy, 8 showed excellent results, 5 good results, and 7 no change. (130 ref)
Kehrer, Hans E. (Westfälische Wilhelms-U Münster, Psychiatrische und Nervenklinik, West Germany) Zeitschrift für Kinder-

und Jugendpsychiatrie, 1974, Vol 2(3), 233-247. [PA, Vol 61:04186]

1874. Increasing spontaneous play by suppressing self-stimulation in autistic children.
Studied appropriate play with toys in 2 autistic children (an 8-yr-old boy and a 6-yr-old girl) with high occurrences of self-stimulatory behavior. Each child participated in the experimental sessions in an A-B-A design, where "A" refers to baseline sessions and "B" refers to self-stimulation suppression sessions. Results show that (a) during the baseline sessions, the children exhibited low levels of play and high levels of self-stimulatory behavior; (b) the percent of unreinforced, spontaneous, appropriate play increased when self-stimulatory behavior was suppressed; and (c) when the suppression of self-stimulation was discontinued, the percent of self-stimulation and that of appropriate play approached their presuppression levels. Results identify a set of conditions under which spontaneous appropriate behavior, uncommon in autistic children, occurs at an increased level. (24 ref)
Koegel, Robert L.; Firestone, Paula B.; Kramme, Kenneth W. & Dunlap, Glen. (U California, Inst for Applied Behavioral Science, Santa Barbara) Journal of Applied Behavior Analysis, 1974(Win), Vol 7(4), 521-528. [PA, Vol 53:10184]

1875. [A survey on child psychiatric practices during the five year period in a child guidance center.] (Japn)
Describes changes in child psychiatric practices at child guidance centers and other welfare institutions occasioned by a grass roots movement of parents of autistic and severely retarded children. Because of the organization of the health system, autistic and severely mentally retarded children without diagnosable physical dysfunctions were often denied admission to health care institutions and to special classes at public schools for children with developmental difficulties. The Hokusei Child Guidance Center initiated a special counseling program for the mothers of autistic children and encouraged nursery schools, kindergartens, and administrators of community agencies to provide better care for severely retarded and autistic children. Community-wide upgrading of facilities and increasing staff specialists are being promoted. A problem still to be resolved is that of increasing the duties and activities of doctors, now extremely limited by the bureaucratic structure.
Koike, Kiyoyuki; Kurube, Takao; Shigemori, Masao & Fujimaki, Takako. (Kyoto Prefectural Rakuto Hosp, Japan) Japanese Journal of Child Psychiatry, 1974(Sep–Nov), Vol 15(5), 258–269. [PA, Vol 60:12273]

1876. Social adjustment and placement of autistic children in Middlesex: A follow-up study.
Collected data on a follow-up study of 32 autistic children identified in an epidemiological survey when they were 8-10 yrs old and investigated 8 yrs later (in 1972). Outcome is described in terms of general social adjustment, employment, and placement history. Results are contrasted with those for a comparison group identified in the original survey and those reported for comparably defined children in other studies. Only one autistic child was employed, and outcome was in general worse for the autistic group in which 62% required extensive care and supervision. There does not seem to be a direct relationship between employability and amount of schooling. It is concluded that expectations with respect to outcome can be indicated with some confidence for comparable groups. (22 ref)
Lotter, Victor. (U Guelph, Canada) Journal of Autism & Childhood Schizophrenia, 1974(Jan-Mar), Vol 4(1), 11-32. [PA, Vol 56:10030]

1877. A behavior modification approach to the treatment of autistic children.
Since C. B. Ferster (see PA, Vol 4FD37F) presented the first theoretical article which attempted a behavioral analysis of autism, behavior modification has contributed in a major way to the education of the autistic child. It is the only intervention which has been empirically demonstrated to offer help for autistic children. Numerous studies reporting recent develop-

ments in (a) the analysis of self-destructive behavior, (b) self-stimulatory behavior, (c) the teaching of appropriate behaviors, and (d) building language are discussed. Generalization and follow-up results, contemporary research, classroom treatment, and new directions for research are also considered. (29 ref)
Lovaas, O. Ivar; Schreibman, Laura & Koegel, Robert L. (U California, Los Angeles) Journal of Autism & Childhood Schizophrenia, 1974(Mar), Vol 4(2), 111-129. [PA, Vol 56:10328]

1878. Graded change in the treatment of the behaviour of autistic children.
Discusses a method of introducing slight and gradual changes into the autistic child's environment. The case histories of a 5-yr-old and a 7-yr-old boy are presented in which this technique was used to reduce the attachment to objects, at the same time working on increasing sociability and attachment to people. Theoretical implications of such attachments are discussed together with more general applications of such a treatment technique.
Marchant, Rosemary; Howlin, Patricia; Yule, William & Rutter, Michael. (U London, Inst of Psychiatry, England) Journal of Child Psychology & Psychiatry & Allied Disciplines, 1974(Jul), Vol 15(3), 221-227. [PA, Vol 53:01369]

1879. A language training program for nonverbal autistic children.
Describes a nonspeech language training program for nonverbal autistic children. On completing the program 2 Ss responded differentially to a limited number of social transactions, demonstrated inter-E and intersetting generalizations, and retained the training responses.
McLean, Linda P. & McLean, James E. (Tennessee Dept. of Mental Health, Nashville) Journal of Speech & Hearing Disorders, 1974(May), Vol. 39(2), 186-193. [PA, Vol 52:10548]

1880. [The treatment of autistic children using operant conditioning techniques.] (Japn)
Outlines a method for introducing operant conditioning techniques and describes various programs for using these techniques to promote the social development of autistic children. Methods for determining the primary and secondary reinforcers (positive and negative) tailored to the reactions of each child are described. The use of operant conditioning in programs to teach and evolve linguistic behavior is presented, starting with individual sounds and working up to words and sentence-level communication. Children are taught syllables and then expected to respond correctly to words by indicating the picture the word describes. Later they are actively encouraged to make use of words and express basic needs. The interaction between the child and the therapist covers a progressively broader range of activities. (49 ref)
Nakayama, Osamu & Nakayama, Tomie. (Kawasaki City Rehabilitation Ctr, Japan) Japanese Journal of Child Psychiatry, 1974(Dec–Feb), Vol 15(1), 29–40. [PA, Vol 62:14256]

1881. The acquisition of simple and compound sentence structure in an autistic child.
Used contingent reinforcement and imitative prompts to teach an autistic 8-yr-old male to use simple and compound sentences to describe a set of standard pictures. When imitative prompts and reinforcement were discontinued, correct use of simple sentences declined, but increased again when imitative prompts and reinforcement were reinstated. When imitative prompts and reinforcements were used to teach compound sentence structure, correct use of simple sentences declined, and correct use of compound structure increased. At the end of training, the child also used novel compound sentences to describe a set of pictures on which he had received no direct training.
Stevens-Long, Judith & Rasmussen, Marilyn. (California State U, Los Angeles) Journal of Applied Behavior Analysis, 1974(Fal), Vol 7(3), 473-479. [PA, Vol 53:06221]

1882. An objective measurement of nonspeaking children's performance with a computer-controlled program for the stimulation of language behavior.
Presents a method for recording a child's performance with a computer-controlled audio-visual device designed to stimulate language behavior in nonspeaking children. From the recorded data a child's position can be estimated on a curve derived from normal children, indicating, over time, whether the nonspeaking child is progressing toward more normal behavior, has reached a plateau, or is retrogressing. This position could be of value in planning treatment for a nonspeaking child and assessing his progress. Data collected on the performance of 1-10 yr old children are discussed.
Colby, Kenneth M. & Kraemer, Helena C. (U California Medical School, Ctr for Health Sciences, Los Angeles, CA) Journal of Autism & Childhood Schizophrenia, 1975(Jun), Vol 5(2), 139-146. [PA, Vol 57:01311]

1883. [Psychoanalytic understanding of infantile psychosis.] (Span)
Examines psychoanalytic theories that support the use of such treatment with autistic children. The clinical history of an autistic 3-yr-old male with mutism is briefly described. There is a concise survey of the contributions of various classical authors, focusing mainly on M. Mahler and the symbiotic and separation-individuation processes, on M. Klein and the schizo-paranoid mechanisms, and finally on the technique of treatment based on the transference–countertransference phenomenon analysis.
Cuevas Corona, Pablo A. Neurología, Neurocirugía, Psiquiatría, 1975, 16(3), 177-182. [PA, Vol 57:03795]

1884. Listening: A goal of therapy for the autistic child.
Since the behavior of autistic children indicates that they do not listen, special techniques are required to overcome their apparent resistance. Providing a quiet setting, whispering or using a soft voice, gentle stroking, music, simultaneous speaking and feeding or other pleasant activity, and any other conditions or procedures which encourage or enhance listening receptivity are suggested as potential sources of communication breakthroughs.
Dubner, Harriet W. (Forum School, Waldwick, NJ) Rehabilitation Literature, 1975(Oct), Vol 36(10), 306-307, 332. [PA, Vol 58:01510]

1885. An operant procedure to teach an echolalic, autistic child to answer questions appropriately.
Developed an operant conditioning procedure to teach a 5-yr-old male autistic patient with rapid immediate echolalia to answer questions correctly. The procedure involved positively reinforcing the patient immediately after a correct response (identifying the action in a picture) and preventing incorrect responses. The procedure is simple to implement and eliminates some of the structure and constraints inherent in previously described operant methods. This allows the procedure to be administered by a variety of therapeutic personnel and parents and in a variety of living situations.
Freeman, Betty J.; Rivto, Edward & Miller, Revel. (U California, Neuropsychiatric Inst, Los Angeles) Journal of Autism & Childhood Schizophrenia, 1975(Jun), Vol 5(2), 169-176. [PA, Vol 57:01628]

1886. Modifying the verbal expression of a child with autistic behaviors.
Used the Bell and Howell Language Master in conjunction with the Monterey Language Program to modify the verbal expression of a 9-yr-old boy with autistic behaviors. The goal was to train the child to correctly name up to 10 pictures presented individually. Two training modes were used: the therapist either spoke at the time (live voice) or presented a tape recording of her voice via a Language Master. Results suggest that the child's responses to the Language Master were as good as, if not better than, his responses to the live-voice presentations. His spontaneous speech was also noted to improve in the classroom and the home. Possible reasons for the improvement in verbal expression are considered. (18 ref)

Hargrave, Elizabeth & Swisher, Linda. (Oak Lane Elementary School, Hurdle Mills, NC) Journal of Autism & Childhood Schizophrenia, 1975(Jun), Vol 5(2), 147-154. [PA, Vol 57:01635]

1887. **[Group play communication therapy with autistic children.]** (Japn)
Describes a play therapy program for autistic children that emphasizes promoting development by opening and expanding communication activities. Autism is not a strict diagnosis; it applies to a variety of similar developmental abnormalities that range from almost completely psychogenic to almost completely organic problems. The 3-phase play communication therapy presented here applies almost exclusively to overcoming psychogenic problems. In Phase 1, the therapist seeks to build a warm relationship with the child. Through imitation of the child's activities he or she seeks to subjectively enter into the child's autistic world and understand its limitations and psychodynamics. The therapist also develops a close physical relationship and deep empathy for the child. The matching of therapist to child is based on feelings of mutual compatibility. Phase 2 stresses participation in a number of different play activities. Phase 3 attempts to give the child intuitive insight into the nature of his or her inner world by suggesting some of the latent content apparent in the play activities. The play activities of children are open to symbolic interpretation much like the dreams of adults; play activities have the added advantage of permitting immediate intervention. Developing and improving internal communication has resulted in considerable improvement in some cases. Three cases are discussed. (English summary)
Higashiyama, Hirohisa. (Osaka Kyoiku U, Japan) Japanese Journal of Child Psychiatry, 1975(Jul–Aug), Vol 16(4), 224–236. [PA, Vol 63:03719]

1888. **Psychotherapy and education for autistic children.**
Reports results of a program to counsel and train autistic children. The program is based on early identification and referral, parent counseling and training in childrearing tactics appropriate to autistic children, and socialization experiences. Characteristics of autistic children are discussed, with emphasis on memory functions. Educational strategies should focus on assisting autistic children to develop greater flexibility in applying their skills and expanding their areas of experience. Characteristics of the mental structure of autistic children are described and related to training, socialization, and educational strategies. (3 ref)
Hirai, Nobuyoshi. Hiroshima Forum for Psychology, 1975, Vol 2, 43–48. [PA, Vol 64:01732]

1889. **Stress in families of institutionalized and noninstitutionalized autistic children.**
Explored the relationships between parents' reports of personal and family problems (viewed as stress indicators) in their attempts to deal with an autistic child. 2 variables were examined: institutionalization and the age of the child. Parents in 29 families with autistic children (28 mothers and 22 fathers) were interviewed and completed a questionnaire as part of a larger follow-up study. Children ranged in age from 1 to 18, with 1 aged 24. 78% were male and all but one were Caucasian. The families were evaluated for level of stress by combining parent interview responses. No differences were found between families of institutionalized and noninstitutionalized children. There was some suggestion, however, that among children kept at home, stress ratings were higher for families of older children than of younger children.
Holroyd, Jean; Brown, Nancy; Wikler, Lynn & Simmons, James Q. (U California, Neuropsychiatric Inst, Los Angeles) Journal of Community Psychology, 1975(Jan), Vol 3(1), 26-31. [PA, Vol 53:12340]

1890. **Movement of therapy in the treatment of autistic children: II. Intellectual changes.**
Describes changes in 4 autistic children aged 2 yrs 10 mo-9 yrs in estimates of intellectual development during their period of motor education. Three of the Ss were taken for 2½-hr swimming lessons and 1 ½-hr movement session each week for 10 wks. The 4th S had only movement education--30 sessions of 3½ hrs each week. The physical activity and movement therapy appeared to coincide with an increase in each child's developmental skills, judged by the Fels Behaviour Rating Scale, Merrill Palmer Scale of Mental Tests, Purdue Motor Development Survey, and other measures.
Jones, J. G. & Best, J. F. (U Western Australia, Nedlands) Australian Occupational Therapy Journal, 1975, Vol 22(1), 15-29. [PA, Vol 58:05790]

1891. **[The play therapy program at Aichi Colony Hospital for autistic children.]** (Japn)
Discusses and reviews a play therapy program carried out for 6 yrs at Colony Central Hospital in Aichi Prefecture. During the 1st yr, the children were randomly assigned to different groups for 2 hrs of unstructured play therapy. During the 2nd period, play therapy was structured along the lines of activity in a normal Japanese kindergarten. Groups of autistic children at various stages of development were given individual or group tasks: rhythmic music, physical exercises, mimicking, playing tag, using building blocks, coloring pictures, putting on shoes, playing in the pool, eating, etc. After 4 yrs, children who had made good progress continued in this program, and a special program was instituted for the severely disturbed children. Efforts were concentrated on evaluating the needs and individual interests of each child and using these interests as a base to expand contact with the external world. Close skin contact with the therapist was considered important. The case histories of 2 5-yr-old autistic boys and their progress in the program are presented.
Kawamura, Tomoko & Ishii, Takaaki. (Aichi Prefectural Colony Central Hosp, Kasugai, Japan) Japanese Journal of Child Psychiatry, 1975, Vol 16(5), 307–315. [PA, Vol 63:03914]

1892. **The use of fantasy enactment in the treatment of an emerging autistic child.**
Describes the therapy of an autistic child. Several techniques were employed, of which the most important were following and enacting the child's fantasies, limit-setting to release perseverative fantasies, reflection of feeling contained in the fantasies, and limited interpretation of unconscious processes.
MacDonald, Rita T. & Allan, John A. Journal of Analytical Psychology, 1975(Jan), Vol 20(1), 57-68. [PA, Vol 54:05770]

1893. **Peculiarities in the endocrine response to insulin stress in early infantile autism.**
11 4-13 yr old autistic children subjected to the stress of insulin-induced hypoglycemia showed slower recovery of blood glucose and faster and intractable cortisol response in the 3 hrs following the stress. Data suggest that autistic children overreact to this stressor and support clinical evidence of stress intolerance. It is suggested that this peculiarity may be implicated in an explanation of the abnormal behavior seen in this disorder. (15 ref)
Maher, Kevin R.; Harper, Juliet F.; Macleay, Allan & King, Maurice G. (U Newcastle, Australia) Journal of Nervous & Mental Disease, 1975(Sep), Vol 16(3), 180-184. [PA, Vol 55:04749]

1894. **Brief time-outs as consequences for errors during training programs with autistic and retarded children: A questionable procedure.**
Studied the relative effectiveness of several brief time-out durations as punishers for error responding in applied learning tasks in 3 experiments with 4 autistic and 8 retarded 8-20 yr old Ss. The tasks included antonym learning, picture naming, and drawing. Time-out durations ranged from zero to 30 sec. In all cases Ss made either the same or fewer errors on the lowest time-out duration, or, if they did make fewer errors on a longer time-out condition, its use was not warranted when considered in terms of efficient use of training time. This finding occurred even though the experiments utilized 3 different tasks, different Ss and Es both within and across experiments, different token exchange ratios, and different experimental settings. Results question the value of brief time-outs as consequences for errors during training programs with these populations.

Martin, Garry. (U Manitoba, St Paul's Coll, Winnipeg, Canada) Psychological Record, 1975(Win), Vol 25(1), 71-89. [PA, Vol 54:01679]

1895.   [Group therapy of autistic children at an outpatient clinic.] (Japn)
To overcome autistic tendencies and achieve successful socialization, autistic children must be given regular contacts with normal children. Although an autistic child may be able to achieve a successful rapport with a therapist in a therapeutic environment, he can make only limited progress there. Autistic and mentally retarded children were divided into 3 groups of 6–8 members depending on age, mental and physical development, and social abilities. The most advanced group was periodically taken to a local school to play with normal children. This stimulation helped some children to markedly increase their social skills and their ability to interact emotionally and physically with normal children. It provided both positive and negative motivation for overcoming autistic habits, and spontaneous behavior was improved. Social prejudice of teachers and of parents of normal children must be countered to permit the expansion of this program to include the more severely retarded and emotionally disturbed children. (English summary) (3 ref)
Masumura, Mikio et al. (Niigata Prefectural Yukyoso Hosp, Nagaoka, Japan) Japanese Journal of Child Psychiatry, 1975(Nov), Vol 16(5), 316–324. [PA, Vol 63:03727]

1896.   [Educational therapy for severely retarded children.] (Japn)
Emotionality plays a crucial role in the development of severely retarded children and in their communication with therapists. Severely retarded children may exhibit withdrawn, autocentric behavior patterns which are underdifferentiated in their human relationship and object perception responses. Such children must be helped to develop on both the emotional and the cognitive level and to integrate the human-directed and object-directed responses in a practical way. The principles stressed in this program were (1) to gain a clear picture of the child's developmental state; (2) to participate in and expand any of the child's behavior patterns, to ensure a response from the external environment and condition the child to be aware of this response; (3) to assure and expand the child's intentionality; and (4) to overcome entrenched behavior patterns and encourage more flexible responses, using various original devices and concepts. Case histories and success of the program for 3 microencephalic children are presented. (English summary) (2 ref)
Matsuyama, Kunihiro; Tanimura, Satoru; Shibata, Chosei & Ogawa, Yoshiko. (Mukogaoka Day Training Ctr for Handicapped Children, Nagaokakyo, Japan) Japanese Journal of Child Psychiatry, 1975(Nov), Vol 16(5), 282–295. [PA, Vol 63:03765]

1897.   Perceptual-motor training and the autistic child.
Describes a perceptual-motor program consisting of 8 groups of activities, ranging from running to swimming to arts and crafts. The program gives autistic children a summer experience of 5 hrs/day, 5 days/wk, which is designed to involve them in many of the cognitive, motor, and recreational activities pursued by average children. The time each child spends in each group of activities, called a station, is determined by that child's needs and characteristics. It is hoped that mastering the needed skills will assist in developing a more positive self-concept, which ideally encourages increased socializing. This program is a pioneering effort to apply the scientific principles and techniques developed by practitioners and researchers in the neglected area of perceptual-motor training for this special group of children. (17 ref)
Mosher, Richard. (U Ottawa, Canada) Journal of Leisurability, 1975(Jul), Vol 2(3), 29-35. [PA, Vol 57:03769]

1898.   [A group therapy for autistic children based on volunteer activities.] (Japn)
Describes programs and activities of a volunteer group in providing a group therapy class for autistic children. The volunteer group presently consists of 2 child psychiatrists, 1 pediatrician, 1 teacher, 1 medical student, 5 graduate educational psychology students, 8 educational psychology undergraduates, 1 nurse, 5 student nurses, 3 psychologists, and 3 nonprofessionals. There are presently 20 3–9 yr old children attending the therapy sessions. An individual therapist is assigned to each child. Based on the theories of M. K. DeMyer, H. Wallon, and H. Bucher concerning the autistic child's developmental inability to perform imitative physical movements, the treatment program was designed to promote the child's awareness of his body and to encourage physical coordination. After 1 hr of free play therapy, the children complete basic kinesthetic training exercises in jumping, climbing, and balancing. The case history of an 11-yr-old autistic boy, the oldest member of the group, is presented. (English summary)
Murata, Toyohisa et al. (Fukuoka U School of Medicine, Japan) Japanese Journal of Child Psychiatry, 1975(Mar–Apr), Vol 16(2), 152–163. [PA, Vol 62:14192]

1899.   [Day care for preschool children at the outpatient department psychiatric hospital.] (Japn)
Reports on the daycare therapy and treatment programs at a hospital for autistic, mentally retarded, hyperkinetic, and aphasic preschool children. For treatment purposes, the children were divided into 2 groups of 6–8 members depending on age but without regard to diagnosis. The staff consisted of psychiatrists, psychologists, nurses, and social workers. The therapy program emphasized free expression and participation in a variety of activities. Interaction between the children was particularly encouraged. The main purpose of the program was to prepare children for entrance into normal kindergartens. A follow-up of several children in the program found they were coping adequately with the kindergarten environment. The mothers found that a great advantage of the program was their opportunity to exchange views and feelings with mothers who had children with similar problems. Fathers were instructed, with the use of videotapes, concerning their child's problems and progress at special meetings. The case histories of 7 children who participated in the program are presented in detail. (English summary)
Nakane, Akira & Kato, Hiroko. (Umegaoka Metropolitan Hosp, Tokyo, Japan) Japanese Journal of Child Psychiatry, 1975(Mar–Apr), Vol 16(2), 125–137. [PA, Vol 62:14407]

1900.   Directiveness and compliance behavior in a preschool autistic-like child.
Percentage and latency of compliances to verbal directives were recorded for 5 target behaviors in a 4½-yr-old autistic-like boy. Repeated vs single directive presentation methods were compared to assess their relationship to compliance behavior. During the repeated directive condition the highest percentage of compliances occurred after a single directive. The single directive condition produced a shorter compliance latency in all target behaviors. Over 75% of all compliances during this study were emitted after a single directive.
Neumann, Albert J.   Research & the Retarded, 1975(Spr), Vol 2(2), 15-24. [PA, Vol 58:03862]

1901.   Day care treatment for autistically inclined preschool children.
Discusses a daycare treatment program for preschool children with autistic tendencies. Children are divided into 4 groups depending on developmental level, with 4–6 members in each group. The treatment schedule consists of 2 sessions/wk for a 9-mo period. During a daycare treatment session, the child undergoes 1 hr of group play therapy and 1 hr of educational therapy. To promote stabilized social behavior, themes pertaining to everyday life are constantly repeated and expanded. Since the developmental stage of each child is slightly different in regard to responsiveness of sense organs, perceptual and speech impediments, and cognitive abilities, the type and strength of stimulus and the patient–therapist relationship must be individually adapted to the child's exact needs. Camping excursions and working with the child during a 1-wk hospitalization period permits the staff to come into direct contact with the child over a prolonged period and to compare the child's behavior patterns with those reported by his parents. (English summary)

Okuno, Koji. (Mie Prefectural Takachaya Hosp, Tsu, Japan) Japanese Journal of Child Psychiatry, 1975(Mar–Apr), Vol 16(2), 138–151. [PA, Vol 62:14057]

1902. Reacting to autistic children: The danger of trying too hard.
Recent work has revealed that autistic children's predominating tendency to avoid social interactions is actually enhanced by the "friendly" approaches of others. To investigate this finding, the reactions of 8 autistic children to 4 styles of adult behavior were videotaped. The adult reacted to the child's looks at her by (a) smiling, (b) gaze averting, (c) gaze averting plus other "timid" behaviors and (d) doing nothing except continuing to look back. For condition "d," it was found that autistic children showed less avoidance behavior after eye contact and spent more time within 1 meter of the adult. The implications for treatment are contrary to much modern practice and to what seems to be adults' "natural" response. Reactivity by others appeared to enhance the child's avoidance, and it is suggested that adults should be circumspect in the degree of sociability with which they respond to autistic children. (16 ref)
Richer, John & Richards, Barry. (Reading U, England) British Journal of Psychiatry, 1975(Dec), Vol 127, 526-529. [PA, Vol 55:07315]

1903. Setting generality and stimulus control in autistic children.
Assessed the transfer of treatment gains of 10 6½-13½ yr old autistic children across settings. In Phase I each S learned a new behavior in a treatment room, and transfer to a novel extra-therapy setting was assessed. 4 of the Ss showed no transfer to the novel setting. Therefore, in Phase 2, each S who failed to transfer participated in an analysis of stimulus control to determine the variables influencing the deficit in transfer. Each of the Ss who did not transfer was selectively responding to an incidental stimulus during the original training in the treatment room. Utilizing a reversal design, each of the 4 Ss responded correctly in the extra-therapy setting when the stimulus that was functional during training was identified and introduced into the extra-therapy setting. The extreme selective responding and the resulting bizarre stimulus control found are discussed in relation to the issue of setting generality of treatment gains. (19 ref)
Rincover, Arnold & Koegel, Robert L. (U California, Inst for Applied Behavior Science, Santa Barbara) Journal of Applied Behavior Analysis, 1975(Fal), Vol 8(3), 235-246. [PA, Vol 54:12341]

1904. Increasing isolate and social play in severely disturbed children: Intervention and postintervention effectiveness.
Exp I instituted a group treatment procedure to increase the isolate and social play of 4 severely disturbed 5–7 yr olds. Results indicate that play behavior could be increased significantly by the use of food and social reinforcement and by the use of passive shaping, but that it quickly declined when the intervention was terminated. Social play, however, did remain above baseline levels during extinction. Exp II, using 4 severely disturbed 10–12 yr olds, replicated the results of Exp I. However, results show that the procedure of fading adult intervention proved an effective method for increasing the resistance of social play to extinction.
Romanczyk, Raymond G. et al. (State U New York, Binghamton) Journal of Autism & Developmental Disorders, 1975(Mar), Vol 5(1), 57–70. [PA, Vol 59:01582]

1905. An autistic child in residential treatment.
Describes the case history and residential treatment of a boy 4½ yrs old at the Sonia Shankman Orthogenic School of the University of Chicago. The dynamics of the child's behavior are interpreted in the light of B. Bettelheim's work with autistic children. The interpersonal relationships of the facility are related to the positive treatment effects.
Sanders, Jacquelyn. (U Chicago, Sonio Shankman Orthogenic School) Reiss-Davis Clinic Bulletin, 1975(Fal), Vol 12(2), 97-106. [PA, Vol 55:10516]

1906. [Psychiatric day care for mentally and emotionally disturbed children in the University of Tokyo Hospital.] (Japn)
Summarizes the history of treatment programs for autistic and severely disturbed children at the Tokyo University Hospital from 1952 to the present. Originally the daycare unit had a relatively unstructured and permissive atmosphere in which the therapists attempted to relieve the children of intrapsychic anxiety and other emotional conflicts in hopes of establishing affective contact with them. After 1959, an individualized, well-structured, therapeutic educational program was instituted to better achieve these goals using behavior modification techniques in the areas of self-care, feeding, and educational and social development. Education and social development was best promoted when autistic children were integrated with normal children in a nursery school or kindergarten. It was observed that children diagnosed as suffering from childhood autism without primary mental retardation often evinced multiple clinical disorders such as aphasia, retardation, epilepsy, and other CNS dysfunctions. (English summary)
Sasaki, Masami. (U Tokyo Faculty of Medicine, Japan) Japanese Journal of Child Psychiatry, 1975(Mar–Apr), Vol 16(2), 112–124. [PA, Vol 62:14414]

1907. Imitative speech training of an autistic child in the home.
Describes the use of conditioning procedures, modeled after the method of O. I. Lovaas, with a nonverbal 6-yr-old girl to help her to speak. The procedure was conducted in 5 phases of approximately 90 1-hr sessions in the home, to establish verbal imitation in the child. Some progress in communicative behavior was made, but success was lower than hoped because (a) medication often made the patient drowsy, (b) she was often not hungry so that food was not useful as a reinforcer, and (c) the parents were unwilling to take part in the therapy.
Shigley, R. Hal & Shigley, Judy K. (Western Carolina U) Western Carolina University Journal of Education, 1975(Spr), Vol 7(1), 38–42. [PA, Vol 59:03906]

1908. [On a therapeutic and nursing method dealing with autistic children.] (Japn)
Discusses therapeutic methods and the coordination of the professional and nonprofessional staffs in the treatment and education of autistic children. A program is described in which a conference of all professional staff members (e.g., psychiatrists, special education teachers, and pediatricians) was held twice a month and reports were made on the children's behavior and therapeutic progress. An innovative attempt was made to mix autistic children with normal kindergartners as a part of the play therapy program. Although it was initially feared that the erratic behavior patterns of the autistic children might create unfavorable responses in the normal children, actual practice proved that these fears were unfounded. The mothers of autistic children learned to overcome some of their overanxious reaction patterns by observing the interactions between normal children and their mothers. Children interacted most successfully with each other in an unstructured playground environment. (English summary)
Shimada, Shozo. (Kobe U School of Medicine, Japan) Japanese Journal of Child Psychiatry, 1975(Mar–Apr), Vol 16(2), 91–96. [PA, Vol 62:14064]

1909. Optometric care for a child manifesting qualities of autism.
Presents the case history of a sickly 4.75-yr-old male esotrope referred to the author by a family physician and subsequently diagnosed autistic by a developmental examiner and a psychologist. The child's behavior during the initial and several followup interviews is described, and some personality development is noted over a period of about a year. Optometric care included prismatic rectification of the esotropia and prescription of spherical lenses corrective of mild hyperopia. When last interviewed, the child still seemed autistic and limited in his visual sampling of distant objects. Binocular functioning, rudimentary personal interrelationships, and "longer periods of meaningful attentiveness" are listed as persistent improvements initiated and maintained during the period described.

Streff, John W. (Southern Coll of Optometry, Memphis, TN) Journal of the American Optometric Association, 1975(Jun), Vol 46(6), 592-597. [PA, Vol 56:04546]

1910. [An application of group therapy for autistic children in the Child Unit, Seiryoin, Sapporo Municipal General Hospital.] (Japn)
Describes the general principles and methods used in the group therapy program for autistic children at the general hospital in Sapporo, Japan. Children, ages 2.10–6.0 yrs, are assigned to different groups depending on their age and level of development. The guidance program for each group can be divided into 6 distinct periods: (a) behavioral observation period; (b) continued observation and an attempt to determine the children's personal interests; (c) introduction of the individual guidance system; (d) introduction of thematic situations with particular emphasis on group activities and the individual's participation in the group; (e) examination of the play-therapy themes and their relevance to the therapy; and (f) reexamination of play-therapy themes. It is noted that not only is it important to observe the children carefully, but the actions of the therapist and the quality of interaction with the child must also be observed, noted, and discussed. (English summary)
Yamazaki, Kosuke et al. (Sapporo Municipal General Hosp, Child Unit, Japan) Japanese Journal of Child Psychiatry, 1975(Mar–Apr), Vol 16(2), 103–111. [PA, Vol 62:14204]

1911. [The ethological theory of infantile autism.] (Ital)
Describes how N. Tinberger's theory of the ethological origin of childhood autism is supported by data from its application to these children in their homes and schools. Treatment consists of a progressive enlargement of the relational space of the child. The therapist's background and imagination in creating stimulating new situations is fundamental to this process.
Zappella, Michele. (Hosp Regionale St Maria della Scala, Servizio di Neuropsichiatria Infantile, Siena, Italy) Archivio di Psicologia, Neurologia e Psichiatria, 1975(Apr-Jun), Vol 36(2), 119-143. [PA, Vol 55:12654]

1912. Differences between mentally retarded and normal intelligence autistic children.
Compared 17 autistic children with an IQ below 70 and 19 with an IQ above 70. Mean ages were 8 yrs 7 mo and 8 yrs 5 mo, respectively. The 2 groups differed somewhat in the pattern of symptoms, but were closely similar in terms of the main phenomena specifically associated with autism. The low IQ and high IQ Ss differed more substantially, however, in terms of other symptoms such as self-injury and stereotypies, and there were major differences in outcome. It is concluded that the possibility that the nature of the autistic disorder may differ according to the presence or absence of associated mental retardation needs to be taken into account in planning studies of etiology. (19 ref)
Bartak, Lawrence & Rutter, Michael. (U London, Inst of Psychiatry, England) Journal of Autism & Childhood Schizophrenia, 1976(Jun), Vol 6(2), 109-120. [PA, Vol 57:03431]

1913. Crisis and diagnosis: Infantile autism.
Outlines a theoretical model for presenting diagnoses to parents of autistic children. The model is based on crisis theory. Actual professional practice, as determined by interviews with the parents of 22 autistic children aged 4–23 yrs, is compared with the theoretical model. This study demonstrated that professional practice did not seem to have given adequate recognition to mourning reactions but did show a tendency toward increased involvement of parents in treatment. The failure to recognize or encourage adaptive mourning is seen as fostering denial which might impair the ability of the parents to cope effectively with the problem.
Bonnefil, Margaret. (Los Angeles Psychiatric Service, Didi Hirsch Community Mental Health Ctr, CA) Clinical Social Work Journal, 1976(Win), Vol 4(4), 276–288. [PA, Vol 61:13987]

1914. Sign language acquisition in a mute autistic boy.
Reports the case of a mute autistic boy who learned to communicate extensively through American Sign Language. Over a 6-mo period he produced many spontaneous signs and sign combinations, and analyses of these combinations indicated the presence of a full range of semantic relations. Further evidence of conceptual progress was provided by his increased score on the Peabody Picture Vocabulary Test. Parents' and teacher's reports indicated that the child's social behavior improved. The extent of the boy's linguistic and behavioral progress markedly exceeds that usually reported for mute autistic children. (21 ref)
Bonvillian, John D. & Nelson, Keith E. (Vassar Coll) Journal of Speech & Hearing Disorders, 1976(Aug), Vol 41(3), 339-347. [PA, Vol 57:03437]

1915. [Double-focus treatment of a psychotic young girl and her parents.] (Fren)
Reports on the psychotherapy of an autistic girl 3½ yrs old and of her parents. The child was in individual analytic psychotherapy with one therapist. During the 1st phase, the mother had weekly talks with the other therapist, the father refusing to participate. Autism grew less pronounced, and a fantasy communication between mother and child developed. In a 2nd phase, the parents were treated as a couple, causing them to realize (a) their culpability in regard to their psychotic child; (b) the fact that pre-existent communication disorders were aggravated by this culpability; and (c) the fact that cessation of communication itself exerted a psychogenic influence on the child. The treatment restored a certain degree of communication, both on a fantasy and reality level, among the family members. (German & Spanish summaries)
Boudry, Cl. & Pfaehler, P. (U Lausanne, Ctr de Psychiatrie Infantile, Switzerland) Revue de Neuropsychiatrie Infantile et d'Hygiene Mentale de l'Enfance, 1976(Jan-Feb), Vol 24(1-2), 25-33. [PA, Vol 58:03715]

1916. [Musical aids to assist therapy in mentally retarded and autistic children.] (Fren)
Discusses the use of musical aids as a part of therapy with mentally retarded and autistic children. From 1955 to 1960 the number of mentally deficient, trisomic, encephalitic, and cerebrally disordered children has increased, and music has assumed an important social and educational place in their lives. Psycho-motor and perceptual (sensory) exercises have been set to music with success. The language of music is shown to be an effective tool for communication in the psychotic child. Music is utilized as a therapeutic aid, akin to projective tests. The problems of musical therapy are discussed, including the rapidly changing response of the psychotic child to music and the possible facilitation of a psychotic child's return to autism. Although musicotherapy is not an exact science, it is proving to be a beneficial treatment for various psychological disorders.
Brauner, Alfred & Brauner, François. (Groupement de Recherches Pratiques pour l'Enfance, Paris, France) Vie médicale au Canada français, 1976(Oct), Vol 5(10), 1024–1026, 1037–1039. [PA, Vol 59:05984]

1917. Integrating the environment in therapy.
Studied the effects of an integrated treatment program and environmental modification on the behavior of 24 institutionalized severely disturbed autistic children and their caretakers. Within 1 wk of full implementation of the program, (a) there was an increase in social eye-contact between the children and the adults; (b) 4 previously nontalking children began using a few words, communicatively and spontaneously; (c) there was an observable increase in the amount of smiling, both by children and adults; and (d) there was a decrease in the children's destructive behavior.
Clancy, Helen G. (U Queensland, Brisbane, Australia) Man-Environment Systems, 1976(Sep), Vol 6(5), 305–312. [PA, Vol 59:01702]

1918. Evaluating autistic children.
A review of the literature is presented, supporting the conclusion that IQ tests are of prognostic value with autistic children. To facilitate testing such children, several behavioral techniques are recommended, including using positive reinforcement, optimizing the sequence of item presentation, ignoring interfering behaviors, and employing short testing sessions. The advantages of such techniques are discussed, and the inclusion of courses in behavioral techniques in the training of clinical child psychologists is stressed. (14 ref)
Freeman, B. J. (U California Medical School, Div of Mental Retardation & Child Psychiatry, Los Angeles) Journal of Pediatric Psychology, 1976, Vol 1(3), 18–21. [PA, Vol 62:03753]

1919. Effect of duration of time out in suppressing disruptive behavior of a severely autistic child.
Evaluated the effectiveness of either a 3-min, a 15-min, or a 1-hr time out from positive reinforcement in reducing the disruptive behavior of a severely autistic 4-yr-old male. Behavior was best suppressed with the 15-min duration. However, the pitfalls of arbitrarily setting a duration of time out for a child without assessing the effect on him are examined. In addition, the uselessness of group experiments and the problems inherent in long time-out durations are discussed.
Freeman, B. J.; Somerset, Tom & Ritvo, E. R. (U California Medical School, Los Angeles) Psychological Reports, 1976(Feb), Vol 38(1), 124–126. [PA, Vol 56:02618]

1920. Acquisition of American sign language by a noncommunicating autistic child.
Experiments on the perception and language abilities of autistic children have indicated that these children have auditory–visual association problems. These findings, combined with evidence showing that autistic communication is primarily gestural, led to the teaching of elements of American Sign Language (Ameslan) to a 5-yr-old nonverbal autistic boy. Results after 20 hrs of training indicate that (a) the child did acquire signs, (b) increasing signing led to increasing vocal speech, and (c) the child had rudimentary English syntax. The use of Ameslan spontaneously generalized to other situations and the training resulted in increased social interaction. (23 ref)
Fulwiler, Robert L. & Fouts, Roger S. (U California, Langley Porter Neuropsychiatric Inst, San Francisco) Journal of Autism & Developmental Disorders, 1976(Mar), Vol 6(1), 43–51. [PA, Vol 59:01432]

1921. [Advantages of behavior therapy with serious forms of childhood autism.] (Fren)
Reports behavior therapy with 8-yr-old autistic male. Observation by medical personnel and parents emphasized preferred activities, potential reinforcers, desirable behaviors to encourage, and constricted behaviors selected for extinction. A therapeutic team provided continuity, stability, and security in patient's environment; an observer kept records which the team discussed weekly. The patient met following criteria: (a) difficulty since early infancy, (b) autistic behavior, (c) absence of language, (d) aggressiveness and behavioral stereotypy, and (e) no response to psychotherapy, or chemotherapy. He presented serious eating problems, difficulty relating to adults, incessant crying, and poor attention span. Of a total of 90 sessions of behavior therapy, 10 are reported in detail. Post-treatment behavior indicated considerable learning. Improvement was noted in sensorimotor functions (grasping and seizing), in the ability to keep 2 objects in mind while obtaining a 3rd, and the ability to perceive a complete structure. Activity became goal-directed, verbal behavior increased, and rapport with adults was strengthened. The behavioral approach is recommended as quantifiable, objective, flexible, and applicable by teams, including parents.
Gault, C. et al. (Service d'Explorations Fonctionnelles Psychopathologiques, Tours, France) Perspectives Psychiatriques, 1976, No 58, 282-284. [PA, Vol 58:03836]

1922. Advising parents of severely atypical children.
Discusses the family physician as the primary source of continuing guidance for the parents of autistic, schizophrenic, or brain-damaged children. It is essential to anticipate problems in areas such as the medication, early education, reactions of siblings, and stresses within the lives of the parents. The family physician can help parents find the resources to cope with the multitude of problems confronting them and their children. Case histories illustrating the help of the family physician with such problems are presented. (16 ref)
Harris, Sandra L. (Douglass Coll, Rutgers State U) Journal of Family Practice, 1976(Aug), Vol 3(4), 381-383. [PA, Vol 56:10405]

1923. Employing electric shock with autistic children: A review of the side effects.
The use of electric shock in a punishment paradigm has continued to be a highly controversial issue in the treatment of autistic children. While the experimental literature argues for the effectiveness of the procedure for reducing maladaptive behaviors, some clinicians and researchers have expressed fear of possible negative side effects. The reported side effects of contingent electric shock are reviewed in an attempt to evaluate the validity of these fears. The review indicates that the majority of reported side effects of shock were of a positive nature, including response generalization, increases in social behavior, and positive emotional behavior. The few negative side effects reported included fear of the shock apparatus, negative emotional behavior, and increases in other maladaptive behavior. Implications for the use of the shock procedure are discussed in terms of correct usage of the shock, therapist reservations, and alternative procedures. (34 ref)
Lichstein, Kenneth L. & Schreibman, Laura. (Memphis State U) Journal of Autism & Childhood Schizophrenia, 1976(Jun), Vol 6(2), 163-173. [PA, Vol 57:01642]

1924. Control of self-stimulatory behavior of an autistic child through brief physical restraint.
Tested the effectiveness of restraint in controlling self-stimulation in a 7-yr-old autistic boy enrolled in a special education class. Restraint took the form of a light touch by the teacher on the boy's body or hands whenever self-stimulatory behavior occurred. Restraint was shown to be more effective in controlling this behavior than either prompts, reinforcement, or continuous praise for periods of no self-stimulation. At 7-wk follow-up, self-stimulation remained at low, posttreatment levels. The authors report anecdotally that the boy's general level of arousal was more controlled and that he was more responsive to verbal stimuli following treatment.
Luiselli, James K.; Reisman, John; Helfen, Carol S. & Pemberton, Bruce W. (Crosby School, Behavioral Intervention Project, Arlington, MA) SALT: School Applications of Learning Theory, 1976(Nov), Vol 9(2), 3–13. [PA, Vol 63:01575]

1925. [A functional concept of language: Theoretical and methodological considerations.] (Fren)
Presents a functional view of verbal behavior, in which particular aspects of speech are held to be subject to augmentation through the principle of selective reinforcement. Several strategies are described for the application of this principle to the abnormal speech generated by retarded or psychotic children, autistic or schizophrenic children, a case of mutism, and children with problems in speech articulation. On balance, the evidence drawn from the literature supports the efficacy of behavior modification techniques for the normalization of aberrant speech in quite different kinds of patients. A continuing problem exists, however, in obtaining corrected verbal responding that will be generalized to life outside the laboratory. For this reason it is urged that the laboratory situation be made to resemble a more usual environment wherever possible and that appropriate behaviors acquired in the laboratory be reinforced socially in the more habitual home setting of the patient. (21 ref)
Mear-Crine, A.-M. & Lafleur, L. (U Montréal, Canada) Annales Médico-Psychologiques, 1976(Dec), Vol 2(5), 775–785. [PA, Vol 63:08113]

1926.   Reinforcement of autistic children's responses to music.
Appropriate and inappropriate behaviors of a 10-yr-old and 2 7-yr-old autistically labeled males were observed and recorded during alternating individual and group sessions under 2 conditions: Condition A, one-to-one reinforcement and shaping, and Condition B, differential reinforcement. Music served as an effective curriculum (to teach appropriate musical responses) and as a context to shape and alter other individual and social behaviors. Increases in appropriate behaviors were accompanied by variable decreases in inappropriate behaviors. (16 ref)
Schmidt, David C.; Franklin, Robert & Edwards, Joseph S. (U Missouri, Kansas City) Psychological Reports, 1976(Oct), Vol 39(2), 571-577. [PA, Vol 57:08762]

1927.   The acquisition and generalization of compound sentence structure in an autistic child.
Trained a 6-yr-old autistic boy, whose language consisted primarily of 2-word phrases, to describe verbally a standard set of training pictures using both simple and compound sentences. Training included imitative prompts, differential reinforcement, and time-out. Probe trials presenting a set of novel stimuli were used to examine the extent of stimulus generalization for both sentence types in the experimental setting, and S used simple and compound sentences spontaneously in a classroom setting at the end of the training period.
Stevens-Long, Judith; Schwarz, Jane L. & Bliss, Deborah. (California State U, Los Angeles) Behavior Therapy, 1976(May), Vol 7(3), 397-404. [PA, Vol 57:01663]

1928.   The intensive treatment team: Delivering behavioral treatment in a residential setting.
Views the simple lack of time as one of the major problems in implementing behavior therapy programs and describes an intensive team approach to behavior therapy that was used in a center for autistic children. The team concept was developed to (a) provide more specific responses to prevailing problems, (b) increase the probability of success of behavioral programs, and (c) provide nursing staff with practical experience in using behavior modification techniques. Some of the methods used by the team are illustrated in 2 case examples.
Streifel, John A.; Smith, Paul A. & Savino, Lawrence J. (Camarillo State Hosp, CA) Hospital & Community Psychiatry, 1976(Oct), Vol 27(10), 697-698. [PA, Vol 57:10879]

1929.   Cognitive-perceptual treatment of exceptional children.
Based on the belief that cognitive operations consist of multiple stages of information-processing, cognitive-perceptual treatment is designed to specify the locus and nature of the child's deficits in information processing and to compensate for them. Clinical and empirical observations at the Illinois Institute, as well as the findings of others, demonstrate that this treatment program can be applied to exceptional children of many different diagnoses, including emotionally disturbed, learning disabled, autistic, and mentally retarded. The case study of a 7-yr-old autistic male is presented to illustrate the technique, process, and effectiveness of the treatment program.
Tong-He Koh. (Illinois Inst for Developmental Disabilities, Chicago) Child Care, Health & Development, 1976(Oct), Vol 2(5), 251-259. [PA, Vol 57:13138]

1930.   Behavioristic procedures in the treatment of autistic children: A review of the literature. MS. 1473 (17 pp/paper: $4; fiche: $2).
Akiyama, Robert M. (U California, Davis) Catalog of Selected Documents in Psychology, 1977(May), Vol 7, 42. [PA, Vol 58:05874]

1931.   Problems of dependence and development in an excessively passive autistic boy.
Describes a 10-yr interrupted period of psychoanalytic therapy with an autistic boy that began when he was 7 yrs of age. His intolerance of anxieties about separation led frequently to states of psychic dissolution and mindlessness. As he improved, he employed 2 different methods for achieving contact: One was designed to prevent innovation and development, while the other permitted change and growth in himself and his internal objects.

The author discusses the technical difficulty of distinguishing between this withdrawn boy's real need to be sought out in the transference and his passive exploitation of this situation. (9 ref)
Alvarez, Anne. Journal of Child Psychotherapy, 1977, Vol 4(3), 25–46. [PA, Vol 64:01499]

1932.   Training autistic children to urinate in the toilet through operant conditioning techniques.
Evaluated the use of operant conditioning techniques to toilet train children in an autism ward of a hospital for developmentally disturbed children. Five profoundly retarded males with clear clinical manifestations of autism were selected as Ss. Records of their urination behavior were kept during a baseline period and throughout the application of procedures. Appropriate urination behavior was immediately followed by positive reinforcers, such as candy, verbal praise, and physical affection. Inappropriate urination behavior was immediately followed by negative reinforcers, verbal as well as physical. Results show that operant conditioning techniques can be used to change the urination behavior of profoundly retarded autistic children even where other methods have failed. Factors requiring further investigation for their possible impact on the effectiveness of these procedures in toilet training autistic children are also discussed. (16 ref)
Ando, Haruhiko. (Aichi Prefectural Colony Central Hosp, Kasugai, Japan) Journal of Autism & Developmental Disorders, 1977(Jun), Vol 7(2), 151–163. [PA, Vol 59:10402]

1933.   [Behavioral modification psychotherapies in the autistic child.] (Fren)
Describes the use of behavioral modification psychotherapies, largely diffused in the Anglo-Saxon countries, for treating severely autistic children hospitalized in a child psychiatry service for at least 1 yr. Using L. Kanner's (1958) clinical study on childhood autism, the same syndrome is described in behavioral terms. This new approach is the basis for the therapeutic project, both on practical and theoretical grounds. To illustrate the method and its application, 3 observations of children hospitalized between 1976 and 1977 are presented. (Dutch, German, Italian, & Spanish summaries) (2½ p ref)
Barthelemy-Gault, C. & Larmande, C. (Centre Hosp Régional de Tours, France) Acta Psychiatrica Belgica, 1977(Sep–Oct), Vol 77(5), 549–586. [PA, Vol 64:10720]

1934.   Sign language and multisensory input training of children with communication and related developmental disorders.
Investigated simultaneous communication and multisensory input in the treatment of 6 autistic and communication disordered 5–12 yr olds. Ss were taught manually signed English and speech using a multisensory–intrusion approach. The hypothesis was that such a technique would alleviate the Ss' difficulties in information processing, organization of experience, and affect. The dependent measures were behavioral ratings derived from both structured (teaching) and unstructured (free play) sessions. Results indicate that the Ss manifested a consistent acquisition of sign language, which in some cases transferred into verbal communication skills. Statistical analyses of some of the observed socio-affective behaviors (i.e., nonsolitary play, interaction with peers and adults, exploration, and detachment) revealed tendencies supportive of the hypothesis. The variability of the data preclude any categorical statement in relation to the hypothesis. The preliminary results, however, strongly support continuation of the study. (19 ref)
Benaroya, S. et al. (Douglas Hosp, Children's Services, Verdun, Canada) Journal of Autism & Developmental Disorders, 1977(Mar), Vol 7(1), 23–31. [PA, Vol 59:01415]

1935.   Considerations in analysis and treatment of dietary effects on behavior: A case study.
Scientific and public interest in the effects of diet on behavior disorders has recently increased. This paper argues that, (a) the experimental analysis of behavior offers an effective scientific methodology for assessing the effects of dietary substances on behavior problems, and (b) such analysis permits behavioral consequences to be considered as an alternative treatment to

dietary control. A case study of a 9-yr-old retarded boy (IQ 40) with autistic behaviors is presented. Suspected dietary substances were demonstrated not to be effective influences on the child's behavior, whereas a simple behavior modification program improved his problem behaviors. Also discussed are issues and problems which arise in research on dietary effects on behavior and in selection of effective and ethical treatments. (15 ref)
Bird, Bruce L.; Russo, Dennis C. & Cataldo, Michael F. (John F. Kennedy Inst, Baltimore, MD) Journal of Autism & Childhood Schizophrenia, 1977(Dec), Vol 7(4), 373–382. [PA, Vol 60:12059]

1936. A relationship between motor control and language development in an autistic child.
Notes that recent work in both experimental and clinical psychology indicates that an important link exists between the development of motor control and language development. Diagnostic and therapeutic work with autistic children reveals a high incidence of gross motor dysfunction along with language deficits. A study to evaluate the effectiveness of behavior modification techniques in eliciting speech from nursery-age autistic children yielded new data to confirm the importance of the relationship. Results from a case study of one autistic 4.6 yr old female demonstrate that the S most frequently vocalized when motorically quiet, and engaged in motor activity when not speaking and especially prior to speech. Data from 30 behavior modification sessions and an intensive clinical interview indicate that limiting the S's gross motor activity was effective in increasing the frequency of vocalization. Theoretical interpretations of this phenomenon and implications for teatment and further research are offered. (29 ref)
Bram, Susan; Meier, Mila & Sutherland, Pamela J. (New York U Medical Ctr) Journal of Autism & Developmental Disorders, 1977(Mar), Vol 7(1), 57–67. [PA, Vol 59:01553]

1937. Current status of drug research and treatment with autistic children.
Presents a critical overview of the literature, with particular emphasis on methodology and with suggestions for future research. The importance of diagnosis, classification, and definition of subgroups within the etiologically heterogeneous population of autistic children is discussed in terms of response to drug treatment. Further research into the biological process(es) underlying this clinical picture should aid the development of a more rational pharmacological approach—an adjunct to the total treatment of the individual child. (61 ref)
Campbell, Magda; Geller, Barbara & Cohen, Ira L. (New York U Medical Ctr) Journal of Pediatric Psychology, 1977, Vol 2(4), 153–161. [PA, Vol 62:06732]

1938. [On the treatment of an autistic child at an institution for the severely mentally retarded.] (Japn)
Reports the case history of an autistic child who was hospitalized in a large institution for the severely mentally retarded. The child (K) was diagnosed as autistic at age 7 yrs and had been attending a special school; on weekends he was enrolled in a play therapy program for autistic children. K was accepted at the institution for the mentally retarded because his mother was sick, she had 2 other children, and the family lived in a densely populated area. At the time of K's admission he lacked emotional expression, was fidgety and hyperkinetic, exhibited compulsive activities, had nonverbal lalorrhea, had eccentric eating habits, and had no contact with other children. As a general treatment plan it was decided he should learn to play freely; be given practice in verbal communication; and have warm, physical contact with the staff. Factors at this institution that were particulary supportive of K's development include spacious grounds permitting great freedom of movement, a receptive and easy-going staff that worried less about a particular diagnosis than about promoting each child's development, and a long-term treatment plan for steady, continuous development without changes or interruptions. During his 5-yr stay, K was administered daily doses of a tranquilizer in small amounts. Without medication he developed insomnia, vagrancy, and other regressive behavior patterns. K made progress in

speech communication, social contacts, and exhibited no restlessness.
Chou, Tatsuo. (Osaka U, Japan) Japanese Journal of Child Psychiatry, 1977(Dec–Feb), Vol 18(1), 42–44. [PA, Vol 62:09322]

1939. Observations on a therapeutic residential setting for autistic children.
Describes a therapeutic milieu for children labeled with a diagnosis of early infantile autism. This study, conducted in a residential setting, discusses the various procedures adopted for alleviating the problems encountered with these children, such as the formation of social relationships, language formation, and compulsive behavior.
Cooper, Nicolas A. (London Hosp Medical Coll, England) Child Care, Health & Development, 1977(Nov–Dec), Vol 3(6), 437–441. [PA, Vol 61:09092]

1940. The search for help of parents of autistic children: or Beware of professional "groupthink."
Reports on interviews with 10 parents and families of autistic children. Questions dealt particularly with the parents' contacts with professionals, recommendations made for treatment, treatment followed, and professional attitudes encountered. Most of the professionals based their treatment on the "family as a problem" model, did not listen to parents' concerns about lack of progress by a child and lack of schooling, and displayed rigid and stereotyped attitudes. Parental dissatisfaction led to the establishment of a children's center that provides schooling and home skills. (15 ref)
Culbertson, Frances M. (U Wisconsin, Whitewater) Journal of Clinical Child Psychology, 1977(Win), Vol 6(3), 63–65. [PA, Vol 62:06439]

1941. [Operant conditioning with autistic children: A survey of the literature.] (Duth)
Summarizes 35 reports on the results of operant conditioning used with autistic children. The studies analyzed involved a total of 81 Ss. The procedures applied in operant conditioning include aversive therapy, chaining, contingency management, direct support, extinction, fading, modeling, positive physical contacts, prompting punishment, shaping, supportive management, time-out from positive reinforcement, and token economy. The mean CA of the Ss of these studies was about 23 mo. Practically all of the cases included speech difficulties, interaction disorders, and stereotyped behavior. The desired therapeutic goals were achieved with 78% of the Ss and partially achieved with 21%. Training sessions took place twice a week for 6 mo. According to these reports, the techniques that were most successful in eradicating undesirable behavior were chaining, direct support, extinction, punishment, shaping, and token economy. A follow-up study of 38% of the Ss indicated that only 6% suffered relapses. (48 ref)
Dullaart-Pruyser, E. (Zeikenhuis Amsterdam-Noord, Netherlands) Nederlands Tijdschrift voor de Psychologie en haar Grensgebieden, 1977(Jul), Vol 32(5), 307–332. [PA, Vol 61:04175]

1942. Group therapy with autistic/schizophrenic adolescents.
Describes a group therapy program for severely disturbed 12–14 yr olds at a psychiatric center. Using behavior modification, the highly structured program stressed a nonpermissive atmosphere. Such inappropriate behaviors as physical agitation and nonsensical speech were aggressively identified as "crazy." Appropriate behavior, including sensible speech and the identification of inappropriate behavior in others were positively reinforced with pats, hugs, hand shaking, and group applause. Videotaping of sessions helped group members confront their behaviors and showed that these severely disturbed children made considerable gains in demonstrating behavior appropriate to the group discussion setting.
Epstein, Norman. (Community Mental Health Ctr, Children's Psychiatric Ctr, Eatontown, NJ) Social Casework, 1977(Jun), Vol 58(6), 350–358. [PA, Vol 62:11482]

1943. Attention training: The use of overcorrection avoidance to increase the eye contact of autistic and retarded children.
A crucial 1st step in teaching and training the retarded and autistic involves developing and maintaining eye contact with the therapist. Functional movement training (an overcorrection procedure) plus edibles and praise were compared with edibles and praise alone as a method of developing eye contact in 3 such children: an 8-yr-old autistic boy, an 8-yr-old severely retarded girl, and a 6-yr-old severely retarded boy. In both conditions, the S was given food and praise when eye contact occurred within 5 sec of the therapist's verbal prompt. Functional movement training avoidance plus edibles and praise produced about 90% attention for the 3 Ss, while edibles and praise alone were less effective (eye contact never exceeded 55%). Functional movement training avoidance combined with edibles and praise appears to be an effective method of teaching eye contact and possibly other forms of instruction-following to behaviorally disordered children who are not always responsive to positive consequences.
Foxx, R. M. (U Maryland Baltimore County, Catonsville) Journal of Applied Behavior Analysis, 1977(Fal), Vol 10(3), 489–499. [PA, Vol 60:07878]

1944. Thumbsucking in an autistic child overcome by overcorrection.
An overcorrection procedure was employed to suppress thumbsucking in a 24-mo-old autistic boy. The procedure involved holding the child's hands down to his side for 30 sec on each occurrence of thumbsucking. Thumbsucking was reduced from a rate of 200 instances in a 2-hr period to 0 over 13 sessions. The suppression of thumbsucking was maintained for 14 mo, and was generalized to a ward setting where the intervention was never made.
Freeman, B. J.; Moss, Debbie; Somerset, Tom & Ritvo, E. R. (U California Medical School, Los Angeles) Journal of Behavior Therapy & Experimental Psychiatry, 1977(Jun), Vol 8(2), 211–212. [PA, Vol 59:12737]

1945. [Behavior therapy approach to the therapeutic education of an autistic child: A process of speech training.] (Japn)
Describes the verbal behavior training given to an 8-yr-old mute autistic male, employing behavior therapy techniques. Attempts to develop speech had little success, but sensory motor training improved coordination and discrimination ability. S learned to match objects to pictures and objects to written characters and to use the characters to represent the objects. (English summary) (36 ref)
Hirata, Akitsugu. Japanese Journal of Educational Psychology, 1977(Jun), Vol 25(2), 104–115. [PA, Vol 64:12985]

1946. Behavioral treatment of self-stimulation: An examination of alternatives to physical punishment.
Reviews the use of behavioral procedures other than physical punishment in treating the noninjurious self-stimulatory behaviors of retarded and autistic individuals. Evidence is presented that suggests that the combination of positive reinforcement for functional responses with deceleration techniques such as extinction or overcorrection may provide an effective means of reducing self-stimulation and teaching appropriate behaviors. (24 ref)
Hobbs, Steven A. & Goswick, Ruth A. (U Tulsa) Journal of Clinical Child Psychology, 1977(Spr), Vol 6(1), 20–23. [PA, Vol 61:08944]

1947. Generalization of "curiosity" questioning behavior in autistic children.
Four minimally verbal autistic children (ages 8–10 yrs) were first trained in question-asking behavior of the forms "What is . . . for?" and "What is/are . . . doing?" in a summer camp. The study then examined the variables controlling generalization of these 2 behaviors across settings (from training to nontraining), across response classes (from asking the questions to correctly answering the questions), and across time (maintaining correct answers at follow-up). Data show that there was little generalization of spontaneous question-asking outside the sessions until token reinforcement for spontaneous question-asking in nontraining times was increased. Ss seldom answered the questions correctly until contingent modelling for correct answers was given. 11 mo after the camp period, 3 Ss still showed maintenance of correct answers to the 2 question forms but asked no questions spontaneously under a no-reinforcement condition. The implications of training and generalizing the 2 forms of "curiosity" questions in autistic children are discussed. (18 ref)
Hung, David W. (Rotary School Autistic Program, Toronto, Canada) Journal of Behavior Therapy & Experimental Psychiatry, 1977(Sep), Vol 8(3), 237–245. [PA, Vol 60:12178]

1948. Self-stimulation and learning in autistic children: Physical or functional incompatibility?
Four self-stimulating autistic children were taught 2 discrimination tasks. One task required a response that physically interfered with their self-stimulation; the other did not. All Ss responded similarly across tasks. The 3 Ss with higher MA scores learned both tasks without external suppression of self-stimulation. None of the Ss showed an inverse relationship between self-stimulation and learning. Results show that elimination of self-stimulation is not a prerequisite for the acquisition of a new behavior in all autistic children.
Klier, Jolynn & Harris, Sandra L. (Rutgers U, Graduate School of Applied & Professional Psychology, Busch Campus) Journal of Applied Behavior Analysis, 1977(Sum), Vol 10(2), 311. [PA, Vol 59:12473]

1949. [A consideration of the effectiveness of therapeutic camping for autistic children.] (Japn)
Conducted therapeutic camping for 45 4–12 yr old autistic children. Follow-ups showed improvements in numerous types of behavior. Group activities were thought to be primarily responsible for the improvement, and it is suggested that they are most effective when conducted in isolation from the settings of daily life. (English summary) (11 ref)
Kobayashi, Ryuji & Murata, Toyohisa. (Fukuoka U, Japan) Japanese Journal of Child Psychiatry, 1977(Jul–Aug), Vol 18(4), 221–234. [PA, Vol 64:12857]

1950. Research on the difference between generalization and maintenance in extra-therapy responding.
Many authors have reported that the development of programs for producing durable extra-therapy responding lags behind the development of programs for producing initial behavior change. In Exp I with 3 autistic 7–11 yr olds (estimated IQ below 10), responding was recorded continuously in both the therapy and extra-therapy settings. One S did not generalize to the extra-therapy setting, but other Ss did. For Ss who generalized, however, extra-therapy responding was not maintained. A 2nd experiment was conducted, using 6 male autistic children (average CA 10.2 yrs; IQ range untestable to 35). Two variables affecting the durability of extra-therapy responding were assessed and found to be influential: the use of partial reinforcement schedules in the original treatment environment, and the presence of noncontingent reinforcers in the extra-therapy environment. Results suggest there are 2 distinct parameters of extra-therapy responding: generalization and maintenance. A technology for producing durable extra-therapy responding is discussed in terms of different treatment procedures required for different deficits in extra-therapy responding. (24 ref)
Koegel, Robert L. & Rincover, Arnold. (U California Social Process Research Inst, Santa Barbara) Journal of Applied Behavior Analysis, 1977(Spr), Vol 10(1), 1–12. [PA, Vol 59:01570]

1951. Teaching autistic children to respond to simultaneous multiple cues.
A number of studies have shown that autistic children tend to learn new discriminations by responding to only a restricted number of available cues and that this may be responsible for some of their abnormal behavior. Therefore, this investigation assessed the feasibility of teaching autistic children to respond to multiple cues. Results show that 4 autistic children (mean CA, 6 yrs and 9 mo) could learn a conditional discrimination requiring

them to discriminate a multiple-cue complex from each of its 2 component cues. However, the children did not learn this discrimination in the same manner as 4 normal children. In the early trials, the autistics responded at a higher level to 1 of the 2 component cues. Only after many trials did the autistics respond equally on the basis of both component cues. Results of an initial attempt to teach a general set to respond to multiple cues showed that, when an autistic child was taught a series of successive conditional discriminations, the child eventually learned a set to approach new discriminations by responding equally on the basis of both component cues. Results are discussed in terms of understanding and treating autistic children's abnormal development. (25 ref)
Koegel, Robert L. & Schreibman, Laura. (U California Social Process Research Inst, Santa Barbara) Journal of Experimental Child Psychology, 1977(Oct), Vol 24(2), 299–311. [PA, Vol 60:05376]

1952. Simultaneous communication with autistic and other severely dysfunctional nonverbal children.
Suggests that despite its widespread application, the teaching of speech does not appear to be effective with all autistic and other severely dysfunctional, nonverbal children. A body of recent evidence points to the peculiarities in the information processing of these children and to the importance of gestures as aids or alternatives to speech. The present study reports on the use of simultaneous communication (gestures plus speech) with 5 such children, all of whom were males, ages 5 yrs 3 mo–9 yrs 4 mo. Two of the Ss were diagnosed as autistic and severely mentally retarded; 1 was autistic and mentally retarded; 1 had congenital rubella syndrome, brain damage, bilateral hearing loss, and autistic features; and 1 had childhood schizophrenia at the symbiotic stage. The fact that 4 of the Ss showed marked gains in their ability to communicate over a 5-wk period raises some theoretical and methodological issues pertinent to the treatment of autistic and autistic-like children and to a general understanding of the processes involved in nonverbal communication. Improvements that were significant at the .001 level were found in the areas of interaction with peers, positive behaviors, awareness, and self-care skills. (29 ref)
Konstantareas, M. Mary; Oxman, Joel & Webster, Chris D. (Clarke Inst of Psychiatry, Child & Adolescent Service, Toronto, Canada) Journal of Communication Disorders, 1977(Sep), Vol 10(3), 267–282. [PA, Vol 60:03615]

1953. Communication training in mute autistic adolescents using the written word.
Taught the expressive and receptive use of 3 written words to 3 mute autistic adolescents using a procedure based on H. S. Terrace's errorless discrimination model and D. Premack's language training with chimps. Expressive language was measured by the S's selection of the appropriate word card from among the available alternatives when the corresponding object was presented. Receptive language was measured by the S's selection of the appropriate object from among the available alternatives when the corresponding word card was presented. The sequence of the presentations and the order of placement of the available alternatives were randomized. The 3 subjects required 979, 1,791, and 1,644 trials, respectively, to master both the expressive and receptive use of the 3 words. The correct response rates for the 3 Ss over the entire training program were 92, 92, and 90%, respectively. It is concluded that, as concrete visual symbols, written words may provide a viable communication system for the mute autistic. (33 ref)
LaVigna, Gary W. (Camarillo State Hosp, Behavior Development & Learning Ctr, CA) Journal of Autism & Developmental Disorders, 1977(Jun), Vol 7(2), 135–149. [PA, Vol 59:10276]

1954. [On pre-requirements to the use of audio-visual techniques in deviant children: Thoughts from the psychoanalytical treatment of a thirteen month aged child.] (Fren)
Discusses the analytic cure of a child, hospitalized since birth, which took place between the 13th and 21st mo of age. The discussion raises the question of the use of audiovisual techniques for psychotic and autistic Ss and argues for the pedagogic use of

imagery for such Ss. The primary importance of symbolic function on imagery function is demonstrated. (Flemish, German, Italian, & Spanish summaries)
Lefort, Rosine. Acta Psychiatrica Belgica, 1977(Jul–Aug), Vol 77(4), 446–467. [PA, Vol 64:08393]

1955. Reply to reader comments on "Employing electric shock with autistic children."
Reactions to a 1976 article by the author on the use of electric shock with autistic children indicate that despite the effectiveness of the treatment with autistic children and the absence of major undesirable side effects, there exists a very strong spirit in the US which abhors punishment with this or any other patient population.
Lichstein, Kenneth L. (Memphis State U) Journal of Autism & Childhood Schizophrenia, 1977(Sep), Vol 7(3), 303–306. [PA, Vol 60:05641]

1956. Treatment of obsessive-compulsive neurosis with history of childhood autism.
Presents a detailed case report of a 17-yr-old male, followed over 3 yrs, who had severe obsessive-compulsive rituals and ruminations, interpersonal deficits, complicating depression, and a history of childhood autism. Intensive behavioral treatment was given in an operant framework, with in vivo exposure modeling, response prevention, and social skills training. Compulsive rituals improved markedly and lastingly, but ruminations and social defects persisted. When intercurrent depression occurred, dothiepin (50–300 mg/day) facilitated behavioral treatment. Adjustment remained fragile. Minimum maintenance treatment in the community could not be adequately arranged, so that gains made in hospital were partly lost at follow-up, despite continuing improvement in rituals.
Lindley, Peter; Marks, Isaac; Philpott, Robin & Snowden, John. (Bethlem Royal Hosp, London, England) British Journal of Psychiatry, 1977(Jun), Vol 130, 592–597. [PA, Vol 59:10438]

1957. Communicating with autistic children.
The delayed and disordered language of autistic children is discussed as it affects the delivery of health care and other services in interdisciplinary settings. Current research is reviewed in terms of 4 major areas of communication-related deficits associated with early childhood autism: language delay, need for sameness, and impairments in social and information processing skills. Within the framework of each deficit area, methods for communicating with autistic children in health-care settings are presented. (45 ref)
Lord, Catherine & Baker, Ann F. (U Minnesota, Inst of Child Development) Journal of Pediatric Psychology, 1977, Vol 2(4), 181–186. [PA, Vol 62:06463]

1958. The elimination of a child's in-class masturbation by overcorrection and reinforcement.
Attempts at modifying the masturbation of an 8-yr-old autistic mentally retarded boy through the reinforcement of incompatible behaviors were unsuccessful. When the child was required to "practice" a series of overcorrection responses contingent on masturbation, all masturbation was eliminated after 8 days of overcorrection treatment. The behavior remained absent at 1-, 6-, and 12-mo follow-ups.
Luiselli, James K.; Helfen, Carol S.; Pemberton, Bruce W. & Reisman, John. (Crosby School Behavioral Intervention Project, Arlington, MA) Journal of Behavior Therapy & Experimental Psychiatry, 1977(Jun), Vol 8(2), 201–204. [PA, Vol 59:12749]

1959. The use of psychedelic drugs in the treatment of severely disturbed children: A review.
Reviews clinical reports on the therapeutic effects of LSD, its derivatives, and psilocybin on autistic schizophrenic children. Daily administration of 10–100 mg LSD improves the functions of the autonomic system, resulting in good gastrointestinal regulation, normalized sleep pattern, and weight gain. Stereotyped motor responses are reduced, and comprehension of speech is improved. However, the objectivity of clinical observations is questionable in at least one study. The drug effects lasted 5 yrs in one study, but were only transient in other studies. There is no

evidence to indicate any chromosomal abnormality after repeated administration of LSD. (54 ref)
Rhead, John C. (Maryland Psychiatric Research Ctr, Baltimore) Journal of Psychedelic Drugs, 1977(Apr–Jun), Vol 9(2), 93–101. [PA, Vol 61:04254]

1960.   Problems of dependence and development: Discussion.
Comments on several aspects of the case of Bobbie, an autistic boy treated by A. Alvarez (see PA, Vol 64:1479). The present author notes the relative absence of direct material concerning jealousy and rivalry, especially as compared with material from other autistic children, who often seem preoccupied with these problems.
Riley, Charlotte.   Journal of Child Psychotherapy, 1977, Vol 4(3), 47–48. [PA, Vol 64:01550]

1961.   Personal distance in play therapy with an autistic and a symbiotic psychotic child.
Compared the personal distance behaviors of 2 severely disturbed male children, a 9-yr-old autistic Mexican American and a 7-yr-old symbiotic psychotic Caucasian. Naturalistic observation was employed, with each of the Ss being videotaped during sessions of individual play therapy. Data included measurement of distance between therapist and patient each 15 sec, durations of periods spent within 1 ft personal distance or physically touching, initiation of movement into specific zones of distance, and direction and magnitude of zone changes initiated by each participant. Results support the hypotheses that (a) the autistic child would maintain an average personal distance from the therapist that was significantly greater than the average distance maintained by the symbiotic child, and (b) the autistic child would demonstrate a significantly heightened motility pattern when compared to that of the symbiotic child. Both children were significantly prone to increase the distance between themselves and the therapist, while the therapist was more likely to decrease the personal distance, although not significantly so. Suggestions for therapeutic use of personal distance phenomena with disturbed children are discussed.
Rogers, Alan L. & Fine, Harold J. (U Tennessee) Psychotherapy: Theory, Research & Practice, 1977(Spr), Vol 14(1), 41–48. [PA, Vol 61:06482]

1962.   Acquisition of modified American Sign Language by a mute autistic child.
Attempted to teach a modified version of American Sign Language to a mute 5-yr-old boy who had been diagnosed autistic and who had a Merrill-Palmer IQ of 65. Previous attempts to teach imitative spoken language had failed, and baseline data indicated that S's signing vocabulary was also nonexistent. Data were collected during 20 structured sessions involving presentation of stimuli, prompting and manual guidance when necessary, and reinforcement. Continuous use of signs as communication in class and at home was emphasized. S had mastered 12 signs at the end of the study. Spontaneous signing frequency as recorded by parents and teachers during several 48-hr periods rose from 15 to 42 emitted signs over the 3 mo of the study. S made a half year's developmental progress during this time, as measured by a sign-language adaptation of the Alpern-Boll Communication Scale. S, however, made no apparent progress in acquiring spoken language.
Salvin, Ann; Routh, Donald K.; Foster, Robert E. & Lovejoy, Karen M. (U North Carolina, Chapel Hill) Journal of Autism & Childhood Schizophrenia, 1977(Dec), Vol 7(4), 359–371. [PA, Vol 60:12088]

1963.   A reply to the comments on "Employing electric shock with autistic children: A review of the side effects."
Replies to criticisms of K. L. Lichstein and L. Schreibman's (1976) paper defending the use of electric shock with autistic children. It is pointed out that the paper only concentrated on one specific issue—side effects—and that there are many other issues involved in this procedure that need to be clarified. Misuses of contingent electric shock are discussed, and characteristics of good behavior therapists are described.

Schreibman, Laura. (Claremont Men's Coll, CA) Journal of Autism & Developmental Disorders, 1977(Jun), Vol 7(2), 203–204. [PA, Vol 59:10447]

1964.   Some thoughts about developing programs for autistic adolescents.
Describes the procedures and underlying philosophy of the TEACCH (Treatment and Education of Autistic and related Communications-Handicapped Children) program, emphasizing the role of parents as cotherapists. The concerns of older autistic persons and their families are reviewed, including residential, employment, and social adjustment needs. It is concluded that an individualized intervention program in which parents have primary responsibility for decisions made about their child and adolescent will provide the best, most responsive treatment approach. (24 ref)
Sloan, Jerry L. & Schopler, Eric. (U North Carolina Medical School, Chapel Hill) Journal of Pediatric Psychology, 1977, Vol 2(4), 187–190. [PA, Vol 62:06817]

1965.   Some determinants of the reinforcing and punishing effects of timeout.
Conducted 2 experiments to investigate some determinants of the reinforcing and punishing properties of time-out (TO). Exp I began as an attempt to reduce the frequency of tantrums of a 6-yr-old autistic girl by using TO. Unexpectedly, the result was a substantial increase in the frequency of tantrums. Using a reversal design, subsequent manipulations showed that the opportunity to engage in self-stimulatory behavior during the TO period was largely responsible for the increase in tantrums. Exp II was initiated following the failure of TO to reduce the spitting and self-injurious behavior of a 16-yr-old retarded boy. Using a multiple-baseline design, the nature of the time-in environment was shown to be an important determinant of the effects of TO. When the time-in environment was enriched with new toys, continuous prompting, and praise, TO was effective as a punisher. A conception of TO is discussed in terms of the relative reinforcing properties and clinical implications of TO and time-in.
Solnick, Jay V.; Rincover, Arnold & Peterson, Christa R. (U North Carolina, Chapel Hill) Journal of Applied Behavior Analysis, 1977(Fal), Vol 10(3), 415–424. [PA, Vol 60:07913]

1966.   A negative reaction to the use of electric shock with autistic children.
Responds to K. L. Lichstein and L. Schreibman's (1976) paper which defended the use of electric shock to prevent autistic children from harming themselves and/or others. The need to find alternatives to punishment for these children is discussed.
Webster, C. D. (U Victoria, British Columbia, Canada) Journal of Autism & Developmental Disorders, 1977(Jun), Vol 7(2), 199–202. [PA, Vol 59:10456]

1967.   Effects of a procedure derived from the overcorrection principle on manipulated and nonmanipulated behaviors.
Positive practice overcorrection (OC) has been shown to be effective in reducing self-stimulatory behaviors displayed by retarded and autistic individuals. In addition, the procedure may increase the occurrence of appropriate behavior through intensive practice. In the present study, several stereotypic behaviors and an appropriate behavior (appropriate toy play) displayed by a pair of autistic 10-yr-old male twins were measured before and during treatment by a positive-practice-in-appropriate-toy-play OC procedure. OC was introduced for each of the targeted inappropriate behaviors in succession for both Ss. Results show that OC reduced all stereotypic behaviors displayed by both Ss. In addition, 1 S displayed marked increases in the behavior practiced during OC, relative to its baseline rate of occurrence. Results indicate that for some individuals, OC may be effective in teaching and motivating appropriate forms of behavior as well as reducing stereotypy.
Wells, Karen C.; Forehand, Rex; Hickey, Kevin & Green, Kenneth D. (U Georgia) Journal of Applied Behavior Analysis, 1977(Win), Vol 10(4), 679–687. [PA, Vol 61:01579]

1968. **Establishing generalization effects among autistic children.**
Notes that, although elusive, generalization of behavior change in autistic children is essential to obtaining maximum treatment effects. Using behaviorally based treatment and teachers and parents as trainers, generalization effects between home and school were measured on 4 behaviors: following instructions, washing, wiping bottom, and sharing toys. Ss were 12 boys aged 9–14 yrs whose WISC scores were greater than 30 but less than 90. Results indicate that both settings were effective in establishing generalization. Behaviors treated in one setting generalized to another when Ss were provided with an opportunity for daily practice.
Zifferblatt, Steven M.; Burton, Stephen D.; Horner, Rob & White, Trudy. (NIH, National Heart, Lung & Blood Inst, Bethesda, MD) Journal of Autism & Childhood Schizophrenia, 1977(Dec), Vol 7(4), 337–347. [PA, Vol 60:12217]

1969. **Triiodothyronine (T₃) concentration and therapy in autistic children.**
Investigated the clinical and biochemical status of the thyroid function of 13 7–21 yr old patients with an autistic syndrome. There was no clinical evidence for hypothyroidism in any S, and triiodothyronine (T₃), thyroxine, and thyrotropin concentrations were within the normal range. Two Ss who had retarded bone ages were treated with T₃ (beginning dosage, 25 mcg/day) for 6 mo. Hyperthyroidism developed when T₃ levels exceeded physiologic concentrations in these patients. The concept that the clinical response to T₃ in autistic patients results from correction of thyroid dysfunction is not supported by these findings. (9 ref)
Abbassi, V.; Linscheid, Thomas R. & Coleman, M. (Georgetown U Medical Ctr) Journal of Autism & Developmental Disorders, 1978(Dec), Vol 8(4), 383–387. [PA, Vol 62:06721]

1970. **Case study: Art expression as a guide to music therapy.**
Describes the use of music therapy in the case of a 14-yr-old institutionalized autistic girl. The child, whose verbal expression was limited, was willing to communicate through drawing, thus giving her therapist information on her feelings, likes, and dislikes. Music sessions mediated by drawing helped the girl to lengthen her attention span, modify compulsive drawing habits, broaden the range of her feelings, and gain a firmer hold on reality.
Blasco, Serafina P. (Princess Sofia Ctr for Special Education, Madrid, Spain) American Journal of Art Therapy, 1978(Jan), Vol 17(2), 51–56. [PA, Vol 63:05805]

1971. **A controlled crossover study of triiodothyronine in autistic children.**
Conducted a placebo-controlled crossover study of the behavioral effects of triiodothyronine (T₃) in 30 2.3–7.2 yr old clinically euthyroid autistic children. Ss' intelligence was determined by the Gesell Developmental Schedules or the Wechsler Preschool and Primary Scale of Intelligence. Optimal dosages of T₃ ranged from 12.5 to 75 mcg daily. Multiple independent raters and multiple rating scales (including Clinical Global Impressions, Children's Psychiatric Rating Scale, Children's Behavior Inventory, Nurses' Global Impressions Scale, and Connors Parent–Teacher Questionnaire) were used. Except for a few symptoms that were reduced on T₃, the drug did not differ from placebo. Time appeared to account for most of the improvement in the whole sample. As a group, the lower IQ Ss responded to T₃. The individual Ss who were responders could not be defined by any parameter. (21 ref)
Campbell, Magda et al. (New York U Medical Ctr) Journal of Autism & Developmental Disorders, 1978(Dec), Vol 8(4), 371–381. [PA, Vol 62:06731]

1972. **Acquisition of sign language by autistic children: I. Expressive labelling.**
There has been growing interest in teaching sign language to autistic children who have failed to develop speech. However, controlled experimentation in this area is nonexistent. In the present study, 4 nonverbal autistic children (ages 10, 14, and 15 yrs) were taught expressive sign labels for common objects, using a training procedure that consisted of prompting, fading, and stimulus rotation. The efficacy of the procedure was demonstrated in a multiple-baseline design across objects. The results were reliable, replicable across Ss, and generalizable across therapists. A stimulus control analysis demonstrated that, for 3 Ss, correct signing was controlled solely by the visual cues associated with the presentation of a given object and was independent of the auditory cues related to the same object. These latter results are discussed with respect to the known perceptual and linguistic deficits of autistic children. (18 ref)
Carr, Edward G.; Binkoff, Jody A.; Kologinsky, Eileen & Eddy, Michael. (State U New York, Stony Brook) Journal of Applied Behavior Analysis, 1978(Win), Vol 11(4), 489–501. [PA, Vol 64:03761]

1973. **The use of contingent music to increase appropriate conversational speech.**
Contingent "preferred" music was investigated as a reinforcer to increase appropriate conversational speech in a mentally retarded and autistic-like 14-yr-old boy. Results of an ABAB reversal-design study demonstrate that music, when applied contingently, can be used as a tool to increase appropriate speech and decrease inappropriate speech.
Deutsch, Marilyn & Parks, A. Lee. (Nisonger Ctr, Columbus, OH) Mental Retardation, 1978(Feb), Vol 16(1), 33–36. [PA, Vol 61:08932]

1974. **The effect of environmental stimulation upon the stereotyped behavior of autistic children.**
Observed 2 groups of 3 autistic children, equated for CA but differing in IQ and performance MA, for 20-min sessions. The high-IQ group had a mean CA, MA, and IQ of 49 mo, 35 mo, and 73.3, respectively, while the low-IQ group had means of 49 mo, 16.2 mo, and 34.7, respectively. Total duration of time Ss engaged in stereotyped behavior was recorded for each minute. During Minutes 6–15, Ss were provided with either minimal or high environmental stimulation. High environmental stimulation was found to increase the mean duration of time the low-IQ group engaged in stereotyped behavior but to decrease the duration for the high-IQ group. (10 ref)
Frankel, Fred; Freeman, B. J.; Ritvo, Edward R. & Pardo, Rosina. (U California, Los Angeles) Journal of Autism & Developmental Disorders, 1978(Dec), Vol 8(4), 389–394. [PA, Vol 62:06643]

1975. **Using self-stimulation as reinforcement for autistic children.**
Examined the effects of using self-stimulatory behavior as reinforcement for spontaneous appropriate sentences in 2 autistic boys, ages 11.9 and 10.2 yrs. Ss were put on a token system and always received 1 token for every spontaneous appropriate sentence they made. An ABABA design was employed. In Condition A, the opportunity to self-stimulate was contingent on the payment of tokens (2 tokens for 2 min of self-stimulation). In Condition B, no tokens were required for self-stimulation. Results show that both Ss exhibited a much higher rate of spontaneous appropriate sentences during the contingent self-stimulation (A) condition, demonstrating that self-stimulation functioned as an effective reinforcement. The possibility of using self-stimulation as reinforcement in the treatment of autistic children is discussed. (17 ref)
Hung, David W. (Florida Mental Health Inst, Tampa) Journal of Autism & Childhood Schizophrenia, 1978(Sep), Vol 8(3), 355–366. [PA, Vol 62:04145]

1976. **Summer camp treatment program for autistic children.**
Describes a 3-wk residential treatment program for 18 autistic children (mean age 9 yrs 6 mo). Camp staff consisted of university students who focused the training on 4 major areas: self-help skills, language training, generalization of language from training to nontraining settings, and reduction of undesirable behaviors. Results suggest that out of 145 training programs given to the children, 115 produced improvement of 15% or more. Every child improved 15% or more in at least one area of

treatment during the camp, and there was some generalization from training to nontraining settings.
Hung, David W. & Thelander, Mary J. (Rotary School Autistic Program, Willowdale, Canada) Exceptional Children, 1978(Apr), Vol 44(7), 534–536. [PA, Vol 61:11421]

1977. Food refusal in an autistic type child treated by a multi-component forced feeding procedure.
A multicomponent forced feeding procedure involving shaping, negative reinforcement, and the use of preferred foods for positive reinforcement was used to teach a 5-yr-old autistic type boy to accept a wide variety of foods. Following a baseline during which all solid foods were refused, the treatment within a multiple baseline design led to rapid acceptance of a number of foods in school and then at home. In cases where shaping and positive reinforcement alone are not possible because the child refuses to sample new foods, this forced feeding procedures may lead to significant improvement in eating behavior. (7 ref)
Ives, Clifford C.; Harris, Sandra L. & Wolchik, Sharlene A. (Rutgers U Graduate School of Applied & Professional Psychology, New Brunswick) Journal of Behavior Therapy & Experimental Psychiatry, 1978(Mar), Vol 9(1), 61–64. [PA, Vol 62:14234]

1978. The use of physical contact as a positive reinforcer.
In a study with 2 boys selected from 24 children (3–10 yrs old) with diagnoses of brain damage, retardation, or autism it was demonstrated that tactile contact could serve as the sole reinforcer in behavioral modification training. Physical contact also accelerated and maintained preexisting behaviors. Anecdotal data suggested that physical contact generalized to other persons and situations.
Johnson, Claudia A. & Frankel, Alan. (VA Hosp Day Treatment Ctr, Salem, VA) Behavior Therapy, 1978(Nov), Vol 9(5), 969–970. [PA, Vol 62:09149]

1979. A home-based program for a preschool behaviorally disturbed child with parents as therapists.
Evaluated the effects of a set of reinforcement procedures on the autistic behaviors of a 4-yr-old girl. The study was carried out entirely in a home setting with the mother and father as change agents. The parents were trained to use, in a semistructured play setting with written and verbal instructions, a treatment program consisting of positive attention and time-out. Each parent independently applied the training procedures to the child's compliance, inappropriate vocalization, and noncompliance behaviors. Both multiple baseline and reversal procedures were employed to assess treatment effects. Results indicate that the parents' use of the positive attention and time-out procedures was responsible for a substantial improvement in their daughter's compliance with instructions and a marked decrease in the 2 inappropriate responses. Comparisons across parents indicated no marked differences in the procedures' effects on the child's behaviors. (17 ref)
Johnson, Moses R.; Whitman, Thomas L. & Barloon-Noble, Rebecca. (U Notre Dame) Journal of Behavior Therapy & Experimental Psychiatry, 1978(Mar), Vol 9(1), 65–70. [PA, Vol 62:14237]

1980. Generalization of parent-training results.
Conducted 2 experiments to assess the generalized effects of several different parent/teacher training programs. In Exp I with 4 mothers of autistic children, it was found that a brief demonstration of how to teach the autistic child new behaviors was sufficient to teach parents how to teach those children those behaviors. However, generalization to new child-target behaviors did not take place. Another parent training program, which did not demonstrate how to teach any one specific child behavior, but was based on teaching the use of general behavior-modification procedures, was effective in teaching the parents how to teach new child-target behaviors. Exp II, with 3 adults of varying professional backgrounds and 6 autistic children, provided analyses of the individual effect of several components of the generalized training program. Results show that videotape illustrations of the procedures, without the presence of a master

teacher, were sufficient to teach the adults. However, sub-parts of the videotapes produced highly specific training results, with each component changing corresponding areas of the adults' behaviors. Viewing of the entire package was necessary before the adults were able to improve the autistic children's behaviors. Overall results suggest the importance of obtaining multiple measures of the effects of parent and teacher training programs, including measures of acquisition and generalization of both adult and child behaviors. (32 ref)
Koegel, Robert L.; Glahn, T. J. & Nieminen, Gayla S. (U California Social Process Research Inst, Santa Barbara) Journal of Applied Behavior Analysis, 1978(Spr), Vol 11(1), 95–109. [PA, Vol 61:11364]

1981. Treatment of an autistic child's fear of riding a school bus through exposure and reinforcement.
A 7-yr-old boy, fearful of riding a school bus, was reinforced for spending short periods of time on the bus while it was parked near the school and later for riding the route from home to school. S's mother was present to provide reinforcement. After 9 treatment days, S was capable of riding the bus independently, and over the course of a 1-yr follow-up, he continued independent riding without difficulties. (10 ref)
Luiselli, James K. (Arlington Public Schools, Behavioral Intervention Project, MA) Journal of Behavior Therapy & Experimental Psychiatry, 1978(Jun), Vol 9(2), 169–172. [PA, Vol 63:01576]

1982. An experimental analysis of side effects and response maintenance of a modified overcorrection procedure: The case of the persistent twiddler.
Used a 3- and 5-min modified overcorrection procedure to suppress a high-frequency hand stereotypic behavior, twiddling, exhibited by a 10-yr-old autistic girl. As demonstrated through the use of an ABCB design, both durations of overcorrection were immediately successful in reducing twiddling to near 0 levels during 20-min classroom training sessions. Neither overcorrection procedure resulted in a great deal of response maintenance during a 10-min, free-play probe period immediately following the training sessions. Approach and proximity to the trainer were also assessed during the free-play probe sessions. Neither of these behaviors varied significantly from baseline measures when the overcorrection procedures were instituted. The 3-min overcorrection duration (B), however, produced slightly more response maintenance than the 5-min duration (C). This small effect reversed when the 3-min duration was reinstated. (22 ref)
Marholin, David & Townsend, Nancy M. (Boston U) Behavior Therapy, 1978(Jun), Vol 9(3), 383–390. [PA, Vol 62:04151]

1983. [A therapeutic treatment for pre-school children with developmental handicaps: Therapeutic treatment and its effectiveness for younger pre-school children.] (Japn)
11 developmentally impaired preschoolers completed twice weekly, 60-min treatment sessions that included free play and structured play (e.g., playing ball, drawing, and completing puzzles). Developmental change was assessed with standardized measures. It is concluded that the integration of general treatment and special treatment is effective in improving the development of impaired children. (English abstract) (14 ref)
Matsusaka, Kiyotoshi. (Mie U Faculty of Education, Japan) Japanese Journal of Child Psychiatry, 1978(Sep–Nov), Vol 19(5), 313–333. [PA, Vol 64:12868]

1984. Behavior therapy for autistic children: A study of acceptability and outcome.
An inpatient program for autistic children which used behavior modification methods is described, and a follow-up study of the 1st 15 children discharged from the program is reported. Mean age of the 10 boys and 5 girls at admission was 65.9 mo. In general, the outcome results appear to be comparable to those of other treatment methods. It is noted, however, that there was a relatively high proportion of children (53%) living at home at follow-up (mean follow-up time 23 mo). A 2nd main purpose of the study was to assess the acceptability of this program to

parents and to document their impressions regarding their child's period of inpatient care. Overall, a high level of acceptability was found. (5 ref)
Mazuryk, Gregory F.; Barker, Philip & Harasym, Lisa. (Thistletown Regional Ctr for Children & Adolescents, Toronto, Canada) Child Psychiatry & Human Development, 1978(Win), Vol 9(2), 119–125. [PA, Vol 62:06678]

1985.   Behavior of withdrawn autistic children: Effects of peer social initiations.
Evaluated positive social initiations by a behaviorally disordered age-peer as an intervention for 3 withdrawn, autistic children. During baseline, the peer trainer (a 10-yr-old boy) made few social approaches to target Ss (an 8-yr-old girl and 2 9-yr-old boys). The peer trainer greatly increased his rate of positive social initiations during the 1st intervention, decreased social approaches during a 2nd baseline, and increased social approaches again in a 2nd intervention phase. To evaluate whether increased social initiations toward a target S would affect the social behavior of other children in the setting, intervention was begun at different times for each S. Increases in peer trainer initiations resulted in an immediate acceleration in the frequency of all Ss' positive social behavior. For 2 of the 3 Ss, negative social behaviors increased marginally during intervention sessions. Intervention applied to 1 S did not produce any "spillover" of treatment effect on the behavior of children not under intervention procedures at that time. (16 ref)
Ragland, Elizabeth U.; Kerr, Mary M. & Strain, Phillip S. Behavior Modification, 1978(Oct), Vol 2(4), 565–578. [PA, Vol 64:01660]

1986.   The effect of high doses of Vitamin B₆ on autistic children: A double-blind crossover study.
Used data from an earlier nonblind study to identify 16 autistic-type child outpatients who had apparently improved when given vitamin B₆ (pyridoxine). In a double-blind study each child's B₆ supplement was replaced during 2 separate experimental trial periods with either a B₆ supplement or a matched placebo. Behavior was rated as deteriorating significantly during the B₆ withdrawal.
Rimland, Bernard; Callaway, Enoch & Dreyfus, Pierre. (Inst for Child Behavior Research, San Diego, CA) American Journal of Psychiatry, 1978(Apr), Vol 135(4), 472–475. [PA, Vol 61:06638]

1987.   Sensory extinction: A procedure for eliminating self-stimulatory behavior in developmentally disabled children.
Investigated the role of sensory reinforcement in the motivation of self-stimulation. If self-stimulatory behavior is maintained by its sensory consequences, such as the proprioceptive, auditory, or visual stimulation it produces, then such behavior should extinguish when those sensory consequences are not permitted. A new procedure is introduced—sensory extinction—in which certain sensory consequences are masked or removed, to examine whether self-stimulation is operant behavior maintained by sensory reinforcement. The effectiveness of sensory extinction was assessed by a reversal design for each of 3 autistic children, and the results show the following: (a) Self-stimulation reliably extinguished when a certain sensory consequence was removed, then increased when that consequence was permitted. This was replicable within and across Ss. (b) Different sensory extinction procedures were required for different self-stimulatory behaviors, since the sensory reinforcers supporting them were idiosyncratic across Ss. (c) Regarding clinical gains, the data suggest that sensory extinction may be a relatively convenient and rapid alternative for the treatment of self-stimulation. Present findings extend the efficacy of extinction as a behavior-modification technique to instances in which the reinforcer is purely sensory. Implications for the treatment of other forms of deviant behavior are discussed. (38 ref)
Rincover, Arnold. (U North Carolina, Greensboro) Journal of Abnormal Child Psychology, 1978(Sep), Vol 6(3), 299–310. [PA, Vol 64:01662]

1988.   Kaspar Hauser's recovery and autopsy: A perspective on neurological and sociological requirements for language development.
Feral children have frequently been studied to understand historical antecedents of autism. Hauser, who appeared in Nuremberg, Germany, in 1828, is one of these children, raised under conditions of extreme deprivation. His case history and gradual acquisition of language after age 17 are summarized. Findings of a postmortem examination that indicated pathology patterns due to malnutrition, are discussed. It is concluded that Hauser's postadolescent recovery of language contradicts the concept of a "critical period" for language development. (18 ref)
Simon, Nicole. (American Science & Engineering Inc, Cambridge, MA) Journal of Autism & Developmental Disorders, 1978(Jun), Vol 8(2), 209–217. [PA, Vol 62:03810]

1989.   [On our experience in using pentoxifylline for abnormal behavior and the autistic syndrome.] (Japn)
Describes the successful use of pentoxifylline (150–600 mg/day) with 3–15 yr old children with abnormal behavior (e.g., self-mutilation, aggressiveness, and hyperkinesis) and with autism. It is noted that while the drug was effective in reducing symptoms of autism, developmental factors in the disorder should not be ignored. (English abstract) (9 ref)
Sogame, Shiro. (Takachaya Mental Hosp, Asunaro Gakuen Children's Dept, Japan) Japanese Journal of Child Psychiatry, 1978, Vol 19(3), 137–144. [PA, Vol 64:13081]

1990.   Effects of *l*-5-hydroxytryptophan in autistic children.
Evaluated the behavioral effects of levo-5-hydroxytryptophan (L-5-HTP), administered in combination with carbidopa, in 3 male autistic children, aged 4.9–8.0 yrs, using direct behavioral observation, parent ratings, and the Connors Abbreviated Rating Scale. Ss were also rated by the Gesell Development Schedule. Ss were assessed under each of 4 conditions—baseline, placebo I, L-5-HTP (50–500 mg/day) plus carbidopa (100 mg/day), and placebo II. During the 20-wk study, 2 Ss showed behavioral changes that appeared to be unrelated to drug treatment. Results do not support the hypothesis that a functional deficit in brain serotonin underlies the autistic syndrome. (20 ref)
Sverd, J. et al. (Long Island Research Inst, Health Sciences Ctr, Stony Brook, NY) Journal of Autism & Childhood Schizophrenia, 1978(Jun), Vol 8(2), 171–180. [PA, Vol 62:04221]

1991.   Early childhood autism and structural therapy: Outcome after 3 years.
Examined the effect of 3 yrs of structural therapy on 21 inpatient cases of early childhood autism (ECA). Treatment resulted in the discharge of 12 patients. Details of treatment procedure, therapeutic progress, and their effects on diagnostic and prognostic conceptualizations are presented. Comparisons are made among previous reports of attempted treatment of ECA, as well as the results of 2 other treatment units in the same setting. Results support the hypothesis that the high stimulation, physically intrusive, gamelike, novelty filled, and developmentally oriented treatment approach of structural therapy is capable of producing a significant improvement in cases of ECA.
Ward, Alan J. (Henry Horner Children's Ctr, Chicago, IL) Journal of Consulting & Clinical Psychology, 1978(Jun), Vol 46(3), 586–587. [PA, Vol 61:13887]

1992.   An indirect method for increasing the rate of social interaction in an autistic child.
Describes the treatment of a 9-yr-old autistic boy who manifested a low rate of social interaction with his parents and older sister. Previous attempts to persuade the parents to devote more time to interacting with the child had failed. The parents then were instructed to give the child training in handwriting. A dramatic improvement in S's ability to reproduce the alphabet was observed. More importantly, a great increase in the rate of interaction between the child and the members of his family was documented. The percent of 10-sec intervals in which S spoke to his family or they spoke to him jumped from 19% during baseline to 89% during the intervention phase. Postintervention

rates of interaction continued to be higher than during baseline. (20 ref)

Wildman, Robert W. & Simon, Steven J. (Central State Hosp Forensic Services Ctr, Milledgeville, GA) Journal of Clinical Psychology, 1978(Jan), Vol 34(1), 144–149. [PA, Vol 61:06594]

1993.   Sign language and multisensory input training of children with communication and related developmental disorders: Phase II.

Results from the 2nd yr of the author's (see PA, Vol 59:1415) study show that the 5 children, who were developmentally disordered with dominant autistic features and lack of speech, continued to augment their signing vocabulary after being taught sign language with audiovisual devices. Overall findings of the study demonstrate significant improvement in receptive and expressive language, acquisition of rudimentary steps in abstraction and concept formations, better impulse control, and increased interaction with objects in the environment. (1 ref)

Benaroya, S. et al. Journal of Autism & Developmental Disorders, 1979(Jun), Vol 9(2), 219–220. [PA, Vol 62:11338]

1994.   Teaching autistic children to use sign language: Some research issues.

Discusses 3 questions concerning the use of sign language as an alternative system of communication for nonverbal autistic children. The first issue is whether teaching a child to sign facilitates speech development. The literature indicates that following simultaneous communication training, mute children are not likely to learn to talk; however, a combination of simultaneous communication training and separate vocal training may have a synergetic effect on speech development. In contrast, those who initially have good verbal imitation skills apparently show gains in speech following simultaneous communication training alone. The second issue pertains to the upper limit of sign acquisition; research data suggest that abstract concepts, syntax, and generative skills can be taught. Procedures used in the operant conditioning of speech may prove useful in training complex signing skills. The 3rd issue concerns whether sign acquisition results in a general inprovement in adaptive functioning. It appears that following sign training, some children do show increases in spontaneous communication, decreases in self-stimulatory behavior, and improvement in social skills. These outcomes, however, are often difficult to interpret. (38 ref)

Carr, Edward G. (State U New York, Stony Brook) Journal of Autism & Developmental Disorders, 1979(Dec), Vol 9(4), 345–359. [PA, Vol 63:08111]

1995.   Establishing functional language in an autistic child: A cooperative approach.

Describes procedures used by a teacher of the severely emotionally disturbed, a speech pathologist, and the S's parents over a 2.5 yr period to facilitate behavior change and language development in an autistic boy (4 yrs 3 mo of age) who made no attempts to communicate. His parents were instructed in behavior management techniques and were encouraged to bombard him with talking, reading, singing, and sharing play experiences. Later, more specific language procedures were demonstrated. Behavior management techniques were used with the S in a class of 6 3–6 yr olds who were experiencing similar adjustment problems. Language therapy concentrated on developing both receptive and expressive skills. At age 6 yrs 10 mo, the S's receptive language scores were within the norms for children aged 5–5.5 yrs. On the Peabody Picture Vocabulary Test, the S scored 5.5 yrs on receptive vocabulary; informal language samples suggest that his expressive skills were at approximately the same level. (14 ref)

Coppage, Kay W. & Veal, Michael C. (Comprehensive Psycho-Educational Services for South Georgia, Valdosta) Journal of Communication Disorders, 1979(Nov), Vol 12(6), 447–460. [PA, Vol 66:08490]

1996.   Beginning psychoanalysis of a 16 year old autistic girl: The first three months.

Describes the 1st 3 mo of psychoanalysis of a 16-yr-old female diagnosed as autistic. Various aspects of expulsion, projection,

separation anxiety, and mirroring are discussed. The difficulties of instituting psychoanalysis with such a patient are delineated. (English & French abstracts) (8 ref)

Eyre, Dean P. (U Ottawa, Canada) Canadian Journal of Psychiatry, 1979(Nov), Vol 24(7), 652–660. [PA, Vol 66:01705]

1997.   Suppression of self-stimulation: Three alternative strategies.

Four boys (ages 5–7 yrs) with autistic–like behavior were treated for self-stimulatory behavior with timeout (TO), DRO, and overcorrection. All Ss showed a rapid response to overcorrection. Three Ss demonstrated some evidence of decrement in responding with TO. During DRO, 1 S showed a modest decrease, 2 showed no change, but 1 exhibited a consistent increase in responding. A multiple baseline applied to 1 S failed to reveal any generalization of suppression from one setting to another. A strong but not perfect relationship was found between a frequency and a duration measure of self-stimulation. There was evidence of negative side effects for 1 S during overcorrection and for another during TO, but none was enduring. There was also indirect evidence that overcorrection facilitated appropriate play. (17 ref)

Harris, Sandra L. & Wolchik, Sharlene A. (Rutgers U, Douglass Coll, New Brunswick) Journal of Applied Behavior Analysis, 1979(Sum), Vol 12(2), 185–198. [PA, Vol 65:10913]

1998.   Teaching autistic children to follow instructions in a group by a firm physical prompting procedure.

Proposes a procedure of graded, firm physical prompting to increase instruction-following behavior of nonverbal autistic children. Results from 4 6–11 yr olds suggest that some autistic children may not learn to follow instructions consistently in a training procedure that uses guidance or gesture. The firm prompt procedure could serve as an effective and practical training alternative. The merits of using the procedure in group training of noncompliant children and the possibility of its application to training various motor behaviors are discussed. (27 ref)

Hung, David W.; Cosentino, Angela & Henderson, Ellen. (Florida Mental Health Inst, Tampa) Journal of Behavior Therapy & Experimental Psychiatry, 1979(Dec), Vol 10(4), 329–338. [PA, Vol 65:08481]

1999.   Psychopharmacological treatment of psychotic children: A survey.

A review of controlled investigations shows the following: Children with infantile autism might benefit from psychopharmacological medication when they grow older (e.g., above the age of 7 yrs). Learning might be facilitated when psychoactive medication is able to inhibit psychotic preoccupations and idiosyncratic reactions. Schizophrenia and manic-depressive psychosis in children are treated as in adults. Special attention must be paid to the toxic effects of imipramine. (51 ref)

Jørgensen, Ole S. (Frederiksborg County Hosp, Dept of Child Psychiatry, Hillerød, Denmark) Acta Psychiatrica Scandinavica, 1979(Feb), Vol 59(2), 229–238. [PA, Vol 64:01689]

2000.   Motivating autistic children.

A major problem encountered in the field of autism is the children's characteristic lack of motivation. This problem is especially apparent when autistic children attempt to complete learning tasks. The purpose of this study was to investigate the influence of correct vs incorrect task completion on children's motivation to respond to such tasks. Ss were 3 autistic children aged 6 yrs 1 mo, 11 yrs 11 mo, and 12 yrs 3 mo. Results demonstrate that when Ss worked on tasks at which they were typically incorrect, their motivation for those tasks decreased to extremely low levels. However, designing treatment procedures to prompt Ss to keep responding until they completed the tasks correctly served to increase Ss' motivation to respond to those tasks. The implications of these findings are that (a) autistic children's learning handicaps (which typically lead to low levels of correct responding) may result in few or inconsistent rewards for attempting to respond at all, thus decreasing the children's motivation; and (b) treatment procedures designed to keep the

children responding until they complete a task correctly may result in coincidental reinforcement for perseverance, increasing the children's motivation to respond to those tasks. Results are discussed in relation to the literature on learned helplessness. (22 ref)
Koegel, Robert L. & Egel, Andrew L. (U California Social Process Research Inst, Santa Barbara) Journal of Abnormal Psychology, 1979(Aug), Vol 88(4), 418–426. [PA, Vol 62:13799]

2001. Manual language acquisition and its influence on other areas of functioning in four autistic and autistic-like children.
Four nonverbal 8–10 yr old autistic children received simultaneous (speech and sign) communication training over a 9-mo period. The most pronounced change observed in the Ss was in the area of communication. On admission, Ss' productive communication repertoires (either in speech or in sign) were either totally absent or only minimal. By the end of the 1st 2 mo of training, considerable gains were evident in their signing ability, although their sign production was only approximately correct. By the end of the 9-mo program, progress was pronounced and noticeable, particularly in view of the total lack of success of previous speech training with all of the Ss. Although social, self-care, and related abilities were not the main focus of intervention, all Ss demonstrated measurable gains in these areas as well. (32 ref)
Konstantareas, M. Mary; Webster, Christopher D. & Oxman, Joel. (Clarke Inst of Psychiatry, Child & Family Studies Ctr, Toronto, Canada) Journal of Child Psychology & Psychiatry & Allied Disciplines, 1979(Oct), Vol 20(4), 337–350. [PA, Vol 65:03922]

2002. Contrasting illness and behavioral models for the treatment of autistic children: A historical perspective.
The disease model views autism as an illness and the child's behaviors are considered symptoms. One school of thought, based on Freudian and psychodynamic theory, postulates illness caused by environmental factors; the other perspective arises from organic psychiatry, which postulates an illness caused by nutritional, genetic, or structural damage to the nervous system. Treatment focuses on identifying and removing "autism"; the child's behavior as such is not considered the prime target for intervention. In the behavioral or learning approach, the child's behaviors are taken apart into smaller units, which are studied separately in relation to separate and easily indentifiable parts of the child's environment. Behavioral studies have generally used a single-S or a within-S design; this emphasis is seen as the main strength of the behavioral approach to treatment. Behavioral work with autistic children allows for an exchange of information and treatment techniques across many different kinds of children with different kinds of problem behaviors. (21 ref)
Lovaas, O. Ivar. (U California, Los Angeles) Journal of Autism & Developmental Disorders, 1979(Dec), Vol 9(4), 315–323. [PA, Vol 63:07921]

2003. The effects of progressive muscle relaxation on the behavior of autistic adolescents: A preliminary analysis.
Trained 5 autistic Ss (aged 11–19 yrs) in the use of progressive muscle relaxation to determine the effects of the relaxation training on task-oriented, disruptive, and stereotypic behavior, in a structured 12-min academic session. Prior to each session, Ss engaged in 1 of 2 activities with the relaxation trainer for 10 min (i.e., the practice at relaxation or a Simon-says game). Measures of disruption, on-task, and academic rate were gathered in the academic session. In addition, a relaxation checklist was used to determine the extent to which the S was relaxed in the relaxation sessions. Results give little evidence of differential effects as a consequence of the relaxation procedures on any of the dependent measures. The addition of relaxation cues during academic sessions failed to produce any change in Ss' behaviors. (36 ref)
Marholin, David et al. Child Behavior Therapy, 1979(Spr), Vol 1(1), 75–84. [PA, Vol 65:06016]

2004. Adapted melodic intonation therapy: A case study of an experimental language program for an autistic child.
Presents the case report of a 3-yr-old nonverbal autistic boy who received an experimental language treatment. Consisting of signing plus an intoned rather than spoken verbal stimulus, this adaptation of melodic intonation therapy enabled the child to produce trained, imitative, and finally spontaneous intoned verbalizations which generalized to a variety of situations. (15 ref)
Miller, Shifra B. & Toca, Jan M. (Louisiana State U School of Medicine, New Orleans) Journal of Clinical Psychiatry, 1979(Apr), Vol 40(4), 201–203. [PA, Vol 64:08367]

2005. A question of autism.
Describes the case of a 3-yr-old boy, David, who had an autistic 7-yr-old brother and was beginning to show signs of autism. A detailed metapsychological understanding of the case, based on A. Freud's diagnostic profile, is presented. It is concluded that while David was not yet autistic, there were indications that he might progress to a point where he would appear as if he were. Among several such indications, the diagnostician singled out as especially significant the boy's weak ego and tendency to fall back on an identification with his autistic brother's behavior whenever threatened with aggressive feelings toward his brother. The 1st 8 mo of psychotherapy produced marked improvement in David's contact with external reality. (21 ref)
Radford, Patricia. (Hampstead Clinic, London, England) Journal of Child Psychotherapy, 1979, Vol 5, 5–23. [PA, Vol 66:06267]

2006. Treatment report of an autistic child: Monozygotic twin concordant to autism.
Describes an attempt to treat an autistic 5.5-yr-old boy using behavior modification in a set-up milieu. The techniques used were intrusion, interruption, and relationship development. Initially, the S was totally controlled; in the midphase, he was partially controlled; and in the final phase, he was not controlled at all. Verbal appreciation, praise, and the "relationship" were used as rewards and reinforcements. In the last phase, the child was partially "released" from his autistic world and able to relate to others. (2 ref)
Shivarathnamma, N. (Victoria Hosp, Bangalore, India) Indian Journal of Clinical Psychology, 1979(Sep), Vol 6(2), 95–100. [PA, Vol 65:08513]

2007. Effects of peer-mediated social initiations and prompting/reinforcement procedures on the social behavior of autistic children.
Evaluated peer-mediated social initiations and prompting/reinforcement procedures (in training and generalization sessions) as interventions for increasing the positive social behavior of 4 autistic 9–10 yr olds. During baseline, the peer trainer made few social initiations and did not prompt or socially reinforce Ss. For 2 Ss, baseline was followed by social initiation intervention; and for the other 2, baseline was followed by prompting and social reinforcement. Both interventions produced dramatic and comparable increases in positive social behavior during training sessions. Posttreatment responding was not observed for either intervention. When interventions terminated in a 2nd baseline period, Ss' behavior returned to the level observed during the initial baseline. Ss were then exposed to the intervention procedure they had not yet experienced. Again, there were positive and comparable behavior changes in the treatment setting, but no increase in positive social behavior was observed during generalization assessment. (17 ref)
Strain, Phillip S.; Kerr, Mary M. & Ragland, Elizabeth U. (Middle Tennessee Mental Health Inst, Nashville) Journal of Autism & Developmental Disorders, 1979(Mar), Vol 9(1), 41–54. [PA, Vol 62:11515]

2008. Sign language as a means of communicating with autistic and mentally handicapped children.
Briefly describes the simultaneous communication program at the Sir James Douglas School. Simultaneous communication (the speaker uses signs as well as speaking) worked well for some

children who could not be taught to express themselves by other means. It is suggested that parents and workers can be taught to use simultaneous communication, and some helpful teaching films are listed. (23 ref)
Stull, Stephanie et al. (Sir James Douglas Elementary School, Victoria, Canada) Child Care Quarterly, 1979(Sum), Vol 8(2), 143–147. [PA, Vol 62:06771]

2009.   Immobilization: Effects and side effects on stereotyped behavior in children.
Reduced self-stimulatory responses of 4 retarded/autistic children (6–13 yrs old) using brief immobilization. A reversal design was employed such that immobilizing was systematically applied and withdrawn in one category of responses while the effects of collateral responses were also assessed. In 3 cases, the suppressive effects of immobilization generalized to collateral responses of similar topography, but in one of these cases there were undesirable side effects. In the 4th case, where generalized suppression did not occur, the collateral responses were of dissimilar topography from the target response. The emergence of an incompatible response appeared to be responsible for most of the response generalization effects. (34 ref)
Bitgood, Stephen C.; Crowe, Michael J.; Suarez, Yolanda & Peters, R. Douglas. (Jacksonville State U) Behavior Modification, 1980(Apr), Vol 4(2), 187–208. [PA, Vol 65:10897]

2010.   Motivating autistic children through stimulus variation.
Evaluated the differential effectiveness of 2 methods of presenting discrimination tasks to 2 autistic girls (aged 7 yrs 3 mo and 5 yrs 3 mo). In a constant task (CT) condition, the common method of presenting a single task throughout a session was used. In a varied task (VT) condition, the same task was interspersed with a variety of other tasks from the Ss' clinic curricula. Results show declining trends in correct responding during the CT condition, with substantially improved and stable responding during the VT condition. In addition, naive observers judged the Ss to be more enthusiastic, interested, happier, and better behaved during the VT sessions. Results suggest that "boredom" may be an important variable to control in the treatment of autistic children and that care may be necessary when defining criteria for task acquisition. Results are discussed in relation to the literature on increased responsivity to stimulus novelty and variation. (23 ref)
Dunlap, Glen & Koegel, Robert L. (U California, Speech & Hearing Ctr, Santa Barbara) Journal of Applied Behavior Analysis, 1980(Win), Vol 13(4), 619–627. [PA, Vol 65:05998]

2011.   Effects of praise and reprimand on the topography and probability of occurrence of stereotypies in autistic children.
Observed 7 autistic children (mean age 8.2 yrs) while they participated in discrimination learning tasks. Ratings of the topography of their stereotypies were recorded following the administration of praise or reprimand for performance on each trial. Ratings were also made following reprimands for misbehavior. Stereotypies followed reprimanded trials significantly more often than praised trials and were most likely to occur following reprimands for misbehavior. No differences were found in overall topographic change as a function of praise or reprimand. (7 ref)
Ferrari, Michael. (Rutgers U, New Brunswick) Psychological Reports, 1980(Apr), Vol 46(2), 519–522. [PA, Vol 65:13272]

2012.   Adjunctive hypnotherapy with an autistic boy.
Describes the use of adjunctive hypnotherapy in a 16-yr-old autistic male and discusses the need for specialized techniques of induction and treatment. The use of music in hypnosis allowed S to maximize the value of a special skill in his uneven developmental repertoire. He not only achieved specific behavior change but extended gains in broader areas of social and cognitive skills. (10 ref)
Gardner, G. Gail & Tarnow, Jay D. (U Colorado School of Medicine, Denver) American Journal of Clinical Hypnosis, 1980(Jan), Vol 22(3), 173–179. [PA, Vol 66:01882]

2013.   Training and generalization of yes and no as mands in two autistic children.
A nonverbal boy (CA 8 yrs 3 mo, MA 2 yrs 6 mo) and a previously echolalic girl (CA 10 yrs 8 mo, IQ range 30–50) were first trained to use "yes" and "no" to mand 3 food items, following the stimulus question "Do you want . . .?" and presentation of a food item. Ss were then tested for generalization of the 2 mands to successive sets of new food items. Results show that the boy needed to be trained on 5 sets of food items before generalization occurred. The girl generalized and maintained the 2 mands after being trained on only 1 set of items. Specific response patterns and the importance of intermittent modeling and arrangement of reinforcers in the training are discussed. (15 ref)
Hung, David W. (Florida Mental Health Inst, Tampa) Journal of Autism & Developmental Disorders, 1980(Jun), Vol 10(2), 139–152. [PA, Vol 64:12990]

2014.   Behavioral contrast and generalization across settings in the treatment of autistic children.
Previous research on the generalization of treatment gains across settings focused on the question of whether generalization does or does not occur. However, the literature suggests that behavioral contrast may occur in extra-therapy settings if the reinforcement procedures in the therapy setting are highly discriminable from those in other settings. Therefore, the present study examined (a) whether a highly discriminable treatment procedure in one setting would produce a behavioral contrast effect in other unmanipulated settings, and (b) if such contrast-like trends could be eliminated if initially different reinforcement procedures in 2 settings were subsequently made similar. Results for 8 5–9 yr old autistic Ss show that (a) when very different reinforcement procedures (primary rewards or punishment in therapy settings and no rewards or punishment in extra-therapy settings) were in effect, Ss showed contrast-like behavior changes in the untreated extra-therapy settings; and (b) such trends in responding could be eliminated, resulting in generalization of treatment gains, if the reinforcement procedures were subsequently made relatively similar in the 2 settings, even when the procedures consisted essentially of noncontingent reinforcement. (30 ref)
Koegel, Robert L.; Egel, Andrew L. & Williams, Julie A. (U California, Social Process Research Inst, Santa Barbara) Journal of Experimental Child Psychology, 1980(Dec), Vol 30(3), 422–437. [PA, Vol 65:06012]

2015.   Direct versus indirect response-reinforcer relationships in teaching autistic children.
Three severely autistic children, ages 4–6 yrs, were taught a total of 6 new target behaviors (in a multiple baseline design) employing 2 different response-reinforcer relationships: (a) those in which the target behaviors were a direct part of the response chain required to procure a reinforcer (e.g., opening the lid of a container to obtain a food reward inside the container); and (b) those in which the target behavior was an indirect part of the chain leading to the reinforcer (e.g., the therapist handing the S a food reward after S had opened the lid of an empty container). In all cases, results show rapid acquisition only when the target behavior was a direct part of the chain leading to the reinforcer. Several conceptualizations concerning efficient reinforcement contingencies are discussed. (28 ref)
Koegel, Robert L. & Williams, Julie A. (U California, Social Process Research Inst, Santa Barbara) Journal of Abnormal Child Psychology, 1980(Dec), Vol 8(4), 537–547. [PA, Vol 65:08489]

2016.   [The mental hospital: Is treatment feasible? Experiences from a psycho-social treatment program with younger schizophrenics.] (Norg)
Describes the restructuring of a 30-bed unit in a psychiatric hospital. Care was initially provided for withdrawn, passive, and autistic young schizophrenics who were referred to staff in 4 small groups. Activity, general care, and individualized treatments programs were developed. The program ended during its 5th yr, primarily because of an inability to obtain control of intake and the lack of some degree of patient selection. The

importance of developing different treatment milieus according to the needs of the patients is stressed. It is argued that the smaller unit should replace the psychiatric hospital since the hospital contains so many other elements that are detrimental to the patient's needs. (31 ref)
Lorentzen, Steinar. (Ullevål Sykehus, Oslo, Norway) Tidsskrift for Norsk Psykologforening, 1980(Sep), Vol 17(9), 442–451. [PA, Vol 66:06506]

2017. Use of a visual stimulus fading procedure to teach color naming to an autistic child.
An 8-yr-old autistic boy was taught to sight read the name of each of 5 colors, which were superimposed over a card of the respective color. In a series of graduated steps, the color word was then faded out until independent naming was achieved. During posttest assessments conducted 1 day, 10 days, and 7 mo after training, correct responding was maintained and generalization of color naming was observed. (5 ref)
Luiselli, James K. & Donellon, Sally. (Thompson School, Behavioral Intervention Project, Arlington, MA) Journal of Behavior Therapy & Experimental Psychiatry, 1980(Mar), Vol 11(1), 73–76. [PA, Vol 66:01805]

2018. [Therapist variables in treatment of autistic children: Analysis and summary of attribution relationships.] (Germ)
Conducted 5 treatment sessions with 9 autistic children (As) using therapists (Ts) with 3 levels of expertise—professionals, mothers, and inexperienced students. Before and after the sessions, Ts completed an attribution questionnaire. After each session, Ts self-rated their behavior with the As as either relationship-enhancing or task-structuring and rated As according to their readiness for cooperation and capability. The 130 sessions were videotaped and were judged by a nonparticipants. Results show that professionals but not students and mothers attributed modification of the child's autistic behavior to their own efforts and abilities. Students increased their belief that their degree of success in working with autistic children was primarily determined by their abilities. Results suggest that for younger As, relationship-enhancing T behavior is indicated while for older As, cooperation and capability may be increased with task-structuring T behavior. (32 ref)
Pesta, Thekla; Kellersmann, Jürgen & Miller, B. (U Wien, Psychologisches Inst, Austria) Zeitschrift für Klinische Psychologie. Forschung und Praxis, 1980, Vol 9(2), 102–128. [PA, Vol 66:04249]

2019. Platelet uptake of serotonin in psychotic children.
Found constant and significantly different platelet serotonin uptake values in 10 long-term hospitalized children in 2 groups—"autistic" and "other psychotic." Three weekly assays on 6 parents suggest the possible importance of genetic factors in these diseases. (9 ref)
Rotman, Avner; Caplan, Rochelle & Szekely, George A. (Weizmann Inst of Science, Rehovot, Israel) Psychopharmacology, 1980(Mar), Vol 67(3), 245–248. [PA, Vol 65:10596]

2020. Treatment programs and strategies for psychotic children.
Comments that the role of a physician as healer and scientist leads to a confusion of aims, just as his/her attention to the deviant child is split between the person and the organism. Parental perplexity is reviewed in relation to the study of the meaning of diagnosis and matched by professional perplexity concerning realism and hope. A study by M. Sherman et al (1979) indicated that 30 pairs of parents of psychotic children had a good cognitive grasp of a variety of professional terms and yet were confused about the meaning of "a diagnosis." It is suggested, therefore, that the parents as well as the child be considered more thoroughly in the therapeutic approach. (27 ref)
Shapiro, Theodore. (Cornell U Medical Coll, New York) Family & Child Mental Health Journal, 1980(Fal–Win), Vol 6(2), 118–129. [PA, Vol 66:13192]

2021. The effects and side-effects of an overcorrection procedure applied by parents of severely emotionally disturbed children in a home environment.
Investigated overcorrection procedures applied by teachers and parents to treat self-stimulatory behavior of 2 autistic elementary school age children. The experimental design had 4 conditions during which observations were collected in the home. Following baseline, overcorrection was implemented in a public school classroom by a teacher, in the home by parents, and in both environments simultaneously. This permitted (a) examination of the effects of treatment on the target behaviors across environments and (b) determination of whether overcorrection would lead to desirable side effects. For this purpose, proximity to others and playing appropriately were identified as positive behavioral correlates for both Ss. Three behaviors were identified for each S as negative behavioral correlates. Results show that in each setting, overcorrection procedures were associated with statistically significant differences in the target behaviors. However, two-thirds of untreated behaviors changed in desirable and significant directions. Lowest levels of target behaviors were attained when the procedures were applied simultaneously at school and at home. (19 ref)
Simpson, Richard L. & Swenson, Carl R. (U Kansas Medical Ctr, Kansas City) Behavioral Disorders, 1980(Feb), Vol 5(2), 79–85. [PA, Vol 65:01812]

2022. Transfer factor immunotherapy of an autistic child with congenital cytomegalovirus.
Administered transfer factor to an autistic child to improve his specific immunocompetence to cytomegalovirus. S was 20 mo old at the start of treatment and 38 mo old at completion. Although motor development improved, the age-span of treatment was during a period when motor development is accelerated in normal development. It is recommended that a trial of transfer factor treatment be utilized only if the specific viral agent can be identified. (10 ref)
Stubbs, E. Gene; Budden, Sarojini S.; Burger, Denis R. & Vandenbark, Arthur A. (U Oregon Health Sciences Ctr, Crippled Children's Div, Portland) Journal of Autism & Developmental Disorders, 1980(Dec), Vol 10(4), 451–458. [PA, Vol 65:06107]

2023. Decreasing self-stimulatory behavior with physical exercise in a group of autistic boys.
Observed 5 autistic boys (9.5–11.7 yrs old) during 27 language training sessions. Each session followed 1 of 3 periods: (a) physical exercise, (b) TV watching, or (c) regular academic work. It was found that (a) the lowest levels of self-stimulation followed physical exercise, (b) there were no differences in the levels of self-stimulation following TV watching and following academics, and (c) the levels of correct question answering were not affected by the 3 different previous periods. (25 ref)
Watters, Robert G. & Watters, Wilhelmina E. (U Ottawa, Canada) Journal of Autism & Developmental Disorders, 1980(Dec), Vol 10(4), 379–387. [PA, Vol 65:06406]

2024. An in vivo approach to the desensitization of a retarded child's toilet phobia.
Eliminated a 5.8-yr-old retarded, autistic male's toilet phobia over a period of 33 school days by using a gradual approximations approach with a mastery model being used on a number of trials. The program produced generalization to nontreatment settings, enabling S to be taken into situations without a potty, something never before possible. (9 ref)
Wilson, B. & Jackson, Henry J. (Frankston Special Developmental School, Australia) Australian Journal of Developmental Disabilities, 1980(Sep), Vol 6(3), 137–140. [PA, Vol 66:08567]

2025. Applying psycholinguistic concepts to the treatment of an autistic child.
Describes a language program designed to allow an autistic 4-yr-old boy to acquire, in a near simultaneous manner, skill across a variety of sentence types. The training, which was focused on teaching the combinatorial and semantic properties of grammatical morphemes, resulted in S's developing and using sentences, whereas he had previously been limited to single words and rote

phrases. The improvement occurred across a variety of settings and encompassed both elicited and spontaneous language. As expected from the autistic syndrome, those areas of language functioning requiring social skill (e.g., sustained dialog) showed continued deficits. (22 ref)
Blank, Marion & Milewski, Janet. (Coll of Medicine & Dentistry of New Jersey-Rutgers Medical School, Piscataway) Applied Psycholinguistics, 1981(Feb), Vol 2(1), 65–84. [PA, Vol 66:06431]

2026. Development of language behavior in an autistic child using total communication.
Demonstrated the effectiveness of a procedure employing behavior modification techniques (e.g., modeling, stimulus control) in conjunction with a total communication approach in the training of verbal labeling behavior and rudimentary telegraphic speech, while simultaneously decreasing echolalia in an autistic 4-yr-old girl. (8 ref)
Cohen, Morris. (Middle Georgia Psychoeducational Ctr, Macon) Exceptional Children, 1981(Feb), Vol 47(5), 379–381. [PA, Vol 65:08466]

2027. Normal peer models and autistic children's learning.
Research and legislation regarding mainstreaming autistic children into normal classrooms have stressed the importance of studying whether autistic children can benefit from observing normal peer models. The present investigation systematically assessed whether autistic children's learning of discrimination tasks could be improved if they observed normal children perform the tasks correctly. In the context of a multiple baseline design, 4 autistic Ss (5–7.9 yrs old) worked on 5 discrimination tasks that their teachers reported were posing difficulty. Throughout the baseline condition, Ss evidenced low levels of correct responding on all 5 tasks. In the subsequent treatment condition, when normal peers modeled correct responses, Ss' correct responding increased dramatically. In each case, the peer modeling procedure produced a rapid achievement of the acquisition criterion that was maintained after the peer models were removed. (58 ref)
Egel, Andrew L.; Richman, Gina S. & Koegel, Robert L. (U Maryland, College Park) Journal of Applied Behavior Analysis, 1981(Spr), Vol 14(1), 3–12. [PA, Vol 66:08982]

2028. The effectiveness of operant language training with autistic children.
Studies of operant language therapy with autistic children have indicated that behavioral techniques may be of value in increasing the language skills of such children. A review of recent studies, however, suggests that in the absence of adequate experimental controls, misleading conclusions may be drawn about the effectiveness of treatment. It is also apparent that the effects of therapy vary according to the linguistic competence of the children involved, and to the different aspects of language ability being taught. The implications of recent findings for understanding the basic deficit underlying early childhood autism are discussed. (3 p ref)
Howlin, Patricia A. (U London, Inst of Psychiatry, England) Journal of Autism & Developmental Disorders, 1981(Mar), Vol 11(1), 89–105. [PA, Vol 66:06338]

2029. Effects of pyridoxine and magnesium on autistic symptoms—initial observations.
In an open trial, a heterogeneous group of 44 children aged 3–16 yrs (IQs 20–70) with autistic symptoms were treated with large doses of vitamin B_6 (600–1,125 mg) and Mg (400–600 mg). Clinical improvement with worsening on termination of the trial was observed in 15 Ss. 13 responders and 8 nonresponders were retested in a 2-wk, crossover, double-blind trial, and the responses to the open trial were confirmed. (13 ref)
Lelord, G. et al. (Ctr Hospitalier Regionale de Tours, France) Journal of Autism & Developmental Disorders, 1981(Jun), Vol 11(2), 219–230. [PA, Vol 66:10931]

2030. The relative efficiency of two orders for training autistic children in the expressive and receptive use of manual signs.
Four nonverbal autistic children (10 yrs 9 mo to 16 yrs of age) learned with simultaneous communication (speech plus gesture) the receptive and expressive use of 8 signed words. In a within-S comparison, each S was first taught 4 words expressively (signing) and then receptively and the other 4 words receptively and then expressively. Results indicate that (1) it took fewer trials to teach expressive and receptive use when teaching was done in the order expressive then receptive; (2) the teaching of expressive use facilitated the learning of receptive use; (3) the teaching of receptive use interferred with the learning of expressive use; and (4) by the end of training, good receptive control by the spoken word alone had developed. (34 ref)
Watters, Robert G.; Wheeler, Linda J. & Watters, Wilhelmina E. (U Ottawa, School of Psychology, Canada) Journal of Communication Disorders, 1981(Jul), Vol 14(4), 273–285. [PA, Vol 66:06216]

2031. Response–reinforcer relationships and improved learning in autistic children.
To affect more rapid response acquisition for autistic children, researchers have begun to investigate the functional relationships of reinforcers to other components of the operant conditioning paradigm. Previous research suggested that functional relationships between target behaviors and reinforcers might be especially effective. The present experiment assessed, within a multiple baseline design, the possibility of improving 3 autistic children's (4, 4.5 and 7 yrs of age) learning by changing arbitrary response-reinforcer relationships (while holding target behaviors and reinforcers constant) so that the target behaviors became functional (i.e., direct part of the response chain required for S to procure the reinforcer). Results show that (1) arranging functional response-reinforcer relationships produced immediate improvement in Ss' learning and resulted in rapid acquisition of criterion level responding; and (2) high levels of correct responding initially produced by functional response-reinforcer relationships were continued even when previous ineffective arbitrary response-reinforcer conditions were reinstated. (20 ref)
Williams, Julie A.; Koegel, Robert L. & Egel, Andrew L. (West Virginia U) Journal of Applied Behavior Analysis, 1981(Spr), Vol 14(1), 53–60. [PA, Vol 66:08565]

Mental Retardation

2032. Identifying and modifying behavioral deficits.
Develops the proposition that the major focus in behavior modification should be on procedures of instruction rather than on the process of learning itself. In the area of retarded development, this focal difference stresses analyses of defects in the program of instruction and how to eliminate these defects rather than analyses of the defects inherent in the child's nervous system. However, several changes must be made in current behavior modification technology if the techniques derived from this approach to developmental retardation are to have broad and important consequences. These recommended changes include means for generalizing repertoires, establishing the validity, replicability, and efficiency of training programs, and using training programs as diagnostic instruments. (24 ref.)
Bricker, William A. (George Peabody Coll. for Teachers) American Journal of Mental Deficiency, 1970(Jul), Vol 75(1), 16-21. [PA, Vol 45:01190]

2033. A thirty-day residential training program for retarded children.
Describes an intensive training program in which retarded children are institutionalized for 30 days in order to assist parents in home management of their children. 3 example cases are presented. Through a joint effort of nursing and psychology personnel, behavior modification programs are developed for each child while their parents receive training and guidance in developing and carrying out behavior modification programs.

Follow-up contact by the training team is maintained after the children are discharged.
Fingado, Marta L.; Kini, Joanne F.; Stewart, Kathryn & Redd, William H. (U. Arizona) Mental Retardation, 1970(Dec), Vol. 8(6), 42-45. [PA, Vol 48:05124]

2034.   Intellectual and social development in relation to family functioning: A longitudinal comparison of home vs. institutional effects.
Tested 42 mentally retarded children before entering an institution and 1 yr. later on measures of social quotient (SQ) (Vineland Social Maturity Scale) and IQ (Stanford-Binet, Form L or Cattell Infant Intelligence Scale). Ss' families were pre- and postinterviewed to assess the adequacy of family functioning. 27 community-based families and their children who were of similar CA and IQ were compared. Family functioning, SQ, and IQ/SQ discrepancy were found to be related to family decisions to seek long-term residential placement. Community families and children showed decreases over the year on all measures taken, whereas institutional families tended to improve in functioning. In the community group, significant positive correlation was found between IQ decrement and family pre-posttest losses. In the institution group, significant negative correlation was found between low initial SQ and family increments in functioning. Results illustrate the important reciprocal relations existing between the retarded child and his family. (32 ref.)
Kershner, John R. (U. California, Los Angeles) American Journal of Mental Deficiency, 1970(Nov), Vol. 75(3), 276-284. [PA, Vol 46:03608]

2035.   The "shopping" behavior of parents of mentally retarded children: The professional person's role.
Describes the diagnostic and therapeutic "shopping" of parents of retarded children as a learned response to unsatisfactory contacts with professional people regarding their child. The role of the professional person in initiating or preventing, and in stopping shopping behavior is discussed, with special emphasis on the informing interview. The need for research in this area is underscored, and areas for research are suggested.
Anderson, Kathryn A. (U. Oregon, Medical School, Child Development & Rehabilitation Center) Mental Retardation, 1971(Aug), Vol. 9(4), 3-5. [PA, Vol 49:11529]

2036.   Vocational theories and work habits related to childhood development.
Discusses several theories of vocational development as they relate to skill-teaching in childhood by the occupational therapist. Certain work habits are traced to early development: attitude to work, punctuality, regular attendance, appearance, attitude to supervisor, attitude to fellow workers, speed of work, manual dexterity, concentration, cleanliness, and social skills. Problems encountered when working with clients, especially the retarded, who have not developed these work habits are noted.
Bailey, Diana M. (Walter E. Fernald State School for the Mentally Retarded, Waltham, Mass.) American Journal of Occupational Therapy, 1971(Sep), Vol. 25(6), 298-302. [PA, Vol 48:03418]

2037.   The mentally retarded child in the home and the family cycle.
Considers the problem of managing a retarded child in the home could be made routine by emulating conventional parenthood. Results of interviews of 103 women with moderately retarded children living at home are reported. The mother's role performance is (a) skewed in the direction of expressive vs. instrumental activities (and is reversed when normal children are considered); (b) based on the advocacy of recipes that contrast sharply with her behavior (and are intended mainly for claiming that conventional routines are being followed); and (c) based on the capacity to meet expectations of other family members. Routine domestic life is possible, it is argued, so long as normal-appearing activity is both available and congruent with conventional parental roles. In both senses, it becomes less so during the retarded child's later years. (15 ref.)

Birenbaum, Arnold. (Wheaton Coll.) Journal of Health & Social Behavior, 1971(Mar), Vol. 12(1), 55-65. [PA, Vol 47:07405]

2038.   [A behavioral approach to life in a group among children: The token economy.] (Fren)
Presents a review of the literature on behavior modification techniques for use with youngsters. All the techniques reviewed use the approach of the token economy. General characteristics of the token system are described as it is used with retarded, delinquent, and emotionally disturbed youngsters, and youngsters with varied behavioral problems. (112 ref.)
Boisvert, Jean M. & Trudel, Gilles. (U. Quebec, Hosp. Saint-Jean-de-Dieu, Montreal, Canada) Bulletin de Psychologie, 1971, Vol 25(14-17), 872-881. [PA, Vol 51:03676]

2039.   Generalization of punishment effects in the deviant behavior of a psychotic child.
Used punishment with brief electric shock to suppress a specific costly form of destructive behavior in an 11-yr-old male retarded schizophrenic. Touching a forbidden object was punished in a series of experimental situations, which included differences in experimental rooms, the objects presented, presession experiences, persons present during the session, and timing of shock delivery. Change in experimental conditions was typically followed by a renewal of the punished response. Previous findings of the specificity of punishment effects were thus supported. As more conditions were introduced, suppression was obtained with fewer punishments. The importance is emphasized of consistent application of a punishment procedure in a variety of contexts to produce suppression for nonspecific stimulus conditions.
Bucher, Bradley & King, Larry W. (U. California, los Angeles) Behavior Therapy, 1971(Jan), Vol. 2(1), 68-77. [PA, Vol 47:09063]

2040.   [Clinical history of an adolescent with behavior problems.] (Span)
Describes the case history of a 13-yr-old girl with behavior problems. Since the S was mentally subnormal, the question of whether her problems were due to her intelligence level or other factors was considered. Psychotherapeutic approach was comprehensive, involving medication as well as pedagogical, familial, and educational guidance.
Castro Penalver, Pedro E. (Children's Hosp., Mexico, D. F.) Revista de la Clínica de la Conducta, 1971(Feb), Vol. 4(8), 49-53. [PA, Vol 48:03538]

2041.   Stabilization of the retarded child for dental procedures.
Discusses an appliance developed as a splinting device for injured body extremities in its modified usage as a stablizing support for the child-patient during the period of dental treatment. It adds to the comfort of the child and allows for the most ideal placement of the child's head for optimal vision of the dentist. Adaptation usually requires less than 1 min. and may be immediately remolded for the patient in the chair and the patient who follows.
Corcoran, John W. & Bender, Paul A. (Medical U. South Carolina, Coll. of Dental Medicine, Charleston) Mental Retardation, 1971(Dec), Vol. 9(6), 26-28. [PA, Vol 47:11467]

2042.   [Investigation of 200 cases of request for placement in specialized residential accommodation drawn from consultations at the Committee for the Study & Care of Severely Retarded (CESAP).] (Fren)
Examined the case histories of 200 children (median age = 4 yr.) with multiple handicaps and IQs < 50 whose parents had requested residential treatment for their child during their 1st consultation at the CESAP. Variables studied included (a) characteristics of the child, family, and siblings; (b) socioeconomic status; and (c) context of the request. Results were compared with control data obtained in a previous study in which the parents of 1,000 children requested other services (e.g., educational guidance) during their 1st consultation. Certain characteristics of the child were found with much greater frequency than in the control population, including IQ < 35, uncontrolled epilepsy, and behavior disturbances. These children also tended to come from larger families, lower socioeconomic levels, and immigrant families. (German & Spanish summaries)

Dano, Cl. & Lopez, E. Revue de Neuropsychiatrie Infantile et d'Hygiene Mentale de l'Enfance, 1971(Mar), Vol. 19(3-4), 151-158. [PA, Vol 49:09570]

2043. Treated phenylketonuria: Intelligence and blood phenylalanine levels.
Analysis of 113 phenylketonurics (age range = a few days to 5½ yr.) on treatment with a low phenylalanine diet showed: (a) a decrease in performance on tests of intelligence in Ss younger than 18 mo. when blood phenylalanine levels were below 5 mg/100 ml, raising the question of whether phenylalanine needs of phenylketonuric infants are greater than normal infants and older children; (b) dietary regimens producing phenylalanine levels above 5 mg/100 ml were not followed by a decrease in IQ; and (c) discontinuation of dietary treatment was more deleterious to the IQ of those Ss whose phenylalanine intake had been more limited (blood phenylalanine level less than 9 mg/100 ml) in the year immediately prior to discontinuation than in those Ss kept on more liberal intake (phenylalanine greater than 9 mg/100 ml). (35 ref.)
Fuller, Renée & Shuman, Joyce. (Rosewood State Hosp., Owings Mills, Md.) American Journal of Mental Deficiency, 1971(Mar), Vol. 75(5), 539-545. [PA, Vol 46:05347]

2044. Counseling the mentally retarded: A behavioral approach.
Discusses the efficacy of verbal counseling with mental retardates from a theoretical viewpoint. It is obvious that mentally retarded adolescents lack the verbal controls over nonverbal behavior. Instead of using verbal controls, it is suggested that counseling with the mental retardates should emphasize behavioral approach by the use of token reinforcements administered in variable schedules in social situations. Further research is needed to determine answers to the questions "Which technique works best, under what circumstances, and with whom?"
Gardner, William I. & Stamm, John M. (U. Wisconsin) Rehabilitation Counseling Bulletin, 1971(Sep), Vol. 15(1), 46-57. [PA, Vol 47:09723]

2045. Behavioral management services for the retarded: Applications of operant training procedures in the home.
Describes the basic principles underlying a program of operant training in the homes of retarded children. Success was found to occur at a high rate when control of the children's behavior was effectively transferred from the original therapist to the parents.
Hislop, M. W. (Mental Retardation Center, Toronto, Ontario, Canada) Ontario Psychologist, 1971, Vol. 3(4), 226-233. [PA, Vol 47:11514]

2046. Establishing use of crutches by a mentally retarded spina bifida child.
Taught a 5-yr-old mentally retarded spina bifida child to walk with the aid of crutches. This behavior was developed through fading of physical prompting within a 10-step successive approximation sequence. Preliminary training to establish gait consisted of developing use of parallel bars through fading of physically modelled responses within a 6-step successive approximation sequence. Use of parallel bars ceased during an extinction period and completely recovered upon being primed with 1 "free" reinforcement. Systematic use of natural reinforcers was employed as an aid in maintaining use of crutches.
Horner, R. Don. (Parsons State Hosp. & Training Center, Parsons Research Project, Kan.) Journal of Applied Behavior Analysis, 1971(Fal), Vol. 4(3), 183-189. [PA, Vol 47:11478]

2047. [On the problems of aimed pharmacotherapy of depressions in imbecile children and juveniles.] (Germ)
Reports the therapy of 31 imbecile juveniles showing depressive symptoms with 5-(2-dimethylamino ethoxy-imino) -5H-dibenzo[a,d] cyclohepta-1,4-diene hydrochloride, (noxiptilin, agedal). The physical compatibility of noxiptilin proved satisfactory so that it is considered suitable for prolonged treatment. Noxiptilin showed a favorable influence on the depressive symptoms of children, especially those with inhibited and anxious depressive symptoms. Noxiptilin is regarded as less suited for the depressions of such imbecile children whose psychopathologic symptoms are aggravated by a deep-rooted psychopathic predisposition.
Jacobs, Rolf. (Schleswig National Hosp., Inst. of Child Psychiatry, W. Germany) Arzneimittel-Forschung, 1971(May), Vol. 21(5), 607-609. [PA, Vol 48:03545]

2048. The mentally retarded, psychotic child.
Discusses diagnosis, management, and treatment of 3 types of combined retardation-psychosis in children. It is noted that a child may be both psychotic and mentally retarded when there is a common cause, or when the psychosis is an additional or secondary complication. Treatment and management will depend on diagnosis. The primary mentally retarded child may be poorly physically endowed, clumsy, dysplastic, with neurological defects, poor perception, and poor motor ability. The primary psychotic child may have no neurological signs, and abundant energy.
Jennings, A. N. (Marsden Hosp., Westmead, New South Wales, Australia) Australian Journal of Mental Retardation, 1971(Mar), Vol. 1(5), 145-149. [PA, Vol 48:09203]

2049. Problems reported by parents of mentally retarded children: Who helps?
Interviewed parents of 171 community-labeled retardates with IQ < 79 regarding their problems with their retarded child, and the resources—personal, private, and public—used to help with these problems. Perceived availability and effectiveness of services were also investigated. It was found that parents did not receive assistance from public or private resources for most problems. Further, a large proportion of parents, especially those from minority groups reported that they did not know of additional services or that no services were needed. (15 ref.)
Justice, R. S.; O'Connor, Gail & Warren, Neil. (Social Rehabilitation Services, Region X, Seattle, Wash.) American Journal of Mental Deficiency, 1971(May), Vol. 75(6), 685-691. [PA, Vol 47:01458]

2050. Shopping parents: Patient problem or professional problem?
Defines the term "shopping parent" and tests the hypothesis that parents who seek at least 3 professional evaluations of their retarded child are looking for a "magical" cure. On a basis of 218 families surveyed, less than 3% were seen as shopping parents and these parents were making a specific request of the clinic. Several suggestions as to how parents can be assisted are offered and it is concluded that the term shopping parent is a misnomer.
Keirn, William C. (U. California, Neuropsychiatric Inst., Los Angeles) Mental Retardation, 1971(Aug), Vol. 9(4), 6-7. [PA, Vol 49:11646]

2051. Shock as punishment in a picture-naming task with retarded children.
Taught 2 5- and 6-yr-old retarded children to name pictures according to a standardized procedure. In Exp. I, correct responses were positively reinforced on a 5-1 ratio under 1 stimulus condition, incorrect responses were followed with a sharp "no," and the S was ignored for inattentive behavior. Under another stimulus condition, correct responses were reinforced as in the 1st condition, but incorrect responses and 5-sec periods of inattentive behavior were followed by "no" and an electric shock. Less inattentive behavior was exhibited and more words were learned to a preset criterion in the shock condition than in the no-shock condition. In Exp. II, the ratio of inappropriate responses to shock was varied. The amount of inattentive behavior tended to increase in the shock condition, relative to that in the no-shock condition, as this ratio was increased. 2 other measures of performance used were the ratio of errors to correct responses and the number of correct responses. Shock tended to produce better performance on these measures also. (19 ref.)
Kircher, Alfred S.; Pear, Joseph J. & Martin, Garry L. (Child Guidance Clinic, Winnipeg, Manitoba, Canada) Journal of Applied Behavior Analysis, 1971(Fal), Vol. 4(3), 227-233. [PA, Vol 48:01514]

2052. [Testing of sulpiride in infantile psychiatry.] (Fren)
Administered daily oral doses of 120-200 mg/kg sulpiride to
hospitalized 3-7 yr. old mental retardates, neurotics, or psychotics (N = 26). Treatment duration ranged from 20 days to 1 yr.
Positive or medium drug effects were found in 14 cases. Sulpiride
had incontestable action on neurotic reactions (phobias and
obsessions) and produced little change in mental retardates. No
conclusions could be reached for psychotics due to the small
number of Ss (n = 3). Sulpiride produced no contraindications,
was compatible with other medications, and was beneficial in
prolonged usage. Results indicate the drug is best utilized for
thymic regulation, incoherent thought processes, and excessive
fatigue. It is concluded that sulpiride usage is appropriate in
infantile psychiatry because of its incisive, rapid action and
exceptional tolerance.
Kohler, C.; Marcon, G. & Maritan, C. (St. Eugenie Hosp., Jean
Dechaume Wing, Saint-Genis-Laval, France) Revue de Neuropsychiatrie Infantile et d'Hygiene Mentale de l'Enfance,
1971(Dec), Vol. 19(12), 751-758. [PA, Vol 50:01521]

2053. [Evaluation of the clinical effects of sulpiride in medical-
educational day school and day hospital for children.] (Fren)
Describes the pretreatment symptoms, sulpiride dosage, and
treatment effects for each of 23 6-13 yr. old severely retarded,
mildly retarded, or psychotic children. Positive or medium drug
effects were found in 14 cases; 7 out of 9 mildly retarded Ss
showed affective and intellectual improvement. No side effects
were found, although there was a slight tendency for the drug to
accentuate certain symptoms (e.g., impulsive reactions) in severe
retardates. Possible reasons for the lack of success with severe
retardates include the presence of a neurological syndrome and
the nonparticipation of parents (who had to administer the drug
on weekends). Symptom analysis indicates that sulpiride was
most effective in releasing intellectual and affective inhibitions,
had very little effect on psychomotor disturbances and character
disorders, and had indeterminable effect on depressive and
dissociative reactions. It is concluded that sulpiride can be
effectively used in an open institution or day hospital setting.
Lang, J. L. & Le Strat, M. Revue de Neuropsychiatrie
Infantile et d'Hygiene Mentale de l'Enfance, 1971(Dec), Vol.
19(12), 759-772. [PA, Vol 50:01530]

2054. Clinical comparison of haloperidol with chlorpromazine
in mentally retarded children.
In an 8-wk double-blind comparison in 61 mentally retarded
children, haloperidol reduced the severity of the target symptoms
impulsiveness, hostility, and aggressiveness in significantly more
Ss than did chlorpromazine. Global results with haloperidol were
also significantly better than those with chlorpromazine. Among
the chlorpromazine Ss, there was a trend toward improvement,
but it did not achieve significance in the time of the study. At the
dose levels used, adverse reactions were equal and minimal for
the 2 groups. No abnormal laboratory results that could be
attributed to the drugs occurred in either group.
Le Vann, Leonard J. (Alberta School Hosp., Red Deer, Canada)
American Journal of Mental Deficiency, 1971(May), Vol. 75(6),
719-723. [PA, Vol 47:01108]

2055. Toilet training of normal and retarded children.
Trained early elements in an operant chain of toilet behaviors in
3 normal 18-21 mo. old infants and 5 retarded male 4 and 9 yr.
olds. Following that, eliminative behaviors were conditioned by
operant procedures. Each S was equipped with an auditory
signalling device that gave cues to the learner. Base-line behavior
was recorded for a period of 5 days. The procedure for training
consisted of 2 steps: (a) a response was obtained through
physical, verbal, and auditory prompts; and (b) prompts were
faded until the S responded in the presence of the auditory signal.
When the device was removed the S performed without the
auditory prompt. Parents were instructed in a similar procedure
to enhance generalization in the home. 7 of the Ss reached a
criterion and maintained that behavior during 3 criterion
sessions.

Mahoney, Kurt; Van Wagenen, R. Keith & Meyerson, Lee.
(Arizona State U.) Journal of Applied Behavior Analysis,
1971(Fal), Vol. 4(3), 173-181. [PA, Vol 48:01536]

2056. [Treatment with dipiperon in an outpatient department
for children and adolescents.] (Germ)
Discusses treatment with a neuroleptic of the butyrophenones
(dipiperon) in an outpatient department of children and adolescents. 85 patients diagnosed as neurosis and reactive behavior
disturbances (26), early brain damage (41), and mental deficiency
(18) were examined. 76% of the patients showed good results,
but the mentally deficient (83%) and the brain-damaged (76%)
responded better to the drug than the behaviorally disturbed
(73%). The average dosage was 60-100 mg. Side effects were
minimal; extrapyramidal reactions not noted. The new liquid
medium lends itself to easier administration.
Müller-Küppers, M. (U. Heidelberg, Psychiatric-Neurological
Clinic, W. Germany) Acta Paedopsychiatrica, 1971(Feb), Vol.
38(2), 40-46. [PA, Vol 47:07027]

2057. Reduction of self-abusive behavior in a blind child by
using a feeding response.
Treated an 11-yr-old retarded male, blind from age 2, for self-
abusive behavior (head beating) by creating a feeding response
incompatible with it. When head beating had been eliminated at
feeding time, additional techniques were used to extend its
elimination beyond the eating situation. A 3-phase program
involved intermittent primary rewards, "timeout," and rewarding incompatible responses. 9 mo. after the program began the
previously continual self-abusive responses were down to 3 or 4 a
day and of so little intensity that they could be overlooked.
Myers, James J. & Deibert, Alvin N. (Hope School, Springfield,
Ill.) Journal of Behavior Therapy & Experimental Psychiatry,
1971(Jul), Vol. 2(2), 141-144. [PA, Vol 47:05478]

2058. Effects of reinforcement contingencies on attention span
and task related stimulus control in retarded children.
During training with an adult, 3 retarded boys were presented 3
tasks, each associated with a different training regime (extinction, contingent, or noncontingent reinforcement). The contingent task acquired discriminative properties, whereas other tasks
did not. Control was maintained in familiar and unfamiliar
settings and with novel adults. When the contingent task was
introduced following the presentation of extinction and noncontingent tasks, Ss manipulated the contingent task; when the other
2 tasks were presented after the contingent task, Ss ignored them
and continued working on the contingent task. Results were
replicated when assignments of reinforcement contingencies to
tasks were removed.
Redd, William H. (Massachusetts General Hosp., Boston)
Proceedings of the 79th Annual Convention of the American
Psychological Association, 1971, Vol. 6(Pt. 2), 671-672. [PA, Vol
46:05367]

2059. Functions of parental attention in an oppositional,
retarded boy.
2 experiments analyzed the interaction of punishment and
positive reinforcement. Contingent parental attention could not
maintain cleanup behavior in a retarded oppositional boy. When
a blast from a bicycle horn was used to eliminate disruptions,
cleaning increased greatly. However, praise was now necessary to
maintain the high level of cleaning. Furthermore, the praise had
to come from the parent using the horn. These results suggest
that the horn prompted the child to look more to a parent, thus
attenting to the parent's praise. Exp. III demonstrated a transient
punishment effect of praise. This suggests that a response-
consequence linkage may have discriminative functions.
Sajwaj, Thomas & Hedges, Donald. (U. Mississippi, Medical
Center) Proceedings of the 79th Annual Convention of the
American Psychological Association, 1971, Vol. 6(Pt. 2), 697-
698. [PA, Vol 46:05368]

2060. Preliminary considerations in psychotherapy with
retarded children.
Psychotherapy for the retarded child with emotional problems
may be the responsibility of the school psychologist. Because the

literature dealing with the most profitable techniques and procedures is sparse, an overview of the special needs and characteristics of retarded children has been made. The child brings a language deficit, emotional attitudes related to retardedness, and social experiences to the therapeutic situation. Group and individual therapy are discussed with suggestions for successful implementation.
Selwa, Barbara I. (U. Northern Iowa) Journal of School Psychology, 1971, Vol. 9(1), 12-15. [PA, Vol 47:05659]

2061. Group psychotherapy: Its effects on mothers who rate social performance of retardates.
Results indicate that mothers who underwent psychotherapy rated the retardates significantly higher in security and appearance than they did before therapy, while the mothers in the control group saw no changes in their retarded children.
Siegel, Bess; Sheridan, Kathleen & Sheridan, Edward P. (Oakland Counseling Service, Pontiac, Mich.) American Journal of Psychiatry, 1971(Mar), Vol. 127(9), 1215-1217. [PA, Vol 47:01465]

2062. Response cost effects on echoic responding of mentally retarded.
In an experimental study, removal of tokens for no response proved more effective than rewards in learning echoic responses of low-verbal mentally retarded children. It appears that failure-avoidance leads in motivating these retarded children over reward for success. Implications for motivating mentally retarded children using failure avoidance techniques are briefly discussed.
Talkington, Larry W. & Hall, Sylvia M. (Fairview Hosp. & Training Center, Salem, Ore.) Australian Journal of Mental Retardation, 1971(Jun), Vol. 1(6), 188-190. [PA, Vol 47:09523]

2063. Token economy and motivating environment for mildly retarded adolescent boys.
Describes a token economy program with 20 12-18 yr. old mildly and moderately retarded boys whose days were controlled through a system of positive and negative reinforcement and timeout procedures. Preliminary results indicate that all but 1 S significantly improved behaviorally and socially after 5 mo. of the program. Other results indicate a change in status hierarchy among the Ss and improvement of aide attendance.
Tymchuk, Alexander J. (George Peabody Coll.) Mental Retardation, 1971(Dec), Vol. 9(6), 8. [PA, Vol 47:11497]

2064. [Trampoline gymnastics with learning-disabled and mentally retarded children.] (Germ)
Describes a method by which gymnastics are aided through rhythmical-musical exercises. As a medium to regulate breathing the children are taught rhymes, songs, and dances in which the metric concentrations are coupled with the body impact and landing positions.
Zu Stolberg, Elisabeth & Kerkhoff, Winfried. (Albert-Schweitzer-Sonderschule, Münster, W. Germany) Vierteljahresschrift für Heilpädagogik und ihre Nachbargebiete, 1971(Sep), Vol. 40(3), 207-212. [PA, Vol 48:05683]

2065. Social aspects of medical care for the mentally retarded.
Considers the varied complex social issues associated with mental retardation which affect its clinical management: the family's sense of rejection, potential social isolation, and anxiety about caring for the child's unusual health needs. The physician plays a key role in ameliorating these stresses by working with the family as cooperative equals and using supportive community resources to avoid risk to their physical, mental, and social health. Treatment of these issues in mental retardation is discussed as a model for chronic illness in general.
Adams, Margaret. (Walter E. Fernald State School, Eunice Kennedy Shriver Center, Waverley, Mass.) New England Journal of Medicine, 1972(Mar), Vol. 286(12), 635-638. [PA, Vol 48:12032]

2066. The role of the special school in the integration of mentally retarded children into the community.
Discusses evidence confirming the deleterious effects of prolonged institutionalization of retarded children on their cognitive and linguistic functioning and on their personal and social adjustment. The argument that educational segregation in a specialized and separate school environment militates against future social integration is viewed as unsupported by research. Early identification of the severely retarded is often the case, and this permits early intervention in a program designed to integrate the child in the community. Intervention in the social and cognitive areas can be effective, despite the wide differences in these Ss. The school must work with the parents providing guidance so the parent can work effectively with the child. There is evidence that the retardate's learning rate of semiskilled work is less dependent on intellectual limitations than on distractibility, social adjustment pressures, or difficulties in emotional interaction. The need for the community to be educated as to the needs of the retarded is stressed. (16 ref.)
Andrews, R. J. & Apelt, Winifred C. (U. Queensland, St. Lucia, Australia) Australian Journal of Mental Retardation, 1972(Jun), Vol. 2(2), 54-58. [PA, Vol 49:07352]

2067. Comparative effects of a token economy in nursery school.
Used reinforcement with tokens and "time-out" procedures to control the disruptive or negative behavior of 9 retarded children in a nursery school setting. Experimental Ss were selected by their teachers as behavior problems and were compared with 10 controls of similar age and IQ who attended a similar program, but without tokens. Base lines were taken in both groups before the introduction of tokens into the experimental setting, and a suspension of treatment procedure was used to test for the effectiveness of the token economy. The experimental group displayed more negative behavior than controls during base line, but demonstrated superior performance during token economy phases. Suspension of treatment produced a significant return to higher levels of negative performance. The efficacy of the use of lay volunteers as behavior modification technicians is discussed.
Baker, J. Garry; Stanish, B. & Fraser, B. (Mental Retardation Center, Toronto, Ontario, Canada) Mental Retardation, 1972(Aug), Vol. 10(4), 16-19. [PA, Vol 49:03092]

2068. Teaching the retarded to swim.
Describes the testing of a modified form of the Gabrielsen's Total Push-Kick Method for teaching preschool children to swim in order to determine its applicability to mentally retarded children. 90% of 14 trainable and 26 educable retarded children learned how to swim.
Bundschuh, E. L. et al. (U. Georgia, Retardation Center) Mental Retardation, 1972(Jun), Vol. 10(3), 14-17. [PA, Vol 49:01272]

2069. A double-blind comparison of haloperidol (Haldol) and thioridazine (Mellaril) in outpatient children.
Conducted a double-blind comparison of haloperidol and thioridazine with 38 male and 19 female 5-11 yr olds who exhibited the symptomology of childhood psychiatric disorders. Ss received identical-appearing capsules containing .5 mg haloperidol or 10 mg thioridazine. The maximum allowed dosage was 10 mg haloperidol or 200 mg thioridazine. Ss were evaluated before, during, and after drug therapy. Physical and laboratory determinations were obtained, and symptomological evaluation was based on a specially designed "Checklist of Home Behavior" and global physician ratings. While some beneficial changes were noted for behavior during homework, results indicate that haloperidol and thioridazine were essentially the same in treatment effectiveness.
Claghorn, James L. (Texas Research Inst. of Mental Sciences, Houston) Current Therapeutic Research, 1972(Dec), Vol. 14(12), 785-789. [PA, Vol 51:01570]

2070. The first ten months of the Rubella Living-Unit.
Describes operation of a Rubella living unit, established to halt regression and teach basic self-help skills to a group of preschool deaf, blind, mentally retarded children, mostly confined to beds

in a residential school. Originally 6, then 10 children with 9 staff members working 12 hr. 7 days/wk., formed this unit. Improvement of the child's life style, helping him reach his maximum potential, and determining the most effective teaching techniques with this type of child were the objectives. Means for achieving them were instructing the children in daily living skills, enlarging experiences by field trips, improving interactions with peers and staff, and evaluating the educational potential. 6 case histories are presented, emphasizing that progress was much greater than expected. It is believed that such children are able to learn "if someone believes in the child's potential and gives enough of himself to the learning situation."
Dolan, William S. (Sunlight House, Deaf-Blind Program, Scituate, Mass.) New Outlook for the Blind, 1972(Jan), Vol. 66(1), 9-14. [PA, Vol 48:07565]

2071. Factors determining residential placement of mentally retarded children.
Selected 143 children, all identified as mentally retarded by a variety of agencies in 1 community. 30 Ss institutionalized at some time during the follow-up period were compared to those not so admitted. Results show that the 5 most significant variables which discriminate between retarded Ss with high and low probabilities of institutionalization represent characteristics of the patients themselves. Those likely to be admitted generally had IQs less than 53, were younger, had more physical disabilities and adaptive behavior failures, and were of Anglo-American background. (41 ref.)
Eyman, R. K.; O'Connor, G.; Tarjan, G. & Justice, R. S. (Pacific State Hosp., Socio-Behavioral Lab., Pomona, Calif.) American Journal of Mental Deficiency, 1972(May), Vol. 76(6), 692-698. [PA, Vol 48:12039]

2072. Prophylactic physiotherapy with young retarded children.
Discusses the general duties and functions of physical therapists in relationship to the mentally retarded who have physical handicaps. Several case studies and the relative successes of these cases are described.
Fisher, Glenice. (Challinor Centre, Ipswich, Queensland, Australia) Australian Journal of Mental Retardation, 1972(Dec), Vol. 2(4), 122-126. [PA, Vol 50:05334]

2073. [Use of a cerebral oxygenating drug in chronic mental retardation: Report of a trial of vincamine.] (Fren)
Discusses recent progress made in understanding the circulation system in the brain, the discovery of vascular anomolies in numerous mentally retarded patients, and the encouraging results obtained by M. Salmon on 150 cases of carotid sinus irritation. 34 cases of mental retardation treated by the cerebral oxyginator, vincamine, are reported. In 11 cases, an improvement was obtained in the infant's psychomotor system. It is thus considered that cerebral vasoregulators can be useful in the treatment of infant mental retardation, an area in which medicine is particularly ineffective. (34 ref.)
Fossey, F. & Pasquier, Ch. (Regional Hosp. Center, Angers, France) Revue de Neuropsychiatrie Infantile et d'Hygiene Mentale de l'Enfance, 1972(Nov), Vol. 20(11-12), 887-891. [PA, Vol 50:05340]

2074. The effect of positive and negative reaction tendencies on receptive language development in mentally retarded children.
Investigated the effects of experiential and life history variables on acquisition of receptive vocabulary responses in 2 studies with 42 8-18 yr. old retardates in each. Exp. I examined the effects of the positive reaction tendency and found that conditions which provided for maximum social reinforcement were more effective than those providing the minimum. Exp. II examined the effects of the negative reaction tendency and found that conditions which provided for negative prior interaction resulted in slower learning than conditions providing either positive prior interaction or none. Results lend partial support to E. Zigler's formulations concerning acquisition of new responses. (16 ref.)

Gayton, William F. & Bassett, John E. (U. Rochester, Medical Center) American Journal of Mental Deficiency, 1972(Mar), Vol. 76(5), 499-508. [PA, Vol 48:12064]

2075. Stimulus factors in skill training of retarded adolescents on a complex assembly task: Acquisition, transfer, and retention.
64 moderately and severely retarded Ss enrolled in 4 sheltered workshops learned to assemble a 15-piece bicycle brake and were then tested for transfer to a 24-piece bicycle brake. 53 Ss were retested on both tasks after 1 yr. ½ of the Ss worked with parts of the training task brake as they came from the factory (form-only), and the others with parts that were color-coded (color-form). All worked with parts of the transfer task brake as they came from the factory (form-only). Half of the Ss learned the tasks to a criterion of 6 correct out of 8 consecutive trials, the others to 20 trials beyond criterion on the training task brake (overlearning). Results show the color-form Ss learned the training task brake significantly faster than the form-only, and overlearning did not affect transfer. The 1-yr retention study yielded significant retention effects. (30 ref.)
Gold, Marc W. (U. Illinois) American Journal of Mental Deficiency, 1972(Mar), Vol. 76(5), 517-526. [PA, Vol 48:12065]

2076. Development and validation of a mediated package for training parents of preschool mentally retarded children.
Describes a 4-unit parent training program that emphasized teaching self-care skills to their preschool mentally retarded children. An evaluation of the program by parents suggests that the program has the potential to make significant changes in the behavior repertoires of preschool mental retardates.
Hofmeister, Alan M. & Latham, Glenn. (Utah State U) Improving Human Performance, 1972(Mar), Vol 1(1), 3-7. [PA, Vol 53:05671]

2077. [A study of promotional activity for social adaptability of the mentally retarded: Children's group.] (Japn)
Describes a program in which the parents of mentally retarded children participated in guidance sessions designed to improve their understanding of the abilities and limitations of their children. The children were given training for the kinetic function, group play, and musical play.
Iida, M. et al. (National Inst. of Mental Health, Div. of Mental Deficiency Research, Ichikawa, Japan) Journal of Mental Health, 1972(Mar), Vol. 46(20), 145-179. [PA, Vol 49:09635]

2078. Increase and maintenance of verbal behavior of a mentally retarded child.
Used operant and imitative techniques to program generalization of verbal behavior in 1 female 11-yr-old mental retardate. In the training sessions, a high rate of phoneme imitation and tacting sounds with pictures was established using contingent positive reinforcement. A self-programming procedure enabled S to practice independently sounds and words learned with the therapist. In addition, 2 of S's peers, who were mentally retarded but verbal, were trained to practice words with S. Data indicate that the program (a) increased phoneme imitation from 41% during base line to 95% during treatment, and (b) increased the rate of classroom verbalizations from 15% during base line to 46% during treatment. Classroom follow-up data indicate S's average rate of verbalization decreased slightly from the treatment phase, but remained substantially above base-line level. (24 ref.)
Jeffrey, D. Balfour. (U. Utah) Mental Retardation, 1972(Apr), Vol. 10(2), 35-40. [PA, Vol 48:09569]

2079. Extinction of vomiting behavior in a retarded child.
Komechak, Marilyn G. (Child Study Center, Fort Worth, Tex.) Catalog of Selected Documents in Psychology, 1972(Spr), Vol. 2. [PA, Vol 49:07520]

2080. Behavior management training for parents of the mentally retarded.
Discusses 2 assumptions which underlie efforts to train parents of mentally retarded children in the management of behavior: (a) parents generally prefer to care for their retarded child at home rather than committing him to an institution and (b) parents

frequently request institutionalization for behavioral reasons. A project is reported that was designed to train parents of the retarded, many of whom were considering institutionalization of their child at the time of the referral. 66 referrals were studied. Problems were specified and parents were asked to keep records of their occurrence and frequency. Follow-up contact was done either by telephone or home visits. 10 cases are presented with success to some extent in all of them. Selecting appropriate behaviors to maximize parental involvement and reinforcing, through successive approximations the parents' data recording and contingency management is seen as the way to success of this sort of project.

Kurtz, Paul S.; Cook, Carolyn & Failla, Jack. (Mount Pleasant State Home & Training School, Mich.) Michigan Mental Health Research Bulletin, 1972(Win), Vol. 6(1), 5-16. [PA, Vol 52:05693]

2081.   Domiciliary programmes for intellectually handicapped children.
Examines home programs for the intellectually handicapped. It is noted that care at home is important, but that assessment of the child's capabilities and the attitudes of the parents are necessary. Home programs may consist of actual therapy, suitable methods of handling the child in specific situations, and suggestions of daily routine. In designing the program, it is suggested that the following factors must be taken into consideration: (a) those which describe the child in his environment, (b) those concerning the child's own abilities, (c) minor structural changes in the house and yard, (d) design of the house, and (e) one to one relationships. A brief example of a program is given, with a description of some equipment used.

Lee, Lesley. (Challinor Center, Ipswich, Queensland, Australia) Australian Journal of Mental Retardation, 1972(Sep), Vol. 2(3), 80-84. [PA, Vol 50:03518]

2082.   Effects of group procedure with parents of MR children.
Assigned 31 parents of mentally retarded children to 3 experimental discussion groups which met for 10 wk. Compared to 31 controls, the experimental Ss showed a significant improvement in knowledge of retardation and child-rearing attitudes (p = .001 and .002, respectively).

Lewis, Juliet. (Miami-Dade Junior Coll. South, Div. Intercurricular Studies) Mental Retardation, 1972(Dec), Vol. 10(6), 14-15. [PA, Vol 50:01538]

2083.   [Acquisition of grammatical rules through verbal training: An example of verbal conditioning.] (Germ)
Conducted a psycholinguistic experiment with 12 5-9 yr old mentally handicapped children with severe speech retardation. Ss were exposed to 3 experimental phases: Phase 1, in which they were divided into 3 groups on the basis of their vocabulary and type of utterances: 4 with lowest level, 4 with higher level, and control group of 4 mixed level; Phase 2, a training phase in which the 1st group was rewarded for the use of verbs, the 2nd group for the use of adjectives, and the control group without reward; and Phase 3, an examination phase checking the results of the training session by comparing the tests of Phase 1 and Phase 2 in regard to the number and variety of verbs and ajectives used, length, complexity, syntactical correctness, and general competence of utterances. Results indicate (a) a significant difference between Group 1 vs Groups 2 and 3 in regard to the number and variety of verbs used; (b) a significant difference between Group 2 vs 1 and 3 in regard to the number and variety of adjectives used; and (c) between Groups 1 and 2 vs 3 in regard to the complexity of construction and syntactical competence. 2 tables with experimental data are presented and the experimental procedures and problems are discussed. (English summary) (21 ref)

List, Gudula. (U. Constance, Div. of Psychology, W. Germany) Zeitschrift für Klinische Psychologie. Forschung und Praxis, 1972, Vol. 2(1), 164-176. [PA, Vol 51:07453]

2084.   Assessing and increasing descriptive communication skills in retarded children.
Reviews recent developments in research methodology and discusses the use of a 2-person communication paradigm to assess and increase the descriptive skills of retarded children. Preliminary results suggest that the technique is an objective method for observing and modifying interpersonal communication behaviors of these children. Uses of the paradigm in the laboratory and classroom are suggested. (24 ref.)

Longhurst, Thomas M. (Kansas State U.) Mental Retardation, 1972(Apr), Vol. 10(2), 42-45. [PA, Vol 48:09572]

2085.   An interdisciplinary program for retarded children and their families.
Describes the work in the past 2 yr. of the Center for Developmental and Learning Disorders' staff (an interdisciplinary team) in helping parents cope with daily living with their retarded child. Initially, families may be so overwhelmed by problems that the family strengths are not apparent. Parents are given staff guidance and support, in an atmosphere encouraging free communication, on dealing with the problems of mental retardation and assuming appropriate roles to help their child. The occupational therapist responsible for the assessment of the child's development and function establishes an ongoing relationship with the family and is frequently able to channel the parents' energies positively through home treatment programs.

McKibbin, Elsie H. (U. Alabama, Center for Developmental & Learning Disorders) American Journal of Occupational Therapy, 1972(Apr), Vol. 26(3), 125-129. [PA, Vol 48:09558]

2086.   Issues in the application of reinforcement theory in the treatment of a child's self-injurious behavior.
Discusses theoretical, clinical, and teaching issues that evolve when reinforcement theory is used to treat self-injurious behavior in children. The case of an 8-yr-old mute, mentally retarded girl with over a 1-yr history of head banging (resulting in large hematomas) illustrates the following issues: (a) the emotional reaction that an S's self-injurious behavior and the use of punishment procedures may arouse in many people, (b) the limitations and advantages of punishment procedures, and (c) the importance of collaboration among personnel involved in the treatment program.

Morrison, Delmont. (Langley Porter Neuropsychiatric Inst., San Francisco, Calif.) Psychotherapy: Theory, Research & Practice, 1972(Spr), Vol. 9(1), 40-45. [PA, Vol 50:05464]

2087.   The different remedial motor training programs and the development of mentally retarded pre-schoolers.
27 mentally retarded children (average CA = 49 mo.) participated in 1 of the following programs for 6 mo.: (a) randomly selected activities with social attention, (b) social reinforcement for casually selected gross-motor activities, or (c) social reinforcement for gross-motor activities prescribed from a developmental assessment of sensorimotor deficiencies. Full scale, gross-motor, fine motor, language, and personal-social, pre- and posttest scores from the Denver Developmental Screening Test were obtained. Statistical analysis demonstrated that Ss participating in the prescribed training program had significantly greater increments over the interval in gross-motor, language, and full-scale scores than did the others. The study demonstrates the advantage of using a detailed developmental analysis of sensorimotor defects as a basis for the selection of remedial sensorimotor activities.

Morrison, Delmont & Pothier, Patricia. (U. California, Medical School, San Francisco) American Journal of Mental Deficiency, 1972(Nov), Vol. 77(3), 251-258. [PA, Vol 50:03852]

2088.   Retarded infants and their parents: A group for fathers and mothers.
Discusses the lack of continuity and the fragmentation of services offered to retarded children and their parents. The organization, members, and themes discussed in a group for the parents of retarded children are described.

Nurse, John. (U. Exeter, England) British Journal of Social Work, 1972(Sum), Vol. 2(2), 159-174. [PA, Vol 49:07590]

2089. Training psychiatrists in mental retardation.
Reviews some approaches to training psychiatrists in mental retardation and describes a program begun in the District of Columbia to provide consultation for mental retardation. In addition to teaching the physical aspects of retardation, this program attempts to incorporate training in family interaction and its relationship to the social environment. The resident sees the retarded child not only as a genetic product, but also as he affects and is affected by his interpersonal environment. *Raskin, David E.* (National Inst. of Mental Health, Rockville, Md.) American Journal of Psychiatry, 1972(May), Vol. 128(11), 1443-1445. [PA, Vol 48:09211]

2090. Symposium on the treatment of behavioural problems: IV. Manic-depressive illness in retarded children.
Reviews the literature on the incidence of manic-depressive illness in children and in mentally retarded patients. The relationship between manic-depressive illness and "affective storms" is considered. It is suggested that manic-depressive illness in mentally retarded patients may be present as "manic-depressive equivalents." Criteria for diagnosis of manic-depressive illness are presented and the case of a manic-depressive equivalent in a 13-yr-old mentally retarded boy is described. Arguments concerning why mentally retarded patients should have a higher or lower rate than normals of affective illness are considered. (15 ref.)
Revill, M. G. (Queen Mary's Hosp. for Children, Carshalton, England) British Journal of Mental Subnormality, 1972(Dec), Vol. 18(35, Pt. 2), 89-93. [PA, Vol 50:05155]

2091. A case study in the remediation of severe self-destructive behavior in a 6-year-old mentally retarded girl.
Reports a case history of a girl who began to display a type of autistic withdrawal and noncommunicativeness with others after the sudden loss of her close association with her grandmother. The program for treatment was based on the principle of an expanding hierarchy of positive interests. Self-destructive tendencies were shaped and modified through this treatment program and the child's life-space was expanded.
Rubin, Gerald; Griswald, Karen; Smith, Ira & De Leonardo, Concetta. (Glassboro State Coll.) Journal of Clinical Psychology, 1972(Jul), Vol. 28(3), 424-426. [PA, Vol 51:03715]

2092. Effects of concurrent and serial training on generalized vocal imitation in retarded children.
Conditioned 2 retarded 8-yr-old females by operant shaping techniques to imitate vocal items presented by the E. Ss were reinforced for increasingly accurate imitations of the training items. Training was done alternately by (a) a serial method in which 1 item was trained to criterion before the next was introduced in a series of 3 items; and (b) a concurrent procedure in which 3 words were shaped into accurate imitations at the same time. Immediately after reaching criterion, the CRF schedule was gradually reduced to an intermittent one and unreinforced untrained probe items introduced among the accurately imitated training items. Response to these probe items was later rated for imitation accuracy. There was no significant difference in the number of trials required to reach criterion performance through concurrent and serial training procedures. As the number of correct imitations increased, the accuracy of the unreinforced probe items also generally increased. However, the increase in probe accuracy was consistently greater following concurrent training. Results suggest that teaching verbal imitations concurrently may be advantageous in establishing a functional behavioral class of accurate imitation without increasing training trials.
Schroeder, Gerald L. & Baer, Donald M. (U. Kansas) Developmental Psychology, 1972(Mar), Vol. 6(2), 293-301. [PA, Vol 47:11511]

2093. A modeling approach to changing parent-child interactions.
Describes a paradigm wherein a mother was reinforced for observing and modeling her 4-yr-old child's therapist, producing significant changes in a maladaptive Parent × Child interaction

pattern. The changes were measured over a 3-mo period; behavior was monitored by time sampling in a standarized setting before and after treatment. This approach is contrasted with traditional behavior therapy. An important contrast is that the child is not considered a passive recipient under control of reinforcement contingencies, but is viewed as an active participant in the interaction eliciting responses from the mother, as well as responding to her.
Seitz, Sue & Terdal, Leif. (National Regional Resource Center of Pennsylvania, Harrisburg) Mental Retardation, 1972(Jun), Vol. 10(3), 39-43. [PA, Vol 49:01226]

2094. Television as a language training medium with retarded children.
A review of the literature indicates that TV is a potentially useful but largely unexplored training medium for mentally retarded children. Research in the use of TV for training prelanguage and language skills and the development of training tapes for national viewing is suggested. (17 ref)
Striefel, Sebastian. (Parsons State Hosp., Bureau of Child Research, Kan.) Mental Retardation, 1972(Apr), Vol. 10(2), 27-29. [PA, Vol 48:09579]

2095. Modification of vocational behavior in a community agency for mentally retarded adolescents.
Applied operant techniques to 19 noninstitutionalized, moderately to severely retarded late adolescents whose multiple behavioral problems and very low levels of productivity precluded them from working in sheltered workshops. Techniques used in the study, performed over a period of 15 mo. at the Work Experience Center of the St. Louis Jewish Employment and Vocational Service, included token reinforcement, cueing lights, and punishment. While these procedures were generally successful in raising production and eliminating or reducing work-interfering behaviors, it was found that these operant methods had to be continued in order to maintain the improvements noted.
Trybus, Raymond J. & Lacks, Patricia B. (Gallaudet Coll., Counseling & Placement Center, Washington, D.C.) Rehabilitation Literature, 1972(Sep), Vol. 33(9), 258-266. [PA, Vol 49:07669]

2096. Multiple effects of a procedure to increase sitting in a hyperactive, retarded boy.
Used a prompting and differential reinforcement procedure to increase sitting in a hyperactive, 4-yr-old retarded boy in a remedial preschool. This procedure not only increased sitting, but had the additional effects of decreasing posturing while leaving normal walking unaffected, and increasing the use of toys and proximity to children. Results suggest that preschool programs can be designed that will treat several behaviors simultaneously in order to maximize a teacher's effectiveness.
Twardosz, Sandra & Sajwaj, Thomas. (U. Kansas) Journal of Applied Behavior Analysis, 1972(Spr), Vol. 5(1), 73-78. [PA, Vol 48:09584]

2097. Programed instruction: Teaching coinage to retarded children.
Used programed instruction presented by a teaching machine which required a specific response pattern in an attempt to teach coin equivalencies to 8 mentally retarded children. The initial success of the program suggested the development of further programs of coinage instruction. A theoretical interpretation of the proficiency of the particular response technique used in the study within the context of attention theory is provided.
Wunderlich, Richard A. (Catholic U. of America) Mental Retardation, 1972(Oct), Vol. 10(5), 21-23. [PA, Vol 49:09814]

2098. The extinction of a self-injurious behavior in an epileptic child.
Describes a contingency reinforcement behavior modification program to eliminate the falling behavior of a 14-yr-old retarded girl with a history of grand- and petit-mal epilepsy. No falls occurred after the 1st 6 wks of the program, and staff ratings of the patient's behavior before and after the program indicated that the program was successful in eliminating the maladaptive

behaviors and increasing self-maintenance and appropriate social activities.
Adams, Kenneth M.; Klinge, Valerie K. & Keiser, Thomas W. (Lafayette Clinic, Detroit, Mich.) Behaviour Research & Therapy, 1973(Aug), Vol. 11(3), 351-356. [PA, Vol 52:08288]

2099.   Behavior therapy with emotionally disturbed and retarded Filipino children: II.
Presents several studies on behavior therapy with emotionally disturbed and retarded children (a) in the school setting, with individual targets, and (b) in the home setting, with parents as mediators. Appended are behavior inventories for use in the home and school. (9 p ref)
Ahmed, Mohiuddin et al. (Philippine Mental Health Association, Quezon City) Philippine Journal of Mental Health, 1973(Jul–Dec), Vol 4(2), 69–110. [PA, Vol 61:08924]

2100.   Mothers of retarded children: Satisfaction with visits to professional people.
Describes interviews with 23 mothers concerning their experiences with professional people in regard to their retarded children from the time the child was born until the time of the interview. Results indicate that specific professions and visits made for diagnoses generate a low degree of maternal satisfaction.
Anderson, Kathryn A. & Garner, Ann M. (Mental Health Center, Children & Adolescent Services, Meadville, Pa.) Mental Retardation, 1973(Aug), Vol. 11(4), 36-39. [PA, Vol 51:05458]

2101.   [Application of the principles of the experimental analysis of behavior to the rehabilitation of developmentally retarded children.] (Span)
Reports that 3 types of behavior were successfully modified, i.e., attention, imitation, and socialization. Reinforcement was food and/or social reinforcement. It is considered that the low cost of rehabilitation programs makes it feasible for developing countries with a shortage of personnel and resources.
Anzures, Rafael; Naranjo, César & Calderón, Héctor A. (National Autonomous U. Mexico, Mexico City) Revista Latinoamericana de Psicología, 1973, Vol. 5(3), 325-354. [PA, Vol 52:01616]

2102.   Camp Freedom: Behavior modification for retarded children in a therapeutic camp setting.
Compared the progress of 25 retarded children who attended an experimental summer camp (Camp Freedom) based on principles of behavior modification, with a matched group of 15 retarded Ss who did not attend camp. The campers showed significantly greater progress than did controls in predetermined target areas, suggesting that a camping experience may have beneficial effects, and that a program of behavior modification may provide even further benefits.
Baker, Bruce L. (Nichols House, Cambridge, Mass.) American Journal of Orthopsychiatry, 1973(Apr), Vol. 43(3), 418-427. [PA, Vol 51:01636]

2103.   Prevention of mental retardation.
Reports that there are almost 16½ million mentally retarded (MR) persons in India, 3,500 institutionalized in 68 institutions. It is recommended that MR be in part prevented by (a) early testing and treatment for phenylketonuria, (b) prevention of prenatal infections, (c) professional assistance (e.g., from a midwife) at time of delivery of infant, and (d) family planning to reduce family size. Preventive measures must be directed toward the Indians who live in small villages and constitute most of the population.
Banerji, B. S. Indian Journal of Mental Retardation, 1973(Jan), Vol 6(1), 33-42. [PA, Vol 53:09984]

2104.   Music therapy with retarded children.
Demonstrated behavior changes and general responsiveness of retarded children with the aid of music. The music ranged from very simple rhythms and beats involving the child, to more complex and free flowing rhythms, dance movements to music, singing and listening to mechanical and natural sounds. Interest and concentration (usually an upper limit of 1 min) have been noticeably increased. The children increased their vocabulary through music activities, responding with the words, music, dance, parts of the body, social greetings, with this learning observed at other times than during music sessions. Cases are included to demonstrate the findings.
Barber, Eleanor. (Red Cross, Victorian Div., Australia) Australian Journal of Mental Retardation, 1973(Sep), Vol. 2(7), 210-213. [PA, Vol 51:09432]

2105.   Dilemmas in the training of clinical child psychologists in mental retardation.
Suggests that the training of clinical psychologists interested in retardation should begin with a thorough grounding in general and clinical psychology before more specialized training is given.
Barclay, A. (St. Louis U.) Journal of Clinical Child Psychology, 1973(Win), Vol. 2(1), 32-33. [PA, Vol 50:03108]

2106.   The psychiatric halfway house.
Discusses the diminishing importance of the large institution and strong augmentation of small community-based residential facilities commonly known as halfway houses or community residences. These facilities are being established in great numbers, not only for the emotionally troubled, but also for the mentally retarded, the drug dependent and alcoholic, youths from broken homes, youthful and adult offenders, and other handicapped people. It is noted that there has been a large increase in the number of psychiatric community residences over the last decade. Being an alternative to institutionalization is a new concept for the community residence, which had initially been conceptualized as a transitional facility from an institution to home living. The community residence movement arose from the desire to alleviate 4 basic deficiencies of the traditional institution: largeness, universal medical model, a closed society, and isolation from the community. The community residence also has a potential for goal orientation, according to the changing needs of the population it serves.
Budson, Richard D. (McLean Hosp., Belmont, Mass.) Psychiatric Annals, 1973(Jun), Vol. 3(6), 64-83. [PA, Vol 51:03739]

2107.   [Surgical treatment of epilepsy and mental disorders in children.] (Slok)
Performed massive surgical interventions on 22 epileptic 3-14 yr olds whose seizures could not be medically controlled and who were severely brain damaged and mentally retarded. The operations consisted of removal of different amounts of cortical matter, lobectomy, and in one case hemispherectomy. The mental status was determined clinically and with a battery of psychological tests. 37% of Ss remained free of seizures, 18.5% were considerably improved, and 44.5% showed no change. No correlation between etiology and the results of surgery was found. However, all those who did not change showed, prior to the operation, secondary bilateral synchronic epileptic discharges in EEG, and all Ss with temporal lobe epilepsy were cured or improved. Where surgery removed seizures, there was no further mental deterioration. Ss who continued having seizures also continued to deteriorate mentally. It is concluded that surgery of untreatable epilepsy is indicated at any age when progressive or irreversible mental defects are likely. (Russian & English summaries)
Cigánek, L.; Benko, J. & Cačková, M. (U Komenského, Bratislava, Czechoslovakia) Československá Psychiatrie, 1973(Dec), Vol 69(6), 363-365. [PA, Vol 54:10312]

2108.   Chronic drug intoxication causing pseudoretardation in a young child.
Describes the development of a young girl who in her preschool years appeared to be mildly retarded. The cause of her pseudoretardation seemed to be chronic intoxication with phenobarbital. Reevaluation of intellectual ability at 7½ yr. revealed a normal intellectual ability on the basis of WISC verbal, mathematical, and other test results. Results imply that since children are vulnerable at an early age to any interference with their developmental and maturational processes, administration to them of potent sedatives should be avoided.

Cordes, Charles K. (Letterman General Hosp., Child Psychiatry Service, San Francisco, Calif.) Journal of the American Academy of Child Psychiatry, 1973(Apr), Vol. 12(2), 215-222. [PA, Vol 50:09130]

2109. Psychological management of the retarded child and its family.
Proposes that the later functioning of most retarded persons depends more on socialization than IQ. Early relationships between physician and such families are instrumental in providing the necessary home support.
Freeman, Roger D. (U. British Columbia, Health Sciences Center, Vancouver, Canada) Psychiatric Annals, 1973(Jul), Vol. 3(7), 11-22. [PA, Vol 52:05689]

2110. Parent-child training for the MR.
Carried on a parent-child training program for 8 mentally retarded preschool children and their mothers, with 3 objectives: (a) to devise and test an individualized educational program for such children; (b) to develop their mothers' abilities to act as educational therapists; and (c) to help the mothers examine their children's needs and feelings by clarifying their own needs, feelings, and expectations.
Freeman, Stephen W. & Thompson, Charles L. (U. Tennessee, Memorial Research Center & Hosp., Birth Defects Center) Mental Retardation, 1973(Aug), Vol. 11(4), 8-10. [PA, Vol 51:05937]

2111. Input deficit and stimulus enrichment: A replication-with-expansion.
Conducted 2 studies based on a methodological criticism of J. E. Gordon and H. C. Haywood's (see PA, Vol. 43:8582) research on stimulus enrichment procedures with cultural-familial and brain-damaged retarded persons. The criticism focused on the confound of etiological group and order of similarities task presentation. A repeated measures design was used in the present studies, as well as in a reanalysis of Gordon's data, to isolate these order effects. The following variables were analyzed with 48 institutionalized retardates: etiology (cultural-familial vs organic), age (late childhood vs young adult), condition (regular similarities task *A* vs enriched similarities task *B*), and order (*AB* vs *BA*). In the noninstitutional study ($n = 36$) the same variables were investigated with the exception of age. The findings of 3 analyses, including significant Order $\times$ Condition interactions, seriously question the results and conclusions of Gordon and Haywood.
Friedrich, Douglas; Libkuman, Terry & Thomas, Arthur. (Central Michigan U.) American Journal of Mental Deficiency, 1973(May), Vol. 77(6), 687-693. [PA, Vol 51:07987]

2112. [Behavior therapy of children in their natural environment.] (Germ)
Discusses the application of operant conditioning to the modification of child behaviors in 3 areas: (a) parental training of retarded children, (b) the application of token-economy procedures by parents and teachers, and (c) the modification by parents of their own and their children's behavior within the family. A "model of rules" is proposed as an alternative to the operant model for intervention in the school and in the families of deviant children. (French summary) (32 ref)
Gottwald, Peter. (Max Planck Inst. of Psychiatry, Munich, W. Germany) Psychologie - Schweizerische Zeitschrift für Psychologie und ihre Anwendungen, 1973, Vol. 32(3), 220-239. [PA, Vol 51:07692]

2113. The modification of meal-time spitting behaviour.
Reports on a case study which demonstrates that withdrawal of a positive reinforcer contingent upon an undesirable response can act as an effective behavior modification technique. This program was used to modify undesirable spitting responses of a retarded 9-yr-old girl at the meal table. Prior to the program, behavior was apparently maintained by removal from the meal table as a result of the spitting response. In the program the S was required to stay at the table and the meal was removed. The meal was returned only after 1 min of nonspitting behavior. The program continued for 31 days with mealtime spitting responses declining to zero.

Kemp, Briony M. (Strathmont Centre, Gilles Plains, Southern Australia) Australian Journal of Mental Retardation, 1973(Dec), Vol. 2(8), 222-225. [PA, Vol 52:10697]

2114. [On the effects of stimulus flooding on mentally retarded children.] (Germ)
Argues that stimulus flooding, by which is meant the "ubiquitous, epochal excessive stimulation" or the "urbanization trauma" to which children are exposed, has different effects depending upon intelligence. In normal children, it is implied, this flooding often results in somatic and mental acceleration with few negative consequences. In the moderately retarded (IQ 70-89) permanent flooding supposedly leads to chronic feelings of failure and exhaustion. In the severely retarded the "mental defects of resonance" are seen as preventers of ill effects of flooding.
Nissen, Gerhardt. Praxis der Kinderpsychologie und Kinderpsychiatrie, 1973(Aug), Vol. 22(6), 195-199. [PA, Vol 51:07711]

2115. Altering territoriality through reinforcement.
Measured the base-line spatial and aggressive behavior of 22 5-10 yr. old retarded boys (IQ 50 or less) in 2 groups. After 14 wk., 4 "Habitats" (enhanced territorial environments) were introduced into each room along with videotape playlets illustrating their use. Group 2 had 2 social reinforcers in addition to the teacher for 7 wk.; Group 1 had the social reinforcers for the 8th wk. While base-line environments were highly territorialized, the territories were abandoned with the introduction of the habitats which many children shared. Time spent in the habitats was related to the time adults spent in them. Aggression was reduced during treatment and fluctuations were associated with adult deviation from random use of the habitats. Results indicate that designed environments and spatial availability of adults can be important variables in the control of aggression in this population.
O'Neill, Susan M. & Paluck, Robert J. (Hunter Coll., City U. New York) Proceedings of the 81st Annual Convention of the American Psychological Association, 1973, Vol 8, 903–904. [PA, Vol 50:05808]

2116. Teaching attendants the applied aspects of behavior modification: An empirical approach.
Gave 3 female attendants in an institution for the retarded instructions, videotape playback, and a videotaped model for teaching 10 commands to a retarded child. Instructions and videotape playback had little effect in improving Ss' training proficiency, but modeling resulted in an increase of mean scores. In a subsequent study with 15 newly hired attendants, it was found that film and live modeling were equally effective in teaching adequate reinforcement procedures.
Panyan, Marion C. & Patterson, Earl T. (Lubbock State School for the Mentally Retarded, Tex.) Proceedings of the 81st Annual Convention of the American Psychological Association, 1973, Vol 8, 903–904. [PA, Vol 50:05816]

2117. The effects of punishment on the acquisition and maintenance of reading behavior in retarded children.
Examined reading progress as a function of punishment (slapping) for incorrect responding after social reinforcement proved ineffective. Ss were 3 retarded children: a 12-yr-old boy, a 9-yr-old girl, and an 8-yr-old boy. Punishment procedure proved effective for maintenance and acquisition of reading repertoire. Results contradict frequent suggestions that punishment effects are at best transient, since the repertoire remained functional 10 additional days after punishment was discontinued. No negative side effects were observed. A more extensive evaluation of punishment effects in learning of retarded children is suggested. (English & Spanish abstracts)
Ribes, Emilio; Galesso-Coaracy, Salvador A. & Durán, Lilia. (U. Veracruz, Mexico) Revista Interamericana de Psicología, 1973, Vol. 7(1-2), 33-42. [PA, Vol 51:05477]

2118. An experimental evaluation of tokens as conditioned reinforcers in retarded children.
Reviews literature on implementation of token systems in human Ss since the publication of experimental reports in 1936 by Wolfe

and 1937 by Cowles indicating that tokens could be established as conditioned reinforcers. It is shown that tokens have been successfully used as prosthetic motivational devices in a great variety of situations and subjects, e.g., retarded children, adult psychotics, delinquent children and adolescents, low achievers in schools, emotionally disturbed children, and in normal classroom settings. In these reports, administration of tokens usually produced an increase in the frequency of desirable social and productive behavior. However, none showed that the effect of the tokens depended on their role as conditioned reinforcers based on the standard exchange systems being used. No assessment was provided about the separate contribution of the social reinforcement operations involved in dispensing tokens in a social setting. It is suggested that there may be confounding effects of social reinforcement in token administration based on the failure to establish token systems in Ss who are partially unresponsive to social reinforcement.
Ribes-Inesta, E., et al. (U. Veracruz, Xalopa, Mexico) Behaviour Research & Therapy, 1973(Feb), Vol. 11(1), 125-128. [PA, Vol 50:03579]

2119. Demonstration versus instructions in concept attainment by mental retardates.
Compared the effectiveness of training by silent demonstrations with that of providing equivalent verbal instructions, using 3 age and ability groups of 48 adult mental retardates-adolescent group (mean age = 15.8 yrs), work skills group (mean age = 26.8 yrs), and prevocational group (mean age = 27.2 yrs). Ss were required to coordinate the number and color of plastic discs with 3-marble triangles on a Chinese checkerboard. At all age and ability levels, demonstration was superior to verbal instructions in promoting concept attainment and transfer. Providing candy reinforcement for correct answers had no effect on performance.
Rosenthal, Ted L. & Kellogg, Jeffrey S. (U. Arizona) Behaviour Research & Therapy, 1973(Aug), Vol. 11(3), 299-302. [PA, Vol 52:08369]

2120. Socioepidemiological analysis of admissions to a state-operated outpatient clinic for retarded children.
Reports on a socioepidemiological analysis of cases admitted to a state-operated outpatient clinic for retarded children between 1962 and 1970. Male admissions predominated over the 8-yr period. Admissions tended to be young (i.e., under 10 yrs of age). Admissions in the early years showed a middle-class utilization pattern and a significant increase in lower-class admissions over time. Although medical referrals predominated over the 8 yrs, there was a substantial increase in public medical referrals in the later years.
Rowitz, Louis. (Illinois State Pediatric Inst., Chicago) American Journal of Mental Deficiency, 1973(Nov), Vol. 78(3), 300-307. [PA, Vol 52:03390]

2121. NARC's "patterning" study described.
Reports a National Association for Retarded Children (NARC) sponsored study of Doman-Delacato sensorimotor training techniques utilized in a remediation program at Denton (Texas) State School. 76 Ss were assigned to 3 treatment groups in the NARC study. Treatment program and activities are described and illustrated with a case study.
Savage, Dorothy; Kroeger, Margaret & Chapman, Darral. (Dallas Academy, Tex.) Academic Therapy, 1973(Fal), Vol. 9(1), 71-76. [PA, Vol 51:11415]

2122. Rehabilitation of mentally retarded children.
Notes that of those who visit child guidance clinics, 60% come with the problem of mental retardation (MR). Parents hope that a drug will cure their child and bring him to a normal range of intelligence. It is suggested that parents must learn to accept MR and to train the child with consistency, allowing and encouraging him to develop self-help skills when possible.
Shukla, T. R. & Pershad, Dwarka. (Hosp for Mental Diseases, Postgraduate Training Ctr, Ranchi, India) Indian Journal of Mental Retardation, 1973(Jan), Vol 6(1), 28-32. [PA, Vol 53:09906]

2123. [Application of operant conditioning technique upon a mentally retarded child developing symptoms like obsession-neurosis.] (Japn)
Used Yates' theoretical model of stimulus generalization as the basis for successfully treating a 12-yr-old boy for his phobia of the therapy room. Small-step operant conditioning technique was employed as follows: the boy (a) established rapport with the therapist, (b) went out of the dormitory with him, (c) approached, and (d) entered the treatment building, and finally (e) entered the therapy room. Children's books were the reinforcers chiefly used. (English summary)
Suzumura, Kenji. Japanese Journal of Special Education, 1973(Dec), Vol. 11(2), 15-20. [PA, Vol 52:08378]

2124. Using video tape with the mentally retarded.
Discusses the use of a video tape recorder to assist in staff training, increase parental involvement, and isolate and eliminate specific inappropriate behaviors of the mentally retarded.
Weisbord, Hyman F. (Miriam Home for the Exceptional, Laval, Quebec, Canada) Canada's Mental Health, 1973(Nov), Vol. 21(6), 12-18. [PA, Vol 52:01300]

2125. Early intervention: Being better prepared for the special education classroom.
Describes the Infant, Toddler, and Preschool Research and Intervention Project in Tennessee, currently serving 70 families, 40 with mentally retarded children. The project consists of 5 units. The Coordination Unit provides administration, family social services, and evaluation. The Toddler Unit involves both delayed and normal children 18-36 mo old. The Preschool Unit concentrates on preparation for the child's entry into public school. The Parent Training Program includes parents or guardians as integral parts of the overall project, providing training, consultation, and help with problems.
————. Education & Training of the Mentally Retarded, 1974(Feb), Vol. 9(1), 30-32. [PA, Vol 52:08286]

2126. Note on "Effect of motor development on body image scores for institutionalized mentally retarded children."
Discusses the evaluation by W. C. Chasey et al (see PA, Vol 52:8002) of the use by M. P. Maloney et al (see PA, Vol 44:11088) of 2 measures of body image-the Eye, Hand, and Ear Test and the Personal Orientation Test-with mentally retarded children. Although Chasey et al stated that these measures did not meet their criteria of effectiveness, it is argued that both measures are appropriate to the assessment of the therapeutic effects of N. C. Kephart's (1971) sensorimotor training program as it has been adapted for retarded persons.
Ball, Thomas S. (Neuropsychiatric Inst-Pacific State Hosp Research Group, Pomona, CA) American Journal of Mental Deficiency, 1974(Sep), Vol 79(2), 225-226. [PA, Vol 53:03423]

2127. Foster homes: Alternatives to institutions?
Examined 36 foster home child units to examine factors which may be related to the outcome of most foster care programs for retarded and handicapped children. Over half of the children resided in foster homes which needed substantial improvement.
Browder, J. Albert; Ellis, LuAnn & Neal, Judith. (U Oregon, Medical School, Portland) Mental Retardation, 1974(Dec), Vol 12(6), 33-36. [PA, Vol 53:09885]

2128. Counseling process with mentally retarded clients: A behavioral exploration.
Examined behavioral aspects of the process of counseling with 28 adolescent mentally retarded clients. Transcripts from an early and a late counseling session were rated according to the initial client statement (dependent, hostile, or other), therapist response (approach or avoid), and client continuation of the topic. Results indicate that counselors varied significantly in approach-avoidance response style with respect to client IQ level and type of client statement, and retarded clients varied significantly in continuation response style with respect to therapist approach-avoidance behavior and client IQ level.
Browning, Philip L.; Campbell, David R. & Spence, Joyce T. (U Oregon, Rehabilitation Research & Training Ctr in Mental

Retardation) American Journal of Mental Deficiency, 1974(Nov), Vol 79(3), 292-296. [PA, Vol 53:10234]

2129. Improving the physical fitness of retarded boys.
Compared the physical fitness performance of 20 mentally retarded 10-14 yr old boys who participated in an adapted version of the Royal Canadian Air Force Physical Fitness Training Program conducted under contingency conditions and 20 10-14 yr olds who participated in the program on a noncontingent basis. The contingency management condition involved a point system based on token economy principles. Results indicate that Ss in the contingency group performed better on most of the 5 exercises in the program than Ss in the noncontingent group. (19 ref)
Campbell, Jack. (U. Nevada, Reno) Mental Retardation, 1974(Jun), Vol. 12(3), 31-35. [PA, Vol 52:12944]

2130. Genetic counseling and mental retardation.
Considers the role of medical genetics in prevention and its chief tool as genetic counseling. Diagnostic techniques (e.g., metabolic screening, chromosome analysis, differential chromosome stains, and amino centers is) are described. Indications for metabolic screening include psychomotor retardation; failure to thrive; unusual odor; cutaneous changes; eye abnormalities; enlargement of liver, spleen, or kidneys; than deficits. The need to study chromosome abnormalities (e.g., Down's, Patau's, deletion, Turner's or Klinefelter's syndromes) is discussed. Single gene mutations cause 20% of the genetic types of mental retardation, and they may be inherited as autosomal dominant, recessive, or x-linked traits. Less than 50% of the families with a retarded child ever receive genetic counseling. Better planning and prevention are needed. It is concluded that genetic services should be reorganized in order to include and provide diagnosis throughout the country. (29 ref)
Crandall, Barbara F. & Pancoe, Michael. (U. California, Los Angeles) Psychiatric Annals, 1974(Feb), Vol. 4(2), 70-95. [PA, Vol 52:10768]

2131. Instrumental modification of hypernasal voice quality in retarded children: Case reports.
Used the Oral Nasal Acoustic Ratio (TONAR) to reduce the hypernasality of 3 mental retardates during a 3-wk treatment period; concomitant improvements in speech intelligibility occurred in 2 Ss.
Daly, David A. & Johnson, Hettie P. (U Michigan) Journal of Speech & Hearing Disorders, 1974(Nov), Vol 39(4), 500-507. [PA, Vol 53:10508]

2132. Training generalized receptive prepositions in retarded children.
Used prompting and reinforcement in 2 experiments to teach 3 retarded children (3, 4, and 11 yrs old) to respond correctly to 3 categories of prepositional requests. Training sessions were alternated with probe sessions. During training, a child was trained to respond to 1 request (e.g., "put the doll next to the cup"); during probing, the child was tested for generalization of this training to untrained requests. Responses to untrained requests were never prompted nor reinforced. Results show that, as requests from 1 category were trained, the children's responses to the untrained requests of that category became increasingly correct. As discriminations among 2 or more categories were trained, the children's responses to the untrained requests of those categories also became increasingly correct.
Frisch, Sue A. & Schumaker, Jean B. (Woolley Wood School, Sheffield, England) Journal of Applied Behavior Analysis, 1974(Win), Vol 7(4), 611-621. [PA, Vol 53:10512]

2133. [Adaptation of the mentally handicapped to a working life.] (Fren)
Studied the work productivity and social acceptance of retarded adults working in a protected workshop. 30 men, aged 19-25 yrs, whose average IQ was 54, were asked to perform 3 simple manual tasks. 2 instructors rated the number and quality of completed tasks. The social popularity of Ss was assessed through informal interviews with Ss and their instructors. Results indicated a significant relationship between intelligence level and work productivity. Most Ss were neither accepted nor rejected by the group as a whole, and the percentage of Ss with high popularity was small. Instructors were only slightly successful in rating the social acceptability of Ss. It is suggested that protected workshops create an exceptional environment, and that this must be taken into account in studies of the working retarded. (English, German, & Spanish summaries)
Galkowski, T. (National Inst of Health & Medical Research, Montrouge, France) Revue de Neuropsychiatrie Infantile et d'Hygiene Mentale de l'Enfance, 1974(Jan), Vol 22(1-2), 121-131. [PA, Vol 54:07889]

2134. The training and generalization of a conversational speech form in nonverbal retardates.
Differential reinforcement and imitation were used with 2 retarded children to train 3 sequential verbal responses associated with the display of a picture and questions related to that picture. 2 types of generalization sessions were conducted: (a) general sessions, during which 10 pictures never used during training were displayed, with reinforcement on a noncontingent basis; and (b) intermixed sessions, during which 10 pictures never used during training were displayed, but a picture having received training was also shown, and correct responses to this picture were reinforced on a variable schedule. Both Ss learned the sentences being training, but little generalization was evident from this training when the 3 Es conducted general probe sessions. Generalization occurred with 1 E only after that E conducted intermixed probe sessions. Generalization to a 3rd E was then observed (i.e., after the 1st 2 Es had conducted intermixed probe sessions) without the use of intermixed probe sessions by this 3rd E. (15 ref)
Garcia, Eugene. (U. Utah) Journal of Applied Behavior Analysis, 1974(Spr), Vol. 7(1), 137-149. [PA, Vol 52:08320]

2135. Media stimulation and exceptional children.
Describes a media stimulation project which utilizes 2 categories of video equipment—live video systems and prerecorded video tapes—as a therapeutic aid. The project is based on the assumption that a retarded child who is functioning at a medium to high level can recognize his self-image and will respond favorably. Pilot studies at a mental retardation institute indicate the validity of this presumption.
Greelis, Michael. (Mental Retardation Inst, Valhalla, NY) Mental Retardation, 1974(Dec), Vol 12(6), 30-31. [PA, Vol 53:10515]

2136. [The value of pyritinol in the treatment of retarded children: Trials made in a school for mentally subnormal children.] (Fren)
Studied the psychostimulant effects of pyritinol chlorhydrate (pyrithioxin). 20 retarded girls (IQ 55-75) were selected for study because of their pronounced slowness and passivity. Ss were given 400 mg of pyritinol a day for 3 mo. The behavior of each S was rated by her teachers, and her performance was measured on a test of attention and motor performance. 8 Ss showed clear improvement in behavior and attention, 7 Ss showed no effects, and 5 Ss showed increased psychostimulation expressed in aggressive and impulsive behaviors. It is concluded that pyritinol can be useful in counteracting the apathy and conceptual slowness of mentally retarded children.
Hugonenq, H.; Espinas, A. & Saias, Mme. Revue de Neuropsychiatrie Infantile et d'Hygiene Mentale de l'Enfance, 1974(Jan), Vol 22(1-2), 133-139. [PA, Vol 54:08060]

2137. Stimulus fading and schedule learning in generalizing and maintaining behaviors.
Attempted to determine whether experimentally verified conditions for generalization and maintenance could be applied in a music therapy clinic. The Ss were 2 retarded boys at a state hospital and training center. A music preference test (Cotter and Toombs, 1966) was given to each. Both Ss preferred music to white or ambient noise, and both selected children's music and rock-and-roll music. Initial therapy goals were achieved: (a) to increase accuracy of color discriminations, and (b) to increase on-task behaviors, defined as proximity to the task and absence

of vocalizations. Results demonstrate that the amount of therapist time and attention required to establish desired behaviors could be gradually decreased if specific plans for maintaining behaviors were applied.
Johnson, Janet M. & Zinner, Carol C. (Ohio State U, Faculty for Exceptional Children) Journal of Music Therapy, 1974(Sum), Vol 11(2), 84-96. [PA, Vol 53:07701]

2138.   Dance therapy with retarded children.
Describes, in the context of other therapeutic efforts with retarded children, the difficulty of determining experimentally, in 1 study, the general effectiveness of short-term dance therapy even when individual changes were clearly apparent. (32 ref)
Kavaler, Susan I. (Postgraduate Ctr for Mental Health, New York, NY) International Mental Health Research Newsletter, 1974(Spr), Vol 16(1), 9-11. [PA, Vol 53:07839]

2139.   [Reflections on the problems posed by children of mentally handicapped parents.] (Fren)
Presents a longitudinal study of 5 children of mentally retarded parents. It is noted that the sparse literature available on normal children of retarded couples focuses on their affective and character problems, and their slowness in language development. Case histories of the 5 Ss revealed a high incidence of instability in the parental relations and of general disinterest in the child. It is suggested that disturbances in the parent-child relations in families with retarded parents make the children highly vulnerable to ego disorders. It is concluded that social service agencies need to be more aware of the problems of mentally handicapped couples and their normal children. (English, German, & Spanish summaries)
Kohler, C. & Didier, P.   Revue de Neuropsychiatrie Infantile et d'Hygiene Mentale de l'Enfance, 1974(Jan), Vol 22(1-2), 53-64. [PA, Vol 54:07893]

2140.   [Medical readaptation in mental retardation.] (Fren)
Discusses the integration of the mentally retarded into society. Data are presented on etiological and socioeconomic factors for 1,500 mentally retarded children treated at the Center for Readaptation in Sao Paulo, Brazil. It is suggested that many cases of retardation could be prevented by family planning, genetic counseling, and adequate prenatal and postnatal care. In a country such as Brazil, which has limited funds available for mental health, the scientific establishment of priorities for the treatment of the mentally retarded is considered essential. It is concluded that prevention and early diagnosis are of primary importance in the treatment of the retarded, and that attempts to educate the retarded should be focused on mildly and moderately retarded children. (English, German, & Spanish summaries)
Krynski, R.   Revue de Neuropsychiatrie Infantile et d'Hygiene Mentale de l'Enfance, 1974(Jan), Vol 22(1-2), 85-101. [PA, Vol 54:07895]

2141.   Building and maintaining self-feeding skills in a retarded child.
Used operant conditioning techniques to teach a 4-yr-old echolalic female with severe behavior problems to accept an increasing variety and texture of foods while concurrently developing appropriate self-feeding skills. S had existed for 3 yrs on a diet consisting primarily of cinnamon toast, bacon, milk, and eggnog. 15 working days were required to teach her to self-feed and accept nutritionally balanced meals. Progress in other self-help areas accompanied the acquisition of self-feeding skills, which were still present 5 mo after termination of treatment.
Leibowitz, J. Michael & Holcer, Pauline. (U Nebraska, Medical Ctr, C. Louis Meyer Children's Rehabilitation Inst) American Journal of Occupational Therapy, 1974(Oct), Vol 28(9), 545-548. [PA, Vol 53:07965]

2142.   Self-abusive behavior in the mentally retarded.
Reviews the literature on sensory deprivation in both animals and humans and presents a theoretical basis for treating self-abuse in the mentally retarded. The use of operant conditioning procedures and structured graded tactile stimulation, and the need of the child for a nurturing relationship are considered. A case study of a 9-yr-old mentally retarded girl is presented to illustrate the success of various kinds of treatment. (24 ref)
Lemke, Haru. (Lehigh U.) American Journal of Occupational Therapy, 1974(Feb), Vol. 28(2), 94-98. [PA, Vol 52:06009]

2143.   Elimination of middle-of-the-night tantrums in a blind, retarded child.
Applied behavioral techniques to the treatment of a mentally retarded 4-yr-old girl with a long history of middle-of-the-night tantrums. 15 days of ignoring this behavior failed to eliminate the tantrums. Thereafter, the child was kept awake each evening until midnight and gradually her night-time tantrums disappeared. No remission was observed in 3- and 6-mo follow-ups.
Martin, Jerry A. & Iagulli, Diane M. (U. Minnesota, Medical School) Behavior Therapy, 1974(May), Vol. 5(3), 420-422. [PA, Vol 52:10705]

2144.   [The mentally retarded child in the family.] (Srcr)
Mental retardation is defined as lack of ability to learn and mature socially at the usual rate because of factors that have existed before and at the time of conception, during pregnancy and birth, and during the developmental period until 16 yrs of age. Societal attitudes toward the mentally retarded are discussed. The importance of allowing a mentally retarded child to establish a meaningful relationship with his/her mother (which takes a longer time than for the mentally nonretarded) is emphasized. The institutionalization of the mentally retarded is seen as the least desirable way to deal with them. The preferred way is to keep them in their families whenever possible.
Morić-Petrović, Slavka.   Psihijatrija Danas, 1974, Vol 6(2–3), 179–184. [PA, Vol 62:01321]

2145.   Three cases of jargon.
Describes case studies of 3 2-5 yr olds who were functioning below normal on standard language and intelligence tests, had not crept on hands and knees as infants, and who spoke jargon with the flow of conversation, but unintelligibly. The apparent value of enforced creeping on the children's development, as shown by improved tests scores, is discussed.
Mosier, Kay.   Academic Therapy, 1974(Spr), Vol 9(5), 377-380. [PA, Vol 54:05775]

2146.   Mental retardation: Scope for prevention: I. Nutrition.
Briefly reviews literature (chiefly research in India) on the relationship between retardation and malnutrition; the studies indicate a causal link. Recommended preventative measures are (a) improved agricultural methods, (b) curtailing population growth, (c) public education, and (d) intensive research into fetal and infantile brain development. (20 ref)
Murthy, R. S.   Indian Journal of Mental Retardation, 1974(Jul), Vol 7(2), 49-57. [PA, Vol 53:11955]

2147.   Developmental retardation and the family physician.
Discusses the formidable problem of the family with a developmentally retarded child with particular reference to the role of the family physician as organizer-coordinator of the highly complex multidisciplinary requirements of this medical problem. A case is presented illustrating numerous aspects of diagnosis and management, as well as pitfalls to be avoided. The quality of the family physician as one who is concerned, accepting, open, and honest, as well as accessible to the families under his care, is taxed to the fullest in this instance. Regular joint family visits, together with monitoring of this problem during routine medical visits, are effective means of anticipating and meeting the family's needs.
Neal, Edward M.   Journal of Family Practice, 1974 No(Nov-Dec), Vol 1(3-4), 14-17. [PA, Vol 54:03544]

2148.   [System of vocational preparation of mentally retarded youth.] (Slok)
A description of a special apprenticeship program geared to the mentally retarded (blacksmith, carpenter, plumber, upholsterer, etc.)
Ostrý, Bohumil. (Charles U, Prague, Czechoslavakia) Československá Defektologie, 1974, Mono, 125-149. [PA, Vol 57:09148]

2149. Report on a home-management project at Rideau Regional Centre.
Describes a project which demonstrates that many retarded children could function outside an institution after the parents have been trained to act as therapists for the child.
Pulvermacher, Gerald D. (Rideau Regional Ctr, Smith's Falls, Ontario, Canada) Ontario Psychologist, 1974(Oct), Vol 6(4), 19-23. [PA, Vol 53:08075]

2150. Shaping the future: Home management: The past six years.
Traces the development of a program designed to help parents cope with the behavior of their mentally retarded children at home.
Ramsden, Marna. Ontario Psychologist, 1974(Oct), Vol 6(4), 14-17. [PA, Vol 53:08076]

2151. The family training center: An experiment in normalization.
Suggests that preventing institutionalization may mean training parents to be teachers of adaptive behavior. The family training center provides a model in which parents and children learn new ways to interact with one another through effective use of precise behavior management. Case examples are presented.
Ray, Joel S. (George Peabody Coll.) Mental Retardation, 1974(Feb), Vol. 12(1), 12-13. [PA, Vol 52:03758]

2152. Reducing stereotypic responding of retarded persons by the differential reinforcement of other behavior.
Reports that the stereotypic responding of 3 retarded persons (a 12-yr-old female, 22-yr-old female, and 23-yr-old male) was reduced when reinforcement was delivered for specified periods of time in which the behavior did not occur. In an ABAB design in which "No." was used in all 4 phases and in which each S was reinforced for not emitting stereotypic responding during the "B" phases, responding was decreased for the 3 Ss to an average of $\frac{1}{100}$ of baseline levels. The method of differentially reinforcing behavior other than the specified one is discussed as an alternative to extinction. (32 ref)
Repp, Alan C.; Deitz, Samuel M. & Speir, Nancy C. (Georgia Retardation Ctr, Atlanta) American Journal of Mental Deficiency, 1974(Nov), Vol 79(3), 279-284. [PA, Vol 53:10200]

2153. Behavioral therapy of phobias: A case with gynecomastia and mental retardation.
Describes the use of systematic desensitization for trichophobia in a 13-yr-old mentally retarded boy (IQ = 42) with slight gynecomastia and anxiety about his sexual identity.
Rivenq, Bernard. (Anbar Inst., Montreal, Quebec, Canada) Mental Retardation, 1974(Feb), Vol. 12(1), 44-45. [PA, Vol 52:03763]

2154. Group work with parents of retarded adolescents.
Discusses the sources of difficulty parents face in coping with retarded children and suggests ways of ameliorating these problems. 2 principal causes for such difficulty are the emotional impact of having a retarded child, and the lack of knowledge about the child's condition. Work with parents includes education, counseling, therapy, or various combinations of these. Advantages are cited for providing services for groups of parents. An illustrative short-term group of parents of vocational students is described in some detail. As the group progressed, parents became more willing to let their children grow up, and thus became more cooperative with the vocational school in its efforts to promote independent functioning.
Robinson, Lillian H. (Tulane U, Medical School) American Journal of Psychotherapy, 1974(Jul), Vol 28(3), 397-408. [PA, Vol 53:10270]

2155. Training parents in groups as behavior modifiers of their mentally retarded children.
Natural and foster parents' groups were taught a number of principles of behavior modification and how to apply them to their retarded children. Group leaders used programed booklets, modeling and behavior rehearsal, lecturing and discussion, weekly assignments, and positive reinforcement. As weekly assignments, the parents read a programed text, counted and charted their children's behavior, and intervened with reinforcement, extinction, time outs, modeling, cueing, and rehearsal procedures. Following completion of training in 11 groups, 27 of the 33 families entering the program successfully modified 55 of the 58 behaviors for which plans were initiated. (24 ref)
Rose, Sheldon D. (U Wisconsin, School of Social Work, Madison) Journal of Behavior Therapy & Experimental Psychiatry, 1974(Sep), Vol 5(2), 135-140. [PA, Vol 53:07982]

2156. Training adolescents to use behavior modification with the severely handicapped.
Describes a 4-wk project in which 13 high school students learned to train 5 mentally retarded children. After intensive instruction for 1 wk on theoretical and practical aspects of working with the retarded, groups of 2 or more students met with each mother and her child for interviews and observation. Target behaviors and the steps to achieve them were set up by the students. Behavior modification was then carried out with minimal supervision by the project coordinator, and the progress of each child was recorded daily. Results suggest that high school students trained to use behavior modification methods can effect significant behavioral changes in handicapped children. The benefits of developing such paraprofessionals as teacher aides are discussed.
Rouse, Bobbye M. & Farb, Joel. (U. Texas, Medical Branch, Galveston) Exceptional Children, 1974(Jan), Vol. 40(4), 286-288. [PA, Vol 52:01679]

2157. Generalization of self-referent speech established in a retarded adolescent by operant procedures.
Taught a severely retarded 13-yr-old boy who did not use personal pronouns in his spontaneous speech to use pronouns in answering training questions. A control procedure demonstrated that it was the reinforcement contingency that increased the correct use of pronouns. After initial training, S used these pronouns infrequently in his spontaneous speech, so 3 procedural changes (using sentences instead of phrases, moving the training from an experimental room to the classroom, and having the teacher's aide ask S about his activities) were introduced to increase generalization of the new responses. During this time and a follow-up period, the S's spontaneous use of correct self-referent speech increased ($p = .001$). Collateral improvements were a decrease in idiosyncratic speech ($p = .01$) and an increase in normal speech ($p = .001$), which included new combinations of pronouns used correctly with other words not included in the training. That these changes occurred only with procedural revision suggests the need for explicit programing to increase generalization. (15 ref)
Rubin, Beverly K. & Stolz, Stephanie B. (American U.) Behavior Therapy, 1974(Jan), Vol. 5(1), 93-106. [PA, Vol 52:06030]

2158. Community services: Legitimate at last.
Describes the development of a mental retardation unit within the child and adolescent outpatient department of a large metropolitan psychiatric hospital and how it functions as a community resource for clients and agencies.
Rubino, C. A. Ontario Psychologist, 1974(Oct), Vol 6(4), 9-13. [PA, Vol 53:08083]

2159. Modeling as a training tool for retarded children and their parents.
Describes a clinical training program in which a modeling approach is used for teaching retarded children and their parents new ways of interacting and for increasing the children's use of verbal communication. Results on the 4 parent–child pairs discussed carry implications for making the parents an integral part of the child's language development process. (22 ref)
Seitz, Sue & Hoekenga, Robert. (U. Wisconsin, Waisman Center for Research in Mental Retardation & Human Development) Mental Retardation, 1974(Apr), Vol. 12(2), 28-31. [PA, Vol 52:10732]

2160.   Early language intervention: A contingent stimulation model.
Presents data from a review of research findings on learning and conditioning in normal infants in order to generate intervention strategies for developmentally retarded infants. Contingent stimulation is proposed as a model to promote both specific and generalized effects in prelinguistic vocal behavior. The approach is compatible with current concerns regarding infant-caretaker relationships and parent training and also lends itself to demands for evaluation and accountability. (50 ref)
Simeonsson, Rune J. & Wiegerink, Ronald. (U. Nebraska, Omaha) Mental Retardation, 1974(Apr), Vol. 12(2), 7-11. [PA, Vol 52:10736]

2161.   Treatment and care of the mentally retarded.
Discusses 3 factors which may have prevented psychiatry from exerting an influence on mental retardation: (a) the shift to an educational focus following the introduction of intelligence testing in Paris by A. Binet, (b) the eugenic alarm of the late 19th and early 20th centuries, and (c) the intense preoccupation of psychiatry with the intrapsychic dynamics of the neuroses. A survey is provided of some of the problems that the mentally retarded individual and his parents encounter in coping with the environment. Intellectual and behavioral deficits may result in the learning of responses maladaptive to the environment. Parental reaction and perhaps rejection of the retarded child is discussed. Society's reaction and rejection are likewise detailed. The treatment of mental retardation via drugs (anticonvulsants, stimulants, and tranquilizers), psychotherapy, and behavior modification is described. (45 ref)
Simmons, James Q.; Tymchuk, Alexander J. & Valente, Mario. (U. California, Neuropsychiatric Inst., Mental Retardation Research Center, Los Angeles) Psychiatric Annals, 1974(Feb), Vol. 4(2), 38-69. [PA, Vol 52:10555]

2162.   Noncitizen: Plight of the mentally retarded.
Considers that the mentally retarded have been denied their human and civil rights by the public and by professionals. It is proposed that most programs for the retarded are, at best, dehumanizing and that professionals have an ethical obligation to refuse to refer children to such programs. (15 ref)
Skarnulis, Ed. (Eastern Nebraska Community Office of Retardation, Family Resource Services, Omaha) Social Work, 1974(Jan), Vol. 19(1), 56-62. [PA, Vol 52:03392]

2163.   Group counseling with parents of the MR: Leadership selection and functioning.
Describes the various roles and functions of the leader of a parents group, and argues for a maximum of flexibility in accordance with the aims and objectives of the particular group. The concept of several leaders is explored, and the objectives of diverse types of groups discussed.
Sternlicht, Manny & Sullivan, Ina. (Willowbrook Developmental Ctr, Queens Unit, Staten Island, NY) Mental Retardation, 1974(Oct), Vol 12(5), 11-13. [PA, Vol 53:06005]

2164.   The effect of contingent music on establishing imitation in behaviorally disturbed retarded children.
Studied the effectiveness of music as a functional reinforcer in a comprehensive treatment program which might be generalized to other environments. The use of music to increase imitative behavior of 4 retarded 9-13 yr olds was evaluated. The treatment effects were substantial and in the expected direction for virtually all imitative tasks.
Underhill, Karen K. & Harris, Lawrence M. (Cameron-Elk-McKean-Potter Counties Mental Retardation Services, Bradford, PA) Journal of Music Therapy, 1974(Fal), Vol 11(3), 156-166. [PA, Vol 54:05979]

2165.   A stress-stength model for nurse-social worker collaboration.
Describes the evolution of a stress-strength model for nurse-social worker collaboration in a mental health clinic serving retardates and their families in the community. Traditional role differentiation difficulties experienced by nurses and social workers in interdisciplinary settings are analyzed. Taking profes-sional training and areas of expertise into consideration, plus the predominant stress situation presented by the patient/client and family, a categorizing scheme for major treatment responsibility was evolved which set the stress locus in child management and development (nurse), family relationships and interaction (social worker), or complex combinations of these factors (joint). (50 ref)
Veeder, Nancy W. (Boston Coll. Graduate School, Research Sequence) Mental Retardation, 1974(Apr), Vol. 12(2), 39-42. [PA, Vol 52:10790]

2166.   Parent training technology: A potential service delivery system.
Describes the Parent Training Technology System (PTTS), an operant-type behavior modification system that utilizes parents as behavior modification technicians. The program has been used to eliminate undesirable behavior and to teach self-help, language, motor coordination, social-recreational, and academic skills to mildly, moderately, severely, and profoundly retarded children, as well as psychotic and "emotionally disturbed" children. It is suggested that because parents, siblings, peers, and teachers are involved in the program, and training takes place in the child's natural environment, many stimulus control problems inherent in more traditional intervention clinical strategies are avoided. (27 ref)
Watson, Luke S. & Bassinger, Joan F. (Illinois Dept of Mental Health, Chicago) Mental Retardation, 1974(Oct), Vol 12(5), 3-10. [PA, Vol 53:05950]

2167.   Parental compliance with postdischarge recommendations for retarded children.
Used parental compliance with postdischarge recommendations as the criterion for successful intervention in a study conducted on a short-term inpatient ward for retarded children. A study of 217 recommendations to 80 families was based on the hypothesis that parents will be more likely to follow through on recommendations if they (a) feel comfortable with the diagnosis of the child's problem, (b) feel that the professional caretakers are concerned about the child both during and after hospitalization, and (c) feel relieved of stress and helped by the therapy. Parents' attitudes and the extent to which they had followed the recommendations were assessed in telephone interviews at least 3 mo after the child was discharged. Results indicate that 3 variables were significantly correlated with compliance: agreement with the diagnosis, postdischarge contact with the ward, and preadmission stresses of caring for the child.
Wikler, Lynn & Stoycheff, Judy. (Neuropsychiatric Inst, Los Angeles, CA) Hospital & Community Psychiatry, 1974(Sep), Vol 25(9), 595-598. [PA, Vol 53:03906]

2168.   Automated reinforcement of head posture in two cerebral palsied retarded children.
Used a transistor radio activated by a mercury switch to reinforce head posture in a 17-yr-old girl and a 9-yr-old boy who were nonambulatory and unable to communicate verbally. Under the contingent music condition dropping the head forward automatically terminated the broadcast (music). A comparison of baseline and treatment phases showed that head orientation was strongly controlled by contingent music.
Ball, Thomas S.; McCrady, Richard E. & Hart, Archibald D. (Neuropsychiatric Inst-Pacific State Hosp Research Group, Pomona, CA) Perceptual & Motor Skills, 1975(Apr), 619-622. [PA, Vol 54:09812]

2169.   The use of play therapy with the mentally retarded.
Reports that research on play therapy with mentally retarded children is a recent phenomenon. The available studies have shown that play therapy yielded positive results in behavior and social organization of the mentally retarded child. In most instances, intelligence scores did not show gains comparable to those in behavioral growth and maturity. L. Mundy's study, however (see PA, Vol 32:5605), showed large intellectual gains and an increase in school readiness.

Bernhardt, Marcia & Mackler, Bernard. (Hunter Coll, City U New York) Journal of Special Education, 1975(Win), Vol 9(4), 409-414. [PA, Vol 56:04374]

2170. Behaviour modification with the mentally retarded: A staff training programme.
Describes an in-service training course in behavior modification for staff at a residential training center for mentally retarded children and adults. It involved a combined lecture-discussion and practical format with continual feedback for participants. Group projects with real therapeutic aims were supervised by a team of psychologists, and completion of the course resulted in certificates for the participants and publication of reports for use during future courses. A number of problems are discussed which must be taken into account during course development. 4 full project reports are included.
Bettison, S. & Garlington, W. (Strathmont Ctr, Gilles Plains, Australia) Australian Journal of Mental Retardation, 1975(Mar), Vol 3(5), 131-145. [PA, Vol 54:11856]

2171. Johnny's bird is dead and gone: Remedial work with a retarded pre-schooler.
Reports on an intervention undertaken with a 5-yr-old retarded male child who had become increasingly anxious, hostile, and frustrated after the death of his pet bird. The child had a severe defect in the area of speech and language and had been enrolled for 5 mo in a preschool program for difficult or atypical children. The pet bird died during a period when the mother of the child was hospitalized, and the child subsequently showed increased concern about things and people that were "gone." A remedial approach was developed on the basis of assumptions that the child was concerned with the possible loss of objects or people, that he was not adequately aware of different meanings of the word "gone," and that his emotional difficulties were symptoms of an inadequate working through of the original loss experience. An interest taken by the child in a toy bird provided staff members with an opportunity to talk with the child about the differences between a toy bird and a live bird. The remainder of the approach involved making use of opportunities that permitted distinguishing between something being gone forever and something being gone for a short time and encouraging the child to verbalize this distinction. An improvement in overall functioning became evident about 3–4 wks after initiation of the specific programs.
Brandt, Elisabeth P. & Bower, Patricia J. (U Regina, Canada) Canada's Mental Health, 1975(Jun), Vol 23(2), 19–20. [PA, Vol 61:04054]

2172. The effects of varying schedules of time-out on aggressive behavior of a retarded girl.
Timeout scheduled after every 2nd aggressive act or after every such act produced significant positive results in a 7-yr-old retarded female. Timeout after every 5th act had no effect. It appears that timeout may be effective proportionate to the percentage of target behaviors it follows.
Calhoun, Karen S. & Matherne, Paula. (U Georgia) Journal of Behavior Therapy & Experimental Psychiatry, 1975(Aug), Vol 6(2), 139-143. [PA, Vol 55:05088]

2173. Training pre-school children to modify their retarded siblings' behavior.
In a demonstration project, 3 3-6 yr old females were taught to be modifiers of their retarded younger siblings' behavior by means of a short training film. Their ability to teach the handicapped siblings was observed 3 wks before, immediately after, and 6 wks after exposure to the filmed models. It is concluded that preschool children could be taught instructional skills such as prompting, modeling, giving verbal information, calling attention, and the appropriate use of reinforcement. (16 ref)
Cash, Wanda M. & Evans, Ian M. (U Hawaii) Journal of Behavior Therapy & Experimental Psychiatry, 1975(Apr), Vol 6(1), 13-16. [PA, Vol 54:05668]

2174. [Teaching problem children mathematics and language.] (Fren)
Used a graphic method of teaching mathematics to 16 educationally retarded boys and girls, 8-17 yrs old. Instruction was essentially nonverbal. The child described a situation mathematically by means of diagrams, representing each object by a point and relationships by different colors. Considerable progress was made, especially by the younger children. General verbal facility (an area in which they were all deficient) developed, mathematical understanding increased markedly, and behavior in general and attitudes toward school showed noticeable improvement. (English summary)
Cordier, J.; Lowenthal, F. & Heraux, C. (U Libre, Bruxelles, Belgium) Enfance, 1975(Jan-Apr), No 1, 111-125. [PA, Vol 55:03194]

2175. Psychotherapy with mentally handicapped children in a day school.
Describes individual psychotherapy with 3 mentally handicapped boys attending a special school for English-speaking retarded children living in Paris. It is maintained that the mentally retarded child can use play therapy to unblock troublesome feelings and to bring about more adequate behavioral responses, just as the neurotic child does.
Davidson, Claire D. Psychotherapy: Theory, Research & Practice, 1975(Spr), Vol 12(1), 13-21. [PA, Vol 55:10205]

2176. Cooperation of the MR child during dental procedures with some associated variables.
Dicks, Joseph L. (Georgia Retardation Ctr, Dental Program, Atlanta) Mental Retardation, 1975(Jun), Vol 13(3), 28. [PA, Vol 54:08175]

2177. Treatment of childhood encopresis: Full cleanliness training.
Describes the use of full cleanliness training in combination with positive reinforcement as a treatment for encopresis with an 8-yr-old retarded male who demonstrated a toilet phobia. Soiling was effectively eliminated at the end of 16 wks of treatment but recurred when the parents became inconsistent in their use of the procedure during follow-up. The merits of the treatment program are discussed as are some procedural difficulties.
Doleys, Daniel M. & Arnold, Susan. (U Alabama, Medical School) Mental Retardation, 1975(Dec), Vol 13(6), 14-16. [PA, Vol 55:10330]

2178. Sensory-motor stimulation for slow-to-develop children: A home-centered program for parents.
Describes a program for parents to help their slow developing child develop to the fullest potential. This program is carried out in the home so as to give parents a feeling of participation in their child's fate. A developmental stimulation suggestion chart is presented. Results of the program are discussed.
Eddington, Connie & Lee, Teresa. (Developmental Disabilities, Inc, Salt Lake City, UT) American Journal of Nursing, 1975(Jan), Vol 75(1), 59-62. [PA, Vol 54:10038]

2179. The children's hour: II. Parents as teachers.
Reports that new methods of behavior modification teaching have shown promise in dealing with the retarded child. These methods can often be taught easily to parents of retarded children. A series of manuals have been tested by 128 families in the Boston area. Results show that parents of this middle-class sample who made a commitment to using the manuals found them easy to integrate into a daily routine.
Fields, Suzanne. Innovations, 1975(Fal), Vol 2(3), 9-11. [PA, Vol 56:08393]

2180. An experiment in the pre-occupational education of mentally retarded students on the junior high school level.
Conducted a program to provide realistic simulated career exploration opportunities to mentally retarded adolescents. Students were paid "school dollars" to perform services as a nurse's aide, printer's helper, gas station attendant, manicurist, and electronics assembly worker. Dollars earned, according to their performance, were deposited in the students' checking

accounts to be used in purchasing items from the class store, thereby introducing the concept of banking. 8 of 10 students responding to an oral questionnaire said they felt earning money has been worth the effort regardless of their feelings about working at a particular job. 9 said they were happy to have participated, and 6 said they thought they had found an occupation to pursue in the future. Oral testing indicated that all students learned the fundamental concept of banking.

Fleres, Carol N. (U South Carolina) Education & Training of the Mentally Retarded, 1975(Feb), Vol 10(1), 26-29. [PA, Vol 54:04188]

2181. A survey of marriages among previously institutionalized retardates.

Notes that the ability of retardates to handle the responsibilities of marriage and parenthood has been seriously questioned, but few studies have explored the realities of this problem. The present report, part of an ongoing study, investigated the marital status of 80 previously institutionalized retardates. Results show that about 50% of the couples studied could sustain a marriage for several years with a reasonable degree of competence and that children did not, at least in the first few years, serve as an overwhelming burden. It is concluded, however, that the numerous difficulties encountered by many of these couples emphasize the importance of preparing institutional residents to assume the responsibilities of marriage. Recommendations are made.

Floor, Lucretia; Baxter, Donald; Rosen, Marvin & Zisfein, Laura. (Elwyn Inst, PA) Mental Retardation, 1975(Apr), Vol 13(2), 33-37. [PA, Vol 54:05564]

2182. Parental management of inappropriate hyperactivity in a young retarded child.

Describes a procedure used by parents of a 3-yr-old boy to eliminate inappropriate hyperactive behavior at mealtime and after meals, using a multiple baseline procedure and contingent attention and time-out. A sharp decrease in inappropriate behaviors is reported.

Frazier, James R. & Schneider, Henry. (North Carolina Memorial Hosp, Child Development Inst, Chapel Hill) Journal of Behavior Therapy & Experimental Psychiatry, 1975(Oct), Vol 6(3), 246-247. [PA, Vol 55:10333]

2183. An experimental analysis of response acquisition and elimination with positive reinforcers.

Presents the case of an 11-yr-old retarded female with a history of deviant behaviors who underwent an extensive experimental-therapeutic program to decrease deviant behavior and increase appropriate behavior. The program provided an experimental analysis of omission procedures for the reduction of deviant behaviors, and positive reinforcement for the acquisition and maintenance of appropriate play behavior. Response covariation of deviant behaviors was demonstrated. The study included a time period when the child was physically ill and under medical isolation. At the end of a 2-yr follow-up, the child had significantly advanced her overall behavioral repertoire, thus improving her physical health and living conditions.

Garcia, Eugene E. & deHaven, Everett D. (U Utah) Behavioral Neuropsychiatry, 1975(Apr-Mar), Vol 7(1-12), 71-78. [PA, Vol 56:10308]

2184. The effect of sheltered work adjustment training on vocational sophistication of educable retarded adolescents.

Administered Vocational Interest and Sophistication Assessment (VISA) to 10 male and 8 female retardates in a 20-wk sheltered workshop program and compared the pre- and postresults with those of 8 males and 9 females in special education classes who received some vocational instruction. The males, but not the females, made significantly greater gains in the experimental workshop than in the special education classes. However, the workshop program included more intensive training in the 7 vocational categories for males than in the 4 categories for females. Suggestions are offered for further research.

Gordon, Robert A. Vocational Evaluation & Work Adjustment Bulletin, 1975(Dec), Vol 8(4), 9-20. [PA, Vol 57:04430]

2185. Public attitudes toward mentally retarded children.

Argues that the recent trend toward integrating mentally retarded children in the community and public school warrants examination of public attitudes toward these children. Factor analysis of questionnaire responses of 430 adults revealed 4 factors underlying attitudes toward retarded children: Positive Stereotype, Segregation in the Community, Segregation in the Classroom, and Perceived Physical and Intellectual Handicap. Older respondents, parents of school-aged children, and people with no previous contact with a retarded person tended to favor segregation of retarded children in the community. Results suggest that attitudes of these groups must be addressed if retarded persons are to be successfully integrated into society.

Gottleib, Jay & Corman, Louise. (Research Inst for Educational Problems, Cambridge, MA) American Journal of Mental Deficiency, 1975(Jul), Vol 80(1), 72-80. [PA, Vol 54:09480]

2186. The social work function in the EarlyHelp program for preschool handicapped children.

Discusses the role of the school social worker in Project EarlyHelp, a demonstration project for 3-8 yr olds that is designed to evaluate and help the physically, mentally, or emotionally handicapped child. The project provides a multidisciplined, differential diagnosis and prepares educational prescriptions to minimize learning disabilities.

Highfill, Thomas J. & Anderson, Richard J. (Peoria Public Schools, Project EarlyHelp, IL) Child Welfare, 1975(Jan), Vol 54(1), 47-52. [PA, Vol 54:06072]

2187. Imitation as a consequence for children's behavior: Two experimental case studies.

Presents 2 case studies showing how an adult's imitation of 2 retarded children's inappropriate classroom behavior was effective in reducing the behavior. In one case imitation served as an aversive stimulus (rapid eating) and in the other as a positive reinforcer (animal-like yelping was accelerated). (19 ref)

Kauffman, James M.; LaFleur, N. Kenneth; Hallahan, Daniel P. & Chanes, Cyd M. (U Virginia) Behavior Therapy, 1975(Jul), Vol 6(4), 535-542. [PA, Vol 55:01525]

2188. Physicians' awareness and attitudes toward the retarded.

Community-based services for retarded citizens are increasing as alternatives to institutional care. For community services to reach their potential they must be recognized and utilized by all professional groups, including physicians. Questionnaires were sent to 37 general practitioners and 23 pediatricians and to 175 parents of children attending local developmental centers. 74% of the pediatricians, 61% of the general practitioners, and 71% of the parents responded. Results show that the sample was fairly unfamiliar with the local services for the mentally retarded, in spite of the fact that the area had gained national recognition for its programs.

Kelly, N. Karen & Menolascino, Frank J. Mental Retardation, 1975(Dec), Vol 13(6), 10-13. [PA, Vol 55:10466]

2189. [The handicapped child.] (Fren)

Cites estimates that children with handicaps (physical or mental deficiencies, behavior problems, and chronic conditions) constitute 5–10% of the total child population, depending on the country. A program of screening, evaluation, and therapy is the more effective the earlier in the child's life it begins—if possible, soon after birth, especially in cases of congenital handicaps. Besides treatment of the handicap, rehabilitation must involve the family, the academic milieu, and appropriate professional workers. Finally, prevention should include not only genetic counseling, prenatal and obstetrical supervision, health education, and prevention of accidents, but the fight against alcoholism, slums, and prostitution. It should also include programs of information, family education and legislative changes.

Manciaux, M. & Deschamps, J. P. (Ctr International de l'Enfance, Paris, France) Vie médicale au Canada français, 1975(Mar), Vol 4(3), 248-252. [PA, Vol 57:05950]

2190. Teaching behaviour modification procedures to parents of retarded and psychotic children: Practical problems and issues.
Discusses practical problems and issues which arise in training parents of retarded and psychotic children in the use of behavior modification techniques. The discussion is based on both individual and group attempts at training 14 parent-sets over a 2-yr period. It is concluded that much empirical research is needed to determine the conditions which must be present for (a) maximally training parents on behavior modification procedures and (b) generalizing their training to the treatment of new behavior problems. (22 ref)
Morris, Richard J. (Syracuse U) Scandinavian Journal of Behaviour Therapy, 1975, Vol 4(4), 169-180. [PA, Vol 57:06356]

2191. Training correct utensil use in retarded children: Modeling vs. physical guidance.
Compared modeling and physical guidance for teaching 24 retarded males (mean age = 13.5 yrs, mean IQ = 25.3) to use a knife, fork, and spoon. Initial premeal training methods resulted in no improvement over baseline. The methods were revised to extend throughout meals, and a 3rd method (physical guidance with praise) replaced a former control procedure. Methods involving physical guidance produced significant improvement while modeling did not. All groups then received physical guidance with praise which resulted in their achieving similar levels of performance. Follow-up observations revealed that correct utensil use continued under maintenance conditions. (15 ref)
Nelson, Gary L.; Cone, John D. & Hanson, Christopher R. (West Virginia U) American Journal of Mental Deficiency, 1975(Jul), Vol 80(1), 114-122. [PA, Vol 54:09970]

2192. Psychopathology of mental retardation: A study of 100 mentally retarded children: I. Psychopathology.
Studied 100 mentally retarded children of all ages referred to a psychiatric clinic in regard to the severity of their retardation, their ages at the time of referral, their social class, presenting symptoms and diagnoses, and the effects of organicity on their clinical pictures. It was found that 38 Ss were psychotically disturbed, 13 had no evidence of psychiatric disorder, and 49 showed symptoms of characterologic, neurotic, behavioral, or situational disorders. Although the incidence of emotional disorder was high among Ss, their symptoms did not differ in kind from those found in a group of nonretarded children referred to the clinic. (22 ref)
Philips, Irving & Williams, Nancy. (U California, Medical School, San Francisco) American Journal of Psychiatry, 1975(Dec), Vol 132(12), 1265-1271. [PA, Vol 55:10071]

2193. [Proposal for teaching sign language to the mentally retarded.] (Fren)
Contends that sign language should be taught to severely and moderately mentally retarded children to provide an additional and alternative form of communication. Both theory and empirical evidence suggest that sign language and oral language would enhance each other. Specific indications for the use of sign language are described.
Rondal, Jean A. & Hoffmeister, Robert J. (U Liège, Belgium) Revue Belge de Psychologie et de Pédagogie, 1975(Jun-Sep), Vol 37(150-151), 51-60. [PA, Vol 58:01408]

2194. Conditioning prosocial behaviors in a mentally retarded child without using instructions.
Used operant conditioning with physical reinforcers to increase prosocial behaviors in a hyperactive, mentally retarded 3-yr-old female. The prosocial behavior included increased attention and immobile behavior. No instructions were given the child regarding expected behavior or possible rewards for such behavior. It is suggested that achieving instructionless conditioning in a young retarded child has implications for other children who have difficulty absorbing verbal instructions.
Stoudenmire, John & Salter, Leo. (North Mississippi Medical Ctr, Mental Health Complex, Tupelo) Journal of Behavior

Therapy & Experimental Psychiatry, 1975(Apr), Vol 6(1), 39-42. [PA, Vol 54:05974]

2195. Relative effectiveness of behavioral and reflective group counseling with parents of mentally retarded children.
Evaluated the relative effectiveness of behavioral and reflective group parent counseling. Ss were 51 mothers of mentally retarded children who were assigned to behavioral, reflective, or waiting-list control groups. 6 success criteria, including direct observations, attitudinal scales, maternal reports, and frequency counts, were used to measure outcome (e.g., Hereford Parent Attitude Survey and the Missouri Behavior Problem Checklist). Both types of counseling had a beneficial effect relative to the untreated controls, but the behavioral method resulted in a significantly greater magnitude of improvement. The consistency of these results across measures strongly suggests that the behavioral technique was the treatment of choice for counseling parents of the retarded. (29 ref)
Tavormina, Joseph B. (U Virginia) Journal of Consulting & Clinical Psychology, 1975(Feb), Vol 43(1), 22-31. [PA, Vol 53:12122]

2196. A longitudinal assessment of clinical services to the mentally retarded.
Evaluated the impact of changes in a university child development clinic's services from 1966 to 1972 using data from 1,295 cases and comparisons with data from a similar, 1960-66 study. Results reveal no significant differences in the clinic's client population over this 12-yr period.
Barclay, Allan; Endres, Jan; Kelly, Tom & Sharp, Austin R. (St Louis U Child Development Ctr) Mental Retardation, 1976(Oct), Vol 14(5), 10-11. [PA, Vol 57:08575]

2197. Job training placement for retarded youth: A survey.
A survey of the types of jobs to which 1,438 mentally retarded youth were assigned for on-the-job training in a work-study program in 1972-1974 showed assignments to 185 different jobs in 14 major industries and a miscellaneous classification.
Becker, Ralph L. (Orient State Inst, Ohio Div of Mental Retardation & Developmental Disabilities, Columbus) Mental Retardation, 1976(Jun), Vol 14(3), 7-11. [PA, Vol 57:04137]

2198. Family-level interventions for retarded children: A multivariate approach to issues and strategies.
Considers issues and strategies of household-level interventions for families of retarded children. A perspective regarding retardation and a statement of the relevant levels of analysis is set forth. Section 1 considers the specific issues facing families with retarded children. Section 2 (a) reviews the literature concerning interventions aimed at families with retarded children, and (b) offers suggestions for future research and intervention efforts. (88 ref)
Berger, Michael & Foster, Martha. (Georgia State U) Multivariate Experimental Clinical Research, 1976, Vol 2(1), 1–21. [PA, Vol 59:12634]

2199. The role of the clergy in serving the mentally retarded.
Points out that clergy are frequently the people to whom parents turn when a mentally retarded child is born. The pastoral care required in such situations includes dealing with the parents' shock, grief, and emotional disorganization, removing their fantasies that the child is evil, and reiterating the message that all children are God's children. The authority of the clergy is seen as helpful in correcting distorted perceptions and providing motivation for parenthood. (45 ref)
Bergman, Charles C. Journal of Religion & Health, 1976(Apr), Vol 15(2), 100-107. [PA, Vol 57:11011]

2200. [Aid to the mentally handicapped child and its family at an early stage.] (Fren)
Deplores the fact that many physicians, in dealing with mentally handicapped patients, are still content with diagnosis; i.e., with establishing existing defects. Such an attitude inhibits the child's developmental possibilities and causes resentment by the parents. The purpose of a specialized consultation for the mentally handicapped is not just to establish an accurate somatic and

psychological diagnosis, but also to emphasize the favorable aspects so that the parents and child are helped to emerge from their sense of inferiority and defeat. Diagnosis should be the starting point of parental inspiration and patient rehabilitation. (German & Spanish summaries)
Bettschart, W.; Bridel, S.; Ingignoli, J.-P. & Papilloud, J. (U Lausanne, Ctr de Psychiatrie Infantile, Switzerland) Revue de Neuropsychiatrie Infantile et d'Hygiene Mentale de l'Enfance, 1976(Jan-Feb), Vol 24(1-2), 35-45. [PA, Vol 58:03674]

2201.   The effects of a systematic physical fitness program on clients in a comprehensive rehabilitation center.
Developed and validated a Physical Fitness (PF) Training Package for use with rehabilitation clients. The package does not require specially trained personnel or special equipment. 20 males, aged 16-35 yrs, from a rehabilitation center participated in the validation. Seven of these had behavioral problems; 4 were mentally retarded; 1 had epilepsy; 1 had a cardiovascular condition; 1 had visual impairments; and 6 clients had other disabling conditions. Although all had attended high school, only 5 had graduated. Ss were divided into 2 groups according to fitness; the less fit group was not required to do as many repetitions of the exercises. Groups exercised for 1 hr, 3 times/wk for 8 wks. Each exercise class included a 5-min audio cassette lecture and a 50-min exercise period involving 6 activities. Substantial improvement and measurable "carry over" effects were noted in all areas of fitness. The program did not produce any significant increase in self-reported personal adjustment; however, this may have been due to the instability of the measurement scales.
Bolton, Brian & Milligan, Tim. (U Arkansas) American Corrective Therapy Journal, 1976(Mar-Apr), Vol 30(2), 41-46. [PA, Vol 57:10647]

2202.   Teaching adaptive interpersonal behavior: Group techniques in residential treatment.
Describes an approach to group treatment of mildly retarded and borderline adolescents in a residential school setting, which attempts to develop the necessary interpersonal skills for a successful return to community life. The approach is characterized by its use of (a) action techniques, (b) skill building activity, (c) a strong reality orientation, and (d) a high degree of structure. (12 ref)
Crenshaw, David A. (Rhinebeck Country School, NY) Child Care Quarterly, 1976(Fal), Vol 5(3), 211–220. [PA, Vol 62:09122]

2203.   [Specific aspects of a recent technique: The development group for children.] (Fren)
Describes the structure and techniques used in a group formed to foster the psychomotor, intellectual, and emotional development of psychotic and mentally deficient 5–10 yr olds. Groups of 6–8 children were given toys which encouraged movement, manipulation of objects, or projective activity (e.g., designs), and were told they could do what they wanted, either alone or with other children. Ss also acted out their fantasies using procedures similar to psychodrama. The permissive attitude of the 2 therapists during the sessions contrasted with the limit-setting provided by rules about putting the room in order at the end of the session. The way in which the therapists' interpretation of fantasy and provision of realistic limits interacted in the group is discussed, as well as the children's reactions to the therapists' rules. The group provided gradual frustrating experiences, a multiplicity of transference phenomena, and the opportunity to test limits. Out of 70 participants, 56 showed at least some improvement in development. Unusual features of this type of group are examined.
Decherf, Gérard.   Perspectives Psychiatriques, 1976, Vol 57(3), 205-214. [PA, Vol 57:06285]

2204.   Neurological disorders of school-age children.
Discusses the problems surrounding diagnosis and treatment of neurologically disabled children and the attitudes of teachers and parents toward handicapped children. Three major categories encountered in child neurology are mental retardation, cerebral

palsy, and epilepsy. Patterns of development in normal and retarded children (both static and progressive encephalopathy) are depicted. Initially, families react to the problem of mental subnormality by feeling overwhelmed; they then exhibit denial, anger, intellectual acceptance, and finally, emotional acceptance. Anger may be expressed against the doctor, although it is usually the mother who is blamed and who blames herself. Rejection of the child, and frequently of the mother, by the father is not uncommon. Reactions of overprotectiveness and of unrealistic expectations by both parents and teachers are common behaviors.
Dodge, Philip R. (Washington U Medical School) Journal of School Health, 1976(Jun), Vol 46(6), 338–343. [PA, Vol 62:01351]

2205.   The effects of social punishment on noncompliance: A comparison with timeout and positive practice.
The effects of social punishment, positive practice, and timeout on the noncompliant behavior of 4 mentally retarded 8- and 10-yr-old children were assessed in a multitreatment withdrawal design. When programmed, the experimental procedure occurred contingent on noncompliance to E-issued commands. Commands were given at 55-sec intervals throughout each experimental session. Results show (a) lower levels of noncompliance with social punishment than with the positive-practice or timeout conditions, and (b) relatively few applications of social punishment required to obtain this effect. The advantages of social punishment over other punishment procedures, considerations to be made before using it, and the various aspects of the procedures that contribute to its effectiveness are discussed. (40 ref)
Doleys, Daniel M. et al. (U Alabama Medical School, Birmingham) Journal of Applied Behavior Analysis, 1976(Win), Vol 9(4), 471-482. [PA, Vol 57:13285]

2206.   The grief reaction of parents of the retarded and the counsellor's role.
Discusses the 5 stages of grief suffered by parents of the intellectually handicapped. Suggestions are offered for counselors when working with the handicapped child and his/her parents. It is noted that counselors should (a) inform the parents about available social services and special education, (b) be sensitive to both implicit and explicit questions asked, and (c) be prepared to deal with problems incidental to but resultant of the grief process. It is concluded that by understanding the grief process the counselor can enhance his/her effectiveness in helping the parents achieve increased comfort in living with and managing a mentally retarded child.
Evans, Eryl C.   Australian Journal of Mental Retardation, 1976(Dec), Vol 4(4), 8–12. [PA, Vol 59:01686]

2207.   A program for high school students in a facility for the retarded.
Describes a program at a state hospital in which 28 high school students worked with blind mentally retarded residents. To date, more than 160 students have worked in the program each semester in 9 of the hospital's 10 treatment programs. The students are a valuable source of one-to-one assistance. They increase the amount of personal care and attention that each resident receives, and they free staff members for other activities.
Fountain Valley High School Community Services Program. (Fountain Valley High School, CA) Hospital & Community Psychiatry, 1976(Oct), Vol 27(10), 721-723. [PA, Vol 57:11024]

2208.   Self-injurious behavior in schizophrenic and retarded children.
Self-injurious behavior is a problem with some children who are primarily nonverbal and low-functioning. This behavior has resulted in management difficulties far out of proportion to its incidence. In the present paper, possible operant and respondent paradigms instrumental in the acquisition and maintenance of several different topographies of self-injurious behavior are examined. Support for these paradigms is gathered from existing epidemiological literature dealing with humans and primates and from the literature concerned with treatment of self-injurious behavior. Immediate outcome and results of subsequent follow-

up are presented as a function of type of intervention, the nature of positive reinforcement utilized, and the topography of the self-injurious response involved. (60 ref)
Frankel, Fred & Simmons, James Q. (U California, Los Angeles) American Journal of Mental Deficiency, 1976(Mar), Vol 80(5), 512-522. [PA, Vol 56:06194]

2209.   Double-blind clinical trial of 5-hydroxytryptophan in a case of Lesch-Nyhan syndrome.
5-Hydroxytryptophan (5-HTP) treatment of a case of Lesch-Nyhan syndrome in a 6½-yr-old male showing compulsive self-mutilation, athetoid movements, and characteristic clinical bio-chemical picture was studied on a double-blind basis. 5-HTP (100 mg/day) in conjunction with a peripheral decarboxylase inhibitor (Carbidopa, 50 mg/day) or placebo was administered for 7 fortnightly treatment blocks. 5-HTP produced a significant reduction in athetoid movement and a sedative effect but did not improve the patient's mood or reduce self-mutilation. (25 ref)
Frith, C. D. (MRC Div of Psychiatry & Inherited Metabolic Diseases, Clinical Research Ctr, Middlesex, England) Journal of Neurology, Neurosurgery & Psychiatry, 1976(Jul), Vol 39(7), 656-662. [PA, Vol 57:01683]

2210.   [On the therapy of a severe eating disorder of a 7 year old retarded girl.] (Germ)
Reports a case study of a 7-yr-old girl with a retardation-malfunction syndrome. S had shown a severe eating disorder with a sole fixation on bottle-feeding. Behavior modification with the goal of normal eating is described, including the subtle exercises for the development of eating skills. Therapy was successful, and S has progressed in her socioemotional development. (30 ref)
Gutezeit, Günter; Delfs-Heuer, Frauke & Grosse, Rainer. (Christian-Albrechts-U Kiel, Kinderklinik, West Germany) Praxis der Kinderpsychologie und Kinderpsychiatrie, 1976(Jul), Vol 25(5), 161–173. [PA, Vol 65:01780]

2211.   Treating self-injurious behavior of a retarded child by overcorrection.
Reports a case history in which overcorrection procedures applied to chronic self-injurious behavior of an 8-yr-old rubella syndrome boy produced rapid suppression of self-injury. The procedure was implemented at school and at home with control maintained 24 hrs/day. Results suggest that overcorrection may be useful in certain cases of self-injurious behavior and is a procedure that can be consistently applied by staff and parents.
Harris, Sandra L. & Romanczyk, Raymond G. (Rutgers State U, Douglass Coll) Behavior Therapy, 1976(Mar), Vol 7(2), 235-239. [PA, Vol 56:06409]

2212.   Teaching mute retarded children vocal imitation.
Describes a system used by 8 institution staff members to teach vocal imitative responses to 3 nonvocal 11-13 yr old retarded children. The system may be characterized by a response classification scheme and a recording and graphing procedure which give detailed information regarding the nature and progress of the shaping, the use of objective criteria to guide the trainer in applying differential reinforcement and in shifting reinforcement schedules during the course of training, and the use of specific prompting techniques. Data are presented to illustrate the progress of the Ss. It is concluded that the system appears practical and explicit enough to be adopted by child care staff without involving a great deal of professional supervision.
Hung, David W. (Rotary School Program for Autistic Children, Toronto, Canada) Journal of Behavior Therapy & Experimental Psychiatry, 1976(Mar), Vol 7(1), 85-88. [PA, Vol 56:08398]

2213.   Adoption of the at risk child in W. A.
Surveys the issues and problems of the placement for adoption of an "at risk" child (the child who may be retarded or present other problems) in Western Australia. The possible repercussions of an incorrect placement are discussed, and the need for a placement officer to be as informed as possible about the child's background, diagnosis of mental condition, and prognosis of development is stressed. When an "at risk" child is placed,

consideration must be given to the ability of the adopting parents to cope with the child's possible mental retardation.
Kagi, Carole. (U Western Australia, Nedlands) Australian Journal of Mental Retardation, 1976(Mar), Vol 4(1), 5-7. [PA, Vol 57:04097]

2214.   [Parents as participants in the behavior therapy of their mentally retarded children.] (Fren)
Reports a program involving 16 couples who were parents of retarded children aged 4-9 yrs. Etiology of the retardation included cerebral lesions, autism, encephalitis, phenylketonuria, and petit mal epilepsy. All children lived at home, 13 had siblings, and 10 attended nursery school or kindergarten part-time. Children were assessed at the Max Plank Psychiatric Institute, with parents assisting, for comprehension of commands, dressing, continence, and language. Exercises were chosen which would teach self-feeding, imitation, and language. Preconditions for treatment were established (e.g., imitation training required that child remain seated). Treatment proceeded by small sequential steps with each correct response rewarded. Generalization integrated exercises into daily life; the child who had learned dressing and undressing was required to perform these actions morning and night. After training, parents took over the therapy sessions, under supervision. Four couples passed an intensive course conducted while the family and child were hospitalized together; 12 couples received less intensive training. All conducted 15-min sessions with the children 4 times daily for 60 sessions. Parents were successful in meeting objectives of ensuring continuation of therapy, averting relapses, and charting responses. Additional target modification arose from parental behavior changes. (20 ref)
Kane, Gudrun; Kane, John F.; Amorosa, Hedwig & Kumpmann, Sibylle. Perspectives Psychiatriques, 1976, No 58, 293-303. [PA, Vol 58:03847]

2215.   [On medical and educational remediation under microcephaly.] (Russ)
Treatment of microcephalic children was begun by working toward the development of steady attention and ability to differentiate processes that were severely hampered in these children. The success of corrections depended not only on the degree of mental retardation encountered but also on the motor potential of the children. It was important to develop the children's ability to imitate, allowing instruction in elementary actions as well as playing an important role in the reconstruction of their behavior. Assuming relative preservation of mechanical and visual memory, it is necessary to accustom them to their own and other peoples' names, their place in the residential environment, and recognition of people and pictures. All these children require long and numerous repetitions of exercises and assignments as well as continual teacher assistance. (6 ref)
Knyazeva, M. P. (Child Neurological Hosp #6, Moscow, USSR) Defektologiya, 1976(Jun), No 6, 53–58. [PA, Vol 63:08440]

2216.   Parents' experiences of official help and guidance in caring for a mentally handicapped child.
A sample of 97 parents of mentally handicapped children replied to a postal questionnaire asking about the effects their child had on various aspects of family life and their attitudes toward services provided. Contacts with services were a major source of problems, which often assumed greater importance than problems arising more directly out of the child's handicap.
Lloyd-Bostock, Sally. (U Oxford, Wolfson Coll Ctr for Socio-Legal Studies, England) Child Care, Health & Development, 1976(Nov-Dec), Vol 2(6), 325-338. [PA, Vol 58:01401]

2217.   Alternatives to the principle of normalization.
Discusses the role of normalization in directing community-based services for retarded children. Alternate principles which place more importance on individual clients and enduring goals are endorsed along with direct evaluation of service systems. (19 ref)
Mesibov, Gary B. (U North Carolina, Learning of the Biological Sciences Research Ctr, Chapel Hill) Mental Retardation, 1976(Oct), Vol 14(5), 30-32. [PA, Vol 57:08849]

2218. Employing task arrangements and verbal contingencies to promote verbalizations between retarded children.
Investigated the effects of arranging task events for interdependence, to increase the probability of social responding. Two experiments employed 4 10–12 yr old males, one of whom was moderately retarded and 3 mildly retarded. During task interdependence, the Ss, participating in dyads and a 4-person group, obtained task materials (a puzzle piece) from their partner before completing their task (appropriately placing the puzzle piece). The verbal contingency required a verbal request to precede an S's receiving a task material from his partner. The verbal contingency yoked with task interdependence made task completion contingent on the appropriate verbalization. Findings suggest that task interdependence was sufficient to increase partner-directed verbalizations for 3 of the 4 Ss. When the verbal contingency was added, all Ss increased their requests and other verbalizations to partner. Applied to a 4-person group, the verbal contingency yoked with varying levels of task interdependence correspondingly affected the pattern and level of group communications. The greater the task interdependence, (i.e., the more members each S depended on to complete his task), the more complex the social network of verbal contacts and the higher the level of both requests and other verbalizations for the group. (17 ref)
Mithaug, Dennis E. & Wolfe, M. S. (U Washington Child Development & Mental Retardation Ctr, Seattle) Journal of Applied Behavior Analysis, 1976(Fal), Vol 9(3), 301-314. [PA, Vol 57:06355]

2219. Judgments of educators and child-care personnel about appropriate treatment for mentally retarded or normal, overactive or withdrawn, boys.
30 special educators and 28 child-care personnel ranked the appropriateness of various psychological treatments for a 7-yr-old male described as either mentally retarded or of normal intelligence and whose behavior was described either as withdrawn or overactive. The predicted IQ Level × Behavior interaction was found only for drug treatment, which was ranked as relatively more appropriate for the retarded overactive child. Drug treatment and behavior modification were perceived as more appropriate for the overactive child. Play therapy, family therapy, and no treatment were deemed more appropriate for the withdrawn child. Educators favored behavior modification and school consultation more than did child-care personnel.
Morrison, Thomas L. & Thomas, M. Duane. (U California, Davis) Journal of Clinical Psychology, 1976(Apr), Vol 32(2), 449-452. [PA, Vol 57:03838]

2220. Modified time-out procedures for controlling tantrum behaviors in public places.
Recommends 3 methods of modified isolation procedures for parents to use with retarded and brain damaged children. The methods, to be supplemented with positive reinforcement, are taking the child to a quiet corner for 2 min before resuming normal activities, taking him to the car and waiting outside the car till he ceases the behavior, and placing a coat or blanket over his head and shoulders till he stops the tantrum.
Murray, Michael E. (U Texas Health Science Ctr, Dallas) Behavior Therapy, 1976(May), Vol 7(3), 412-413. [PA, Vol 57:01648]

2221. The effectiveness of speech training techniques based on operant conditioning: A comparison of two methods.
Four retarded and speech-deficient children were taught to imitate 24 verbal stimuli by 2 methods based on operant conditioning principles. After pretesting on 3 lists of stimuli, 2 children were trained on List A by the method of O. I. Lovaas (1966), given a midtest, trained on List B by the method of R. O. Nelson and I. M. Evans (see PA, Vol 43:11488), and given a posttest. List C was a control list, given without training. The other 2 children received the same training in reverse order. Training required 1 yr. The 2 methods were equally effective in increasing the number of correct responses, but for 3 of the 4 children, fewer training trials were required to meet criterion for the 2nd training method and training list. (21 ref)

Nelson, Rosemery O. et al. (U North Carolina, Greensboro) Mental Retardation, 1976(Jun), Vol 14(3), 34-38. [PA, Vol 57:04036]

2222. [Recent research in mental retardation.] (Fren)
Discusses changes in France since World War II in the concept of mental deficiency (MD) and its treatment. Special teachers, classes, and teaching methods have greatly expanded. Sharp disagreement exists, however, as to what shall be included in the concept of MD, and these differences are important because of their bearing on therapeutic methods. Three psychological approaches to the study of MD children are described: (a) comparison with normal children of the same CA; (b) comparison with normals of the same MA; and (c) comparison of groups of MD children of the same MA but differing in the etiology of the disorder. Other approaches are physiological and sociological. The relationship between the social environment and MD is considered a central problem, and the most desirable study method would therefore be to define representative samples of the general population and then to compare the MD children found in each sample. Whether the conceptual diversity of MD study will eventually be coordinated is uncertain. Recent work has focused on severe MD and on the mechanisms of MD production. An English translation of the article is included. (49 ref)
Netchine, S. & Netchine, Gaby. (CNRS Lab de Psycho-biologie de l'Enfant, Paris, France) Revue de Psychologie Appliquée, 1976, Vol 26(Spec Issue), 295–319. [PA, Vol 61:03902]

2223. New directions for work with parents of retarded children.
Discusses how social workers should use techniques of special education and behavioral psychology in working with parents of retarded children. Earlier attitudes which encouraged resignation can prevent a child from reaching his full potential. Social workers must help parents gain realistic yet more optimistic expectations and equip them with more effective skills for teaching their children. The children should be encouraged in self-help and social skills, but should be expected to learn only one skill at a time. Ways of teaching parents include didactic counseling, use of programmed texts, modeling, rehearsal, and use of videotapes.
Proctor, Enola K. (Washington U, St Louis) Social Casework, 1976(Apr), Vol 57(4), 259-264. [PA, Vol 58:01772]

2224. Therapeutic tutoring of retarded adolescents by medical students.
Describes a program designed to provide both help for retarded adolescent girls who were too depressed to involve themselves in vocational training, and an opportunity for medical students to have a supervised patient contact as a basis for studying the interrelationship of emotional and intellectual development. The medical students, acting as tutor-therapists, met weekly with the girls to help improve their capacities and to assist them with painful feelings regarding their incapacities. The girls improved in school and job performance, ability to relate, and ability to manage frustration and anxiety. Two case studies illustrate the success of the program. (27 ref)
Robinson, Lillian H. (Tulane U Medical School) Journal of the American Academy of Child Psychiatry, 1976(Spr), Vol 15(2), 343–356. [PA, Vol 59:06009]

2225. Sign language as an alternative language system for the mentally retarded.
Recommends sign language, particularly American Sign Language (ASL), as an alternative or adjunct way of communicating with severely and moderately retarded children. Sign language can be used as a prosthetic device when oral communication is prevented or made difficult by defective articulation, voice quality, or stuttering. When used as a complementary language system, it interacts positively with oral language development. Use of sign language can enhance vocal language development because messages use spatial means, which involve less complex grammatical structure, and because sign language allows more reduplications than does spoken language. To put this proposal

into effect, ASL would have to be offered as an option in the regular school curriculum. (47 ref)
Rondal, Jean A. & Hoffmeister, Robert J.   Philippine Journal of Mental Health, 1976, Vol 7(2), 57–62. [PA, Vol 64:01322]

2226. Psychiatric disorder in children with birth anomalies: A retrospective follow-up study.
Studied 273 8–19 yr olds who had been treated for a congenital malformation during their 1st mo of life, using psychiatric interviews with the S and at least one of his/her parents. The S was also given the WISC and Bender Gestalt test. The rate of psychopathological disturbance was as high as 49% (the classification used included organic brain disorder and mental retardation). Developmental deviations, psychoneurotic disorder, and reactive disorder were the commonest types of disturbance (in 18, 17, and 11%, respectively). 11% were suffering from organic brain disorder, and 8% had an IQ of no more than 50. Ss were also compared with 509 8–19 yr olds from the general population in terms of behavior disturbance as rated by their teacher. Approximately 1 child in 5 in both groups presented behavior problems, and behavior was labeled as antisocial in 10% of Ss in both groups. The 2 groups did not differ significantly in regard to the family's social class, annual income, father's education or number of children in the family, but parents of the malformed Ss had received psychiatric treatment more often than the control group parents. (43 ref)
Sandberg, Seija. (Inst of Psychiatry, London, England) Acta Psychiatrica Scandinavica, 1976(Jul), Vol 54(1), 1-16. [PA, Vol 57:05954]

2227. Emotional problems of the handicapped.
Discusses some of the emotional problems experienced by the mentally and physically handicapped child. It is noted that frequently these problems begin in the home where parents and siblings pass on feelings of resentment toward the child for his/her inadequacies. Such feelings are reinforced by teachers and other adults, schoolmates, and friends who do not understand his/her special needs and limitations. It is suggested that the solution to the emotional problems of the handicapped may be in helping them to increase their tolerance for and acceptance of the disability in order to (a) reduce the frustration which they are bound to have and (b) reduce the external forces which impel them to strive for goals that are difficult for them to attain.
Shanker, Uday. (Kurukshetra U, India) Asian Journal of Psychology & Education, 1976(Mar), Vol 1(1), 38-40. [PA, Vol 58:11786]

2228. [Stimulating the activity of mentally retarded schoolchildren by means of the Young Pioneer Club.] (Russ)
Young Pioneer clubs require and create suitable situations for certain desirable types of behavior, therefore providing an opportunity to help retarded students to correct or improve their behavior. A special summer camp was set up for 17 5th–7th grade students where getting together, conversation, distribution of assignments, and different practical deeds took place. It was found that the Pioneer clubs can be used very effectively to assist retarded children.
Shisha, V. I. (Ministry of Education, Kiev, USSR) Defektologiya, 1976(Feb), No 2, 41–46. [PA, Vol 64:10956]

2229. Parents participate in clinical care of retarded children.
A survey of 60 parents of mentally retarded children indicates that parents' participation in clinical team meetings was a good experience for all concerned and had, in fact, produced some desirable behavioral changes on the part of both the parents and the staff.
Sieffert, Allan; Hendricks, Carmen O.; Marks, Jill & Gutierrez, Philip B. (Kansas Neurological Inst, Topeka) Social Work, 1976(May), Vol 21(3), 238-239. [PA, Vol 56:02548]

2230. A Machiavelli for planners: Community attitudes and selection of a group home site.
Adult survey respondents were supportive of the rights of the mentally retarded to equal employment opportunity and marriage, but were somewhat unfavorable toward group homes and strongly opposed to the right to bear children. Age, ethnicity,

home ownership, and self-styled ideology were consistently related to respondents' attitudes.
Sigelman, Carol K. (Texas Tech U Research & Training Ctr) Mental Retardation, 1976(Feb), Vol 14(1), 26-29. [PA, Vol 56:01181]

2231. [Techniques of behavior modification.] (Span)
Presents 5 papers, given at the Fifth National Convention of Psychology in Valladolid, Spain, in April 1976, which deal with (a) the modification of homosexual behavior, (b) the modification of behavior in infants, (c) the treatment of obsessive behavior, (d) the modification of behavior in a mentally retarded girl, and (e) controlling migraines through controlling body temperature with biofeedback.
Spanish Society of Psychologists. (Madrid, Spain) Revista de Psicología General y Aplicada, 1976(Jul–Oct), Vol 31(141–142), 607–624. [PA, Vol 62:01640]

2232. Helping parents to accept.
Asserts that the way in which a professional team approaches the parents of a mentally handicapped child influences the parents' acceptance of that child. It is emphasized that methods of telling the parents about their child's handicap, including who should tell, how much, and when, must be carefully weighed. Professionals should, in a nonjudgmental way, encourage parents to identify emotions (e.g., guilt, anger, anxiety, or grief) in their reactions. It is important to stress how normal these feelings are. Parents may benefit from group therapy sessions in working through feelings. Efforts should be made to educate parents about their child's handicap and to encourage them to direct their need for more information to experts rather than to family or friends. Involvement with the child and the passing of time are acknowledged as the major ways in which the grief of parents is relieved and acceptance of the child is achieved. The conclusion is drawn that early action, diagnosis, and involvement are critical factors in "helping parents to accept."
Stokes, B. M. (St Michael's House, Dublin, Ireland) Child Care, Health & Development, 1976(Feb), Vol 2(1), 29-33. [PA, Vol 57:01757]

2233. Participant evaluations of the effectiveness of their parent counseling groups.
Evaluations by 45 mothers of a retarded child as to the effectiveness of an 8-wk behavioral, reflective, or combination group counseling treatment indicated that, while all Ss endorsed the group counseling procedure, more satisfaction was voiced for the behaviorally oriented groups (including the behavioral and combination methods) than the purely reflective group.
Tavormina, J. B.; Hampson, Robert B. & Luscomb, Richard L. (U Virginia) Mental Retardation, 1976(Dec), Vol 14(6), 8-9. [PA, Vol 58:01624]

2234. A comparison of the adaptive behavior of retarded individuals successfully and unsuccessfully placed in group living homes.
Compared the adaptive behavior patterns of 47 retarded individuals successfully and 25 unsuccessfully placed in group living homes, using the Adaptive Behavior Scale developed by the American Association of Mental Deficiency. Results show that there was a significant difference between the 2 groups. Adaptive behavior domains that tended to create many problems in group living homes, resulting in the return of the individual to the institution, were untrustworthy behavior, economic activity, number and time concept, and hyperactive tendencies. Behavioral domains that were tolerated, even though it would seem that they would cause problems, were inappropriate interpersonal manners, psychological disturbances, and rebellious behaviors.
Taylor, James R. (Orange Grove Ctr for the Retarded, Chattanooga, TN) Education & Training of the Mentally Retarded, 1976(Feb), Vol 11(1), 56-64. [PA, Vol 57:04085]

2235. Environmental maintenance of retarded behavior: A behavioral perspective.
Suggests that retarded behavior in children is maintained by certain events in the environment and their relationship to an individual's behavior. Maintenance of these behaviors is attrib-

uted to positive reinforcement, avoidance behavior, and contingency schedules. Several examples of the maintenance effects of each of these paradigms are given.
Thurman, S. Kenneth. (Temple U) Education, 1976(Win), Vol 97(2), 121-125. [PA, Vol 57:10583]

2236. Selection of play materials for the severely handicapped: A continuing dilemma.
Surveys existing studies on the development of play materials for the severely handicapped and explores the feasibility of a taxonomy of play materials. The following key points are made regarding the selection of play materials for severely retarded preschoolers, school age children, and adolescents and adults: (a) Exploratory play activity that is consistent with the developmental norm should be used whenever possible with these preschoolers. However, objects can be presented more frequently and social or tangible reinforcers may be required initially to encourage such activity. (b) For the severely and profoundly retarded school age child, play materials must be selected that can function both as toys for play and tasks for learning, preacademic, academic, and social interaction skills. (c) Play materials for adolescents or adults must assist them in the development of exploratory, social, and game playing skills.
Wehman, Paul. (U Wisconsin, Madison) Education & Training of the Mentally Retarded, 1976(Feb), Vol 11(1), 46-50. [PA, Vol 57:03648]

2237. Early diagnosis and intervention of retardation: A survey of parental reactions concerning the quality of services rendered.
Attempted to provide an estimate of the degree to which the early intervention model has been assimilated into supportive services for mentally retarded infants and children. 215 families (47% of those sampled) completed a questionnaire which was developed to provide the Connecticut Department of Mental Retardation with a compendium of parental reactions to the types of services their mentally retarded infant or child received. Results show that professional advice was sought almost unanimously from doctors (94%); advice consisted of an objective and clinical portrayal of the situation (27%), another referral (24%), or an attempt to minimize the symptoms (14%). 14% received either a bleak prognosis or misinformation. 51% were very dissatisfied, dissatisfied, or uncertain about the advice they received; 49% were satisfied or very satisfied. 77% were either satisfied or very satisfied with the medical treatment their children received. Each family who contacted one of the specific early intervention programs at a regional facility felt the quality of services was exceptional. (23 ref)
Abramson, Paul R.; Gravink, Marilyn J.; Abramson, Linda M. & Sommers, Dave. (U California, Los Angeles) Mental Retardation, 1977(Jun), Vol 15(3), 28–31. [PA, Vol 59:08380]

2238. The volunteer model of vocational habilitation as a component of the deinstitutionalization process.
Presents a volunteer model for vocational habilitation program. The model is discussed as a component of the deinstitutionalization process emphasizing the need for linkage mechanisms between large residential facilities and community settings. A demonstration of the model is presented in which 5 mentally retarded adolescents and adults served as community volunteers within a nonprofit organization.
Andriano, Timothy A. (U Wisconsin, Waisman Ctr on Mental Retardation & Human Development, Madison) Mental Retardation, 1977(Aug), Vol 15(4), 58–61. [PA, Vol 59:12815]

2239. Experi-mental: A simulation of the distribution of services to mentally deficient children.
Introduced a formal analytical technique in a typical planning operation of the Quebec Ministry of Social Affairs. The mental deficiency sector of the province was chosen because important changes were imminent in both the orientation and types of services provided to children in this sector. A simulation model was constructed according to system dynamics methodology to provide an integrated description of the social impact of these changes. The immediate result of the simulation model was to focus a reevaluation by government planners on certain opera-

tional features of the system of services and on the implementation schedule of the ministry's policy. In a broader context, the model demonstrated that simulation is a viable approach to planning social services. Similar social services studies have been initiated to familiarize government planners with the methodology and have been used in the preparation of precise implementation plans.
Bernard, J. C.; Camirand, F.; Hosios, A. J. & Rousseau, J. M. (Ecole des Hautes Commerciales, Montreal, Canada) Behavioral Science, 1977(Sep), Vol 22(5), 356–366. [PA, Vol 60:09870]

2240. Intervention with handicapped infants: Correlates of progress.
Explored the possibility that certain groups of children were more likely than others to benefit from a large-scale early intervention program in which parents served as the primary intervention agents. Longitudinal data for a sample of 37 male and 36 female infants with various handicaps were related to a number of organismic and psychological-sociological factors. Children were administered the Bayley Scales of Infant Development upon entry to the treatment program and at intervals of 4–5 mo after that time. Developmental progress was related to organic damage in infants with biological impairments. In general, the impact of intervention appeared to depend on the degree of intellectual handicap. About 90% of the infants who made substantial increases in developmental rate had mothers rated high in terms of parent–child interaction, in contrast to only 37% of the infants whose rates did not increase following intervention.
Brassell, William R. (Western Carolina Ctr, Morganton, NC) Mental Retardation, 1977(Aug), Vol 15(4), 18–22. [PA, Vol 60:01383]

2241. [Psychiatry of the young child: Experience of four years in a nursery.] (Fren)
Attempted to improve the behavior of 60 3–5 yr olds in a day-care center in a low income area of a Canadian city. The Ss included retarded children and those with behavioral problems. A psychiatrist and a psychomotor educator, invited as consultants, observed the groups and made recommendations to day-care workers to eliminate disruptive behavior. Initial services involved diagnosis and treatment; later services included consultation. Some of the Ss were treated individually with food and social reinforcement. It is suggested that day-care workers need better understanding of young children and the family milieu; otherwise the occasion of the child's first parting from his or her mother may induce workers to try to replace the "bad" parent or to refuse responsibility for such a young child. The value of having mental health professionals present in nurseries as a preventive measure is emphasized. (German & Spanish summaries) (5 ref)
Breton, J.-J. & Sabatier, C. (Hosp Ste-Justine, Montreal, Canada) Revue de Neuropsychiatrie Infantile et d'Hygiene Mentale de l'Enfance, 1977(May–Jun), Vol 25(5–6), 311–318. [PA, Vol 63:06066]

2242. [Psychological and social picture of children at their placement in institutional care.] (Slok)
Performed psychological examinations of 170 institutionalized children, aged 6–15 yrs. Results show the following: (a) Boys and girls were placed in institutions in equal numbers during the 1st yr of school. Boys gradually gained prevalence at these institutions, however, ultimately accounting for 60% of the children. (b) Of the truant and delinquent children with normal family backgrounds, 19.4% revealed neurotic disorders, signs of minimal brain dysfunction, and psychopathological development. (c) The institutionalized children were retarded in their reading ability by an average of 1 standard deviation from the mean. The need to develop special classes to improve children's reading techniques and their attitudes toward reading is suggested. Such classes, it is argued, will have a positive effect on the children's total personality development. (Russian summary) (20 ref)
Čulen, Jozef & Hanzelyová, Eva. (U Komenského, Bratislava, Czechoslovakia) Psychológia a Patopsychológia Dieťaťa, 1977, Vol 11(5), 419–438. [PA, Vol 62:11647]

2243. **Video editing and medication to produce a therapeutic self-model.**
Self-modeling requires the production of a videotape in which the S is seen to perform in a model way. A 4-yr-old "hyperactive" boy, initially under psychotropic medication, was unable to role play suitable behaviors. Video editing was used to produce a videotape that, when watched by the S, had therapeutic effects as compared with an unedited film.
Dowrick, Peter W. & Raeburn, John M. (U Auckland Medical School, New Zealand) Journal of Consulting & Clinical Psychology, 1977(Dec), Vol 45(6), 1156–1158. [PA, Vol 60:07755]

2244. **Current problems in severe mental handicap.**
Presents a sociocultural discussion of the problems encountered in providing appropriate services for the mentally handicapped in different countries. Issues related to views of retardation as "eternal childhood," the influence of technological progress, normalization, the need for early intervention, the role of parents, approaches to special education, manpower and consumer needs, and the special problems of developing countries are considered.
Dybwad, Gunnar & Dybwad, Rosemary. International Child Welfare Review, 1977(Mar), No 32, 62–86. [PA, Vol 59:12821]

2245. **Clinical group work with multi-handicapped adolescents.**
Describes successful use of unstructured, feelings-oriented group psychotherapy with late adolescents who had mild to moderate intellectual impairment with other major handicaps. Based on the premise that with therapeutic support group members could achieve normal psychological goals, the groups explored many issues successfully. The nondirective therapist provided reflection, support, and clarification of ideas and distortions. Major themes included rejection and abandonment by families and others, fears of exclusion, dependency issues, and anger toward parent figures.
Empey, L. Jane. Social Casework, 1977(Dec), Vol 58(10), 593–599. [PA, Vol 63:03711]

2246. **Conceptual tempo and mother-child interaction: Results from a longitudinal intervention program.**
Assessed (a) the effects of the child's participation in longitudinal intervention upon his conceptual tempo, and (b) the relation of maternal and child latencies to their structured teaching interaction. Ss in the 2 studies were 39 low socioeconomic status "high-risk" Black children aged 40–66 mo and their mothers. The children were selected from a population of new offspring born to mothers of below-average intelligence (WAIS IQ below 75). Results indicate some effects of treatment upon tempo but ruled out the effect of mother/child matching or differing latencies upon patterns of interaction. Instead, both maternal and child behaviors were affected by maternal latency. Mothers with short latencies and children of mothers with short latencies exhibited more positive interactions and fewer negative interactions. Findings are interpreted in terms of the general dimension of tempo. (20 ref)
Falender, Carol A. & Heber, Rick. (U Wisconsin, Madison) Psychological Reports, 1977(Dec), Vol 41(3, Pt 1), 995–1002. [PA, Vol 60:12066]

2247. **Clinical issues on the physical restraint experience with self-injurious children.**
Discusses characteristics of the self-injurious behavior of retarded and emotionally disturbed children regularly confined to physical restraint devices. Issues are raised on the relationship between the uses of physical restraint and self-injurious behavior. An argument is presented that the experience of being physically restrained can acquire reinforcing properties such that, when a self-injurious child is released from restraint, self-injury is exhibited in order to obtain the replacement of restraint. Furthermore, if physical restraint replacement has reinforcing properties to a child, it may be amenable for manipulation as such, in the context of a behavioral treatment intervention. Further investigations are encouraged on the current and alternative uses of physical restraint devices with self-injurious children. (18 ref)

Friedin, Bruce D. (Brooklyn Developmental Ctr, NY) Research & the Retarded, 1977, Vol 4(1), 1–6. [PA, Vol 59:12648]

2248. **The effect of experimenter facial orientation during imitation maintenance.**
Investigated the roles played by less conspicuous but functionally important components of a training "package" of imitative responding. Results from 3 retarded children indicate that imitation of 2 topographical types of models ("standing" and "sitting") was dependent on the presence of experimenter facial orientation within the experimental procedure.
Garcia, Eugene E. & Trujillo, Alex. (U Utah) Journal of Applied Behavior Analysis, 1977(Spr), Vol 10(1), 95. [PA, Vol 59:01557]

2249. **A durable enuresis alarm.**
Describes an enuresis alarm, especially designed for use with highly destructive mentally retarded children, that is relatively inexpensive and can be made by persons with no specialized skills. After approximately 8 mo of continuous use, it has proven to be very durable and a reliable indicator of bedwetting.
Hanson, Ronald H.; Myers, Carol J. & Schwarzkopf, Karl H. (Minnesota Learning Ctr, Brainerd) Behavioral Engineering, 1977, Vol 4(2), 51–54. [PA, Vol 62:04138]

2250. **Behavioral training for parents of retarded children: Alternative formats based on instructional manuals.**
Tested a series of instructional manuals about behavior modification with retarded children as a self-contained resource, and as part of 3 larger training programs involving different amounts of professional assistance to parents: telephone consultations, training groups, and training groups plus home visits. 160 families with retarded children were randomly assigned to the 4 training conditions or to a delayed-treatment control group. The 20-wk treatment period emphasized the programing of self-help skills, but also provided an introduction to programing language skills and managing behavior problems. Results show that the manuals-alone format was as effective as the more expensive training formats in producing gains in children's self-help skills and fostering knowledge of behavioral principles in mothers. The 2 group-training formats produced more efforts at behavior-problem management, greater gains in knowledge of principles by fathers, and higher self-confidence as teachers. Telephone consultation was generally the least effective training format. Implications of the results for future strategies of family intervention are discussed. (32 ref)
Heifetz, Louis J. (Yale U) Journal of Autism & Childhood Schizophrenia, 1977(Sep), Vol 82(2), 194–203. [PA, Vol 60:05640]

2251. **Institutionalized adolescents' perceptions of a summer camp program.**
51 of 80 institutionalized adolescents, average age 16.5 yrs, responded to open-ended questionnaires sent 1-mo post-camp. Ss' diagnostic classifications ranged from mental retardation and brain damage to schizophrenia and adjustment problems. Results suggest that Ss perceived camp as an excellent experience, from which they learned much.
Herr, David E. (James Madison U) Adolescence, 1977(Fal), Vol 12(47), 421–431. [PA, Vol 60:12286]

2252. **Suppression of a retardate's tongue protrusion by contingent imitation: A case study.**
A case study of a 12-yr-old retarded boy treated for tongue protrusion demonstrated that contingent imitation can be used to suppress a persistent inappropriate behavior and that cues associated with imitation can be used to maintain the level of suppression once the model's mimicry is withdrawn.
Kauffman, James; Hallahan, Daniel P. & Ianna, Susan. (U Virginia) Behaviour Research & Therapy, 1977, Vol 15(2), 196–197. [PA, Vol 59:03881]

2253. **Dance therapy.**
Summarizes the state of the art for dance therapy. Aimed at channeling tension toward bodily integration, appropriate affect, insight into behavior, and improved social interaction, dance therapy combines principles from bioenergetics and Gestalt

therapy while also emphasizing body activity. Particularly helpful when verbal communication is blocked, it has succeeded with psychotics, normal neurotics, and children with emotional disturbances, learning disabilities, and mental retardation. The little research thus far, while indicating dance therapy's effectiveness, has been inconclusive. Nonetheless, the dance therapy movement has yielded several body movement diagnostic instruments and has made therapists more aware of body movement's importance. (23 ref)
Kavaler, Susan & Riess, Bernard F. (Postgraduate Ctr for Mental Health, New York, NY) Transnational Mental Health Research Newsletter, 1977(Spr), Vol 19(1), 2–5. [PA, Vol 59:12659]

2254. Overcorrection: An effective procedure that failed.
Reports on an overcorrection procedure used to modify the high rate of head-striking behavior of a 10-yr-old retarded girl. While the treatment was effective in reducing the behavior, the staff ultimately abandoned it because it could not be implemented in their applied setting. It is suggested that while technically effective treatments are available for such disorders, greater attention must be paid to staff response, cost, and implementation factors, which may make even effective treatments impractical. (16 ref)
Kelly, Jeffrey A. & Drabman, Ronald S. (U Mississippi Medical Ctr, Jackson) Journal of Clinical Child Psychology, 1977(Win), Vol 6(3), 38–40. [PA, Vol 62:06665]

2255. The modification of socially detrimental behavior.
Notes that maladaptive behaviors of retarded persons which lead to immediately self-injurious or disruptive consequences have received much clinical/experimental attention. However, there is a broader class of behaviors which, while not so immediately dramatic, can exert a seriously detrimental influence on the social adjustment of retarded individuals because other people find the actions unpleasant or disquieting. In an own-control paradigm, the high frequency tongue-extension of a poorly functioning 34-mo-old female was the target for modification. Results show that modification employing lemon juice as an aversive substance reduced the target behavior to low levels. Results also show that when tongue thrusts were reduced, the child showed greatly increased social responsiveness and others showed more positive reactions to her.
Kelly, Jeffrey A. & Drabman, Ronald S. (U Mississippi Medical Ctr) Journal of Behavior Therapy & Experimental Psychiatry, 1977(Mar), Vol 8(1), 101–104. [PA, Vol 59:06136]

2256. Human sexuality: Expanding self-awareness in a leisure setting.
Describes the operation and goals of Camp Kohai, a program for children, adolescents, and adults who are mentally retarded or have learning disabilities or emotional and behavioral problems. The program integrates learning and living with a program of sex education which includes teaching self-awareness, concern for others, and basic sensitivity.
Lebrun, Simone & Hutchinson, Peggy. (Kohai Educational Ctr, Toronto, Canada) Journal of Leisurability, 1977(Apr), Vol 4(2), 6–8. [PA, Vol 60:01397]

2257. Group work with mentally retarded foster adolescents.
Describes a group formed for mentally retarded adolescents who were in foster care. Members were a behaviorally heterogeneous group of boys and girls from ages 13 to 18. Initial preparation and interviews were viewed as important in helping the children overcome initial fears. Simple games and crafts served as a bridge to sharing, expressing feelings, and ego-building. As intimacy developed, an empathic worker encouraged greater verbal expression and communication of feelings about such life problems as being in foster care. Members learned to support each other. With caring and acceptance, along with clear limits, these adolescents overcame isolation, attained a sense of their own worth, and learned to help and be helped.
Lee, Judith A. (New York U School of Social Work) Social Casework, 1977(Mar), Vol 58(3), 164–173. [PA, Vol 60:09906]

2258. Group therapy for parents of mentally retarded children.
Describes a program that gave parents of mentally retarded children an opportunity to explore their own needs and difficulties. The program involved 6 couples in group settings. The leaders concluded that the most effective approach was an eclectic one including Rogerian reflection, Freudian interpretation, A. Ellis's reality therapy, Gestalt techniques, and learning-theory-based behavior modification. Most parents proved to be compassionate and insightful group members with a great deal to offer each other. (22 ref)
Loeb, Roger C. (Lehigh U) Journal of Marital & Family Therapy, 1977(Apr), Vol 3(2), 77–83. [PA, Vol 59:03829]

2259. Case report: An attendant-administered contingency management programme for the treatment of a toileting phobia.
A 15-yr-old mentally retarded male, institutionalized for 11 yrs, displayed an intense fear of urinating in a toilet. As a result, he wet his pants at a frequent rate. In an attempt to eliminate this fear a variety of response-contingent consequences were programmed (token reinforcement, social reinforcement, and time-out). The effects of introducing structured contingencies resulted in a steady reduction in the frequency of pants wettings. During a follow-up phase of evaluation, when programmed contingencies were discontinued, the problem behavior had been completely eliminated. At that time the S was initiating his own bathroom visits and toileting himself in an appropriate manner.
Luiselli, J. K. (Crosby School, Behavioural Intervention Project, Arlington, MA) Journal of Mental Deficiency Research, 1977(Dec), Vol 21(4), 283–288. [PA, Vol 61:06569]

2260. Teaching a picture language to a non-speaking retarded boy.
Reports the case of a 14-yr-old retarded boy with unreliable hearing (which ruled out spoken language) who was unable to learn receptive or expressive sign language after extensive operant training, but who rapidly acquired a limited symbolic language (pictorial representations of objects) after an identical training method. (17 ref)
Murphy, G. H. et al. (U London Inst of Psychiatry, England) Behaviour Research & Therapy, 1977, Vol 15(2), 198–201. [PA, Vol 59:03890]

2261. Assessing the intellectual consequences of early intervention with high-risk infants.
Infants at risk for mental retardation were divided into a group that received early day-care intervention and a matched control group that did not. The purpose was to prevent sociocultural retardation. 23 Ss were tested at 7 mo and 24 at 18 mo of age on a simple 2-choice visual-discrimination task and on the Bayley Scales of Infant Development to assess the impact of the intervention on their development. The experimental group's performance was reliably superior to that of the control group on both measures, and experimental Ss scoring high on the Bayley Scales reached criterion on the discrimination task on fewer trials than low Bayley scorers. The relationship was particularly strong at 18 mo.
Ramey, Craig T. & Smith, Barbara J. (U North Carolina) American Journal of Mental Deficiency, 1977(Jan), Vol 81(4), 318–324. [PA, Vol 58:05986]

2262. Community services for developmentally handicapped children: To value or evaluate.
Contends that it is not enough to develop a new range of community services for developmentally handicapped children; these services must be subjected to continued evaluation to ensure that their intended quality is realized. All programs must be evaluated, problems inherent in an evaluative process must be acknowledged and identified, and all existing evaluation resources must be utilized.
Ramsden, Marna. Ontario Psychologist, 1977(Jul), Vol 9(3), 36–38. [PA, Vol 61:11477]

2263. Mentally retarded, hyperkinetic and psychotic.
Presents the case of an 18-yr-old mentally retarded hyperkinetic female who experienced 3 acute psychotic episodes. Treatment with phenothiazines was discontinued because the patient lost

control of all sphincter muscles, experienced muscle restlessness and flailing limbs, and developed woody muscle rigidity without affectual response. Following her 3rd psychotic episode, the use of molindone (5 and 10 mg) produced no undesirable side effects, and the patient was able to function socially. Possible reasons for this latter response and the need for clinical study of phenothiazine-sensitivity in adolescents and adults are discussed.
Renshaw, Domeena C. (Loyola U of Chicago) Diseases of the Nervous System, 1977(Jul), Vol 38(7), 575–576. [PA, Vol 60:03604]

2264.　Contributions of dance therapy in a treatment program for retarded adolescents and adults.
Presents a condensed version of a more complex study of how mentally retarded persons communicate nonverbally. Nonverbal communication is a particularly effective form of intervention with those whose verbal ability is limited. The method of observation and scoring was based on R. Laban's "effort/shape" system. It was found that people with higher cognitive ratings showed greater movement complexity. There was a tendency, too, for movement complexity to increase as the social skill level rose. Three clinical examples of the therapeutic applications of these findings are presented.
Rogers, Susan B. (Hahnemann Medical Coll, Philadelphia, PA) Arts in Psychotherapy, 1977, Vol 4(3–4), 195–197. [PA, Vol 62:09056]

2265.　Intensive feeding training with retarded children.
An intensive feeding program previously developed for adult retardates was modified for use with 6 low functioning retarded children under 4 conditions: baseline, training, maintenance, and follow-up. (Ss had CAs ranging from 3.5 to 13.5 yrs and social or mental ages ranging from .75 to 1.62 yrs, according to the Vineland Social Maturity Scale or the Cattell Infant Intelligence Scale.) Ss were given 6 meals/day with a maximum eating time of 15 min/meal. A spoon was the only utensil used in training. Graduated guidance faded from hand to shoulder was used to establish correct feeding responses. Restitutional and positive practice overcorrection were used for incorrect responses, and tray time-out and restitutional overcorrection were used for inappropriate behaviors. In all Ss, correct eating responses increased to nearly optimal levels, incorrect eating responses were reduced to minimal levels, and inappropriate or disruptive behaviors were virtually eliminated. Follow-up data on intervals up to 1 yr indicate that the effects were durable and justified the approximately 173 training sessions that were required for each S. (17 ref)
Stimbert, Vaughn E.; Minor, Jane W. & McCoy, James F. (U Tennessee Child Development Ctr, Behavior Modification Clinic, Memphis) Behavior Modification, 1977(Oct), Vol 1(4), 517–530. [PA, Vol 60:07914]

2266.　Why no guidelines for behavior modification?
Reviews the guidelines for behavioral programs published by the National Association of Retarded Children, and discusses several reasons why guidelines should not be enunciated for behavior modification. Alternative methods for protecting the rights of clients in behavioral programs (e.g., professional ethics codes) are recommended. (28 ref)
Stolz, Stephanie B. (NIMH Small Grants Section, Rockville, MD) Journal of Applied Behavior Analysis, 1977(Fal), Vol 10(3), 541–547. [PA, Vol 60:08110]

2267.　Informing parents about mental retardation: A study of professional communication and parent acceptance.
Examined the nature and outcome of professional communication with parents of 37 mentally retarded children. The research was conducted at a multidisciplinary, diagnostic clinic for children with developmental disabilities. Data collection steps included interviewing parents before and after they received a report of the diagnostic findings, observing professional–parent interaction during the so-called "informing interview," and reviewing medical records and questionnaires. Results indicate that the professionals discussed the diagnosis of mental retardation with varying degrees of frankness, explained the concept of

mental retardation in less than one-third of the cases, and discussed certain test results in about half of the cases. There was a significant relationship between the nature of professional communication and the parents' willingness to accept the diagnosis of mental retardation; parents who received specific, clear, and frank communication were more apt to accept the diagnosis. Parental acceptance was not significantly related to the characteristics of the child, the parents, or the professional who informed them.
Svarstad, Bonnie L. & Lipton, Helene L. (U Wisconsin) Social Science & Medicine, 1977(Sep), Vol 11(11–13), 645–651. [PA, Vol 61:01286]

2268.　The evolution of programs for blind mentally retarded children in residential facilities.
A review of the literature reveals that for the 1st quarter of the 20th century, most of the discussion centered on who was responsible for mentally retarded blind children—educators of the blind or educators of the mentally retarded. There are currently 44 institutions in the US for blind mentally retarded children, and program development is proceeding rapidly in response to pressure from parents, professionals, and the community. (43 ref)
Tretakoff, Maurice I. Journal of Visual Impairment & Blindness, 1977(Jan), Vol 71(1), 29–33. [PA, Vol 61:06765]

2269.　Survival skills for community-bound retarded youths.
Argues that removing retarded individuals from large institutions and placing them in community settings has significant social and economic advantages. Unfortunately, few programs have been developed to aid residents in their difficult transition from the institution to the community. The mechanics are described for developing self-paced programs to teach community skills, using as an example a system that was developed for teaching shopping skills to retarded adolescents. (10 ref)
Weitz, Steven E. & Roll, David L. (Children's Psychiatric Ctr/Community Mental Health Ctr, Red Bank, NJ) Journal of Clinical Child Psychology, 1977(Win), Vol 6(3), 41–44. [PA, Vol 62:06819]

2270.　Theory and practice of art therapy with the mentally retarded.
Describes the use of art therapy with a 22-yr-old mentally retarded female to illustrate some of the features of pathology associated with mental retardation and the practical application of art therapy to many of the problems. It is noted that since art therapy is particularly adept with nonverbal approaches, the intellectual impairment of the mentally retarded does not present a substantial obstacle to treatment. In 2 yrs of art therapy with the S, gradual progression was apparent, in both art expression and general behavior, from an infantile dependency to greater maturity. By partially satisfying some of her needs both artistic and personal (object fixation and the need for constant reassurance), she became more flexible and independent. It is argued that the frequency of pathological or arrested ego development among the mentally retarded clearly supports a mode of treatment such as art therapy, which appears to foster ego development through the development of a mature body image.
Wilson, Laurie. (New York U) American Journal of Art Therapy, 1977(Apr), Vol 16(3), 87–97. [PA, Vol 61:01462]

2271.　Durable, efficient, and economical electronic toilet-training devices for use with retarded children.
Describes the construction of 2 sets of electronic devices to aid in training correct toileting behavior in retarded children. Two sets of units are involved: a body-worn alerting unit in vest or harness form which monitors the child's elimination as he or she moves through the environment, and a toilet-installed unit which monitors elimination on a commode. Both devices contain moisture detection circuits and have been shown to be reliable and efficient in over 3 yrs of testing.
Yonovitz, A. & Michaels, Robert. (U Texas Health Science Ctr, Speech & Hearing Inst, Houston) Behavior Research Methods & Instrumentation, 1977(Aug), Vol 9(4), 356–358. [PA, Vol 59:11399]

2272.   Punishment of self-injurious behavior in natural settings using contingent aromatic ammonia.
Used contingent aromatic ammonia to suppress the self-injurious behavior (SIB) of 2 retarded children (aged 3 and 4 yrs) in clinic, home, and school settings. In Study 1, several reversals demonstrated the effectiveness of a 3-sec ammonia contingency in the deceleration of hair-pulling in the clinic. A momentary ammonia contingency was found to be no different from differential reinforcement of other behavior. Family members and school personnel suppressed the behavior in the home and school in a multiple baseline fashion. Difficulties in long-term maintenance were encountered. Study 2 demonstrated the effectiveness of response-duration ammonia in eliminating hand-biting. Complete suppression was maintained at a 1-yr follow-up. These studies replicate the suppressive effects of aromatic ammonia, extend the findings to children with different SIBs in natural settings, demonstrate the necessity for different durations of ammonia, and suggest that maintenance must be assessed and programmed rather than assumed. (29 ref)
Altman, Karl; Haavik, Sarah & Cook, J. William. (U Kansas Medical Ctr, Children's Rehabilitation Unit, Kansas City) Behaviour Research & Therapy, 1978, Vol 16(2), 85–96. [PA, Vol 62:11474]

2273.   The Croydon workshop for parents of pre-school mentally handicapped children.
A multidisciplinary team of professionals met the parents of 25 preschool handicapped children for a series of evening meetings to discuss how professionals and parents could help the development of the child. The workshop was well-attended by parents who received practical advice from both the professionals and other parents. Multidisciplinary parents workshops appear to be an effective community service for the parents of handicapped children. (19 ref)
Attwood, Tony. (St Lawrence's Hosp, Caterham, England) Child Care, Health & Development, 1978(Mar–Apr), Vol 4(2), 79–97. [PA, Vol 62:01724]

2274.   Toilet training the retarded: An analysis of the stages of development and procedures for designing programs.
The developmental sequence of bladder and bowel control is outlined, and the deficiencies in the sequence, which are frequently experienced by the retarded, are described. Guidelines are provided for designing toilet training programs that are appropriate to the developmental stage and the requirements of the S and his or her environment. (65 ref)
Bettison, Sue. (U Adelaide, Mental Health Services, Australia) Australian Journal of Developmental Disabilities, 1978(Sep), Vol 5(3), 95–100. [PA, Vol 63:08032]

2275.   A clarification of sensory integrative therapy and its application to programming with retarded people.
Sensory integrative therapy as described by A. J. Ayres (1972) is being applied and modified for use with retarded children and adults. This paper clarifies the theoretical base of sensory integrative therapy, discusses appropriate target populations, and reviews pertinent research findings with retarded persons. A bibliography that lists resources in order of technical difficulty is included. (31 ref)
Clark, Florence A. & Shuer, Julie. (U Southern California) Mental Retardation, 1978(Jun), Vol 16(3), 227–232. [PA, Vol 62:08948]

2276.   Techniques for recruiting foster homes for mentally retarded children.
Investigated how a mass media campaign affected the manner in which individuals became aware of the Lancaster (Nebraska) Office of Mental Retardation (LOMR) program and were influenced to become foster parents of retarded children. Data were collected from 37 families who had begun foster parenting since the initiation of the campaign. Results show the following: (a) 32 LOMR parents either knew foster parents or were themselves foster parents for another agency before they became foster parents for LOMR; (b) only 8 Ss knew another LOMR foster parent before being recruited; (c) 22 Ss who were new to foster parenting and who had been made aware of LOMR by mass media already knew other foster parents before they became one for LOMR; (d) LOMR foster parents and those from another agency were highly influenced by interpersonal communication. It is concluded that it is unrealistic to expect to recruit foster parents from the general population by media campaigns if they have had no previous contact with foster parents.
Coyne, Ann. (U Nebraska School of Social Work, Omaha) Child Welfare, 1978(Feb), Vol 57(2), 123–131. [PA, Vol 61:06251]

2277.   Teaching janitorial skills to the mentally retarded: Acquisition, generalization, and maintenance.
A task analysis of janitorial skills required for cleaning a restroom yielded 6 subtasks with a total of 181 component responses. Six 13–15 yr old Ss (IQs 40–50) were required to progress through a series of 4 prompt levels ordered generally from more to less direct assistance for 20 of the most difficult components. Another series of 4 prompts, ordered from less to more direct assistance, was used to teach the other 161 responses. Ss progressed to the next more intense prompt level contingent on failure to respond appropriately with less assistance. A multiple baseline across Ss and subtasks was employed to evaluate the efficacy of the procedures. Ss were trained in their public school. Results show rapid response acquisition, skill generalization to a 2nd restroom, and maintenance of the newly learned behavior. The present research provides evidence of a model for analyzing vocational skills and teaching them to the mentally retarded. (8 ref)
Cuvo, Anthony J.; Leaf, Ronald B. & Borakove, Larry S. (Southern Illinois U, Rehabilitation Inst, Carbondale) Journal of Applied Behavior Analysis, 1978(Fal), Vol 11(3), 345–355. [PA, Vol 63:08412]

2278.   Teaching change computation to the mentally retarded.
Instructional procedures for teaching change computation skills were developed and evaluated on 3 mentally retarded adolescents (MA 8–9 yrs, CA 17, 13, and 17 yrs). A multiple baseline across Ss combined with a multiple baseline across responses was employed. Four response classes, each defined by a different manner of computing change, were taught. Instructional techniques involved (a) training problems in which the proper responses were modeled, (b) practice problems in which correct responses were reinforced and incorrect responses resulted in corrective feedback, and (c) review problems in which previously trained response classes were rehearsed prior to instruction on a new class. Retraining was provided when Ss' performance fell below the designated criterion. Shaping, chaining, and modeling were the principal antecedent conditions; information feedback and tangible reinforcers were used as consequences. The results show virtually 100% performance on a posttest and follow-up test. Idiosyncratic patterns of generalization across response classes are noted. (16 ref)
Cuvo, Anthony J.; Veitch, Vicky D.; Trace, Michael W. & Konke, Janis L. (Southern Illinois U, Carbondale) Behavior Modification, 1978(Oct), Vol 2(4), 531–548. [PA, Vol 64:01638]

2279.   Hospital care of the ill child with mental retardation.
Suggests that hospital personnel can respond to the needs of the mentally retarded child who is hospitalized by determining the child's level of independence and methods of communication at home. Professionals must initiate interactions with the child and must be prepared to give progress reports to parents. An advocacy role is recommended. (6 ref)
Erickson, Marcene P. (U Utah Graduate School of Social Work) Developmental Medicine & Child Neurology, 1978(Oct), Vol 20(5), 674–677. [PA, Vol 63:10350]

2280.   Sharing the caring: A Swedish approach to short-term care of mentally handicapped children.
Describes the establishment of a short-stay home, which offers temporary care for mentally handicapped children living with their parents in one Swedish county. An approach is presented that parents, care staff, and the supervising psychologist have all found satisfactory in contrast to the provision previously available in hospital units.

Evans, Rosemary & Fyhr, Gurli. (Charing Cross Hosp, Child Development Ctr, London, England) Child Care, Health & Development, 1978(Mar–Apr), Vol 4(2), 69–78. [PA, Vol 62:01741]

2281. Stability and attitudes of primary caregivers in the community.
48 primary caregivers in community living facilities (foster, group, and adult homes) were interviewed personally to examine both stability and attitudes toward mentally retarded persons. Job interests and attitudes among all Ss reflected a strong humanistic orientation. Most wished that their jobs would allow more time for interacting with and/or instructing residents. *Felsenthal, D. & Scheerenberger, R. C.* (U Wisconsin, Harry A. Waisman Ctr on Mental Retardation & Human Development, Madison) Mental Retardation, 1978(Feb), Vol 16(1), 16–18. [PA, Vol 61:09047]

2282. Foster home care for mentally retarded children: Can it work?
Investigated whether retarded children reared in foster care program could adjust to life in the community. Only children who were so damaged organically that they were unlikely to move beyond the stage of needing complete care and those whose organic damage interfered with developing control were restricted from the program. Of 40 children studied, 12 tested as trainable to low trainable, 14 tested as educable, and 14 had recorded IQs of over 70 but were functioning at an extremely low level and had serious organic problems that interfered with personality functioning. The 1st complete physical, mental, and social evaluation revealed that although 1 S showed some regression on the IQ test, all but 4 other Ss showed increases up to 10 or 11 points, several moving from trainable to educable. Much of the improvement was, as expected, pseudoimprovement, with subsequent progress predicted to be much slower. *Freeman, Henry.* (Family & Children's Service, Pittsburgh, PA) Child Welfare, 1978(Feb), Vol 57(2), 113–121. [PA, Vol 61:06254]

2283. ["Feeblemindedness" and its treatment.] (Germ)
Recent research has shown that mental retardation is not due solely to hereditary factors; rather, it is determined in large part by the social environment. It is suggested that as early as in utero, one's social surroundings can have an effect and that the retardate is born with the stigma of being a pariah. Possibilities for treatment are discussed, and it is argued that more attention should be given to largely unused areas of personal development and interpersonal communication. (German summary) (20 ref) *Gastager, Susanne.* Zeitschrift für Klinische Psychologie und Psychotherapie, 1978; Vol 26(1), 54–61. [PA, Vol 65:05687]

2284. Early intervention: A personal view.
Expresses doubts about some aspects of early intervention (EI) programs for handicapped children and cites A. Gesell's (1944, 1966) findings that development depends on maturation of the CNS. Questions are raised concerning (a) the emotional effects of EI on child and family, (b) the theory of normalization, and (c) the emphases of some EI programs on IQ. The importance of parental involvement and etiological diagnosis is noted. (13 ref) *Graves, Philip.* Australian Journal of Mental Retardation, 1978(Sep), Vol 5(3), 85–87. [PA, Vol 63:07911]

2285. A special foster care program: Reimbursement for parents and consultants.
Describes the reimbursement-determination component of a community placement program for retarded children. This population makes special demands on foster parents and requires services of consultants in order to insure continued success of placement. Reimbursement of selected parents must be high enough to recognize the extra effort they expend and low enough to be acceptable to funding sources. The formula used by the program includes the child's level of functioning, special placement circumstances, parents' need for consultative services, and program overhead costs, to arrive at the total placement cost and to allocate money to program, parents, and consultants. The

actual fee structure of the program is described, and an example of the use of the formula is given. (5 ref) *Hampson, Robert B.; Tavormina, J. B.; Naiman, Rubin & Kriendler, Jack.* (Southern Methodist U) Administration in Mental Health, 1978(Win), Vol 6(2), 147–153. [PA, Vol 66:06462]

2286. Psychotic behavior in children under the institutions for the mentally retarded in Denmark.
Attempted to identify children with psychotic behavior in the institutions for the mentally retarded in Denmark and to use the data for an analysis of psychotic behavior. The 392 Ss consisted of 2 groups selected from a central register: (a) 217 representative Ss (i.e., every 4th child between the ages of 3.5 and 13.5 yrs), and (b) 175 psychotic Ss selected from the remaining children. A combined observation and interview scheme with 17 behavioral items and 6 developmental scales was constructed. After a 3-wk observation period, Ss were evaluated on the scheme by the adult who had the closest contact with each S. The observer was then interviewed by one of the investigators. Scoring systems for psychotic behavior were constructed and their consistency was analyzed by the Rasch item-analysis model. Two major behavioral dimensions—bizarre behavior and psychotic withdrawal—were used for the diagnostic grouping of the Ss. The distributions of the Ss with regard to developmental retardation, organic brain damage, and psychiatric diagnoses were investigated. Conclusions regarding guidelines for reorganization of present services and establishment of new services are proposed. (23 ref) *Haracopos, Demetri & Kelstrup, Anders.* (Sofieskolen, Bagsvard, Denmark) Journal of Autism & Developmental Disorders, 1978(Mar), Vol 8(1), 1–12. [PA, Vol 61:13631]

2287. Working with parents of mentally handicapped children on a longterm basis.
Discusses some of the problems which occurred over a 4.5-yr period in working with a group of parents of preschool and school age mentally handicapped children. *Harris, John.* (Trent Polytechnic, Nottingham, England) Child Care, Health & Development, 1978(Mar–Apr), Vol 4(2), 121–130. [PA, Vol 62:01608]

2288. Teaching an artificial language to nonverbal retardates.
Taught 8 nonverbal retarded Ss to communicate utilizing a technique developed by D. Premack (1970, 1972). Ss were moderately to profoundly retarded and had not responded to other forms of remedial language therapy. A behavioral approach was used in which plastic shapes represented words of varying degrees of abstractness. All 8 Ss learned some words within a 4-mo training period. Six of the 8 Ss learned to construct 3- to 7-word sentences. The rate of learning and level of difficulty attained varied greatly, and was not correlated with MA or CA. Children in a normal nursery school comparison group learned all words and constructed 3- to 7-word sentences within a 3-wk period. (34 ref) *Hodges, Patricia M. & Deich, Ruth F.* (California State U, Los Angeles) Behavior Modification, 1978(Oct), Vol 2(4), 489–509. [PA, Vol 64:01648]

2289. Behaviour therapy in clinical child psychiatry: A preliminary report.
Conducted behavioral therapy with 33 children and their families in a clinical setting. Six of the children were severely subnormal (IQ below 50); all the others were in the range of normal or superior intelligence (IQs of 70 or more). Treatment techniques included desensitization, immediate reinforcement, token economies, and self-monitoring. For 21 of the Ss, ratings of improvement were made by the therapist; for the others, ratings were made by the parents, using the same criteria as the therapists. Results show that 24 of the Ss had improved, suggesting that behavior therapy can be used across a wide range of children, with a variety of ages, intelligence levels, social classes, or behavior problems. (18 ref)

Levere, Ruth H. (Hosp for Sick Children, Dept of Psychological Medicine, London, England) Child Care, Health & Development, 1978(Jul–Aug), Vol 4(4), 261–272. [PA, Vol 62:14247]

2290. Controlling self-inflicted biting of a retarded child by the differential reinforcement of other behavior.
Controlled the self-inflicted biting of a retarded child in 3 classroom settings using a program of differential reinforcement of other behavior. The functional control of the reinforcement contingency was demonstrated through use of a multiple-baseline design.
Luiselli, James K. et al. (Behavioral Intervention Project, Arlington, MA) Psychological Reports, 1978(Apr), Vol 42(2), 435–438. [PA, Vol 62:01620]

2291. Effects and side-effects of a brief overcorrection procedure in reducing multiple self-stimulatory behaviour: A single case analysis.
Describes the use of positive practice overcorrection to reduce the classroom self-stimulatory behavior of a 10-yr-old mentally retarded child. An initial attempt to reduce 4 stereotyped hand movements through reinforcement of incompatible behavior resulted in a decrease in 3 types of behavior and an increase in the 4th. When 1 minute of positive practice overcorrection was then made contingent upon the increased behavior, it was immediately reduced to near-zero levels with accompanying low occurrences of all other behavior forms. Response suppression was durable following evaluation of the procedure at 2- and 3.5-mo follow-ups. (10 ref)
Luiselli, James K.; Pemberton, B. W. & Helfen, Carol S. (Boston U) Journal of Mental Deficiency Research, 1978(Dec), Vol 22(4), 287–293. [PA, Vol 64:06164]

2292. Family therapy in child and adolescent psychiatry: A review of 35 families.
A retrospective study of 35 families who received family therapy revealed that 40% dropped out after the 1st 6–10 sessions despite precautions taken to accept only motivated families. The clinical impression is that family therapy with families having antisocial children proved a failure. Suggested reasons for this outcome include the fact that these families came from the lower socioeconomic levels and members could not be motivated for therapy. Very poor intrafamilial interpersonal relationships further hindered them from coping in an open and objective manner. Family therapy among the problematic retardates and the problematic adolescents is considered to have been helpful. Both groups came from higher socioeconomic levels and were deemed better motivated to take an interest in the patient and improve family interaction. The families who successfully completed the treatment communicated better, developed mutual understanding, and grew in tolerance for each other. Pathological hatred and rejection were replaced by acceptance and adequate amounts of love and family harmony.
Master, Roshan S. Child Psychiatry Quarterly, 1978(Jul–Sep), Vol 11(3), 70–82. [PA, Vol 63:10166]

2293. Utilization of a multidisciplinary center by bilingual clients.
Reports a preliminary investigation of the uses made of specialized bilingual clinical services for mentally retarded children by a group of Cubans. The extensive engagement as consumers seemed to be related to their relatively greater availability. Typical procedures are also noted. (Spanish abstract) (3 ref)
McGrath, Frances C.; Montiel, Pedro A.; Shellhase, Leslie J. & Silva, Maria. (U Miami, FL) Revista Interamericana de Psicología, 1978, Vol 12(1), 59–65. [PA, Vol 65:13386]

2294. The blind and visually handicapped mentally retarded: Suggestions for intervention in infancy.
Presents a rationale for implementing early transdisciplinary intervention in behalf of blind and visually handicapped, mentally retarded infants. A program is described that stresses normal developmental goals, a holistic approach to the child and family, and techniques for enhancing the development of the child's reflexes and gross motor skills; sensory, cognitive and fine motor skills; language; and affective personality and independence. The

roles of professionals and parents receive special emphasis. (43 ref)
Mori, Allen A. & Olive, Jane E. (U Nevada, Las Vegas) Journal of Visual Impairment & Blindness, 1978(Sep), Vol 72(7), 273–279. [PA, Vol 63:06407]

2295. Public transportation training: In vivo versus classroom instruction.
Evaluated a classroom program to teach public transportation usage (bus riding skills) to retarded persons. Based on a task analysis of specific skills, 5 retarded male students (CAs 18–24 yrs, IQs 46–85) were taught each of the components of locating, signaling, boarding and riding, and exiting a bus. Skills were taught sequentially, using training procedures consisting of role playing, manipulating the actions of a doll on a simulated model, and responding to questions about slide sequences. Before, during, and after training, Ss were tested on generalization probes in the classroom and in the natural environment. Results of a multiple-baseline design across Ss indicate that up to 12 mo after training, each S exhibited appropriate bus riding skills on actual city buses. Two other Ss were trained on each skill component in vivo, on city buses, in order to compare the relative effectiveness and efficiency of classroom vs in vivo training. Both Ss acquired appropriate bus riding skills; however, the in vivo training procedure was more time consuming and expensive than classroom training. (20 ref)
Neef, Nancy A.; Iwata, Brian A. & Page, Terry J. (Western Michigan U) Journal of Applied Behavior Analysis, 1978(Fal), Vol 11(3), 331–344. [PA, Vol 63:08447]

2296. The effects of self-recorders' training and the obtrusiveness of the self-recording device on the accuracy and reactivity of self-monitoring.
To evaluate the effects of training in self-recording, 4 adolescent retarded Ss (mean IQ 64) received intensive training in self-monitoring, while 5 comparable Ss received minimal training. To evaluate the effects of the obtrusiveness of the self-recording device, all 9 Ss self-recorded appropriate classroom verbalizations, sometimes with a hand-held counter and sometimes with a belt-worn counter. Self-monitoring was reactive, producing increases in appropriate verbalizations. Training increased the accuracy but not the reactivity of self-monitoring. The hand-held counter tended to produce more accurate self-recordings and higher frequencies of appropriate verbalizations, although these latter findings were not significant. Results are useful in enhancing both the assessment and therapeutic functions of self-monitoring.
Nelson, Rosemery O.; Lipinski, David P. & Boykin, Ronald A. (U North Carolina, Greensboro) Behavior Therapy, 1978(Mar), Vol 9(2), 200–208. [PA, Vol 61:08965]

2297. Program for developmentally disabled children.
Children who are developmentally disabled are more often handicapped by a lack of social skills than by intellectual limitations. A pilot program that improved the psychosocial functioning of such children by involving them in one-to-one relationships with caring adults is described.
Panzer, Barry M.; Wiesner, Leslie C. & Dickson, William D. (Downstate Medical Ctr, Div of Child & Adolescent Psychiatry, Brooklyn, NY) Social Work, 1978(Sep), Vol 23(5), 406–411. [PA, Vol 64:01739]

2298. Imitation training with a 4-year-old retarded person: The relative efficiency of time-out and extinction in conjunction with positive reinforcement.
A 4-yr-old patient in a hospital for the educationally subnormal was taught to imitate motor responses modelled by the experimenter (E). With 2 of the behaviors, correct imitation was followed by reinforcement (praise and cuddles), and failure to imitate had no consequences. However, with a further 2 behaviors, not only was correct imitation followed by reinforcement, but failure to imitate resulted in 30 sec of time-out during which the E refused all social interaction with the S. Results suggest that a more efficient imitation training program might be

constructed if a punishing consequential event rather than extinction is used to modify inappropriate responses.
Parsons, Jill & Davey, Graham C. Mental Retardation, 1978(Jun), Vol 16(3), 241–245. [PA, Vol 62:09174]

2299. Tay-Sachs and related storage diseases: Family planning.
Discusses family planning and the choices available to those families where a child has previously died from Tay-Sachs or related lipid storage diseases. Findings are based on interviews with 24 families and show that birth order of the diseased child affects family planning.
Schneiderman, Gerald; Lowden, J. Alexander & Rae-Grant, Quentin. (Hosp for Sick Children, Toronto, Canada) Mental Retardation, 1978(Feb), Vol 16(1), 13–15. [PA, Vol 61:08338]

2300. Elimination of echolalic responding to questions through the training of a generalized verbal response.
Echolalia, the parroting of the speech of others, is a severe communication disorder frequently associated with childhood schizophrenia and mental retardation. Two echolalic children, 1 schizophrenic and 1 retarded (ages 7 and 15 yrs, respectively) were treated in a multiple-baseline design across Ss. Each S was taught to make an appropriate, nonecholalic verbal response (i.e., "I don't know") to a small set of previously echoed questions. After such training, this response generalized across a broad set of untrained questions that had formerly been echoed. Results obtained were the same irrespective of the specific experimenter who presented the questions. Further, each S discriminated appropriately between those questions that had previously been echoed and those that had not. Follow-up probes showed that treatment gains were maintained 1 mo later. The procedure is economical, in that it produces a rapid and widespread cessation of echolalic responding. (13 ref)
Schreibman, Laura & Carr, Edward G. (Claremont Men's Coll) Journal of Applied Behavior Analysis, 1978(Win), Vol 11(4), 453–463. [PA, Vol 64:03808]

2301. Rapid reduction of lengthy pausing during vocal responding by nonverbal retarded children.
Results of a study with 6 retarded children (ages 3–10 yrs) indicate that the use of a mildly aversive consequence in escape-avoidance paradigm rapidly reduced lengthy pauses during Ss' vocal responding and also increased Ss' verbal response rates.
Singer, Fredric L.; Pasnak, Robert; Drash, Philip W. & Baer, Richard. (Catholic U of America) Behavior Therapy, 1978(Sep), Vol 9(4), 669–670. [PA, Vol 62:04161]

2302. Task analysis in recreation programs for mentally retarded persons.
Explores the use of task analysis with retarded children: breaking down individual behaviors, teaching them individually, and chaining them together to produce the whole skill. Although task analysis is highly accepted by educators, the difficulty is to break down various behavioral objectives to determine when the child achieves mastery in each step. Each step should require increased precision, speed, or some other quantitative improvement. The advantage of this system is that the child is able to achieve mastery many times while learning, and therefore the rewards of mastery, both while accomplishing a realistic task and while working up to a higher level of goals.
Wehman, Paul. (Virginia Commonwealth U) Journal of Leisurability, 1978(Jan), Vol 5(1), 13–20. [PA, Vol 62:11626]

2303. Improving free play skills of severely retarded children.
Examined the effects of a behavioral training program on the autistic, independent, and social types of play of 4 severely and profoundly retarded children. The training program involved the use of instructions, modeling, physical guidance, and verbal reinforcement. Results indicate that a marked increase in independent and social play occurred with the introduction of the training program with all 4 children. Occupational therapists can play an increasingly important role in helping educators formulate relevant educational programs for severly retarded children, particularly in the areas of play and motor skill development. (19 ref)

Wehman, Paul & Marchant, Jo A. (Virginia Commonwealth U) American Journal of Occupational Therapy, 1978(Feb), Vol 32(2), 100–104. [PA, Vol 61:06592]

2304. Neighbourhood centres: An experimental project in the psycho-educational care of mentally handicapped children in Algiers.
Discusses changing socioeconomic conditions in Algeria and their effect on mentally handicapped children. Efforts to provide assistance and care for such children are noted, especially those of the *Association Aide aux Inadaptés,* a group of parents, teachers, psychologists, and educators with overall responsibility for initiation and management of neighborhood care centers. The physical characteristics, aims, staff makeup, and financial arrangements of 4 day care centers set up by the association are discussed. The centers are viewed as representing a nonmedical approach to the task of caring for mentally handicapped persons; keeping children in their own neighborhoods and ensuring early detection and treatment of maladjustments are seen as important benefits of the program.
Yaker, Annette. (National Inst of Public Health, Psychology Section, Algiers, Algeria) International Child Welfare Review, 1978(Sep–Dec), No 38–39, 61–66. [PA, Vol 64:01496]

2305. Prader-Willi Syndrome: Two case studies.
Examines the medical data and behavioral characteristics of 2 boys born with Prader-Willi Syndrome. Accompanying developmental behavior patterns resulted in the cooperative use of behavior modification techniques that produced a negative and positive response, respectively. Psychological assessment of the syndrome shows similar and consistent characteristics for both boys throughout the study. It is advised that precautionary dietary measures be used as the medical treatment for appetite control.
Bahling, Elizabeth F. (Edinboro School System, Intermediate Unit #5, PA) Bulletin of the British Psychological Society, 1979(Win), Vol 8(1), 133–136. [PA, Vol 62:13919]

2306. [A standardized program for developing play behavior in retarded children.] (Germ)
A 14-step program for developing play behavior in retarded children was designed for use at home, in nursery school, and in kindergarten. The goal of the program was to teach children to play with structured and unstructured materials and to increase their frustration tolerance for withdrawal of the adult. Data collected before, during, and after treatment indicated that the play behavior of 9 brain-damaged children improved in frequency and exactness, regardless of whether or not the therapist was present. Success was evident in play with familiar and unfamiliar materials. Based on the learning curves, conjectures are made as to further treatment. (15 ref)
Brack, Udo B. & Lederer, P. (Klinik des Kinderzentrums München, West Germany) Zeitschrift für Kinder- und Jugendpsychiatrie, 1979, Vol 7(1), 43–54. [PA, Vol 65:06385]

2307. Effects of L-5-hydroxytryptophan on monoamine and amino acids turnover in the Lesch-Nyhan syndrome.
Found decreased spinal fluid 5-hydroxyindoleacetic acid (5-HIAA), the major metabolite of serotonin, and decreased homovanillic acid, the major metabolite of dopamine, indicating a decrease in monoamine metabolism in a male infant with the Lesch-Nyhan syndrome. Administration of 5-hydroxytryptophan and carbidopa produced an increase in spinal fluid 5-HIAA, indicating that it might be possible to correct the serotonin deficiency in this syndrome, but there were no changes in the marked mental retardation and neurological deficits. Self-mutilation appeared to be suppressed by therapy, but the effectiveness of the drugs decreased with time. There were also changes in the spinal fluid concentration of amino acids that might affect brain protein synthesis. These changes were corrected during the administration of 5-hydroxytryptophan and carbidopa. (24 ref)
Castells, Salvador et al. (State U New York, Downstate Medical Ctr) Journal of Autism & Developmental Disorders, 1979(Mar), Vol 9(1), 95–103. [PA, Vol 62:11529]

2308. Deinstitutionalization and community placement: Clinical and environmental factors.
Examined the literature concerning client adaptation after placement into community-based residences from institutions. Findings are as follows: (a) The occurrences of maladaptive behavior in community settings were predictive of institutional readmission, (b) demographic and functional behavior characteristics were inconstantly related to success in the community, (c) sociophysical environmental characteristics of residential alternatives influence behavior in the community, and (d) the concept of successful placement needs to be more explicitly and consistently defined. (31 ref)
Crawford, Jeffrey L.; Aiello, John R. & Thompson, Donna E. (Rockland Research Inst, Orangeburg, NY) Mental Retardation, 1979(Apr), Vol 17(2), 59–63. [PA, Vol 66:08686]

2309. Counseling with handicapped children.
Traditional school counseling practices need to be modified when working with specific subgroups of handicapped children. The learning disabled, for example, often manifest process disorders of attention span and visual/auditory retention that can be barriers to ordinary verbal interchange. Similarly, the mentally retarded and behaviorally disordered/emotionally disturbed frequently exhibit handicap-related impairments that limit their capacity for benefiting from individual or group counseling based on conventional counselor-counselee interaction. Specific counseling strategies, techniques, and skills appropriate to the needs and abilities of disability subgroups are proposed. (10 ref)
DeBlassie, Richard R. & Lebsock, Marjean S. (New Mexico State U) Elementary School Guidance & Counseling, 1979(Feb), Vol 13(3), 199–206. [PA, Vol 63:08461]

2310. [Treatment with carbamazepine of epilepsy with behavioral disorders in mentally retarded children in a medicopedagogic institution.] (Fren)
35 mentally retarded girls with epilepsy associated with behavior disorders were treated with carbamazepine for 4 mo–7 yrs. 50% of the Ss improved, 30% showed a disappearance of the epileptic spells, and 67% showed an aggravation of EEG. Improvement of behavior and absence of spells were observed more frequently in primary generalized epilepsy than in secondary partial epilepsy and were seen least often in secondary generalized epilepsy. Results were also better in dementia epileptica than in epilepsy without dementia. The aggravation of EEG, consistent with the disappearance of epileptic crises and behavioral improvement, is most often observed in Ss with epileptic absences or progressive dementia. (Dutch, German, Italian, & Spanish abstracts) (15 ref)
D'Hollander, Luc. Acta Psychiatrica Belgica, 1979(Sep–Oct), Vol 79(5), 557–569. [PA, Vol 65:10949]

2311. Suppression of chronic drooling in mentally retarded children and adolescents: Effectiveness of a behavioral treatment package.
A treatment package consisting of positive reinforcement for dryness and overcorrection for wetness was used to reduce drooling in 2 populations. Exp I assessed the effectiveness of the procedure with 3 profoundly retarded and physically handicapped Ss, aged 7, 12, and 15 yrs. Exp II examined the effectiveness of the procedure with 2 nonhandicapped moderately and mildly retarded Ss, aged 14 and 15 yrs. In both experiments, the treatment package was effective in reducing or eliminating long-term chronic drooling. Maintenance of gains over a 6-mo period was found for 4 of the 5 Ss. (16 ref)
Drabman, Ronald S.; Cordua y Cruz, Glenn; Rosse, James & Lynd, R. Sterling. (U Mississippi Medical Ctr, Jackson) Behavior Therapy, 1979(Jan), Vol 10(1), 46–56. [PA, Vol 62:06633]

2312. Relationship between community environments and resident changes in adaptive behavior: A path model.
Investigated the relationship between environmental ratings of community homes using factor scores derived from W. Wolfensberger and L. Glenn's Program Analysis of Service Systems (PASS) and changes in adaptive behavior of residents living in those facilities. A path analysis was used to relate resident characteristics (e.g., age, IQ, and initial score on adaptive behavior) with 6 PASS environmental ratings and both of these sets of variables with average annual change in adaptive behavior over a 3-yr period. The 245 Ss varied in age from young children to adults (most Ss were over 18 yrs) and in level of retardation from profound to mild (fewer than 25% were profoundly retarded). Results show that a number of PASS scores were significantly associated with positive change in adaptive behavior for specified types of residents. Older, less retarded Ss improved in all aspects of adaptive behavior in conjunction with positive ratings on items dealing with comfort and deployment of staff, access to the home, local proximity of services, and blending with the neighborhood. (19 ref)
Eyman, Richard K.; Demaine, Gail C. & Lei, Tzuen-jen. (U California Neuropsychiatric Inst–Pacific State Hosp Research Group, Pomona) American Journal of Mental Deficiency, 1979(Jan), Vol 83(4), 330–338. [PA, Vol 62:11614]

2313. Development of articulatory competence in mentally retarded children.
22 mentally retarded children participated in a verbal stimulation program developed at the Institute for Psychophysiological and Speech Disorders in Belgrade, Yugoslavia. Intensive home therapy was associated with an increase in articulatory competence in both moderately and profoundly retarded Ss. The development of articulation differed between retardate groups as well as with the sequence of normal phonological production. Results suggest that the order in which sounds are introduced into the therapeutic program may be a critical factor in the overall development of competent articulation. (27 ref)
Fitzgerald, Hiram E.; Brajović, Cvjetko; Djurdjić, Slavoljub & Djurdjević, Miladin. (Michigan State U) Perceptual & Motor Skills, 1979(Jun), Vol 48(3, Pt 2), 1175–1182. [PA, Vol 64:13095]

2314. The therapeutic use of edited videotapes with an exceptional child.
A 7-yr-old mentally retarded girl with habitual tantrums and considerable off-task behavior was videotaped in class. Training began with a 5-day baseline session during which both tantrums and on-task behaviors were recorded. Next the child was taken to the media room to view a 30-sec sequence of herself engaged in on-task behavior, followed by a 60-sec segment of a cartoon chosen by the child. The videotaped on-task behavior and cartoon were repeated. Then a 30-sec segment of the S in a tantrum was followed by a 60-sec segment on a blank screen. Training continued for 24 min on 5 days; after training there was a 1-day reversal period. Tantrums decreased during intervention and remained low during reversal; on-task behavior was slightly increased.
Greelis, Michael & Kazaoka, Katsushige. (New York Medical Coll, Valhalla) Academic Therapy, 1979(Sep), Vol 15(1), 37–44. [PA, Vol 66:04051]

2315. Training parents of retarded children as behaviour therapists: A review.
Reviews the literature on behaviorally oriented parent training programs where the children involved are mentally retarded. Attention is given to the variety of behavior problems encountered, both in case studies and in group programs. It is suggested that the procedures used with retarded children have been successful, at least in the short term, and that they are similar to those used with nonretarded children. (3 p ref)
Griffin, Michael W. (Queen Victoria Medical Ctr, Melbourne, Australia) Australian Journal of Mental Retardation, 1979(Mar), Vol 5(5), 18–27. [PA, Vol 66:08509]

2316. The potential of relaxation training for the mentally retarded.
Relaxation training has several potential applications for the mentally retarded: eliminating specific phobias, reducing general anxiety, facilitating group and individual psychotherapy, preparing for covert therapies, reducing behavioral difficulties, and coping with specific academic problems. (55 ref)
Harvey, John R. (U Nebraska Medical Ctr, Meyer Children's Rehabilitation Inst, Omaha) Mental Retardation, 1979(Apr), Vol 17(2), 71–76. [PA, Vol 66:08513]

2317. Evaluation of a regional resource center for multiply handicapped retarded children.
Evaluated a demonstration program for multiply handicapped children, using a treatment group of 30 Ss (mean CA 5 yrs 6 mo) and 26 similarly handicapped control Ss (mean CA 6 yrs 7 mo) selected from outside the 100-mile limit of the program. Major program impact was in the area of coordination of services. A significant change to a more negative attitude on the part of treatment group parents with regard to some aspects of normalization was found. (39 ref)
Hetherington, Robert W.; Suttill, Joanne; Holmlund, Cleo & Frey, Douglas D. (HEW National Ctr for Health Service Research, Hyattsville, MD) American Journal of Mental Deficiency, 1979(Jan), Vol 83(4), 367–379. [PA, Vol 62:11617]

2318. Group skills training to increase the conversational repertoire of retarded adolescents.
10 mentally retarded adolescents lacked appropriate social interaction skills and were referred for group conversational skills training. Group treatment consisted of an instruction-modeling-rehearsal procedure sequentially targeting 3 classes of conversational skills: (a) eliciting information from others; (b) appropriate self-disclosing of interests and personal information; and (c) using reinforcing-complimentary conversational behaviors. During baseline and following each training group, social behavior was assessed by recording unstructured 8-min dyadic conversations between randomly-paired Ss. Weekly generalization probes consisted of unstructured 8-min conversations between each S and a different nonretarded, unfamiliar partner. Results indicate that contingent on group targeting of a specific conversational skill, the frequency of that skill increased in both the unstructured dyadic interactions between pairs of retarded Ss and the generalization interactions between retarded Ss and novel nonretarded persons. Follow-up maintenance of skill increases was obtained. The utility of a "single group" multiple baseline design in applied social skills research is discussed. (18 ref)
Kelley, Jeffrey A.; Wildman, Beth G.; Urey, Jon R. & Thurman, Clarence. (U Mississippi Medical Ctr, Jackson) Child Behavior Therapy, 1979(Win), Vol 1(4), 323–336. [PA, Vol 65:08485]

2319. [Ethical problems in the use of behavior modification procedures with the mentally handicapped.] (Fren)
Intervention in mental retardation entails 2 broad ethical considerations whose interdependence is indisputable. The first concerns the status of the therapy; the second is linked to special traits of members of the population to which the therapy is addressed, especially as intensity of handicap decreases the S's control of environment. Ethical problems specific to behavior modification can be subsumed under 2 categories of concern: (a) the philosophy of behavior modification, which directs control of the behavior of the individual and his/her environment; and (b) the punitive techniques that are an accepted part of the behavior modification repertoire. Two steps are suggested when using behavior modification with the mentally handicapped: (a) inform the public, whether specialists or not, about the scope of behavior modification, its methods, principles, and theoretical base; and (b) include behavior therapists as members of multidisciplinary teams working in the area of mental handicap. (6 ref)
Lambert, Jean-Luc. (U de Liège, Lab de Psychologie Expérimentale, Belgium) Bulletin de Psychologie, 1978–79(Sep–Oct), Vol 32(18), 951–956. [PA, Vol 66:01803]

2320. Utilization of manipulative behavior in a retarded asthmatic child.
Used hypnotic techniques with an 11-yr-old mentally retarded asthmatic boy who coughed at night and had other behavior with which his parents could not cope. The 1-session intervention utilized and capitalized on ego-syntonic feelings and behavior and channeled them into more adaptive activity, respected his need for control, reduced the attention-getting value of his misbehavior, and helped his parents handle his attempts to manipulate them. The patient's responses to these techniques were compared with hypnotic phenomena. (25 ref)
Lazar, Billie S. & Jedliczka, Zofia T. (U Illinois Medical Ctr, Chicago) American Journal of Clinical Hypnosis, 1979(Apr), Vol 21(4), 287–292. [PA, Vol 64:10912]

2321. Training in conceptual tempo: Its effects on mentally retarded children's responding style to questionnaire items.
23 "impulsive" mentally retarded adolescents were assigned to 3 conditions: visual discrimination, question-answering, and no treatment control. Nonsignificant differences between groups on some tasks indicate that the training effect on conceptual tempo is task specific.
Lee, Dong Y. & Cottreau, Ruby. (U Western Ontario, Faculty of Education, London, Canada) Psychological Reports, 1979(Feb), Vol 44(1), 198. [PA, Vol 64:03532]

2322. Variables related to progress in a parent infant training program for high-risk infants.
The efficacy of a parent-infant training program was evaluated in terms of S's sex, age, and initial severity of cognitive impairment. Data collected on 32 high-risk infants, over a 1-yr time span, show substantial gains on cognitive and language (expressive and receptive) indices. The relative degree of success on these measures was related to the initial age and initial severity of the infants under study. Results are discussed in terms of effective early intervention strategies that employ parents as the primary intervention agents for high-risk infants. (27 ref)
Maisto, Albert A. & German, Michael L. (U North Carolina, Charlotte) Journal of Pediatric Psychology, 1979(Dec), Vol 4(4), 409–419. [PA, Vol 63:05178]

2323. Involving parents in extending the language development of their young mentally handicapped children.
The parents of 10 3.3–5.8 yr old mentally handicapped children (mean Griffiths General Quotient 53) were solely responsible for carrying out language learning activities at home. Parents were effective in teaching their child to identify and name objects and to structure 2-word sentences. It is argued that a parent-centered approach not only makes more effective use of professional resources but that it may overcome the generalization problems encountered by previous approaches. (17 ref)
McConkey, Roy; Jeffree, Dorothy M. & Hewson, Simon. (St Michael's House, Dublin, Ireland) British Journal of Disorders of Communication, 1979(Dec), Vol 14(3), 203–218. [PA, Vol 66:08406]

2324. Training parents of retarded children as behaviour therapists: What we know. I.
Summarizes research on the efficacy of behaviorally oriented training programs for parents of retarded children. Advantages of this approach are noted: (1) It enables the planned intervention to take place in the milieu where the problem occurs. (2) The potential for the application of preventive strategies rather than curative or ameliorative ones is enhanced. (3) Communication between institutions (e.g., universities, colleges, schools) and parents is facilitated. (37 ref)
Molloy, Geoffrey N. (Monash U, Faculty of Education, Clayton, Australia) Mental Retardation Bulletin, 1979, Vol 7(3), 109–122. [PA, Vol 66:08541]

2325. Use of relaxation in the short-term treatment of fetishistic behavior: An exploratory case study.
An 8-yr-old boy was treated for inappropriate and excessive sexual response in the presence of barefoot women. The boy also suffered from phenylketonuria resulting in mild to moderate mental retardation and hyperactivity. Relaxation training was used for 1 wk of intensive training, followed by approximately 6 mo training via tape recordings in the patient's home. A significant decrease was noted in the target behaviors at the end of Week 1. At 6-, 12-, and 18-mo follow-up, the behavior was reported to be virtually eliminated. (2 ref)
Shaw, William J. & Walker, C. Eugene. (Oklahoma Dept of Corrections, Oklahoma City) Journal of Pediatric Psychology, 1979(Dec), Vol 4(4), 403–407. [PA, Vol 63:05984]

2326.   Self-injury in the de Lange syndrome.
Examined the use of behavioral procedures to treat minor self-injury in a male 13-yr-old de Lange syndrome patient. Results show the effectiveness of mild punishment together with time-out and differential reinforcement of other adaptive behaviors. (23 ref)
Singh, Nirbhay N.   & Pulman, Ruth M. (Mangere Hosp & Training School, Auckland, New Zealand) Journal of Mental Deficiency Research, 1979(Jun), Vol 23(2), 79–84. [PA, Vol 66:06362]

2327.   [Structured grief therapy with children.] (Duth)
Behavioral treatment of pathological grief in a 9-yr-old mentally retarded girl is described as an example of short-term therapy, in which the emotional responses of the child and the mother–child interactions were the focuses of therapy. The pathological aspects of the grieving behavior are considered to be, in part, an analog to phobic behavior and in part as being an element in the mother–child and family interaction. As the number of parental divorces is still growing, grief therapy for children might become increasingly important in the future. (11 ref)
Tieken, Hans M. (U Amsterdam, Netherlands) Tijdschrift voor Psychotherapie, 1979(Mar), Vol 5(2), 85–93. [PA, Vol 65:01815]

2328.   A controlled double-blind study of haloperidol versus thioridazine in the treatment of restless mentally subnormal patients: Serum levels and clinical effects.
Examined the efficacy and side effects of haloperidol (HAL) and thioridazine in the treatment of 30 17–46 yr old moderately and severely retarded patients. Results indicate that the differences between HAL and thioridazine were few, and that drug holidays or withdrawal of medication for 1–3 days/week may benefit patients. (French, Dutch, German, Italian & Spanish abstracts) (8 ref)
Väisänen, K.; Rimón, R.; Räisänen, P. & Viukari, M. (Central Inst of Vaalijala for the Mentally Retarded, Nenonpelto, Finland) Acta Psychiatrica Belgica, 1979(Nov–Dec), Vol 79(6), 673–685. [PA, Vol 66:01876]

2329.   Group treatment of characterologically damaged, developmentally disabled adolescents in a residential treatment center.
Describes the treatment of developmentally disabled, characterologically damaged adolescents through group psychotherapy. While progress was slow, most youngsters developed some capacity for empathy and became supportive of one another. Behavioral improvements were also obvious. Major alterations in the format and techniques used in leading the groups were needed in order to maintain behavioral control and help the youngsters compensate for their social and developmental deficits. (13 ref)
Weinstock, Anne. (Southgate Residential Training Ctr, Behavioral Treatment Unit, MI) International Journal of Group Psychotherapy, 1979(Jul), Vol 29(3), 369–381. [PA, Vol 66:11028]

2330.   Behavioral training for parents of mentally retarded children: One-year follow-up.
Followed up 95 families who had completed a 20-wk behavioral-training program for parents of retarded children (L. J. Heifetz; see PA, Vol 60:5640). Parents had retained their knowledge of programming principles, and children had retained their skill gains. Many families had initiated some teaching of new skills, although few carried out regular formal teaching sessions; 44% of families had continued "useful" or "very useful" teaching. (18 ref)
Baker, Bruce L.; Heifetz, Louis J. & Murphy, Diane M. (U California, Los Angeles) American Journal of Mental Deficiency, 1980(Jul), Vol 85(1), 31–38. [PA, Vol 64:08450]

2331.   A model for psychological consultation to rural development centers.
Presents a consultation model oriented toward serving retarded children in rural child development centers that has 4 components ranging from direct to indirect services and that requires the psychologist to exercise a variety of functions ranging from the traditionally clinical to the more programmatic and community oriented. The model is also seen to address special needs of rural teachers and parents and to require modifications in traditional consultation theory and practice. (9 ref)
Curry, John F.; Anderson, David R. & Munn, Duncan E. (Duke U Medical Ctr) Journal of Rural Community Psychology, 1980(Fal), Vol 1(2), 24–33. [PA, Vol 66:06457]

2332.   Generalization and transfer between comprehension and production: A comparison of retarded and nonretarded persons.
With 10 mentally retarded (MR) Ss (mean CA 16 yrs, mean IQ 44) and 10 nonretarded Ss (mean CA 4 yrs, mean IQ 108), the 2 levels of the IQ Level factor were combined factorially with 2 levels of a training condition factor: Comprehension-Production and Production Only. Ss in the former groups were trained to comprehend coin labels and then produce verbally the correct coin label. Ss in Production Only groups were trained on the latter response only. Both groups attained a high level of acquisition and maintained it on 1- and 4-wk follow-up tests. No difference occurred between groups in magnitude of acquisition, but MRs took 3 times as many trials to complete training. Contrary to past research, generalization from comprehension to production was bidirectional, with no difference in magnitude between groups. Transfer from comprehension to production occurred in both groups; comprehension training facilitated a savings of trials in production training. Results show that language differences between MR and non-MR persons are quantitative rather than qualitative. (30 ref)
Cuvo, Anthony J. & Riva, Maria T. (Southern Illinois U Rehabilitation Inst, Behavior Modification Program, Carbondale) Journal of Applied Behavior Analysis, 1980(Sum), Vol 13(2), 315–331. [PA, Vol 65:13269]

2333.   Lithium therapy in aggressive mentally subnormal patients.
In a series of 15 17–63 yr old aggressive mentally retarded patients treated with lithium, there was an improvement in aggressive behavior in 11 cases, 3 Ss showed no change, and 1 S became worse during treatment. Treatment had to be discontinued in 1 S who developed tardive dyskinesia, but side effects generally were not a problem. (15 ref)
Dale, P. G. (Coldeast Hosp, Southampton, England) British Journal of Psychiatry, 1980(Nov), Vol 137, 469–474. [PA, Vol 66:08574]

2334.   Chronic vomiting and rumination in intellectually normal and retarded individuals: Review and evaluation of behavioral research.
Reviews 26 studies investigating behavioral procedures used to treat the chronic vomiting and rumination of normal children and adolescents and mentally retarded children, adolescents, and adults. The studies were evaluated with respect to several dimensions: target behavior, measurement techniques, reliability of measurement, S characteristics, unsuccessful treatments, side effects, experimental design, maintenance and generalization, and successful behavioral procedures. On the basis of the critique, recommendations are made to service providers concerning treatments to use and the conditions under which they may be appropriate. (31 ref)
Davis, Paula K. & Cuvo, Anthony J. (Southern Illinois U, Behavior Modification Program, Carbondale) Behavior Research of Severe Developmental Disabilities, 1980(May), Vol 1(1), 31–59. [PA, Vol 66:08492]

2335.   The use of self-modeling to improve the swimming performance of spina bifida children.
Investigated the use of edited videotape replay (which showed only "positive" behaviors) to improve the water skills of 3 spina bifida children, aged 5–10 yrs. Using a multiple baseline across Ss design, behavioral changes were observed to occur in close association with intervention. One S was given successive reapplications of videotaped self-modeling with continuing improvements. (19 ref)
Dowrick, Peter W. & Dove, Cynthia. (U London, Birkbeck Coll, England) Journal of Applied Behavior Analysis, 1980(Spr), Vol 13(1), 51–56. [PA, Vol 65:08471]

2336.   The empirical selection of a punisher for a retarded child's self-injurious behavior: A case study.
Finger gnawing behavior in a 5-yr-old retarded boy was greatly reduced using a lemon juice punisher. This technique was empirically selected by sequentially implementing 4 punishment procedures that gradually increased in level of aversiveness of the consequence stimulus. The advantages of using a multiple baseline design to select an effective punishment technique are discussed. (5 ref)
Gross, Alan M.; Wright, Becky & Drabman, Ronald S. (U Mississippi Medical Ctr, Jackson) Child Behavior Therapy, 1980(Fal), Vol 2(3), 59–65. [PA, Vol 66:10876]

2337.   Tardive dyskinesia and other drug-induced movement disorders among handicapped children and youth.
Neuroleptic drugs are used with substantial numbers of mentally retarded children and youth. These drugs can exert untoward effects on many biological systems, and movement disorders or dyskinesia are among the most important consequences of neuroleptic use. The literature concerned with tardive dyskinesia, the most serious of these movement disorders, is examined. Neuroleptic-induced movement disorders, withdrawal-emergent symptoms, and acute extrapyramidal effects are discussed. Studying abnormal drug-induced movements in a population already prone to abnormal movements (e.g., stereotypies) even without drugs is necessary to establish proper guidelines for neuroleptic use. (57 ref)
Gualtieri, C. Thomas & Hawk, Barbara. (North Carolina Memorial Hosp, Dept of Child Psychiatry, Chapel Hill) Applied Research in Mental Retardation, 1980, Vol 1(1–2), 55–69. [PA, Vol 66:08582]

2338.   Parent support groups for the families of mentally handicapped children.
Describes a model of parent support group that has as its aim the provision of an effective clinical service to the handicapped child and his/her family. An evaluation is made of the effectiveness of the group after a period of 6 mo. (12 ref)
Holland, J. M. & Hattersley, J. (Royal Albert Hosp, Lancaster, England) Child Care, Health & Development, 1980(May–Jun), Vol 6(3), 165–173. [PA, Vol 64:06160]

2339.   Operant techniques in the analysis and modification of self-injurious behavior: A review.
Major studies relevant to modification of self-injurious behavior in the retarded are evaluated with respect to treatment procedure (extinction, time-out from positive reinforcement, differential reinforcement of other behavior, overcorrection, required relaxation, aversive stimulation, and combinations of these). Experimental design, behavioral definitions, reliability, and generality are discussed. (5 p ref)
Horner, R. Don & Barton, Elizabeth S. (U Kansas, Bureau of Child Research, Lawrence) Behavior Research of Severe Developmental Disabilities, 1980(May), Vol 1(1), 61–91. [PA, Vol 66:08517]

2340.   The opportunity to earn oneself off a token system as a reinforcer for attentive behavior.
Separate token reinforcement contingencies were compared with 2 mentally retarded children, an 8-yr-old boy (IQ 79) and a 9-yr-old girl (IQ 83), in a special education classroom. Each received tokens contingent upon attentive behavior while working on academic tasks. The separate contingencies consisted of providing Ss with token reinforcement that included the opportunity to earn their way off the system vs a similar contingency that did not provide this opportunity. The 2 contingencies were compared in separate simultaneous-treatment designs for each S. The contingencies were implemented daily and were balanced across different time periods. Providing Ss with the opportunity to earn their way off the system led to higher levels of attentive behavior than did the contingency without this added back-up event. Results suggest that opportunities to earn one's way off the system can reinforce behavior and perhaps provide an initial step in weaning clients from a highly structured reinforcement program. (17 ref)

Kazdin, Alan E. & Mascitelli, Sally. (Pennsylvania State U, University Park) Behavior Therapy, 1980(Jan), Vol 11(1), 68–78. [PA, Vol 63:06400]

2341.   Trichotillomania in childhood: A case of successful short-term treatment.
Trichotillomania (compulsive hair pulling) in children is a complex symptom for which no single psychodynamic conceptualization has yet been identified. An important predisposing factor for this symptom appears to be an inconsistent, depriving relationship between mother and child. Some therapists have applied the concept of the "transitional" (soothing) object in treating young children with this disorder. A case of a 5-yr-old retarded boy is presented in which hair pulling occurred in response to psychological trauma (threatened loss of and/or injury to a beloved grandfather). Treatment was carried out through the mother and consisted of her clarifying the traumatic events and the child's anxious and angry feelings about them. Child psychologists and pediatricians, as primary caregivers, should be aware that hair pulling can represent a traumatic neurosis and should take a careful psychosocial history before instituting any physical treatment or referring on to a dermatologist. (6 ref)
Litt, Carole J. (Case Western Reserve U School of Medicine) Journal of Pediatric Psychology, 1980(Mar), Vol 5(1), 37–42. [PA, Vol 64:01472]

2342.   Relaxation training with the developmentally disabled: A reapprasial.
Reviews applications of relaxation training with the developmentally disabled to evaluate whether its use is justified. Studies are evaluated in terms of whether adequate controls for internal validity were imposed, whether the relaxation procedures were compared to other interventions, and whether attempts were made to determine if Ss achieved a state of relaxation. Results indicate that in the majority of controlled studies, the effects of relaxation training procedures were no more effective than other interventions. In other studies, claims to the efficacy of relaxation training were obscured by methodological shortcomings. Several recommendations are presented for controlled experimental evaluation of relaxation training with developmentally disabled populations. (41 ref)
Luiselli, James K. (Behavioral Intervention Project, Concord, MA) Behavior Research of Severe Developmental Disabilities, 1980(Nov), Vol 1(3), 191–213. [PA, Vol 66:08534]

2343.   Programming response maintenance of differential reinforcement effects.
A mentally retarded, behaviorally disturbed 11-yr-old male who exhibited several inappropriate motor responses was successfully treated with a differential reinforcement program in 2 special classroom settings. The program consisted of reinforcing S with tokens for the absence of inappropriate responding during prescribed intervals measured by a mechanical timer. (19 ref)
Luiselli, James K.; Colozzi, Gail A. & O'Toole, Kathleen M. (Thompson School, Behavioral Intervention Project, Arlington, MA) Child Behavior Therapy, 1980(Sum), Vol 2(2), 65–73. [PA, Vol 66:06346].

2344.   Some variations in the use of differential reinforcement procedures with mentally retarded children in specialized treatment settings.
Examined the use of time-based schedules of reinforcement to effect problem response reduction. These procedures are described as delivering reinforcement of other behavior immediately following a specified interval of nonresponding or a specified interval of responses occurring in less than or equal to a prescribed limit. In the present single-S, multiple baseline studies, variations in the usual application of these methods were examined with 3 mentally retarded children in specialized treatment settings. The variations were (1) providing reinforcement on a delayed rather than an immediate basis and (2) not having the change-agent present with Ss during the interval for reinforcement. In 2 studies, the treatment programs were effective in reducing problem responses—one with the disruptive

behavior of a child (13 yrs of age and Vineland Social Quotient of 50) within 3 training sessions and the other with the aggressive and disruptive behaviors of 2 children (6 and 8 yrs of age and IQs of approximately 50) during a free-play activity. (17 ref)
Luiselli, James K. & Reisman, John. (Behavioral & Educational Resource Assoc, Concord, MA) Applied Research in Mental Retardation, 1980, Vol 1(3–4), 277–288. [PA, Vol 66:08535]

2345.   Vitamins: The get-smart pills?
Of 22 4th–6th graders in a class of the slowest readers in the school, the 11 Ss who received multiple vitamin tablets for 5 mo improved their learning, test scores, and classroom behavior. The other 11 Ss, on a candy regime, did not improve.
Maseck, Daryl.   Journal of Orthomolecular Psychiatry, 1980, Vol 9(1), 58–65. [PA, Vol 65:10964]

2346.   The Pilot Parent Program: Helping handicapped children through their parents.
Describes a program to help the parents of children recently identified as mentally retarded or developmentally delayed. Other parents who have children with similar problems visit them offering crisis guidance, emotional support, knowledge about the child's condition, and information about community services and programs that are available. Referrals are made mainly through physicians. The members also engage in advocacy and social activities. The sense of community generated among the parents is very valuable, as is the development of appreciation for the children's abilities and progress. Thus, the Pilot Parent Program has been very successful. (6 ref)
Menolascino, Frank J. & Coleman, Robert. (U Nebraska Medical Ctr) Child Psychiatry & Human Development, 1980(Fal), Vol 11(1), 41–48. [PA, Vol 64:10945]

2347.   Training parents of retarded children as behaviour therapists: What we need to know: II.
Asserts that the case for training parents of retarded children in behavior modification techniques is far from proven. Reference to the literature indicates that training programs of this kind have inherent flaws and that research methods have been defective. Specific recommendations are made for improving research into parent training: comprehensive reporting of descriptive data, such as demographic information about the parents; precise description of the childrens' presenting problems, degree of retardation, and type of disability; precise description of parent–child behavior; reliability of parents' observations; treatment procedures; and designs. Researchers should consider the generalizability, durability, and cost of any changes attributable to treatment, and whether these changes represent any appreciable difference to the child or the family. Five specific problems for investigation are described. (16 ref)
Molloy, Geoffrey N. (Monash U Faculty of Education, Clayton, Australia) Mental Retardation Bulletin, 1980(Spr), Vol 8(1), 3–12. [PA, Vol 66:08542]

2348.   Wanted: Some guidelines for investigating, reporting and evaluating parent training interventions.
Suggests that some of the practical implications of the no-difference-in-treatment conclusion (M. W. Griffen, 1979) are questionable and that parents of retarded children need assistance that is different from that required of parents of nonretarded children. Further, the claimed efficacy of such programs must be considered within the context of carefully defined characteristics of the particular target group. (27 ref)
Molloy, Geoffrey N. (Monash U, Faculty of Education, Clayton, Australia) Australian Journal of Developmental Disabilities, 1980(Jun), Vol 6(2), 71–77. [PA, Vol 66:08470]

2349.   Serotonergic approaches to the modification of behavior in the Lesch-Nyhan syndrome.
In 9 5–14 yr old patients with Lesch-Nyhan syndrome, a pharmacologic attempt was made to alter the balance of biogenic amines in the CNS by increasing the level of serotonin. Ss were treated with 5-hydroxytryptophan in combination with the peripheral decarboxylase inhibitor carbidopa and with imipramine. Most Ss had a striking alteration in self-mutilative behavior. However, within 1–3 mo, each became tolerant, and

this pharmacologic effect could not be produced again even 1 yr later. These observations suggest that the characteristic behavior of the Lesch-Nyhan syndrome patient is related to neurotransmitter balance, and that there may be ways to modify it. (19 ref)
Nyhan, William L.; Johnson, Harold G.; Kaufman, Irving A. & Jones, Kenneth L. (U California-San Diego, La Jolla) Applied Research in Mental Retardation, 1980, Vol 1(1–2), 25–40. [PA, Vol 66:08596]

2350.   The effects of protective equipment on self-injurious behavior.
Evaluated a restraint apparatus, a foam-padded helmet, using a 17-yr-old mentally retarded male with a history of head hitting as well as other self-injurious behavior (SIB). On test days when initial baseline rates of SIB were high, the protective gear had an immediate suppresive effect; the difference between baseline and restraint conditions on these days showed a 90–99% reduction in SIB. When baseline rates of SIB were low, the helmet had a slight or no effect. (5 ref)
Parrish, John M.; Aguerrevere, Luis; Dorsey, Michael F. & Iwata, Brian A. (John F. Kennedy Inst, Baltimore, MD) Behavior Therapist, 1980, Vol 3(5), 28–29. [PA, Vol 66:06987]

2351.   Generalization and maintenance of skills acquired in Non-Speech Language Initiation Program training.
31 nonverbal children who had completed training on the Non-Speech Language Initiation Program designed by J. Carrier and L. Peak (1975) were pre- and posttested on a generalization test battery involving number matching, color matching, sentence imitation, command-following, receptive and expressive vocabulary, and spontaneous speech in an unstructured setting. 90% of the Ss showed 6 mo of maintenance and generalization that were unrelated to age, sex, or presence of siblings. However, less generalization occurred among institutionalized Ss, who were more severely retarded and more organically handicapped, than among Ss who resided in the community. These differences were most apparent on subtests involving production of speech. (22 ref)
Porter, Patricia B. & Schroeder, Stephen R. (U North Carolina, Chapel Hill) Applied Research in Mental Retardation, 1980, Vol 1(1–2), 71–84. [PA, Vol 66:08608]

2352.   Suppression of self-injurious behaviour: Determining the least restrictive alternative.
Compared the effects of DRO, overcorrection (OC), lemon juice (LJ), and aromatic ammonia (AM) on the rate of self-poking in a 5-yr-old deaf, blind retarded child. DRO and OC were both ineffective. Although LJ suppressed and stabilized the rate of poking, AM produced greater suppression. (22 ref)
Rapoff, M. A.; Altman, K. & Christophersen, Edward R. (Pediatric Research Inst, Kansas City, KS) Journal of Mental Deficiency Research, 1980(Mar), Vol 24(1), 37–46. [PA, Vol 66:06356]

2353.   Toward a Christian perspective of developmental disability.
Two models of habilitation and several concepts linked with the habilitation of mentally retarded and developmentally disabled persons are compared with biblical views. (18 ref)
Ratcliff, Donald. (Gallipolis Developmental Ctr, OH) Journal of Psychology & Theology, 1980(Win), Vol 8(4), 328–335. [PA, Vol 66:13444]

2354.   The effects of antecedent vestibular stimulation on the receptive language learning of retarded toddlers.
Monitored the receptive language learning of 3 mentally handicapped toddlers (approximately 12–18 mo delayed in expressive and receptive language—Bayley Scales of Infant Development). The total number of trials to criterion system was employed during the baseline and intervention conditions. During intervention, Ss were exposed to 90 sec of intense vestibular stimulation immediately prior to the language tasks. Results indicate that vestibular stimulation, when applied systematically as an antecedent to the receptive language tasks, decreased the total trials needed to reach criterion for each S. Although Ss displayed varied reactions to the vestibular activities, a negative reaction

bore no effect on the concomitant change in rate of learning. (20 ref)
Raver, Sharon A.   Child Study Journal, 1980, Vol 10(2), 77–86. [PA, Vol 64:03537]

2355.   [Elimination of eating with the hands in a retarded adolescent using removal of positive reinforcement.] (Span)
Describes an aversive training procedure that aimed at altering a retarded adolescent's eating behavior. Food was removed whenever the inappropriate response appeared. The functional role of the independent variable was demonstrated with the use of an ABAB design. Proper eating behavior was maintained at a 4-mo follow-up. (English abstract) (5 ref)
Reid, Rubén & Ugalde B., Francisco.   Revista Chilena de Psicología, 1980, Vol 3(1), 37–41. [PA, Vol 66:13305]

2356.   The effects of physician counseling technique on parent reactions to mental retardation diagnosis.
Conducted a structured interview to identify and evaluate circumstances and counseling techniques that 26 mothers of mentally retarded children felt influenced their reactions to the initial diagnostic interview. Significant physician behaviors were an attitude of concern, appreciation of the handicapped child's value to the parents as a love object, planning an uninterrupted and unhurried discussion of the findings, allowing parent contact with the child before the diagnosis was told, sharing extensive information with the parents but without absolute predictions, and making specific practical recommendations. Satisfied parents were more likely to follow the physician's recommendations. The degree of dissatisfaction did not correlate with lag time before parents enrolled in an early childhood special education program. (19 ref)
Rubin, Annette L. & Rubin, Richard L.   Child Psychiatry & Human Development, 1980(Sum), Vol 10(4), 213–221. [PA, Vol 64:05905]

2357.   Self-management of classroom behavior with retarded/disturbed children.
A current trend in classroom behavior analysis is the exploration of self-management procedures. The present paper describes self-management on-task behavior that was achieved by 4 6–9 yr old mentally retarded/emotionally disturbed Ss. A series of verbal and gestural cues were used to teach self-assessment and self-reinforcement. The prompts were gradually faded until complete self-management was attained. The effect upon task performance, accuracy, and disruptive behavior was examined when on-task behavior was reinforced. Results show that performance and accuracy increased for most Ss while disruptive behavior declined. (18 ref)
Shapiro, Edward S. & Klein, Roger D. (U Pittsburgh School of Medicine, Western Psychiatric Inst & Clinic) Behavior Modification, 1980(Jan), Vol 4(1), 83–97. [PA, Vol 65:06196]

2358.   An analysis of self-assessment and self-reinforcement in a self-managed token economy with mentally retarded children.
Examined the effects of training self-assessment and self-reinforcement in the self-management of a token economy with 5 moderately to mildly retarded children (mean CA 10 yrs, mean IQ 60). The separate effects of the self-assessment and self-reinforcement components were evaluated. Results show that all Ss displayed substantially improved levels of on-task behavior and maintained these levels throughout training in self-management. Four Ss were successful in achieving highly accurate self-assessment. It was also found that training in both components of self-management, self-assessment and self-reinforcement may not be necessary to maintain accurate self-management with mentally retarded children. (30 ref)
Shapiro, Edward S.; McGonigle, John J. & Ollendick, Thomas H. (Lehigh U) Applied Research in Mental Retardation, 1980, Vol 1(3–4), 227–240. [PA, Vol 66:08556]

2359.   Posture training as a means of normalization.
Emphasizes the need for posture assessment and training as an integral part of individualized educational programming. Findings of several posture studies with mentally retarded persons are summarized. Methods are suggested for cooperative implementa-

tion of posture programming by special educators, physical educators, parents, and significant others. (13 ref)
Sherrill, Claudine. (Texas Women's U) Mental Retardation, 1980(Jun), Vol 18(3), 135–138. [PA, Vol 66:08741]

2360.   Treatment of self-injurious behaviour: A three year follow-up.
Six mentally retarded children (ages 6–13 yrs) who had been successfully treated with a multi-element treatment program were observed yearly for 3 yrs. Results show complete response suppression in 2 Ss and a near-zero frequency of self-injurious behavior in 3. The other S had died, through natural causes, after the 1st followup. (10 ref)
Singh, Nirbhay N.; Gregory, P. R. & Pulman, Ruth M. (Mangere Hosp & Training School, Auckland, New Zealand) New Zealand Psychologist, 1980(Nov), Vol 9(2), 65–67, 84. [PA, Vol 66:10900]

2361.   [Psychodiagnostics in the preventive care of a district child centre.] (Czec)
Presents data on 77 retarded preschool children followed at a child care center. The author considers questions regarding the screening and care of children with suspected retardation, and analyzes the most frequent difficulties to be taken into account at the individual developmental stages. Practical procedures by which the pediatrician and children's nurse may help not only the somatic but also the psychological development of the children concerned are suggested. (Russian abstract) (16 ref)
Stolaříková, Dagmar.   Psychológia a Patopsychológia Dieťaťa, 1980, Vol 15(2), 139–144. [PA, Vol 66:04175]

2362.   Therapy with families of a mentally retarded child.
Identifies major treatment goals, crisis periods, family reactions, and basic techniques for therapy with families of mentally retarded children. Primary goals focus on counseling and educating the family to deal more effectively with potential and actual problems. Therapy with these families has a dual function: (a) coping with immediate crisis interventions and (b) long-term counseling involving goal-setting and family role development for flexibility in future problem periods. (4 ref)
Turner, Andrew L. (U Missouri, Columbia) Journal of Marital & Family Therapy, 1980(Apr), Vol 6(2), 167–170. [PA, Vol 65:10886]

2363.   Group news watching and discussion to increase the current affairs awareness of retarded adolescents.
Assessed the news awareness of 8 predelinquent or delinquent mentally retarded (MA) Ss (CA 13–17 yrs, IQ 40-70) using daily verbal news quizzes. In multiple baseline fashion, group TV newswatching plus brief discussion was sequentially introduced with 4 Ss and a TV news exposure-only condition was used with 4 Ss. While passive TV newswatching alone resulted in little change in news awareness, contingent upon the introduction of TV newswatching plus brief discussion, all Ss showed substantial improvement in their current affairs awareness. On several probe days, news quiz performance of the MR Ss was compared to the performance of 10 nonretarded high school students who viewed the same network news program; retarded Ss who received the TV plus discussion intervention performed at levels comparable to their nonretarded agemates on these probe days. (9 ref)
Wildman, Beth G. & Kelly, Jeffrey A. (Jackson Mental Health Ctr, MS) Child Behavior Therapy, 1980(Spr), Vol 2(1), 25–36. [PA, Vol 66:06522]

2364.   A progress report on Australian practice and research in intellectual handicap.
Summarizes conditions in Australia relevant to understanding the development of service-delivery systems and research in intellectual handicap. The main areas of applied research are reviewed—early intervention, service delivery to metropolitan and isolated communities, and intervention studies with school-age children and adults. The majority of work in Australia is either derivative or parallels that of the US or UK and, in particular, reflects common concerns with the achievement of normalization and the development of more effective compensatory programs. (53 ref)

Birnbrauer, Jay S. & Leach, David J. (Murdoch U, School of Social Inquiry, Australia) Applied Research in Mental Retardation, 1981, Vol 2(2), 165–180. [PA, Vol 66:08613]

2365. The direct and indirect effects of positive reinforcement on on-task behavior.
Results of 2 experiments with 8 learning disabled and/or mentally retarded children show that praise of an on-task pupil in the presence of an off-task pupil was ineffective in improving the behavior of the 1st pupil. If reinforcement tokens were added to the procedure, the indirect praise technique was sometimes effective. It is concluded that direct praise is needed to maintain large improvements in behavior. (18 ref)
Boyd, L. Adlai; Keilbaugh, William S. & Axelrod, Saul. (Florida Mental Health Inst, Tampa) Behavior Therapy, 1981(Jan), Vol 12(1), 80–92. [PA, Vol 65:08462]

2366. Teaching laundry skills to mentally retarded students.
Five 19–21 yr old mentally retarded Ss (IQs 36–69) were taught 3 subtasks—sorting laundry and using a washer and a dryer—using 3 prompt sequences and praise and response-contingent feedback. Rapid acquisition and maintenance of skills were obtained. (4 ref)
Cuvo, Anthony J.; Jacobi, Liz & Sipko, Ronald. (Southern Illinois U, Rehabilitation Inst, Carbondale) Education & Training of the Mentally Retarded, 1981(Feb), Vol 16(1), 54–64. [PA, Vol 66:08491]

2367. Prevention of incorrect responding for establishing instruction following behaviours.
Compared 2 techniques for teaching instruction-following to 3 mentally retarded children (7–10 yrs of age): the experimental technique in which incorrect responses were prevented by interruption and the trial-and-error technique. A cross-over design was used. Results favor the experimental technique, thereby providing further support for the notion of errorless-discrimination learning. (12 ref)
Duker, Pieter C. (Catholic U of Nijmegen, Netherlands) Journal of Mental Deficiency Research, 1981(Mar), Vol 25(1), 25–32. [PA, Vol 66:06069]

2368. Physical restraint as positive reinforcement.
Analyzed the reinforcing function of physical restraint for 3 retarded individuals (CAs 15–30 yrs) who had a history of restraint and appeared to enjoy it. Using a preference paradigm with 1 S and a reversal design with 2 others, the authors found that an arbitrary response systematically increased for each when followed by brief periods of restraint. No comparable increases occurred in conditions in which responses were not consequated or were followed by stimuli designed to control for the nonrestraint components of the restraint consequence. Results are discussed in terms of 3 clinical issues: determining the possible role of restraint in maintaining behavior problems such as self-injury in natural settings, preventing or eliminating the reinforcing function of restraint, and using restraint reinforcement in treating behavior problems when this consequence is the only identifiable reinforcer for an individual. (8 ref)
Favell, Judith E.; McGimsey, James F.; Jones, Michael L. & Cannon, Preston R. (Western Carolina Ctr, Morganton, NC) American Journal of Mental Deficiency, 1981(Jan), Vol 85(4), 425–432. [PA, Vol 65:08475]

2369. Tourette syndrome in mentally retarded children.
Describes a study in which 6 mentally retarded Ss (CA 6 yrs 4 mo–12 yrs 5 mo) originally manifesting symptoms of Gilles de la Tourette syndrome were first thought to have manneristic behavior. Prompt response to treatment with haloperidol (0.5–2 mg) exposed their true nature as tics associated with Tourette syndrome. (7 ref)
Golden, Gerald S. & Greenhill, Lawrence. (U Texas Medical Branch, Galveston) Mental Retardation, 1981(Feb), Vol 19(1), 17–19. [PA, Vol 66:08579]

2370. What is a human rights committee?
The origin of the human rights committee arises from the need to monitor program conditions in residential facilities serving mentally disabled individuals. Confusion exists as to the role and responsibilities of these committees. Some critical elements for consideration in establishing such a committee are proposed. (13 ref)
Griffith, Robert G. & Henning, Dana B. (Temple U) Mental Retardation, 1981(Apr), Vol 19(2), 61–63. [PA, Vol 66:08637]

2371. Factors contributing to normalization in residential facilities for mentally retarded persons.
Examined the influence of 4 types of variables on the level of environmental normalization (EN) achieved by 144 community residential facilities (CRF) for the mentally retarded. Results show that characteristics of the CRF (e.g., size, number of disability groups served, and type of experience provided) are more important than characteristics of the residents in determining EN. (16 ref)
Hull, John T. & Thompson, Joy C. (Province of Ontario Ministry of Community & Social Services, Toronto, Canada) Mental Retardation, 1981(Apr), Vol 19(2), 69–73. [PA, Vol 66:08639]

2372. Problems involved in the use of ammonia in the treatment of self injurious behaviour.
Ammonia has been suggested to be an effective aversive stimulus for the treatment of self-injurious behavior. However, the authors' experience in using ammonia in aversive therapy programs with a 13-yr-old female (moderately retarded) and an 8-yr-old male (IQ 69), who were also able to manipulate social situations to their advantage, suggests that ammonia was neither as easy to use nor as effective in suppressing the behavior as had been claimed. Not only were there problems in administering ammonia, but there was the possibility of physical side effects. For these reasons, ammonia cannot be recommended as an aversive stimulus. (3 ref)
Jones, Megan & Andersen, Margaret. (Gladesville Hosp, Australia) Australian Journal of Developmental Disabilities, 1981(Mar), Vol 7(1), 27–31. [PA, Vol 66:08522]

2373. Play and the mentally retarded child.
Provides a description of some of the play characteristics of mentally retarded (MR) children and arguments for the importance of play for them. A brief and critical review of the sparse literature on play with MR children strongly indicates the need for more research on play for this particular group. Procedures for the therapeutic use of play with MR children with emotional or behavior problems are suggested. (29 ref)
Li, Anita K. (U Calgary, Canada) Mental Retardation, 1981(Jun), Vol 19(3), 121–126. [PA, Vol 66:08250]

2374. Services for the mentally handicapped in Denmark.
Outlines some aspects of the Danish system of delivering services to the mentally retarded that contrast sharply with the UK system. Implications of instituting a philosophy of normalization are discussed from both the administrative and client viewpoints. (6 ref)
Malin, N. A. (U Sheffield, Evaluation Research Group, England) Child Care, Health & Development, 1981(Jan–Feb), Vol 7(1), 31–39. [PA, Vol 66:01922]

2375. Introductory trade training for slow learners and mildly retarded young adults.
Over a 5-yr period, 38 16–21 yr old mentally retarded males (WAIS IQs 51–90) employed at an industrial work center for handicapped persons were given additional training in woodwork and cabinet making and attended special classes for 1 yr that were similar to those for 1st-yr apprentices. The outcome was evaluated by comparing the performance of Ss in end-of-year tests with that of normal 1st-yr apprentices, by seeking the opinions of instructors and trainees involved about changes in general work and social skills, and by following the progress of Ss subsequent to their participation in the scheme. On test pieces, most Ss produced work of a satisfactory quality, while taking significantly longer than 1st-yr apprentices to complete the test. A quarter of those completing this training have entered a normal apprenticeship, supported by special arrangements for remedial education. The consensus of opinion among instructors and trainees was that the scheme was successful, despite some

problems that arose regarding selection, continuing participation, and the subsequent employment of trainees. (5 ref)
Nettelbeck, Ted & Kirby, N. H. (U Adelaide, Australia) Australian Journal of Developmental Disabilities, 1981(Mar), Vol 7(1), 3–8. [PA, Vol 66:08733]

2376. Effects of self-instructional training on cognitive impulsivity of mentally retarded adolescents.
Assessed the cognitive styles of 27 retarded adolescents (mean CA 16 yrs; mean MA 7.5 yrs) using the Matching Familiar Figures Test. The most impulsive subsequently received training in self-instruction while observing a reflective model or observed the model without specific training in self-instruction. Posttraining measures indicated that the self-instruction procedure produced significantly more reflective responding than the model-alone procedure. Results also suggest the presence of a developmental lag in cognitive style among these Ss compared to recent norms for nonretarded children. The finding that the present Ss were responsive to self-instructional training is inconsistent with A. R. Luria's (1961) contention that retarded individuals are incapable of using the language-based 2nd signaling system to influence and control their own behavior. (15 ref)
Peters, R. D. & Davies, K. (Queens U, Kingston, Canada) American Journal of Mental Deficiency, 1981(Jan), Vol 85(4), 377–382. [PA, Vol 65:08504]

2377. Public attitudes and community acceptance of mentally retarded persons: A review.
Suggests that strategies to facilitate the development of improved public attitudes toward the mentally retarded appear necessary as increasing numbers of this population leave institutions and enter the community. Research on the effects of contact and information upon attitudes toward mentally retarded persons is reviewed, and implications for efforts to improve public attitude toward community integration of mentally retarded people are presented. (54 ref)
Sandler, Allen & Robinson, Rick. (Ken-Crest Growth & Development Ctr, Philadelphia, PA) Education & Training of the Mentally Retarded, 1981(Apr), Vol 16(2), 97–103. [PA, Vol 66:08655]

2378. Public residential facilities: Status and trends.
Results of a survey of 278 operational public residential facilities for the retarded indicate an effort to meet the challenge of the more difficult-to-manage or emotionally disturbed resident by the heightened interest in recruiting psychologists and psychiatrists. Definite movement towards both deinstitutionalization and institutional reform was also evident. (1 ref)
Scheerenberger, R. C. Mental Retardation, 1981(Apr), Vol 19(2), 59–60. [PA, Vol 66:08657]

2379. Is isolation room time-out a punisher?
Disputes the commonly held assumption that timeout (TO) intervention, as represented by use of an isolation room, constitutes a punisher on empirical and theoretical grounds. Consistent, unemotional use of TO, without ancillary punishers, was found to result in typical extinction curves (rather than the steeper gradient of punishment curves) for both autistic (11.5-yr-old female and 10.5-yr-old male) and mentally impaired (8-yr-old male and 13 yr-3-mo-old male) children with widely different abrasive behaviors. Such curves ordinarily result from withdrawal of either a positive or a negative reinforcer. But "maladaptive" classroom behaviors are thought to be maintained by negative reinforcement, the reduction of stress (an aversive stimulus) following aggression. Thus, extinction of "maladaptive" behavior will result from withdrawal of the aversive stimulus, (i.e., escape from classroom-induced stress). The danger of using punishers and the therapeutic value of reduced environmental stimulation are pointed out. (13 ref)
Smith, Donald E. (U Michigan School of Education, Ann Arbor) Behavioral Disorders, 1981(Aug), Vol 6(4), 247–256. [PA, Vol 66:11313]

2380. Child-rearing expectations of families with atypical children.
Assessed the childrearing expectations of 101 Australian parents of intellectually handicapped children with mean CAs between 4 yrs 6 mo and 8 yrs 5 mo, and IQs of 28–68. Parents were given the Parent As A Teacher Inventory (PAAT). The overall PAAT index for Ss scoring at either the upper or lower extremes proved to be valuable in identifying those parents who would be the most and least successful teachers in a home-based language training program. (16 ref)
Strom, Robert; Rees, Roger; Slaughter, Helen & Wurster, Stanley. (Arizona State U, Parent–Child Lab, Tempe) American Journal of Orthopsychiatry, 1981(Apr), Vol 51(2), 285–296. [PA, Vol 66:09050]

2381. Genetic screening for mental retardation in Michigan.
Describes the Michigan Department of Mental Health's genetic screening laboratory, which was established in 1977 to provide diagnostic information on retarded patients. Of 727 patients screened during a 2-yr period, a genetic diagnosis was established for 121 moderately to severely retarded patients. Genetic counseling was provided for 40% of their parents. A wide variety of chromosomal abnormalities, inborn errors of metabolism, and dysmorphic syndromes was discovered, including 16 instances of previously unknown familial conditions. This program has demonstrated a cost-effective method for determining genetic etiology in mental retardation and, in some instances, has led to prevention of mental retardation. (10 ref)
Thoene, Jess et al. (U Michigan Medical Ctr, Ann Arbor) American Journal of Mental Deficiency, 1981(Jan), Vol 85(4), 335–340. [PA, Vol 65:08597]

2382. Cognitive development in retarded and nonretarded persons: Piagetian tests of the similar structure hypothesis.
Surveys 30 studies involving 104 separate tests of the similar-structure hypothesis with Piagetian conceptual measures. The present authors distinguish between studies that did and did not screen organically impaired Ss from their mentally retarded samples. Studies that did not meet this requirement yielded findings inconsistent with the similar-structure hypothesis; retarded groups were significantly inferior to nonretarded groups matched on MA. Studies that did meet the requirement, yielded findings supporting the hypothesis. Findings have implications for the developmental vs difference controversy and for diagnosis and training of the mentally retarded. (3 p ref)
Weisz, John R. & Yeates, Keith O. (U North Carolina, Chapel Hill) Psychological Bulletin, 1981(Jul), Vol 90(1), 153–178. [PA, Vol 66:08282]

2383. A plea to end the use of the patterning treatment for retarded children.
Maintains that the treatment program for brain-damaged children known as "patterning" should be discontinued because (1) empirical evidence does not support it, (2) it adds unnecessary financial and emotional burdens onto already frustrated and drained families, and (3) it is too rigid a program to be practically followed. Also reviewed is the debate over the patterning rationale (i.e., if a child makes certain motions frequently enough, previously unused brain cells will become programmed to take over the function of the damaged ones.) Other therapeutic alternatives, such as behavioral modification, are advocated. (11 ref)
Zigler, Edward. (Yale U) American Journal of Orthopsychiatry, 1981(Jul), Vol 51(3), 388–390. [PA, Vol 66:10795]

Downs Syndrome

2384. Mental and motor development in young mongol children.
A 2-yr longitudinal study of 45 mongol babies reared at home and 9 placed in foster homes and institutions with a matched (age, sex, and social class) normal control group revealed that the mongol children were significantly below the control group on

the Bayley Infant Scales of Mental and Motor Development at 6 wk., declined rapidly to 10 mo., and less rapidly after that to 2 yr. Mean scores of boarded-out mongols were significantly below those who were reared in the home. Mean mental scale scores of mongol boys were significantly ($p < .05$) below those of the girls.
Carr, Janet. (U. London, Inst. of Education, England) Journal of Mental Deficiency Research, 1970(Sep), Vol. 14(3), 205-220. [PA, Vol 46:11371]

2385.   [Attempt at reeducation of syntactic structuration in the adolescent mongol.] (Fren)
Notes that a number of studies have confirmed experimentally that at equal intellectual and social levels mongols have a level of speech inferior to those who are retarded but not mongols. This defect affects syntax as well as articulation and rhythm. A method of reeducation was developed which was inspired by the principles of structural linguistics and the techniques of programmed teaching. An experiment in reeducation, involving a group of 10 adolescent mongols, showed improvement in the level of syntactic structuration. The significance of this improvement is discussed. (German & Spanish summaries)
Castellan-Paour, M. T. & Paour, J. L. (Les Cypres Medico-Professional Inst., Salon-de-Provence, France) Revue de Neuropsychiatrie Infantile et d'Hygiene Mentale de l'Enfance, 1971(Jul), Vol. 19(7-8), 449-461. [PA, Vol 50:01436]

2386.   Infantile spasms associated with 5-hydroxytryptophan administration in patients with Down's syndrome.
A seizure syndrome closely resembling infantile spasms has been found in 15% of a series of patients with down's syndrome who were receiving long-term 5-hydroxytryptophan (5-HTPN) therapy. In 5 of 9 patients, the seizures were stopped by decreasing the oral dose of 5-HTPN, the precursor amino acid of the serotonin metabolic pathway. The role of this pathway in seizure disorders, particularly in the infantile spasm syndrome, is discussed.
Coleman, Mary. (Children's Hosp. of the District of Columbia, Washington) Neurology, 1971(Sep), Vol. 21(9), 911-919. [PA, Vol 47:07406]

2387.   The effects of own-home and institution-rearing on the behavioural development of normal and mongol children.
Replaced early, simple types of behavior that were little related to the external world by locomotion and manipulatory types of behavior in both mongols and normal children (MA below 2 yr.). Manipulatory behaviors were at 1st oriented at least partly toward the S's own body, but later principally toward the external world. The focus of the S's visual attention at different ages reflected the changing incidence of different types of behavior. Normal Ss were more active than mongols of the same development level, and paid more attention to ongoing events. Behavioral differences were found for both mongols and normal Ss, between those who lived at home with their parents and those in institutions. Differences were evident in the frequency with which different types of behavior were performed, and the distribution of visual attention to different factors in the environment. The lower developmental level of the institution-reared Ss did not adequately account for these behavioral differences. By altering institutional environmental conditions to resemble more closely the home, the behavior of the institution-reared Ss became more like that of the home-reared children. The behavioral differences between home- and institution-reared mongols were greater than those between home- and institution-reared normal Ss. There were also differences between the care given to home-reared mongols and that given to home reared normal children. (43 ref)
Francis, Sarah H. (Australian National U., Canberra, Australian Capital Territory) Journal of Child Psychology & Psychiatry & Allied Disciplines, 1971(Oct), Vol. 12(3), 173-190. [PA, Vol 48:05464]

2388.   Verbal operant conditioning with young institutionalized Down's syndrome children.
3 groups of 6 institutionalized Down's syndrome children were drawn from 2 comparable state schools. Pre- and postexperimental evaluations were made with 2 language measures, the Stanford-Binet (Form L-M), and a social rating scale. Group 1 received 7 wk of verbal operant conditioning in an experimental environment. Group 2 spent 7 wk. in the same environment without conditioning. Group 3 remained in the institution. Significant positive changes were noted for Group 1 on the Stanford-Binet and 1 language measure. (15 ref.)
MacCubrey, Jean. (Boston Children's Hosp., Medical Center, Mass.) American Journal of Mental Deficiency, 1971(May), Vol. 75(6), 696-701. [PA, Vol 47:01475]

2389.   Mental growth in noninstitutionalized mongoloid children.
Compared a mental growth curve for noninstitutionalized mongoloid children with those curves presented for institutionalized mongoloid patients. While arguments have been advanced for the intellectual and social superiority of home-rearing as opposed to institutional rearing for mongoloid retardates, studies concerning mental growth curves for mongoloid children have been limited largely to institutionalized populations. Ss were drawn from the outpatient register of a child development clinic and a residential school for exceptional children. Marked differences in mental growth after age 9 yr. were noted between the curves presented for institutionalized and noninstitutionalized Ss.
Meindl, Joseph L.; Barclay, Allan G.; Lamp, Robert E. & Yater, Allan C. (Indiana U., South Bend) Proceedings of the 79th Annual Convention of the American Psychological Association, 1971, Vol. 6(Pt. 2), 621-622. [PA, Vol 46:05366]

2390.   [The effect of early psychological training of mentally retarded children.] (Swed)
Matched 2 groups of mongoloid children with respect to age (16-69 mo) and sex (2 boys and 6 girls in each group). One group received the following types of training: (a) sensory functions (exposure to musical instruments, tactile stimuli, and games involving color and form discrimination); (b) bodily needs (table manners, toilet training, etc); (c) intellectual functions (jigsaw puzzles, verbal games); (d) motorics: gross (e.g., climbing stairs), and fine (e.g., sewing); (e) memory (of location of toys); (f) control of aggressive behavior; (g) social functions (setting a table, serving food); (h) attention. The Ss were trained twice a week for an unspecified period of time; no details on teaching methods are offered. All were tested 4 times with Griffiths Mental Development Scales, 0-8 years. The trained children showed significantly greater increments in mental age (mean = 10.5 mo) than the matched controls (mean = 3.5 mo). Training improved performance on all subscales.
Fällström, K. & Aronson, M. Nordisk Psykiatrisk Tidsskrift, 1972, Vol 26(8), 467-473. [PA, Vol 53:07700]

2391.   A communication program for children with Down's syndrome.
Discusses the need for a variety of effective speech and language therapies for children diagnosed as Down's syndrome. Recommendations are considered with respect to 3 groups divided according to CA: 5-10, 11-16, and 17-40 yr. old. Within the symptom complex of Down's syndrome, difficulties in all areas of language are confounded by sensory and perceptual deficits. Communication programs have to maintain elasticity offering stimulation for the nonverbal to providing techniques for children with unique language handicaps.
Glovsky, Leon. (American Inst. for Mental Studies, Training School Unit, Vineland, N.J.) Training School Bulletin, 1972(May), Vol. 69(1), 5-9. [PA, Vol 49:01137]

2392.   Effects of genetic counseling on parental self-concepts.
Administered a semantic differential self-concept scale to 18 pairs of parents of children with Down's syndrome before and after genetic counseling. Genetic counseling was effective in improving parental self-concepts, with greatest improvement shown by mothers. It is hypothesized that mothers may feel closer to the children, and thus need more reassurance to alleviate feelings of guilt and self-blame.

Antley, Mary A.; Antley, Ray M. & Hartlage, Lawrence C. Journal of Psychology, 1973(Mar), Vol. 83(2), 335-338. [PA, Vol 50:07160]

2393. Modeling and shaping by parents to develop chewing behavior in their retarded child.
Butterfield, William H. & Parson, Ronal. (Washington U., George Warren Brown School of Social Work) Journal of Behavior Therapy & Experimental Psychiatry, 1973(Sep), Vol. 4(3), 285-287. [PA, Vol 52:03717]

2394. Treatment of encopresis in a mongol with operant conditioning.
Describes the case of an 11½-yr-old boy with Down's syndrome who developed a problem of encopresis associated with a change in his school environment. The patient was encouraged by the parent and teacher to sit on the toilet seat in the morning and was rewarded if he defecated. No punishments were used. He showed improvement after 6 wks of consistent training and after 5 mo was fully retrained.
Chopra, H. D. Indian Journal of Mental Retardation, 1973(Jan), Vol 6(1), 43-46. [PA, Vol 53:10163]

2395. Group work with parents of children with Down's syndrome.
Describes group treatment of families of children with Down's syndrome. Two developments reported are an educational program for professionals on the needs of parents who had given birth to such a child and a program of information and support for the siblings of such children.
Murphy, Ann; Pueschel, Siegfried M. & Schneider, Jane. (Children's Hosp. Medical Center, Boston, Mass.) Social Casework, 1973(Feb), Vol. 54(2), 114-119. [PA, Vol 50:07450]

2396. Tryptophan treatment of infants with Down's syndrome.
5-hydroxytryptophan (5HTP) has been reported to increase the muscle tone and the blood 5-hydroxytryptamine (5HT) content in infants with Down's syndrome (DS). In this study levotryptophan (10-50 mg/kg/day) was given chronically for up to 2 yrs to 9 newborn infants with DS. 14 untreated infants with DS served as controls. The muscle tone of tryptophan-treated Ss with DS improved most clearly during the 1st half year of life. During the 1st yr the mean level of 5HT in the platelet-rich plasma of treated Ss was significantly higher than that in untreated controls but did not reach the level found in 22 healthy infants. Side-effects resembling those of 5HTP occurred, and 1 of the 9 patients developed an infantile spasm syndrome. (25 ref)
Airaksinen, E. M. (U Helsinki, Finland) Annals of Clinical Research, 1974(Feb), Vol 6(1), 33-39. [PA, Vol 53:10079]

2397. An experimental parent-assisted treatment program for preschool language-delayed children.
Used parents as the primary language trainers for 6 preschool children with Down's syndrome. The program applied the environmental language intervention strategy to effect a generalized functional language in children who primarily were capable of only single-word utterances. The 5-mo program ran in 2 stages—2 mo with professionals and mothers as language trainers and 3 mo in the home with parents as the sole language trainers. Results from the 2-mo stage indicate marked increases in utterance length and grammatical complexity in imitation and conversation for all 3 experimental Ss but negligible changes for the 3 controls. Follow-up assessment indicates continued language increments for the experimental Ss over 3 mo of home programing with parents as the sole language trainers. The experimental language growth in the mean length of utterance over 3 mo of home programing for the retarded children was comparable to growth for normally developing children.
MacDonald, James D. et al. (Nisonger Ctr, Columbus, OH) Journal of Speech & Hearing Disorders, 1974(Nov), Vol 39(4), 395-415. [PA, Vol 53:09898]

2398. Acceleration of vocal behavior in developmentally retarded children.
Describes changes in vocal behavior of 10 Down's syndrome children during a 4-mo experimental training program. Ss' total vocal behavior increased over the period; they emitted more utterances and used more different words in the utterances than before the program. Analysis of results indicates that some Ss were beginning to use longer and possibly more complex vocal chains. Among the factors that may have contributed to these changes were the highly structured character of the program, the individualized or small group format of instruction, immediate correction of errors, the practice of increasing performance requirements as soon as a task was mastered, and reciprocal reinforcement of Ss and teachers.
Tawney, James W. (U. Kentucky) Education & Training of the Mentally Retarded, 1974(Feb), Vol. 9(1), 22-27. [PA, Vol 52:08695]

2399. A clinical nursing study: Failure to thrive in a child with Down's syndrome.
Examined the impact of an individually tailored developmental nursing program on a 5-yr-old male with Down's syndrome and severe failure to thrive. Investigation of the child and his family suggested that the failure to thrive was the result of masked deprivation, and a study was designed to measure the effect of a 17-day program of developmental nursing care on specific parameters of growth and behavior: height, weight, amount of sleep, caloric intake, active mobility, awareness of the environment, prelanguage vocalizations, self-stimulation behavior, and play activity with toys. Data on these criteria were gathered before, during, and after the nursing care program. Findings support the assumptions that there would be an increase in height, weight, amount of sleep, active mobility, awareness of the environment, prelanguage vocalizations and a decrease in self-stimulation. Findings do not support the assumptions that there would be an increase in caloric intake and play activity with toys. The study supports the use of nursing care as the primary therapeutic modality for children with this condition and illustrates an approach to systematic evaluation of the effects of nursing care. (74 ref)
Durand, Barbara. (U California, Nursing School, San Francisco) Nursing Research, 1975(Jul-Aug), Vol 24(4), 272-286. [PA, Vol 55:01156]

2400. Social and play behaviors of institutionalized mongoloid and nonmongoloid retarded children.
Observed 24 retardates, 12 mongoloid (Down's syndrome) and 12 nonmongoloid (mean ages, 10 yrs 3 mo and 9 yrs 11 mo, respectively), in dyadic interaction with peers in a free-play situation. A number of specific peer-social and nonsocial behaviors were recorded as they occurred. Differences between mongoloid and nonmongoloid Ss were most apparent on several social behavior categories, which support the stereotypic conception of mongoloids as more sociable and gregarious. Differences were most apparent for the mongoloid males. The possible influence of tranquilizer drugs and cottage placements on the observed differences is discussed.
Schlottmann, Robert S. & Anderson, Victor H. (Oklahoma State U) Journal of Psychology, 1975(Nov), Vol 91(2), 201-206. [PA, Vol 55:07404]

2401. Immediate and long-term effects of developmental training in children with Down's syndrome.
Determined whether the rate of development of a group of mentally retarded children could be improved by early, systematic mental training. Eight children with Down's syndrome, aged 21–69 mo, were trained systematically, following the pattern of normal development, over a period of 1½ yrs. The MA (Griffith's Mental Development Scales) of the trained children was compared with that of 8 matched controls before, during, and after the training period. Both groups were living in a small institution offering a homogeneous environment. Results show that training had a significant effect on the MA of the trained Ss. However, in a follow-up study 1 yr after the completion of training, the effect was reduced in the trained group, although still higher overall than the control group. This finding indicates that while early training is effective for mentally retarded children, it must be a continuous process to achieve long-term benefit. (French, German & Spanish summaries)

Aronson, Marita & Fällström, Kerstin. Developmental Medicine & Child Neurology, 1977(Aug), Vol 19(4), 489–494. [PA, Vol 60:03299]

2402.   [The Grenoble Guidance Center: Results after one year of operation.] (Fren)
Reports the work done by a multidisciplinary treatment staff (psychiatrists, educators, psychoanalysts, psychologists, and pediatricians) with seriously disturbed children, primarily cases of Trisomy 21 or childhood psychosis, at the Guidance Center recently established in Grenoble, France. (English summary) (17 ref)
Boucharlat, J. et al. (Centre Hosp Universitaire de Grenoble/Hosp Sud, France) Annales Médico-Psychologiques, 1977(Jul), Vol 2(2), 209–227. [PA, Vol 64:10972]

2403.   Continuous measurement of progress in infant intervention programs.
Argues for the use of a criterion-based continuous strategy (as opposed to a norm-based periodic method) in which an infant's daily performance of targeted skills is recorded as a means of assessing treatment effects of intervention efforts. A simple method of continuous measurement is described, along with experiences from a parent-implemented research program for Down's Syndrome infants in which a consultant assists parents in designing individual treatments.
Hanson, Marci J. & Bellamy, G. Thomas. (U Oregon) Education & Training of the Mentally Retarded, 1977(Feb), Vol 12(1), 52–58. [PA, Vol 58:09816]

2404.   Treatment of a Down's syndrome child with multiple behaviour problems in a ward setting.
Presents a case in which a combined reinforcement and punishment procedure was used to eliminate self-injury, a shaping procedure was used to overcome feeding problems, and a manual guidance procedure was used to initiate walking in an institutionalized 3.8-yr-old severely retarded boy. (17 ref)
Jones, Judith; Singh, N. N.; White, A. J. & Astwood, Christine. (Mangere Hosp & Training School, Auckland, New Zealand) Australian Journal of Mental Retardation, 1977(Dec), Vol 4(8), 16–19. [PA, Vol 61:08951]

2405.   Increasing a Down's child's attending behavior with attention from teachers and normal preschool children.
Describes the modification of the attending (i.e. on-mat) behavior of a 5.5-yr-old hyperactive Down's syndrome boy during an individual activity time period when children engaged in independent activities on separate mats. Results show that the S's on-mat behavior changed as a direct function of contingent teacher and/or peer attention. (Spanish abstract) (23 ref)
Reiber, Joan L.; Goetz, Elizabeth M.; Baer, Donald M. & Green, Donald R. (U Kansas) Revista Mexicana de Análisis de la Conducta, 1977(Jun), Vol 3(1), 75–85. [PA, Vol 61:13867]

2406.   Application of Foxx and Azrin toilet training for the retarded in a school program.
Describes the successful use of a modified version of R. M. Foxx and N. H. Azrin's (1973) toilet training procedure, which requires that the child remain in the bathroom until he or she begins to initiate going to the toilet by him- or herself, with an 11-yr-old boy with Down's syndrome who had never been toilet trained.
Trott, Maryann C. (Española Elementary School, NM) Education & Training of the Mentally Retarded, 1977(Dec), Vol 12(4), 336–338. [PA, Vol 61:06588]

2407.   Behavior modification of retarded preschool children.
Applied operant conditioning to 2 Down's syndrome children: a 5-yr-old boy with autistic behavior and a 4-yr-old girl whose behavior problem was rejecting other children. The boy was involved in a "ball game play," in which music was played on a cassette recorder as a reinforcer. His responses to the game increased remarkably during the experiment, and his autistic behavior was modified substantially. In about 3 yrs, he could play in the field with social reinforcement. For the girl, social reinforcement from the teacher (praise, physical contact) was

used, and every response related to the target behaviors (laughing, clapping her hands, approaching the boy discussed above, giving him a toy, or touching him) was immediately reinforced. In 20 sessions, the girl's approach behaviors toward the boy improved both in quality (from passive to positive responses) and in frequency. (5 ref)
Yamaguchi, Kaoru. (Tokyo Gakugei U, Japan) RIEEC Research Bulletin, 1977(Nov), No 8, 14 p. [PA, Vol 65:06047]

2408.   Teaching a severely retarded child to stand by rewarding successive approximations.
Attempted to determine whether a severely retarded 4-yr-old child who was unable to stand or walk alone could be taught to stand with minimal support. The training procedure involved rewarding successive approximations of weight bearing. The child was trained to support almost all of her weight for a substantial part of a training session. (12 ref)
Cass, Susan & Zimmer-Hart, Charles L. (Flinders U of South Australia, Bedford Park) Australian Journal of Mental Retardation, 1978(Dec), Vol 5(4), 142–145. [PA, Vol 64:01634]

2409.   Parental education and rate of intellectual development of Down's syndrome (Trisomy-#21) individuals.
W. Golden and H. Pashayan (1976) recently reported a "trend" between 4 ordinal categories of parental education and the IQs of their Down's syndrome children. The lack of statistical analyses and other methodologial flaws made reinvestigation of their reported phenomenon necessary. This investigation used only Trisomy-#21 type Down's syndrome children as Ss ($N = 94$). Stanford-Binet Intelligence Scale scores of males, females, and a composite group were correlated with the educational levels of their parents. Parental education data were divided into 3 categories—mothers' and fathers' educations, and a composite education score. Of the 9 possible relationships between IQ data and parental education, all were positive and 8 were statistically significant. Implications of these relationships are discussed. (2 ref)
Clements, Paul R.; Hafer, Marilyn & Pollock, Jonathan L. (O'Berry Ctr, Goldsboro, NC) Research & the Retarded, 1978, Vol 5(1), 15–19. [PA, Vol 63:01217]

2410.   Improving the generalized mnemonic performance on a Down's syndrome child.
A training program was conducted to improve the generalized mnemonic performance, or memory, of a Down's syndrome child (CA 6 yr 7 mo, IQ 50). Training was directed at digit-span performance, with generalization from training determined by responses to untrained mnemonic performance probes. The digit-span items varied in length from 3 to 5 digits. Each length constituted an item class, with each class trained within the framework of a multiple-baseline design. Probes consisted of untrained digit-span items, grammatical sentences, nongrammatical sentences, and match-to-sample items. A training procedure, in which 15 items from each class varied continually from trial to trial and from day to day, resulted in the percentage of correct responses to both training and probe items increasing to levels substantially above baseline. These findings were replicated in a 2nd study with 2 other mentally retarded children. (13 ref)
Farb, Joel & Throne, John M. (Lakemary Ctr for Exceptional Children, Paola, KS) Journal of Applied Behavior Analysis, 1978(Fal), Vol 11(3), 413–419. [PA, Vol 63:08418]

2411.   Teaching functional reading to the TMR.
L. Brown et al (1972) developed programs to teach trainable mentally retarded (TMR) children to read a few words and phrases. The present paper provides information on the generalizability of Brown's results to a 2nd group of 3 6–8 yr old Down's syndrome children. The teaching procedure is described: (a) Ss were given candy reinforcement for correctly picking out their own name and the names of their classmates. (b) The words "boy" and "girl" were introduced and appropriately connected to each classmate's name via worksheets. (c) Further words specific to each S's vocabulary were learned. (d) Noun phrases, verbs, and finally sentences were introduced. (e) More complex words, consonant sounds, and for one child, vowel sounds, were

taught. Results show that one S learned to read 132 words with complete accuracy and to read stories from a preprimer, another learned 65 words, and the 3rd learned 30 words. Findings suggest that TMR students can be taught functional reading skills by the classroom teacher without expensive or sophisticated methods. (3 ref)
Folk, Mary C. & Campbell, Jack. (Picollo School, Reno, NV) Education & Training of the Mentally Retarded, 1978(Oct), Vol 13(3), 322–326. [PA, Vol 63:08419]

2412.   A multidisciplinary approach to early intervention strategies for the education of the developmentally handicapped 0–3 year old: A pilot study.
Describes a program for developmentally handicapped children which was established to demonstrate the desirability of a more extensive center for the detection of developmental handicaps and the planning of early intervention strategies for under 3-yr-olds. Essentially, 6 children have received the comprehensive service. The program has been functioning for 12 mo, and data collected during that period support the benefit of such input. The paper suggests an ideal situation of sensorimotor stimulation from as early as 3 mo of age, followed by more cognitive stimulation from approximately 12 mo of age. (16 ref)
Ford, Jacquie.   Australian Journal of Mental Retardation, 1978(Mar), Vol 5(1), 26–29. [PA, Vol 62:03997]

2413.   Down's infants: An interdisciplinary approach involving parents.
Describes a program designed to provide parents of children with Down's syndrome and the children themselves with regular contact with other families in a similar situation in the hope that the contact itself would prove therapeutic. The group was initially given factual information about government and local authority provisions for handicapped children; however, it was quickly realized that their emotional needs and fears had to be allayed before further education could take place. This was achieved by visits to special schools, talks to overcome parents' initial shock at seeing Down's adults, and explanations of the clinical syndrome and its implications, including genetic counseling. The parents then became less apprehensive and began to consider their children as having special needs. It was possible to involve many professional disciplines to answer parents' questions. The interdisciplinary approach has so far involved pediatricians, general practitioners, health visitors, social workers, psychologists, physiotherapists, teachers, student teachers, lecturers in education, and community health specialists, some of whom have yet to learn the art of communication with each other and all of whom effectively communicated with the group. (German & French abstracts)
Sinson, Janice C. (City of Leeds Society for Mentally Handicapped Children, England) International Journal of Rehabilitation Research, 1978, Vol 1(1), 59–69. [PA, Vol 61:06403]

2414.   Parental speech to young Down's syndrome children: An intervention study.
Parents of 7 Down's syndrome children who were at the 1–2 word stage of expressive language development were given a language objective to work toward with their child, but no instructions on how to attain this goal. The parents spontaneously altered their language strategies in their attempts. Some parents were more successful and differed in their strategies, using more target words in shorter "statement" utterances. Parents who used a questioning or imitating strategy were less successful. The less successful parents were then shown how to alter their language strategies more appropriately to produce greater improvement in their child's use of the target words. (20 ref)
Cheseldine, Sally & McConkey, Roy. (Victoria U of Manchester, Hester Adrian Research Ctr, England) American Journal of Mental Deficiency, 1979(May), Vol 83(6), 612–620. [PA, Vol 62:08857]

2415.   The effect of early intervention and pre-school stimulus on the development of the Down's syndrome child.
Describes the effect of early and continuous parental counseling, together with intensive preschool stimulation in which the parents were fully involved, on 3 groups of Down's syndrome Ss born between 1960 and 1969. The stimulated group was compared with a similar group who developed unaided in their own homes and with a 3rd group who were institutionalized before their 2nd birthday. Developmental clinics in East Kent (England) providing the stimulus are described. The effects of social class, parental age, and family pattern are noted. The tests used were the Griffiths Developmental Scale and Stanford-Binet Intelligence Scale—Revised, and the school placement at 5 yrs was studied. Results show that the stimulated group scored higher on the IQ and developmental tests, particularly on personal, social, and speech development. School placement acted as an unbiased measurement of progress and suggests that Ss were more easily integrated into the normal community. (13 ref)
Ludlow, Joyce R. & Allen, L. M.   Journal of Mental Deficiency Research, 1979(Mar), Vol 23(1), 29–44. [PA, Vol 66:06468]

2416.   A parent–teacher administered weight reduction program for obese Down's syndrome adolescents.
Six moderately retarded adolescents (mean age 17.5 yrs) with Down's syndrome participated in a parent–teacher-administered behavioral weight reduction program. The program involved graduated exposure to a number of weight reduction techniques combined with external and self-administered reinforcement components over a 19-wk treatment and maintenance period. All Ss achieved significant weight loss during treatment and maintenance phases. Follow-ups revealed that weight loss was maintained. (8 ref)
Rotatori, Anthony F.; Fox, Robert & Switzky, Harvey N. (Northern Illinois U, DeKalb) Journal of Behavior Therapy & Experimental Psychiatry, 1979(Dec), Vol 10(4), 339–341. [PA, Vol 65:08511]

2417.   The progress of developmentally delayed pre-school children in a home-training scheme.
Compared the rates of development of 35 preschool children in a home training program. Ss entered the service at different ages and suffered from different disabilities. The families received weekly visiting from a home advisor, who was specially trained to develop skills in the parents to help their children. Those who developed most rapidly were the group of environmentally deprived Ss. The nonspecific developmentally delayed and Down's syndrome Ss progressed well during the study period. Ss who suffered from cerebral palsy and those with visual handicaps developed at a very slow rate, despite the training that they were receiving. This finding may reflect the severity of their handicaps, but it also suggests that the needs of these particular groups should be further examined. The age of entry to the scheme did not seem to be an important variable. The individual variability within each specified group was wide. (9 ref)
Barna, S. et al. (Welsh National School of Medicine, Cardiff) Child Care, Health & Development, 1980(May–Jun), Vol 6(3), 157–164. [PA, Vol 64:06224]

2418.   Facilitating syntax acquisition.
Demonstrated the effectiveness of a miniature linguistic systems approach to teaching the subject–verb–object structure to 2 6-yr-old Down's syndrome children. Ss were taught to produce selected examples of that structure from a Subject by Verb–Object matrix. Both Ss generalized their production of the structure to all remaining examples in the matrix. (3 ref)
Holdgrafer, Gary. (U Alberta, Edmonton, Canada) Psychological Reports, 1980(Apr), Vol 46(2), 498. [PA, Vol 65:13597]

2419.   Elimination of assaultive and inappropriate sexual behavior by reinforcement and social-restitution.
The assaultive behavior, inappropriate interpersonal-sexual behavior, and genital self-stimulation of a 13-yr-old Down's syndrome male were successfuly eliminated in a school setting through the use of a naturalistic social-restitution procedure and

DRO descriptive verbal praise. While the DRO procedure alone was partially successful in reducing target responses, the combined procedures eliminated all problem behavior. Generalization of behavior control to teachers was achieved, and results were maintained at 1 and 6 mo posttreatment follow-ups. Social validation of behavior improvement was provided. (29 ref)
Polvinale, Robert A. & Lutzker, John R. (University of the Pacific, Socialization Ctr, CA) Mental Retardation, 1980(Feb), Vol 18(1), 27–30. [PA, Vol 66:08548]

2420. Effects of physicians' early parental counseling on rearing of Down syndrome children.
A survey of the feelings of 37 couples with a school-age Down's syndrome child born since 1970 suggested a diminished influence of physicians' early counseling on parental decisions, attitudes, and rearing practices. In contrast, undefined "personal feelings," own research, and input from community parent groups were major influences. (8 ref)
Springer, Alice & Steele, Mark W. (U Pittsburgh School of Medicine, Children's Hosp) American Journal of Mental Deficiency, 1980(Jul), Vol 85(1), 1–5. [PA, Vol 64:08594]

Institutionalized Mentally Retarded

2421. Social intelligence and the institutionalized adolescent retardate: The influence of the informal social system.
One of the many factors that affects the institutionalized retardate's desire and ability to learn—the influence of the peer group— has not been adequately explored. This paper describes such a group in a state institution serving about 300 mildly and moderately retarded adolescents and young adults, housed in cottages of approximately 75-80 residents each. Attention is focussed on how group participation enhanced the retardates' learning of specific social skills. Some strategies are suggested by which institutions can capitalize on the learning potential that exists in these groups. (20 ref.)
Forman, Mark. (Rutgers State U., Graduate School of Social Work) Mental Retardation, 1970(Apr), Vol. 8(2), 12-16. [PA, Vol 47:11506]

2422. The therapeutic role of visits and vacations for institutionalized retarded children.
Attempted to provide empirical support for the assumption that visits and vacations are of therapeutic value for institutionalized retarded children. A group of 39 familial retarded children divided into developmental levels with mean MAs of 7, 8.8, and 11.8, respectively, were given a task on which performance reflects dependence upon adults and wariness of them. Ss, especially at younger MA levels, who received more visits and went on more vacations were found to be more independent and less wary. Results also indicate that it may be possible to predict from preinstitutional social histories which children are likely to be visited and be taken on vacations.
Balla, David & Zigler, Edward. (Yale U., Child Study Center) Mental Retardation, 1971(Jun), Vol. 9(3), 7-9. [PA, Vol 49:11535]

2423. Behavior changes in mentally retarded children following the initiation of an experimental nursing program.
An experimental nursing care unit was set up for a random sample of 8 severely retarded children showing self-destructive and often disturbed behaviors. A combination of nurturant nursing and conditioning principles were utilized in developing individualized programs for these childen. 8 randomly selected controls remained under the usual care. Testing with the Central Wisconsin Colony Scales of Adaptive Behavior before and approximately 3-4 mo. after treatment revealed significant experimental control group differences on 3 social behavior factors: unskilled verbalization, failure to respond to contact by others, and passive response to contact by others. There was a trend toward improved nonverbal communication. There were no significant differences on the behaviors listed under: resistive responses to others, posturing and stereopathy, or inappropriate responses to others.
Balthazar, Earl E.; English, George E. & Sindberg, Ronald M. (Central Wisconsin Colony & Training School, Madison) Nursing Research, 1971(Jan), Vol. 20(1), 69-74. [PA, Vol 47:01452]

2424. Effect of staff ethnocentrism on the rating of self-help skills of minority group mentally retarded patients.
Administered Ross' Fairview Self-Help Scale to 49 Mexican-American, 48 Negro, and 98 Caucasian, mentally retarded institutionalized adolescents matched for mean MA and CA. 46 nursing staff Ss rated the patients' self-help skills. Results indicate that, contrary to expectations, scores were not rated as lower than would be expected from MA, but were in fact higher.
Boroskin, Alan & Giampiccolo, James S. (Fairview State Hosp., Costa Mesa, Calif.) American Journal of Mental Deficiency, 1971(Sep), Vol. 76(2), 249-251. [PA, Vol 47:09527]

2425. Modeling and environmental generalization by mentally retarded subjects of televised aggressive or friendly behavior.
Matched 20 aggressive and 20 nonaggressive 8-38 yr old institutionalized mentally retarded Ss on age, sex, and IQ. Ss were shown either an "aggressive" or a "friendly" television film of a child playing with a large inflatable doll. Results indicate that friendly Ss modeled the aggressive film behavior in the experimental room, while aggressive Ss did not. Friendly behavior increased and aggressive behavior decreased after the friendly film. Later, in the ward, Ss who had seen the aggressive film were more aggressive, and Ss who had seen the friendly film were more friendly. However, results apply mainly to friendly Ss' behavior, since they were more friendly even after the aggressive film than aggressive Ss were after the friendly film. Specific modeling was incomplete, the behavior in the ward being more related to the general mood of the film than to the specific actions seen in the film.
Fechter, John V. (U. South Dakota) American Journal of Mental Deficiency, 1971(Sep), Vol. 76(2), 266-267. [PA, Vol 47:09501]

2426. The role of nonprofessional persons in teaching language skills to mentally retarded children.
Reviews a 2-yr research project in which 2 former psychiatric aides were trained to serve as language developmentalists for small groups of institutionalized severely retarded children. 40 Ss participating in the program were compared with a matched control group on variables of IQ, language, age, and social quotient. Ss attending language classes met daily for approximately 1 hr. They were taught from the Peabody Language Development Kits and a series of lessons developed during the project. Results show significantly greater language scores made by the language training group. IQ score increases were equivocal, but again favored those Ss attending language classes.
Guess, Doug; Smith, James O. & Ensminger, E. Eugene. (Kansas Neurological Inst., Topeka) Exceptional Children, 1971(Feb), Vol. 37(6), 447-453. [PA, Vol 46:05362]

2427. [Value of small doses of neuroleptics in the severe states of hospitalism in the severely mentally retarded child.] (Fren)
Reports the frequent occurrence and the treatment of "hospitalism syndromes" (i.e., severe reactions to being hospitalized) in severely retarded children. 6 cases are discussed. While the more severe forms can endanger life, less marked forms are characterized by sleep disturbances, refusal of food, and various manifestations of agitation or aggression. The risk to life increases in proportion to the degree of impairment in psychological development. The introduction of neuroleptic drugs from the time of admission considerably diminished the incidence of these disturbances. Dosage and duration of treatment are of little importance. This chemotherapy is combined with psychotherapeutic and institutional measures, which are described in detailed. (German & Spanish summaries)
Midenet, M. (Stephansfeld Psychiatric Hosp., Brumath, France) Revue de Neuropsychiatrie Infantile et d'Hygiene Mentale de l'Enfance, 1971(Jun), Vol. 19(6), 289-294. [PA, Vol 49:07570]

2428. [Elements of institutional psychotherapy for disturbed mentally defective patients.] (Fren)
Describes the type of psychotherapy considered suitable for mentally defective children showing developmental disturbances or symptoms of deficiency in a full care institution and a day hospital. A better understanding of the specific psychopathological mechanisms underlying the deficiency structure is needed, along with their interdependence with relational mechanisms in neurosis or psychosis. It is argued that theories which emphasize purely mechanistic or psychogenetic factors should be discounted. For each patient it is essential to distinguish between a specific task (e.g., education or guidance care) and complex sensory relationships. This emphasis may occasionally lead to psychotherapy (in the strict sense) which may then prove impossible to separate from the total institutional care necessary for it. (German & Spanish summaries)
Mises, R. (Departmental Center of Infantile Neuropsychiatry, 7 Benserade St., Gentilly, France) Revue de Neuropsychiatrie Infantile et d'Hygiene Mentale de l'Enfance, 1971(May), Vol. 19(5), 253-258. [PA, Vol 49:07574]

2429. Longitudinal assessment of the relation between measured intelligence of institutionalized retardates and hospital age.
Studied the Stanford-Binet Intelligence Scale, WAIS, and WISC scores on the admission records of 122 institutionalized retardates. The relationship between IQ scores and length of hospitalization was examined. A significant positive change of IQ scores with length of hospitalization was found. Only 37 Ss showed IQ decreases over time. Results are contrasted with opposite findings in cross-sectional studies. It is suggested that the educational program at the institution studied may have contributed to the IQ increases.
Sachs, Lewis B. & Frisk, Guy C. (West Virginia U.) Developmental Psychology, 1971(Nov), Vol. 5(3), 541. [PA, Vol 47:05483]

2430. Transference toward the child therapist and other parent surrogates.
Hypothesized that true transference occurs in child psychoanalysis. The attitudes of a 7-yr-old institutionalized male retardate toward his male therapist, teachers and cottage workers of both sexes were assessed. The participant adults inferred the S's attitudes before, during, and following 2 mo. of psychotherapy. Similarly, 3 examining psychologists described the S's attitudes toward his mother and father before and after therapy. The obtained Q sorts were intercorrelated and factor analyzed. Results support the transference hypothesis. Sex similarity was a potent but not exclusive determinant of transference. Both the male therapist and a male teacher were "father figures." (39 ref.)
Subotnik, Leo. (Veterans Administration Hosp., St. Cloud, Minn.) Journal of Genetic Psychology, 1971(Dec), Vol. 119(2), 215–231. [PA, Vol 48:01081]

2431. A treatment program for a self-destructive child.
Presents a case study with a detailed account of a treatment program for the modification of the self-destructive behavior of a boy residing in an institution for the mentally retarded. The 13-mo intensive treatment program employed a variety of approaches (restraints, hydrotherapy, human contact, etc.) and emphasized the development of an interpersonal relationship. The program ultimately resulted in a marked reduction in self-destructive behavior and elimination of restraining apparatus.
Thomas, Richard L. & Howard, Gail A. (U. Washington) Mental Retardation, 1971(Dec), Vol. 9(6), 16-18. [PA, Vol 47:11492]

2432. [About psychological aids to the families of severely retarded children: Its importance for treatment of these children.] (Fren)
Discusses variables which affect the adjustment of parents and retarded children to resident care, and describes attempts to ease this adjustment. Analysis is based on observations of 40 2-6 yr. old residents of a Parisian center for the observation and care of severely retarded children. No correlation was found between the degree of neuropathological injury and the development of the

child, indicating that both primary and elaborated neuropathological deficiencies can be compensated. The evolution of the child largely depends upon the capacity of the mother or her substitute to overcome anguish, and on the help she receives. The importance of the child's relationship with his family during resident treatment is stressed. (German & Spanish summaries)
Villechenoux-Bonnafé, Y. (Comite d'Etude et de Soins aux Arriérés Profonds, Paris, France) Revue de Neuropsychiatrie Infantile et d'Hygiene Mentale de l'Enfance, 1971(Mar), Vol. 19(3-4), 159-164. [PA, Vol 49:07675]

2433. To what behaviors do attending adults respond?
Recorded the responses of 15 attending adults to more than 800 samples of behavior of 49 ambulatory institutionalized young retarded children. The attending adults usually failed to respond at all to either appropriate or inappropriate child behaviors. When responses were made to appropriate behaviors, they were likely to be encouraging, and thus were probably positively reinforcing. Responses to inappropriate behaviors were discouraging about twice as often as encouraging, providing potential positive reinforcement for unacceptable behaviors. For all behaviors, adult behavior appeared to offer children infrequent, variable ratio reinforcement schedules.
Warren, Sue A. & Mondy, Lewis W. (Boston U.) American Journal of Mental Deficiency, 1971(Jan), Vol. 75(4), 449-455. [PA, Vol 46:03638]

2434. Play therapy conducted by mentally retarded inpatients.
Reports a study in which 6 young retarded inpatients served as assistants in treating 10 younger retarded inpatients in a pyramid therapy approach in training and play sessions. Assistant behaviors during unstructured play sessions were examined and compared with behaviors representative of successful child treatment. Results indicate that the assistants (a) provided models of both simple and complex role relationships, (b) provided varied verbal stimulation, (c) initiated setting limits, (d) established expectations, and (e) facilitated self-awareness in both body image and self-concept, thereby engaging in behavior designated as important ingredients in successful child therapy. (33 ref.)
Whale, Carol K. & Henker, Barbara A. (U. California, Irvine) Psychotherapy, 1971(Fal), Vol. 8(3), 236-245. [PA, Vol 47:11060]

2435. Pyramid therapy in a hospital for the retarded: Methods, program evaluation, and long-term effects.
Describes a 9-mo hospital program with 5 16-24 yr. old female retarded "therapists" and 10 6-10 yr. old retarded "trainees." The program had 3 interrelated objectives: (a) extending the use of nonprofessional therapists to retarded patients in a hospital setting, (b) developing behavior modification procedures that could be taught to and used by mentally retarded persons, and (c) evaluating the effectiveness of this "therapeutic pyramid" approach. Children in 1 group were given 60 individual training sessions, then 60 play sessions; simultaneously, the matched control group was given play, then training. The training groups gained significantly in basic social behaviors over the play groups in each phase of the investigation. Children in the 1st play group also showed significant gains which were attributed to the general effects of participation in the program. Follow-up measures indicate that response acquisitions of the trainees and behavior modification skills of the therapists were durable. (18 ref.)
Whalen, Carol K. & Henker, Barbara A. (U. California, Irvine) American Journal of Mental Deficiency, 1971(Jan), Vol. 75(4), 414-434. [PA, Vol 46:03626]

2436. The "mother system" in an institution for the retarded.
Presents an approach called the "mother system," which has been found to be effective in getting active cooperation from psychiatric aides. Under this system aides become "mothers" with "families" of "children" for whom they are both responsible and accountable. 2 basic types of "mother" systems are discussed, 1 involving partial and the other involving total responsibility for a child. 3 areas are noted which need special attention

for successful mother systems: responsibility, guidance, and reinforcement.
David, Michael K. (Napa State Hosp., Imola, Calif.) Mental Retardation, 1972(Feb), Vol. 10(1), 17-19. [PA, Vol 48:03225]

2437. Direct measurement of psychopharmacologic response: Effects of chlorpromazine on motor behavior of retarded children.
Administered graded doses of chlorpromazine (CPZ) to 4 11-14 yr. old institutionalized developmentally retarded children. Using direct, continuous, and automatic measurements, the effects of CPZ on 3 types of motor movements (hand, leg, and stereotyped rocking) and several types of control (free-operant, discriminated-operant, fixed-ratio, variable-interval, and patellar-reflex) were studied. Results support the hypotheses that (a) CPZ decreases the rate of motor responding, (b) graded doses of CPZ have a graded effect on response rate, and (c) CPZ response data curves obtained from children are similar to those obtained with animals. (28 ref.)
Hollis, John H. & St. Omer, Vincent V. (U. Kansas) American Journal of Mental Deficiency, 1972(Jan), Vol. 76(4), 397-407. [PA, Vol 48:05484]

2438. Segregation: The case for.
Emphasizes the necessity of segregating into institutions mental defectives who are (a) a menace to society; (b) unable to care for themselves; and (c) a physical, mental, and financial drain on the family and community. Several individual cases are cited to indicate that segregation would be more beneficial for the child, family, and/or society. One study is cited where 102 inmates of an institution for the retarded were released against the advice of the doctors in charge. Only 13 made satisfactory adjustment, and many others had to be returned to institutions.
Parker, Neville. Australian Journal of Mental Retardation, 1972(Mar), Vol. 2(1), 16-18. [PA, Vol 49:01204]

2439. [Effects of pyritinol on retarded adolescents and young adults: Clinical and long-term study.] (Fren)
Administered pyrithioxin to 23 16-24 yr. old Ss institutionalized for mental retardation, many of whom suffered from additional difficulties. The pyrithioxin was in a concentration of 80.5 mg. per 5 ml., and the dose was 2 tablespoons per day for from 3-6 mo. The purpose was to improve psychomotor operations, openness, and stability. Permanent improvement was noted in 87% of the cases. The drug was well tolerated, and improvement was noted after 2 mo.
Rossignol, Cl. (U. Tours, Children's Medical Clinic, France) Revue de Neuropsychiatrie Infantile et d'Hygiene Mentale de l'Enfance, 1972(Sep), Vol. 20(8-9), 707-711. [PA, Vol 49:11741]

2440. Differential reactions to frustrations of adolescent and adult institutionalized retardates.
Administered the Rosenzweig Picture-Frustration Study to 52 12-44 yr. old institutionalized retardates. Results indicate that adolescents and adults direct their frustrations in essentially the same manner, in an essentially extra- or impunitive manner. However, the adult retardates tended to focus upon the frustrating situation itself, while the adolescents also focused their energy on attempts to finding solutions to the frustrating problem. Length of institutionalization is discussed as a possible variable to account for this.
Siegel, Louis, et al. (Willowbrook State School, Staten Island, N.Y.) Journal of Psychology, 1972(Mar), Vol. 80(2), 193-196. [PA, Vol 48:05478]

2441. A parent involvement program for institutionalized retarded children in need of behavior training.
Describes a program to involve parents in the behavior training of their institutionalized child to increase the likelihood that the child might once again live at home and attend community programs. Parents are asked to come to the institution to observe, participate in, and discuss the play-therapy, behavior training techniques being used with their child. Counseling is provided the parents individually and in projected groups. Written program guidelines are provided parents when the child goes home weekends or vacations.
Smith, Ira A.; Rubin, Gerald; DiLeonardo, Concetta M. & Griswold, Karen N. Training School Bulletin, 1972(Nov), Vol. 69(3), 115-120. [PA, Vol 50:01628]

2442. Segregation: The case against.
Asserts that segregation of the intellectually handicapped child is neither necessary, nor good. This assertion is based on the following points: (a) the impersonalization of an institution vs. home and community, (b) the traumatization of separation for the child as well as the family, (c) the lower cost of home care and special financial assistance which is available if the child is at home, and (d) often better care found in the home rather than at the institution. In many situations segregation of the mentally retarded is a means of passing the responsibility of care. It is also contended that segregation because of mental handicap involves other aspects of discrimination.
Urquhart, G. S. (Psychiatric Services, Brisbane, Queensland, Australia) Australian Journal of Mental Retardation, 1972(Mar), Vol. 2(1), 19-21. [PA, Vol 49:01244]

2443. Timeout duration and the suppression of deviant behavior in children.
Investigated the effects of 3 timeout durations in a group of 20 7-21 yr. old retarded, institutionalized Ss. Each S received 1, 15, and 30 min. of timeout in a design counterbalanced in terms of the order in which timeout durations were presented. Displays of deviant behavior (aggression, tantrums, and self-destruction) were followed by periods of isolation in a timeout room. A reversal design was employed such that return-to-base-line periods were instituted after each timeout. Rate of deviant behavior was significantly reduced, with 15 and 30 min. producing a 35% decrease in deviant behavior. Range of effects in all timeout conditions varied widely. The sequence in which the 1-min. duration was presented affected the direction of its effect. When it preceded the use of longer durations, 1 min. was most effective. As it came later in the sequence, its suppressive characteristics became less reliable. (39 ref.)
White, Geoffry D.; Nielsen, Gary & Johnson, Stephen M. (Oregon Research Inst., Eugene) Journal of Applied Behavior Analysis, 1972(Sum), Vol. 5(2), 111-120. [PA, Vol 49:01252]

2444. Social relationships of the mentally retarded.
Describes a project in which 42 mental retardates 9–12 yrs old (IQ 50–70) were placed in a special protective and growth-producing environment for 2 yrs to foster and stimulate their social interactions, using the help of psychiatric social workers on the one hand and endeavoring to educate the parents on the other hand. The behavior patterns of the children in 8 areas of social relationships (e.g., participation in family responsibilities, class programs, group activities) were measured at the beginning of the project, at the end of the 1st yr, and at the end of the project in terms of the degree and frequency of independence shown by each child. Results in the 8 areas of social behavior studied support the assumption that mentally retarded children can grow and develop in an environment specially designed to help them.
Banerji, B. S.; Misra, A. K. & Singh, S. N. Indian Journal of Mental Retardation, 1973(Jul), Vol 6(2), 81–96. [PA, Vol 60:01585]

2445. Observational study of ward staff behavior.
Describes a behavioral observation procedure for the study of ward staff behavior in a fairly typical state school ward for young children with primary retardation and secondary physical disabilities. 2 Os recorded 60 different behaviors of the staff over a 3-wk period. Similar behaviors were grouped to obtain a final list of 10 behaviors. Data indicate that more than half of the ward personnel's time was spent on activities away from the children and, of the time spent with the children, most went toward nonsocial types of interactions. Time spent at nonchild related tasks, e.g., housekeeping, paperwork, tended to be more visible to superiors. It is suggested that child related behavioral goals be made highly visible and the staff be rewarded for accomplishment of those goals.
Harmatz, Morton G. (U. Massachusetts) Exceptional Children, 1973(Apr), Vol. 39(7), 554-558. [PA, Vol 50:11747]

2446.   Intellectual and conceptual acquisition in retarded children: A follow-up study.
Conducted a follow-up study of 25 institutionalized retarded children (mean CA = 118 mo) 13 mo after their participation in a behavior modification program. The objective of the original experimental program was to provide training in the acquisition of conceptual and intellectual skills using modeling, information feedback, and social and material reinforcement. A control condition was evaluated also, in which Ss received 10 hr of social interaction but no experimental training. It was found that Ss who had participated previously in the experimental program functioned at a high level on the concept attainment task. In addition, original gains in IQ reported for the Ss in the experimental condition were retained, and the initially severely retarded Ss continued to increase their IQ scores during the 13-mo interval.
Jacobson, Leonard I.; Bernal, Guillermo; Greeson, Larry E. & Rich, John J. (U. Massachusetts) Bulletin of the Psychonomic Society, 1973(May), Vol. 1(5-B), 340-345. [PA, Vol 51:03808]

2447.   Increasing mentally retarded adolescents' verbalizations about current events.
Examined the effects of antecedent and consequent events on the verbal behavior of 3 institutionalized mentally retarded male adolescents. Verbal statements related to current national and international events were recorded after exposures to TV news programs. The accuracy of verbalizations was examined as a function of: (a) exposures to TV news presentations in massed form (i.e., viewing the entire news program before an opportunity to describe it) vs distributed form (i.e., viewing each news item separately with each followed by an opportunity to describe it), and (b) contingent tokens and social praise for correct verbal responses (i.e., statements corresponding to news items presented). Both the temporal distribution of news presentations and the reinforcement procedures improved the accuracy of verbal statements by the Ss. (24 ref)
Keilitz, Ingo; Tucker, Dennis J. & Horner, R. Don. (Parsons State Hosp. & Training Center, Kan.) Journal of Applied Behavior Analysis, 1973(Win), Vol. 6(4), 621-630. [PA, Vol 52:03741]

2448.   Primitive, atypical, and abnormal-psychotic behavior in institutionalized mentally retarded children.
Presents case histories to illustrate primitive, atypical, and abnormal (or psychotic) behaviors, the 3 most common types seen in institutionalized mentally retarded children and adolescents. Behavioral manifestations and specific approaches to management and treatment are related to the histories of 5 6-14 yr old boys exhibiting 1 of the following: (a) primitive behavior amidst delayed development, (b) atypical intrafamilial communication patterns, (c) atypical behavior response in a closely knit family, (d) childhood psychosis, or (e) the rumination syndrome. Administrative implications and suggested guidelines for implementing specific diagnostic and treatment approaches to emotionally disturbed young patients are discussed within the context of redirected goals for appropriate institutions. It is suggested that such institutions should provide regional resource programs and facilities as back-up services for community-based programs for the mentally retarded. (15 ref)
Menolascino, Frank J. (Nebraska Psychiatric Inst., Omaha) Journal of Autism & Childhood Schizophrenia, 1973(Jan), Vol. 3(1), 49-64. [PA, Vol 51:09457]

2449.   Effects of institutionalization on retarded children: A longitudinal cross-institutional investigation.
Administered the Peabody Picture Vocabulary Test, the Social Deprivation Scale by E. Zigler et al, and 3 tasks measuring verbal dependency, wariness of adults, imitation, and behavior variability to 103 familially and organically retarded children in 4 residential institutions. The measures were administered twice with a 2.5-yr interval. Results indicate that the response to institutionalization is a complex function of preinstitutional life experiences, the environments of the particular institution, and the sex and diagnosis of the Ss. Ss became less verbally dependent, less imitative, and more variable in their behavior

during the 2.5 yrs. While IQ did not change, MA increased from a mean of 7.15 to 7.57 (p < .01). Ss who showed greater behavior variability and who had a home to which to return were discharged more frequently. Objective characteristics of the institutions (e.g., size and cost) were not related to behavior or development of the children. (76 ref)
Balla, David A.; Butterfield, Earl C. & Zigler, Edward. (Yale U.) American Journal of Mental Deficiency, 1974(Mar), Vol. 78(5), 530-549. [PA, Vol 52:08489]

2450.   Attendant behavior and attitudes toward institutionalized retarded children.
Reports that 14 20-50 yr old institutional aides' perceptions of the attractiveness, likability, and mental level of 37 5-15 yr old retarded residents were related to the affective tone, content, and frequency of aide-resident interactions. Residents who were seen favorably on these attitudinal dimensions tended to receive more positive, more social, and more overall interactions with aides, as measured by reliable behavioral observations on the ward. Suggestions for research on contingency training and staff-patient ratios, as well as implications for inservice programs, are discussed. (15 ref)
Dailey, Wayne F.; Allen, George J.; Chinsky, Jack M. & Veit, Steven W. (U. Connecticut) American Journal of Mental Deficiency, 1974(Mar), Vol. 78(5), 586-591. [PA, Vol 52:08495]

2451.   Aide-resident ratio and ward population density as mediators of social interaction.
Observed various types of interpersonal interaction between 37 institutionalized retarded children (mean age = 9 yrs) and 18 attendants under different ward populations and resident-aide ratios. High population density alone was not associated with decreases in the general quality of aide-initiated interactions with residents when resident-aide ratio was held constant. Lowering the resident-aide ratio by adding a 2nd attendant to a moderately populated ward did not change the behavior of either aide. Decreasing the resident-aide ratio when 1 aide was present, by decreasing the resident population, was associated with significant increases in the frequency of desirable types of aide behavior. These findings suggest that attendants might be most effective when working alone with a small group of residents.
Harris, Joan M.; Veit, Steven W.; Allen, George J. & Chinsky, Jack M. (U Connecticut) American Journal of Mental Deficiency, 1974(Nov), Vol 79(3), 320-326. [PA, Vol 53:10353]

2452.   Effects of programed social interaction on the measured intelligence of institutionalised moderately and severely retarded children.
Evaluated the effect of sociomotivational factors on performance on the Stanford-Binet Intelligence Scale. 18 of 27 institutionalized moderately and severely retarded children were assigned to a 10- or 20-hr social interaction condition in which experimentally controlled interactions between Es and Ss occurred. The Stanford-Binet was administered to Ss before and after participation. 9 Ss were assigned to a no-treatment control condition, in which the Stanford-Binet was administered twice, with 1 mo between administrations. Small but significant increases in IQ were found for Ss in the experimental conditions, but not in the control condition. Initial degree of retardation was unrelated to IQ change.
Jacobson, L. I.; Bernal, G. & Greeson, L. E. (U. Miami) Journal of Mental Deficiency Research, 1974(Mar), Vol. 18(1), 87-91. [PA, Vol 52:12845]

2453.   Training and education of the mentally retarded children: A survey report.
Notes that Indian institutions for educating and training the mentally retarded can provide care for only 2,400 patients out of the estimated 5-19 million retarded in the country. In a New Delhi home serving 87 mildly and moderately retarded children, 73 came from homes on the lower socioeconomic level. 40 had serious speech defects and 41 were retarded in motor development. It is felt that institutional care is preferable to home care for such children, since trained therapists and teachers achieve

improvement in behavior and learning that overprotective parents cannot. (17 ref)
Kaur, Ravinder & Sen, Arun K. Indian Journal of Mental Retardation, 1974(Jul), Vol 7(2), 65-71. [PA, Vol 53:12526]

2454. Play therapy with institutionalized mentally retarded children.
Assigned 12 5-11 yr old institutionalized retarded children to either individual play therapy, group play therapy, or a no-treatment control. The Denver Developmental Screening Test (DDST) was administered by 2 separate testers as a pretest and after each of 3 10-session blocks of therapy. The 1st and 3rd blocks were directive therapy; the 2nd was nondirective. DDST scales for Fine Motor-Adaptive, Language, and Personal-Social skills showed a main effect for treatment group. The Gross Motor scale and the other scales revealed a Treat-ment × Measurement Period interaction. All scales had a similar pattern: the no-treatment group did not change while scores for individual and group therapy groups increased across sessions. There were no differences between group and individual therapy. (18 ref)
Newcomer, Barbara L. & Morrison, Thomas L. (U. Washington, Child Development & Mental Retardation Center) American Journal of Mental Deficiency, 1974(May), Vol. 78(6), 727-733. [PA, Vol 52:08517]

2455. Reducing aggressive and self-injurious behavior of institutionalized retarded children through reinforcement of other behaviors.
Reduced aggressive and self-injurious behaviors of 4 8-13 yr old retarded children by combining various techniques with the differential reinforcement of other behaviors (DRO). In 1 study, aggressive responses of a severely retarded child were reduced when DRO was combined with a 30-sec timeout. In a 2nd study, various aggressive classroom behaviors were reduced when a child was told "no" for an inappropriate response but earned puzzle pieces for periods of time when inappropriate responses did not occur. Exchangeable tokens were given to a 3rd S for every 15 min in which aggressive responding did not occur, while each inappropriate response resulted in the loss of all tokens accrued. Responding was decreased to a level far below baseline. For a 4th child, self-injurious responses were followed by "no," and intervals of time in which no self-injurious responding occurred earned candy. The rate of this behavior was reduced significantly. (29 ref)
Repp, Alan C. & Deitz, Samuel M. (Georgia Retardation Center, Atlanta) Journal of Applied Behavior Analysis, 1974(Sum), Vol. 7(2), 313-325. [PA, Vol 52:12976]

2456. Programming the generalization of a greeting response in four retarded children.
Used reinforcement techniques of prompting and shaping to develop handwaving in 4 10-13 yr old institutionalized retarded Ss. A multiple-baseline design across Ss demonstrated the reliable functioning of the training procedures. Specifically, it showed that training and maintenance of the greeting response by 1 E was not usually sufficient for generalization of the response to the more than 20 other members of the institution staff who had not participated in the training of the response. However, high levels of generalization to staff members were recorded for 3 Ss over periods ranging from 1 to 6 mo after a 2nd E trained and maintained the response in conjunction with the 1st E. The 4th S, although never receiving training by a 2nd E, showed similar results following a 2nd training by the 1st E.
Stokes, Trevor F.; Baer, Donald M. & Jackson, Robert L. (U Kansas) Journal of Applied Behavior Analysis, 1974(Win), Vol 7(4), 599-610. [PA, Vol 53:10138]

2457. Interactions between residents and staff: A qualitative investigation of an institutional setting for retarded children.
Reports on an investigation of types of interactions occurring between retarded individuals and staff, and frequency of occur-rence per type. Results indicate that the setting did not provide sufficient occasions for learning.

Blindert, H. Dieter. (Behavior Clinic, CPRI, London, Canada) Mental Retardation, 1975(Oct), Vol 13(5), 38-40. [PA, Vol 55:05245]

2458. Therapists' approach and avoidance responses and the verbal behavior of mentally retarded clients.
Investigated the effect of therapists' approach-avoidance re-sponses on the elicitation of mentally retarded client dependent and hostile statements. Transcripts from early and late counsel-ing sessions were rated according to initial client statement, therapist response, and client continuation of the topic. Results, based on 28 institutionalized mentally retarded adolescents (mean IQ, 66), indicated that Ss did not respond differentially to therapist approach-avoidance behavior in the early counseling session but did respond differentially in the late session. Findings are compared with results of previous studies that investigated this research question with nonretarded clients.
Campbell, David R. & Browning, Philip L. (U Oregon, Rehabilitation Research & Training Ctr in Mental Retardation) Journal of Counseling Psychology, 1975(Jul), Vol 22(4), 320-323. [PA, Vol 54:05727]

2459. Effects of combining methylphenidate and a classroom token system in modifying hyperactive behavior.
Studied the combined effects of methylphenidate (0.3 mg/kg/day) and a token reinforcement program in controlling the classroom behavior of 16 hyperactive, institutionalized retarded 9-15 yr olds. A within-S, placebo-controlled, double-blind design was employed. Results from 13 Ss indicate that the behavior modification procedures in the presence of placebo medication produced significant increases in work-oriented and related decreases in disruptive behaviors. Few effects from the addition of active medication to the treatment program were found on any of the dependent measures (seat activity, teachers' ratings, and academic performance). Findings suggest that behavior modification is a viable alternative to drug therapy for hyperactivity in retarded persons. (36 ref)
Christensen, Donald E. (Portsmouth Psychiatric Ctr, VA) American Journal of Mental Deficiency, 1975(Nov), Vol 80(3), 266-276. [PA, Vol 55:10171]

2460. Training mentally retarded adolescents to brush their teeth.
The need for self-care by retarded individuals led to the development and evaluation of a comprehensive toothbrushing program that included a task analysis and training procedure specific to each component of the task analysis. 8 9-17 yr old institutionalized retardates, in 2 groups, individually received acquisition training that included scheduled opportunities for independent performances, verbal instruction, modeling, demon-stration, and physical assistance. The 1st group received token plus social reinforcement; the 2nd received only social reinforce-ment. All Ss showed improved toothbrushing behaviors when compared to baseline. 6 Ss correctly performed all toothbrushing steps in 2 of 3 consecutive sessions. Results emphasize the need for systematic program development and evaluation.
Horner, R. Don & Keilitz, Ingo. (U Kansas) Journal of Applied Behavior Analysis, 1975(Fal), Vol 8(3), 301-309. [PA, Vol 54:12329]

2461. Resident-care practices in institutions for retarded persons: A cross-institutional, cross-cultural study.
Institution- and resident-oriented case practices for institutional-ized retarded persons were investigated in 166 living units in 19 institutions in the US and 11 institutions in a Scandinavian country. Living units in the Scandinavian country were more resident-oriented than those in the US. Large central institutions were characterized by the most institution-oriented care prac-tices, group homes by the most resident-oriented practices, with large and small regional centers falling between these extremes. Within type of institution, care practices were generally homoge-neous. Living units for more severely retarded residents were characterized by more institution-oriented practices. Large liv-ing-unit size was predictive of institution-oriented practices while cost/resident/day, number of aides/resident, and number of

professional staff/residents did not predict care practices. Characteristics of the Child Management Inventory, which assesses resident care practices, are examined. (29 ref)
McCormick, Mark; Balla, David & Zigler, Edward. (Yale U) American Journal of Mental Deficiency, 1975(Jul), Vol 80(1), 1-17. [PA, Vol 54:10386]

2462.   Foster home adjustment of retardates.
Tested the hypothesis that there are 4 factors that influence the adjustment of a previously institutionalized retardate to a foster home: (a) length of the retardate's stay in an institution before foster-home placement, (b) his home environment before institutionalization, (c) his ability to control his impulses, and (d) his capacity for social communication. A study of 52 female and 20 male placements (ages 1-57 yrs) in foster homes of which only half were successful, showed that only factors (a) and (d) had predictive validity. (22 ref)
Miller, Steven I. et al. (Loyola U, Chicago) Indian Journal of Social Work, 1975(Jul), Vol 36(2), 145-154. [PA, Vol 55:07401]

2463.   A reply to Zigler and Seitz.
In response to E. Zigler and V. Seitz's critique (see PA, Vol 54:3454), it is conceded that there should be (a) multivariate analyses, where applicable, in studies having more than 1 dependent variable; (b) definition of the population for which sensorimotor training procedures may be appropriately prescribed; and (c) validation of the profile measure as a tool to assess neurological disorganization. (30 ref)
Neman, Ronald. (National Assn for Retarded Citizens, Arlington, TX) American Journal of Mental Deficiency, 1975(Mar), Vol 79(5), 493-505. [PA, Vol 54:03437]

2464.   Birth order, maternal age, and mental retardation.
Presents a statistical comparison between 2 groups of mentally retarded individuals selected from an institution and a community-based center. The 378 individuals had CAs of 3-69 yrs and IQs of 6-90. Birth order, mother's age at birth of the child, and etiology of mental retardation were analyzed using a chi-square for 2 independent samples. Results identify 2 high-risk populations—very young mothers, CAs 16-20 yrs, and mothers aged 35-45 yrs—and reveal that both mother's age and cause of retardation are related to whether or not the child will remain in the community. It is concluded that results present a strong case for preventive emphasis as part of the long-range goals of mental retardation services.
Sternlicht, Manny; Staaby, Judy & Sullivan, Ina. (Willowbrook Developmental Ctr, Staten Island, NY) Mental Retardation, 1975(Dec), Vol 13(6), 3-6. [PA, Vol 55:10076]

2465.   Dance therapy and education program.
Describes a dance therapy program for the mentally retarded residents of the Muskoka Center in Ontario, established in 1973 to improve their physical, mental, and social skills. The program involved 150 residents in classes of 8-12 members, who met for 1 hr twice a week. Music was used to stimulate the individual to feel, think, and act in a specific way. The program included tap, ballet, acrobatic, and ball-room dancing to improving basic body movements, muscle coordination, balance, and especially social skills. As the Center has 300 retardates, predominantly female, 8-80 yrs old, ranging from educable to profoundly retarded, a wide variety of programs was necessary. As a reward for those who achieved success, a series of skits were produced for the benefit of the community. Main results of the program included improvement in everyday posture, walking, and general level of confidence and poise.
Tipple, Blanche. (Muskoka Ctr, Gravenhurst, Canada) Journal of Leisurability, 1975(Oct), Vol 2(4), 9-12. [PA, Vol 57:10674]

2466.   On "An experimental evaluation of sensorimotor patterning": A critique.
Discusses the method of sensorimotor training for retarded children that was described in a study by R. Neman et al (1975) emphasizing the theoretical rationale underlying the method of treatment, S selection, statistical analyses, and interpretation of findings. Problems raised by the premature release of the findings to the press are noted. (29 ref)

Zigler, Edward & Seitz, Victoria. (Yale U) American Journal of Mental Deficiency, 1975(Mar), Vol 79(5), 483-492. [PA, Vol 54:03454]

2467.   Integrating remedial methods into child care practice.
Often there are special communication problems found in working with emotionally disturbed and/or retarded children. Therapeutic methods are described that are used at a residential treatment center for children who often suffer from perceptual distortions and may be unable to learn through verbal instruction. Typical problems include the child who cannot follow instructions because normal grammar is confusing, the child who cannot remember more than one thing at a time, and the child with disorders related to spatial orientation and sequencing. Special ways of teaching these skills are presented. For example, a child who is unable to learn the sequence involved in making a bed may be able to use a list of instructions broken down into very small steps. Although such children usually try the counselor's patience, they need to be taught that they are acceptable, capable of learning, and worth teaching.
Adler, Jack & Finkel, William. (Jewish Child Care Assn of New York, NY) Child Care Quarterly, 1976(Spr), Vol 5(1), 53–62. [PA, Vol 62:04306]

2468.   Social adaptation assessment as a tool for prescriptive remediation.
Focuses on the evaluation of social adaptation in the mentally retarded and on the use of data from the Adaptive Behavior Checklist (ABCL) in prescriptive remediation. The ABCL is a tool for assessing the degree of social adaptiveness of residents in a state-supported residential facility for mentally retarded children and adults at all levels of measured intelligence, physical handicap, and educational, vocational, and training potential. Suggestions for remedial programs include physical therapy, audiological assessment, opthalmological evaluation, and behavioral programs in toileting, eating, table manners, personal cleanliness, dressing, oral hygiene, grooming, and acquisition of attending behaviors.
Allen, Robert M.; Loeffler, Frank J.; Levine, Martin N. & Alker, Leslie N. (U Miami, FL) Mental Retardation, 1976(Feb), Vol 14(1), 36-37. [PA, Vol 56:01200]

2469.   Steady and transition states: Effects of alternative activity on body-rocking in retarded children.
Reports 2 experiments in which steady and transition states were observed for 2 independent operants (body-rocking and ball-manipulandum) in 1 male and 4 female institutionalized, 120-185 mo old retarded children. First, stable FR response rates were successively obtained for body-rocking and ball-manipulandum responding. Second, transition states were obtained for the 2 operants simultaneously. Results indicate that the independent operants under standardized experimental conditions showed moderately correlated and stabler response rates. The method of simultaneous operants provided a valid technique for analysis of transition states, i.e., the functional separation of stereotyped acts (body-rocking) and alternative activity (ball manipulandum). The effects of experimental manipulations were reversible. (25 ref)
Hollis, John H. (U Kansas) Psychological Reports, 1976(Aug), Vol 39(1), 91-104. [PA, Vol 57:03926]

2470.   Attendant staff speech to the institutionalized retarded: Language use as a measure of the quality of care.
An observational measure of adult speech to children, developed by B. Tizard et al (see PA, Vol 48:11260) was modified and applied to residences for retarded adults. The measure categorizes the major functions of staff talk to residents as "control" and "information." Results resemble the findings of Tizard et al i.e., "informative" staff speech was more complex and its frequency was associated with resident language comprehension abilities. The speech measure was related to another index of the quality of care provided in such facilities. Ability (mental age) of resident speech "targets" was also found to affect the frequency of informative remarks by staff.

Pratt, Michael W.; Bumstead, Dennis C. & Raynes, Norma V. (Rockefeller U, New York, NY) Journal of Child Psychology & Psychiatry & Allied Disciplines, 1976(Apr), Vol 17(2), 133-143. [PA, Vol 56:04573]

2471. Success expectancy and achievement expectancy in trainable mentally retarded and in nonretarded children.
Attempted to determine (a) whether there is a difference between the success expectation and the achievement expectation of nonretarded and trainable mentally retarded children of the same MA, and (b) whether there is any difference in action output and verbal output of the motivation of the 2 groups. Ss were 15 institutionalized severely retarded males and 15 nonretarded males who were rewarded for accurately estimating the number of jumps they could make. The performance level of retarded Ss was lower than that for normal Ss, but their aspiration levels were higher. The lower performances may be accounted for either by lower motor proficiency in retarded Ss or by their lesser bodily effort (weaker action output). Results suggest, however, that the achievement expectation of mentally retarded Ss is stronger than that of nonretarded Ss. (Czechoslovakian & Russian summaries) (18 ref)
Révi, Jeno & Illyes, Sandor. (Hungarian Academy of Sciences, Inst of Psychology, Budapest) Studia Psychologica, 1976, Vol 118(3), 222-228. [PA, Vol 57:11535]

2472. Effects of price manipulations on consumer behavior in a sheltered workshop token economy.
When the price of frequently purchased goods in a workshop store was increased, it was observed that 22 16–46 yr old institutionalized retardates displayed discriminative purchasing behavior, reducing the frequency of acquisition and amount spent on more expendable items, irrespective of relative modal unit price of item classes.
Schroeder, Stephen R. & Barrera, Francisco J. (U North Carolina, Chapel Hill) American Journal of Mental Deficiency, 1976(Sep), Vol 81(2), 172-180. [PA, Vol 57:06519]

2473. New long-stay patients in a hospital for mental handicap.
Tested the prediction made in the 1971 policy document, *Better Services for the Mentally Handicapped,* that the number of beds in hospitals for mental handicaps will decrease. This can be achieved only by admitting fewer new long-stay patients. A study was made of 50 such cases admitted to a mental hospital in the 5 yrs 1970-1974. Of these admissions 54% had WISC scores under 25, and 42% were children. 62% were admitted for behavior problems and 38% for physical infirmity and helplessness. It is concluded that there are some mentally handicapped people who have problems of profound mental retardation and high nursing dependency with which only a hospital can cope.
Spencer, Douglas A. (Meanwood Park Hosp, England) British Journal of Psychiatry, 1976(May), Vol 128, 467-470. [PA, Vol 56:10445]

2474. A national trend: The impact of educating and training formerly institutionalized children and adults in the community.
Examines the responsibilities of various institutions and community organizations in educating formerly institutionalized mentally retarded and physically hndicapped individuals. It is argued that in order for such individuals to make an adequate adjustment in the community at large, specialized training must begin in the institutional setting, where the individual should be provided with a comprehensive, graduated transitional program terminating in semi-independent, or independent community living. Group homes are also a means of normalizing the life of these individuals. Adults assigned to group homes assist in the general maintenance of the home; children are taught basic self-help skills and also assist in the maintenance of the home. Programs designed by special schools, community colleges, the public schools, and vocational schools are described.
Thornley, Margo L. (Northwest Ctr for the Retarded, Seattle, WA) Education & Training of the Mentally Retarded, 1976(Apr), Vol 11(2), 152-155. [PA, Vol 56:08498]

2475. Interpersonal interactions between institutionalized retarded children and their attendants.
Developed an observational method to enable detailed analysis of the behavioral and situational components of aide-resident interpersonal interactions in an institutional ward for retarded children. The mode of communication, interpersonal affect, response to the initiator of an encounter, the context within which the interaction occurs, and a mand/tact dimension were measured for 37 institutionalized retarded children (mean CA, 9.3 yrs; mean IQ, 23.0). The development and validation of the scale, including data on its reliability, utility, and communicability in training novice observers, are reported. Interrater agreement in each dimension exceeded 80%, averaging 89% over all categories. Observations over a 7-wk period indicated that the dormitory was consistently characterized by child-care and ward-management activities and a neutral affective atmosphere in which aides initiated most of the interactions. The observational method appears appropriate for evaluating interventions designed to improve the quality of residential treatment.
Veit, Steven W.; Allen, George J. & Chinsky, Jack M. (U Connecticut) American Journal of Mental Deficiency, 1976(Mar), Vol 80(5), 535-542. [PA, Vol 56:06549]

2476. Drug treatment: Factors contributing to high risk in institutions.
Reviews the reasons that drugs administered to institutionalized mentally retarded individuals do not always have the intended beneficial effects. Inadequately trained staff, the number and complexity of drugs employed, and the vulnerability of the child are discussed. Recommendations are made for new directions in drug administration.
Greer, John G.; Davis, Tara B. & Yearwood, Kenneth. (Memphis State U) Exceptional Children, 1977(Apr), Vol 43(7), 451–453. [PA, Vol 59:01606]

2477. Social interaction between caregivers and profoundly retarded children.
Observed the interaction between 77 nonambulatory, profoundly retarded young people and the staff members in 4 wards of a residential institution to determine what conditions influenced the quality of care given. The amount and kind (verbal vs nonverbal, task-related vs non-task-related) of staff-initiated activity directed toward the child was observed during feeding and recreation periods. It was found that on the average, the staff spent 8% of the time in social (non-task-related) interaction, a figure that, though low, compares favorably with a figure of 1% reported elsewhere. There were significant differences between wards in the amount of staff–child interaction observed, especially verbal interaction. To investigate whether the child's level of functioning was a factor in the differences in care found among wards, the children were rated on a scale which measured their (a) need for nursing care, (b) physical development, (c) awareness, and (d) ability to help themselves. Scores on these scales were correlated with the staff-interaction figures, and it was found that although the staff did, as expected, interact more with the more able children, the child's level of adaptive functioning did not consistently predict the amount or kind of interaction with the staff. It was believed that administrative action could help create a more child-oriented atmosphere in the lowest interacting wards.
Hermanson, Colleen & Das, J. P. (Eric Cormack Ctr, Edmonton, Canada) Mental Retardation Bulletin, 1977, Vol 5(3), 101–114. [PA, Vol 61:11506]

2478. Self-perception of intrinsic and extrinsic motivation: Effects on institutionalized mentally retarded adolescents.
Self-perception theory predicts that the introduction of extrinsic rewards for behavior that is intrinsically rewarding may decrease rather than enhance overall motivation. This hypothesis was tested on 44 institutionalized mentally retarded adolescents (median CA 15 yrs 4 mo, median IQ 61). Intrinsic (high and low task interest) and extrinsic (high- and low-incentive objects) motivation were both manipulated as independent variables, and the dependent variable was task persistence during a free-play period. For a high intrinsically interesting task, the task

persistence was greater under the external reward of low- rather than high-incentive value conditions. The opposite trend was revealed for the low intrinsically interesting task. Results provide some evidence that the greater the amount of the reward for an interesting activity, the greater the degree to which the intrinsic interest is undermined. (24 ref)
Lee, Dong Y.; Syrnyk, Randal & Hallschmid, Claus. (Alberta School Hosp, Red Deer, Canada) American Journal of Mental Deficiency, 1977(Jan), Vol 81(4), 331-337. [PA, Vol 58:05628]

2479.   The effects of environmental design on adolescents in an institution.
Reports a time-sampling study of 31 retarded adolescents' behavior before and after a day hall in a state institution was redesigned to provide an enriched environment. The new design, which included a large-group area for gross-motor activities and a small-group area with learning booths, promoted purposeful activity and reduced passive use of the day room.
Levy, Ellen & McLeod, William. Mental Retardation, 1977(Apr), Vol 15(2), 28–32. [PA, Vol 59:01709]

2480.   [Reeducative techniques in a hospital environment.] (Fren)
650 mentally deficient hospitalized children were exposed to an innovation in re-education: The "materiatheque" service provides materials and explanatory matter in 4 areas (autonomy, communication, occupation, and socialization) corresponding to the child's level of utilization, and catalogues them by a card system. Adolescents, young adults, and 5-yr-olds were re-educated in knowledge (e.g., sensory and academic prerequisites), motility (e.g., discovery and appropriation of space), and communication (e.g., language, breathing, and lip movement). Efforts focused on (a) adaptation of those Ss below the level of semi-educables, who were taught acceptance of contacts with the world, language, comprehension of orders, and practical matters such as eating and dress; (b) re-education of those stable enough to accept a work structure; and (c) apprenticeship to learn skills for a protected workshop situation. (German & Spanish summaries)
Masurel, C. & Moley, J. (Hosp Rivière-des-Prairies, Montreal, Canada) Revue de Neuropsychiatrie Infantile et d'Hygiene Mentale de l'Enfance, 1977(May–Jun), Vol 25(5–6), 339–346. [PA, Vol 63:06103]

2481.   Increasing institutional staff to resident interactions through in-service training and supervisor approval.
Investigated effects of supervisor approval on staff–resident interactions in a state retardation center for multihandicapped persons. Following baseline, an in-service training program designed to teach staff members appropriate methods of interacting with and stimulating residents was instituted along with contingent supervisor approval. After a return to baseline, supervisor approval alone was instituted. Ss were the 15 attendants (mean age 39.3 yrs, mean education 11.2 yrs) in a unit housing 54 profoundly retarded adolescents and adults. The main supervisor was the unit director, who had 24-hr supervisory responsibilities over the unit. Results show that when the unit supervisor commended and attended to staff members for interacting with residents, staff–resident interactions increased 25 to 50% above baseline rates. It is concluded that supervisor approval was an inexpensive and readily available process to change institutional staff behavior. (18 ref)
Montegar, Carol A.; Reid, Dennis H.; Madsen, Charles H. & Ewell, Marion D. (Western Michigan U) Behavior Therapy, 1977(Sep), Vol 8(4), 533–540. [PA, Vol 60:03694]

2482.   The value and practical use of behavior modification programmes: A nurse's viewpoint.
Behavior modification programs, conducted by nurses, focus attention on the institutionalized retarded person's individual needs and become significant personal experiences for both the people involved. Special knowledge and intensive staff training are needed so that nurses can apply and incorporate behavior modification programs into their daily work schedules. Details of 5 behavior modification programs, designed to reduce unaccept-

able behavior and conducted by nurses, are presented. Case reports of 6 mildly and severely retarded female adolescents and adults in an institution are included for illustration. It is concluded that acceptable behavior patterns can be established and retained through simple programs organized and conducted by the nursing staff.
Scott, Anne. (Strathmont Ctr, Gilles Plains, Australia) Australian Journal of Mental Retardation, 1977(Mar), Vol 4(5), 14–17. [PA, Vol 60:07911]

2483.   Parental visitation of the institutionalized retarded.
Investigated factors relating to parental visitation of the mentally retarded. Data including CA, MA, sex, and length of institutionalization were obtained from files of 512 residents at a state institution. The mean age of the Ss was 23.9 yrs; 60% of them were males, and 66% had been institutionalized prior to 1965. Results for a 3-yr period, show an inverse relationship between the number of parental visits and the distance of the parental home from the institution. When the natural parents were living together, the retarded child received more visits than when the child's parents were separated or one parent was deceased. Single mothers were living significantly closer to the facility than single fathers. Single fathers appeared to put more effort into visiting, since they visited just as often as the mothers, but had to travel further distances than the mothers to do so. Visitation frequency followed a curvilinear pattern, decreasing uniformly from 20–60 miles (from 0–20 miles visitation frequency was uniform), and then leveling off.
Sechrest, Lee B. & Sukstorf, Steve. (Florida State U) Journal of Applied Social Psychology, 1977(Oct–Dec), Vol 7(4), 286–294. [PA, Vol 60:12324]

2484.   Residential care for the mentally handicapped.
Since there are different kinds and degrees of mental handicap, certain general principles have evolved on which current thinking about the mentally handicapped child in residential care is based. Three interacting sets of factors are considered in the present paper: (a) the relevance of changes in public and professional attitudes to mental handicap, (b) the evidence of differences in the effects on children of different kinds of residential environment, and (c) individual differences in mentally handicapped children which may result in different needs. (56 ref)
Segal, Stanley S. Educational Research, 1977(Jun), Vol 19(3), 199–216. [PA, Vol 60:03702]

2485.   Chronological age and social age as factors in intensive daytime toilet training of institutionalized mentally retarded individuals.
Data for intensive daytime toilet training programs carried out with 13 retarded trainees were retrospectively analyzed. Evidence is presented for CA and social age (Vineland Social Maturity Scale) as factors affecting progress on such programs. Children below age 20 yrs were trained significantly faster than adults over the age of 25; and children with social ages of 2.0–2.5 yrs progressed significantly faster than children with social ages between 1.5 and 2 yrs.
Smith, Paul S. & Smith, Linda J. (Prudhoe Hosp, England) Journal of Behavior Therapy & Experimental Psychiatry, 1977(Sep), Vol 8(3), 269–273. [PA, Vol 60:11975]

2486.   Linking young and old institutionalized people.
Suggests that engaging older people in service to young mentally retarded people can benefit each group. A demonstration of such a program is presented in which residents of a nursing home and institution for the retarded engaged in a number of visits. The implementation of the program is discussed as well as observations regarding the outcome. It is believed that the elderly are a resource for serving the children, leading to the mutual benefit of each group.
Solon, Jerry A.; Amthor, Rebecca P.; Rabb, Margaret Y. & Shelley, James C. (NIH, National Inst on Aging, Bethesda, MD) Public Health Reports, 1977(Jan–Feb), Vol 92(1), 57–64. [PA, Vol 61:01671]

2487. Establishing words and objects as functionally equivalent through manual sign training.
Investigated whether sign–object and sign–word training would lead to acquisition of word–object associations, and tested the proposal that if 2 stimuli control the same response, training a new response to 1 of the stimuli would increase the probability of the 2nd stimulus also controlling that response. The Ss were 6 institutionalized retarded 11–21 yr old males, each having some receptive and productive speech and imitative motor and verbal skills. Nonsense words, signs, and objects were used as stimuli. All Ss were sequentially trained to (a) pair the objects with their identical matches, (b) imitate the manual signs, (c) pair the manual signs with the objects, (d) imitate the nonsense words, and (e) pair the manual signs with the words. Following this training, Ss were given receptive and productive word–object association probes. All Ss performed at an 87% correct level or better on the 1st receptive probes and at a 73% correct level or better on the 1st productive probes. These Ss demonstrated that following sign–object and sign–word training, they could correctly associate the word with the object. (22 ref)
VanBiervliet, Alan. (U Kansas, Bureau of Child Research) American Journal of Mental Deficiency, 1977(Sep), Vol 82(2), 178–186. [PA, Vol 60:05484]

2488. Individual and group contingencies and collateral social behaviors.
Individual and group contingencies were implemented in a sorting task employing 9 institutionalized retarded men aged 19–24 yrs. A higher frequency of appropriate social behaviors and a lower frequency of inappropriate social behaviors occurred under group task and reward conditions than under individual task and reward conditions. These effects were maintained in a subsequent snack period in which no experimental contingencies were in effect. No difference in task performance was found under the 2 different contingencies, as it was completed at almost maximal efficiency under both. (18 ref)
Frankosky, Richard J. & Sulzer-Azaroff, Beth. (Paul Devers State School, Taunton, MA) Behavior Therapy, 1978(Jun), Vol 9(3), 313–327. [PA, Vol 62:04316]

2489. Environmental noise in a residential institution for mentally retarded persons.
Assessed the noise characteristics in residence halls housing young mentally retarded children and tested the effects of this noise on speech-discrimination performance of 21 9–14 yr old residents. Results of the noise survey indicate that the mean level of the noise was 75 db, with the level greater than 70 db during 71% of the sampling time. The spectrum was similar in configuration to the longtime speech spectrum. Selected residents were tested for speech discrimination in quiet and noise conditions. Mean scores on the Word Intelligibility by Picture Identification test were 73.9% correct in the quiet and 44% correct in the noise conditions. It is concluded that the residents, who already had a primary language-learning handicap, were being subjected to a possible secondary impediment resulting from their living environment.
Glenn, Larry E.; Nerbonne, G. Patrick & Tolhurst, Gilbert C. (Southern Connecticut State Coll) American Journal of Mental Deficiency, 1978(May), Vol 82(6), 594–597. [PA, Vol 62:01807]

2490. Drug treatment: Factors contributing to high risks in institutions.
Because of the widespread use of drugs in the treatment of exceptional children, investigators are currently studying the efficacy, suitability, and safety of the drugs employed. This paper examines an aspect of pharmacological management that has been largely neglected in the literature—the administration of prescribed drugs. Focusing on the institutional setting, the following 3 factors contributing to high risk of drug error or misuse are delineated: (a) staff training and sophistication, (b) number and complexity of drugs employed, and (c) vulnerability of the exceptional child. An attempt is made to clarify these issues, to report some preliminary programs that appear to be effective, and to offer concrete suggestions for persons who are involved in the pharmacological management of exceptional children. (German & French abstracts) (15 ref)
Greer, John G.; Davis, Tara B. & Yearwood, Kenneth. (Memphis State U) International Journal of Rehabilitation Research, 1978, Vol 1(1), 19–26. [PA, Vol 61:08996]

2491. The management of obesity in the post-adolescent developmentally disabled client with Prader-Willi syndrome.
Discusses the problem of obesity control in 2 retarded residents (17 and 21 yrs old) who were diagnosed as having Prader-Willi syndrome, with a description of the syndrome, a brief case history of one of the residents with the syndrome, and an outline of the program used by a residential facility for exceptional young adults in managing this difficult problem.
Heiman, Michael F. (Stockton Residential Facility, Exceptional Young Adults Program, CA) Adolescence, 1978(Sum), Vol 13(50), 291–296. [PA, Vol 62:04139]

2492. Some negative side effects of a punishment procedure for stereotyped behavior.
Punished 2 profoundly retarded 16- and 18-yr-old adolescents for engaging in stereotyped self-stimulatory behavior. A within-Ss reversal design was used. One S also experienced a differential reinforcement of other behavior condition to reduce his self-stimulatory behavior. Both Ss exhibited what could be interpreted as negative side effects of the punishment condition. For one S this was seen in experimenter directed aggression, while for the other the side effect was a decrease in social behavior. These behaviors were not seen in the other experimental conditions. The data suggest that punishment may result in negative side effects, and when it is the treatment of choice, a careful, systematic monitoring of a variety of behaviors should be made. In this way any deleterious effects of the procedure are more likely to be detected. (17 ref)
Mayhew, Gerald L. & Harris, Francis C. (Colin Anderson Ctr, St Mary's, WV) Journal of Behavior Therapy & Experimental Psychiatry, 1978(Sep), Vol 9(3), 245–251. [PA, Vol 64:03787]

2493. Use of Moos' Ward Atmosphere Scale in a residential setting for mentally retarded adolescents.
Administered a modified version of the Ward Atmosphere Scale to 14 staff members and 10 students at a residential center for mildly and moderately retarded adolescents. Differences between staff's perceptions of the environment and their image of an ideal environment, and between staff's and students' perceptions of the school environment are noted. (2 ref)
McGee, Mark G. & Woods, Donald J. (Texas A&M U) Psychological Reports, 1978(Oct), Vol 43(2), 580–582. [PA, Vol 63:10364]

2494. The relation of length of institutionalization to the intellectual functioning of the profoundly retarded.
Measured the effect of institutionalization in relation to performance on the Cattell Infant Intelligence Scale by 103 profoundly retarded residents with a mean CA of 20.3 yrs, mean MA of 18.1 mo, mean IQ of 12.7, and mean number of years in the institution of 10.6. After partialing out CA and MA, years in the institution was negatively correlated with success in visually directed object manipulation (Cattell items below an MA of 9 mo), social imitation (9–12 mo), and purposeful, constructive activities (over 20 mo). Findings are compared with previous studies on retarded and nonretarded infants and children. (19 ref)
Ohwaki, Sonoko & Stayton, Samuel E. (Lynchburg Training School & Hosp, VA) Child Development, 1978(Mar), Vol 49(1), 105–109. [PA, Vol 62:01828]

2495. Mentally retarded child: Institutional care and life style.
Describes the Rome Developmental Center, a New York State institution for the severely mentally retarded, particularly its policy and procedures with respect to a group of 140 children, CA 2–21 yrs, residing in 10 living units. Physicians who help make decisions regarding institutionalization of children should know about the quality of care given in local facilities.
Wilkie, Ormond L. (Rome Developmental Ctr, NY) New York State Journal of Medicine, 1978(Jun), Vol 78(7), 1142–1146. [PA, Vol 62:14419]

2496.   The effects of institutionalisation on retardates' social independence.
Administered the Adaptive Behavior Scales to 40 mentally retarded Ss (mean CA 13–20 yrs; mean MA 4–8 yrs). Results suggest that the longer proportion of life-time institutionalized, the more likely the S is to be socially dependent. (24 ref)
Burkhart, Gary & Seim, R. (U Western Ontario, University Hosp Psychology Dept, London, Canada) Journal of Mental Deficiency Research, 1979(Sep), Vol 23(3), 213–218. [PA, Vol 66:06492]

2497.   The relationship of visitation to adaptive behavior of institutionalized mentally retarded persons.
Adaptive Behavior Scale scores for 896 5–71 yr old institutionalized Ss (IQs 0–69) indicated that, in general, the frequency of visitation that typically occurs in most institutions was not significantly related to the behaviors that were expected to be most readily affected by such visitation—adaptive behavior and socialization. (5 ref)
Fletcher, Donna N. (Florida State U, Coll of Education, Tallahassee) Mental Retardation, 1979(Jun), Vol 17(3), 152–154. [PA, Vol 66:08692]

2498.   Language differences between institutionalized and noninstitutionalized retarded children.
The linguistic performances of 15 noninstitutionalized (mean CA 12 yrs 6 mo; mean IQ 51.60) and 15 institutionalized (mean CA 13 yrs 4 mo; mean IQ 50.15) retarded children were compared on use of grammatical categories and structure of spoken language (Length–Complexity Index) and for underlying subskills (Illinois Test of Psycholinguistic Abilities). Differences were not found between the groups for use of grammatical categories or structures but were found for subskills of Auditory Reception, Auditory Sequential Memory, Verbal Expression, and Auditory Closure. Further analysis by multiple stepwise regression indicated that noninstitutionalized and institutionalized children may be differentiated by examining a number of linguistic variables. The grammatical structure of language appeared less affected by environment than were the semantic and auditory elements. (25 ref)
McNutt, James C. & Leri, Susan M. (McGill U, School of Human Communication Disorders, Montreal, Canada) American Journal of Mental Deficiency, 1979(Jan), Vol 83(4), 339–345. [PA, Vol 62:11238]

2499.   Treatment of self-injurious behaviour with a GABA (gamma-aminobutyric acid) analogue.
Describes self-injurious and other undesirable behavior in 28 institutionalized mental defectives (aged 16–37 yrs). The effect of treatment with a GABA analog, baclofen (20–300 mg), is given. There was significant improvement in the behavior of many of the Ss. In some the improvement seems to be dependent on continuing the baclofen, while in others it has been maintained after stopping the drug, thus indicating that behavior modification has taken place. It has been possible to discontinue, or reduce, other medication in some of the Ss. (9 ref)
Primrose, D. A. (Royal Scottish National Hosp, Stirling) Journal of Mental Deficiency Research, 1979(Sep), Vol 23(3), 163–173. [PA, Vol 66:06406]

2500.   Verbal interactions between staff and residents in an institution for the young mentally retarded.
Examined patterns of verbal interaction between staff and 29 residents (aged 8–32 yrs) in a training center for young mentally retarded persons. Ss were moderately to profoundly retarded. Five undergraduate psychology students observed interactions in 2 structured and 2 unstructured settings (35 hrs of data). Conversation type initiations from staff elicited more verbal responses from residents than other types of verbal stimuli. Structured situations provided more verbal interactions than unstructured situations. There was a high frequency of ignore-type responses to resident-initiated verbal interactions. It is suggested that some features of the environment could be developed to improve language competence in mentally retarded people. (14 ref)

Prior, M. et al. (La Trobe U, Bundoora, Australia) Mental Retardation, 1979(Apr), Vol 17(2), 65–69. [PA, Vol 66:08706]

2501.   Prevalence of drug therapy for institutionalised mentally retarded children.
Investigated the prevalence of the use of drugs for behavior problems and emotional disorders among 435 retarded children residing in an institution. 60% of the Ss were on drug therapy, and of these, 47% were on psychotropic drugs. 65% of those on medication received 2 or more drugs, and 78% of the drugs had been prescribed within 2 yrs of the survey date. Thus, the high proportion of patients on medication for behavior problems indicates that drug therapy, and not behavior modification, is the treatment of choice. (6 ref)
Pulman, Ruth M.; Pook, Rosemary B. & Singh, Nirbhay N. (Mangere Hosp & Training School, Auckland, New Zealand) Australian Journal of Mental Retardation, 1979(Jun), Vol 5(6), 212–214. [PA, Vol 66:08600]

2502.   Resident abuse: A continuing dilemma.
Proposes that institutions implement a more precise system for handling and preventing child abuse in facilities for the retarded and mentally ill. An example is presented of standardizing system procedures, as well as variables that influence action to be taken when these procedures are violated. A table demonstrates the relationships between such variables as medical findings, client/witness/suspect reports, and recommended disciplinary action. (7 ref)
Sluyter, Gary V. & Cleland, Charles C. (Sluyter & Assoc, Corpus Christi, TX) American Corrective Therapy Journal, 1979(Jul–Aug), Vol 33(4), 99–102. [PA, Vol 64:08637]

2503.   The future forms of residential services for mentally retarded people in Australia: A Delphi study.
50 significant persons in the field of mental retardation in Australia were sampled by means of a three-round Delphi probe to determine their expectations concerning the future forms of residential services for mentally retarded people in Australia. The changes predicted represented significant departures from most historical and even many current approaches. Generally, Ss were optimistic in their outlook but cautious in citing the date of widespread implementation of their predictions. (14 ref)
Annison, John E. & Young, William H. (Minda Inc, Brighton, Australia) Australian Journal of Developmental Disabilities, 1980(Dec), Vol 6(4), 167–180. [PA, Vol 66:13405]

2504.   Visiting the mentally handicapped in residential care.
Various characteristics of 100 residents (aged 5–22 yrs) of a large hospital for the mentally handicapped were investigated in order to find any associations between these characteristics and the frequency of visiting by parents. Findings suggest that early attachment of the parents to the Ss was of more importance for visiting than present skills and behavior. The most frequently visited Ss were more likely to recognize people, have some speech, and have had a normal appearance as a baby. The unvisited Ss were more likely to have been born with an abnormal appearance and into homes with pre-existing social and emotional problems. (15 ref)
Colledge, Julian. (Maudsley Hosp, London, England) British Journal of Psychiatry, 1980(Oct), Vol 137, 313–318. [PA, Vol 66:08683]

2505.   Factors related to contact between mentally retarded persons and their parents during residential treatment.
Significant bivariate correlations were found between the duration of family visits and 11 parent or offspring variables among 180 residents (2% nonretarded, 10% mildly, 23% moderately, 43% severely, and 22% profoundly mentally retarded; average CA 23 yrs) of a state-owned residential facility. A linear combination of years of prior institutionalization, parents living together, presence of convulsive disorders, and the Adaptive Behavior Scale Psychological Disturbances domain results in a multiple correlation of .42 with the duration of parental visits. A weak correlation was shown between client adaptive behavior and parental contact. (6 ref)

D'Onofrio, Antonia et al. (Woodhaven Ctr, Woodhaven Program, Philadelphia, PA) Mental Retardation, 1980(Dec), Vol 18(6), 293–294. [PA, Vol 66:08687]

2506.   The stabilization of adaptive behavior ratings for institutionalized clients in two settings.
Administered the Adaptive Behavior Scale, Part 1 to 46 mentally retarded residents (mean CA 18.32 yrs, mean IQ 49.9) in a state institution: 23 Ss were examined in their cottages and 23 in their classrooms. A significant overall setting effect was not evident in the MANOVA for repeated measures. This finding supports the hypothesis that "Part 1" behavioral ratings remain relatively stable across settings for older adolescents and young adults. (11 ref)
Epstein, Howard R. & Weber, Donald B. (Miami U, OH) Mental Retardation, 1980(Aug), Vol 18(4), 177–179. [PA, Vol 66:07006]

2507.   Parental opposition to deinstitutionalization: A challenge in need of attention and resolution.
Examines parental opposition to the deinstitutionalization (DI) of mentally retarded persons in Nebraska, using a tripartite conceptual framework that historically describes the national and state social–legal context within which parental opposition has emerged; identifies the bases of the opposition; and recommends how these concerns can be resolved by offering directions for future research and policy analysis based on applicable psychological theories and studies and on legal decisions and principles. 23 parents opposed to DI were interviewed. Information from these interviews, public hearings, and legal files was classified in terms of 4 major concerns behind parental opposition to DI: (a) the adequacy of the community-based service delivery system vs DI; (b) the ideology underlying the provisions of community-based services to mentally retarded citizens; (c) the process utilized to implement DI; and (d) parents' ability to cope with their mentally retarded offspring in the community or at home. (4 p ref)
Frohboese, Robinsue & Sales, Bruce D. (American Assoc for the Advancement of Science, Washington, DC) Law & Human Behavior, 1980, Vol 4(1–2), 1–87. [PA, Vol 65:01191]

2508.   Punishment of self-injurious behavior: Issues of behavior analysis, generalization, and the right to treatment.
Conducted a long-term, multifaceted behavioral analysis of severe self-injurious behavior in a 13-yr-old institutionalized retarded boy. Adult attention was not a significant controlling variable. However, avoidance of task/demands was found to be a critical determinant of self-injurious behavior, aggression, and screaming. Results support the avoidance hypothesis concerning self-injurious behavior and point to the need for its continued investigation. Treatment intervention employed physical punishment (a thigh slap) in a multiple-stimulus, multiple-baseline design. Suppression of self-injurious behavior, aggression, and disruptive behavior was rapid and virtually complete. Generalization to the residential setting was actively programmed, resulting in continued suppression without further need of physical punishment. Ethical, legal, and procedural problems associated with the treatment of self-injurious behavior are discussed. (14 ref)
Romanczyk, Raymond G.; Colletti, Gep & Plotkin, Ronald. (State U New York, Children's Units, Binghamton) Child Behavior Therapy, 1980(Spr), Vol 2(1), 37–54. [PA, Vol 66:06358]

2509.   Elimination of chronic self-injurious behavior by withdrawal of staff attention.
Self-injurious behavior is frequently noted in institutionalized persons. Several treatment techniques have been attempted including medication, timeout, shock, aromatic ammonia, and adaptive clothing. Several authors have suggested extinction as an alternative technique though self-injury may occur during the extinction period. The present case study of a 19-yr-old retarded male suggests that staff attention may maintain self-abusive behavior since withdrawal of this attention resulted in a rapid reduction of self-injurious behavior. (7 ref)

Rose, Vincent; Sloop, Wayne & Baker, Phyllis. (Lynchburg Training School & Hosp, VA) Psychological Reports, 1980(Feb), Vol 46(1), 327–330. [PA, Vol 65:11052]

2510.   A comparison of physical restraint and positive practice overcorrection in treating stereotypic behavior.
Three mentally retarded, severely disturbed female children in a psychiatric facility received physical restraint or positive practice overcorrection to reduce their stereotypic mouthing or face-patting behavior. Physical restraint consisted of a verbal warning and manually restraining the child's hands. Positive practice involved the same verbal warning followed by manual guidance in appropriate manipulation of the task. Both methods were of equal effectiveness for all Ss. Immediate and dramatic reductions in stereotypic mouthing were evident when the treatments were implemented. Under a reversal to baseline procedure, 2 Ss showed an immediate return to pretreatment levels, and the 3rd S's mouthing behavior gradually increased across the reversal phase. Reinstating treatment for all Ss reduced the behavior to near zero levels. (21 ref)
Shapiro, Edward S.; Barrett, Rowland P. & Ollendick, Thomas H. (U Pittsburgh School of Medicine, Western Psychiatric Inst & Clinic) Behavior Therapy, 1980(Mar), Vol 11(2), 227–233. [PA, Vol 63:10220]

2511.   Development of spontaneous manding in language deficient children.
Six institutionalized children, ages 7–11 yrs, with little or no spontaneous vocal manding, were trained to request food items under natural conditions when snacks were presented. "I want a" was appropriate when an adult presented food in the playroom. "Out" was appropriate when the items were displayed in the hallway, across a half-door barrier from the child. The 2 mands were trained in sequence. To encourage "spontaneous" productions, no vocal cuing was provided by the adult. After criterion performance in each step, several probe sessions were conducted for various cuing conditions, adults, and settings. Probes after imitation training showed no spontaneous manding. In probes after training for "approximately" natural cues, most Ss showed little transfer to the natural cues. However, good transfer generally occurred across persons and from training room to playroom. Most Ss did not use one of the trained mands in the stimulus conditions that were appropriate for the other mand. At the end of training, extinction training was given for 1 mand in 1 setting. Performance of the other mand was little affected. (7 ref)
Simic, Joan & Bucher, Bradley. (U Western Ontario, London, Canada) Journal of Applied Behavior Analysis, 1980(Fal), Vol 13(3), 523–528. [PA, Vol 64:13156]

2512.   The characteristics of institutional settings which influence residents' development.
Reviews studies supporting the view that demographic variables such as size of the institution and cost per patient/day are important determinants of the effects an institution will have on the behavior of its residents (e.g., mentally retarded children). Other studies are cited in which sociopsychological characteristics rather than demographic variables influence the residents' behavior and development. Studies such as those of B. Tizard et al (see PA, Vol 48:11260) and M. W. Pratt et al (see PA, Vol 56:4573) are seen to represent an important advance because they suggest specific connections between institutional setting, staff workers' behavior, and residents' development. Because their approach penetrates beyond a general demonstration that institutions detrimentally affect development, such inquiries permit clinicians and administrators to begin considering ways in which residential environments might be altered to foster development. (18 ref)
Towfighy-Hooshyar, Nahid. (U Alberta, Edmonton, Canada) Mental Retardation Bulletin, 1980, Vol 8(3), 122–133. [PA, Vol 66:11025]

Mild Mental Retardation

2513.   The effect of institutionalization on educable mental retardates' expectancy of failure.
Previous research has established that mildly retarded youngsters have a higher expectancy of failure than normal children of the same MA. It has been assumed that this heightened expectancy of failure is a consequence of the higher incidence of failure experienced by retardates. The present study with 60 10-20 yr old institutionalized retardates sought to determine if institutional placement would alter Ss' experience of failure in such a way as to decrease their expectancy of failure. This was confirmed for long- and short-term Ss, but between group differences were not significant.
Payne, James E. (U. Texas, Graduate School of Social Work) Training School Bulletin, 1971(Aug), Vol. 68(2), 77-81. [PA, Vol 47:05480]

2514.   Incentives affecting behavior changes in the retarded.
Rated 24 educable adolescents (mean IQ = 64.4) 5 times at 2-mo intervals on a scale of dependent-independent and extroverted-introverted behavior. Ss received daily verbal feedback based on their behavior ratings. At the end of each week they received a monetary incentive according to their ratings (from $.33 at 1st to $1.33 at the end of the project). Analyses of variance indicate significant improvement in the dependency-independency and extroversion-introversion scores (ps < .01). Whether the size of change in behavior was important enough for permanent community placement is an object of further inquiry.
Rapp, John; Lemke, Elmer A. & Landis, John. (Livingston County Special Education Supervisor, Pontiac, Ill.) Exceptional Children, 1971(Nov), Vol. 38(3), 229-232. [PA, Vol 49:07609]

2515.   An analysis of timeout and response cost in a programmed environment.
Exposed 6 15-19 yr. old mildly retarded institutionalized boys with high rates of antisocial behavior to 2 parameters of timeout and response cost within the context of a programmed environment. For 5 of the 6 Ss, the 2 higher values (30 tokens response cost or 30 min. timeout) were significantly more suppressive than the lower values (5 tokens or 5 min.). For the 1 remaining S, there was a strong relationship in the opposite direction. Also, the timeout and response cost of higher value became increasingly more suppressive over time, whereas those of lower value did not. There were few appreciable differences between the timeout and response cost of similar magnitude. A discussion of these results is presented in support of the notion that the functional aversiveness of timeouts (and response costs) appears to be critically dependent upon interactions with the environmental conditions in which they are implemented and the Ss' reinforcement histories. (23 ref.)
Burchard, John D. & Barrera, Francisco. (U. Vermont) Journal of Applied Behavior Analysis, 1972(Fal), Vol. 5(3), 271-282. [PA, Vol 49:04958]

2516.   Habilation of the retarded child: A remedial program.
Utilized operant procedures with a 4½-yr-old Negro male with a diagnosis of mild mental retardation and delayed speech. The child's father learned reinforcement techniques and conducted sessions at home in addition to weekly sessions conducted by the E. After 1 yr. of language development training, the program was modified to include arithmetic skills, concept development, memory skills, and other behavioral requirements tested by the WISC and Stanford-Binet. After 2 yr. the S was progressing normally and had an IQ in the average range. He was promoted from 1st to 2nd grade and on follow-up was still doing well. It is concluded that training in speech, language, and other cognitive skills may be helpful in developing normal behaviors in children diagnosed as retarded.
Drash, Philip W. (Johns Hopkins U., John F. Kennedy Inst. for Habilitation of the Mentally & Physically Handicapped Child) Journal of Special Education, 1972(Sum), Vol. 6(2), 149-159. [PA, Vol 50:11969]

2517.   Social reinforcement of weight reduction: A case report on an obese retarded adolescent.
Delivered social reinforcement in the form of attention and praise by the E to an obese, mildly retarded, 14-yr-old female for weight loss per week at or below a specified level. Her initial weight was 239 lbs. Over a 42-wk period, of which the 1st 15 wk. involved reinforcement, the next 15 wk. an extinction period, and the last 10 wk. the reinstatement of reinforcement, S lost 79 lbs. Weight loss per week was greatest during the 2 reinforcement phases; weight loss per week decreased below the base-line period during extinction. Rapid weight loss is attributed to social reinforcement delivered by the E as other environmental aspects were unaltered during the experiment. (20 ref.)
Foxx, Richard M. (Anna State Hosp., Behavior Research Lab., Ill.) Mental Retardation, 1972(Aug), Vol. 10(4), 21-23. [PA, Vol 49:02854]

2518.   Maternal participation in a preschool project for disadvantaged handicapped children.
Describes a 10-mo program in which 10 inner city mothers and their educable mentally retarded children participated. Issues surrounding the raising of a handicapped child were confronted. Basic principles of early education were taught to all mothers. Regular opportunities for group and individual counseling were also provided.
Nellans, Teresa A.; Reinsel, Michael; Binder, Barbara & Burrow, Will H. Training School Bulletin, 1972(Feb), Vol. 68(4), 207-211. [PA, Vol 48:12048]

2519.   A short-term inpatient program for mildly retarded adolescents.
Describes the admission of mildly retarded (IQ = 50-80) adolescents who are having difficulty getting along in the community to a 2-mo inpatient program at UCLA's Neuropsychiatric Institute. Deviant behavior is treated through milieu programs based on a merit system and an interactional approach, structured activities, and psychotherapy or play therapy. Therapy is conducted by trainees from various disciplines, who also work with the parents.
Yusin, Alvin S.; Reardon, Diane; Henry, Anita & Whiter, Peggy. (U. Southern California, Medical School, Los Angeles) Hospital & Community Psychiatry, 1972(Oct), Vol 23(10), 315-318. [PA, Vol 49:07695]

2520.   The effects of reinforcement on perseverative speech in a mildly retarded boy.
Used differential reinforcement (pennies and praise) to eliminate repetitive, unintelligible speech which often followed appropriate verbalizations in a 7-yr-old mildly retarded boy. Strong control over the behavior was produced by contingent reinforcement.
Butz, Robert A. & Hasazi, Joseph E. (U. Vermont) Journal of Behavior Therapy & Experimental Psychiatry, 1973(Jun), Vol. 4(2), 167-170. [PA, Vol 51:03680]

2521.   Modification of mother-child interactions: A modeling approach for groups.
Taught a group of 4 mothers to respond differentially to selected behaviors that their mildly retarded 4-9 yr old children exhibited, using live demonstrations and directed discussion. The altered response repertoires of the mothers resulted in behavior change on the part of their children in a task-oriented situation. Some evidence for change in other situations is presented. Results support the usefulness of working with child-care agents as a vehicle for modifying child behavior, and the need for refining the technology for such intervention is noted. It is suggested that mothers can learn techniques of child management by observing and discussing critical interactions occurring in another mother-child pair.
Mash, Eric J.; Lazere, Richard; Terdal, Leif & Garner, Ann. (U. Calgary, Alberta, Canada) Child Study Journal, 1973, Vol. 3(3), 131-143. [PA, Vol 51:11408]

2522.   Modification of mother-child interactions: Playing with children.
Taught 5 groups (n = 8-10) of mothers how to use behavior modification principles to generate effective play behavior be-

tween themselves and their 4-10 yr old mentally retarded children. A shift in the free play interaction occurred both in terms of a change in the cues which the mothers gave, as well as a change in the way in which they consequated various child behaviors. Commensurate with the change in the mothers' behavior the children also showed an increase in the appropriateness of their play behavior. Results point out the importance of developing parent training methods which deal with nondeviant types of behavior. Evaluating parent training programs in terms of parent-child behavior as a unit is emphasized.
Mash, Eric J. & Terdal, Leif. (U. Calgary, Alberta, Canada) Mental Retardation, 1973(Oct), Vol. 11(5), 44-49. [PA, Vol 51:09734]

2523. Rhythm training for educable mentally retarded children.
Used intentional training and modeling procedures to teach rhythm skills to 14 educable mentally retarded children (CA range, 87-118 mo; MA range, 57-89 mo) in the context of small group rhythm bands, predance-movement activities, games, and stories. The 14 Ss in the experimental group participated in an intensive, 4-wk program while 14 control Ss (of similar CA and MA) spent time in a traditional primary music program; control Ss also participated in an unrelated project under motivational conditions similar to those in the rhythm program. Results of the posttest rhythm measure show that the experimental Ss significantly improved over their pretest performance ($p < .0005$). The control group showed no improvement in rhythm skills. (25 ref)
Ross, Dorothea M.; Ross, Sheila A. & Kuchenbecker, Shari L. (U. California, San Francisco) Mental Retardation, 1973(Dec), Vol. 11(6), 20-23. [PA, Vol 52:04083]

2524. Intentional training vs observational learning of mediational strategies in EMR children.
Obtained measures of ability to learn paired associates and of mediational skill for 36 86-120 mo old educable mentally retarded children. 12 Ss in the intentional training condition over a 5-wk period were given 5 hrs of explicit training in formulating mediational links within the context of a story and table game program. The 12 Ss in the observational learning condition were exposed to the same materials and to live and symbolic models who formulated mediational links. The controls participated in a story and table game program with no direct training or modeling of mediational links. Posttraining measures show that mediational skills were acquired as effectively through observational learning as through intentional training. (19 ref)
Ross, Dorothea M.; Ross, Sheila A. & Downing, Martha L. (U. California, San Francisco) American Journal of Mental Deficiency, 1973(Nov), Vol. 78(3), 292-299. [PA, Vol 52:04084]

2525. Enhancing group discussion skills of educable children: A case study.
Conducted group discussions structured as a game in 2 classes of 8 boys each categorized as educable mentally retarded or as learning disabled. Ss received points for complying with the teacher's request to exhibit 1 of 7 specified discussion behaviors. The game was played twice a wk for 3 wks, and 3 baseline and 3 posttreatment discussions were held for comparison. Improvement in some discussion behaviors occurred during treatment, and some improvements continued afterward. Other behaviors did not change, perhaps because too many complicated behaviors were introduced at once, forcing the Ss to disregard some of them. Since control groups were not established, results of the game procedure must be interpreted with caution.
Glass, Raymond M. & Goldgraber, Jacob. (Indiana U., Center for Innovation in Teaching the Handicapped) Exceptional Children, 1974(Jan), Vol. 40(4), 289-291. [PA, Vol 52:01865]

2526. Prediction of work adjustment for adolescent male educable retardates.
Hypothesized that the client's perception of a positive relationship with his staff supervisor is predictive of a favorable work adjustment rating in a rehabilitation workshop. Both work adjustment and the client-perceived relationship were evaluated

twice with a 1-mo interval using the Social Self-Esteem Scale, 20 items from the Barrett-Lennard Relationship Inventory, and the Minnesota Employment Satisfactoriness Inventory. Work adjustment and the client-perceived relationship were not related in 25 16-yr-old male educable retardates. However, high work adjustment ratings at the time of the 1st evaluation were predictive of staff-rated frequency of positive verbal interactions at the time of the 2nd evaluation. Additional findings of a relationship between social self-esteem and work adjustment were as predicted. An 18-mo follow-up indicated that good work adjustment in the workshop was predictive of successful placement in competitive employment.
Hollender, John W. (Emory U.) Journal of Counseling Psychology, 1974(Mar), Vol. 21(2), 164-165. [PA, Vol 52:08459]

2527. Producing generative sentence usage by imitation and reinforcement procedures.
3 retarded Ss aged 32, 12, and 6 yrs and 2 developmentally normal toddlers aged 2.5 yrs were trained, using imitation and reinforcement procedures, to use correct sentences. The experimental task was to use sentences with correct subject-verb agreement to describe pictures that were presented to the Ss. 2 classes of sentences were taught: those involving a plural subject that required the use of the verb "are" (e.g., "the boys are running") and those involving a singular subject that required the use of the verb "is" (e.g., "the boy is running"). The basic design of the study involved multiple baselines for each class of sentences. 4 of the Ss began to produce novel, untrained sentences of a particular type to generalization probe pictures when that particular class of sentence was currently being trained. Thus, the imitation and reinforcement procedures appeared to be functional in producing generative sentence usage for both types of sentences. One S produced correct sentences to both singular and plural probe pictures when only "is" sentences had been taught. A reversal procedure and retraining phase indicated that for this S, imitation and reinforcement procedures for training one class of sentence behavior seemed functional in producing generative responses of the other class of sentences. (15 ref)
Lutzker, John R. & Sherman, James A. (U of the Pacific) Journal of Applied Behavior Analysis, 1974(Fal), Vol 7(3), 447-460. [PA, Vol 53:06215]

2528. [Value of 1035 MD in the psychomotor re-education of slightly and moderately mentally retarded children treated in a school for mentally subnormal children.] (Fren)
34 girls and 16 boys 7-10 yrs old were given 6 ml of 1035 MD daily for 6 mo. Evaluation was based on clinical observation and performance on tests of psychomotor development. It was found that Ss receiving 1035 MD showed faster psychomotor improvement than did a group of matched Ss who received no medication. Improvement was most remarkable in the areas of rhythm comprehension and spatiotemporal organization, and was more pronounced in moderately than in mildly retarded Ss. It is concluded that the prolonged use of 1035 MD can produce significant and permanent increases in the psychomotor levels of moderately retarded children.
Parente, C. & Colombel, J. C. Revue de Neuropsychiatrie Infantile et d'Hygiene Mentale de l'Enfance, 1974(Jan), Vol 22(1-2), 141-150. [PA, Vol 54:08066]

2529. Teaching retarded persons to rehearse through cumulative overt labeling.
20 educable mentally retarded children (mean age = 11 yrs), divided into 2 treatment groups, were given a pretest, 14 training sessions, and a posttest on a 7-position serial memory task. Experimental Ss were given specific instructions in cumulative overt labeling and practiced this technique with prompting during the 14 training sessions. On the posttest with no accompanying instructions to rehearse, all experimental Ss continued to engage in cumulative overt labeling and performed significantly better than controls. Findings are discussed in terms of a production deficiency model with comparisons made to other rehearsal and training investigations.

Turnbull, Ann P. (North Carolina Memorial Hosp, Div for Disorders of Development & Learning, Chapel Hill) American Journal of Mental Deficiency, 1974(Nov), Vol 79(3), 331-337. [PA, Vol 53:10535]

2530. Development of cooperative and competitive play responses in developmentally disabled children.
Studied the usefulness of a behavior management procedure for training cooperative and competitive social play. Ss were 5 8-10 yr old educable mentally retarded children who had marked behavior and communication disorders. Baseline data indicated that the Ss exhibited no competitive responses and low levels of cooperative play. Upon instituting a token-praise-feedback procedure, increases in cooperative play as well as small increases in competitive play were observed. Reinstating the token-feedback procedure after reversal resulted in high levels of competitive play with no change in cooperative play. (24 ref)
Knapczyk, Dennis R. & Yoppi, Judith O. (Indiana U, Developmental Training Ctr) American Journal of Mental Deficiency, 1975(Nov), Vol 80(3), 245-255. [PA, Vol 55:10357]

2531. A case study of a 12-year-old schizophrenic mildly retarded boy.
Presents the case study of a severely disturbed 12-yr-old male who received treatment through a nondirective, humanistic treatment approach. Overall improvement was noted, and a total education and rehabilitation plan for future development is discussed. The employment of these humanistic techniques on a ward-wide basis as they relate to the special problems of an institutional setting is also discussed.
Rubin, Gerald & Castle, Melvin. (Lynchburg Training School & Hosp, VA) Journal of Clinical Psychology, 1975(Jan), Vol 31(1), 119-120. [PA, Vol 56:04421]

2532. Using a pictorial job training manual in an occupational training program for high school EMR students.
Conducted a 6-wk program to teach educable mentally retarded high school girls the skills necessary to gain employment in motels and hotels as maids. 8 girls of varying intellectual ability served as Ss. Specific community needs and job qualifications were the guiding targets, and a locally developed pictorial training manual was the central feature of the approach. The manual, including 149 illustrations, was developed from slides of experienced maids performing routine tasks; low-readability captions were included. Experienced maids were timed on their tasks for S evaluation purposes. Results of the program, which involved on-site experience, show that all Ss experienced a 50-75% reduction in time on many job phases following 6 wks involvement. 6 were able to approximate or better the target time required to clean a room and were considered work ready.
Weisenstein, Greg R. (U Kansas, Habilitation Personnel Training Project) Education & Training of the Mentally Retarded, 1975(Feb), Vol 10(1), 30-35. [PA, Vol 54:04222]

2533. Acquisition and retention of a mediational strategy for PA learning in EMR children.
The ability of educable mentally retarded (EMR) children to acquire and retain a mediational strategy for paired associate learning was demonstrated by a training procedure which consisted of the sequencing of consecutive lists under varying degrees of mediational facilitation. The components of the training procedure included training interval, overt verbalization, and verbal context combined with imagery instruction. 45 EMR children (mean CA, 11.26; mean IQ, 63.33) were randomly assigned to 1 of 3 groups: mediation, standard, and control. Analyses of data show significantly superior performance of the mediation group in acquisition and retention of the mediational strategy. The pedagogical implications of the study are discussed. (15 ref)
Burger, Agnes L. & Blackman, Leonard S. (New York U) American Journal of Mental Deficiency, 1976(Mar), Vol 80(5), 529-534. [PA, Vol 56:06221]

2534. Visual memory training of digit recall in educable mentally retarded children.
Spatial grouping and schematic redundancy supplemented by external cueing were employed in an intensive training program incorporating structured digit strings presented visually. The program was administered individually to 5 experimental educable mentally retarded (EMR) children (MA, 5.66 yrs; WISC) while unstructured random digit strings were presented to 4 MA-matched control EMRs. At the completion of training, all experimental Ss gained at least 2 digits above their initial baseline measures whereas only 1 control evidenced any gain (1 digit) in digit recall. Results are interpreted to support H. H. Spitz's (1966) input organization schema, and they dispute the developmental prerequisite hypothesis related to digit recall capacity. (15 ref)
Burger, Agnes L. & Blackman, Leonard S. (New York U) Education & Training of the Mentally Retarded, 1976(Feb), Vol 11(1), 5-10. [PA, Vol 57:03623]

2535. Adolescent group for mentally retarded persons.
Established a personal growth group for 8 adolescent educable mentally retarded males and females to enhance their social and emotional development in 4 areas: development of self-awareness, enhancement of self-image, consideration of future goals and plans, and development of problem-solving skills. Three study units—feelings and behavior, growing up, and relationships—were established to help group members (a) identify, define, and express feelings; (b) understand the interrelationship between feelings and behavior; (c) develop an awareness of their own maturation; (d) develop a sense of identity; (e) understand and consider choices they will face as adults; and (f) express their feelings about difficulties in family relationships, develop social skills, and improve relationships with friends and family. The use of concrete (vs abstract) material such as drawings, and audiovisual equipment, field trips, and parent and school staff involvement is recommended for such groups.
Hynes, Jane & Young, Joyce. (Emerson School, Minneapolis, MN) Education & Training of the Mentally Retarded, 1976(Oct), Vol 11(3), 226-231. [PA, Vol 57:10800]

2536. Lithium carbonate in juvenile manic-depressive illness.
Presents the case history of a mildly mentally retarded manic-depressive 15-yr-old female who was successfully treated with lithium carbonate. During 4 yrs of maintenance treatment with daily doses of 600-900 mg of the drug, disruptive manic behavior was controlled, and a subjective leveling out of mood allowed the patient to develop more fully her cognitive and psychomotor capacities. (20 ref)
Kelly, John T.; Koch, Michael & Buegel, Dale. (U Minnesota Medical School, Minneapolis) Diseases of the Nervous System, 1976(Feb), VOL 37(2), 90-92. [PA, Vol 56:01117]

2537. Psychotherapy with mentally retarded children.
Discusses the applicability of modified psychoanalytic psychotherapy in treating mentally retarded children with neurotic symptoms. The problem of differentiating emotional disturbance due to maternal deprivation from organic retardation is examined. The case of a 7½-yr-old girl suffering from multiple neurotic symptoms and mild mental retardation is presented, and specific guidelines for therapists working with such children and their parents are described. (27 ref)
Smith, Edith; McKinnon, Rosemary & Kessler, Jane W. (Case-Western Reserve U, Mental Development Ctr) Psychoanalytic Study of the Child, 1976, Vol 31, 493-514. [PA, Vol 58:07877]

2538. Video-tape feedback and behavioral change.
The presentation of videotaped material of a 19-yr-old educable mentally retarded male during interviews with an E significantly reduced the S's headshaking behavior both during subsequent conversations with the E and in general conversations. Some of the factors in the reduction of the behavior are discussed.
Weisbord, Hyman F. Education & Training of the Mentally Retarded, 1976(Feb), Vol 11(1), 18-20. [PA, Vol 57:03961]

2539.   Training a parent to teach communication skills: A case study.
Describes the procedure involved in training a mother to teach 2 communication skills to her 15-yr-old mentally retarded daughter (IQ 56). Use of a multiple baseline design across skills indicated that training of each skill was associated with increases in that skill. The increases were maintained at a 2-mo follow-up. (17 ref)
Arnold, Susan; Sturgis, Ellie & Forehand, Rex. (U Georgia) Behavior Modification, 1977(Apr), Vol 1(2), 259–276. [PA, Vol 59:12723]

2540.   Behaviour modification, normalization and person-orientedness.
Contends that behaviorist models are incompatible with the concept of normalization for mentally retarded persons, both directly and more generally in terms of the orientation of consciousness that normalization fosters. It is suggested that institutions committed to normalization goals should reject behaviorist models, which are object-oriented, in favor of a person-oriented approach. Ways of structuring residential unit environments are suggested that are person-oriented and that present as normalized an experience as is possible within the institution. The discussion is illustrated with a description of a 30-person unit for mildly and moderately retarded adolescents that strives for eventual community placement of residents.
Briton, John. (Victoria Mental Health Dept, Middle Park Hostel, Bundoora, Australia) Australian Journal of Mental Retardation, 1977(Dec), Vol 4(8), 4–13. [PA, Vol 61:09090]

2541.   Maintenance and generalization of trained metamnemonic awareness by educable retarded children.
The majority of 68 educable retarded children (young group, MA 6 yrs; older group, MA 8 yrs) required to estimate their memory span were found to be unrealistic estimators. Following training in span estimation the older Ss improved under both explicit and implicit feedback conditions, while younger Ss only benefited from explicit feedback. Three posttests of the effects of training revealed long-term (1-yr) maintenance of training for older Ss, but younger Ss showed posttest improvement only on an immediate test. While long-term maintenance was found for older Ss, generalization to similar span-estimation tests was not found. The utility of training metamnemonic knowledge which does not generalize was questioned and alternate training procedures are proposed. (20 ref)
Brown, Ann L.; Campione, Joseph C. & Murphy, Martin D. (U Illinois Ctr for the Study of Reading) Journal of Experimental Child Psychology, 1977(Oct), Vol 24(2), 191–211. [PA, Vol 60:05455]

2542.   The responsiveness of mentally retarded children to psychotherapy.
Studied 20 children aged 5–15 yrs diagnosed as mild or borderline familial retardates, and 20 children of normal or higher intelligence and compared the responsiveness of the 2 groups in psychoanalytic psychotherapy. In an ex post facto design the groups were matched for diagnosis, presenting problems, age, sex, socioeconomic status, length of treatment, and combinations of treatment methods. The outcome variable measured was improvement in the presenting problem rated along a 5-point scale. Therapists rated their own patients. Examination of the descriptive statistics presented suggests that familially retarded patients are at least as responsive to psychoanalytic psychotherapy as are normals. (3 p ref)
Hayes, Michael.   Smith College Studies in Social Work, 1977(Mar), Vol 47(2), 112–153. [PA, Vol 60:09575]

2543.   A comparison of singing ranges of mentally retarded and normal children with published songbooks used in singing activities.
Found that the mean range and midpoints of the voices of a sample of educable mentally retarded children 7 and 8 yrs old were significantly lower than those of normal children of the same CA and were also significantly lower than those in published songbooks used by children.
Larson, Betsy A. (Loyola University Coll of Music, LA) Journal of Music Therapy, 1977(Fal), Vol 14(3), 139–143. [PA, Vol 63:01227]

2544.   [Cognitive restructuring as a behavior modification technique with a mildly retarded individual.] (Span)
Cognitive restructuring was used to modify the verbal behavior of a mildly retarded 12-yr-old boy. He was given a calendar, the desired response being to identify the correct date. After a 10-day baseline, he was presented with a rationale for responding correctly. The S's incorrect responses decreased from 3.1 to .5 per session. Results are discussed within the framework of using cognitive restructuring for behavior modification in mental retardates. (English summary) (17 ref)
Prieto, Alfonso G. & Zcrer, Stanley H. (U Arizona) Análisis y Modificación de Conducta, 1977, Vol 3(4), 33–41. [PA, Vol 61:11379]

2545.   Imagery and verbal mediation in paired-associate learning of educable mentally retarded adolescents.
Studied 60 educable mentally retarded (EMR) adolescents to investigate paired associate learning as a function of variations in image-evoking potential of the response members and of instructions to utilize a verbal mediation strategy. Results indicate that performance with verbal mediation instruction surpassed that under nonmediation instruction conditions regardless of imagery level. Results are discussed in terms of A. Paivio's (1971) conceptual peg hypothesis as well as the EMR's deficiency in input organization. (13 ref)
Burger, Agnes L. & Blackman, Leonard S. (New York U) Journal of Mental Deficiency Research, 1978(Jun), Vol 22(2), 125–130. [PA, Vol 63:01215]

2546.   Situation generality of overcorrective functional movement training.
A multiple baseline design across situations was employed with an 8-yr-old institutionalized educable mentally retarded boy to assess the effects of an overcorrective functional movement training procedure on stereotypic head-turning and the generality of behavioral change to 2 nontreatment situations. Results indicate that the overcorrection procedure was immediately effective in reducing head-turning in the treatment situation. Head-turning initially increased in the 2 nontreatment situations and then gradually declined. (10 ref)
Doleys, Daniel M. & Wells, Karen C. (U Alabama School of Medicine, Birmingham) Psychological Reports, 1978(Dec), Vol 43(3, Pt 1), 759–762. [PA, Vol 64:08457]

2547.   Reactivity of self-monitoring procedures with retarded adolescents.
Investigated the reactivity of self-monitoring procedures with 2 mildly retarded adolescents using single-case designs. The effects of 2 variables, social reinforcement and feedback, on the degree of reactivity were also examined. Both Ss monitored a socially undesirable behavior and were asked to self-record for extended periods of time with minimal cues from the environment. Self-monitoring produced reactive decreases in the target behavior. Reinforcement had a differential effect across Ss, further altering the target behavior for only 1 S. Feedback decreased the behavior for the 2nd S. The Ss' accuracy in self-recording was quite low.
Zegiob, Leslie; Klukas, Nancy & Junginger, John. (Memphis Ecumenical Children's Assn, TN) American Journal of Mental Deficiency, 1978(Sep), Vol 83(2), 156–163. [PA, Vol 62:06719]

2548.   Imitation in EMR boys: Model competency and age.
The effects of model age and competence on the imitation behavior of 80 educable mentally retarded (EMR) boys (mean CA 12.2 yrs; mean IQ 61) were investigated. Ss viewed a videotape in which either an adult or a peer performed a motor task with either high or low competence. In addition, the models engaged in 4 kinds of off-task social behavior. Ss imitated the off-task social behavior emitted by high-competent and peer models more than low-competent and adult models. In addition, high-competent models were imitated more than were low-competent models on the motor-skill task, but no significant age effect was found. The efficacy of modeling as an instructional strategy is

discussed, and it is concluded that EMR boys should be exposed to competent models, especially peers, who emit a repertoire of adaptive behaviors. (19 ref)
Becker, Stephen & Glidden, Laraine M. (Greater Hartford Assn for Retarded Citizens Inc, CT) American Journal of Mental Deficiency, 1979(Jan), Vol 83(4), 360–366. [PA, Vol 62:11222]

2549. Gilles de la Tourette syndrome.
Reports a case of Gilles de la Tourette syndrome in a 16-yr-old mildly mentally subnormal female (IQ 70). The literature on the condition is briefly reviewed, and the effectiveness of haloperidol is discussed. (15 ref)
Izmeth, A. (Greaves Hall Hosp, Southport, England) Journal of Mental Deficiency Research, 1979(Mar), Vol 23(1), 25–27. [PA, Vol 66:06388]

2550. Vigilance performance of mildly retarded children.
Studied the contribution of developmental factors to the vigilance performance of 9 mildly mentally retarded (IQ 53–81) children, 13 nonretarded children of the same CA (11–13 yrs), and 12 younger nonretarded children of about the same MA. The retarded Ss showed an earlier and faster decline in vigilance performance than the CA control group. The MA control group performed in a way similar to that of the retarded Ss, suggesting that the more rapid decline in vigilance performance was largely a developmental phenomenon. (3 ref)
Kirby, N. H.; Nettelbeck, T. & Thomas, P. (U Adelaide, Australia) American Journal of Mental Deficiency, 1979(Sep), Vol 84(2), 184–187. [PA, Vol 63:01224]

2551. Levels of political knowledge of mildly mentally retarded adults.
Administered the Civic Awareness Questionnaire to 62 institutionalized and 55 noninstitutionalized retarded adults (CA 22–46 and 17–22 yrs, respectively) and to 5th- and 8th-grade children and nonretarded CA-matched low socioeconomic status college students. On all 4 knowledge indices, the retarded adults' performance closely resembled that of nonretarded 5th-grade children. Results indicate that in both retarded groups Ss had acquired minimal political knowledge, even though none had been exposed to any voter education. (12 ref)
Klein, Nancy K. & Green, Barbara B. (Cleveland State U, Specialized Instructional Programs) American Journal of Mental Deficiency, 1979(Sep), Vol 84(2), 159–164. [PA, Vol 63:01225]

2552. [Vocational rehabilitation of educable mentally retarded (EMR) children.] (Hebr)
Compared adjustment measures for students who took part in 2 programs for EMR graduates of special schools. 50 Ss participated in a work program (direct placement in the work) and 50 in a work-study program (studying 3 days and the rest of the week getting on-the-job training and then working as regular employees). Ss, their parents, and their employers were interviewed regarding levels of satisfaction and adjustment. The work-study Ss were significantly more stable, satisfied, and adjusted than were the work-program Ss, and their professional opportunities (reflected in the number of different jobs) were less limited. (4 ref)
Margalit, Malka & Schuchman, Rachel. Israeli Journal of Psychology & Counseling in Education, 1979(Sep), Vol 11, 43–48. [PA, Vol 65:11237]

2553. Developmental effects of social reinforcement on eye-contact and speech in mildly intellectually handicapped children.
Investigated the developmental effects of social reinforcement on the interview behavior of 58 children 8–15 yrs old, mean IQ 75. High and low social reinforcement for eye contact was given at the interview. Findings indicate a feedback rather than a reward model in explaining the effects of social reinforcement. No evidence was found for significant variations in eye contact as a function of age, sex, or IQ. (9 ref)
McGregor, Harvey & Berry, Paul. (U Queensland, Brisbane, Australia) Exceptional Child, 1979(Nov), Vol 26(3), 117–126. [PA, Vol 66:06351]

2554. Living with a child who is mentally retarded: A course in parent education.
Parents of educable mentally retarded children above age 6 yrs were taught to use (a) developmental checklists to observe the child's behavior and generate realistic expectations, (b) a knowledge of the child's learning inabilities, and (c) behavioral analysis techniques to analyze the home learning situation of the child. The program changed the parents' approach to problem areas exhibited by the child and increase their effectiveness in managing the child's behavior and learning in the home situations. (13 ref)
Munro, John K. (Melbourne State Coll, Carlton, Australia) Australian Journal of Mental Retardation, 1979(Dec), Vol 5(8), 303–306. [PA, Vol 66:08410]

2555. A chaining procedure to teach a retarded deaf girl to wear her hearing aid.
A 5-yr-old mildly retarded female with severe hearing loss and extreme fear of her hearing aid was successfully taught, after 3 mo, to wear the aid by means of a chaining procedure. This involved introducing the component parts of the equipment separately and teaching her to accept one part before introducing another. (3 ref)
Wilson, Barbara & Moore, Patricia. (Bethlem Royal Hosp, Hilda Lewis House, Croydon, England) British Journal of Mental Subnormality, 1979(Dec), Vol 25(49, Pt 2), 88–90. [PA, Vol 65:13291]

2556. [Individual differences in pupils and the collective character of teaching.] (Polh)
Discusses how teachers should modify their instructional procedures for children who are classified as superior, mentally retarded, or slow learners. All teaching should be a stimulating process directed toward optimizing the development of the child. (English & Russian summaries)
Włodarski, Ziemowit. (U Warsaw, Poland) Psychologia Wychowawcza, 1979(Jan–Feb), Vol 22(1), 68–80. [PA, Vol 64:13288]

2557. Control of disruptive behavior by manipulation of reinforcement density and item difficulty subsequent to errors.
Proposed that programs carefully arranging reinforcement contingencies to maximize the learning of developmentally delayed children have neglected variables inherent in task sequencing. In 3 experiments with 3 mildly mentally retarded 3-yr-old boys, the effects of manipulating item difficulty and reinforcement density were examined. Contingent upon errors, delayed Ss were shifted to items of differing difficulty resulting in low or high, medium or high, and low, medium, or high densities of reinforcement. Results demonstrate that, as reinforcement density subsequent to errors increased, disruption decreased. Findings indicate that trainers can control disruptive behavior by programming reinforcement densities through sequencing of item difficulty subsequent to errors. (9 ref)
Altman, Karl; Hobbs, Steven; Roberts, Mark & Haavik, Sarah. (U Kansas Medical Ctr, Children's Rehabilitation Unit, Kansas City) Applied Research in Mental Retardation, 1980, Vol 1(3–4), 193–208. [PA, Vol 66:08483]

2558. Teaching a high-avoidance motor task to a retarded child through participant modeling.
Investigated the effectiveness of participant modeling as a technique for teaching a 12-yr-old educable mentally retarded boy (Slosson Intelligence Test score of 54) a high-avoidance task (a modified forward dive). Self-directed performance was employed at each step during target behavior achievement. Results show that this technique was successful; the target behavior was maintained at a 3-wk follow-up. (12 ref)
Feltz, Deborah L. (Pennsylvania State U, Coll of Health, Physical Education & Recreation, University Park) Education & Training of the Mentally Retarded, 1980(Apr), Vol 15(2), 152–155. [PA, Vol 66:10869]

2559. Teaching assertive and commendatory social skills to an interpersonally-deficient retarded adolescent.
A mildly retarded 16-yr-old girl was referred for treatment of interpersonal skills deficits (e.g., inability to handle peers'

derogatory comments and to respond to other peers' friendly approaches). A behavioral social skills training procedure was used to teach refusal assertive skills and commendatory prosocial behavior during role-plays of situations that had been troublesome. Behavioral skill training approaches for remediating the social deficits of retarded persons are discussed. (12 ref)
Geller, Marilyn I.; Wildman, Hal E.; Kelly, Jeffrey A. & Laughlin, Carl S. (West Virginia U) Journal of Clinical Child Psychology, 1980(Spr), Vol 9(1), 17–21. [PA, Vol 63:12430]

2560.   Effects of modification of conceptual tempo on acquisition of work skills.
On the basis of Matching Familiar Figures Test (MFFT) scores, 41 mildly intellectually retarded (WISC) Ss were assigned to 2 subgroups—reflective and impulsive. They were further assigned, randomly, to control and experimental conditions. The 2 experimental groups received a training program designed to promote self-generation of strategies, using self-verbalization to induce a more reflective approach. The control groups received the normal training program of a work preparation center. The criterion measure taken at pre- and posttest was a collation task standardized to provoke response uncertainty. Analysis of residual gain scores derived from the 2 testing occasions indicated that the experimental groups improved significantly more than the controls and that the improvement generalized to their performance on the Porteus Maze and MFFT. Contrary to expectations, however, the effect of training did not bring about significant differential improvement for impulsive over reflective Ss. Both benefited from the training. (18 ref)
Gow, Lyn & Ward, James. (Macquarie U School of Education, Sydney, Australia) Perceptual & Motor Skills, 1980(Feb), Vol 50(1), 107–116. [PA, Vol 65:11058]

2561.   Program development for the acquisition of work and social skills.
Describes the development of a series of experimental programs for intellectually handicapped adolescents within the Granville (Australia) Work Preparation Center (GWPC) with the cooperation of the GWPC Research and Development Project, based at Macquarie University in New South Wales. Programs cover social competency, language development, instruction following, skill development, conceptual style, reading, and task construction. Principles of instruction, training strategies, and techniques are discussed in relation to programs developed to run concurrently with regular GWPC programs. (12 ref)
Hauritz, Margory; Riches, Vivienne; Parmenter, Trevor R. & Ward, James. (Macquarie U, North Ryde, Australia) Australian Journal of Developmental Disabilities, 1980(Mar), Vol 6(1), 11–16. [PA, Vol 66:08727]

2562.   Completing job applications: Evaluation of an instructional program for mildly retarded juvenile delinquents.
Seven males (aged 15–18 yrs) from a residential treatment facility for juvenile offenders served as Ss in a study designed to train minimally literate individuals to read and complete job applications. A Master Employment Application (MEA) was created to be representative of a typical job application; it required 35 separate items of biographic information from the prospective employee. The training program progressed from matching items projected by the teacher to writing responses to biographic items on overhead projector transparencies of the MEA. A multiple baseline design across sets of biographic items was used to evaluate the program's effectiveness. All Ss' scores on the MEA increased as a function of the training program and were maintained in a 2-wk follow-up. Ss also increased their performance on 3 real job applications used to assess generalization. (16 ref)
Heward, William L.; McCormick, Sandra H. & Joynes, Yvonne. (Ohio State U, Faculty for Exceptional Children, Columbus) Behavioral Disorders, 1980(Aug), Vol 5(4), 223–234. [PA, Vol 66:06518]

2563.   Small group behavioral training to improve the job interview skills repertoire of mildly retarded adolescents.
Four retarded male adolescents (WISC IQs of 45–74) in a short-term residential treatment program received behavioral job interview skills training. Treatment consisted of behavioral group sessions using instructions, modeling, and rehearsal procedures to increase, in multiple baseline fashion, the Ss' ability to disclose positive information about their experience and background, convey interest in the position, and direct relevant questions to an interviewer. Treatment was assessed by objective ratings of individual, structured role-play job interviews following each treatment session; objective ratings of pre–posttraining performance during tape-recorded in-vivo generalization job interviews at a fast-food restaurant; and global evaluations of pre–posttraining in-vivo generalization interviews made by experienced personnel interviewers unfamiliar with the treatment. Results indicate that potentially employable retarded citizens can be successfully taught appropriate job interview behavior using a small-group behavioral procedure. (14 ref)
Kelly, Jeffrey A.; Wildman, Beth G. & Berler, Ellen S. (U Mississippi Medical Ctr, Jackson) Journal of Applied Behavior Analysis, 1980(Fal), Vol 13(3), 461–471. [PA, Vol 64:13171]

2564.   Community placement stability of behavior problem educable mentally retarded students.
Follow-up community placement data were collected for 186 behavior problem educable mentally retarded students (CA 5–23 yrs; IQ 40–95) at 6, 12, and 18 mo after discharge. Greatest stability throughout the follow-up period was observed for Ss initially placed in their natural homes. Comparable data for foster home and group home placements indicated decreasing placement stability throughout this period. (4 ref)
Reagan, Michael W.; Murphy, Robert J.; Hill, Yvonne F. & Thomas, Don R. (Brainerd State Hosp, Minnesota Learning Ctr) Mental Retardation, 1980(Jun), Vol 18(3), 139–142. [PA, Vol 66:08650]

2565.   The efficacy of social interventions on the personal adjustment of mildly handicapped adolescents.
Investigated the type of interventions that would best facilitate the adjustment of mildly intellectually handicapped adolescents in personal, social, and vocational areas. 23 male and 7 female 15–18 yr old Ss (IQ 48–96) were assigned to 1 of 6 groups: work skills training, social skills training, social followed by work skills training, work followed by social skills training, work concurrent with social skills training, and control (no training). Results indicated that differential effects did occur, yet independent measures such as full scale IQ, age, sex, and background contributed only minimally to these changes. Thus, significant gains appeared to have been associated with the actual interventions themselves such that some claims for the efficacy of program prototypes can be made. It is concluded that the content and sequence of components within intervention programs may be important in the modification of individual incompetencies and skill deficits. (44 ref)
Riches, Vivienne. (Macquarie U, School of Education, North Ryde, Australia) Australian Journal of Developmental Disabilities, 1980(Sep), Vol 6(3), 119–129. [PA, Vol 66:08735]

2566.   Group psychotherapy with mildly retarded, emotionally disturbed adolescents.
Based on the authors' experience with on-going groups conducted on an inpatient ward for developmentally disabled adolescents, the advantages and difficulties of group psychotherapy with emotionally disturbed, mentally retarded adolescents (MRAs) are discussed. The groups generally consist of 6–8 patients, ages 12–18 (WISC IQs 53–80); most patients remain in the group for approximately 4 mo. A major treatment problem is the discrepancy between CA and MA, which is not found in normal adolescents. Many groups of MRAs present with complex problems of a greater variety than is typical of non-MR groups. In agreement with other researchers, it is noted that the therapist with MRA groups must be a very active leader. Talk therapy must often be supplemented with additional forms of verbal and nonverbal therapy. Advantages of group treatment for

MRAs include (a) contact with peers and a sense of belonging to a peer group, (b) the availability of numerous behavior models, (c) greater opportunities for feedback, and (d) improvement in participants' verbal skills. (18 ref)
Welch, Veronica O. & Sigman, Marian. (U California, Los Angeles) Journal of Clinical Child Psychology, 1980(Fal), Vol 9(3), 209–212. [PA, Vol 65:08454]

Moderate Mental Retardation

2567.   Effects of music on performance of manual tasks with retarded adolescent females.
Assigned 16 institutionalized moderately retarded adolescent females to contingent and noncontingent music groups on the basis of work performance of manual tasks in a simulated workshop situation. Each matched pair of Ss received the same music (yoked) through headphones; however, the music was dependent on the work rate of only the contingent S. During each 75-min session, 15-min yoked music periods were alternated with 15-min silent periods. It was found that contingent music resulted in significantly higher mean work rate than silence. This difference occurred in early sessions and responding was stable over sessions. Noncontingent music did not result in significantly higher mean work rate. Overall responding decreased during early sessions and gradually improved. (15 ref.)
Cotter, Vance W. (Texas Woman's U.) American Journal of Mental Deficiency, 1971(Sep), Vol. 76(2), 242-248. [PA, Vol 47:09528]

2568.   Verbal mediation in moderately retarded children: Effects of successive mediational experiences.
Tested 40 16-18 yr. old mentally retarded adolescents using a 3-stage mediational paradigm. In the mediational condition (A-B, B-C, A-C), verbal associative links (A←B←C) could be used to aid A-C learning while in the control paradigm (A-B, D-C, A-C) no such mediation was possible in 3rd-stage learning. In 2 separate mediational sessions, results indicate pronounced facilitation of A-C learning due to utilization of A-B and B-C links. Recall data following A-C learning suggest that during Session II, A-C learning was enhanced by the employment of mediational strategies developed during Session I. Verbal mediation in retarded persons is likely restricted to a limited range of procedural variations with the length and nature of test trials and degree of task difficulty of critical importance.
Borkowski, John G. & Kamfonik, Allan. (U. Notre Dame) American Journal of Mental Deficiency, 1972(Sep), Vol. 77(2), 157-162. [PA, Vol 49:07734]

2569.   Communicative skills for trainables.
Describes a specific approach developed over 4 yr. to teach trainable children communicative skills within a wide scope of social behavior.
Happ, F. William & Lyon, Susan. Mental Retardation, 1972(Oct), Vol. 10(5), 38-39. [PA, Vol 49:09625]

2570.   Effects of accelerating and decelerating consequences on the social behavior of trainable retarded children.
Observed the free-play interactions of 14 trainable retarded children. It was predicted that responses followed by positive or negative social consequences would immediately be repeated or changed, respectively. This prediction was not supported in the majority of cases. An alternative hypothesis was tested on the same data and was supported. The new analyses showed that aversive consequences tended to facilitate the immediate recurrence of aggressive responses but to inhibit conversational and directive suggestion-type responses. This finding is explained in terms of differences between pro- and antisocial behaviors and between reinforcing-punishing and accelerating-decelerating functions of consequences.
Kopfstein, Donald. (Emory U.) Child Development, 1972(Sep), Vol. 43(3), 800-809. [PA, Vol 49:02664]

2571.   Vibration as positive reinforcement for retarded children.
Contends that previous studies investigating vibration as a positive reinforcer did not provide: adequate controls for touch and noise; a sufficient number of Ss; or comparisons of vibration with other reinforcers. In the present study, 4 groups of 40 trainable, institutionalized, retarded 8-12 yr. olds were exposed to an operant button-pressing paradigm. Results indicate that vibration compared favorably with a food reinforcer and that vibration was significantly more effective as a reward than the touch or the noise emitted by the vibrator. It is suggested that vibration may be used as an effective reinforcer to train retarded children.
Rehagen, Nicholas J. & Thelen, Mark H. (U. Missouri) Journal of Abnormal Psychology, 1972(Oct), Vol. 80(2), 162-167. [PA, Vol 49:04826]

2572.   Language training: A program for retarded children.
Placed 3 moderately- to severely-retarded 9-13 yr. olds who demonstrated a limited expressive noun vocabulary in a language program to be trained to produce the basic grammatical relations (subject-verb-object responses). Intermediate and terminal linguistic goals were in part based on L. Bloom's developmental data, and the program used behavior modification techniques. Posttraining generalization tests show that Ss were able to produce appropriate subject-verb-object responses to novel pictures which represented trained and untrained constructions. 2 Ss produced a large number of subject-verb, verb-object, and subject-verb-object responses in their spontaneous speech after training was completed.
Stremel, Kathleen. (Parsons State Hosp. & Training Center, Kan.) Mental Retardation, 1972(Apr), Vol. 10(2), 47-49. [PA, Vol 48:09578]

2573.   The impact of speech therapists on moderately retarded children in an institutional environment.
Assessed changes in the behavior of 12 7-14 yr. olds in a home-school community for the retarded who received speech therapy for 5 mo. Ss were compared with a group matched for age, IQ, etiology of retardation (Down's syndrome or brain damage), language age, and pattern of Illinois Test of Psycholinguistic Abilities (ITPA) scores. Ss were given pre- and post-speech therapy testing with the ITPA and the 4 factor scales of the Progress Assessment Chart. Speech therapy did not appear to lead to impressive language age gains. Language age gains were associated in both experimental and control groups with IQ, CA, and etiology of retardation. Clinical observations regarding the effect of personal relationships, hearing impairment, and nurse expectations on language gains are discussed.
Viney, Linda. (Macquarie U., North Ryde, New South Wales, Australia) British Journal of Mental Subnormality, 1972(Dec), Vol. 18(35, Pt. 2), 94-100. [PA, Vol 50:05586]

2574.   Development of interpersonal language responses in two moderately retarded children.
Used instructional guidance and operant reinforcement procedures to increase the interpersonal language behavior of 2 moderately retarded, institutionalized children. The generalized effects of these procedures upon the interpersonal and nonsocial language behavior of these 2 Ss and 2 other Ss not involved in training were rated in a free-play group situation. In addition to programed changes in the language behavior, unprogramed changes in the nonverbal social behavior were also recorded in these rating sessions, which occurred during Base Line 1, Training 1, Base Line 2, and Training 2 periods. Results indicate that while both the trained and nontrained Ss showed marked increments in interpersonal language behavior during both training periods and precipitous decrements during the Base Line 2 period, no substantial changes in their nonsocial language behavior occurred. Changes in the nonverbal social behavior of 3 Ss were positively correlated with their interpersonal language behavior.
Whitman, Thomas L.; Burish, Thomas & Collins, Carol. (U. Notre Dame) Mental Retardation, 1972(Oct), Vol. 10(5), 40-45. [PA, Vol 49:09803]

2575. The use of token reinforcement with trainable mentally retarded in a work activity setting.
Evaluated the effects of an experimental token economy on the target behaviors of attendance, punctuality for work, quality and quantity of work output, and social responsiveness in a work activities behavior modification program for the mentally retarded. These target behaviors have previously been considered as highly necessary for successful adjustment to a vocational setting. Ss were 16 16-21 yr old trainable mental retardates. The focal tasks included ceramics finishing, wood finishing, and small-parts assembly. The 4 target behaviors were recorded by staff for a 10-day baseline period. During the token economy, tokens that could be exchanged for goods at the workshop store were given for appropriate behavior. An extinction period similar to the baseline period was followed by return to token reinforcement for another 2 wks. While all target behaviors improved as a result of this program, social responsiveness improved most. (15 ref)
Close, Daniel W. (New Day Products Evaluation & Training Unit, Pocatello, Ida.) Vocational Evaluation & Work Adjustment Bulletin, 1973(Dec), Vol. 6(4), 6-14. [PA, Vol 52:08452]

2576. A lexical approach to the remediation of final sound omissions.
Tested the hypothesis that a language training (vocabulary building) or lexical approach to the remediation of final sound omissions may be for some children an effective method of therapy. A 6-yr-old trainable mentally retarded boy with a vocabulary of 5 understandable words, all of which contained final consonant omissions, was taught by a lexical method. He was required to use the final consonant to differentiate between word alternatives not previously present in his vocabulary. This method of training brought obvious improvement in the use of final consonants and should offer an alternative to the traditional approach to therapy for some children who omit final consonant sounds.
Ferrier, E. E. & Davis, Marilyn. (Indiana State U.) Journal of Speech & Hearing Disorders, 1973(Feb), Vol. 38(1), 126-130. [PA, Vol 52:03405]

2577. Video taped modeling: The development of three appropriate social responses in a mildly retarded child.
Taught 3 social responses—use of grammatically correct questions, smiling, and speaking about appropriate topics—to a moderately retarded 7-yr-old boy. A modified multiple baseline design was employed, using 3 treatment procedures: modeling, instructions plus social reinforcement, and modeling plus instructions plus social reinforcement, all shown on videotape. Although it was impossible to assess individually the effects of the 3 procedures, results indicate that the training sessions did produce a significant increase in the target behaviors. The theoretical superiority of the modeling plus instructions plus social reinforcement procedure is discussed, along with the feasibility of model presentation by videotape and the use of nonretarded peers as models. (33 ref)
Nelson, Rosemery; Gibson, Frank & Cutting, D. Scott. (U. North Carolina, Greensboro) Mental Retardation, 1973(Dec), Vol. 11(6), 24-28. [PA, Vol 52:03750]

2578. Graduation: What happens to the retarded child when he grows up?
Collected information to assess the quality of community life experienced by 120 moderately retarded adults after graduation from school. Interviews were held with their parents or guardians who were administered the Depth Interview Schedule. Recommendations are made for (a) new criteria for evaluation of community adjustment of the moderately retarded, emphasizing comprehensive postschool programing to meet their recreational and social needs and providing occupational and vocational training; and (b) community-based residential facilities to provide such programing as an alternative to the parent-child model and the permanent parent-child relationship which it reinforces.
Stanfield, James S. (California State U., Los Angeles) Exceptional Children, 1973(Apr), Vol. 39(7), 548-552. [PA, Vol 50:11878]

2579. Conjugate control of motor activity in mentally retarded persons.
Used motion pictures on a conjugate schedule of reinforcement to modify rates of gross motor activity in 18 moderately retarded institutionalized adolescents and adults (mean age = 23 yrs). Ss learned to increase and decrease their activity rates relative to baseline conditions. Within noncontingent conditions, increasing the level of sensory stimulation decreased activity rates.
Switzky, Harvey N. & Haywood, H. Carl. (George Peabody Coll. for Teachers) American Journal of Mental Deficiency, 1973(Mar), Vol. 77(5), 567-570. [PA, Vol 51:07474]

2580. Effect of motor development on body image scores for institutionalized mentally retarded children.
Investigated the effects of a physical development program on body-image concepts of 44 trainable mentally retarded 10-19 yr olds, as measured by Barrier and Penetration variables from the Holtzman Inkblot Technique. Ss were randomly assigned to 1 of 3 groups: Group 1 (experimental) participated in a daily 5-wk physical development program; Group 2 (Hawthorne control) participated in a daily 5-wk sedentary recreation program; and Group 3 (control) was pre- and posttested but received no specialized program. A comparison of pre- and postprogram scores showed a significant decrease in the number of Ss giving Penetration responses on the Holtzman Inkblot Technique for the experimental group only, indicating a more positive body-image as a result of the physical development program. (23 ref)
Chasey, William C.; Swartz, Jon D. & Chasey, Carol G. (George Peabody Coll.) American Journal of Mental Deficiency, 1974(Jan), Vol. 78(4), 440-445. [PA, Vol 52:08002]

2581. Follow-up study of retarded clients from a training workshop.
Presents the results of a follow-up of 268 18–54 yr old retardates trained in the workshop of a voluntary agency between 1957 and 1970. Findings indicate that workshop programs should be expanded to prepare its graduates to meet crisis situations (e.g., unemployment, the draft, children, or marriage).
Stabler, Elizabeth M. (Stamford Aid for Retarded, Conn.) Mental Retardation, 1974(Jun), Vol. 12(3), 7-9. [PA, Vol 52:13035]

2582. The possible use of sociodrama as a training technique for the moderately mentally handicapped in school, half-way training centre, and sheltered workshop.
Discusses sociodrama as a technique to help children with moderate mental handicaps develop social skills in which they often become deficient. With a modification of the procedure toward the practicing of response patterns and away from problem solving, sociodrama would provide opportunities for learning both by conditioning and through cognitive modification for all but the most profoundly retarded. Its dramatization process of role playing involves movement, language, and convergent and divergent thinking. Sociodrama provides the individual with a picture of how he operates in real life situations, and such feedback could be increased through the use of videotape. The behavioral outcome of acquiring and developing personal interrelationship values through dependency learning is described as an example of how the social skills of the retarded could be enhanced by participation in sociodrama.
Foster, S. E. (Mt Gravatt Teachers' Coll, Brisbane, Australia) Slow Learning Child, 1975(Mar), Vol 22(1), 38–44. [PA, Vol 59:08837]

2583. Teaching TMR children and adults to dial the telephone.
Summarizes 2 studies, one with trainable mentally retarded (TMR) children and the other with TMR adults, in which 90% of Ss learned to dial a telephone with only a few min of instruction. Procedures with a device called the Dial-A-Phone are described.
Leff, Ruth B. Mental Retardation, 1975(Jun), Vol 13(3), 9-11. [PA, Vol 54:08202]

2584. [Experience in social adjustment of trainable retarded children in the day center of the Warsaw Psychoneurological Institute.] (Russ)
In a review of a book by H. Olechnowicz, *Studies in the Socialization of the Retarded* (1973), the work of the day center at the Warsaw Psychoneurological Institute is described. The 20 retarded children, 9–22 yrs old, live at home and spend 6–10 hrs daily at the center, depending on their parents' working day. One of the goals of the center is to educate parents how to teach and train their children to work. The center also provides a collective for children who otherwise must stay at home. The upbringing of these children begins with purposeful, socially controlled and organized behavior in order to develop self-control.
Sumarokova, V. & Yavkin, V. Defektologiya, 1975(Jun), No 6, 84–86. [PA, Vol 64:10958]

2585. Improvement of cognitive functioning in the trainable mentally retarded through visual-motor tutoring.
Gave to 8 trainable mentally retarded public school children (CA 7-17 yrs) 27 individual, 3-dimensional, visual-motor tutoring experiences based on certain psychological correlates of the communications process and their inability to perform specific tasks required on the Leiter International Performance Scale. Eight children matched for CA and Leiter IQ served as controls and received 27 individual art and craft experiences. Pre- and posttest consisted of the Leiter and the Hiskey-Nebraska Test of Learning Aptitude. On the posttest the experimental group made significant gains in Leiter IQ and Hiskey MA, when compared to their pretest scores, while the control group did not make similar gains. Similarly, the experimental group made significant gains over the control group on posttest Leiter IQ. There had been no significant difference between the 2 groups on their Leiter or Hiskey. (17 ref)
Thrapp, Robert W. Child Study Journal, 1975, Vol 5(4), 211-220. [PA, Vol 55:13510]

2586. Learning devices for mentally retarded children.
Conducted a pilot study with 8 trainable mentally retarded children (CA, 4-9 yrs; MA, 18 mo to 3½ yrs) to develop and test learning devices for mentally retarded children. Two products, the dressing smock and a figure reproduction stencil board, were developed to aid Ss in the development of (a) self-care, fine and gross motor, and cognitive and perceptual skills; and (b) figure reproduction, cognitive, perceptual, and manipulative skills. Results are significant in the degree of skill increase and knowledge attainment of both products, suggesting the desirability of interdisciplinary activity.
Bartholomew, Robert. (Northern Illinois U) Education & Training of the Mentally Retarded, 1976(Feb), Vol 11(1), 37-39. [PA, Vol 57:03620]

2587. Televison programs as socializing agents for mentally retarded children.
Broadcast over commercial TV channels 4 half-hour television dramas employing mentally retarded children as actors in everyday situations. Home interviews with 144 trainably retarded children and their parents conducted after the series indicate that such programs plus parental involvement offer hope for the socialization and development of self-esteem in mentally retarded children.
Baran, Stanley J. (U Texas, Austin) AV Communication Review, 1977(Fal), Vol 25(3), 281–289. [PA, Vol 60:12668]

2588. The integration of moderately retarded children into regular residential camps: A demonstration program.
Placed 38 mentally retarded children in 17 vacation camps with nonretarded children. 39% of the retarded children were rated highly successful in integration with the camp society, 27% moderately successful, and 13% unsuccessful. The researchers conclude that integrated camp experience can be a highly functional, useful, and enjoyable experience for both retarded and nonretarded children. A follow-up study rated 65% of the children as successful, 20% unsuccessful, and 15% as having mixed outcomes.

Braaten, June. (Ontario Assn for the Mentally Retarded, Toronto, Canada) Journal of Leisurability, 1977(Jul), Vol 4(3), 27–31. [PA, Vol 62:11223]

2589. The effect of an isometric strength program on the intellectual and social development of trainable retarded males.
Examined the effect of muscular strength on the development of the intellectual, physical, and social skills of trainable mental retardates (TMRs). Ss were 40 TMR males, aged 12 yrs, with IQ 30–50 and a minimum development level of 3 yrs, who were randomly divided into experimental and control groups. Experimental Ss performed 12 isometric exercises for 10 sec each, daily for 6 wks, administered by the same experimenter. Control Ss spent the same amount of time merely walking and talking with the experimenter. All Ss were evaluated at the beginning and end of the 6-wk period with the Stanford-Binet Intelligence Test and the Vineland Social Maturity Scale. The posttest revealed significant gains in strength, social skills, and intelligence by the experimental TMRs.
Brown, B. J. (Virginia Polytechnic Inst & State U) American Corrective Therapy Journal, 1977(Mar–Apr), Vol 31(2), 44–48. [PA, Vol 59:08457]

2590. An experimental analysis of language training generalization across classroom and home.
Investigated the effects of several procedures aimed at increasing the use of trained speech outside the speech training environment. Two trainable mentally retarded 16-yr-olds (MAs, 4.4 and 4.2 yrs, respectively) were trained using imitation and reinforcement procedures to label a series of pictures with complex sentences containing 5-word chains. Concurrently, the use of this trained repertoire was monitored in a classroom setting and at home. Results indicate that Ss did not begin to use the trained instances in the classroom or at home until some instances were actually trained in these settings. Implications for efficient speech therapy and research are discussed. (20 ref)
Garcia, Eugene E.; Bullet, John & Rust, Frank P. (U California, Santa Barbara) Behavior Modification, 1977(Oct), Vol 1(4), 531–550. [PA, Vol 60:07963]

2591. Effects of two variable-ratio schedules of timeout: Changes in target and non-target behaviors.
VR8 and VR4 schedules of time-out were applied to the high-rate inappropriate verbal behavior of a 10-yr-old retarded boy (IQ 35). Results show that both schedules were effective in suppressing the target behavior, the VR4 schedule being slightly more effective.
Jackson, Joan L. & Calhoun, Karen S. (U Georgia) Journal of Behavior Therapy & Experimental Psychiatry, 1977(Jun), Vol 8(2), 195–199. [PA, Vol 59:12740]

2592. A counseling program for TMR students.
Describes a program of group counseling for trainable mentally retarded students (CA range 13–21 yrs, MA range 4–5 yrs). Groups of 8 met weekly with the counselor, and later in the year parent groups were formed. The school district psychologist was called in to discuss with the parents the sexual feelings of the students (who were physically mature). Both group endeavors were judged successful. It was shown that the severely retarded can learn the rudiments of group process, that they can be trained to think through simple problems, and that they can learn to interact in new ways. Parents shared each other's fears, experiences, and ideas.
Norman, Margie L. (Austin Elementary/Opportunity School, TX) School Counselor, 1977(Mar), Vol 24(4), 274–277. [PA, Vol 60:08361]

2593. Stimulus selection and tracking during urination: Autoshaping directed behavior with toilet targets.
Describes a simple procedure for investigating stimuli selected as targets during urination in the commode. 10 normal males aged 21–30 yrs preferred a floating target that could be tracked to a series of stationary targets. This technique was used to bring misdirected urinations in a severely retarded 15-yr-old male under rapid stimulus control of a floating target in the commode. The float stimulus was also evaluated with 9 institutionalized,

moderately retarded 8–14 yr old males, and results indicate rapid autoshaping of directed urination without verbal instructions or conventional toilet training. The technique can be applied in training children to control misdirected urinations in institutions for the retarded, in psychiatric wards with regressed populations, and in certain male school dormitories. (16 ref)
Siegel, R. K. (U California Ctr for Health Sciences, Los Angeles) Journal of Applied Behavior Analysis, 1977(Sum), Vol 10(2), 255–265. [PA, Vol 59:12766]

2594. Direct and vicarious effects of social praise on mentally retarded preschool children's attentive behavior.
Examined the effects of social praise on the attentive behavior of reinforced and nonreinforced children. Two pairs of mentally retarded preschool boys (CA 42–53 mo, IQ 37–51) served as Ss. Employing a reversal design, 1 S from each pair was differentially reinforced for attending to manipulative toys. Results show that (a) the intervention procedure increased the attentive behavior of the target Ss; (b) nonreinforced Ss also increased their attentive behavior during both reinforcement conditions; and (c) this "spillover" of reinforcement effect was transient, as the nontarget Ss', level of attentive behavior decelerated during the final half of each 20-day reinforcement period.
Strain, Phillip S. & Pierce, James E. (Children & Youth, Nashville, TN) Psychology in the Schools, 1977(Jul), Vol 14(3), 348–353. [PA, Vol 59:12769]

2595. Applied behavior analysis in the treatment of mealtime tantrums and delay in self feeding in a multi-handicapped child.
Describes the use of applied behavior analysis to treat the feeding problem of mealtime tantrums (crying and self-injurious behavior) and delay in self-feeding in a moderately retarded 6-yr-old girl with microcephaly and microphthalmia. Treatment was conducted by a 2nd-yr medical student without previous experience with this approach, and subsequently by family members. The case and its treatment are discussed in terms of the needs of the family and its problems. (8 ref)
Thompson, Robert J. (Duke U Medical Ctr, Div of Medical Psychology) Journal of Clinical Child Psychology, 1977(Win), Vol 6(3), 52–54. [PA, Vol 62:06710]

2596. The acquisition of classification skills by trainable mentally retarded children.
The performance of 22 6–12 yr old trainable mentally retarded (TMR) Ss given training in the identification and utilization of dimensional properties of form, size, and color in object sorting was compared with 19 nontrained controls. The study investigated whether classification skills could be induced in TMR children through individualized experiential training, whether multiple as well as single classification skills could be acquired, and whether gains associated with training would be sustained following an interval of no training. Trained Ss were found to perform significantly more single and multiple classifications on both the immediate and the deferred posttest than controls. (7 ref)
Klein, Nancy K. & Safford, Philip L. (Cleveland State U) Education & Training of the Mentally Retarded, 1978(Oct), Vol 13(3), 272–277. [PA, Vol 63:08439]

2597. Self-regulation in retarded persons: Acquisition of standards for performance.
24 trainable mentally retarded children (mean Slosson Intelligence Test IQ 40.1, mean MA 46.4 mo) were divided into 3 groups equated by stratified assignment on IQ, MA, and CA. One group was then randomly assigned to each treatment condition: (a) Training 1 (live/film), (b) Training 2 (film/live), and (c) control. In the 1st phase of the study, both training groups watched 5 clown models set their standard at 6 on a bowling game. Subsequent standards set by the training and control groups indicated that these retarded Ss did base their standards on the models' standards (i.e., social referent). A training program including both live and filmed demonstrations was developed in order to teach the Ss a concept (i.e., "between") that would allow them to set their standards based on their own past performance. Both training groups acquired, retained, and

generalized the concept as evidenced by the standards they set. (9 ref)
Litrownik, Alan J.; Cleary, Catherine P.; Lecklitner, Gregory L. & Franzini, Louis R. (San Diego State U) American Journal of Mental Deficiency, 1978(Jul), Vol 83(1), 86–89. [PA, Vol 62:03892]

2598. Self-regulation in mentally retarded children: Assessment and training of self-monitoring skills.
Assessed self-monitoring skills in 30 7–11 yr old trainable mentally retarded (TMR) children (MAs 3–5 yrs; IQs 30–50) and then developed and evaluated a demonstration-training program aimed at teaching these skills. Ss were divided into 3 groups equated by stratified assignment on IQ, MA, and CA. One group was randomly assigned to each of 3 treatment conditions: (a) training, (b) attention control, and (c) no-contact control. Ss' ability to observe and monitor differentially the consequences of their performance was assessed, as well as the type of task they had worked on. Self-monitoring skills were similarly assessed after a 1-hr demonstration-training program or yoked experience, following a 1-wk retention interval, and on a transfer task. It was found that none of the Ss could self-monitor at the preassessment, but these skills were acquired, retained, and transferred as a function of training. Results suggest that TMR students can be given more responsibility for monitoring their own behavior (including consequences), and future researchers should focus on evaluating the reactive effects on self-monitoring skills.
Litrownik, Alan J.; Freitas, Janet L. & Franzini, Louis R. (San Diego State U) American Journal of Mental Deficiency, 1978(Mar), Vol 82(5), 499–506. [PA, Vol 61:08956]

2599. Training and generalization of a greeting exchange with a mentally retarded, language-deficient child.
Modeling, fading, and reinforcement procedures were used to teach a moderately mentally retarded 10-yr-old boy how to respond to adult-initiated questions within the context of a greeting exchange. Following acquisition of each of 4 responses, an assessment session was conducted in a nontraining setting to measure stimulus and response generalization. For 3 of 4 responses, consistent stimulus generalization was observed. S produced previously acquired responses in the nontraining setting, both during and following training, and while in the presence of individuals who were not associated with training. A 4th response did not generalize until a modified version was taught. No response generalization was observed. (3 ref)
Luiselli, James K. et al. (Boston U) Education & Treatment of Children, 1978(Sum), Vol 1(4), 23–29. [PA, Vol 63:12437]

2600. Reduction of undesired classroom behavior by systematically reinforcing the absence of such behavior.
Employed differential-reinforcement-of-other-behavior (DRO) reinforcement schedules in which the delivery of a reinforcer (a bit of food or a token) was contingent on the nonoccurrence of the undesired behavior during a specified time interval with 3 moderately retarded children. The 1st S was a 19.2-yr-old female, the 2nd a 17.2-yr-old male, and the 3rd a 16.8-yr-old female. All possessed rudimentary verbal skills. Leaving an assigned seat without permission, throwing objects, and hitting others was reduced in the 1st S, drooling (excessive salivation) was reduced in the 2nd S, and placing the hand(s) near the mouth was reduced in the 3rd S. The advantages of DRO reinforcement schedules over corporal punishment and time-out are discussed. (12 ref)
Poling, Alan D.; Miller, Kathy; Nelson, Neal & Ryan, Charlotte. (U South Carolina) Education & Treatment of Children, 1978(Spr), Vol 1(3), 35–41. [PA, Vol 63:06409]

2601. The effects of varying types of reinforcement on gross motor skill learning and retention in trainable mentally retarded boys.
Five trainable mentally retarded boys aged 14–17, IQs 25–39, participated in 48 treatment sessions during a 12-day period. Four different reinforcing conditions were applied to the gross motor skills of underhand beanbag throw and a ring toss. While

learning of these 2 motor skills did not occur as such, the most consistent response occurred under the Social plus Token Reinforcement treatment condition, followed by the Social Reinforcement treatment, the Token Reinforcement treatment, and the Instruction Only condition. (30 ref)
Schack, Fred K. & Ryan, Terry. (George Mason U) American Corrective Therapy Journal, 1978(Sep–Oct), Vol 32(5), 135–140. [PA, Vol 63:08064]

2602.　The use of overcorrection with artificial nails in the treatment of chronic fingernail biting.
Developed an overcorrection procedure that completely eliminated nailbiting in a 9-yr-old moderately mentally retarded female. The procedure was easy to administer because (a) only 1 person was needed to conduct the overcorrection training, (b) S's parents were the major behavior-change agents, and (c) physical force during training was never required. (7 ref)
Barmann, Barry C. (University of the Pacific, CA) Mental Retardation, 1979(Dec), Vol 17(6), 309–311. [PA, Vol 66:08485]

2603.　Teaching mending skills to mentally retarded adolescents.
Presents a model for analyzing community living skills and teaching them to trainable mentally retarded Ss. A task analysis of 3 mending skills was developed and validated, aided by consultation with persons having expertise in home economics and mental retardation. Five trainable retarded Ss (17.2–20.6 yrs of age) received training on sewing hems, buttons, and seams; skills were acquired rapidly and maintained. The behavior generalized from trained to untrained tasks on their common components for all Ss. A multiple baseline across participants combined with a multiple baseline across responses demonstrated the combined effectiveness of an objectively validated, detailed task analysis; graduated sequence of prompts; and response consequences in training and maintaining community living skills with mentally retarded adolescents. (5 ref)
Cronin, Kathleen A. & Cuvo, Anthony J. (Southern Illinois U, Carbondale) Journal of Applied Behavior Analysis, 1979(Fal), Vol 12(3), 401–406. [PA, Vol 65:01935]

2604.　Teaching conversational skills to retarded adolescents.
Used a modeling-coaching-rehearsal procedure to teach conversational skills to 2 moderately retarded adolescents (13 and 20 yrs old). A structured conversation format with a nonretarded peer partner was used. Several social components (fully answering questions asked by a peer, asking the partner questions, and extending social invitations) were sequentially trained in a multiple baseline design. Conversational skills were successfully trained, and they generalized to novel nonretarded peers and to free play interactions with retarded peers. Improvement was largely maintained at 3-wk followup. (15 ref)
Kelly, Jeffrey A. et al. (U Mississippi Medical Ctr, Jackson) Child Behavior Therapy, 1979(Spr), Vol 1(1), 85–97. [PA, Vol 65:06011]

2605.　The effects of modeling and verbal cues on concept acquisition of moderate retardates.
Conducted an experiment to determine if D. Meichenbaum and J. Goodman's (see PA, Vol 46:3785) procedure (modeling and instructional variables that significantly reduced error rates and increased response times with impulsive children) would reduce errors and increase performance latency in 25 moderately retarded 9–14 yr olds (IQs 36–54). Results indicate that modeling and modeling combined with low-meaning verbalizations, conceptual verbalizations, and self-instructions produced a reflective cognitive tempo in the Ss when compared with no-model controls. Findings support research describing an inverse relationship between number of errors and time to completion. (12 ref)
Norton, G. Ron & Lester, Carolyne J. (U Winnipeg, Canada) Cognitive Therapy & Research, 1979(Mar), Vol 3(1), 87–90. [PA, Vol 64:03536]

2606.　Restitution and positive practice overcorrection in reducing aggressive–disruptive behavior: A long-term follow-up.
Few overcorrection studies have reported long-term follow-up data. Those that have reported such data investigated either encopretic or self-stimulatory behavior. Long-term follow-up in the reduction of aggressive–disruptive behavior has not been reported. The present investigation used combined restitution and positive practice overcorrection to reduce paper-tearing by a 5-yr-old moderately retarded, nonverbal girl. 18-mo follow-up data indicate continued response suppression. Issues related to teaching socially appropriate behaviors as part of overcorrection procedures are discussed. (12 ref)
Shapiro, Edward S. (U Pittsburgh School of Medicine, Western Psychiatric Inst & Clinic) Journal of Behavior Therapy & Experimental Psychiatry, 1979(Jun), Vol 10(2), 131–134. [PA, Vol 64:13022]

2607.　A comparison of three strategies for teaching object names.
Three experiments with 30 undergraduates, 36 moderately retarded Ss (mean CA 18 yrs, mean IQ 47), and 30 preschoolers, respectively, examined the relative efficacy of 3 methods of presenting stimuli in object-naming tasks. Stimuli were introduced successively, simultaneously (SI), and using a combination (CO) of the 2 procedures. Adults, retarded Ss, and preschoolers were taught to produce the names of 5 Hebrew letters, English words, or American coins, respectively. Presentation method was a between-Ss treatment in a factorial design. Results from the series of systematic replications were consistent in showing better posttest performance for Ss in the SI and CO conditions. Further, follow-up data in Exp III showed that retention was also superior for Ss trained by the SI or CO methods. Although the acquisition criterion was met in fewer trials by Ss in the successive condition, only several minutes more training time was required by the SI and CO conditions. From a cost effectiveness point of view, either of the latter 2 techniques should be favored over the successive procedure for teaching verbal naming skills. (6 ref)
Cuvo, Anthony J. et al. (Southern Illinois U Rehabilitation Inst, Behavior Modification Program, Carbondale) Journal of Applied Behavior Analysis, 1980(Sum), Vol 13(2), 249–257. [PA, Vol 65:13268]

2608.　Training trainable mentally retarded adolescents in delay behavior.
Seven out of 10 trainable mentally retarded individuals (mean CA 18.9 yrs; mean IQ 36.8) who had been unable to exhibit sufficient delay behaviors in a workshop setting were taught to defer gratification via a behaviorally based intensive training program. (3 ref)
Franzini, Louis R.; Litrownik, Alan J. & Magy, Martin A. (San Diego State U) Mental Retardation, 1980(Feb), Vol 18(1), 45–47. [PA, Vol 66:08503]

2609.　The effect of music ear training upon the auditory discrimination abilities of trainable mentally retarded adolescents.
Found equivocal results in a study that tested the hypothesis that music ear training would enhance auditory discrimination abilities (as measured by the Goldman-Fristoe-Woodcock Test of Auditory Perception). However, the authors suggest that the results should not be generalized, but established by additional research in other situations. (6 ref)
Humphrey, Terrence. (Hammond State School, LA) Journal of Music Therapy, 1980(Sum), Vol 17(2), 70–74. [PA, Vol 66:10769]

2610.　Self-monitoring in moderately retarded adolescents: Reactivity and accuracy as a function of valence.
To determine the effects of valence on the accuracy and reactivity of self-monitoring, 40 adolescent moderately retarded students were divided into 4 groups: self-record a positive aspect of their performance (i.e., finish a bead-string task within the time limit), self-record a negative aspect (i.e., not finish within the time allowed), self-record a neutral aspect (i.e., when they strung the beads), and string beads without self-recording. Acquisition of

the self-monitoring skills was not differentially affected by the aspect of the behavior (i.e., positive, negative, or neutral) that cued recording, nor were there any differences in accuracy during postassessments. Results indicate that (a) the group monitoring when they finished significantly surpassed the group monitoring when they did not finish, and (b) the positive and neutral monitoring groups significantly outgained the negative and control groups. The reactive effects of self-monitoring are determined, in part, by the aspect of performance that cues the self-recording response. (26 ref)
Litrownik, Alan J. & Freitas, Janet L. (San Diego State U) Behavior Therapy, 1980(Mar), Vol 11(2), 245–255. [PA, Vol 63:10203]

2611.   Training interpersonal skills among mentally retarded and socially dysfunctional children.
Two moderately retarded boys (aged 11 and 12 yrs) who resided in an inpatient unit for emotionally disturbed children were treated for deficits in social skills (e.g., facial mannerisms, eye contact, and intonation and content of speech). The treatment package consisted of instructions, performance feedback, social reinforcement, modeling, and role-playing. The effects of the treatment in developing appropriate social performance were evaluated in separate multiple-baseline designs across behaviors for each S. The training improved social skills and brought Ss up to or beyond the level of normal controls. (18 ref)
Matson, Johnny L.; Kazdin, Alan E. & Esveldt-Dawson, Karen. (U Pittsburgh School of Medicine, Western Psychiatric Inst & Clinic) Behaviour Research & Therapy, 1980, Vol 18(5), 419–427. [PA, Vol 65:01793]

2612.   Mimicry versus imitative modeling: Facilitating sentence production in the speech of the retarded.
Randomly assigned 12 trainable mentally retarded children (CAs 6–19 yrs; MAs 2.1–4.3 yrs) at the 2-word stage of language development to mimicry and imitative modeling language instruction classes. Ss in the mimicry group imitated agent–action–object (AAO) constructions immediately after presentation, while Ss in the imitative modeling group first heard the AAO presentation and later produced the AAO construction in response to a verb question. Imitative modeling Ss achieved as many correct AAO responses during training as did the mimicry Ss and more correct responses on a generalization task and in a free play setting. They also displayed more novel response behavior (selective imitations) and spontaneously corrected productions. Results support the use of modeling procedures for inducing language production in the retarded. (18 ref)
Prelock, Patricia A. & Panagos, John M. (Norton City Schools, OH) Journal of Psycholinguistic Research, 1980(Nov), Vol 9(6), 565–578. [PA, Vol 66:13442]

2613.   Behavioral treatment of food refusal and selectivity in developmentally disabled children.
The highly selective food refusal of 2 moderately mentally retarded girls (CAs 6 and 9 yrs; IQs 41 and 42) was reduced using procedures consisting of delivery of preferred foods as reinforcers, extinction, and fading. Results of a multiple baseline design show increased consumption of all selected foods and decreased food expulsion for both Ss. Findings suggest that behavioral methodology and principles may be useful in assessing and treating a variety of eating disorders. (20 ref)
Riordan, Mary M.; Iwata, Brian A.; Wohl, Marianne K. & Finney, Jack W. Applied Research in Mental Retardation, 1980, Vol 1(1–2), 95–112. [PA, Vol 66:08552]

2614.   The effectiveness of a behavioral weight reduction program for moderately retarded adolescents.
30 moderately mentally retarded adolescents were assigned to either a behavior therapy, a social–nutrition, or a waiting list control group. Behavior therapy Ss lost significantly more weight than did nutrition and control Ss. Behavior therapy Ss continued to lose weight during maintenance and follow-up conditions. (12 ref)

Rotatori, Anthony F. & Fox, Robert. (Northern Illinois U) Behavior Therapy, 1980(Jun), Vol 11(3), 410–416. [PA, Vol 64:13018]

2615.   The effects of goal setting on the manual performance rates of moderately retarded adolescents.
Hypothesized that (a) goal setting would significantly increase the number of successful trials on each prevocational training task completed by 5 moderately retarded adolescents (CA 15–18 yrs, IQ 56–40) within a 90-min period and (b) informing Ss of their previous performance level would significantly improve performance over conditions in which knowlege of results was not provided. Results support the hypotheses. (14 ref)
Warner, Dennis A. & Mills, William D. (Washington State U, Pullman) Education & Training of the Mentally Retarded, 1980(Apr), Vol 15(2), 143–147. [PA, Vol 66:11044]

2616.   Treatment of stereotyped toe-walking with overcorrection and physical therapy.
Reports on the successful integration of a behavior therapy technique (positive practice overcorrection) within a traditional physical therapy program for reducing stereotyped toe-walking in a 9-yr-old moderately mentally retarded boy (MA 3 yrs 8 mo) with bilateral heel cord tightening. The integration of therapies was effected following the unsuccessful long-term use of a therapeutic exercise program alone. Follow-up data for 6 wks are reported. (19 ref)
Barrett, Rowland P. & Linn, Dorothy M. (U Pittsburgh School of Medicine, Western Psychiatric Inst & Clinic) Applied Research in Mental Retardation, 1981, Vol 2(1), 13–21. [PA, Vol 66:11031]

2617.   Vocational interest evaluation of TMR adults.
52 trainable mentally retarded adults (mean CA 24 yrs) participated in a 3-stage job-training and placement program over a 5-yr period. Vocational inventoried interest and expressed interest were correlated, as were relationships between inventoried interest and such variables as CA and IQ (WISC or Stanford-Binet Intelligence Scale). Results show that (a) Ss could discriminate between occupational likes and dislikes when using pictorial inventoried interest assessment techniques, (b) a positive relationship existed between expressed and inventoried interest, (c) inventoried interest was independent of CA and IQ, (d) there was a general consistency in inventoried occupational choice over a 6-mo interval, and (e) the Reading-Free Vocational Interest Inventory has predictive and status validity, as evidenced by job incumbents' success and their inventory cluster profiles. (26 ref)
Becker, Ralph L.; Schull, Caryl & Cambell, Ken. (Orient State Inst, OH) American Journal of Mental Deficiency, 1981(Jan), Vol 85(4), 350–356. [PA, Vol 65:08659]

Severe Mental Retardation

2618.   Behavioral engineering: Two apparatuses for toilet training retarded children.
Describes a training procedure for eliminating daytime incontinence which provides an immediate signal when the child voids so that the trainer can react immediately. 2 apparatuses were developed for this purpose: (a) a toilet-chair apparatus to signal proper toileting, and (b) a portable pants-alarm apparatus to signal wetting of the pants. A reprimand was given when pants wetting occurred whereas positive reinforcement was given for proper toileting. Results with 4 profoundly retarded 3-6 yr. old females indicate the reliability of the apparatuses in practice and the effectiveness of a toilet training program that used the 2 apparatuses.
Azrin, N. H.; Bugle, C. & O'Brien, F. (Anna State Hosp., Ill.) Journal of Applied Behavior Analysis, 1971(Fal), Vol. 4(3), 249-253. [PA, Vol 47:11513]

2619.   Reinforcement therapy for behavior problems in severely retarded children.
6 severely retarded 6-9 yr. old children (IQ below 25) were treated in a small home-like living unit. The project emphasized

the "total milieu" use of reinforcement techniques by regular attendants trained as therapists, and the behavioral measurement of both Ss and matched ward controls. Ss were evaluated by results obtained on the Peabody Picture Vocabulary Test and the Denver Developmental Screening Inventory. Treatment was generally effective, with less success obtained for retarded Ss who also presented psychotic behavior. (23 ref.)
Baker, Bruce L. & Ward, Michael H. (Harvard U.) American Journal of Orthopsychiatry, 1971(Jan), Vol. 41(1), 124-135. [PA, Vol 46:11367]

2620.   Behavioral differences among an institution's back ward residents.
Studied 55 5-15 yr. old severely and profoundly retarded children over many mo. Rates of working for various consequences were recorded, and disrupting behaviors were noted. Ss worked in cubicles with automatically programmed sequences. Ss were drawn from 2 purportedly similar custodial buildings of a large public institution. Unexpected behavioral differences between the 2 groups proved to be associated with differences in characteristics and practices of building employees. This finding raises important questions for habilitators, researchers, and administrators seeking to improve residential services for retarded people.
Barrett, Beatrice H. (Walter E. Fernald State School, Behavior Prosthesis Lab., Waverly, Mass.) Mental Retardation, 1971(Feb), Vol. 9(1), 4-9. [PA, Vol 48:05459]

2621.   A comparison of procedures for eliminating self-injurious behavior of retarded adolescents.
Attempted to eliminate the self-injurious behaviors of 4 institutionalized, profoundly retarded adolescents. Some of the behaviors studied were: face-slapping, face-banging, hair-pulling, face-scratching, and finger-biting. 3 remediative approaches are reported: (a) elimination of all social consequences of the self-injurious behavior was not effective with the 2 Ss with whom it was attempted, (b) the same 2 Ss were exposed to reinforcement of non-self-injurious behavior which was ineffective under no food deprivation and effective with 1 of the 2 Ss under mild food deprivation, and (c) electric-shock punishment eliminated the self-injurious behaviors of all 4 Ss. Results suggest that punishment was more effective than differential reinforcement of non-self-injurious behavior which, in turn, was more effective than extinction through elimination of social consequences. The effects of the punishment, however, were usually specific to the setting in which it was administered. (16 ref.)
Corte, Henry E.; Wolf, Montrose M. & Locke, Bill J. (Plymouth State Home, Northville, Mich.) Journal of Applied Behavior Analysis, 1971(Fal), Vol. 4(3), 201-213. [PA, Vol 47:11468]

2622.   Symposium on the educational problems of the severely mentally handicapped child: II. The age of admission to hospital of severely subnormal children.
Compared the frequeucy of certain medical and social variables in 285 mentally retarded patients admitted to a children's hospital to determine whether any of the variables were associated with earlier or later admission. Although some of the factors considered did not show a statistically significant increase relating to particular age groups, certain trends were seen and 3 significant factors concerning the 38 under 1-yr-old admissions were observed.
Donoghue, E. C.; Abbas, K. A. & Gal, E. (Queen Mary's Hosp. for Children, Carshalton, England) British Journal of Mental Subnormality, 1971(Dec), Vol. 17(33, Pt. 2), 94-100. [PA, Vol 48:03540]

2623.   Operant audiometry with severely retarded children.
Describes procedures for establishing stimulus control with an operant audiometric program. The procedures were applied to 18 severely retarded children using both ascending and descending methods for establishing thresholds. Various pretest stimulus control criteria were used to determine their effect on threshold variability. Results indicate that (a) the described procedure provides reliable thresholds, (b) ascending-descending measurement methods are not a critical variable in threshold variability,

and (c) stimulus control criteria have a major effect on threshold variability. (French summary)
Fulton, R. T. & Spradlin, J. E. (U. Kansas) Audiology, 1971(Jul), Vol. 10(4), 203-211. [PA, Vol 47:05473]

2624.   The effectiveness of time-out in reducing maladaptive behavior of autistic and retarded children.
4 profoundly retarded girls (mean age, 10.7 yr.), 3 of whom displayed obvious autistic behaviors, underwent 14 mo. of intensive behavioral modification therapy with time-out from positive reinforcement as the basic procedure. Attempts were made to reduce 3 types of behavior: aggressiveness towards self, aggressiveness towards others, and running from their living unit. The frequency of these behavioral patterns was reduced by more than 98% in all 4 Ss during the therapy period. Although Ss were able to sustain these behavioral patterns, eliminating the inappropriate behaviors in the therapy sessions to a variable interval reinforcement schedule of 360-1, very little of this behavior generalized from therapy to Ss' everyday patterns. 4 procedures to facilitate generalization were all unsuccessful. It was found, however, that time-out did seem to sensitize the Ss to the response-stimulus sequence which facilitated acquisition of more basic self-help behaviors.
Husted, John R.; Hall, Patricia & Agin, Bill. (Warren G. Murray Children's Center, Centralia, Ill.) Journal of Psychology, 1971(Nov), Vol. 79(2), 189-196. [PA, Vol 47:07278]

2625.   [Experience of CESAP: From medico-social action to research and clinical considerations.] (Fren)
Describes the Committee for the Study and Care of the Severely Retarded (CESAP) which was created in 1966 to (a) organize services for the specialized care of Parisian children with IQs of less than 50; and (b) conduct information, research, and teaching activities. The options incorporated in the organization of the care services seem to have stimulated and increased the effectiveness of clinical study, if not research efforts. Diverse categories of children are accepted into equally diverse structures (e.g., residential institutions and family placements), and partially overlapping teams are used for these different services. These factors have helped the CESAP rapidly collect a sizable core of observations and define a number of fundamental questions concerning severe mental deficiency. (German & Spanish summaries)
Launay, Cl. & Zucman, E. (Herold Hosp., Paris, France) Revue de Neuropsychiatrie Infantile et d'Hygiene Mentale de l'Enfance, 1971(Mar), Vol. 19(3-4), 109-113. [PA, Vol 49:07529]

2626.   Behavior modification in a profoundly retarded child: A case report.
Describes 3 behavior modification programs used with a profoundly retarded 7-yr-old boy. The programs developed a self-feeding operant, taught S to respond appropriately to a verbal command, and greatly increased his ability to stand without support. Side effects included an apparent increase in S's responsiveness to his environment, and independent mobility by crawling or using a walker. Observational follow-up information indicates that S's behavior gains have been maintained in his home. Questions raised by the training techniques used are considered.
Miller, Harold R.; Patton, Mary E. & Henton, Karel R. (Marshall State School & Hosp., Mo.) Behavior Therapy, 1971(Jul), Vol. 2(3), 375-384. [PA, Vol 48:03167]

2627.   Crying and laughing in imbeciles.
Compared 90 severely retarded children living at home and attending local training centers with 15 Ss living in a hospital and attending hospital school. The study covered 10 consecutive school days. It was found that (a) Ss living at home laughed more than those living in hospital (and more than a comparison group of 10 normal children); (b) Ss with Down's Syndrome laughed more than others; and (c) no significant differences in frequency of crying occurred.
Norris, David. (Bournemouth Coll. of Technology, England) Developmental Medicine & Child Neurology, 1971(Dec), Vol. 13(6), 756-761. [PA, Vol 48:07642]

2628. Promotion of positive social interaction in severely retarded young children.

Used prompting and reinforcement to train severely retarded young institutionalized children to imitate novel social responses of a model as a means of facilitating positive social interaction with peers. Matched pairs of Ss (10 experimental, 10 control) were rated on the level of social behavior emitted in the ward setting both before and after the experimental Ss were trained. After training, the experimental Ss exhibited a significantly higher level of social behavior, which generalized to the ward setting. Controls showed no change in level of social behavior.—*Paloutzian, Raymond F.; Hasazi, Joseph; Streifel, John & Edgar, Clara L.* (Claremont Graduate School, Calif.) American Journal of Mental Deficiency, 1971(Jan), Vol. 75(4), 519-524. [PA, Vol 46:03617]

2629. Music therapy: An effective solution to problems in related disciplines.

Reports 2 studies exemplifying the extension of the music therapist's services outside his own particular program. The 1st describes the collaborative work of a music therapist and a preschool teacher at an inner city settlement house; the 2nd a program by a speech therapist and a music therapist for a child in an institution for the mentally retarded. The procedures of Exp. I and II show that duration of hand movement and rocking was decreased in a profoundly retarded child. When verbal stimuli and preferred music were presented contingent upon response, they functioned as reinforcing stimuli. Music can be presented and withdrawn immediately contingent on specific responses; the music lasts for the duration of appropriate behavior. It is concluded that music could be a potent reinforcer for a variety of behaviors in many different situations.—*Steele, Anita L. & Jorgenson, Helen A.* (Cleveland Music School Settlement, O.) Journal of Music Therapy, 1971(Win), Vol. 8(4), 131-145. [PA, Vol 49:07656]

2630. [Specialized family placement for severely retarded children: Analysis of four years of activity.] (Fren)

Describes the 1st family placement for 39 11.2-12 yr. old severely retarded children with a wide range of handicaps: 17% were not testable, and 15% with IQs > 50 presented psychotic symptoms or severe social problems. 32 foster families cared for the Ss for a period of 6 mo. to 21.2 yr., supported and guided by a social worker, nursery school supervisor, and physiotherapist. 3 doctors and 1 psychologist assisted on a part-time basis. The foster homes were visited regularly, and team members met weekly to discuss the child's progress. The child was seen at the hospital once a month. Data indicate that the program has been successful. The adjustment of the child's natural parents is discussed. (German & Spanish summaries)—*Tomkiewicz, S.; Biny, Y. & Zucman, E.* (National Inst. of Health & Medical Research, Paris, France) Revue de Neuropsychiatrie Infantile et d'Hygiene Mentale de l'Enfance, 1971(Mar), Vol. 19(3-4), 165-175. [PA, Vol 49:09789]

2631. Reducing hyperactive behavior in a severely retarded child.

Investigated a procedure for controlling the hyperactive behavior of a severely retarded 6-yr-old female. During a 4-wk training period reinforcement (food and verbal procedures) was administered contingent upon the occurrence of a sitting response which was incompatible with continuous "nonadaptive" locomotive behaviors displayed by the S. A 3-wk followup indicated a substantial improvement in the S's general sitting behavior. During this 5-day posttreatment period the S remained sitting for an average time of about 5½ min. in comparison with 1 min. during the 5-day pretreatment period.—*Whitman, Thomas L.; Caponigri, Vicki & Mercurio, Joseph.* (U. Notre Dame) Mental Retardation, 1971(Jun), Vol. 9(3), 17-19. [PA, Vol 48:05491]

2632. Effects of reinforcement and guidance procedures on instruction-following behavior of severely retarded children.

Used positive reinforcement, physical guidance, and fading procedures to teach motor responses to a variety of verbal instructions to a 4.5-yr-old male and a 7-yr-old female who were severely retarded. Ss' responses to 1 set of instructions provided the focus for the training procedures. Their responses to a 2nd set of instructions were used to assess the generalized effects of training. The frequency of responses to both sets of instructions was evaluated during and after the daily training sessions when no training procedures were in effect. Ss showed pronounced increases in instruction-following behaviors (both trained and untrained) during training periods with decreases in such behavior occurring during the Base-line 2 period. Findings demonstrate the applicability of the training procedures for producing and maintaining instruction-following behaviors in severely retarded children and for facilitating appropriate responding to instructions not directly involved in training. (15 ref.)—*Whitman, Thomas L.; Zakaras, Michael & Chardos, Stephen.* (U. Notre Dame) Journal of Applied Behavior Analysis, 1971(Win), Vol. 4(4), 283-290. [PA, Vol 48:05492]

2633. [Operant conditioning modification of severely retarded children through conditions of material reinforcement.] (Germ)

Reports that operant conditioning procedures improved mastery in self-help (the putting on and taking off of jackets) in 6 6-12 yr. old profoundly retarded children. 3 Ss received material reinforcement (food) and the other 3 received social reinforcement (contacts with the E). Considerable learning success was made in both groups after 35 sessions. The social reinforcement group was slightly better than the material reinforced group.—*Alt, Christa & Bloschl, Lilian.* (U. Dusseldorf, Inst. of Psychology, W. Germany) Zeitschrift für Klinische Psychologie und Psychotherapie, 1972, Vol. 20(1), 33-42. [PA, Vol 50:01395]

2634. Intensive play: A technique for building affective behaviors in profoundly mentally retarded young children.

Describes the technique of intensive play used with profoundly mentally retarded young children in whom unawareness, fearfulness, and unresponsiveness are general characteristics. Intensive play is the building, through close body contact and physical stimulation, of positive responses to normally pleasurable experiences. The method was developed to break through the barriers of unawareness, fearfulness, and unresponsiveness and is used for building affective behavior.—*Bradtke, Louise M.; Kirkpatrick, William J. & Rosenblatt, Katherine P.* (Sunland Training Center, Miami, Fla.) Education & Training of the Mentally Retarded, 1972(Feb), Vol. 7(1), 8-13. [PA, Vol 49:07386]

2635. Assessment and modification of verbal imitation with low-functioning retarded children.

Gave a speech sound imitation test composed of 25 consonant-vowel combinations to 30 7-16 yr. old severely and profoundly retarded institutionalized children. Results indicate that although the retarded Ss made more errors than preschoolers, the pattern of errors was similar. The most frequent type of error made by low-functioning Ss as well as normal preschoolers was in place of articulation. Subsequently, 10 low-functioning Ss were divided into component and speech-sound training groups. The difference in these procedures was the units of behavior that served as the training stimuli. Results indicate that the speech-sound group emitted fewer errors than the component group on the posttest.—*Bricker, William A. & Bricker, Diane D.* (George Peabody Coll. for Teachers) Journal of Speech & Hearing Research, 1972(Dec), Vol. 15(4), 690-698. [PA, Vol 50:07202]

2636. Development and maintenance of a behavior modification repertoire of cottage attendants through T.V. feedback.

Investigated the use of commercial trading stamps as token reinforcers in combination with an on-ward training program for 9 female attendants who worked with 5 severely retarded children. Base-line interaction was recorded for a 2-wk period followed by 6 wk. of both direct and indirect delivery of stamps for time and quality of interaction. Time of interaction increased 700%. This increase was associated with a progressive increase in the suitability of tasks selected by the attendants for use with the

children. Individual training with 4 attendants produced an increase in their use of tangible reinforcers, an increase in fading of motor prompts, and a reduction in use of punishment.
Bricker, William A.; Morgan, David G. & Grabowski, John G. (George Peabody Coll.) American Journal of Mental Deficiency, 1972(Sep), Vol. 77(2), 128-136. [PA, Vol 49:09231]

2637. Modifications of language situations in an institution for profoundly retarded children.
49 mentally retarded children (CA 3.7-15.9 yr., MA 50-129 wk.) with diverse diagnoses were given individual and group training to stimulate naming behavior. Each S served as his own control in a comparison between learning through a Normal Language Corpus (NLC) and a Reduced Language Corpus (RLC). The simplified (RLC) technique was not superior to the NLC but individual training was superior to group training, particularly in the MA range of 50 and 120 wk. (21 ref.)
Fraser, William. (Lynebank Hosp. for Mental Defectives, Dunfermline, Scotland) Developmental Medicine & Child Neurology, 1972(Apr), Vol. 14(2), 148-155. [PA, Vol 49:05019]

2638. Controlling the behavior of a profoundly retarded child.
Describes the case of a 12-yr-old profoundly retarded, self-abusive, and assaultive child who did not feed himself. An operant conditioning program motivated the S to feed himself and to modify undesirable responses within 8 days. Training occurred during mealtime using bites of his meal as a reinforcer.
Lemke, Haru & Mitchell, Robert D. (Hamburg State School & Hosp., Pa.) American Journal of Occupational Therapy, 1972(Jul), Vol. 26(5), 261-264. [PA, Vol 50:07401]

2639. The effect of incongruent instructions and consequences on imitation in retarded children.
Conducted a 13-phase experiment with 3 severely retarded boys. In 8 phases, E's instructions before demonstrating a behavior and the consequences for imitative behavior were incongruent. Consequences rather than instructions controlled imitative behavior when (a) Ss were instructed not to imitate but received reinforcers if they imitated, (b) Ss were instructed to imitate but were differentially reinforced for other behavior, and (c) Ss were instructed to imitate but were verbally reprimanded for imitation. Although Ss were highly imitative at the beginning of the study, when there was no reinforcement for imitation Ss gradually stopped imitating when instructed not to imitate. Instructions seemed to control imitative behavior when there was no reinforcement for imitation and Ss were instructed to imitate. Results indicate a need for further investigation of antecedent and consequent variables in imitation experiments and point out that certain techniques may be more efficient than others in eliminating well-established responses.
Martin, Jerry A. (Eunice Kennedy Shriver Center for Mental Retardation, Waltham, Mass.) Journal of Applied Behavior Analysis, 1972(Win), Vol. 5(4), 467-475. [PA, Vol 49:11441]

2640. Training profoundly retarded children to stop crawling.
Describes a study of the profoundly retarded child who continues to crawl even though he can walk. Crawling and walking were viewed as 2 alternative response modes, both reinforced by movement. A training program was designed to increase ease and speed of walking relative to that of crawling and consisted of restraint-for-crawling and priming-of-walking. With the program, 4 profoundly retarded 4-7 yr. olds reduced crawling and began to walk instead. When training was discontinued, 2 Ss with moderate walking impairment continued to walk rather than crawl. 2 Ss with severe impairment, however, required occasional use of the restraint procedure to maintain walking as the dominant mode of locomotion. The program was easily administered, required little time, and was effective for all 4 Ss.
O'Brien, F.; Azrin, N. H. & Bugle, C. (Anna State Hosp., Ill.) Journal of Applied Behavior Analysis, 1972(Sum), Vol. 5(2), 131-137. [PA, Vol 49:01199]

2641. Training and maintaining a retarded child's proper eating.
Explored whether motivational procedures are needed to maintain a retardate's continued use of previously trained eating skills.

A profoundly retarded 6-yr-old who ate food with her hands was trained by a manual guidance procedure to eat properly with a spoon, but the S still did not use the spoon after having learned to do so. When a motivational-maintenance procedure was applied, the S did begin to eat properly. When maintenance was discontinued, S returned to eating with her hands. Proper eating returned when maintenance was applied again; when discontinued, S returned to eating with her hands. Results demonstrate that continued motivational procedures are needed after training to maintain the retardate's continued use of proper eating skills.
O'Brien, F.; Bugle, C. & Azrin, N. H. (Anna State Hosp., Behavior Research Lab., Ill.) Journal of Applied Behavior Analysis, 1972(Spr), Vol. 5(1), 67-72. [PA, Vol 48:09581]

2642. The potential for language acquisition of illiterate deaf adolescents and adults.
Studied the extent to which 16 institutionalized, hearing-impaired, nonverbal mental retardates could acquire communication skills through the use of sign language. Tutors assigned to Ss taught sign language during 24 2 ½-hr weekly sessions. 2 Ss had good working knowledge of sign language at the start of the program; however, 4 of the remaining 14 increased their knowledge of receptive and expressive vocabulary by over 200 signs. 6 Ss increased their knowledge by 75-150 signs, 1 learned 10 signs, and 2 learned no signs at all. A follow-up 1 yr. later revealed that sign-language classes had been established on a daily basis, there were many reports of self-sufficiency and reduced behavior problems, and 4 of the original Ss had been attending a community sheltered workshop. Further investigation into the use of sign language with deaf retardates is recommended. (15 ref.)
Spidal, David A. & Pfau, Glenn S. (National Education Association, Project LIFE, Washington, D.C.) Journal of Rehabilitation of the Deaf, 1972(Jul), Vol. 6(1), 27-41. [PA, Vol 50:09686]

2643. Teaching productive noun suffixes to severely retarded children.
Used differential-reinforcement and imitation procedures to teach 4 mental retardates (CAs = 11, 13, 16, and 16 yrs) productive noun suffixes when labeling stimuli exemplifying the verb form of an action or activity. Specifically, Ss were taught to convert verbs to nouns by adding the *er* morpheme. Training continued until Ss required a minimum number of trials to reach criterion for each verb presented, at which point they consistently produced the correct response on the 1st presentation of each new verb. Experimental control of the training procedures was demonstrated by teaching the grammatical misuse of the *ist* morpheme, rather than the *er* morpheme, when labeling verbs.
Baer, Donald M. & Guess, Doug. (U. Kansas) American Journal of Mental Deficiency, 1973(Mar), Vol. 77(5), 498-505. [PA, Vol 51:07426]

2644. [A test of 1035 MD on a population of institutionalized mentally deficient and severely retarded children.] (Fren)
1035 MD, a cerebral vasodilator previously used in cases of senility, was administered as part of ongoing therapy for retarded children in conjunction with other medications. This was not a rigorous experiment as dosages, duration, and method of administration varied. 17 of 38 cases showed improvement.
Besançon, G. & Blineau-Vecchierini, M. F. (U. Nantes, Hosp. Center, France) Revue de Neuropsychiatrie Infantile et d'Hygiene Mentale de l'Enfance, 1973(Sep), Vol. 21(9), 565-568. [PA, Vol 51:07630]

2645. Developing verbal imitative behavior in a profoundly retarded girl.
Describes the use of food reinforcement to develop verbal imitative behavior in a mute profoundly retarded 14-yr-old girl. The study comprised 9 phases (99 sessions). The 1st 4 phases alternated conditions of noncontingent and contingent reinforcement, bringing the S's vocalizations under the control of E-vocalizations. The remaining phases aimed at developing correct imitation of 5 training sounds. All sounds were presented within each session, but reinforcement contingent upon imitation was

introduced for 1 sound at a time in a multiple baseline design. Correct imitation of training sounds developed rapidly with some evidence of generalized imitative responding. Results are discussed in light of previous research with other populations and the implications of the present paradigm for further research on language development in the profoundly retarded child.
Butz, Robert A. & Hasazi, Joseph E. (U. Vermont) Journal of Behavior Therapy & Experimental Psychiatry, 1973(Dec), Vol. 4(4), 389-393. [PA, Vol 52:08000]

2646. Evaluation of self-help habit training of the profoundly retarded.
Measured behavioral changes in 3 self-help areas (dressing, feeding, and toileting) for 47 profoundly retarded 4-16 yr olds admitted to a short-term residential facility in Louisiana. Checklist scales were developed to measure performance on each self-help area; items were arranged from simple to complex skills. Inter-rater reliability for the dressing, feeding, and toileting scales was .99, .95, and .96, respectively. Results show an average institutional stay of 7.1 mo, average MA gain of 3.36 mo on the Cattell Infant Intelligence Scale, and significant performance gains in each area. Advantages of intensive self-help training are discussed.
Colwell, Cecil N.; Richards, Eileen; McCarver, Ronald B. & Ellis, Norman R. (Northwest State School, Bossier City, La.) Mental Retardation, 1973(Jun), Vol. 11(3), 14-18. [PA, Vol 51:01642]

2647. Haloperidol for control of severe emotional reactions in mentally retarded patients.
Reviewed case reports of 27 severely retarded 5-15 yr old children, in order to determine the effectiveness of haloperidol in improving 7 symptoms of emotional and motor disturbance. Dosages of haloperidol began low and were increased to a maximum level of effectiveness. Concomitantly, a prophylactic dose of benztropine mesylate was given to prevent extrapyramidal reactions. Evaluations of patient status, and clinical laboratory tests were given periodically during treatment. Improvement was noted in all areas of behavior except disorders of speech and communication. In addition, no adverse reactions or signs of liver, kidney, or blood abnormalities were linked with optimal haloperidol dosages. The use of benztropine mesylate was thought to be important in successful use of haloperidol. The need for more well-controlled, double-blind studies with mental retardates is stressed.
Grabowski, Stanislaw W. (Ellisville State School, Miss.) Diseases of the Nervous System, 1973(Aug), Vol. 34(6), 315-317. [PA, Vol 51:07643]

2648. Nonverbal communication: An alternate mode of communication for the child with severe cerebral palsy.
Investigated the feasibility of teaching 4 10-12 yr old severely mentally retarded cerebral-palsied children to use an electromechanical communication device. Ss easily learned to use the device to signal distress and indicate the need for attention. The extent to which they used the communication system depended heavily on the attitude of the staff.
Hagen, Chris; Porter, Wyne & Brink, Joyce. (Rancho Los Amigos Hosp., Downey, Calif.) Journal of Speech & Hearing Disorders, 1973(Nov), Vol. 38(4), 448-455. [PA, Vol 51:07510]

2649. [Psychotherapy with severely mentally handicapped children.] (Germ)
Asserts that however severe the handicaps, individual psychotherapy must be tried. Severely mentally handicapped children show the same "behavior disorders" as normally intelligent children. Some symptoms cannot be explained by the mental retardation or the diagnosis of cerebral lesion, but require individual human therapeutic approaches. This therapy requires a special technique, adapted to the handicap. Psychological and behavioral theories inadequately explain therapeutic procedures, but this does not mean that therapy is impossible. Theoretical bases must be created in accordance with the specific reality of this group of patients. (91 ref.)

Herzka, H.; Teichmann, A.; Wintsch, H. & Venetianer, E. (Child Psychiatric Service, Winterthur, Switzerland) Acta Paedopsychiatrica, 1973, Vol. 39(12), 318-335. [PA, Vol 51:07600]

2650. Effects of behavioral training on the functioning of a profoundly retarded microcephalic teenager with cerebral palsy and without language or verbal comprehension.
Jacobson, Leonard I.; Bernal, Guillermo & Lopez, Gerardo N. (U. Miami) Behaviour Research & Therapy, 1973(Feb), Vol. 11(1), 143-145. [PA, Vol 50:03486]

2651. Operant methods of toilet-behavior training of the severely and profoundly retarded: A review.
Reviews studies concerning the application of operant techniques to the problems of toilet-training severely and profoundly retarded children. It is concluded that no specific determinations can be made concerning the relative effectiveness of the operant procedure at this time, owing to multiple design weaknesses in much of the research reported. Suggestions are offered for improving future research in the area. (34 ref)
Osarchuk, Michael. (Adelphi U.) Journal of Special Education, 1973(Win), Vol. 7(4), 423-437. [PA, Vol 52:08362]

2652. Skill centers: A model program for young severely retarded children.
Reports results of an education project for institutionalized, severely retarded children which employed a skill center curriculum and behavior modification techniques. Significant progress was achieved in motor skills, vocabulary, communication, and social behavior.
Smeets, Paul M. & Manfredini, Dianne C. (California School for the Deaf, Riverside) Education & Training of the Mentally Retarded, 1973(Oct), Vol. 8(3), 124-127. [PA, Vol 52:01294]

2653. Instruction-following behavior of a retarded child and its controlling stimuli.
Used a combination of positive reinforcement and fading of physical guidance to teach a profoundly retarded 11-yr-old boy specific responses to specific verbal instructions. The design consisted of a multiple baseline of probe data across different verbal instructions. S started responding correctly to each verbal instruction as that item was trained in a multiple-baseline order. Generalization did not occur to items that had not yet been trained, nor to items included to assess generalization. Probes of variations in the verbal instructions, conducted after training was completed, revealed that generalization was minimal except when the variation consisted of the verb only, the noun only, the noun plus preposition, or when the verb of the instruction was presented last. The training did not develop a generative instruction-following capability, nor did all verbal elements of the instruction control a specific response.
Striefel, Sebastian & Wetherby, Bruce. (Parsons State Hosp., Research Center, Kan.) Journal of Applied Behavior Analysis, 1973(Win), Vol. 6(4), 663-670. [PA, Vol 52:03773]

2654. Use of a peer modeling procedure with severely retarded subjects on a basic communication response skill.
Gave basic communication training to 2 groups of 25 severely retarded children under experimental conditions of peer model demonstrating the correct response or verbal instruction only. 25 control retardates were given equal activity time with no training. The modeling group significantly outperformed the verbal instruction group, who in turn outperformed controls. Implications of modeling as a relatively unexplored procedure with retardates are discussed. (16 ref.)
Talkington, Larry W.; Hall, Sylvia M. & Altman, Reuben. (Fairview Hosp. & Training Center, Salem, Ore.) Training School Bulletin, 1973(Feb), Vol. 69(4), 145-149. [PA, Vol 51:05483]

2655. Acute effect of section of the corpus callosum upon "independent" epileptiform activity.
Reports the case of a severely mentally retarded 9-yr-old boy who had had a right hemiparesis and convulsive seizures since infancy. Convulsions could not be controlled in spite of large doses of the anticonvulsant drugs phenobarbital, methylphenyl-

succinimide, and primidone. A pneumoencephalogram revealed a large porencephalic cyst and generalized atrophy of the left hemisphere. EEG recordings revealed multiple spike foci discharging independently on both hemispheres. Scalp electrodes were applied to the right side before exposing surgically the left hemisphere. Simultaneous recording was performed from right scalp and left cortical electrodes. Active spikes were recorded independently from both sides. After section of the corpus callosum, the spikes from the right disappeared; the left side showed no changes. Left hemispherectomy was then performed. Results are discussed in the context of (a) criteria for definition of independent spikes in the EEG and (b) the existence of mirror foci in humans. (27 ref.)
Torres, Fernando & French, Lyle A. (U. Minnesota, Medical School) Acta Neurologica Scandinavica, 1973, Vol. 49(1), 47-62. [PA, Vol 51:07814]

2656. Training two severely retarded adolescents to ask questions.
Taught 2 severely retarded 16-yr-old boys to discriminate items they knew how to label (training items) from items they did not know (probe items), to respond appropriately by naming any training items, and to ask a question about any probe items. The Ss did not learn to question when appropriate questioning was modelled by the E; however, when they were prompted and rewarded for asking questions about some training items, they began to ask questions about probe items. Both the modelling- and prompting-reinforcement procedures were introduced in an across-S, multiple baseline design.
Twardosz, Sandra & Baer, Donald M. (U. Mississippi, Medical Center, Jackson) Journal of Applied Behavior Analysis, 1973(Win), Vol. 6(4), 655-661. [PA, Vol 52:03776]

2657. Using attendants to build a verbal repertoire in a profoundly retarded adolescent.
Describes an attendant-administered program for developing imitative speech through reinforcement techniques which was used with a 16-yr-old profoundly retarded female. Improvement in imitative control over the course of training was demonstrated, and this control generalized to situations outside of sessions. Implications for implementing institutional training procedures are discussed.
Wheeler, Andrew J. (Massachusetts Dept. of Mental Health, Walter E. Fernald State School, Waverley) Training School Bulletin, 1973(Nov), Vol. 70(3), 140-144. [PA, Vol 52:06190]

2658. An alternative to representative day care centers.
Describes Programmed Environments for the Developmentally Retarded, a project carried out by J. W. Tawney at the University of Kentucky and designed to meet the expected demands for services to the severely developmentally retarded. Since the existing system of day care centers provides only limited instructional time for the children, other possible methods suggested by Dr. Tawney for attacking the problem of educating the retarded population are discussed. Specific factors to be considered, and major questions needing to be answered before intervention models can be devised, are examined.
————. Education & Training of the Mentally Retarded, 1974(Feb), Vol. 9(1), 41-43. [PA, Vol 52:08662]

2659. Behavior therapy of pica with a profoundly retarded adolescent.
Used a 4-phase time-out procedure to treat a nonverbal 14-yr-old severely retarded, ambulatory male, who had a lengthy history of pica. Results indicate that after 9 mo of treatment, S's pica had been contained to a significant degree.
Ausman, James; Ball, Thomas S. & Alexander, Dean. (Pacific State Hosp, Intensive Behavioral Intervention Ward, Pomona, CA) Mental Retardation, 1974(Dec), Vol 12(6), 16-18. [PA, Vol 53:10155]

2660. A special feeding technique for chronic regurgitation.
Employed same-S experimental designs to compare rates of voluntary regurgitation in 1 6- and 1 11-yr-old male profoundly retarded lay-down patients when fed by a standard institutional and a special feeding method. Experimental controls included

times and amounts of food and the rate at which they were fed to the S. In both cases regurgitation markedly decreased under the special feeding method. With 1 S, reversion to the standard method was associated with a lapse into a state of listlessness and apathy from which he recovered when the special method was restored. The common denominator between the special feeding method and other clinical techniques is the promotion of the S's active participation in the feeding process. (28 ref)
Ball, Thomas S.; Hendricksen, Helen & Clayton, Jean. (Pacific State Hosp., Pomona, Calif.) American Journal of Mental Deficiency, 1974(Jan), Vol. 78(4), 486-493. [PA, Vol 52:08488]

2661. Use of behaviour modification techniques in behaviour training of severely and profoundly retarded children.
Discusses the techniques used by researchers to modify behavior problems of the severely and profoundly retarded. Unfortunately, it is punishment which seems to have had some measure of success when severe self-injurious behavior has been involved. Mild and moderate punishment has been found ineffectual if there were no alternate responses which would produce reinforcement. Severe punishment suppressed a response totally and for a long time, inhibited other responses, and increased frequency of response if it produced reinforcement. Aggressive behavior, including self-inflicted wounds, is dealt with by technological innovations, environmental alterations, and other means. Training methods sometimes used are said to be either too lenient or too cruel, but no one workable system has yet been established.
Foster, S. E. (Mt Gravatt Teachers' Coll, Brisbane, Qld, Australia) Slow Learning Child, 1974(Mar), Vol 21(1), 24-37. [PA, Vol 53:03727]

2662. Head hitting in severely retarded children.
Presents a nursing-care approach to head-hitting behavior in severely retarded children. Interpretations about the source and nature of this symptom are made. Instead of the conventional approach of restraining the child, an alternative is suggested involving 3 general principles: nurturant nursing care through the fostering of warm, close relationships; interruption and prevention of destructive behavior; and reinforcement of more acceptable behaviors. 2 case histories are detailed to illustrate this approach.
Geiger, Jane K.; Sindberg, Ronald M. & Barnes, Charles M. American Journal of Nursing, 1974(Oct), Vol 74(10), 1822-1825. [PA, Vol 54:03736]

2663. Transfer of operantly conditioned visual fixation in hyperactive severely retarded children.
Following operant conditioning of visual fixation responses to objects of known preference, 10 hyperactive, severely retarded 6-10 yr old children were given a series of transfer tests: (a) a distracting testroom, (b) neutral (unconditioned) stimuli, (c) E replacement, (d) simple play tasks presented in the testroom and the classroom, (e) Seguin formboard, (f) beat manipulation, and (g) classroom assessment involving prescribed tasks. Results show consistent improvement for most Ss in the majority of tests for frequency and duration of visual fixation. No improvement was shown on the Seguin formboard, and a significant practice effect was obtained on the bead manipulation task.
Hogg, J. & Maier, I. (U Manchester, Hester Adrian Research Ctr, England) American Journal of Mental Deficiency, 1974(Nov), Vol 79(3), 305-310. [PA, Vol 53:10179]

2664. Operant conditioning of feeding in a blind profoundly retarded girl.
Describes the successful use of behavior modification procedures to restore feeding behavior in a recently blind 11-yr-old profoundly retarded female. The patient was rewarded by being allowed to play a music box. Despite the girl's progress, she was withdrawn from the program after 14 days of treatment when her mother observed one of the nurses scolding and shaking her. The importance of staff cooperation is emphasized.
Hymowitz, Arthuree E. & Hymowitz, Norman. (Coll of Medicine & Dentistry of New Jersey) Indian Journal of Mental Retardation, 1974(Jul), Vol 7(2), 58-64. [PA, Vol 53:12207]

2665. The modification and generalization of voice loudness in a fifteen-year-old retarded girl.

Treated a 15-yr-old severely disturbed girl for aphonia. Because of the extent of her withdrawal, the S was conditioned in a laboratory setting and received tokens for speaking loudly enough to operate a voice-operated relay. Conditioning at first consisted of saying 100 monosyllabic words, with the possibility of reinforcement on each word. Later, the S was required to say a polysyllabic word, and finally, 5 or 6 words per token. The S was shaped to speak with normal loudness in the laboratory, and generalization to a reading situation in the laboratory was measured and observed to occur, at first for a few minutes, and later for a longer period. Generalization to a reading situation in the classroom did not occur, but the S's voice loudness also increased in the classroom when several new reinforcement contingencies were put into effect there. (25 ref)

Jackson, Donald A. & Wallace, R. Frank. (U Kansas) Journal of Applied Behavior Analysis, 1974(Fal), Vol 7(3), 461-471. [PA, Vol 53:05918]

2666. Behavior modification in a sheltered workshop for severely retarded students.

Conducted a study of 10 severely retarded 16-19 yr olds to investigate the effects of a token system and a prosthetic modification (screening of a sheltered workshop area) on Ss' work behavior. Task-specific performance measures of average error and production in each of 5 nursery-can production tasks and the generalized work performance measure of average visual inattendance-verbal prompt were observed during baseline, training, and follow-up. Grouped data reveal differences in task difficulty, a reduction in average error, and an increase in average production with the tokens. Average visual inattendance-verbal prompt decreased irrespective of the tokens, and there were individual differences in average error, production, and visual inattendance-verbal prompt.

Karen, Robert L.; Eisner, Melvin & Endres, Robert W. (California State U, San Diego) American Journal of Mental Deficiency, 1974(Nov), Vol 79(3), 338-347. [PA, Vol 53:10520]

2667. [Acquisition of autonomous social behavior by two profoundly retarded children.] (Fren)

Examines factors related to successful behavior modification of children's eating habits. Learning to eat properly is not simply the acquisition of a series of movements; it is social learning in the midst of environmental contingencies more complex than merely taking in food. Procedures used with 2 Ss enrolled in a special day school rather than in a closed institution are described in detail. Positive reinforcement supplanted aversive methods. The roles of teachers, peers, and especially parents, are given special attention. Part of the task is helping teachers and parents to accept their proper roles not only in the acquisition of good habits but especially in maintaining them. (15 ref)

Lambert, J.-L. (U Liège, Lab de Psychologie Expérimental, Belgium) Revue de Psychologie et des Sciences de l'Education, 1974, Vol 9(4), 475-488. [PA, Vol 58:01658]

2668. A method for home training an incontinent child.

Describes a home training method for incontinent children utilizing a signal apparatus. Effective toilet training was accomplished through simple conditioning procedures using an auditory signal apparatus in a profoundly retarded 7-yr-old male for whom traditional training methods had failed. These procedures involved pairings of first the buzzer and running to the bathroom, and then bladder distension and the buzzer. After a number of such pairings the child began to indicate when his bladder was distended. This served as a cue for the parents to prompt the appropriate toileting response. Independent toileting behavior was effected within a 7-wk period and maintained over a 5-mo follow-up with generalization to new situations.

Litrownik, Alan J. (San Diego State U) Journal of Behavior Therapy & Experimental Psychiatry, 1974(Jul), Vol 5(1), 77-80. [PA, Vol 53:03749]

2669. Community alternatives to institutional care for severely retarded children.

Lubach, John E. (U. Houston) Catalog of Selected Documents in Psychology, 1974(Win), Vol 4, 21. [PA, Vol 52:08426]

2670. Operant conditioning of sustained visual fixation in hyperactive severely retarded children.

The relative preferences of each of 10 hyperactive, severely retarded institutionalized 6-10 yr old children for a set of stimulus objects were assessed prior to use of the objects as discriminant stimuli in an operant program aimed at increasing the duration of visual fixation through the use of social and edible reinforcers. Increases contingent upon reinforcement in both percentage of time per session spent fixating the objects and frequency of visual fixation were demonstrated for most Ss by the use of reversal procedures, while analyses of variance of group results confirm these trends statistically. The present study confirms other findings that the behavior of the hyperactive child is amenable to modification through the appropriate management of discriminative stimuli and reinforcement contingencies.

Maier, I. & Hogg, J. (U Manchester, Hester Adrian Research Ctr, England) American Journal of Mental Deficiency, 1974(Nov), Vol 79(3), 297-304. [PA, Vol 53:10190]

2671. Hazardous voluntary falling: A treatment approach.

Prior to treatment, a nonverbal, 8-yr-old severely retarded child was confined in an enclosed crib 17 hrs/day to prevent hazardous voluntary falling. The treatment program involved the technique of developing a small rug as a cue and, concurrently, a conditioned reinforcer for sitting. The rug, when placed on a stool or bed, served the dual function of controlling falling and reinforcing appropriate sitting or lying. It was demonstrated that bed- and stool-falling changed as a function of rug placement and control over falling was retained even after the rug was no longer in use.

Marks, Patricia & Ball, Thomas S. (Pacific State Hosp, Pomona, CA) Mental Retardation, 1974(Oct), Vol 12(5), 36-39. [PA, Vol 53:06063]

2672. Observed versus potential behavior in the follow-up results in a typical behavior modification program.

McNamee, S. & Peterson, J. (Case Western Reserve U) Catalog of Selected Documents in Psychology, 1974(Fal), Vol 4, 131. [PA, Vol 53:12219]

2673. Developing cooperative play in socially withdrawn retarded children.

Compared 3 approaches (high-low dyad, low-low dyad, and experimenter-low shaping) to the development of cooperative play in 6 severely retarded 4-12 yr olds. Results show that pairing a high and low interacting child and the shaping procedure produced the greatest amount of cooperative play. No appreciable increase in cooperation was found by pairing 2 low interacting children or in the no-treatment condition. These results were maintained at the 3-wk follow-up evaluation.

Morris, Richard J. & Dolker, Michael. (Syracuse U) Mental Retardation, 1974(Dec), Vol 12(6), 24-27. [PA, Vol 53:10529]

2674. [Shaping appropriate eating behavior of a profoundly retarded boy.] (Japn)

A profoundly retarded 9-yr-old boy underwent 47 training sessions to shape appropriate eating behavior. After 5 baseline periods, his hand was manually guided by a trainer for 10 sessions. For the next 20 sessions, verbal punishment and time-out were delivered contingent upon finger feeding. For the last 12 sessions, time-out was used when he threw utensils or food, and verbal praise was given after every 2 successful spoon feedings. The progress record indicated that both positive and negative reinforcements were effective in maintaining appropriate self-feeding. During the training, the S began to interact with others in nontraining situations. (English summary)

Oshio, Chikamori; Tomiyasu, Yoshikazu & Komiya, Mitsuya. (Inst for Developmental Research, Aichi Prefectural Colony, Japan) Japanese Journal of Special Education, 1974(Jun), Vol 12(1), 1-9. [PA, Vol 53:12530]

2675. Remote-control aversive stimulation in the treatment of head-banging in a retarded child.
Response-contingent shock has been demonstrated to reduce the rate of head-banging, but poor generalization has frequently resulted. The treatment of a 9-yr-old profoundly retarded, head-banging female demonstrated similar problems with generalization when stationary shock equipment was used, but remote-control apparatus was able to overcome generalization problems and reduce head-banging to zero.
Prochaska, James et al. (U Rhode Island) Journal of Behavior Therapy & Experimental Psychiatry, 1974(Dec), Vol 5(3-4), 285-289. [PA, Vol 53:12232]

2676. [Effects of punishment on multiple behaviors in a human subject.] (Span)
Studied punishment effects in a severely retarded child under a multiple-concurrent design, using 6 different responses in 2 successive stimulus situations. Differential reinforcement of other behavior and fixed interval reinforcement schedules were also used to evaluate interaction with punishment. Results show that many of the assumptions about punishment are unjustified and that its effects are complex and dependent on multiple variables. (15 ref)
Ramirez, Luis & Ribes, Emilio. (Ctr de Modificacion de Conducta B. F. Skinner, Bogata, Colombia) Revista Latinoamericana de Psicología, 1974, Vol 6(2), 161-178. [PA, Vol 53:05937]

2677. Parent-child interactions as the therapy target.
Presents results of an experimental language therapy program for a severely retarded Hindu child and her parents. The treatment target was the parent-child interactions. Immediate results show changes in the desired direction in these interactions, with some of these changes being documented over 3 mo. Immediate improvement was seen in nonverbal child behaviors such as positively responding to parents and engaging in independent play such that parents viewed the child as more competent and were able to support independent play and reduce their physical contact and interruptive behavior. Improvement in the child's verbal behavior was reported in follow-ups at 3 mo and again at 1 yr. It is argued that parent-child interactions constitute the child's language environment, and that it is the quality of this environment that will most affect the verbal behavior of the slow developing child. (24 ref)
Seitz, Sue & Riedell, Gail. (U Wisconsin, Madison) Journal of Communication Disorders, 1974(Dec), Vol 7(4), 295-304. [PA, Vol 57:13362]

2678. An analysis of behavior during the acquisition and maintenance phases of self-spoon feeding skills of profound retardates.
Describes several problems encountered during the course of teaching self-feeding skills to a group of 4 profoundly retarded children. The primary technique used was the 7-step shaping technique with reinforcement and fading procedure. Factors such as maintenance of posttraining eating behavior, length of time taken to reach successive steps of training, choice of specific training procedure, use of physical restraints, readiness of the children, and motivating variables for the trainers are discussed.
Song, A. Y. & Gandhi, R. (Southern Wisconsin Colony & Training School, Union Grove) Mental Retardation, 1974(Feb), Vol. 12(1), 25-28. [PA, Vol 52:03770]

2679. A study of the interactions between nursing staff and profoundly mentally retarded children.
Observed 16 9-18 yr old ambulant children (mental age 18-24 mo or less) in 5 hospital wards for interactions promoting positive, negative, or neutral patient behavior. An extreme poverty of interpersonal exchange between Ss and staff was noted and a lack of Ss' attempts to relate to staff. Findings suggest a need to (a) revise training for nurses caring for mentally retarded children; and (b) consider other types of staff training, other forms of long-term care, and the need for larger staffs.
Wright, E. C.; Abbas, K. A. & Meredith, C. (Queen Mary's Hosp for Children, Carshalton, England) British Journal of Mental Subnormality, 1974(Jun), Vol 20(38, Pt 1), 14-17. [PA, Vol 53:06084]

2680. A community-oriented center for severely and profoundly retarded children: Elisabeth Ludeman Center, Park Forest, Illinois.
Describes a 3-yr-old community center which has developed programs that give the residents a high level of interaction with direct-care staff members and with the community. Features of the program include small groups of children living together in 4-bedroom homes served by the center, vocational training for high school students, the use of the center's facilities by community residents, and an audiovisual service for inservice training and staff communication.
————. Hospital & Community Psychiatry, 1975(Oct), Vol 26(10), 667-670. [PA, Vol 55:02735]

2681. A new method for toilet training developmentally disabled children.
Trained 20 profoundly retarded 4-12 yr olds, using a variety of relaxation and tension activities designed to help them differentiate and gain control of the toileting musculature. Operant techniques were used to reinforce appropriate urination. Posttraining scores of the experimental and control groups differed significantly for both accidental and appropriate urination.
Edgar, Clara L.; Kohler, Hugh F. & Hardman, Scott. Perceptual & Motor Skills, 1975(Aug), Vol 41(1), 63-69. [PA, Vol 55:07611]

2682. Adolescent retardates in a therapy group.
Describes a 6-8 wk program of behavior modification used in a psychiatric unit designed to treat 12-18 severely retarded (IQ, 50-65) adolescents 12-19 yrs old who are too disturbed for parents or schools to handle. Patients are individually awarded points for successful participation in the 30-min/day group therapy sessions. Sessions focus on (a) building trust and rapport between participants and the therapist and (b) helping participants to effectively communicate daily needs and emotions. The program uses the patient's desire for success and adult and peer approval, and rewards him or her for approximate performance (on increasing discriminating bases) until acceptable functioning within the group is achieved. As patients learn to solve problems in a more socially approved manner, they are further reinforced by massive praise. It is concluded that this program helps retarded, disturbed adolescents assume more productive approaches to human relationships, and these are evidenced by reduced interpersonal friction in the unit.
Etters, Lloyd E. (U California Ctr for Health Science, Neuropsychiatric Inst, Los Angeles) American Journal of Nursing, 1975(Jul), Vol 75(7), 1174-1175. [PA, Vol 58:03829]

2683. Manual language with the severely and profoundly retarded: A pilot study.
Reviews the literature on speech deficits and treatment programs for the nonspeaking retarded. Related studies with normal infants and with chimpanzees are also discussed. The procedures and results of an exploratory study with 24 profoundly and severely retarded residents (CA range 11-46 yrs, IQs 10-35) are described. The results are promising and demonstrate the feasibility of teaching manual language to the nonspeaking retarded, corroborating other recent findings. (22 ref)
Ferguson, Sandra J. (North Carolina Div of Mental Health Services, Raleigh) Research & the Retarded, 1975(Sum), Vol 2(3), 32-40. [PA, Vol 58:03682]

2684. Teaching dressing skills to a severely retarded child.
Describes how an 8-yr-old, severely retarded boy was taught to remove his shirt independently in 16 training sessions using operant techniques. Reinforcement was dispensed contingent upon successful independent performance on each of 5 undressing subtasks which were used in a backward chaining method. S was given dry cereal as a reinforcer for successful task completion; completion was considered independent only if performed without physical or verbal prompting.
Ford, Lana J. American Journal of Occupational Therapy, 1975(Feb), Vol 29(2), 87-92. [PA, Vol 54:01658]

2685. Developing generalized behavior-modification skills in high-school students working with retarded children.
7 high-school trainees each conducted training sessions with 2 profoundly retarded children. Each trainee was asked to teach one child to follow the instruction "Bring ball" and the other child to follow the instructions "Sit down" and "Come here." During baseline sessions, before the trainees had been instructed in behavior modification techniques, no trainee successfully taught either child to follow the instructions. After differing numbers of baseline sessions, trainees were exposed to training procedures designed to teach them to teach one child to follow the instruction "Bring ball." The training procedures consisted of videotaped modeling, rehearsal, and corrective feedback and praise. Following the training procedures, 4 of the 7 trainees successfully taught their child to follow the instruction "Bring ball." Further, all trainees were able to teach their other children to follow the instructions "Sit down" and "Come here," even though they had received no modeling, rehearsal, or feedback on how to teach the children to follow these instructions. The ability of the trainees to teach new behaviors to different children indicates the development of generalized skills in behavior modification. (19 ref)
Gladstone, Bruce W. & Sherman, James A. (Carleton U, Ottawa, Canada) Journal of Applied Behavior Analysis, 1975(Sum), Vol 8(2), 169-180. [PA, Vol 54:08440]

2686. Toward automated physical therapy with the non-ambulatory profoundly retarded via operant conditioning.
Presents data which indicate the feasibility of automated physical therapy for the crib-bound profoundly retarded via operant conditioning techniques. The eliciting properties of tactile stimulation were determined with 3 childen (31/2 and 5 yrs old) involved in daily 30-min training sessions for 40 days. An inexpensive manipulandum, which has been field tested and which reliably records responsers from a crib-bound S, was used. Each S's idiosyncratic rate of responding dictated the most effective procedure to increase his rate of gross physical movement. Implications are stated concerning the possibilities of automated physical therapy.
Griffin, James C.; Patterson, Earl T.; Locke, Bill J. & Landers, William F. (Western Carolina Ctr, Morgantown, NC) Behavioral Engineering, 1975(Spr), Vol 2(3), 72-75. [PA, Vol 55:01032]

2687. Social interactions of a group of severely retarded people with staff and peers in a ward setting.
In a small hospital, the social interactions of 12 adult and 1 12-yr-old severely retarded persons were observed with each other and with staff. There were marked individual differences in susceptibility to social interaction. The frequency of peer interaction was very low. In terms of interaction with the staff, Ss could be grouped as high, moderate, and low scorers. Aversive behavior (e.g., hitting and scratching) was emitted spontaneously by some high scorers, thereby achieving interaction from staff, and by the low scorers in response to approaches from the staff, thereby decreasing the likelihood of such attempts at interaction.
Harzem, Peter & Damon, S. G. (University Coll North Wales, Bangor) Psychological Reports, 1975(Jun), Vol 36(3), 959-966. [PA, Vol 54:09964]

2688. [The reduction of a stereotyped behavior of a seriously retarded child: A comparison of five methods.] (Fren)
Presents the case study of a severely mentally retarded 13-yr-old child who was exhibiting undesirable stereotyped gestures. 5 behavioral methods were used in succession to eliminate the gestures: manipulation of objects, physical contact, aversive conditioning, reinforcement of other behavior, and overcorrection. The latter, which consisted of teaching the child more desirable gestures, proved to be the least effective method. Manipulation of objects and physical contact were most effective. Applications of these methods to a classroom situation are discussed. (English & German summaries) (20 ref)
Lambert, J. L.; Bruwier, D. & Cobben, A. (U Liège, Lab de Psychologie expérimentale, Belgium) Psychologie - Schweizerische Zeitschrift für Psychologie und ihre Anwendungen, 1975, Vol 34(1), 1-18. [PA, Vol 54:12333]

2689. Neurodevelopment and sensory integration for the profoundly retarded multiply handicapped child.
Reports a 9-mo study of 3 profoundly retarded, multiply handicapped Ss less than 5 yrs of age, who received mother-administered, clinic-supervised treatment for neurodevelopmental sensory integration. The emergence of more advanced postural reactions, changes in affect, and responses to objects were recorded. Results suggest that new engrams may be established with the aid of normalized muscle tone and feedback, which in turn can be used to activate formerly precluded neurons. Trends toward early cognitive emergence are discussed in terms of the development of interest and affect, as related to the concept of "fixation attention" of normal 9-mo-old infants. (18 ref)
Norton, Yvonne. (Hitchcock Rehabilitation Ctr, Aiken, SC) American Journal of Occupational Therapy, 1975(Feb), Vol 29(2), 93-100. [PA, Vol 54:01541]

2690. [Change in stereotype following hypothalamus operation in idiocy.] (Slok)
Reports a change of motor stereotypes from patterns similar to the UCR of food acceptance to movements resembling masturbation, after stereotactic bilateral hypothalamotomy of a 7-yr-old profound oligophrenic. The possibility is mentioned that the original oral stereotype was replaced by a still older sexual mechanism of phylogenetic origin. (Russian & English summaries)
Šramka, M.; Nádvorník, P. & Patoprstá, G. (Lab klinickej stereotaxie pri Neurochirurgickej klinicke LFUK, Bratislava, Czechoslovakia) Československá Psychiatrie, 1975, Vol 71(5), 306–307. [PA, Vol 60:01412]

2691. Increasing social play of severely retarded preschoolers with socio-dramatic activities.
Conducted a study to determine whether sociodramatic activities would increase the social play of severely retarded preschool children during a free-play period. Ss were 8 severely retarded 48-52 mo olds with a mean IQ of 37. Social play was observed across baseline and intervention (sociodramatic play provided) conditions in an ABAB design. Results suggest that the opportunity to engage in sociodramatic activities and increased social play are functionally related.
Strain, Phillip. (American U) Mental Retardation, 1975(Dec), Vol 13(6), 7-9. [PA, Vol 55:10262]

2692. The use of omission training to reduce self-injurious behavior in a retarded child.
Used omission training (OM), a response elimination technique which specifies reinforcement for the nonoccurrence of a designated response, to treat a 14-yr-old severely retarded boy with a long-standing self-injurious behavior of headbanging. 50 OM sessions reduced self-injurious responding to a near-zero rate and facilitated the emergence of new, more appropriate social behaviors. None of the undesirable side effects previously reported with aversive conditioning resulted from the OM procedure. (17 ref)
Weiher, Richard G. & Harman, Roger E. (Utah State U, Exceptional Child Ctr) Behavior Therapy, 1975(Mar), Vol 6(2), 261-268. [PA, Vol 54:01712]

2693. Comparison of two procedures for fostering the development of the object construct.
To determine the extent to which training can affect acquisition and retention of the object construct, 21 institutionalized severely mentally retarded children were, exposed to training or control conditions for about 10 min/day on 8 days. There were 2 training procedures: the 1st seemed typical of previous efforts to foster the object construct and the 2nd differed primarily in the size of the steps in the systematic chain of tasks required of the Ss. Both procedures affected acquisition significantly and equally but neither appeared to result in long-term retention. (15 ref)
Brassell, William R. & Dunst, Carl J. (Western Carolina Ctr Infants' Program, Morganton, NC) American Journal of Mental Deficiency, 1976(Mar), Vol 80(5), 523-528. [PA, Vol 56:06220]

2694.   Brief physical restraint to control Pica in retarded children.
Pica, the ingestion of inappropriate food and small objects, was treated in 2 6-yr-old profoundly retarded children by use of brief physical restraint as a punisher. Generalization was observed by training 1st in 1 setting, then in others. Location and presence or absence of a caretaker were varied. One S showed some suppression in the trained setting but no generalization. Extraneous factors required termination of the case. The 2nd S showed near complete suppression in each trained setting but no generalization. Complete suppression was obtained only when restraint was made contingent on the earliest detectable part of the pica response. The effectiveness and economy of the treatment, and the requirements for effective maintenance, are discussed.
Bucher, Bradley; Reykdal, Beverly & Albin, Jack. (U Western Ontario, London, Canada) Journal of Behavior Therapy & Experimental Psychiatry, 1976(Jun), Vol 7(2), 137-140. [PA, Vol 56:10295]

2695.   [Behavioral approach to stereotypies in a profound retardate.] (Fren)
Briefly reviews explicative theories of stereotypic behavior and methods used by previous researchers to eliminate these behaviors. The use of behavioral techniques to modify stereotypies of the hands and mouth in an 11-yr-old profoundly retarded male are described. Five methods were used: manipulation of objects, social contact with the experimenter, differential reinforcement of other behaviors, aversive conditioning, and overcorrection. The effectiveness of each method is described, as well as its ease of application in the classroom setting. Results indicate that while all methods reduced the incidence of stereotypies, manipulation of objects and social contact also produced more adaptable social behavior in the S. After 1½ mo, gestural stereotypies were reduced to 18% from a baseline of 60%; mouth stereotypies showed greater variability. The necessity of continual reinforcement of adapted responses such as social contact is stressed. (23 ref)
Cobben, A. (U Liège Service de Psychologie Experimentale, Belgium) Feuillets Psychiatriques de Liège, 1976, Vol 9(2), 202–211. [PA, Vol 59:03867]

2696.   Behaviour modification: Toilet-training procedures in a special care unit.
Describes the design and implementation of a behavior modification program for toilet training of 9 severely mentally retarded children (mean age 6.3 yrs; mean IQ 30). The following parameters of behavior were recorded: wetting, soiling, and successful use of pot or toilet following an accident-free period. Two of the Ss were successfully trained.
Connolly, John A. & McGoldrick, Maureen. (St Augustine's, Child Development Clinic, Blackrock, Ireland) Child Care, Health & Development, 1976(Oct), Vol 2(5), 267-272. [PA, Vol 57:13281]

2697.   Case study: Use of differential reinforcement to suppress self-injurious and aggressive behavior.
Used a program of differential reinforcement of other behavior to reduce the rates of aggression and head-banging in a profoundly retarded female aged 6 yrs, 8 mo. Although 2 different time-out procedures were not associated with stable decreases in aggressive behavior, this program was associated with immediate and dramatic decreases in aggression and head-banging. Results suggest that (a) initial values of such programs may be situation-specific and (b) either the procedure or the inclusion of contingencies for all maladaptives within one program may be superior to a time-out program which focuses on a subset of all maladaptive behavior. (18 ref)
Frankel, Fred; Moss, Debra; Schofield, Susan & Simmons, James Q. (U California, Los Angeles) Psychological Reports, 1976(Dec), Vol 39(3, Pt 1), 843-849. [PA, Vol 58:01648]

2698.   Stimulus control of generalized imitation in subnormal children.
Established generalized imitation in 3 subnormal children (2 5-yr-olds and a 7-yr-old) by reinforcing their imitations of a limited set of modeled actions in the presence of a large ball. A discrimination was then established by training nonimitation in the presence of a small ball. Imitation was then tested for various other ball sizes. Rate of imitation decreased as the test stimuli increasingly differed in size from the large ball. Imitations that were never reinforced occurred at about the same rate as those that were reinforced when in the presence of the large ball in training.
Furnell, J. R. & Thomas, G. V. (Stirling Royal Infirmary, Scotland) Journal of Experimental Child Psychology, 1976(Oct), Vol 22(2), 282-291. [PA, Vol 57:06927]

2699.   Retardate trace classical conditioning with pure tone and speech sound CSs.
Compared retardate trace conditioning performance with a 200-msec trace CS and a 450-msec CS-offset-UCS-onset interval under pure-tone (slow and fast rise-time) and speech sound (a synthesized voiced stop consonant-vowel) conditions. Ss were 48 undergraduates and 24 severely and profoundly retarded residents of a training school (CA, 15-24 yrs). There was no effect of type of CS, but the retardates showed a bimodal performance distribution atypical for single-cue conditioning. Additional data collected under the same CS and interstimulus interval conditions with normal Ss demonstrated an essentially unimodal performance distribution, again with no effect of type of CS presented.
Guminski, Margaret M. & Ross, Leonard E. (U Wisconsin, Madison) Bulletin of the Psychonomic Society, 1976(Feb), Vol 7(2), 199-201. [PA, Vol 56:06230]

2700.   Drugs in use in schools for severely subnormal children.
Reviews drug therapy used in the management of 42 severely subnormal children in 2 special schools in Birmingham, England, following the introduction of the 1970 Education Act. Diagnoses of children on medication included (a) epilepsy, and (b) hyperkinesis and rage reactions. The 4 drugs dispensed most often by the staff were haloperidol, procyclidine HCl, phenobarbitone, and phenytoin. Problems encountered in such a program are discussed in terms of (a) the responsibilities of the teaching and nonteaching staff who must monitor side effects of medication; (b) parents who do not wish their children to have medication and thus will not administer weekend doses, causing their children to come to school disorderly, and disrupting long-term therapy; and (c) the need for trained nurses in schools having such drug therapy programs.
May, Elsie. Child Care, Health & Development, 1976(Oct), Vol 2(5), 261-266. [PA, Vol 57:13332]

2701.   Treatment of self-injurious behavior by a combination of reinforcement for incompatible behavior and overcorrection.
In 2 related studies, a combination of reinforcement for incompatible behavior and positive practice overcorrection was applied to the elimination of head-slapping and head-banging behavior exhibited, respectively, by 2 profoundly retarded 14- and 16-yr-old males. The design for both studies also included a period in which only reinforcement for incompatible behavior was applied. The results from Study 1 indicate that, while reinforcement had little effect in reducing the frequency of the S's head slapping, the combination of reinforcement and overcorrection had an immediate effect in significantly reducing and eventually eliminating that behavior. A 4-mo follow-up indicated no significant recurrence of the behavior. In Study 2, on the other hand, both reinforcement and the combination of reinforcement and overcorrection resulted in a significant increase in the frequency of the S's head-banging behavior, possibly because some element of the program itself was being perceived as rewarding. Discussion centers on several research questions left unanswered by the differing effects of the procedures applied in both studies, such as how overcorrection produces desired behavioral change when it is, indeed, effective.

Measel, C. Julius & Alfieri, Peter A. (Cresson State School, PA) American Journal of Mental Deficiency, 1976(Sep), Vol 81(2), 147-153. [PA, Vol 57:06351]

2702. Teaching selected telephone related social skills to severely handicapped students.
Developed a program for teaching severely handicapped students the skills necessary for appropriate interaction with their peers via the telephone and how to initiate and receive requests to engage in social interactions across many social situations. Instructional procedures utilized were modeling, priming, chaining of responses, and rehearsal. Four of 7 students (CA 12-16 yrs; IQ 35-53) completed the program. Another student was completing the last phase when instruction was terminated. Failure to incorporate the required expressive language (i.e., expand the student's mean utterance length) is postulated as an explanation for the program's ineffectiveness with one student. Similarly, a failure to build in attention to the task appeared to explain the program's ineffectiveness with the other student. Observations made subsequent to the program indicated that the skills were maintained and transferred to actual telephone and social situations.
Nietupski, John & Williams, Wes. (U Wisconsin) Child Study Journal, 1976, Vol 6(3), 139-153. [PA, Vol 57:04444]

2703. A sociometric technique for use with moderately to severely retarded persons.
Describes a pictorial sociometric technique for use with retarded persons. Findings from an evaluation of the measure with 6–17 yr olds at a school for exceptional children are presented to show the utility of the measure for planning and maintaining group change in the treatment of retarded persons.
Pack, Peggy L. & McCaffery, Leonard J. (Murray State U) Group Psychotherapy, Psychodrama & Sociometry, 1976, Vol 29, 127–129. [PA, Vol 61:03903]

2704. Promoting recreation skills in severely retarded children.
Four studies using behavior modification procedures were carried out in a summer camp attended by 60 5–15 yr old mentally and physically retarded children. Ss ranged from single Ss to entire classrooms, and camp personnel served as experimenters. Taken together, results of the 4 studies show the following: (a) Day camps can be significant teaching settings for young handicapped children. (b) Childrens' participation in healthy, physical activities can be increased by employing behavior modification procedures. (c) Indigenous camp personnel with proper training and supervision can carry out behavior modification techniques without disrupting the normal camp routine and as a result have more time to supervise children's activites. (d) Behavior modification practices executed by existing personnel, can be carried out with a small monetary cost (e.g., the total cost of the above interventions was $15, used for purchase of reinforcers such as candy and trinkets).
Rosen, Howard S. (U Illinois) Revista Mexicana de Análisis de la Conducta, 1976(Jan), Vol 2(1), 85–99. [PA, Vol 61:13872]

2705. Visual-motor performance and receptive language learning in a visually impaired profoundly retarded boy.
An 8-yr-old, profoundly retarded (IQ unmeasurable), nonverbal, institutionalized boy with severe strabismus and nystagmus was trained in 2 experiments. In Exp I, vocal responses, object identification, and discrimination of objects were shaped, and fixation training was done to correct as much as possible the eye conditions. Since the fixation training had increased S's discrimination from 1 to 15 objects, Exp II investigated the use of eye movement parameters to differentially process information. A visual discrimination device was used to present stimuli. The data show a correlation between fixation frequency and error rate; fixation frequency decreased with correct choices. The finding that distinctive fixation patterns were correlated with a rational solution to a discrimination problem has important implications for mental retardation theories.
Schroeder, Steve. (U North Carolina) Research & the Retarded, 1976, Vol 3(1), 1-13. [PA, Vol 58:07732]

2706. Toilet training a severely retarded nonverbal child.
Describes a learning procedure used to toilet train a severely retarded nonverbal child in 13 days. After training, accidents decreased to a near-zero level and remained so during 10 wks of posttraining. Results suggest that intensive learning procedures can be used to toilet-train retarded persons.
Singh, Nirbhay N. (U Auckland, New Zealand) Australian Journal of Mental Retardation, 1976(Mar), Vol 4(1), 15-18. [PA, Vol 57:03957]

2707. Stimulus box for the profoundly mentally retarded.
Describes a stimulus box adapted from a packing crate. One end was left open; the floor was padded, a window was cut out, toys and bells hung from the ceiling and walls. The box was stimulating, therapeutic, and safe for children with severe physical and mental impairment.
White, Jeanine. (Pacific State Hosp, Pomona, CA) American Journal of Occupational Therapy, 1976(Mar), Vol 30(3), 167. [PA, Vol 56:06327]

2708. Some variables influencing the maintenance of acquired self-feeding behavior in profoundly retarded children.
Describes a program to teach 3 7-, 8-, and 11-yr-old profoundly retarded children to feed themselves. Shaping, fading, and behavioral consequences were employed to develop long-term maintenance of the acquired behavior. A series of probes was attempted. The training indicated that long-term maintenance of acquired self-help skills in the retarded may relate more to program design features than to deficits in the individuals.
Albin, Jack B. Mental Retardation, 1977(Oct), Vol 15(5), 49–52. [PA, Vol 61:08925]

2709. Economical procedures for the reduction of aggression in a residential setting.
29 8–19 yr old females on a residential unit for the severely and profoundly mentally retarded were exposed to a series of procedures to assess effects on aggression. The procedures involved the manipulation of amount of living space, presence or absence of toys, and presentation of noncontingent reinforcers on a variable-time schedule. The presence or absence of toys had no effect on the amount of aggression, enlarging the living space significantly reduced the amount of aggression, and presentation of noncontingent edible reinforcers reduced aggression even further.
Boe, Rodlyn B. (John F. Kennedy Inst, Baltimore, MD) Mental Retardation, 1977(Oct), Vol 15(5), 25–28. [PA, Vol 61:09089]

2710. Effects of varying schedules of timeout on high- and low-rate behaviors.
Examined the effects of identical VR time-out schedules on the high- and low-rate disruptive behaviors of a 19-yr-old mentally retarded female (IQ below 30). A VR 8 schedule was only moderately effective with a low-rate behavior, but rapidly and significantly suppressed an independent high-rate behavior after eliminating the low-rate behavior with a continuous schedule of time-out.
Calhoun, Karen S. & Lima, Paul P. (U Georgia) Journal of Behavior Therapy & Experimental Psychiatry, 1977(Jun), Vol 8(2), 189–194. [PA, Vol 59:12729]

2711. Establishing walking by severely retarded children.
Examines the implications of independent ambulation for severely retarded children and reviews the literature describing behavioral interventions which facilitate walking. Findings from applied behavior analysis of single Ss support the value of operant techniques in the acquisition of walking. An operationally defined, data-based, 4-level sequence for training walking beginning with momentary standing and ending with independent walking on command is described. Representative data from 5 severely retarded 2½-3 yr old children are presented. (19 ref)
Haavik, Sarah & Altman, Karl. (U Kansas Medical Ctr, Children's Rehabilitation Unit, Kansas City) Perceptual & Motor Skills, 1977(Jun), Vol 44(3, Pt 2), 1107–1114. [PA, Vol 59:10424]

2712. Training instrumental symbolic communication among profoundly retarded children: An exploratory study.
Nine 16–18 yr old profoundly retarded Ss (IQ range 1–7) were tutored in grasping and placing felt shapes as an initial step to learning symbolic language. The Ss and their foster grandparent tutors participated in 30-min training sessions each weekday for approximately 2 mo, supervised by a research assistant. The foster grandparents prompted the Ss toward a symbol and guided their hands, with a symbol in grasp, to the language tray. Reinforcement of food or drink was given immediately upon a grasp and place response and was varied systematically across training sessions. Grasping behavior was performed by all the Ss, but did not vary from food reinforcement except for 3 Ss. Three Ss were never seen to place symbols. Three other Ss began to place more frequently (independent of experimental conditions), and 2 of the remaining 3 showed no variation as a function of food reinforcement, while 1 S placed more frequently under food conditions. Interobserver reliability for grasping behavior averaged 92.5%; for placing behavior, 81.6%. (15 ref)
Haskett, G. J.; Bost, Loujeania; Hawkins, Mary & Hawley, Elizabeth. Research & the Retarded, 1977, Vol 4(2), 30–37. [PA, Vol 61:03890]

2713. A comparison of manual and oral language training with mute retarded children.
Investigated whether sign language training would be more effective than verbal language training in teaching 12 nonverbal normal-hearing severely and profoundly retarded 4.5–8.5 yr olds to communicate. Ss were matched in threes and randomly assigned to a verbal language group, a sign language group, or a placebo group. Results indicate that both language groups showed progress while the placebo group did not show any progress. Results also demonstrate that it is possible for sign language to transfer to verbal language. The significance of this finding and the direction of future research are discussed. (26 ref)
Kahn, James V. (U Illinois Coll of Education, Chicago Circle) Mental Retardation, 1977(Jun), Vol 15(3), 21–23. [PA, Vol 59:08112]

2714. Reducing self-injurious behavior of severely retarded individuals through withdrawal of reinforcement procedures.
Self-injurious behavior is a serious problem among some of the profoundly and severely retarded. Exp I employed a nonverbal severely retarded 16-yr-old male who scored near the basal level on the Vineland Social Maturity Scale (VSMS); he was exposed to a contingent withdrawal of reinforcement procedure in an attempt to suppress his self-abusive behavior. Vibratory stimulation was used as the reinforcer. In Exp II, differential reinforcement of other behavior and contingent withdrawal of vibration were used to decrease the self-injurious behavior of a 12-yr-old severely retarded female who scored at the basal level of the VSMS. Results of both experiments indicate that (a) vibratory stimulation can serve as an effective reinforcer for severely retarded individuals, and (b) the contingent withdrawal of reinforcement can produce response suppression similar to that found under an application of aversive stimulus procedure. (22 ref)
Nunes, Dennis L.; Murphy, Robert J. & Ruprecht, Michael L. (St Cloud State U) Behavior Modification, 1977(Oct), Vol 1(4), 499–516. [PA, Vol 60:07906]

2715. [Behavior modification in an individual with organically based profound mental deficiency.] (Span)
Presents a long-term case study on a profoundly retarded child with organic brain damage, to whom a variety of behavioral shaping procedures were applied during 6 mo. The results show that the treatment was not only effective in the experimental situation, but also in other daily-life situations within the clinic routine. Interesting generalization effects appeared not only in situations prior to the experimental sessions, but also in other and more remote moments. Follow-up data suggest, however, that to maintain such gains it is necessary to counteract the adverse external conditions in a normal psychiatric ward. Some considerations are offered about difficulties which arise among members of the medical and psychological staff in a neurologic clinic. (English summary)
Pelechano, Vicente & Massieu, M. P. (U de La Laguna, Tenerife, Canary Islands) Análisis y Modificación de Conducta, 1977, Vol 3(4), 69–87. [PA, Vol 61:11377]

2716. Voluntary control of stereotyped behaviour by mentally retarded children: Preliminary experimental findings.
Rhythm is a typical feature of many of the stereotyped behaviors shown by mentally retarded, autistic, and blind children. The rhythm of stereotyped behavior was conceived neurologically as an expression of involuntary activity of the CNS. To test this hypothesis, operant conditioning methods were used in an attempt to synchronize the rhythm of chronic body rocking to a visual pacemaker in 3 severely retarded children. Under comparable experimental conditions, complete synchronization of the rocking rhythm was demonstrated for 1 child, no synchronization for the 2nd, and intermittent synchronization for the 3rd. Results suggest that different children with the same form of stereotyped movements may vary extremely in the extent of voluntary control they can exert on the rhythm of their body rocking. Furthermore, a child may also produce extreme variations in the volitional control of rhythm during body rocking, independent of his motivational state. The theoretical implications and clinical significance of these findings are discussed. (French, German & Spanish summaries)
Pohl, Peter. (Ludwig-Maximilians-U München, Inst für Sozialpädiatrie und Jugendmedizin, West Germany) Developmental Medicine & Child Neurology, 1977(Dec), Vol 19(6), 811–817. [PA, Vol 60:11973]

2717. Auditory reinforcement in profoundly retarded multiply handicapped children.
Four profoundly retarded multiply handicapped children (mean age CA 12.8 yrs, mean MA 5.4 mo) were placed in a situation where auditory stimulation was made contingent on a visually directed leverpulling response. Two experiments were performed. In Exp I, a technique for establishing an effective reinforcer from a range of possible reinforcing stimuli was evaluated. In Exp II, a multiple schedule was used to compare the effectivenesss of a reinforcer whose efficacy was established in Exp I with a 2nd auditory stimulus. The selection of auditory reinforcers and an evaluation of their relative potency was achieved using these techniques. Results show the feasibility of systematic measurement of operant-conditioning effects with very severely handicapped Ss in a laboratory situation. The information gained concerning the effectiveness of auditory reinforcers has implications for behavior-modification programs with these children.
Remington, R. E.; Foxen, T. & Hogg, J. (U Southampton, England) American Journal of Mental Deficiency, 1977(Nov), Vol 82(3), 299–304. [PA, Vol 61:01284]

2718. Operant training of head control and beginning language for a severely developmentally disabled child.
Contingent social reinforcement was applied differentially to aid the behavioral and educational development of a 9-yr-old severely retarded nonverbal female with quadriplegic spastic cerebral palsy. Four behaviors prerequisite and collateral to beginning language development were defined and measured: eye contact, head control, imitative vocalization, and cessation of drooling. Treatment was administered in multiple baseline design, and improvements in all behaviors were observed over the 20-wk program. The experimenters found the improvements maintained during follow-up periods 1 and 12 mo after the initial training had ceased.
Richman, Joel S. & Kozlowski, Nancy L. (U Illinois, Chicago Circle) Journal of Behavior Therapy & Experimental Psychiatry, 1977(Dec), Vol 8(4), 437–440. [PA, Vol 61:06580]

2719. Evaluating the Foxx and Azrin toilet training procedure for retarded children in a day training center.
Compared R. M. Foxx and N. A. Azrin's (1973) overcorrection and repeated positive practice toilet training procedure with a no-training group and a scheduling method which required the trainees to be taken to the toilet 4 times/day. Data from 14 7–12

yr old severely and profoundly retarded children indicate that the Foxx and Azrin method virtually ended accidental daytime wetting in the school setting and that there was considerable generalization of self-initiation into the home setting even without parental involvement. These results, however, did require considerable cost to staff in terms of time and energy. *Sadler, Orin W. & Merkert, Faythe.* (Comprehensive Mental Health Ctr, Savannah, GA) Behavior Therapy, 1977(Jun), Vol 8(3), 499–500. [PA, Vol 59:06163]

2720. Behavioural control of self-injury in the mentally retarded.
Notes that self-injury is a common problem among retarded children and the most effective treatment has been aversive (pain or shock) punishment. In the present study, alternative treatment techniques were used to control such behavior in 2 severely retarded children (11.5 and 14.4 yrs of age). In the 1st case, each self-injurious response resulted in (a) verbal reprimand, (b) arms being restrained in Treatment I and mild punishment and arms being restrained in Treatment II, and (c) differential reinforcement of other behavior. In the 2nd case, the child received noncontingent attention for 6 hrs/day. Self-injury was eliminated in both cases with lasting effects. (20 ref)
Singh, Nirbhay N. (Mangere Hosp & Training School, Auckland, New Zealand) New Zealand Psychologist, 1977(Apr), Vol 6(1), 52–58. [PA, Vol 60:01514]

2721. The use of positive practice training in work adjustment with two profoundly retarded adolescents.
Employed with 2 retardates a positive practice training (PPT) procedure that used repetition, reeducation, and aversive training. With one, a 16-yr-old nonverbal male with an IQ of 21, the work was assembling drapery pulleys. After establishing a baseline for 6 days, the PPT was introduced and increased output greatly. Return to baseline conditions reduced work output, but reintroduction of PPT restored the gains. The 2nd S, an 18-yr-old male with IQ of 18, was noncompliant. Four frequently used commands were the successive targets for PPT. Once the noncompliant behavior to the 1st command was reduced, the training was applied to the next 3 commands in turn. Compliance was heavily praised; noncompliance was followed by repeated guided practice in obeying. Results, including response generalization, are reported in detail, and the advantages and drawbacks of PPT are discussed.
Wehman, Paul; Schutz, Richard; Renzaglia, Adelle & Karan, Orv. (Virginia Commonwealth U) Vocational Evaluation & Work Adjustment Bulletin, 1977(Sep), Vol 10(3), 14–22. [PA, Vol 61:04227]

2722. Teaching buttoning to severely/profoundly retarded multihandicapped children.
Provides a detailed guide to teaching buttoning as one aspect of learning dressing skills. Descriptions of a suitable garment and ways to teach the child to find and grasp the button, pull the button, find the hole, put the button in the hole, and button his/her own clothing are included along with words of encouragement for the teacher.
Adelson-Bernstein, Nancy & Sandow, Lynda. (Suffolk Developmental Ctr, Melville, NY) Education & Training of the Mentally Retarded, 1978(Apr), Vol 13(2), 178–183. [PA, Vol 61:14515]

2723. Suppression of repetitive self-injurious behavior by contingent inhalation of aromatic ammonia.
Two institutionalized children who exhibited high rates of severely self-injurious behaviors were punished with aromatic ammonia inhalation on a response-contingent basis. Ss were a 4-yr-old microcephalic severely retarded girl and a 7-yr-old severely retarded girl with an unspecified congenital defect. The contingency was applied throughout all aspects of each S's institutional program, which focused on teaching of self-help skills. Suppression of the self-injurious responses was both rapid and general. The contingency was maintained for 2 mo although there was no responding after the 1st 5 days. Follow-up sessions, conducted 4 mo after the punishment contingency was removed, revealed that suppression effects were highly durable. Aromatic

ammonia inhalation appears to be an effective alternative for decelerating extremely maladaptive behaviors that do not yield to more conventional nonaversive forms of therapy. It is suggested, however, that the procedure should be used with great caution, for it may involve risk to the S.
Baumeister, Alan A. & Baumeister, Alfred A. (George Peabody Coll for Teachers) Journal of Autism & Developmental Disorders, 1978(Mar), Vol 8(1), 71–77. [PA, Vol 61:13829]

2724. Multiple behavioral effects of the use of lemon juice with a ruminating toddler-age child.
Long-standing rumination in a profoundly retarded 3-yr-old girl was treated using lemon juice as a consequence of the rumination. Rumination was nearly eliminated and weight was increased as a function of the use of lemon juice while the child was in a daycare center. Concurrent with treatment, positive and negative behaviors were observed to occur. Six-month follow-up in the home found a maintenance of the reduced rate of rumination, negative behaviors decreased or "disappeared," while socially desirable behaviors were maintained or continued to increase, even though none was systematically treated.
Becker, Judith V.; Turner, Samuel M. & Sajwaj, Thomas E. (U Tennessee, Ctr for the Health Sciences, Memphis) Behavior Modification, 1978(Apr), Vol 2(2), 267–278. [PA, Vol 61:13830]

2725. Workshop supervision: Evaluation of a procedure for production management with the severely retarded.
Reports that the production capacity of 3 19–26 yr old profoundly retarded (MAs 2.6–3.2 yrs) woman employees at a community workshop was significantly increased over baseline data by use of a timer and bell. If S finished the task before the bell rang, she received 2 pennies instead of the usual one. The gains were long-lasting and approached the standard industrial production time for the task studied. (6 ref)
Bellamy, G. Thomas; Inman, Dean P. & Yeates, John. (U Oregon Ctr on Human Development) Mental Retardation, 1978(Aug), Vol 16(4), 317–319. [PA, Vol 63:01787]

2726. Using generalized imitation to expand verbal imitative repertoires in nonspeaking retarded children.
Developed a simplified training procedure (fading, modeling, prompting, and reinforcement) which does not require shaping and which can be used by ward staff without extensive instruction. The procedure was applied successfully by ward staff in individual sessions to extend verbal imitation in 4 severely retarded children who could imitate only a few vocal models.
Clark, Hewitt B. & Dameron, David W. (Children's Behavioral Services Ctr, Oasis Group Home & Family Training Program, Las Vegas, NV) Behavior Therapy, 1978(Nov), Vol 9(5), 966–967. [PA, Vol 62:09117]

2727. Use of contingent lemon juice to eliminate public masturbation by a severely retarded boy.
Reduced public masturbatory responses in a severely retarded 7.8-yr-old boy by contingent oral lemon juice. The S had a 4-yr history of this behavior, and other procedures (ignoring, hand spanking) had been ineffective. The lemon juice contingency was effective in 13–16 days in both home and schooland was easily implemented by parents and teachers. (12 ref)
Cook, J. William; Altman, Karl; Shaw, Jeanne & Blaylock, Marsha. (U Kansas Medical Ctr, Childrens Rehabilitation Unit, Kansas City) Behaviour Research & Therapy, 1978, Vol 16(2), 131–134. [PA, Vol 62:11478]

2728. Effective treatment of self-injurious behavior through a forced-arm exercise.
Investigated a forced arm exercise as a means of eliminating head-hitting in 2 profoundly retarded boys (5 and 12 yrs old). During sessions restraints used to manage Ss were removed. After a baseline measure, required practice of repeated vertical arm movements was made contingent on each response. Later, this procedure was combined with reinforcement under a DRO schedule. Arm exercise alone produced a substantial decrease in head-hitting, while the combination treatment engendered near-zero levels. Subsequently, reduction of head-hitting was extended to several contexts by regular ward staff. This type of treatment

appears as effective with self-injurious behavior as it is with stereotyped behavior.

DeCatanzaro, Denys A. & Baldwin, Graham. (U British Columbia, Vancouver, Canada) American Journal of Mental Deficiency, 1978(Mar), Vol 82(5), 433–439. [PA, Vol 61:08931]

2729.   Retarded children as observers, mediators, and generalization programmers using an icing procedure.

Treated a 2.5-yr-old profoundly retarded blind child who engaged in mild forms of self-injurious behavior by using other retarded children as mediators and generalization programmers. In the 1st phase, 3 14–15 yr old retarded children served as observers and mediators in an icing (placing an ice cube in the target child's mouth and simultaneously holding his hands down while counting to 3) procedure designed to decrease shirt and/or finger sucking-chewing behavior. Results indicate that the procedure was effective but did not generalize outside of a 30-min treatment session. In a 2nd generalization programming phase, observations were taken every 7.5 min through the entire day. After baseline, the retarded peers were brought in for 5 10-min periods spaced throughout the day. During these periods, they delivered icing contingent upon the target S's shirt and/or finger sucking-chewing behavior. Results demonstrate that 50 mins of icing led to generalization throughout the entire 8-hr day. (11 ref)

Drabman, Ronald S.; Ross, James M.; Lynd, R. Sterling & Cordua, Glen D. (U Mississippi Medical Ctr, Jackson) Behavior Modification, 1978(Jul), Vol 2(3), 371–385. [PA, Vol 63:01550]

2730.   The timeout ribbon: A nonexclusionary timeout procedure.

Recently, the use of timeout rooms has been questioned by various agencies, and some have adopted policies that prohibit or greatly restrict exclusionary timeout. The present study developed a timeout procedure that did not require removal of the misbehavior from the learning environment. The procedure was applied to the disruptive behaviors of 5 severely retarded children in an institutional special-education classroom. An observer prompted all teacher behaviors related to the procedures to assure their precise implementation. After baseline, a reinforcement-only condition was implemented. Each child was given a different colored ribbon to wear as a tie and received edibles and praise every few minutes for good behavior and for wearing the ribbon. When timeout was added, a child's ribbon was removed for any instance of misbehavior and teacher attention and participation in activities ceased for 3 min or until the misbehavior stopped. Reinforcement continued at other times for appropriate behavior. An ABCBC reversal design was used to demonstrate control of the behavior by the conditions applied. On average, the children misbehaved 42 and 32% of the time during the baseline and reinforcement conditions, respectively, but only 6% of the time during the timeout conditions. The practicality and acceptability of the procedure were supported further by the successful implementation of the procedure by a teacher in another state and by responses to a questionnaire given to 40 mental health professionals. (18 ref)

Foxx, R. M. & Shapiro, S. T. (U Maryland, Baltimore) Journal of Applied Behavior Analysis, 1978(Spr), Vol 11(1), 125–136. [PA, Vol 61:11353]

2731.   Assessment, modification, and generalization of social interaction among severely retarded, multihandicapped children.

To maximize the development and generalization of social responses among 2 severely retarded, multihandicapped children and their classroom peers, a continuous observation system was used to select target responses according to their initiator–responder units. (P. S. Strain et al, 1977). Prompting and reinforcement tactics were implemented to increase the social responses of the Ss. The results demonstrate that social behaviors that previously occurred at extremely low rates could be significantly accelerated and maintained across time. Generalization of trained behaviors to a nontraining setting was documented and replicated across behaviors and Ss. The results point out the importance of target behaviors being selected on the basis of their consistency in setting the occasion for positive social behaviors by peers. (21 ref)

Gable, Robert A.; Hendrickson, Jo M. & Strain, Phillip S. (George Peabody Coll for Teachers) Education & Training of the Mentally Retarded, 1978(Oct), Vol 13(3), 279–286. [PA, Vol 63:08421]

2732.   A retrospective evaluation of pipamperone (Dipiperon®) in the treatment of behavioural deviations in severely mentally handicapped.

19 severely mentally handicapped female patients (CA 15–24 yrs, IQ less than 36) were treated with pipamperone because of behavioral disturbances. The dose varied from 40 to 180 mg/day orally spread over 1–3 intakes. Duration of treatment was 2–10 mo. Therapeutic effect, evaluated by means of a 12-item rating scale, showed that significant improvement was obtained from 9 of the 12 items. Overall improvement was very good in 2, good in 10, moderate in 5, and insufficient in 2 Ss. Serious side effects were not observed. (French, Dutch, German, Italian, & Spanish summaries) (5 ref)

Haegeman, J. & Duyck, F. (Medisch Pedagogisch Inst St-Vincentius, Viane, Belgium) Acta Psychiatrica Belgica, 1978(Mar–Apr), Vol 78(2), 392–398. [PA, Vol 65:06061]

2733.   Effects of imitation training on immediate and delayed imitation by severely retarded children.

Used contingent reinforcement in training 8 severely retarded children aged 4–14 yrs who were previously judged to be nonimitative. A yoked control group was given comparable training, but with noncontingent reinforcement. (Experimental Ss had a mean score of 10.9 on the Fairview Self-Help Scale; control Ss had a mean score of 12.0. It is noted that nonretarded children average 100 on this scale.) Posttests of imitation of new behavior of a reinforced model showed significant immediate and delayed (15 min) imitation only in the contingent-reinforcement group.

Hekkema, Nancy & Freedman, P. E. (U Illinois, Chicago) American Journal of Mental Deficiency, 1978(Sep), Vol 83(2), 129–134. [PA, Vol 62:06657]

2734.   Negative preference management: Behavioral suppression using Premack's punishment hypothesis.

Inappropriate behaviors that occurred often in 3 severely retarded adolescents were identified, measured, and designated as more preferred; behaviors seldom observed in the Ss were identified and designated as less preferred. When the less preferred behaviors were made contingent on the emission of the more preferred behaviors, there was an immediate, substantial, and consistent suppression of the more preferred behaviors. The procedure, based on D. Premack's (1971) punishment hypothesis, is called negative preference management. Some possible advantages of the technique as an applied behavioral reduction procedure are discussed. (7 ref)

Krivacek, Dennis & Powell, J. (California State Coll, PA) Education & Treatment of Children, 1978(Sum), Vol 1(4), 5–13. [PA, Vol 63:12435]

2735.   Brief hospitalization for the behavioral treatment of feeding problems in the developmentally disabled.

Describes the use of short-term hospitalization for the treatment of long-standing feeding problems in developmentally disabled children. Two cases are presented in which a physically handicapped girl (4 yrs 7 mo old) and a severely retarded boy (2 yrs 10 mo old) were taught to accept new foods and textures through the use of applied behavior analysis techniques. Hospitalization provided the controlled setting necessary to accomplish the training as rapidly as possible and allowed for parent training so that the procedures could be maintained at home. Criteria for determining need for hospitalization vs treatment as an outpatient are presented. (12 ref)

Linscheid, Thomas R.; Oliver, Judith; Blyler, Elaine & Palmer, Sushma. (Georgetown University Hosp, Div of Psychology) Journal of Pediatric Psychology, 1978, Vol 3(2), 72–76. [PA, Vol 62:06847]

2736. Social reinforcement and the naturally occurring social responses of severely and profoundly retarded adolescents.
Studied 18 severely and profoundly institutionalized females (mean CA 14 yrs 7 mo) to investigate the hypothesis that the deficits in social behavior is due, in part, to the failure of their environment to maintain that behavior. Using an ABAB design, the investigators systematically ignored Ss and gave them social reinforcement for appropriate social behavior. Social behavior decreased during nonreinforcement conditions and increased during reinforcement conditions. Thus, data support the hypothesis. (19 ref)
Mayhew, Gerald L.; Enyart, Patience & Anderson, John. (Colin Anderson Ctr, St Marys, WV) American Journal of Mental Deficiency, 1978(Sep), Vol 83(2), 164–170. [PA, Vol 62:06677]

2737. Are profoundly and severely retarded people given access to the least restrictive environment? An analysis of one state's compliance.
Primarily in the last decade, a large number of court decisions and federal guidelines have sought to provide retarded persons access to the least restrictive treatment environment. A set of 9 questions were asked of respondents representing 3 mental health facilities for severely and profoundly handicapped populations ranging from 3 to 21 yrs in 1 state. Results indicate that (a) placement staffings are appropriately conducted, (b) parents abrogate their right to monitor their children's services and placements, (c) a small percentage of students who could be placed in less restrictive environments are so placed, and (d) public schools resist placement of the severely or profoundly retarded student. (9 ref)
Miller, Sidney R.; Miller, Ted L. & Repp, Alan C. (Illinois Regional Resource Ctr, Northern Illinois U) Mental Retardation, 1978(Apr), Vol 16(2), 123–126. [PA, Vol 62:09282]

2738. Manual communication for the severely handicapped: An assessment and instructional strategy.
Describes the use of a manual communication system with 2 severely handicapped males. A classroom teacher and an occupational therapist assessed individual skills across social, cognitive, motor, and communication domains, and signs were presented during settings in which they normally occurred. A data collection system was developed to document acquisition and monitor program success. It is suggested that the CA and the relative amount of success in past therapy or language instruction programs are of primary importance in the selection of candidates for such a program. (6 ref)
Salisbury, Christine; Wambold, Clark & Walter, Gail. (Kansas City Regional Ctr, MO) Education & Training of the Mentally Retarded, 1978(Dec), Vol 13(4), 393–397. [PA, Vol 63:13012]

2739. Home intervention with parents of severely subnormal, pre-school children: An interim report.
Conducted a 3-yr program of home-based intervention with 2 groups of preschool severely subnormal children and their parents: 16 children (mean CA 29.8 mo, mean IQ 44.5) visited every 2 wks and 16 children (mean CA 30.4 mo, mean IQ 42.5) visited every 8 wks. 11 had Down's syndrome, 8 had cerebral palsy, and 13 had other diagnoses. The program had apparently contradictory results: Frequently visited children, after initial superiority over infrequently visited children, later showed a deceleration in intellectual growth. Less frequently visited children conversely showed a rise in performance after an initial decrement. The interpretation is advanced that parents in the latter group were less dependent on the visiting therapist and more able to take positive action to assist their children and improve their own situation. (14 ref)
Sandow, Sarah & Clarke, A. D. (U Hull, England) Child Care, Health & Development, 1978(Jan–Feb), Vol 4(1), 29–39. [PA, Vol 62:04292]

2740. A simple procedure for training and maintenance of proper mealtime behaviour in severely retarded children.
Trained 4 severely/profoundly mentally-retarded teenage girls (social age 1.5–1.8 yrs) to use acceptable mealtime behaviors after as little as 10 days' training. The training procedure consisted of a combination of mild punishment and physical restraint applied to inappropriate behaviors. Training resulted in a rapid increase in the proportion of appropriate mealtime behaviors to a level close to unity. Follow-up observation at 10-day intervals showed no reduction in appropriate behaviors under a simple maintenance procedure. (6 ref)
Singh, Nirbhay N. & Beale, Ivan L. (Mangere Hosp & Training School, Auckland, New Zealand) Australian Journal of Mental Retardation, 1978(Jun), Vol 5(2), 46–48. [PA, Vol 63:01593]

2741. Practice makes perfect: The elimination of stereotyped body-rocking through positive practice.
Used a positive practice procedure in a public school classroom to reduce the frequency of body-rocking in a 16-yr-old severely retarded girl. Although previous interventions (i.e., differential reinforcement of other behavior, time out, verbal instructions) had proven ineffective, positive practice rapidly reduced the frequency of body-rocking to near zero levels in 7 days of treatment. The procedures were easily carried out and cost-effective, requiring approximately 9 min of staff time/day during 20 days of treatment and 1.4 min/day during a 135-day follow-up period. Results of a 6-mo follow-up show that response suppression was durable. Little generalization of suppression was observed from the training setting to other settings. (16 ref)
Townsend, Nancy M. & Marholin, David. (Boston U School of Education) Scandinavian Journal of Behaviour Therapy, 1978, Vol 7(3), 195–201. [PA, Vol 63:13016]

2742. Control of selective echolalia via the instatement of a general alternative response.
Treatment for echolalic responding has been limited to the training of a small number of correct responses and limited stimulus verbalizations by the experimenter, leaving the possibility that the introduction of novel stimuli could result in the re-occurrence of echolalia. In the present study, an 11-yr-old severely retarded male's echolalic responding to questions that he could not answer correctly was controlled by instituting a general alternative response, "I don't know." The S continued to respond correctly to questions that he could answer, indicating that the general alternative response had been appropriately discriminated. A Baseline, Treatment I, Differential Reinforcement of Other Behavior, and Treatment II design indicated that the S's echolalic responding and the appropriate use of the general alternative response were under experimental control. Generalization of the experimental results to the S's regular daycare setting was accomplished by having the staff verbally punish all echolalic responses and then restate the question to the S until a noncholalic answer had been emitted. Suggestions for combining previous treatment procedures for echolalia with the general alternative response procedure are offered. (4 ref)
Tucker, George H.; O'Dell, Stan L. & Suib, Michael R. (U Mississippi) Behaviour Research & Therapy, 1978, Vol 16(4), 302–306. [PA, Vol 63:10224]

2743. Effects of different environmental conditions on leisure time activity of the severely and profoundly handicapped.
Studied the efficacy of 3 environmental conditions—Toy Proximity, Modeling, and Instructions plus Modeling—on the independent leisure activity of 3 severely and profoundly handicapped individuals (CAs 16, 18, 34 yrs; IQs 18, 15, 31). The effects of the conditions were evaluated in a combination of simultaneous treatment and ABA reversal, with each of the experimental conditions presented in a Latin square sequence. It was found that each of the 3 antecedent events resulted in substantially higher levels of independent play than did baseline activity. Instructions plus Modeling led to the highest level of independent play, while Toy Proximity and Modeling resulted in lower but almost equivalent rates of responding. Implications include more systematic approaches to behavioral assessment and stimulus-fading maintenance strategies in recreation settings. (27 ref)
Wehman, Paul. (Virginia Commonwealth U) Journal of Special Education, 1978(Sum), Vol 12(2), 183–193. [PA, Vol 62:11695]

2744. An introduction to behavioural principles in teaching the profoundly handicapped.
Summarizes the author's principles for implementing behavioral modification treatments with severely handicapped subnormal children: (a) Precede any teaching by a thorough assessment, including behavioral assets, deficits, and excesses. (b) Pinpoint realistic targets relevant to the child's development of independence and attainable in the short term. (c) Use consequences that are *effective* as reinforcers by determining exactly which events will reinforce the child's learning. Teach the child sensitivity to people as reinforcers. (d) Monitor progress by objective recording of specific teaching targets. (e) Change the teaching targets in the light of progress, enabling the child to acquire increasingly sophisticated skills. (f) Be consistent, both within the teaching procedure and between different teachers. (6 ref)
Williams, Chris. (Royal Western Counties Hosp, Starcross, England) Child Care, Health & Development, 1978(Jan–Feb), Vol 4(1), 21–27. [PA, Vol 62:04173]

2745. Egocentric speech: An adaptive function applied to developmental disabilities in occupational therapy.
Discusses egocentric speech as it relates to the structures of assimilation and accommodation in Piaget's earlier sensorimotor stage, then as it appears in the preoperatory level of the concrete operations stage of intelligence. The importance of the behavior as a foundation for the inner language and thinking capacities of the adult is supported by the research of Soviet scientists L. S. Vygotsky and A. R. Luria, who argued that egocentric speech affects the child's future cognitive and behavioral activity by promoting self-stimulating and self-regulating complex problem-solving abilities. Three case studies are presented in which egocentric speech is used in conjunction with problem-solving tasks in occupational therapy. Ss were a 40-yr-old severely retarded man, a 26-yr-old brain damaged woman, and a 21-yr-old man with a self-inflicted gunshot wound in the temple. (14 ref)
Burnell, Diana P. (San Jose State U) American Journal of Occupational Therapy, 1979(Mar), Vol 33(3), 169–174. [PA, Vol 64:01843]

2746. The effects of overcorrection: A case study.
The effects of overcorrection on multiple problems were studied in the case of a severely mentally handicapped 11-yr-old boy. While the techniques proved effective, they were extremely time-consuming, and during treatment periods there were large increases in collateral behavior. (13 ref)
Clements, J. & Dewey, M. (Ely Hosp, Psychology Dept, Cardiff, Wales) Behaviour Research & Therapy, 1979, Vol 17(5), 515–518. [PA, Vol 65:10900]

2747. Suppression of self-stimulatory behavior of a profoundly retarded boy across staff and settings: An assessment of situational generalization.
Examined the direct and generalized effects of positive reinforcement and modified arm overcorrection on the occurrence of appropriate play and self-stimulatory behaviors of a 17-yr-old profoundly retarded boy. A multiple baseline design was employed to assess the effects of treatment across 10 teachers in 2 settings. Results indicate that the procedure directly increased play behavior and suppressed self-stimulation. There was no evidence of generalized changes in the S's behavior across teachers and settings. The failure of the treatment program to produce such changes is examined with reference to the procedures employed. (40 ref)
Coleman, R. Steven; Whitman, Thomas L. & Johnson, Moses R. (U Notre Dame) Behavior Therapy, 1979(Mar), Vol 10(2), 266–280. [PA, Vol 62:06624]

2748. The effect of activation therapy on severely subnormal children.
Assessed 11 severely subnormal children (CA, 4–12 yrs; social age, 11 mo–5 yrs) for various developmental skills and social competence, after which Ss were put on a regular program throughout the day. This began with basic hygiene in the early morning and continued through physical exercise and recreational and musical programs in the evening. All Ss were involved in as many activities as possible. Comparison of pre–postprogram assessments indicated that Ss were able to learn various skills as a result of being actively involved in programs throughout the day. (7 ref)
Embar, Padma; Kinker, Ramesh; Rudra, Rajini & Murthy, Pramila. Indian Journal of Clinical Psychology, 1979(Sep), Vol 6(2), 105–110. [PA, Vol 65:08472]

2749. Treatment of a retarded child's feces smearing and coprophagic behaviour.
The daily rearrangement of a 7-yr-old profoundly retarded male's (IQ less than 20) routine shower was effective in eliminating his low-frequency feces smearing and coprophagic behavior during the late afternoon/early evening part of the day. The effects appeared to generalize in that both types of behavior were reduced at other times of the day and night. A model for analyzing the motivations and reinforcing conditions for rectal digging, coprophagy, and smearing feces is presented. (8 ref)
Friedin, Bruce D. & Johnson, Helene K. (New York State Dept of Mental Hygiene, Brooklyn Developmental Ctr) Journal of Mental Deficiency Research, 1979(Mar), Vol 23(1), 55–61. [PA, Vol 66:06332]

2750. Time delay: A technique to increase language use and facilitate generalization in retarded children.
Manipulated institutional breakfast-serving procedures to assess what effect changes in that aspect of the environment would have on requests for food. During baseline, 6 severely retarded children (11.10–15.7 yrs) were required to pick up their food trays and return to their seats. The 1st manipulation, delaying the giving of the food tray for 15 sec, served as a cue to evoke meal requests by 3 Ss. Two Ss required a model of an appropriate meal request (i.e., "Tray please.") at the end of the 15-sec delay before they began their meals. To evoke meal requests from the 6th S, an intensive training procedure, consisting of massed trials of delay and modeling, was required. Three different probes were administered to assess generalization across the people serving the meals, across mealtimes, and across both people and mealtimes. Typically, generalized responding in these new situations could be prompted by use of the 15-sec delay procedure. Functional aspects of the delay procedure and its potential usefulness for evoking speech and facilitating generalization are discussed. (10 ref)
Halle, James W.; Marshall, Ann M. & Spradlin, Joseph E. (U Kansas, Lawrence) Journal of Applied Behavior Analysis, 1979(Fal), Vol 12(3), 431–439. [PA, Vol 65:01782]

2751. Reduction of inappropriate verbalizations in an emotionally disturbed adolescent.
Compared the effectiveness of timeout vs extinction and provided evidence as to the usefulness of timeout in the area of speech disfluencies in a severely retarded 15-yr-old female whose retardation was associated with autism. Results show the efficacy and practicality of the timeout procedure in that control was markedly improved over extinction and was obtained rapidly. (3 ref)
Herdman, Marcia A. (North Jersey Training School, Totowa, NJ) Mental Retardation, 1979(Oct), Vol 17(5), 251–252. [PA, Vol 66:08515]

2752. Acquisition and generalization of instruction following behavior in profoundly retarded individuals.
Four profoundly retarded 17–24 yr old male residents of a state institution learned to comply with the instructions "come here," "stay," and "sit" in a special therapy room where instructions were presented in a fixed sequence. Testing occurred in the S's ward dayroom, where instructions were presented in a random sequence. Despite dramatic changes in the stimulus conditions associated with the transfer to the testing situation, Ss performed close to their asymptotic level. Three experimentally naive Ss participated in a 2nd experiment, which was similar to the 1st, except that the number of acquisition sessions and the number of trials per session were reduced. The reduction did not appear to affect performance in the testing environment. (10 ref)

Ivy, Robert & Dubin, William. (J. N. Adam Developmental Ctr, Perrysburg, NY) Perceptual & Motor Skills, 1979(Aug), Vol 49(1), 163–139. [PA, Vol 65:03788]

2753.   Eliminating rumination behavior in a profoundly retarded adolescent: An exploratory study.
Food satiation was successful in eliminating rumination in a profoundly retarded 17-yr-old boy. Results were immediate and were maintained over several months on a modified satiation diet. S also became more sociable, curious, and amenable to programming. (2 ref)
Libby, Dorothy G. & Phillips, Elizabeth. (Central Wisconsin Ctr for the Developmentally Disabled, Madison, WI) Mental Retardation, 1979(Apr), Vol 17(2), 94–95. [PA, Vol 66:08529]

2754.   Teaching table games to severely retarded children.
Parents and paraprofessionals were trained to teach a hierarchy of Lotto table games to 4 children (CA 8–10 yrs, MA 21–46 mo), 3 of whom were nonverbal and were receiving sign language instruction. Ss acquired approximately 80% of the steps in task analyses. Adaptations of commercially produced games permit severely retarded students to participate with nonhandicapped siblings. (7 ref)
Marchant, JoAnn & Wehman, Paul. (Richmond Public Schools, VA) Mental Retardation, 1979(Jun), Vol 17(3), 150–152. [PA, Vol 66:08404]

2755.   Decreasing self-injurious behavior: Punishment with citric acid and reinforcement of alternative behavior.
A profoundly mentally retarded 19-yr-old male received contingent citric acid applied to his mouth for engaging in self-injurious behavior (SIB) and tantrum screaming. A combination multiple baseline across behaviors and reversal design was used. Citric acid was first introduced for screaming and then for SIB. When the solution was delivered for screaming, this behavior decreased while SIB remained high. Presentation of citric acid for SIB was also associated with a decrease in that behavior. Withdrawal of punishment for the SIB was associated with an increase in the behavior, while reintroduction of the citric acid decreased the behavior. Following this condition, proximity to and orientation toward the trainer was positively reinforced in addition to the punishment contingency. Reinforcement for these behaviors was then withdrawn and reintroduced. Those conditions in which positive reinforcement was presented and SIB was punished were associated with the most consistently low levels of SIB. (15 ref)
Mayhew, Gerald & Harris, Francis C. (Tidewater Community Coll) Behavior Modification, 1979(Jul), Vol 3(3), 322–336. [PA, Vol 64:10871]

2756.   A comparison of different methods of toilet training the mentally handicapped.
A number of different toilet training methods have recently been described. N. R. Ellis's (1963) model of toilet training is used to provide a simple basis for classifying these methods. Two main differences, timing vs regular potting and intensive individual training vs group training, are distinguished. Three toilet training programs (intensive individual, regular potting; intensive individual, timing; group training, regular potting) are compared in 5 severely or profoundly mentally retarded children for each method. It is concluded that intensive individual training is more cost-effective than group training and that although there is no significant difference between the intensive individual regular potting and timing methods, the former is the method of choice as it is slightly less complex. Various practical and theoretical issues arising from these toilet training programs are discussed, including the need for more detailed study of bladder function and other factors related to the development of continence in such children. (26 ref)
Smith, Paul S. (Prudhoe Hosp, Psychology Dept, England) Behaviour Research & Therapy, 1979, Vol 17(1), 33–43. [PA, Vol 64:03811]

2757.   Acquisition and use of Blissymbols by severely mentally retarded adolescents.
Four nonverbal adolescents (MAs between 2 yrs 2 mo and 2 yrs 11 mo) with CAs between 15 and 18 yrs were given the Peabody Picture Vocabulary Test (PPVT), a self-help scale, and an environmental language inventory 1 wk prior to a class on Blissymbols. Results question the practicality of teaching Blissymbols to the severely/profoundly retarded nonverbal individual with a mental and behavioral age of about 2 yrs unless the person has the desire to communicate, can respond to the PPVT, and acquires Blissymbols at a fairly rapid rate in the early stages of teaching. (2 ref)
Song, Agnes. (Central Wisconsin Ctr for the Developmentally Disabled, Madison) Mental Retardation, 1979(Oct), Vol 17(5), 253–255. [PA, Vol 66:08742]

2758.   Operant control of pathological tongue thrust in spastic cerebral palsy.
Observable tongue thrust in a 10-yr-old retarded male was modified during mealtime using a procedure consisting of differential reinforcement (presentation of food contingent upon tongue in) and punishment (gently pushing the tongue back into the mouth with a spoon). Results show substantial decreases in tongue thrust and food expulsion and a large increase in observed chewing. Findings suggest that operant techniques may be an effective means of treating tongue thrust and its associated problems and that further development and evaluation of behavioral interventions may provide a desirable alternative to more intrusive surgical or mechanical procedures. (35 ref)
Thompson, George A.; Iwata, Brian A. & Poynter, Holly. (Western Michigan U) Journal of Applied Behavior Analysis, 1979(Fal), Vol 12(3), 325–333. [PA, Vol 65:01814]

2759.   Reduction of stereotyped body-rocking using variable time reinforcement: Practical and theoretical implications.
Describes 2 experiments with 7 profoundly retarded Ss (aged 17–45 yrs). Results indicate that the variable time schedule of reinforcement was effective in reducing stereotypy. It is tentatively concluded that stereotypies in ward and laboratory environments differ in function. (30 ref)
Tierney, I. R.; McGuire, R. J. & Walton, H. J. (U Edinburgh, Scotland) Journal of Mental Deficiency Research, 1979(Sep), Vol 23(3), 175–185. [PA, Vol 66:06367]

2760.   The sexual behaviour of the institutionalised severely retarded.
A survey of observed sexual behavior in a unit of 30 severely retarded residents aged 10–33 yrs showed that most behavior was "appropriate." Homosexual activity was not greater than in the normal population. Sexual behavior directed toward staff was rare. Masturbation was the most common sexual behavior observed, but sex play (between both prepubertal and postpubertal residents) was also common. Sexual activity was often the only spontaneous cooperative mutual behavior observed and the only interresident interaction apart from aggression. (2 ref)
West, R. R. (Kingsbury Training Ctr, Bundoora, Australia) , 1979(Mar), Vol 5(5), 11–13. [PA, Vol 66:08715]

2761.   Assertion training with institutionalized severely retarded women.
Five 17–35 yr old females (IQs 22–50) were trained in assertiveness based on instances commonly occurring in their institutional life. Results show that significant generalization of the assertiveness response took place; however, some response decrement was evident at 6-mo follow-up. (9 ref)
Wortmann, Helga & Paluck, Robert J. (U Houston, Clear Lake City) Behavior Therapist, 1979(Jan–Feb), Vol 2(1), 24–25. [PA, Vol 65:05862]

2762.   Use of contingent vibration in the treatment of self-stimulatory hand-mouthing and ruminative vomiting behavior.
Describes the treatment of self-stimulatory hand-mouthing and ruminative vomiting in a 6-yr-old profoundly retarded boy using vibratory stimulation during a complete ABAB reversal design. Complete elimination of both target behaviors occurred after only 11 days of treatment. Treatment gains generalized to nontreatment settings were maintained over a 1-yr follow-up period. (12 ref)
Barmann, Barry C. (U California, Counseling Psychology Program, Santa Barbara) Journal of Behavior Therapy &

Experimental Psychiatry, 1980(Dec), Vol 11(4), 307–311. [PA, Vol 66:13267]

2763. The use of contingent-interrupted music in the treatment of disruptive bus-riding behavior.
To treat the disruptive bus-riding behavior of an 8-yr-old profoundly retarded female, music was played during each bus ride as long as the S was sitting appropriately; the music was interrupted contingent upon each response defined as disruptive. A significant reduction in disruptive riding occurred with each introduction of contingent-interrupted music. (13 ref)
Barmann, Barry C.; Croyle-Barmann, Carol & McLain, Bill. (U California, Counseling Psychology Training Clinic, Santa Barbara) Journal of Applied Behavior Analysis, 1980(Win), Vol 13(4), 693–698. [PA, Vol 65:05985]

2764. Treatment of stereotyped hair-pulling with overcorrection: A case study with long term follow-up.
Reports the successful use of a positive practice overcorrection procedure for reducing stereotyped hair-pulling in a 7½-yr-old severely mentally retarded female. This procedure was implemented after the unsuccessful use of a response prevention "treatment" by her parents. In addition, a verbal warning procedure was used to maintain the near-zero rate of hair-pulling achieved through overcorrection. Follow-up data for 1 yr are reported. (7 ref)
Barrett, Rowland P. & Shapiro, Edward S. (U Pittsburgh School of Medicine, Western Psychiatric Inst & Clinic) Journal of Behavior Therapy & Experimental Psychiatry, 1980(Dec), Vol 11(4), 317–320. [PA, Vol 66:13268]

2765. The use of awareness and omission training to control excessive drooling in a severely retarded youth.
Awareness and omission training resulted in a significant reduction in drooling and remnants of drool and an increase in wiping by an 11-yr-old severely mentally retarded boy. Training effects were maintained 20 wks after treatment termination and were generalized to other settings. (11 ref)
Barton, Edward J. & Madsen, Jennifer J. (Northern Michigan U) Child Behavior Therapy, 1980(Spr), Vol 2(1), 55–63. [PA, Vol 66:06317]

2766. Elimination of habitual vomiting using DRO procedures.
Describes a DRO procedure that was used to decrease the habitual vomiting of an 8.2-yr-old ambulatory, severely retarded male. Reinforcers (food, praise, and hugs) eliminated the vomiting in 10 1-hr sessions. The DRO is contrasted with aversive procedures that have been used to treat vomiting. (10 ref)
Bennett, Debra. Behavior Therapist, 1980(Jan–Feb), Vol 3(1), 16–18. [PA, Vol 66:04039]

2767. Parents as behavior modifiers: Intervention for three problem behaviors in a severely retarded child.
Assessed the efficacy of training parents as behavior modifiers of problem behaviors displayed by their 7-yr-old severely retarded son. The targeted problem behaviors included throwing objects, refusing to comply with parental commands, and refusing to sit in a chair at a table. The case is unique in that the S's retardation resulted from a rare chromosomal aberration previously unexplored in the behavioral therapy literature. Parents were instructed in a simple behavioral treatment package consisting of verbal punishment and reinforcement. Treatment was assessed according to a multiple-baseline-across-behaviors design. Results show significant improvement on all 3 target behaviors after intervention. Transfer of training to the natural environment was assessed at 2-mo follow-up; results show maintenance of behavioral improvement. (20 ref)
Brehony, Kathleen A.; Benson, Betsey A.; Solomon, Laura J. & Luscomb, Richard L. (Virginia Polytechnic Inst & State U) Journal of Clinical Child Psychology, 1980(Fal), Vol 9(3), 213–216. [PA, Vol 65:08463]

2768. [Diagnosis—developmental arrest: A therapeutic program.] (Germ)
Describes a behavior modification program used with a profoundly retarded 10-yr-old girl who was unable to swallow food, play, or socialize and who apparently did not understand speech. After acquiring some basic behavior patterns, the S learned to feed herself and to play on her own, became able to verbalize her needs in a simple way, showed emotional reactions, and attempted to learn to walk. (English abstract) (8 ref)
Bronder, Gisela; Böttcher, Käte & Rohlfs, Sigrid. Praxis der Kinderpsychologie und Kinderpsychiatrie, 1980(Apr), Vol 29(3), 95–99. [PA, Vol 65:13264]

2769. Stereotyped behaviour, alternative behaviour and collateral effects: A comparison of four intervention procedures.
Assessed the effects of 4 procedures (i.e., a mild slap to the forearm, differential reinforcement, overcorrection plus DRO, and a mild slap plus DRO), on a stereotyped behavior, an alternative behavior, and collateral self-injurious behaviors of a profoundly retarded 5-yr-old girl. The most effective procedure was a mild slap plus DRO. Near zero suppression of the stereotyped behavior was attained on the 1st day of implementation, collateral self-injurious behaviors were virtually eliminated, and alternative behavior increased dramatically. There was some evidence for generalization across trainers, settings, and time. (27 ref)
Cavalier, A. R. & Ferretti, R. P. (Partlow State School & Hosp, Tuscaloosa, AL) Journal of Mental Deficiency Research, 1980(Sep), Vol 24(3), 219–230. [PA, Vol 66:08488]

2770. Treatment by overcorrection of self-injurious eye gouging in preschool blind children.
Used positive practice overcorrection to treat the self-injurious eye gouging behaviors of an average intelligence 5-yr-old blind male and a severely retarded 7-yr-old blind female. An A-B treatment design was used, and the overcorrection was administered in the absence of other techniques. The treatment established rapid control over the eye gouging behaviors, bringing the rates of the behaviors to zero levels by the 3rd day of treatment. These findings indicate short positive practice may be a viable treatment alternative for the self-injurious eye gouging of young blind retarded and nonretarded children. (8 ref)
Conley, O. Stephen & Wolery, Mark R. (Regional Child Development Ctr, Big Stone Gap, VA) Journal of Behavior Therapy & Experimental Psychiatry, 1980(Jun), Vol 11(2), 121–125. [PA, Vol 66:06324]

2771. Autism reversal: A method for reducing aggressive-disruptive behavior.
Data for a 17-yr-old severely retarded male (MA 2.7 yrs) show that his aggressive-disruptive behavior was reduced through the autism reversal procedure, which consisted of a forced-arm exercise. Implications for therapists include the achievement of a reduced maladaptive behavior that had been resistant to change through other programmatic means and the broad generality of the autism reversal technique. (7 ref)
Davidson-Gooch, Lyn. (Lurleen B. Wallace Developmental Ctr, Decatur, AL) Behavior Therapist, 1980(Mar–Apr), Vol 3(2), 21–23. [PA, Vol 66:04044]

2772. The use of omission training to reduce stereotyped behavior in three profoundly retarded adults.
The present study examined the patterns of topographically different stereotyped responses and demonstrated the use of a positive approach for decreasing stereotyped behavior. Experimental control was demonstrated while examining multiple effects with 3 profoundly retarded males aged 18–21 yrs. They had all been institutionalized for more than 10 yrs. The effective use of omission training in controlling stereotyped acts and in producing multiple effects is demonstrated. (16 ref)
Dehaven, Everett D.; Rees-Thomas, Anthony H. & Benton, Shawn V. (Kansas Neurological Inst, Topeka) Education & Training of the Mentally Retarded, 1980(Dec), Vol 15(4), 298–305. [PA, Vol 66:10864]

2773. Generalization effects of newly conditioned reinforcers.
Examined (a) the effect of music and approval as reinforcers for following a command; (b) the effect of a food-pairing procedure on an approval alone condition, an approval plus music condition, and an ignore condition; (c) the durability of newly conditioned reinforcers; and (d) the strength of the new reinforcers as contingencies for following a 2nd command. Results with a severely retarded, nonambulatory, nonverbal 15-yr-old female indicate that the approval and music, which initially had not functioned as reinforcers, were conditioned as reinforcers by pairing with food. Maintenance over a 10-wk period demonstrated that the newly conditioned reinforcers continued to reinforce the original behavior. In addition, the approval and music generalized as reinforcers for a new behavior. (21 ref)
Dorow, Laura G. (Columbia U Teachers Coll) Education & Training of the Mentally Retarded, 1980(Feb), Vol 15(1), 8–14. [PA, Vol 65:10903]

2774. Treatment of self-injurious behavior using a water mist: Initial response suppression and generalization.
Two experiments evaluated the effects of a fine mist of water applied to the face contingent upon self-injurious behavior (SIB) exhibited by profoundly retarded persons. In Exp I with 7 5–37 yr old profoundly mentally retarded Ss, results of individual reversal designs showed substantial reductions in a variety of SIBs (mouthing, hand biting, skin tearing, and head banging). In Exp II, 2 hand biters, aged 21 and 26 yrs, were each observed in 2 settings. Following initial baselines in each setting, a series of manipulations was undertaken to compare the effects of mild verbal punishment ("No") with those of a combined treatment ("No" plus mist procedure). Results in one setting indicate that "No" suppressed SIB only after it was first paired with the water mist. Once acquired, the punishing properties of "No" could be extended to a 2nd setting in which the mist was never applied, and these effects could be generalized across therapists. The water mist procedure may be an effective alternative to traditional punishment techniques. (19 ref)
Dorsey, Michael F.; Iwata, Brian A.; Ong, Pamela & McSween, Terry E. (John F. Kennedy Inst, Div of Behavioral Psychology, Baltimore, MD) Journal of Applied Behavior Analysis, 1980(Sum), Vol 13(2), 343–353. [PA, Vol 65:13270]

2775. Rapid eating in the retarded: Reduction by nonaversive procedures.
Four profoundly retarded rapid eaters (CAs 9–21 yrs and average Vineland Social Maturity Scale age of 1 yr 8 mo) were taught to spoon dip at normal rates with a nonaversive treatment package that included 2 major components: (1) praise and food reinforcement for successively longer independent pauses between bites (up to 5 sec) and (2) steadily diminishing physical prompts for pausing when Ss attempted to eat rapidly. A multiple baseline experimental analysis documented that this treatment package was responsible for a reduction in rate from an average of 10.5 bites/30 sec during baseline to 3 bites/30 sec following treatment. This improvement persisted under a maintenance regime in which one-to-one attention was gradually withdrawn, Ss were intermittently reinforced for pausing, and prompts for pausing were successfully eliminated. (7 ref)
Favell, Judith E.; McGimsey, James F. & Jones, Michael L. (Western Carolina Ctr, Morgantown, NC) Behavior Modification, 1980(Oct), Vol 4(4), 481–492. [PA, Vol 66:08501]

2776. Teaching generalized speech: Reestablishing a previously trained repertoire of functional speech in a profoundly retarded adolescent.
Completed a 6-yr follow-up to assess a profoundly retarded child's (at follow-up: CA 16 yrs, MA 2 yrs 11 mo) previously trained language skills. No retention of the trained language was observed. The same training procedures were found to be effective in promoting generalized speech, although extensive training was required to reinstate the language skills. (10 ref)
Garcia, Eugene E. & DeHaven, Everett D. (Arizona State U, Coll of Education, Tempe) Behavior Research of Severe Developmental Disabilities, 1980(Oct), Vol 1(2), 147–160. [PA, Vol 66:08505]

2777. An analysis of antecedent, response, and consequence events in the treatment of self-injurious behavior.
Attempted to replicate and extend the findings of E. Carr et al (1976) on the effects of antecedent events on self-injurious behavior (SIB). A 16-yr-old severely retarded female who frequently bit herself on both hands and arms served as S. Each experimental session was divided into 3 subconditions in which S was presented with a puzzle; a sorting task; or a free choice of puzzle, sorting, or coloring tasks. The rate of instructional directives (mands) was systematically varied. Findings indicate an antecedent by response interaction: SIB increased when mands were delivered during the sorting task but did not increase during the puzzle task or when no mands were given during the sorting task. Although the SIB appeared to be maintained by negative reinforcement, the negative reinforcement in this context appeared to be characterized as an escape rather than avoidance conditioning phenomenon. Contingent application of verbal praise for correct task responses had a minor but systematic effect in reducing SIB, suggesting that differential reinforcement of incompatible behavior may be a less effective treatment for behavior maintained by negative reinforcement. (14 ref)
Gaylord-Ross, Robert J.; Weeks, Marian & Lipner, Carol. (San Francisco State U) Education & Training of the Mentally Retarded, 1980(Feb), Vol 15(1), 35–42. [PA, Vol 65:10908]

2778. A comparison of passive and active music reinforcement to increase preacademic and motor skills in severely retarded children and adolescents.
Compared the effectiveness of passive music reinforcement (contingent music listening, CML) and active music reinforcement (contingent instrument playing, CIP) in increasing preacademic and motor skills of 8 severely retarded Ss 8–18 yrs old. Because the established criteria included a consistent increase in behavior, both types of reinforcement were effective by definition. No significant differences were found between CML and CIP as to average number of sessions to criterion or average frequency of improved behavior. The similar positive effects of passive and active music reinforcement support the conclusions of the only previous study in this area. (19 ref)
Holloway, Martha S. (Florida State U) Journal of Music Therapy, 1980(Sum), Vol 17(2), 58–69. [PA, Vol 66:10768]

2779. The effects of an environmental enrichment program on the behavior of institutionalized profoundly retarded children.
Determined the effects of procedures designed to enrich the physical and social environment of an institutional ward on the adaptive (ADP) and maladaptive (MADP) behaviors of 5 profoundly retarded ambulatory females (ages 9.0–13.1 yrs). Behavior observed in an environment "enriched" with toys and objects and an "enriched" environment coupled with differential reinforcement of ADP behavior was compared to that occurring in corresponding baseline or "austere" conditions and during a period of noncontingent reinforcement. Results show (a) little change in ADP and MADP child and adult-directed behavior across conditions, (b) an overall higher incidence of ADP object-directed behavior and reduced self-directed MADP behavior in each treatment condition compared to corresponding control conditions, and (c) a reduction in MADP self-directed behavior and an increase in ADP object-directed behavior in the enriched-plus-differential-reinforcement conditions compared to the enriched environment alone. These behavioral gains were largely maintained during a follow-up condition by continuing the "enriched" environment and transferring the responsibility for differential reinforcement to direct-care staff. (54 ref)
Horner, R. Don. (U Kansas, Bureau of Child Research, Lawrence) Journal of Applied Behavior Analysis, 1980(Fal), Vol 13(3), 473–491. [PA, Vol 64:13144]

2780. Teaching independent toileting to profoundly retarded deaf-blind children.
Trained 9 profoundly retarded deaf-blind children (mean age 14.3 yrs) to initiate and execute toileting activities independently. The training procedure included increasing the Ss' intake of liquid, food reduction, positive reinforcement for independent

and partially independent toileting as well as for remaining dry between toileting actions, punishment for pants wetting, limitation of environmental stimulation, and increasing distance between Ss' position and toilet bowl. All Ss were able to achieve independence, and the rate of accidents dropped to zero. The acquired skills were also displayed for that part of the day during which training was not applied and were retained, with the exception of 1 case, after the intervention was discontinued. (9 ref)
Lancioni, Giulio E. (Katholieke U Nijmegen, Inst of Orthopedagogics, Netherlands) Behavior Therapy, 1980(Mar), Vol 11(2), 234–244. [PA, Vol 63:10201]

2781. Response-contingent taste-aversion in treating chronic ruminative vomiting of institutionalised profoundly retarded children.
In 2 experiments, a 16-yr-old (Exp I) and a 12-yr-old (Exp II) were treated with lemon juice and/or Tabasco sauce. Each program eliminated rumination, with effects maintained 1–9 mo following treatment. For the S who exhibited major weight-loss prior to intervention, substantial weight gain was also demonstrated. (24 ref)
Marholin, David; Luiselli, James K.; Robinson, Margaret & Lott, Ira T. Journal of Mental Deficiency Research, 1980(Mar), Vol 24(1), 47–56. [PA, Vol 66:06347]

2782. Treatment of compulsive hand in mouth behaviour in a profoundly retarded child using a sharp pinch as the aversive stimulus.
Results from a 13-yr-old profoundly retarded girl show that a sharp pinch on the back of the hand, contingent upon hand-in-mouth behavior was an economical and effective aversive stimulus in a program that successfully reduced compulsive hand-in-mouth behavior related to vomiting and rumination over a 3-mo period. (16 ref)
Minness, Patricia M. (York U, Downsview, Canada) Australian Journal of Developmental Disabilities, 1980(Mar), Vol 6(1), 5–10. [PA, Vol 66:08540]

2783. An interlocking progressive-ratio procedure for determining the reinforcer preferences of multihandicapped children.
It is important to those working directly with retarded populations to be able to successfully identify strong reinforcers for these persons. Data are presented demonstrating that an interlocking progressive-ratio schedule of reinforcement can be used to determine reinforcement preference for severely retarded children. Five multihandicapped students (aged 10.8–18.4 yrs) were assessed across 6 stimulus events. The 2 severely retarded Ss preferred visual reinforcers to both tactile and auditory reinforcers. The 3 profoundly retarded Ss did not exhibit preferences among the reinforcers. The significance of the differences in performance generated by the 2 groups is discussed. (18 ref)
Nunes, Dennis L.; Murphy, Robert J. & Doughty, Neil R. (St Cloud State U) Behavior Research of Severe Developmental Disabilities, 1980(Nov), Vol 1(3), 161–174. [PA, Vol 66:08545]

2784. Social milieu of a residential treatment center for severely or profoundly handicapped young children.
39 severely or profoundly handicapped young children who lived in a residential treatment center were Ss in a modified time-sampled observation study of social behavior, state, and physical context. The study was conducted for 3 successive years. Although system-level changes in the ecology of the institution over the 3 yrs did not appear to affect the social-interaction indices, the developmental ages of the Ss were positively related to social opportunities and social behavior. (16 ref)
Reuter, Jeanette; Archer, Frances M.; Dunn, Virginia & White, Colleen. (Kent State U, First Chance Project/Outreach) American Journal of Mental Deficiency, 1980(Jan), Vol 84(4), 367–372. [PA, Vol 63:08198]

2785. Prerequisite vs. *in vivo* acquisition of self-feeding skill.
Separating the acquisition of prerequisite skills from the learning of skills in vivo may be a more efficacious procedure for self-help training of low-functioning developmentally delayed children. Two procedures for training independent use of a fork at meals

were compared with 6 96–144 mo old severely and profoundly retarded Ss in 2 groups. Using previously accepted procedures, control Ss were trained during meals while experimental Ss received prerequisite training making use of simulated food (styrofoam pieces). Data were collected during training, generalization-to-meal, and follow-up. For 6 mo following training, the efficacy of prerequisite training was upheld. The complexity of individual responses to the singular or conjunctive use of social and edible reinforcement for self-feeding skill generalization and maintenance is discussed. (16 ref)
Richman, Joel S.; Sonderby, Tina & Kahn, James V. (U Illinois, Chicago Circle) Behaviour Research & Therapy, 1980, Vol 18(4), 327–332. [PA, Vol 64:13016]

2786. Music listening versus juice as a reinforcement for learning in profoundly mentally retarded individuals.
Motivation and rewards are 2 phases of learning wherever it takes place. Research with 12 profoundly retarded Ss demonstrates the difficulty of choosing any one reinforcer. The difference between music and juice as reinforcers was not statistically significant. Psychologically, "reward" itself should be considered the factor that affects learning. The result could predictably be similar at other intellectual levels. The confounding factor to definitive research is the wide variety of personal preferences for the rewards tested. (26 ref)
Saperston, Bruce M.; Chan, Ruby; Morphew, Christy & Carsrud, Karen B. Journal of Music Therapy, 1980(Win), Vol 17(4), 174–183. [PA, Vol 66:10899]

2787. The effects of facial screening on infant self-injury.
Treated an 11-mo-old mildly microcephalic, severely retarded male who bit his thumb to the bone by facial screening, covering his face with a terrycloth bib for about 3 sec contingent on thumb-biting. Self-injury was rapidly suppressed; monthly follow-ups for 12 mo showed that improvement was maintained. Results suggest that facial screening may be useful in certain cases of self-injurious behavior when other techniques cannot be used for ethical or pragmatic reasons. (14 ref)
Singh, Nirbhay N. (Mangere Hosp & Training School, Auckland, New Zealand) Journal of Behavior Therapy & Experimental Psychiatry, 1980(Jun), Vol 11(2), 131–134. [PA, Vol 66:06363]

2788. Self-injury in the profoundly retarded: Clinically significant versus therapeutic control.
In the 1st of 2 experiments with profoundly retarded girls, response-contingent aromatic ammonia was used to reduce the high frequency of face-slapping and face-hitting in a 15-yr-old deaf, blind S. In Exp II, an overcorrection procedure was used to control jaw-hitting in a 16-yr-old. These treatments resulted in near-zero levels of self-injury. (25 ref)
Singh, Nirbhay N.; Dawson, Maryan J. & Gregory, P. R. (Mangere Hosp & Training School, Auckland, New Zealand) Journal of Mental Deficiency Research, 1980(Jun), Vol 24(2), 87–97. [PA, Vol 66:08558]

2789. Transfer of instructional control from loud tone to normal tone in profoundly retarded adolescents.
Three profoundly retarded adolescents (CAs 13–16 yrs; MA less than 2 yrs) did not respond to verbal instructions unless the instructions were presented very loudly (shouted). A time-delay procedure was used for the transferring of a limited set of verbal instructions in all 3 Ss from loud tone to normal tone control. The normal tone control training for each instruction consisted of establishing loud tone control by means of differential reinforcement procedures. Thereafter, normal tone control training trials consisted of 2 presentations—a normal tone presentation (1st) and a loud tone presentation (2nd) of the same instruction. The time-delay between the 2 presentations was increased systematically from 0 sec to a maximum of 10 sec. All Ss learned to follow the normal tone instructions after the time-delay procedure had been introduced. Transfer from loud tone to normal tone control or from one normal tone instruction to another was not observed. By contrast, transfer did occur across people and settings. (20 ref)

Smeets, Paul M. & Striefel, Sebastian. (State U of Leiden, Netherlands) Behavior Research of Severe Developmental Disabilities, 1980(Oct), Vol 1(2), 105–121. [PA, Vol 66:08559]

2790. Assessment and selection of leisure skills for severely handicapped individuals.
Describes leisure skill competency areas that can be assessed in severely handicapped individuals: proficiency with which objects or materials are engaged, length of self-initiated action, material preferences, and the frequency and direction of social interactions. Guidelines for selecting leisure skills are presented. (29 ref)
Wehman, Paul & Schleien, Stuart. (Virginia Commonwealth U, Div of Educational Services) Education & Training of the Mentally Retarded, 1980(Feb), Vol 15(1), 50–57. [PA, Vol 65:11245]

2791. Training eye-pointing behavior in a nonambulatory profoundly mentally retarded child using contingent vibratory stimulation.
Used contingent vibration to train a precommunication response in a spastic-quadriplegic profoundly mentally retarded 11-yr-old male. Results indicate an increase in S's eye-pointing behavior subsequent to the administration of response contingent vibration. (6 ref)
Zucker, Stanley H.; D'Alonzo, Bruno J.; McMullen, Michael R. & Williams, Ronald L. (Arizona State U, Tempe) Education & Training of the Mentally Retarded, 1980(Feb), Vol 15(1), 4–7. [PA, Vol 65:10940]

2792. Teaching three severely retarded children to follow instructions.
An analysis of teaching simple instruction-following behavior was completed with 3 6–14 yr old Ss (MA $\leq$ 2 yrs 5 mo) with Down's syndrome. Two approaches were compared to determine the extent to which they yielded effective instructional control. One involved the continual use of a model: the other involved withdrawing the model following its initial use in training. In comparing the effects of the 2 approaches, an alternating treatments design was applied within a multiple baseline. Results indicate that Ss did not consistently follow those instructions taught with continual modeling. Ss did follow those instructions trained with the modeling component discontinued. Findings suggest that modeling should be discontinued when teaching instruction-following behavior to severely retarded children. (23 ref)
DeHaven, Everett. (State of Kansas Social & Rehabilitation Services, Kansas Neurological Inst, Topeka) Education & Training of the Mentally Retarded, 1981(Feb), Vol 16(1), 36–48. [PA, Vol 66:08981]

2793. A follow-up of severely and profoundly mentally retarded children after short-term institutionalization.
Conducted a follow-up study of 100 mentally retarded children (average MA 18.78 mo; average CA 8.62 yrs) after an average of 10.5 mo of institutionalization. Ss were administered the American Association on Mental Deficiency Adaptive Behavior Scale. It is concluded that the institutional/training experience seems to lead some parents to keep their child at home and others to place their child in an institution on a long-term basis, contrary to early plans and intent. (1 ref)
Ellis, Norman R.; Bostick, George E.; Moore, Sheila A. & Taylor, Janine J. (U Alabama, University) Mental Retardation, 1981(Feb), Vol 19(1), 31–35. [PA, Vol 66:08690]

2794. Nonexclusionary timeout: Maintenance of appropriate behavior across settings.
Sought to (a) replicate the findings of R. M. Foxx and S. T. Shapiro (see PA, Vol 61:11353), (b) examine the utility of modifying the basic reinforcement schedule of the original study, and (c) demonstrate control across settings and maladaptive behaviors using a multiple baseline design. S was a 19-yr-old severely retarded male. Findings indicate that a signaled timeout can be employed successfully in more than 1 setting and that it can be used in conjunction with DRO reinforcement schedule. (20 ref)

Huguenin, Nancy H. & Mulick, James A. (U Massachusetts, Amherst) Applied Research in Mental Retardation, 1981, Vol 2(1), 55–67. [PA, Vol 66:10880]

2795. Evaluating a supervision program for developing and maintaining therapeutic staff–resident interactions during institutional care routines.
Evaluated a program to teach and maintain language training interactions between institutional staff and 5 profoundly handicapped children (3–7 yrs old). Following baseline observations of bath sessions, staff were sequentially taught to vocalize more during the bath, praise child vocalizations, imitate sounds, and provide sound prompts. Procedures included a brief in-service meeting followed by a series of supervisory prompts and feedback. Results indicate that staff acquired the interaction skills in the bath sessions and that the skills generalized to another direct care task, dressing. The number of days on which components of supervision were implemented decreased from 47% of all days during the experimental conditions to 19% of the days during a 19-wk maintenance period, with no decrease in staff behavior. The interactions did not interfere with the quality of the direct care task or increase the time necessary to complete it. Some increases were noted for child vocalization frequencies. (36 ref)
Ivancic, Martin T. et al. Journal of Applied Behavior Analysis, 1981(Spr), Vol 14(1), 95–107. [PA, Vol 66:08694]

2796. A comparison of sign and verbal language training with nonverbal and retarded children.
12 nonverbal, hearing, retarded children (mean CA 69 mo; IQs below 20) were matched and assigned to sign language training, speech training, and placebo groups. Results indicated no significant difference between the verbal and sign language groups, though the sign and verbal groups learned significantly more than the placebo group. Findings are interpreted as indicating that some nonverbal retarded children will benefit more from sign language than speech training. (29 ref)
Kahn, James V. (U Illinois, Chicago Circle) Journal of Speech & Hearing Research, 1981(Mar), Vol 24(1), 113–119. [PA, Vol 66:13365]

2797. Improving needed food intake of profoundly handicapped children through effective supervision of institutional staff.
Evaluated a program to increase the prescribed food intake of 2 profoundly mentally retarded males, CAs 4 yrs 5 mo and 5 yrs 10 mo, by improving institutional staff performance. The supervision program, consisting of a brief inservice followed by a series of supervisory prompts, supervisory feedback, and staff self-recording was implemented with 11 18–52 yr old staff members. Using a multiple baseline design, the program appeared effective in increasing the intake of targeted food categories for both Ss at supper and lunch. (24 ref)
Korabek, Cynthia A.; Reid, Dennis H. & Ivancic, Martin T. (Northern Indiana State Hosp & Developmental Disabilities Ctr, South Bend) Applied Research in Mental Retardation, 1981, Vol 2(1), 69–88. [PA, Vol 66:11010]

2798. Application of contingent physical restraint to suppress stereotyped body rocking of profoundly mentally retarded persons.
Investigated the effectiveness of contingent restraint in reducing stereotyped body rocking of 7 profoundly retarded Ss (8.75–31.75 yrs) to determine (a) whether restraint reduced stereotyped body rocking and (b) the degree to which the effectiveness of restraint depended on where in the behavioral sequence it was administered. Results show that restraint reduced the amount of body rocking and was judged to be generally more effective if applied when the S was bent over in the middle of the response sequence rather than when S was sitting upright at the end of the response sequence. Results are interpreted in terms of response chaining and postural feedback. Implications for the utilization of physical restraint as a behavioral intervention are discussed. (24 ref)

Reid, J. Gordon; Tombaugh, Tom N. & Heuvel, Kees V. (Carleton U, Ottowa, Canada) American Journal of Mental Deficiency, 1981(Jul), Vol 86(1), 78–85. [PA, Vol 66:08551]

2799. Stimulus control of stereotypic responding: Effects on target and collateral behavior.
Established inhibitory stimulus control over stereotypic responding of 2 profoundly retarded adults (19- and 28-yr-old males). Discrimination training using the overcorrection technique was carried out under conditions where a light on one end of a series of 5 lights signaled the presence of the punishment contingency and the light on the other end signaled nonpunishment. Tests for generalization of inhibition were made to all 5 lights in the series, resulting in generalization gradients. A multiple-baseline procedure was employed in which both target (punished) and nontarget stereotypies were recorded. Steep generalization gradients were obtained, indicating that Ss were able to make sharp discriminations between safe and unsafe conditions. Deceleration of the target stereotypy was accompanied by marked increases in rates of nonpunished stereotypies. Orderly generalization gradients were obtained for the collateral behavior as well. (27 ref)
Rollings, J. Paul & Baumeister, Alfred A. (U Alabama) American Journal of Mental Deficiency, 1981(Jul), Vol 86(1), 67–77. [PA, Vol 66:08553]

2800. Home intervention with parents of severely subnormal pre-school children: A final report.
Two experimental groups of a total of 32 severely subnormal preschool children, 1 visited individually at 2-wk intervals and 1 at 8-wk intervals, were compared with a 3rd distal contrast group of 15 Ss who received no intervention. Analyses of successive IQ changes, measured by the Cattell Infant Intelligence Scale and the Vineland Social Maturity Scale, in all 3 groups showed that the less frequently visited group made greater progress after 2 yrs but that this difference disappeared after 3 yrs. The contrast nonintervention group made fewer gains overall than the 2 experimental groups. Four questions are discussed: the maintenance of early gains, the influence of social class, the optimal level of intervention, and the meaning of successful intervention to parents. (7 ref)
Sandow, S. A.; Clarke, A. D.; Cox, M. V. & Stewart, F. L. (West London Inst of Education, England) Child Care, Health & Development, 1981(May–Jun), Vol 7(3), 135–144. [PA, Vol 66:13661]

2801. Effects of thioridazine dosage on the behavior of severely mentally retarded persons.
Conducted a double-blind, placebo-controlled trial of thioridazine (1.28–17.54 mg/kg) with 20 severely retarded patients (mean CA 15.7 yrs). Ss were assessed on a relatively low standardized dose (2.5 mg/kg) as well as on the individual dosage that had previously been determined clinically as most effective. Both active drug conditions caused a reduction in hyperactivity, bizarre behavior, and self-stimulation. The standardized dose, which was less than half the mean titrated level, resulted in an equivalent therapeutic response. The need for more attention to dosage levels in future investigations is emphasized. (28 ref)
Singh, Nirbhay N. & Aman, Michael G. American Journal of Mental Deficiency, 1981(May), Vol 85(6), 580–587. [PA, Vol 66:06409]

2802. Training severely and profoundly mentally handicapped nocturnal enuretics.
Describes a feasible program for the treatment of nocturnal enuresis in the institutionalized mentally handicapped, using an enuresis alarm in conjunction with increased fluids, rewards for dryness, and some punishments for wetness. Five severely and profoundly mentally handicapped Ss (mean CA 19 yrs; mean MA 3 yrs) were successfully trained over periods of 18–92 wks. (26 ref)
Smith, Linda J. (Northumberland Area Psychology Service, Prudhoe Hosp, England) Behaviour Research & Therapy, 1981, Vol 19(1), 67–74. [PA, Vol 65:08514]

2803. Increase in adaptive behavior level after residence in an intermediate care facility for mentally retarded persons.
Residence for approximately 10 mo in an Intermediate Care Facility for the Mentally Retarded (ICF/MR) led to a substantial increase in the adaptive behavior level of 95 14–46 yr old severely and profoundly mentally retarded (Vineland Social Maturity Scale scores 1.62–2.01) former residents of a large state institution. Certain advantages provided by ICF/MR residence that could have provided this increase are discussed (e.g., improved environmental conditions and training) along with other variables. (17 ref)
Witt, Sandra J. (Sunland Ctr, Gainesville, FL) Mental Retardation, 1981(Apr), Vol 19(2), 75–79. [PA, Vol 66:08717]

Educational Issues

Autism

2804. Recent innovations in teaching the autistic child.
Discusses several hypotheses which have been advanced to explain the cause of autism including: (a) psychogenic causation; (b) a predisposition of the autistic child to instability or an unusually developed sensitivity that requires more maternal care; (c) a biological cause, e.g., a rare recessive gene; and (d) perceptual inconsistency. Recent programs and studies dealing with autism are reported. Programs discussed include those: (a) "based on the assumption that autism is a disorder which pervades the entire range of ego functioning, the child having problems with speech, language, and general communication"; (b) teaching reading to autistic children; and (c) teaching reading using programmed instructional materials. Studies discussed include: (a) an attempt to determine if the autistic child's language development revealed any features distinctive from that of the normal child; (b) an attempt to develop speech in a 4½-yr-old boy; (c) compliance and resistance and using operant conditioning procedures to teach; (d) using a behavior modification approach; and (e) determining the effect of auditory control on operant behavior in mute autistic children. Many schools and institutes are attempting to develop more effective methods for helping these children in school settings. "The prognosis for children with infantile autism looks somewhat better today than in the past."
Mordock, John B. (Astor Home for Children & Astor Guidance Center, Rhinebeck, N.Y.) Devereux Schools Forum, 1970(Fal), Vol. 6(1), 3-15. [PA, Vol 48:01351]

2805. Emotional characteristics of learning disability.
Studied 3rd and 4th graders to explore relationships between emotional disturbance and learning disability. 226 Ss, rigidly defined and selected as having a learning disability, were compared with a control group of 168. Factorial analysis of variance disclosed that Ss with learning disabilities exhibited greater emotional stress on only 4 out of 14 scores on the Children's Personality Questionnaire. Despite marked deficiencies in verbal learning and cognitive functions, they were comparable to normal Ss in emotional status. It is suggested that deficits in social (nonverbal) perception may be more critical to the onset of autism. Further implications for the study of autism are made by questioning the validity of equating learning disabilities with emotional disturbance. (18 ref.)
Myklebust, Helmer R.; Killen, James & Bannochie, Margaret. (U. Illinois, Chicago) Journal of Autism & Childhood Schizophrenia, 1972(Apr), Vol. 2(2), 151-159. [PA, Vol 50:11558]

2806. Special educational treatment of autistic children: A comparative study: I. Design of study and characteristics of units.
Conducted a follow-up study over a 3½-4 yr period, with 50 autistic children (age at outset = 3.5-15 yrs) attending 3 different special units, to assess changes in educational, cognitive, linguistic, social, and behavioral status. The units varied in

amount of structure and orientation to educational goals. Details of the study design, methods used, and results of an objective examination of staff behavior in the 3 units are described. Results demonstrate significant differences in the amount and character of staff interactions with children, both between units and between individual staff. (27 ref.)
Bartak, Lawrence & Rutter, Michael. (U. London, Inst. of Psychiatry, England) Journal of Child Psychology & Psychiatry & Allied Disciplines, 1973(Sep), Vol. 14(3), 161-179. [PA, Vol 51:05788]

2807. Immediacy of feedback: Its effects on academic performance.
Compared the effectiveness of immediate vs end-of-task consequation. S was an autistic, mentally retarded 6-yr-old male. The task was to draw a line for dot-to-dot in an appropriate sequence from 1-22. The numbers were separated into 3 groups, and considered a multiple base line design with each group available for comparison. Scoring was correct minus incorrect. During the base-line phase, the S received feedback for each response only after the entire task was completed. In the immediate consequation phase, feedback was administered immediately after each response. Results show that immediate consequation is more effective. However, only moderate generalization is indicated across groups of numbers. Improvements seemed to be short-lived. It is concluded that effectiveness of end-of-task is questionable, and that effort should be made to provide immediate consequation with similar Ss.
Harrison, Darryll R. (Western Michigan U.) SALT: School Applications of Learning Theory, 1973(Mar), Vol. 5(2), 4-14. [PA, Vol 51:07279]

2808. On structuring a lesson.
Discusses the needs of seriously handicapped brain-damaged and autistic children who require that a teacher provide a highly structured lesson and environment. The elements which contribute to a well-organized lesson and the factors which might militate against a good lesson are outlined. It is suggested that less handicapped children could benefit from a modification of the same structuring procedures, adapted to their levels of disability and strengths.
Lettick, Amy. Journal of Learning Disabilities, 1973(Jan), Vol. 6(1), 10-15. [PA, Vol 50:03522]

2809. The case for "special" children.
Describes procedures used in acclimating children with emotional problems to a new environment. At the special school, autistic children have individual one-to-one teachers. Overall teacher ratio is 8:1 with the average child obtaining 15 hrs of schooling per week. Emphasis is on children doing things to feel good about themselves before development of cognitive abilities.
Lewis, Eleanore G. (Lexington Nursery & Kindergarten School, Mass.) Young Children, 1973(Aug), Vol. 28(6), 369-374. [PA, Vol 52:01871]

2810. Special educational treatment of autistic children: A comparative study: II. Follow-up findings and implications for services.
50 autistic children (7-9 yrs old at the beginning of the study) attending 3 different special units were followed up over a 3½-4 yr period to assess changes in educational, cognitive, linguistic, social, and behavioral status. Tests employed included the Merrill-Palmer Scale of Mental Tests and the Performance scale of the WISC. The group as a whole had made considerable progress in all spheres and it is concluded that the results amply justify the provisions of special education for autistic children. Comparisons between the units suggests that large amounts of specific teaching in a well-controlled classroom situation is likely to bring the greatest benefits in terms of scholastic progress. Findings are used to consider a variety of specific questions in relation to the optimum types of schooling required for autistic children. (25 ref)
Rutter, Michael & Bartak, Lawrence. (Inst. of Psychiatry, U. London, England) Journal of Child Psychology & Psychiatry &

Allied Disciplines, 1973(Dec), Vol. 14(4), 241-270. [PA, Vol 51:11988]

2811. Programming for severely disturbed youngsters in a public school.
Describes a program for autistic or schizophrenic children based on behavior modification theories. After a child is admitted to the program, a prescription is formulated detailing individualized instruction. Prescriptions are regularly reviewed, and revised or replaced as needed. Samples of improved behavior are given.
Carter, Ronald D. & Poeschel, Susan M. (U Wisconsin, Oshkosh) SALT: School Applications of Learning Theory, 1974(Apr), Vol 6(3), 39-42. [PA, Vol 53:01966]

2812. Special education as the basic therapeutic tool in treatment of severely disturbed children.
Describes a school which initiated a therapeutic approach in 1953 for autistic, schizophrenic, and psychotic children by substituting the special day school for the mental hospital. The staff viewed the disturbances of these children as disorders of the CNS that resulted in severe cognitive and language deficits; not as disorders caused by parental mishandling. Diagnostic labels were discarded and replaced by an interdisciplinary psychoeducational assessment of each child's strengths and deficits. Each child's individualized program has short- and long-range goals aimed at achieving the highest possible academic or vocational placement. Children who make no academic progress are trained in life skills to prepare them for community living. This program of special education succeeded in advancing many children to regular or special classes in the public schools, to jobs, and to more meaningful and useful lives.
Fenichel, Carl. (League School, Brooklyn, NY) Journal of Autism & Childhood Schizophrenia, 1974(Mar), Vol 4(2), 177-186. [PA, Vol 56:10743]

2813. Treatment of psychotic children in a classroom environment: I. Learning in a large group.
Investigated the feasibility of modifying the behavior of autistic children in a classroom environment. In Exp I, 8 autistic children were taught certain basic classroom behaviors, assumed to be necessary for subsequent learning to take place in the classroom, in one-to-one sessions. However, behaviors taught in a one-to-one setting were not performed consistently in a classroom-sized group, or even in a group as small as 2 children with 1 teacher, and the Ss evidenced no acquisition of new behaviors in a classroom environment over a 4-wk period. Therefore, Exp II introduced a treatment procedure based upon "fading in" the classroom stimulus situation from the one-to-one stimulus situation. Such treatment was highly effective in producing both a transfer in stimulus control and the acquisition of new behaviors in a kindergarten 1st-grade classroom environment. (30 ref)
Koegel, Robert L. & Rincover, Arnold. (U. California, Inst. of Applied Behavioral Science, Santa Barbara) Journal of Applied Behavior Analysis, 1974(Spr), Vol. 7(1), 45-59. [PA, Vol 52:08339]

2814. [Research on adjustment in groups of autistic children.] (Japn)
Investigated the adjustment of 13 Japanese autistic children to participation in groups in kindergarten or elementary school for periods of over a year, using at the end of each term (a) Nagoya University Autistic Child's Developmental Scale (NAUDS) and (b) Nagoya University Autistic Child's Adjustment Scale (NAGA). The former is a 5-point rating scale classifying 11 features of autistic behavior on a diagrammatic profile; the latter is a rating of adjustment based on teacher's description of child's behavior in groups. Results indicate that adjustment to groups is not always improved with increasing CA but depends on features of child's syndrome. It is predicted that group experiences will be more effective for those who have developed beyond the 3rd stage (a measure of individual initiative) on the NAUDS. Numerous benefits to autistic children from group participation are described. However, it has no effect on stereotyped behavior, perseveration, or pathological language. (English summary)

Marui, Fumio et al. Bulletin of the Faculty of Education, U. Nagoya, 1974(Jul), Vol 21, 105-150. [PA, Vol 58:09654]

2815. [A study of children in special classes: A discussion in relation to mental deficiency.] (Fren)
Explored the traditional criteria of mental deficiency continuing other work carried out by the same group of workers on different types of severe intellectual deficiency. Results demonstrated the complexity and diversity of the progressive structural traits that the usual classifications do not take into account in slightly deficient children. (German & Spanish summaries)
Misès, R.; Breon, S. & Fuchs, F. Revue de Neuropsychiatrie Infantile et d'Hygiene Mentale de l'Enfance, 1974(Jul-Aug), Vol 22(7–8), 457-502. [PA, Vol 56:04918]

2816. The musical life of an autistic boy.
A hyperactive 8-yr-old autistic male who had exceptional musical ability and absolute pitch but who was unable to read music was given training in several aspects of music in individual lessons 2 or 3 times/wk during a 4-yr period. He now reads piano music moderately well and can read melodies and accompany himself with chords at the piano. His behavior improved steadily as he became more competent in musical activities, and his ability to concentrate improved as he was brought to read music and perform it in rhythm without letting his attention wander. His comprehension of music was aided considerably by practice in taking dictation and learning to write the notes of the melodies with the correct rhythmic values.
O'Connell, Thomas S. (Marshall U) Journal of Autism & Childhood Schizophrenia, 1974(Sep), Vol 4(3), 223-229. [PA, Vol 56:10040]

2817. Key variables determining the acquisition of speech by autistic five year olds.
Utilized a teaching program to assist 2 5-yr-old autistic-type males in developing speech and making other improvements in their condition. In addition to lacking speech ability, both Ss showed an inability to develop interpersonal relations and scored in the range of possible autism on the Rimland Check List for Behavior Disturbed Children (Form E2) and the Sameness Questionnaire of M. Prior and M. B. MacMillan (1973). The program was designed to (a) establish a warm helping relationship with each child; (b) reduce hyperactivity while taking the associated "figure-ground" problem into account; (c) provide fine and gross motor training linked to language training (e.g., drawing and letter matching); (d) help the socialization of Ss by engaging them in simple physical activities (e.g., walks and ball throwing exercises); and (e) provide language and speech training, involving the naming of stimuli and the formation of simple sentences. One S acquired normal speech, but the other did not, and a possible explanation of this differential response to the program is offered in terms of differences in the stimulation and support provided by their home environments. (34 ref)
Rees, R. J. (Canberra Coll of Advanced Education, Australia) Exceptional Child, 1975(Nov), Vol 22(3), 159–172. [PA, Vol 59:11155]

2818. A multi-axial classification for the education of autistic children.
Suggests that the term "education of autistic children" is too broad and should be dropped from the vocabulary of multidisciplinary care for the handicapped. Following the World Health Organization tri-axial classification of mental disorders, complementary axes are offered upon which a child broadly classified as autistic might be more accurately assessed and that would facilitate a specific educational approach. The diagnostic differentiation into Kanner and Mahler syndromes is accepted as the basis for these axes. (21 ref)
Dyer, Christopher & Hadden, Angela J. (Whitefield School, Dept for Non-communicating Children, London, England) Child Care, Health & Development, 1976(May-Jun), Vol 2(3) 155-164. [PA, Vol 56:08764]

2819. [Teaching children with autistic-syndrome in a special school for trainable mentally retarded children.] (Germ)
Findings of a 4-yr program for autistic children in a school for the trainable mentally retarded show that children with severe early infantile autism and in some cases with brain damage can be adequately helped in such a setting. Isolated therapy of single symptom complexes (e.g., speech and perception) does not do justice to the autistic child. More important for the first special educational help for these children are elements of nondirective therapy, play therapy that is based on psychoanalysis, and behavior therapy according to the individual needs of the child. Autistic isolation may be overcome if autistic and other trainable children, who are less emotionally disturbed, are taught together. (71 ref)
Feuser, Georg. Praxis der Kinderpsychologie und Kinderpsychiatrie, 1976(Feb–Mar), Vol 25(2), 57–67. [PA, Vol 65:04158]

2820. Systematic observation of classroom behavior of retarded and autistic preschool children.
Observed 6 autistic Ss (mean CA, 44.7 mo; mean MA, 24.3 mo) and 6 retarded Ss (mean CA, 56.2 mo; mean MA, 27.5 mo) for 7 20-min sessions. The following environmental parameters were manipulated: teacher-to-child ratio, presence of food reinforcement, and skill area being presented. Behavior under observation fell into 3 classes: adaptive performance (percentage response and percentage correct), attention, and maladaptive behavior. Results suggest that food reinforcement and the 1:1 teacher-to-child ratio may not generally enhance adaptive performance but may have an effect upon attention and tantrum behavior; attention to task is more predictive of adaptive behavior than attention to teacher; and interactions were generally lacking between the above parameters and diagnostic group, while level of functioning did show such interactions. Results support the practice of individual behavioral assessment of autistic and retarded children. The present procedure, coupled with statistical analysis for individual Ss, may provide educational prescriptions for individual children. (1 p ref)
Frankel, Fred & Graham, Vicki. (U California, Los Angeles) American Journal of Mental Deficiency, 1976(Jul), vol 81(1), 73-84. [PA, Vol 56:10744]

2821. Alternative to therapy: Garden Program.
Suggests, on the basis of a questionnaire study, that there are beneficial effects from including a gardening program in the school curriculum for emotionally disturbed, autistic, and mentally retarded children. Changes were reported in self-awareness, self-esteem, responsibility, practical knowledge, work concepts, and communication skills.
Kaiser, Marge. (Novato Human Needs Ctr, CA) Journal of Clinical Child Psychology, 1976(Fal), Vol 5(2), 21–24. [PA, Vol 62:02288]

2822. The development and functional control of reading-comprehension behavior.
Reading comprehension, indicated by motor behavior and multiple-choice picture selection called for in written instructions, was taught to an autistic 12-yr-old girl, using verbal prompts, modelling, and physical guidance. S was rewarded for correct behaviors to training items; nonrewarded probes were used to assess generalization. Probable maintaining events were assessed through their sequential removal in a reversal design. Results show that (a) following acquisition, performance was maintained at a near-100% level when candy, praise, attention, and training were removed; (b) absence of other persons was correlated with a marked decrease in performance, whereas their presence was associated with performance at near 100%; and (c) performance generalized to probes and across experimenters. Rewards, which may have been reinforcing during acquisition, did not appear necessary to maintain later performance. Instead, presence of others (a setting event) was demonstrated to have control over maintained performance. (19 ref)
Rosenbaum, Michael S. & Breiling, James. (Georgia State U) Journal of Applied Behavior Analysis, 1976(Fal), Vol 9(3), 323-333. [PA, Vol 57:06364]

2823. An observational investigation of two elementary-age autistic children during free-play.
Used 2 observational systems (Social Interaction and Behavior Repertoire) to measure the behavior patterns of 2 autistic children (1 male and 1 female, 9 and 8 yrs old) and their classroom peers during a free-play period. Results obtained from the total Behavior Repertoire system indicate that the Ss spent the majority of the free-play period manipulating various toys and objects. Data obtained from the Social Interaction system revealed that Ss' encounters with peers typically were negative. Additionally, Ss were observed to respond more frequently to vocal-verbal social behavior by peers, than they were to motor-gestural responses. The observational methodology employed and the results obtained are discussed in terms of their significance for the clinical treatment of autistic behavior, and the evaluation of such treatment. (19 ref)
Strain, Phillip S. & Cooke, Thomas P. (American U) Psychology in the Schools, 1976(Jan), Vol 13(1), 82-91. [PA, Vol 56:06179]

2824. A multielement design model for component analysis and cross-setting assessment of a treatment package.
The applied problem necessitating this design was a cross-setting and component analysis of a special school's natural treatment package for an 8.5-yr-old autistic boy's self-stimulatory behavior. The S's school day was viewed as a multielement baseline with 4 alternating elements—classroom, play area, small room, and large room—each with a different procedure. Conditions were held constant in the classroom and the play area, the normal school settings, so that manipulations for this one S did not disrupt the rest of the class. Components of the treatment package were manipulated in 2 experimental settings designated as small and large rooms. The design allowed (a) reversal comparisons of procedures (experimental rooms) over time, and (b) daily comparisons of procedures across all 4 settings (multielement baseline). The assumption that procedures in the natural and the experimental settings were comparable was supported by the findings that the behavioral effects were comparable in natural and experimental settings when corresponding procedures were in effect. It is concluded that daily comparisons of the multielement baseline seem most desirable when the applied problem requires comparison of several procedures and settings (e.g., component and cross-setting analyses) and as a result, when the possibility of time-correlated artifacts is greatest.
Bittle, Ron & Hake, Don F. (Anna Mental Health & Development Ctr, IL) Behavior Therapy, 1977(Nov), Vol 8(5), 906–914. [PA, Vol 60:08282]

2825. Development of communicative behavior in autistic children: A parent program using signed speech.
Studied the value of a parents' signed-speech program to aid the development of appropriate communicative behavior and to deter ritualistic and disruptive motor behavior of autistic children. Mothers of 4 autistic classmates (aged 6 and 7 yrs) used manual signs in conjunction with verbalizations to extend a group-oriented classroom program into the home. After a baseline period, experimental treatments were initiated using a multiple baseline design. Children were encouraged and reinforced for using either or both forms of communication. Results indicate improvement of communicative behavior in each child's total environment. Observations indicate that ritualistic and destructive behavior was practically eliminated in all of the children without direct treatment. The manual signs made an acceptable motor behavior readily available to replace undesirable and nonreinforced behavior, and they also served as visual prompts for attending and responding behavior. (17 ref)
Casey, LaDeane. (Human Resource Assoc, Tempe, AZ) Devereux Forum, 1977(Sum), Vol 12(1), 1–15. [PA, Vol 61:07289]

2826. Effects of social deprivation upon operant behavior in mentally retarded and autistic children.
Made repeated observations of the reinforcer effectiveness of voice recordings of the judged preferred teacher of 16 retarded and autistic children (54–140 mo old). Observations were conducted under typical classroom conditions or after more than 24 hrs in which each S was deprived of the attention of the judged preferred teacher. Results demonstrate that (a) deprivation increased the rate of response with played back voice recordings; (b) the response rate increase came from sources other than the information value of social reinforcement, novelty, or anxiety; and (c) autistic and retarded Ss showed equivalent effects of the experimental manipulations. Implications for the nature of social reinforcement and deficits in autistic children are discussed. (17 ref)
Frankel, Fred; Simmons, James Q. & Olson, Sandra. (U California, Los Angeles) Journal of Pediatric Psychology, 1977, Vol 2(4), 172–175. [PA, Vol 62:07343]

2827. A new look at childhood autism: School–parent collaboration.
Describes problems of families with autistic children and the school's relationships with these families. Suggestions are made for school–parent collaboration in managing the child and problems such as the family's guilt, withdrawal, frustration, and lack of understanding. Parent discussion groups, social events for parents and the autistic child, individual conferences, and referral to community agencies are ways the schools can assist these families. A program that involves parents as well as professionals in every aspect of diagnosis and treatment is described. It is based on the concept that human growth may be interrupted or delayed at one of several points. Remediation of specific areas of developmental delay is the basis of the educational therapeutic program.
Kelley, John B. & Samuels, Marian. (Brentwood Ctr for Educational Therapy, Pacific Palisades, CA) Journal of School Health, 1977(Nov), Vol 47(9), 538–540. [PA, Vol 65:12918]

2828. Assessing and training teachers in the generalized use of behavior modification with autistic children.
Investigated the feasibility of developing reliable, valid criteria for measuring and training the skills necessary to teach autistic children. The behaviors of 11 teachers (10 of whom were under age 30) and 12 autistic 5–13 yr olds were recorded in a series of different teaching situations. Teacher-training was initiated at different times for different teachers. Results show the following: (a) It was possible to assess empirically whether a teacher was correctly using defined behavior-modification techniques. (b) Generally, for any given session, systematic improvement in the child's behavior did not occur unless the teacher working in that session had been trained to use the techniques to a high criterion. (c) All 11 teachers were rapidly trained to use these techniques. (d) The teachers learned generalized skills effective with a variety of children and target behaviors. (16 ref)
Koegel, Robert L.; Russo, Dennis C. & Rincover, Arnold. (U California, Social Process Research Inst, Santa Barbara) Journal of Applied Behavior Analysis, 1977(Sum), Vol 10(2), 197–205. [PA, Vol 59:13058]

2829. [The preschool treatment of mentally retarded children and autistic ones.] (Japn)
Six mentally retarded and 2 autistic children were trained in a preschool program that employed operant conditioning and social imitation learning to treat cognitive disabilities, language delays, and social relationships. Response to treatment seemed to depend on reinforcer effectiveness rather than on autism vs retardation. (English summary) (35 ref)
Nakayama, Osamu & Nakayama, Tomie. (Rehabilitation Ctr of Kawasaki City, Japan) Japanese Journal of Child Psychiatry, 1977(Jul–Aug), Vol 18(4), 247–261. [PA, Vol 64:13393]

2830. Functional considerations in the use of procedural timeout and an effective alternative.
Conducted 2 single-S experiments with students in special preschool classes. In Exp I, the disruptive, appropriate, and inappropriate play behaviors of an autistic 5-yr-old girl were measured as a function of 3 independent variables: reinforcement, a typical time-out procedure, and regularly paced teacher instructions. In an ABA reversal within a multiple baseline across 2 teachers, all 3 independent variables comprised the A conditions and procedural time-out was omitted in B. Exp II

examined the appropriate and inappropriate eating of a 5-yr-old male—variously diagnosed as autistic, retarded, and brain damaged—as a function of the same 3 variables. Two teachers conducted baseline and paced instruction-plus-reinforcement conditions in multiple baseline across teachers. Subsequently, 1 teacher performed a series of reversals and replications with various combinations of a typical time-out procedure and reinforcement mixed with paced instructions. Results suggest that time-out did not produce response decrement in a punishment paradigm, but rather response increment in a negative reinforcement paradigm. Paced instructions appears to be an alternative when time-out is not effective and, in conjunction with reinforcement, reduces inappropriate behavior to near zero. (39 ref)
Plummer, Sandi; Baer, Donald M. & LeBlanc, Judith M. (U Kansas) Journal of Applied Behavior Analysis, 1977(Win), Vol 10(4), 689–705. [PA, Vol 61:02310]

2831.   A method for integrating an autistic child into a normal public-school classroom.
Investigated, in 2 experiments, the feasibility of using behavioral techniques to integrate an autistic 5-yr-old girl into a normal public-school class with 1 teacher and 20–30 normal children. In both experiments, initial treatment was given by a therapist who then trained the classroom teacher to continue treatment. Overall results show that (a) during treatment by a therapist in the classroom, the S's appropriate verbal and social behaviors increased and autistic mannerisms decreased; and (b) training teachers in behavioral techniques was apparently sufficient to maintain the S's appropriate school behaviors throughout kindergarten (Exp I) and the 1st grade (Exp II). (28 ref)
Russo, Dennis C. & Koegel, Robert L. (Johns Hopkins U Medical School, John F. Kennedy Inst) Journal of Applied Behavior Analysis, 1977(Win), Vol 10(4), 579–590. [PA, Vol 61:02313]

2832.   A simultaneous comparison of three methods for language training with an autistic child: An experimental single case analysis.
In a single-case, simultaneous-treatment design, 3 methods for experimental language acquisition in a 6 yr 4 mo old autistic boy were compared using a Latin square design and trend-line analysis. Results show that a total communication approach was significantly superior to sign-based and verbalization approaches. The verbalization treatment resulted in decreased performance. Results indicate that use of a cross-modality inhibitory process to explain the alleged superiority of the sign-based approach is questionable. Variation among autistic children indicates a need for further research and for caution against premature acceptance of a given treatment approach or theoretical explanation. (14 ref)
Brady, Douglas O. & Smouse, Albert D. (Child Study Ctr, Ft Worth, TX) Journal of Autism & Developmental Disorders, 1978(Sep), Vol 8(3), 271–279. [PA, Vol 62:04796]

2833.   Development of communicative behavior in autistic children: A parent program using manual signs.
Mothers of 4 6- and 7-yr-old autistic classmates were taught to use manual signs with verbalizations to aid development of appropriate communicative behavior and to deter undesirable behavior in their children. The experimental treatment was initiated in a daily mother–child laboratory session using a multiple-baseline design across Ss. The preschool classroom program remained unchanged. Data were recorded for each child daily over a 5-wk period, in the classroom and in a mother–child session, on 4 types of communicative behavior and 4 types of inappropriate behavior. Communicative behaviors increased and inappropriate behaviors decreased in relation to baseline conditions for each child. The manual sign program facilitated generalization of communicative behavior to the child's total environment. Desirable behaviors were maintained and had improved in the classroom 3 mo after initiation of the program. (16 ref)
Casey, LaDeane O. (Human Resource Assoc, Tempe, AZ) Journal of Autism & Developmental Disorders, 1978(Mar), Vol 8(1), 45–59. [PA, Vol 61:14518]

2834.   Developmental assessment as a basis for planning educational programs for autistic children.
The Psychoeducational Profile (PEP), an instrument that provides a comprehensive evaluation of developmental functioning and behavior in autistic children, is described. The importance of integrating information about the child's unique learning characteristics with measured skill levels is emphasized. Factors involved in programming from assessment data are considered, including understanding the child's abilities, selecting realistic goals and methods, and anticipating potential management problems. Two case studies demonstrate the process of developing a teaching program based on information derived from the PEP. It is concluded that viewing the autistic child as developmentally disabled with specifiable handicaps and determining a starting point for educational goals from a comprehensive assessment can reduce initial uncertainty and provide a framework for ongoing education. (10 ref)
Marcus, Lee M. (Piedmont TEACCH Ctr, Chapel Hill, NC) Behavioral Disorders, 1978(May), Vol 3(3), 219–226. [PA, Vol 64:13391]

2835.   [Specificities of education of a psychotic child.] (Srcr)
Attempted to change the social behavior of 3 psychotic children (1 autistic and 2 schizophrenics). Three methods were used in the learning process: (a) long-term hospitalization within an organized therapeutic community and reeducation of psychomotor functioning, (b) day hospital and school attendance in a protected environment, and (c) treatment in a community setting with outpatient therapy. Results suggest that the level of primary relationship with an object or objective reality determined the success of the teaching methods and approaches used. (3 ref)
Radulović, Koviljka; Bojanin, Svetomir; Stefanović, Tatjana & Povše, Violica. (Zavod za Mentalno Zdravlje, Belgrade, Yugoslavia) Psihijatrija Danas, 1978, Vol 10(2), 213–220. [PA, Vol 65:06401]

2836.   Some recent behavioral research on the education of autistic children.
Discusses several research issues concerned with educating autistic children within existing family and community resources. The literature review is divided into 2 major areas: advances in parent and teacher training; and issues and findings pertaining to classroom instruction, including group instruction, individualized instruction, motivation, and the generalization and maintenance of treatment gains. Educating autistic children is viewed as an ever changing process, rather than as a single, circumscribed program: Educational techniques evolved from the results of research and will continue to be revised as a function of new research findings. Sufficient data are now available, reporting several benefits for parents, teachers, and students, to encourage the use of these behavior modification techniques in the treatment of autistic children. (3½ p ref)
Rincover, Arnold; Koegel, Robert L. & Russo, Dennis C. (U North Carolina, Greensboro) Education & Treatment of Children, 1978(Sum), Vol 1(4), 31–45. [PA, Vol 63:13011]

2837.   A comparison of human and automated instruction of autistic children.
Compared the effects of automated vs teacher-controlled instruction in the education of autistic children. Four autistic children, ages 9–13 yrs, each with extreme deficits in language, social, and self-care behaviors, were trained on a matching-to-sample task under 3 instructional situations within an intra-S replication design and multiple baseline procedure. Analysis of the data showed the following results: (a) The teacher, manually operating the teaching machine, was able to teach and maintain the matching-to-sample task. (b) The same autistic children did not acquire or maintain the task when taught by the machine alone. (c) The teacher alone (without the machine) was able to teach and maintain the task. Results suggest that automated instruction may, at least, serve as a valuable aid to teachers of autistic children. However, before machines can be used without the participation of a trained teacher, further research appears necessary. Several areas of primary concern in the development

of automated instruction for autistic children are discussed. (29 ref)

Russo, Dennis C.; Koegel, Robert L. & Lovaas, O. Ivar. (Johns Hopkins U School of Medicine, John F. Kennedy Inst) Journal of Abnormal Child Psychology, 1978(Jun), Vol 6(2), 189–201. [PA, Vol 64:04200]

2838.   A summer program for autistic children.
Describes a 3-summer program that enrolled 15–30 3–18 yr old autistic children each summer. The need for year-round programming for severely handicapped children and the importance of interagency cooperation in the provision of these services are discussed. The prescriptive diagnostic and evaluation procedures and sample data from an individual participant are also presented. (1 ref)

Van Wert, Margie & Reitz, Andrew L. (Pressley Ridge School, Pittsburgh, PA) Education & Treatment of Children, 1978(Win), Vol 1(2), 47–55. [PA, Vol 63:06417]

2839.   A developmental approach to educating the disturbed young child.
The Developmental Therapy curriculum for emotionally disturbed and autistic children is described, and evidence of progress is presented for handicapped preschool children. The curriculum includes 146 developmental milestones clustered into stages reflecting social and emotional growth in children from approximately age 2 to 12 yrs. Within each stage, 4 curriculum areas are defined: Behavior, Communication, Socialization, and (Pre) Academics. Long-range goals and short-term objectives for social-emotional growth are established and incorporated into a child's individualized education program. To explore the hierarchical validity of the Developmental Therapy Objectives Rating Form (DTORF), 87 children were evaluated over a 9-mo period, with positive results. Subsequently, DTORF data were collected on 106 severely emotionally disturbed, autistic, or mixed handicapped young children. Results in 1 school year indicate progress in each area and reflect a hierarchical integration across stages. (16 ref)

Wood, Mary M. & Swan, William W. (U Georgia, Coll of Education, Athens) Behavioral Disorders, 1978(May), Vol 3(3), 197–209. [PA, Vol 64:13403]

2840.   Autistic children in school.
Presents a definition of autism, evidence documenting the education of autistic children, a description of issues related to classroom behavior, and training suggestions for school personnel. An empirical and functional approach to a description of autism is recommended. Several comprehensive treatment programs, employing mainly behavior modification techniques and applied in a one-to-one setting, have resulted in marked generalized improvement and cessation of autistic behaviors. These techniques may be transferable to the classroom following a period of intervention in which the learning group size is gradually increased and the reward schedule is reduced. Preliminary steps have been taken regarding mainstreaming; further investigation is indicated. Educators are encouraged to become acquainted with issues in the contemporary research literature pertaining to specific autistic behavior, including disruptive activity, self-stimulation, lack of motivation, stimulus overselectivity, and inability to generalize and maintain classroom gains. Teachers should also be specially trained in certain empirically evaluated teaching techniques. (79 ref)

Dunlap, Glen; Koegel, Robert L. & Egel, Andrew L. (U California, Santa Barbara) Exceptional Children, 1979(Apr), Vol 45(7), 552–558. [PA, Vol 62:12266]

2841.   A rebus system of non-fade visual language.
Describes the successful use of the Peabody Rebus Reading Program with normal preschool children (Ss in the rebus group were more able to identify printed words as equivalents of spoken words, were more able to identify the correspondence between the serial position of a word and a location in linear space, and performed better on tests of shape and directional discrimination than Ss in normal playgroups or those using the Peabody Language Development Kit). Because of these results, the rebus

program was incorporated into an experimental program, "nonfade visual language," for autistic and severely mentally handicapped children. Theoretical bases of this approach are outlined, and the necessary skills that the children must have are described (visual attention, visually directed reaching, and prehensility). No receptive language or signing skills are required. The equipment and teaching procedures used to teach some sample rebuses are described. Spoken language, although not necessary, is used to support and reinforce children's progress. (17 ref)

Jones, K. R. (Bristol Polytechnic, School of Special Education, England) Child Care, Health & Development, 1979(Jan–Feb), Vol 5(1), 1–7. [PA, Vol 62:04819]

2842.   Case-history and clinical observations: Valuable material for teachers.
Attempts to educate teachers in the reading and distilling of important features of case reports; the case of an autistic boy is used as an illustration. It is stressed that teachers should learn how to read such material and ferret out important issues to help in planning classroom strategies. It is suggested that this type of training be included in the education of teachers for the severely emotionally disturbed.

Morgan, Sharon R. (U New Mexico, Albuquerque) Behavioral Disorders, 1979(Nov), Vol 5(1), 48–52. [PA, Vol 65:04055]

2843.   Management and education of autistic children.
Recent federal legislation has posed a new kind of challenge—the low-functioning autistic child—for the public schools. Some of the most troublesome behaviors that autistic children present are discussed: disruptive behavior (tantrums, self-injury, self-stimulation); learning problems (stimulus overselectivity, motivational problems); and difficulties functioning in a group-oriented program. Recent advances in behavioral treatment procedures that have enabled autistic children to benefit from educational opportunities in the public schools despite their pervasive developmental disabilities are described. It is noted that there has been a proliferation of research in this area over the past 10 yrs and that new teaching techniques are being developed at a very rapid rate. Teachers and school psychologists are urged to keep abreast of new developments. (63 ref)

Rincover, Arnold & Tripp, Jill K. (U North Carolina, Greensboro) School Psychology Digest, 1979(Fal), Vol 8(4), 397–411. [PA, Vol 63:06412]

2844.   Teaching spontaneous-functional speech to autistic-type children.
A variety of behavioral techniques have been applied to the remediation of speech and language skills in autistic children. A methodology is still needed for teaching functional speech that is self-initiated. The authors present a program for increasing spontaneous functional speech that is applicable in individual and group settings and emphasizes the use of language skills beyond the circumscribed world of the classroom. (13 ref)

Sosne, Jeffrey B.; Handleman, Jan S. & Harris, Sandra L. (Rutgers U) Mental Retardation, 1979(Oct), Vol 17(5), 241–245. [PA, Vol 66:09048]

2845.   A simultaneous treatment comparison of three expressive language training programs with a mute autistic child.
Simultaneously compared the relative effectiveness of 3 language training models (total communication sign training, nonverbal "sign-alone" training, and oral [vocal] training) for teaching expressive language skills to a 4½-yr-old mute autistic boy. A single-S, alternating-treatment (multi-element) design with replication within S was used to compare the rate of expressive word acquisition across training models. Results show the total communication model was substantially superior to both oral and sign-alone training models, and place in question the theory of an intersensory integration disability to explain the success of sign language. Alternatively, the data suggest that the use of physical prompts combined with multisensory inputs provided a basis for the demonstrated success. (15 ref)

Barrera, Ricardo D.; Lobato-Barrera, Debra & Sulzer-Azaroff, Beth. (U Massachusetts, Amherst) Journal of Autism & Developmental Disorders, 1980(Mar), Vol 10(1), 21–37. [PA, Vol 64:04193]

2846.   Evaluation of a language program for young autistic children.
Presents retrospective data comparing an individualized language development program for preschool autistic children receiving language remediation (experimental Ss) with a group receiving the basic school curriculum only (controls). All findings favor the language remediation group (e.g., experimental Ss made significant gains in 1 yr while controls required 2 yrs). Results support the hypothesis that an individualized language remediation program facilitates the acquisition of prelinguistic and linguistic skills. (23 ref)
Bloch, Judith; Gersten, Elayne & Kornblum, Susan. Journal of Speech & Hearing Disorders, 1980(Feb), Vol 45(1), 76–89. [PA, Vol 65:08822]

2847.   The effects of constant vs varied reinforcer presentation on responding by autistic children.
The autistic child's characteristic lack of motivation can create considerable problems for educators. Since there is some evidence that stimulus variation may influence motivation, this study assessed the differential effects of constant vs varied reinforcer presentation. The study examined whether differences would occur (a) in the total number of responses emitted by autistic children when the reinforcer was held constant as opposed to varied and (b) in the interresponse interval for constant vs varied reinforcer presentation. 10 4–13 yr old autistic children made significantly more and faster responses when the reinforcer presentation was varied as opposed to constant. Results are discussed in terms of the effects of stimulus variation on satiation and implications for teachers of autistic children. (34 ref)
Egel, Andrew L. (U Maryland, College Park) Journal of Experimental Child Psychology, 1980(Dec), Vol 30(3), 455–463. [PA, Vol 65:06389]

2848.   Generalization from school to home with autistic children.
Assessed the generalization of verbal behavior from school to home with 3 autistic boys (6, 7, and 9 yrs old). The present study attempted to expand on previous research by J. S. Handleman (1979) by analyzing the effects of single vs multiple trainers on generalization. Ss were taught responses to common questions in 2 school settings and were probed to determine transfer of learning to their homes. All Ss demonstrated greater generalization when they received training at varied locations as opposed to instruction in a single setting. Results suggest that manipulating the school environment to more closely simulate home conditions may facilitate transfer of treatment gains to the natural setting. (18 ref)
Handleman, Jan S. & Harris, Sandra L. (Rutgers U, Douglass Coll, New Brunswick) Journal of Autism & Developmental Disorders, 1980(Sep), Vol 10(3), 323–333. [PA, Vol 65:04160]

2849.   Behavioral writing for an autistic-like child.
A 12-yr-old boy in a classroom for the emotionally disturbed was treated for 1 semester using a combined fading-tracing handwriting program and behavior modification. Results show a significant decrease in size and an increase in quality of letters written. The S also received some positive attention from his classmates. (8 ref)
Hartley, Steven T. & Salzwedel, Kenneth D. Academic Therapy, 1980(Sep), Vol 16(1), 101–110. [PA, Vol 66:08998]

2850.   Intertrial interval duration and learning in autistic children.
Investigated the influence of intertrial interval (ITI) duration on the performance of autistic children during teaching situations. Three 7–11 yr old Ss were taught under the same conditions existing in their regular programs, except that the length of time between trials was manipulated. With both multiple baseline and repeated reversal designs, 2 lengths of ITIs were employed: short intervals with the discriminative stimulus (SD) for any given trial presented approximately 1 sec following the reinforcer for the

previous trial vs long intervals with the SD presented 4 or more sec following the reinforcer for the previous trial. Results show that (a) the short ITIs always produced higher levels of correct responding than the long intervals; and (b) there were improving trends in performance and rapid acquisition with the short ITIs in contrast to minimal or no change with the long intervals. Results suggest that manipulations made between trials influence autistic children's learning. (27 ref)
Koegel, Robert L.; Dunlap, Glen & Dyer, Kathleen. (U California, Speech & Hearing Ctr, Santa Barbara) Journal of Applied Behavior Analysis, 1980(Spr), Vol 13(1), 91–99. [PA, Vol 65:08829]

2851.   Public school programing for autistic children.
Describes a North Carolina program for autistic children, featuring parental involvement, carefully structured, explicit teaching methods, and improvement of attitudes toward autistic children. Autistic children can benefit from a proper public school environment and can enhance the experience of teachers and other children. (7 ref)
Schopler, Eric & Olley, J. Gregory. (U North Carolina Coll of Medicine, Div of TEACCH, Chapel Hill) Exceptional Children, 1980(Mar), Vol 46(6), 461–463. [PA, Vol 63:13013]

2852.   Academic performance in the classroom as a function of a parent applied home management program with severely emotionally disturbed children.
Conducted an analysis of specific individual measures of classroom academic performance as a function of a parent applied procedure for reducing self-stimulatory responses in 3 autistic and autistic-like males (mean age 9.06 yrs). Results indicate that although there were a number of significant differences in academic performance among and across the experimental conditions, none of the differences could be directly associated with the home intervention procedures applied by the parents. It is concluded that generalization effects of treatment across settings, time, and dependent variables must be specifically programmed with severely emotionally disturbed children. (23 ref)
Simpson, Richard L.; Swenson, Carl R. & Thompson, Thomas N. (U Kansas Medical Ctr, Kansas City) Behavioral Disorders, 1980(Nov), Vol 6(1), 4–11. [PA, Vol 66:08557]

2853.   Treatment of atypical anorexia nervosa in the public school: An autistic girl.
Because of the increase in public school programs for severely handicapped children, teachers are more likely than ever to be confronted with serious medical or psychological problems like anorexia nervosa. In the case study presented, desensitization successfully treated the eating disorder of a preadolescent autistic girl. The case also accentuates the problems teachers face in making appropriate decisions due to conflicting literature findings, traditional role responsibilities, and lack of expert resources and supportive services in the public school settings. If programs are to meet the needs of these children in the future, service and resource models for the public school settings must be developed. (13 ref)
Stiver, Richard L. & Dobbins, John P. (U Wisconsin, Oshkosh) Journal of Autism & Developmental Disorders, 1980(Mar), Vol 10(1), 67–73. [PA, Vol 64:04204]

2854.   Using sign language to remediate severe reading problems.
Discusses remedial techniques that are successful with disabled readers and notes that American sign language and the manual alphabet combine several desirable characteristics of remedial reading techniques. Successful use of sign language with aphasics, autistic children, and a group of learning disabled students is described. A summary of an experimental program using the manual alphabet to improve learning disabled children's spelling skills (J. H. DuBois and E. P. O'Brien, 1977) is provided. Suggestions for implementing the method in classrooms and a list of activities and materials available are presented. (24 ref)

Vernon, McCay; Coley, Joan D. & DuBois, Jan H. (Western Maryland Coll) Journal of Learning Disabilities, 1980(Apr), Vol 13(4), 215–218. [PA, Vol 64:11217]

2855. Issues in the modification of American Sign Language for instructional purposes.
The use of manual communication and sign languages for language education of autistic, deaf retarded, and mentally retarded individuals is receiving increasing attention by educators. A better understanding of the physical and linguistic bases of sign languages is needed. Preliminary evidence from studies of oral-only, manual-only, and oral-manual modes of communication suggests that flexibility in utilizing all modes is the most effective teaching method. The present paper considers the possible utilization of modifications of the American Sign Language for use in 3 general areas: (1) instruction of deaf students in the classroom, (2) communication between hearing parents and young deaf children, and (3) communication with individuals with handicaps other than deafness. (29 ref)
Moores, Donald F. (Gallaudet Coll) Journal of Autism & Developmental Disorders, 1981(Mar), Vol 11(1), 153–162. [PA, Vol 66:06203]

2856. The Autism Attitude Scale for Teachers.
Describes the Autism Attitude Scale for Teachers, a 32-item list developed as a means of assessing the attitudes of teachers whose schools would receive autistic pupils for the 1st time. The scale also evaluates the effect of inservice training for those teachers. Reliability was verified by data from 95 regular education teachers. (6 ref)
Olley, J. Gregory et al. (U North Carolina, Chapel Hill) Exceptional Children, 1981(Feb), Vol 47(5), 371–372. [PA, Vol 65:06858]

Mental Retardation

2857. Revised perspectives in academic and vocational programming for culturally advantaged mentally retarded children.
Distinguishes between the characteristics of culturally advantaged and disadvantaged mentally retarded children. Considering these differences, the critical role of parental aspirations in planning their children's programs is noted. A variety of "continuous education" programs designed to accelerate academic instruction for the mentally retarded is described.
Blackman, Leonard & Maizes, Isaac. (Teachers Coll., Columbia U.) Mental Retardation, 1970(Aug), Vol. 8(4), 16-19. [PA, Vol 47:11666]

2858. The uses of music to enhance the education of the mentally retarded.
Suggests that the use of music instruction by those oriented in psychopathology of children and psychopathology of the retarded may enhance the learning ability of the retarded. Basic learning abstractions may be practiced and promoted circuitously by the application of intrinsic music symbols, starting with learning at the most elementary level. Through the social encounter, in a unique 1:1 relationship with an instructor who utilizes the attractions of music, many social and disciplinary skills will be practiced and promoted.
Cameron, Rosaline. Mental Retardation, 1970(Feb), Vol. 8(1), 32-34. [PA, Vol 47:11668]

2859. The influence of temperament on education of mentally retarded children.
Compared 52 retarded children, ranging in MA from 4-6 yr and in CA from 5-12 yr., with a group of 5-yr-old normal children. Comparison on 9 categories of temperament reveals that the retarded children were, in general, more intensely responsive, more distractible, less persistent, and limited to shorter attention spans than normals. Administration of the Wide Range Achievement Test to the retarded children 3 yr after initial data collection, and subsequent comparison of achievement and temperament in the 12 highest and 12 lowest scoring Ss reveals that MA and threshold of responsiveness, but not CA, IQ, or the

other 8 categories of temperament, were related to achievement scores.
Chess, Stella & Korn, Sam. (New York U. Medical School) Journal of Special Education, 1970(Win), Vol. 4(1), 13-27. [PA, Vol 47:03659]

2860. The effect of context on the reading of mentally retarded and normal children at the first grade level.
Hypothesized that facilitation of word recognition by context would be significantly greater for normal than for retarded Ss. 40 words were presented to Ss in the context of a story or excerpted and Ss were required to read the words. Results indicate that the context condition improved performance significantly for both normal and retarded Ss. The interaction between condition and population type was not significant, thus failing to support the original hypothesis. Both retardates and normals were equally helped by the context condition.
Levitt, Edith. (Columbia U.) Journal of Special Education, 1970(Fal), Vol. 4(4), 425-429. [PA, Vol 47:05655]

2861. Role play with retarded adolescent girls: Teaching and therapy.
Describes the use of role play in classes of retarded adolescent girls in a vocational school setting, both for teaching appropriate job behavior and for improving interpersonal relationships. No difficulties were encountered over a 2-yr period and several advantages are cited. This experience leads to agreement with those who suggest that more use should be made of psychodramatic techniques with retarded youngsters; however, the need for more formal studies to test whether the method is as effective as it appears to be is suggested.
Robinson, Lillian. (Tulane U., Medical School) Mental Retardation, 1970(Apr), Vol. 8(2), 36-37. [PA, Vol 47:11677]

2862. Training generative verb usage by imitation and reinforcement procedures.
3 retarded children (1 18-yr-old boy, and 1 16-yr-old and 1 14-yr-old girl) were trained, using imitation and reinforcement procedures, to produce past and present tense forms of verbs in response to verbal requests. 2 types of experimental sessions were arranged: training and probe. During training sessions, S was trained to produce 1 verb in both the past and the present tense. Then, in a probe session, the generalization of this training was tested by presenting to the S a series of untrained verbs interspersed with previously trained verbs. Responses to untrained verbs were never reinforced. Training sessions alternated with probe sessions throughout a multiple base-line design involving 4 classes of verb inflections as the base lines. The results showed that, as past and present tense forms of verbs within an inflectional class were trained, Ss correctly produced past and present tense forms of untrained verbs within this class. When verbs from 2 or more classes were trained, Ss correctly produced the verb tenses from each of these classes. Thus, the imitation and reinforcement procedures were effective in teaching generative use of verb inflections. (15 ref.)
Schumaker, Jean & Sherman, James A. (U. Kansas) Journal of Applied Behavior Analysis, 1970(Win), Vol. 3(4), 273-287. [PA, Vol 46:05375]

2863. Programming for special class misfits.
The behaviorally disruptive, withdrawn, or seriously disturbed child has often been excluded from special education programs for the retarded despite a functioning level concomitant with participating peers. An engineered classroom program is described wherein specific response patterns leading to exclusion were subjected to behavior modification techniques. Ss were 15 9-17 yr. old students classified as disruptive or nonparticipative and rejected from special classrooms. Results of the pilot project are evaluated and discussed regarding implications for future programming. It is concluded that the 20-wk project demonstrated the feasibility of programming for emotionally disturbed retarded children.
Talkington, Larry & Watters, Lenore. (Austin State School, Tex.) Mental Retardation, 1970(Apr), Vol. 8(2), 27-29. [PA, Vol 47:11682]

2864. Sex education: Fact and fancy.
Responds to S. Gordon's (see PA, Vol.49:Issue 3) discussion of the role of sex education in special education. The point is not denied that sex education is important for handicapped young people, however, it is pointed out that proponents of sex education often have varied and multiple reasons for their support, and that the results of sex education have not yet been shown to change sexual behavior patterns. It is also emphasized that the advocates of sex education have the responsibility of clearly stating what are the valid expectations and limitations of their procedures, especially when used with youngsters who require special education.
Balester, Raymond J. (Case Western Reserve U.) Journal of Special Education, 1971(Win), Vol. 5(4), 355-357. [PA, Vol 49:05300]

2865. An exploratory study of prevalence of mental retardation in Mysore City.
Screened 4,218 3-17 yr old children in 13 schools for hearing, speech, and intelligence. Seguin Form Board was individually administered to measure IQ. The mean IQ was 94.28, standard deviation 19.95. The distribution of IQ scores is positively skewed. Government schools had more retarded children than did private schools.
Bharath Raj, J. (All India Inst. of Speech & Hearing, Mysore) Journal of the All-India Institute of Speech & Hearing, 1971(Jan), Vol. 2, 117-127. [PA, Vol 51:09434]

2866. Symposium on the educational problems of the severely mentally handicapped child: IV. The hospital school for the mentally subnormal.
Discusses the multiple handicaps and behavioral deviancies found in mentally subnormal children in hospital schools. Problems associated with training teachers to deal with these areas of difficulty and plan suitable curriculum are noted. A case history of a subnormal boy is presented to illustrate the skills necessary for a teacher in hospital schools.
Bland, G. A. (Brookhall Hosp., Blackburn, England) British Journal of Mental Subnormality, 1971(Dec), Vol. 17(33, Pt. 2), 107-116. [PA, Vol 48:03710]

2867. Some considerations about the neglect of sex education in special education.
Expresses general agreement with the point of view stated in S. Gordon's (see PA, Vol. 49:Issue 3) paper emphasizing the need for greater sex education among handicapped youngsters. 3 additional difficulties in formulating a successful program are suggested: (a) overcoming the discomfort that many teachers have in dealing with sex education, (b) revising the curriculum so that it meets the needs of the students, and (c) permitting alternatives for children who do not wish to participate because of parental objection or other reasons.
Blom, Gaston E. (U. Colorado, Medical Center, Denver) Journal of Special Education, 1971(Win), Vol. 5(4), 359-361. [PA, Vol 49:05315]

2868. Responses of mentally retarded children on a visual discrimination task involving concept formation.
Evaluated 3 groups of mentally retarded children on a visual discrimination reading readiness task. Ss included 75 mentally retarded persons residing at a state institution divided into 5 MA groups ranging from 3-8 yr. 3 different groups of 25 Ss were matched on CA, MA, and IQ and 2 of these were paired on perceptual functioning on the basis of Gellner classifications. The 3rd group included 25 Ss diagnosed as having genetic mechanisms. The task consisted of 100 cards of 3 colored pictures with 2 of them being associated. Results showed that the minimally handicapped visual group performed higher than the other 2 groups. MA was highly related to success especially for the highest MA group. Implications of these data are discussed.
Bradley, Betty H. (Columbus State Inst., O.) Slow Learning Child, 1971(Mar), Vol. 18(1), 34-41. [PA, Vol 47:01612]

2869. Sex education for the handicapped.
Responds to S. Gordon's (see PA, Vol. 49:Issue 3) article on the lack of sex education among handicapped children, essentially agreeing with all of the important points made.
Delp, Harold A. (Temple U.) Journal of Special Education, 1971(Win), Vol. 5(4), 363-364. [PA, Vol 49:05365]

2870. Academic achievement and minimal brain dysfunction in mentally retarded children.
Investigated the performance of 68 minimal brain dysfunction (MBD) children on standardized tests of academic achievement for mentally retarded (MR) children. Ss were classified into 4 groups depending on presence of neurological and visual-motor impairment. Dependent variables were standard scores on word recognition, arithmetic, and spelling subtests of the WRAT. Results were analyzed using t tests. It is concluded that (a) academic achievement of MR Ss in arithmetic and spelling "is related to visual-motor impairment, but not to soft neurological signs"; (b) signs of MBD do not have a direct relationship to the reading achievement of MR Ss; and (c) differences in academic achievement among MR Ss "may become apparent only when test scores are controlled for MA."
Edwards, R. Philip; Alley, Gordon R. & Snider, Bill. (Western Carolina U.) Exceptional Children, 1971(Mar), Vol. 37(7), 539-540. [PA, Vol 47:03661]

2871. Effects of perceptual-motor training on the educable mentally retarded.
54 educable children (mean age = 9.6 yr.; mean IQ = 68.1), deficient in perceptual-motor abilities according to the Perceptual Motor Survey (PMS), took part in 3 training conditions: (a) a structured program of perceptual motor training twice each week for 4½ mo. (Kephart group), (b) table games (Hawthorne group), or (c) regular classroom schedules (control). Before and after training each child responded to the PMS, WISC, Wide Range Achievement Test (WRAT), and Stanford Achievement Test (SAT). For those children under 10 the Kephart group produced higher PMS scores than the control group (p < .05). Neither WISC, WRAT, nor SAT scores varied as a function of training conditions.
Fisher, Kirk L. (School District of Lancaster, Pa.) Exceptional Children, 1971(Nov), Vol. 38(3), 264-266. [PA, Vol 49:07798]

2872. Implicit criteria used to determine promotion for normal and retarded students.
Administered the Elementary School Adjustment Scale (ESAS) to 61 retarded elementary students and 61 randomly selected normal students. Their mean grade placements were 3.3 and 4.6, respectively. The ESAS used by 114 teachers is a 30-item multiple-choice behavioral observation scale. Specific items related to promotion were identified by discriminant analysis. It is concluded that retention was used as a remedial technique as well as punishment for students who exhibited undesirable behavior.
Flynn, Timothy M. (Southern Illinois U.) Psychology in the Schools, 1971(Jul), Vol. 8(3), 204-208. [PA, Vol 47:09672]

2873. Psychoeducative considerations of physical handicapping conditions in children.
Surveyed 44,943 school-aged children to ascertain the prevalence of psychologically and educationally relevant physical handicaps. Of 195 physically handicapped Ss identified and evaluated, 83 (43%) showed some degree of mental retardation. 7% of 103 Ss given hearing examinations showed incidence of hearing loss, and approximately 25% were felt to display some degree of psychological maladjustment. It is concluded that educational programs for the physically handicapped must also consider intellectual and emotional disturbances.
Friedman, Ronald J. & MacQueen, John C. (U. Iowa) Exceptional Children, 1971(Mar), Vol. 37(7), 538-539. [PA, Vol 47:03651]

2874. Okay, let's tell it like it is (instead of just making it look good).
Discusses the need for sex education among the mentally retarded. 8 important facts are listed as necessary to include in

any sex education campaign or curriculum: (a) masturbation is a normal expression of sex, (b) all direct sexual behavior involving the genitals should be in privacy, (c) any time a physically mature girl and boy have sexual relations they risk pregnancy, (d) birth control should be used unless children are desired and the responsibility for them accepted, (e) society feels that intercourse should not be engaged in until age 18, (f) adults should not be permitted to use children sexually, (g) the only way to discourge homosexuality is to risk heterosexuality, and (h) sexual behavior between consenting adults should be no one else's business.
Gordon, Sol. (Syracuse U.) Journal of Special Education, 1971(Win), Vol. 5(4), 379-381. [PA, Vol 49:05410]

2875. Missing in special education: Sex.
Discusses the role of sex education in special education. It is observed that handicapped children have the same emotions and sexual drives as their normal counterparts, but less knowledge. Along with disadvantaged young people, the handicapped are by far the most vulnerable segment of the youth population with regard to sexual exploitation and pathology. Even the isolated among them cannot afford to be naive about sex. It is concluded that the retarded and their families must be prepared early to make decisions about contraception and voluntary sterilization.
Gordon, Sol. (Syracuse U.) Journal of Special Education, 1971(Win), Vol. 5(4), 351-354. [PA, Vol 49:05409]

2876. Differences in attitude of educationally handicapped, mentally retarded and normal students: A study of attitudes toward school, teachers and academics.
Administered Burke's School Attitude Survey to 3 study groups drawn from a middle-class elementary school district: 85 normals, 47 educationally handicapped, and 16 mentally retarded students. Responses to the 3 attitudinal dimensions of teacher, school, and academics were tabulated. Chi squares were then computed. Results indicate significant differences between normal and educationally handicapped Ss in all 3 dimensions, and a significant difference between normal and mentally retarded Ss in the dimensions of school and academics. The educationally handicapped and the mentally retarded Ss expressed more negative attitudes than the normals for all 3 dimensions.
Guthery, George H. Journal of Learning Disabilities, 1971(Jun), Vol. 4(6), 330-332. [PA, Vol 47:09726]

2877. [The psychological problems of education and treatment of mentally retarded children in the United States of America.] (Polh)
Presents a report on the educational system in the United States and the education and treatment of the emotionally disturbed, mentally retarded, and children with specific reading problems. Existing theories and their application in psychological and pedagogical practice are considered. The role of behavior therapy in the psychotherapy of maladjusted children is discussed. Detailed examinations of institutions in the United States which treat these children are presented. Similar methods of reeducation of dyslexic children in Poland are described. (Russian summary)
Hornowska, Stanislawa. Przeglad Psychologiczny, 1971, Vol. 1(21), 205-224. [PA, Vol 46:07468]

2878. Learning deficiency versus developmental conceptions of mental retardation.
Critically reviews descriptions of the mentally retarded and learning deficiency concepts of education. Objections are made to the assumptions that mental retardation (a) automatically entails learning deficiency, (b) is equivalent to learning deficiency, or (c) can be accounted for in terms of learning deficiency. An alternative developmental view is presented which assumes that learning ability is primarily based on level of intellectual development, with mentally retarded Ss viewed as being slow in development rather than in learning. Implications for teaching and for educational research are discussed. (36 ref.)
Iano, Richard P. (Temple U., Coll. of Education) Exceptional Children, 1971(Dec), Vol. 38(4), 301-311. [PA, Vol 49:11950]

2879. Effect of classroom noise on number identification by retarded children.
Using number recognition tasks displayed at $\frac{1}{10}$ and $\frac{1}{100}$ sec. duration, the effects of 4 classroom auditory environments were examined (no noise, typical classroom background noise, typical classroom background noise + noise episodes, and noise episodes). The presence of a 1st order interaction between auditory environment and display rate support research findings indicating the suppressing effect of meaningful noise on performance. Earlier findings that the effects of noise were greatest when display durations are increased are supported.
Joiner, Lee M. & *Kottmeyer, Wayne A.* (Southern Illinois U.) California Journal of Educational Research, 1971(Sep), Vol. 22(4), 164-169. [PA, Vol 48:01707]

2880. [An investigation of the social background of mental retardates.] (Danh)
Compares the educational-occupational stratification of 53 diagnosed mental retarded in special classes (n = 46) and special education groups with the 2,790 students from Grades 1-7 in the schools of a local community. Lower strata were overrepresented among retardates. Findings are discussed in terms of deprivation and teacher expectancies.
Kruuse, Emil. (Office of School Psychology, Herstederne, Denmark) Skolepsykologi, 1971, Vol. 8(6), 455-461. [PA, Vol 49:11975]

2881. Spina bifida children in school: Preliminary report.
Briefly discusses 28 spina bifida children in primary or special schools. Problems encountered range from (a) difficulty in finding suitable physical locations, to (b) teachers' apprehensions, and (c) lack of specialized consultants.
Laurence, E. Rose. (Welsh National School of Medicine, Pediatric Pathology Lab., Cardiff) Developmental Medicine & Child Neurology, 1971, Vol. 13(6, Suppl. 25), 44-46. [PA, Vol 48:07772]

2882. The relationship between the Wechsler Intelligence Scale for Children and the Slosson Intelligence Test.
Administered the WISC and Slosson Intelligence Test (SIT) to a total of 50 11-14 yr. olds in the 6th grade and special education classes. A high positive correlation was obtained between the SIT and WISC Verbal and Total scales, especially for extreme intelligence classifications of mental defective and superior. It is concluded that while the WISC is preferable for placement, the SIT is adequate for screening purposes.
Maxwell, Michael T. (Washington School, Miles City, Mont.) Child Study Journal, 1971(Spr), Vol. 1(3), 164-171. [PA, Vol 48:01709]

2883. Symposium on the educational problems of the severely mentally handicapped child: III. On the education of the subnormal pupil.
Examined 786 subnormal children in training centers and hospital schools. Data is presented on numbers, grading, etiology and secondary diagnostic factors, psychotic and major personality disorders, adaptive behavior, social incompetence, chronic illness, and custodial responsibilities. It is concluded that the total treatment of the mentally subnormal child is multidisciplinary. The place of "medicine" in the instruction of teachers of the subnormal is discussed.
McCoull, G. British Journal of Mental Subnormality, 1971(Dec), Vol. 17(33, Pt. 2), 101-106. [PA, Vol 48:03719]

2884. Resource centers for teachers of handicapped children.
Describes a model of a resource center for the instruction of handicapped children which will be primarily a service to teachers. Children will be enrolled in the center for short periods only, for the purposes of diagnosis and program development. When children leave the center, they leave with an educational package which has been developed specifically for them. The services of the center will be available to all teachers experiencing problems with children who are mentally retarded, emotionally disturbed, visually handicapped, speech impaired, deaf, crippled, or other wise health impaired.

Moss, James W. (Office of Education, Bureau for the Handicapped, Washington, D.C.) Journal of Special Education, 1971(Win), Vol. 5(1), 67-71. [PA, Vol 48:03686]

2885.   [Special Education and child psychiatry: School medical work at a school for retarded.] (Germ)
Reports on personal experience in child psychiatric work in special education. The examined students were found to have many and multiple handicaps; uniform, simple intellectual defects were seldom found. Child psychiatric advice is considered necessary for special educators to counteract therapeutic resignation and to delineate possibilities for educational work and medical treatment. Professional problems are indicated, and organizational plans for the necessary teamwork between special educators and child psychiatrists are discussed. (18 ref.)
Muller, Peter. (U. Göttingen, Psychiatric Clinic, W. Germany) Praxis der Kinderpsychologie und Kinderpsychiatrie, 1971(Aug), Vol. 20(6), 193-197. [PA, Vol 48:09716]

2886.   [A study of the development of self-assessment in mentally retarded 5th and 8th grade schoolchildren.] (Russ)
47 11-16 yr. old mentally retarded 5th (20 Ss) and 8th (27 Ss) graders from 2 Moscow auxiliary schools, along with 40 normals as controls from a regular school, participated in a study of changes in the self-assessment of personal and mental capacities by oligophrenics in the adolescent period, utilizing a modification of self-rating scales first devised by T. Dembo. It was shown that adolescent oligophrenics equated mental ability with success in school. Character was not viewed as separated from behavior. Ratings of character were based more often on assessment by self than on that by others. Ratings of mental ability, however, were based more on assessment by others than on that by self.
Namazbaeva, Zh. I. (Inst. of Defectology, Moscow, USSR) Defektologiya, 1971(Jan), Vol. 3(1), 24-30. [PA, Vol 47:01625]

2887.   [Thoughts on the mental education for mentally retarded in schools.] (Germ)
Explored the close relationship of orientation in the environment, mother tongue development, and comprehension of quantity. The education of mentality is not an isolated effort within the educative process of mentally handicapped children, nor is it a mere additive to existing educational curricula.
Obholzer, Rudolf.   Vierteljahresschrift für Heilpädagogik und ihre Nachbargebiete, 1971(Jun), Vol. 40(2), 126-131. [PA, Vol 48:03720]

2888.   The child oriented resource room program.
Describes a program in which 19 school districts in the Buffalo, New York area established resource rooms which included special education classes for children classified as mentally retarded or as having serious learning difficulties. A child evaluation center to help children from regular classes was also established. The program was generally considered to be successful.
Reger, Roger   & Koppmann, Marion. (Board of Cooperative Education Services, Buffalo, N.Y.) Exceptional Children, 1971(Feb), Vol. 37(6), 460-462. [PA, Vol 46:05525]

2889.   [Increase in cognitive activity and independence in pupils of the auxiliary school in programmed teaching.] (Russ)
Argues for the incorporation of elements of programmed instruction in teaching Russian to mentally retarded children in order to increase both cognitive activity and self-reliance. Presents a detailed illustration of a programmed lesson.
Salova, Zh. S. (Auxiliary School No. 18, Leningrad, USSR) Defektologiya, 1971(Jan), Vol. 3(1), 60-64. [PA, Vol 47:01626]

2890.   Developmental trends in the vocational interests of special education and normal students.
Attempted to analyze the development of vocational interests in special education and normal students. 45 normal and 45 retarded Ss ranging in age from 9-18 yr. were tested on a pictorial measure of vocational interests. Significant age and group differences were noted on a number of occupational clusters derived on the basis of Ss' response to the measure. Group differences were interpreted in terms of differential early experi-

ence between retardates and normals. Significant developmental trends were analyzed in terms of general to specific response trends, developmental lag, and the differential educational experiences of the 2 groups.
Silverman, Mitchell. (U. South Florida) Journal of Genetic Psychology, 1971(Jun), Vol. 118(2), 157-172. [PA, Vol 46:09641]

2891.   Development of complex sentence structure in a retarded girl using a multiple baseline technique.
Multiple base-line techniques were used to demonstrate that prompts and differential positive reinforcement (praise and tokens) increased complex language in a retarded girl. These procedures were extremely effective when used by her preschool teacher. However, these same procedures, when used by the child's mother with comparable accuracy were considerably less effective. Reversals showed that the teacher's praise alone could maintain the complex speech as effectively as praise and tokens together. The differential effectiveness of the mother and teacher may be ascribed to subtle differences in praising or to possible differences in the child's reinforcement history with these individuals.
Twardosz, Sandra & Sajwaj, Thomas. (U. Kansas) Proceedings of the 79th Annual Convention of the American Psychological Association, 1971, Vol. 6(Pt. 2), 663-664. [PA, Vol 46:05369]

2892.   A problem of involvement with parents of mildly retarded children.
About 94% of the 6,000,000 retarded individuals in this country are a little-studied group that is offered negligible service on special education programs of the schools. The parents of these mildly or borderline retarded children have not organized in an effort to receive better services. Several reasons are suggested for this lack of involvement by the parents: (a) unwillingness to admit to a significant intellectual problem with their child, (b) indifference, and (c) dependence on special education programs of the school. Questionnaires were sent to parents of mildly retarded children in special education classes to try to involve these parents in their child's education. 2 conclusions are discussed: (a) Significant differences were found between respondents and nonrespondents on socioeconomic status and children's IQ level. The possible reasons for this are discussed and some selected questions are presented and response examples given. (b) Those who did respond evidenced intense feelings toward the problem the classificatory labeling of the children. Parental responses reinforced changes planned by the school and showed a need for parent education programs to provide an opportunity for increased involvement and to strike at many misconceptions of retardation.
Wadsworth, H. G.   & Wadsworth, Joanna B. (Community Consolidated School District 59, Ridge School, Elk Grove Village, Ill.) Family Coordinator, 1971(Apr), Vol. 20(2), 141-147. [PA, Vol 46:11553]

2893.   Validity of the Slosson Drawing Coordination Test with adolescents of below-average ability.
Administered to a total of 114 black and white 14-19 yr. olds with IQs of below 90 the (a) Slosson Drawing Coordination Test, (b) WISC or WAIS, (c) Benton Visual Retention Test, and (d) Raven's Progressive Matrices. Moderate to low correlations of the Slosson with the other tests indicate that the Slosson aids in the identification of visual-perceptual or motor coordination problems with adolescents of below-average ability. Some racial differences were reflected in the correlations. It is suggested that the Slosson be used only for screening.
Alcorn, Charles L.   & Nicholson, Charles L. (North Carolina Central U., Durham) Perceptual & Motor Skills, 1972(Feb), Vol. 34(1), 261-262. [PA, Vol 48:07779]

2894.   Representational modes as they interact with cognitive development and mathematical concept acquisition of the retarded to promote new mathematical learning.
Suggests that during certain periods of a child's mental and cognitive development, the use of selected representational modes in the instructional presentation of ideas would be better than others in promoting mathematical learning. In 2 related

studies the mathematical learning of 20 trainable mentally retarded (TMR) and 67 educable mentally retarded (EMR) children was examined under 2 modes of representational presentation: manipulative (enactive) and nonmanipulative (pictorial-symbolic). The TMR Ss did significantly better under the manipulative representational mode. The EMR Ss also learned better under the manipulative mode, but only on certain types of mathematical ideas.
Armstrong, Jenny R. (U. Wisconsin) Journal for Research in Mathematics Education, 1972(Jan), Vol. 3(1), 43-50. [PA, Vol 47:11663]

2895.   Special education and the pediatrician.
Briefly considers some areas of mutual interest to pediatric medicine and special education mental retardation, learning disabilities, reading problems, and parent groups. Selected aspects of appropriate working relationships among medical and educational personnel are discussed from the vantage point of some educators. The implications of certain changes in special education replacing the medical framework with behavioral systems, deemphasis of etiology, and a thrust to maintain exceptional children in mainstream educational programs are presented.
Bateman, Barbara & Frankel, Herman. (U. Oregon, Coll. of Education) Journal of Learning Disabilities, 1972(Apr), Vol. 5(4), 178-186. [PA, Vol 48:07780]

2896.   Designing instructional settings for children labeled retarded: Some reflections.
Discusses the fallacy of teaching the retarded in terms of simplistic ideas, e.g., having an inferior ability to learn. Teaching the retarded has frequently been subject to a self-fulfilling prophecy by which they are tested on untaught skills and consequently considered mentally inferior. The curriculum for the retarded should not be a watered-down revision of the normal academic program. Instead, it should emphasize social competence, which is not consistently related to intelligence until the IQ drops below about 40. Since the retarded have difficulty in transferring symbolic knowledge to concrete situations, they should have more direct experience in different social situations to equip them for postschool life. It is emphasized that retarded children present wide variations in learning rate and style, perseverance and ability to attend to and comprehend the nature of the learning task.
Bauer, David H. & Yamamoto, Kaoru. (Chico State Coll.) Elementary School Journal, 1972(Apr), Vol. 72(7), 343-350. [PA, Vol 48:12185]

2897.   The librarian and the exceptional child.
Discusses exceptionality in children, particularly the mentally retarded. The role of the librarian in dealing with such children is delineated. 3 guidelines are offered: (a) exploring one's own reaction to exceptional children in an effort to develop a positive attitude; (b) informing oneself about community services available to such children, then acting as a resource person; and (c) learning about exceptionality through reading, consultation with other professionals, and familiarity with various media that stimulate and sustain an exceptional child's interest in learning.
Duplica, Moya M. (U. Washington, School of Social Work) Rehabilitation Literature, 1972(Jul), Vol. 33(7), 198-203. [PA, Vol 49:05376]

2898.   The mildly retarded as casualties of the educational system.
Considers that some children in public schools merit special education placement and subsequent status as mentally retarded primarily because of faults inherent in the organizational and instructional system in the regular grades and not necessarily because of any inherent limitations in themselves. Among the reasons why such children become casualties of the educational system are ignorance of motivational and situational aspects of mental retardation, lack of systematic early identification, misapplication of social reinforcement techniques, lack of administrative support, and the organizational structure of special educa-

tion itself. These aspects are discussed and possible remedies are proposed. (50 ref.)
Forness, Steven R. (U. California, Medical School, Los Angeles) Journal of School Psychology, 1972(Jun), Vol. 10(2), 117-126. [PA, Vol 49:07803]

2899.   Reinforcement overkill: Implications for education of the retarded.
Research evidence on the motivation of mentally retarded persons seems to indicate the considerable potency of social reinforcement in the form of adult attention and approval. The use of token economy systems in classes for retarded children appears to be a form of overkill in that checkmarks, tokens, and back-up reinforcers are largely unnecessary when all that is needed is a more systematic form of social reinforcement from the teacher. Social praise and approval, morever, represent more "natural" consequences for appropriate behavior than tokens or checkmarks. It is noted that teachers may often unintentionally ignore or misuse social-reinforcement techniques to the particular disadvantage of the retarded child. A burgeoning research effort in the area of social-reinforcement approaches to classroom management and motivation has demonstrated the effectiveness of systematic teacher attention and approval.
Forness, Steven R. & MacMillan, Donald L. (U California, Los Angeles) Journal of Special Education, 1972(Fal), Vol 6(3), 221-230. [PA, Vol 53:04048]

2900.   Integration of the handicapped: What demands will be made?
Summarizes arguments for and against integration of the handicapped into regular classes. 3 types of integration (organizational, educational, and social) are examined. A favorable educational setting, a level-adapted teaching program, and educational therapy are presented as criteria for special education. It is emphasized that administrative procedures must be simplified and coordinated in order to serve the handicapped. It is noted that great demands are placed on teachers of the handicapped. (17 ref.)
Gjessing, Hans J. Family & Child Mental Health Journal, 1972(Mar), Vol. 19(1), 28-39. [PA, Vol 49:09908]

2901.   The effects of various classroom environments on performance of a mental task by mentally retarded and normal children.
Investigated whether performance of a mental task by 14 brain injured mentally retarded children, 14 cultural familial mentally retarded children, and 14 normal children of comparable mental age would be differentially affected by various classroom environmental conditions. It was found that both normal Ss and cultural familial mentally retarded Ss performed the experimental task best when secluded visually. There was no particular advantage to complete seclusion. The brain injured mentally retarded Ss, however, performed best when completely secluded. Since there was no significant difference in overall performance between the brain injured and cultural familial mentally retarded Ss, the important factor seems to be the type of environmental control.
Gorton, Chester E. (Texas Woman's U., Coll. of Education) Education & Training of the Mentally Retarded, 1972(Feb), Vol. 7(1), 32-38. [PA, Vol 49:07822]

2902.   Attitudes toward school by segregated and integrated retarded children: A study and experimental validation.
The attitudes toward school of retarded children in various school placements were investigated in 2 studies. The 1st study compared the attitudes of nonretarded children, and retarded children in segregated and integrated class placements. Results indicate that the segregated group posited significantly less favorable attitudes than the other groups. Since S selection was not random, a 2nd study was undertaken in which retarded children were randomly assigned to integrated and segregated classes and on whom preintegration data were collected. Results are similar to those in Study 1, and are discussed in terms of the labeling process and its consequences for behavior.

Gottlieb, Jay & Budoff, Milton. (Harvard Medical School, Research Inst. for Educational Problems, Boston, Mass.) Proceedings of the 80th Annual Convention of the American Psychological Association, 1972, Vol. 7(Pt. 2), 713-714. [PA, Vol 48:05665]

2903.   The role of instruction in the acceleration of development of logical abilities in children.
Investigated the effect of training on the development of the classificatory ability in 196 4-7 yr. old normal and in 45 9-11 yr. old mentally retarded children. ½ of these Ss were trained for 6 successive days in logical classification. The effects of instruction were tested both immediately and 1 mo. afterwards. Progress due to instruction was noted in Ss of all age groups, including the retarded ones, as compared with untrained Ss. Whereas practically all 6- and 7-yr-old Ss passed on from the pre- to the operational stage in classification, the 4 yr. olds proved ineducable in that respect. It is concluded that logical classification ability cannot be developed by instruction below the age of 4-5, for reasons of maturational insufficiency. (23 ref.)
Grzywak-Kaczyńska, Maria & Walesa, Czesław. (Catholic U. Lublin, Poland) Polish Psychological Bulletin, 1972, Vol. 3(1), 17-23. [PA, Vol 48:07783]

2904.   [A special occupational therapy day school: A one year experience.] (Fren)
Describes a day school in the Val-de-Marne Department which is intended to take 50 slightly and moderately retarded 16-20 yr. old adolescents of both sexes. A number of decisions was made prior to opening concerning: (a) the criteria for admission of the adolescents, (b) the composition of the staff (medical and educational), and (c) the principles of education. During the 1st few months a quantitative and qualitative study was made of the first intake of adolescents. It is noted that results at the end of the 1st yr. are difficult to evaluate precisely due to the brief period the school has been in existence, but some trends are reported. (German & Spanish summaries)
Illien, F.; Ribon, J. F. & Haviotte, L. R. (Union pour la defense de sante mentale dans la Region Est, Fontenay-sons-Bois, France) Revue de Neuropsychiatrie Infantile et d'Hygiene Mentale de l'Enfance, 1972(May), Vol. 20(5), 477-489. [PA, Vol 50:12017]

2905.   [Investigations about the possibilities of early detection of learning-disabled Students in Special Education by means of objective test procedures.] (Germ)
42 children who did not pass the school entrance examination were tested with 12 psychometric scales after being placed in a special education class. 33 were transferred to regular school after 1 yr., while the remaining ones remained in special education (mentally retarded). The transfer (successful) children showed significantly better performances on 11 out of 12 scales when compared with the special education children. Tests included the Peabody Picture Vocabulary Test, bead stringing, spatial relations, tracing, and others.
Kornmann, Reimer. (Inst. for Special Education, Heidelberg, W. Germany) Zeitschrift für Entwicklungspsychologie und Pädagogische Psychologie, 1972, Vol. 4(1), 17-26. [PA, Vol 48:09714]

2906.   [Psycho-pedagogical premises of reading-writing acquirement by mental deficients.] (Romn)
Demonstrates the insufficiencies of academic selection and orientation of mental deficients. Examinations of 61 8-13 yr olds in the 1st form of a special school indicated Ss' success or lack of success in reading-writing. Findings suggest the necessity and possibility of reducing the exaggerated degree of heterogeneity in special classes.
Kulcsár, Tiberiu. (Babes-Bolyai U., Cluj, Romania) Revista de Psihologie, 1972, Vol. 18(1), 77-87. [PA, Vol 51:09949]

2907.   [The Zaire child 3-7½ years old: Contribution to the understanding of his development in relationship to influences and characteristics of family milieu.] (Fren)
Trained 764 Zaire children for 6 mo. in a pre-primary school setting in Kinshasa. Training consisted, e.g., of crayon drawing,

the use of geometric objects, carrying objects, and following orders. Testing indicated that an experimental group of 100 overcame physiological, psychological, and sociological retardation due to the family milieu. The 2 most important findings were that the experimental group was superior and the means on all tests were augmented from 3-6½ yr. old.
Mpiutu ne Mbodi. (Free U. Brussels, Belgium) Revue Belge de Psychologie et de Pédagogie, 1972(Jun), Vol. 34(138), 33-44. [PA, Vol 50:05794]

2908.   Effects of social reinforcement on the retarded child: A review and interpretation for classroom instruction.
Reviews the literature on social reinforcement effects with emphasis on its informative role. Research is summarized and critically examined, and implications are drawn for classroom teachers, particularly those who teach the retarded. It is concluded that studies affirm the importance of social reinforcement in the control of performance in children generally, and retarded children in particular. A research deficiency is noted in the failure to use more complex cognitive tasks. It is suggested that teachers of the retarded need to strike a fine balance between minimum motivating feedback well distributed over time and a full measure of informative feedback, both negative and positive. Random or indiscriminate feedback is concluded to impede learning and, sometimes, also to lead to inattention in a complex learning task. (2 p. ref.)
Panda, Kailas C. & Lynch, William W. (Virginia Commonwealth U.) Education & Training of the Mentally Retarded, 1972(Oct), Vol. 7(3), 115-123. [PA, Vol 49:10015]

2909.   [The role of concreteness in the mental activity of mentally retarded schoolchildren.] (Russ)
Investigated the use of pictures to stimulate thinking in the solution of riddles by mentally retarded schoolchildren. 20 1st- and 2nd-grade special education students were asked to solve riddles of 3 degrees of logical complexity and to explain their answers. If S could not answer a riddle or answered it incorrectly, it was read again accompanied by 3 pictures. One picture depicted the solution object; each of the others depicted an object which had 1 of the characteristics stipulated in the riddle. The use of pictures increased correct answers and decreased the instances in which S had no explanation or a logically absurd explanation for an incorrect answer. Ss' explanations of correct answers were divided into 6 groups according to quality (e.g., explanation focuses on 1 stipulated characteristic, explanation focuses on 2 stipulated characteristics) and the use of pictures increased the number of better explanations. It is concluded that, since no help other than the pictures were offered, their use did stimulate active, independent thinking.
Protsko, T. A. (Minsk Pedagogical Inst., USSR) Defektologiya, 1972, Vol. 2, 26-31. [PA, Vol 50:11586]

2910.   Educations rhythmics: An interdisciplinary approach to mental and physical disabilities.
Describes the philosophy, method, and structure of educational rhythmics, education in the synchronization of individual levels of motor and cognitive ability through rhythmic exercises. Results from research studies of this approach are presented. Instructional materials and programs are outlined.
Robins, Ferris & Robins, Jennet. (Oberer Schooren, Uerikon, Switzerland) Journal of Learning Disabilities, 1972(Feb), Vol. 5(2), 104-109. [PA, Vol 48:03688]

2911.   Side effects of extinction procedures in a remedial preschool.
Undertook behavior-modification procedures with a 7-yr-old retarded boy who engaged in excessive conversation with his preschool teacher. When the teacher ignored his initiated conversation during free-play periods, it decreased. In addition, social behavior relative to children increased, and use of girls' toys decreased during free play. Also appropriate behavior at group academics declined, while disruptions rose. In a 2nd study, the teacher alternated conditions of praise and ignoring for talking with children. Talking with children varied accordingly. In addition, use of girls' toys and group disruptions rose during

the ignoring condition. Appropriate behaviors dropped. Lastly, a time-out procedure was used to eliminate the undesirable side effects of disruptions and of use of girls' toys. Apparently, a response class may have member behaviors that covary directly and/or inversely. Some covariations may be socially desirable, others undesirable. The appearance of undesirable side effects can be controlled using behavior modification techniques.
Sajwaj, Thomas; Twardosz, Sandra & Burke, Marianne. (U. Mississippi, Medical Center) Journal of Applied Behavior Analysis, 1972(Sum), Vol. 5(2), 163-175. [PA, Vol 49:01356]

2912.   A close look at a variety of reinforcers.
Examines several positive reinforcers that can be used in the classroom to reinforce children when they exhibit appropriate social and academic behaviors. 5 general categories discussed are edible, nonedible, activity, social, and token. The advantages and disadvantages of using each reinforcer are outlined. The importance of selecting appropriate reinforcers for each child also is discussed.
Stainback, William C. & Stainback, Susan B. (Virginia State Coll.) Training School Bulletin, 1972(Nov), Vol. 69(3), 131-135. [PA, Vol 50:01954]

2913.   [Situational pedagogy.] (Fren)
Notes that since mentally retarded children are less inclined to use defense mechanisms, it is easier to perceive their somatizations and transferences. In order to offer these children other adult models, it is important that the members of the treatment team know and recognize one another. The thesis is defended that the teacher cannot be sensitized to the reactions of the microgroup (his class) and will not be able to assume his responsibility within the team unless he masters the cognitive processes of the instrument which he is transmitting (knowledge). It is then quite beneficial to analyze the transferences.
Stassart, J.   Information Psychiatrique, 1972(Mar), Vol 12(45), 73-82. [PA, Vol 54:12611]

2914.   A note on the semantic structures of the school-related attitudes in exceptional children.
Administered a semantic differential form to a total of 620 retarded, disturbed, blind, and deaf students. 4 people (classmates, teacher, parent, and myself) and 4 curricular areas (social studies, language, science, and mathematics) were rated, respectively, on 9 and 8 bipolar scales. On people concepts, 3 factors merit, movement, and security were found among normal middle school Ss. 2 factors were identified in the retarded and disturbed, 4 in the blind, and 3 in the deaf. The deaf group's semantic space was essentially identical with that of the normal group; the blind also exhibited high correspondence with the normal. 1 factor for the blind, deaf, and retarded coincided with merit, while another factor in the disturbed, blind, and deaf corresponded with movement. In the case of the security factor, the blind and deaf corresponded with normals, but in the case of the disturbed and retarded the security factor split with 1 of the other 2 in normals. Correspondence among groups was less convincing with curricular ratings. The 1st factor, excluding the retarded, was easily identified as the vigor factor in normal Ss. The certainty factor was also clearly evident among the blind, deaf, and disturbed. The retarded group appeared to split its loading among the vigor, certainty, and nameless factors with normal Ss. It is suggested that the semantic space of school-related attitudes in various exceptional groups is not structured in a manner radically different from normal middle school age children. (18 ref.)
Thomas, Elizabeth C. & Yamamoto, Kaoru. (U. Arkansas) Journal of Psychology, 1972(Jul), Vol.81 (2), 225-234. [PA, Vol 49:01377]

2915.   Personality and sociocultural retardation.
Presents research evidence indicating the importance of noncognitive variables in determining how well the socioculturally retarded child will achieve in structured testing and scholastic situations. Socioculturally retarded children come from intellectually and experientially restricted environments, and such environmental restrictions appear to influence the personality structures of these children. They approach formal testing and scholastic situations with poor achievement motivation, little expectation for success and high expectation of failure, heightened anxiety, poor self-concepts, and a need for emotional nurturing. Since these noncognitive variables influence learning, consideration must be given these factors along with cognitive variables in formal academic programs. (61 ref.)
Tymchuk, Alexander J. (U. California, Medical School, Los Angeles) Exceptional Children, 1972(May), Vol. 38(9), 721-728. [PA, Vol 50:05873]

2916.   [Problems in the special education of exceptional children in the USSR.] (Russ)
Presents a brief summary, by the Director of the Institute of Defectology of the Academy of Pedagogical Sciences, of the history of special education in the USSR, and describes the Institute's work with exceptional children of various categories. Each of the current 5-yr plans for the study of pupils with delays in development (learning disabilities), hearing disorders, visual disturbances, mental retardation, and speech problems is presented, and the current 5-yr plan for exceptional children of preschool age is described.
Vlasova, T. A. (USSR Academy of Pedagogical Sciences, Inst of Defectology, Moscow) Defektologiya, 1972, No 6, 3-13. [PA, Vol 54:04220]

2917.   Sex education for the mentally retarded: An analysis of problems, programs, and research.
Analyzes the literature and critically examines specific programs of sex education. It is noted that most of the literature presents theorizations rather than scientific data. Topics examined include (a) the need for sex education, (b) the schools, (c) the teacher's role, and (d) the marriage potential of the mentally retarded. The status of research is discussed and future guidelines suggested. (18 ref.)
Vockell, Edward L. & Mattick, Pamm. (Purdue U., Hammond, Ind.) Education & Training of the Mentally Retarded, 1972(Oct), Vol. 7(3), 129-134. [PA, Vol 49:10097]

2918.   Effects of a music enrichment program in the education of the mentally retarded.
Studied the effects of a music-enrichment program on the measured intelligences, basic knowledges, communicative abilities, and social behaviors of 10 retarded children in an educational setting, compared to 10 control Ss at the same school. A program of musical activities was conducted for a 40-min period, twice weekly, for 18 wk.,36 sessions, and approximately 24 hr. of time. Controls, although having some musical participation in their regular classroom settings, did not receive the additional music treatment. Pretest and posttest administration of the Peabody Picture Vocabulary Test measured intelligence, and pretest and posttest evaluations with the Trainable Mentally Retarded Performance Profile were used as measures of change in basic knowledge, communication, and social behavior for each S. It is concluded that there was a significant gain in the measured intelligence of the experimental group engaged in the music enrichment program and a significant difference in favor of the experimental group in the amount of change in intelligence. Both groups made significant gains in basic knowledge, communication, and social behavior; however, there was no significant difference between the 2 groups in the amount of mean change in these areas.
Wingert, M. Lucille. (Warren County School System, McMinnville, Tenn.) Journal of Music Therapy, 1972(Spr), Vol. 9(1), 13-22. [PA, Vol 49:08029]

2919.   The application of operant principles to mentally retarded children.
Presents case studies of 6 mentally retarded children (ages 5-15 yrs) with multiple handicaps such as epilepsy, physical handicap due to cerebral palsy, behavior problems, and autistic behavior. Operant procedures with contingency management were applied to establish self-care abilities, modify deviant behavior, and teach academic skills. The most effective results were achieved in the training of self-care and the modification of deviant behavior. Although better results were also obtained in the teaching of

certain reading skills, compared to conventional teaching, it was not shown that language and number concepts which involve higher mental process could be taught by the same operant principles.
Yamaguchi, Kaoru. (Tokyo Gakugei U, Research Inst for the Education of Exceptional Children, Japan) RIEEC Research Bulletin, 1972(Sep), No 1, 27 p. [PA, Vol 54:10257]

2920.   Year one of a research program: Special reading instructional procedures for mentally retarded and learning disabled children.
Presents 31 articles describing the 1st year's activities of a reading research program. The work is in 5 subprograms: codification of the knowledge base, codification of reading skills, organization of specifications and recommendations, formulation of prototypes, and evaluation of prototypes. The research program, projects within subprograms, and evaluation studies are described. Year 1 focused on mentally retarded pupils. 6 reading skills were selected as priority skills: identifying main ideas, identifying supporting ideas, using context clues, learning synonyms, learning homonyms, and learning concepts. Evaluation studies were designed to examine the relative effectiveness of 2 or more teaching treatments and of amounts of a treatment.
Blake, Kathryn et al. (U. Georgia) Journal of Research & Development in Education, 1973, Vol. 6(Mono.), 177. [PA, Vol 51:07984]

2921.   The effect of kinesthetic and visual-motor experiences in the creative development of mentally retarded students.
Notes evidence from recent research suggesting that a more complete understanding of the abilities of mentally retarded students may result from assessing their creative development. Indications that the mentally retarded may achieve as highly or even excel the normal child in creative ability are considered. 2 programs of creative training for mentally retarded students were evaluated in a study with 7-16 yr olds (IQ = 40-85). Results suggest that visual-motor creative training may enhance the creative production of these children. (17 ref.)
Carter, Kyle R.; Richmond, Bert O. & Bundschuh, Ernest L. (U. Georgia) Education & Training of the Mentally Retarded, 1973(Feb), Vol. 8(1), 24-28. [PA, Vol 51:03934]

2922.   [Problems of instruction and education for the mentally retarded child and those with neurogenic defects.] (Fren)
Presents 10 case histories exemplifying the nature and range of the medical, psychological and educational disorders among children and adolescents of low intelligence. The sample includes cases drawn from the lower end of the distribution of intelligence in the general population and others rooted in faulty development within the CNS. It is argued that the educational needs of these children, who are already working under a handicap, are not properly met by the current concepts governing public education in France. A more humane and realistic approach to the instruction of those attempting to cope, with a lower mental capacity, first with the demands of school and later the demands of adult economic life would center on practical instruction (e.g., manual arts or crafts) to provide "a substitute for intelligence" (in Kuhlmann's phrase). It is suggested that this would allow for the formation of a satisfying metier for adult life, reducing the needless and chronic sense of failure and inadequacy now induced by their unavailing efforts to cope with an educational program designed for those of normal intelligence.
Chatagnon, P. A. (Maison-Blanche Hosp., Lab. of Genetic Biochemistry & Nerve Biology, Marne, France) Annales Médico-Psychologiques, 1973(Feb), Vol. 1(2), 177-213. [PA, Vol 51:01898]

2923.   Mental age: Bedrock or quicksand of IQ?
Considers that the normal child's intellectual growth generally reaches its highest level by the age of 16 yrs; most individuals who have a CA older than 16 yrs have an MA of 16 yrs. However, a retarded person whose development lags behind that of a normal person, may not stop growing mentally at the CA of 16, and higher-level retardates may continue to develop until their 4th decade of life. Implications for the continuing education

of retardates beyond the age of 16 yrs are drawn, and strategies for teaching the retarded child some of the problem solving techniques used by the normal child are outlined. It is suggested that future research should concentrate on remedial teaching programs based on a rational model explaining how information is processed in children at different stages of their mental development.
Das, J. P. (U Alberta, Ctr for the Study of Mental Retardation, Edmonton, Canada) Mental Retardation Bulletin, 1972–73, Vol 1(3), 68-72. [PA, Vol 58:03572]

2924.   How to teach retardates to control their behaviour.
Summarizes a symposium on the development of control in mentally retarded children, held at the 20th International Congress of Psychology at Tokyo, August 1972. S. W. Bijou discussed the application of operant conditioning principles to teaching retardates, and K. Yamaguchi described 3 teaching areas in which he had used behavior modification. V. I. Lubovosky explained his "motor conditioning" method for developing verbal control in retardates. K. Amano reported that rhythm training has been found to contribute to the acquisition of reading skills, and P. E. Bryant discussed differences in the perceptual strategies used by normals and retardates.
Das, J. P. (U Alberta, Interdisciplinary Research Ctr, Edmonton, Canada) Indian Journal of Mental Retardation, 1973(Jan), Vol 6(1), 5-20. [PA, Vol 53:10509]

2925.   Attention: Where it's at.
Discusses the importance, in educating retarded children, of training them in efficiency in maintaining the orienting response to important stimuli (i.e., in "paying attention"). The author's studies in this area are summarized and suggestions offered for specially designed instruction in attention for retarded children. Findings have demonstrated no general defect in the orienting response of the retarded child, as compared with the nonretarded, and indicate that distractibility is not unmanageable in a retarded population.
Das, J. P. (U Alberta Ctr for the Study of Mental Retardation, Edmonton, Canada) Mental Retardation Bulletin, 1972–73, Vol 1(2), 29-32. [PA, Vol 58:02175]

2926.   The use of a fading technique in paired-associate teaching of a reading vocabulary with retardates.
Trained two groups of 9 nonreading retarded children (MA range, 4.2-6.11 yrs) with a paired-associates technique to compare the effects of a fading procedure and a standard (simultaneous presentation) method on reading-vocabulary acquisition. For the 1st 8-word list, the groups received either faded or nonfaded training and were tested on the number of words learned. Both groups were then given nonfaded training on a 2nd 8-word list and were again tested. Results indicate that the group which was given faded training on the 1st word list learned significantly more words from both lists than the nonfaded training group ($p < .05$). Educational significance was seen in the fact that the fading procedure could itself be faded. The efficacy of fading is interpreted with an attentional explanation: the salience of the picture stimuli was reduced by fading, which increased the relative salience of the words.
Dorry, George W. & Zeaman, David. (U. Connecticut) Mental Retardation, 1973(Dec), Vol. 11(6), 3-6. [PA, Vol 52:04068]

2927.   The hidden handicap: Attitudes toward children and their implication.
Contends that many special education programs for the retarded fail to accomplish their purpose because teacher attitudes are negative and inflexible. Some of these damaging attitudes are described, their causes and their effects on children are analyzed, and remedies are suggested.
Ensher, Gail L. (Syracuse U.) Mental Retardation, 1973(Aug), Vol. 11(4), 40-41. [PA, Vol 51:05842]

2928.   [Are workers' children less intelligent-or really just "die Dummer?"] (Germ)
Compared the socioeconomic status (SES) of 2,600 pupils in schools for the mentally handicapped with the status of an unselected sample of pupils in schools for normal children. Only

6.3% of the children in the special schools came from middle-class families, compared to 29.4% of the children in normal schools. 265 of the pupils in special schools had normal IQs (90-116), but of this group 98% were children of skilled and unskilled workers, craftsmen, and minor clerks. Of the special school students with lower IQs (42-89), over 90% came from lower socioeconomic levels. It is concluded that children of lower SES are grossly overrepresented in special schools, and that lift courses should be offered in normal schools, at least for all children of average intelligence and low achievement, to avoid their placement in special schools. (English summary) (19 ref) *Ferdinand, W. & Uhr, R.* Psychologie in Erziehung und Unterricht, 1973, Vol 20(1), 31-35. [PA, Vol 53:12518]

2929. Comparison of separately administered and abstracted WISC short forms with the full scale WISC.
Administered the Devereux Short Form and the standard WISC in counterbalanced order to 26 6-15 yr old mentally retarded children. Neither form of test nor order of administration resulted in significant differences in IQ scores. Correlation between the administered short form and the standard WISC was significant. Results are interpreted as further demonstration of the usefulness of this short form with retarded children.
Finch, A. J.; Childress, W. B. & Ollendick, T. H. (Virginia Treatment Center for Children, Richmond) American Journal of Mental Deficiency, 1973(May), Vol. 77(6), 755-756. [PA, Vol 51:07994]

2930. The learning of difficult visual discriminations by the moderately and severely retarded.
Designed an efficient and effective procedure for training moderately and severely retarded individuals to make fine visual discriminations. A test of the model was conducted with 16 adolescent and adult retardates. Results suggest that expectancies for such individuals are in need of examination. Implications for sheltered workshops, work activity centers, and classrooms are discussed.
Gold, Marc W. & Barclay, Craig R. (U. Illinois, Children's Research Center) Mental Retardation, 1973(Apr), Vol. 11(2), 9-11. [PA, Vol 51:01902]

2931. The effect of vicarious reinforcement on attentive behavior in the classroom.
Examined the effect of social reinforcement delivered to target Ss on the attentive behavior of adjacent peers in a classroom setting. In a combined reversal and multiple base-line design, 2 pairs of 8-12 yr. old mentally retarded children were sequentially exposed to 3 reinforcement phases. After base-line rates of attentive behavior were obtained, praise was delivered to the target S in each S pair for attentive behavior. After a reversal phase, praise was delivered contingently to target Ss for inattentive behavior. In a final phase, contingent praise for attentive behavior was reinstated for the target Ss. Throughout the study, nontarget Ss received no direct reinforcers. Results indicate a vicarious reinforcement effect. Reinforcing attentive behavior of target Ss increased this behavior in adjacent peers. However, reinforcing inattentive behavior of target Ss also increased the attentive behavior of adjacent peers. The effects obtained through vicarious reinforcement were considered to reflect the discriminative stimulus properties of reinforcement, which may serve as a cue for the performance of nonreinforced peers. (20 ref.)
Kazdin, Alan E. (Pennsylvania State U.) Journal of Applied Behavior Analysis, 1973(Spr), Vol. 6(1), 71-78. [PA, Vol 50:09906]

2932. Adaptation of a concepts-reading program to the retarded.
Discusses The Kindergarten Program, designed to develop the communication skills of young children in general, with special reference to its 2 instructional subsystems, the Instructional Concepts Program and the Beginning Reading Program, as these have been used in special education classes. Materials for each program are described, the general mode of lesson presentation is outlined, needed adaptations for retarded children are indicated, and the advantages and disadvantages are listed. Use of the Beginning Reading Program may not be feasible with children whose learning problems are complicated by, e.g., imperfect visual or auditory perception, and alternatives in such cases are suggested. Both programs enable the teacher to evaluate learning, and can produce a high success rate in the appropriate population. It is concluded that their effectiveness will depend on the teacher's skill in adapting and modifying the materials to meet pupil needs.
Kokaska, Sharen M. (Palos Verdes Unified School District, Rolling Hills, Calif.) Education & Training of the Mentally Retarded, 1973(Dec), Vol. 8(4), 211-216. [PA, Vol 52:06353]

2933. [A study on the educational thought of Édouard Séguin.] (Japn)
Discusses the place of Édouard Séguin in the history of education. One of his greatest contributions was his program for "idiotic children"—a term in which he included several types of children, from the severely handicapped to the mentally retarded—whose right to education had been ignored. He proposed physical education for them to encourage their harmonious overall development and to train their senses. He also emphasized the importance of vocational education to help them become self-sufficient and socially independent.
Matsuya, Katsuhiro. (Taisho U., Tokyo, Japan) Japanese Journal of Special Education, 1973(Dec), Vol. 11(2), 27-42. [PA, Vol 52:08682]

2934. The school psychologist and mild retardation: Report of an ad hoc committee.
Reports that the school psychologist identifies more persons as "retarded" than any other agent and is central in the current allegations of inappropriate school educable mentally retarded (EMR) labeling of children whose slow learning is associated with disadvantage. Court orders and legislative mandates have caused wholesale return of EMRs to regular programs. This legal activity is predicted mostly on the assumption that labeling is chiefly by IQ, but generally the child must fail class first before psychological referral. Thus return to regular class still leaves a learning problem, requiring a different role for both psychologist and teacher, whatever the child's label. (29 ref.)
Meyers, C. Edward. (U. Southern California) Mental Retardation, 1973(Feb), Vol. 11(1), 15-20. [PA, Vol 50:03844]

2935. CEC ERIC's the new way to know: Mental retardation in the Soviet Union.
Reports the impressions of U.S. special educators invited to observe programs for educating mentally retarded children in the Soviet Union. Methods of diagnosis and child placement are discussed, and the basic curriculum is examined.
Nazzaro, Jean. (Council for Exceptional Children, Information Center, Reston, Va.) Education & Training of the Mentally Retarded, 1973(Oct), Vol. 8(3), 166-171. [PA, Vol 52:01877]

2936. WISC profiles: Above average and MR good and poor readers.
Examined WISC profiles of 62 intellectually above average and 35 mentally retarded children in terms of their performance on a reading achievement test. No specific WISC subtests were found to differentiate good vs poor readers consistently for both intellectual groups. Some mentally retarded Ss read significantly better than above average Ss of comparable mental ages. It is concluded that reading disability should not be considered a phenomenon confined to those of average or above average IQ since there are good and poor readers at all intellectual levels. This has implications for acceptance of retardates into remedial reading programs from which they are usually excluded.
Ramanauskas, Sigita & Burrow, Will H. (U. Connecticut) Mental Retardation, 1973(Apr), Vol. 11(2), 12-14. [PA, Vol 51:01906]

2937. Guide posts to functional ability: A curriculum for the moderately and severely retarded.
Notes that education of mentally retarded children has moved progressively from health care and training orientation to an educational enterprise. There has been uncertainty among teachers as to what should be taught to retarded children. As a

consequence teachers have tended to cling to familiar primary school practices, resulting in a "watered down" version of a normal school curriculum. To overcome these practices, a curriculum was developed with 5 levels of teacher planning. The levels involve the development of philosophy, curriculum, syllabus, work program, and lesson plans. The curriculum is based on present and future "usefulness" to the retarded child.
Reynolds, A. R. (Queensland Sub-Normal Children's Assn., Brisbane, Australia) Australian Journal of Mental Retardation, 1973(Dec), Vol. 2(8), 232-235. [PA, Vol 52:11043]

2938. Occupational exploration practices: A pilot study to increase the vocational sophistication of slow learners.
Investigated the effects of exploring occupational possibilities on the vocational sophistication of slow learners. Ss were 40 high school students in special classes; treatment consisted of field trips for 1 group and lectures for another, with a 3rd group as controls. The Vocational Interest and Sophistication Assessment Inventory was administered to all Ss before and after treatment and showed gains in vocational sophistication after the occupational experience exposure. (32 ref.)
Salomone, Paul R.; Lehmann, Elizabeth & Green, Alan J. (Syracuse U., Div. of Special Education & Rehabilitation) Mental Retardation, 1973(Aug), Vol. 11(4), 3-7. [PA, Vol 51:05950]

2939. Teacher retention of stereotypes of exceptionality.
165 special and general education undergraduates rated a typical retarded, normal, or gifted child on 5 dimensions (attitude toward adults, tasks, own performance, motor reactions, and verbalizations) and then rated a videotape of a normal child who was labeled either retarded, gifted, or normal. Results suggest that Ss comprehended experimentally induced stereotypes but when faced with performances of normal children, selectively retained portions of the stereotype and discarded some components of the label in light of conflicting perceptions.
Salvia, John; Clark, Gary M. & Ysseldyke, James E. (Pennsylvania State U.) Exceptional Children, 1973(May), Vol. 39(8), 651-652. [PA, Vol 51:03827]

2940. Classroom techniques: A program for training children in coordination and perceptual development.
Suggests that 1 area in special education which suffers from a lack of attention is the child's physical development. A program is described which is geared toward (a) meeting each child's needs regardless of ability and (b) developing both the child's gross and motor coordination as well as improving his perceptual problems.
Thelen, David C. (Varina Elementary School, Va.) Education & Training of the Mentally Retarded, 1973(Feb), Vol. 8(1), 29-35. [PA, Vol 51:03950]

2941. [Special characteristics of performance behaviors of boys who are difficult to educate.] (Germ)
Compared about 1,400 high school students who had difficulties in performance in schools and social adjustment with adequately performing and adjusting youths of the same age. Main criteria for selection of the sample included nonpromotion from 1 grade to the next. More than ⅔ of the boys difficult to train failed to obtain the educational goals of their classes. Negative social attitudes were other required criteria. In some cases, mental retardation was a concomitant trait. Results show that nearly all boys showed physical-psychological retardation (from 1-3 yrs). This retardation is significant ($p < .01$) when compared to the "normal" group. Retarded motor development correlated .63 with the criterion of difficult to train. Means and standard deviations of teacher ratings were examined. It was found that boys difficult to train possessed age-inappropriate knowledge: did not concentrate well; were superficial in observations; disinterested in schools; slow in learning; had short memory; tendency to falsify in the direction of their fantasies; and were slow in language, thought, and judgments.
Topel, Wilhelm. Probleme und Ergebnisse der Psychologie, 1973, Vol. 44, 57-72. [PA, Vol 51:09937]

2942. Stability of IQ of immigrant and non-immigrant slow-learning pupils.
Referred all West Indian immigrant children entering a city over a period of 16 mo. who were suspected by teachers as being possible slow learners to a psychologist. The 14 Ss who obtained Verbal WISC scores of less than 80 were retested after a period of 1½-2½ yr. A control group of 12 nonimmigrant pupils of similar ability was reassessed after a similar period. Increases for the immigrants ranged from 2-21 (mean = 8.2), while the mean rise for controls was .25 (t = 3.7). In the case of every immigrant there was a rise in score, the mean rise being over 8 points of IQ. For the immigrants the test-retest coefficient was .76. There was a significant positive correlation between score rise and time between tests.
Watson, P. (Leeds Child Guidance Center, England) British Journal of Educational Psychology, 1973(Feb), Vol. 43(1), 80-82. [PA, Vol 50:10057]

2943. Art curricula and MR preschoolers.
Studied the effect of an art specialist on an art curriculum for retarded preschoolers. Ss were 33 retarded 2-7 yr olds and 11 normal 3-4 yr olds from lower and middle class families. A rating system was devised to evaluate paintings collected initially and 5 mo later. All groups made statistically significant gains ($p < .10$) with no effect attributable to the art specialist. The paintings of normal 3 yr olds and retarded children appeared similar, but the normal 4 yr olds were at a higher level of artistic development.
Winkelstein, Ellen; Shapiro, Bernard J. & Shapiro, Phyllis P. (Rhode Island Coll.) Mental Retardation, 1973(Jun), Vol. 11(3), 6-9. [PA, Vol 51:01911]

2944. Systematically and precisely arranged: An instructional program for low performance children.
Describes the work of the Experimental Education Unit of the University of Washington and its model preschool center for handicapped children. Children are grouped into 4 classes: infant learning, early preschool, advanced preschool, and kindergarten. Many of the children have very low performance levels in developmental areas, and instruction must be arranged precisely and systematically; when this is done, acquisition rates may increase markedly. A case history illustrates procedures and results.
————. Education & Training of the Mentally Retarded, 1974(Feb), Vol. 9(1), 33-36. [PA, Vol 52:08664]

2945. Pre-student teaching practicum with exceptional children: A program description.
Describes a newly developed teaching experience for the educable-mentally-retarded teacher trainee at the junior year level. The program represents a commitment on the part of teacher educators at the university level to provide relevant experiences for students and to improve the quality of training programs even when student enrollment is large.
Anderson, Robert H. & Hemenway, Robert E. (Memphis State U) Education & Training of the Mentally Retarded, 1974(Oct), Vol 9(3), 152-157. [PA, Vol 53:06092]

2946. Early education for mentally retarded children.
Reviews selected United Kingdom early education programs for handicapped children that illustrate recent developments in the field. Some of the concepts of the nature of early childhood education considered important in the future development of services for the handicapped are discussed, and suggestions for a model of early education for the mentally retarded are presented.
Andrews, R. J. & Andrews, Jeanette G. (U Queensland, Fred & Eleanor Schonell Educational Research Ctr, St Lucia, Australia) Australian Journal of Mental Retardation, 1974(Mar), Vol 3(1), 1-5. [PA, Vol 53:01963]

2947. Descriptive concepts for preschool retarded children.
Details the direct instruction method, teaching materials, and measurement procedures used in teaching descriptive concepts to 4 4-yr-old retarded boys. All Ss learned correct responding to tasks used during teaching and developed concepts, as evidenced by performance on novel tasks. Replication of the program with

3 2- and 3-yr-old retarded children was equally successful. Results support the view that preschool retarded children can be taught many of the skills with which other children enter public schools.
Bellamy, G. Tom & Bellamy, Terry T. (U Oregon, Ctr on Human Development) Education & Training of the Mentally Retarded, 1974(Oct), Vol 9(3), 115-122. [PA, Vol 53:06198]

2948.   [Adaptation classes in secondary education.] (Fren)
Examines the problems posed by the recruitment of "difficult" pupils and by their regrouping into a class where there is close psychopedagogic collaboration between doctors, psychotherapists, reeducators, social workers attached to a center for retarded children, and the responsible teachers in the high school or secondary school. (German & Spanish summaries)
Bley, R.   Revue de Neuropsychiatrie Infantile et d'Hygiene Mentale de l'Enfance, 1974(Jul–Aug), Vol 22(7–8), 503-516. [PA, Vol 56:04894]

2949.   [Rhythmic exercise in physical education of mentally defective youth.] (Slok)
Description and illustration of exercises used with mentally retarded youth.
Černá, Marie. (Charles U, Prague, Czechoslovakia) Československá Defektologie, 1974, Mono, 114-124. [PA, Vol 57:09130]

2950.   Outdoor education for the retarded child.
Discusses an outdoor education program for the mentally retarded child which involved 50 10-13 yr old children and 10 adults and was continued at the behest of parents, educators, and children. The objective of the program was to provide a central theme for the intermediate special curriculum. From the children's point of view the program was an unqualified success; they appreciated it not only because it was fun but because they found the work interesting. Administrators found it a success because none of the anticipated problems arose; children did not become sick and need to be taken home, and no one became lost or was seriously injured. Most important, it was a success because the children learned and retained what they learned.
Cormany, Robert B. (West Shore School District, Lemoyne, PA) Education & Training of the Mentally Retarded, 1974(Apr), Vol 9(2), 66-69. [PA, Vol 53:10505]

2951.   [The influence of questions on the time of study of narrative texts: Comparative study of normal and retarded children.] (Fren)
Investigated the relation between the use of questions and the time of study of narrative texts. Ss were 42 normal and 42 retarded children with IQs (Stanford-Binet or WISC scores) ranging from 60 to 85. Within populations, Ss were separated into 2 experimental and 1 control groups. The experimental material consisted of prepared short texts of varying lengths accompanying study questions. Results indicate that the combined factors (length of text and nature of questions) affected the time of study differently in the 2 groups. (16 ref)
Denhière, Michèle & Denhiere, Guy. (U Paris VIII, Lab de Psychologie, France) Bulletin de Psychologie, 1974, Vol 28(1-6), 280-294. [PA, Vol 54:12598]

2952.   [The pedagogical study of mentally retarded 2nd and 3rd grade students.] (Russ)
Describes the heterogeneity of 40 2nd and 3rd graders in Moscow school for the mentally retarded and discusses the best educational methods for the various types of children. Ss were divided into 5 groups on the basis of how well they were succeeding with the school program, whether or not they showed a disturbance of the dynamics of the nervous processes, and if such a disturbance was present, whether there was a predominance of inhibition or of excitation. The description of each group is based on data gathered through medical documents, school records, conversations with parents, conversations with Ss, psychological testing, and observation of Ss in various school activities. It is concluded that the educational progress of a mentally retarded child depends both on the structure of his defect and on the type of instruction that he receives.

Em, Z. B. (Academy of Pedagogical Sciences, Inst of Defektologiya, Moscow, USSR) Defektologiya, 1974, Vol 1, 33–39. [PA, Vol 56:04901]

2953.   Breaking down the IQ walls: Severely retarded people can learn to read.
Describes a system to teach reading to children who experience difficulty with traditional methods. The letters are constructed using a circle ("ball"), a line ("stick"), and an angle ("bird"). Reading is begun when 2 letters are learned. The stories are science fiction and grow in complexity as the child learns. The method was used to teach retarded students with IQs of 33-72. The Ss learned to read so well that they were getting 100% on achievement tests. As they learned to communicate, their self-esteem increased.
Fuller, Renée.   Psychology Today, 1974(Oct), Vol 8(5), 97-102. [PA, Vol 53:08362]

2954.   Comparison of classroom behavior of special-class EMR, integrated EMR, low IQ, and nonretarded children.
Compared the classroom behavior of 12 segregated and 14 integrated educable mentally retarded (EMR) children—who were all formerly segregated and then randomly assigned to their present class placements—with that of 18 low-IQ children who had never been identified for special-class placements and 11 intellectually average children. The method was a time-sampling observational one, using 12 behavior categories. Data indicate that 4 mo after the school year began, the integrated EMR children behaved more similarly to nonlabeled EMR children than to their segregated peers. Results are discussed in terms of appropriate peer models influencing classroom behavior of EMR children.
Gampel, Dorothy H.; Gottlieb, Jay & Harrison, Robert H. (U Massachusetts, Boston) American Journal of Mental Deficiency, 1974(Jul), Vol 79(1), 16-21. [PA, Vol 53:01971]

2955.   [Differential effects of verbal praise, feedback of results, and verbal praise combined with feedback of results on the maintenance of arithmetic response rate.] (Span)
Studied the role of verbal praise and feedback of results in maintaining and increasing arithmetic performance previously achieved by a combination of token economy, verbal praise, and feedback of results in 5 elementary school slow learners who were especially deficient in arithmetic performance. Verbal praise was an effective method for improving performance in 3 Ss and ineffective in 1 S. The remaining S showed an increase in performance as a function of time in all conditions. (English summary)
Garcia, Cirilo H. et al. (U Monterrey, Mexico) Revista Interamericana de Psicología, 1974, Vol 8(1-2), 41-52. [PA, Vol 53:01916]

2956.   Teacher expectancy for academic achievement of mentally retarded pupils.
Investigated whether knowledge of a hypothetical retarded child's socioeconomic status (SES) and sex would influence 72 experienced special education teachers' expectations of the ultimate academic achievement level possible for that child at the end of formal schooling. The 72 teachers each completed a questionnaire which described a hypothetical boy or girl from a high or low SES family; teachers estimated the probability of the child's being able to read each item at the end of schooling. While SES and sex did not influence teacher expectations, a good deal of variability in expectancy levels was observed. (15 ref)
Heintz, Paul. (New York U., School of Education, Div. of Behavioral Sciences) Mental Retardation, 1974(Jun), Vol. 12(3), 24-27. [PA, Vol 52:13221]

2957.   [A study of the effects of a resource-room service program for mentally retarded children and slow learners.] (Japn)
Compared 9 retarded 1st graders in a resource-room program with 10 similar children in regular classes. After a year of the program the experimental group showed a greater increase in IQ and greater progress in Japanese than the control group, and 2

experimental Ss attained the normal achievement level. (English summary)
Iida, Sadao. (Yamanashi U, Kofu City, Japan) Japanese Journal of Special Education, 1974(Mar), Vol 11(3), 62-75. [PA, Vol 53:04051]

2958.   [Use of problem-solving help on the Kohs-Goldstein test by the mentally retarded.] (Fren)
300 male and female retarded special education students 15-21 yrs old received 4 levels of help in solving the Kohs-Goldstein tests on items they had previously failed. Individual differences in use of help were found, and a scoring procedure was devised to distinguish among items spontaneously solved, those corrected with help, and those unsolved despite help. This procedure yields a profile more capable of revealing individual differences than the conventional scoring.
Ionescu, S.; Radu, V.; Solomon, E. & Stoenescu, A. (Academia de Stiinte Sociale si Politice, Inst de Psihologie, Bucharest, Romania) Revue Roumaine des Sciences Sociales - Série de Psychologie, 1974, Vol 18(1), 75-92. [PA, Vol 54:06336]

2959.   The use of a contingent music activity to modify behaviors which interfere with learning.
Behaviors which interfere with learning are common among retarded children and those diagnosed as emotionally disturbed. A child who demonstrates behaviors such as not following directions, short attention span, and self-destructive and stereotyped behaviors presents a difficult problem for his teacher and parents. The use of music activity to decrease behaviors which interfere with learning is described, and an example of the multiple baseline techniques is included. Data indicate that music activity contingent on following directives and on the absence of stereotyped behavior is an effective consequence of the method.
Jorgenson, Helen. (Ohio State U.) Journal of Music Therapy, 1974(Spr), Vol. 11(1), 41-46. [PA, Vol 52:13225]

2960.   [Learning without errors: Applications in mental retardation.] (Fren)
Describes an apparatus and a set of discrimination problems that can be used to study errorless learning in retarded children. The apparatus consists of a response unit, a reinforcement unit, and a control unit. Programed presentation of stimuli consists of progressive introduction of the negative stimulus while the trial-and-error method consists of presentations of both positive and negative stimuli from the outset. 5 Ss (average chronological age 11 yrs 1 mo and average IQ 47) were assigned to the programed condition, and 5 Ss (average chronological age 11 yrs 5 mo and average IQ 48) were assigned to the trial-and-error condition. 3 types of discriminations were used: left-right, number-numeral matching, and syllable discriminations. The programed condition resulted in errorless learning in most cases, while trial-and-error method produced many errors. The superiority of the programed method is discussed in terms of its applicability to special education. (English abstract)
Lambert, Jean-Luc. Psychologica Belgica, 1974, Vol 14(2), 105-113. [PA, Vol 54:01947]

2961.   Language training for retarded-deaf children in a state institution.
Describes an ongoing program in language training for a nonvocal group of 8 12-19 yr old retarded-deaf children at the Rosewood State Hospital School, Owings Mills, Maryland. Rating scales were used to evaluate the Ss' communication skills and classroom adjustment. A teacher rating form was also used to collect pre- and poststudy data for determining the efficacy of the program. Procedural steps are presented for teaching 3 different components of language skills (i.e., sentence structure, vocabulary, and reading comprehension). Data indicate that the program increased the vocabulary and the usage of words in phrases and sentences to statistically significant levels. Ss also showed substantial gains in reading in terms of grade levels.
Mitra, Sudhansu B. (Coppin State Coll) Training School Bulletin, 1974(May), Vol 71(1), 41-48. [PA, Vol 53:01977]

2962.   Progress and problems in the education of the mentally handicapped in the U.K.
Briefly summarizes recent progress and problems in the education of the mentally retarded in the United Kingdom. In 1971 responsibility for the education of mentally handicapped children was transferred from the health to the education authorities. No child is now regarded as "ineducable" or unsuitable for education in school and all children are included, regardless of severity of the mental handicap. The following areas are discussed: early education of the child, the content of education, planning for the individual child, teacher training, experiments in integration, and post-school education. Each area is considered in terms of past practices, present status, problems encountered, and future goals.
Mittler, Peter. (U Manchester, Hester Adrian Research Ctr, England) Slow Learning Child, 1974(Nov), Vol 21(3), 140-154. [PA, Vol 53:12528]

2963.   The young E.S.N./S. in education: 1963-1973.
Describes a system of educational provisions for educationally subnormal children of nursery and infant school age who could not be accommodated within an ordinary program. An observational rating scale has been developed to assess the children, guide their teaching, and possibly help evaluate the program at the end of its 1st decade.
Preston, P.   AEP (Association of Educational Psychologists) Journal, 1974(Fal), Vol 3(7), 26-28. [PA, Vol 54:01954]

2964.   Use of electric shock in the classroom: The remediation of self-abusive behavior.
Describes the successful use of a portable shock apparatus to eliminate the self-abusive behavior of an 11-yr-old retarded child in the classroom. Several other positive side effects were noted: a decrease in aggression by the child toward others, improvement in academic performance, and an increase in command-following behavior. However, the effects were severely limited in that there was no generalization beyond the classroom. No negative side effects were observed for either the child or the other children in the class.
Ramsey, Gregory. (Hogan Regional Ctr, Hathorne, MA) Behavioral Engineering, 1974(Fal), Vol 1(2), 4-9. [PA, Vol 53:12233]

2965.   Research and implementation of CAI in elementary and secondary schools.
Presents the results of 3 programs of Computer Assisted Instruction (CAI), carried on as part of a county project. The high school study, involving 137 students, indicated that it was possible, with computer support, to provide an individualized program in geometry for greater numbers of students per class with no significant differences in achievement. In the secondary school study, involving 58 matched pairs of students, individualized computer-based programs produced significantly greater achievement gains in arithmetic than traditional classroom drill. The 3rd study showed that 10 mentally retarded high school students benefited significantly from a CAI arithmetic diagnostic and drill program developed for the regular school population.
Richardson, William M.   Viewpoints, 1974(Jul), Vol 50(4), 39-51. [PA, Vol 53:12461]

2966.   Pointers for teachers as counselors of the moderately and severely mentally retarded: Patterson revisited.
Conducted a survey to learn how parents regard practices and trends in educationally oriented teacher-parent encounters. Included in the questionnaire were pointers for professionals suggested by L. L. Patterson (1956). 63 parents of retarded children and 3 associations for retarded children participated. Results identify (a) the agreement among parents regarding pointers and trends, (b) background factors related to parent opinion, and (c) implications to guide professional practice. (18 ref)
Sellin, Donald & Gallery, Michael. (Western Michigan U) Education & Training of the Mentally Retarded, 1974(Dec), Vol 9(4), 215-221. [PA, Vol 54:04213]

2967.   Zone planning for accelerating adaptive behavior in the retarded.
Describes an innovative teaching environment developed to serve a heterogeneous population of mentally retarded children excluded from other treatment programs. A period of individual therapy designed to increase attending behaviors and decrease self-destructive, aggressive, or other interfering responses is followed by programing each child into a therapy-zone plan of treatment. The zones of special education, self-help, language skills, socialization, and motor skills are used. Children move from one prescribed zone to another upon completing daily goals, thereby avoiding the interfering stimuli of other zones and the distracting social stimuli of large groups. The zone approach is discussed as a viable community-based model.
Stabler, Brian; Gibson, Frank W.; Cutting, D. Scott & Lawrence, P. Scott. (U. North Carolina, Medical School, Chapel Hill) Exceptional Children, 1974(Jan), Vol. 40(4), 252-257. [PA, Vol 52:01879]

2968.   Determining TV preference and its implications for educating retarded children.
Describes a 10-session study with 6 low-level and 6 high-level retarded children in which Ss could choose among 3 videotaped programs or a no-program consequence. Results show that Ss chose programs more often than the no-program consequence and suggest that low-level retarded children can watch the same program on several occasions without satiation occurring but that high-level retarded children need more varied presentations.
Striefel, Sebastian & Smeets, Paul M. (Parsons Research Center, Bureau of Child Research, Kan.) Exceptional Children, 1974(Jan), Vol. 40(4), 285-286. [PA, Vol 52:01858]

2969.   Integrating mentally retarded with normal children: An experiment.
Describes the successful integration of 5 mentally retarded children into a regular class of a New Delhi, India, private school. The individual and community benefits of integration are specified.
Varma, Satish C. & Varma, Chandra K. (State U New York, Downstate Medical Ctr, Brooklyn) Indian Journal of Mental Retardation, 1974(Jul), Vol 7(2), 81-85. [PA, Vol 53:12536]

2970.   Children tutoring children.
In 2 parts, reviews literature on children tutoring other children. Part 1 presents tutorial models for non-mentally-retarded children; Part 2 discusses literature on the retarded tutoring other retarded children. (32 ref)
Wagner, Patricia. (Bronx Developmental Services, Model Rehabilitation Program, NY) Mental Retardation, 1974(Oct), Vol 12(5), 52-55. [PA, Vol 53:06224]

2971.   The efficacy of the resource room for educating retarded children.
Evaluated a resource room program over a 2-yr period. Ss were 29 10-yr-old children (mean IQ, 69.0; reading level, preprimer) in the experimental group and 41 9.8-yr-old matched controls in self-contained special classes. Analysis of variance performed on the data at the end of the 1st and 2nd yrs showed no significant differences in self-concept between the groups. Ss in the resource room program were better academically and socially than controls. Residual gains over the 2-yr period in self-concept, social adjustment, and arithmetic showed no significant differences between groups, but the experimental group made better residual gains in word reading and vocabulary.
Walker, Valaida S. (Pennsylvania Dept. of Public Welfare, Southeastern Region, Philadelphia) Exceptional Children, 1974(Jan), Vol. 40(4), 288-289. [PA, Vol 52:01881]

2972.   Reduced versus nonreduced models in language training of MR children.
Used a highly structured training program to provide language training to 10 mentally retarded children (based on scores on the Peabody Picture Vocabulary Test) in 2 groups. During training, one group received only reduced (telegraphic) imitation models, while the other group received only nonreduced imitation models. Results indicate that language training with reduced models increased Ss' performance during the lessons and on posttesting. Performance differences were also found to generalize from the use of pictures as stimulus materials to the use of real objects. Neither form of language training was found to influence Ss' comprehension of the concepts taught.
Willer, Barry. (Lakeshore Psychiatric Hosp, Toronto, Canada) Journal of Communication Disorders, 1974(Dec), Vol 7(4), 343-355. [PA, Vol 57:13965]

2973.   Special reading instructional procedures for mentally retarded and learning disabled children: Overview of research program activities.
Briefly summarizes the problem, goals, target groups, organizing dimensions, specific program activities, and strategies used in conducting research during the 1st 2 yrs of an experimental reading instructional program for retarded and learning-disabled children.
Williams, Charlotte L. & Blake, Kathryn A. (U Georgia, Special Reading Instructional Procedures for Mentally Retarded & Learning Disabled Children Research Program) Education & Training of the Mentally Retarded, 1974(Oct), Vol 9(3), 143-149. [PA, Vol 53:06225]

2974.   Early childhood educational objectives for normal and retarded children.
Presents a model for early childhood education where the objectives are viewed as the same for normal and retarded children with variations only in the degree of achievement. The means by which the classroom teacher can construct educational objectives that cover various behaviors is discussed.
Winkelstein, Ellen; Shapiro, Bernard J.; Tucker, Dorothy G. & Shapiro, Phyllis P. (Rhode Island Coll) Mental Retardation, 1974(Oct), Vol 12(5), 41-45. [PA, Vol 53:06227]

2975.   Effects of physical stigmata and labels on judgments of subnormality by preservice teachers.
102 randomly selected full-time students in a teacher training program participated in a study to determine the influence that the label "mentally retarded" and physical attractiveness had on individual judgments of subnormality. Ss examined a series of photographs of children that had been selected along a continuum of physical attractiveness with the 2 extremes of the physically attractive and the physically unattractive photographs being utilized in the design. Analysis of data indicated that the presence of physical stigmata in the unattractive photographs influenced judgments of subnormality. Results fail to support the hypothesis that a label appended to a photograph could influence judgments of subnormality. The impact of the physical appearance and teacher judgments on the educational outcome of the child are discussed. (19 ref)
Aloia, Gregory F. (U California, School of Education, Riverside) Mental Retardation, 1975(Dec), Vol 13(6), 17-21. [PA, Vol 55:10646]

2976.   Environment-based language training with mentally retarded children.
Analyzed the language behavior of 9 retarded 12-13 yr olds (ranging from mild to borderline retardation) before and after a 6-wk summer camp type activity to test the hypothesis that rate of verbal behavior could be increased through a systematic program in which the children would experience an environmental event and concurrently verbalize the experience. A 72-item picture-stimulus instrument was developed and administered individually to all Ss by the same examiner. The instrument was designed to sample 3 language processes: receptive, integrative, and expressive. Results indicate that total number of words, total number of sentences, sentence length, and total number of nouns expressed increased significantly. Also, the immediate gains were still significant 1 yr later. (17 ref)
Baum, Dale D.; Odom, Mildred & Boatman, Rex D. (New Mexico State U) Education & Training of the Mentally Retarded, 1975(Apr), Vol 10(2), 68-73. [PA, Vol 54:08434]

2977. [A study of the behavior modification of slow-learning pupils based on client-centered concepts.] (Germ)
Evaluated 25 8-12 yr olds in a school for slow learners with an IQ above 79. Ss received individual client-centered therapy for 20 min once a week for 5 wks, and therapy in groups of 3-4 for 30 min each week. A control group of 21 members was comparable in age, sex (57% male), IQ, and other factors. Pre- and posttest data showed that the counseled Ss became significantly less anxious and more self-reliant. Even the least bright ones learned self-exploratory behavior, though with some delay. Social maturity increased significantly, but not social desirability. (English & German summaries)
Bommert, Hanko et al. (Westfalische Wilhelms-U Munster, Psychologisches Inst, W Germany) Psychologie in Erziehung und Unterricht, 1975, Vol 22(3), 129-136. [PA, Vol 58:06348]

2978. Communication and curriculum process in special education.
Considers ways in which problem-solving skills might be communicated to moderately and severely mentally handicapped children who lack the necessary verbal and language skills. The models of several theorists are discussed with respect to their conceptualizations of the instruction phase of the curriculum process. Because the mentally handicapped child tends to show high field dependence, poor discrimination, poor memory, poor generalization, failure to understand what is being learned, and failure to undergo incidental learning, it is contended that proper instruction requires highly structured arrangements of the stimulus situation that isolate the critical features upon which the mentally handicapped child must act in order to learn. Such instruction would emphasize the more concrete media of creative representation and iconic representation rather than the more abstract media of language and other symbolic forms.
Cooper, G. M. & Bennetts, L. N. (Flinders U of South Australia, Bedford Park) Exceptional Child, 1975(Nov), Vol 22(3), 143-152. [PA, Vol 59:11125]

2979. The organization and structure of workshops for parents of mentally handicapped children.
Describes a workshop approach that has proven feasible in securing the involvement of the parents of mentally handicapped children. The primary objective of the approach is to assist parents to internalize a teaching model for their child's learning and behavior. Assistance given in the phases of observation, assessment, and analysis is described, and the precourse activity and course structure are discussed.
Cunningham, Cliff C. & Jeffree, Dorothy M. (U Manchester, England) Bulletin of the British Psychological Society, 1975(Oct), Vol 28, 405-411. [PA, Vol 61:08800]

2980. Effects of letter-reversals training on the discrimination performance of EMR children.
90 mentally retarded elementary school children who committed letter-reversal errors on a pretest were randomly assigned to 1 of 3 (1 experimental and 2 control) training conditions consisting of 7 sessions given over a 5-wk period. Subsequent statistical analyses revealed that for 1 of 4 letter-discrimination posttests, experimental Ss performed significantly better than the placebo controls. Differences between the experimental and the method-specific control Ss were in the expected direction but not statistically significant. Aptitude × Treatment interactions for 3 of the 4 posttests revealed the training effect on the most pronounced with younger and more retarded children.
Evans, Ross A. & Bilsky, Linda H. (U Wisconsin, Madison) American Journal of Mental Deficiency, 1975(Jul), Vol 80(1), 99-108. [PA, Vol 54:10615]

2981. Attitudes toward retarded children: Effects of labeling and behavioral aggressiveness.
Examined effects of the label "mentally retarded" on attitudes of peers among 48 3rd graders. Half of the Ss were shown a videotape of an actor displaying acting-out behavior, while the remaining half were shown a videotape with the same actor engaging in passive behavior. Half of the Ss in each of these 2 groups were told that the actor was a 5th grader, and the other half were told that he was a mentally retarded boy in a special class. Analysis of variance results revealed a significant interaction between label and behavior, which indicated that Ss responded more negatively to the "mentally retarded" actor who displayed acting-out behavior than to the same actor who exhibited identical behavior but was not labeled. It is concluded that labels should be considered only as they interact with specific behavior.
Gottlieb, Jay. Journal of Educational Psychology, 1975(Aug), Vol 67(4), 581-585. [PA, Vol 54:12581]

2982. Placement in regular programs: Procedures and results.
48 9-10 yr old students classified as mentally retarded and living in an economically depressed area were randomly divided into matched experimental and control groups and placed in 4 classrooms of 12 students each. The objective was to initiate an experimental, individualized, instruction program that would facilitate the return of special education students to regular classes. After 1 yr's intervention, 13 students from the experimental group were placed in regular classes. A 1-yr follow-up study was done to determine the academic and social adaptation of the 13 students. Outcome measures included the Wide Range Achievement Test, Gray Oral Reading Test, and teacher ratings of social and academic behavior. Results show that a high percentage of the Ss could acquire basic skills at a rate to allow regular class placement. Once placed, these students maintained their academic and behavioral adjustments.
Haring, Norris G. & Krug, David A. (U Washington, Child Development & Mental Retardation Ctr, Experimental Education Unit) Exceptional Children, 1975(Mar), Vol 41(6), 413-417. [PA, Vol 54:04193]

2983. Teacher-rated impulsivity and achievement among mildly retarded youth.
Studied the relationship between academic performance of slightly retarded students and their degree of impulsivity. Ss were 235 students 8-17 yrs old, whose teachers rated their reflectivity-impulsivity and their ability in reading, arithmetic, and spelling. Results indicate that the more reflective students tended to perform better academically.
Hayes, Charles S. & Prinz, Robert J. (U Iowa, Hosp School, Child Development Clinic) Psychology in the Schools, 1975(Jan), Vol 12(1), 100-102. [PA, Vol 54:10618]

2984. The educational needs of the mentally handicapped.
Studied the educational needs of mentally handicapped children in the new day special schools from 3 major perspectives as a result of examinations of (a) questionnaires received from headteachers of 88 schools, (b) the skills of 151 mentally handicapped children in 44 of these schools, and (c) questionnaires completed by 52 parents of mentally handicapped children. Results highlight the effect of these schools being in an "educational wilderness" until 1971 and indicate a low level of achievement in certain social skills and parental problems and attitudes. (16 ref)
Hughes, John M. (Caerleon Coll of Education, Wales) Educational Research, 1975(Jun), Vol 17(3), 228-233. [PA, Vol 55:05649]

2985. [The aspiration level of mental retardates.] (Czec)
Tested 200 pupils in regular schools (9, 12, and 15 yrs old) and 50 pupils in special schools to determine their ideas about their future professions. Most of the mentally retarded chose a manual profession, particularly the older ones; none chose intellectual work. The normal children showed the opposite tendency, but their interest in jobs requiring higher education decreased with age. There was no difference between boys and girls among the retardates; among the normals, boys chose occupations requiring basic school education and girls chose jobs requiring a high school education.
Langer, Stanislav. (Pedagogická fakulta, Hradec Králové, Czechoslovakia) Psychológia a Patopsychológia Dietata, 1975, Vol 10(2), 123-138. [PA, Vol 55:10066]

2986. Identifying children's abilities in classes for the MR.
Evaluated 24 male and 10 female 6-13 yr olds from 3 intermediate classes for the retarded—utilizing the Illinois Test of Psycholinguistic Abilities and the Slosson Intelligence Test—to denote inter- and intravariability of their learning abilities. Results discriminate 4 groups: mentally retarded, 12%; mentally retarded with specific psycholinguistic disabilities, 44%; specific psycholinguistic disabilities, 35%; and average children, 9%. Implications for curriculum design are presented. (20 ref)
Lombardi, Thomas P. (West Virginia U) Mental Retardation, 1975(Feb), Vol 13(1), 3-6. [PA, Vol 54:04202]

2987. Generalizing the use of descriptive adjectives through modelling.
2 retarded children, 6 and 8 yrs old, were exposed to daily imitation training in which a teacher or nurse modeled and instructed each child to imitate 12 sentences containing 1 of 6 animal names. Ss were praised for correct verbal imitation. Across 3 phases of a multiple-baseline design, sentences varied as to the presence or absence of size and/or color adjectives describing the animals. In probe sessions at another time of day and in a different setting, E twice asked each S to describe 12 different animal pictures. Ss' use of descriptive adjectives (color and/or size) greatly increased during probe sessions as a function of the sentence content (presence or absence of color and/or size adjectives) in modeling and imitation training sessions. Generalization to descriptions of animals not used in imitation training sentences was also obtained.
Martin, Jerry A. (U Minnesota, Children's Rehabilitation Ctr) Journal of Applied Behavior Analysis, 1975(Sum), Vol 8(2), 203-209. [PA, Vol 54:08446]

2988. Pre-school mentally handicapped children.
Examined the characteristics of the preschool mentally handicapped child. Information was collected on 150 mentally handicapped children who were under 5 yrs of age. Many of the children had additional handicaps and all showed marked retardation in their physical, social, play, and language development. The majority of parents expressed a willingness to take part in a parental involvement project. Their main concerns were with the child's speech and language development and in coping with management problems. The implications of these findings for services provided for these parents and children are discussed.
McConkey, R. & Jeffree, Dorothy M. (U Manchester, Hester Adrian Research Ctr, England) British Journal of Educational Psychology, 1975(Nov), Vol 45(3), 307-311. [PA, Vol 55:10983]

2989. Teaching beginning reading skills to retarded children in community classrooms: A programmatic case study.
Examined the effectiveness of an experimental program for teaching functional beginning reading skills to severely disabled learners. Instruction with an experimental phonic decoding skills program was given to 2 special school classes totaling 19 children ranging in chronological age from 7-12 yrs who had severe reading disabilities. Intragroup and intrasubject comparison of pretest-posttest data on a phonic skills test show: (a) Both classes made significant pretest-posttest gains. (b) All children showed pretest-posttest increments. (c) In particular, both classes achieved competence in skill generalization tasks that are prerequisite to the functional application of phonics. It is concluded that the experimental program offers an effective method for imparting functional decoding skills to disabled learners.
Richardson, Ellis; Oestereicher, Mary H.; Bialer, Irv & Winsberg, Bertrand G. (New York State Dept of Mental Hygiene, New York) Mental Retardation, 1975(Feb), Vol 13(1), 11-15. [PA, Vol 54:04209]

2990. Operant approaches to group therapy in a school for handicapped children.
To determine the effectiveness of operant approaches to group therapy with children with cerebral palsy or mental retardation, a total of 23 30-min sessions were administered to 4 5-6 yr old males. There was considerable improvement in Ss' attention to tasks, and they showed some increase in social interactions,

though to a lesser degree. Teacher ratings also showed some improvement in classroom behavior. (French, German, & Spanish summaries)
Schofield, Leon J. & Wong, Sandralawae. (Hobart & William Smith Coll) Developmental Medicine & Child Neurology, 1975(Aug), Vol 17(4), 425-433. [PA, Vol 55:05122]

2991. Teacher attitudes and the labeling process.
Tested 3 assumptions which appear to underlie the decision-making process that permits the systematic labeling of the so-called 6-hr retarded child. Ss were 36 randomly selected teacher clusters (8 teachers/cluster) in the field-test network of the Curriculum Research and Development Center in Mental Retardation (Yeshiva University). Total sample consisted of 288 teachers from 16 states. Each cluster was randomly assigned 1 of 9 hypothetical but realistic profiles of students. Teachers were then asked to evaluate the adaptiveness of the child and the appropriateness of a mental retardation label. Results, based on 67% of questionnaires returned, support the notion that teachers' labeling decisions tend to be biased against the lower socioeconomic levels and thus contribute to the inappropriate labeling of these children.
Smith, I. Leon & Greenberg, Sandra. (Yeshiva U, Ferkauf Graduate School of Humanities & Social Sciences) Exceptional Children, 1975(Feb), Vol 41(5), 319-324. [PA, Vol 54:01959]

2992. Teacher bias and the evaluation of retarded children.
Reviews the major research in the area of teacher bias, especially as it applies to retarded children. It is noted that strong resistance to the use of test results for identifying children with learning problems has been developing over the past few years. This resistance has grown to the extent that many educators and psychologists tend to reject the use of such testing. Much of the basis for condemning the use of tests is based on sociological grounds (e.g., the tests are not relevant for Black people). Some of the criticism, however, is due to the popular acceptance of the "Rosenthal" effect which suggests that test results tend to become self-fulfilling prophecies and that the performance of children is affected in the direction indicated by psychological reports based on these test results. This review presents some evidence that the negative effects of testing may have been overestimated. (43 ref)
Soule, Don. Research & the Retarded, 1975(Sum), Vol 2(3), 7-20. [PA, Vol 58:04455]

2993. Action-concept learning in retarded children using photographic slides, motion picture sequences, and live demonstrations.
Investigated the relative effectiveness of 3 action-concept instructional techniques with 30 retarded 12-yr-old children. Ss viewed slides, movies, or live demonstrations of 20 actions. The 3 different instructional approaches yielded higher adjusted posttest than pretest recognition scores. The highest posttest score was yielded by the motion picture sequence technique.
Stephens, Wyatt E. & Ludy, Isa E. (Southern Illinois U, Carbondale) American Journal of Mental Deficiency, 1975(Nov), Vol 80(3), 277-280. [PA, Vol 55:10994]

2994. Raising intelligence levels of the mentally retarded: An overlooked educo-legal implication.
Studies by investigators at the University of Iowa Child Welfare Station before World War II demonstrated that the intelligence levels of the mentally retarded could be raised, often up to and beyond normalcy (IQ 100). Yet, the implications were never seriously followed up on anything approaching broad-gauged scale. The juridical climate now supports the position that because the evidence is that all the retarded can learn under proper conditions, they are all entitled to public schooling. It is suggested that the public schools may soon be confronted with an even more far-reaching educo-legal thrust based on the kind of evidence first reported by the Iowa investigators; that is, the public schools have a responsibility not only to educate or train the retarded to achieve their retarded potentialities, but to increase those potentialities (i.e., raise their intelligence levels).

Throne, John M. (U Kansas) Journal of Education, Boston, 1975(Feb), Vol 157(1), 43-53. [PA, Vol 57:03645]

2995.   Year two of a research program: Special reading instructional procedures for mentally retarded and learning disabled children.
Reports findings of evaluation studies designed to examine whether reading instructional procedures vary in effectiveness among groups and whether groups vary in attainment of reading skills after the use of the procedures. Ss were retarded and nonretarded pupils and learning disabled and nonlearning disabled children.
U Georgia, Coll of Education. (Athens, Georgia) Journal of Research & Development in Education, 1975, Vol 8(Mono), 138 p. [PA, Vol 54:12612]

2996.   Symbol communication for the mentally handicapped.
Describes briefly the individual progress of 5 11-16 yr old nonvocal mentally retarded children with cerebral palsy in a program utilizing Bliss Symbols, an alternate communication mode for nonvocal, motorically impaired persons of near- or above-normal intelligence. 5 graduate students met weekly with 1 child each for 8 wks and a total of 15-20 hrs teaching time. Results indicate that Bliss Symbols were effectively implemented as a means of respondent and limited expressive communication for the population sampled.
Vanderheiden, Deborah H. et al. (U Wisconsin, Cerebral Palsy Communication Group, Research & Evaluation, Madison) Mental Retardation, 1975(Feb), Vol 13(1), 34-37. [PA, Vol 54:04219]

2997.   Mothers of retarded children review a parent education program.
Describes mothers' evaluations of a program that provided extensive opportunities for parents to become informed about mental retardation and child development, to observe the program provided for their children, and to discuss family and personal problems with one or more professional staff persons. Findings are based on interviews conducted with 61 mothers selected from a group of 123 families, all of whom had a child in the program for 2 yrs or more. Mothers were asked about the effects of the program, how the organizational features (e.g., lectures, staff conferences, and parent participation) contributed to the stated goals of the program, what information they found particularly useful, and the relative importance of the staff's contributions. Results show that the mothers learned a great deal of factual information relating to the resolving of everyday living problems with their children, and that the mothers' needs to understand and deal with realities were closely linked to the effort to maintain self-esteem and handle negative feelings about their children. Implications for teaching, the importance of the teacher's role for parental understanding, and types of parental concerns are also discussed.
Warfield, Grace J. (U Minnesota, Minneapolis) Exceptional Children, 1975(May), Vol 41(8), 559-562. [PA, Vol 54:12198]

2998.   Short-term memory: Curricular implications for the mentally retarded.
Maintains that research on short-term memory and the mentally retarded has generally failed to find practical application in educational settings. This article highlights selected studies in this area and focuses on instructional techniques likely to enhance the intellectual-academic performance of retarded children, irrespective of the setting in which these objectives are pursued. Strategies in which the retarded are deficient (e.g., labeling and grouping) are discussed in terms of current research findings, and possible avenues of remediation are presented. It is contended that extensive application of these techniques should result in reducing the "exaggerated deficiency" characteristics of the performance of many retarded children. (50 ref)
Winschel, James F. & Lawrence, Elizabeth A. (Syracuse U) Journal of Special Education, 1975(Win), Vol 9(4), 395-408. [PA, Vol 56:04934]

2999.   Effects of labeling as educable mentally retarded on teachers' expectancies for change in a student's performance.
Studied the effects of alleged bias on teachers' perceptions of a child labeled mentally retarded (EMR). An equal number of 40 regular class elementary and 40 EMR teachers from a large urban inner city school district were randomly assigned to groups of 20 viewing a videotape in which a Black child was said to be either in a 6th-grade or an EMR classroom. At 4 intervals, Ss predicted the future achievement level of the child on concept formation tasks, shown in the tape to be administered by a teacher. Results of a repeated measures analysis of variance indicated that the EMR label did not elicit lower mean expectancy scores than the regular class label, while the trend of increasing expectancies over trials suggests that a teacher's personal evaluation of a student's performance may contribute more than an educational-diagnostic label such as EMR to the behavioral expression of expectancies. There was no difference between EMR and regular class teachers nor interaction of trials with label or teacher group. (30 ref)
Yoshida, Roland K. & Meyers, C. Edward. (Neuropsychiatric Inst, Pacific State Hosp, Pomona, CA) Journal of Educational Psychology, 1975(Aug), Vol 67(4), 521-527. [PA, Vol 54:10626]

3000.   The target groups: Description of subjects participating in Year 3 evaluation studies.
Selection criteria and S characteristics are presented for all groups studied in the research program, Special Reading Instructional Procedures for Mentally Retarded (MR) and Learning Disabled (LD) Children (University of Georgia, Athens). 444 students enrolled in regular classes or in classes for MR and LD students were selected from 5 Georgia counties and 1 Florida county. For the target populations of MR and LD Ss, normal and non-LD Ss were matched by MA and reading level or CA and IQ or CA or IQ.
Allen, Jerry. (U Georgia) Journal of Research & Development in Education, 1976, Vol 9(Mono), 4–8. [PA, Vol 60:01910]

3001.   Special schools or special schooling for the handicapped child? The debate in perspective.
Maintains that emphasis in the education of children with either physical or mental handicaps should be on the method of education (special schooling) rather than on the location (special schools) of the facility. A continuum of the provision of education ranging from placement of a child in an ordinary class with no modifications to placement in highly specialized institutions is seen as a more useful approach to the education of exceptional children. The main points along this continuum and results of evaluative studies of the different forms of special educational provision are discussed.
Anderson, Elizabeth M. (Thomas Coram Research Unit, London, England) Journal of Child Psychology & Psychiatry & Allied Disciplines, 1976(Apr), Vol 17(2), 151–155. [PA, Vol 56:04891]

3002.   Toward a noncategorical approach: Suggested course work for teachers of the retarded.
Argues that many existing programs for teachers of the retarded are redundant, and a description is presented of a state university's program designed to eliminate some of these redundancies. The program contains 2 major components. The first is a 2-course sequence which presents the essence of 3 traditional characteristics courses (mentally retarded, emotionally disturbed, learning disabled). The second part, a generic methods course, uses a 2-course sequence to incorporate and synthesize the content and competencies traditionally offered in the 3 separate methods courses and which all students interested in any 1 of the 3 disability categories would enroll. A model for the development of such a program is presented.
Anderson, Robert M.; Dietrich, Wilson L. & Greer, John G. (Memphis State U) Education & Training of the Mentally Retarded, 1976(Feb), Vol 11(1), 73-76. [PA, Vol 57:04287]

3003.   Vicarious effects on the creative behavior of retarded and nonretarded children.
The effects of observing a model's overt display of a creative drawing response and hearing a description of these actions were

assessed with 54 retarded (mean CA, 11.4 yrs; IQ, 48-79) and 68 nonretarded (mean age, 11.3 yrs; IQ, 89-111) children. The modeled creative strategy was designed to be high in the dimension of elaboration. A multivariate research design was employed to assess the target dimension of elaboration, as well as to determine transfer to tasks of varying degrees of similarity to the model's task and to creative dimensions other than elaboration. The overt modeling of a creative strategy was most effective in improving elaboration, although verbal descriptions also aided performance. Retarded children were less able than nonretarded children to discriminate the essential elements of the model's elaboration strategy and displayed less acquisition of the elaboration strategy but showed comparable gradients of transfer. (21 ref)
Arem, Cynthia A. & Zimmerman, Barry J. (Pima Community Coll, Tucson, AZ) American Journal of Mental Deficiency, 1976(Nov), Vol 81(3), 289-296. [PA, Vol 58:04362]

3004.   Effects of a response-cost procedure on the academic performance of retarded students.
Examined the effectiveness of a response-cost procedure for facilitating the academic performance (arithmetic problems) of 3 noninstitutionalized female adolescent (ages, 13, 15, and 16 yrs) retardates, using a multiple baseline across individuals. The response-cost procedure resulted in a significant increment in the percentage of problems completed correctly by all 3 Ss, suggesting that inferior academic performance of the retarded is, in part, a motivational deficit.
Arnold, Susan C.; Forehand, Rex & Sturgis, Ellie T. (U Georgia) Journal of Behavior Therapy & Experimental Psychiatry, 1976(Jun), Vol 7(2), 191-192. [PA, Vol 56:10736]

3005.   Story repetition as an educational technique for young mental retardates.
An adult read individually to 6 mentally retarded children (CA, 6 yrs 1 mo to 7 yrs 8 mo; MA, 1 yr 9 mo to 3 yrs 8 mo) over a period of 6 wks. Verbal interaction between the adult and each child was examined under 2 story presentation procedures: daily presentations of the same children's story vs a control procedure in which a new story was presented each day. Results demonstrate greater potential for the repeated story procedure in terms of providing opportunities for increased verbal interaction and improved language facility. The most dramatic finding was evidence for interactional continuity in the form of increasing complexity of language usage by the children as stories were repeated.
Baron, Richard L. & Ackerman, Paul D. (Wichita State U) Child Study Journal, 1976, Vol 6(3), 155-163. [PA, Vol 57:04419]

3006.   The relationship between selected physical environment variables and the behavior of MR youth in a learning setting.
Outlines a project which will provide environmental data for the use of designers and educators in developing and implementing desirable learning experiences for mentally retarded youth. The data will also be applicable to environmental design for normal youth.
Bartholomew, Robert. (Northern Illinois U) Man-Environment Systems, 1976(May), Vol 6(3), 183-184. [PA, Vol 58:12707]

3007.   Teacher strategies in dyadic communication.
Investigated the use of language teachers in one-to-one teaching of mentally handicapped children. Three teachers and 3 children were Ss. Four principal units of communication behavior were examined: segment, demand, unit, and series. It was found that there is an initial "tuning in" period, irrespective of task complexity or differences between children, and that teachers have the ability to "tune into" the child. There is variation in the production of segments. Teachers are more likely to give positive feedback than negative, and children succeed more than they fail, possibly because teachers select tasks on which the child can succeed; this is additional evidence that teachers are "tuned in" to the child. (1 ref)

Berry, Paul & Conn, Philip. (U Queensland, Schonell Educational Research Ctr, Brisbane, Australia) Exceptional Child, 1976(Jul), Vol 23(2), 99–112. [PA, Vol 63:08408]

3008.   Massed and distributed practice and retarded and normal pupils' learning sight vocabulary.
Examined 36 14-yr-old retarded, 36 9½-yr-old normal, and 36 14-yr-old normal students' use of massed and distributed practice in learning sight vocabulary. Within both treatments the groups differed. The normal groups exceeded the retarded but did not differ from each other. Within groups the treatments differed. All Ss using massed practice reached a higher level at a slightly faster rate than those using distributed practice.
Blake, Kathryn. (U Georgia) Journal of Research & Development in Education, 1976, Vol 9(Mono), 12–13. [PA, Vol 60:01913]

3009.   The special school pupil as a motor car user.
Examined the records of 221 young male motor vehicle drivers from special schools for the mentally retarded in Australia, especially in relation to their road offenses and criminal convictions. Findings were compared with previous studies of 2 groups of high school students (N = 800), one group with IQs over 100 and the other under 90. The drivers from the special schools had fewer driving licenses and fewer that had expired or been suspended. Of those with licenses, the number having both traffic and criminal offenses was higher in the special school group. However, the total number of criminal offenders was less for this group than for the 2 high school groups. The relationship between driving difficulties and illiteracy was also examined. It is concluded that the number of drivers from special schools is so small that they do not constitute an appreciable danger on the roads.
Boyce, Lorinne & Dax, E. Cunningham. (Community Health Services, New Town, Australia) Australian Journal of Mental Retardation, 1976(Jun), Vol 4(2), 53-61. [PA, Vol 57:10565]

3010.   Teachers' behaviors in classes for severely retarded-multiply trainable mentally retarded, learning disabled and normal children.
The behaviors of 21 teachers in classes for severely retarded/multiply handicapped, trainable mentally retarded, learning disabled, and normal children were recorded using an interaction process analysis. This time-sampling technique allowed recording of such behaviors as teachers' verbalizations to individual children and to the group, teachers' emission of positive and negative reinforcements, and the responses of children to the teachers. Significant differences were found among the 4 groups of teachers in a number of interaction categories. The differences in interaction patterns are discussed in terms of their effects on children and current notions about educational placements for handicapped children.
Bryan, Tanis H. & Wheeler, Roslyn A. (Bureau of Educationally Handicapped, Chicago, IL) Mental Retardation, 1976(Aug), Vol 14(4), 41-45. [PA, Vol 57:04422]

3011.   Teacher attitudes toward integration of children with handicaps.
Describes changes in the attitudes of teachers who were untrained in special education but had mentally or physically handicapped preschoolers placed into their normal classroom. Attitudes changed toward favorable agreement with the following proposals: (a) Modification of class routines is necessary to accommodate integration. (b) Similar instructional competencies are effective with both normal and exceptional children. (c) All exceptional children in a particular category will not necessarily respond in concert to a particular educational methodology. (d) Staff insight will not necessarily enable a child to respond with the parameters of normalcy. (e) Physically impaired children are not necessarily easier to accommodate than mentally impaired children.
Clark, E. Audrey. (California State U, Preschool Lab, Northridge) Education & Training of the Mentally Retarded, 1976(Dec), Vol 11(4), 333-335. [PA, Vol 58:01955]

3012. The effects of labeling of special education students on the perceptions of contact versus noncontact peers.
In a 2 × 2 factorial design, 150 7th and 8th graders in 3 contact conditions (contact with educable or trainable mentally retarded pupils or no contact) responded to a short sketch of a 12-yr-old boy. Utilizing 3 dependent variables, half the Ss rated the person described to them without a label present, while the other half rated the identical sketch with the added information that the person attended special education classes for the mentally retarded. Results reveal both a significant Labeling effect and a significant Label × Contact interaction for all 3 dependent variables. Additional analyses supported the conclusion that a label tends to be evaluated realistically and suggested that it is not contact per se, but the quality of contact which is important in predicting responses toward the mentally retarded. (25 ref)
Cook, J. William & Wollersheim, Janet P. (U Montana) Journal of Special Education, 1976(Sum), Vol 10(2), 187-198. [PA, Vol 56:06778]

3013. Comparison of Slosson and Peabody IQs among candidates for special education.
Three White female examiners individually administered the Peabody Picture Vocabulary Test, Forms A and B, and the Slosson Intelligence Test to 50 Black and White 72-132 mo olds who were suspected of being mentally retarded. Product-moment correlations between the Slosson and Peabody Forms A and B were .41 and .51, respectively. Correlations and *t*s were computed for stratifications by race and by sex.
Covin, Theron M. Psychological Reports, 1976(Dec), Vol 39(3, Pt 1), 814. [PA, Vol 58:02172]

3014. Upbringing and education of the special child in USSR.
Presents an overview of the Soviet team-approach to the treatment of the mentally retarded and other exceptional children, including the learning disabled and those with visual, hearing, motor, or speech defects. Prenatal preventive care, early and ongoing diagnoses, and educational interventions provided by the Institute of Defectology are described, and recent research efforts are outlined.
Das, J. P. (U Alberta, Ctr for the Study of Mental Retardation, Edmonton, Canada) Mental Retardation Bulletin, 1976, Vol 4(1), 3-9. [PA, Vol 58:01509]

3015. Counseling with the mentally handicapped child.
Handicapped children have a larger number of personal problems than nonhandicapped children because they face larger numbers of frustrations, are misunderstood and rejected more often, and have greater difficulty in developing healthy self-concepts. Developing parental acceptance; stimulating productivity, achievement, independence, and interest in the client's environment; and counseling within the limits of a short attention span are problems faced by the counselor of mentally handicapped children. Dealing with these problems requires adoption of a nontraditional counseling milieu. Counseling effectiveness can be increased by (a) teaching aspects of counseling, (b) use of a behavioral-based approach rather than reliance on verbal expressions, and (c) use of group counseling sessions with children who are overly sensitive about their handicap. Many counselors are trained in skills that do not take into account client intellectual ability. Counseling should be emphasized at the elementary school level to avoid serious maladjustments at a later time.
DeBlassie, Richard R. & Cowan, Mary A. (New Mexico State U) Elementary School Guidance & Counseling, 1976(May), Vol 10(4), 246-253. [PA, Vol 61:07362]

3016. Path analysis of parents' conservatism toward sex education of their mentally retarded children.
Investigated 3 probable reasons why parents of mentally retarded children would be opposed to sex education being offered as a school subject: general sexual attitudes, specific sexual attitudes, and prejudices against the retarded children's own sexuality. A 5-section questionnaire including scale adaptations from I. Reiss's (1967) questionnaire on sexual permissiveness and R. W. Libby's (1970) liberalism scale on sex education was given to 60 parents of retarded children and 62 parents of nonretarded children, matched with respect to child/parent ages and religious affiliation. A correlation analysis revealed evidence of all 3 variables and led to a causal model of conservatism on sex education. A path analysis revealed that (a) sexual prejudices are a major obstacle to sex education and (b) each group of parents represents a specific dynamic of conservatism on sex education. Methods of pedagogical intervention to modify parental attitudes towards sex education of handicapped children are considered relevant to the observation that both specific values and prejudices, rather than general negativism, were found to be directly related to conservatism. (16 ref)
Dupras, Andre & Tremblay, Rejean. (U Quebec, Montreal, Canada) American Journal of Mental Deficiency, 1976(Sep), Vol 81(2), 162-166. [PA, Vol 57:06925]

3017. Expectancy and halo effects as a result of artificially induced teacher bias.
Examined the effects of deviancy labels on 100 elementary grade and special education teachers' expectations of child behavior and their ability to evaluate child behavior objectively. Ss were assigned to 1 of 4 label groups, each of which dealt with one label (emotionally disturbed, learning disabled, mentally retarded, normal), and each group participated in 2 treatment phases. During Phase 1, Ss identified behaviors they expected to be displayed by hypothetical children characteristic of the label condition. They were asked to complete a referral form for either a hypothetical normal, mentally retarded, learning disabled, or emotionally disturbed child. During Phase 2, each group saw the same videotape of normal 4th-grade boy and completed a 2nd referral form based on the behaviors displayed during this presentation. Each group was told the boy was a member of a different category. Results indicate that Ss held negative expectancies toward children categorized with a deviancy label and maintained expectancies even when confronted with normal behavior. Maintenance of this bias was sufficient to cause Ss to misinterpret actual child behavior, resulting in a halo effect. Results further indicate that the label of educable mentally retarded generated a greater degree of negative bias than did the labels learning disabled or emotionally disturbed, although all 3 deviancy labels produced negative expectancies and halo effects significantly different from those found under control conditions.
Foster, Glen & Ysseldyke, James. (Model Learning Disabilities Systems, State College, PA) Contemporary Educational Psychology, 1976(Jan), Vol 1(1), 37-45. [PA, Vol 58:04174]

3018. The developmental class: Best of both worlds for the mentally retarded.
Argues that retarded children should be grouped in school by developmental level rather than by CA or IQ. The potential advantages of placing retardates with normal children of similar MA are enumerated. It would make the classroom more homogeneous, prevent the development of negative teacher expectations (by removing the "mental retardation" label), enhance the social position of the retarded child, provide models (normal, able students) for the retarded, and encourage parents to prolong regular class attendance by retardates.
Goodman, Joan F. (U Pennsylvania, Graduate School of Education) Psychology in the Schools, 1976(Jul), Vol 13(3), 257-265. [PA, Vol 57:02006]

3019. Imitation in language training.
Reviews research concerning language acquisition and language training by imitation. It is maintained that, regardless of the controversy surrounding the role of imitation in normal language acquisition, imitation is a necessary component in teaching children language rules that govern the production of grammatical regularities. Implications for intervention with language deficient children are considered. (27 ref)
Holdgrafer, Gary. (U Alberta School of Rehabilitation Medicine, Edmonton, Canada) Mental Retardation Bulletin, 1975-76, Vol 3(23), 202-215. [PA, Vol 58:06365]

3020. [Primary geographic imagery and concepts in students in special schools.] (Russ)
Mentally retarded children perceive new phenomena very flatly and one-sidedly; they do not notice details, traits, differences, and likenesses of things and are unable to see causes and consequences of events. A special 4-yr course in geography for 5th–8th grade children was set up to help them overcome these defects. Special schoolchildren were found to have insufficient knowledge of geographic notions which, as a rule, were distorted and reflected reality very superficially. In real life they seldom used these notions and always hesitated over which of them to choose for any given occasion. Since ordinary geographic courses failed to help these children, it is recommended that research in this field be continued. A combination of geographic and verbal forms of control was found to be very helpful.
Kaffemanas, R. B. (USSR Academy of Sciences, Inst of Defectology, Moscow) Defektologiya, 1976(Jan), No 1, 32–37. [PA, Vol 64:11191]

3021. [Teaching of preschool retardates by play using demonstrations and verbal instructions.] (Russ)
Studied the relationship of imitation of an adult's action, action according to a pattern, and verbal instruction in teaching mentally retarded preschool children. It was found that the combination of the 3 methods is effective in teaching students to differentiate between 2 geometric figures visually and by name, and to perform actions according to instructions. Experiments showed that acquisition of names of geometric figures is very difficult for retarded children, while visual differentiation is learned rather quickly; substitution of the geometric figure for its name results in very successful completion of a rather difficult assignment. Teaching of mentally retarded preschool children is most effective when it provides a large amount of repetition of the material, yet keeps the students' interest alive.
Kataeva, A. A. & Davydova, S. I. (USSR Academy of Sciences, Inst of Defectology, Moscow) Defektologiya, 1976(Jan), No 1, 69–74. [PA, Vol 64:11192]

3022. Imitating children during imitation training: Two experimental paradigms.
Two experiments with 1 profoundly mentally retarded (age 7 yrs) and 2 educable mentally retarded (ages 3 and 4 yrs) children explored the utility of adult imitating during imitation training. Both experiments used an ABAB design to determine the effects of reinforcing specific responses with a "modeling only" condition (traditional operant methods of shaping, fading, prompting, and verbal praise) and an "imitation" condition (traditional operant methods plus immediate imitation of the child's response by the teacher). Overall results show that acquisition of imitative skills occurred slightly more rapidly during the imitation condition. (16 ref)
Kauffman, James M.; Snell, Martha E. & Hallahan, Daniel P. (U Virginia) Education & Training of the Mentally Retarded, 1976(Dec), Vol 11(4), 324-332. [PA, Vol 58:02187]

3023. Who are all the children?
In this 7th article of a series commemorating the American Bicentennial, 6 short vignettes (1817-1980) from the history and projected future of special education are presented to reflect revolutionary strides in the move for educational opportunity. A discussion of changing attitudes and changing children describes the historical development of special education, focusing on recognition and labeling, social indictment, the "happiness first" motto, mainstreaming, evidence for needed reform, and the responsibility of the advocacy function. It is pointed out that there are more than 9 million mentally and/or physically handicapped 0-21 yr olds in this country who have difficulties in adjustment or learning and to whom the concept of exceptionality applies. This dynamic and expanding concept is viewed as interacting along 3 dimensions: (a) chronological age, (b) degree of variation from the norm in education-related performance, and (c) environmental and cultural factors affecting the learner's accommodation to school programs. Finally, achieving the goal of education of all is considered in light of federal support, local assistance, the role of technology and the commitment of individual teachers. (38 ref)
Lance, Wayne D. (U Oregon) Exceptional Children, 1976(Oct), Vol 43(2), 66-76. [PA, Vol 57:11528]

3024. Survey of art programs and art experiences for the mentally retarded in Indiana.
Results of a survey of 415 special education teachers indicate a need for more art training for classroom teachers and more knowledge of exceptional children for art teachers. However, the greatest need seems to be for more effective art programs designed specifically to meet the needs of exceptional students.
Lovano-Kerr, Jessie & Savage, Steven L. (San Diego State U) Education & Training of the Mentally Retarded, 1976(Oct), Vol 11(3), 200-211. [PA, Vol 57:11530]

3025. The application of brief time-out to control classroom talk-out behavior.
Utilized a reversal design to assess the effectiveness of 2 contingencies in modifying the inappropriate classroom verbalizations of 2 mentally retarded adolescent boys. During extinction phases, inappropriate verbalizations were ignored by the teacher, whereas during time-out phases, inappropriate verbalizations led to a brief period during which the boys were unable to receive otherwise continuously available positive reinforcement for on-task behavior. Frequency of inappropriate verbalizations was much lower during time-out served as an effective punishing stimulus without students losing a substantial amount of academic time. Such procedures are efficient and easily included in the classroom structure.
Luiselli, James K.; Helfen, Carol S. & Anderson, Donald F. (Walter E. Fernald State School, Waltham, MA) SALT: School Applications of Learning Theory, 1976(Aug), Vol 9(1), 16–24. [PA, Vol 62:14828]

3026. Use of sociometric techniques with mentally retarded and learning disabled children.
Suggests that with the current emphasis on mainstreaming mentally handicapped persons, 2 components of the community should be analyzed: the social-legal value system and the functional, day-to-day value system. Although legal action can result in the development of general community services for the handicapped, analysis of the functional value system is needed to develop strategies for full community integration.
McCaffery, Leonard J. (Ed)
(Ed). Group Psychotherapy, Psychodrama & Sociometry, 1976, Vol 29, 111–112. [PA, Vol 62:02298]

3027. Use of sociometric techniques with mentally retarded and learning disabled children.
Discusses how the social/legal value system and the functional, day-to-day value systems of community institutions undergoing change or expansion affect the integration of mentally retarded and learning disabled children in regular educational activities. Effects on service delivery, children's self-perceptions, and sociometric issues are examined.
McCaffery, Leonard J. Group Psychotherapy, Psychodrama & Sociometry, 1976, Vol 29, 111–112. [PA, Vol 61:04802]

3028. Content analysis of basal reading texts for normal and retarded children.
Analyzed 120 stories from 4 basal readers for normal and retarded children in terms of themes of achievement imagery, dependent behaviors, and occupational roles of characters. Chi-square analyses revealed no significant differences between the readers for normal and retarded children in examples of achievement imagery, dependent behaviors, or occupational roles. Some sex differences were observed. Implications of research variables related to story content are presented. (30 ref)
McCloud, Barbara K.; Mitchell, Marlys M. & Ragland, Gilbert G. (North Carolina Central U) Journal of Special Education, 1976(Fal), Vol 10(3), 259-264. [PA, Vol 57:06768]

3029. Retarded and normal pupils' learning attributes of conjunction, inclusive disjunction, and exclusion concepts.
Compared the effect of a conjunction, an inclusive disjunction, and an exclusion concept on 54 14-yr-old retarded, 54 9½-yr-old normal, and 54 14-yr-old normal students' attribute identification. The 3 groups differed in performance on the attribute identification tasks; older normals performed better than either of the other groups. All Ss receiving the conjunction concept performed better than Ss receiving the exclusion concept. Ss receiving the conjunction and Ss receiving the inclusive disjunction concepts performed similarly; so did Ss receiving the inclusive disjunction and the exclusion concepts. All Ss performed better across 4 trials.
McLaughlin, Phillip. (Virginia Commonwealth U) Journal of Research & Development in Education, 1976, Vol 9(Mono), 35–36. [PA, Vol 60:01937]

3030. Retarded and normal pupils' learning rules for conjunction, inclusive disjunction, and exclusion concepts.
Compared the effect of a conjunction, an inclusive disjunction, and an exclusion concept on rule learning of 54 retarded 14-yr-old, 54 normal 9½-yr-old, and 54 normal 14-yr-old students. Ss receiving the conjunction concept and the inclusive disjunction concept performed better than those receiving the exclusion concept. Ss did not differ over 4 trials in learning the conjunction and inclusive disjunction concepts, but all Ss showed a significant increase in performance across trials. Both normal groups exceeded the retarded group in amount learned and rate of learning, and there was a significant Groups by Trials interaction.
McLaughlin, Phillip. (Virginia Commonwealth U) Journal of Research & Development in Education, 1976, Vol 9(Mono), 33–34. [PA, Vol 60:01935]

3031. Retarded and normal pupils' complete learning of conjunction, inclusive disjunction, and exclusion concepts.
Explored the effect of a conjunction, an inclusive disjunction, and an exclusion concept on the complete learning of 54 14-yr-old retarded, 54 9½-yr-old normal, and 54 14-yr-old normal students. Findings show a significant main effect for Groups and significant Groups by Trials and Treatments by Trials interactions. Older normals exceeded the other 2 groups in amount learned and rate of learning; retarded and younger normal Ss did not differ in these areas. Ss receiving conjunction problems exceeded Ss receiving the other 2 types of problems in amount learned and rate of learning. Ss receiving inclusive disjunction problems performed similarly to Ss receiving exclusion problems.
McLaughlin, Phillip. (Virginia Commonwealth U) Journal of Research & Development in Education, 1976, Vol 9(Mono), 37–38. [PA, Vol 60:01936]

3032. Special child—special growth: Developmental art therapy.
Describes the progress of 8 children with multiple handicaps and retarded development in a program of creative developmental therapy. The Ss, ranging in age from 42–66 mo, were enrolled in a special educational preschool program. A creative developmental level was determined for each S through ratings of his/her art work, and a program for creative therapy was individually designed. At the end of the semester their art works were again rated. Of the 7 Ss who completed the semester, 1 showed no change while 6 advanced developmentally in their creative abilities from 5 to 33 mo. Implications for the education of the atypical, handicapped child are discussed.
Musick, Patricia L. (U Houston) Art Psychotherapy, 1976, Vol 3(3–4), 135–144. [PA, Vol 61:02306]

3033. Number and percent of mentally retarded students in public school classes.-700 R.
Surveyed the state education agencies of 49 states and the District of Columbia to examine trends in enrollment of mentally retarded students in public education. (Alaska indicated that since that state uses a noncategorical approach to student placement, enumeration of mentally retarded persons in the public school system was not possible.) 39 states and the District of Columbia increased enrollment of these students, while a decline was seen in 10 states. The overall enrollment increased from 1.43% to 1.87% between the school year 1970-1971 and 1972-1973, and the largest increases occurred in the southeastern and south central states.
Neman, Ronald S. & Luckey Robert E. (National Assoc for Retarded Citizens, Arlington, TX) Education & Training of the Mentally Retarded, 1976(Apr), Vol 11(2), 158-160. [PA, Vol 56:08766]

3034. A motoric approach to teaching multiplication to the mentally retarded child.
Administered an author-developed diagnostic test to 25 mentally retarded males (CA, 8-10 yrs) in a lower socioeconomic school as a first step in developing and implementing a sequential program for teaching multiplication tables. The diagnostic test indicated that the class generally lacked knowledge and immediate recall of multiplication facts above 3. In order to demonstrate the concept that multiplication is a process of commutative addition with equal addends and that addition is the culmination of counting, Ss participated in class sessions that used (a) motoric review of the tables; (b) manipulative objects (e.g., beans and toothpicks) which Ss sorted into factorial combinations; and (c) visual and numerical worksheets and flash cards. At the end of 2½ wks, 16 Ss showed marked improvement; the other 9 remained almost unchanged. (17 ref)
Ogletree, Earl J. & Ujlaki, Vilma. (Chicago State U) Education & Training of the Mentally Retarded, 1976(Apr), Vol 11(2), 129-134. [PA, Vol 56:08767]

3035. Disturbed classroom behaviour: A comparison between mentally retarded, learning-disabled and emotionally disturbed children.
Attempted to identify and measure the nature and prevalence of disturbed classroom behavior in 56 mentally retarded children and to compare them with 51 learning disabled and 65 emotionally disturbed children. 11 types of disturbed classroom behavior (defined as behavior which interfered with learning) were studied. Ss were rated by their teachers on the Devereux Elementary School Behavior Rating Scale. Results show that the 3 groups exhibited significant differences on their profiles of the cumulative 11 disturbed classroom behavior factors. They also differed on the individual factors of Classroom Disturbance, Disrespect-Defiance, External Blame, Achievement Anxiety, Comprehension Disorders, Irrelevant Responsiveness, and Lack of Creative Initiative. The mentally retarded Ss exhibited more Comprehension Disorders than did Ss of the other 2 groups. The emotionally disturbed Ss showed higher Classroom Disturbance, Disrespect-Defiance, External Blame, Achievement Anxiety, Inattentive-Withdrawal, and Irrelevant-Responsiveness but lower Comprehension Disorders and Lack of Creative Initiative than did the mentally retarded. (31 ref)
Parashar, Om D. (Virginia Commonwealth U) Journal of Mental Deficiency Research, 1976(Jun), Vol 20(2), 109–120. [PA, Vol 59:11153]

3036. [Efficacy and differential effects of social reinforcement on the behavior modification of a mental retardate.] (Span)
A single-case study of classroom behavior modification is presented in which a 12-yr-old mentally retarded female with a long history of classroom disturbance and physical harm to peers was treated. The child's parents were unemployed; her father was alcoholic, and the mother suffered from extensive neurological damage. The girl, her parents, and 6 siblings lived in an unsanitary 2-room house. After a baseline was established, the following S behaviors were monitored: frequency of talking with peers, frequency with which the child observed the experimenter, frequency of child leaving seat, and total time of disruptive behavior. Positive reinforcements were social reinforcement by teacher and a promise of admission to certain programs. Negative reinforcements were private reprimands, restriction of time spent with peers, and elimination of privileges. All disruptive behavior decreased over time. Additionally, this generalized to progress in school work (spelling). The wider use of behavior

modification in the classroom to decrease disturbances and increase productivity is discussed.
Pelechano, Vicente & Vinagre, J. (Universidad de la Laguna, Tenerife, Spain) Análisis y Modificación de Conducta, 1976, Vol 2(2), 133–144. [PA, Vol 63:02074]

3037.   [On motives for reading literary books in students in special schools.] (Russ)
Studied the motives stimulating students to borrow certain literary books from the library. A questionnaire investigation showed that only 42% of 5th-grade students and 48% of 8th-grade students from a school for the mentally retarded were motivated by a desire to learn, compared to 80% of 5th-grade students from a normal school. The retarded students were motivated more by practical, class-oriented reasons, entertainment, or no stated motive.
Pobrein, V. B. (Pedagogical Inst, Kaunas, USSR) Defektologiya, 1976(Mar), No 3, 18–22. [PA, Vol 64:11207]

3038.   [Questionnaire on Vocational Interests of the Mentally Deficient (QVIMD): Experimental variant, 1974.] (Romn)
Describes the elaboration of the QVIMD-74, based on a previous study of the vocational interests of 269 mentally retarded students and the range of occupations for which they can be qualified. The method of elaborating and testing the QVIMD-74 is described, and all the items are presented. The questionnaire and the Raven Standard Progressive Matrices were administered to 262 Ss. The 2 final forms (B for boys and G for girls) may be used for vocational guidance when Ss graduate from special schools, or when they are in the last class of the general school for the mentally retarded, to indicate the educational steps that could be taken. (French summary) (20 ref)
Radu, Valentina; Catina, Ana & Ionescu, Şerban. (Inst of Pedagogical & Psychological Research, Bucharest, Romania) Revista de Psihologie, 1976(Oct–Dec), Vol 22(4), 419–438. [PA, Vol 61:07407]

3039.   Play and reality: Essentials of educational planning for blind retarded children.
Discusses the importance for perceptual and conceptual development in blind retarded children of planned educational play activities focusing on stimulating auditory and tactile sensory systems. Emphasis is placed on the use of (a) careful planning, sequences of activities, and easily managed materials to engage children in play; (b) spoken language, rhythm, and music to encourage communication and listening skills; (c) body awareness, sound localization, and posture, and kinesthetic exercises to stimulate orientation and mobility skills; and (e) dramatic play and interactions with others to facilitate social development.
Rogow, Sally M. (U British Columbia, Vancouver, Canada) Education & Training of the Mentally Retarded, 1976(Dec), Vol 11(4), 314-317. [PA, Vol 58:02205]

3040.   Teaching language to mentally retarded deaf children: A review of the literature and a description of one classroom program.
Developed a special language program for intermediate level multi-handicapped deaf students at a state school for the deaf. The program's basic components are emergency words, practical experience vocabulary, and highly structured activities for concept development and drill procedures. This "survival language" features a variety of student options, focusing on the needs of this special population for management of attention and individualization of instruction. These options include drill work towards meeting specific objectives, with particular attention paid to written language. Reference is made to selected language programs, objectives, and goals developed by other educators to meet the needs of deaf students who are mentally retarded and/or have severe language impairment. (16 ref)
Shepard, Charlotte H. (Oregon State School for the Deaf) American Annals of the Deaf, 1976(Aug), Vol 121(4), 366-369. [PA, Vol 57:02014]

3041.   Sexuality, sex education and the mentally retarded: One educational approach.
Presents a model of sex education whose basic premise is that parents and teachers must be knowledgeable and comfortable with their own sexuality as well as that of others. They must also be sensitive in dealing openly with various expressions of human sexuality. Although this program is designed for those involved with mentally retarded children, it can be generalized to all instructional programs in sex education.
Thurman, Richard L.; Bassin, Jeff & Ackermann, Teel. (U Missouri School of Education, St Louis) Mental Retardation, 1976(Feb), Vol 14(1), 19. [PA, Vol 56:01486]

3042.   Amount of training and retarded and normal pupils' learning new words and transformations.
Studied the effect of training in learning transformations on 36 14-yr-old retarded, 36 9½-yr-old normal, and 36 14-yr-old normal students' discrimination between new words and their transformations. Normal groups performed equally well, and both were better than the retarded group. The performance of all Ss improved across trials, and 1 training practice was as effective as 4 practices.
Tucker, Jacqueline. (U Georgia) Journal of Research & Development in Education, 1976, Vol 9(Mono), 11. [PA, Vol 60:01947]

3043.   Contiguity of transformations and retarded and normal pupils' learning of sight vocabulary.
Investigated the relative effectiveness of 2 amounts of contiguity of transformations in 36 14-yr-old retarded, 36 9½-yr-old normal, and 36 14-yr-old normal students' sight vocabulary learning. The older and younger normal groups performed equally well, and both were superior to the retarded group. All Ss improved across trials, and Ss receiving 1 contiguous list learned as well as those receiving 4 lists.
Tucker, Jacqueline. (U Georgia) Journal of Research & Development in Education, 1976, Vol 9(Mono), 10. [PA, Vol 60:01949]

3044.   Coding transformations and retarded and normal pupils' sight vocabulary learning.
Tested the effectiveness of 2 amounts of coding on 36 14-yr-old retarded, 36 9½-yr-old normal, and 36 14-yr-old normal students' sight vocabulary learning involving new words and transformations. Both groups of normals were better than the retarded Ss, older normals were better than younger normals, there was no improvement across trials, and the 2 amounts of coding did not produce significantly different results.
Tucker, Jacqueline. (U Georgia) Journal of Research & Development in Education, 1976, Vol 9(Mono), 9. [PA, Vol 60:01948]

3045.   Demonstration and explication as modes of instruction.
The relative value of different modes of instruction for the acquisition of certain skills was tested on 1,683 Ss aged 4-22 yrs (including 333 mentally retarded children). Simple (reproductive) skills and skills that require some modifications in performance were studied. The modes of instruction were: demonstration (visual) combined with explication (verbal), demonstration alone, and explication alone. The data were analyzed for the effects of 3 kinds of variables: (a) type of skill, (b) attributes of Ss and (c) features of the instructional mode. Findings indicate that Ss acquired a skill more effectively when a demonstration of that skill was combined with a verbal explication of the activity. The relative value of demonstration and explication changed with types of activity, age of the S, and level of mental development. Compared with explication, demonstration was generally more effective for stereotyped activities than for those requiring modifications in performance.
Wlodarski, Ziemowit. (U Warsaw Inst of Psychology, Poland) Polish Psychological Bulletin, 1976, Vol 7(2), 85-93. [PA, Vol 57:11541]

3046.   [Level of some spatial orientation skills in mentally retarded schoolchildren.] (Russ)
Argues that from the first days of their school attendance, the poor spatial orientation of mentally retarded children can deter them from successful learning, especially by hampering their ability to cope with graphic assignments. Corrective measures

that can overcome the difficulties of correct orientation while drawing on paper are offered, such as (a) placing a set of objects on the sheet of paper via verbal instructions, (b) placing the same set of objects by memory, (c) reproducing figures with the help of points, (d) drawing lines according to given directions, and (e) drawing an imaginary route. It has been discovered that spatial orientation skills can be successfully developed when the principles are acquired through actions with objects. Drawing, in this case, is the best way to gain this experience. Other kinds of activities such as sports may also be useful.
Abbasov, M. G. (Scientific Research Inst of Pedagogy, Baku, USSR) Defektologiya, 1977(Jan), No 1, 38–42. [PA, Vol 64:11180]

3047. The priory parents workshop.
A multidisciplinary team conducted a 16-session workshop, attended by 18 mothers of handicapped children, that enabled both parents and professionals to discuss the problems associated with handicapped children and possible practical solutions. Topics included child development, observation methods, and behavior modification; specific remedial programs were designed and carried out at home.
Attwood, Tony. (St Lawrence's Hosp, Caterham, England) Child Care, Health & Development, 1977(May–Apr), Vol 3(2), 81–91. [PA, Vol 59:10868]

3048. Some problems associated with achievement testing of the mentally retarded.
Discusses problems that occur when nationally normed achievement tests are used to evaluate mentally retarded students, focusing on issues related to test content, standardization, personality influences, and instructional relevance. Although criterion-referenced tests are alternative methods of achievement measurement, they also have some limitations when used with retarded individuals. Guidelines for administering, scoring, and interpreting normative achievement tests are presented. (16 ref)
Baine, David. (U Alberta, Edmonton, Canada) Mental Retardation Bulletin, 1977(Fal), Vol 5(2), 49–61. [PA, Vol 61:02325]

3049. Teaching adult retarded persons reading through mental effectiveness training.
Describes teaching techniques used and reports achievement progress of 33 adult mentally retarded Ss (2 classes, IQ range 30-80, CA 18-57 yrs) taught with L. Bjorgum's Basic Training in Mental Effectiveness. Ss were pre- and posttested on the Wide Range Achievement Test. Results indicate that retarded Ss can achieve at a rate comparable with other classes of handicapped learners when taught with specifically designed materials. These retarded Ss were also able to achieve month for month progress comparable to other nonretarded students (educationally handicapped, vocational rehabilitation, and summer school) when all were taught with the Mental Effectiveness Training program. A sample lesson plan is included.
Bjorgum, Louise & Hudler, Mary N. (Sierra Schools Language Arts Developmental Ctr, Sacramento, CA) Mental Retardation, 1977(Feb), Vol 15(1), 18-20. [PA, Vol 58:06346]

3050. Facilitative effects of coin displacement on teaching coin summation to mentally retarded adolescents.
Compared 2 methods of teaching coin summation to retarded adolescents; one method involved a coin-displacement procedure, the other did not. Displacement was designed to compensate for retarded persons' attention and retention deficits. A pretest-posttest matched-groups design, as well as a multiple baseline across coin-counting responses, was used. 14 Ss (mean CA 15.36 yrs, mean IQ 46.20) were assigned to either displacement or nondisplacement conditions. Ss in both groups were first taught to count a single coin and then sum that coin in combination with coins previously taught. Both groups used the same finger-counting procedure; however, Ss in the displacement condition were also required to move each coin aside systematically after it was counted. The training methods were modeling, modeling with S imitation, and independent counting by the S. Both groups improved from pre- to posttest; however, the displacement group performance was significantly better. Skill mainte-

nance for both groups was evident on follow-up. Displacement Ss required fewer trials and less time to complete training. It is concluded that coin displacement may compensate for attention and retention deficits of retarded persons.
Borakove, Larry S. & Cuvo, Anthony J. (Brooklyn Developmental Ctr, NY) American Journal of Mental Deficiency, 1977(Jan), Vol 81(4), 350-356. [PA, Vol 58:06349]

3051. [The influence of vicarious reinforcement on asking questions: An experiment in observational learning.] (Germ)
In 4 classes of retarded 8th graders, a male and female role model were selected based on a sociogram, teachers' agreement, and the frequency with which the pupil asked questions. During 12 hrs of teaching at least 6 questions per hour were asked. Teachers praised the models in front of the class. When a model later asked a question praise was again given, while other students were answered but not praised. The amount of praise was doubled for the last 8 hrs. The controls in 4 classes were praised only at the start, but not later. In the experimental classes questioning increased from 5 to 62 questions, in the controls it decreased from 7 to 5. A generalization of the behavior to other students and later situations was evident. (4 ref)
Borchert, Johann. (Pädagogische Hochschule Ruhr, Fachbereich II, Dortmund, West Germany) Psychologie in Erziehung und Unterricht, 1977, Vol 24(5), 306–309. [PA, Vol 63:10668]

3052. What's in a name? Some reflections on the possible consequences of labelling children educationally subnormal.
Questions the value of integrating moderately and severely educationally subnormal children in the same school because of the problem of stigmatizing the children. It is suggested that the majority of the moderately subnormal might better be educated in ordinary schools.
Burden, Robert L. AEP (Association of Educational Psychologists) Journal, 1977(Sum), Vol 4(5), 37–42. [PA, Vol 61:04783]

3053. Effects of self-monitoring, token reinforcement and different back-up reinforcers on the classroom behaviour of retardates.
Nine mentally retarded boys monitored and recorded their own behavior as on- or off-task. Self-monitoring alone produced a significant increment in the externally assessed level of on-task behavior. Only when access to back-up consequences were introduced was there a further significant increment. Provision of high-value consumption consequences was followed by a loss of accuracy in self-monitoring and reduction in on-task behavior to baseline levels. (19 ref)
Coleman, Peter & Blampied, Neville M. (U Canterbury, Christchurch, New Zealand) Exceptional Child, 1977(Jul), Vol 24(2), 95–107. [PA, Vol 64:08854]

3054. Leisure skills instruction for the moderately and severely retarded: A demonstration program.
Describes a 2-mo summer recreation program designed to provide the 30 severely and moderately retarded participants with recreational skills that they could use without adult supervision. Results show that 38% of all skills begun were mastered and 66% of the subtasks were successfully completed.
Day, Robert M. & Day, H. Michael. (George Peabody Coll for Teachers) Education & Training of the Mentally Retarded, 1977(Apr), Vol 12(2), 128–131. [PA, Vol 59:02099]

3055. Comprehension of printed sentences by children with reading disability.
Studied sentence comprehension in children with different types of reading disability in relation to their other reading skills. Ss were 34 8–17 yr olds whose primary problem was in reading and 31 8–12 yr olds whose reading problems were associated with learning disorders, language disorders, and mental retardation. All Ss were administered the sentence comprehension test and 31 other reading tests. For the types of reading problems assessed, sentence comprehension was at the same level of proficiency, relative to normal readers, as was oral word reading. Significantly higher correlations were observed between sentence comprehension and 4 tests involving oral word reading than between sentence comprehension and almost all of the remaining 27 tests.

Results are discussed with regard to mechanisms underlying sentence comprehension in normal readers and children with reading disability.
Doehring, Donald G. (McGill U, Montreal, Canada) Bulletin of the Psychonomic Society, 1977(Oct), Vol 10(4), 350–352. [PA, Vol 60:08298]

3056.   [Remedial education in medical and educational settings.] (Germ)
Discusses personnel, facilities, and methods used in the *Heilpädagogik* (therapeutic pedagogy, remedial education) approach. This approach provides special assistance for preschool children who have physical handicaps, mental retardation, learning disabilities, or certain behavior disorders. (42 ref)
Ehrhardt, Françoise & Ehrhardt, K. J. (Johann Wolfgang Goethe-U Frankfurt, Zentrum der Psychiatrie, West Germany) Zeitschrift für Kinder- und Jugendpsychiatrie, 1977(Jun), Vol 5(2), 165–183. [PA, Vol 63:04172]

3057.   A transition model for placement of handicapped children in regular and special classes.
Mainstreaming and deinstitutionalization are current phenomena which call for a variety of handicapped children to be "transitioned" to a range of educational settings not previously available to them. A model is presented in which critical transition parameters are conceived as functionally related continua, indicating degrees of readiness for both special and regular classroom settings. The model is based upon actual experience in placement of disturbed, learning disabled, and retarded children of nearly all ages and levels of functioning into school settings after discharge from a psychiatric hospital. (28 ref)
Forness, Steven R. (U California Ctr for the Health Sciences, Los Angeles) Contemporary Educational Psychology, 1977(Jan), Vol 2(1), 37-49. [PA, Vol 58:04373]

3058.   A comparative longitudinal analysis of special education groups.
The reading and mathematics performance of 5 groups of primary school age children—4 of which were receiving special education in various forms—were compared longitudinally using a nationally representative sample (12,684). Data were drawn from the National Child Development Study, a multidisciplinary longitudinal study of the physical, social, and educational development of all the children in England, Scotland, and Wales born in 1 wk of March 1958. The children were evaluated at ages 7 and 11 yrs (R. Davie et al, 1972 and K. Fogelman and H. Goldstein, 1976). The various educational provisions were evaluated taking into account the earlier placement and performance of the children. There was little difference in the reading progress of educationally subnormal children in ordinary and special schools, although the latter made more progress in mathematics. Results also suggest that children receiving some help within normal schools made most progress. (20 ref)
Ghodsian, M. & Calnan, M. (National Children's Bureau, London, England) British Journal of Educational Psychology, 1977(Jun), Vol 47(2), 162–174. [PA, Vol 60:01925]

3059.   Piaget and normalization: Developmental humanism.
The technology of behaviorism and the social consciousness of normalization have produced monumental changes for developmentally handicapped children. Both, however, lack an intrinsic developmental perspective and as pragmatic approaches they do not provide conceptual bases to distinguish the means–end aspects of "normality." J. Piaget's cognitive-developmental theory is proposed as a framework to provide content, direction, and structure for educational and habilitative intervention. The specific contributions of (a) competency focus, (b) cognitive stages, (c) invariance of development, (d) construction of reality, (e) assimilation–accommodation, and (f) decentration are considered within the context of mainstreaming and other normalization efforts. An interface between the sequences of "guiding environments" and the Piagetian construct of stages in the construction of reality is specified. The juxtaposition of common themes promotes the systematic analysis of environments and

experiences of the developmentally handicapped to meet developmental as well as humanistic criteria. (18 ref)
Grunewald, Karl; Simeonsson, Rune J. & Scheiner, Albert. (Swedish Board of Health & Welfare, Div of Care of the Mentally Retarded, Stockholm) Scandinavian Journal of Educational Research, 1977, Vol 21(4), 181–195. [PA, Vol 60:11439]

3060.   Spina bifida children in ordinary schools.
Conducted a 6-yr follow-up of 155 spina bifida children born in 1967–1969. 62 Ss had been placed in ordinary schools. Ss' handicaps were relatively mild overall, and placements were generally successful. However, discussions with school staff and parents indicated that not all placements had been trouble-free. In agreement with previous research, a need for better communication between schools, medical authorities, and other support services was revealed, as was the desirability of welfare assistance provisions where handicaps were appreciable. Suggestions are made about the support that education and community medical services will need to consider if they wish to implement a more radical integration policy. The appointment of an advisory teacher to effect liaison and to mobilize support for ordinary schools accepting a handicapped child is recommended, particularly to ensure that the resources and expertise concentrated in special schools be made more widely available. (26 ref)
Halliwell, Miles D. & Spain, Bernie. (Inner London Education Authority, Research & Statistics Group, England) Child Care, Health & Development, 1977(Nov–Dec), Vol 3(6), 389–405. [PA, Vol 61:09304]

3061.   [Experimental method of compensating for developmental deficits in children not ready for school.] (Polh)
Describes the development of a course of studies for children whose IQ is less than 70. A pilot group of 14 students was used to evaluate the curricular aspects of the program. Results suggest that with some modifications, the course of studies could be implemented in a regular school.
Hornowska, Stanisława. (Professional Education Council, Poznań, Poland) Psychologia Wychowawcza, 1977(Sep–Oct), Vol 20(4), 402–409. [PA, Vol 64:13385]

3062.   Simultaneous-treatment design comparisons of the effects of earning reinforcers for one's peers versus for oneself.
The influence of different methods of dispensing reinforcers earned by a target S on that S's behavior was examined with 2 mentally retarded boys, a 7-yr-old and a 9-yr-old, in a special education classroom. In separate experiments, each S received tokens contingent upon attentive behavior. The different methods of dispensing reinforcers consisted of exchanging the tokens for back-up events for oneself or for the entire class. The 2 methods of exchanging tokens were compared in separate simultaneous-treatment designs for each S. The simultaneous-treatment design permits a comparison of different treatments with an individual S. The treatments are administered in the same phase but are balanced across different time periods during which they are implemented. In each experiment, earning tokens that purchased back-up events for the entire class was more effective in altering the S's behavior than was earning tokens that purchased back-up events for oneself. In addition, the simultaneous-treatment design was demonstrated to be a useful technique to compare treatments with individual Ss. (28 ref)
Kazdin, Alan E. & Geesey, Sally. (Pennsylvania State U) Behavior Therapy, 1977(Sep), Vol 8(4), 682–693. [PA, Vol 60:04151]

3063.   The sexual adolescent who is mentally retarded.
Describes adolescents who are mentally retarded and discusses the current trend of accepting them as social-sexual persons in comparison to past practices of suppressing their freedom because they are sexual. The importance of sex education is emphasized; it should be included in a broader program of preparation for skills in social living because of recent innovations in mainstreaming the mentally retarded individual into the community. Issues on birth control are discussed and methods of teaching sex education outlined. (16 ref)

Kempton, Winifred. (Planned Parenthood Assn of Southeast Pennsylvania, Philadelphia) Journal of Pediatric Psychology, 1977, Vol 2(3), 104–107. [PA, Vol 62:01317]

3064. Influence of "mentally retarded" label on teachers' nonverbal behavior toward preschool children.
Examined the effect of labeling a preschool child as "mentally retarded" on the nonverbal behavior of 12 student teachers. The student teachers were assigned to 1 of 12 preschool children, either an experimental (labeled) or control (nonlabeled) child. All children were, in fact, nonhandicapped and had no diagnosis or record of mental retardation. After reading a description (labeled or nonlabeled) of their child's developmental status, each student teacher read their child a story. Results of analysis of the videorecorded reading sessions indicated that teachers were more immediate (i.e., showed less social distance) to children bearing the "mentally retarded" label.
Kurtz, P. David; Harrison, Michael; Neisworth, John T. & Jones, Russell T. (U Tennessee School of Social Work, Nashville) American Journal of Mental Deficiency, 1977(Sep), Vol 82(2), 204–206. [PA, Vol 60:05946]

3065. [Hierarchization of pre-arithmetic tasks of mentally retarded children.] (Fren)
In a study of 108 Belgian schoolchildren, moderately and severely mentally retarded, in special learning classes, it was found that the order of difficulty in learning to use figures was the same as that of normals. The retardates did differ from normals in the order in which they acquired figures and counting. Results are discussed from the teacher's point of view.
Lambert, Jean-Luc. (U Liège, Belgium) Revue Belge de Psychologie et de Pédagogie, 1977(Sep–Dec), Vol 39(159–160), 65–74. [PA, Vol 63:12993]

3066. Would it smell sweeter with any other name? An integrated education for educationally sub-normal pupils.
Describes the integration of severely and moderately handicapped educationally subnormal pupils in the same primary school, with the provision that at age 10 or 11 yrs the latter would transfer to a normal secondary school. The promise of transfer seemed to minimize the stigma of integration for parents of the moderately subnormal pupils.
Love, Peter C. AEP (Association of Educational Psychologists) Journal, 1977(Sum), Vol 4(5), 42–44. [PA, Vol 61:04800]

3067. Weaknesses, strengths, or a dual approach? A case for capitalizing on talent.
Argues that teachers should emphasize the particular talents of children and use those talents as vehicles for instruction in other areas as well. The case of Shyoichiro Yamamura, who, although labeled mentally retarded at an early age, became famous for his artwork on insects, is presented as an example of this approach. (16 ref)
Morishima, Akira. (U Iowa Coll of Education) Education & Training of the Mentally Retarded, 1977(Feb), Vol 12(1), 36–41. [PA, Vol 58:10542]

3068. The effects of known-item interspersal on acquisition and retention of spelling and sightreading words.
Results from 6 mentally retarded adolescents in a study on the effects of interspersing known items during training on new items show that (a) both acquisition and retention of spelling and sight reading words were facilitated by the interspersal procedure, and (b) all Ss acquired more words during the interspersal condition than either the high-density social reinforcement or baseline conditions. It is suggested that the procedure's effectiveness might be attributed to better maintenance of attending behavior of unknown items as a function of the inclusion of known items, which directly increase the amount of reinforcement for correct responses during the early stages of skill acquisition.
Neef, Nancy A.; Iwata, Brian A. & Page, Terry J. (Western Michigan U) Journal of Applied Behavior Analysis, 1977(Win), Vol 10(4), 738. [PA, Vol 61:02307]

3069. [Contribution to employment of past experiences by mentally retarded schoolchildren.] (Russ)
The problem of transfer of past experience by mentally retarded children is very important for the proper organization of school teaching and learning. Investigation shows that mentally retarded children tend to use their past experience in unchanged form; they cannot gear it to new conditions. This is partially attributable to impaired regulatory speech functions and interword connections. Unlike normal children, mentally retarded children cannot analyze an assignment given to them; they usually start performing it without any contemplation. It is concluded that in learning how to generalize new experience, mentally retarded schoolchildren learn how to transfer their past experience to new conditions.
Pinsky, B. I. (USSR Academy of Sciences, Inst of Defectology, Moscow) Defektologiya, 1977(Jan), No 1, 43–47. [PA, Vol 64:11206]

3070. [Self-concept of intelligence with pupils in special and normal schools: A group effect.] (Germ)
Compared 165 mentally retarded children (70 < IQ ≤ 85) in special and normal schools with respect to self-concept of mental ability, test-anxiety, and achievement motivation. As predicted, children in special schools had a better self-concept of mental ability and less test-anxiety. Both groups manifested a remarkable decrease in hope of success from Grade 4 through Grade 9. Results support W. U. Meyer's (1972) theory of self-concept of mental ability and do not support the stigmatism theory of expectancy. (17 ref)
Rheinberg, Falko & Enstrup, Birgit. (Ruhr-U Bochum, Psychologische Inst, West Germany) Zeitschrift für Entwicklungspsychologie und Pädagogische Psychologie, 1977(Jul), Vol 9(3), 171–180. [PA, Vol 61:14546]

3071. Brief report on the WISC-R: III. WISC-R and PPVT scores for Black and White mentally retarded children.
Administered the Peabody Picture Vocabulary Test (PPVT) and the WISC-R in counterbalanced order to 39 8.0–14.11 yr old Black and White children referred for psychoeducational evaluation. Results suggest that the WISC-R intelligence score is significantly and positively correlated to the PPVT intelligence score.
Richmond, Bert O. & Long, Marvin. (U Georgia) Journal of School Psychology, 1977(Fal), Vol 15(3), 261–263. [PA, Vol 60:08617]

3072. The von Restorff effect as a teaching technique with trainable retardates.
Rogers, George W. & Richmond, Bert O. (Northern Kentucky U) Catalog of Selected Documents in Psychology, 1977(Nov), Vol 7, 116–117. MS. 1606 (13 pp/paper: $4; fiche: $2). [PA, Vol 61:04812]

3073. Integrated settings at the early childhood level: The role of nonretarded peers.
Recent trends toward early intervention and mainstreaming have resulted in a growing number of preschool programs that integrate retarded and nonretarded children. These programs are generally based on the assumption that nonhandicapped peers function as behavioral models and/or reinforcing agents for handicapped youngsters within the context of positive social interaction. A review of the relevant empirical literature, however, indicates that such benefits do not necessarily result from integrated programing. The implications of recent studies that have investigated procedures for structuring peer imitation and peer reinforcement at the preschool age level are discussed, and specific suggestions are offered for maximizing the potential long-range benefits of integrated early childhood programs. (28 ref)
Snyder, Lee; Apolloni, Tony & Cooke, Thomas P. (U Kansas Bureau of Child Research) Exceptional Children, 1977(Feb), Vol 43(5), 262–266. [PA, Vol 58:06381]

3074. Early intervention via educational programs for parent–infant–young children with developmental delays and disabilities.
Discusses a model of preschool education in which the parents of children with developmental disabilities are involved as educators in teaching their children at home and/or at school. Use of the method with a 13-mo-old Down's syndrome boy is presented as an example.
Tein, R. G. Australian Journal of Mental Retardation, 1977(Jun), Vol 4(6), 10–12. [PA, Vol 59:11161]

3075. Unified programming procedures for the mentally retarded.
Describes Unified Programming Procedures (UPP) developed at the Lakemary Center for Exceptional Children, a private residential facility and school for mentally retarded children in Paola, Kansas. The UPP is designed to coordinate functionally the planning, implementation, and evaluation of individual program plans for each student. The discussion of the UPP focuses on 7 areas: (a) assessment, (b) behavioral objectives, (c) written programs, (d) time-framing, (e) names of staff, (f) methods, and (g) measures.
Throne, John M. et al. (Lakemary Ctr for Exceptional Children, Paola, KS) Mental Retardation, 1977(Feb), Vol 15(1), 14-17. [PA, Vol 58:06385]

3076. Children's knowledge of time and money: Effective instruction for mentally retarded.
Assessed the effectiveness of instructional units designed to promote the acquisition of time and money concepts by retarded children. The units were developed to start at levels not requiring counting and other number skills; they are based on language and vocabulary rather than number concepts. The Time unit was given to 112 nonretarded and 69 educable mentally retarded (EMR) children. The Money unit was given to 117 nonretarded, 64 EMR, and 115 trainable mentally retarded (TMR) children. Nonretarded Ss were from kindergarten to Grade 3. EMR Ss were approximately the same age as the 3rd graders, and their MA was similar to that of the kindergartners. TMR Ss were older than the nonretarded (mean CA 14.5 yrs); their MA level, however, was slightly below that of the nonretarded kindergartners. The average IQs of the EMR and TMR Ss were 71.1 and 42.4, respectively. Results show that the Time and Money units increased retarded Ss' scores significantly on most test items. Generally, the instruction brought retarded Ss up to a level above that of the MA peers, although still below that of their CA peers. Implications for instruction in other content areas are noted.
Thurlow, Martha L. & Turnure, James E. (U Minnesota, Research Development & Demonstration Ctr in Education of Handicapped Children) Education & Training of the Mentally Retarded, 1977(Oct), Vol 12(3), 203–212. [PA, Vol 61:02320]

3077. Teaching coin equivalence to the mentally retarded.
A program was designed to teach coin equivalence to mentally retarded adolescents. Coin equivalence was defined as choosing several different combinations of coins to equal specified target values. A pretest–posttest matched-groups design was employed with an experimental group receiving the monetary training, and a no-training control group. A multiple baseline across coin-counting responses was also incorporated in the experimental group. Ss were 7 males and 7 females aged 14–18 yrs; their MA ranged from 6 yrs 4 mo to 10 yrs 10 mo. Training was divided into 6 stages, each teaching one specific method of combining coins to equal 10 target values from $.05 through $.50. A 3-component response chain was used, requiring (a) naming, (b) selecting and counting, and (c) depositing target monetary values into a coin machine. Experimental Ss improved significantly in coin equivalence performance and maintained their skill on follow-up tests; control Ss did not.
Trace, Michael W.; Cuvo, Anthony J. & Criswell, Judith L. (Southern Illinois U) Journal of Applied Behavior Analysis, 1977(Spr), Vol 10(1), 85–92. [PA, Vol 59:02132]

3078. A multimodality language program for retarded preschoolers.
Eight retarded preschoolers (CA 26–37 mo; Gesell Developmental Quotient 47–68) placed in a day activity center setting were selected for inclusion in a multimodality receptive language program. The program is described, and teacher training procedures are discussed. Results indicate that all children made substantial gains in receptive language skills over the 7-mo period and half showed advances in expressive language functioning.
Wolf, Judith M. & McAlonie, Mary L. (U Minnesota Inst of Child Development) Education & Training of the Mentally Retarded, 1977(Oct), Vol 12(3), 197–202. [PA, Vol 61:02323]

3079. Results of an intensive developmental curriculum with moderately and severely retarded children.
Reports findings from an intensive developmental intervention over an 11-mo period with 29 moderately and severely retarded children and adolescents (3.8–16.2 yrs). The intervention emphasized 6 rehabilitative-educational skill areas: gross motor, fine motor, social skills, self-help, cognitive, and language. Classroom space was organized around 6 learning stations, 1 for each of the curriculum areas. Based on entering performance in each curriculum area (Learning Accomplishment Profile), a specific developmental intervention plan was established for each child. Results show that the amount of developmental growth over the intervention period was significant in each of the skill areas. On the average, pupils were progressing at the rate of about half the rate for nonretarded children. Summative evaluation data were collected on a pre–post basis using the Behavior Maturity Check List and the Trainable Achievement Record. It is concluded that a developmental rather than psychometric approach to identification, intervention, and evaluation appears to be differentially sensitive to the needs and abilities of retarded children. (German & French summaries)
Wyne, Marvin D. & Stuck, Gary B. (U North Carolina School of Education, Chapel Hill) International Journal of Rehabilitation Research, 1977(Jan), Vol 1(0), 51–57. [PA, Vol 61:04820]

3080. The assessment of minority students: Are adaptive behavior scales the answer?
Discusses the use of adaptive behavior scales (e.g., American Association on Mental Deficiency Adaptive Behavior Scale) in the assessment of minority children. Positive and negative characteristics of such scales are discussed. Recommendations include cautions for the use of such scales in the evaluation of culturally different minority children. (16 ref)
Baca, Leonard & Cervantes, Hermes. (U Colorado) Psychology in the Schools, 1978(Jul), Vol 15(3), 366–370. [PA, Vol 62:09832]

3081. Teaching through imitation: Industrial education for the moderately and severely retarded.
Analyzed the changes in behavior of 25 boys (mean CA 11.64 yrs, mean IQ 44.84) after a visual-imitative instructional method was used to teach industrial education psychomotor tasks. It was hypothesized that visual instruction followed by imitation was appropriate for teaching psychomotor skills and would evoke positive changes of behavior. Results indicate that severely retarded children can learn psychomotor tasks through imitation. (17 ref)
Bender, Michael. (John F. Kennedy Inst for Handicapped Children, Baltimore, MD) Education & Training of the Mentally Retarded, 1978(Feb), Vol 13(1), 16–21. [PA, Vol 61:09661]

3082. An approach to the planning and evaluation of a parental involvement course.
Describes the organization, content, and evaluation of a parental involvement course. The course was designed to fulfil the expressed needs of parents whose children attended a local-authority day school for the educationally subnormal. 13 families with children attending the school were interviewed. The course was directed by educational psychologists working closely with the school staff. Data on the effectiveness of such a course were collected on 3 levels, and are discussed: (a) parental subjective

evaluation of course methods, (b) assessment of objectives, and (c) evaluation of changes in parental behavior. (4 ref)
Bevington, Pat; Gardner, Jill M. & Cocks, Roger P. (Old Hall School, Willenhall, England) Child Care, Health & Development, 1978(Jul–Aug), Vol 4(4), 217–227. [PA, Vol 62:14811]

3083. Low-income children's attitudes toward mentally retarded children: Effects of labeling and academic behavior.
Examined the effects of the label "mentally retarded" and of academic competence on 96 low-income 6th graders' attitudes toward peers. Attitude was defined in terms of Ss' affective feelings and behavioral inclinations. Results show that Ss expressed more favorable attitudes toward a competent than an incompetent child and, paradoxically, toward a labeled than a nonlabeled child. The data also reveal that an academically incompetent child who was not labeled as retarded evoked negative attitudes, especially from boys, whereas an incompetent child who was labeled as retarded evoked positive attitudes. Findings are discussed in terms of the pros and cons of the current trend toward delabeling. (16 ref)
Budoff, Milton & Siperstein, Gary N. American Journal of Mental Deficiency, 1978(Mar), Vol 82(5), 474–479. [PA, Vol 61:09604]

3084. Affective response to exceptional children by students preparing to be teachers.
A semantic differential was administered to 56 Ss majoring in early childhood, elementary, and middle school education at the University of Georgia. Ss' affective response to exceptional children was higher when they perceived having only a single exceptional child vs many in a regular classroom.
Buttery, Thomas J. (U Georgia) Perceptual & Motor Skills, 1978(Feb), Vol 46(1), 288–290. [PA, Vol 61:09341]

3085. [Personality characteristics under the influence of labeling and reference group effects: A reinterpretation.] (Germ)
A reinterpretation of studies by S. Krug et al (see PA, Vol 61:14536) and by F. Rheinberg et al (see PA, Vol 61:14546) leads to the following conclusion. The labeling effect incurred by mentally retarded children when they must enroll in a special school seems to weaken and reverse itself under the influence of a reference-group effect, if these children are among the more intelligent in the special class. However, when they are about to leave the special school, the relevance of the original label seems to increase once again, effecting a lowering of self-concept. The crucial factor intervening between labeling- and reference-group effect is probably the varying relevance that different social groups acquire for the individual. (8 ref)
Casparis, Claudio. (U Zürich Pädagogische Inst, Switzerland) Zeitschrift für Entwicklungspsychologie und Pädagogische Psychologie, 1978(Jul), Vol 10(3), 265–268. [PA, Vol 65:02145]

3086. Competencies of persons responsible for the classification of mentally retarded individuals.
Placement decisions concerning mentally retarded persons rest heavily on the assessment data generated by school psychologists and related psychological personnel, but critics contend that current tests do not accurately measure or predict learning and that large numbers of children are incorrectly classified. The present article delineates the training and competencies individuals should possess if they have primary responsibility for classification and placement decisions.
Cegelka, Walter J. (U Missouri, St Louis) Exceptional Children, 1978(Sep), Vol 45(1), 26–31. [PA, Vol 62:04862]

3087. Confusion confounded: A teacher tries to use research results to teach math.
Reviews research relevant to the needs of special education teachers working to teach math to mentally retarded children. What mathematical skills should the learning disabled youngster be encouraged to master, what problems are encountered in teaching these skills, and what methods have proven useful in imparting these skills are among the questions asked. It is noted that research offers few and/or conflicting answers. It is concluded that (a) use of Piagetian theory may help a teacher decide when to teach a child what; (b) a task-analysis approach

can be useful if it is kept in mind that absolute precision may be impossible; and (c) teachers should start with those techniques and materials with which they feel comfortable, and if they do not work, try something else. (33 ref)
Chandler, Harry N. (McMinnville Senior High School, OR) Journal of Learning Disabilities, 1978(Jun–Jul), Vol 11(6), 361–369. [PA, Vol 62:04803]

3088. Visual Symbol Communication Instruction with nonverbal, multiply-handicapped individuals.
Visual Symbol Communication Instruction provides a specific methodology for teaching a chosen visual symbol system and facilitating its usage in nonspeech communication by nonverbal handicapped people. The program's novelty lies in its allowing either a gestural or a visual response using a visual communication display. Receptive instruction is designed to teach and enhance retention of visual symbols by individuals having receptive language. Blissymbol instruction through a series of sequential tasks was implemented with 5 nonverbal, mentally retarded individuals: 2 males (ages 16 and 17 yrs) and 3 children (ages 3 yrs 9 mo, 7 yrs 1 mo, and 8 yrs 3 mo). The protocol design and methodology promoted rapid systematic learning and high retention of symbols in all clients responding with a directed eye gaze. Three of the Ss achieved step criterion with only 1 attempt per step on all 14 compulsory steps; the other 2 Ss had a similar performance on 13 of the 14 compulsory steps. The performances of clients receiving instruction by an aide suggested the program may also be implemented effectively by paraprofessionals. (18 ref)
Elder, Pamela S. & Bergman, Joan S. (U Alabama, Ctr for Developmental & Learning Disorders, Birmingham) Mental Retardation, 1978(Apr), Vol 16(2), 107–112. [PA, Vol 62:09779]

3089. So you don't have any money for your token economy.
A token system, which used community donated reinforcers, was designed to improve the academic performance of students in a 7th-grade language arts class for slow learners. A teacher-designed behavioral proclamation and a contract were negotiated with students as part of treatment. The mean class average of the experimental group increased 7 points above baseline and 19% above that of a control group. (2 ref)
Eller, B. F.; Ideker, J. S. & Holben, M. M. (East Tennessee State U) Psychological Reports, 1978(Aug), Vol 43(1), 322. [PA, Vol 63:08416]

3090. Signing program for non-speaking and minimal speaking retarded children.
Describes a program to teach nonspeaking or minimally speaking retarded children to express their basic needs using sign language based on the Victorian method. Diagrams of signs and a list of vocabulary stages are included.
Kaufmann, Pat. (Minda School, Brighton, Australia) Australian Journal of Mental Retardation, 1978(Jun), Vol 5(2), 72–79. [PA, Vol 63:02063]

3091. The rights of the mentally ill and the mentally retarded: Are sexual rights included?
Discusses current trends relating to rights of the mentally ill and the mentally retarded as they pertain to sex education and sexual roles. Very little work has been done in the area of sexuality and the mentally ill. There has been a spurt of interest in the field of mental retardation because the need for sex education is so blatant. New laws and principles have been introduced to improve the lives of the mentally retarded, such as normalization, by offering more opportunity for social living. However, some mentally retarded individuals are being returned to the community without being adequately prepared for the move. The need for social-sexual training is evident. Likewise, there is a need to train professionals to provide such services as well as to develop policies. Sexual rights of the mentally retarded, including training in social-sexual behavior, knowledge about sexuality, right to birth control services, right to marry, and right to have a voice in whether or not to have children, are listed.

Kempton, Winifred. (Philadelphia Planned Parenthood Assn, PA) Devereux Forum, 1978(Win), Vol 13(1), 45–49. [PA, Vol 62:01187]

3092. Least restrictive alternative: An educational analysis.
Discusses the history of public school education and how various reforms and strategies have affected the status of children with special needs. Compliance with Public Law 94-142 and the availability of "least restrictive alternatives" for these children are examined. Children cannot continue to be arbitrarily divided between special and regular education, because such practices are restrictive and allow few if any alternative choices. (29 ref)
Klein, Nancy K. (Cleveland State U, Coll of Education) Education & Training of the Mentally Retarded, 1978(Feb), Vol 13(1), 102–114. [PA, Vol 61:09691]

3093. [Remedial education or education?] (Germ)
Discusses whether the placement of a mentally retarded child should serve primarily educational or therapeutic goals. In a presented case, medical therapy was the dominant purpose. The 2 goals should be combined and given due attention. (English summary) (6 ref)
Lempp, R. (Eberhard-Karls-U Tübingen, West Germany) Zeitschrift für Kinder- und Jugendpsychiatrie, 1978, Vol 6(2), 142–151. [PA, Vol 64:03533]

3094. Role of strategy in reading by mentally retarded persons.
Tested 21 12–16 yr old and 3 32–49 yr old mentally retarded individuals who could read on their ability to pronounce words and produce meaningful associates. Analyses of Ss' responses indicated an overuse of a strategy of memorizing words as a way to recognize words in print and an inability to consider word meanings in terms of abstract referents. A comparison of these results with responses given by nonretarded 2nd and 5th graders suggests that retarded persons use cognitive strategies that lead to inefficient reading and even interfere with the development of effective reading skills. (20 ref)
Mason, Jana M. (U Illinois, Ctr for the Study of Reading) American Journal of Mental Deficiency, 1978(Mar), Vol 82(5), 467–473. [PA, Vol 61:09699]

3095. Effects of contingency management on academic achievement and conduct of mentally retarded Arab students.
An experimental group of 11 mentally retarded Arab children (mean CA 8.8 yrs; mean IQ 48.2) was involved in a contingency-management program based on successful completion of academic work. A control group of 11 retarded Ss with approximately equal mean CA and IQ scores was exposed only to the regular teaching routine. Results indicate that academic achievement was greatest in Phase B of an ABA design. In addition, experimental Ss made achievement gains beyond those of the controls, and there were some generalization effects stemming from the treatment phase. Also, good conduct, although not directly manipulated in the study, was observed in the 3 phases of the study. Experimental Ss displayed more attending behavior and decreased their amount of nonattending and disruptive behavior during the treatment phase. Results also indicate that contingency management is a viable technique for retarded children living in a culture substantially different from that in the US.
Moracco, John C. & Fasheh, Violet. (Auburn U School of Education) American Journal of Mental Deficiency, 1978(Mar), Vol 82(5), 487–493. [PA, Vol 61:09706]

3096. [The education of the mentally handicapped child.] (Fren)
Mental handicaps are defined as alterations that simultaneously affect intelligence, emotions, and physical abilities (e.g., motor skills). The classification systems of such handicaps are both complex and imperfect. For retardation, the classification system is based on characteristics of different stages of arrested mental development. A table presents the characteristics of maturation and development for preschool children (from birth to 5 yrs), the educational and learning abilities of school age individuals (ages 6–21), and the social and professional abilities of adults (21 yrs and older). The development of specialized programs in Belgium

for the mentally handicapped is described. The involvement of parents in the stimulation of their children is discussed, as are changing attitudes toward the problems and treatment of the retarded. The results of a study reflecting the concern of adolescents in France for the retarded are mentioned. (9 ref)
Pasquasy, R. Bulletin de Psychologie Scolaire et d'Orientation, 1978(Jan), Vol 27(1), 3–11. [PA, Vol 66:09035]

3097. Teaching retarded preschoolers to imitate the free-play behavior of nonretarded classmates: Trained and generalized effects.
Applied 2 peer-imitation training procedures to increase the imitation between 3 36–38 mo old retarded and 3 49–59 mo old nonretarded children in integrated preschool settings. Baseline observations revealed low rates of imitation and social interaction between the 2 groups under naturalistic conditions. A simple training procedure, consisting of adult-delivered prompts and social reinforcement, was employed to increase the retarded Ss' imitation of their nonretarded classmates' free-play behavior. Demonstrations of training effects were made using multi-element baseline and multiple baseline designs. Data collected under nontraining conditions indicated maintenance of peer-imitation effects. Increases in reciprocal social interaction between the groups were also noted under training and nontraining conditions.
Peck, Charles A.; Apolloni, Tony; Cooke, Thomas P. & Raver, Sharon A. Journal of Special Education, 1978(Sum), Vol 12(2), 195–207. [PA, Vol 62:12101]

3098. Use of multiple discriminant function analysis in evaluation of a state-wide system for identification of educationally handicapped children.
The assessment information upon which diagnostic specialists based their classification decisions was used concurrently to predict the classification decisions that the diagnosticians made for 477 children in Grades 2–6 representing school districts throughout Utah. The rationale for this procedure was to manifest the variables along with their relative weights upon which the diagnostic classifications were based, to gain evidence of consistency with which diagnostic standards were followed, and to examine how accurately the diagnostic classifications made in Utah could be duplicated statistically. Results indicate that the "mentally retarded," "culturally disadvantaged," "slow learner," and "no-significant-problem" groups could be efficiently identified statistically, but the distinctions between those groups were based almost entirely on the variables of WISC Full Scale IQ and race. The other 2 classifications of "learning disabled" and "emotionally handicapped" could not be efficiently identified statistically; the consistency of standards employed for those classifications is questioned. (14 ref)
Petersen, Calvin R. & Hart, Darrell H. Psychological Reports, 1978(Dec), Vol 43(3, Pt 1), 743–755. [PA, Vol 64:08897]

3099. Dental health education for the mentally and physically handicapped.
Discusses research showing that dental disease is more frequent among children who are physically and mentally handicapped than among the nonhandicapped. Educational interventions that may help remedy this situation are suggested. (27 ref)
Price, James H. (Kent State U) Journal of School Health, 1978(Mar), Vol 48(3), 171–174. [PA, Vol 62:12293]

3100. Overview of language remediation.
Dissatisfaction with the global "language-bath" approach to language training for children with severe communication deficits led to the development of more structured programs, but many of these failed in the area of generalization. Recent approaches are overcoming this problem, and strategies based on the cognitive and interpersonal reality of the child are succeeding in teaching handicapped children to communicate. Focus on the active role of the child and on how the basis of meaning is established early in interaction with primary care-givers has led to a change in emphasis in research away from language as structure to language as meaning, with stress on the functions it serves and the content or settings in which these interactions take

place. Implications for new language intervention programs are discussed, and current programs are reviewed. It is concluded that the base of knowledge, technology, and methodology for the development of effective intervention strategies exists. Increasingly fine-grained research is necessary to monitor existing procedures and develop new approaches. (33 ref)
Price, Penelope. (Macquarie U, Sydney, Australia) Australian Journal of Mental Retardation, 1978(Dec), Vol 5(4), 126–133. [PA, Vol 64:02163]

3101. Developing nonretarded toddlers as verbal models for retarded classmates.
Two 28-mo-old retarded toddlers were separately taught to imitate words emitted by nonretarded age-mates through application of a peer-imitation-training procedure. A within-S multiple baseline design across responses was employed. Generalization data were collected under structured and free-play conditions. Results indicate that Ss' imitative verbal behavior increased concurrently with the application of the training procedure. Moreover, Ss' levels of verbal peer imitation increased under structured generalization conditions, even for responses never directly trained. Ss did not increase their levels of verbal peer imitation under free-play conditions. Increases in rates of spontaneous verbalizations to classmates were apparent in the free-play setting once the intervention was in effect. (18 ref)
Rauer, Sharon A.; Cooke, Thomas P. & Apolloni, Tony. (Santa Rosa Junior Coll) Child Study Journal, 1978, Vol 8(1), 1–8. [PA, Vol 61:12035]

3102. Gestural facilitation of expressive language in moderately/severely retarded preschoolers.
Nine moderately retarded young children (CAs 3 yrs 6 mo to 6 yrs 11 mo, MAs 20–30 mo) attending a preschool, received informal language training involving 2 methods. In one method, gestures accompanied the oral presentation of words. In the second method, words were presented without gestures. Both methods involved modeling, accompanying, prompting, and shaping the desired responses with positive feedback. Results indicate that gestures facilitated the children's spontaneous use of the target words. A significant mean difference was observed between the acquisition of control and experimental target words, but no significant mean difference was observed between the children's imitation of experimental and control words. (18 ref)
Reich, Rosalyn. (State U New York, Albany) Mental Retardation, 1978(Apr), Vol 16(2), 113–117. [PA, Vol 62:09811]

3103. [Reference group change: Acceptance of a stigma or new comparison standard for self evaluation? Reply to Casparis.] (Germ)
Comments on C. Casparis's (see PA, Vol 65:2145) reinterpretation of some effects of special schooling. His concept and the concept of the reference group can be used to explain decreases in self-concept at the beginning of special schooling. Casparis's assumption that labeling effects increase at the end of special schooling is not supported by the data. (English summary) (8 ref)
Rheinberg, Falko & Krug, Siegbert. (Ruhr-U Bochum Psychologische Inst, West Germany) Zeitschrift für Entwicklungspsychologie und Pädagogische Psychologie, 1978(Jul), Vol 10(3), 269–273. [PA, Vol 65:02160]

3104. Comparison of the performance of first-grade and mentally retarded students on the Peabody Mathematics Readiness Test.
The Peabody Mathematics Readiness Test was developed to assess mathematics readiness and identify children who would encounter difficulty in 1st-grade mathematics. In the present study, the performance of 175 mentally retarded (mean CA 10 yrs 7 mo; mean MA 6 yrs—Stanford-Binet Intelligence Scale and the WISC) Ss and 737 1st-grade Ss were compared on this test. Retarded Ss' mean scores were significantly lower than those of the nonretarded Ss on the drawing test; however, there were no significant differences between the mean scores of the groups on the other 5 subscales (Number, Containment, Size, Shape, and Configuration). (8 ref)

Richardson, Lloyd I.; Thurman, Richard L. & Bassler, Otto C. (U Missouri, St Louis) American Journal of Mental Deficiency, 1978(Jul), Vol 83(1), 83–85. [PA, Vol 62:04906]

3105. Test-retest reliability of the Quick Test for mentally retarded children.
Data from 24 male and 26 female retarded children aged 6–16 yrs indicate that the Quick Test is suitable for screening the intelligence of retarded children in this age range. Findings of the study, which involved teaching 10 special education teachers how to administer the test, also indicate that special education teachers can master the technique.
Rotatori, Anthony F. (Northern Illinois U) Perceptual & Motor Skills, 1978(Feb), Vol 46(1), 162. [PA, Vol 61:09820]

3106. Possibilities of influencing short-term memory output through training.
Trained 30 mentally retarded children (mean WISC IQ 72) in 4 memory functions daily for 2 mo. Memory performance was measured at 1, 3, 5, 7 and 8 wks, and compared with that of a control group of children who were tested at the beginning and end of the experiment but did not receive the memory training. On all 4 functions (memory span for words, memory span for sentences, episodic short-term memory, and recognition of visual and acoustic material), performance was significantly improved as the result of training. (14 ref)
Ruisel, Imrich & Droppová, Zdena. (Slovak Academy of Sciences, Inst of Experimental Psychology, Bratislava, Czechoslovakia) Studia Psychologica, 1978, Vol 20(2), 143–148. [PA, Vol 64:02166]

3107. The effectiveness of resource programming.
Reviewed the results of 17 studies of resource programs and their effects on the academic achievement and personal–social development of exceptional children. Only those studies that included relevant comparison groups were reviewed. Problems in efficacy research are discussed; many of the limitations of studies of special class placement are applicable to research on resource room programing. Results were not definitive in either domain. In the academic domain, programs for learning disabled and mildly disturbed children proved generally more effective than programs for retarded children. In the personal–social domain, positive effects of resource programing have not been established. In general, the most carefully designed studies supported the effectiveness of resource programing. The incorporation of formative evaluation procedures into resource program development as a supplement to traditional summative methodology is recommended. (38 ref)
Sindelar, Paul T. & Deno, Stanley L. (Pennsylvania State U) Journal of Special Education, 1978(Spr), Vol 12(1), 17–28. [PA, Vol 61:09714]

3108. Counseling the special education student: A developmental approach.
The job of the developmental counselor who works with special education students involves counseling and consultation with these youngsters, their families, teachers, and prospective employers. A developmental guidance and counseling program is needed for mentally retarded youngsters as much as for "normal" children. Another crucial component is to counsel and guide the normal students, regular school staff, and community more fully to accept, understand, and help mentally retarded youngsters toward becoming more adequate in dealing with the world. (22 ref)
Smaby, Marlow & Briski, John. (U Minnesota, Duluth) Pupil Personnel Services Journal, 1978, Vol 7(1), 69–76. [PA, Vol 63:10686]

3109. The effects of musical stimulation on distractibility and activity level among retarded subjects.
Investigated the effects of music on activity and academic performance among retarded children. 36 children (IQs 47–84; ages 11 yrs 2 mo–18 yrs 8 mo) were divided into low, medium, and high distractible groups on the basis of teacher ratings. Ss performed arithmetic problems under each of 3 conditions: calming music, exciting music, and no music. There were no

significant differences in math performance that could be attributed to the different conditions of music. The only significant finding was that the low distractible group performed significantly better than medium and high distractible groups. (5 ref)
Spudic, Thomas J. & Somervill, John W. (Mansfield Training School, CT) Education & Training of the Mentally Retarded, 1978(Dec), Vol 13(4), 362–366. [PA, Vol 63:13014]

3110.   [Physical education for spina bifida children in special schools for the physically handicapped.] (Germ)
Maintains that the shortage of environmental experience of children with spina bifida is due mainly to their inadequate motor development, which cannot be recovered by individual physical therapy alone. However, specifically selected and organized physical education makes possible the necessary mobility and social experiences. By giving the children exercises suitable for their ages, it is possible to achieve late maturation and personality stabilization. (English & French abstracts) (63 ref)
Strohkendl, H. & Schüle, K. (German Superior Sports Coll, Cologne, West Germany) International Journal of Rehabilitation Research, 1978, Vol 1(1), 39–58. [PA, Vol 61:07329]

3111.   [A comparative study between heuristic and explanative instructions in mentally retarded children.] (Japn)
27 mentally retarded students received instructions regarding the properties of magnets under heuristic (a technique in which the basic contents of a subject are provided by means of hypothesis verification) or explanatory instructions. Four male teachers asked Ss comprehension questions before and after each instruction and rated Ss' motivation and style of inquiry. Results show that heuristic instruction resulted in better performance by Ss on postinstruction test questions. There was no difference between Ss in terms of Ss' motivation and style of inquiry. (22 ref)
Taguchi, Noriyoshi.   Japanese Journal of Educational Psychology, 1978(Mar), Vol 26(1), 12–22. [PA, Vol 64:13399]

3112.   Differences in reading achievement between spina bifida children attending normal schools and those attending special schools.
Administered the Neale Analysis of Reading Ability to (a) a total of 55 spina bifida children from normal and special schools and controls matched for age, sex, social class of father, and position in the family. A multiple regression equation was used to compare observed scores with the expected scores. Results show that the spina bifida Ss receiving a normal school education were reading up to the level expected from their intelligence test scores, but the children in special schools had significant differences between observed and expected scores. The discrepancies may be accounted for by more profound physical handicap among the special school children but teachers' expectations may also be important in influencing reading achievement. (25 ref)
Tew, Brian & Laurence, K. M. (Welsh National School of Medicine, Dept of Child Health, Cardiff) Child Care, Health & Development, 1978(Sep–Oct), Vol 4(5), 317–326. [PA, Vol 62:14839]

3113.   Can mental retardation be reversed?
Recent research is summarized that suggests that reversing mental retardation may be successfully undertaken when 5 conditions are satisfied: (a) Retardation is defined behaviorally. (b) The behavior in question is identified by performances on tasks such as those found on standardized intelligence tests. (c) Performances are deliberately and systematically trained to improve proficiency. (d) The gains are maintained over time. (e) The results generalize from trained to untrained tasks. Training research in memory, vocabulary, and spatial relations is reviewed. (19 ref)
Throne, John M. & Farb, Joel. (U Kansas) British Journal of Mental Subnormality, 1978(Dec), Vol 24(2, No 47), 67–73. [PA, Vol 64:04206]

3114.   [A consideration on clinical evaluation and diagnosis in the remedial education of young mentally retarded children.] (Japn)
Based on clinical data for 44 mentally retarded children, a diagnostic profile was developed to measure the process of remedial education. Some problems with the profile are discussed, and the results of collaboration with parents and staff members of a day nursery and kindergarten are discussed. (18 ref)
Usagawa, Hiroshi. (Shukutoku Coll, Inst for Social Welfare, Chiba, Japan) Japanese Journal of Child Psychiatry, 1978, Vol 19(3), 201–214. [PA, Vol 64:13401]

3115.   Referential communication in normal and educationally subnormal children.
A series of 5 referential description tasks was performed by 76 normal and educationally subnormal (5 1–80 IQ range) children of equivalent MAs (5 and 7 yrs). General aspects of their performance and suggestions for improving their communication skills are discussed (e.g., by explicit instructions to the Ss to compare items, and by combining visual and tactual experiences before item descriptions).
Watson, Judith M. (Moray House Coll, Edinburgh, Scotland) Educational Research, 1978(Feb), Vol 20(2), 109–113. [PA, Vol 61:12041]

3116.   Educability revisited: Curricular implications for the mentally retarded.
Argues that the greater accommodation of mild and moderately retarded children into regular school settings requires changes in both general and special education. Deficiencies of typical curricular approaches to the education of the retarded are discussed, and instruction more clearly focused on fundamental cognitive abilities and related learning strategies is proposed. The cumulative effect of intensive instruction in learning skills, as opposed to the casual, isolated, or sporadic development of any specific ability, is suggested. The limits of any curricular method are acknowledged, and the study of the ecology of special education is proposed. (20 ref)
Winschel, James F. & Ensher, Gail L. (Syracuse U) Education & Training of the Mentally Retarded, 1978(Apr), Vol 13(2), 131–138. [PA, Vol 61:14553]

3117.   Colored chalk and messy fingers: A kinesthetic-tactile approach to reading.
Utilized the Fernald technique (VAKT; G. M. Fernald and H. Keller, 1921)—a multisensory approach to teaching reading and spelling that incorporates visual, auditory, kinesthetic, and tactile elements—that helped 3 young boys, all considered slow learners, learn to read and improved their attitudes toward reading. (7 ref)
Witman, Carolyn C. & Riley, James D. (William M. Hampton School, Greensboro, NC) Reading Teacher, 1978(Mar), Vol 31(6), 620–623. [PA, Vol 66:09059]

3118.   Making retarded children literate: A five year study.
Administered a battery of measures (e.g., Peabody Picture Vocabulary Test) to 12 Ss (average CA at beginning of study, 10 yrs; IQs 35–55) in the Distar language program. The direct instruction model used with these Ss emphasized modern behavioral principles and logical systematic programming. Results strongly indicate that the Ss who have been on all levels of the Distar language and reading programs demonstrated mastery of most of the basic literacy skills. (11 ref)
Booth, Alan; Hewitt, Don; Jenkins, Warren & Maggs, Alex. 1979(Sep), Vol 5(7), 257–260. [PA, Vol 66:08966]

3119.   Using logic in special classrooms: I.
At all levels of schooling, there is no formal instruction in logic for the mentally retarded. Nonlogical, illogical, and extra-logical reasoning dominate in the mental processes of such students. However, they can be taught logical reasoning. This is done by requiring them to use evidence in discourse and to make inferences, draw implications, and make deductions and inductions. Examples illustrate how such aspects of logic as "if–then" and negation arguments can replace nonlogical explanations.

Cherkes, Miriam. (U Connecticut, Storrs) Academic Therapy, 1979(Nov), Vol 15(2), 165–171. [PA, Vol 66:04381]

3120.   A preliminary investigation of the role of logic in special class instruction.
Classrooms for the mentally retarded (MR), emotionally disturbed (ED), learning disabled (LD), and average (A) were studied to ascertain which rules of formal logic teachers and students employ. The purpose was to delineate specific rules of logic; then to examine their use in classrooms at the primary, intermediate, and junior high levels and in classrooms for the MR, ED, LD, and A. Results indicate that the use of extralogical forms of reasoning was significantly greater than the use of valid, formal, logical rules. This was found to be true of teachers and students, at all levels and for all diagnostic labels. Implications for further research and for classroom needs are discussed. (26 ref)
Cherkes, Miriam. (U Connecticut) Contemporary Educational Psychology, 1979(Jan), Vol 4(1), 67–80. [PA, Vol 64:02147]

3121.   The blind nursery school child.
Describes the developmental experiences of normal blind children and a retarded blind child in a nursery school. The author, one of the teachers, noted the importance of early verbal and physical contact with blind children. Instances of separation anxiety are discussed, as is the school's policy of having the mothers stay until the child feels secure. Many blind children enjoy rhythmic, repetitive movements, which are safe outlets for the child's physical energy. These movements can become intense, thus indicating the child's withdrawal from the world. To counteract this tendency, close involvement with a caring adult is required to make the world more attractive and meaningful and to motivate the child to participate in constructive games. Blind children's use of language to express their own sensory perceptions is discussed, and observations of group interactions among sighted and blind children are described. (1 ref)
Curson, Annemarie. (Hampstead Child-Therapy Course & Clinic, Nursery School for the Blind, London, England) Psychoanalytic Study of the Child, 1979, Vol 34, 51–83. [PA, Vol 64:12732]

3122.   Strategic behavior in the mentally retarded.
Reviews research findings that compare the performance of normal and mentally retarded persons on tasks where strategic and planning behaviors are required. The deficits (if any) of the retardates in the specific control processes underlying learning, attention, and memory paradigms are discussed. Also provided is a brief outline of the implications for educational practices. (23 ref)
Dash, Udaya N. (U Alberta, Edmonton, Canada) Mental Retardation Bulletin, 1979(Sum), Vol 7(1), 17–30. [PA, Vol 66:08232]

3123.   Education for problem children.
Recommends that education of mentally retarded children should utilize concrete media, such as perceptual knowledge and sensory training (visual, auditory, motor). Techniques for delinquent children include reeducation and improvement of home and school environment. Gifted children must also have educational methods designed specifically for them.
Dutta, Tapash S.   Indian Psychological Review, 1979, Vol 18(1–4, Spec Iss), 31–34. [PA, Vol 65:08824]

3124.   Changing teachers' negative expectations.
Teachers are sometimes unable to accept the handicaps of the slow learner or to change their views that such children can succeed. To determine if teachers are responsive to a change procedure, teachers from 32 primary schools were randomly assigned to treatment or control groups. Each completed a satisfaction scale about 3 children in his or her class requiring academic help and 3 who required none. The children received the Peabody Individual Achievement Test before and after experimental intervention. This consisted of selecting limited objectives for children in need of help and using teacher-identified strategies: programming, patterning, and focusing. Although no ability or achievement gains by the children were noted during the month in which the study took place, teachers in the treatment group did change their views of the slow learner. It was found that teacher satisfaction was related to judgment of student capability.
Dworkin, N. (Temple U) Academic Therapy, 1979(May), Vol 14(5), 517–531. [PA, Vol 66:04273]

3125.   Cognitive modifiability in retarded adolescents: Effects of instrumental enrichment.
Compared the 2-yr progress of 57 matched pairs of 12–15 yr old mentally retarded, socioculturally deprived Ss who were exposed to 2 different programs. One group in a residential center and 1 group in a day center received Instrumental Enrichment (IE), a program designed by the 1st author to modify the cognitive functions of retarded adolescents in Israel; another group from each of the 2 settings received General Enrichment (GE). Results show significantly better performance by the IE groups than by the GE groups on tests of specific cognitive functions, on scholastic achievement, and on some classroom interaction scales. (13 ref)
Feuerstein, Reuven et al. (Hadassah-Wizo-Canada Research Inst, Deitcher Ctr, Jerusalem, Israel) American Journal of Mental Deficiency, 1979(May), Vol 83(6), 539–550. [PA, Vol 62:09783]

3126.   Effect of labeling and teacher behavior on children's attitudes.
78 4th graders from a school containing an integrated special education program viewed 1 of 2 videotapes depicting a child performing various behaviors. On one tape the teacher reacted positively to the child's behavior, on the other negatively. Ss were told that the child was either "normal," mentally retarded, or learning disabled. Across all labeling conditions, Ss rated the child higher on a peer-acceptance questionnaire when the child was reacted to positively by the teacher. Further, the "mentally retarded" label led to significantly higher peer-acceptance ratings than did the other labels. (19 ref)
Foley, James M. (Capital Area Intermediate Unit, Harrisburg, PA) American Journal of Mental Deficiency, 1979(Jan), Vol 83(4), 380–384. [PA, Vol 62:12217]

3127.   Attitudes of educators toward handicapped and non-handicapped children.
Previous research has shown that teachers generally perceive handicapped children more negatively than nonhandicapped children. The present study, in which 111 educators completed the Personal Attribute Inventory for 4 target groups (gifted, normal, retarded, and handicapped children), supports this notion. In addition, present results do not vary across different groups of educators or by whether they taught in institutional or public school settings. (4 ref)
Green, Sara C.; Kappes, Bruno M. & Parish, Thomas S. (Kansas State U, Manhattan) Psychological Reports, 1979(Jun), Vol 44(3, Pt 1), 829–830. [PA, Vol 64:11089]

3128.   Regular teacher concerns with mainstreamed learning handicapped children.
Examined the affective components of regular teachers' interactions with special education students assigned to their classrooms. Teachers who were the primary instructors for 51 educable mentally retarded pupils and 196 educationally handicapped children in Grades 1–8 were asked to express the degree of comfort or discomfort they experienced while responsible for the special child in a variety of school-related situations. Teachers consistently reported more comfort with activities involving supervision and academics than with activities that involved public display of the child's competence. Five teacher response patterns were identified, and teachers were found to be somewhat less comfortable with the retarded than with the educationally handicapped child. (1 ref)
Guerin, Gilbert R. (San Jose State U School of Education) Psychology in the Schools, 1979(Oct), Vol 16(4), 543–545. [PA, Vol 65:04050]

3129. The effects of self-management procedures on the study behavior of two retarded children.
A single-S design with one replication was used to assess the effects of self-monitoring and self-delivered reward with retarded children. Results indicate that the 2 educably retarded boys, aged 10 and 13 yrs, who served as Ss were highly responsive to self-management procedures. On-task behavior improved for both Ss during self-monitoring of study behavior. This effect was short-lived, however, and not as dramatic as the changes found with self-delivered reward procedures. (14 ref)
Horner, Robert H. & Brigham, Thomas A. (U Oregon Ctr on Human Development) Education & Training of the Mentally Retarded, 1979(Feb), Vol 14(1), 18–24. [PA, Vol 64:04196]

3130. Manual communication systems: A comparison and its implications.
Manual communication has been successfully used to teach many nonverbal children to express themselves; however, little research is available regarding the comparative efficiency and effectiveness of different sign systems. 30 undergraduate speech students participated in a study to compare the intelligibility of American Sign Language (AMESLAN) and American Indian Sign (AMERIND) prior to and after an instructional unit. Statistical analyses showed that AMERIND signs were more intelligible to the untrained viewer, were more intelligible after training, and were more intelligible after a 2-wk time delay when compared to AMESLAN signs for the same concepts. (35 ref)
Kirschner, Alison; Algozzine, Bob & Abbott, Thomas B. (Sarasota Public Schools, FL) Education & Training of the Mentally Retarded, 1979(Feb), Vol 14(1), 5–10. [PA, Vol 64:04197]

3131. Educational placement of children with spina bifida.
Studied procedures of school placement for 38 5–18 yr olds with spina bifida in 23 school districts in western New York State 5 yrs after a mandated process was enacted. Data were gathered by conference interview and questionnaires from school district administrators, parents, and teachers. Findings reveal that placement procedures varied among school districts and often did not meet state mandated requirements. (13 ref)
Lauder, Calvin E.; Kanthor, Harold; Myers, Gary & Resnick, Jacqueline. (City School District, Student Educational Services, Rochester, NY) Exceptional Children, 1979(Mar), Vol 45(6), 432–437. [PA, Vol 62:07355]

3132. Treatment of stereotyped and aggressive behaviors of retarded children using reinforcement and response-contingent restraint.
Two studies examined the effect of combining brief physical restraint (holding arms by sides of body for 20 sec) with differential reinforcement in reducing classroom problem behaviors of 2 retarded children. In Exp I, the restraint procedure was effective in reducing the frequency of face-touching by a 10-yr-old moderately retarded boy in 2 training settings. In Exp II, restraint led to reduction of an 11-yr-old severely retarded boy's physical aggression (pinching, grabbing clothing) in class. (21 ref)
Luiselli, James K. et al. (Boston U) Scandinavian Journal of Behaviour Therapy, 1979, Vol 8(2), 103–113. [PA, Vol 65:04168]

3133. The Derbyshire Language Scheme: Remedial teaching for language delayed children.
Describes the content of the Derbyshire Language Scheme (DLS), a collection of activities aimed at teaching language skills to mentally retarded children. At every level, there are "comprehension only" and "expression only" activities that are graded in difficulty and organized into teaching groups. Role-reversal techniques are used to teach expressive language. The DLS emphasizes child-centered teaching, carefully programmed tasks, a clear statement of the skills to be taught, and a deliberate attempt to teach these skills in a manner in which the child is likely to use them in his or her normal environment. The contents of each of the 3 main DLS sections—single word level, 2–4 word level, and levels 5–10—are described. (9 ref)

Masidlover, M. (Derbyshire County Council Educational Psychology Service, Ripley, England) Child Care, Health & Development, 1979(Jan–Feb), Vol 5(1), 9–16. [PA, Vol 62:04828]

3134. Guidance and counseling practices with mentally retarded youth.
Presents results of an Iowa survey of counselors to determine problems that interfere with the provision of counseling services to retarded youth. Essentially, it was found from responses that (a) only vague indications are made by special education staff as to what is needed from the counselor, (b) that only partial responsibility is given to the counselor for the total counseling and guidance role, (c) more than 50% of counselors do not have access to the handicapped or are not assigned to serve the handicapped, and (d) counselors are not trained to serve retarded youth.
Morley, Raymond E. & Kokaska, Charles. (Iowa Dept of Public Instruction, Des Moines) Mental Retardation, 1979(Aug), Vol 17(4), 201–202. [PA, Vol 66:09108]

3135. Parents of the gifted lag.
Surveyed the attitudes of 50 parents of mentally retarded children and 50 parents of gifted children toward funding for special education. Parents of the retarded strongly supported such funding, but parents of gifted children neither knew about giftedness nor favored special educational facilities for their children. (7 ref)
Napolitano, Helen S. (Marymount Manhattan Coll) Creative Child & Adult Quarterly, 1979(Spr), Vol 4(1), 58–61. [PA, Vol 64:11200]

3136. Evaluation of a transitional training program for mentally retarded, multiply handicapped high school students.
A comparative study showed that when transitional vocational services are provided during the last years of school, rather than the traditional academic program, the experimental students progressed better than the controls on all criteria measured, even though the latter were less handicapped.
O'Brien, Patrick J. (Illinois Inst for Developmental Disabilities, Chicago) Rehabilitation Literature, 1979(Aug), Vol 40(8), 232–235. [PA, Vol 66:04397]

3137. Early childhood education for psychosocially disadvantaged children: Effects on psychological processes.
26 Black children at high risk for sociocultural retardation attended, from infancy, a day-care center with educational treatment in the form of systematic curriculum; 24 control Ss were educationally untreated. The McCarthy Scales of Children's Abilities were administered to both groups at 42 mo of age. The educationally treated group's scores were superior to the educationally untreated group on the Verbal, Perceptual-Performance, Quantitative, and Memory Scales but not on the Motor scale. (10 ref)
Ramey, Craig T. & Campbell, Frances A. (Frank Porter Graham Child Development Ctr, Chapel Hill, NC) American Journal of Mental Deficiency, 1979(May), Vol 83(6), 645–648. [PA, Vol 62:09651]

3138. A home training service for pre-school developmentally handicapped children.
Developed and evaluated a home training service for 19 preschool developmentally handicapped children. The service was based on the Portage model of early childhood education and involved parents as the major teaching resource (M. Shearer and D. E. Shearer, 1972). Ss served as their own controls. Data included details of skills taught through the Portage service, monthly scores on the Portage checklist, and 2-monthly scores on the Griffiths Mental Development Scale. Results show that 88.2% of tasks taught through the Portage service were learned, 67.3% being learned within one wk. In both experimental groups there was an increase in the rate of acquisition of checklist skills coinciding with the introduction of the Portage service. Most Ss also showed increased gains on mental development test scores after the introduction of the service. (15 ref)

Revill, Susan & Blunden, Roger. (Ely Hosp, Mental Handicap in Wales/Applied Research Unit, Cardiff) Behaviour Research & Therapy, 1979, Vol 17(3), 207–214. [PA, Vol 64:08866]

3139.   Self-control and generalization procedures in a classroom of disruptive retarded children.
Attempted to decrease disruptiveness by increasing self-evaluative skills and programing generalization in a class of 12 5–11 yr old mentally retarded children (IQ 33–64). Ss were observed 5 days/wk during a morning experimental period and several times per week in the afternoon as a measure of generalization. Behavior was recorded according to an interval sampling observational code. Results show that systematic feedback was effective in significantly reducing disruptiveness; greater reductions resulted from the token program and the subsequent matching and fading phases. Decreased levels of disruptiveness were maintained throughout self-evaluation and the phases that followed. Decreased levels of disruption also generalized to afternoon sessions, to days when the experimental procedures were not in effect, and to days when substitute teachers taught the class. In ability to self-evaluate, the class initially matched the teacher's ratings with about 50% accuracy; this gradually increased to consistently above 90% during the latter phases. (23 ref)
Robertson, Stephen J.; Simon, Steven J.; Pachman, Joseph S. & Drabman, Ronald S. (U Mississippi Medical Ctr, Jackson) Child Behavior Therapy, 1979(Win), Vol 1(4), 347–362. [PA, Vol 65:08839]

3140.   Performance of mentally retarded children on a hierarchically sequenced introductory mathematics curriculum.
16 moderately and severely retarded children took diagnostic tests to assess their understanding of number concepts. Eight Ss (experimentals) were trained with a hierarchically sequenced mathematics curriculum and the other 8 Ss (controls) were trained toward the same objectives using traditional methods. After 1 yr, the experimental group mastered 32 and the control group 15.5 objectives, suggesting that a hierarchically sequenced mathematics curriculum may provide an effective approach to the teaching of number concepts to retarded children. (10 ref)
Singh, Nirbay N. & Ahrens, Michael G. (Mangere Hosp & Training School, Auckland, New Zealand) Exceptional Child, 1979(Mar), Vol 26(1), 27–33. [PA, Vol 66:04402]

3141.   The concurrent validity of the 1965 Wide Range Achievement Test with neurologically impaired and emotionally handicapped pupils.
Administered the Wide Range Achievement Test (WRAT) concurrently with the Stanford Achievement Test (SAT) to 296 neurologically impaired and emotionally handicapped children to determine the content validity and reliability of the WRAT. Correlation coefficients between the 2 measures were statistically significant, but there was a significant overestimation of grade equivalent scores on the WRAT when compared to all administered test levels of the SAT. The younger the pupil, the higher the correlation between the 2 instruments and the lower the overestimation of scores; the older the pupil, the lower the correlation and the higher the overestimation of WRAT scores. It was found that 7 of the 14 administrators of the WRAT significantly overestimated their scores in relation to the SAT. It is concluded that the WRAT is an adequate instrument for a broad one-time screening and placement device for severely handicapped pupils, provided the scores are interpreted with caution, but it is not recommended as a test of academic achievement on a longitudinal basis. The possibility that the SAT may be underestimating pupils' scores is also discussed. (2 ref)
Williamson, Wayne E. (Bronx Regional Office for Special Education, NY) Journal of Learning Disabilities, 1979(Mar), Vol 12(3), 201–203. [PA, Vol 62:07377]

3142.   [Self-instructional training used as vocal overcorrection.] (Norg)
Describes a treatment program given to a 17-yr-old mentally retarded pupil. The majority of self-instructional training programs have been applied to Ss within the normal intellectual range. In the present case it was necessary to develop preparatory procedures in 4 stages prior to the onset of treatment. Treatment led to an effective reduction of target behavior and some positive side effects. It is suggested that the complex contingencies established in self-instructional training be clarified. (5 ref)
Wright, Jan & Larsen, Kjell-Arne. (Emma Hjort School, Sandvika, Norway) Scandinavian Journal of Behaviour Therapy, 1979, Vol 8(4), 191–198. [PA, Vol 65:06408]

3143.   Mainstreaming: The proof is in the implementation.
Warns that mainstreaming, or the practice of educating handicapped children in the "least restrictive environment," must be carefully monitored. Mainstreaming could proceed along the same lines as deinstitutionalization, which has often amounted to the trading of inferior care for no care at all. Research is desperately needed, the authors assert, to determine which children, with which handicaps, are likely to benefit from mainstreaming. To date, the data on the merits of educating mentally retarded children with their normal peers are inconclusive. Without appropriate teacher training and support services, mainstreaming appears doomed to fail. Thus, any mainstreaming worthy of the name is no bargain for taxpayers. Finally, the authors question the sanctity of normalization, the principle behind mainstreaming. (13 ref)
Zigler, Edward & Muenchow, Susan. (Yale U) American Psychologist, 1979(Oct), Vol 34(10), 993–996. [PA, Vol 63:10617]

3144.   Generalization of learning among the mentally retarded.
Surveys selected experimentally established methods of achieving generalization with the mentally retarded. These methods include (a) using multiple training environments; (b) using multiple trainers; (c) modifying the training environment to approximate the natural environment in terms of materials, reinforcement, and language cues; (d) modifying the natural environment; (e) discrimination training; (f) teaching functional skills; and (g) teaching self-monitoring and reinforcement. (3 p ref)
Baine, David. (U Alberta, Edmonton, Canada) Mental Retardation Bulletin, 1980(Sum), Vol 8(2), 51–66. [PA, Vol 66:08956]

3145.   Parent training: A school-based model for enhancing teaching performance.
Reports the results of a school-based remedial program that attempted to increase the programming knowledge and teaching skills of nonproficient families. Participants were 16 parents who had completed a standardized parent training course but had not met the program's criteria for proficiency. Nine parents received additional action-oriented training in conjunction with a 3-wk mini-camp educational program for their retarded children. Seven parents comprised a comparison group. Mini-camp parents demonstrated significant improvement in knowledge and skills relative to their own performance following standardized training and relative to the performance of comparison group parents. The feasibility of incorporating components of the mini-camp training program into ongoing educational programs for retarded children is discussed. (10 ref)
Brightman, Richard P.; Ambrose, Stephen A. & Baker, Bruce L. (U California, Los Angeles) Child Behavior Therapy, 1980(Fal), Vol 2(3), 35–47. [PA, Vol 66:11270]

3146.   Sexual knowledge and education of ESN students in centers of further education.
Reports data from a 1979 survey concerning the level of sexual awareness among educationally subnormal (ESN) students (IQs of 60–100) attending 2 "Further Education Colleges" operated by the British Spastic Society. Findings from 50 respondents indicate that they had limited access to sexual information both from parents and peers, that all welcomed the prospect of formal sex education courses, and that the greatest lack of knowledge concerned conception and contraception. Suggestions for small-group sex education/personal relationship programs for such students are included.
Brown, Hilary. (Spastic Society, London, England) Sexuality & Disability, 1980(Fal), Vol 3(3), 215–220. [PA, Vol 66:04379]

3147.   Public school principals' attitudes toward mainstreaming retarded pupils.
Investigated the perceptions of 345 Maine public school principals toward the effective mainstreaming of handicapped children according to type and level of handicapping condition. Compared with other handicapped pupils, mentally retarded students were generally viewed by Ss as having the poorest prognosis for successful mainstreaming. Even mildly retarded pupils were seen as possessing relatively poor chances for successful integration within the regular classroom setting. (9 ref)
Davis, William E. (U Maine, Orono) Education & Training of the Mentally Retarded, 1980(Oct), Vol 15(3), 174–178. [PA, Vol 66:08980]

3148.   Can helping hurt? Effects of constraining and nonconstraining retrieval cues on list transfer by mentally retarded adolescents.
Gave 64 retarded adolescents (mean CA 14.66 yrs; mean MA 10.07 yrs) constraining and nonconstraining retrieval cues on 1 of the 4 presentation and recall trials. Ss were cued on either Trial 2 or 3, and half of each group received either blocked or random presentation over the 1st 2 trials. Lists for the last 2 trials were randomly arranged. On Trial 4, recall for all Ss was uncued. Ss who received nonconstraining cues showed significantly more recall transfer than did those in the constraining condition; there were no significant differences on Trials 1–3. Blocking facilitated clustering but not recall. Improvement over trials was associated with increases in both the number of categories and the mean number of words per category recalled. Results suggest that the provision of constraining retrieval cues may have encouraged Ss to adopt a passive role in list learning, a tendency that proved to be detrimental to subsequent uncued list processing. (17 ref)
Evans, Ross A. (U Wisconsin, Madison) American Journal of Mental Deficiency, 1980(Nov), Vol 85(3), 299–305. [PA, Vol 65:03519]

3149.   Effects of time-out from auditory reinforcement on two problem behaviors.
A 9-yr-old severely retarded boy (MA 2.8 yrs) and a 11-yr-old moderately retarded girl (MA 5.4 yrs) exhibiting high rates of inappropriate verbal/vocal behavior or out-of-seat behavior were treated using time-out. Results across 3 settings support the effectiveness of the technique. (9 ref)
Ford, John E. & Veltri-Ford, Anita. (Dept of Human Resources, Caswell Ctr, Kinston, NC) Mental Retardation, 1980(Dec), Vol 18(6), 299–303. [PA, Vol 66:08985]

3150.   Effects of a remedial program on visual-motor perception in spina bifida children.
Results of an assessment of the perceptual functioning of spina bifida patients (mean age 82.9 mo) after a multidisciplinary remedial program show that 12 experimental Ss improved significantly on a global index of visual perception and on the 5 subtests of the Frostig Development Test of Visual Perception, compared to 24 control and attention-placebo Ss. (26 ref)
Gluckman, Sandra & Barling, Julian. (U of the Witwatersrand, Johannesburg, South Africa) Journal of Genetic Psychology, 1980(Jun), Vol 136(2), 195–202. [PA, Vol 64:08855]

3151.   Improving attitudes toward retarded children by using group discussion.
Hypothesized that (a) nonhandicapped children who participated in a discussion of retardation would improve their attitudes significantly more than children who did not participate; (b) children having positive attitudes would cause greater improvement in attitudes of negative children than would those having neutral attitudes; and (c) high sociometric status children would be more resistant to attitude change than would low status children. 339 3rd–6th graders were pretested on a 30-adjective checklist and a sociometric questionnaire, and on the basis of their responses were assigned to 1 of 3 experimental discussion-group conditions or a control condition (discussion of a nonrelevant topic). Data analyzed through a regression analysis of covariance showed significant support for the 1st hypothesis. However, positive Ss did not serve as more effective change

agents than neutral Ss, and low status Ss were not more inclined to change attitudes than were high status Ss. At the least, however, the findings indicate that it is possible through directed discussion to improve the attitudes of nonhandicapped children toward retarded children and suggest that if the treatment precedes the mainstreaming experience, normal children may be prepared to accept their handicapped peers. (8 ref)
Gottlieb, Jay. (New York U) Exceptional Children, 1980(Oct), Vol 47(2), 106–111. [PA, Vol 64:13380]

3152.   Influence of iconicity and phonological similarity on sign learning by mentally retarded children.
Studied the acquisition of sign–word pairs by 36 moderately to severely retarded (mean IQ 41) 9–13 yr olds as a function of the iconicity and cheremic (phonological) similarity of the signs, and the vocabulary age (Peabody Picture Vocabulary Test) of Ss. A recall format (alternate learning and test trials) paired-associates paradigm was employed. Results of an ANOVA revealed that iconicity enhanced learning, similarity interfered with acquisition, and there was no effect of vocabulary age within the range studied. There were no interactions among the above variables. (21 ref)
Griffith, Penny L. & Robinson, Jacques H. (Kent State U) American Journal of Mental Deficiency, 1980(Nov), Vol 85(3), 291–298. [PA, Vol 65:03521]

3153.   Social interactions among preschool children.
Investigated the nature and extent of social interactions among 37 4–6 yr old preschool children at different developmental levels. Communicative and parallel play interactions of mildly, moderately, severely, and nonhandicapped Ss were observed during free play across 2 time periods. Nonhandicapped and mildly handicapped Ss interacted with each other more frequently than expected on the basis of availability, and they interacted with moderately and severely handicapped Ss less frequently than expected. Moderately and severely handicapped Ss interacted with all 4 groups as expected by availability. The potential value of integrated programs for children of varying developmental levels is discussed. (11 ref)
Guralnick, Michael J. (Ohio State U, Nisonger Ctr, Columbus) Exceptional Children, 1980(Jan), Vol 46(4), 248–253. [PA, Vol 63:08425]

3154.   Personality factors and ability groups.
21 academically handicapped (AH) and 35 academically gifted (AG) students were administered the Children's Personality Questionnaire and the results were subjected to a stepwise discriminant analysis. It is tentatively concluded that AG Ss were excitable, assertive, enthusiastic, venturesome, and forthright whereas AH Ss were phlegmatic, obedient, sober, shy, and shrewd. (4 ref)
Hunt, Dennis & Randhawa, Bikkar S. (U Saskatchewan Coll of Education, Saskatoon, Canada) Perceptual & Motor Skills, 1980(Jun), Vol 50(3, Pt 1), 902. [PA, Vol 66:04389]

3155.   Assessment of retarded student achievement with standardized true/false and multiple-choice tests.
The relative efficacy of content-appropriate, orally administered true–false and multiple-choice testing was examined with 653 retarded adolescents. Three of the 9 original true–false tests of the Social and Prevocational Information Battery were transformed into an orally administered multiple-choice format. Both approaches demonstrated utility and psychometric adequacy. (8 ref)
Irvin, Larry K.; Halpern, Andrew S. & Landman, Janet T. (U Oregon, Research & Training Ctr in Mental Retardation, Eugene) Journal of Educational Measurement, 1980(Spr), Vol 17(1), 51–58. [PA, Vol 66:06764]

3156.   Is it necessary to decide whether to use a nonoral communication system with retarded children?
Reviews the literature and maintains that teachers of retarded children should not refrain from using oral–nonoral communication, regardless of whether or not the child's hearing is normal. In fact, nonoral systems are considered essential for many

retarded learners (e.g., Manual English paired with speech for a language-delayed child). (13 ref)
Jones, Thomas W. (Texas Tech U) Education & Training of the Mentally Retarded, 1980(Apr), Vol 15(2), 157–160. [PA, Vol 66:11291]

3157.   Enhancing classroom attentiveness by preselection of back-up reinforcers in a token economy.
Examined the effects of 2 methods of selecting and exchanging back-up reinforcers with 2 mentally retarded 6- and 7-yr-old boys participating in a token economy in a special education class. In separate experiments, each S received tokens contingent upon attentive behavior. Methods of selecting and exchanging back-up reinforcers (i.e., free time, a recess, selection of a small toy, playing with a valued toy) consisted of preselecting back-up events that were to be purchased in advance of earning the tokens vs selecting back-up events only after tokens had been earned. The 2 methods were compared in separate simultaneous-treatment designs for each child. In each experiment, preselecting back-up reinforcers led to higher levels of attentive behavior than selecting back-up events after the tokens had been earned. The possible influence of making back-up events less remote in relation to the token-earning behaviors and the prompting function of the preselected procedure are discussed. (19 ref)
Kazdin, Alan E. & Geesey, Sally. (Pennsylvania State U, University Park) Behavior Modification, 1980(Jan), Vol 4(1), 98–114. [PA, Vol 65:06392]

3158.   The influence of receptive training on rate of productive language acquisition in mentally retarded children.
Examined the relative efficiency of 2 tactics for teaching spoken picture labeling to 4 mild-to-moderately retarded Ss (CAs 5 yrs 11 mo to 10 yrs 4 mo). Each S's rate of acquisition of spoken picture labels was compared for 2 training conditions. Each condition was repeated 10 times for 5 Ss. In one condition, Ss were first trained to identify the pictures when given the spoken label as a cue; and then productive labeling was trained. In the other condition, only productive training was given. No uniform pattern of results emerged across the 5 Ss. For 3 Ss, no facilitation effect of prior receptive training was shown. For 2 Ss, there appeared to be an interaction between training tactic and S's level of echolalia and misarticulations. One S echoed the experimenter cues accurately during receptive training. This S showed significantly faster acquisition for the Reception-then-Production sequences. The other S echoed receptive cues inaccurately, although he was able to imitate the cues without error. This S showed a significantly slower rate of acquisition in the Reception-then-Production sequences. (15 ref)
Keller, Martha F. & Bucher, Bradley. (U Western Ontario, London, Canada) Behavior Research of Severe Developmental Disabilities, 1980(Oct), Vol 1(2), 93–103. [PA, Vol 66:09015]

3159.   A direct measure of adaptive behavior.
Discusses the discrepancies sometimes found between children's academic status and their social competence, and the implications of these discrepancies for educational programing, psychological assessment, diagnosis, and treatment. In an attempt to empirically record and define such differences, B. O. Richmond and R. H. Kicklighter (1980) developed a self-report evaluation instrument, the Children's Adaptive Behavior Scale (CABS), that measures 5 adaptive domains: language development, independent functioning, family role performance, economic-vocational activity, and socialization, in 6–10 yr olds. The present paper reports on an examination of the scale's performance with 60 slow learners (SL) and 60 educable mentally retarded (EMR) 7–10 yr olds. Reliability for the 5 domains ranged from .63 to .83, with an overall reliability of .91. Mean raw scores were found to increase steadily with CA, as expected. The overall correlation between CABS and WISC-R scores was .51, with EMRs scoring lower on all domains than the SLs. No significant effects of race or sex (with the exception that boys scored higher than girls on economic-vocational activity) were found. Difficulties in measuring adaptive behavior and the advantages of the CABS over other scales are described. (21 ref)

Kicklighter, Richard H.; Bailey, Brenda S. & Richmond, Bert O. (State Dept of Education, Atlanta, GA) School Psychology Review, 1980(Spr), Vol 9(2), 168–173. [PA, Vol 64:02185]

3160.   Recent advances in mnemonic strategy training with mentally retarded persons: Implications for educational practice.
Reviews a portion of the empirical literature on training mentally retarded people to use mnemonic strategies, specifically, strategy maintenance, strategy generalization, and metamemory. It is concluded that although significant gains have resulted from the past 2 decades of research, many questions of educational significance remain unanswered. (49 ref)
Kramer, Jack J.; Nagle, Richard J. & Engle, Randall W. (Fort Hays State U) American Journal of Mental Deficiency, 1980(Nov), Vol 85(3), 306–314. [PA, Vol 65:03525]

3161.   Computer assisted development of number conservation in mentally retarded school children.
10 9–14 yr old retarded schoolchildren (IQs 40–72) participated in a program aimed at helping them acquire the ability to conserve number. During training sessions, Ss were required to make judgments concerning the numerosity of differently colored sequences of squares that displayed in various orientations. A significant number of Ss acquired the ability to conserve number; however, this ability was to some degree dependent upon the form of questioning used. (14 ref)
Lally, Mike. (Australian National U, School of Physical Sciences, Canberra) Australian Journal of Developmental Disabilities, 1980(Sep), Vol 6(3), 131–136. [PA, Vol 66:09016]

3162.   Intra-individual discrepancy in diagnosing specific learning disabilities.
Studied the relationship between intraindividual discrepancy and exceptionality in 248 1st–6th graders. Categories of exceptionality included gifted/creative; sensory impairment, behavior disorder; physical handicap, mental retardation, and learning disability. The discrepancy between S's expected and actual level of functioning was computed by 9 formulas commonly used in special education. Data reveal a significant relationship between discrepancies and exceptionalities, although a relatively low strength of association was found. Results also indicate that intraindividual discrepancy is questionable when used as the defining characteristic of special learning disabilities; such a discrepancy is equally likely to occur in Ss classified as sensory impaired, behavior disordered, and learning disabled. (23 ref)
O'Donnell, Linda E. (U Missouri, Special Education Program, Kansas City) Learning Disability Quarterly, 1980(Win), Vol 3(1), 10–18. [PA, Vol 65:08835]

3163.   Increasing parent involvement.
Discusses the importance of parental involvement in individualized education programs for retarded children and describes a project that stresses such home–school cooperation. Presented are suggestions for obtaining parental assistance at school, informing parents of their legal rights, supplying material and support for home programs, and dealing with overbearing parents. (2 ref)
Porcella, Ann. Education & Training of the Mentally Retarded, 1980(Apr), Vol 15(2), 155–157. [PA, Vol 66:11303]

3164.   Effect of vocational instruction on academic achievement.
A study of vocational instruction for 70 mentally handicapped junior high school students showed that (a) career development models can foster academic growth, (b) Ss may have had skills that were not developed because of lack of reinforcement, and (c) internalized motivation may be an important factor for achievement gains. Development of external locus of control is important to promote learning effectiveness. (5 ref)
Porter, Mahlon E. Exceptional Children, 1980(Mar), Vol 46(6), 463–464. [PA, Vol 63:13008]

3165.   Medical training and mentally retarded citizens: An enrichment program.
In cooperation with a pediatrician, junior level medical students were exposed to mentally retarded individuals, and a seminar

was conducted regarding expected roles of physicians as stated in Public Law 94-142, The Education of All Handicapped Children Act. Guidelines regarding appropriate roles, appropriate interventions, and useful communication to the schools are discussed. (4 ref)
Retish, Paul M. (U Iowa, Coll of Education, Iowa City) Mental Retardation, 1980(Oct), Vol 18(5), 253–254. [PA, Vol 66:08795]

3166. Sex education for the mentally retarded.
Maintains that through the inclusion of sex education programs, the trainable and educable retarded can better understand both themselves and others and can develop into adults who respond appropriately to the feelings of love and affection. A brief review of the literature is included. (15 ref)
Russell, Tommy & Hardin, Patricia. (U Alabama, Program of Mental Retardation, University) Education & Training of the Mentally Retarded, 1980(Dec), Vol 15(4), 312–314. [PA, Vol 66:11306]

3167. A word list of essential career/vocational words for mentally retarded students.
J. Pfeiffer's (1968) Delphi Technique was used with 100 professionals interested in career/vocational education to ascertain the primary 100 words with which mentally retarded students should be conversant prior to their formal entry into the work world. These 100 words are presented. (19 ref)
Schilit, Jeffrey & Caldwell, Mary L. (Florida Atlanta U) Education & Training of the Mentally Retarded, 1980(Apr), Vol 15(2), 113–117. [PA, Vol 66:11309]

3168. Current issues and problems: A conversation with Jeptha V. Greer and Betty A. Hare about the challenges facing educators of mentally retarded students.
Thomas, M. Angele
(Ed). (Council for Exceptional Children, Reston, VA) Education & Training of the Mentally Retarded, 1980(Dec), Vol 15(4), 284–290. [PA, Vol 66:11314]

3169. Generalization of naming responses to objects in the natural environment as a function of training stimulus modality with retarded children.
Picture cards, photographs, and real objects were compared as training stimuli in facilitating the generalization of naming responses learned in a special training room to real objects in the natural environments of 4 retarded children (5, 6, 9, and 14 yrs old). The amount of transfer of naming behavior between the 3 stimulus modes and the average amount of training time required for each stimulus mode were also assessed. Three of the 4 Ss displayed more generalization to the real objects in the natural environment when they were trained with real objects. The 4th S displayed substantial generalization regardless of the training mode. No particular mode clearly facilitated the transfer of naming responses to other modes or greatly reduced training time. Results of 2 supplementary procedures conducted with 1 S show that (a) training in several environments facilitated generalization to real objects in the natural environment when real objects were used as training stimuli but not when picture cards were used, and (b) transfer from picture cards to real objects was facilitated by training other picture cards and the real objects portrayed by them at the same time. (25 ref)
Welch, Steven J. & Pear, Joseph J. (U Manitoba, Winnipeg, Canada) Journal of Applied Behavior Analysis, 1980(Win), Vol 13(4), 629–643. [PA, Vol 65:06407]

3170. Teaching moderately and severely handicapped adolescents to shop in supermarkets using pocket calculators.
Reports how 6 of 7 moderately and severely handicapped adolescents (CA 13–17 yrs, IQ 38–53) were taught to use a calculator (for subtraction), locate the price of each item (on a given list of 10 nontaxable items), determine which items they have enough money to purchase, and actually purchase the items in a community supermarket. (10 ref)
Wheeler, Jill et al. (Madison Metropolitan School District, Div of Specialized Educational Services, WI) Education & Training of the Mentally Retarded, 1980(Apr), Vol 15(2), 105–112. [PA, Vol 66:11319]

3171. Research issues in training interpersonal skills for the mentally retarded.
Presents a multidimensional model of interpersonal behavior designed to facilitate the systematic examination and development of research on teaching interpersonal skills to the mentally retarded. (21 ref)
Bernstein, Gail S. (U South Dakota, Ctr for the Developmentally Disabled, Vermillion) Education & Training of the Mentally Retarded, 1981(Feb), Vol 16(1), 70–74. [PA, Vol 66:08960]

3172. Concepts of learning and behavior disorders: Implications for research and practice.
Two major factors seem to have contributed to the current transformation of special education. The 1st has to do with evidence for or against the special class model of service delivery; the 2nd, which is less widely acknowledged, concerns the increasingly complex ways of viewing children with learning and behavior problems. A brief review of the 2nd factor suggests that ecological concepts in mental retardation, learning disabilities, and emotional disorders have begun to characterize current thinking. (73 ref)
Forness, Steven R. (U California, Mental Retardation & Child Psychiatry Program, Los Angeles) Exceptional Children, 1981(Sep), 48(1), 56–64. [PA, Vol 66:13645]

3173. Functions of the Illinois Test of Psycholinguistic Abilities (ITPA): Are they trainable?
Presents a meta-analysis for the literature assessing the effectiveness of psycholinguistic training using the Illinois Test of Psycholinguistic Abilities (ITPA) as the criterion measure. The analysis established the efficacy of psycholinguistic training since the average child receiving psycholinguistic training performs better than 65% of untrained children. Additional data delineating results for ITPA subtests and various study characteristics support the primary finding. It is concluded that extant research, contrary to previous research reviews that were found to underestimate the positive effects of intervention, has demonstrated the effectiveness of psycholinguistic training. (44 ref)
Kavale, Kenneth. (U California School of Education, Riverside) Exceptional Children, 1981(Apr), Vol 47(7), 496–510. [PA, Vol 65:13599]

3174. The abused mentally retarded child.
Reviews the literature on the relationship of child abuse to mental retardation which suggests a higher incidence of mental retardation for abused children than might be expected in the general population. Problems concerning inconsistent and inadequate definitions of abuse and retardation within the literature are also discussed. Implications are drawn for the expanded role of educators in the prevention, identification, and treatment of abused children with intellectual deficiencies. (17 ref)
Rose, Ernest & Hardman, Michael L. (U Utah, Salt Lake City) Education & Training of the Mentally Retarded, 1981(Apr), Vol 16(2), 114–118. [PA, Vol 66:08114]

3175. Teaching the handicapped to eat in public places: Acquisition, generalization, and maintenance of restaurant skills.
Evaluated classroom-based instruction in restauranting skills for 3 male students (CAs 17–22 yrs, IQs 46–75) who were taught 4 components in sequential order: locating, ordering, paying, and eating and exiting. Training was implemented in a multiple baseline design across Ss and consisted of modeling and role playing in conjunction with photo slide sequences and a simulated ordering counter. The use of a menu containing general item classes and a finger matching procedure for identifying errors in the delivery of change greatly reduced the reading and math skills necessary to enter and complete the program. Periodic probes were conducted in a McDonald's restaurant prior to, during, and up to 1 yr following the termination of training. In addition, 2 probes (overt and covert observation) were conducted in a Burger King restaurant to assess further generalization to a location different from the one depicted throughout training. Results show that Ss' performance on restaurant probes improved as a result of training, generalized to novel settings, maintained over an extended period of time,

and was comparable to that of a normative sample of nonretarded persons. (15 ref)
Van den Pol, Richard A. et al. Journal of Applied Behavior Analysis, 1981(Spr), Vol 14(1), 61–69. [PA, Vol 66:08743]

Downs Syndrome

3176.   [Children with Down's syndrome and some features of their cognitive activity.] (Russ)
27 10-14 yr old Ss with Down's syndrome participated in a psychopedagogical study of their behavior and cognitive activity in the 2nd and 3rd yr of auxiliary (special) schooling. Ss were imbeciles characterized by the traits of "obedience, docility, good nature, and sometimes affectionateness." their emotions were positively toned. Contrary to many other mentally retarded children, those with Down's syndrome exhibited relatively stable attention. They appeared also to perform truly at the level of their mental capacities, whereas many of the mentally retarded children with organic lesions of the CNS did not fulfill their potential. Children with Down's syndrome were shown to be capable of learning very simple games and some elementary manual skills.
Lur'e, N. B. (Inst. of Defectology, Moscow, USSR) Defektologiya, 1971(Jan), Vol. 3(1), 30-36. [PA, Vol 47:01623]

3177.   Teaching functional reading to young trainable students: Toward longitudinal objectives.
Taught 2 5-yr-old Mongoloid students to read functionally 12 nouns and 12 adjective-noun phrases. A "whole word method" was employed. After 50 hrs of instruction, results show that Ss had already progressed beyond the reading level expected of many older Mongoloid students. The program presented here, as well as others cited, draws attention to the need for longitudinal instructional programs for trainable-level retarded students.
Brown, Lou et al. (U Wisconsin, Madison) Journal of Special Education, 1972(Fal), Vol 6(3), 237-246. [PA, Vol 53:04046]

3178.   Some effects of token rewards on school achievement of children with Down's syndrome.
Tested the effectiveness of a token economy system in producing improvement in the academic performance of 13 6-14 yr old children with Down's syndrome. 1 group was given programed instruction in language and arithmetic and received token reinforcement for correct responses. Ss showed significant improvement in both subject areas. A 2nd matched group received only verbal praise for correct responses to the same instructional materials. These Ss failed to improve in arithmetic but showed significant gains in language. Retest scores 1 yr later revealed that the token group maintained its gains in both subject areas whereas the language performance of the no-token group showed a significant decline.
Dalton, A. J.; Rubino, C. A. & Hislop, M. W. (Mental Retardation Centre, Toronto, Ontario, Canada) Journal of Applied Behavior Analysis, 1973(Sum), Vol. 6(2), 251-259. [PA, Vol 51:01644]

3179.   Visual feedback in word acquisition behaviour in moderately retarded subjects.
Taught 12 moderately retarded children (mean age 122 mo, mean IQ 41.6) to discriminate 6 words of 3 letters each. The words were presented orally and the child was to select the printed word. 9 of the 12 Ss were able to reach criterion, indicating that such children are able to make the kind of discrimination associations necessary for reading behavior. The finding that there was no difference between the Down's syndrome Ss and the others is considered important and may serve to dispel some misgivings about their educational possibilities. Analysis of Ss who failed showed that some had not understood the association principle. (15 ref)
Jackson, Merrill. (Monash U, Clayton, Vic, Australia) Slow Learning Child, 1974(Nov), Vol 21(3), 155-163. [PA, Vol 53:12525]

3180.   Early childhood education for children with Down's syndrome.
Describes a successful preschool program for children with Down's syndrome that is aimed at providing the family with specific skills and information needed to establish an optimal environment for the development of the child. It is suggested that the effectiveness of the program rests on the following factors: (a) early identification of children with Down's syndrome, (b) specific task analysis of objectives which the child can be expected to achieve in typical development, (c) provision of precision teaching of skills and positive reinforcement techniques for parents and teachers to use with the children, and (d) provision of a means of assessing the influence of such instructional procedures on the child's growth and learning abilities.
Kysela, G. M. (U Alberta, Edmonton, Canada) Mental Retardation Bulletin, 1973–74, Vol 2(2), 58-63. [PA, Vol 58:04384]

3181.   Modifying maternal teaching style: Effects of task arrangement on the match-to-sample performance of retarded preschool-age children.
Observed 21 mothers and their retarded preschool-age children during 6 teaching sessions. After the 1st 3 sessions, each mother-child dyad was assigned to one of the 3 groups, which were matched on measures of mother and child behavior and on measures of various mother and child background factors. Before the last 3 teaching sessions, mothers received instructions to modify certain aspects of their teaching style. Children of mothers who had been instructed to present the materials of the task systematically obtained significantly higher performance scores during training than did children of mothers who either received no instruction or had been told to increase positive feedback for correct responses. Further, 6 of 7 children whose mothers had altered the manner in which they presented the task materials showed improvement on a test administered after training. These results suggest that nonverbal activities which precede responding are critical aspects of teaching style and deserve more attention than they have received in the past.
Filler, John W. (George Peabody Coll for Teachers) American Journal of Mental Deficiency, 1976(May), Vol 80(6), 602-612. [PA, Vol 56:06814]

3182.   Individual variability among children with Down's syndrome.
Six Down's syndrome children (IQs 47–73) who had shared the same preschool for 3–4 yrs were administered psychological tests to see whether there were characteristics of mental functioning held in common. When the Ss were 66– 75 mo of age, they were given the Wechsler Preschool and Primary Scale of Intelligence (WPPSI) and the Reading Subtest of the Wide Range Achievement Test. Results show no uniformity in level of mental retardation, stability of IQ, reading achievement, relationship of mental to motor development, and relationship of Verbal to Performance IQ. Similarity was observed in the performance of 2 of the 10 subtests of the WPPSI. (10 ref)
LaVeck, Beverly & Brehm, Sharon S. Mental Retardation, 1978(Apr), Vol 16(2), 135–137. [PA, Vol 62:09804]

3183.   Underestimating the educability of Down's syndrome children: Examination of methodological problems in recent literature.
Considers that for many years, the educational capabilities of Down's syndrome persons have been underestimated, because a large number of studies purporting to give an accurate picture of Down's syndrome persons' developmental capabilities have had serious methodological flaws. A close examination of that literature and a look at findings from 2 current early education projects (J. E. Rynders and J. M. Horrobin, 1975; A. H. Hayden and N. G. Haring, 1976) for Down's syndrome children reveal that psychometrically defined educability is far more common in Down's syndrome persons than a cursory review of the literature would lead one to believe. (35 ref)
Rynders, John E.; Spiker, Donna & Horrobin, J. Margaret. (U Minnesota) American Journal of Mental Deficiency, 1978(Mar), Vol 82(5), 440–448. [PA, Vol 61:08720]

3184.   Situational influences on assessment performance.
Investigated the effects of 2 situational factors—setting (i.e., classroom or small testing room) and familiarity of the examiner (i.e., mother or unknown female)—on the assessment performance of developmentally disabled preschool age children. Ss were 8 16–36 mo olds: 5 girls and 3 boys. Four Ss had Down's syndrome, 1 S had hydrocephalus, 1 S had cerebral palsy, and 2 Ss had less common syndromes associated with delayed development. Ss were administered a 7-item instrument with 4 items involving motor imitation skills and 3 involving fine motor-manipulative skills. The unfamiliar examiners were female graduate students in special education and psychology who had experience and training in working with young handicapped children. A Treatment by Treatment by S ANOVA yielded significant main effects for Examiner and Setting. Ss scored significantly higher when examined by their mothers than by unfamiliar women. They also scored significantly higher in the small testing room than in their own classroom. (16 ref)
Stoneman, Zolinda & Gibson, Sara. (U Georgia, Georgia Retardation Ctr, Athens Unit) Exceptional Children, 1978(Nov), Vol 45(3), 166–169. [PA, Vol 62:03978]

3185.   Accelerating the development of Down's syndrome infants and young children.
Evaluated the progress of 36 Down's syndrome children, aged 3–37 mo, who had participated in an early education development project for 4–24 mo. Results show that the development of all Ss was accelerated, with achievements at and above normal levels for some of the Ss. (21 ref)
Clunies-Ross, Graham G. (Preston Inst of Technology, Bundoora, Australia) Journal of Special Education, 1979(Sum), Vol 13(2), 169–177. [PA, Vol 66:08976]

3186.   The effects of two teaching strategies on the acquisition and recall of an academic task by moderately and severely retarded preschool children.
10 moderately and severely handicapped preschoolers were Ss in a pre- and posttest design to evaluate the effects of cumulative and successive pairs programming strategies. Ss were taught to identify 5 functional words. Performance was measured by the number of presentations required to learn all of the words and the number of words recalled correctly on the posttest. Two Mann-Whitney tests were employed to determine the significance of the treatment effects. The 5 Ss who received the cumulative programming strategy learned the words in significantly fewer trials and identified more words correctly on the posttest. Results are consistent with literature on the learning performance of nonhandicapped children and infra-human Ss. (9 ref)
Fink, William T. & Brice-Gray, Kathleen J. (U Oregon Preschool for Multihandicapped Children) Mental Retardation, 1979(Feb), Vol 17(1), 8–12. [PA, Vol 64:02151]

3187.   Performance characteristics of preschool Down's syndrome children receiving augmented or repetitive verbal instruction.
Compared 20 Down's syndrome 3-yr-olds (IQs 53–78) with 15 nonretarded 3-yr-olds on their ability to respond to typical preschool learning tasks when given either augmented or repetitive verbal instruction. Augmented verbal instruction began with (a) a verbal prompt followed, as needed, by (b) verbal instruction, (c) verbal instruction plus modeling, and (d) verbal instruction plus manual guidance. Repeated verbal instruction involved the verbal repetition of task directions up to 3 times after the initial verbal prompt. Results indicate that Down's syndrome Ss experienced serious acquisition problems despite either the augmented or the repeated verbal-instruction series. (19 ref)
Rynders, John E.; Behlen, Katherine L. & Horrobin, J. Margaret. (U Minnesota) American Journal of Mental Deficiency, 1979(Jul), Vol 84(1), 67–73. [PA, Vol 62:12297]

3188.   Role expectations of parents of intellectually handicapped children.
Tested the assumption that many attitudes about appropriate parental response to child behaviors related to learning in normal populations would be relevant to effective parent education for parents of intellectually handicapped children. The Parent As A Teacher Inventory (PAAT) was administered to 101 parents of handicapped (predominantly Down's syndrome and brain-damaged) children (mean CA 5 yrs 8 mo; mean IQ 40) at the beginning of a 3-yr program to teach the parents how to develop language skills in their children. Analysis of PAAT data showed that (a) in the 2 largest subgroups, there were more positive attitudes in parents of Down's syndrome children than in those with brain-damaged children; (b) Ss held PAAT expectations closely resembling those of parents with children of normal intellect; (c) Ss expressed reservations about their abilities as teachers but were willing to learn teaching skills; and (d) total PAAT scores of Ss at lower or upper extremes served as excellent guides to identify those who would be least and most successful as teachers for their children. (6 ref)
Strom, Robert; Rees, Roger; Slaughter, Helen & Wurster, Stanley. (Arizona State U, Parent–Child Lab, Tempe) Exceptional Children, 1980(Oct), Vol 47(2), 144–147. [PA, Vol 64:13397]

Institutionalized Mentally Retarded

3189.   Teaching efficiency of a responsive versus a nonresponsive environment.
Administered Woolman's Reading in High Gear, Student Helper Progress Test to 60 institutionalized mentally retarded adolescents before and after Ss were taught in the (a) Edison Responsive Environment, or (b) conventional classroom. A statistical analysis of the data showed that the responsive environment was no more effective for learning than the nonresponsive environment, but was more efficient in that the same amount of material was learned in less time.
Brown, Raymond C. (Medical U. South Carolina, Charleston) American Journal of Mental Deficiency, 1971(Sep), Vol. 76(2), 225-229. [PA, Vol 47:09517]

3190.   Relationships among three measures used in screening mentally retarded for placement in special education.
Examined the relationship between WISC and Stanford-Binet IQ scores, Wide Range Achievement Test (WRAT) scores, and Nihira et al Adaptive Behavior Scale (ABS) scores for 129 institutionalized mentally retarded children and adolescents in a special education program (mean age, 14 yrs). Significant but small to moderate correlations (.26-.50) were obtained between WRAT and IQ scores and between ABS scores and IQ. Each measure differentiated between special education training levels. Use of the ABS may provide an important supplement to more frequently used screening procedures such as IQ and achievement scores.
Christian, Walter P. & Malone, Daniel R. (Central State Hosp., Mental Retardation Unit, Milledgeville, Ga.) Psychological Reports, 1973(Oct), Vol. 33(2), 415-418. [PA, Vol 51:09439]

3191.   The application of generalized correct social contingencies: An evaluation of a training program.
2 female aides operating a kindergarten-style program for 6 institutionalized mental retardates (mean age = 9.4 yrs) were trained, using O feedback, to apply generalized correct social contingencies to 10 defined classes of appropriate and inappropriate child behaviors. A multiple baseline design was used to demonstrate, sequentially, the effects of the training procedure upon the attending behavior of each aide. After withdrawal of feedback, a posttraining follow-up assessed the durability of training. It was found that training increased the proportion of appropriate child behaviors to which both aides attended, compared with baseline data, and a follow-up over a number of weeks indicated that the effects of training were apparently durable.
Parsonson, Barry S.; Baer, Ann M. & Baer, Donald M. (U Waikato, Hamilton, New Zealand) Journal of Applied Behavior Analysis, 1974(Fal), Vol 7(3), 427-437. [PA, Vol 53:06123]

3192.   Camp counseling with emotionally disturbed adolescents.
Analyzed the effect of a week-long camping experience with 73 institutionalized adolescents on 54 undergraduate special education students serving as camp counselors. Ss included 33 majors in the mentally retarded (MR) and 21 in the emotionally disturbed (ED) fields; they ranged from sophomores to seniors. Specifically, the investigation sought to determine whether Ss would view the emotionally disturbed more positively or negatively at the end of the camp session than at the beginning. Results show there were significant positive differences between pre- and postcamp perceptions for all groups except the seniors. The greatest changes were made by the junior ED group who perceived the emotionally disturbed less positively than did all MR groups prior to camp. It is suggested that the seniors, from their greater experience and course work, had a more stable and realistic perception of handicapped persons prior to camp. It would appear that the combination of course work and direct work with the emotionally disturbed is the important factor in helping students acquire a more positive perception. Practicum courses, such as camping, are recommended in conjunction with characteristics and methods courses.
Herr, David E. (Pennsylvania State U, Coll of Education) Exceptional Children, 1975(Feb), Vol 41(5), 331-332. [PA, Vol 54:01941]

3193.   Sexual knowledge and attitudes of institutionalized and noninstitutionalized retarded adolescents.
61 noninstitutionalized and 61 institutionalized mentally retarded adolescents were psychometrically assessed on 3 measures: sexual knowledge, sexual attitudes, and self-concept. Results show that the 2 groups differed on total score on sex knowledge only, with the noninstitutionalized group being more knowledgeable. With regard to sexual attitudes and self-concept, the 2 groups did not differ in terms of total correct statements. Internal consistency demonstrated on all the measures ranged from .50 to .90. Intercorrelations of relevant variables for each group (10 for the noninstitutionalized, 13 for the institutionalized) produced several significant correlations. Results are discussed with reference to the development of a standardized instrument for assessing sex education programs for mentally retarded persons.
Hall, Judy E. & Morris, Helen L. (U Alabama Medical School, Birmingham) American Journal of Mental Deficiency, 1976(Jan), Vol 80(4), 382-387. [PA, Vol 56:00879]

3194.   Symposium on structured teaching and training: II. An individualised prescriptive teaching programme for institutionalised retarded children.
Investigated the effectiveness of an individualized prescriptive teaching (PT) program based on a task analysis approach as contrasted with ability training instruction in the traditional special education program. Data were obtained from 16 PT Ss (mean CA 11.5 yrs, mean IQ 34.0) and 19 control Ss (mean CA 12.0 yrs, mean IQ 37.0). Significant gains were made in reading, mathematical concepts, and linguistic development skills. (19 ref)
Peniston, Eugene G. (Virginia State Coll) British Journal of Mental Subnormality, 1976(Dec), Vol 22(43, Pt 2), 93-98. [PA, Vol 58:06376]

3195.   Consistency of teaching: An observational study in an institutional setting for retarded children.
Observations were made of 14 staff (teachers) interacting with the same learner toward the same teaching objective using the same program. Teachers used a mean of 8.34 different types of stimulus presentation per program even though each program specified one type. Low levels of consistency were also observed across teachers in the categories of use of material (28.16% consistency), use of reinforcers (28.4%), and use of schedules of reinforcement (57.8%).
Blindert, H. Dieter & Lawrence, Cheryl. (Canadian Peace Research Inst, Behavior Clinic, London) Mental Retardation, 1977(Dec), Vol 15(6), 13-15. [PA, Vol 61:04781]

3196.   Retention of MR children in a community school program: Behaviors and teacher ratings as predictors.
In an effort to extend the works of E. Lessing and M. Oberlander (1974), who evaluated 3 school re-entry programs for elementary school age severely disturbed children, an evaluation was made of the behavioral status of 9 11-17 yr old institutionalized developmentally disabled adolescents at the point of their entry into a community school program and after a 3-4 mo follow-up period. Teacher and parent attitudes toward the student were also assessed at both times. Instruments utilized included the 5 scales used by Lessing and Oberlander and a behavior development survey. Commission of asocial behaviors by the student was predictive of teacher ratings of poor outcome after 3-4 mo. Teacher's initial impression of the student was also predictive of later outcome ratings. Comparison of this group with a mentally ill population indicated that factors which are predictive of extrusion of the mentally ill population are the same as those for developmentally disabled populations.
Peterson, Carol P. (Illinois Inst for Developmental Disabilities, Chicago) Mental Retardation, 1977(Feb), Vol 15(1), 46-49. [PA, Vol 58:10548]

3197.   Experience effects in the acceleration of number conservation in mentally retarded children.
Studied the differential effects of prior experience on conservation of number with 10 8-16 yr old moderately retarded long-stay residents and 10 7-14 yr old mildly retarded short-stay residents of a state institution for the mentally retarded. All Ss were given pre- and posttests of conservation of number. The moderately retarded Ss were given pretraining on hierarchically structured arithmetic tasks, and the mildly retarded were instructed on traditional arithmetic tasks. Both groups were then taught the concepts of "same," "more," and "less" by a learning set method. A significant interaction was observed between type of training and gains in conservation ability. Results show unequivocally that moderately retarded Ss' ability to conserve number was accelerated by appropriate teaching methods. (29 ref)
Singh, Nirbhay N. (U Auckland, New Zealand) Australian Journal of Mental Retardation, 1977(Mar), Vol 4(5), 22-28. [PA, Vol 60:08321]

Mild Mental Retardation

3198.   Meaningfulness in school tasks for EMR children.
Investigated the influence of meaningfulness on the acquisition and retention of a school-like task by educable mentally retarded and normal children. Retarded Ss and normals matched for CA and MA were given either a meaningful or nonmeaningful task to learn. Original learning and retention after 30 days were measured. Results indicate that (a) meaningfulness increased performance in original learning for all groups, (b) meaningfulness was more important for retardates than for normals matched for CA in original learning, and (c) retardates did significantly better in the retention task with high meaningfulness than normal Ss matched for MA. It is suggested that the classroom teacher can facilitate learning for both retardates and normals by incorporating familiar cues into the material to be learned. (27 ref.)
Elliott, Raymond N. (Pennsylvania State U.) Journal of Special Education, 1970(Spr), Vol. 4(2), 189-197. [PA, Vol 45:10719]

3199.   The influence of the teacher expectancy phenomenon on the academic performances of educable mentally retarded pupils in special classes.
Reviews the notion of the expectancy phenomenon (that individuals behave as they are expected to behave). An experiment was conducted to test the effect of expectancy on academic performance in classes of mentally retarded children. The experimental group included a group of children whose names had been given to their teachers as having had hidden potential, but who did not differ from the control group. After an academic year, both experimental and control groups were given tests in a number of

different subjects and their scores were compared with similar tests which had been given before the start of the experiment. No significant differences between the experimental and control groups were found. It is concluded that the expectancy phenomenon is not strong enough to influence the academic performance of educable mental retardates. (29 ref.)
Gozali, Joav & Meyen, Edward L. (U. Wisconsin, Milwaukee) Journal of Special Education, 1970(Fal), Vol. 4(4), 417-424. [PA, Vol 47:05647]

3200. Maintaining social acceptance gains made by mentally retarded children.
Investigates the permanence of gains made by 95 educable mentally retarded (EMR) students in an extension of a study by M. Chennault (see PA, Vol. 42:7766) in which the social acceptability of EMR students was increased by pairing them with popular students in a school skit. Ss were given the Ohio Social Acceptance Scale (OSAS) as a pre-, post-, and post-posttest measure. Ss in the experimental condition put on a carnival for their class, while other Ss served as controls. OSAS results show a significant difference in social acceptability between the 2 groups for the pre- and posttest comparison, but not for the pre- and post-posttest comparison (1 mo. later). This indicates that the acceptance of EMR Ss can be enhanced, but diminishes when treatment ceases.
Rucker, Chauncy N. & Vincenzo, Filomena M. (U. Connecticut) Exceptional Children, 1970(May), Vol. 36(9), 679-680. [PA, Vol 46:05526]

3201. Information processing behaviors related to learning disabilities and educable mental retardation.
All the elementary school age children failing in a county school system were administered a battery of psychoeducational tests to determine their information processing behaviors. Of the 472 Ss who successfully completed audiometric and visual screening and had no school record or medical history of acute physical, chronic health, or social personal problems, 1 group (N = 185) had average and above verbal intelligence. These Ss were considered to have learning disabilities on the basis of their perceptual deficits. The remaining Ss with below average intelligence (educable mental retardation) seemed to work to predicted grade equivalent in some academic achievement areas. The principal components obtained from an orthogonal rotation of the behavioral variables indicate that these 2 S groups had many similar perceptual and language deficits, but decided behavioral differences.
Sabatino, David A. & Hayden, David L. (Pennsylvania State U.) Exceptional Children, 1970(Sep), Vol. 37(1), 21-29. [PA, Vol 46:05527]

3202. Effects of readiness on incidental learning in EMR, normal, and gifted children.
Investigated the effects of readiness on incidental learning among 30 educable mentally retarded (EMR), 30 normal, and 30 gifted Ss who were equated on CA (84-119 mo.). Ss were divided into readiness and nonreadiness treatment groups. The incidental learning stimuli were presented with the intentional learning materials. The criterion measure was based on the incidental learning task. When readiness was given, EMR, normal, and gifted Ss did not differ in incidental learning; when readiness was not given, they did. Readiness was found to benefit EMR and normal Ss while it had no effect on gifted Ss.
Williams, Eddie H. (U. Southern California) American Journal of Mental Deficiency, 1970(Sep), Vol. 75(2), 117-119. [PA, Vol 45:07895]

3203. Informational determinants of social reinforcement effectiveness among retarded children.
Administered a concept identification task under 1 of 6 verbal reinforcement conditions to 72 children in primary or intermediate special education classes. 2 classes of outcome events (social reinforcers and unfamiliar foreign words) were used in conjunction with 3 levels of informational structure. Results indicate that common expressions of social approval, whether defined or not, were virtually ineffective in facilitating learning. The unfamiliar terms, however, were highly susceptible to information induction. When the foreign words were defined and used as outcome events, performance was significantly enhanced.
Cairns, Robert B. & Paris, Scott G. (Indiana U.) American Journal of Mental Deficiency, 1971(Nov), Vol. 76(3), 362-369. [PA, Vol 48:01534]

3204. The relationship between sequences of instruction and mental abilities of retarded children.
40 educable mentally retarded adolescents randomly assigned to 2 groups received 2 different sequences of programed instruction. The 2 sequences (1 ordered, 1 random) consisted of 612 identical frames but the frames were placed in different orders for the 2 groups. No differences were found between the 2 groups on immediate learning, retention, or transfer. Results of correlational analyses were equivocal but there was some indication that different aptitudes were required by the 2 groups in order to make equivalent learning test scores.
Cartwright, G. Phillip. (Pennsylvania State U.) American Educational Research Journal, 1971(Jan), Vol. 8(1), 143-150. [PA, Vol 46:07490]

3205. Effects of a physical developmental program on psychomotor ability of retarded children.
The Oseretsky Tests of Motor Proficiency were administered to 27 73-146 mo. old educable mentally retarded (EMR) children before and after participating in a 15-wk physical developmental program, and to 20 EMR children not enrolled in the developmental program. A comparison of pre- and postprogram performances on the Oseretsky tests indicated that: (a) EMR children receiving a concentrated physical education program improved significantly in the gross motor skill components of the Oseretsky tests, and (b) these improvements resulted in the experimental EMR group surpassing the control group on the majority of items of the posttest. (19 ref.)
Chasey, William C. & Wyrick, Waneen. (U. Texas) American Journal of Mental Deficiency, 1971(Mar), Vol. 75(5), 566-570. [PA, Vol 46:05515]

3206. Influence of a model of commitment in mild retardation.
Reviews the research literature supporting the need for models of commitment, discusses problems in defining and measuring commitment, and offers programming suggestions. A variety of models of adult commitment, e.g., parents and teachers, is considered helpful in developing achievement motivation in mildly retarded children. (18 ref.)
Christoplos, Florence. (Coppin State Coll.) Mental Retardation, 1971(Feb), Vol. 9(1), 26-28. [PA, Vol 48:05659]

3207. Changing classroom behavior of retarded children: Using reinforcers in the home environment and parents and teachers as trainers.
Using 6 6-16 yr. old educable mentally retarded Ss living at home and attending public school, a procedure was established for making reinforcers available in the home environment for cooperative and attentive classroom behavior. Throughout the program, both parents and teachers of the Ss served as trainers. All Ss were found to exhibit marked improvement in both academic performance and classroom behavior.
Edlund, Calvin V. (San Juan Unified School District of Carmichael, Calif.) Mental Retardation, 1971(Jun), Vol. 9(3), 33-36. [PA, Vol 49:11591]

3208. Parent-school collaboration via educational merit badges?
Describes 3 problems: (a) discontinuity in the training of our youth; (b) segregation of youth from the adult world; and (c) values and behavior fostered by peer cultures, that sociologists and social anthropologists have identified as intensifying the stresses of adolescence. These problems are related to the retarded. It is proposed that parents of the educable mentally retarded (EMR) and educators, could collaborate to minimize these problems. Trial use of a merit badge system in conjunction with a well structured and shareable (clearly communicable) curriculum or course of study for the EMR is suggested. (29 ref.)

Edmonson, Barbara & Cegelka, Walter J. (U. Oregon) Training School Bulletin, 1971(Aug), Vol. 68(2), 97-105. [PA, Vol 47:05643]

3209. Learning potential and vocational aspirations of retarded adolescents.
The learning potential (LP) hypothesis states that the educable mentally retarded who profit from training sessions in LP assessment are educationally retarded students, while those who do not profit function as the mentally retarded are typically described to function. An interview, examining present vocational status and development of vocational goals in low income, special, and regular-class adolescents, tended to support this hypothesis. While the educable students with a low LP tended to respond initially like their nonretarded peers, they generally appeared to be functioning in a fantasy period of vocational development. Educable students with a high LP aspired low, had specific knowledge and/or experience with the job they chose, and had discussed it with their families.
Folman, Rosalind & Budoff, Milton. (Research Inst. for Educational Problems, Cambridge, Mass.) Exceptional Children, 1971(Oct), Vol. 38(2), 121-130. [PA, Vol 48:03713]

3210. Ethnic and social status characteristics of children in EMR and LD classes.
Determined the ethnic and social status characteristics of 274 educable mentally retarded (EMR) and 215 learning disability (LD) children representing 11 school districts. Questionnaires forwarded to the teachers of each S were returned for 66.79% of the EMR sample and 86.51% of the LD sample. Ss' social status was converted into a prestige score according to the Occupational Scale. It was found that the percentage of Afro-Americans was 34.21% for EMR Ss and 3.22% for LD Ss. The absence of Spanish-Americans is explained.
Franks, David J. (U. Missouri) Exceptional Children, 1971(Mar), Vol. 37(7), 537-538. [PA, Vol 47:03662]

3211. Who are the retarded?
Compared 11-yr-old children in educable (n = 378) and regular (n = 319) classes on the Slosson Intelligence Test for Children and Adults, the Auditory Reception and Verbal Expression subtests from the 1968 Illinois Test of Psycholinguistic Abilities, and adaptations of the Test of Social Inference and the Temple Informal Reading Inventory. Ss scoring above and below a T score of 45 (equivalent to IQ 75) on each of the variables were identified. 25% of the Ss in educable classes fell above the cutting point on at least 4 of the 5 criteria. Only 31% of those in educable classes failed either 4 or 5 of the criteria. Findings support efforts to place most children in educable classes into regular classrooms.
Garrison, Mortimer & Hammill, Donald D. (Temple U.) Exceptional Children, 1971(Sep), Vol. 38(1), 13-20. [PA, Vol 47:07598]

3212. The parents' role in sex education for the retarded.
Presents results of the social work section of an interdisciplinary survey concerned with selected aspects of the sexual development and education of the mildly retarded. 15 parents of retarded adolescents (8 girls and 7 boys with IQ ranges from 55-70) were interviewed in depth. An attempt was also made to synthesize extensive clinical experience in dealing with the problem. The necessity for parent participation in programs concerned with sex education is highlighted.
Goodman, Lawrence; Budner, Stanley & Lesh, Betty. (Mental Retardation Center of New York Medical Coll., Flower-Fifth Avenue Hosp., N.Y.) Mental Retardation, 1971(Feb), Vol. 9(1), 43-45. [PA, Vol 48:05664]

3213. Verbal problem solving among educable mentally retarded children.
Administered a verbal problem-solving test to 2 samples of 31 educable mentally retarded (EMR) children, differentiated by high or low IQ level, to identify the effect of 3 parameters on performance. Results indicate that presence of a distractor (extraneous information) in the verbal problem was significant (p < .01). Higher-IQ EMRs significantly outperformed lower-

IQ EMRs on the tasks (p < .01), but failed to sustain expected superior performance on problems with extraneous information. Findings suggest a rote computation habit, rather than active processing of verbal information, as the problem solving style of many EMRs at all IQ levels. The need for carefully developed programs in verbal problem solving is indicated. 4
Goodstein, H. A.; Cawley, J. F.; Gordon, S. & Helfgott, J. (Indiana U.) American Journal of Mental Deficiency, 1971(Sep), Vol. 76(2), 238-241. [PA, Vol 47:09724]

3214. Increasing descriptive language skills in EMR students.
Describes a classroom project using visual and tactile stimuli designed to increase the use of descriptive words by 12 educable mentally retarded 16-19 yr. old high school students. Class discussions, exercises, and homework assignments in writing, speaking, spelling, and explaining elaborative words were planned for each day with a variety of interests, abilities, and personalities. Subjective evaluation by the teacher indicates that most of these Ss could increase their immediate use of elaborative language as a result of the program.
Henderson, Lorraine J. Mental Retardation, 1971(Jun), Vol. 9(3), 13-16. [PA, Vol 48:05667]

3215. The problem of motivation in the education of the mentally retarded.
1 possible reason for the failure to demonstrate the efficacy of self-contained classes for the educable mentally retarded lies in the failure of such classes to balance the emphasis on motivational and cognitive variables. Several motivational variables have been isolated experimentally and the research findings have been interpreted to suggest that children who have experienced excessive amounts of failure dramatically differ from children with little history of failure on these variables. 3 specific motivational variables are discussed and the related research evidence presented: (a) expectancy for failure, (b) outer-directedness, and (c) positive and negative reaction tendencies. Implications are drawn and suggestions made regarding ways of dealing with these behaviors. (35 ref.)
MacMillan, Donald L. (U. California, Riverside) Exceptional Children, 1971(Apr), Vol. 37(8), 579-586. [PA, Vol 47:01624]

3216. Flexibility training with educable retarded children.
Tested the hypothesis that training in perceptual and cognitive shifts would improve the performance of educable mentally retarded children on flexibility measures and on the Stanford-Binet and WISC scales. The Cognitive Flexibility Test was also administered to 28 Ss the results of which were compared to a control group of 28 that was matched on mental age. Instruction facilitated performance on variables measuring verbal fluency and concept formation; however, significant improvement was generally limited to those variables which shared content with the training exercises.
McKinney, James D. & Corter, Harold M. (U. North Carolina, Chapel Hill) Journal of School Psychology, 1971(Win), Vol. 9(4), 455-461. [PA, Vol 48:01711]

3217. Effects of delay of reinforcement on retarded children's learning.
No study has investigated delays of reinforcement of more than 30 sec. in the classroom, although many classroom delays exceed 30 sec. A study designed for a 4-way analysis of variance investigated (a) delays of reinforcement of 0, 5, and 15 min.; (b) returning test stimuli before reinforcement vs. not returning test stimuli; (c) primary vs. intermediate grade range; and (d) trials. Ss were educable retarded students in public schools. All main effects were found to be significant as well as the interactions between range and procedure and delay and procedure.
Piper, Terrence J. (U. Wisconsin, Milwaukee) Exceptional Children, 1971(Oct), Vol. 38(2), 139-145. [PA, Vol 48:03721]

3218. [North American Mexican students and mild mental retardation.] (Span)
Discusses the inadequate evaluation procedures used on minority groups in schools which measure IQ, but fail to account for adaptive behavior. The historical precedent of Mexican-Americans provides illustration, noting clinical and socioeconomic

aspects. The high incidence of leaving school is attributed to erroneous diagnostics (due to language problems) which place children in groups for retarded students. The problem of measuring the capabilities of Ss from different sociocultural backgrounds is discussed.

Share, Jack. (U. California, Los Angeles) Revista de la Clínica de la Conducta, 1971(Feb), Vol. 4(8), 38-48. [PA, Vol 48:03727]

3219.   Study of verbal behavior in special and regular elementary school classrooms.
Used the Flanders Interaction Analysis Category System to observe 27 public school classrooms (9 intermediate educable mentally retarded, 9 intermediate intellectually-average, and 9 primary intellectually-average) to study the relationship between classroom type and teacher-pupil verbal interaction. The basic question under investigation concerned whether teacher-pupil verbal behavior in special classes differed significantly from teacher-pupil verbal behavior in regular classes. A multivariate analysis of variance yielded no significant differences between the verbal interaction of special classes and that of regular classes. (19 ref.)

Stuck, Gary B. & Wyne, Marvin D. (U. North Carolina, Chapel Hill) American Journal of Mental Deficiency, 1971(Jan), Vol. 75(4), 463-469. [PA, Vol 46:03756]

3220.   Achievement and intelligence in primary and elementary classes for the educable mentally retarded.
Correlated the Wide Range Achievement Test (WRAT) scores of 192 children in primary and elementary classes for the educable mentally retarded with their Stanford-Binet Intelligence Scale or WISC IQ scores. It was found that the WISC was a better differential predictor of achievement in reading, spelling, and arithmetic at the elementary level only. The use of an Educational Quotient, computed by dividing WRAT standard scores by IQ scores and multiplying by 100, is discussed. The reliability of the WRAT (split-half) was excellent with this sample.

Sundean, David A. & Salopek, Thomas F. (Erie County Public Schools, Pa.) Journal of School Psychology, 1971, Vol. 9(2), 150-156. [PA, Vol 47:07610]

3221.   Effects of goal setting upon learning in educable retardates.
Administered 10-item spelling tasks at 2 difficulty levels to 40 public school and 40 institutionalized educable mental retardated (EMR) adolescent males. Each S repeated his test 10 times. Before each trial, experimental Ss predicted the number of words they expected to spell correctly on the upcoming trial. Controls were not asked to estimate performance. Each S was told his score (number of correctly spelled words) at the end of each trial. Analysis of variance on criterion scores (total number of correct responses on 10 trials) show that (a) the mean of Ss who performed the easier of the 2 tasks was significantly greater ($p < .01$) than the mean of Ss who performed the more difficult task; (b) the mean of Ss who made estimates exceeded the mean of Ss who did not ($p < .01$); (c) the means of the public school and institutionalized subsamples did not differ significantly; and (d) none of the interaction effects reached significance.

Warner, Dennis A. & de Jung, John E. (Washington State U.) American Journal of Mental Deficiency, 1971(May), Vol. 75(6), 681-684. [PA, Vol 47:01629]

3222.   Measuring the Self Concept of Ability as a Worker.
Discusses the relationship of self-concept of ability to performance and the need for a measurement device for the self-concept of work ability for educable mentally retarded adolescents. The Self Concept of Ability as a Worker Scale is described which employs an interview technique and is intended to be used by teachers and vocational workers. Data concerning statistical evidence of reliability and internal consistency are derived from the responses of 84 Ss. (18 ref.)

Burke, Donald A. & Sellin, Donald F. (Michigan State U.) Exceptional Children, 1972(Oct), Vol. 39(2), 126-132. [PA, Vol 50:06959]

3223.   Effects of contingency management upon reading achievement of junior high educable mentally retarded students.
Attempted to increase the reading achievement of 13 12.4-15.11 yr. old educable mentally retarded students through systematic use of contingency management techniques. Ss participated in a 50-min reading session daily throughout the 17-wk study. Pre- and posttesting of reading achievement demonstrated a mean advancement of 1.3 yr. 7 Ss were subsequently placed in regular reading classes. Followup 1 yr. later indicates all were achieving success in the regular program.

Busse, Larry L. & Henderson, Hyrum S. (U. Washington) Education & Training of the Mentally Retarded, 1972(Apr), Vol. 7(2), 67-73. [PA, Vol 49:09869]

3224.   School attendance areas as a factor in attitudes of EMR adolescent students toward school and school related activities.
Administered a semantic differential to compare expressed attitudes of 37 male and 13 female educable mentally retarded adolescents who attended school outside their normal attendance area with attitudes of 25 male and 12 female educable mentally retarded adolescents who attended school within their attendance area. The nonlocal group expressed significantly higher attitude scores on 5 of the 6 concepts. Most of this difference is accounted for by the males. (19 ref.)

Dick, Herman F. & Lewis, Mary E. (Oakland Schools, Pontiac, Mich.) Education & Training of the Mentally Retarded, 1972(Apr), Vol. 7(2), 82-87. [PA, Vol 49:09888]

3225.   Discrimination training on the identification of reversible letters by EMR adolescents.
Administered oddity or matching directionality training problems to 48 educable mentally retarded Ss (aged 11 yr., 10 mo. to 17 yr., 10 mo.). Half of the Ss were trained with lower-case b's and d's; the other half were trained with a directionally reversible drawing of a sock. Ss were divided into above- and below-median reading grade subgroups. After training, Ss were administered a letter reversals transfer task. Analyses of variance on training errors reveal that matching training produced significantly fewer errors than oddity training. In addition, high readers performed significantly better than low readers on the transfer task. Significant interactions between reading level and stimulus factors on both training and transfer performance are discussed.

Evans, Ross A. & Bilsky, Linda. (Teachers Coll., Columbia U.) American Journal of Mental Deficiency, 1972(Sep), Vol. 77(2), 169-174. [PA, Vol 49:07791]

3226.   [Several characteristics of the drawing activities of mentally retarded preschoolers.] (Russ)
Administered a drawing test to mentally retarded students of a special nursery school for children with CNS disorders. 4 groups of 30 Ss each, 1st- through 4th-yr students, drew a picture of their choice, a house, a tree, and a person. Ss' performance improved with increasing age and education, the most salient changes occurring between the 1st and 2nd school years. While some of the 1st-yr students-not understanding what was asked of them-produced no drawings, all 2nd-yr students attempted the tasks. An evaluative relation toward one's work appeared first among the 2nd-yr Ss. Depicting spatial relations was difficult even for 4th-yr students.

Gavrilooshkina, O. P. (Moscow Nursery School No. 468, USSR) Defektologiya, 1972, Vol. 4(1), 69-72. [PA, Vol 50:09169]

3227.   Social acceptance of EMRs integrated into a nongraded elementary school.
Administered the Peer Acceptance Scale to 16 1st-3rd graders and 20 4th-6th graders of both sexes with average IQs. Ss' social acceptance of 3 groups was assessed: educable mentally retarded (EMR) children integrated into the academic routine of a nongraded school, EMRs who remained segregated in the nongraded school's only self-contained class, and normal controls. Results indicate that (a) both integrated and segregated EMRs were rejected significantly more often than controls, (b) younger Ss were more accepting of others than older Ss, (c) males expressed more overt rejection than females, and (d) integrated

EMRs were rejected significantly more often than segregated EMRs by males but not by females.
Goodman, Hollace; Gottlieb, Jay & Harrison, Robert H. (Research Inst. for Educational Problems, Cambridge, Mass.) American Journal of Mental Deficiency, 1972(Jan), Vol. 76(4), 412-417. [PA, Vol 48:05663]

3228. A group contingency for individual misbehaviors in the classroom.
Replicates and extends an earlier study (see PA, Vol. 42:19208) of a procedure to eliminate disruptive classroom behaviors. A total of 100 institutionalized retarded adolescents (mean age = 15.4 yr.; mean IQ = 65) in 11 academic classes were given a ½-hr reward period to use as they wished, but were informed that their class would lose 1 min. of this period for misbehaviors of individuals during the day. A significant decline in misbehavior rate resulted. This system was well received by the students, and was considered by teachers and administrators to be an asset to the educational program.
Greene, Robert J. & Pratt, Janie J. (E. R. Johnstone Training & Research Center, Bordentown, N.J.) Mental Retardation, 1972(Jun), Vol. 10(3), 33-35. [PA, Vol 49:01142]

3229. Retardates' reading achievement in the resource room model: The first year.
Hammill, Donald; Iano, Richard; McGettigan, James & Wiederholt, J. Lee. (Temple U.) Training School Bulletin, 1972(Nov), Vol. 69(3), 104-107. [PA, Vol 50:01800]

3230. Training and transfer of word definitions by retarded children.
Trained 10 7-11.6 yr. old educable retardates, matched for total acceptable responses (naming, formal, and functional description) to picture noun-objects with 10 controls, in a 14-day program during which these features were specified for 3 objects in 10 class categories. The most pronounced result was a significantly greater reduction of unacceptable responses by the experimental Ss to training and transfer items. Greater increases in formal description responses to training items were obtained for experimental Ss, while both groups displayed significant formal description increases on transfer items. Training failed to produce clearcut effects for either naming or functional description responses.
Haugen, David M. & McManis, Donald L. (Eastern Washington State Coll.) American Journal of Mental Deficiency, 1972(Mar), Vol. 76(5), 594-601. [PA, Vol 48:12069]

3231. Labels and stigma in special education.
Considers that in the delivery of services to disadvantaged, deprived, and mildly retarded children (a) insufficient attention has been given to the fact that certain special education labels imply deficiencies and shortcomings in children and (b) no systematic inquiry has been made of children's perceptions of the labels and services offered them. Data from several studies were analyzed which involved more than 10,000 public school students, graduates, and dropouts; college students; prospective and inservice teachers; and counselors. Children rejected the labels culturally disadvantaged and culturally deprived as descriptive of themselves, acceptance of such labels was associated with lowered school attitudes, and teachers held lowered expectations for their performance. The educable mentally retarded reported (and teachers confirmed) stigma associated with special class placement. Few strategies for the management of stigma in classes for the educable mentally retarded had been developed by teachers. (23 ref.)
Jones, Reginald L. (U. California, Riverside) Exceptional Children, 1972(Mar), Vol. 38(7), 553-564. [PA, Vol 50:05742]

3232. Group structures in retarded adolescents.
Analyzed sociometric data obtained over a 3-yr period from a total of 124 educable mental retardates in special schools and classes (mean CA = 11 yr. at the beginning of the study). It was found that some of the features were not directly comparable to those obtained with nonretarded children of similar age. Reasons for these differences are discussed. It is concluded that programs

specifically designed to encourage the development of interpersonal skills are required in special schools and classes.
Laing, Alice F. (University Coll., Swansea, Wales) American Journal of Mental Deficiency, 1972(Jan), Vol. 76(4), 481-490. [PA, Vol 48:05672]

3233. Higher-order and lower-order reading responses of mentally retarded and nonretarded children at the first-grade level.
Tested hypotheses that the reading processes of retarded children, as inferred from responses to a reading task, would be qualitatively inferior to those of nonretarded children matched for reading achievement (based on Wide Range Achievement Test scores). Ss were 20 educable mental retardates (CA = 8-14 yr.) and 24 nonretarded children at the 1st-grade level. Data were based on 10 error categories, as well as repetitions, self-corrections, and regressions that occurred during reading. Results provide support for 2 of the 3 hypotheses; retarded Ss made more "search for closure" responses and "simple" or "inferior" errors. It is concluded that there is a need for development and evaluation of a curriculum to facilitate reading strategies of retarded children. (21 ref.)
Levitt, Edith. (Columbia U., Teachers Coll.) American Journal of Mental Deficiency, 1972(Jul), Vol. 77(1), 13-20. [PA, Vol 49:01321]

3234. Incremental art curriculum model for the mentally retarded.
Reviews the relative position of art in special education curriculums, summarizes existent research literature related to art and the mentally retarded, and presents the beginnings of a structured, sequential, behaviorally based art program for educable retarded children. The curriculum model proposed includes a method of assessing the individual's increment of learning in the areas of visual analysis, perceptual discrimination, self-awareness, and self-concept. Brief descriptions of 3 introductory lesson plans and an abbreviated synopsis of activities from the unit on self-awareness and self-concept are included as illustrative material.
Lovano-Kerr, Jessie & Savage, Steven. (Indiana U.) Research Bulletin, Institute of Education, U. Helsinki, 1972(Nov), Vol. 39(3), 193-199. [PA, Vol 50:07781]

3235. Motivational style: An important consideration in programs for EMR-labeled children.
Discusses the conclusion of educators that the special learning needs of educable mentally retarded children are cognitive in nature, and that activities recommended for their special classes have reflected this conclusion. In questioning this assumption, however, it is posited that low IQ, low socioeconomic status, minority children have learning problems based on emotional and/or motivational differences rather than cognitive. It is concluded that unless needs for attention are satisfied, the failure set reversed, and dysfunctional problem-solving approaches altered, the probability of academic success is low regardless of the administrative arrangement in which the child's education is provided. (16 ref.)
MacMillan, Donald L. (U. California, Riverside) Journal of School Psychology, 1972(Jun), Vol. 10(2), 111-116. [PA, Vol 49:07888]

3236. Classroom techniques.
Explored the fact that normal kindergarten and older retarded children's behaviors in number development have some developmentally analogous identities. 120 8-10 yr. old educable retarded and 60 nonretarded kindergartners served as Ss in an experimental task to determine the effects of materials and transformations, given that preoperational thought and judgments about number are influenced heavily by perceptual cues. It is concluded that since most nonconserving responses can be ascribed to denial of certain principles of number, the teaching activities in number should reinforce those principles continuously.
McGettigan, James F. (Temple U.) Education & Training of the Mentally Retarded, 1972(Dec), Vol. 7(4), 183-188. [PA, Vol 50:03836]

3237.   Developmental study of the acquisition and utilization of conceptual strategies.
Tested the effects of instruction in 2 formally different strategies on conjunctive concept attainment and problem-solving efficiency at 2 developmental levels. A total of 90 educable retarded 9-11 yr. olds with MAs of 5-6 and 7-8 yr. served as Ss. Treatments consisted of instruction in conservative focusing, successive scanning, or no instruction. It was found that with the 5-7 MA level, training in focusing failed to facilitate performance; scanning instruction increased problem-solving efficiency but did not facilitate concept attainment. At the 7-8 MA level, instruction in both strategies facilitated performance, although focusing was more effective than scanning. Results indicate that the acquisition of complex cognitive operations in young children is a function of both the logical structure and informational demands of the task. (24 ref.)
McKinney, James D. (U. North Carolina, Chapel Hill) Journal of Educational Psychology, 1972(Feb), Vol. 63(1), 22-31. [PA, Vol 48:01710]

3238.   Physical activities for mentally retarded school children.
Reviews 4 broad stages in the development of recreation for the mentally retarded between 1920 and 1968. Previous studies indicate that significant gains were made in tasks for which children were trained but that there was little follow-up of aftereffects of training. Specific training programs, e.g., the Doman-Delacato approach as well as more general programs, are discussed. Physical education principles and techniques are identified as essential for teachers of the mentally retarded. A survey in 1970 in Saskatchewan, Canada, indicates that physical education and recreation can help the social and emotional development of the mentally retarded. (51 ref.)
McLeod, J.; Gittens, J. A. & Leong, C. K. (U. Saskatchewan, Saskatoon, Canada) Slow Learning Child, 1972(Mar), Vol. 19(1), 40-52. [PA, Vol 49:09998]

3239.   Language behavior of EMR children.
Describes language behavior of educable mentally retarded (EMR) children in special classes as a function of IQ, sex, socioeconomic status, CA and MA, and special treatment effects. A representative sample of 182 EMR children between 6.9-12.8 yr. old, with IQ between 50-69, served as Ss. Findings indicate that language behavior of children in special classes is below every reasonable expectation according to MA, and that language deficiency evidenced by children may lead to referral and eventual placement in EMR classes.
Ogland, Vanetta S. (U. Wisconsin, River Falls) Mental Retardation, 1972(Jun), Vol. 10(3), 30-32. [PA, Vol 49:01344]

3240.   An experimental and ethological analysis of social reinforcement with retarded children.
Assessed the effectiveness of positive and negative evaluative comments for learning by 56 6-12 yr. old educable mentally retarded Ss in a 2-choice discrimination task. Negative comments after incorrect responses greatly facilitated learning, while positive comments after correct responses had little effect. A naturalistic analysis of the use of evaluative expressions in 6 special education classrooms indicates that positive evaluations were used more frequently and indiscriminately and were less contingent upon behavior than negative comments. Results indicate that the 2 forms of evaluations differ in their effectiveness and in their functions in everyday interactions. (17 ref.)
Paris, Scott G. & Cairns, Robert B. (Indiana U.) Child Development, 1972(Sep), Vol. 43(3), 717-729. [PA, Vol 49:03280]

3241.   The responsiveness of cloze readability measures to linguistic variables operating over segments of text longer than a sentence.
Tested the hypothesis that cloze would be sensitive to linguistic constraints using as Ss 58 mentally retarded junior high school students who scored at a grade level equivalent of 2.5 or above on the Wide Range Achievement Test. Ss were administered 2 cloze tasks, 1 containing sentences in natural order, the other in modified or randomly rearranged order. Therefore, availability of

linguistic constraints was the same within sentences but not between sentences for the 2 passages. Analysis of variance using a Latin Square design with repeated measures over 1 type of material controlled by counterbalancing indicated significantly more correct cloze responses for sentences in the natural order. This was contrasted with the assumption that other formulas of readability would assign equivalent ratings to both types of materials. (French & Spanish summaries) (33 ref.)
Ramanauskas, Sigita. (U. Connecticut) Reading Research Quarterly, 1972(Fal), Vol. 8(1), 72-91. [PA, Vol 50:05826]

3242.   Group time-out from rock and roll music and out-of-seat behavior of handicapped children while riding a school bus.
Reports on the reduction of out-of-seat behavior, a universal and potentially dangerous problem among children on school buses, under a group time-out procedure from rock and roll music. Ss were 6-15 yr. olds from educable mentally retarded classes. Their classroom teachers acted as Os, recorders, and implementers of the contingencies. Music was played while the bus was moving, as long as all Ss were sitting in their bus seats and shut-off for 5 sec. for each out-of-seat observed. Reversals to base line were introduced to assess the effects of the music and group time-out. A marked reduction of out-of-seats occurred with each introduction of the music and group time-out contingency. Results demonstrated the applicability of reinforcement procedures in modifying these behaviors in a moving environment and are consistent with research on reinforcement procedures in modifying out-of-seat behaviors in the closed environment of the classroom.
Ritschl, Carlo; Mongrella, John & Presbie, Robert J. (Nanuet Public Schools, Behavior Modification-Learning Disability Program, N.Y.) Psychological Reports, 1972(Dec), Vol. 31(3), 967-973. [PA, Vol 50:01922]

3243.   The efficacy of listening training for educable mentally retarded children.
Taught listening skills to 82-120 mo. old educable mentally retarded children within the context of small-group games. The procedures used in the 10-wk training program included intentional teaching, peer modeling, and tangible, social, and symbolic rewards. The experimental group (n = 17) showed marked improvement. Although their posttraining total score was still below that of an average group (n = 16) of the same CA, on 1 subtest they surpassed the average group and on 3 subtests equalled it. A control group (n = 16) showed no improvement which suggests that the traditional special class program effects little improvement in listening skills. (18 ref.)
Ross, Dorothea M. & Ross, Sheila A. (U. California, San Francisco) American Journal of Mental Deficiency, 1972(Sep), Vol. 77(2), 137-142. [PA, Vol 49:10043]

3244.   Teacher expectancy as it relates to the academic achievement of EMR students.
Teachers in charge of 18 special classes for educable mentally retarded (EMR) children (N = 136 6-12 yr. old Ss) were asked to indicate their expectations for each of the Ss for the year ahead. Ss were rated on academics (subject matter skills), social behavior (class adjustment), and language (self-expression, written and verbal). Tests administered at the beginning and end of a 3-semester period disclose no statistical relationship between expectations and academic achievement.
Schwarz, Robert H. & Cook, John J. (U. Wisconsin, Center on Mental Retardation) Journal of Educational Research, 1972(May), Vol. 65(9), 393-396. [PA, Vol 49:01364]

3245.   [Failures in speech comprehension of young mentally retarded schoolchildren.] (Russ)
Investigated whether mentally retarded Ukrainian children in 1st and 2nd grade special education classes understand grammatical concepts, e.g., "sex of adjective". Ukrainian nouns are either masculine, feminine, or neuter. An adjective modifying a noun must agree with the noun's sex, the sex of the adjective being indicated by its ending. Ss were presented a row of cards depicting red objects of all sexes and yellow objects of all sexes and were asked, e.g., "Where is the red (ending specifies male

noun) one?", "Where is the yellow (ending specifies neuter noun) one?" Only 8.7% of the 1st grade answers and 20% of the 2nd grade answers were correct. Ss tended to ignore the adjectival endings denoting the grammatical concept of sex, answering solely on the basis of the meaning of the adjective, in this case, the color it specifies.
Smirnova, L. A. (A. M. Gorky Government Pedagogical Institute, Kiev, USSR) Defektologiya, 1972, Vol. 4(1), 19-24. [PA, Vol 50:10020]

3246.   Reward anticipation and performance expectancy on the learning rate of EMR adolescents.
Assigned 60 noninstitutionalized educable mentally retarded adolescents to 1 of 4 treatment conditions combining 4 types of reward and performance expectancy in a learning task situation. A significant interaction of variables was obtained. Performance was inferior under the reward-failure condition and superior under the no reward-failure condition. (25 ref.)
Welch, Russell F. & Drew, Clifford J. (Abilene Public Schools, Tex.) American Journal of Mental Deficiency, 1972(Nov), Vol. 77(3), 291-295. [PA, Vol 50:03940]

3247.   Instructional treatments based on learning strategies and the recognition memory of retarded children.
Compared the effectiveness of 3 different treatment conditions in 2 recognition tasks, recognition of displays or groups and recognition of individual pictures. The 1st treatment, elaboration, involved relating pictures to a short story designed to place the 2 in meaningful context. The 2nd treatment utilized instructions which were developed to highlight characteristics of pictures the Ss were asked to look at and name. The 3rd treatment was primarily a control condition involving no special clues or instructions in presentation of pictures. 74 junior high school educable mentally retarded Ss were assigned randomly to 1 of 3 treatment conditions. Planned comparisons were made to test differences between the treatments on the 2 recognition tasks. Elaboration was found to be significantly superior to highlighting or the no-special-instructions control in recognition of displays, but no significant difference was found between highlighting or control conditions. Highlighting condition showed significantly fewer false recognitions of individual pictures. It is concluded that well-structured instruction can lead to most effective performance.
Bender, Nila N. & Taylor, Arthur M. (U. California, Riverside) American Educational Research Journal, 1973(Fal), Vol. 10(4), 337-343. [PA, Vol 51:07983]

3248.   The special child in the regular classroom.
Integrated 3 educable mentally retarded children who had previously been placed in special self-contained classrooms with 22 nonhandicapped children in a 3rd grade classroom during the 1st yr. of the North Sacramento model program. A similar number were integrated into a 4th grade classroom during the 2nd yr. of the project. A precision teaching procedure was used with both experimental groups. Control groups of educable mentally retarded and educationally handicapped Ss in regular classrooms were maintained. Results indicate that the handicapped and nonhandicapped Ss in the integrated setting improved as much or more than did their controls in academic skills, social behavior, and attitude change.
Bradfield, Robert H., et al. (California State U., San Francisco) Exceptional Children, 1973(Feb), Vol. 39(5), 384-390. [PA, Vol 50:07657]

3249.   Performance of EMRs on the Let's Look at Children Written Exercises for first graders.
Investigated the suitability of the Let's Look at Children Written Exercises for intermediate level educable mentally retarded (EMR) children. The 141 Ss ranged in mental age (MA) from 6 to 9 yrs. It is concluded that the Exercises are most appropriate for use with EMR children with MAs of 6. Advantages for use with EMR children include numerous demonstration exercises with high success expectancies and coordination of the Exercises with specified instructional strategies. In the latter case the

Exercises appear to be a definite improvement over conventional IQ tests; however, a rigorous task analysis has yet to be done.
Brantley, John C. & Mitchell, Marlys M. (U. North Carolina, Chapel Hill) Mental Retardation, 1973(Oct), Vol. 11(5), 41-43. [PA, Vol 51:09942]

3250.   Use of the "College Bowl" format to increase silent reading comprehension.
Manipulated performance variables to improve the reading performance of 16 educable mentally retarded public school students (IQs 51-88). Incentives consisting of a team competition format and the contingent use of money appeared to result in a dramatic increase in reading skill.
Brown, Lou; Huppler, Barbara; VanDeventer, Pat & Sontag, Edward. (U. Wisconsin) Child Study Journal, 1973, Vol. 3(4), 181-193. [PA, Vol 52:06345]

3251.   Educational materials: Use of reinforcement principles to increase comprehension of instructional filmstrips.
Showed 5 educable mentally retarded 12-15 yr olds in a public school special class 4 different instructional filmstrips. Ss were then given 4 tests of comprehension. Baseline measures suggest that the Ss answered from 18-24% of the comprehension questions correctly. Performance charts and money were then manipulated in an attempt to increase comprehension scores. A multiple baseline design was used to measure the effectiveness of the instructional procedures. Results suggest that correct responding was a function of the contingent consequences presented and that initial responding might have been due to inappropriately programed performance variables rather than to the intrinsic difficulty level of the instructional materials.
Brown, Lou, et al. (U. Wisconsin, Madison) Education & Training of the Mentally Retarded, 1973(Feb), Vol. 8(1), 50-56. [PA, Vol 51:03933]

3252.   Timeout as a punishing stimulus in continuous and intermittent schedules.
Investigated the effectiveness of a brief period of isolation (timeout) in the control of disruptive behavior emitted by an 8-yr-old retarded girl in a preschool classroom setting. Timeout was shown to be an effective punishing stimulus (Exp I), and its control of the child's disruptive behavior was investigated under 4 schedules of intermittent timeout (Exp II). Results suggest that as a larger percentage of responses were punished, a greater decrease in the frequency of that response occurred. This inverse relationship between the percentage of responses punished and the frequency of the response appeared to be a nonlinear function. This function suggests that some schedules of intermittent punishment may be as effective as continuous punishment, at least in the case of the continued suppression of a response that has already been reduced to a low frequency. (31 ref)
Clark, Hewitt B.; Rowbury, Trudylee; Baer, Ann M.. & Baer, Donald M. (Johnny Cake Child Study Center, Mansfield, Ark.) Journal of Applied Behavior Analysis, 1973(Fal), Vol. 6(3), 443-455. [PA, Vol 51:11974]

3253.   Clinical studies of teachers and children in selected public school educable special classes.
Conducted a diagnostic study of cognitive and affective characteristics of children, teacher practices, and the relationship between these variables and low performance in 48 7-11 yr olds in 6 public school educable special classes. Probabilities for change of these determinants of learning were also examined. Over a 2-yr period, Ss' cognitive performances and emotional behavior were evaluated on the basis of 7 clinical tests (e.g., the Stanford Binet) and direct classroom observations. Resulting from these evaluations, prescriptive intervention programs were pursued. Data reveal that the majority of Ss changed in substantially positive directions over the 2 yrs and that behavior and performances among and within Ss were extremely variable. (25 ref)
Ensher, Gail L. (Syracuse U.) Training School Bulletin, 1973(Aug), Vol. 70(2), 93-105. [PA, Vol 51:07986]

3254. Visual self-confrontation and the self-concept of the exceptional child.
Conducted a pilot study to investigate methods and effects (photography, mirrors, films, and videotape) of extending a child's self-awareness during a 7-mo period. 8 preadolescents (mean age = 116.6 mo) with specific learning disabilities, 58 children (mean age range = 109.3-133 mo) of above average intelligence (mean IQ range = 141.8-145.8), and 14 educable mentally retarded (EMR) boys (mean age range = 172.5-174 mo) served as Ss. Pre- and posttests included visual recognition tests, identification of self from a series of gradually focused slides, the Self-Esteem Inventory, and the Self-Concept as a Learner test. Tests were administered in September and April. All groups except the EMR boys showed significant improvement at recognizing themselves on at least one of the self-recognition tests. Findings also support the effectiveness of videotape self-confrontation experiences. The EMR boys appeared to have the poorest self-concepts. Possible improvements in the methodology used and intergroup differences are discussed. (33 ref.)
Gill, Newell T. & Messina, Robert. (Florida Atlantic U.) Florida Journal of Educational Research, 1973, Vol 15, 18-36. [PA, Vol 51:05939]

3255. The influence of typewriting on selected language arts skills and motor development of the educable mentally handicapped.
Studied the influence of typewriting on academic achievement (Metropolitan Achievement Test) and motor development (Lincoln-Oseretsky Motor Development Scale) of 60 educable mentally retarded 8-15 yr olds (IQ range 55-84). Ss received 45 min of language arts instruction daily for 20 wks in addition to regular reading lessons; 30 Ss used electric typewriters to complete the reading exercises and 30 Ss used pencils or pens. Posttest achievement scores indicate that reading and spelling performance of the typing Ss did not significantly exceed that of the other Ss, but did so in 2 of the motor development subtests. There was no significant difference in vocabulary development.
Gladis, Paulette. (U. North Dakota) American Journal of Mental Deficiency, 1973(Jan), Vol. 77(4), 451-454. [PA, Vol 51:05940]

3256. The performance of educable mentally retarded children on subtraction word problems.
Recorded the performance of 118 educable mentally retarded (EMR) Ss (mean MA = 8 yrs 2 mo) on subtraction work problems written in various linguistic formats. Results indicate the difficulty encountered by many of the Ss in solving problems whose format differs from a standard action sequence. This deficit is interpreted as representing the use of scanning rather than comprehension strategies when Ss attempt to solve problems. Findings suggest that the teaching of problem solving to EMR children requires changes in curricula and methods.
Goodstein, Henry A. (U. Connecticut) Education & Training of the Mentally Retarded, 1973(Dec), Vol. 8(4), 197-202. [PA, Vol 52:06349]

3257. Social acceptability of retarded children in nongraded schools differing in architecture.
Compared the social position of integrated and segregated educable mentally retarded (EMR) children (*n* = 56) in a traditional school building to that of EMR children (*n* = 80) in a no-interior-wall school. Results indicate that while EMR Ss in the unwalled school were known more often by their non-EMR peers, they were least likely to be chosen as friends. Retarded Ss in the unwalled school were rejected more often than retarded in the walled school. Also, integrated EMR Ss were rejected more than segregated EMR.
Gottlieb, Jay & Budoff, Milton. (Research Inst. for Educational Problems, Cambridge, Mass.) American Journal of Mental Deficiency, 1973(Jul), Vol. 78(1), 15-19. [PA, Vol 51:05941]

3258. Social acceptance of EMR children during overt behavioral interactions.
Attempted to determine (a) whether educable mentally retarded (EMR) children are rejected during overt interactions with non-EMR children and (b) whether EMR children integrated full-time in a nongraded school are perceived by their non-EMR peers to be similar to segregated EMR or non-EMR children. 42 4th, 5th, and 6th graders (9-12 yrs old) were asked to select 1 of 2 children as a partner to help them win a prize at a bean-bag toss game. Depending upon the treatment, the other 2 children were either (a) a segregated EMR child and a non-EMR child, (b) an integrated EMR child and a non-EMR child, or (c) a segregated EMR child and an integrated EMR child. Results indicate that both integrated and segregated EMR children were chosen less often than non-EMR children and that integrated and segregated EMR children were selected equally often. Findings are discussed in terms of the competence vs liking dimension. Also, it is suggested that the effects of physical deviance on EMR children's social acceptability should be examined.
Gottlieb, Jay & Davis, Joyce E. (Research Inst. for Educational Problems, Cambridge, Mass.) American Journal of Mental Deficiency, 1973(Sep), Vol. 78(2), 141-143. [PA, Vol 52:01866]

3259. Effects of total body movement training on EMR's ability to understand geometric forms.
Greer, Rachel D. (U. Arkansas, Pine Bluff) Mental Retardation, 1973(Oct), Vol. 11(5), 40. [PA, Vol 51:09946]

3260. Tempo modification in visual perception of EMR children.
Gave nonintellectual tasks which involved visual perception and spatial relationships to 45 White and 42 Black 7-12 yr old educable mental retardates in urban schools. Ss copied visible patterns and also reproduced patterns from memory after tachistoscopic exposure. The major variable was perceptual tempo, manipulated by instructions to adopt a reflective rather than impulsive style of responding. Other variables were sex and race. Perceptual accuracy was increased by instructions to adopt a reflective attitude, presumably because the latency of responding was increased. Blacks improved more than Whites with reflective instructions, showing superior performance afterward.
Harcum, Phoebe M. & Harcum, E. Rae. (Magruder School, Williamsburg, Va.) Perceptual & Motor Skills, 1973(Aug), Vol. 37(1), 179-188. [PA, Vol 51:09446]

3261. WISC and reading achievement of children referred back to the regular classroom or to a special education class after psychological evaluation.
Brain-injured 7-8 yr olds did not differ significantly from educable retardates on WISC Performance subtests and did not differ from Ss returned to regular classrooms on WISC Verbal subtests. Returned Ss were reading at grade level on the Wide Range Achievement Test, whereas brain-damaged and retarded Ss averaged well below grade level.
Jansen, David G. (Willmar State Hosp., Minn.) Perceptual & Motor Skills, 1973(Aug), Vol. 37(1), 203-204. [PA, Vol 51:09947]

3262. Self-concept measurement and placement of adolescent inner-city EMRs.
Administered the Illinois Index of Self Derogation (IISD) and Brookover's General Self-Concept of Ability scale (GSCA) to 2 groups of 31 Black, 14-16 yr old educable mental retardates who were either partially integrated academically with equal-CA peers or were academically segregated. The partially-integrated Ss exhibited higher self-concepts than the segregated Ss on both scales. The difference was significant on the GSCA but not on the IISD. The 2 measures were correlated +.50. Findings are discussed in light of research on academic achievement and self-concept, different possible class placements, and the possibility of different types of self-concept (i.e., global and specific).
Kahn, James V. & Garrison, Mortimer. (U. Illinois, Chicago) Training School Bulletin, 1973(Aug), Vol. 70(2), 80-83. [PA, Vol 51:07988]

3263. Functional analysis of WISC performance of learning-disordered, hyperactive, and mentally retarded boys.
Investigated patterns of WISC performance of children with serious school learning and adjustment problems. Ss were 26 boys in public school classes for educable mentally retarded, 24

private school children with serious learning and behavior problems, and 26 boys referred to a pediatric learning disability clinic for evaluation of hyperactivity and learning problems. Analysis of the data from the various WISC subtests suggests that remedial programs should be individualized rather than based on preconceived concepts.
Keogh, Barbara K.; Wetter, Jack; McGinty, Ann & Donlon, Genevieve. (U. California, Los Angeles) Psychology in the Schools, 1973(Apr), Vol. 10(2), 178-181. [PA, Vol 50:09908]

3264.   [Late reading experiments with mentally retarded youths.] (Germ)
Conducted experiments with 14 mentally Test 17-20 yr olds. The various disturbing variables of the reading process were analyzed. Mentally retarded children often show good ability to learn in the postpubescent phase which should be utilized for again trying to teach them reading. Results of life-relevant and marked successes can be obtained in an estimated 20-30% of such youths. No statistical evaluation was attempted for the data obtained but 4 different groups of poor readers were isolated and analyzed. Hypotheses for further investigation are suggested.
Kobi, Emil E. (U. Basel, Switzerland) Vierteljahresschrift für Heilpädagogik und ihre Nachbargebiete, 1973(Sep), Vol. 42(3), 279-288. [PA, Vol 51:11983]

3265.   The isolate child.
A controlled experiment attempted to improve the interaction of the moderately retarded "isolate" child with his/her normal peers in a classroom situation. Videotape recordings were used which showed nonretarded children participating in the same activities (reading, group playing, gymnastic exercises, and getting ready to leave the classroom) as the retarded children. Findings strongly support the use of peer models within observational learning paradigms as a means of changing classroom behavior and increasing the social interaction of isolate children.
Kysela, G. M. (U Alberta, Learning & Development Clinic, Edmonton, Canada) Mental Retardation Bulletin, 1972–73, Vol 1(1), 8-10. [PA, Vol 58:04385]

3266.   The pod in a summer program for exceptional children.
Describes a 5-wk summer pilot program for mildly retarded children, 7 at primary and 9 at intermediate level, located in a pod, or open classroom, in which the instructional space is not divided by walls but is flexibly organized as the needs of individual pupils or small groups require. The program was conducted by 2 teachers with the participation of 7 interns. Teacher reactions at the end of the project listed both advantages and disadvantages in the arrangement. Ss seemed to react to that factor of the arrangement—structure, freedom, or attention—which more directly satisfied their personal needs, and these factors seemed to be related to their previous experiences.
Mitchell, Marlys; Wheeler, Kay & Hoover, Roberta. (U. North Carolina, Chapel Hill) Education & Training of the Mentally Retarded, 1973(Dec), Vol. 8(4), 203-206. [PA, Vol 52:06354]

3267.   The relationship between Bender Gestalt performance and achievement among retardates.
Computed the Pearson product moment coefficients between error scores of 76 9-15 yr old mental retardates on the Bender Visual Motor Gestalt Test for Children (BG) and Reading and Arithmetic scores on the Wide Range Achievement (WRAT). BG performance was not related to reading achievement but did covary with WRAT Arithmetic scores. Partial correlation, used to control for variations in CA and IQ, reduced the magnitude of the correlation between BG performance and arithmetic achievement significantly. The small amount of variance accounted for by the adjusted correlation raises questions relating to the utility of the Bender Gestalt as a predictor of academic achievement in a mentally retarded population.
Morgenstern, Murry & McIvor, William. (New York Medical Coll., Mental Retardation Inst., N.Y.) Training School Bulletin, 1973(Aug), Vol. 70(2), 84-87. [PA, Vol 51:07990]

3268.   Improving oral language skills in a classroom for the educable mentally retarded.
Describes a classroom project utilizing the Bell & Howell Language Master audiovisual instruction system to improve oral communication skills in 6 preadolescent educable mentally retarded Ss. Standardized test scores and linguistic analyses of pre- and post-treatment speech samples revealed improved quantity and quality of oral language.
Odom, Mildred; Longhurst, Thomas M. & Boatman, Rex R. (Bluemont School, Unified School District No. 383, Manhattan, Kan.) Education & Training of the Mentally Retarded, 1973(Dec), Vol. 8(4), 187-193. [PA, Vol 52:06355]

3269.   Teacher ratings and self concept reports of retarded pupils.
Examines the relationship between self-ratings and teacher ratings of 100 9-15 yr old children in classes for the educable mentally retarded. Each S completed a self-report on the Coopersmith Self-Esteem Inventory. Results indicate that the self-images of these pupils are positively related to the teachers' image of their academic ability. The teachers' ratings of each pupil's social and emotional behavior were not correlated significantly with the child's perception of his social or emotional relationship. The educable mentally retarded Ss did not perceive their standing among peers to be positively correlated to academic success. Implications for the pupils' educational program are suggested. (15 ref)
Richmond, Bert O. & Dalton, J. Leon. (U. Georgia) Exceptional Children, 1973(Nov), Vol. 40(3), 178-183. [PA, Vol 51:09951]

3270.   Storage and utilization of previously formulated mediators in educable mentally retarded children.
Attempted to determine whether the educable mentally retarded child is capable of the long-term retention of mediational links that he had formulated previously on a paired-associate task. Following pretraining measures of paired-associate learning and retention and of mediational skills, the experimental group Ss (12 6-10 yr olds) were given long-term mediation training within the context of a story and table game program, while the control group Ss (*n* = 2) participated in a similar program with no mediational instruction. Posttraining measures provided evidence of the long-term retention of specific mediational links as well as substantial support for the efficacy of long-term mediation training. (15 ref.)
Ross, Dorothea M. & Ross, Sheila A. (U. California, San Francisco) Journal of Educational Psychology, 1973(Oct), Vol. 65(2), 205-210. [PA, Vol 51:05948]

3271.   Cognitive training for the EMR child: Situational problem solving and planning.
Conducted 2 studies to evaluate the efficacy of training in situational problem solving and planning. The 6-wk programs were presented within the context of small group discussions, table games, and craft activities. The specific training procedures used included intentional training, direct and vicarious reinforcement, peer modeling, and brainstorming. In both studies the experimental groups' (*n* = 15 and 14) posttest scores were far superior to those of the control groups (*n* = 15 and 14). Results suggest an important experiential component in the educable mentally retarded child's deficit in cognitive skills and provide strong support for the efficacy of early intensive cognitive training. (23 ref.)
Ross, Dorothea M. & Ross, Sheila A. (U. California, San Francisco) American Journal of Mental Deficiency, 1973(Jul), Vol. 78(1), 20-26. [PA, Vol 51:05947]

3272.   Factors in special class placement.
Identified factors associated with placement in classes for the educable retarded. Tests administered to determine grouping included the WISC, Metropolitan Readiness Tests Wide Range Achievement Tests, and Stanford Achievement Tests. Comparisons were made between a group of 17 low IQ (<80) regular class Ss and 3 groups of special class Ss: (a) 18 low IQ (<80) Ss, (b) 9 average IQ (>80) Ss, and (c) the total group of 32 special class Ss. No differences were found between regular and special

class Ss on preschool readiness and language development or on achievement prior to differential placement. Significant socioeconomic status differences favored the regular class Ss. Both low socioeconomic status and poor school behavior were associated with special class placement of average IQ Ss. At 9 yrs of age, significant differences favoring regular class Ss were found on measures of academic achievement. These differences were attributed to the effects of differential school placement. (19 ref.) *Rubin, Rosalyn A.; Krus, Patricia & Balow, Bruce.* (U. Minnesota) Exceptional Children, 1973(Apr), Vol. 39(7), 525-532. [PA, Vol 50:12089]

3273.   Diagnostic-prescriptive perceptual training with mentally retarded children.
Attempted to ascertain the extent to which the learning efficiency (language and perceptual and academic skills) of 106 educable mentally retarded children would be increased when the stronger of 2 perceptual modalities (auditory or visual) was matched to a unisensory auditory or visual perceptual curriculum. The study consisted of an auditory perceptual training phase and a visual perceptual training phase. There were no significant differences in the adjusted mean scores between a Hawthorne group and the 2 groups receiving prescriptively matched unisensory visual and auditory perceptual curricula. All groups demonstrated significant gains on the criterion posttest measures. There were no significant interactions between measured perceptual strengths and the 2 types of perceptual interventions. Diagnostic prescriptive teaching utilizing the perceptual modality of greater measured strength (or weakness) failed to achieve initial teaching success. (24 ref.)
Sabatino, David A.; Ysseldyke, James E. & Woolston, Joan. (Pennsylvania State U.) American Journal of Mental Deficiency, 1973(Jul), Vol. 78(1), 7-14. [PA, Vol 51:05949]

3274.   Pictures and the indefinite quantifier in verbal problem solving among EMR children.
Compared 2 groups of 36 educable mentally retarded children differentiated on the basis of MA (mean MA = 87.94 and 106.19 mo) for solving verbal arithmetic problems under various conditions. The problems were varied by the presence or absence of extraneous information and the use of an indefinite quantifier as opposed to numerals. All problems were accompanied by pictures. Both MA groups demonstrated significantly inferior performance on problems with extraneous information. However, the higher-MA group evidenced superior performance on problems with the indefinite quantifier and extraneous information than on problems with numerals and extraneous information. The possibility of using the indefinite quantifier for verbal problem-solving instruction is suggested.
Schenck, William E. (U. Connecticut) American Journal of Mental Deficiency, 1973(Nov), Vol. 78(3), 272-276. [PA, Vol 52:04085]

3275.   [Which pupils are offered special education in Denmark?] (Danh)
Compares the achievement of 142 pupils in Grades 5-10 from classrooms for educable mentally retarded or reading retardates with 138 6th graders and 139 7th graders in regular classrooms. Using the sentence silent-reading test, it is demonstrated that special class pupils may be characterized as slow readers; with some pupils possessing functional reading skills sufficient for regular classrooms if slowness in reading and behavior deviations were accepted. Oral and silent reading tests measure different aspects of the reading process. Special education in reading should be offered if the pupil is unable to follow regular teaching. When pupils are selected on basis of national norms the spirit of the previous statement is violated; bad teaching would be a dominant feature in this group.
Soegard, Arne. (Office of School Psychology, Lyngby-Taïk, Denmark) Skolepsykologi, 1973, Vol. 10(2), 94-107. [PA, Vol 51:05952]

3276.   Elaboration instruction and verbalization as factors facilitating retarded children's recall.
Compared 2 types of elaboration training (imagery and sentence elaboration) over 2 levels of verbalization (none and overt). 32 elementary, educable mentally retarded children were randomly assigned to 1 of the 4 elaboration treatment conditions of the resulting 2×2 factorial design. Results indicate that verbalization greatly influenced the degree of effectiveness of elaboration training. However, no support was found for the secondary hypothesis that overt verbalization would result in relatively greater facilitation with one type of elaboration (imagery) than with the other type (sentence elaboration). 2 sets of explanations are examined. In addition, educational applications of elaboration are discussed, with special attention given to the implications of the verbalization findings. (25 ref.)
Taylor, Arthur M.; Josberger, Marie & Whitely, Susan E. (U. Minnesota, Research & Development Center in Education of Handicapped Children) Journal of Educational Psychology, 1973(Jun), Vol. 64(3), 341-346. [PA, Vol 50:12117]

3277.   Special education at the crossroad: Class placement for the EMR.
Considers that class placement for educable mentally retarded children has created a controversy in the field of special education. Approaches justifying class placement, as reported by recent research, are outlined. Critical issues in the integration and/or segregation system are explored, as well as the application of guidelines to schools and other institutions serving educable mentally retarded children.
Taylor, George R. (Coppin State Coll.) Mental Retardation, 1973(Apr), Vol. 11(2), 30-33. [PA, Vol 51:01909]

3278.   Special-class placement and suggestibility of mentally retarded children.
Compared the suggestibility characteristics of educable mentally retarded (EMR) children with special class experience ($n = 30$) with those of EMR children who remained in the regular grades ($n = 30$). Both groups were found to be suggestible to some degree, but the regular grade EMR Ss were more so. Suggestibility is defined as the degree to which one is uncritically amenable to outside influence. It is noted that this study was conducted in a school setting and may not apply to EMR children in other situations. (16 ref)
Trippi, Joseph A. (State University Coll. New York, New Paltz) American Journal of Mental Deficiency, 1973(Sep), Vol. 78(2), 220-222. [PA, Vol 52:01880]

3279.   Verbal elaboration and the promotion of transfer of training in educable mentally retarded children.
Tested the ability of 23 educable retarded children (mean CA = 9 yr.) to transfer verbal elaboration techniques to a standard paired-associate task following 1, 2, or no elaboration experiences. An additional 18 Ss were tested in 2 outside control conditions which were used to identify the effects of reversal experience on acquisition and transfer. Since analyses revealed no differences in performance attributable to reversal experience, the 2 outside control conditions were combined with the appropriate experimental conditions for further statistical analyses. Relative to the performance of Ss not receiving elaboration experience, those receiving 1 elaboration experience showed little evidence of transfer while those receiving 2 experiences revealed quite clear transfer performance. The relevance of these findings to previous failures to find transfer and their implications for educational practice are discussed. (25 ref.)
Turnure, James E. & Thurlow, Martha L. (U. Minnesota) Journal of Experimental Child Psychology, 1973(Feb), Vol. 15(1), 137-148. [PA, Vol 50:10047]

3280.   The sociometric status of educable mentally retarded students in regular school classes.
Administered a sociometric test to 39 educable mentally retarded (EMR) students and their normal classmates in selected school districts in rural northern Idaho. The EMR students were in the regular class the entire day. There was an assumption that because of the togetherness of the EMR students with their

classmates that they would be socially accepted. EMR students were divided into two groups on the basis of IQ range: 45-65 and 66-80. It was found that EMR students tended to be rejected by their normal classmates. Normal students realize that EMR students are not functioning as normal students. Recommendations are made to develop a program to improve social acceptance.
Van Osdol, Bob M. & Johnson, Dale M. (U. Tulsa, Coll. of Education) Australian Journal of Mental Retardation, 1973(Sep), Vol. 2(7), 200-203. [PA, Vol 51:09955]

3281.   Language for mentally retarded deaf children: Project LIFE.
Reported the progress of mildly retarded children with severe or profound hearing impairment on hierarchical programed units provided by Project LIFE (Language Improvement to Facilitate Education). Ss (8-12 yrs old) were from the summer programs of a semiresidential school in a large midwestern city, and were chosen on the basis of a staff prediction of their success. One group of 5 Ss participated in the Perceptual Training Program, and another group of 5 Ss participated in both the Perceptual Training Program and the Thinking Activities Program. Both groups showed improvement from pre- to posttests provided for the programs by Project LIFE. No information is provided on any other outcomes of participation in the program(s). (21 ref.)
Vockell, Karen; Vockell, Edward L. & Mattick, Pamm. (Purdue U.) Volta Review, 1973(Oct), Vol. 75(7), 431-439. [PA, Vol 51:05954]

3282.   Attitudes of children toward their special class placement.
Conducted personal interviews with 369 8-17 yr old children in classes for the educable mentally retarded. Results show that (a) younger Ss had a more favorable attitude toward being in a special class, (b) less than 10% of all Ss viewed themselves as being "mentally retarded," and (c) Ss were capable of communicating their attitudes effectively.
Warner, Frank; Thrapp, Robert & Walsh, Suzanne. (California State U., San Francisco) Exceptional Children, 1973(Sep), Vol. 40(1), 37-38. [PA, Vol 51:05955]

3283.   Overt verbalization and the continued production of effective elaborations by EMR children.
Trained 40 junior high school educable mentally retarded (EMR) children to generate elaborations, but only 20 were required to verbalize their elaborations overtly on an initial paired-associate (PA) list. A 2nd PA list was administered in which 10 of the Ss, required to verbalize on the 1st list, were not permitted to verbalize their elaborations on a 2nd list; the remaining 10 Ss continued to verbalize. Initial PA list results replicated previous findings that Ss permitted to verbalize overtly recall significantly more than Ss forced to keep their elaboration activities covert. However, 2nd-list results reveal that Ss no longer permitted to verbalize maintained the same level of recall as those Ss who continued to verbalize their elaborations overtly. It is concluded that overt verbalization served to train EMR children to generate elaborations, but that it need not be maintained once training is completed. The relevance of these findings to classroom elaboration training is discussed. (21 ref)
Whitely, Susan E. & Taylor, Arthur M. (U. Minnesota, Measurement Service Center) American Journal of Mental Deficiency, 1973(Sep), Vol. 78(2), 193-198. [PA, Vol 52:01884]

3284.   The dimensional effects of instructional materials.
Taught 6 money concepts to 2 groups of educable mentally retarded public school students. For 50 Ss the teachers used only 2-dimensional materials; for 33 Ss only 3-dimensional materials. Learning performance was the same for both groups.
Whorton, James E. & Shaw, Leland G. (U. Florida) Journal of Special Education, 1973(Fal), Vol. 7(3), 251-260. [PA, Vol 52:04092]

3285.   [Transfer of motor skills in mentally retarded school children.] (Russ)
Determined the influence of 2 training methods on the transfer of motor skills in mentally retarded school children. Mildly

retarded 4th graders learned to assemble a metal model. The training of Group 1 consisted only of a preparatory demonstration. Group 2 Ss were given detailed explanations and recommendations as part of their preparatory demonstration and also while they were building their models. Half the Ss in each group assembled chairs and the other half assembled tables. When Ss had mastered the skill of assembling one model, they were shown a pattern of a 2nd model and were asked to assemble it without any assistance. Ss who had done a chair were given a table and vice versa. Group 2 Ss needed fewer repetitions and less time to master assembling their 2nd model. It is concluded that the type of training given to retardates does influence the transfer of motor skill.
Abdurasulov, D. A. (Academy of Pedagogical Sciences, Inst of Defektology, Moscow, USSR) Defektologiya, 1974, Vol 1(29-33), 151-155. [PA, Vol 56:04890]

3286.   Sensitivity and validity of learning-potential measurement in three levels of ability.
Hypothesized that learning-potential assessment is more sensitive than traditional IQ tests in tapping the intellectual potential of disadvantaged children. The Series Learning Potential Test (SLPT) was administered 3 times to 126 bright-normal, dull-to-average and subnormal 3rd, 4th, and 5th graders with training in problem-relevant strategies interpolated following the 2nd administration in Exp I. Both low-IQ groups gained more than the high-IQ group from the training, and the dull group gained more than the other groups from repeated administrations without training. In Exp II with 207 3rd graders, IQ was found to predict teacher ratings of school achievement for all groups and the SLPT was found to predict teacher ratings for the bright group; however, the SLPT was superior to IQ (Test of General Ability) as a predictor in the dull-to-average and the subnormal groups. Substantial proportions of subnormal Ss reached the average reasoning level of their nonretarded peers following the short training session.
Babad, Elisha Y. & Budoff, Milton. (Research Inst. for Educational Problems, Cambridge, Mass.) Journal of Educational Psychology, 1974(Jun), Vol. 66(3), 439-447. [PA, Vol 52:11054]

3287.   Social acceptance of mildly retarded pupils in resource rooms and regular classes.
Administered sociometric questionnaires to 1,234 nonretarded peers to determine the social acceptance of 65 mildly retarded children enrolled in regular classes and resource centers within urban and suburban school settings. When rated by peers of the same sex, mildly retarded urban Ss achieved significantly higher peer ratings than nonretarded Ss, whereas suburban mildly retarded Ss received significantly lower ratings than nonretarded Ss. However, no appreciable differences were obtained between retarded and nonretarded samples in level of peer acceptance in either setting when ratings of boys and girls were combined. Variations in personal characteristics and in value orientations of suburban and urban school children, as well as differences in methods of analyzing peer choices, are cited as possible explanations for differences between these results and those of previous reports. Implications are discussed for future research and educational practice involving the peer acceptance of retarded children in normalized school settings. (23 ref)
Bruininks, Robert H.; Rynders, John E. & Gross, Jerry C. (U. Minnesota) American Journal of Mental Deficiency, 1974(Jan), Vol. 78(4), 377-383. [PA, Vol 52:07997]

3288.   A closer look at labeling children who are mildly handicapped.
Reviews the labeling controversy in the field of special education and notes that many changes are being made in the makeup of public school programs serving the mildly handicapped child. The role of the regular class teacher is examined, and it is contended that the teacher's role is an important variable left out of much educational planning. It is concluded that regular class teachers have not been trained to manage individual differences in a class and that, in the case of borderline children, a

differentiation ought to be made between the need for special education and the need for remediation. (36 ref)
Childs, Ronald E. (Valdosta State Coll) Education & Training of the Mentally Retarded, 1974(Dec), Vol 9(4), 179-182. [PA, Vol 54:04183]

3289.   Classroom integration: Concerns & cautions.
Argues that special educators and school administrators should not make decisions regarding the integration of the mildly mentally handicapped child into the regular classroom without first assessing the needs and attitudes of the regular classroom teacher.
Doll, G. F. (U Calgary, Canada) Mental Retardation Bulletin, 1973-74, Vol 2(3), 108-111. [PA, Vol 58:06357]

3290.   Modification of conceptual impulsivity in retarded children.
105 educable mentally retarded (EMR) pupils in 9 primary-level classes who were found to be conceptually impulsive received 1 of 3 randomly assigned treatments: (a) visual discrimination training with extended teacher praise for correct responding, (b) visual discrimination training without extended verbal reinforcement, or (c) no specific intervention. Results using the class mean as the experimental unit support the prediction that impulsively responding young EMR pupils can be taught to delay responses and to make significantly fewer errors than similar pupils who receive no specific intervention. (27 ref)
Duckworth, Susanna V.; Ragland, Gilbert G.; Sommerfeld, Roy E. & Wyne, Marvin D. (Winthrop Coll) American Journal of Mental Deficiency, 1974(Jul), Vol 79(1), 59-63. [PA, Vol 53:01969]

3291.   Long-term effects of conservation training with educationally subnormal children.
22 nonconserving educationally subnormal–educable mentally retarded (EMR)–children (MA, 4 yrs 11 mo to 11 yrs 9 mo; CA, 8 yrs 7 mo to 14 yrs 2 mo) were divided into 3 groups matched for MA. Two groups received training in number and length, while the 3rd was a control. The learning set (LS) group was trained by a discrimination learning method, and the verbal rule (VR) group was trained with a verbal didactic method. VR group posttest scores were significantly superior to those of the LS and control groups. 16 mo later, posttests from 21 Ss showed that original differences were still apparent, but not significant. One retraining session was given to each S, using the original methods. A 3rd posttest disclosed that although all 3 groups showed improvement in conservation skills, the VR group was still superior to the LS and control groups. Nonconserving Ss remaining were given VR training. Their posttest scores were better than their past performance and were comparable to those of the VR group. It is concluded that (a) it is possible to train EMR children in conservation skills, and these skills can be retained over time; (b) although the LS method appears to offer advantage, its effects are not maintained; and (c) the VR method produces generalizability, transfer, and long-term retention.
Field, Dorothy. (U London Inst of Education, Dept of Child Development, England) Journal of Special Education, 1974(Fal), Vol 8(3), 237-245. [PA, Vol 56:04903]

3292.   Regular-class adjustment of EMR students attending a part-time special education program.
Investigated the effect of a part-time special education program in promoting the personal and social development of elementary educable mentally retarded (EMR) students in the regular class. 122 teachers used a descriptive scale to rate 61 normal students in regular classes, 61 EMR students attending regular class part-time as well as a part-time special education program, and 61 students in regular class who were eligible for EMR class but put on the waiting list pending placement. The normal students were rated significantly higher than both EMR groups. No difference was found between the ratings of EMR special-class and EMR waiting-list students. (16 ref)
Flynn, Timothy M. (Southern Illinois U) Journal of Special Education, 1974(Sum), Vol 8(2), 167-173. [PA, Vol 53:01970]

3293.   Attitudes of Norwegian and American children toward mildly retarded children in special classes.
Investigated the attitudes of 285 Norwegian and 231 American 10-14 yr olds toward educable mentally retarded (EMR) children. It was hypothesized that Norwegian Ss would express more favorable attitudes than would the American Ss because they have more opportunity for social interaction with EMR children and because Norwegian EMR children are less deviant than American EMRs. Data indicate that American Ss reported significantly more favorable attitudes than did Norwegian Ss, contrary to the prediction. Findings are discussed in terms of the effects of social contact on attitudes toward the retarded, perceptions toward EMRs in relation to perceived deviance, and methodological difficulties in cross-national sampling techniques.
Gottlieb, Jay. (Research Inst for Educational Problems, Cambridge, MA) Journal of Special Education, 1974(Win), Vol 8(4), 313-319. [PA, Vol 56:04850]

3294.   Social contact and personal adjustment as variables relating to attitudes toward EMR children.
Studied the attitudes of 284 intellectually average 3rd-6th graders toward educable mentally retarded (EMR) pupils, and replicated the study 4 mo later in schools serving and not serving EMR pupils ($n = 114$ and 101 3rd and 4th graders, respectively). Both sets of findings indicate that attitudes toward EMR pupils were most favorable when the raters had little school contact with the EMR children. The 2nd purpose of the study was to test the prediction that well adjusted nonEMR pupils would express more favorable attitudes than poorly adjusted children. Results did not support this prediction. Results are discussed in terms of the difficulties of the contact hypothesis to predict attitudes toward retarded persons.
Gottlieb, Jay; Cohen, Lenore & Goldstein, Laurie. (Research Inst for Educational Problems, Cambridge, MA) Training School Bulletin, 1974(May), Vol 71(1), 9-16. [PA, Vol 53:01972]

3295.   Scouting for the retarded: A potential school curriculum.
Proposes a curriculum for the retarded educable 11-15 yr old student based on the regular program of the Boy Scouts of America. The program has all the elements desirable as an educational program for the adolescent retarded, including involvement of home and community, group activities, individual reinforcers, and individual instruction.
Gourley, Theodore J. (Woodstown-Pilesgrove Regional School District, NJ) Education & Training of the Mentally Retarded, 1974(Dec), Vol 9(4), 191-193. [PA, Vol 54:04190]

3296.   Sociometric status of retarded children in an integrative program.
Determined the sociometric status in elementary school regular classes of 40 former special class educable mentally retarded children who had participated in an integrative resource room program. The educable Ss were no better accepted in regular classes than were educable children in previous studies for whom such supportive resource room services had not been made available. However, considerable overlap in sociometric acceptances and rejections were found between the educable Ss and other pupils in the regular classes. (19 ref)
Iano, Richard P., et al. (Temple U.) Exceptional Children, 1974(Jan), Vol. 40(4), 267-271. [PA, Vol 52:01869]

3297.   Academic performance of mentally handicapped children as a function of token economies and contingency contracts.
Investigated the effects of several incentive systems on the reading and arithmetic performances of 12 6-11 yr old educable mentally retarded children. Normal (nonsystematic) classroom management was compared with a token economy plus superimposed contracts over an 8-wk period. Both reversal and multiple baseline designs were employed. Results show that reading and arithmetic performances were highest when the token economy was combined with a superimposed contract. Performance was lowest when neither the token economy nor the combination of tokens and contracts were in effect.

Jenkins, Joseph R. & Gorrafa, Sheila. (U Illinois) Education & Training of the Mentally Retarded, 1974(Dec), Vol 9(4), 183-186. [PA, Vol 54:04194]

3298.   Student views of special placement and their own special classes: A clarification.
Administered a school morale inventory by L. Wrightman et al to 341 junior high school mental retardates and 717 nonretarded students, to study the school attitudes of the students and to contrast the attitudinal findings with earlier data on stigma reported by teachers and by mental retardates. Results reveal as many positive responses were given by special class students to various questions as were given by the nonretarded group. Since other investigations indicate overwhelmingly that retarded students reject special class placement, it is suggested that retarded students reject the stigma of special placement but hold many positive attitudes toward their classroom and school experiences. An analysis of responses from 114 suburban mental retardates and 227 inner-city retardates reveals more positive attitudes held by the suburban retarded. It is suggested that retarded students cannot be considered a homogeneous group and that the educational problems of the inner-city retardates are particularly acute.
Jones, Reginald L. (U California, Berkeley) Exceptional Children, 1974(Sep), Vol 41(1), 22-29. [PA, Vol 53:06209]

3299.   Effects of group reinforcement and punishment on classroom behavior.
Used group token reinforcement and punishment procedures to alter appropriate behaviors in a class of educably retarded students. Baseline observations were made to determine the rate with which 6 11-12 yr old students were performing appropriate behaviors. A group token program was implemented where students could earn points if the entire class was paying attention when a timer sounded at various time intervals. Points earned could be exchanged at the end of each day for a special event. This program was removed and points were given to the group independent of performance. In the final phase a punishment procedure was used in which points were given at the beginning of the class session and withdrawn from the group if anyone was not attending when the timer sounded. Results show that appropriate behaviors increased over baseline during the reinforcement and punishment phases. Performance tended to decline when the tokens were delivered without requiring appropriate behavior. Practical advantages of group procedures are discussed. (19 ref)
Kazdin, Alan E. & Forsberg, Sara. (Pennsylvania State U) Education & Training of the Mentally Retarded, 1974(Apr), Vol 9(2), 50-55. [PA, Vol 53:10521]

3300.   Increasing response frequency with a token economy: An experimental analysis.
Educable mentally retarded children in an intermediate level special education classroom (mean IQ = 68.3) performed academic mathematics tasks in several types of token economies. Contingent tokens produced significantly higher response rates than noncontingent tokens. Group contingent tokens were as effective in maintaining high response as were individual contingent tokens. Delay of reward from a daily to a weekly basis had no detrimental effect on response rate.
Krug, David A. (Portland State U) Improving Human Performance, 1974(Fal), Vol 3(3), 128-136. [PA, Vol 54:04196]

3301.   What parents can do to help their special preschoolers.
Provides educational activity recommendations for parents of special preschoolers with learning disabilities, language lags, and mild mental retardation. Suggestions are divided into areas of visual-motor, language, and cognitive development.
Lowenthal, Barbara. Academic Therapy, 1974(Win), Vol 10(2), 181-185. [PA, Vol 54:07901]

3302.   A comparison of two methods of improving prose comprehension in educationally subnormal children.
Conducted a study of 100 educationally subnormal 9-16 yr olds to compare 2 methods of facilitating Ss' aural reception. Under the 1st method, an attempt was made to improve Ss' listening

comprehension by providing images of the concepts in prose detail to facilitate recoding; the 2nd method decreased the rate of presentation to allow more time for Ss to analyze and store the material. Both methods produced similar significant improvements in recall performance. Ways of studying the recoding performance of educationally subnormal children to provide information to enable further improvement in reception are examined. (15 ref)
Riding, R. J. & Shore, J. M. (U Birmingham, School of Education, England) British Journal of Educational Psychology, 1974(Nov), Vol 44(3), 300-303. [PA, Vol 53:10533]

3303.   Social acceptance of EMR adolescents in integrated programs.
Randomly assigned 400 nonretarded 9th-grade students from 3 suburban junior high schools to experimental and control groups of equal size. In the experimental condition, nonretarded children and 30 educable mentally retarded (EMR) adolescents from the special classes in each school were integrated in nonacademic classes, clubs, and social and athletic activities. Control groups were not integrated. An acceptance scale was devised and administered to all Ss at midyear. A 3-way analysis of variance revealed that the experimental groups consistently gave more positive ratings to EMR adolescents than did the control groups and that female Ss gave more positive ratings than males in all groups. (16 ref)
Sheare, Joseph B. (Pennsylvania State U.) American Journal of Mental Deficiency, 1974(May), Vol. 78(6), 678-682. [PA, Vol 52:08691]

3304.   Elimination of subtraction errors by contingent self-correction in retarded children.
3 institutionalized educable mentally retarded children who added subtraction problems served as Ss. 4 experimental conditions were used in conjunction with a combination of a multiple baseline and reversal design. Identification of the type of error and reduction of subtraction errors was observed as a result of a contingent self-correction procedure.
Smeets, Paul M. & Striefel, Sebastian. (California School for the Deaf, Riverside) Journal of Psychology, 1974(Mar), Vol. 86(2), 269-275. [PA, Vol 52:13232]

3305.   Statistical realities of special-class distributions.
Examined the informational value contained in the 1st 2 moments (mean and standard deviation-SD) of special-class distributions. A canonical correlation model applied to data on 36 primary level, EMR classrooms to determine whether classroom means and SDs on a criterion variable were predictable from classroom means and SDs on input measures confirmed the independent information contained in these 2 classroom descriptors. (28 ref)
Smith, I. Leon. (Yeshiva U., Curriculum Research & Development Center in Mental Retardation) American Journal of Mental Deficiency, 1974(May), Vol. 78(6), 740-747. [PA, Vol 52:08693]

3306.   Acceptance of responsibility for school work by educationally subnormal boys.
Tested the hypothesis that mentally retarded children educated in an informal school offering opportunities to choose and to experience the outcome of choice, in a supportive atmosphere, would be able to accept more responsibility for their own successes and failures in school. Increased awareness of the relationship between personal striving and outcome was expected to result in higher attainment scores on a measure of reading ability. 2 groups of 20 boys, matched for age and home background, were chosen to represent the extremes on a formal-informal dimension. Ss were tested by a group reading assessment and on the Intellectual Achievement Questionnaire. Greater acceptance of responsibility for academic achievement was found in informal school Ss, who also scored significantly higher on the reading test. Comparison on measures of locus of control and reading ability supported both hypotheses.
Wooster, Arthur D. (U Nottingham, School of Education, England) British Journal of Mental Subnormality, 1974(Jun), Vol 20(38, Pt 1), 23-27. [PA, Vol 53:06229]

3307.   Placement of Black and White children in educable mentally handicapped classes and learning disability classes.
Data from the WISC and WAIS scores (used for placement) of 107 educable mentally handicapped students and 73 learning disabled students in middle and high schools suggest that there is a trend toward increased placement in learning disability classes of Blacks with learning problems. Findings on the overall and separate racial composition of each placement category are also presented.
Burke, Arlene A. (School District 162, Huth Upper Grade Ctr, Matteson, IL) Exceptional Children, 1975(Mar), Vol 41(6), 438-439. [PA, Vol 54:04181]

3308.   An evaluation of the Peabody Individual Achievement Test with primary age retarded children.
Studied the convergent and discriminant validity of the Peabody Individual Achievement Test (PIAT) with primary aged children who were classified educable mentally retarded. Ss were 55 children who were given the PIAT, Wide Range Achievement Test, and the Peabody Picture Vocabulary Test. Convergent validity was found for PIAT mathematics, reading, recognition, and spelling subtests. Discriminant validity was not found for the PIAT mathematics and spelling subtests.
Burns, Edward. (Ohio U) Psychology in the Schools, 1975(Jan), Vol 12(1), 11-14. [PA, Vol 54:10630]

3309.   Positive reinforcers for modification of auditory processing skills in LD and EMR children.
Reports results of a study indicating that double reinforcement (token reinforcement and teacher enrichment) brought about increased development of auditory skills in a group of Ss using Science Research Associates Listening Skills Level IIA Tapes. Observations made during the limited 3-group comparison study are recounted.
Bussell, Carol; Huls, Beth & Long, Linda. (Eisenhower Elementary School, Lake Park, FL) Journal of Learning Disabilities, 1975(Jun-Jul), Vol 8(6), 373-376. [PA, Vol 54:10613]

3310.   Intelligence and reading achievement of EMR children in three educational settings.
Reports on a study with retarded 3rd graders in regular, segregated self-contained, and Plan A "mainstream" classes. Results indicate that there was no evidence to support differences in reading achievement among the 3 systems, although Plan A provided considerable supportive resources.
Carter, John L. (U Houston) Mental Retardation, 1975(Oct), Vol 13(5), 26-27. [PA, Vol 55:05642]

3311.   Auditory discrimination and training effects for educable retarded children.
Conducted an investigation in 2 parts: Part 1 utilized 90 retarded 7-17 yr olds to determine the relationship between mental age, IQ, and auditory discrimination; Part 2 focused on effects of training to enhance discrimination. From the original 90 Ss, 32 were randomly selected and placed in a program; the remaining Ss were used as controls. It was found that auditory discrimination was directly related to mental maturity, but could be enhanced.
Carter, John L. (U Houston) Education & Training of the Mentally Retarded, 1975(Apr), Vol 10(2), 94-95. [PA, Vol 54:07884]

3312.   A classroom program teaching disadvantaged youths to write biographic information.
Little attention has been given to how formal classroom instruction can be adapted to teach youths everyday skills, such as the correct writing of biographic information frequently requested in transactions like applying for a job or a social security number and cashing a check. In this study, 6 delinquents or mildly retarded 14-16 yr olds in a special education classroom were taught to complete job application forms with the date, their name, signature, address, telephone number, date of birth, and a reference's name, address, and occupation. Each S was trained on 1 item of biographic information at a time, after which he was tested on 4 application forms, including 1 on which he had not been trained. The tests showed that after an item had been taught, it was correctly used in completing application forms on which the Ss had been trained and forms on which they had never been trained. Results demonstrate the feasibility of teaching community-living, vocation-related skills to special education youths in a classroom setting. (24 ref)
Clark, Hewitt B.; Boyd, Sandra B. & Macrae, John W. (Johnny Cake Child Study Ctr, Mansfield, AR) Journal of Applied Behavior Analysis, 1975(Spr), Vol 8(1), 67-75. [PA, Vol 54:04184]

3313.   The efficacy of a social learning curriculum with borderline mentally retarded children.
A social learning curriculum based on Function III of H. Goldstein's (1964) curriculum for the educable mentally retarded was tested for its effectiveness in an urban setting. The Adaptive Behaviour Scale (Part I), the Vineland Social Maturity Scale, the Primary Assessment Chart of Social Development, and a specially devised Checklist were used to contrast the attainments of 12 educable mentally retarded Ss (CA, 6-12 yrs) utilized a social learning curriculum and matched controls who worked with a language skills program. Multivariate analyses of covariance, with pretest social maturity measures as covariates, revealed no significant differences between adjusted posttest criterion means after an 18-wk experimental period. The univariate tests were consistent with the multivariate analyses. (15 ref)
Cole, P. G. (U Western Australia, Nedlands) Australian Journal of Mental Retardation, 1975(Sep), Vol 3(7), 191-199. [PA, Vol 56:01470]

3314.   Intelligence, creativity, and performance abilities of EMR pupils.
Administered Figural Form A of the Torrance Tests of Creative Thinking and the WISC to 217 6-12 yr old children in classes for the educable mentally retarded (EMR). The Young Educable Mentally Retarded Performance Profile was completed by each child's teacher. Results show that creativity is as important as intelligence, or more so, in determining their rated performance scores. Implications for educational programs for EMR pupils are discussed.
Cooper, Joel B. & Richmond, Bert O.   Psychology in the Schools, 1975(Jul), Vol 12(3), 304-309. [PA, Vol 54:10614]

3315.   [Contribution to the study of adolescents with minimal intellectual deficit.] (Fren)
Compared 36 normal adolescent male students 17-18 yrs old with a similar sample of adolescent male students with minimal intellectual deficit attending a special school. Comparisons between and within the 2 groups were based on data which included (a) scores on the WISC or Wechsler-Bellevue Intelligence Scale, (b) sociocultural information, and (c) questionnaire responses of instructors regarding Ss' performances and attitudes. Results prove that a wide variety of mental conditions are subsumed under the concept of "mental deficiency."
Dégréaux, A. & Dégréaux, M.   Bulletin de Psychologie, 1974-75, Vol 28(1-6), 118-144. [PA, Vol 54:12599]

3316.   Increasing on-task behavior of a retarded boy: Contingent use of tokens and teacher attention.
Used tokens and time-outs to control the disruptive behavior of an 8-yr-old boy in a public school class for the trainable retarded. The phases of the study included (a) a baseline period; (b) a token phase, during which praise accompanied by tokens and other students received attention during undesirable behavior by the S; and (c) a token time-out phase for disruptive behavior. The data show that both the teachers' and the S's behavior changed through simple contingency management in a token economy framework. It is emphasized that interventions should be economical and that procedures to control disruptive behavior should focus upon social contingencies.
Feindler, Eva L.; Taylor, Cindra & Wilhelm, Patricia. (West Virginia U) SALT: School Applications of Learning Theory, 1975(Oct), Vol 8(1), 10-26. [PA, Vol 58:04372]

3317. Classroom behavior of retarded children before and after integration into regular classes.
Compared the classroom behavior of 11 segregated and 11 integrated educable mentally retarded (EMR) children (aged, 8-11 yrs) on a 12-category observation schedule at 3 times: (a) when all EMR Ss were in special classes, (b) 4 mo after some Ss had been integrated, and (c) at the conclusion of an academic year. Results indicate that integrated Ss differed from segregated ones on a factor that included prosocial behavior, with the integrated group exhibiting more of these behaviors. A comparison of Ss behavior with that of their normal classmates indicated that the integrated EMRs displayed more prosocial and verbally aggressive behaviors and fewer physically aggressive behaviors than the normal children.
Gottlieb, Jay; Gampel, Dorothy H. & Budoff, Milton. (Research Inst for Educational Problems, Cambridge, MA) Journal of Special Education, 1975(Fal), Vol 9(3), 307-315. [PA, Vol 56:04908]

3318. Reading comprehension skills vis-á-vis the mentally retarded.
Conducted a comprehensive review of the literature concerning reading comprehension skills of educable mentally retarded (EMR) children. From about 75 pieces of literature yielded by the search, 6 provided embryonic answers to 3 guiding questions concerning (a) which comprehensive skills should to taught to mentally retarded children, (b) the age or level at which these skills should be taught, and (c) the hierarchy of these skills. What the literature says in answer to these questions is discussed, and other questions are posed. It is concluded that there is a surprising dearth of specificity in research relative to reading comprehension skills for the EMR.
Hurley, Oliver L. (U Georgia, Coll of Education, Div for Exceptional Children) Education & Training of the Mentally Retarded, 1975(Feb), Vol 10(1), 10-14. [PA, Vol 54:03431]

3319. Programming response maintenance after withdrawing token reinforcement.
Evaluated a strategy designed to maintain behavior after withdrawing a token reinforcement program. In a special education classroom, 4 6-8 yr old educable retarded children received token reinforcement for attentive classroom behavior throughout the day. Using a multiple-baseline design across morning and afternoon class sessions, the following phases were presented: Baseline, Token Reinforcement, Tokens plus Peer Praise and Delayed Reinforcement, and Teacher and Peer Praise with a Group Contingency. Phases after the initial token program were designed to gradually fade tokens and substitute "natural" reinforcers (peer praise and activities available in the setting) without a loss of behavior gains. In the last phase, tokens were no longer used in the classroom. 2 follow-up phases, conducted 2 and 9 wks after all contingencies had been withdrawn, showed that inappropriate behavior had been maintained at the low levels achieved during the initial program. Data at the end of the last follow-up phase (approximately 12 wks after any contingency had been in effect) failed to show recovery of inappropriate behavior. (37 ref)
Jones, Russell T. & Kazdin, Alan E. (Pennsylvania State U) Behavior Therapy, 1975(Mar), Vol 6(2), 153-164. [PA, Vol 54:01946]

3320. Standardization of a public school version of the AAMD Adaptive Behavior Scale.
Notes that the California State Department of Education has supported the standardization of a public school version of the American Association on Mental Deficiency's Adaptive Behavior Scale as an appropriate measure of adaptive behavior for children being considered for educable mentally retarded (EMR) classes and other special education programs. The public school version has been approved by the California State Board of Education for use in California schools. The present article describes the research carried out to attain standardization: the work of a multi-ethnic advisory board; the cooperation of selected school districts; a pilot study of 60 3rd and 4th graders of regular, EMR, and educationally handicapped classes; data analysis; and results.
Lambert, Nadine M.; Windmiller, Myra; Cole, Linda & Figueroa, Richard A. (U California, Berkeley) Mental Retardation, 1975(Apr), Vol 13(2), 3-7. [PA, Vol 54:06338]

3321. Locus of control: Implications for special education.
Reviews the definition and measurement of locus of control, emphasizing that although there has been much research on this concept in both education and psychology, it has had little impact on current trends in special education. The possible effect of locus of control on the mainstreaming of mildly retarded children is described, and the relationship of locus of control to achievement and the promotion of internality in children are discussed. Implications for classroom implementation and further research are suggested. (34 ref)
Lawrence, Elizabeth A. & Winschel, James F. (Western Michigan U) Exceptional Children, 1975(Apr), Vol 41(7), 483-490. [PA, Vol 54:04199]

3322. Cognitive skills underlying an inductive problem-solving strategy.
Examined the cognitive skills underlying an inductive problem solving method which has been used to develop critical reasoning skills in a major curriculum program for educable mentally retarded (EMR) children. A total of 112 EMR Ss were given 2 broadly-based measures of cognitive ability (the Social Learning Curriculum Survey Test survey and the Cognitive Abilities Test) and a hierarchically-ordered measure of inductive problem solving (Children's Analysis of Social Situations-CASS). Canonical correlation and multivariate regression analysis revealed 3 factors, Detailing, Inferring, and Generalizing, underlying the inductive process defined by CASS. The cognitive skills represented by these factors are elaborated upon in terms of a defined hierarchy, and implications for curriculum development are discussed. (19 ref)
Lehrer, Barry & Schimoler, Gregory. (Yeshiva U) Journal of Experimental Education, 1975(Spr), Vol 43(3), 13-21. [PA, Vol 54:12607]

3323. Phonological pairing as a reading aid for retarded children.
Exposed 33 educable mentally retarded children (CA, 8 yrs 3 mo to 10 yrs 9 mo; IQ, 51–75) to 1 of 3 modes of word presentation: (a) phonologically paired words in the content-function order, (b) phonologically paired words in the function-content order, and (c) serial list with words randomly assigned. Results indicate that the Ss' demonstrated learning performance was significantly enhanced by phonological pairing of words, with the content-function word order being superior to the function-content word order. It is concluded that the incorporation of new words into the educable mentally retarded child's reading vocabulary can be enhanced by the phonological pairing of content and function words. (18 ref)
Miller, Brenda B. (Indiana U Developmental Training Ctr, Bloomington) Journal of Reading Behavior, 1975(Sum), Vol 7(2), 181-186. [PA, Vol 57:06932]

3324. Functional similarities of learning disability and mild retardation.
Discusses descriptions of educable mentally retarded and learning disabled children as they relate to similarities and differences in assumed cause and educationally relevant problems. The terms "genotype" and "phenotype" are presented to conceptualize the distinction between underlying condition and objectively assessed psychoeducational repertoire. The argument is made that real or assumed differences in the underlying conditions of the educable mentally retarded and learning disabled are somewhat irrelevant to the analysis and design of instructional programs. A tentative schema is provided that illustrates appreciable overlap of the educable retardation and learning disability classifications with respect to instructional objectives and instructional intervention. (18 ref)

Neisworth, John T. & Greer, John G. (Pennsylvania State U, Coll of Human Development) Exceptional Children, 1975(Sep), Vol 42(1), 17-21. [PA, Vol 55:05658]

3325. The assessment class: An organizational approach to assist the development of exceptional children within a regular school system.
Reviews the development in New Zealand of a class for the assessment of educable mentally retarded 5–7 yr old children. This class is intended to determine the most appropriate educational placements for 5 to 10 children while providing them with a stimulating environment in which to work. The need for such a class is discussed, and various facets of its operation—including equipment, staffing, transportation, and support services—are described. Advantages consist of early intervention, deferment in labeling, low staff–pupil ratio, and increased contact with parents. Difficulties encountered have been a shortage of suitably trained personnel, inadequate support services, and lack of objective evaluation. Downward and upward extensions of the assessment concept are expected, and it is predicted that assessment classes will become the main special education facility in New Zealand.
Page, David G. (Dept of Education, Palmerston North, New Zealand) Exceptional Child, 1975(Nov), Vol 22(3), 131–142. [PA, Vol 59:11152]

3326. An analysis of placement factors in classes for the educable mentally retarded.
Examined the policies and practices of the placement of children in classes for the educable mentally retarded (EMR) and attempted to determine the extent to which children are misplaced in these classes. Data were collected on 7,427 children in primary and intermediate EMR classes in Virginia public schools. It was found that (a) on a statewide basis, there were more Blacks than Whites enrolled in EMR classes, even though Whites constituted a decided majority of the total population in the state; (b) there was a high percentage of males enrolled in EMR classes; (c) a majority of children came from low socioeconomic environments; and (d) some special classes for the EMR had become places for assignment of children with a variety of handicapping and nonhandicapping conditions. Recommendations for the placement of EMR children are presented.
Prillaman, Douglas. (Coll of William & Mary) Exceptional Children, 1975(Oct), Vol 42(2), 107-108. [PA, Vol 55:10991]

3327. The experimental validation of a graded word list by EMR children.
A published graded word list was read by 137 educable mentally retarded intermediate, junior high, and senior high students (mean mental age, 123 mo) in 4 towns. Results indicate that sex, school level, and word list grade level, as well as the interaction of these factors, affected the student's reading ability. Thus, the relative readability of the words at the designated graded levels was experimentally validated. Implications for the use of such a list in evaluation and teaching are discussed.
Ramanauskas, Sigita & Kahn, Harris. (U Connecticut) Mental Retardation, 1975(Apr), Vol 13(2), 27-31. [PA, Vol 54:06344]

3328. Categorization of material following transfer from serial to free recall lists with EMRs.
Serial-trained 18 educable mental retardates who had Stanford-Binet scores ranging from 63-81, a mean IQ of 75.05, and a mental age of 8.0 yrs. A 12-item, 3-category list was used. The number of sequential occurrences of items from the same category was compared with the number of category repetitions that would be expected by chance as determined by computer simulation of 2,000 trials. Results show Ss had a combined total of 69 repetitions of categories during free recall, which was significantly greater than expected by chance ($p < .0001$). Ss also placed new items next to old items from the same categories more frequently than would be expected by chance. It is concluded that training a child on a serial task requiring little conceptual ability can accelerate his performance on a higher-level organization task.

Sitton, Sarah C. (Southeast Missouri State U) Mental Retardation, 1975(Feb), Vol 13(1), 28-29. [PA, Vol 54:04216]

3329. Social participation and special class attendance in mildly-retarded children.
Results of a study with a total of 50 normal and mildly retarded children indicate that the assumption that placement of mildly retarded children in special classes is more beneficial to such children than is their retention in regular classes may not be well founded and that admission to a special class may actually inhibit rather than facilitate a young mildly retarded child's social adjustment.
Smart, Rosemary F. & Wilton, Keri M. (U Canterbury, Christchurch, New Zealand) New Zealand Journal of Educational Studies, 1975(May), Vol 10(1), 66-74. [PA, Vol 55:03219]

3330. [Theoretical and methodological problems connected with research into difficulties of reading and writing instruction of mildly retarded children.] (Polh)
Reviews various methods of diagnosing retardation and their relationship to theory. The teaching of retarded children in Poland is described.
Szurek, Ewa. (U Warsaw Inst of Psychology, Poland) Psychologia Wychowawcza, 1975, Vol 18(2), 193–201. [PA, Vol 60:08323]

3331. Training cognitive strategies in the mildly retarded: An applied approach.
Compared the effects of verbal and imaginal mediation strategies on the paired-associate learning of educable mentally retarded preadolescent and adolescent Ss, who were divided into 3 matched experimental groups and a control group. Results indicate that the strategy-supplied Ss performed significantly better than the controls. There was little indication of carry-over of training by the experimental groups on a subsequent paired-associate task. Results and possible solutions for shortcomings are discussed. (17 ref)
Wambold, Clark L. & Hayden, Cathy. (U Wisconsin, Waisman Ctr on Mental Retardation & Human Development, Madison) Education & Training of the Mentally Retarded, 1975(Oct), Vol 10(3), 132-137. [PA, Vol 55:07410]

3332. Improving locus of control through direct instruction: A pilot study.
Conducted a study with 13 experimental and 14 control 9-12 yr old educable mentally retarded children to determine whether retardates could learn adaptive behavioral responses and an awareness of the consequences of behavior as a result of a sequential instructional program. Teaching techniques for 12 consecutive wks included role playing, pictorial representations of inappropriate behaviors, and follow-up group discussions. Praise and social reinforcers were used to increase incentive for group participation. Results show that on each of the dependent measures, the mean scores of the experimental group were significantly better than the control. (18 ref)
Wicker, Patricia L. & Tyler, J. Larry. (Hinds County Schools, Jackson, MS) Education & Training of the Mentally Retarded, 1975(Feb), Vol 10(1), 15-18. [PA, Vol 54:03451]

3333. Intentionality judgement and adaptive behaviour in mildly retarded children.
Studied the relationship between ability to take account of intention and social adaptation in mildly retarded children. Ss were 10 males and 10 females attending primary school special classes (SC) and 10 males and 10 females attending regular classes (RC), all of whom had scored in the 50–75 IQ range and were 117–127 mo old. A total adjustment score for each S was derived from ratings on the Adaptive Behavior Scales, Part II. Intentionality scores were derived from responses to modified versions of 7 pairs of simple stories taken from P. M. Crowley's scale (1968). As expected, the SC Ss were significantly more maladjusted than the RC Ss, with males more maladjusted than females. Results further indicate that the SC Ss took account of intentionality significantly less often than the RC Ss. The correlation between social adjustment and level of intentionality judgments, however, was not significant. It is concluded that the

2 variables appear to have an important but complex relationship in mildly retarded children.

Wilson, Clive; Wilton, Keri & McGeorge, Colin. (U Canterbury, Christchurch, New Zealand) Slow Learning Child, 1975(Mar), Vol 22(1), 5–12. [PA, Vol 59:08864]

3334. Current provisions and research needs in the education of mildly retarded children in New Zealand.
Describes existing special educational facilities for mildly retarded children in New Zealand, and outlines some problems which need to be solved if these facilities are to adequately meet the needs of these children. Programs related to the integration of the children and the provision of work experience for them are outlined, along with teacher training and advisory services and specific research projects that should be conducted.
Wilton, Keri M. (U Canterbury, Christchurch, New Zealand) Australian Journal of Mental Retardation, 1975(Jun), Vol 3(6), 149-151. [PA, Vol 55:01544]

3335. A pilot program for language development in the educable adolescent.
Describes goals and methodologies of a 2-yr program involving 14 15-18 yr old educable mentally retarded boys. Although school staff felt that the Ss developed a greater facility with language, the need for developing objective measures in these areas is noted.
Alson, Leila B. & Swidler, Arleen G. (West Chester State Coll, Speech & Hearing Clinic) Language, Speech, & Hearing Services in Schools, 1976(Apr), Vol 7(2), 102-105. [PA, Vol 58:10505]

3336. Role and the teacher of educable mentally retarded elementary children.
Examined the "position" of the teacher of educable mentally retarded elementary school children. Expectations held by 34 teachers and by 30 principals for 4 roles within that position are described to identify those specific teacher functions considered appropriate or inappropriate by the 2 role-defining groups. Relatively strong agreement in terms of teacher-principal expectations existed for 22 of 52 role norm statements. The 4 roles described are administration and organization, curriculum and instruction, guidance and evaluation, and school-community relations.
Anderson, Richard D. (North Slope Borough School District, Barrow, AK) Journal of Special Education, 1976(Win), Vol 10(4), 383-391. [PA, Vol 57:13583]

3337. Cognitive processes and academic achievement in EMR adolescents.
12 cognitive process variables, including memory and oddity discrimination, were investigated as predictors of Reading and Arithmetic test performance on the Wide Range Achievement Test and were studied for internal structure by means of stepwise regression and factor analyses, respectively. In 115 educable mentally retarded adolescents (mean CA, 177.86 mo), memory variables were the most important predictors of reading and were also involved in arithmetic but to a lesser extent. The data suggest that the ability to generate and utilize strategies facilitating the recall of unstructured material as well as the capacity to be sensitive to strategy-relevant structure embedded in stimuli are important prerequisites for the development of decoding skills required in beginning reading. An oddity task, measuring the ability to maintain the same relational focus for successive applications to new stimulus material, was most pertinent for predicting arithmetic computational skills. It is concluded that cognitive processes are related to or predictive of reading and arithmetic achievement. (26 ref)
Blackman, Leonard S.; Bilsky, Linda H.; Burger, Agnes L. & Mar, Harvey. (Teachers Coll, Columbia U) American Journal of Mental Deficiency, 1976(Sep), Vol 81(2), 125-134. [PA, Vol 57:06917]

3338. Eye movements and conservation acceleration in mildly retarded children.
30 mildly retarded elementary-school children, 15 of whom had received perceptual/attentional training, were tested on 4 Piagetian conservation tasks (number, length, and continuous quantity solid/liquid) presented on 16 mm movie film with taped instructions. Eye movements were recorded during the response period for each task. Subsequent analyses of eye-movement patterns showed clear differences between the training and control groups. Trained conservers showed more visual exploratory activity and less perceptual centration than control group Ss. Moreover, the eye-movement patterns of trained conservers closely approximated those shown by natural (i.e., untrained) retarded conservers in a previous study. Findings are discussed in terms of possible cognitive structural changes resulting from training and possible cognitive structural differences between mildly retarded and nonretarded children. (20 ref)
Boersma, Frederic J. & Wilton, Keri M. (U Alberta, Edmonton, Canada) American Journal of Mental Deficiency, 1976(May), Vol 80(6), 636–643. [PA, Vol 56:04895]

3339. Effectiveness of a learning potential procedure in improving problem-solving skills of retarded and nonretarded children.
Determined the effectiveness of learning potential training on improving children's problem-solving skills on Raven's Coloured Progressive Matrices. 379 nonretarded 6-11 yr old and 174 educable mentally retarded 5.5-14 yr old students were pretested, randomly assigned to trained or nontrained groups, and posttested. Analyses of variance on factor scores derived from a varimax rotation of item responses revealed that learning potential training was effective in increasing the ability to reason by analogy of both retarded and nonretarded children. The learning potential procedure provided learning experiences related to reasoning skills that may not have been previously acquired in school.
Budoff, Milton & Corman, Louise. (Research Inst for Educational Problems, Cambridge, MA) American Journal of Mental Deficiency, 1976(Nov), Vol 81(3), 260-264. [PA, Vol 58:04365]

3340. Special-class EMR children mainstreamed: A study of an aptitude (learning potential) × treatment interaction.
Compared academic, personal, and social growth for 31 special-class educable mentally retarded 93-168 mo olds who were assigned randomly to regular grades or retained in special classes at 3 time intervals: prior to the assignment, 2 mo after assignment, and at the end of the school year. There were no significant differences between the 2 groups prior to or 2 mo after reintegration. After 1 school year, reintegrated Ss were more internally controlled, had more positive attitudes toward school, and were more reflective in their behavior. Results support the hypothesis that the more able students by the learning potential criterion would benefit more from regular than special-class placement. These Ss expressed more positive feelings toward themselves as students, felt others perceived them as more competent, and behaved more reflectively when they were integrated. The high-able (learning potential) Ss performed more competently academically than the low-able (learning potential), regardless of placement. (29 ref)
Budoff, Milton & Gottlieb, Jay. (Research Inst for Educational Problems, Cambridge, MA) American Journal of Mental Deficiency, 1976(Jul), Vol 81(1), 1-11. [PA, Vol 56:10741]

3341. Test-retest reliability of the Singer Vocational Evaluation System.
Examined for the 1st time the test-retest stability of the Singer Vocational Evaluation System (SVES), a work-sample method of measuring vocational aptitudes, interests, and attitudes. A random sample of 30 educable mentally retarded Pittsburgh public high school students took the SVES during 1973-1974. Correlation analysis tested reliability, and *t* tests measured pre-post changes of vocational aptitude (time needed and errors made in completing tasks) and vocational interests. Both aptitude-error and aptitude-time scores significantly improved from pre- to posttest; interest scores showed no significant changes. Test-retest stability for aptitude-error, aptitude-time, and interest were .71, .61, and .61 respectively. The pre-posttest increases probably resulted from intervening vocational training. The moderate stability coefficients indicate that changes were consis-

tent within the sample, and support continued clinical use of the SVES.

Cohen, Charles & Drugo, John. (Pittsburgh Public Schools, Project Liaison, PA) Vocational Guidance Quarterly, 1976(Mar), Vol 24(3), 267-270. [PA, Vol 57:09363]

3342.   Measuring mathematical attitudes of EMH children.
Describes an instrument which requires educable mentally handicapped (EMH) children to match their attitudes about a particular mathematics problem with either a happy or sad face. By tallying the children's responses to each exercise, the evaluator or teacher can learn the child's attitude toward each exercise and toward mathematics in general. Unlike the traditional "attitude toward mathematics" scale, this instrument eliminates the need for the EMH child, who often has difficulty reading, to read several words or sentences prior to making an attitude response.

Dunlap, William P. (U Louisville School of Education) Education & Training of the Mentally Retarded, 1976(Oct), Vol 11(3), 225. [PA, Vol 57:11523]

3343.   Developing the creative potential of educable mentally retarded students.
To study whether the creative abilites of retarded children can be developed through training, the New Directions in Creativity (NDC) program was administered in 18 classes of educable mentally retarded middle-grade and high-school level students. 12 classes served as controls. The NDC activity materials had a strong effect in changing the behavior of the retardates. The experimental group performed significantly better than the control on a battery of 4 Christensen and Guilford tests of creativity: Ideation, Fluency, Word Fluency, Alternate Uses, and Consequences. It was also found that the children in the experimental group had a significantly better general attitude toward school. Experimental Ss were rated by their teachers as exhibiting significantly more behavioral characteristics of creativity. (23 ref)

Ford, Barbara G. & Renzulli, Joseph S. (Northern Illinois U) Journal of Creative Behavior, 1976, Vol 10(3), 210–218. [PA, Vol 63:12979]

3344.   Effects of visual perception and language training upon certain abilities of retarded children.
Research on visual perception training and language training suggests that selective measures of the 2 abilities are correlated with certain measures of reading and intelligence as well as visual perception and psycholinguistic abilities. The present study investigated the effects of short-term training programs in visual perception and language (lessons from the Frostig Program for the Development of Visual Perception and the Peabody Language Development kit, respectively) as they affected the visual perception, language, reading, and intellectual growth of 83 young educable retarded children, aged 7-11 yrs. Results indicate that Ss did increase their visual perceptual abilities as a result of training in visual perception. Visual perception training had no significant effect upon growth in reading, language, or intelligence. Language training was found to have no significant effect on the variables studied. (24 ref)

Forgnone, Charles. (U Florida) Education & Training of the Mentally Retarded, 1976(Oct), Vol 11(3), 212-217. [PA, Vol 57:11524]

3345.   Effects of verbal and pictorial materials on retarded youngsters' memory for information.
Examined the effects of full and partial verbalization of information contained in pictures and of full verbalization without pictures on retarded youngsters' memory for information. 30 13-15 yr old educable retardates (IQs, 50-75) and 30 8-11 yr old normal controls (IQs, 90-115) were tested. Results indicate that facilitation of recall for 13- to 15-yr-old mentally retarded youngsters will occur with the use of pictures only if the aspects of the picture which are to be remembered are verbalized. The relevance of the findings for high-interest low-vocabulary textbooks for the retarded is discussed.

Gagne, Eve E. & Burns, Edward. (State U New York, Binghamton) Perceptual & Motor Skills, 1976(Dec), Vol 43(3), 1288-1290. [PA, Vol 58:03579]

3346.   The achievement of educable mentally retarded children on the Key Math Diagnostic Arithmetic Test.
Administered the Key Math Diagnostic Arithmetic Test (Key Math) individually to a random sample of 227 educable mentally retarded (EMR) children (mean CA 11 yrs 4 mo, mean MA 7 yrs 6 mo). Results suggest that while the difficulty level of the basal items in most subtests was acceptable for EMR Ss, the Ss tended to ceiling quite rapidly in many of the subtests. It is noted that a lack of items in the mid-range of the test prevents the fullest use of the data to provide diagnostic information that will affect programming decisions for EMR children. It is also suggested that the Key Math would tend to lose power to discriminate achievement changes for EMR children. Significant factorial validity was found for the claim of uniqueness of the 14 Key Math Subtests. Profile analysis of Ss' performance revealed a pattern of slight underachievement on the majority of the subtests. The incremental deficit in performance found as Ss progressed through school suggests that academic achievement fails to grow as expected over a longer term in school.

Goodstein, H. A.; Kahn, H. & Cawley, J. F. (U Connecticut) Journal of Special Education, 1976(Sep), Vol 10(1), 61-70. [PA, Vol 58:08652]

3347.   The two-directional resource room: Report on a pilot project.
Discusses the current trend toward regular class placement of exceptional children in light of the logic and research related to the self-contained special class. Connecticut's approach to this problem in special education is outlined, and a local program in Darien is described. Four brief case studies are included to demonstrate the potential impact of a flexible "2-directional" resource room.

Hartman, Robert K. & Hartman, Joyce A. (Regional Educational Assessment & Diagnostic Services, Lakeville Hosp, MA) Education & Training of the Mentally Retarded, 1976(Dec), Vol 11(4), 296-303. [PA, Vol 58:02184]

3348.   Reflection-impulsivity and reading recognition ability among mildly retarded children.
The Matching Familiar Figures Test (MFFT) of reflection-impulsivity and the Standard Reading Inventory (SRI) test of reading recognition ability were administered to 236 8-17 yr olds enrolled in programs for educable mentally retarded students. As expected, age correlated with reading recognition, but there was no relationship between MFFT and SRI scores with age and IQ controlled. This finding casts doubt on the association of reflection-impulsivity as defined by performance on the MFFT and the ability of retarded children to decode words. A possible lack of correspondence between the assessment instruments is considered.

Hayes, Charles S.; Prinz, Robert J. & Siders, Cathie. (U Iowa Hosp School, Child Development Clinic) American Journal of Mental Deficiency, 1976(Sep), Vol 81(2), 194-196. [PA, Vol 57:06107]

3349.   Use of minicourse instruction with student teachers of educable mentally retarded children.
Investigated whether 11 randomly assigned student teachers who received minicourse instruction would increase their use of skills taught by the minicourse compared with 10 student teachers who had not had the minicourse. Also investigated whether the oral language of the 27 educable mentally retarded children (mean CA 123 mo, mean MA 89 mo, and mean language age 75 mo) in the classes of the experimental group student teachers changed. Post-minicourse videotapes of both groups showed significant increases by the experimental group on only 2 of 14 skills. Audiotapes of the children's language showed increases only in the use of action words. It is suggested that the minicourse format will need revision to be an effective training mechanism for use with preservice teachers.

Katz, Gwynne. (Madison Public Schools, WI) Journal of Educational Research, 1976(Jul-Aug), Vol 69(10), 355-359. [PA, Vol 57:01898]

3350.   [Remedial therapy of reading difficulties in special school children.] (Slok)
Examined the effectiveness of using the simultaneous reading method with mildly retarded children. 39 Ss with and without reading difficulties were studied both individually and in groups. Results show that the method led to significant improvement in Ss' reading performance, both in speed and quality. This improvement was also evidenced at 2–4 mo follow-up. (Russian summary)
Kondáš, Ondrej; Slivková, Katarina & Žalondeková, Edita. (U Komenského, Bratislava, Czechoslovakia) Psychológia a Patopsychológia Dietata, 1976, Vol 11(5), 456–464. [PA, Vol 62:12282]

3351.   Social acceptance of the EMR in different educational placements.
Reviews the literature concerning the social consequences of various educational placements of educable mentally retarded (EMR) children. A general conclusion by a majority of the researchers concerned with the problem gave support to the special classroom as being the most efficacious placement for the social and personal development of the EMR child. It is stressed that further study is needed before firm conclusions can be reached. Prescriptive teaching programs based on thorough diagnostic testing should be generated with the optimal development of the individual EMR child in mind. (15 ref)
Lax, Bernard & Carter, John L. (U South Florida, Coll of Education) Mental Retardation, 1976(Apr), Vol 14(2), 10–13. [PA, Vol 56:04916]

3352.   The utility of self-management procedures in modifying the classroom behaviors of mentally retarded adolescents.
Applied self-management procedures (including the self-recording of points, the self-graphing of progress, and the self-selecting of free time activities) to the classroom behaviors of 4 12-yr-old educable mentally retarded Ss. Ss were first awarded points for specified appropriate behaviors. Then during the last 2 treatment phases, they graphed their points earnings and used these points to earn free time activities. A multiple baseline design was used in comparing the effects of these treatment conditions during spelling and reading periods. All 3 treatments produced higher rates of appropriate behavior than did baseline conditions; however, the highest levels of appropriate behavior were achieved during the self-selected free time phases.
Long, James D. & Williams, Robert L. (Appalachian State U) Adolescence, 1976(Spr), Vol 11(41), 29-38. [PA, Vol 58:12714]

3353.   Mainstreaming the mildly retarded: Some questions, cautions and guidelines.
Discusses the integration of mildly handicapped learners with their peers in regular education programs and expresses concern that such "mainstreaming," without adequate precautionary measures, might be harmful to the exceptional child. The principle of mainstreaming and its implementation are distinguished, and roadblocks to the implementation that exist in general education are examined. It is noted that children other than the mainstreamed are affected by such action. The experience of the California State Board of Education in removing educable mentally retarded children from special education classes, delabeling them, and returning them to regular programs, is described, and several of the problems inherent in mainstreaming are illustrated by the "resource teacher" model. In light of this experience, it is stressed that (a) emphasis be given to change agentry with respect to the makeup of each school district and the characteristics of the children involved, (b) the needs of individual mentally retarded children and the effects of their mainstreaming be considered, (c) priority be placed on the outcomes desired by mainstreaming, and (d) attention be given to the preparation of regular teachers for dealing effectively with mentally retarded students. (33 ref)

MacMillan, Donald L.; Jones, Reginald L. & Meyers, C. Edward. (U California, Riverside) Mental Retardation, 1976(Feb), Vol 14(1), 3-10. [PA, Vol 56:01480]

3354.   Teachers on reading: II. Rehabilitating a class of slow learners.
Expands on the philosophy that if reading is to be learned, children must want to learn and know that they can, and teachers must know that the child can learn to read and must expect him to do so. Teaching methods and materials are viewed as less important than these attitudes. The philosophy was demonstrated in action with 15 slow-learning 8-10 yr old children who were "turned off to" reading. Effective techniques included oral language with a tape recorder, language experience activities, rhythmic poetry, choral reading, silent reading periods, and a variety of other activities calling for active participation. The class atmosphere was informal, and IOUs (for free time) were given as reinforcers for learning successes. After the school year's reading rehabilitation program, all but one child gained 1-3 grade levels in reading, and all were "turned on" to reading.
McInnis, Mary. (Mary Lawson Elementary School, Dartmouth, Canada) Urban Review, 1976(Sum), Vol 9(2), 100-104. [PA, Vol 58:08385]

3355.   Increasing generalization in a token program for adolescent retardates: A methodological comment.
Describes procedures used to maximize the probability of achieving generalization of appropriate behavioral change. Results with 11 educable mentally retarded middle-school Ss suggest it is possible to maintain appropriate behavior from token to nonprogram conditions when an array of methodological strategies are combined to facilitate generalization.
Nay, W. Robert & Legum, Louis. (U Illinois) Behavior Therapy, 1976(May), Vol 7(3), 413-414. [PA, Vol 57:01988]

3356.   Letter discrimination in mildly retarded beginning first graders.
Performance on letter discrimination tasks by 38 mildly retarded and normal children of the same MA indicated that the difficulties experienced by retardates in learning to read are probably influenced only to a relatively minor extent by letter discrimination difficulties.
Neville, Donald D. & Vandever, Thomas R. (U South Florida Coll of Education) Mental Retardation, 1976(Dec), Vol 14(6), 48-49. [PA, Vol 58:01405]

3357.   The influence of examiner verbal comments on WISC performances of EMR students.
Applied the methodology used by J. M. Witmer et al (see PA, Vol 47:9668) in their study of the effects of verbal approval-disapproval on WISC scores of normal and average children to a group of 40 educable mentally retarded (EMR) Ss (mean CA, 12.4 yrs; mean IQ, 63.4). Ss were assigned to 1 of 2 treatment groups which either did or did not receive verbal approval; each of these 2 groups was then subdivided into 4 groups. One group in each of the approval and neutral groups was randomly assigned to an examiner. A significant overall effect for the verbal comment procedures was found. Significant differences were also found between the approval and neutral comment groups on the Digit Span and Block Design subtests, but not for the Picture Completion or Arithmetic subtests. Results suggest that EMR test performances are sensitive to examiner praise.
Saigh, Philip A. & Payne, David A. (U Georgia Coll of Education) Journal of School Psychology, 1976(Win), Vol 14(4), 342-345. [PA, Vol 58:03602]

3358.   A peer counseling experiment: High school students as small-group leaders.-700 R.
16 peer counselors (high school juniors) were trained in human relations techniques, group dynamics, and decision-making skills applied to 122 potential dropouts (53 counseled and 69 controls). Peer counseling was conducted in small groups at approximately 20 1-hr meetings. Gain scores on 16 variables were analyzed using a 5-way factorial multivariate analysis. Although the counselees improved significantly in attendance and decisiveness

over the controls, results are inconclusive in demonstrating the efficacy of this program on counselees. (18 ref)
Schweisheimer, William & Walberg, Herbert J. (High School District 211, Palatine, IL) Journal of Counseling Psychology, 1976(Jul), Vol 23(4), 398-401. [PA, Vol 56:06862]

3359. Classroom techniques: A developmental curriculum for the mildly retarded of intermediate and high school age.
Discusses some of the issues involved in developing a work-study curriculum for mildly retarded intermediate and high school age students in a suburban school system. It is concluded that the overall goal of such programs should be to train this group for employment in the 4 general fields (i.e., curricular, instructional, personnel, and logistics) best suited to their capacities. A model is presented to demonstrate how this program could improve the student's communication skills, vocational training, social and personal attitudes, and in general help the student to experience an economically and socially useful adulthood. Also presented is a sample survey for use with administrators, teachers, or parents on validating the goals of the program.
Sharpes, Donald K. (Virginia Polytechnic Inst & State U, Reston) Education & Training of the Mentally Retarded, 1976(Apr), Vol 11(2), 118-125. [PA, Vol 56:08771]

3360. A classroom timeout procedure for retarded children.
Investigated time-out from positive reinforcement as a punishment procedure for the disruptive behavior of 2 male educably retarded children in a classroom setting. Ss were 12 and 14 yrs old, respectively, at the start of the study. Time-out was defined as the interruption of an ongoing reinforcement system, for a fixed time period, contingent upon the emission of inappropriate behavior. Rewards were distributed on a predetermined, random time schedule as the means for establishing the necessary reinforcement environment. Within a reversal and multiple baseline design, time-out from positive reinforcement was an effective and relatively specific reinforcer.
Spitalnik, Robert & Drabman, Ronald. (Bronx Children's Hosp, NY) Journal of Behavior Therapy & Experimental Psychiatry, 1976(Mar), Vol 7(1), 17-21. [PA, Vol 56:08426]

3361. Three approaches to beginning reading instruction for EMR children.
Assigned 15 classes of primary-age educable mentally retarded children to Edmark, Sullivan, or Merrill reading programs to determine whether programs of reading instruction affect the development of word recognition in this population. At the beginning of the school year students were pretested on 2 measures—a 150-word list from the reading program to which they were assigned and a 50-word list to measure learning and transfer. At the end of the school year, posttests administered to 107 children on the 150-word measure revealed differences in achievement among the programs, favoring Edmark.
Vandever, Thomas R.; Maggart, William T. & Nasser, Sheffield. (Metropolitan Nashville-Davidson County Public Schools, TN) Mental Retardation, 1976(Aug), Vol 14(4), 29-32. [PA, Vol 57:04450]

3362. Transfer as a result of synthetic and analytic reading instruction.
Investigated the relationship of synthetic and analytic presentation to the identification of inconsistent transfer words and attempted to determine whether there are differences between retarded and nonretarded children's ability to learn words and to demonstrate transfer to words of varying degrees of inconsistency. 50 educable mentally retarded children and 50 nonretarded 1st and 2nd graders were paired on the basis of WISC vocabulary scores; Ss were also administered Raven's Progressive Matrices (sets A, AB, and B). Pairs were then randomly assigned to 1 of 2 conditions (synthetic or analytic). Ss in the analytic condition learned to read words printed in a contrived alphabet by a whole-word method, and Ss in the synthetic condition learned the same words by a parts-to-whole method. At the end of each of 3 learning sessions, Ss identified transfer words, including some which were consistent with those taught in phoneme-grapheme relationships and some that were inconsistent. The synthetic method promoted identification of both consistent and inconsistent transfer words for both retarded and nonretarded Ss.
Vandever, Thomas R. & Neville, Donald D. (Metropolitan Schools, Nashville, TN) American Journal of Mental Deficiency, 1976(Mar), Vol 80(5), 498-503. [PA, Vol 56:06831]

3363. Quantitative abilities of mentally retarded children.
Distinguishes between mathematics and arithmetic as a basis for discussing the literature on the ability of educable mentally retarded (EMR) children to think in symbolic or abstract terms. One area of research indicates that while EMR children achieve up to their MA expectancy in arithmetical computations, they are below average in their understanding of basic mathematical concepts and problem solving. Literature based on a developmental view of mental retardation argues that the degree of cognitive development of EMRs makes them capable of conceptual learning. Piagetian researchers maintain that like all children, mentally retarded children progress through the same developmental stages, but at a slower rate, and depending upon the degree of retardation, appear to asymptote at the normal stages. It is suggested that the curriculum for EMRs in the area of quantity be expanded to include a balance of conceptual mathematical learnings as well as rote arithmetical learnings. (34 ref)
Vitello, Stanley J. (Pennsylvania State U) Education & Training of the Mentally Retarded, 1976(Apr), Vol 11(2), 125-129. [PA, Vol 56:08773]

3364. Out-of-level testing of special education students with a standardized achievement battery.
Analyzed the feasibility of using teachers' recommendations rather than students' age/grade placement for selecting the level of a standardized achievement test. 359 former and current educable mentally retarded students were tested either with the Primary I, Primary II, or Elementary levels of the Metropolitan Achievement Test (MAT), selected by their current teachers after copies of test booklets for all MAT levels had been presented to them. Results indicate that (a) most of the sample responded above chance levels on all MAT subtests chosen for them, (b) reliability coefficients were comparable to those of the standardization sample, and (c) generally moderate to high positive point-biserial correlations were found for all subtest/level combinations. It is concluded that the teacher selection method of choosing test levels was appropriate for selecting a reliable instrument to assess academic performance for this group of students.
Yoshida, Roland K. (HEW, Bureau of Education for the Handicapped, Washington, DC) Journal of Educational Measurement, 1976(Fal), Vol 13(3), 215-221. [PA, Vol 57:09209]

3365. Pygmalion in reverse.
The effects of learning potential (LP) and teacher expectancies on IQ, school achievements, and teacher ratings were studied in 8 special classes for the retarded. 58 educable mentally retarded 7–15 yr olds (mean WISC IQ 68.2) were divided into 4 groups in a 2 × 2 design, first according to their true unrealized intellectual potential (high and low LP) and then at random into expectancy groups (high and low). Ss were tested at the beginning and end of the school year. IQ, and particularly its reasoning component, was affected by learning potential, but not by teacher expectancies. A consistent interaction was found between changes in most of the teacher ratings and some of the objective achievement scores, characterized by unexpected inferiority of the high-LP/high-expectancy group. (20 ref)
Babad, Elisha Y. (Hebrew U of Jerusalem School of Education, Israel) Journal of Special Education, 1977(Spr), Vol 11(1), 81–90. [PA, Vol 59:02093]

3366. Improving the social status of mainstreamed retarded children.
37 mainstreamed educable mentally retarded (EMR) children in Grades 3, 4, and 5 were randomly assigned to a control group or to an experimental treatment given during regular class activities for the purpose of improving their social status among nonretarded classmates. On the average, Ss were 8–10 mo older than their

normal classmates. Each experimental S worked in a small cooperative group with 4–6 nonretarded classmates on highly structured, manipulative tasks using multimedia materials. The treatment was provided in 2 cycles which lasted a total of 8 wks. Sociometric tests were given before and after treatment to pupils in classes with experimental and control EMR Ss. By 2–4 wks following completion of treatment, nonretarded Ss' social acceptance of their experimental peers improved significantly more than that of control Ss. (17 ref)
Ballard, Maurine; Corman, Louise; Gottlieb, Jay & Kaufman, Martin J. Journal of Educational Psychology, 1977(Oct), Vol 69(5), 605–611. [PA, Vol 60:01912]

3367. Comparison of the effectiveness of adult and peer models with EMR children.
Investigated the effects of model similarity on the behavior of 39 educable mentally retarded (EMR) Ss (CA range 11–14 yrs, IQ range 50–78). An age- and sex-matched peer-model group, an adult sex-matched model group, and a no-model control group were used. All groups were presented 9 test items from the Leiter International Performance Scale. Retention was sampled by repeating the tasks without models in a 2nd session a day later. A significant main effect was found for modeling conditions. A Neuman-Keul procedure revealed that only the peer and control groups were significantly different across both sessions. Examination for 1st-session results revealed significant differences between the peer- and adult-model groups and the peer and control groups. Findings indicate that EMR children respond differentially to peers and adults as models and that peer modeling could be a very effective method for teaching EMR children, particularly in a regular classroom. (18 ref)
Barry, Norman J. & Overmann, Phyllis B. (Xavier U) American Journal of Mental Deficiency, 1977(Jul), Vol 82(1), 33–36. [PA, Vol 59:11117]

3368. Teaching basic math facts to EMR children through individual and small group instruction, pupil teaming, contingency contracting, and learning center activities.
Describes a basic facts program used with 18 educable mentally retarded Ss (CAs 11–14 yrs, IQs 57–90) in a special education class. Results show that the greatest gains were realized in multiplication and division. The large amount of student time involved is noted as a limitation of the project; greater emphasis on individual student progress is recommended.
Broome, Kay & Wambold, Clark L. (Madison Public Schools, Early Childhood Programs, WI) Education & Training of the Mentally Retarded, 1977(Apr), Vol 12(2), 120–124. [PA, Vol 59:02097]

3369. Training strategic study time apportionment in educable retarded children.
Two groups of educable retarded children differing in functioning level served as Ss. One group, the High group, consisted of 31 children drawn from the upper 2 classes of a 5-class stream. The Low group consisted of 39 children drawn from the lowest 2 classes. During pretesting, on each trial but the 1st of a multitrial free recall procedure, Ss were allowed to select half of the to-be-remembered items to see if they would strategically select missed items for extra study. Following pretesting, Ss were divided for training into 3 groups for which the experimenter selected items for study: in the Standard group, missed items; in the Creeping group, recalled items plus one missed item; and in the Random group, half missed and half recalled items. Children in the High group improved in the Standard condition, and those in the Low group benefited from Creeping training. There was no evidence of maintenance of training in the Low group, but children in the High group given training in the standard strategy selected missed items for recall on the posttests. Results are discussed in terms of the stability of trained strategies in retardates, and the question of what constitutes an optimal strategy is considered. (15 ref)
Brown, Ann L. & Campione, Joseph C. (U Illinois Ctr for the Study of Reading) Intelligence, 1977(Jan), Vol 1(1), 94–107. [PA, Vol 61:12003]

3370. Self concept and academic achievement of educable retarded and emotionally disturbed pupils.
Compared the self-concept and academic achievement of educable mentally retarded and emotionally disturbed Ss in regular classrooms and in special classrooms over a 3-yr period. Data from the Piers-Harris Children's Self-Concept Scale and the Stanford Achievement Test show that for these Ss regular classrooms were significantly more effective than special classrooms.
Calhoun, George & Elliott, Raymond N. (California State Coll, Bakersfield) Exceptional Children, 1977(Mar), Vol 43(6), 379–380. [PA, Vol 58:08373]

3371. The effects of a group guidance program on the self-concepts of EMR children.
Studied 211 8-12 yr old educable mentally retarded (EMR) children in 20 randomly selected intermediate-level special education classes. Two independent variables were included and were examined using analysis of covariance for a randomized complete block design. The main independent variable consisted of 2 treatments: One group received 85 sessions of work with a DUSO (development of understanding of self and others) group guidance program, and the 2nd group was a recipient of individual teacher methods to improve self-concept. The blocking variable, the 2nd independent variable, was the county in which the child was located. Pre- and posttesting were completed using the Piers-Harris Children's Self-Concept Scale. No statistical evidence was found indicating that the standardized group guidance program was significantly different or more effective than techniques selected by teachers for improving the self-concept of the EMRs. (23 ref)
Eldridge, Mary S.; Witmer, J. Melvin; Barcikowski, Robert & Bauer, Linda. (Sheperd Coll) Measurement & Evaluation in Guidance, 1977(Jan), Vol 9(1), 184-191. [PA, Vol 58:06359]

3372. Increasing the speech intensity of a retarded-emotionally disturbed student in a public school classroom.
Treated a 14-yr-old "retarded/emotionally disturbed" male public school student for low intensity speech. The speech was of such a low intensity that it presented serious instructional problems to his classroom teacher. The program was divided into 4 instructional phases: imitation of individual words, imitation of phrases, answering questions, and answering questions in a natural classroom setting. Phases 1, 2, and 3 were tutorial in nature and were implemented in the school's instructional materials center. Phase 4 was implemented in the natural classroom setting and was designed to facilitate the generalization of improved speech intensity. Results indicate increased speech intensity in all instructional phases and generalization of those increases to a natural classroom setting.
Evans, Tom; Pierce, Laura; York, Robert & Brown, Lou. (Madison Public Schools, WI) Child Study Journal, 1977, Vol 7(3), 131–144. [PA, Vol 60:08300]

3373. Teacher reactions to the label of educable mentally retarded.
Investigated connotations of the label of educable mentally retarded (EMR) and the ability of this label to influence 50 elementary teachers' (mean age 36 yrs) perceptions of child performance. Data show that teachers held negative expectancies toward children labeled EMR and that these expectations were sufficient to bias interpretations of videotaped behavior. These results are related to the T. Barber et al (1969) model of the expectancy phenomenon; the label of EMR meets at least 3 of the criteria necessary for the establishment of a self-fulfilling prophecy. It is concluded that labeling a child EMR may well reduce the effectiveness of the services made available through such labeling. The development of noncategorical programs is recommended.
Foster, Glen & Keech, Valerie. (Pennsylvania State U) Education & Training of the Mentally Retarded, 1977(Dec), Vol 12(4), 307–311. [PA, Vol 61:06966]

3374.   Labels, categories, behaviors: ED, LD, and EMR reconsidered.
Uses a behavioral rather than a categorical framework to discuss children traditionally labeled learning disabled, mildly emotionally disturbed, and mildly mentally retarded. A historical analysis reveals that the three areas have evolved from highly similar foundations. In addition, no behavioral characteristics can be found that are associated exclusively with any one of the three areas. Children who are usually identified as learning disabled, mildly disturbed, or mildly retarded reveal more similarities than differences. Consequently, successful teaching techniques do not differ among the three areas. A noncategorical orientation is recommended in which children are grouped for instruction according to their specific learning deficits rather than their assignment to traditional categories. (47 ref)
Hallahan, Daniel P. & Kauffman, James M. (U Virginia) Journal of Special Education, 1977(Sum), Vol 11(2), 139–149. [PA, Vol 59:11134]

3375.   The effects of teacher-delivered social reinforcement on the task persistent behavior of educable mentally retarded children.
Studied the effects of teacher-delivered social reinforcers on the task-persistent behavior of 14 11–13 yr olds (MAs 8–10 yrs) enrolled in an intermediate class for the educable mentally retarded. These Ss were grouped with a regular 4th-grade class during a social studies period in which the study was conducted. The special education Ss were randomly divided into 2 groups. Using a reversal design, social reinforcers were delivered contingent on the task-persistent behavior of the 7 target Ss. The 7 in the control, or nonreinforcement, group were essentially ignored as they engaged in appropriate task-related behaviors. Results clearly show that increases in the level of task-persistent behavior and the administration of social reinforcement were functionally related. The level of task-persistent behavior emitted by the controls was not affected by reinforcement delivered to their peers.
Hill, Ada D. & Strain, Phillip S. (Virginia Commonwealth U) Psychology in the Schools, 1977(Apr), Vol 14(2), 207–212. [PA, Vol 59:02105]

3376.   [Learning in mildly retarded children: An attempt at characterization.] (Polh)
Reviews literature dealing with the question of how mentally retarded children who can be admitted to special schools learn. The research includes the following aspects: (a) methodological considerations, (b) classical conditioning and delayed response, and (c) the learning organization of mildly retarded children. A set of teaching postulates appropriate for these children is suggested. (English & Russian summaries) (26 ref)
Janiak, Ewa. (U Warsaw, Poland) Psychologia Wychowawcza, 1977(Nov–Dec), Vol 20(5), 478–492. [PA, Vol 64:12741]

3377.   Vicarious reinforcement and direction of behavior change in the classroom.
Examined the effect of verbal approval delivered to a target S on the behavior of an adjacent nonreinforced peer in a special education class of educably mentally retarded children. Ss were a 6-yr-old boy (IQ 74) and an 8-yr-old boy (IQ 78). The experiment assessed whether behavior changes in the nonreinforced peer resembled the behavior changes of the reinforced target S. In separate phases of a reversal design, target S was praised either for inattentive or attentive behavior. Praising target S altered the behavior of both target S and the nonreinforced peer. The behavior of target S changed, depending upon the specific behavior (i.e., inattentive or attentive behavior) that was associated with praise; however, attentive behavior of the nonreinforced peer increased when target S was praised independently of the specific behavior performed and praised on the part of target S.
Kazdin, Alan E. (Pennsylvania State U) Behavior Therapy, 1977(Jan), Vol 8(1), 57-63. [PA, Vol 58:04381]

3378.   The influence of behavior preceding a reinforced response on behavior change in the classroom.
Examined the influence of behavior that immediately precedes a reinforced target response on the effectiveness of a reinforcement contingency in 2 experiments with mentally retarded children in a special-education classroom. Two reinforcement schedules were examined in each experiment. For each schedule, a prespecified period of attentive behavior served as the target response. The schedules differed in whether inattentive or attentive behavior was required immediately to precede the target response. These schedules were examined with an 8-yr-old boy (IQ 75) in a simultaneous treatment design using praise as the reinforcer (Exp I), and with an 8-yr-old boy (IQ 73) and a 9-yr-old girl (IQ 68) in separate reversal designs using tokens as the reinforcer (Exp II). While attentive behavior increased under each schedule, the increase was greater when attentive rather than inattentive behavior preceded the reinforced response. Results indicate that the effect of a contingency may be determined not only by the specific response reinforced but also by the behavior that immediately precedes that response. (15 ref)
Kazdin, Alan E. (Pennsylvania State U) Journal of Applied Behavior Analysis, 1977(Sum), Vol 10(2), 299–310. [PA, Vol 59:13285]

3379.   Learning economy: A practical approach to prevocational training of money management.
Describes a classroom program for training money management skills in educable mentally retarded 12–17 yr olds in a junior high school special education classroom. Students were trained to maintain daily records of class work and were paid monetary wages based on their accuracy of performance. The wages could be used to buy high interest learning activities. Results indicate that the students learned many of the concepts of money management. This procedure also reduced the amount of absences from school.
Knapczyk, Dennis R. & Livingston, Gary. (Indiana U) Research & the Retarded, 1977, Vol 4(1), 7–17. [PA, Vol 59:13287]

3380.   Expressive verbal behavior of Appalachian mentally retarded students.
Evaluated the verbal expressive abilities of 34 children in classes for the mentally retarded with the Illinois Test of Psycholinguistic Abilities. Results indicate a greater coordination between the retarded Ss' verbal expression and overall psycholinguistic abilities than those obtained for the test's normative population. The importance of categorical analysis of the verbal expression ability for remedial efforts is discussed.
Lombardi, Thomas P. (West Virginia U) Research & the Retarded, 1977, Vol 4(2), 26–29. [PA, Vol 61:03898]

3381.   Effects of music-listening contingencies on arithmetic performance and music preference of EMR children.
A 5-phase experiment investigated (a) whether contingent music-listening would act as a reinforcer to increase arithmetic performance of educable mentally retarded children and (b) whether this contingent reinforcement would affect preference for that reinforcer. The 30 Ss had a CA range of 9 yrs 10 mo to 14 yrs and an IQ range of 50-75. During the 3 baseline (no reinforcement) phase, Ss returned to their classrooms at the end of the arithmetic work period. During the 2 treatment phases, experimental Ss meeting criterion were permitted to remain and listen to either rock (high preference) or music classics (low preference). Statistical analyses revealed significant differences between the no-reinforcement and contingent-reinforcement conditions and between the control and 4 experimental groups during the contingent-reinforcement phases. No differential effect between the more or less preferred contingencies was found. Analyses of the music-selection data indicated that the contingencies did not influence music preference. (23 ref)
Miller, D. Merrily. (Fordham U) American Journal of Mental Deficiency, 1977(Jan), Vol 81(4), 371-378. [PA, Vol 58:06374]

3382. Parental influence on maladaptive behavior of mentally retarded children in the classroom.
Determined the degree of parental influence on maladaptive behavior of 33 mentally retarded children in the classroom. Data were collected from the Ss' parents by means of sociometric questionnaires and from their teachers by means of a maladaptive behavior checklist. Data indicate that the number of parents in the home and the parents' levels of education, sex, socioeconomic status, and attitudes toward their retarded children significantly correlated with the children's maladaptive behavior in the classroom.
Peniston, Eugene G. & McLean, Marian G. (PHS Indian Health Services, Roosevelt, UT) Research & the Retarded, 1977, Vol 4(2), 38–44. [PA, Vol 61:04809]

3383. Cross-age helping for the EMR child.
A review of experimental literature as well as tentative findings from a research project with 14 5-9 yr old educable mental retardates suggest that cross-age tutoring can be an effective strategy for slow-learning children. Successful implementation of such a project depends on a careful internship, development of materials, solid commitment, careful assignment of tutors and tutees, and encouragement of flexible modifications. Within-class tutoring appeared to be effective when basic skills and drills were student-taught but teacher-guided.
Smith, Linda M. & Pfeiffer, Isobel L. (Young Elementary School, Akron, OH) Education & Training of the Mentally Retarded, 1977(Feb), Vol 12(1), 32-35. [PA, Vol 58:10560]

3384. Special education class achievement and an experiential taxonomic curriculum.
Tested the hypothesis that educationally handicapped (EH) and junior high educable mentally retarded (EMR) classes using an experiential taxonomic-based curriculum would achieve higher gains than would EH and EMR classes using other curricula. 15 students in experimental and control EMR classrooms and students in the 2 EH classrooms were administered the project pretest–posttest assessing reading, mathematics, social responsibilities, and written communication skills, and the Wide Range Achievement Test Spelling subtest. Experimental classes then employed the experiential taxonomic curriculum while control classes used any other curricula. Students in the experimental EMR class showed significant gains in reading and communication. The experimental EH class showed a signficant gain in communication. The hypothesis was supported in several areas of the curriculum.
Steinaker, Norman & Harrison, Marilyn. Educational Research Quarterly, 1977(Fal), Vol 2(3), 13–21. [PA, Vol 60:10465]

3385. Context utilization in reading by educable mentally retarded children.
Reviews literature to determine how well educable mentally retarded (EMR) children use context in a typical reading situation. Findings from studies employing the cloze procedure suggest that (a) EMR children can use contextual cues to predict missing words accurately, providing the context is sufficiently constrained; (b) when the context is not constrained enough to determine the exact word, EMR children are (or might be) less likely than nonretarded children to produce appropriate word substitutions; (c) at least some EMR children are able to utilize information in the context beyond sentence boundaries; and (d) differences between EMR and nonretarded children in their use of context in reading may be quantitative, rather than qualitative. (French & Spanish summaries) (1½ p ref)
Streib, Rachel. (U Kansas Neurological Inst) Reading Research Quarterly, 1976-77, Vol 12(1), 32-54. [PA, Vol 57:13960]

3386. Response strategies and stimulus salience with learning disabled and mentally retarded children on a short-term memory task.
Studied 10 learning-disabled and 10 educable mentally retarded Ss to investigate whether 3-dimensional items (objects) are easier to remember than 2-dimensional items (pictures). As previous research found 3-dimensional stimuli more salient among educable mentaly retarded children, the possibility exists that the differential salience of 3-dimensional stimuli might even be greater among the learning disabled. While the number of Ss was small, the finding that objects facilitated recall by learning-disabled children even more than the 3rd dimension did for mentally retarded children has potential implications for teachers. (25 ref)
Swanson, H. Lee. (U Northern Colorado) Journal of Learning Disabilities, 1977(Dec), Vol 10(10), 635–642. [PA, Vol 61:02318]

3387. Vocabulary development of educable retarded children.
Three approaches to vocabulary instruction were developed based on research on the training of elaboration strategies with retarded children, and these approaches were tested with 1 mo of vocabulary instruction given to 9 classes of educable mentally retarded Ss. Data related to vocabulary development and strategy indicate that the instructional conditions were differentially affected. Findings provide guidelines as to how elaborations can be incorporated into classroom instruction. (15 ref)
Taylor, Arthur M.; Thurlow, Martha L. & Turnure, James E. (St Paul Public Schools, Special Education Dept, MN) Exceptional Children, 1977(Apr), Vol 43(7), 444–450. [PA, Vol 59:02131]

3388. Mainstreaming: Implications for training regular class teachers.
Data from a survey of 2,186 elementary school teachers in 124 school systems show that (a) teachers' perceptions of their abilities to deal with mildly handicapped children by means of individualized instruction, remediation techniques, or behavior management increased with experience and training, and (b) these competencies were seen as weakest by bachelor degree teachers. Stronger preservice programs are advocated.
Alberto, Paul A.; Castricone, Nicholas R. & Cohen, Sandra B. (Georgia State U) Education & Training of the Mentally Retarded, 1978(Feb), Vol 13(1), 90–92. [PA, Vol 61:09329]

3389. Increasing initial interactions among integrated EMR students and their nonretarded peers in a game-playing situation.
Examined 2 ways of increasing the initial interaction among integrated EMR students and their nonretarded classmates in a game-playing situation. 304 randomly assigned 7th and 8th graders observed classmates about to play a simple game and were asked to select partners and opponents from 2 pairs of students matched on sex and grade. The experimental pair had 1 EMR student and 1 nonretarded student; the control pair had 2 nonretarded students. The Ss' past knowledge of the pair members served as a covariate in the design to determine whether past knowledge influenced their selections of pair members. Each S was also provided information regarding the competency level of each pair member in relation to the particular game. Results indicate that the covariate was not a significant factor in the selection process; however, the appended competency statement and the game-playing option were significant in influencing selection of the pair members and increasing the selection of the EMR child by his nonretarded classmate.
Aloia, Gregory F.; Beaver, Robert J. & Pettus, William F. (U Arizona) American Journal of Mental Deficiency, 1978(May), Vol 82(6), 573–579. [PA, Vol 62:02271]

3390. Learning characteristics of educationally handicapped and retarded children.
During the past 10 yrs, special educators have been debating the merits of mixing learning disabled and emotionally disturbed children. Recently, this debate has taken on a broader focus. Some special educators now advocate the use of generic categories and programs that include educable mentally retarded, learning disabled, and emotionally disturbed children. The efficacy of this new trend is addressed in this article. The learning characteristics of 40 educationally handicapped (learning disabled and emotionally disturbed) and 20 educable mentally retarded children were compared using 5 problem-solving tasks (Digit Span, Raven Progressive Matrices, Matching Familiar Figures Test, a puzzle task, and the rod-and-frame test). Based on the results of this study, several concerns are raised about the use of generic categories and programs in special education. (23 ref)

Becker, Laurence D. (U California Medical Coll, Irvine) Exceptional Children, 1978(Apr), Vol 44(7), 502–511. [PA, Vol 61:11997]

3391.   Pictures, imagery, and retarded children's prose learning.
96 10–16 yr old educable mental retardates were randomly assigned to 1 of 4 experimental conditions to listen to a 20-sentence story: Picture Ss viewed illustrations of the story, imagery Ss were instructed to generate mental pictures of the story, repetition control Ss heard each sentence of the story twice, and control Ss simply listened to the story once. Planned comparisons revealed that picture Ss recalled more story information than did Ss in all other groups. Differences among the other conditions, age by conditions interactions, and age differences per se were not statistically significant. A number of theoretically and practically interesting issues are discussed in the context of recent prose learning findings with normal children. (21 ref)
Bender, Bruce G. & *Levin, Joel R.* (U Colorado Medical Ctr, John F. Kennedy Child Development Ctr) Journal of Educational Psychology, 1978(Aug), Vol 70(4), 583–588. [PA, Vol 62:04794]

3392.   Facilitation of class-inclusion performance in mildly retarded adolescents: Feedback and strategy training.
Two experiments explored the feasibility of training mildly retarded adolescents to solve class-inclusion problems. In Exp I, using 42 Ss (mean CA 177.80 mo; mean MA 107.91 mo), the effects of training consisting primarily of feedback were investigated. In Exp II, using 72 Ss with CA and MA similar to Ss in Exp I, training with feedback alone vs training with feedback plus a counting strategy were compared. Both experiments assessed the generality of training effects to specific training and/or posttest formats. Results suggest that training was generally effective in improving performance with untrained class-inclusion problems on immediate and delayed posttests. Feedback training with pictorial stimuli appeared to be effective regardless of posttest format. The effects of the other training method/format combinations varied according to posttest format.
Bilsky, Linda H.; Gilbert, Lucy & Pawelski, Christine E. (Columbia U Teachers Coll) American Journal of Mental Deficiency, 1978(Sep), Vol 83(2), 177–184. [PA, Vol 62:07330]

3393.   An investigation of the Goodenough-Harris Drawing Test and the (Coopersmith) Self-Esteem Inventory.
Two groups of educable mentally retarded (EMR) primary and secondary pupils ($N = 16$) were compared on measures of self-esteem and IQ to determine whether scores on a self-drawing test and those on a self-perception test were related. The results of the Pearson product-moment correlations revealed for the secondary EMR Ss a significant relationship between scores on the Goodenough-Harris Drawing Test and those on the Self-Esteem Inventory. (8 ref)
Calhoun, George; Whitley, Jim D. & Ansolabehere, Elaine M. (California State Coll, Bakersfield) Educational & Psychological Measurement, 1978(Win), Vol 38(4), 1229–1232. [PA, Vol 64:01303]

3394.   An intervention strategy for teachers of the mildly handicapped.
Describes an intervention strategy to modify academic and social behaviors. The strategy is sequenced into 3 stages: (a) modification of instructional techniques, (b) reinforcement of academic tasks, and (c) modification of social behaviors. Research is cited to support the contention that the most efficient method to achieve increased academic performance and decreased off-task social behaviors is to first modify instructional techniques and then reinforce academic performance. If these 2 steps are taken, the frequency with which teachers need to resort to modification of social behaviors will be reduced. (24 ref)
Darch, Craig B. & Thorpe, Harold W. (Longfellow School, Oskosh, WI) Education & Training of the Mentally Retarded, 1978(Feb), Vol 13(1), 9–14. [PA, Vol 61:09670]

3395.   Teacher–student interaction in special education classrooms.
Observed each of 12 teachers for a minimum of 10 hrs' codable interaction time in 2 randomly selected self-contained special education classrooms—5 for educable mentally retarded and 7 for educationally handicapped. Results show that the basic teacher–student communication pattern was the teacher's attempt to maximize success and minimize failure. Similar interaction patterns were found in both types of classrooms. (4 ref)
Dembo, Myron H.; Yoshida, Roland K.; Reilly, Tom & Reilly, Vera. (U Southern California) Exceptional Children, 1978(Nov), Vol 45(3), 212–213. [PA, Vol 62:04805]

3396.   Comparison of potential reinforcer ratings between slow learners and regular students.
Investigated whether slow learners differed from regular students in their evaluation of reinforcers that had been classified on a continuum from concrete to abstract. The Ss were 297 girls and boys: 136 13–16 yr olds (slow learners) from a vocational junior high school and 161 11–13 yr olds from a regular junior high. Ss were given a revision of the Reinforcement Survey Schedule, and the responses of the slow learners were compared to those of the regular students within the 7 levels of reinforcers: food, pasttime activities, sports, social reinforcers, being right, school subjects, and reinforced processes. As predicted, there was no significant difference between the groups for food and pasttime reinforcers, but significant differences were found for the remaining levels. Because slow learners valued fewer secondary reinforcers, the customary reinforcers available in regular classrooms may not be effective for this group. (16 ref)
de Scholz, Helvia C. & McDougall, Daniel. (U Calgary, Canada) Behavior Therapy, 1978(Jan), Vol 9(1), 60–64. [PA, Vol 61:01275]

3397.   Ratings of educable mentally handicapped students by regular and special teachers.
16 special class and 35 regular class teachers rated the adjustment of 61 randomly selected educable mentally handicapped children (ages 8–14 yrs), using the Flynn Elementary School Adjustment Scale. The children participated in a special education program in which they were assigned to the regular classroom and were also provided a daily supplemental class period for small group and individual tutoring. Results indicate that special class teachers rated the special class students significantly higher than the regular class teachers. Differences in students' behavior in the 2 situations are discussed.
Flynn, Timothy M. (Virginia Polytechnic Inst & State U, Coll of Home Economics) Exceptional Children, 1978(Apr), Vol 44(7), 539–540. [PA, Vol 61:12012]

3398.   Goal-setting and learning in the high school resource room.
Conducted a study to illustrate how goal-setting procedures can be applied in a classroom, especially to facilitate learning by students with learning problems. Ss were 16 educable mentally retarded or learning disabled students aged 15–18 yrs, who were assigned to a remedial resource room. Ss individually gave the teacher their goals for correctly spelled and defined words in a weekly test. Goal-setting was found to be superior to no-goal-setting for both spelling and vocabulary tasks. (13 ref)
Gardner, David C. & Gardner, Paula L. (Boston U School of Education) Adolescence, 1978(Fal), Vol 13(51), 489–493. [PA, Vol 62:09789]

3399.   Correlates of social status among mainstreamed mentally retarded children.
Explored the relative contributions of misbehavior, academic incompetence, and exposure to nonretarded children to the explanation of retarded children's sociometric status. Teachers and peers rated retarded children on the dimensions of misbehavior and academic performance. The results indicate that perceived academic incompetence was associated with educable mentally retarded children's level of social acceptance, whereas perceived misbehavior was associated with retarded children's social rejection by peers. Amount of exposure to nonretarded

children did not relate significantly to retarded children's social status. The data are discussed in terms of the assumptions underlying the mainstreaming of retarded children into regular classes. (24 ref)
Gottlieb, Jay; Semmel, Melvyn I. & Veldman, Donald J. (Northern Illinois U) Journal of Educational Psychology, 1978(Jun), Vol 70(3), 396–405. [PA, Vol 62:02223]

3400. The impact of work/study programs on development of the mentally retarded: Some findings from two sources.
Examined the employment success of both graduates and early terminators from high school work/study programs for educable retarded young adults 16–21 yrs old. Employment levels were also studied. Data sources included the vocational placement results of students who terminated from work/study programs in 14 Oregon school districts, along with analogous information about work/study terminators from 43 federally funded work/study projects conducted in the US between 1955 and 1972. Both the Oregon and the federal program participants demonstrated that mentally retarded persons who finished their work/study programs had substantially higher employment levels than did similar retarded persons not completing or only partially served by their programs. Also, work/study program completors had employment levels comparable to those of same age non-White adults in the general population. (French & German summaries) (3 ref)
Halpern, Andrew S. (U Oregon Coll of Education, Rehabilitation Research & Training Ctr in Mental Retardation) International Journal of Rehabilitation Research, 1978, Vol 1(2), 167–175. [PA, Vol 62:12272]

3401. Imitating children's errors to improve their spelling performance.
Compared the effectiveness of 2 methods of correcting spelling errors in 2 experiments with 2 educable mentally retarded 8-yr-olds and 1 learning disabled 12-yr-old, respectively: showing the S a correct model vs imitating the S's errors and then showing the correct model. In both, the method including imitation of the S's errors was more effective, especially for nonphonetic words. Results are interpreted in the light of research on concept learning and attention.
Kauffman, James M. et al. (U Virginia) Journal of Learning Disabilities, 1978(Apr), Vol 11(4), 217–222. [PA, Vol 62:02289]

3402. Effect of EMR placement models on affective and social development.
Investigated the effects of 3 educable mentally retarded (EMR) placement models on children's social and affective development. The Barclay Classroom Climate Inventory (BCCI) was administered to 45 randomly selected classes from a population of 115 classes representing self-contained (SC), selected academic placement (SAP), and learning center (LC) models. For SAP and LC children, BCCI assessments were obtained in both EMR and regular class settings. The BCCI data comprised self, peer, and teacher expectations. Results indicate that the SC setting resulted in the strongest support in terms of acceptance, and the SAP–EMR settings resulted in the fewest suspected problems. This it appears that stronger social support systems exist and fewer problems emerge for the children who are placed with others of similar cognitive ability.
Kehle, Thomas J. & Guidubaldi, John. (Kent State U) Psychology in the Schools, 1978(Apr), Vol 15(2), 275–282. [PA, Vol 62:02290]

3403. Teacher attitudes toward the educable mentally retarded.
Studied teacher attitudes held toward one group of exceptional children, the educable mentally retarded (EMR), prior to the implementation of the California Master Plan for Special Education. 60 experienced majority and minority EMR and regular class teachers completed a questionnaire containing the Multidimensional Attitude Scale on Mental Retardation. EMR and regular class teachers as groups did not differ in their attitudes toward retarded pupils, a finding consonant with other research. ANOVA revealed, however, ethnic group differences in certain areas of attitudes within the regular class and EMR

teachers. In addition, regular class teachers with previous experience with the retarded were more positive toward them than teachers with little contact with EMR children and adults. Results are discussed with reference to plans to educate EMR pupils in regular rather than in self-contained, nonintegrated classrooms.
Kennon, Adah F. & Sandoval, Jonathan. (U Maryland) Education & Training of the Mentally Retarded, 1978(Apr), Vol 13(2), 139–145. [PA, Vol 61:14534]

3404. Regular class teachers' perceptions of transition programs for EMR students and their impact on the students.
Obtained data on the perceptions of 252 regular class teachers who taught children who had been in for the educable mentally retarded (EMR) programs but had been decertified (D) and returned to regular classes in response to court cases and recent legislation. A cohort of regular class (RC) students from 12 unified school districts were selected for comparative purposes. It was found that D students were placed into low ability classes; yet teachers perceived D Ss to be significantly lower than RC students in both academic achievement and social acceptance. Only a small proportion of teachers indicated that the enrollment of D students had much impact on the regular class instructional program. The teachers, however, were rather critical of the services received under the auspices of a transitional program, indicating in large part that the services were either not apparent or ineffective.
MacMillan, Donald L.; Meyers, C. Edward & Yoshida, Roland K. (U California School of Education, Riverside) Psychology in the Schools, 1978(Jan), Vol 15(1), 99–103. [PA, Vol 61:01947]

3405. Vocational adjustment of EMR youth in a work-study program and a work program.
Compared adjustment measures for students who took part in 2 work programs for EMR graduates of special schools. 50 students took part in a work program (direct placement in the work) and 50 students, a work-study program. Age range of the 2 groups was 16–22 yrs; IQ was 60–80. The students, their parents, and their employers were interviewed regarding vocational satisfaction and adjustment. Results show that the work-study program graduates were significantly more stable, satisfied, and adjusted than were the work program graduates, but their professional opportunities (reflected by the number of different jobs held) were limited.
Margalit, Malka & Schuchman, Rachel. (Tel-Aviv U School of Education, Israel) American Journal of Mental Deficiency, 1978(May), Vol 82(6), 604–607. [PA, Vol 62:02297]

3406. Preparing teachers of the mildly retarded: An instructional module on reading.
Reports on the development, implementation, and evaluation of an instructional module in reading as part of a competency based program to prepare teachers of mildly handicapped children. The module, used in a 15-wk methods course for 66 graduate students, was divided into 5 content areas: (a) students read articles about reading and were tested on their knowledge; (b) students were equipped with basic procedures and techniques in reading assessment; (c) instructional strategies for teaching reading to the mildly handicapped were taught; (d) instructional materials in reading were presented; and (e) students were required to organize and design a reading program for 6 children. Participants rated the module after the course was over. Two main findings emerged: (a) few of the students had been previously prepared in reading methodology despite the fact that many of them were employed as teachers, and (b) partly because of this lack, the course could profitably be expanded to a full semester. General evaluative comments reflected overall satisfaction with the module.
Martinez, David H.; Odle, Sara J. & Anderson, Robert M. (Portland State U) Education & Training of the Mentally Retarded, 1978(Apr), Vol 13(2), 218–224. [PA, Vol 61:14220]

3407.   An evaluation of the teacher consultant model as an approach to mainstreaming.
Contrasted 2 special education resource service models for their effects on student achievement and on teacher and pupil behavior. A total of 547 mildly handicapped children (mean age 8.4 yrs) participated in the study—261 Ss in the teacher consultant model, 219 in the resource room model, and 67 controls. Dependent measures of academic achievement were the Word Recognition and Arithmetic subtests of the Wide Range Achievement Test and the Reading Comprehension subtest of the Peabody Individual Achievement Test. Academic performance gains were equivalent for both models, while teacher behaviors were judged slightly better under the teacher consultant model. Both approaches were superior to controls (no service). The parallel academic gains coupled with improved teacher behaviors suggest the utility of having both models in operation within a continuum of services. Data support increased instruction in the regular classroom, thereby promoting many of the goals of mainstreaming through education in the least restrictive alternative, improved regular teacher skills, and attenuation of the effects of labeling. (14 ref)
Miller, Ted L. & Sabatino, David A. (U Tennessee, Chattanooga) Exceptional Children, 1978(Oct), Vol 45(2), 86–91. [PA, Vol 62:07358]

3408.   Integration: The need for a systematic evaluation of the socio-adaptive aspect.
A review of the literature suggests that the impetus for the current trend toward the integration of the mentally handicapped child into regular classes stems, in part, from the disappointing results obtained with special class placement. As such, from an academic as well as an economic point of view, integration would seem to be a viable alternative. However, from the socio-adaptive perspective, data suggest that normal peer group attitudes toward educable mentally retarded children are not positive and can lead to the social isolation of these children. These attitudes have implications for the "modeling" that is assumed to operate within integrated educational programs. It is concluded that there is a need for a systematic evaluation of peer group and teacher attitudes within integrated educational programming. (31 ref)
Mosley, James L. (U Calgary, Canada) Education & Training of the Mentally Retarded, 1978(Feb), Vol 13(1), 4–8. [PA, Vol 61:09708]

3409.   Social acceptance of elementary educable mentally retarded pupils in the regular classroom.
Assessed the effectiveness of mainstreaming in a Tennessee school system in terms of the social acceptance or rejection of 32 educable mentally retarded (EMR) students by 32 of their non-EMR classmates. Results indicate that 5th- and 6th-grade EMR students received significantly lower sociometric ratings than a randomly selected sample of their non-EMR classmates. (17 ref)
Reese-Dukes, Judson L. & Stokes, Elizabeth H. (Middle Tennessee State U) Education & Training of the Mentally Retarded, 1978(Dec), Vol 13(4), 356–361. [PA, Vol 63:13010]

3410.   Test of the generality of Bobrow and Bower's comprehension hypothesis.
In a test of the generality of S. A. Bobrow and G. H. Bower's (see PA, Vol 43:12226) hypothesis, 36 educable mentally retarded (EMR) children (mean CA 101.8 mo; mean MA 71.3 mo) were assigned, following pretraining measures, to experimental and control conditions. The experimental group was given intensive training with both self-generated and supplied links, while the control group participated in the same training format but without mediational instruction. Posttraining measures strongly supported the applicability of the comprehension hypothesis to the associative learning of EMR children. Superior associative learning and greater comprehension occurred under generated as compared to supplied conditions.
Ross, Dorothea M. & Ross, Sheila A. American Journal of Mental Deficiency, 1978(Mar), Vol 82(5), 453–459. [PA, Vol 61:09712]

3411.   Facilitative effect of mnemonic strategies on multiple-associate learning in EMR children.
Following pretraining measures of multiple-associate learning and general memory skills, 33 educable mentally retarded children (mean CA 102 mo; mean MA 68.1 mo) were randomly assigned to 1 of 3 conditions: imagery, rote repetition, or control. Each group participated in a story and game program for 5 hrs over a 2-wk period that, depending on condition, involved intensive training in the use of either imagery or rote repetition or no direct mnemonic training. Posttraining measures of Ss who received mnemonic training showed marked improvement, with imagery being significantly superior to rote repetition.
Ross, Dorothea M. & Ross, Sheila A. American Journal of Mental Deficiency, 1978(Mar), Vol 82(5), 460–466. [PA, Vol 61:09711]

3412.   A comparison of intellectual, achievement, and adaptive behavior levels for students who are mildly retarded.
Argues that identification of retarded children and decisions on their educational placement should not necessarily be made on the basis of the same test data. To determine the statistical relationships between data used to identify retarded children and their academic achievement, 75 mildly retarded children (mean CA, 10 yrs; mean IQ, 62) were tested on the WISC, Adaptive Behavior Scales, and 3 subscales of the Wide Range Achievement Test and were scored for Expectancy Age (A. J Harris, 1970). The results suggest that adjusted expectancy level (based on MA) may be a better predictor of achievement than IQ. (7 ref)
Whorton, James E. & Algozzine, Robert F. (U Florida) Mental Retardation, 1978(Aug), Vol 16(4), 320–321. [PA, Vol 63:02086]

3413.   Special class exit criteria: A modest beginning.
Adaptive Behavior Scales, WISC Full-Scale IQ, and Wide Range Achievement Test scores were used to predict program placement for 75 educable mentally retarded Ss (mean CA 151 mo; mean IQ 61). Actual class placement was correctly predicted for 84% of the sample. (19 ref)
Algozzine, Robert; Whorton, James E. & Reid, William R. (U Florida) Journal of Special Education, 1979(Sum), Vol 13(2), 131–136. [PA, Vol 66:09063]

3414.   Adaptive behavior of retarded, slow-learner, and average intelligence children.
Scores on the WISC-R and the Adaptive Behavior Scales (ABS) were obtained for 94 elementary school children referred for psychological services in a southeastern rural area. Some of the adaptive behavior scores differentiated among Ss classified as educable mentally retarded, slow-learners, or average intelligence. Some of the domain subscores of the ABS seem to be of questionable validity and reliability. (9 ref)
Bailey, Brenda S. & Richmond, Bert O. (State Dept of Education, Atlanta, GA) Journal of School Psychology, 1979(Fal), Vol 17(3), 260–263. [PA, Vol 65:02166]

3415.   A drastically different analysis.
With regard to R. E. Childs's (see PA, Vol 66:8974) article on drastic changes in the education of the educable mentally retarded child, the present author suggests that hardly anything has changed for these children and that almost everything has changed in the way in which mental retardation is viewed. Therefore, although change has not taken place in the education of the retarded, it probably will during the next decade. Without taking a stand either for or against mainstreaming, the author concludes that people and society as a whole should, on the strength of their values, make the decision as to the degree to which they want society integrated. (3 ref)
Blatt, Burton. (Syracuse U) Mental Retardation, 1979(Dec), Vol 17(6), 303–306. [PA, Vol 66:08961]

3416.   Academic self-concept change in special education students: Some suggestions for interpreting self-concept scores.
Studied changes in academic self-concept, as measured by the Student's Perception of Ability Scale, in 50 severely learning disabled pupils (average WISC) and 18 educable mentally retarded pupils (WISC IQs 55–75) receiving full-time remedial placement and in 83 children in regular classroom. Ss were aged

8–12 yrs. Pre–post data were collected over a 12-mo period. Results reveal that full-time placement was accompanied by significant increases in academic self-concept, especially in the areas of reading/spelling and confidence. (13 ref)

Boersma, Frederic J.; Chapman, James W. & Battle, James. (U Alberta, Edmonton, Canada) Journal of Special Education, 1979(Win), Vol 13(4), 433–442. [PA, Vol 66:08965]

3417. The zone of potential development: Implications for intelligence testing in the year 2000.

Discusses the practice and interpretation of intelligence testing of educable retarded children. The current and future state of intelligence testing are discussed in terms of 3 criteria: their predictive, diagnostic, and remedial functions. Individual testing formats are considered within a framework of L. S. Vygotsky's (1978) theory of potential development and the underlying assumptions of that theory concerning task analysis and transfer of training. The social nature of the testing situation and the degree of contextual support provided for the learner are described. U. Neisser's (1976) distinction between academic intelligence and everyday thinking is discussed, with particular reference to the life adjustment of mildly retarded citizens. (54 ref)

Brown, Ann L. & French, Lucia A. (U Illinois) Intelligence, 1979(Jul–Sep), Vol 3(3), 255–273. [PA, Vol 64:11220]

3418. Effects of relaxation and EMG training on academic achievement of educable retarded boys.

Compared the effects of prerecorded relaxation tapes with EMG muscle relaxation exercises in 16 educable retarded boys. Results of a 10-wk study show that EMG-based relaxation resulted in significant gains in cognition, reading achievement, coordination, memory, and handwriting. All dependent measures for the tape group were in the positive direction but did not reach significance except for handwriting legibility. (4 ref)

Carter, John L.; Lax, Bernard & Russell, Harold L. (U Houston at Clear Lake City, Diagnostic Education Ctr) Education & Training of the Mentally Retarded, 1979(Feb), Vol 14(1), 39–41. [PA, Vol 64:04090]

3419. A drastic change in curriculum for the educable mentally retarded child.

Discusses the changes in education that educable mentally retarded (EMR) children have received—from a regular class curriculum approach, to an arts and crafts one emphasizing handwork, to a vocational emphasis where jobs were the major emphasis, to a curriculum emphasizing practical skills for independent living. It now appears that many educators have decided that EMR children are capable of handling regular class curriculums, supporting the position that they do not need special education but rather a remedial approach that assumes that the children have normal potential and only need correctional education. Problems associated with this drastic change in the educational curriculum are discussed. For example, curriculums designed for normal children are not meant for EMR children because they have different educational needs and the 2 groups cannot be equated. (14 ref)

Childs, Ronald E. (U Northern Colorado, Greeley) Mental Retardation, 1979(Dec), Vol 17(6), 299–301. [PA, Vol 66:08974]

3420. Rebuttal.

Responds to S. A. Warren's (see PA, Vol 66:9057) and B. Blatt's (see PA, Vol 66:8961) criticisms of the present author's (see PA Vol 66:8974) article on changes in the curriculum for the educable mentally retarded child. The author stands by his position that mentally retarded children need a special curriculum that accents practical skills for independent living, not regular class academics.

Childs, Ronald E. (U Northern Colorado, Greeley) Mental Retardation, 1979(Dec), Vol 17(6), 306. [PA, Vol 66:08975]

3421. Clinical criteria for mainstreaming mildly handicapped children.

Although integrating handicapped children into regular classrooms is a well-established educational practice, the clinical decision to mainstream a given child should be based on systematic consideration of several factors, such as age, degree of handicap, curriculum, social skills, class size, teacher competency, and family resources. These criteria are discussed, along with various approaches to and evidence for and against mainstreaming. (32 ref)

Forness, Steven R. (U California, Neuropsychiatric Inst, Los Angeles) Psychology in the Schools, 1979(Oct), Vol 16(4), 508–514. [PA, Vol 65:04159]

3422. Relationship between classroom behavior and achievement of mildly mentally retarded children.

Although the relationship between classroom behavior and academic achievement is well established for nonretarded children, the nature of this relationship is not clear for retarded children. Behavioral observations of 133 students (mean CA 11.3 yrs, mean IQ 66.1) in classrooms for educable mentally retarded children and for 44 educationally handicapped children (mean CA 10.7 yrs, mean IQ 77.2) were compared to the Ss' achievement scores on the Wide Range Achievement Tests Reading and Arithmetic subtests and the Stanford-Binet Intelligence Scale. Although significant correlations were found between some categories of behavior and achievement in arithmetic, the general absence of strong correlations was noteworthy when compared to previous findings on nonretarded Ss. (22 ref)

Forness, Steven R.; Silverstein, Arthur B. & Guthrie, Donald. (U California, Neuropsychiatric Inst, Los Angeles) American Journal of Mental Deficiency, 1979(Nov), Vol 84(3), 260–265. [PA, Vol 63:06397]

3423. Teaching number-word equivalences: A study of transfer.

Investigated whether retarded adolescents and nonretarded preschool children would generalize to other tasks involving printed number names if they were taught the number names in an auditory-receptive task. Four nonretarded preschool children (CAs 3 yrs, 3 mo [3-3], 3-7, and 4-7) and 3 retarded children (CAs 7-11, 8-4, and 11-1; IQs 50, 53, and 67) participated. All Ss could count and use spoken and printed numerals; none of the Ss could adequately perform any task involving printed number words. After receiving training on an auditory-receptive task involving printed number words, all Ss improved their performance on tasks involving matching printed number words and numerals and printed number words and sets and improved in their ability to name printed number words. (5 ref)

Gast, David L.; VanBiervliet, Alan & Spradlin, Joseph E. (U Kentucky) American Journal of Mental Deficiency, 1979(Mar), Vol 83(5), 524–527. [PA, Vol 62:07346]

3424. Comparison of response cost and timeout in a special education setting.

Compared 2 punishment procedures to determine their effectiveness in reducing rates of noncompliance among 11 educable mentally retarded Ss (CA 6–10 yrs, IQ 45–68) in a self-contained classroom at a middle-class suburban elementary school. Response cost consisted of taking tokens away from an S contingent upon noncompliance with teacher commands. Time-out consisted of placing noncompliant Ss outside of the group for 1 min for each noncompliance. Results suggest that response cost was as effective as the response-cost plus time-out contingency and that it was the controlling variable in reduction of noncompliant behavior. The potential of response cost as an effective alternative to the use of time-out is discussed, and ethical and legal ramifications concerning the use of punishment in special education settings are addressed. (27 ref)

Gresham, Frank M. (U South Carolina) Journal of Special Education, 1979(Sum), Vol 13(2), 199–208. [PA, Vol 66:08995]

3425. Psychodrama, creative movement and remedial arts for children with special educational needs.

Compared the effects of training in psychodrama or creative movement added to the regular school curriculum for educationally retarded children aged 11–13 yrs. Both experimental conditions led to more significant improvement in personality growth and achievement than did traditional teaching alone.

Hazelton, Ted; Price, Betty & Brown, George. AEP (Association of Educational Psychologists) Journal, 1979(Sum), Vol 5(1), 32–37. [PA, Vol 65:08826]

3426. Interaction between handicapped and nonhandicapped teenagers as a function of situational goal structuring: Implications for mainstreaming.
The effects of cooperative, individualistic, and laissez-faire goal structures were compared on interpersonal interaction and attraction between 18 13–16 yr old nonhandicapped junior high school students and 12 high trainable mentally retarded peers participating in 6 weekly sessions of a bowling class. Results indicate that considerably more positive interactions took place between nonhandicapped and handicapped Ss in the cooperative condition than in the individualistic or laissez-faire conditions. (18 ref)
Johnson, Roger T. et al. (U Minnesota, Minneapolis) American Educational Research Journal, 1979(Spr), Vol 16(2), 161–167. [PA, Vol 64:08858]

3427. Are retarded children more distractible? Observational analysis of retarded and nonretarded children's classroom behavior.
Retarded children are frequently characterized as more distractible and/or more outerdirected than are nonretarded children. In this study, behavior thought to reflect these processes and its relationship to task demands was examined. 29 educable mentally retarded and 29 nonretarded children aged 9–12 yrs were observed while they worked on academic classroom tasks; retarded Ss were also observed while they worked on nonacademic tasks. Retarded Ss were less attentive than nonretarded Ss during academic periods. They spent less time on task, more time out of their seats, and more time "looking busy" but not working. Little support was found for the notion that retarded children are more outerdirected than nonretarded children. Retarded Ss responded differently in nonacademic and academic situations, suggesting that behavior reflecting attention is task-related. Results are discussed in terms of previous conceptualizations of retarded persons' attention processes. (32 ref)
Krupski, Antoinette. (U California Graduate School of Education, Los Angeles) American Journal of Mental Deficiency, 1979(Jul), Vol 84(1), 1–10. [PA, Vol 62:12283]

3428. The effect of music on retention in a paired-associate task with EMR children.
Measured retention in a paired-associate task embedded in story and song format, using music as a mediator. Ss were 9 boys and 9 girls (7–11 yrs old) classified as educable mentally retarded (EMR) from Grades 2–5 of self-contained special education classes. Two lists of 10 word-pairs each were used, List A providing a warm-up exercise. List B was presented (a) as a list, (b) in story form, and (c) in the form of a song. Total recall scores for List B were higher than for the other 2 conditions, but the differences were not significant. Scores for boys were higher than for girls under all 3 conditions. It is concluded that music, when used in conjunction with training on retention techniques, can vary and enhance the learning situation with EMR children. (16 ref)
Myers, Elizabeth G. (Southwestern Virginia Training Ctr, Hillsville) Journal of Music Therapy, 1979(Win), Vol 16(4), 190–198. [PA, Vol 66:06732]

3429. Regular-classroom teachers' attributions and instructional prescriptions for handicapped and nonhandicapped pupils.
Examined 102 teachers' attributions and prescriptions for normal achieving (NA), educationally handicapped (EH), and educable mentally retarded (EMR) pupils. Ss were provided an experimental packet containing simulated background and current achievement information on an NA, EH, or EMR pupil. Background descriptive information reflected that pupil affected Ss' failure but not success attributions, as well as the manner in which they revised their failure-attribution ratings. It was found that Ss' initial instructional prescriptions were anchored by descriptive information reflecting characteristics of NA, EH, and EMR pupils. However, as Ss continued to receive current achievement information, their instructional decisions appeared to be more weighted on pupils' current performance and less on achievement history. (15 ref)
Palmer, Douglas J. (Texas A&M U) Journal of Special Education, 1979(Fal), Vol 13(3), 325–337. [PA, Vol 66:08844]

3430. A comparison of two methods of teaching a reading task to mildly intellectually handicapped adolescents.
Eight mildly intellectually handicapped trainees (mean age 17.01 yrs, mean IQ 70.88) at a work preparation center were taught to read 2 lists of words of equal difficulty by different methods. A pilot experiment had indicated that trainees had learned to read a list of difficult tool names incidentally while using an auto-instructional device to identify the names of the tools orally. In the present experiment the effectiveness of this approach was compared with a more traditional paired-associate method of teaching word recognition. Results indicate that there were no differences between the methods on the rate of acquisition, nor were there differences between the levels of retention after 6 mo. At least 90% of the words were retained on both lists by all Ss at the end of 6 mo. Results are discussed in the context of theories of attention, associated clustering, and overlearning. (21 ref)
Parmenter, Trevor R. et al. (Macquarie U, North Ryde, Australia), 1979(Mar), Vol 5(5), 28–32. [PA, Vol 66:09034]

3431. Parental influence on maladaptive behaviour of mentally retarded children in the classroom.
Determined the degree of parental influence on maladaptive behavior of 35 educable mentally retarded children (CA 9.65 yrs) in the classroom. Data were collected from the Ss' parents by means of sociometric questionnaires (the Parental Attitudinal Survey, the Hollingshead 2-Factor Index of Social Position) and from their teachers by means of a maladaptive behavior checklist. Results indicate that the parents' level of education, number of parents in the home, socioeconomic status, and the parents' attitude toward their retarded children significantly correlated with the children's maladaptive behavior in the classroom. (14 ref)
Peniston, Eugene & McLean, Marian G. (Virginia State Coll, Petersburg) British Journal of Mental Subnormality, 1979(Dec), Vol 25(49, Pt 2), 70–74. [PA, Vol 65:13048]

3432. Expectancy effects of labels: Fact or artifact?
Predictions were obtained from 36 classroom teachers concerning the performance of a child labeled as either gifted, normal, or educable mentally retarded at 4 intervals during the course of a 40-min period in which the teachers viewed a videotape of the child as he or she responded to tasks requiring reasoning, general information, word recognition skills, or knowledge. A significant interaction between label and length of exposure to the child was found, such that expectancy effects were reduced with increasing exposure. (10 ref)
Reschly, Daniel J. & Lamprecht, Michael J. (Iowa State U, Ames) Exceptional Children, 1979(Sep), Vol 46(1), 55–58. [PA, Vol 63:01928]

3433. The utility of multiple-choice test formats with mildly retarded adolescents.
Determined if 100 mildly mentally retarded secondary school students could respond to a verbally presented multiple-choice test of social and personal knowledge. This was of concern due to the lack of standardized group tests to measure classroom learning within the area of special education. Results indicate that Ss were capable of responding appropriately to 2- and 3-alternative tests. The reliability estimates obtained were moderately high given the number of test items. Validity coefficients were low although statistically significant. Conclusions are drawn as to the applicability of multiple-choice test formats for assessing educational achievement of mildly retarded students. (14 ref)
Reynolds, William M. (State U New York, Albany) Educational & Psychological Measurement, 1979(Sum), Vol 39(2), 325–331. [PA, Vol 64:08899]

3434. The factorial validity of the Piers-Harris Children's Self Concept Scale for a sample of intermediate-level EMR students enrolled in elementary school.
Scores of 117 8–12 yr old educable mentally retarded Ss on the Piers-Harris Children's Self-Concept Scale were factor analyzed. Partial support for the construct validity of the scale was obtained by replicating factors bearing on physical appearance and behavior. Some support was also found for factors reflecting popularity, academic ability, and anxiety. The factor analytic results are compared with those from other studies. Suggestions for future research include more clearly defining emotionally toned factors, broadening the response structure of the scale, considering maturational effects in attempting to replicate factors across age periods, and searching for a general self-concept factor. (7 ref)
Rich, Charles E.; Barcikowski, Robert S. & Witmer, J. Melvin. (Ohio U) Educational & Psychological Measurement, 1979(Sum), Vol 39(2), 485–490. [PA, Vol 64:06873]

3435. Cognitive training for the EMR child: Language skills prerequisite to relevant–irrelevant discrimination tasks.
Reports on the efficacy of a 6-wk training program for teaching educable mentally retarded (EMR) children the language skills prerequisite to distinguishing between the relevant and irrelevant features of a task. For 100 min/wk 20 5–10 yr old experimental (E) group Ss were given practice with the instructions used in relevant–irrelevant discrimination tasks within a story and game context. 20 matched control Ss also participated in story and game activities, but with no training in the discrimination instructions and tasks. The E group showed significant gains in the posttests, and there was subjective evidence of transfer to other classroom and playground activities. (13 ref)
Ross, Dorothea M. & Ross, Sheila A. (U California, San Francisco) Mental Retardation, 1979(Feb), Vol 17(1), 3–7. [PA, Vol 64:02165]

3436. The effect of type of reinforcer and reinforcement schedule on performances of EMR students on four selected subtests of the WISC-R.
A study with 120 educable mentally retarded students (mean age 11.8 yrs) examined the effect on performance of 3 types of test item response reinforcers (token, verbal praise, and verbal neutral) and 2 levels of reinforcement schedule (FR and continuous). Results indicate (a) no Reinforcement × Schedule interaction, (b) no main effect for Type of Schedule, and (c) a statistically significant positive effect on scaled scores for token and verbal praise reinforcers on the WISC-R Arithmetic, Digit Span, and Picture Completion subtests. No effect on Block Design scores was noted. (3 ref)
Saigh, Philip A. & Payne, David A. (U Georgia, Coll of Education, Athens) Psychology in the Schools, 1979(Jan), Vol 16(1), 106–110. [PA, Vol 65:13644]

3437. Special classroom placements for EMR children: Guidelines for community mental health personnel.
Community mental health personnel have become increasingly involved in public school interventions for mildly retarded children. Previous research, legal findings, and ethical principles regarding the most common intervention—special class placement—are reviewed. Advantages and disadvantages of special placement are presented. A process model is proposed as offering guidelines to the mental health professional who is involved in establishing treatment programs for such children. (29 ref)
Smead, Valerie S. & Goetz, Theodore M. (Human Development Ctr, Lubbock, TX) Community Mental Health Journal, 1979(Spr), Vol 15(1), 17–26. [PA, Vol 64:06258]

3438. Hierarchical assessment of social competence.
Examined 3 hypotheses concerning the Test of the Hierarchy of Inductive Knowledge: It was proposed that the processes assessed by the measure are (a) cumulative and hierarchical, (b) developmental, and (c) related to behavioral criteria. Analyses of data collected from 120 educable mentally retarded children (mean IQ 68.9) between the ages of 9 and 14 yrs generally supported the developmental and criterion-related features of the measure, but only partially confirmed the hierarchical component. Discussion focuses on the emphasis necessary in subsequent empirical work and on the measure's potential for instructional applications in relation to current assessment issues in special education. (19 ref)
Smith, I. Leon & Greenberg, Sandra. (New York U, Curriculum Research & Development Ctr in Mental Retardation) American Journal of Mental Deficiency, 1979(May), Vol 83(6), 551–555. [PA, Vol 62:09887]

3439. What is wrong with mainstreaming? A comment on drastic change.
Comments on R. E. Childs's (see PA, Vol 66:8974) article on the changes in curriculum for the educable mentally retarded (EMR) child. Childs suggests that mainstreaming is not beneficial because EMR children and children of normal intelligence have different educational needs. Although Childs makes some valid points in his criticism of this practice, in the absence of an empirical base for making decisions about the education of children, it may be advisable to encourage careful examination of all available data and to promote more research on the effects of mainstreaming. (4 ref)
Warren, Sue A. (Boston U) Mental Retardation, 1979(Dec), Vol 17(6), 301–303. [PA, Vol 66:09057]

3440. School psychology: The post *Larry P.* era.
Proposes 5 scenarios for the practice of school psychology in the post Larry P. era (*Larry P.* v. *Wilson Riles,* a case in which the State of California was enjoined from using IQ tests as a basis for placement of Black children in classes for the educable mentally retarded). It is noted that many other variables are likely to influence school psychology in the future; these include the resolution of differences between psychologists and educators, the outcome of various conferences scheduled for the early 1980's, and the effects of energy shortages and decreased program funds. It is argued that school psychology can survive, improve, and do well if it accepts the challenges posed by the Larry P. case. Conditions that could cause failure are also noted. (22 ref)
Bardon, Jack I. (U North Carolina, Greensboro) School Psychology Review, 1980(Spr), Vol 9(2), 159–167. [PA, Vol 64:01967]

3441. Developing Models for Special Education: Using a multiple time-series/multiple baseline design in the ESEA IV-C Project.
Describes the Developing Models for Special Education, a project designed to produce data for national validation, by presenting the theoretical model and its application in operational terms. Results of the project indicate that 80% of the children would master 80% of the objectives prescribed during a 6-wk evaluation period. It is concluded that this type of evaluation design is useful for projects employing specific behavior objectives and criterion-reference testing. (4 ref)
Bergquist, Constance C. & Graham, Darol L. Evaluation Review, 1980(Jun), Vol 4(3), 307–321. [PA, Vol 66:02147]

3442. *P.* v. *Riles*: Legal perspective.
Presents a descriptive analysis of *Larry P.* v. *Wilson Riles,* the landmark decision in which a federal district court enjoined California from using any standardized intelligence tests to assess Black children for educable mentally retarded (EMR) placement. The early history of school testing litigation is traced, including the initial decision in Larry P. in 1972 that preliminarily enjoined the defendants from using IQ tests until such time as there was a full trial on the merits. That final decision in 1979 is described in detail, including the statutory and constitutional bases the court used in deciding against California and the remedy it imposed on the state for discriminating against Black children incorrectly placed in EMR classes. (7 ref)
Bersoff, Donald N. (U Maryland School of Law, Baltimore) School Psychology Review, 1980(Spr), Vol 9(2), 112–122. [PA, Vol 64:00913]

3443.   A self-instructional package for increasing attending behavior in educable mentally retarded children.
Describes a self-instructional package developed to aid 2 9- and 11-yr-old highly distractible retarded children (WISC IQs 70 and 46, respectively) in increasing their attending behavior in a training and 2 generalization (one-to-one and classroom) situations. Three untrained Ss (9, 10, and 14 yrs old) were monitored for general comparison and social validation purposes. One of these control Ss was distractible and the other 2 (criterion comparison) did not have attentional problems. During training, experimental Ss were taught through self-instruction to focus their attention and to cope with math and printing tasks. After learning the self-instructions the Ss were sequentially exposed to slides of distracting situations, audio distractors (noisy lunchroom peer interactions), and in-vivo distractors (children playing with wooden blocks in the training setting). The entire training procedure was handled in a game-like context. The training package produced direct and generalized changes in self-instructional behavior. A decrease in off-task behavior also occurred during math, printing, and a phonics program in both generalization situations. Reliable changes in academic task performance were not observed, and no changes on any of the dependent measures occurred for the 3 untrained Ss. (31 ref)
Burgio, Louis D.; Whitman, Thomas L. & Johnson, Moses R. (U Notre Dame) Journal of Applied Behavior Analysis, 1980(Fal), Vol 13(3), 443–459. [PA, Vol 64:13375]

3444.   The efficacy of special versus regular class placement for exceptional children: A meta-analysis.
Selected 50 primary research studies of special vs regular class placement for use in a meta-analysis. Each study provided a measure of effect size (ES), defined as the posttreatment difference between special and regular placement means expressed in standard deviation units. ES was used as a dependent variable in order to assess the effects of independent variables such as placement, type of outcome measure, internal validity, and other educational, personological, and methodological variables. Special classes were found to be significantly inferior to regular class placement for students with below average IQs, and significantly superior to regular classes for behaviorally disordered, emotionally disturbed, and learning-disabled children. Other independent variables bore little or no relationship to ES. (85 ref)
Carlberg, Conrad & Kavale, Kenneth. Journal of Special Education, 1980(Fal), Vol 14(3), 295–309. [PA, Vol 66:06721]

3445.   Minimum competency testing: Implications for mildly retarded students.
The rapid adoption of minimum competency tests (MCT) as a necessary condition for a high school diploma has focused attention on a variety of educational and social issues. Of particular significance is the effect of MCT on the mildly mentally retarded high schooler. The present paper reviews the disadvantages, as well as the advantages, of competency tests on this special population. Alternatives to using MCT as a criterion for earning a diploma are suggested within the discussion of the movement's ultimate impact. (14 ref)
Cohen, Sandra B.; Safran, Joan & Polloway, Edward A. (U Virginia, Charlottesville) Education & Training of the Mentally Retarded, 1980(Dec), Vol 15(4), 250–255. [PA, Vol 66:11338]

3446.   Personal reflections on the *Larry P.* trial and its aftermath.
The author, counsel for the defendants, discusses personal opinions about the issues involved in the case of *Larry P.* v. *Wilson Riles,* in which the State of California was ordered to stop using standardized intelligence tests to identify Black children for educable mentally retarded (EMR) placement. It is argued that (a) the court treated the issue of what criteria to use in place of the IQ test as an issue of little importance; (b) there was inappropriate behavior toward Dr. Wilson Riles (the State Superintendent of Public Instruction) on the part of plaintiffs' counsel; (c) an assumption that EMR placement has no advantage over regular class placement has not been substantiated; (d) there is evidence to show that EMR labeling has not been detrimental to employment prospects; and (e) such controversy should not have surrounded a program that was always optional. (1 ref)
Condas, Joanne.   School Psychology Review, 1980(Spr), Vol 9(2), 154–158. [PA, Vol 64:02149]

3447.   Incidental learning in mildly retarded children.
Nine male and 6 female educable mentally retarded children (mean CA 11 yrs, MA 8 yrs, IQ 71) were compared with the same number of both CA- and MA-matched intellectually normal Ss on a Type 1 incidental learning task involving simple recognition and recall skills. Results show that retarded Ss learned incidentally as well as MA-matched normal Ss, but exhibited significantly poorer incidental learning than CA-matched normals. Findings support the hypothesis that an incidental learning deficiency exists for the retarded group compared with the CA- but not the MA-matched controls. (11 ref)
Fox, Robert & Rotatori, Anthony F. (Western Illinois U) Journal of General Psychology, 1980(Jan), Vol 102(1), 121–125. [PA, Vol 65:08207]

3448.   Teaching coin skills to EMR children: A curriculum study.
Attempted to determine the kinds of money skills attained by 100 educable mentally retarded (EMR) children and to construct and field-test a portion of a coin skills curriculum that was judged to be at an appropriate level for elementary-age EMR students. Ss had a mean CA of 116.6 mo and a mean IQ of 72.9. Results indicate that the procedures and materials developed and presented were successful in teaching the selected coin skills. (23 ref)
Frank, Alan R. & McFarland, Thomas D. (U Iowa, Div of Special Education, Iowa City) Education & Training of the Mentally Retarded, 1980(Dec), Vol 15(4), 270–278. [PA, Vol 66:11283]

3449.   Recreation for mildly retarded students: An important component of individualized education plans.
Notes that although the value of recreation, or the wise and constructive use of leisure time, for retarded persons has been recognized in the professional literature for several years, the inclusion of recreation in the development of individualized education plans has not been fully realized. The authors encourage such action by selectively reviewing those suggestions put forth in the literature. In addition, specific intructional goals, such as promoting self-concept, are presented. (26 ref)
Frith, Greg H.; Mitchell, Janet W. & Roswal, Glenn. (Jackson State U) Education & Training of the Mentally Retarded, 1980(Oct), Vol 15(3), 199–203. [PA, Vol 66:08988]

3450.   Improving recall in retarded persons: Consistency of ordering and simultaneity of presentation.
Investigated consistency of ordering (blocked or random) and presentation method (simultaneous or sequential) in a multitrial, free recall task with 60 educable mentally retarded adolescents. In the blocked–simultaneous condition, 5 groups of 3 stimuli were presented consistently in the same groups from trial-to-trial as well as simultaneously (with 3 words on a slide). The blocked–sequential condition maintained the consistent ordering, but only 1 item at a time was presented. In a random–simultaneous condition, stimuli were presented in changing groups of 3. A random–sequential treatment used both inconsistent ordering and sequential presentation. Consistent ordering led to facilitation of organization and recall from both recency and other serial positions. Subjective organization and clustering were also enhanced by simultaneous presentation. It is concluded that if 1 instructional strategy had to be chosen in an applied context, it should be consistent ordering and simultaneous presentation. (12 ref)
Glidden, Laraine M. & Klein, J. S. (St Mary's Coll of Maryland, Div of Human Development) Journal of Mental Deficiency Research, 1980(Dec), Vol 24(4), 299–306. [PA, Vol 66:08992]

3451.   Locus of control and social reinforcement in the motor performance of educable mentally retarded students.
Investigated whether social reinforcement in the form of verbal praise would differentially influence performance on an accuracy motor task in 100 educable mentally retarded elementary students, who were determined to be internal or external by scores on the Children's Locus of Control Scale. ANOVA revealed that social reinforcement was a significant variable in the performance of internally controlled Ss. (15 ref)
Heitman, Robert J. & Justen, Joseph E. (U South Alabama, Coll of Education, Mobile) Education & Training of the Mentally Retarded, 1980(Oct), Vol 15(3), 204–208. [PA, Vol 66:08999]

3452.   A career awareness program for educable mentally retarded students.
Results from a modified version of the Vocational Exploration Group Participant Assessment Form administered to 14 12–16 yr olds (53–72 IQ) indicate that a counselor trainee succeeded in modifying counseling procedures and commercial career education materials to assist Ss. (13 ref)
Johnson, Norbert; Flowers, Andy; Johnson, Sara C. & Johnson, Jerome. (Troy State U) Vocational Guidance Quarterly, 1980(Jun), Vol 28(4), 328–334. [PA, Vol 64:13388]

3453.   Teaching addition and subtraction to mentally retarded children: A self-instruction program.
Two self-instruction procedures were used to teach addition and subtraction regrouping skills to 3 mildly mentally retarded children (CAs of 9 yrs, 2 mo to 10 yrs, 3 mo and WISC IQs of 62, 69, and 74) who had failed to learn addition and subtraction under normal classroom conditions. Number of problems completed and accuracy were monitored during a daily math period, and the effects of the procedures were assessed through a multiple baseline design. For all Ss, increases in accuracy on math problems requiring regrouping were evident during respective training conditions. Correlated but less pronounced increases in accuracy on addition and subtraction problems not requiring regrouping also occurred. A decline in the number of problems completed by each S was noted. (22 ref)
Johnston, Mary B.; Whitman, Thomas L. & Johnson, Moses R. (U Notre Dame) Applied Research in Mental Retardation, 1980, Vol 1(3–4), 141–160. [PA, Vol 66:09011]

3454.   Instructional procedures for teaching reversible passive voice and clause constructions to three mildly handicapped children.
Investigated the application of systematic instructional procedures in simplifying the complex sentence forms of reversible passives and clause constructions. Multiple baselines assessed treatment and maintenance effects in 3 Ss. Findings suggest that applied behavior analysis focusing on antecedent events of comprehension training can teach mildly handicapped children to comprehend complex sentence forms. (14 ref)
Kameenui, Ed; Carnine, Doug & Maggs, Alex. (U Oregon) Exceptional Child, 1980(Mar), Vol 27(1), 29–40. [PA, Vol 66:06727]

3455.   Regular class teachers' attitudes and perceptions of the Resource Specialist Program for educable mentally retarded pupils.
Assessed the perceptions and attitudes of 91 regular classroom teachers toward the Resource Specialist Program (RSP), which is the major transitional program for educable mentally retarded students provided by the California Master Plan for Special Education. Results from a 22-item questionnaire indicate favorable responses for 5 categories assessing various aspects of the program. Differences emerged, however, between grade levels. Lower elementary and secondary Ss revealed approving perceptions and attitudes, while middle school Ss expressed some concern. In contrast to earlier evaluations, findings suggest general satisfaction with the RSP. (6 ref)
Kavale, Kenneth A. & Rossi, Constance. (U California, Riverside) Education & Training of the Mentally Retarded, 1980(Oct), Vol 15(3), 195–198. [PA, Vol 66:09014]

3456.   Differential reinforcement of incompatible behavior (DRI) in treating classroom management problems of developmentally disabled children.
Examined the use of DRI procedures in treating the classroom management problems of 2 developmentally disabled children (a 10-yr-old male and a 6-yr-old female). Each study utilized reinforcement delivered on adjusting schedules. In Study I hallucinatory verbalizing was eliminated by reinforcing S for remaining quiet during specified intervals. In Study 2 out-of-seat behavior was suppressed by reinforcing appropriate sitting. In each case the effects of DRI were immediate and produced stable suppression, but these positive results were restricted to settings in which treatment was applied. Procedures used to maintain the effects of intervention are discussed. (11 ref)
Luiselli, James K.; Colozzi, Gail A.; Helfen, Carol S. & Pollow, Robin S. (Thompson School, Behavioral Intervention Project, Arlington, MA) Psychological Record, 1980(Spr), Vol 30(2), 261–270. [PA, Vol 65:13600]

3457.   The new educable mentally retarded population: Can they be mainstreamed?
Collected data on 151 8–15 yr old educable mentally retarded (EMR) students at the beginning and end of a 2-yr period. At the time of the 2nd data collection, 28 of the Ss were no longer EMR: 14 had returned to regular classes as "normal" students, and 14 were reclassified into one of the special education categories other than EMR. Teachers completed questionnaires concerning the curricular areas in which the Ss were integrated and the amount of time this integration occurred during the course of the week. Integration is defined as spending 135 min or more per day in a regular classroom with nonhandicapped children. Results show that most of the Ss were not integrated for any kind of instruction. Ss were provided instruction in academic subjects in segregated classes; slightly more integration was attempted in art, music, and vocational education classes. (6 ref)
MacMillan, Donald L. & Borthwick, Sharon A. (U California, Riverside) Mental Retardation, 1980(Aug), Vol 18(4), 155–158. [PA, Vol 66:09021]

3458.   Convergent and discriminant validity of Project PRIME's *Guess Who?*
Two forms of the Guess Who?, a peer-assessment instrument, were administered to 1,095 7–14 yr old mildly handicapped learners and 143 teachers. Factor analysis of the student and teacher ratings yielded 3 factors—disruptive, bright, and dull—for both sets of data. Factor scores for the 2 forms were then intercorrelated in a multitrait–multimethod matrix, and the results established the convergent and discriminant validity of the instrument. (6 ref)
MacMillan, Donald L.; Morrison, Gale M. & Silverstein, Arthur B. (U California School of Education, Riverside) American Journal of Mental Deficiency, 1980(Jul), Vol 85(1), 78–81. [PA, Vol 64:08890]

3459.   Correlates of social status among mildly handicapped learners in self-contained special classes.
Studied the contributions of perceived cognitive competence and misbehavior to the variance in the sociometric status of 222 educable mentally retarded (EMR) and 65 educationally handicapped (EH) children in self-contained special classes. Teachers and peers rated Ss on academic competence and misbehavior. Results indicate that the combined teacher ratings of these 2 dimensions accounted for the most variance in both acceptance and rejection of EMR Ss, whereas ratings of academic competence were associated with both acceptance and rejection of EH Ss. Results are discussed in terms of differential factors associated with social status of mildly handicapped learners in special classes vs regular classes. In addition, the data suggest the importance of differences in the characteristics of children doing the rating of both independent and dependent variables. (9 ref)
MacMillan, Donald L. & Morrison, Gale M. (U California School of Education, Riverside) Journal of Educational Psychology, 1980(Aug), Vol 72(4), 437–444. [PA, Vol 64:08862]

3460.   Larry P.: An educational interpretation.
Discusses the educational significance of the decision, in *Larry P.* v. *Wilson Riles,* to permanently enjoin the state of California from using IQ tests as a criterion for placing Black children in EMR (educably mentally retarded) classes. It is argued that the court did not give sufficient weight to the facts that children were not routinely IQ tested before serious school failure singled them out for the assessment process, persons trained to give IQ tests are also trained to make allowances for cultural and linguistic disadvantage in interpreting test results, and a large proportion of children determined to be EMR eligible were never so placed. Additional issues considered are: (a) how predictive tests are related to school curriculum, (b) the debatability of the court's protrayal of special EMR classes as stigmatizing, (c) changes in the EMR population between the original hearing and the final decision, (d) semantic confusion over concepts of mild mental retardation and cognitive capacity, and (e) the impact of the decision on Black children experiencing academic difficulties. (20 ref)
MacMillan, Donald L. & Meyers, C. Edward. (U California, Riverside) School Psychology Review, 1980(Spr), Vol 9(2), 136–148. [PA, Vol 64:02160]

3461.   System-identification of mildly mentally retarded children: Implications for interpreting and conducting research.
Argues that the system of identification of educable mentally retarded (EMR) children is designed to find children for service delivery and is not intended to identify a population with known parameters. Variability in the system derives from several sources: teacher judgment of academic failure, teacher referral, screening of referrals, and factors related to the assessment process. Moreover, recent litigation and sociopolitical forces have compounded this variability to the point of obscuring the population parameters of EMR or mildly mentally retarded children. (14 ref)
MacMillan, Donald L.; Meyers, C. Edward & Morrison, Gale M. (U California School of Education, Riverside) American Journal of Mental Deficiency, 1980(Sep), Vol 85(2), 108–115. [PA, Vol 64:13429]

3462.   Intelligence test on trial.
An attorney for the plaintiff in the *Larry P.* v. *Wilson Riles* case discusses how the major focus of contention came to be the validity of IQ tests. It is stated that the plaintiffs had 2 goals: (a) to stop the placement of disproportionate numbers of Black children in EMR (educable mentally retarded) classes and (b) to prove that IQ tests were improperly used to support the contention that Black people had lower intelligence than White people. In detailing the pretrial history of the case, it is stated that the court acted only after there had been a failure to act by every other responsible agency. The state had the burden of proving that a disproportionate number of Blacks were of limited intelligence. Trial arguments for and against the validity of IQ tests are summarized. It is argued that a fair reviewer of the case would find that Black children were overenrolled in EMR classes, that IQ tests played a substantial role in the decision to send a child to EMR classes, and the difference in IQ scores found for Black and White children is a function of culture rather than intelligence.
Madden, Palmer B. (Morrison & Foerster, San Francisco, CA) School Psychology Review, 1980(Spr), Vol 9(2), 149–153. [PA, Vol 64:00922]

3463.   The effect of educable mental retardation descriptive information on regular classroom teachers' attributions and instructional prescriptions.
Examined the effect of (a) the educable mental retardation (EMR) label, (b) psychometric information, or (c) label and psychometric information on teachers' attributions and instructional prescriptions. Ss were a total of 102 elementary school teachers: 34 received only labeling information on an EMR pupil, 34 received only psychometric data, and 34 received both types of information. Results show that EMR labeling and psychometric information similarly affected Ss' attributions and their instructional prescriptions. However, EMR labeling information affected the manner in which Ss revised their pupil ability attributional ratings. In addition, it was noted that accumulation of EMR information rather than type of information affected teachers' instructional prescriptions. (8 ref)
Palmer, Douglas J. (Texas A&M U, College Station) Mental Retardation, 1980(Aug), Vol 18(4), 171–175. [PA, Vol 66:08845]

3464.   Psychological evidence in the *Larry P.* opinion: A case of right problem—wrong solution?
Presents arguments and counterarguments concerning the issues that surfaced during the court trial of *Larry P.* v. *Wilson Riles.* The history of IQ testing, various definitions of bias in testing (e.g., mean differences, content bias, and predictive validity) and the relative influence of each of these definitions on the trial outcome are presented and explained. The validity of the mild mental retardation placement classification is discussed, and it is noted that changes may be underway and will be welcomed by psychologists. Brief mention is made of the nature vs nurture controversy applied to intelligence, the meaning of IQ test results, the role of IQ tests in the placement process, and recent changes in the percentage of Black pupils in mild mental retardation placement. It is hoped that a focus on test bias will be dropped in favor of broader issues of the usefulness and fairness of assessment procedures in developing effective programs for children. (47 ref)
Reschly, Daniel J. (Iowa State U) School Psychology Review, 1980(Spr), Vol 9(2), 123–135. [PA, Vol 64:00926]

3465.   The diagnostic/instructional link in individualized education programs.
Investigated the extent to which the long-term goals and short-term instructional objectives of the Individualized Education Program (IEP) can be documented as being predicated upon the psychoeducational assessment. The IEPs and corresponding psychoeducational assessments of 243 students identified as educable mentally retarded, emotionally disturbed, or learning disabled were collected and analyzed. Results reveal that the goals and objectives of the IEP have a limited foundation in the psychoeducational assessment. Specific consequences of this situation are discussed in terms of impact on the education of handicapped students, as well as suggestions for strengthening the diagnostic/instructional link in IEPs. (8 ref)
Schenck, Susan J. (Coll of Charleston) Journal of Special Education, 1980(Fal), Vol 14(3), 337–345. [PA, Vol 66:06737]

3466.   Teacher factors and special class placement.
Examined attitudes and personal characteristics of 32 regular class teachers. Of these, 16 had had a 7- or 8-yr-old child transferred from their class to a special class (SC Ss), while the remainder, who had children of comparable age and ability in their classes, did not refer such children to special class placement (NR Ss). NR Ss were more in favor of mainstream provisions for low-ability children; they reported a higher proportion of low achievers in their classes; and a higher proportion of them were married. (23 ref)
Smart, Rosemary; Wilton, Keri & Keeling, Brian. (U Canterbury, Christchurch, New Zealand) Journal of Special Education, 1980(Sum), Vol 14(2), 217–229. [PA, Vol 66:06645]

3467.   Teaching measurements skills to mentally retarded students: Training, generalization, and follow-up.
Three mentally retarded students (CAs 17–23 yrs; IQs 59–61) received instruction in 7 areas related to ruler usage. A task analysis of measurement skills identified the 1st 3 areas as prerequisite skills and the remaining 4 as basic components of measuring. Results show that Ss learned to measure correctly on follow-up tests. Ss also showed improvement in estimating and measuring the length of novel objects. (9 ref)
Smeenge, Merri E.; Page, Terry J.; Iwata, Brian A. & Ivancic, Martin T. (Western Michigan U, Kalamazoo) Education & Training of the Mentally Retarded, 1980(Oct), Vol 15(3), 224–230. [PA, Vol 66:09046]

3468.   [A follow-up study of former pupils of special schools for the educable mentally retarded.] (Norg)
Conducted a follow-up study on 30 adults born during 1937–1943 who attended special schools for the educably mentally retarded upon reaching the age of 14 yrs. Information about education, occupation, and social and personal problems was obtained, and Ss were given the WAIS and other cognitive tests. Results show that it was impossible or difficult to understand written performance in Norwegian for approximately half of the Ss, and 40% grasped some of the elementary rules of multiplication. IQ was related to competence in written Norwegian and to skills in math. Ss with the lowest IQ scores were receiving a disability pension at adult age, and the greatest gain in IQ scores was obtained by Ss who had the most difficult living conditions in childhood. (22 ref)
Svendsen, Dagmund. (U i Bergen, Inst for Kognitiv Psykologi, Norway) Tidsskrift for Norsk Psykologforening, 1980(Jun), Vol 17(6), 270–275. [PA, Vol 65:13053]

3469.   Identification and labelling and the provision for mildly intellectually handicapped in special classes in Queensland.
Criticizes the myriad euphemisms that have been used through the years to identify the child who is below normal in intellectual capacity (e.g., backward, retarded, slow learner, learning disabled, dyslexic) and contends that in time any new such term takes on negative overtones. In addition, the paper reports a study of attitudes of mildly mentally handicapped (IQ 50–80) and nonhandicapped 10–16 yr olds toward special education or "opportunity" classes attached to regular classes. Results show that handicapped Ss viewed their special classes positively but that the attitudes of nonhandicapped Ss toward those in the special classes needed improvement. (18 ref)
Swan, Geoffrey. (Baroona Special School, Brisbane, Australia) Australian Journal of Developmental Disabilities, 1980(Jun), Vol 6(2), 61–70. [PA, Vol 66:09051]

3470.   Sensitivity to orthographic structure in educable mentally retarded children.
Presented 30 educable mentally retarded (EMR) children (mean CA 113.8 mo; mean MA 80.6 mo) with an item selection task to assess their sensitivity to orthographic structure in printed English words. Ss were also administered the Peabody Picture Vocabulary Test and the Peabody Individual Achievement Test. Analyses of performance indicated that Ss acquired implicit knowledge of orthographic rules and that this ability was related to the development of reading skills. (13 ref)
Allington, Richard L. (State U New York, Albany) Contemporary Educational Psychology, 1981(Apr), Vol 6(2), 135–139. [PA, Vol 66:11263]

3471.   Influence of a child's race and the EMR label on initial impressions of regular-classroom teachers.
99 elementary school teachers were shown a photograph of an 11-yr-old Black, Mexican-American, or White child and were told that the child was either educable mentally retarded (EMR) or attended a 5th-grade class. Three dependent measures were used to assess Ss' initial impressions of the child's attractiveness and academic and behavioral potential. Data indicate that the race of the child significantly influenced Ss' initial expectations. The EMR label yielded significant results when Ss assessed the child's intellectual potential. A significant interaction was found on the behavioral measure between race and label, indicating that the race and label of a child can differentially influence a teacher's initial impressions of his or her behavior. (21 ref)
Aloia, Gregory F.; Maxwell, James A. & Aloia, Stephen D. (Arkansas State U, State University) American Journal of Mental Deficiency, 1981(May), Vol 85(6), 619–623. [PA, Vol 66:06628]

3472.   Socioeconomic bias in special education placement decisions.
Analyzed the planning and placement decisions of the Educational Placement and Planning Committees for 973 students (mean CA 10.9 yrs) in Michigan. An attempt was made to determine if evidence suggesting a socioeconomic bias in placement existed. Data included Ss from 5 categories: learning disabled, educable mentally impaired, emotionally impaired, otherwise impaired, and nonimpaired. No statistically significant differences that would indicate a socioeconomic bias were found. However, other factors (sex, age, intelligence, location of district) may contribute substantially to special education placement. Significant agreement was found between school psychologists and teacher consultants with respect to placement decisions. (8 ref)
Bernard, Robert & Clarizio, Harvey. (Michigan State U, Coll of Education, East Lansing) Psychology in the Schools, 1981(Apr), Vol 18(2), 178–183. [PA, Vol 66:11267]

3473.   Generalization of verbal abstraction strategies by EMR children and adolescents.
Compared the effectiveness of strategy-training programs on the verbal abstraction performance of 80 educable mentally retarded (EMR) Ss (mean CA 12.01 yrs; mean MA 7.73 yrs). Training programs differed in the degree of S self-management required. In terms of acquisition, all 3 training conditions, irrespective of the degree of self-management required, were superior to the control condition. At maintenance, the 2 self-managing conditions (self-instruction and modeling) were superior both to more traditional instructor-controlled training (relevant attributes) and to the control condition. All 3 training conditions were more effective in promoting generalization when compared to the control condition. (27 ref)
Burger, Agnes L.; Blackman, Leonard S. & Clark, Henry T. (New York U) American Journal of Mental Deficiency, 1981(May), Vol 85(6), 611–618. [PA, Vol 66:06720]

3474.   Larry P. and the EMR child.
Reviews Judge Peckham's decision in *Larry P.* vs *Riles,* which enjoined the use of standardized IQ tests on Black children for the purpose of educable mentally retarded placement unless the court gives prior approval to the testing. While this decision applies only in California, the potential precedent-setting nature of this decision is discussed. An ecologically oriented classification system is presented as an alternative service delivery model. (16 ref)
Cremins, James J. (Boston Coll) Education & Training of the Mentally Retarded, 1981(Apr), Vol 16(2), 158–161. [PA, Vol 66:09077]

3475.   The attitudes of nonhandicapped students toward the mildly retarded: A consideration in placement decisions.
A review of the literature indicates mixed empirical results regarding the acceptance of mildly retarded students (MMRs) by their nonretarded peers (NRs). Analysis of the surveyed studies suggested several summary statements: (a) Interaction between MMRs and NRs did not necessarily improve acceptance of MMRs and NRs; acceptance increased when contact between MMRs and NRs was limited. (b) NR males displayed more rejection of MMRs than did NR females. (C) Well-adjusted NRs did not accept MMRs better than poorly adjusted NRs. (d) Appropriate social behaviors may be more critical than academic skills in terms of acceptance of MMRs by NR peers. The potential need for "inservice" workshops for NRs to increase their understanding of MMR peers is noted. It is suggested that the role and input of NR peers of individual education plan committees, particularly at the secondary level, be recognized. (18 ref)
Frith, Greg H. & Mitchell, Janet W. (Jacksonville State U) Education & Training of the Mentally Retarded, 1981(Feb), Vol 16(1), 79–83. [PA, Vol 66:08987]

3476.   Computer-assisted teaching of sight-word recognition for mentally retarded school children.
Describes and evaluates a computer-assisted training program used to teach a sight vocabulary to 16 mildly mentally retarded schoolchildren (aged 9–16 yrs). The training program was designed to supplement conventional methods of teaching by using aspects of computer technology to implement various learning principles that would otherwise be difficult to employ. Eight Ss were taught associations between the written and spoken

versions of words by a "talking" computer. These Ss increased their sight vocabularies by an average of 128%; a comparison group had a 34% increase. Furthermore, this increase remained constant for over 23 wks following the completion of the nonintensive 4-wk training program. (13 ref)
Lally, M. (Australian National U, Information Sciences Lab, Canberra) American Journal of Mental Deficiency, 1981(Jan), Vol 85(4), 383–388. [PA, Vol 65:08830]

3477.   Effects of exceptionality status and art instruction on Goodenough-Harris standard IQs.
Results from 72 nonexceptional, learning disabled, and educable mentally retarded Ss (CAs 8–15 yrs) show that exceptionality, art instruction, and time elapsing between test administrations affected Goodenough-Harris Drawing Test composite standard IQs. (6 ref)
Lindsey, Jimmy D. & Frith, Greg H. (Jacksonville State U) American Journal of Mental Deficiency, 1981(May), Vol 85(6), 658–660. [PA, Vol 66:06768]

3478.   Evaluation of the effects of SOMPA measures on classification of students as mildly mentally retarded.
Recent suggestions for changes in classification criteria for mild mental retardation, advocated in the literature and by the courts and federal agencies, were investigated with samples of children from 4 sociocultural groups (149 White, 128 Black, 125 Hispanic, 122 Native American Papago). Application of the requirements of sociocultural background and broadly conceived adaptive behavior, using the System of Multicultural Pluralistic Assessment Adaptive Behavior Inventory for Children and Estimated Learning Potential measures, sharply reduced the number and percentage of children eligible for mild mental retardation classification in all sociocultural groups. Implications for the diagnostic construct of mild mental retardation and for the concept of bias in assessment are discussed. (17 ref)
Reschly, Daniel J. (Iowa State U, Ames) American Journal of Mental Deficiency, 1981(Jul), Vol 86(1), 16–20. [PA, Vol 66:09117]

3479.   Individualization, simulation, and integration: A model secondary program for the mildly mentally handicapped.
Presents an individualized instructional program for promoting self-confidence and functional skills of 30 14–19 yr old mildly mentally handicapped Ss. Simulation was used extensively as an instructional technique as was integration into regular classes on the basis of need and ability. On the Social and Prevocational Information Battery, Ss averaged an 8-point percentile improvement for each year in the program. (7 ref)
Sargent, Laurence R.; Lehman, Regina; Smith, Darrell L. & Hildebrandt, Carol. (Iowa Dept of Public Instruction, Des Moines) Education & Training of the Mentally Retarded, 1981(Apr), Vol 16(2), 162–165. [PA, Vol 66:09041]

3480.   Intergroup contact and social outcomes for mainstreamed EMR adolescents.
Examined the prediction of the hypothesis that contact between nonretarded and educable mentally retarded (EMR) adolescents would result in the EMR adolescents being viewed as more competent, likeable, and socially acceptable. 26 mainstreamed EMR Ss (mean age 16 yrs) participated. Likeability, competence, and acceptability scores were computed for each S on the basis of responses by 438 nonretarded and EMR classmates to a survey questionnaire. Intergroup contact did not significantly modify the attitudes of nonretarded Ss toward the EMR Ss, who were viewed as significantly more competent, likeable, and socially acceptable by EMR classmates in the special class than by nonretarded classmates in the mainstream class. (17 ref)
Stager, Susan F. & Young, Richard D. (Indiana U, Bloomington) American Journal of Mental Deficiency, 1981(Mar), Vol 85(5), 497–503. [PA, Vol 65:13608]

Moderate Mental Retardation

3481.   Behavior incidents in a state residential institution for the mentally retarded.
Behavior incidents continue to be a concern of administrators of large multipurpose institutions. The pattern of unacceptable behavior of 1,260 residents at an institution was studied and compared with that at typical junior and senior high schools with 1,066 student Ss. It was found that misbehavior occurs most often among teenage trainable male retardates on the afternoon shift during the summer months. Twice as many medical problems are reported as behavior problems. It appears that although the behavior criteria varies, the typical junior or senior high school does not seem to have more or less appreciable number of behavior incidents that do retardates in a residential institution.
Dayan, Maurice. (Pinecrest State School, Pineville, La.) Mental Retardation, 1970(Feb), Vol. 8(1), 29-31. [PA, Vol 47:11469]

3482.   The effects of institutionalization upon prescriptive teaching for the moderately mentally retarded.
Analyzes classroom effects of institutionalization based on observations of 180 children in Project 50 at the Columbus State Institute. Prescriptive teaching, involving a systematic approach to the education of children, is viewed as dependent on knowledge of learning characteristics of the retarded, knowledge of the task, and employment of motivational techniques and procedures for teaching specific tasks. Tasks include not only psychological concepts, but also educational concepts, e.g., ability to count blocks. Some specific procedures are discussed.
Bradley, Betty H. (Columbus State Inst., O.) Australian Journal of Mental Retardation, 1971(Mar), Vol. 1(5), 150-153. [PA, Vol 48:09543]

3483.   The effect of a special instructional program on young "non-educable" children.
Explored the nature of the interrelationships between intellectual functioning and language development in an educational and environmental enrichment program. 2 matched groups (n = 12) of young trainable retardates were tested by Stanford-Binet Intelligence Scale, Form L-M, Vineland Social Maturity Scale, and Illinois Test of Psycholinguistic Abilities (ITPA). The experimental group was assigned a project teacher, received language lessons, a special curriculum, and field trips. The control group remained in their classrooms. The Wilcoxon matched-pairs signed-ranks test (a 2-tailed test with a .01 significance level) was employed for a statistical comparison of the 2 groups. At the end of 9 mo., the scores of the experimental group were significantly higher on the total ITPA scores and auditory vocal association. It is concluded that environmental enrichment alone does not make substantial improvement in language development.
Chovan, William L. (Western Carolina U.) Western Carolina University Journal of Education, 1971(Fal), Vol. 3(2), 22-28. [PA, Vol 49:03125]

3484.   Implementing an evaluative-prescriptive approach to curriculum for TMR children.
Describes an evaluative-prescriptive approach to curriculum planning for trainable mentally retarded children, emphasizing the teacher's key role as evaluator-prescriptor-implementer. 13 teachers and 20 assistants participated in the pilot testing phase of the program, and their reactions are reported. Suggestions are made for further direction and purpose for this approach.
Cox, Eunice W. & Winters, Stanley A. (Queens Coll., City U. New York) Education & Training of the Mentally Retarded, 1971(Dec), Vol. 6(4), 156-160. [PA, Vol 50:01727]

3485.   Effects of physical education on fitness and motor development of trainable mentally retarded children.
Determined the effect of a physical education program on the physical fitness and motor development of 36 8-18 yr. old children classified as trainable mentally retarded. An experimental group of 18 Ss had a 30-min planned physical education program for 58 consecutive school days. The control groups had

free play or teacher-directed recreational activity during this time. On 2 fitness test items, the shuttle run and sit-ups, the experimental group improved significantly. No other statistically significant results were obtained. (15 ref.)
Funk, Dean C. (Valley High School, Las Vegas, Nev.) Research Quarterly, 1971(Mar), Vol. 42(1), 30-34. [PA, Vol 46:07500]

3486.   Fundamental educational problems suggested by recent investigations into the characteristics of moderately retarded children.
Presents case histories, specific remedies applied, and examples of programmed reading used. It is observed that a global concept of IQ does not consider areas of proficiency or deficiency. Moderately retarded children are qualitatively different, and this commits the educationist to a training approach which involves the child in repeated exposure. An alternative assumption is that each child has a range of perceptual and emotional characteristics at various levels of development. The child's emotional status colors his relationship with the total environment, and is established before induced learning occurs. It is concluded that assessment in many areas is important in planning the child's educational program.
Johnson, K. E. (Cromehurst Special School, Lindfield, New South Wales, Australia) Australian Journal of Mental Retardation, 1971(Mar), Vol. 1(5), 141-144. [PA, Vol 48:09713]

3487.   Programming for trainable mentally retarded children.
Outlines current views of education for the mentally retarded and presents educational observations based upon these views. Specific goals for a work-play program and broad goals are suggested for guidelines for teachers. The necessity of translating broad goals into specific instruction objectives is emphasized. The focus on the individual child is enhanced through task-analysis approach. (19 ref.)
Leong, Che Kan. (U. Saskatchewan, Inst. of Child Guidance & Development, Saskatoon, Canada) Slow Learning Child, 1972(Jul), Vol. 19(2), 102-108. [PA, Vol 49:09981]

3488.   Mental retardation: Parents' perception of the problem.
Studied parents' perceptions of schooling problems as part of a larger study to evaluate the merits of different forms of schooling. 39 male and 21 female retarded children (average age = 11.8 yr.) at a special school for the mildly retarded were given the WISC performance scale and Vineland Social Maturity Scale early in the academic year, and the 44 Ss who completed 1 yr. of training were retested late in the year. Scores of the 16 dropouts were analyzed, and there was found to be a significant risk (p = .05) that low IQ, low social maturity Ss would be withdrawn early. Parental perceptions of progress were obtained by mail questionnaire, with a return of 34 out of 44. Their ratings generally agreed with test scores showing an average improvement of rank. The hypothesis that parents would harshly evaluate staff efforts was disconfirmed by their liberal evaluation of Ss' progress. It is concluded that good cooperation can be expected from parents in future efforts.
Mazumdar, B. N.   & Prabhu, G. G.   Child Psychiatry Quarterly, 1972(Jan), Vol. 5(1), 13-18. [PA, Vol 49:11995]

3489.   A vocal-motor program for teaching nonverbal children.
Presents a behaviorally-based speech and language training method for multiply handicapped preschool children. Training procedures are based on the echoic motor and vocal responses a nonverbal child emits in response to gross motor and vocal stimuli. No verbal cues are used. The child is presented with gross motor and vocal stimuli, then any echoic motor or vocal response that occurs is reinforced. The thesis is advanced that echoic vocal responses precede the development of imitative vocal responses.
Stewart, Farrell J. (Multnomah County Intermediate Education District, Portland, Ore.) Education & Training of the Mentally Retarded, 1972(Dec), Vol. 7(4), 176-182. [PA, Vol 50:03921]

3490.   Evaluation of the effect of a physical education program upon minimum levels of muscular fitness of trainable mentally retarded boys.
Investigated the effect of an organized physical education program on minimum levels of muscular fitness of trainable mentally retarded (TMR) boys. The Kraus-Weber Test of Minimum Muscular Fitness was administered to 35 10-16 yr. old TMR boys before and after participating in a 6-mo physical education program. Results reveal that an organized physical education program significantly affected the minimum levels of muscular fitness of the TMR Ss. It is recommended that additional studies determine the effects of physical education on social and academic performance, that comparison be made according to sex, retardation differentials, and age, and that other instruments be employed to measure muscular fitness. (21 ref.)
Taylor, George R. (Coppin State Coll.) Training School Bulletin, 1972(Aug), Vol. 69(2), 49-53. [PA, Vol 49:05562]

3491.   Teaching appropriate hallway behavior to an emotionally disturbed, trainably retarded child.
Studied modification of destructive behavior in a relatively unstructured environment. The S was a 10-yr-old black male previously evaluated as hyperactive, trainably retarded, and emotionally disturbed. The target behavior was to refrain from touching any item hanging on the hallway. 5 15-20 min. daily sessions were held during which the hallway was sectioned off in irregular lengths. S was rewarded with praise and cereal after each section of hallway for not touching. After the training period, S was rewarded tangibly only after each regular trip without touching. Results show a drop in mean touches from 1.52/trip during baseline to .17 during the shifting to "natural" consequences period. Follow-up over 5 days indicated a continued low rate. It is concluded that long established destructive behavior can be modified after brief but precise and intensive periods of training.
Willis, Jerry. (Jefferson County Dept. of Health, Birmingham, Ala.) Psychology in the Schools, 1972(Dec), Vol. 5(1), 11-16. [PA, Vol 50:10066]

3492.   Language comprehension in the moderately retarded child.
Administered the Carrow Auditory Test of Linguistic Comprehension to retarded trainable pupils attending public school special education classes. Results suggest that the Carrow test can provide useful information concerning the language comprehension development of trainable retarded children. Results further demonstrate systematic language growth in children with IQ's as low as 20 and 30. Retarded Ss acquired mastery of vocabulary items and aspects of morphology and syntax. When matched on MA, the retarded Ss' use of lexical items did not differ from nonretarded Ss' to a great extent; however, retarded Ss' use of grammatical categories was inferior to that of nonretarded Ss. (27 ref.)
Bartel, Nettie R.; Bryen, Diane & Keehn, Susan. (Temple U.) Exceptional Children, 1973(Feb), Vol. 39(5), 375-382. [PA, Vol 50:07638]

3493.   Reliability and transitivity of pair-comparison sociometric responses of retarded and nonretarded subjects.
Administered 3 pair-comparison sociometric tests in succession to 6 groups of trainable mentally retarded Ss of high school age, 4 groups of nonretarded high school Ss, and 4 groups of nonretarded Ss in Grades 2-3. Each group contained 6 males. The purpose of the tests was to assess the reliability and transitivity of social preferences when mental ability is a confounding factor. For 4 of the 6 retarded groups reliability coefficients were acceptable, though lower than those of nonretarded Ss. Analysis of transitivity indicated that rank-order sociometric tests with retarded Ss must be used with caution insofar as transitivity of preferences cannot be assumed. Possible causes of intransitive social preferences, and the advantages of pair-comparison sociometry with retarded Ss are discussed.

Burns, Edward. (Ohio U., Coll. of Education, School of Curriculum & Instruction) American Journal of Mental Deficiency, 1973(Jan), Vol. 78(4), 482-485. [PA, Vol 52:07999]

3494.   Decreasing classroom misbehavior through the use of DRL schedules of reinforcement.
Reported 3 experiments in which reinforcing low rates of responding reduced inappropriate behaviors. In Exp I, the talking-out behavior of an 11-yr-old trainable mentally retarded (TMR) boy was reduced when the teacher allowed 5 min of free time for a talk-out rate of less than .06/min. In Exp II, the talking-out behavior of an entire TMR class ($N = 10$) was reduced when reinforcement was delivered for a response rate of less than .10/min. In Exp III, successively decreasing the differential reinforcement of low rates (DRL) reduced the off-task verbalizations of 15 female high school students. In each case, DRL proved manageable for the teacher and successful in reducing misbehavior. (15 ref)
Dietz, Samuel M. & Repp, Alan C. (Georgia State U.) Journal of Applied Behavior Analysis, 1973(Fal), Vol. 6(3), 457-463. [PA, Vol 51:11976]

3495.   College juniors' reactions to tutoring adolescent trainable retarded students.
Self-ratings and ratings made by Os indicate that after tutoring mental retardates, special education majors gained confidence in their teaching ability and became more competent in planning and carrying out classroom activities.
Minkoff, Jack & Sellin, Donald. (Gloucester Township Public Schools, Blackwood, N.J.) Education & Training of the Mentally Retarded, 1973(Oct), Vol. 8(3), 146-149. [PA, Vol 52:01873]

3496.   Development of learning devices for retarded children: A report on a pilot reseach project.
Conducted a pilot research project on the development and testing of 2 learning devices for 2 male and 6 female trainable mentally retarded 4-9 yr olds with a mental age range of 18 mo to 3½ yrs. The 2 prototypes which were selected for evaluation were a dressing smock and figure reproduction stencil board. Results indicate a significant increase in the level of skill performance using the 2 learning devices. It is hoped that this pilot study might serve as stimulus or model for other educational devices.
Bartholomew, Robert. (Cornell U.) SALT: School Applications of Learning Theory, 1974(Jan), Vol. 6(2), 31-36. [PA, Vol 52:06343]

3497.   Arithmetic computation for trainable retarded students: Continuing a sequential instructional program.
Taught 4 trainable retarded adolescents who had acquired some addition skills to work mixed addition and subtraction problems. The successful task analysis, teaching procedures, and instructional materials are detailed. The program provides a demonstration that these students can succeed in cumulative sequential instruction which progresses from school year to school year. The implication is drawn that increased attention to longitudinal academic objectives may be warranted in trainable programs.
Bellamy, G. Thomas; Greiner, Charles & Buttars, Kathleen L. (U. Oregon) Training School Bulletin, 1974(Feb), Vol. 70(4), 230-240. [PA, Vol 52:13211]

3498.   Teaching adolescent trainable level retarded students to read a restaurant menu.
Studied the learning of a teacher-made restaurant menu by 4 female trainable retarded adolescents. Ss were taught to label food pictures and word cards and later were able to choose from 15 items from a similar teacher-made menu at a restaurant.
Brown, Lou; Van Deventer, Pat; Johnson, Pat & Sontag, Ed. (Madison Public Schools, WI) SALT: School Applications of Learning Theory, 1974(Apr), Vol 6(3), 1-14. [PA, Vol 53:01965]

3499.   The development of lip reading through generalized conditioned reinforcement in a deaf multiply handicapped child.
Reports the successful use of conditioned reinforcement in teaching lip reading to a 9-yr-old boy, diagnosed as emotionally disturbed and trainable mentally retarded, with an IQ of 45 and a moderate-to-severe hearing loss when wearing an aid. After a

baseline score was obtained, reinforcement, consisting at first of tokens and praise and secondly of smiles, was used after correct choices of fruits voiced by the teacher. Later, the fruits were only mouthed, and reinforcement was given in various fixed ratio schedules. Durability checks produced correct responses of 92% and 97%. It is concluded that clinicians can use tangible immediate reinforcers such as tokens to shape and maintain complex behaviors.
Johnson, Carl M. & Kaye, James H. (Kalamazoo Valley Multihandicap Ctr, MI) SALT: School Applications of Learning Theory, 1974(Jul), Vol 6(4), 21-30. [PA, Vol 53:06208]

3500.   Developing mathematical skills by applying Piaget's theory.
Discusses considerations in developing mathematical skills for the trainable mentally retarded child, using Piaget's ideas of concreteness for developing instructional skills. A curriculum guide is presented for developing mathematic skills, and instructions are included for using the curriculum. It is stressed that abstract thinking is difficult for the trainable retarded; therefore, mathematics skills should be concrete and useful in the everyday life of the child.
Kiraly, John & Morishima, Akira. (U Iowa) Education & Training of the Mentally Retarded, 1974(Apr), Vol 9(2), 62-65. [PA, Vol 53:10523]

3501.   Orientation and mobility instruction for the sighted trainable mentally retarded.
Reports on a program designed for the trainable mentally retarded (TMR) in public school curriculums. Ss were 35 pupils from an inner city TMR program with a mean age of 16 yrs and an IQ mean of 42.7. The group had normal corrected visual acuity. Orientation in the classroom and both classroom and outdoor mobility instruction were initiated. Results show that Ss were able to safely and independently travel within their community after receiving such instruction. After 1 school year of instruction 35 pupils were traveling independently to and from school by public transportation. Adolescents who previously were transported daily from their doorstep by leased vans were initiating their own travel to and from school. It is suggested that orientation and mobility instruction should now be considered an integral part of the total curriculum for TMR pupils in the public schools.
Laus, Michael D. (Pittsburgh School System, PA) Education & Training of the Mentally Retarded, 1974(Apr), Vol 9(2), 70-73. [PA, Vol 53:10524]

3502.   Operant audiometry with the trainable mentally retarded: Implications for the public school speech and hearing clinician.
Describes an operant audiometry technique for use in public schools to condition trainable mentally retarded children. The conditioning procedure consists of reinforcing a child with a sweet when he responds to a tone by placing a block in a box and withdrawing reinforcement when he responds in the absence of a signal. The initial tone must be loud enough to encourage S's response, and some prompting may be necessary at the beginning. Audiometric testing follows the conditioning sessions. The successful conditioning of 3 Ss with the technique is described.
Porter, Elaine C. (Dade County Public Schools, Miami, Fla.) Language, Speech, & Hearing Services in Schools, 1974(Jan), Vol. 5(1), 49-54. [PA, Vol 52:04082]

3503.   Teaching trainable level retarded students to count money: Toward personal independence through academic instruction.
Conducted a program for teaching money counting skills to 5 trainable-level 13-20 yr old retarded adolescents with IQs of 46-69. Instructional materials, teaching methods, and evaluation procedures are detailed. The program required 206 trials and approximately 100 hrs of instructional time during 6 mo of school attendance. All Ss learned a sequence of rote counting skills and then learned to apply these skills in counting amounts of change. Results are interpreted as support for the view that

instruction in basic academic skills can be an integral part of practical education.
Bellamy, Tom & Buttars, Kathleen L. (U Oregon) Education & Training of the Mentally Retarded, 1975(Feb), Vol 10(1), 18-26. [PA, Vol 54:04175]

3504. The effects of a direct phonic approach in teaching reading with six moderately retarded children: Acquisition and mastery learning stages.
Used a phonic-based program to teach 6 moderately retarded (IQs 30–40) 7–14 yr olds who had been institutionalized a minimum of 5 yrs. The Distar Reading Level I reading program was used in conjunction with a token reinforcement program. This reading program precedes the onset of reading with the teaching of the child to sequence events, reproduce words, distinguish word parts, and discern similarities and differences between words. Significant improvements from pre- to posttest were found in 14 of the 19 skills evaluated. It is concluded that appropriate instruction enables mildly mentally retarded children to make impressive gains in their ability to read words. (23 ref)
Bracey, Susan; Maggs, Alex & Morath, Philip. (Macquarie U School of Education, North Ryde, Australia) Exceptional Child, 1975(Jul), Vol 22(2), 83–90. [PA, Vol 59:11120]

3505. Teaching arithmetic skills to moderately mentally retarded children using direct verbal instruction: Counting and symbol identification.
Used a highly structured, task analyzed arithmetic program and behavioral techniques to teach arithmetic skills to a group of 6 institutionalized moderately mentally retarded children (IQs approximately 35-50). The aim of the study was to determine whether the Ss made significant gains in 4 types of arithmetical skills: object counting, making lines from numerals, the meaning of plus, and increment additions. Results reveal significant improvement ($p < .05$) in each of the skill areas.
Bracey, Susan; Maggs, Alex & Morath, Phillip. (Macquarie U, North Ryde, Australia) Australian Journal of Mental Retardation, 1975(Sep), Vol 3(7), 200–204. [PA, Vol 56:03012]

3506. A photo-electric pen for producing action feedback to aid development in handicapped children of fine visual-motor skills: Tracing and writing.
Reports on the exploratory use of a photoelectric pen (PEP), designed by the author, as a training device to facilitate tracing behavior. S was a 13-yr-old female attending a school for subnormal children. She had an IQ of 39 (Stanford-Binet Intelligence Scale), very small muscle control, and a history of infantile aphasia and autism. The PEP provided automatic auditory feedback with the production, via headphones or loudspeaker, of a continuous sound when its tip was immediately over a dark trace. S was given 11 25-min sessions during which she used the PEP to trace simple and complex shapes, some letters of the alphabet, and her name. Marked improvements from pre- to posttest were shown in S's ability to trace each type of figure. Comparable results, not reported, have been obtained with 2 male Ss.
Parker, J. L. (James Cook U of North Queensland, Townsville, Australia) Slow Learning Child, 1975(Mar), Vol 22(1), 13–22. [PA, Vol 59:08856]

3507. The uses of a referral and behavior rating scale in an educational setting.
Tested the usefulness of the Primary Grade Retarded Trainable Children's Referral and Behavior Rating Form (PGRC Referral and Rating Form) as a tool for diagnostic educational planning and teacher self-monitoring of progress. 36 children who were participating in a special 3-mo evaluation center underwent psychological testing, and after approximately 5 wks in the program, teachers completed the PGRC Referral and Rating Form for each child. Results indicate that in each of IQ-MA levels (i.e., below 25 mo, 26-35 mo, 36-46 mo, and 40-60 mo), the mean verbal and social development levels increased as tested MA increased. However, this was not true for 10 "untestable" Ss who had a higher modal social mean than the below 25-mo MA group, suggesting that children who are untestable on formal

tests because of language deficits and lack of cooperation may in fact perform quite well on some developmental tasks. The clinical use of the form is demonstrated in 4 sample profiles.
Barker, Roberta & Peterson, Rolf A. (U Chicago, Chicago Circle) Education & Training of the Mentally Retarded, 1976(Oct), Vol 11(3), 218-222. [PA, Vol 57:11514]

3508. Reduction of stereotypic body contortions using physical restraint and DRO.
A 9-yr-old mentally retarded female (Stanford-Binet IQ, 42) displaying high rate stereotypic body contortions of longstanding duration was treated using physical restraint and differential reinforcement of other behavior in her classroom setting. Following the collection on 2 school days of baseline data, the therapist began intensive treatment of the child of the classroom using these techniques. After 2 days of intervention, the S's teacher employed all subsequent treatment procedures for 8 school days in which 8 no-treatment periods occurred. Results indicate that the treatment package was successful in producing immediate and substantial reductions in this moderately self-injurious stereotypy at school. Eventually rate of responding reached a zero level. Although some generalization of treatment effects to the no-treatment periods in school was noted, no systematic, enduring changes in rate of responding at home were observed. Results suggest the treatment package was easily learned and effectively employed by a teacher with no previous experience with behavior modification.
Barkley, Russell A. & Zupnick, Stanley. (U Oregon Health Sciences Ctr, Portland) Journal of Behavior Therapy & Experimental Psychiatry, 1976(Jun), Vol 7(2), 167-170. [PA, Vol 56:10290]

3509. Significant vs meaningful differences in the effects of tangible reinforcement on intelligence test achievement and reliability of TMR subjects.
Investigated the effects of tangible reinforcement on the scores of 72 trainable mentally retarded 9-20 yr olds on the Arithmetic, Picture Arrangement, and Comprehension subtests of the WISC and the Vocabulary subtest of the Lorge-Thorndike Intelligence Test. Performance under a standard and reinforced (M&M) condition, differences in split-half reliability, power estimates, as well as the effect size resulting from treatments, were considered. Reinforced administration resulted in significantly superior performance on all but the Comprehension test, although magnitude of treatment effects was low. Reliabilities under the reinforced condition were higher for all but the Lorge-Thorndike measures. Confidence bounded effect sizes even at their maximal value did not result in "meaningful" differences in performance, however. (28 ref)
Busch, John C. & Osborne, William L. (U North Carolina School of Education, Greensboro) Psychology in the Schools, 1976(Apr), Vol 13(2), 219-225. [PA, Vol 57:11516]

3510. Effects of representation level of materials on transfer of classification skills in TMR children.
Compared the performance of 22 trainable mentally retarded (TMR) children (mean MA 4 yrs 3 mo, mean CA 9 yrs 2 mo) trained in classification skills with that of 19 nontrained controls (mean MA 4 yr 4 mo, mean CA 9 yrs) on a toy-classification task and an object-sorting task. Test materials for the first task comprised toys similar to, yet distinctly different from, those used in the Ss' previous training; materials for the 2nd task comprised abstract multi-dimensional blocks which could be classified according to the same dimensions (form, size, and color) as the toys. Results show that the experimental Ss had superior performance to that of the controls on the toy-sorting task, suggesting that TMR Ss can be taught to classify materials on a conceptual basis when easily manipulated, inherently interesting objects, such as toys, are employed in training and testing. On the object-sorting task, short-term acquisition testing showed no significant differences between the 2 groups; however, long-term testing showed that the experimental Ss performed significantly better than the controls. Overall, there was little evidence that Ss who were taught to classify representational objects on the dimensions of size, shape, and color were able to

transfer their newly acquired skills to the conceptual sorting of multidimensional abstract objects.
Klein, Nancy K. & Safford, Philip L. (Cleveland State U) Journal of Special Education, 1976(Sep), Vol 10(1), 47-52. [PA, Vol 58:09729]

3511.   Social play interaction of retarded children in an integrated classroom environment.
In 2 experiments, 2 different age groups (3–4 and 6–8 yrs) of nonretarded children (*n* = 8) were integrated into a program for trainable mentally retarded children during free play activities. Observations of social play behavior were made for 5 of the trainable children (ages 4–9). Results indicate that when nonretarded children of equivalent CA were integrated, increases in cooperative and parallel play were observed. No changes occurred with the integration of nonretarded children of equivalent MA. (16 ref)
Knapczyk, Dennis R. & Peterson, Nancy L. (Indiana U) Research & the Retarded, 1976, Vol 3(4), 104–112. [PA, Vol 59:02110]

3512.   Effects of direct verbal instruction on intellectual development of institutionalized moderately retarded children: A 2-year study.
Attempted to improve the intellectual development of 28 moderately retarded children (IQ's approximately 30-55) by using direct verbal instruction in classroom settings. A highly structured and task-analyzed concept-language program (the Distar Language 1 Kit), together with positive reinforcement, modeling, and shaping techniques, were used in the 2-yr intervention project. Results reveal significant differences in favor of the experimental treatment conditions on all dependent variables (i.e., the Basic Concept Inventory, Reynell Verbal Comprehension, Stanford-Binet (L-M) Intelligence, Piaget's Class Inclusion, Piaget's Seriation, and Bruner's Matrix) related to the Ss' performance. Ss seemed to be able to maintain approximately a "normal" rate of intellectual development over the 2-yr period. (20 ref)
Maggs, Alex & Morath, Phillip. (Macquarie U Special Education Ctr, North Ryde, Australia) Journal of Special Education, 1976(Win), Vol 10(4), 357-364. [PA, Vol 57:13937]

3513.   Testing pronunciation skill competence of both normal and retarded readers.
Describes a method of testing pronunciation skills so that teachers of special education or reading will have a more systematic means to assess competence. The methodology is based on the assumption that decoding skills can and should be measured independently from comprehension, in order to identify skill deficits and ineffective word-attack strategies. Test construction involves a delineation of words by properties into contrasting sets. Error rates are used to measure skill deficits and analyses of the kind of error that reveals word attack strategies. A summary of test findings compares behavior of moderately retarded adolescents to 24 normal 2nd and 5th graders. Results indicate that both groups were similarly affected by the same word properties.
Mason, Jana M. (Mount St Vincent U, Halifax, Canada) Mental Retardation, 1976(Dec), Vol 14(6), 36-40. [PA, Vol 58:02257]

3514.   A sociometric technique for use with moderately to severely retarded persons.
Mentally retarded children, ages 6 to 17 yrs, were administered a sociometric instrument designed to elicit preferences for work partners among their classmates. Study assignments were based on the results. Ss were seen as having made both social and academic progress as the result of their assignments to work with preferred classmates.
Pack, Peggy L. & McCaffrey, Leonard J. (Murray State U) Group Psychotherapy, Psychodrama & Sociometry, 1976, Vol 29, 127–129. [PA, Vol 62:02305]

3515.   A primary grade retarded-trainable children's referral and behavior rating form: Expectation and referral data.
Peterson, Rolf A. & Gorski, Sally. (U Illinois, Chicago Circle) Catalog of Selected Documents in Psychology, 1976(Feb), Vol 6, 2-3. [PA, Vol 55:08655]

3516.   Improving the sequential memory performance of trainable mentally retarded youngsters: A learning strategies approach.
Attempted to develop techniques for improving sequential memory performance of 3 trainable mentally retarded children (CA 8 yrs 5 mo-10 yrs 11 mo) in a classroom setting by employing two basic learning strategies: labeling and rehearsal by repetition. Labels for 5 objects were taught using stimulus cards; rehearsal was shaped by first presenting 2, then 3, then 4, and finally 5 items. Results of the labeling phase show little difference between the initial baseline and the baseline which followed label teaching, suggesting that labels alone were not sufficient to improve the Ss' performance. Results of the rehearsal training phase show that the Ss' performance improved on each succeeding baseline as items were added, and all Ss performed maximally on the final baseline. These results are consistent with basic research efforts suggesting that (a) the poor recall of the mentally retarded results from a rehearsal strategy deficit and (b) poor recall may be improved by teaching the retarded to use rehearsal strategies.
Wambold, Clark L.; Jedlinski, Kathy & Brown, Lou. (U Wisconsin, Madison) Journal of Special Education, 1976(Sep), Vol 10(1), 41-46. [PA, Vol 58:10567]

3517.   Integration of young TMR children into a regular elementary school.
Two classes of young trainable mentally retarded (TMR) children were moved from a school for the retarded to a regular public school where they interacted with the school population daily, mainly in nonacademic (nonclassroom) situations. Their behavior at 2 times during the year was compared to that of a matched group of TMR children in a school for the retarded. Comparisons of scores on a behavioral checklist, which detailed the relative frequency of 13 kinds of interactions among students, showed no differences between groups. Interactional analysis, however, showed interactions involving only retarded children (at both schools) were predominantly positive in character, but included more provoked aggression and much less teaching, intervening, and comforting than interactions involving nonretarded and retarded children. It is concluded that placement of special classes in a regualr school was effective in promoting interactions between retarded and nonretarded students, thus providing a more normal environment for the retarded children.
Ziegler, Suzanne & Hambleton, Donald. (Board of Education, Toronto, Canada) Exceptional Children, 1976(May), Vol 42(8), 459-461. [PA, Vol 56:04937]

3518.   [On the formation of the act of analyzing the syllabic structure of words and the learning of Japanese syllabic characters in moderately mentally retarded children.] (Japn)
Japanese mentally retarded children, escpecially those with no speech deficiency, were trained to read kanamoji (Japanese syllabic characters) by a procedure that included analyzing the syllabic structure of words (ASSW). 12 out of 19 Ss succeeded at ASSW, and 7 out of 8 who succeeded learned to read. (English summary) (9 ref)
Amano, Kiyoshi.   Japanese Journal of Educational Psychology, 1977(Jun), Vol 25(2), 73–84. [PA, Vol 64:13370]

3519.   Verbal mediation as an instructional technique with young trainable mentally retarded children.
In verbally mediated motor training (VMMT), the S utters the name of the action while performing a response. This procedure was contrasted with a condition in which Ss were trained to perform the response silently (MT) and with an in-class control condition; Ss were 32 4–10 yr old trainable mentally retarded children. Both training treatments were equally facilitative in teaching gross motor movements, but VMMT Ss verbally mediated their responses spontaneously and named the trained action when performed by the examiner in a posttest situation significantly more than MT Ss.
Bender, Nila N. (U California, Riverside) Journal of Special Education, 1977(Win), Vol 11(4), 449–455. [PA, Vol 61:11999]

3520.   Impacts of learning American Indian Sign Language on mentally retarded children: A preliminary report.
Reports the impact of a 10-wk total communication program using American Indian Sign Language (AMERIND) with 32 moderately retarded children. The number of signs learned by Ss ranged from 15 to 200. 27 Ss were observed by the clinician and/or teacher using AMERIND spontaneously for communication purposes, and 15 Ss were reported by their teacher, clinician, or parents to have increased their attempts to communicate by speech.
Duncan, Janice L. & Silverman, Franklin H. (Columbus Special Education Ctr, Kenosha, WI) Perceptual & Motor Skills, 1977(Jun), Vol 44(3, Pt 2), 1138. [PA, Vol 59:11127]

3521.   Experimental evaluation of classroom environments: Scheduling planned activities.
Investigated scheduling of planned activities in a classroom for trainable mentally retarded adolescents using 11 14-20 yr olds (IQ less than 50). 10 classroom activities were scheduled in either a predictable (fixed) or unpredictable (random) order using an ABAB design. Relative to fixed scheduling, random scheduling resulted in significantly lower rates of activity completion and higher rates of disruptions. Lower rates of task completion also generalized to 2 unmanipulated activities. Activity completion and rate of disruptions, while generally inversely related, were significantly correlated for only 2 of 11 Ss. Ss with lower levels of task completion under fixed scheduling showed the largest decrements in performance under random scheduling. Higher rates of disruptions under fixed scheduling were also associated with greater increments in disruptive behavior under random-scheduling conditions.
Frederiksen, Lee W. & Frederiksen, Candace B. (VA Ctr, Dept of Psychology, Jackson, MS) American Journal of Mental Deficiency, 1977(Mar), Vol 81(5), 421-427. [PA, Vol 58:12712]

3522.   Teaching strategy and learning rate of TMRs.
Investigated the effects of a teaching strategy on the learning rate of 18 trainable mentally retarded (TMR) children (mean CA, 14.6; mean WISC IQs 50-51) over a 12-wk period using a curriculum model similar to behavioristic task analysis (S. Englemann, 1969). The teaching strategy required 9 Ss and teacher to share responsibility for control and decision-making, as compared to the traditional approach with 9 Ss in which the teacher assumed full responsibility. All Ss were pre- and posttested on the basis of behavioral objectives (tasks). Findings suggest 2 conclusions: (a) the involvement of TMR Ss in limited control and decision-making roles in the classroom results in higher achievement; and (b) behavioral task analysis as a curriculum approach can be used successfully in the training of mentally retarded persons.
Grigsby, Clifford E. & Harshman, Hardwick W. (Indiana U, Indianapolis) Mental Retardation, 1977(Feb), Vol 15(1), 27-29. [PA, Vol 58:06363]

3523.   Manipulating visual feedback in word acquisition behavior in TMR subjects.
Examined the differential effects of visual-cognitive feedback on the acquisition of word–object association behavior in 12 trainable retarded children (mean CA 122.5 mo; mean MA 51.5 mo). It was hypothesized that word feedback would be the more effective method for teaching associative behaviors. Word and object replica feedback were manipulated. While both forms of feedback facilitated associative behavior, there was a strong, but nonsignificant, tendency for word feedback to be superior. Clinical evidence supporting the hypothesis is considered.
Jackson, Merrill S. (U Tasmania, Hobart, Australia) Journal of Special Education, 1977(Spr), Vol 11(1), 73–79. [PA, Vol 59:02106]

3524.   Use of a pocket calculator to train arithmetic skills with trainable adolescents.
Discusses the rationale for using a calculator to teach arithmetic skills to retarded persons, the results of a pilot study of 6 moderately retarded adolescents who participated in 2 6-wk

training sessions, and the steps that can be followed to use the program with other retarded Ss.
Koller, Elayne Z. & Mulhern, Thomas J. (Latchworth Village Developmental Ctr, Thiells, NY) Education & Training of the Mentally Retarded, 1977(Dec), Vol 12(4), 332–335. [PA, Vol 61:07308]

3525.   Trainable children can learn adjectives, polars, and prepositions!
Presented 6 wks of instruction in the use of adjectives, polars, and locative prepositions to 12 trainable mentally retarded children (IQ 30–55) in 2 groups: younger Ss (CA 6–10 yrs, MA 2.6–3.0 yrs), and older Ss (CA 13–19 yrs, MA 3.6–5.3 yrs). Specially prepared Language Master instruction cards constituted the program. Ss were evaluated pre- and posttreatment on their knowledge of adjectives and prepositions through the use of classroom objects, and on polar concepts using DISTAR Language I exercises developed by S. Englemann, et al (1970). Evaluation exercises were not used in the intervention program. Results indicate that Ss in the older CA group earned significantly higher scores than those in the younger group. Ss in the younger group made significant increases in scores, particularly in learning prepositions. A multisensory approach and active involvement in learning appeared to be major factors in achievement gains.
Mitchell, Marlys; Evans, Carolyn & Bernard, John. (U North Carolina Medical School, Chapel Hill) Language, Speech, & Hearing Services in Schools, 1977(Jul), Vol 8(3), 181–187. [PA, Vol 59:13291]

3526.   Generalizing articulation training with trainable mentally retarded subjects.
Used a multiple-baseline technique to evaluate generalization effects during articulation training with 2 8–9 yr old female trainable mentally retarded students. Four target words were selected for each S on the basis of whether the S could articulate the word correctly when it was modeled but could not articulate the word correctly in response to a picture of it. Five different settings were selected for generalization probing and training for each S. In Setting 1, Experimenter 1 initiated training sequentially on all 4 target words for each S. Other experimenters probed for correct articulation generalization in 4 other settings. Training was initiated in these 4 other settings sequentially only if correct responding failed to generalize to a setting. Results indicate that it was necessary to initiate training on at least 3 of the 4 selected target words in at least 1 additional setting with an additional trainer before correct responding generalized to untrained settings. (21 ref)
Murdock, Jane Y.; Garcia, Eugene E. & Hardman, Michael L. (U New Orleans) Journal of Applied Behavior Analysis, 1977(Win), Vol 10(4), 717–733. [PA, Vol 61:02305]

3527.   Self-concepts of senior TMR students at a semi-integrated setting.
Compared the self-concepts of senior trainable mentally retarded (TMR) students attending a regular high school with TMR students at a segregated school. Structured clinical interviews were conducted with 19 students at each setting. Questions posed were based on those of D. Hambleton and S. Zieglar (1973). The semi-integration plans did not involve any special orientation of regular high school students to the needs of the retarded students. No significant differences were found, and it is suggested that even without planning of semi-integration, such placement does not adversely affect the self-concepts of TMR students.
Nash, B. Chris & McQuisten, Alan. (Ontario Inst for Studies in Education, Midnorthern Ctr, Sudbury, Canada) Mental Retardation, 1977(Dec), Vol 15(6), 16–18. [PA, Vol 61:04807]

3528.   Increasing the compliance of retarded children through simple, systematic consequation.
Describes the use of token reinforcement schedules to increase 2 retarded adolescents' compliance to verbal requests in a classroom setting. Findings from the AB design are presented: During the treatment condition, the 18- and 19-yr-old moderately

retarded Ss complied with 84 and 74% of the requests, compared to 64 and 22% during the baseline condition, respectively.
Poling, Alan; Nelson, Neal & Miller, Kathy. Mental Retardation Bulletin, 1977(Fal), Vol 5(2), 76–81. [PA, Vol 61:02311]

3529.   Retarded children need a special playground.
Argues that a playground for trainable mentally retarded children should be specially designed to meet special needs. Use of the playground should strengthen the children's gross motor as well as conceptual abilities, provide experiences that enhance the development of language, facilitate verbal communication, promote independence, provide an enriching and inviting atmosphere for creative play, and develop self-image. The planning and development of such a playground is described, including before and after photographs and use of the playground by the children attending a special education center near Chicago.
Gillet, Pamela. (Northwest Suburban Special Education Organization, Palatine, IL) Education & Training of the Mentally Retarded, 1978(Apr), Vol 13(2), 160–169. [PA, Vol 61:14527]

3530.   A functional administrative-teaching model for academic programing with the trainable mentally retarded.
The basic components of the diagnostic-prescriptive concept are described as they were implemented into the program structure of an entire instructional unit for 70 trainable mentally retarded children (CAs 6.9–17 yrs, IQs 28–62). The model is referred to as the Functional Analysis Program (FAP). The focus is on the resource materials and operational processes incorporated within the FAP structure. Analysis of Ss progress data on selected standardized tests (Wide Range Achievement Test, Utah Test of Language Development, and Boehm Test of Basic Concepts) indicated that in most areas assessed, significant progress was evident. Results support research suggesting that traditional self-care programs may limit the learning potential of the trainable population. (17 ref)
Hardman, Michael L. (U Utah) Education & Training of the Mentally Retarded, 1978(Feb), Vol 13(1), 23–28. [PA, Vol 61:09681]

3531.   Effects of training conditions on the generalization of manual signs with moderately handicapped students.
Taught 3 moderately retarded 7–8 yr old students with limited spontaneous speech to use signs for 12 food items. Ss were taught some signs in a small-group classroom setting by a student teacher, and other signs were taught to Ss individually by a speech therapist in a separate room. After Ss had reached a criteria of 80% correct responding to the food stimuli, generalization of knowledge was assessed during a probe condition. Results show that Ss met criteria faster when they were trained in small classroom groups rather than in the individual sessions. Response rates dropped considerably when Ss were asked what they had for lunch, suggesting that to insure spontaneous use of trained signs, instructional programs must include training in response to a large variety of materials and language cues. The greatest number of signs produced in the probe condition were those that were trained in the same room that the probe was made, suggesting that teachers and therapists should teach signs in the setting in which they will be used. (13 ref)
Kohl, Frances L.; Wilcox, Barbara L. & Karlan, George R. (U Illinois, Urbana-Champaign) Education & Training of the Mentally Retarded, 1978(Oct), Vol 13(3), 327–335. [PA, Vol 63:08441]

3532.   Group oral language training with TMR children based on *Learning to Think* material.
Reports on the effectiveness of methods used to increase the oral language capacities of 19 7–19 yr old trainable mentally retarded (TMR) Ss. Training materials were adapted from the *Red Book* of the *Learning to Think* series by T. G. Thurstone (1972). Pictures of familiar objects and experiences were projected onto the blackboard and students practiced naming and picture description using phrases and sentences with different grammatical constructions. Ss were instructed in groups of 5 for 30 min twice per week for 8 mo. Pre- and posttest scores were recorded

from the Peabody Picture Vocabulary Test (PPVT), the Northwestern Syntax Screening Test (NSST), and the Sentence Imitation Test. Gains in receptive vocabulary as measured by the PPVT averaged 9.37 mo. Age gains on the NSST averaged 23.79 mo, and there was a significant increase in Ss' ability to imitate sentences. The results are discussed in the context of other instructional methods and assessment procedures frequently used to assess TMR programs. (18 ref)
Lamberts, Frances & Ysseldyke, James E. (Northern Illinois U, Illinois Regional Resource Ctr) Education & Training of the Mentally Retarded, 1978(Oct), Vol 13(3), 309–315. [PA, Vol 63:08443]

3533.   The PREP program: A preschool play program for moderately mentally retarded children.
Describes the 5 major objectives of the PREP program, which is designed to improve the gross-motor play skills of moderately retarded preschool children. A program model is defined that includes individualized instruction in prescribed gross-motor play skills, group activity on selected skills, and free-play activity in a well-planned environment. An individualized teaching model developed by J. A. Wessel (1975) is proposed to implement the PREP model. The teaching model consists of 6 basic steps: planning, assessment, prescribing, teaching, evaluation, and modification. (7 ref)
Watkinson, J. & Wall, A. E. (U Alberta, Edmonton, Canada) Mental Retardation Bulletin, 1978(Sum), Vol 6(1), 1–13. [PA, Vol 62:12308]

3534.   Teaching academic skills to trainable mentally retarded children: A study for tautology.
While it has been demonstrated that through the use of operant procedures, higher level cognitive skills can be taught to trainable mentally retarded children, evidence regarding the generalizability of these skills to the classroom or other open setting is lacking. The value of teaching these skills is questioned in terms of their contribution to Ss' ultimate adjustment in the natural environment. (26 ref)
Hirshoren, Alfred & Burton, Thomas A. (U Georgia, Div for Exceptional Children, Athens) Mental Retardation, 1979(Aug), Vol 17(4), 177–179. [PA, Vol 66:09001]

3535.   Abacus instruction for moderately retarded blind children.
Describes use of the abacus for developing concepts of numbers, addition and subtraction, and money values. An instructional guide is also presented.
Kang, Young W. & Masoodi, Bashir A. (Indiana Public Schools, Gary) Education of the Visually Handicapped, 1979(Fal), Vol 10(3), 79–84. [PA, Vol 64:06501]

3536.   Comparison of two training programs to advance body schema of trainable mentally retarded children.
Compared 2 methods of advancing body schema of 64 trainable mentally retarded 7–17 yr olds. Ss completed the Body-Schema Questionnaire and the Draw-A-Person test before and after the training program and again after 6 mo. Results indicate the advantages of the structural training over the general enrichment curriculum and the advantages of integrating gross motor training with verbal concepts over the use of training in drawing. (12 ref)
Margalit, Malka. (Tel-Aviv U, School of Education, Israel) Israel Annals of Psychiatry & Related Disciplines, 1979(Dec), Vol 17(4), 298–304. [PA, Vol 65:13602]

3537.   Effects of learning to ski on the self-concept of mentally retarded children.
Administered the Self-Concept Scale for Children to 14 trainable mentally retarded students aged 14–20 yrs before and after participation in a 5-wk ski program. A control group of 6 Ss received similar pre- and postmeasures of self-concept but did not participate in the ski program. Significant changes in self-concept occurred among Ss in the experimental but not the control group. The magnitude of success in learning to ski was positively and significantly correlated with magnitude of change in self-concept. (10 ref)

Simpson, H. M. & Meaney, Cheryl. (Traffic Injury Research Foundation of Canada, Ottawa) American Journal of Mental Deficiency, 1979(Jul), Vol 84(1), 25–29. [PA, Vol 62:12299]

3538.   The effects of interspersal training versus high-density reinforcement on spelling acquisition and retention.
Investigated the effects of interspersing known items during spelling instruction on new words for 1 profoundly deaf and 2 trainable mentally retarded males, aged 19–24 yrs. Following a baseline consisting of the presentation of 10 test words/session, a multi-element design was implemented. During interspersal training (IT) sessions, previously mastered words were presented alternately with each of 10 test words. During high-density reinforcement sessions, 10 test words were presented and additional reinforcement was provided for task-related behaviors. Throughout all conditions, test words were deleted and replaced after meeting a mastery criterion. Periodic retention tests were administered over mastered words, and a cumulative retention test was administered at the end of the experiment. High-density reinforcement facilitated performance over baseline; however, IT was superior to the other conditions in terms of both acquisition rate and short- and long-term retention. In addition, Ss preferred the IT condition when offered a choice. (10 ref)
Neef, Nancy A.; Iwata, Brian A. & Page, Terry J.   Journal of Applied Behavior Analysis, 1980(Spr), Vol 13(1), 153–158. [PA, Vol 65:08834]

3539.   Predictive validity of the Revised Stanford-Binet Intelligence Scale with trainable mentally retarded students.
Investigated the predictive validity of the Revised Stanford-Binet Intelligence Scale (SBIS) relative to the Wide Range Achievement Test (WRAT) as a criterion measure. 40 trainable mentally retarded students (CAs 17–20 yrs) were administered both instruments by qualified examiners. Regression analyses were conducted in which scores on the separate measures provided by subtests on Reading, Spelling, and Arithmetic of the WRAT were regressed on SBIS IQs. Results indicated that the SBIS IQs yielded statistically valid predictions of WRAT standard scores for the sample studied. Derived regression equations are reported. (17 ref)
Thiel, Glenn W. & Reynolds, Cecil R. (U Nebraska, Lincoln) Educational & Psychological Measurement, 1980(Sum), Vol 40(2), 509–512. [PA, Vol 64:13445]

3540.   A cognitive skills training program for moderately retarded learners.
Reviews research on problems inherent in curricula for the trainable mentally retarded (TMR), approaches to cognitive training, and similarities between school problems of mentally retarded and minority children. Three TMR Ss (CA 13–14 yrs, IQ 40–50) participated in story exploration sessions during which they were shown they had information that could be brought to bear on the story. Transcript analyses, Gates-MacGinitie Reading Readiness Test scores, and a listening comprehension test showed that Ss were capable of higher order processing that resulted in an increase in performance efficiency over time. (20 ref)
Zetlin, Andrea G. & Gallimore, Ronald. (U California School of Medicine, Mental Retardation Research Ctr, Los Angeles) Education & Training of the Mentally Retarded, 1980(Apr), Vol 15(2), 121–131. [PA, Vol 66:11322]

3541.   Prevalence and pattern of drug treatment for behavior and seizure disorders of TMR students.
The prevalence and pattern of psychotropic and antiepileptic drug treatment for 3,306 trainable mentally retarded (TMR) children and adolescents in public schools were determined from 329 teacher questionnaires and parent interviews. The relationship between drug use and age, race, and sex was also examined. Findings indicate that during the school year, 10% of the students received medication for seizure disorders, and 4.9% were treated for behavior disorders. An additional 1.8% were treated concurrently for both a seizure and a behavior disorder. Data suggest that dosages of methylphenidate, the most frequent-

ly prescribed drug for persons with behavior disorders, were conservative. (32 ref)
Gadow, Kenneth D. & Kalachnik, John. (State U New York, Office of Special Education, Stony Brook) American Journal of Mental Deficiency, 1981(May), Vol 85(6), 588–595. [PA, Vol 66:06724]

3542.   Curriculum for the trainable mentally retarded . . . or "What do I do when the ditto machine dies?"
Discusses problems inherent in implementing an appropriate curriculum for the mentally retarded with respect to simulations, mainstreaming, and skill use. The varying resources a community offers in terms of living/career alternatives are emphasized as crucial considerations a teacher must regard when devising effective programs. (6 ref)
Langone, John. (U Georgia, Athens) Education & Training of the Mentally Retarded, 1981(Apr), Vol 16(2), 150–154. [PA, Vol 66:09017]

3543.   Relationship between home environment and school adjustment of TMR children.
Examined the relationship between the home environment and school adjustment of 104 9–16 yr old trainable mentally retarded (mean WISC IQ 42.4) children. Assessments included Home Observation for Measurement of the Environment Inventory and the Family Environment Scale. Certain child-rearing attitudes and relevant demographic characteristics were also investigated. Measures of school adjustment included the child's social status, self-concept (teacher ratings on the Coopersmith Self-Esteem Inventory and the children's responses on the Primary Self-Concept Inventory), IQ, and teacher ratings of classroom behavior. Results reveal that specific factors of home environment were significantly related to the adjustment of Ss in school, including (a) harmony and quality of parenting, (b) educational and cognitive stimulation available at home, (c) emotional support for learning, and (d) cohesiveness of family members. (42 ref)
Nihira, Kazuo; Mink, Iris T. & Meyers, C. Edward. (Socio-Behavioral Group, Los Angeles, CA) American Journal of Mental Deficiency, 1981(Jul), Vol 86(1), 8–15. [PA, Vol 66:08944]

3544.   Facilitation of interactions between retarded and nonretarded students in a physical education setting.
Examined the effects of pairing trainable mentally retarded (TMR) students with nonretarded students and applying praise for social interaction between TMR and nonretarded students in an integrated physical education program. Nine TMR and 9 nonretarded 7th graders matched on sex and CA were randomly assigned to 1 of 3 treatment conditions. The control group participated in a program of teacher-directed physical activities, and the 1st experimental group participated in teacher-directed physical activities, teacher intervention (pairing TMR with nonretarded Ss), and teacher praise for motor skill performance. The 2nd Experimental Group participated in teacher-directed physical activities, teacher intervention (pairing TMR with nonretarded Ss), and teacher praise for social interaction. The social interaction was videotaped. Findings indicate that pairing TMR with nonretarded Ss in conjunction with teacher praise for social interaction was a highly effective means of increasing the TMR's social interactions. (13 ref)
Santomier, James & Kopczuk, Walter. (U Oregon, Eugene) Education & Training of the Mentally Retarded, 1981(Feb), Vol 16(1), 20–23. [PA, Vol 66:09040]

Severe Mental Retardation

3545.   Symposium on the educational problems of the severely mentally handicapped child: I. The subnormal child: An educational challenge.
Discusses the changes in attitudes which are necessary for the education of the severely subnormal child. It is suggested that the most difficult change to accept may be the acknowledgment that

the educational needs of the subnormal child are similar to those of normal children.
Davie, Ronald. British Journal of Mental Subnormality, 1971(Dec), Vol. 17(33, Pt. 2), 89-93. [PA, Vol 48:03712]

3546.   Severely subnormal children and their parents: An experiment in language improvement.
Matched 2 groups of 15 severely subnormal 11-yr-old children living at home on socioeconomic background, MA, CA, and their scores on the Reynell Language Scales. Mothers of the experimental group carried out a language improvement program under direction. Household tasks, shopping, and excursions were turned into language situations, and storybooks and games were provided. Both groups were pre- and posttested on a number of language measures and a battery of objective experience tests, including the Columbia Mental Maturity Scale, the Reynell Expressive Language and Verbal Comprehension Scales, and the Peabody Picture Vocabulary Test. It was predicted that the experimental group would show greater improvement on the language measures and experience tests than the control group. The experimental group did differ significantly on the Renfrew Articulation Test and on the 3 experience tests; the other language measures showed nonsignificant trends in the expected direction. An appendix on the experience tests is included. (27 ref.)
Jeffree, D. M. & Cashdan, A. (Manchester U., Hester Adrian Research Center, England) British Journal of Educational Psychology, 1971(Jun), Vol. 41(2), 184-194. [PA, Vol 47:09728]

3547.   Problems of diagnosis and placement of the severely subnormal child.
Suggests models relating to the diagnosis and placement of the severely subnormal child, here seen as one whose IQ would generally be expected to be below 50, but who would in all likelihood be attending day training centers. The basic placement of the child is a function of several factors, foremost being the educability of the child and his social and emotional adjustment. Once placed, educational diagnosis and treatment must be continuous and interlocking; and this means that services must be provided within the school itself and that teachers must be trained to become full team members in the diagnostic and placement process.
McLeod, J. (U Saskatchewan, Saskatoon, Canada) Association of Educational Psychologists Journal & Newsletter, 1971(Fal), Vol 2(10), 10-17. [PA, Vol 53:04058]

3548.   Beginning reading discrimination taught at IQ 35 by conditioning.
A simple conditioning method, using cards for control of attention, was tried out on 6 severely retarded children (CA, 6.4-15.11; MA, 2.11-4.3; IQ, 22-47). After 17 workdays the 3 "high-MA" Ss discriminated 8-10 words out of 10 and 9-10 words 24 and 48 days later (with 50-100% transfer to smaller, different print). "Low-MA" Ss retained 10-40% (40% for the 1 S without speech).
Rydberg, Sven. (U. Stockholm, Sweden) Perceptual & Motor Skills, 1971(Feb), Vol. 32(1), 163-166. [PA, Vol 46:03636]

3549.   Teacher bias effects with severely retarded children.
Selected 24 8-16 yr. old severely retarded children who were judged, through extensive testing, to be capable of making further intellectual and social progress. Ss were then divided into experimental and control groups. Optimistic psychological reports on the experimental group were given to their cottage parents to produce, if possible, teacher bias or expectancy effects. From results of posttesting after 6 mo., no effects of teacher bias were found. (19 ref.)
Soule, Donald. (North Carolina Dept. of Mental Health, Raleigh) American Journal of Mental Deficiency, 1972(Sep), Vol. 77(2), 208-211. [PA, Vol 49:07988]

3550.   [Severe retardation: Special education.] (Fren)
Questions present rehabilitation practices which because of their emphasis on teaching skills run the risk of ignoring a more fundamental need, i.e., the need of the retarded person to speak for himself, to reach a sense of identity which is more than just a reflection of what society or his teacher want him to do. A program for adolescents is described in which the emphasis is not on teaching a trade but rather on providing the experiences and giving the youths the support needed to allow them to communicate, and to achieve a sense of identity. (English summary)
Visier, J. P. (Inst. mëdico-professionnel "Les papillons blancs", Belleu, France) Bulletin de Psychologie Scolaire et d'Orientation, 1972(Jan), Vol. 21(1), 1-8. [PA, Vol 48:12084]

3551.   Varied-teacher tutorials: A tactic for generating credible skills in severely retarded people.
Describes the use of varied-teacher tutorial programs for teaching verbal and nonverbal skills to severely retarded children. The program was designed to give pupils the opportunity to learn various skills from several different teachers (primarily student volunteers) thereby eliminating a custodial care program and the often detrimental effects of the intense dependency relationship found in a one-to-one teacher-pupil relationship. Examples of the progress made by specific children in the 4-yr-old program described are presented, and the system for coordinating the various tutorials is outlined. Advantages of the program for the pupils, the student volunteers, and the staff members are discussed. A checklist for assessing the accuracy of the volunteers is described, and suggestions for future research are presented.
Barrett, Beatrice H. & McCormack, James E. (Walter E. Fernald State School, Waverley, Mass.) Mental Retardation, 1973(Dec), Vol. 11(6), 14-19. [PA, Vol 52:04062]

3552.   Training a retarded child as a behavioral teaching assistant.
Describes a behavior modification program used to change the classroom disruptive behavior of 3 retarded children by allowing one of them, a 14-yr-old boy, to serve as a "helper" and distribute candy reinforcers for good behavior. Appropriate behavior by him and the 2 most disruptive children improved through this program.
Drabman, Ronald & Spitalnik, Robert. (Florida Technological U.) Journal of Behavior Therapy & Experimental Psychiatry, 1973(Sep), Vol. 4(3), 269-272. [PA, Vol 52:04069]

3553.   Reduction of stereotypies by reinforcement of toy play.
Recorded the stereotypies (repetitive movements of any part of the body) and toy play of 3 severely retarded 8-14 yr old children in a setting featuring a wide array of toys. High levels of stereotypies and low rates of toy play were initially observed. Prompting and positive reinforcement of toy play markedly increased toy play responses and decreased stereotypies to zero levels. 2 single-S experimental designs confirmed that the treatment procedures were responsible for these results.
Flavell, Judith E. Mental Retardation, 1973(Aug), Vol. 11(4), 21-23. [PA, Vol 51:05464]

3554.   Reinforcement procedures and social behavior in a group context with severely retarded children.
Operant reinforcement procedures were employed by a teacher and a teacher's aide in the classroom to develop simple but sustained social behaviors in 8 severely retarded 6-10 yr olds. The relative effectiveness of social and edible reinforcement was investigated as well as the tendency for these new behaviors to generalize from a group to a free-play situation. Reinforcement procedures were successfully applied in class, providing an effective and economical means for developing social behavior. Edible reinforcement was most effective but the behavior did not generalize.
Guralnick, Michael J. & Kravik, Mark A. (National Children's Center, Washington, D.C.) Psychological Reports, 1973(Feb), Vol. 32(1), 295-301. [PA, Vol 51:03480]

3555.   Employing paraprofessional teachers in a group language training program for severely and profoundly retarded children.
Conducted a study with 42 severely and profoundly retarded children (mean age = 12 yrs) to evaluate the effectiveness of a newly-developed language training program particularly suited for the severely retarded. Designed for use with nonprofessional staff acting as teachers, the program contains a simplified

introduction to operant and modeling procedures, detailed lesson plans, necessary materials, and instructions for testing and evaluation. Ss were assigned to 4 groups based on pretest scores on an identification and a verbalization task. Pairs of Ss were matched within each group according to pretest performance, language equivalence scores, mental classification, age, sex, race, and behavior problems. One member of each matched pair was then randomly designated an experimental or control S. The experimental groups received 2 mo of language training (each group comprising 1 class), with 2 psychiatric aides conducting all activities. Comparison of pre- and posttest performances indicates clear treatment effects, demonstrating the potential for wide-spread institutional use of such programs. (21 ref.)
Phillips, Sheridan; Liebert, Robert M. & Poulos, Rita W. (State U. New York, Stony Brook) Perceptual & Motor Skills, 1973(Apr), Vol. 36(2), 607-616. [PA, Vol 51:03943]

3556. Consultation in a public school for the severely retarded.
Describes a successful 2-yr program in a new school for the severely retarded, in which a consultant worked ½ day/wk with the staff to help solve many severe problems. The consultant's active role in helping the staff establish new behaviors is emphasized. Therefore the consultant reached the children indirectly through the staff. The problems of the system became the focus. Crisis theory and intervention were integral parts of the task. As a desired end result, the consultant became unnecesary.
Pollack, Donald. (California School of Professional Psychology, San Diego) Education & Training of the Mentally Retarded, 1973(Dec), Vol. 8(4), 181-186. [PA, Vol 52:06358]

3557. Assessment of two methods of teaching phonic skills to neuropsychiatrically impaired children.
Gave 18 severely retarded 8-17 yr old readers in a state hospital school 6 hrs of phonic skills instruction in brief, small-group sessions. 9 Ss were taught with a commercially available program. The remaining 9 received an experimentally developed program. Comparison of pre- and posttest scores on a phonic skills test showed instruction had significantly improved phonic skills in both groups. Results also show that the experimental group had learned to generalize the skills, whereas the group that had received the commercial program had not. It is concluded that the experimental program offers possibilities for providing effective instruction in hospital schools.
Richardson, Ellis; Winsberg, Bertrand G. & Bialer, Irv. (New York State Dept. of Mental Hygiene, Child Psychiatric Evaluation Research Unit, Brooklyn) Journal of Learning Disabilities, 1973(Dec), Vol. 6(10), 628-635. [PA, Vol 52:01287]

3558. Public school education for the severely mentally retarded.
Presents the rationale for providing services for the severely and profoundly mentally retarded school age child. Recent research on the education of the trainable mentally retarded and the educable mentally retarded is reviewed. It is suggested that the public school setting can become more democratic in its organization and in its integration of the retarded when a broader range of the retarded is included. (20 ref.)
Risler, Walt P. & Mefford, John P. (Indiana U.) Viewpoints, 1973(Jan), Vol. 49(1), 13-24. [PA, Vol 50:05830]

3559. Assessment and social education of severely subnormal children in a pre-school unit.
Describes the goals, services, facilities, personnel, and activities of a typical day in a school for severely retarded children over 2½ yrs of age. The school is centered around the idea that even severely retarded children can learn social skills if appropriate stimulation and opportunities are provided. The school is staffed with both professional and volunteer workers, the goal being to provide a 1:1 ratio of children and adults. Emphasis is placed on normal activities (e.g., proper eating behavior, painting, and games). Results of an experiment on cue salience in retarded children indicate that retarded children can perform well on identification problems; based on these findings, a program in which children were given a small sum of money and allowed to

go shopping is described. Assessment procedures used in the school are outlined and case histories presented.
Sinson, Janice C. British Journal of Mental Subnormality, 1973(Jun), Vol. 19(36, Pt. 1), 21-32. [PA, Vol 52:01878]

3560. Educational therapy with the severely retarded.
Assigned 18 female and 12 male 6-19 yr old severely retarded children (IQ = 19-39) to 5 heterosexual ability groups for 30-min sessions of educational therapy 5 days/wk for 9 mo. Marked improvement was found in motor, perceptual, and language skills with transference to self-help skills, socialization, and better use of leisure time in the cottage.
Sullivan, June P. & Batarseh, Gabriel J. (Coastal Center, Ladson, S.C.) Training School Bulletin, 1973(May), Vol. 70(1), 5-9. [PA, Vol 51:03490]

3561. Generalized limitation and Orff-Schulwerk.
Describes the "Schulwerk" (schoolwork) method developed by Carl Orff, a contemporary Bavarian composer and conductor, which uses elemental music to aid in learning through discovery. Elemental music involves the use of music, rhythm, movement, voice, speech, or silence to increase conceptual awareness and creativity. "Schulwerk" consists of 4 phases—germ idea, development, exploration, and closure. The extent to which the "Schulwerk" method promoted generalized imitation among 16 severely retarded adolescents was evaluated. The test of generalized imitation (probe) consisted of 4 gross motor and 4 fine motor items scored on a pass–fail basis. Results indicate that generalized imitation was generated by "Schulwerk" but not by a varied schedule of group recreational activities in which a control group of Ss had participated. Limitations of the method and its possible applications are noted.
Bitcon, Carol H. & Ball, Thomas S. (Fairview State Hosp., Costa Mesa, Calif.) Mental Retardation, 1974(Jun), Vol. 12(3), 36-39. [PA, Vol 52:13213]

3562. [Concerning an educational system that assures the development of severely handicapped children.] (Japn)
The delay in the passage of funding for the law assuring the development of severely retarded and multiply disabled children has been costly. Epidemiological studies clearly show a higher death rate among severely handicapped children who do not have the opportunity to attend schools tailored to their needs. Such schools would not only provide for securing the best progress for the individual student but would have medical equipment and a doctor to administer to the special needs of the epileptic, mentally retarded, emotionally disturbed, and physically handicapped child. The schools presently available to the retarded and emotionally disturbed are little better than nurseries that attract low-salaried personnel. Special education programs with enriched curricula must be developed to meet the needs of the multiply handicapped child. The movement for cooperative schools in which handicapped children share the same facilities with normal children deserves encouragement. (English summary) (5 ref)
Fujimoto, Bunro. (Fukui U, Teacher's Coll, Japan) Japanese Journal of Child Psychiatry, 1974(Mar–Apr), Vol 15(2), 96–102. [PA, Vol 63:04175]

3563. Now more than ever: A case for the special class.
Argues for the need for special education classes for the severely and profoundly retarded children. The limitations of existing regular classes and the creation of resource rooms as substitutes for special education programs are discussed, and the need for trained personnel and life-long planning for these children is emphasized. (20 ref)
Smith, James O. & Arkans, Joan R. (U. Washington, Coll. of Education) Exceptional Children, 1974(Apr), Vol. 40(7), 497-502. [PA, Vol 52:13233]

3564. Transfer of stimulus control from motor to verbal stimuli.
Used a transfer of stimulus control procedure to teach 3 profoundly retarded adolescents a series of specific responses to specific verbal instructions. After imitative control of a behavior was established, a verbal instruction was presented immediately

before the behavior was modeled. Each correct response was followed on the next trial by inserting a delay between the verbal instruction and the modeling of the behavior. The delays increased from trial to trial. Transfer of stimulus control was indicated when an S responded correctly on 5 consecutive trials before the behavior was modeled. All 3 Ss responded correctly to each verbal instruction after that item was trained in a multiple-baseline order. Generalization did not occur to items that had not been trained. Probe data revealed that some variations of the verbal instructions controlled responses after training was completed. (18 ref)
Striefel, Sebastian; Bryan, Karen S. & Aikins, Dale A. (Parsons State Hosp., Research Center, Kan.) Journal of Applied Behavior Analysis, 1974(Spr), Vol. 7(1), 123-135. [PA, Vol 52:08694]

3565. Effects of prompting, praise and tokens on the development of counting behavior in a severely retarded boy.
Studied use of reinforcement to improve counting behavior of a male retardate 19 yrs old. 30 sessions of 30 min each were conducted for pointing and counting from 1 through 5. Phases of experiment were the baseline, experimental, second baseline, and reinstatement. Social reinforcement consisted of praise, patting on the shoulders, and kicking under the table. Results suggest a combination of motivational and learning phenomena. Accuracy of counting increased.
Swartz, Frank. (Western Michigan U) SALT: School Applications of Learning Theory, 1974(Oct), Vol 7(1), 25-30. [PA, Vol 54:08458]

3566. Educational services for the severely and profoundly handicapped.
Maintains that until very recently, American society had made no widespread commitment to the educational and social development of the severely/profoundly handicapped. It is argued that the problem of integrating this group into society involves not only a consideration of what the community requires but also what the individual needs and is capable of being. The challenge is to implement wider-ranging quality programs for all severely handicapped children. Recent court decisions have led to increased federal funding and changes in attitudes to provide such programs. Special education personnel need to develop early identification procedures, teacher competencies, better-prepared personnel, parent involvement, community support services, and a national dissemination effort.
Haring, Norris G. (U Washington) Journal of Special Education, 1975(Win), Vol 9(4), 425-433. [PA, Vol 56:04909]

3567. Increasing severely retarded students' participation in group activities via token reinforcement.
Used token reinforcement to increase the participation of 11 severely retarded students (mean CA 13.8 yrs, mean IQ 15.1) in a group musical activity. The behavior measured was the amount of S's continuous participation from the beginning of the activity. The classroom teacher recorded behavior using a tape recorder, and an ABAB design was employed. Results indicate that token reinforcement did cause an increase in participation. Token reinforcement under different schedules, and the feasibility of teachers as ongoing observers of behavior are discussed.
Leon, Jim & Malloy, Diane. Research & the Retarded, 1975(Spr), Vol 2(2), 29-34. [PA, Vol 58:04386]

3568. [Experimental education of severely retarded children in auxiliary school.] (Russ)
Notes that the development of research on abnormal children and upgrading their education in special schools has resulted in many different approaches. Special attention is now paid to severely retarded children, who comprise about 15% of all mentally retarded children. Experience with these children has shown that isolation has a negative impact on their education and upbringing; it is much better for them to remain with their families and to attend school in the daytime. Previous practice, when teachers mainly delivered minimum educational knowledge (writing, counting) and neglected vocational and social adaptation skills, has been recognized as unsatisfactory. Investigation has shown that it is possible to accustom severely retarded

children to work activity lasting 5-6 hrs/day. The first problem is not education, but rather development of self-maintenance and social behaviors, and motor and speech abilities.
Kuz'mitskaya, M. I.; Maller, A. R. & Tskoto, G. V. (Academy of Pedagogical Sciences, Inst of Defectology, Moscow, USSR) Defektologiya, 1976(Jun), No 6, 26–31. [PA, Vol 63:08442]

3569. Special unit care of the preschool child with severe physical or mental handicaps.
Discusses special care units for the severely physically and mentally handicapped preschool child. Types of handicap (cerebral palsy, spina bifida, and Down's syndrome) and ethnic origin (Irish, Indian, and Nigerian) of the children passing through such a unit in a 2-yr period are considered. Management of the unit is described and the need for a multidisciplinary approach to the care of the child is emphasized.
Nowotny, Margaret. Child Care, Health & Development, 1976(Oct), Vol 2(5), 295-303. [PA, Vol 57:13945]

3570. Reducing inappropriate behaviors in classrooms and in individual sessions through DRO schedules of reinforcement.
Differential reinforcement of other behavior (DRO) was used to reduce "hairtwirling," "handbiting," and "thumbsucking" in 2 severely retarded institutionalized children, ages 9 and 11 yrs, and a mildly retarded 4-yr-old in individual settings. This reinforcement schedule was also used to reduce "talk-outs" in 3 mildly retarded children, ages 8, 9, and 13 yrs, in classroom settings. In all 6 cases, responding was reduced substantially, and the reduction was attributed to the DRO schedules under either multiple baseline or ABAB design. (18 ref)
Repp, Alan C.; Deitz, Samuel M. & Deitz, Diane E. (Georgia Retardation Ctr, Atlanta) Mental Retardation, 1976(Feb), Vol 14(1), 11-15. [PA, Vol 56:01482]

3571. Establishing generalized verb-noun instruction-following skills in retarded children.
Used a transfer of stimulus control procedure to establish generalized verb-noun instruction-following skills in 2 severely retarded 12-yr-old boys. Each of 12 verbs was trained, in a multiple baseline order, to criterion with each of 12 nouns in the form of verb-noun verbal instructions. Throughout training, reinforced probes were conducted on both trained and untrained verb-noun combinations. As training progressed, both Ss began to respond correctly to untrained verb-noun instructions. Eventually, a verb needed to be trained in combination with only 1 noun before generalization occurred to the as-yet-untrained 11 verb-noun instructions involving that verb.
Striefel, Sebastian; Wetherby, Bruce & Karlan, George R. (Utah State U Exceptional Child Ctr) Journal of Experimental Child Psychology, 1976(Oct), Vol 22(2), 247-260. [PA, Vol 57:06939]

3572. Teaching students: Teaching teachers.
Describes an in-service course in behavior modification for teachers of severely mentally handicapped children which was offered by student educational psychologists as part of their own training. Problems and possible alternative presentations are discussed.
Thacker, John. (Exeter U, England) AEP (Association of Educational Psychologists) Journal, 1976(Win), Vol 4(3), 23–25. [PA, Vol 59:06472]

3573. Teaching selected social skills to severely handicapped students.
Outlines the process of teaching social skills to the severely handicapped and reviews studies that survey social skill teaching for this population. The present study attempted to teach complex social skills to 11 adolescent students (IQs 38–52). The skills taught included both isolative and cooperative social interactions that were task-related and provided generalizable learning. Components included recognition of appropriate time and place and initiating, sustaining, and terminating interactions. It was found that these basic skills, once learned, were used across environments. It is emphasized that social skills should be integrated into the general curriculum.

Williams, Wes & Hamre-Nietupski, Sue. (U Texas, Austin) SALT: School Applications of Learning Theory, 1976(Apr), Vol 8(3), 1–19. [PA, Vol 61:09722]

3574.   Observing interactions in the severely mentally handicapped.
Preliminary observations were conducted for 4 1-hr sessions in 6 classrooms of a school for the severely mentally retarded: 1 infant class, 1 special care class, 2 junior classes with 5–10 yr olds, and 2 senior groups with 10–16 yr olds. The frequency of interactions ranged from 0 to 10 for the 4 lower classes and was over 100 for each of the senior groups. Part 2 involved observing each member of the senior classes individually for 3 20-min free-play periods. Over 50% of the total number of child-initiated interactions were directed toward the teacher. A positive relationship was found between the interactive behavior for each child in the 3 sessions. 12 categories of behavior were observed, with those of giving and requesting information accounting for about 80% of the initiations. As reported by the 1st author and A. Tatham (1976), 6 of the Ss here observed participated in a structured experimental task requiring them to transmit specific information to each other from behind a screen. As a group, the good performers produced more of the giving and receiving information classroom behaviors than the poor performers. This finding suggests that this methodology may lead to the establishment of connections between classroom behavior and performance in experimental situations. (20 ref)
Beveridge, M. & Berry, Paul. (U Manchester, Adrian Research Ctr, England) Research in Education, 1977(May), No 17, 13–22. [PA, Vol 63:02048]

3575.   Signed English: A language teaching technique with totally nonverbal, severely mentally retarded adolescents.
Reports on a language technique employed with 4 15–19 yr old severely retarded Ss (IQ 30). During the first stage, food items, animals, and common household articles in concrete and pictorial form were used to develop a basic vocabulary of signs. Next, a question or command likely to elicit a 2-word response was added. As vocabulary expanded, Ss generated original sentences and variation of target responses. As Ss improved, declarative sentences, imperative sentences with compound predicates, and less concrete grammatical forms were introduced. Verb negation, tense, and plural noun forms were also included. Results show that after 10 mo, (a) all Ss demonstrated a 200-word receptive sign vocabulary, and 3 Ss showed an expressive sign vocabulary of over 100 words; (b) all Ss showed increases in auditory comprehension of single words and simple commands; and (c) 2 Ss showed stimulation of oral production as a result of the signed English technique.
Linville, Sue E.   Language, Speech, & Hearing Services in Schools, 1977(Jul), Vol 8(3), 170–175. [PA, Vol 59:13289]

3576.   Establishment of controlled arm movements in profoundly retarded students using response contingent vibratory stimulation.
Profoundly retarded multihandicapped individuals are now entering public school programs because of recent legislation and litigation. These students are underserved since systematic effort in providing individualized educational programs for them has no precedent. The present experiment assessed whether operant procedures would be effective in establishing arm movements in 7 nonambulatory profoundly retarded multihandicapped 9–20 yr old males in a public school program. The target behaviors were arm pulling (4 Ss) and arm pushing (3 Ss). Ss were given manual guidance trials followed by vibratory stimulation and free operant procedures with a changing criterion for delivery of vibratory reinforcement. Results show that arm pulling responses increased from fewer than 5/session at baseline to 34/session; arm pushing responses increased from fewer than 1/session at baseline to 86/session.
Murphy, Robert J. & Doughty, Neil R. (St Cloud State U, Coll of Education) American Journal of Mental Deficiency, 1977(Sep), Vol 82(2), 212–216. [PA, Vol 60:06219]

3577.   Designing instructional media for severely retarded adolescents: A theoretical approach to trait-treatment interaction research.
72 severely retarded adolescents (mean CA 197.68 mo, mean IQ 43.70) individually viewed a cartoon, a live action film, and a pixilation film in color or black and white. A distractor method was used to measure frequency and duration of eye movement to visual stimuli. Content of visual stimuli was controlled, presentation of a distractor randomized, and all eye movement monitored to the nearest second. Black and white visual presentations had greater attentional value than color presentations, and use of real human beings appeared to be more salient as an attention-holding technique than was use of animated characters. (19 ref)
Nathanson, David E. (Florida International U, Div of Psycho-Educational Services) American Journal of Mental Deficiency, 1977(Jul), Vol 82(1), 26–32. [PA, Vol 59:11150]

3578.   On presenting pictures and sentences: The effect of presentation order on sentence comprehension in normal and mentally handicapped children.
Tested 39 normal nursery school students (mean age 4 yrs 5 mo) and 48 severely educationally subnormal (ESN) special school students (mean age 12 yrs 6 mo) of similar vocabulary age on a sentence comprehension test under 3 presentation conditions. The test required the S to demonstrate comprehension of spoken sentences by pointing appropriately to 1 of 3 or 4 alternative visual referents. In the 1st condition, the pictures were presented prior to the stimulus sentence; in the 2nd, the pictures and sentence were presented simultaneously; and in the 3rd, the sentence was presented prior to the pictures. Results show that presentation conditions did not affect performance significantly for normal Ss, but performance of ESN Ss was adversely affected by the condition in which sentences were presented prior to pictures.
Wheldall, K. & Mittler, P. (U Birmingham, England) British Journal of Educational Psychology, 1977(Nov), Vol 47(3), 322–326. [PA, Vol 61:06949]

3579.   Classroom interaction: Two studies of severely educationally subnormal children.
An experimental study by P. Evans and J. Hogg (see PA, Vol 55:12505) of go/no-go discrimination learning indicated that individual differences in learning relate to children's scores on the excitation–inhibition factor of the Classroom Assessment Scale. The current paper reports 2 observational studies of 22 ambulant noninstitutionalized severely retarded children (mean CA 11.5 yrs) which show that this scale factor also relates to aspects of the children's classroom behavior. In particular, the frequency of initiation of interaction, amount of speech, number of approaches, and likelihood of interacting with the teacher were positively and significantly related to the degree of excitation of the children. These results are interpreted as indicating that excitable children are more reinforcement-seeking than inhibitable children, and that this tendency leads to the differences observed in the classroom.
Beveridge, Michael & Evans, Peter. (U Manchester, England) Research in Education, 1978(May), No 19, 39–48. [PA, Vol 62:09768]

3580.   Language and social behaviour in severely educationally subnormal children.
In a study of approximately 200 2–17 yr old Ss in 2 schools, there was a strong positive relationship between age and the number of social interactions a child was likely to initiate during a typical classroom free-play period. The type of interaction that showed the largest increase was the verbally initiated child–child interaction. Verbally initiated child–teacher interactions also increased with age, although not so markedly as child–child interactions. There appeared to be no significant change in nonverbal initiations of interactions with age, either to the teacher or to peers. Results support the use of observational techniques for language assessment in that they give further information about the growth of productive language skills as reported in a population survey of language abilities in mentally handicapped school children.

Beveridge, Michael; Spencer, Jenny & Mittler, Peter. (U Manchester, England) British Journal of Social & Clinical Psychology, 1978(Feb), Vol 17(1), 75–83. [PA, Vol 61:07286]

3581. Early receptive language training for the severely and profoundly retarded.
Describes a procedure for teaching object identification to severely and profoundly retarded children. Children are initially asked to discriminate between 2 target words that are phonemically dissimilar. Because some children respond better to visual stimuli than auditory stimuli, the words may be manually signed as well as spoken. The best response was achieved by asking the child to hand the objects to him. Because of physical problems, some children are unable to grasp the objects; in this case, pointing or any signal indicating comprehension is acceptable. Prompts are often necessary, and reinforcements of various kinds are used. Successful use of the technique with a 15-yr-old profoundly retarded boy who demonstrated no oral speech is described.
Booth, Thomas. (Office of Los Angeles County Superintendent of Schools, CA) Language, Speech, & Hearing Services in Schools, 1978(Jul), Vol 9(3), 151–154. [PA, Vol 63:02051]

3582. Curriculum guides for the mentally retarded: An analysis and recommendations.
Examined 227 different curriculum guides for use with the mentally retarded and found that (a) almost no guides for use with severely retarded children existed, and (b) the guides did not appear to be based on any recognizable modern learning theory. General recommendations for the development of new public school curricula are presented.
Cegelka, Walter J. (U Missouri, St Louis) Education & Training of the Mentally Retarded, 1978(Apr), Vol 13(2), 187–188. [PA, Vol 61:14519]

3583. Programming language for severely retarded children.
Describes methods of language programing for profoundly mentally retarded children that are based on linguistic principles. Examples of program contents are drawn from research reports and include cuing procedures, as well as progress from receptive through imitative behaviors, labeling responses, and grammatical sequencing. Materials are included in an appendix. (19 ref)
Davis, Carol M. (Speech & Hearing Ctr, Learning Disabilities Clinic & Educational Testing Services, Mobile, AL) Language, Speech, & Hearing Services in Schools, 1978(Oct), Vol 9(4), 213–219. [PA, Vol 63:12973]

3584. The TMR class and the open space school.
Describes a successful experience in the mainstreaming of severely retarded children into an open space school. Polls of staff and parents indicated that the children's academic progress in the ongoing school remained relatively similar to progress made in the traditional classroom setting, but social behavior greatly improved.
Downing, Charles J. (U Nevada, Reno) Education & Training of the Mentally Retarded, 1978(Feb), Vol 13(1), 64–66. [PA, Vol 61:09673]

3585. Am I right in thinking "education" means more than "training"?
Questions the meaning of mandated "education" for severely educationally subnormal pupils. Is "education" (defined as development of awareness and understanding of principles) a realistic goal, or can the development of such children best be fostered by the narrower goal of "training"? (5 ref)
Edwards, John. AEP (Association of Educational Psychologists) Journal, 1978(Jan), Vol 4(6), 36–37. [PA, Vol 65:11229]

3586. An interest center sensory stimulation program for severely and profoundly retarded children.
Argues that behavioral techniques, which have been extremely effective in training the mildly retarded, are not always appropriate for use with severely retarded nonambulatory children. As an alternative strategy, an interest-center type of classroom organization involving simple sensory input but not an appropriate response from the child is suggested. The classroom can be organized into as many as 5 sensory areas and may include visual, auditory, tactile, kinesthetic, and gustatory–olfactory stimulation centers. Appropriate materials are listed, and advantages and difficulties with the method are described.
Glover, Elayne & Mesibov, Gary B. (Chapel Hill Outreach Project, NC) Education & Training of the Mentally Retarded, 1978(Apr), Vol 13(2), 172–176. [PA, Vol 61:14528]

3587. An educational schema for children with the dual disability of deafness and blindness.
Outlines an educational schema whereby teachers of severely intellectually retarded and multi-handicapped children, including the deaf/blind, can assess the prelanguage levels of children on a hierarchical language schedule that culminates in the acquisition of natural gesture. Appropriate teaching strategies for each prelanguage level are outlined, and the significance of natural gesture as a precursor to the acquisition of symbolic language is discussed. (8 ref)
Hewitt, Heather. (Monnington Ctr, Kew, Australia) Australian Journal of Mental Retardation, 1978(Sep), Vol 5(3), 81–85. [PA, Vol 63:08428]

3588. Improving the independent play of severely mentally retarded children.
Attempted to develop instructional procedures for improving the independent toy play of severely retarded institutionalized children in a classroom setting. Four of 6 4–13 yr old nonverbal children in a self-contained classroom participated. 10 reactive toys (e.g., truck, jack-in-the-box, popcorn popper) and 10 nonreactive toys (block, stuffed animal, ball) were placed randomly about the play area. Interventions took place across 30 school days during each day's play period. Since the goal was to improve independent play, the 3 teachers gradually "faded" from the area: All teachers remained in the play area for the 1st 3 wks, 2 were present for the next 2 wks, and finally one adult supervised the play period for the last week. Pre- and posttests showed that there was little change in 2 of the Ss' play behavior. The other 2 Ss increased their appropriate toy behavior and decreased their stereotypic behavior. None of the Ss showed a preference for reactive or nonreactive toys.
Hopper, Christine & Wambold, Clark. (Madison Metropolitan School District, Early Childhood Program, WI) Education & Training of the Mentally Retarded, 1978(Feb), Vol 13(1), 42–46. [PA, Vol 61:09685]

3589. Assessing classroom environments and prioritizing goals for the severely retarded.
Administered the Balthazar Scales of Adaptive Behavior (II) Scales of Social Adaptation to the female students in 8 classrooms for severely retarded adolescents at a state developmental center. A principal components analysis was applied to this baseline data in order to assess the classroom environments and to then prioritize goals derived from the results. In the analysis, 3 modal classroom types were identified. A method is described for goal setting based on the correspondence between the modal classroom types and the hierarchy of educational goals outlined by D. Krathwohl et al (1964). (10 ref)
Lathey, Jonathan W. (Wassaic Developmental Ctr, Children's Unit, NY) Exceptional Children, 1978(Nov), Vol 45(3), 190–195. [PA, Vol 62:04823]

3590. Instructional strategies for severely language deficient children.
Argues that in some cases, neither manipulation of the environment to approximate the natural conditions of language learning nor exclusive reliance on behavioral technology as the source for instructional procedures is most desirable. In these instances, selective integration of the 2 strategies should be considered. A framework is proposed for decisions relative to instructional techniques—suggestions for choosing between or combining behavioral and developmental training strategies. Instructional decisions must be guided by the idiosyncratic learning characteristics of the target population and specific children. For some children, the most effective approach to language training will be to simulate the tutorial experiences available to the normal child;

but for others, artificial, synthetic, and more structured conditions and a greater degree of control will need to be imposed. (38 ref)
McCormick, Linda P. & Elder, Pamela S. (U Alabama, Birmingham) Education & Training of the Mentally Retarded, 1978(Feb), Vol 13(1), 29–36. [PA, Vol 61:09701]

3591. Effects of serial versus concurrent task sequencing on acquisition, maintenance, and generalization.
Compared effects of serial and concurrent task presentation on skill acquisition, generalization, and maintenance in 2 severely retarded 19- and 22-yr-old females. During serial training, items of 1 response class, tracing, were trained to mastery before those of a 2nd task, vocal imitation. In the concurrent method, training on 2 different tasks, tracing and vocal imitation, alternated within sessions for fixed periods of time. There were no major differences between the serial and concurrent methods of instruction in the number of steps attained per behavior or in the number of trials required to reach criterion levels of performance. It was found, however, that concurrent training resulted in more generalization. Retention results were not consistently related to training method.
Panyan, Marion C. & Hall, R. Vance. (U North Carolina School of Social Work, Charlotte) Journal of Applied Behavior Analysis, 1978(Spr), Vol 11(1), 67–74. [PA, Vol 61:09709]

3592. On shared knowledge: Teachers and severely subnormal children.
Describes the interaction between 1 teacher and 2 severely subnormal children, aged 6 and 8 yrs, in structured teaching sessions. The children differed considerably in verbal comprehension of the crucial task attributes of color, shape, and size, and in the quality and quantity of their participation in the interaction. It was found that the teacher was sensitive to differences between the children and differed in certain aspects of the quality of her interaction, but not in quantity. However, these differences appeared to be a function of relatively static models of the children and did not appear to be adaptive to the particular task involved. (17 ref)
Swann, W. S. (Open U, Faculty of Educational Studies, Hagen, West Germany) British Journal of Educational Psychology, 1978(Nov), Vol 48(3), 340–350. [PA, Vol 64:02168]

3593. Reducing multiple problem behaviours in a profoundly retarded child.
Describes 2 behavior management programs developed for a profoundly retarded 7-yr-old male in a special education classroom. The target behaviors were inappropriate object contact, wild running about the room, and consistent refusal to eat. Literature was reviewed in an effort to find information that would help in the management of these behaviors. However, only a limited number of studies were found to be directly relevant. (3 ref)
Wehman, Paul & Marchant, Jo A. (Virginia Commonwealth U) British Journal of Social & Clinical Psychology, 1978(Jun), Vol 17(2), 149–152. [PA, Vol 62:06715]

3594. A strategy for developing chronological-age-appropriate and functional curricular content for severely handicapped adolescents and young adults.
Points out the inappropriateness of the typical bottom-up or norm-referenced curricula offered to severely handicapped adolescents and young adults. As an alternative, it is proposed that curricula for this population teach CA-appropriate functional skills in natural environments. A curriculum-development strategy is constructed based on these concepts. (5 ref)
Brown, Lou et al. (U Wisconsin, Madison) Journal of Special Education, 1979(Spr), Vol 13(1), 81–90. [PA, Vol 66:08967]

3595. Some further thoughts and clarifications on the education of severely and profoundly retarded children.
Responds to the criticism by E. Sontag et al (see PA, Vol 62:9819) of the present authors' (see PA, Vol 62:9771) position on educational programing for the severely and profoundly retarded. Issue is taken with each of the alternatives proposed by Sontag et al, and questions are raised regarding the interpreta-

tions of the literature and of Public Law 94-142 that Sontag et al propose. (23 ref)
Burton, Thomas A. & Hirshoren, Alfred. (U Georgia Coll of Education) Exceptional Children, 1979(May), Vol 45(8), 618–625. [PA, Vol 62:09770]

3596. The education of severely and profoundly retarded children: Are we sacrificing the child to the concept?
The mandate of Public Law 94-142, The Education of All Handicapped Children Act, has precipitated some divergent thinking among professionals relative to its implementation. The authors develop a position to provide a forum for discussion of this issue as it relates to educational programing for the severely and profoundly retarded. Their position focuses on 3 basic issues involving anticipated levels of learning, personnel training, and the appropriate locus of educational services for the severely and profoundly retarded. (15 ref)
Burton, Thomas A. & Hirshoren, Alfred. (U Georgia Coll of Education) Exceptional Children, 1979(May), Vol 45(8), 598–602. [PA, Vol 62:09771]

3597. Teachers of the severely and profoundly retarded students: What competencies are needed?
Questionnaire data from 33 administrators and 88 teachers indicate that teachers should be trained and employed who demonstrate competence in the learning activities, pupil self-concept, pupil self-discipline, communications development, and parent interaction domains. (2 ref)
Milne, Nidia M. (U Houston) Mental Retardation, 1979(Apr), Vol 17(2), 87–89. [PA, Vol 66:08842]

3598. Multielement designs: An alternative to reversal and multiple baseline evaluation strategies.
A multielement design was used to demonstrate that a procedure involving the response-contingent presentation of music increased upright head positioning with 6 14–19 yr old profoundly retarded pupils who were attending a public school program. The advantages of using multielement designs for the evaluation of educational procedures in general and motivational procedures in particular are discussed with special emphasis on public school settings. (12 ref)
Murphy, Robert; Doughty, Neil & Nunes, Dennis L. (St Cloud State U) Mental Retardation, 1979(Feb), Vol 17(1), 23–27. [PA, Vol 64:02161]

3599. Use of teacher prompts to increase social behavior: Generalization effects with severely and profoundly retarded adolescents.
In a single-S design with replication across Ss, teacher prompts were used to increase the rate of social behavior of 3 severely and profoundly retarded adolescents who were legally blind. Training took place in the classroom on successive school days with the teacher prompting each S to engage in positive social interaction with each peer. Observations for generalization effects immediately followed each training session. The remaining class members were brought into the room, and social interactions were observed in a free-play setting while the teacher was absent. During both phases, observers recorded the behavior of the 3 Ss for 5 min and recorded all units of social exchange that each S initiated or responded to. Increased rates of social behavior were obtained for all 3 Ss during both training and generalization. Factors that contributed to the generalization effects are discussed. (8 ref)
Petersen, Gail A.; Austin, Gloria J. & Lang, Roger P. (Ohio State U, Nisonger Ctr) American Journal of Mental Deficiency, 1979(Jul), Vol 84(1), 82–86. [PA, Vol 62:12292]

3600. The developmental model and its implications for assessment and instruction for the severely/profoundly handicapped.
Contends that normative development sequences cannot provide educational program contents in a direct fashion as educational objectives. Educators are now de-emphasizing "normal development" and are taking a remedial approach to strengthen specific skills regardless of hypothesized developmental sequences and readiness. (28 ref)

Switzky, Harvey; Rotatori, Anthony F.; Miller, Ted & Freagon, Sharon. (Northern Illinois U, DeKalb) Mental Retardation, 1979(Aug), Vol 17(4), 167–170. [PA, Vol 66:09052]

3601. Junior high school students as teachers of the severely retarded: Training and generalization.
Following a multiple baseline design, 4 junior high school students received training and feedback intervention on implementing an instructional program with a severely retarded student. Appropriate teaching behaviors increased on the target program and generalized to other programs. Ss' teaching behaviors increased from 58.8% appropriate responses during baseline to 97.5% during intervention. Results support the efficacy of using school-age tutors when the teacher of the severely handicapped assumes the role of a classroom manager. (18 ref)
Fenrick, Nancy J. & McDonnell, John J. (Mankato State U) Education & Training of the Mentally Retarded, 1980(Oct), Vol 15(3), 187–194. [PA, Vol 66:08983]

3602. Factors which motivate job acceptance among teachers of severely and profoundly mentally retarded children.
Identified factors that motivated job acceptance among 235 S teachers of severely and profoundly mentally retarded children. Survey Responses indicate that challenge and practicum experiences were the 2 most prevalent motivational factors underlying job acceptance. Further evidence suggests that rewarding experience may be a factor in career choice. (22 ref)
Marozas, Donald S. & May, Deborah C. (State U New York, Coll at Geneseo) Education & Training of the Mentally Retarded, 1980(Dec), Vol 15(4), 293–297. [PA, Vol 66:11157]

3603. Delayed and immediate reinforcement: Retarded adolescents in an educational setting.
Two mentally retarded adolescents (a 14-yr-old male and a 17-yr-old female) who had been institutionalized for about 10 yrs and had IQs of 27 and 31, respectively, experienced both immediate and delayed reinforcement when placed in a classroom setting. Appropriate work behavior was triggered using a token reinforcement system. A reversal design was used in which baseline periods alternated with each type of reinforcement period. Both delayed and immediate reinforcement conditions were accompanied by levels of appropriate behavior above baseline. Immediate reinforcement procedures resulted in higher levels of behavior than during delayed reinforcement; delayed reinforcement resulted in greater resistance to extinction after reinforcement had been terminated. No differences in generalization of the appropriate work behavior to another class period occurred as a result of the different reinforcement conditions. (27 ref)
Mayhew, Gerald L. & Anderson, John. (Tidewater Community Coll) Behavior Modification, 1980(Oct), Vol 4(4), 527–545. [PA, Vol 66:09024]

3604. The effect of room management procedures on the engagement of profoundly retarded children.
Investigated whether room management techniques applied to a class of 7 profoundly retarded children (developmental levels 1–12 mo) could successfully improve the relationship between the attention of 4 adults and the engagement levels of the children. Adults interchangeably assumed room manager, mover, and individual worker roles, while researchers rated the children's behavior on a planned activity checklist. Results show that room management changed the quality of attention given to children in such a way as to increase their engagement. (7 ref)
McBrien, Judith & Weightman, Jane. (Victoria U of Manchester, Hester Adrian Research Ctr, England) British Journal of Mental Subnormality, 1980(Jun), Vol 26(50, Pt 1), 38–46. [PA, Vol 66:06730]

3605. Differential reinforcement of correct responses to probes and prompts in picture-name training with severely retarded children.
A systematic sequence of prompt and probe trials was used to teach picture names to 3 severely retarded 4-yr-olds. On prompt trials the experimenter (E) presented a picture and said the picture name for the S to imitate; on probe trials the E did not name the picture. A procedure whereby correct responses to prompts and probes were nondifferentially reinforced was compared with procedures whereby correct responses to prompts and probes were differentially reinforced according to separate and independent schedules (SCH) of primary reinforcement. For all 3 Ss, the FR SCH for correct responses to prompts combined with the CR SCH for correct responses to probes (Phases 3 and 5) generated the highest number of correct responses to probes, the highest accuracy on probe trials, and the highest rate of learning to name pictures. (15 ref)
Olenick, Debra L. & Pear, Joseph J. (U Manitoba, Winnipeg, Canada) Journal of Applied Behavior Analysis, 1980(Spr), Vol 13(1), 77–89. [PA, Vol 65:08836]

3606. Teachers as agents of behavioral change for severely retarded students.
Describes 2 case studies (severely retarded 18- and 11-yr-old females) that employed behavioral modification procedures to decrease problematical behaviors. The studies were carried out in public school settings. Special education teachers under the direction of a school psychologist acted as the agents of behavioral change. (6 ref)
Rotatori, Anthony F.; Switzky, Harvey; Green, Herman G. & Fox, Robert. (Northern Illinois U, DeKalb) Psychological Reports, 1980(Dec), Vol 47(3, Pt 2), 1215–1220. [PA, Vol 66:13659]

3607. Deciding what to teach the severely/profoundly retarded student: A teacher responsibility.
Contends that curricula for the severely/profoundly mentally retarded can be determined only by detailed observation and assessment of the specific behaviors of the group, and by writing behavioral objectives for each member of the class. This task is viewed as a teacher responsibility. (7 ref)
Burton, Thomas A. Education & Training of the Mentally Retarded, 1981(Feb), Vol 16(1), 74–79. [PA, Vol 66:08970]

3608. Analysis and discourse.
Maintains that J. W. Tawney and J. Smith's (see PA, Vol 66:13666) paper was a self-serving interpretation of the literature on the education of severely and profoundly retarded children rather than a professional exchange of information designed to provide stimulation of professional thought. (2 ref)
Burton, Thomas A. & Hirshoren, Alfred. (U Georgia, Coll of Education, Athens) Exceptional Children, 1981(Sep), 48(1), 20–21. [PA, Vol 66:13639]

3609. Rhetoric and respectability.
Contends that J. W. Tawney and J. Smith's analysis (see PA, Vol 66:13666) of the authors' (see PA, Vol 62:9819) paper on the education of severely and profoundly retarded children is neither different from their position nor data-based. It is felt that their time would have been better spent documenting and delineating their own position rather than critiquing the present authors' use of certain phrases. (6 ref)
Sontag, Ed; Certo, Nick & Button, James E. Exceptional Children, 1981(Sep), 48(1), 18–20. [PA, Vol 66:13663]

3610. An analysis of the forum: Issues in education of the severely and profoundly retarded.
Discusses the 3-part forum of issues on the education of severely and profoundly retarded children (T. A. Burton and A. Hirshoren, see PA, Vol 62:9770 and 9771; E. Sontag et al, see PA, Vol 62:9819). Different viewpoints were presented, focusing initially on anticipated levels of learning, personnel preparation, and locus of educational services for this population. The authors of the present article conclude that apparent errors of fact in the 3 articles merit an extensive, critical analysis. These errors are identified and discussed, and views are expressed on these and additional topics related to the education and educability of severely and profoundly retarded children. (56 ref)
Tawney, James W. & Smith, Jonathan. (Pennsylvania State U, Div of Special Education, University Park) Exceptional Children, 1981(Sep), 48(1), 5–18. [PA, Vol 66:13666]

Entries in this Subject Index are derived from the 1982 edition of the *Thesaurus of Psychological Index.Terms*. *See* and *See Also* references direct the user to the preferred terminology or related areas of interest. The numbers which follow each entry refer to the abstract number in this Retrospective.

Educational Placement 2872, 2882, 3277, 2954, 3298, 3547, 2963, 3307, 3326, 1583, 3325, 3374, 3058, 3071, 3060, 3404, 3080, 3086, 3131, 3402, 3412, 3093, 3417, 3437, 3440, 3442, 3446, 3460, 3462, 3464, 1023, 3414, 1654, 3413, 3416, 3444, 3466, 3472, 3474
Educational Process [See Education]
Educational Program Evaluation 3483, 3271, 3555, 2397, 2965, 3313, 3075, 3047, 3107, 2562, 3118, 3136, 3441, 3444
Educational Program Planning 2884, 3486, 2878, 3487, 2904, 2810, 3277, 2967, 3288, 2988, 3507, 3075, 3595, 3596, 2834, 3465
Educational Programs [See Also Project Head Start] 3546, 2516, 3229, 3281, 2652, 3266, 2973, 2997, 2984, 707, 3353, 2817, 3125, 3405, 2295, 2851, 3343, 1888, 3100, 2306, 2552, 2846, 2562, 2800, 2849, 3136, 3145, 3163, 3170, 3441, 3479, 3540
Educational Psychologists [See School Psychologists]
Educational Psychology [See School Psychology]
Educational Television 2587
Educational Toys 2707
EEG (Electrophysiology) [See Electroencephalography]
Ego 1839, 2270
Egocentrism 937, 971, 1049, 1712, 2745, 1146
Egotism 745
Egypt 3095
Eidetic Imagery 785, 1662
Electrical Activity [See Also Alpha Rhythm, Auditory Evoked Potentials, Cortical Evoked Potentials, Evoked Potentials, Somatosensory Evoked Potentials, Theta Rhythm, Visual Evoked Potentials] 367, 957, 177
Electrodermal Response [See Galvanic Skin Response]
Electroencephalography [See Also Alpha Rhythm, Theta Rhythm] 367, 1181, 433, 1196, 1200, 40, 503, 522, 2655, 523, 631, 703, 799, 1242, 213, 161, 1042, 177, 2310, 1061
Electrolytes [See Calcium Ions]
Electromyography 3418
Electrophysiology [See Also Alpha Rhythm, Auditory Evoked Potentials, Basal Skin Resistance, Cortical Evoked Potentials, Electrical Activity, Electroencephalography, Electromyography, Electroretinography, Evoked Potentials, Galvanic Skin Response, Rheoencephalography, Skin Resistance, Somatosensory Evoked Potentials, Theta Rhythm, Visual Evoked Potentials] 4
Electroretinography 631
Elementary School Teachers 2999, 3017, 3373, 3388, 3432, 3128, 3124, 3429, 3455, 3463, 3471
Embedded Figures Testing 452
EMG (Electrophysiology) [See Electromyography]
Emotional Adjustment [See Also Coping Behavior] 2060, 316, 1400, 480, 2809, 3294, 2812, 893, 2256, 964, 642, 1782, 1970, 2297, 1062, 1110, 1383, 1123, 1125, 1179, 2565
Emotional Control [See Coping Behavior]
Emotional Development 403, 2203, 2535, 1228, 1698, 1615, 3402, 1896, 2839, 3121, 1101
Emotional Disorders [See Mental Disorders]
Emotional Insecurity [See Emotional Security]
Emotional Maladjustment [See Emotional Adjustment]
Emotional Responses 368, 2440, 2634, 2647, 1539, 1002, 74, 2010, 1293
Emotional Security 2061
Emotional Stability 2564
Emotional States [See Also Depression (Emotion), Distress, Emotional Trauma, Fear, Loneliness, Pleasure, Restlessness] 3253, 1568, 1638
Emotional Trauma 2341
Emotionally Disturbed 370, 1307, 336, 342, 2863, 326, 1312, 2428, 2914, 473, 498, 2805, 3491, 557, 2038, 2106, 2809, 2959, 545, 2166, 2811, 3499, 2186, 3192, 737, 780, 2219, 2227, 3017, 3057, 3370, 2247, 3035, 3374, 775, 842, 1572, 3372, 944, 2099, 3107, 3390, 970, 979, 1054, 1615, 1906, 2467, 2821, 3141, 1601, 1604, 2309, 1100, 2839, 3120, 1106, 1617, 1651, 1656, 2021, 2357, 2566, 2842, 1629, 1638, 1659, 2378, 3441, 3444, 3465, 3472
Emotions [See Also Related Terms] 1431, 408, 1970, 260
Empirical Methods [See Also Observation Methods] 1155
Employability 1876
Employee Performance Appraisal [See Job Performance]
Employee Productivity 2133, 2725
Employee Selection [See Personnel Selection]
Employee Skills [See Clerical Secretarial Skills]
Employment History 98
Employment Interviews [See Job Applicant Interviews]
Encephalitis 295
Encephalography [See Electroencephalography, Pneumoencephalography, Rheoencephalography]
Encephalography (Air) [See Pneumoencephalography]
Encoding [See Human Information Storage]
Encopresis [See Fecal Incontinence]
Endocrine Disorders [See Diabetes, Endocrine Sexual Disorders, Klinefelters Syndrome, Pituitary Disorders, Thyroid Disorders, Turners Syndrome]
Endocrine Glands [See Thyroid Gland]
Endocrine Sexual Disorders [See Also Klinefelters Syndrome, Turners Syndrome] 738
Endocrine System [See Thyroid Gland]
England 1729, 1157
English Language [See Language]
Enjoyment [See Pleasure]
Enrollment (School) [See School Enrollment]
Enuresis [See Urinary Incontinence]
Environment [See Also Classroom Environment, Communities, Home Environment, Neighborhoods, Rural Environments, School Environment, Social Environment, Suburban Environments, Urban Environments] 1821, 2887, 2115, 577, 2235, 1917, 906, 2495, 1786, 2779, 237, 262, 1110, 3169, 190, 1027, 1280, 2506
Environmental Adaptation 2234, 2312, 2308
Environmental Effects [See Also Noise Effects, Seasonal Variations] 108, 192, 1974
Enzymes [See Also Hydroxylases, Monoamine Oxidases, Transferases] 107, 167
Epidemiology 2120, 638, 645, 1340, 1752, 712, 118, 824, 834, 1758, 2196, 1765, 1776, 1078, 72, 256, 977, 275, 296, 313, 1041, 1056, 1077, 1115, 1157, 1384, 1575
Epilepsy [See Also Epileptic Seizures, Grand Mal Epilepsy, Petit Mal Epilepsy] 367, 389, 2655, 497, 658, 51, 2107, 2201, 2700, 676, 922, 841, 2310, 1061
Epileptic Seizures 2107, 678, 676, 922, 1165, 2310
Epithelium [See Skin (Anatomy)]
Equality (Social) [See Social Equality]
Equipment [See Apparatus]
Errors [See Also Refraction Errors] 658, 891, 3401, 2605, 1642, 266, 2557
Erythrocytes 678

Escape [See Avoidance]
Esteem (Self) [See Self Esteem]
Estimation [See Also Time Estimation] 1610, 1805
Ethics [See Also Experimental Ethics, Professional Ethics, Social Values] 1202
Ethnic Differences [See Racial and Ethnic Differences]
Ethnic Groups [See Also American Indians, Hispanics, Mexican Americans, Blacks] 1077
Ethnocentrism 2424
Etiology 11, 3, 378, 459, 467, 2804, 2883, 1727, 1734, 21, 360, 1446, 1452, 2111, 47, 71, 577, 592, 661, 1203, 637, 699, 73, 3324, 695, 705, 88, 97, 116, 118, 704, 128, 1856, 2227, 106, 132, 173, 889, 775, 1776, 148, 999, 169, 182, 247, 249, 257, 632, 1059, 1553, 1988, 230, 950, 956, 983, 1223, 258, 243, 772, 1057, 1062, 1379, 1762, 2283, 2381, 190, 312, 313, 314, 1090, 1091
Eugenics 716
Europe [See France, Hungary, Ireland, Netherlands, Poland, Scandinavia, Switzerland, Union of Soviet Socialist Republics, United Kingdom, West Germany]
Eustachian Tube [See Middle Ear]
Evaluation [See Also Educational Program Evaluation, Mental Health Program Evaluation, Self Evaluation, Teacher Effectiveness Evaluation] 455, 3017, 3365, 2725, 274, 2370
Evaluation (Educational Program) [See Educational Program Evaluation]
Evaluation (Mental Health Program) [See Mental Health Program Evaluation]
Evaluation (Self) [See Self Evaluation]
Evaluation (Treatment Effectiveness) [See Treatment Effectiveness Evaluation]
Evoked Potentials [See Also Auditory Evoked Potentials, Cortical Evoked Potentials, Somatosensory Evoked Potentials, Visual Evoked Potentials] 40, 1867, 213
Exceptional Children (Gifted) [See Gifted]
Exceptional Children (Handicapped) [See Handicapped]
Excretion [See Urination]
Executives [See Top Level Managers]
Exercise 1497, 2949, 1890, 2589, 2728, 2023
Expectations [See Also Experimenter Expectations, Role Expectations, Teacher Expectations] 356, 1311, 1396, 1405, 2513, 398, 3549, 3246, 518, 579, 521, 1486, 1521, 2471, 876, 3017, 3354, 3365, 1068, 1075, 1140
Expectations (Experimenter) [See Experimenter Expectations]
Expectations (Role) [See Role Expectations]
Experience (Practice) [See Practice]
Experience Level (Job) [See Job Experience Level]
Experiences (Events) [See Also Early Experience, Life Experiences, Vicarious Experiences] 1293
Experiences (Life) [See Life Experiences]
Experiment Controls 872
Experimental Apparatus [See Apparatus]
Experimental Design [See Also Hypothesis Testing] 1708, 2348, 2382
Experimental Ethics 151, 1120
Experimental Instructions 356, 1396, 2632, 2639, 485, 1471, 3260, 530, 1503, 822, 1528, 779, 746, 1559, 958, 993, 1614, 2789
Experimental Methods 1693, 3410, 975, 1004, 250, 1810
Experimentation [See Also Related Terms] 928, 151, 1019, 3087, 943, 2836, 3461, 1145, 299, 1034, 1120, 1155, 1156, 1169, 2364, 3171, 3172
Experimenter Bias 404

tics, Sentence Structure, Sentences, Syllables, Syntax, Transformational Generative Grammar, Words (Phonetic Units)] 2385, 3241, 3256, 3583

Lipid Metabolism Disorders [See Also Amaurotic Familial Idiocy] 2299

Lipreading 3499, 952

Listening [See Auditory Perception]

Listening Comprehension 3243, 514, 3302, 92, 875, 1770, 1082, 307

Literature [See Also Prose] 189

Literature Review 359, 432, 1829, 2908, 529, 2090, 479, 410, 2146, 2970, 3318, 692, 2169, 3351, 724, 795, 3385, 109, 714, 1930, 2992, 3019, 887, 904, 1873, 1941, 2268, 249, 970, 1918, 2275, 242, 915, 2836, 2843, 1999, 3376, 240, 250, 3160, 3173, 160, 272, 297, 299, 306, 310, 1069, 1125, 1155, 1171, 1172, 1795, 2028, 2315, 2334, 2339, 2364, 2373, 2377, 3144, 3172, 3174, 3475

Lithium Carbonate 2536, 2333

Lobotomy [See Psychosurgery]

Localization (Perceptual) [See Perceptual Localization]

Localization (Sound) [See Auditory Localization]

Locus of Control [See Internal External Locus of Control]

Logical Thinking 2903, 2909, 1462, 1578, 1580, 1701, 1645, 3120, 1080, 3119

Loneliness 716

Long Term Memory 3270, 1682, 831

Loudness 1357, 1003, 2789

Loudness Threshold [See Auditory Thresholds]

Lower Income Level 878, 3083

LSD (Drug) [See Lysergic Acid Diethylamide]

Luminance Threshold [See Brightness Perception, Visual Thresholds]

Luria Neuropsychological Tests [See Neuropsychological Assessment]

Lymphatic Disorders [See Blood and Lymphatic Disorders]

Lymphocytes 1236, 170

Lysergic Acid Diethylamide 1959

Magnesium 2029

Mainstreaming (Educational) 3219, 3211, 2902, 3227, 2900, 3248, 3262, 3280, 3258, 3287, 3296, 2954, 2957, 2969, 3310, 2994, 3018, 926, 3333, 3511, 3059, 3366, 2831, 3027, 3052, 3066, 3092, 3116, 3388, 3404, 3408, 3584, 971, 2840, 3026, 3389, 3399, 3407, 1005, 1031, 2851, 3143, 3409, 3151, 3426, 3598, 3128, 3421, 3480, 2027, 3147, 3413, 3416, 3439, 3444, 3457, 3466, 3479

Major Tranquilizers [See Neuroleptic Drugs]

Maladjustment (Emotional) [See Emotional Adjustment]

Maladjustment (Social) [See Social Adjustment]

Male Delinquents 596

Male Genital Disorders [See Klinefelters Syndrome]

Males (Human) [See Human Males]

Malnutrition [See Nutritional Deficiencies]

Mammals [See Primates (Nonhuman)]

Mammillary Bodies (Hypothalamic) [See Hypothalamus]

Management Methods 2795

Management Personnel [See Also Top Level Managers] 2481

Mania [See Pica]

Manic Depression 2536

Manic Depressive Psychosis 2090, 1999

Mannerisms [See Habits]

Manual Communication [See Also Sign Language] 2833, 2738, 952, 2288, 3130, 1810, 3156

Marital Adjustment [See Marital Relations]

Marital Problems [See Marital Relations]

Marital Relations 2181, 919, 1245, 1170

Marital Separation [See Divorce]

Marital Status 2483

Marriage 657, 2181

Married Couples [See Spouses]

Masking [See Auditory Masking, Visual Masking]

Mass Media [See Also Educational Television, Television] 2276

Massed Practice 762, 756, 3008

Masturbation 1958, 2727

Maternal Behavior (Human) [See Mother Child Relations]

Maternal Deprivation [See Mother Absence, Mother Child Relations]

Mates (Humans) [See Spouses]

Mathematical Ability 650, 3363, 3104, 1642

Mathematical Modeling 985

Mathematics (Concepts) [See Also Numbers (Numerals)] 624, 3503, 3050, 3077, 3453

Mathematics Achievement 3267, 624, 3274, 2955, 2965, 3297, 3300, 3337, 1544, 3194, 3346, 3381, 3058

Mathematics Education 2894, 3304, 2965, 3500, 3565, 2174, 3034, 3363, 3505, 3342, 3368, 3524, 3087, 3065, 3535, 3140, 3453

Matriculation [See School Enrollment]

Maturation [See Human Development]

Maturity (Physical) [See Physical Maturity]

Mealtimes [See Feeding Practices]

Meaning [See Nonverbal Meaning, Verbal Meaning, Word Meaning]

Meaningfulness 1305, 3198, 1441, 481, 489, 750

Measurement [See Also Related Terms] 619, 1361, 1540, 2403, 130, 1567, 1582, 1761, 135, 882, 689, 1037, 1049, 201, 820, 968, 1711, 1796, 3458, 300, 1149, 1131, 2506

Media (Educational) [See Instructional Media]

Media (Mass) [See Mass Media]

Mediated Responses 1221

Mediation (Cognitive) [See Cognitive Mediation]

Medical Diagnosis [See Also Electroencephalography, Electromyography, Electroretinography, Galvanic Skin Response, Ophthalmologic Examination, Pneumoencephalography, Rheoencephalography, Urinalysis] 595, 640, 676, 852, 844, 873, 2267, 2305, 1025, 2381, 1056

Medical Education 3165

Medical History [See Patient History]

Medical Model 2002

Medical Patients 2279

Medical Personnel [See Also Attendants (Institutions), Family Physicians, General Practitioners, Nurses, Pediatricians, Physical Therapists, Physicians, Psychiatric Aides, Psychiatric Hospital Staff, Psychiatrists] 2679, 2687, 2457, 2495, 2279

Medical Records Keeping 994

Medical Regimen Compliance [See Treatment Compliance]

Medical Residency 2089

Medical Sciences [See Also Child Psychiatry, Epidemiology, Forensic Psychiatry, Immunology, Neurology, Neuropathology, Obstetrics, Pathology, Pediatrics, Psychopathology] 1172

Medical Students 2224, 3165

Medical Therapeutic Devices [See Also Hearing Aids] 2247

Medical Treatment (General) 2237, 1298

Medication [See Drug Therapy]

Medicine (Science of) [See Medical Sciences]

Melancholia [See Depression (Emotion)]

Melancholy [See Sadness]

Melleril [See Thioridazine]

Memory [See Also Eidetic Imagery, Long Term Memory, Memory Decay, Memory Trace, Short Term Memory, Spontaneous Recovery (Learning)] 1397, 422, 396, 1417, 1676, 511, 535, 448, 594, 618, 1456, 1489, 1503, 409, 575, 2529, 682, 732, 1526, 794, 3337, 3345, 3516, 753, 1552, 774, 1593, 2541, 895, 1571, 1772, 3094, 226, 975, 1004, 1608, 1614, 863, 991, 2410, 260, 1587, 1613, 1631, 1639, 3113, 3418, 1050, 1093, 1168, 1173, 1643, 1657, 3122

Memory Decay 1756

Memory Disorders [See Amnesia]

Memory Trace 1756

Men [See Human Males]

Menarche 535

Menstrual Cycle [See Menarche]

Menstruation [See Menarche]

Mental Age 505, 507, 511, 543, 1198, 486, 527, 602, 668, 1487, 1507, 1512, 2390, 729, 733, 1523, 1526, 730, 1225, 725, 813, 1368, 1543, 817, 1364, 1696, 798, 1563, 1579, 2923, 881, 926, 1552, 1559, 1580, 547, 2401, 1701, 947, 996, 1001, 1586, 1599, 1620, 1653, 2784, 1797, 302, 1112, 1296, 1637

Mental Disorders [See Also Related Terms] 2877, 2873, 2883, 535, 705, 2226, 138, 2251, 1906, 2289, 3091, 2292, 2502, 2853, 1138, 1032, 1056, 1099, 1115, 1127, 1141, 1167, 2501, 3172

Mental Health [See Also Community Mental Health] 1245

Mental Health Centers (Community) [See Community Mental Health Centers]

Mental Health Consultation [See Professional Consultation]

Mental Health Inservice Training 2170, 2481

Mental Health Personnel [See Also Clinical Psychologists, Psychiatric Aides, Psychiatric Hospital Staff, Psychiatrists, School Psychologists] 2436, 2170, 2475, 2219, 944

Mental Health Program Evaluation 1764, 2262, 1782, 2317, 2348

Mental Health Programs [See Also Deinstitutionalization, Home Visiting Programs] 2581, 2658, 2669, 2149, 2150, 2188, 2680, 2207, 2240, 2486, 1782, 1964, 2269, 2302, 2297, 2285

Mental Health Services [See Also Community Mental Health Services] 1875, 2239, 2737, 2374

Mental Hospitals [See Psychiatric Hospitals]

Mental Illness [See Mental Disorders]

Mental Illness (Attitudes Toward) 381, 596, 3192, 944, 2856, 1141

Mental Load [See Human Channel Capacity]

Mental Retardation (Attit Toward) 386, 341, 420, 3227, 3545, 417, 2066, 2077, 2082, 2927, 2450, 2937, 3287, 596, 604, 639, 667, 670, 3294, 1525, 2185, 2991, 3192, 770, 2230, 3012, 3293, 764, 776, 888, 909, 912, 696, 874, 2484, 3064, 944, 1002, 2222, 2281, 3083, 3084, 3403, 3408, 2144, 976, 1005, 3108, 1100, 1134, 1625, 3127, 3151, 719, 1075, 1762, 3431, 3480, 1022, 1141, 1148, 2377, 3147, 3463, 3469, 3475

Metabolism [See Also Metabolites] 333, 51, 102, 138, 167

Metabolism Disorders [See Also Amaurotic Familial Idiocy, Diabetes, Lipid Metabolism Disorders, Phenylketonuria] 333, 1734, 585, 1340, 1517, 692, 771, 2209, 950, 243

Metabolites [See Also Homovanillic Acid, Serotonin Metabolites] 101

Metallic Elements [See Also Calcium Ions, Copper, Lead (Metal), Magnesium] 193

Social Behavior [See Also Aggressive Behavior, Altruism, Assistance (Social Behavior), Attribution, Collective Behavior, Competition, Compliance, Conversation, Cooperation, Eye Contact, Friendship, Group Discussion, Group Participation, Interpersonal Attraction, Interpersonal Communication, Interpersonal Influences, Interpersonal Interaction, Interviewing, Interviews, Involvement, Leadership, Participation, Peer Relations, Praise, Prosocial Behavior, Psychodiagnostic Interview, Reciprocity, Responsibility, Risk Taking, Sharing (Social Behavior), Social Acceptance, Social Adjustment, Social Approval, Social Dating, Social Facilitation, Social Interaction, Social Perception, Social Reinforcement, Social Skills, Verbal Reinforcement] 2435, 340, 1721, 1823, 2063, 374, 1315, 349, 2570, 2911, 2918, 3554, 494, 2652, 2456, 2400, 2823, 2218, 2535, 1355, 1921, 2444, 3580, 3584, 641, 2007, 2548, 2736, 3599, 1653, 1786, 2559, 2784, 1985, 2492, 1075, 1289, 2407
Social Casework 2088, 2223, 1913, 2245, 2297
Social Caseworkers [See Social Workers]
Social Change 496
Social Class [See Also Middle Class, Upper Class] 667, 1481, 3112, 296
Social Dating 657
Social Density 1564
Social Deprivation [See Also Social Isolation] 534, 637, 2826
Social Desirability 1416, 670
Social Discrimination 3442, 3446, 3460, 3462, 3464
Social Environments [See Also Classroom Environment, Communities, Home Environment, Neighborhoods, Rural Environments, School Environment, Suburban Environments, Urban Environments] 1238, 2283, 1575, 2512
Social Equality 2162
Social Facilitation 1606, 1985
Social Groups [See Dyads, Minority Groups]
Social Immobility [See Social Mobility]
Social Influences [See Also Social Approval, Social Desirability, Social Values] 2421, 570, 1471, 577, 632
Social Interaction [See Also Assistance (Social Behavior), Collective Behavior, Conversation, Cooperation, Eye Contact, Friendship, Group Discussion, Group Participation, Interpersonal Attraction, Interpersonal Communication, Interpersonal Influences, Interpersonal Interaction, Interviewing, Interviews, Job Applicant Interviews, Participation, Peer Relations, Physical Contact, Psychodiagnostic Interview, Sharing (Social Behavior), Social Dating] 2628, 1211, 2452, 2687, 2823, 3265, 2479, 2444, 1992, 2477, 936, 987, 1078, 2007, 3097, 2731, 2784, 3153, 268, 2829, 139, 313, 1166, 1710, 3544
Social Isolation 323, 1719, 2443, 1872, 1238, 610, 153, 716, 1985, 3424
Social Learning [See Also Imitation (Learning), Nonverbal Learning] 2421, 1330, 1514, 3313, 2587, 2494, 3398
Social Maladjustment [See Social Adjustment]
Social Mobility 435
Social Perception [See Also Attribution, Impression Formation] 1431, 3488, 1448, 501, 1478, 410, 667, 1687, 3012, 3333, 1568, 971, 974, 2493, 1075, 1297, 248, 1292
Social Processes [See Immigration, Social Deprivation, Social Isolation, Social Mobility, Socialization, Status]
Social Reinforcement [See Also Praise, Verbal Reinforcement] 2891, 323, 2044, 1309, 1328, 2074, 2631, 2632, 3203, 2570, 2908, 3240,

3243, 2087, 2115, 2118, 2633, 2931, 1331, 1855, 2520, 3554, 566, 1494, 2101, 2577, 2670, 2899, 3191, 683, 2168, 2460, 685, 759, 82, 897, 3375, 153, 877, 1791, 1973, 2259, 2718, 2547, 2736, 2826, 2601, 3036, 1064, 1266, 2785, 2611, 1667, 2419, 2553
Social Sciences [See Also Child Psychology, Comparative Psychology, Neuropsychology, School Psychology] 1019
Social Services [See Community Services]
Social Skills 1679, 674, 763, 855, 2582, 2589, 2444, 3384, 1375, 1699, 1775, 3079, 3573, 960, 1049, 2202, 2269, 2467, 2488, 3438, 1895, 2559, 2738, 263, 2297, 3159, 2318, 2603, 2611, 2748, 1269, 1666, 2012, 2329, 2561, 2565, 3175
Social Skills Training 3232, 2702, 2269
Social Structure [See Middle Class, Social Class, Upper Class]
Social Values 2941
Social Work [See Social Casework]
Social Workers 2165, 2186, 1002
Socialization 2101, 2109, 2587, 911, 2480, 2497
Socially Disadvantaged [See Disadvantaged]
Society [See Socioeconomic Status]
Sociocultural Factors [See Also Cross Cultural Differences, Cultural Deprivation, Culture Change] 3218, 2244, 842, 850, 983, 1062, 1661
Socioeconomic Status [See Also Family Socioeconomic Level, Income Level, Lower Income Level, Middle Class, Middle Income Level, Social Class, Upper Class] 2892, 12, 2857, 3210, 3209, 2042, 3239, 3272, 1460, 2120, 2956, 604, 1519, 726, 607, 976, 1272, 2292, 1062, 3431, 1153, 3472
Sociometric Tests 3493, 2703, 3026, 3514
Sociopath [See Antisocial Personality]
Sociopathology [See Antisocial Behavior]
Somatosensory Evoked Potentials 1254
Somesthetic Perception [See Cutaneous Sense, Kinesthetic Perception, Tactual Perception]
Somesthetic Stimulation [See Also Tactual Stimulation] 817, 113, 2354, 1126
Sons 719
Sorting (Cognition) [See Classification (Cognitive Process)]
Sound [See Auditory Stimulation]
Sound Localization [See Auditory Localization]
Sound Pressure Level [See Loudness]
Sourness [See Taste Stimulation]
South Pacific 1270
South Vietnam [See Vietnam]
Southeast Asia [See Philippines, Vietnam]
Space (Personal) [See Personal Space]
Spanish Americans [See Hispanics]
Spasms 1750
Spatial Discrimination [See Spatial Perception]
Spatial Imagery 593
Spatial Organization 42, 450, 1507, 774, 910
Spatial Orientation (Perception) 26, 1207, 2528, 1551, 954, 3046
Spatial Perception [See Also Depth Perception, Distance Perception, Size Discrimination, Spatial Organization, Spatial Orientation (Perception), Stereoscopic Vision] 1319, 1677, 636, 593, 591, 1757, 1551, 774, 1008, 1591, 1602, 3046, 3113, 1285, 3467
Special Education (Aurally Handicap) [See Aurally Handicapped]
Special Education (Emot Disturbed) [See Emotionally Disturbed]
Special Education (Gifted) [See Gifted]
Special Education (Learning Disabil) [See Learning Disabilities]
Special Education (Phys Handicaps) [See Physically Handicapped]

Special Education (Visual Handicap) [See Visually Handicapped]
Special Education Teachers 420, 2927, 2935, 2956, 3495, 2945, 2966, 2999, 2984, 2219, 3002, 3010, 3024, 3336, 764, 3017, 3572, 3195, 3397, 3403, 3406, 3087, 3395, 976, 3007, 3120, 3458, 3592, 3597, 3602, 3606, 3607, 3610
Spectral Sensitivity [See Color Perception]
Speech [See Verbal Communication]
Speech and Hearing Measures 502, 445, 1500, 1882, 567, 135, 1705
Speech Characteristics [See Also Articulation (Speech), Pronunciation, Speech Pauses, Speech Pitch, Speech Rhythm] 326, 379, 1182, 1322, 1218, 2131, 2665, 1523, 53, 1235, 122, 134, 149, 1009, 178, 202, 286, 303, 1277, 1802
Speech Development 1838, 3489, 541, 454, 60, 1763, 92, 115, 1886, 713, 137, 2817, 135, 159, 1244, 232, 1009, 1994, 178, 202, 801, 952, 1260, 240, 2026, 1104, 1135, 1995, 2612
Speech Disorders [See Also Articulation Disorders, Dysphonia, Stuttering] 2884, 349, 2516, 2221, 259, 178, 177, 286, 253, 266, 277, 306, 1104, 2329, 2351
Speech Handicapped 2996, 822, 1952, 1983, 1154, 1629
Speech Measures [See Speech and Hearing Measures]
Speech Pauses 2301
Speech Perception 1436, 445, 629, 1250, 131, 1076, 2489, 803, 303, 886, 1802
Speech Pitch 630, 3372
Speech Processing (Mechanical) [See Compressed Speech, Filtered Speech]
Speech Rhythm 630
Speech Therapists 3531, 1625
Speech Therapy 1820, 2391, 2569, 2573, 541, 2576, 1864, 1866, 2131, 2397, 2665, 2221, 2677, 2817, 1952, 2590, 3372, 2008, 1925, 1945, 2313, 139, 1995, 2025, 2351, 2612, 2796
Speed [See Velocity]
Speed (Response) [See Reaction Time]
Spelling 3221, 3068, 3401, 3538
Spina Bifida 2046, 379, 471, 2881, 479, 919, 920, 865, 3060, 3110, 3112, 3131, 969, 3150, 1122, 2335, 1069, 1170
Spinal Fluid [See Cerebrospinal Fluid]
Spokane Indians [See American Indians]
Spontaneous Recovery (Learning) 413
Sports [See Also Swimming] 3537, 1282
Spouses 2181, 919
Stability (Emotional) [See Emotional Stability]
Stammering [See Stuttering]
Standardization (Test) [See Test Standardization]
Standards (Professional) [See Professional Standards]
Stanford Binet Intelligence Scale 443, 3190, 1347, 1506, 662, 790, 1696, 627, 885, 709, 853, 962, 992, 1589, 1046, 1624, 3539, 1047
Stapedius Reflex [See Acoustic Reflex]
State Hospitals [See Psychiatric Hospitals]
Statistical Analysis [See Also Consistency (Measurement), Factor Analysis, Item Analysis (Statistical), Predictability (Measurement), Statistical Norms] 1680, 666, 3305, 2312, 1116
Statistical Correlation 318, 768, 790, 1554, 3071, 820, 1624, 3393, 1106, 269, 1131, 1647
Statistical Measurement [See Predictability (Measurement), Statistical Norms]
Statistical Norms 385, 1661
Statistical Validity [See Also Factorial Validity, Predictive Validity] 957
Status [See Also Occupational Status, Socioeconomic Status] 3257, 3296, 3459
Stereopsis [See Stereoscopic Vision]
Stereoscopic Vision 1442, 569

3195, 3369, 3394, 3406, 3519, 3530, 3590, 3591, 2832, 2841, 3133, 3187, 3391, 3392, 3401, 3407, 1711, 2836, 3007, 3532, 3583, 3587, 848, 2556, 2605, 2837, 3021, 3111, 3186, 3443, 2835, 3169, 3605, 274, 1241, 2030, 2366, 2367, 2792, 2844, 2855, 3117, 3118, 3144, 3158, 3171, 3429, 3454, 3463, 3479, 3534
Telecommunications Media [See Also Educational Television, Television] 2447
Telencephalon [See Basal Ganglia, Limbic System, Occipital Lobe, Parietal Lobe]
Television [See Also Educational Television] 2094, 1330, 1687
Television Viewing 2968, 654, 875, 851, 2023, 2363
Temperament [See Personality]
Temperature (Body) [See Body Temperature]
Temperature (Skin) [See Skin Temperature]
Terminology (Psychological) [See Psychological Terminology]
Territoriality 2115
Test Administration 2929, 525, 1692, 3509, 3357, 853, 1583, 1576, 1790, 3048, 3184, 1664, 1667, 3477
Test Bias (Cultural) [See Cultural Test Bias]
Test Construction [See Also Cultural Test Bias, Difficulty Level (Test), Item Analysis (Test), Item Content (Test), Test Items, Test Reliability, Test Standardization, Test Validity] 1180, 1401, 3515, 3342, 1355, 135, 882, 1790, 1037, 1031, 3159, 270, 1648, 293
Test Items 3346
Test Normalization [See Test Standardization]
Test Norms 3515, 1109
Test Reliability 1313, 1316, 1419, 478, 502, 469, 1337, 3493, 691, 711, 807, 1516, 3515, 737, 1766, 3341, 3509, 1695, 3346, 1567, 882, 884, 921, 1375, 1699, 3105, 970, 3579, 820, 1788, 291, 3433, 1044, 1082, 1648, 1652, 2856, 293, 1177, 1814, 1815
Test Scores 586, 62, 1538, 768, 920, 1560, 702, 914, 1536, 1554, 1572, 3071, 921, 1603, 1066, 1600, 1624, 1639, 1611, 1177, 1647, 1667
Test Standardization 656, 3320, 743, 1355
Test Validity 322, 1402, 334, 456, 1313, 2893, 446, 463, 1479, 1459, 504, 1484, 3308, 3327, 734, 807, 1516, 89, 816, 1766, 2475, 780, 790, 885, 1544, 1695, 3346, 927, 1567, 135, 914, 1577, 884, 1375, 1377, 1699, 960, 970, 988, 3141, 3579, 955, 279, 291, 1046, 1114, 1799, 3433, 3458, 3462, 1023, 1044, 1047, 1151, 1295, 1611, 1648, 1661
Testes Disorders [See Endocrine Sexual Disorders]
Testing [See Also Cultural Test Bias, Difficulty Level (Test), Item Analysis (Test), Item Content (Test), Rating, Scaling (Testing), Scoring (Testing), Test Administration, Test Items, Test Reliability, Test Standardization, Test Validity] 734, 960, 1604, 1618, 1081
Testing (Hypothesis) [See Hypothesis Testing]
Testing Methods [See Also Multiple Choice (Testing Method)] 1618, 3417, 3155
Tests [See Measurement]
Tests (Achievement) [See Achievement Measures]
Tests (Aptitude) [See Aptitude Measures]
Tests (Intelligence) [See Intelligence Measures]
Tests (Personality) [See Personality Measures]
Text Structure 2951
Thalamic Nuclei 188
Thalamus [See Thalamic Nuclei]
Thematic Apperception Test 1461, 660
Theories of Education 2913
Theories [See Also Related Terms] 231, 943, 951, 1712, 244, 1129, 1154, 1795
Theory Formulation 943

Theory Verification 425
Therapeutic Camps 2102, 3192, 1976, 1949, 2228
Therapeutic Community 2519, 2493
Therapeutic Devices (Medical) [See Medical Therapeutic Devices]
Therapeutic Processes [See Also Psychotherapeutic Processes] 2679, 893, 2481, 2477, 2279, 2356
Therapeutic Techniques (Psychother) [See Psychotherapeutic Techniques]
Therapist Attitudes 14
Therapist Characteristics [See Also Therapist Attitudes] 2458, 2018
Therapist Effectiveness [See Therapist Characteristics]
Therapist Experience [See Therapist Characteristics]
Therapist Patient Interaction [See Psychotherapeutic Processes]
Therapist Personality [See Therapist Characteristics]
Therapy [See Treatment]
Therapy (Drug) [See Drug Therapy]
Therapy (Individual) [See Individual Psychotherapy]
Therapy (Music) [See Music Therapy]
Theta Rhythm 1042
Thinking [See Also Abstraction, Autistic Thinking, Divergent Thinking, Inductive Deductive Reasoning, Inference, Logical Thinking, Reasoning] 324
Thioridazine 2069, 2328, 2801
Thorazine [See Chlorpromazine]
Thought Disturbances [See Also Amnesia, Autistic Thinking, Fantasies (Thought Disturbances), Obsessions, Perseveration] 1825, 551, 152, 200
Threat 119
Thresholds [See Auditory Thresholds, Visual Thresholds]
Thumbsucking 1944
Thyroid Disorders 384
Thyroid Gland 1969
Thyroid Hormones [See Also Thyroxine, Triiodothyronine] 1969, 1971
Thyroid Stimulating Hormone [See Thyrotropin]
Thyrotropic Hormone [See Thyrotropin]
Thyrotropin 267
Thyroxine 267
Tics 2369
Time [See Also Interresponse Time] 3076
Time (Interresponse) [See Interresponse Time]
Time Estimation 531, 1486
Time Perception [See Also Time Estimation] 361, 628, 2528
Tissues (Body) [See Skin (Anatomy)]
Tofranil [See Imipramine]
Toilet Training 2618, 2055, 2651, 2394, 2668, 2681, 2696, 2706, 1932, 2271, 2593, 2719, 2485, 2259, 2406, 2274, 2780, 2756, 2749
Token Economy Programs 2063, 2067, 2515, 2636, 2118, 2038, 2112, 3178, 2575, 2666, 2899, 2460, 3297, 3300, 3319, 2459, 2530, 2472, 3355, 3316, 3567, 1947, 2289, 2340, 3089, 3139, 3157, 2343, 2358, 3603
Token Reinforcement [See Secondary Reinforcement]
Tolerance 2306
Tone (Frequency) [See Pitch (Frequency)]
Tongue 1191, 2252, 2758
Top Level Managers 420
Touch [See Tactual Perception]
Touching [See Physical Contact]
Toxic Disorders [See Also Lead Poisoning] 1734

Toy Selection 666, 2236, 1774, 1012, 268, 1073
Toys [See Also Educational Toys] 3553, 666, 1967, 2709, 2743, 268
Trace (Memory) [See Memory Trace]
Tracking [See Also Rotary Pursuit, Visual Tracking] 1491, 1107, 1108, 1294
Training [See Education]
Training (Clinical Methods) [See Clinical Methods Training]
Training (Mental Health Inservice) [See Mental Health Inservice Training]
Training (Personnel) [See Personnel Training]
Tranquilizing Drugs [See Chlorpromazine, Haloperidol, Neuroleptic Drugs, Phenothiazine Derivatives, Thioridazine]
Transfer (Learning) 1728, 1404, 1326, 2075, 3230, 402, 3279, 542, 558, 1678, 533, 561, 665, 2813, 413, 1221, 2663, 554, 3328, 687, 1690, 574, 1359, 1528, 1694, 3571, 867, 3003, 3510, 934, 2541, 2598, 3423, 800, 2511, 3069, 2332, 2752, 2848, 3148, 3169, 301, 1643, 3144
Transferases 140
Transference (Psychotherapeutic) [See Psychotherapeutic Transference]
Transformational Generative Grammar 163, 751, 828, 829
Transfusion (Blood) [See Blood Transfusion]
Translocation (Chromosome) 146, 815
Transportation [See Public Transportation]
Transposition (Cognition) 1732
Trauma (Emotional) [See Emotional Trauma]
Trauma (Physical) [See Injuries]
Traumatic Neurosis 2341
Traumatic Psychosis [See Reactive Psychosis]
Traveling 3501
Treatment Compliance 2167
Treatment Effectiveness Evaluation 2435, 2035, 2646, 1863, 2138, 2672, 127, 2233, 2403, 1950, 2250, 2824, 2598, 1984, 2317, 1983, 2342
Treatment Facilities [See Also Child Guidance Clinics, Clinics, Community Mental Health Centers, Halfway Houses, Nursing Homes, Psychiatric Hospitals, Therapeutic Camps] 2281
Treatment Methods (Physical) [See Physical Treatment Methods]
Treatment Outcomes [See Also Psychotherapeutic Outcomes] 1863
Treatment [See Also Related Terms] 2043, 1823, 2423, 2431, 1723, 1729, 1821, 2048, 2065, 2089, 2436, 2804, 2625, 38, 2111, 44, 2161, 2178, 2463, 2466, 116, 1929, 2196, 1856, 1884, 842, 2444, 1939, 2222, 169, 1908, 1938, 1940, 2204, 2275, 57, 232, 2002, 2215, 1983, 2004, 2341, 2853, 3093, 243, 772, 2283, 2368, 2827, 160, 297, 313, 1156, 1160, 1171, 1175, 2016, 2020, 2361, 2383, 3174
Trial and Error Learning 2960, 591, 2367
Triiodothyronine 267
Trisomy [See Also Trisomy 21] 1740, 1204, 1717
Trisomy 21 1185, 1199, 1229, 1287
Tryptophan 2386, 167, 2349
Tumors [See Neoplasms]
Turkey 496
Turners Syndrome 645
Tutoring [See Also Peer Tutoring] 3495, 3551, 2585, 2224
Tutors [See Teachers]
Twins [See Also Heterozygotic Twins, Monozygotic Twins] 1187, 155, 190, 1139
Tympanic Membrane [See Middle Ear]
Typing [See Clerical Secretarial Skills]
Typologies (Psychodiagnostic) [See Psychodiagnostic Typologies]

White Blood Cells [See Leucocytes]
White Collar Workers [See Management Personnel, Top Level Managers]
Whites 2424, 435, 1192, 477, 555, 3260, 1497, 3307, 766, 832, 835, 768, 804, 824, 868, 3013, 878, 1064, 1621, 1023, 1178, 1575, 3471, 3478
Wide Range Achievement Test 463, 737, 992, 3141, 1642, 1647
Withdrawal (Defense Mechanism) 216, 222, 262
Withdrawal (Drug) [See Drug Withdrawal]
Withdrawal Effects (Drug) [See Drug Withdrawal]
Women [See Human Females]
Word Associations 1306, 385, 1518, 3323, 3523, 1571

Word Deafness [See Aphasia]
Word Frequency 326, 437, 892, 846, 1630
Word Meaning 1541, 742, 749, 3094
Words (Form Classes) [See Form Classes (Language)]
Words (Phonetic Units) 1305, 1397, 1390, 2860, 663, 1754, 741, 742, 755, 845, 846, 3525, 1561, 3068, 3102, 3423, 183, 1631, 1797, 1630, 3470
Words (Vocabulary) [See Vocabulary]
Work (Attitudes Toward) 2036, 2281
Work Study Programs [See Educational Programs]
Workshops (Sheltered) [See Sheltered Workshops]
Worship [See Religious Practices]

Wounds [See Self Inflicted Wounds]
Writing (Creative) [See Literature]
Writing (Handwriting) [See Handwriting]
Written Language [See Also Handwriting, Handwriting Legibility, Letters (Alphabet), Numbers (Numerals)] 1434, 3244, 1953, 3470

Young Adults 1678, 3264, 445, 605, 614, 1341, 2152, 660, 722, 2133, 2699, 833, 1693, 3045, 1774, 94, 141, 1551, 1556, 1567, 899, 1242, 1244, 1362, 1371, 2487, 2592, 910, 995, 1588, 3591, 129, 1969, 2488, 3400, 1374, 1378, 1786, 2480, 2551, 2725, 848, 1111, 1797, 2584, 2607, 2752, 2761, 140, 1167, 2500, 3594
Youth (Adults) [See Young Adults]

AUTHOR INDEX

The Author Index is intended to be a name index only and not a person index. "Adams, P." will be listed separately from "Adams, Paul" even though the names may refer to the same person; however, two listings for "Adams, P." may refer to two different authors. As many as four authors are listed; if there are more than four, the first author is followed by "et al."

RC570 M4117 1982
+Mental retardation : an abstracte

0 00 02 0229403 9

MIDDLEBURY COLLEGE